W O M E N

and | INTERNATIONAL
HUMAN RIGHTS
LAW

Volume 3
Toward Empowerment

W O M E N
and INTERNATIONAL
HUMAN RIGHTS
LAW

Volume 3

Editors | Kelly D. Askin
Dorean M. Koenig

Transnational Publishers, Inc.
Ardsley, New York

Published and distributed by *Transnational Publishers, Inc.*
Ardsley Park
Science and Technology Center
410 Saw Mill River Road
Ardsley, NY 10502

Phone: 914–693–5100
Fax: 914–693–4430
E-mail: info@transnationalpubs.com
Web: www.transnationalpubs.com

Library of Congress Cataloging-in-Publication Data

Women and international human rights law / edited by Kelly D. Askin and
  Dorean M. Koenig.
    v. cm.
    Includes bibliographical references.
    ISBN 1-57105-093-0
    1. Women's rights. 2. Human rights. 3. Women—Legal status, laws, etc.
  I. Askin, Kelly Dawn. II. Koenig, Dorean Marguerite
  K644.w64   1998
  341.4'81—dc21

                                     98-20643
                                       CIP

Manufactured in the United States of America

This volume is dedicated to Judge Patricia Wald, whose amazing energy, intellect, humor, and commitment serve as such a wonderful role model and inspiration to me and countless others. It is also dedicated to four other dynamic international lawyers who have managed to break through the gender barriers and have their groundbreaking work transform international law. So I also express deep admiration and gratitude to my other role models: Diane Orentlicher, Navi Pillay, Patti Sellers, and Dinah Shelton.

Kelly D. Askin

This volume is dedicated to Eleanor Roosevelt, to the authors of the chapters in these volumes, and to my granddaughter. To Mrs. Roosevelt because my mother honored her, and I do too, for her work to make the world a better place; to the talented and dedicated authors whose work we have been honored to have been entrusted with, because of the fruits of their generosity and perseverence; and to my granddaughter that she may grow up in a world where girls have the opportunity to live full, healthy and active lives as educated women, free of violence and gender apartheid.

Dorean M. Koenig

CONTENTS

Section IV
Regional Issues

Section V
Other Issues

ABOUT THE CONTRIBUTORS

Bina Agarwal is Professor of Economics at the Institute of Economic Growth, University of Delhi, India. Her 1994 book, A FIELD OF ONE'S OWN: GENDER AND LAW RIGHTS IN SOUTH ASIA was awarded the A.K. Coomaraswamy Book Prize (1996) by the Association for Asian Studies, U.S.A.; the Edgar Graham Book Prize (1996), SOAS, University of London; and the K.H. Batheja Award (1995–1996) by the University of Bombay. Other books include: COLD HEARTHS AND BARREN SLOPES: THE WOODFUEL CRISES IN THE THIRD WORLD (1986); and MECHANIZATION IN INDIAN AGRI-CULTURE (1983). Professor Agarwal received a Ph.D. (1978) in Economics from the Delhi School of Economics at the University of Delhi; an M.A. (1977) and B.A. (1972) in Economics, from the University of Cambridge, UK; and a B.A. (Honors, 1970) in Economics from the University of Delhi. Harvard University has invited Professor Agarwal to be the first DHH Ingalls Visiting Professor (Departments of Government and of Sanskrit and Indian Studies). She was a visiting professor at Harvard during 1991–1992; a Bunting Fellow at Radcliffe; visitor at the Princeton Institute for Advanced Study; and visiting fellow at the Institute of Development Studies (Sussex). She is currently Vice President of the International Association for Feminist Economics and a member of the executive committee of the International Economic Association.

Myroslava Antonovych is Associate Professor, Faculty of Law, at the National University of Kyiv-Mohyla, Ukraine. She has written over 60 publications, includ-ing: IMPLEMENTATION OF INTERNATIONAL HUMAN RIGHTS NORMS IN UKRANIAN LEGIS-LATION (Kyiv, 1996); *Rights of National Minorities in Ukraine, in* MINORITY RIGHTS IN NEW EUROPE (P. Kumper and S. Wheatly, eds.1999), and *Human Rights in Ukraine,* LII UKRAINE QUARTERLY (1996). Professor Antonovych received an LL.M. in International Law from McGill University in Montreal (1999); a degree in Law from Lviv University, Ukraine (1995); a Candidate of Sciences degree (the equivalent of the American Ph.D.) in Linguistics from Kyiv Linguistic University, Ukraine (1988); and a degree in English Language and Literature from Dnipropctrovsk University, Ukraine (1981). Professor Anonovych teaches Public International Law, International Human Rights Law, and Constitutional Human Rights.

Azizah al-Hibri is Professor of Law at the T.C. Williams School of Law, University of Richmond, Va. Publications include: *Islamic Jurisprudence and Critical Race Feminism, in* GLOBAL CRITICAL RACE FEMINISM (forthcoming); *An Introduction to Muslim Women's Rights in* WINDOWS OF FAITH (forthcoming); *Is Western Patriarchal Feminism Good for Third World/Minority Women?, in* IS MULTICULTURALISM BAD FOR WOMEN? (1999); *Islamic Law and Muslim Women in America, in* ONE NATION UNDER GOD (1999). Dr. al-Hibri received a J.D. (1985) and Ph.D. (1975) in Philosophy from the University of Pennsylvania; an M.A. in Philosophy from Wayne State University (1968); and a B.A. in Philosophy from the American University of Beirut (1966). She is Founding Editor of HYPATIA: A JOURNAL OF FEMINIST PHILOSOPHY and also founded (and is the current president of) Karamah: Muslim Women Lawyers for Human Rights. Dr. al-Hibri is on the Editorial Boards of THE JOURNAL OF LAW AND RELIGION and THE AMERICAN JOURNAL OF ISLAMIC SOCIAL SCIENCES; and on the Board of Advisors for THE RELIGION AND HUMAN RIGHTS SERIES (Emory University). She is Co-Director of the "Religious Assembly on Uniting America" (Columbia University); a member of the Advisory Board of the Pluralism Project (Harvard University); Religion and Ethics News Weekly (PBS); and on the Board of Directors of the Interfaith Alliance Foundation.

Cynthia L. Ambrose is a Democracy Fellow with the United States Agency for International Development's (USAID) Democracy and Governance Center, serving on the Center's Rule of Law Team. She works with rule of law programs in developing countries worldwide, which promote and strengthen democracy. Her focus area is Human Rights. Ms. Ambrose has been Legal Counsel to the Kosrae Legislature, working for the Federated States of Micronesia. As Legal Counsel, she managed the Legal Department of the Kosrae Legislature. Ms. Ambrose has also been a Legislative Attorney with Cooke & Associates where she represented various organizations before the Maryland General Assembly. She has also worked at the Central and Eastern Europe Law Initiative program of the American Bar Association in the Legal Assessments Division reviewing, among other items, the Nigerian Constitution. She received an LL.M. (1993) from Georgetown Law School in Comparative Legal Systems with a focus on Constitutions and Human Rights; a J.D. (1992) from the Thomas Cooley Law School, and a B.A. (1988) from the University of Maryland.

Penelope Andrews is Associate Professor at the City University of New York Law School, teaching International Human Rights Law, Critical Perspectives on Race and Law, as well as Torts. She is secretary and treasurer of the International Third World Legal Studies Association and is on the Editorial Board of the EAST AFRICA JOURNAL OF PEACE AND HUMAN RIGHTS. She was a Lecturer at La Trobe University in Melbourne, Australia, as well as a visitor at the University of Maryland Law School. Born in Cape Town, South Africa, Professor Andrews held the Chamberlain Fellowship in Legislation at Columbia Law School in 1985, after receiving an LL.M. (1984) from Columbia Law School. She received an LL.B. (1982) from the University of Natal, Durban, where she also received her B.A. She has worked as an Associate at the Legal Resources Centre in Johannesburg, and the NAACP Legal Defense Fund Inc. in New York. Ms. Andrews has served as a consultant to the Ford Foundation and the Community Peace Foundation in South Africa, the Victorian Equal Opportunity Commissioner in Australia and the United Nations Development Fund for Women in New York. She assisted in the Legal Resources Centre with their submission to the Truth and Reconciliation Commission on the role of the legal profession under Apartheid. She is editing (along with co-editor Stephen Ellman) THE SOUTH AFRICAN CONSTITUTION AND THE ENFORCEMENT OF RIGHTS (forthcoming).

Carolyn Patty Blum is Director of the International Human Rights Law Clinic, Boalt Hall Law School, University of California, Berkeley. Professor Blum has taught courses at Boalt Hall on International Human Rights Law and Refugee Law and has taught a Human Rights Writing Seminar, as well as a joint Oxford University-George Washington University Summer Program on Human Rights: International Human Rights Advocacy and Dissemination. She received a J.D. (1976) from Northeastern University Law School and a B.A. (1971) from the University of Arizona. She has served as consultant for asylum appeals and other refugee-related litigation. Her publications include: *Still Missing: The Continuing Search for Accountability for the Crimes of the Pinochet Regime, in* SCREENING JUSTICE (forthcoming); *Images of Lawyering and Political Activism, in* IN THE NAME OF THE FATHER, *in* the UNIVERSITY OF SAN FRANCISCO LAW REVIEW (1996); and *License to Kill: The Principle of the Government's Right to "Investigate Its Enemies," in* WILLIAMETTE LAW REVIEW (1992).

Cynthia Price Cohen is the founder and Executive Director of ChildRights International Research Institute and a research associate at the Ralph Bunche Institute on the United Nations, City University of New York. As the representative of a nongovernmental organization, Dr. Price Cohen participated in the drafting of the United Nations Convention on the Rights of the Child and she systematically follows international activities relating to the rights of the child. Her overviews of status of children's rights can be found in such essays as: *The Developing Jurisprudence of the Rights of the Child*, 6 ST. THOMAS LAW REVIEW 1 (1993); and *Jurisprudence of the Committee on the Rights of the Child: A Guide for Research and Analysis*, 19 MICHIGAN JOURNAL OF INTERNATIONAL LAW 633 (1998), written with Susan Kilbourne. Dr. Price Cohen teaches international child rights law at the Washington College of Law of American University and The University of Tulsa College of Law. She is editor (with Howard A. Davidson) of CHILDREN'S RIGHTS IN AMERICA: U.N. CONVENTION ON THE RIGHTS OF THE CHILD COMPARED WITH UNITED STATES LAW (1990); co-author (with Howard Davidson and Linda Girdner) of ESTABLISHING OMBUDSMAN PROGRAMS FOR CHILDREN AND YOUTH: HOW GOVERNMENT'S RESPONSIVENESS TO ITS YOUNG CITIZENS CAN BE IMPROVED (1993); and co-author (with Susan Bitensky) of UNITED NATIONS CONVENTION ON THE RIGHTS OF THE CHILD: ANSWERS TO 30 QUESTIONS (1997). She recently edited and contributed to HUMAN RIGHTS OF INDIGENOUS PEOPLES (1998). Dr. Cohen received her Doctor of Juridical Science (1994) from the Law Studies Institute of the Polish Academy of Sciences, and is currently a doctoral candidate in Social Policy at the University of Gent, Belgium. She received a J.D. from New York Law School, where she received the Human Rights Award, and her M.S. and B.A. degrees in Political Science from the City College of New York, where she was Phi Beta Kappa.

Rebecca J. Cook is Professor, Faculty of Law, Faculty of Medicine and Joint Centre for Bioethics, University of Toronto, and is Founding Director of the International Human Rights Programme at the law school. She received a J.S.D. (1994) and an L.L.M. (1988) from Columbia Law School; a J.D. (1982) from Georgetown; an M.P.A. (1973) from Harvard; an M.A. (1972) from Tufts; and an A.B. (1970) from Barnard. She has taught at the School of Public Health at Columbia University and continues to lecture there. She is ethical and legal issues co-editor of the INTERNATIONAL JOUR-

NAL OF GYNECOLOGY AND OBSTETRICS, and serves on the editorial advisory board of FAMILY PLANNING PERSPECTIVES, HUMAN RIGHTS QUARTERLY, and THE THIRD WORLD LEGAL STUDIES JOURNAL. She is an occasional adviser to the Commonwealth Medical Association, the Ford Foundation, Profamilia Legal Services for Women and the World Health Organization. Her publications include over one hundred books, articles and reports in the areas of international human rights, the law relating to women's health and feminist ethics. She is author of WOMEN'S HEALTH AND HUMAN RIGHTS (1994), the editor of HUMAN RIGHTS OF WOMEN: NATIONAL AND INTERNATIONAL PERSPECTIVES (1994), and co-author of CONSIDERATIONS FOR FORMULATING REPRODUCTIVE HEALTH LAWS (1998).

Parvin Darabi is a writer, lecturer, human rights activist, and President of the Dr. Homa Darabi Foundation. Parvin Darabi was born in Tehran, Iran. On February 7, 1964, she arrived in San Francisco with $500 to pursue her childhood dream of learning how a radio worked. She received an M.B.A. (1979) from Pepperdine University; an M.S.E.E. (1975) from the University of Southern California; and a B.S.E.E. (1971) from California State University, Northridge. She worked as an electronic system engineer in defense electronic firms until 1994. From 1985–1990, she operated her own company, PT Enterprises, and developed the most sensitive Radar Detector presently on German Naval Vessels. In February 1994, Ms. Darabi's sister, Dr. Homa Darabi, self-immolated, protesting the oppression of women in Iran. Ms. Darabi changed careers, establishing the Dr. Homa Darabi Foundation, in memory of her sister, and has since devoted her time to educating the public on the subjugation of women in Islam and her homeland, Iran. She co-authored with her son, Attorney Romin P. Thomson, RAGE AGAINST THE VEIL, THE COURAGEOUS LIFE AND DEATH OF AN ISLAMIC DISSIDENT (1999). The book was published in German with the title of "du Wolltest fligen" (1997) and in Dutch (1998). Dr. Darabi has published articles in both American and Iranian Journals.

Marcella David is Professor of Law at The University of Iowa College of Law. She received a J.D. from the University of Michigan Law School (1989) and a B.S. from the Rensselaer Polytechnic Institute (1986). Professor David is on the Executive Council of the American Society of International Law and is a member of the Midwest Coalition of Human Rights.

Theresia M. Degener is professor of law, administration, and organization at the University of Applied Sciences (EFH-RWL), Bochum, Germany. She received a doctorate degree in law from Johann Wolfgang Geothe-Universitaet, Frankfurt a.M., Germany; an LL.M. (Master of Laws) from UC Berkeley, Boalt Hall School of Law; and a law degree from Johann Wolfgang Geothe-Universitaet, Frankfurt a.M., Germany. Dr. Degener teaches International Human Rights Law with special focus on Disability Rights Law and has been a guest lecturer at UC Berkeley School of Law. She is affiliated with DPI (Disabled Peoples' International). Working internationally, she teaches disabled women and girls in and outside institutions and trains staff persons in violence prevention. A member of the legal rights working group of the European Disability Forum, she helps to create European Disability Law, and as a member of the German Forum of Disabled Lawyers she helps to create German anti-discrimination laws for disabled persons. Dr. Degener is a Consultant to the German GREENS in law reform on sexual assault. Publications include: *Sterile Without Consent, in* IMPRINTING OUR IMAGE. AN INTERNATIONAL ANTHOLOGY BY WOMEN WITH DISABILITIES (D. Dreidger. & S. Gray eds, 1992); and *Human Rights and Disabled Persons: Essays and Relevant Human Rights Instruments, in* INTERNATIONAL STUDIES IN HUMAN RIGHTS (Y. Koster-Dreese ed., 1995).

Helen Durham is the Australian Red Cross Manager for International Humanitarian Law. She received her Bachelor of Arts from Melbourne University in 1992, and also her Bachelor of Laws with Honours from Melbourne University (1992). She has also submitted for a Doctorate of Judicial Science in 1999. Helen Durham has been a member of the International Committee of the Red Cross delegation to the Diplomatic Conference on the Rome Treaty (1998). She has lectured widely on International Humanitarian Law within Australia, Indonesia, Malaysia, and the Philippines.

Maja Kirilova Eriksson is Professor, Faculty of Law, Uppsala University, Sweden. She received her LL.D. (Juris Doctor, 1984) from Uppsala in Public International Law, and her LL.M. from Leipzig. Dr. Eriksson teaches International Law and directs several advanced courses on Human Rights, Refugee and Humanitarian Law, and Democracy in the European context. Dr. Eriksson is the author of: DAS AUFENTHALTSRECHT VON AUSLÄNDERN (1984); THE RIGHT TO MARRY (1990); AN INTRODUCTION TO THE EUROPEAN CONVENTION ON HUMAN RIGHTS (co-authored) (1993); SKYDD AV MÄNSKLIGA RÄTTIGHETER (1994); and REPRODUCTIVE FREEDOM IN THE CONTEXT OF INTERNATIONAL HUMAN RIGHTS AND HUMANITARIAN LAW (1999). She has also published extensively in journals.

Mahmoud F. Fathalla is Professor of Obstetrics and Gynecology at Assuit University in Egypt. He received a Ph.D. (1967) from Edinburgh University; a Doctorate degree (1962) from the University of Cairo in Obstetrics and Gynecology; and his M.D. (1957) from the University of Cairo. Dr. Fathalla has also received numerous Honorary Degrees: Doctor Honoris Causa (Uppsala University, Sweden 1991); Doctor Honoris Causa (Helsinki University, 1999); Honorary Fellow (American College of Obstetricians and Gynecologists, 1985); and Fellow ad eund. (Royal College of Obstetricians and Gynecologist, 1990). He is former Senior Advisor in Biomedical and Reproductive Health Research for The Rockefeller Foundation, and former Director of the UNDP/UNFPD/WHO/ World Bank Special Program of Research, Research Training and Development in Human Reproduction; and he is also a former President of the International Federation of Gynecology and Obstetrics. Dr. Fathalla authored the book FROM OBSTETRICS AND GYNECOLOGY TO WOMEN'S HEALTH: THE ROAD AHEAD (1997). He is also the Co-Editor of THE FIGO MANUAL OF HUMAN REPRODUCTION (three volumes, 1990); each volume has also been translated into French and Spanish.

Susana T. Fried is a consultant for women's human rights advocacy, policy and research. She has a Masters Degree in City and Regional Planning (1988); a B.A. (1982); and a Ph.D. Ms. Fried is a feminist activist from the United States, currently consulting on women's human rights policy and advocacy. Previously, she worked for eight years with the Center for Women's Global Leadership at Rutgers University, most recently as the Program Director for International Policy and Advocacy. She is currently on the national steering committee for Amnesty International/USA Members for Lesbian and Gay Concerns. Ms. Fried is the Guest Editor, Campaign Section, *The 1998 Global Campaign for Women's Human Rights, in* WOMEN'S HEALTH JOURNAL (1999). She is editor of *The Indivisibility of Women's Human Rights: A Continuing Dialogue* (1996), Center for Women's Global Leadership, New Brunswick, NJ; and the co-author of *Beijing '95: Moving Women's Human Rights from Margin to Center* (with Charlotte Brunch) in 22 SIGNS 1 (1996).

Anne H. Heindel is a Legal Editor for Mathew Bender & Co., and the United Nations Representative from IED/HLP (International Educational Development/ Humanitarian Law Project). She received a J.D. (1994) from Hastings College of Law; a B.A. (1990) from the University of California, Santa Barbara; and is expected to receive her LL.M. (2001) in International Studies from New York University School of Law. Ms. Heindel has done research and writing on armed conflict and self-determination. She is author of ARMED CONFLICT IN THE WORLD TODAY: A COUNTRY BY COUNTRY REVIEW (1995–2000), an annually updated reference report distributed by IED/HLP, Parliamentary Human Rights Group, and the University of d'Oran.

Natalie Hevener Kaufman is on leave from her position as Professor of Government and International Studies at the University of South Carolina, where she teaches Politics of Sex Roles and International Law, and is currently Visiting Professor at The Institute for Family and Neighborhood Life, Clemson University, South Carolina. Professor Kaufman's main research is on gender politics and International Law. Professor Kaufman received a Ph.D. from the University of Virginia and a B.A. from the University of Pennsylvania (Honors). Her books include: IMPLEMENTING THE UN CONVENTION ON THE RIGHTS OF THE CHILD (co-edited); THE PARTICIPATION RIGHTS OF THE CHILD (with Malfrid Flekkoy); HUMAN RIGHTS TREATIES AND THE SENATE: A HISTORY OF OPPOSITION; and INTERNATIONAL LAW AND THE STATUS OF WOMEN. Her articles have appeared in many prominent human and civil rights journals.

Nancy Kelly is an Attorney at the Greater Boston Legal Services; a Clinical Supervisor, Harvard Immigration and Refugee Clinic; and Lecturer in Immigration Law, Boston University School of Law. She is the Co-Founder of Women Refugees Project and the Refugee Law Center. She received a J.D. from Northeastern University School of Law, an M.Ed. from Antioch University, and a B.A. from the University of Massachusetts. Publications include: *Women Whose Government Are Unable or Unwilling to Provide Reasonable Protection from Domestic Violence May Qualify as Refugees under United States Asylum Law,* 11(4) GEORGETOWN IMM. L.J. (1997) (co-authored with Deborah Anker and Lauren Gilbert); *Guidelines for Women's Asylum Claims,* 6(4) INT'L J. REF. L., Oxford University Press (1994); and *Gender-Related Persecution: Assessing the Asylum Claims of Women,* 26 CORNELL INT'L LAW JOURNAL 625 (1993).

Dinorah La Luz is a Commissioner in the International Section of the Commission for Constitutional and Human Rights of the Puerto Rico Bar Association. She received an LL.M. in Comparative Law from the University of San Diego School of Law; a J.D. from the Interamerican University School of Law; an M.A. in Translation from the University of Puerto Rico; a B.A. in Foreign Languages from the University of Puerto Rico; and a B.A. in International Relations from Florida International University. Commissioner La Luz also received a certificate from the Institute of International and Comparative Law (Legal Studies) in Geneva and Strasbourg. She was a participant for CODEM at the NGO Forum in Huarou, China and is the author of The GLOSSARY OF INSURANCE AND LEGAL TERMS, ENGLISH-SPANISH/SPANISH-ENGLISH, 1ST. & 2ND. EDS. (1991–1992) (Supplement 1998); LAS NORMAS DE CONFLICTO ARMADO SEGÚN EL DERECHO INTERNACIONAL, Y SU APLICACIÓN A LOS MOVIMIENTOS DE LIBERACIÓN NACIONAL (The Laws of War as Applied to the National Liberation Movements, forthcoming); and *Mujeres Maltratadas: de victimas a victimarias-aspectos sociales, sicológicos y juridicos* (*Battered Women Who Kill—Social, Psychological and Legal Aspects*) in 63 REV. JUR. U.P.R. 679, No. 3 (1994).

Ilana Landsberg-Lewis is the UNIFEM Advisor on the Convention on the Elimination of All Forms of Discrimination Against Women. She received her Law Degree with a specialization in Human Rights and Union-side Labour Law. She is a feminist activist from Canada, who practiced human rights and union-side labour law in Toronto before joining UNIFEM in 1994. She is also the co-founder and past-President of UNGLOBE (the advocacy group for gay and lesbian employees of the United Nations). Ms. Landsberg-Lewis has written: BRINGING EQUALITY HOME: IMPLEMENTING THE CONVENTION ON THE ELIMINATION OF ALL FORMS OF DISCRIMINATION AGAINST WOMEN (1999).

Janice Love is Associate Professor in the Department of Government and International Studies at the University of South Carolina. She received a Ph.D. (1983) and an M.A. (1977) from Ohio State University, and a B.A. (1975) from Eckerd College. She teaches World Politics, Global Political Economy, and Southern Africa. Complementing her academic life is Professor Love's service with the World Council of Churches, an international ecumenical organization. In 1995, she led the WCC Delegation to the U.N. Fourth World Conference on Women in Beijing and the NGO Forum in Huarou. Dr. Love's books include THE U.S. ANTI-APARTHEID MOVEMENT: LOCAL ACTIVISM IN GLOBAL POLITICS (1985); and SOUTHERN AFRICA IN WORLD POLITICS (Westview, forthcoming)

Ann Elizabeth Mayer is Associate Professor of Legal Studies, Department of Legal Studies, at the Wharton School of the University of Pennsylvania. Professor Mayer received a Ph.D. (1978) from the University of Michigan (1978). She received a Certificate in Islamic and Comparative Law (1977) from the University of London; a J.D. (1975) from the University of Pennsylvania; and an M.A. (1966) and B.A. (1964) from the University of Michigan. Professor Mayer has been a Visiting Lecturer at Yale Law School (1997); Adjunct Professor at the Center for Arab Studies (Georgetown University) (1992); and Visiting Associate Professor at Princeton

University (1983). She has been a member of the Editorial Review Board of HUMAN RIGHTS QUARTERLY, 1994 and Consultant for the Lawyers Committee on Human Rights. Her publications include *Religious Reservations to CEDAW: What Do They Really Mean, in* RELIGIOUS FUNDAMENTALISMS AND THE HUMAN RIGHTS OF WOMEN (Courtney W. Howland ed., 1999); ISLAM AND HUMAN RIGHTS: TRADITION AND POLITICS 3RD EDITION (1999); *Rhetorical Strategies and Official Policies on Women's Rights: The Merits and Drawbacks of the New World Hypocrisy, in* FAITH AND FREEDOM: WOMEN'S HUMAN RIGHTS IN THE MUSLIM WORLD (Mahnaz Afkhami ed., 1995).

Julie Mertus is Professor at Ohio Northern University and serves as a consultant with the Women's Commission for Refugee Women and Children and the Humanitarianism & War Project at Brown University. She received a J.D. (1988) from Yale Law School and a B.S. (1985) from Cornell University in Industrial Labor Relations. Professor Mertus is a MacArthur Foundation Fellow and a Harvard Law School Human Rights Fellow. She is a former Counsel to Human Rights Watch, a Fulbright Scholar, and has been a Visiting Professor at Emory University School of Law. She has written extensively on racism and conflict, human rights, refugees and gender issues. Her most recent book is: KOSOVO: HOW MYTHS AND TRUTHS STARTED A WAR (1999).

Barbara Roblin Mirza is an Associate at Skadden Arps Slate Meagher & Flom LLP. She received an LL.B. from the University of Toronto and a B.A. (Honours) from Queen's University in Kingston, Ontario, Canada. She has served as Co-Editor-in-Chief of the UNIVERSITY OF TORONTO FACULTY OF LAW REVIEW, and is currently an attorney specializing in employee benefits and executive compensation.

Margaret Owen is a barrister called to the bar at Middle Temple, holding also an M.A. Cantab. from Cambridge and a Diploma in Social Administration from the London School of Economics. Following the NGO Forum at Huarou (1985), she founded the international EMPOWERING WIDOWS IN DEVELOPMENT (EWD), an umbrella organization to promote the status of widows, particularly through grass-roots organizations of widows in developing countries, focusing on South Asia and Africa, and involving armed conflict and ethnic cleansing. *See* EWD's *"Widows' Law File" (on its web site: www.oneworld.org/empoweringwidows)*. Ms. Owen was an immigration and refugee lawyer before heading International Planned Parenthood Federation's (IPPF) Law and Policy Division, then moving to RIPA International as Director of Training in Judicial Administration. She is currently consultant to the U.N. Division for the Advancement for Women (UNDAW) on widowhood and human rights; consultant to the UK Department for International Development, the British Council, and has consulted for ILO, WHO, and the Commonwealth Secretariat. Her books include: A WORLD OF WIDOWS (1996); THE WORLD OF THE WIDOW (1994); WIDOWS BANDING TOGETHER (1995); YOUNG WIDOWS, TRAGIC VOICES (1998); and WIDOWHOOD IN 10 COUNTRIES IN SOUTH ASIA AND AFRICA (Oak Foundation, forthcoming).

Karen Parker is an attorney and chief delegate at the United Nations for Humanitarian Law Project/International Educational Development (HLP/IED). Her practice is mainly before the United Nations. She received a J.D. (Honors, 1983) from the University of

San Francisco School of Law; a Diplôme (cum laude, 1982) in International and Comparative Law of Human Rights, Institut International des Droits de l'Homme (Strasbourg); an M.A. (1972) in Comparative Literature; and a B.A. (1971) in Italian Literature from San Francisco State University. She has initiated into the U.N. human rights forums issues on disability (with Disabled Peoples' International); the right to a safe environment (with Sierra Club Legal Defense Fund); weaponry and humanitarian and human rights law (with HLP/IED); sanctions and humanitarian and human rights law (with HLP/IED). She advocates for compensation for Japan's World War II victims. Publications include ARMED CONFLICT IN THE WORLD TODAY: A COUNTRY BY COUNTRY REVIEW (annually since 1994) (Parliamentary Human Rights Group, UK, English) (published also in Arabic, French in preparation by UNESCO Chair, University of Oran, with Anne Heindel); SANCTIONS IN LIGHT OF HUMAN RIGHTS AND HUMANITARIAN LAW (HLP/IED, 1998); MEMORANDUM ON WEAPONS AND THE LAWS AND CUSTOMS OF WAR (HLP/IED, 1997); *Law and Facts of the Tamil Nations Struggle, in* PEACE WITH JUSTICE (Australian Human Rights Foundation, 1996).

Jane Lee Saber is a Lecturer at the University of Ottawa (1999–2000) and a Ph.D. Business Candidate, Marketing, Business Law and Economics at the University of Alberta, where she received a Masters of Law degree (1996). She was awarded a Bachelor of Law (1990) from Queens University and a Bachelor of Commerce (1987) from the University of Alberta. In 1999 she was a co-presenter on "Gender Differences in Search for and Weighting of Communal Information in Choice Tasks" for the Society for Judgement and Decision Making; in 1998 she presented "Gender Differences in Information Processing" at the University of Alberta Ph.D. Research Fair; in November 1998 she presented "Women and the International Monetary Fund" at the American Branch of the International Bar Association; and in 1996 she presented "Poverty, Economics, and The Environment" at the University of Alberta: Interdisciplinary Conference on the Environment. From 1991–1994 Ms. Saber was an Associate Lawyer with Braithwaite, Boyle and Associates. She taught and managed a Suzuki Music School from 1991 through 1997.

Martha L. Schweitz is Professor of International Law, Seinan Gakuin University, Fukuoka, Japan, where she teaches international organizations, international human rights, international economic law, and a seminar on Women and the Law in a Comparative Perspective. She received a J.D. from New York University School of Law (1981); and a B.A. from Stanford University (1976). Her writing has focused on civil society participation in intergovernmental institutions, as well as gender equality and the application of Bahá'i principles to law and social development. She has worked closely with MOVE, the City Women's Center in Kitakyushu, Japan, in its activities to understand and publicize the Convention on the Elimination of All Forms of Discrimination Against Women. Professor Schweitz's books include: CODES OF CONDUCT FOR PARTNERSHIP IN GOVERNANCE: TEXTS AND COMMENTARIES (with co-editor Tatsuro Kunugi), (provisional version, 1999, published by United Nations University, Tokyo, final version forthcoming, 2000).

Patricia Viseur Sellers is a Legal Advisor on Gender-Related Crimes in the Prosecutor's Office of the U.N. International Tribunal for the Former Yugoslavia.. She received a J.D. from the University of Pennsylvania and a B.A. from Rutgers College, Rutgers University. Ms. Sellers' activities include working with the American Society of International Law, the International Prosecutor's Association, the National Conference of Black Lawyers, and the American Bar Association. Her publications include: *The Context of Sexual Violence: Sexual Violence as Violations of International Humanitarian Law, in* SUBSTANTIVE AND PROCEDURAL ASPECTS OF INTERNATIONAL CRIMINAL LAW (Gabrielle Kirk McDonald & Olivia Swaak-Goldman eds., 2000); *The Culture Value of Sexual Violence, in* PROCEEDINGS OF THE 93RD ANNUAL MEETING OF ASIL (1999); and *International Prosecution of Sexual Violence* (with Kaoru Okuizummi) in 7 TRANSNATIONAL LAW & CONTEMPORARY PROBLEMS 1 (1997).

Kathryn Sikkink is Professor of Political Science at the University of Minnesota. She received a Ph.D. and M.A. in Political Science from Columbia University, and a B.A. from the University of Minnesota. Her book ACTIVISTS BEYOND BORDERS: ADVOCACY NETWORKS IN INTERNATIONAL POLITICS (coauthored with Margaret Keck) was awarded the Grawemeyer Award for Ideas Improving World Order (1999) and the International Studies Association's Chadwick Alger Award for best work in the area of international organization (1999). Other publications include IDEAS AND INSTITUTIONS: DEVELOPMENTALISM IN BRAZIL AND ARGENTINA (on development policy in Latin America); and THE POWER OF HUMAN RIGHTS: INTERNATIONAL NORMS AND DOMESTIC CHANGE (co-edited with Thomas Risse and Stephen Ropp). Current research focuses on the influence of international law on domestic politics, human rights, transnational social movements and networks, and on the role of norms in international relations and foreign policy. With the support of the Twentieth Century Fund, she is currently researching the evolution and effectiveness of human rights policies, especially in Latin America. She is a member of the editorial board of INTERNATIONAL ORGANIZATION, the International Advisory Board of INTERNATIONAL STUDIES REVIEW, and the Social Science Research Council/MacArthur Foundation Committee on International Peace and Security.

Adrien Katherine Wing is Professor of Law at the University of Iowa College of Law and teaches Human Rights, Comparative Law, Critical Race Theory, and Constitutional Law. She holds a J.D. from Stanford Law School, an M.A. in African Studies from the University of California at Los Angeles; and an A.B. from Princeton University. She has served on the boards of the Iowa Peace Institute, National Conference of Black Lawyers, Transafrica Forum Scholars Council, International Third World Legal Studies Association, and the American Association of International Law. She was an advisor to the African National Congress Constitutional Committee in the years leading up to the adoption of the first democratic constitution in South Africa. She also served as consultant to the Palestinian Legislative Council with respect to the drafting of the Basic Law in 1996. Author of over fifty publications, she is editor of GLOBAL CRITICAL RACE FEMINISM: AN INTERNATIONAL READER (2000) and CRITICAL RACE FEMINISM: A READER (1997).

ACKNOWLEDGMENTS

This final volume comes after some five years of perseverance from the authors and publishers of these three volumes, all of whom are owed immeasurable appreciation for their professionalism and commitment. Thanks also to the War Crimes Research Office at the Washington College of Law, American University, which was my base during the Fall of 1999 and Winter of 2000, and to the wonderful team at Transnational Publishers, especially Heike Fenton and Maria Angelini. I also extend gratitude to my family, whose support gives me security to venture out into the world with confidence. Finally, I am indebted to new female friends gained during the editing of this last volume, and for the enrichment these friendships added to my personal and professional life, most particularly thanks to Sharelle Aitchison, Julia Baly, Sandy Coliver, Peggy Hicks, Meg Penrose, Jan Perlin, Heather Ryan, Leila Sadat, Gabriela Salgado Gomez, and Martina Vandenberg.

Kelly D. Askin

I wish to acknowledge the authors and our publisher, who have joined Kelly Askin and myself on this long journey to produce these volumes and without whose talents and perseverance in doing their part while under the heavy pressures that so many of them face, we would not have been able to do so. It is a source of great appreciation and gratitude to them and to Kelly Askin that these volumes have attracted the attention and contribution of the very many extremely talented and dedicated women and men who have joined us. My special thanks to Kelly Askin, Heike Fenton, and Maria Angelini.

Dorean M. Koenig

INTRODUCTION

Patricia Viseur Sellers

The third and final volume of *Women and International Human Rights Law* is a worthy component of the trilogy. In less than a decade, scholarly and activist analysis of the human rights of woman has exerted a strong gravitational pull on the normative theory of human rights. Rights protecting reproductive freedom, education of the girl-child, and economic access, together with the negation of the patriarchal divide of rights into the public and private sphere that in practice served to omit women's human rights from the home, during civil emergencies, and in periods of armed conflict, mark strikingly that distinct shift. The chapters in this volume, together with the contributions of the first two volumes, refute any dismissal of women's rights as separate from or inconsequential to human rights. In contemporary society, in order to be legitimate any succeeding theory of rights must first amass the particles germane to female lives.

International humanitarian law and international criminal law have been affected profoundly by the shift. In adjudicating crimes committed during the recent Balkan conflicts and Rwandan genocide, the Chambers of the *ad hoc* International Criminal Tribunals for the former Yugoslavia and for Rwanda have applied a woman-roused human rights perspective to provisions of their respective Statutes. In the *Prosecutor v. Delalić et al.*, a Trial Chamber of the Yugoslavia Tribunal held that the repeated rapes of two female Bosnian Serb detainees, at the hands of their Bosnian Muslim guards, constituted the crime of torture.[1] To support the ruling, the Trial Chamber cited *Fernando and Raquel Mejia* from the Inter-American Commission on Human Rights and *Aydin v. Turkey* from the European Court of Human Rights. The Trial Chamber analogized that the findings of two regional courts that rape violates proscriptions of torture under human rights law were legally relevant to evaluating evidence of rapes in the Bosnian detention camp.

Another woman-centered perspective was contained in the *Delalić* torture jurisprudence. To impose criminal responsibility upon the perpetrator or other person responsible for the crime, torture requires proof beyond a reasonable doubt as to a particular prohibited purpose behind its commission. Purpose can be proven by the perpetrator's motive to elicit information or a confession, or his or her desire to coerce, intimidate, or discriminate against the victim or a third person. The *Delalić* Trial Chamber reasoned that Serbian female detainees had been sexually tortured *inter alia* because they were women, and that this constituted a form of discrimination. As such,

---

1. Prosecutor v. Zejnil Delalić et al., Judgement, IT–96–21–T, Nov. 16, 1998.

Delalić, again gathering the particles of women's lives, held gender discrimination as an actionable purpose behind the crime of torture.

In contrast, forty years prior, the *Cypress v. Turkey* decision of the European Court of Human Rights found that the rapes and enforced prostitution of Greek Cypriot women and girls (victims were between the ages of twelve and seventy-one), did not rise to the level of torture, as it merely constituted inhumane treatment. The case has been cited uncritically, if not approvingly. No consternation was voiced, in part, because at least the Court had examined sexual violence committed against women and girls and had opined that such acts were determinative of a human rights violation. Currently, similar evidence of crimes of rape and sexual slavery are being prosecuted before the Yugoslavia Tribunal in the *Kunarac* case as international crimes of torture, rape, and enslavement.

In the Rwandan Tribunal, the *Akayesu* judgement concluded (for the first time in history) that rape and other forms of sexual violence, including forced nudity, were proscribed by the crime of genocide, and further that the acts were crimes against humanity.[2] The Trial Chamber explicitly noted the physical and mental destruction inherent in these crimes, and implicitly acknowledged that this harm was caused not only to the victims, but also to other members of the targeted group.

Another intractable position for women-centered rights is found in the Yugoslavia Tribunal's *Prosecutor v. Furundzija* judgement.[3] The judgement held that a Bosnian Muslim woman who was forced to submit to oral sex was thus raped. The Trial Chamber synthesized human rights law and humanitarian law:

> The Trial Chamber holds that the forced penetration of the mouth by the male sexual organ constitutes a most humiliating and degrading attack upon human dignity. The essence of the whole corpus of international humanitarian law as well as human rights law lies in the protection of human dignity of every person, whatever his or her gender. The general principle of respect for human dignity is the basic underpinning and indeed the very *raison d'etre* of international humanitarian law and human rights law; indeed in modern times it has become of such paramount importance as to permeate the whole body of international law. This principle is intended to shield human beings from outrages on their personal dignity, whether such outrages are carried out by unlawfully attacking the body or by humiliating and debasing the honour, self-respect or the mental well being of a person. It is consonant with this principle that such an extremely serious sexual outrage as forced oral penetration should be classified as rape.[4]

According to *Furundzija*, a woman's sexual integrity is a fundamental particle of the human right to physical and mental well-being. Women's rights are transported from the shoals of the river into the current, and deemed as inseparable from human rights as wetness is to international waters. But as frequently cautioned by feminist legal theory, such legal mainstreaming is not without peril.

---

2. Prosecutor v. Jean-Paul Akayesu, Judgement, ICTR–96–4–T, Sept. 2, 1998.

3. Prosecutor v. Anto Furundzija, Judgement, IT–95–17/1–T, Dec. 10, 1998.

4. *Furundzija, id.* at para. 183.

Furundzija is enticing, but aren't congratulations, for a corrective alignment of a woman's right to sexual integrity during armed conflict, a pittance when most human rights of women are yet to be identified and identified rights are still not safeguarded? Doesn't *Furundzija*, even in victory, confine or consign emerging woman-centered human rights to re-interpret rather than truly reconstitute norms of human rights? Aren't international law's paramount doctrinal values, *jus cogens* and custom, still gendered? Authors in this and the previous volumes grapple with and raise similar poignant questions even when recounting much recent progress in securing for women their fundamental human rights.

A further danger arises to counter the pull of gravity and to impede the full emergence of either a reformed system or a new system of human rights. The danger is more functional than theoretical. The problem is the "S" word: sensitivity. Governments and civil society are required, in the more progressive societies, to incorporate the hard-won recognition of women's human rights into their laws. And we are so grateful when individuals who implement women's gains are gender sensitive. At first glance, it seems a reasonable stance, but is it truly conducive to enforcement of rights? We persevere to secure woman's rights, yet paradoxically hold individual implementers to a low standard. I speak in particular about state delegates or NGO delegates who are "as sensitive as the next guy" yet who yield to inarticulate rationales that continue to exclude women's human rights in treaties or their subsequent interpretation. I refer to governments that only voice compliance or that deign mere recognition of women's human rights, but not enforcement of those rights, as sufficient compliance. I extend these remarks to international, national, and local civil servants, academics, educational admission committees, police officers, national guards and military personnel, international peace-keeping forces, housing authority officers, loan officers, corporate officers, foundation programme officers, human resource personnel, and others who are not sensitized to gender issues yet make decisions that affect women's lives enormously. Or who are "sensitized" to or aware of gender discrimination, yet fail to competently apply or enforce gender norms.

Sensitivity is not enough. Sensitivity haltingly facilitates compliance of women's human rights by allowing implementers to feel good about what they should be required to do anyway in order to perform their duties in a competent manner. Sensitivity at its worst provides a fluid, lethal escape. Even rationales of "I'm sensitive but my colleagues are not" undermine emerging norms. If women's human rights in international law are to truly be secured, professional *competence* must become the standard. Professional competence in the area of human rights of all people—not just those pertaining to or most affecting men—should be pegged to hiring, promotions, appointments, granting of awards or funds, and annual performance reviews. The higher positioned the individual responsible for putting into operation human rights, the more proven competence he or she must demonstrate. Gender-sensitivity should no longer be merely applauded. Competence should be the minimum standard, not sensitivity or awareness.

Neither states nor individuals, irrespective of their status, are asked to be "sensitive" to torture under humanitarian or human rights law; rather their compliance is mandatory, absolute and non-derogable. *Delalić* held that women can be subjected to sexual torture based on gender discrimination. *Akayesu* determined that sexual violence constitutes genocide as a means of destroying a protected group by causing serious bodily or mental harm to members of the group. *Furundzija* situates one aspect of women's human rights in the central core of human rights and humanitarian law. Similar conduct must also be competently adjudicated and women's human rights competently enforced. We must demand competence and insist on enforcement of the human rights of all people, including the female half of the population marginalized during the first twenty centuries.

Volume 3 of *Women and International Human Rights Law* quantifies other changes and presages the potential of women's human rights. In the first section of this volume, personal rights affecting women are reviewed particularly as these rights affect reproductive rights and freedoms, and women's sexuality; it also considers religious and cultural restrictions on such rights as choice of clothing, freedom to drive, and the right to travel unattended and without permission. The second section looks at specific groups, including children, refugees, widows, the disabled, and armed conflict situations, and details the human rights norms and instruments specifically applicable to the women and children falling within these groups. It also reviews the most common human rights violations of members of these groups, and suggests means of redress.

The third section of this volume focuses on particular issues affecting women of specific religious groups, especially Muslim women, Bahá'i women, and Christian women, and considers how these issues comport with legal and social standards. The fourth section of this volume is geared toward detailing both general and particular issues affecting women in various regions of the world, such as in particular regions of the Middle East, the South Pacific, and Eastern Europe, and describing applicable norms and prescriptions. It also addresses more specific human rights issues of women in particular regions, such as Palestinian women, Ukranian women, and Aboriginal women in Australia.

The fifth section of this volume covers a broad range of issues affecting women's human rights. It considers the impact of the IMF to women, analogizes the historical practice of footbinding of Chinese women to current practices of female genital alterations, reviews property rights of women in South East Asia, discusses the impact of NGOs on the women's movement, and reviews laws and practices of the U.S. government vis-à-vis women.

In the final analysis, enormous progress has been made in recent years to protect and promote women's human rights. The legal, practical, strategic, and informational tools provided in these volumes will undoubtedly be a weapon in this struggle toward full enjoyment of the human rights of all women. These advances have started to permeate the legal norms and institutional policy. But many of these rights are merely words, acknowledged but not respected. We must no longer be satisfied with mere awareness of or sensitivity to women's human rights. We must not even ask whether women's rights are part of human rights; rather individual actors must achieve and maintain competence in the field, given the shift in gravity.

Section I

Personal Rights of Women

ABORTION AND REPRODUCTIVE HEALTH: MAKING INTERNATIONAL LAW MORE RESPONSIVE TO WOMEN'S NEEDS

Maja Kirilova Eriksson

INTRODUCTION

Human rights issues of significance to women have tended to be marginalized and consequently inadequately addressed by the international community. Only recently are women's rights beginning to obtain their long-deserved attention and to become firmly entrenched within, and incorporated into, the international human rights agenda. The slow historical process from disregard to the recognition of women's rights as an integral part of the international human rights movement culminated in the 1993 U.N. World Conference on Human Rights, held in Vienna.[1]

The Vienna Declaration and Programme of Action proclaims: "The human rights of women and the girl child are an inalienable, integral and indivisible part of universal human rights."[2] Nevertheless, several areas crucial for women's status and health, including those related to women's reproductive rights, remain unsettled. Although abortion occurs in every country in the world, and has been practiced for ages throughout the world within or outside the boundaries of law, the issue of abortion remains a sensitive and divisive issue in the realm of human rights law. The extensive discussion of abortion rights in the scholarly literature, and the many controversies which arose in regard to the formulation of declarations regarding abortion, which were supposed to be adopted in the final documents of recent major U.N. thematic conferences held in Vienna,[3] Cairo,[4] and

---

1.   Some 150,000 signatures from 115 countries were submitted by women's groups in 1992 to the United Nations requesting women's rights to be included on the agenda of the Vienna Conference. *See* Gale Binion, *Human Rights: A Feminist Perspective*, 17 Hum. Rts. Q. 515, 524 (1995).

2.   Vienna Declaration, Programme of Action, U.N. Doc. A/CONF.157/21 (1993), at § 18 (hereinafter Vienna Declaration).

3.   The World Conference on Human Rights, held in Vienna in 1993, was the second such U.N. human rights conference. The first International Conference on Human Rights was held in Teheran in 1968. For a review of the achievements of the Vienna Conference, see generally, Donna J. Sullivan, *Women's Human Rights and the 1993 World Conference on Human Rights*, 88 Am. J. Int'l L. 152–67 (1994).

4.   The International Conference on Population and Development (hereinafter ICPD and/or Cairo Conference) was held in Cairo in Sept. 1994. It was the third global conference on popula-

Beijing,[5] witness the difficulties of resolving these complex legal questions in a manner acceptable to the majority of the international community. At the same time, the outcome of the above-mentioned conferences suggests that there is a quest for decriminalization of abortion. Depending upon what position one takes on the issue of induced abortion, the human rights invoked may relate to the right to life of the unborn child or to a woman's rights to control her own body and to reproductive freedom.

This author has earlier taken the position that even though the unborn child is guaranteed a certain degree of protection under international law, it does not possess a legal right to life *per se*.[6] The main focus in this chapter is to analyze whether we can persuasively uphold the argument that access to legal abortion and/or safe abortion services might be considered essential elements of human rights already in force, such as the right to family planning and the right to found a family.

Human rights law has a dynamic character. The content of established international law can be broadened through evolving interpretation,[7] which can stimulate the evolution of laws in ways that enhance the protection of human rights. Women can consequently use the international human rights framework to advance their legal rights and avoid the preservation of a human rights parallel universe for women. Furthermore, provisions of law are not isolated enclaves in a legal system, but instead have an internal coherence, which promotes a system of law. Systematic interpreta-

---

tion issues held under the auspices of the United Nations. Every ten years the U.N. hosts a conference on world population. The first conference was held in Bucharest in 1974, and the second in Mexico City in 1984.

5.   The Fourth World Conference on Women (FWCW) met in Beijing, China, Sept. 4–15, 1995. It was one of the largest global conferences ever organized. Delegations from 181 U.N. member states and eight observers were in attendance. The first conference on women's issues was held in 1975 in Mexico City, the second in 1980 in Copenhagen, and the third in Nairobi in 1985. For a survey on these conferences and their achievements, see THE UNITED NATIONS, THE UNITED NATIONS AND THE ADVANCEMENT OF WOMEN 1945–1995, 33–59 (1995).

6.   Maja K. Eriksson, *The Legal Position of the Unborn Child in International Law*, 36 GYIL 86–130 (1993).

7.   Most of the contemporary human rights norms do not adequately take account of the reality of women's lives. There are a number of major historical barriers to inclusive definitions of human rights, which incorporate the specific needs and concerns of women. Among the barriers mentioned is that international lawmaking institutions have been, and to great extent continue to be, dominated by men, which is reflected in the content and emphasis in international human rights law. The mainstream human rights bodies have in consequence exempted themselves from responsibility in the area of women's rights by the creation of specialized bodies for addressing women's issues. *See* Charlotte Bunch, *Women's Rights as Human Rights: Towards a Re-Vision of Human Rights*, 12 HUM. RTS. Q. 486 (1990); Hilary Charlesworth, *What Are Women's International Human Rights?, in* HUMAN RIGHTS OF WOMEN 58 (Rebecca J. Cook ed., 1994); Charlotte Bunch, *Transforming Human Rights from a Feminist Perspective, in* WOMEN'S RIGHTS HUMAN RIGHTS: INTERNATIONAL FEMINIST PERSPECTIVES 13 (Julie Peters & Andrea Wolper eds., 1995) [hereinafter WOMEN'S RIGHTS HUMAN RIGHTS]; Elisabeth Friedman, *Women's Human Rights: The Emergence of a Movement, in* WOMEN'S RIGHTS HUMAN RIGHTS, *id.* at 20; and Hilary Charlesworth, *Human Rights as Men's Rights, in* WOMEN'S RIGHTS HUMAN RIGHTS, *id.* at 104.

tion can provide clarity on the content of provisions by including related provisions in the evaluation. A holistic approach to family planning provisions based on their interpretation through linkage with other human rights and consideration in the light of recent developments, such as the final documents of international conferences,[8] might propel such an extensive reading.

This chapter will address several legal aspects of abortion in the context of the international community's overall goal to advance the status of women. It is generally accepted that equality between the sexes is central to international human rights law. Physical and mental well-being is the very basis for enhancing equality, as it is vital for the empowerment of women. In other words, this chapter will employ a teleological method of interpretation of the relevant provisions, that is, a method that seeks to realize the objects and purposes of a treaty. A rigid and static approach to the interpretation of human rights treaties would be in conflict with the terms of the Women's Convention, the Vienna Convention on the Law of Treaties, and the modern approach which international bodies take to human rights instruments. Thus, a teleological interpretation of the provisions of the Women's Convention will result in an application encompassing more aspects of reproductive freedom and covering the protection of the individual from any danger of unequal treatment either in public or in private relations.

In regard to reproductive freedom, the unqualified use of several terms of importance is rather confusing. There is, for example, an ongoing debate as to whether abortion is encompassed in the terms "family planning" (which lends itself to differing interpretations), "regulation of fertility," or in both. If abortion is included in the first right, it is protected by human rights law provisions. This will not be the case if abortion is only an element of the term "regulation of fertility," since it has not yet been incorporated as a human right in any judicially binding international instrument. Many of the documents presented in preparation for the Cairo Conference, and thereafter, focus on women's reproductive health. So how does this ambiguous term, "women's reproductive health," relate to the two terms mentioned above? Could this term resolve the criticism of the validity of the rights discourse[9] expressed by many women living in developing countries? Since these terms may be subject to diverse interpretation, the first part of this chapter will be devoted to some terminological clarifications.

As part of the binding legal code of human rights, family planning is recognized by all people, regardless of religion, politics, or ideology. The study undertaken in

---

8. Several experts from CEDAW stressed the need for Bolivia to implement the decisions of the Cairo Conference during the review of its country report under the Women's Convention on Jan. 17, 1995. Press Release WOM/787, CEDAW 263rd mtg. (1995).

9. Rebecca J. Cook, *Women's International Human Rights Law: The Way Forward*, 15 Hum. Rts. Q. 232 (1993). One important issue under debate within feminist jurisprudence is the question of whether rights analysis is useful at all. Arguments have been put forward that the dichotomous and adversarial character of "rights" might be alien to women's experiences. Binion, *supra* note 1, at 525. The traditional sources of international law have been identified as another obstacle for the effective remedy of women's issues. Hilary Charlesworth et al., *Feminist Approaches to International Law*, 85 Am. J. Int'l L. 613 (1991).

this chapter envisages that women's rights are universal, meaning that there cannot be great disparity in their applicability and application in different parts of the world. In other words, it would be incompatible with the principle of the universality of human rights that, depending on where a woman lives, her abortion experiences may "range from a safe, legal method for terminating an unwanted pregnancy to a dangerous, painful and criminal act."[10]

THE CONCEPT OF WOMEN'S REPRODUCTIVE HEALTH

The Vienna Programme of Action includes specific references to women's right to health and to safe maternity. But even though the document recognizes the importance of women's enjoyment of the "highest standard of physical and mental health throughout their life span,"[11] the term reproductive health was not even mentioned during the negotiation process. Though the Vienna Declaration and Programme of Action succeeds in recognizing women's human rights in armed conflicts and in condemning gender-based violence against women, it does not cover the issue of reproductive rights. The Vienna Declaration affirms "a woman's right to accessible and adequate health care and the widest range of family planning services."[12]

The Emergence of Reproductive Health as a Subject of Regulation

Reproductive health is a new subject in the area of international human rights law, and the process of articulating it more clearly is a continuing one. In recent years, governments have slowly but steadily given increased priority to reproductive health, thereby motivating a shift from demographic concerns to concerns about meeting the needs of individuals for reproductive health information and services. In this environment, a new approach towards family planning has evolved: it is now considered in relation to other methods of fertility regulation and women's health, and thus has been incorporated within the concept of women's "reproductive health." This explains to a certain extent why "reproductive health" has been confused with the provisions of family planning and maternal and child health services only, or rather the provisions of family planning and child health services exclusively. The concept is, however, much more complex. While acknowledging the importance of family planning, the broad approach to reproductive health is "not limited to child-bearing ages alone" and further recognizes that reproductive health concerns both men and women.[13]

---

10. KAJSA SUNDSTRÖM, ABORTION—A REPRODUCTIVE HEALTH ISSUE 3 (1993).

11. Vienna Declaration, *supra* note 2.

12. *Id.* at para. 41.

13. U.N. Doc. E/CN.9/1996/2, §4 (1996).

The Cairo Programme of Action

The ICPD Programme of Action was the first universal governmental document[14] to set out the term "reproductive health."[15] There, reproductive health is outlined as a state of complete physical, mental, and social well-being—not merely the absence of diseases or infirmity—in all matters relating to the reproductive system and to its functions and processes. The attainment of reproductive health enables women to go safely through pregnancy and childbirth, which provides couples with the best chance of having a healthy infant. Implicit in that definition, therefore, is that people have the capability of reproducing (prevention and appropriate treatment of infertility) and the freedom to decide if, when, and how often to do so. It would, moreover, include prevention from or cure for an unwanted and mistimed pregnancy. In other words, comprehensive health care must also comprise access to safe abortion services.[16]

Nevertheless, reproductive health services are still generally regarded as a backup to contraceptive failure and a necessary service to avoid complications resulting from unsafe abortions.[17] By considering abortion in the context of health, the controversy

14. In preparation for the Cairo Conference, women's health advocates representing women's networks in Asia, Africa, Latin America, the Caribbean, the United States, and Western Europe adopted a "Women's Declaration on Population Policies," focussing on women's reproductive health. Important aspects of sexual and reproductive health, pregnancy, delivery, and postpartum care were included, as well as "safe and legal abortion services; safe choices among contraceptive methods including barrier methods, information, prevention and treatment of STDs, AIDS, infertility, and other gynaecological problems, child care services; and policies to support men's parenting and household responsibilities." The text of the declaration has been reprinted by the International Women's Health Coalition, New York, Mar. 4, 1993. On the regional level, when adopting the guiding principles for women in development by the OECD/DAC in 1988, a connection between primary health care and family planning was made in § 363 in a way that the latter has been considered an important component of the first. *See* OECD, DAC PRINCIPLES FOR EFFECTIVE AID, DEVELOPMENT ASSISTANCE MANUAL 97 (1992).

15. Programme of Action of the United Nations International Conference on Population and Development (ICPD), U.N. Doc. A/CONF.171/13, Oct. 18, 1994, in Chapter VII, § 7.2 [hereinafter ICPD or Cairo Programme of Action]. (Chapter IV, Gender Equality, Equity and Empowerment of Women, of the Cairo Programme of Action, is reprinted in CENTER FOR THE STUDY OF HUMAN RIGHTS, COLUMBIA UNIVERSITY, WOMEN AND HUMAN RIGHTS: THE BASIC DOCUMENTS 94 (1996) [hereinafter BASIC DOCUMENTS].) *See also* U.N. Doc. E/CN.6/1995/3/Add.3, § 43 (1995).

16. Para. 7.6 of the Cairo Programme of Action, *supra* note 15, states that "All countries should strive to make accessible . . . [a]bortion as specified in paragraph 8.25, including prevention of abortion and the management of the consequences of abortion."

17. Unsafe abortion is defined as a procedure for terminating an unwanted pregnancy either by persons lacking the necessary skills or in an environment lacking the minimal standards or both. WHO, The Prevention and Management of Unsafe Abortion, Report of a Technical Working Group, Geneva, WHO/MSM/92.5. This definition was used in the ICPD's Programme of Action. The Cairo Conference is the first U.N. conference to address unsafe abortion as a major public health concern. However, the first review of the implementation of the Nairobi strategies revealed in 1990 that induced abortions, which were numerous and for the most part carried out clandestinely and adolescent pregnancies, and which were on the rise, constitute a threat to the lives of women and girls. U.N. Doc. E/CN.6/1990/5, § 152 (1990).

on the legal status of abortion was somewhat side-stepped in Cairo. The focus instead turned to the serious health effects[18] of unsafe abortions and aimed to promote the development of safe abortion services to all who need them. It could be concluded that the intention of the drafters of this document was to remove existing legal restrictions, making abortion legal,[19] so that all abortions are safe. In support of this assertion, the U.S. representative at the Cairo Conference, Mr. Timothy E. Wirth, stated: "[O]ur position . . . is that abortion should be safe, legal and rare."[20]

Such an interpretation of the term "reproductive health" has been highly contested by conservatives, who consider it "a euphemism for contraception, sterilization and abortion."[21] The Holy See stated in its reservation to the final document of the ICPD that, on the basis of the preamble, it assumed that the document does not affirm a new internationally recognized right to abortion.[22] Section 1.13 of the preamble does indeed declare that the Cairo Conference "does not create any new international human rights." On the other hand, this author asserts that because of major shifts in attitudes among the world's people and leaders in regard to reproductive health and family planning, "a new comprehensive concept of reproductive health,[23] including family planning and sexual health, as defined in the present Programme of Action" has emerged (section 1.8).

---

18.   In addition, "pregnancies that come too early, too late, too often and too closely spaced intervals in women's reproductive lives" may also affect women's health adversely. Rebecca J. Cook, *Human Rights in Relation to Women's Health*, WHO, 13 (1994).

19.   Argentina underlined that "reproductive health" may not be interpreted as restricting the right to life or abrogating the condemnation of abortion as a method of birth control or an instrument of population policy. U.N. Doc. A/CONF.177/20, 157 (1995). The representative of the Dominican Republic said that the mentioned term does not include abortion or interruption of pregnancy as a component and that the reservation applies to all regional and international agreements referring to these concepts. *Id*. at 159. Peru interpreted "reproductive health" as not including abortion "as a method of birth control or family planning." *Id*. at 171. Venezuela accepts the term solely if it does not include abortion or voluntary interruption of pregnancy. *Id*. at 176.

   The Holy See reaffirmed reservations expressed at the conclusion of the Cairo Conference concerning the interpretation of "reproductive health" and "reproductive rights" in the sense that it does not consider abortion or abortion services to be a dimension of them. *Id*. at 163. Kuwait expressed the view that § 94 contravenes the Islamic Law (Shari'a). *Id*. at 167.

20.   *Id. See also* STANLEY P. JOHNSON, WORLD POPULATION: TURNING THE TIDE, THREE DECADES OF PROGRESS 361 (1994).

21.   Rebecca J. Cook, *The Elimination of Sexual Apartheid: Prospects for the Fourth World Conference on Women*, 5 ISSUE PAPERS ON WORLD CONFERENCES 19 (ASIL 1995).

22.   Cairo Programme of Action, *supra* note 15, at 147.

23.   The Holy See does support the concept of "reproductive health" as a "holistic concept for the promotion of the health of men and women." However, it underlined the necessity to continue work on a more precise definition. Cairo Programme of Action, *supra* note 15, at 147. The Nordic countries consider the ICPD's final document as "breakthrough language concerning reproductive health and reproductive rights—a concept based on the recognition of the basic right of all couples and individuals to decide freely and responsibly the number, spacing and timing of their children and to have means and information to do so." U.N., Information Centre for the Nordic Countries, POP/572, 1 (1994).

The Beijing Declaration and Platform of Action

After the Cairo Conference, the term "reproductive health" has been increasingly used in the international debate. It has been repeated and re-utilized in several regional[24] and global documents, such as the Beijing Declaration, where family planning and regulation of fertility are discussed in the context of reproductive health.[25] However, the wording related to reproductive health in the Beijing Declaration was bracketed[26] before the conference and a few states submitted written statements as to the interpretation of the term "reproductive health." Despite this minor opposition, there is ample support for the concept of reproductive health as described above and as strongly asserted in the final documents of two major U.N. conferences (Cairo and Beijing). While these documents are not legally binding in terms of contemporary international law, they do bear great normative authority since they have been endorsed by the vast majority of governments. Moreover, the Beijing Platform of Action emerged from a preparatory process more participatory and inclusive than any other in history.

It becomes apparent from the above that the phrase "reproductive health" is broader than the rather narrow concepts of fertility regulation and family planning. The phrase includes elements of both,[27] but it expands beyond controlling births. It

---

24. *See* § 30 of the Arab Plan of Action for the Advancement of Women to the Year 2000, adopted in Nov. 1994 in Amman, Jordan. U.N. Doc. E/CN.6/1995/5/Add.5 (1995).

25. U.N. Doc. A/CONF.177/20, § 94 (1995). *See, in addition*, Principle 4 of the Jakarta Declaration for the Advancement of Women in Asia and the Pacific (ESCAP 1994), adopted in preparation for the Beijing Conference. *See* THE RAOUL WALLENBERG INSTITUTE HUMAN RIGHTS GUIDE, A THEMATIC GUIDE TO DOCUMENTS ON THE HUMAN RIGHTS OF WOMEN 50 (Gudmundur Alfredsson & Katarina Tomaševski eds., 1995) [hereinafter THEMATIC GUIDE]. Comprehensive reproductive health, including fertility regulation, has been identified as a major area for U.N. policy, program, and project intervention in the recently proposed "System-Wide Medium-Term Plan for the Advancement of Women 1996–2001," Report of the Secretary-General, Follow-Up to the Fourth World Conference on Women, U.N. Doc. E/CN.6/1996/CRP.2, § 69 (1996).

26. Despite the consensus reached in 1994, by comparison, 35 percent (438 sets of brackets) of the language of the draft Platform for Action at Beijing remained in square brackets, compared to 15 percent of the language, which was in brackets before the Cairo Conference. Much of the bracketed language in the Beijing draft document was the same language, which was agreed upon at Cairo, and almost all of it was related to women's reproductive rights and reproductive health. One of the presented theories is that the opposition was not well organized at Cairo, and it realized afterward the impact that the Cairo document will have on the international community, especially on the lives of women. K. McDonald, *Reproductive Rights Under Attack*, 2 IPPF, CHALLENGES, WOMEN'S HEALTH, WOMEN'S RIGHTS 15 (1995). On the other hand, some key players appeared to shift from earlier positions and signalled early their desire to reach agreement. For example, the Holy See assured that it did not wish to unravel any existing agreements and was not seeking to re-open debates from Cairo.

27. *See* KATARINA TOMAŠEVSKI, HUMAN RIGHTS IN POPULATION POLICIES (1994); *Reproductive Experiences and Needs of Thai Women: Where Has Development Taken Us?, in* POWER AND DECISION, THE SOCIAL CONTROL OF REPRODUCTION 36 (H.H. Pyne, Gita Sen, & Rachel C. Snow eds., 1994) [hereinafter POWER AND DECISION]; *see also* U.N. Doc. CEDAW/C/1996/3/Add.1, § 13 (1995); U.N. Doc. E/CN.6/1996/CRP.2, §§ 69, 84 (1996); U.N. Doc. E/CN.9/1996/2, § 38 (1996); U.N. Doc. E/CN.9/1996/5, § 14 (1996). Access to safe and legal abortion was encouraged by

incorporates an awareness of the social and cultural context in which reproduction and childbearing is carried out and puts it in the context of gender equality and the empowerment of women. As some authors have put it, the notion of reproductive health "is shaped not only by medical conditions, but also by social forces and power relationships that range from the level of the family to that of international institutions."[28] In other words, this term recognizes that to address reproductive health issues successfully, we must address both the reproductive rights of women *and* men and the social behavior and cultural practices that affect reproductive health outcomes. Reproductive rights provide the framework for achieving reproductive health. Again, access to family planning information and services is an important instrument for their exercise.[29] Reproductive health incorporates all of the previous approaches to reproduction and health, focusing only on specific aspects of them, in a comprehensive manner.

THE CONCEPT "REGULATION OF FERTILITY"

The Cairo Programme of Action

Several other definitions of vague terms were discussed and developed at the Cairo Conference. "Regulation of fertility" was one of those newly introduced concepts. Here, it was included for the first time in a universal document, the ICPD Programme of Action.[30] The World Health Organization (WHO), as well as the majority of participants at the ICPD, took the position that "fertility regulation" should be considered as a wider concept than "family planning," since it emphasizes the prevention or the termination of unwanted pregnancy,[31] that is, abortion *per se.* Thus, the term was understood to connote a means of achieving a decline in fertility. At the same time it was also contended that abortion should be used for fertility control when no other means was available. The initial section 7.1 (section 7.2 in the ICPD's final document), proclaimed the right of men and women to obtain access to methods of fertility regulation. More than seventy delegates commented on this paragraph and debated at length the replacement of the phrase "fertility regulation"

members of CEDAW in their discussions on several aspects of women's health issues on Feb. 3, 1995. Press Release WOM/809, 284th Meeting (1995). A couple of years earlier, members of CEDAW asked representatives of Nicaragua's government about the prospects of adopting a general policy for reproductive health in the country and whether the government was carrying out any program to deal with the problem of abortion, which was referred to as the third most common cause of death among mothers. GA Res. A/48/38, § 391,73 (1993).

28. C. M. Obermeyer, *Religious Doctrine, State Ideology and Reproductive Options in Islam, in* POWER AND DECISION, *supra* note 27, at 59.

29. U.N. Doc. A/CONF.171/4, § 110 (1994).

30. Within the NGO community, the Guidelines for the Distribution and Use of Fertility Regulation Methods (WEMOS) of 1989 frequently refers to this phrase as including "hormonal methods, barrier methods such as condoms and diaphragms, natural methods, sterilization and safe abortion services." THEMATIC GUIDE, *supra* note 25, at 249.

31. Abortion is the common, and at times it has been the primary, means for dealing with unwanted pregnancies.

with "family planning." Many delegations assumed that the previous term clearly included abortion.

The WHO proposed that the working definition of "fertility regulation" to be used during the course of the Cairo Conference should include "family planning, delayed childbearing, the use of contraception, treatment of infertility, interruption of unwanted pregnancies and breastfeeding."[32] This definition was presented by WHO in response to a comment on Nigeria's interpretation of "family planning" as viewed as a broader term than "fertility regulation." Thus, family planning today is regarded by the international community as a less comprehensive phrase than fertility regulation and as separate from abortion. This view was subsequently reflected in paragraph 8.25 of the ICPD final document, which emphasizes that: "[i]n no case should abortion be promoted as a method of family planning." This provision was embodied thereafter in section 106(k) of the Beijing Declaration and Platform for Action. Much support for such an interpretation may be found in the reactions (e.g., arguments put forward for the replacement of "fertility regulation" with "family planning") of certain states' representatives to the Cairo Conference, generally known for their strong opposition to abortion. The countries were the Philippines, the Dominican Republic, Libya, Honduras, Argentina, Peru, the Holy See, Malta, and Malaysia. When it became obvious that the phrase "regulation of fertility" would be retained in the final text, reservations were orally expressed by the representatives of El Salvador, Nicaragua,[33] and Honduras.[34] The representative of the latter state based his argument on the Declaration of the Fifteenth Summit of Central American Presidents, adopted in Costa Rica on August 20, 1994.[35] The delegates of Paraguay made it clear that the inclusion of the term "interruption of pregnancy," as part of the concept of regulation of fertility, made the concept unacceptable to their country.[36] The Dominican Republic entered

---

32.   6 EARTH NEGOTIATIONS BULLETIN 2 (Sept. 7, 1994). The term "fertility regulation" has recently been used in similar wording, comprising, among other things, family planning in the Report of the Secretary-General presented to the CSW 14th session, U.N. Doc. E/CN.6/1996/CRP.2, § 85 (1996).

33.   The representative of Nicaragua explained that "[w]e accept the concepts of 'family planning,' 'sexual health,' 'reproductive health,' 'reproductive rights' and 'sexual rights' expressing an explicit reservation on these terms and any others when they include 'abortion' or 'termination of pregnancy' as a component. Abortion and termination of pregnancy can under no circumstances be regarded as a method of regulating fertility or a means of population control." Cairo Programme of Action, *supra* note 15, at 139.

34.   It reads as follows: "As far as reproductive rights, reproductive health and family planning are concerned, we wish to express reservations, as the other Latin American countries have done: we should never include abortion within these concepts, either as service or as a method of regulating fertility." *Id*. at 137. Malta's reservation is very similar.

35.   The statement reads as follows: "As a consequence of this, one accepts the concepts of 'family planning,' 'sexual health,' 'reproductive health,' 'regulation of fertility,' 'reproductive rights,' and 'sexual rights' as long as these terms do not include 'abortion' or 'termination of pregnancy,' because Honduras does not accept these as arbitrary actions; nor do we accept them as a way of controlling fertility or regulating the population." Cairo Programme of Action, *supra* note 15, at 138.

36.   *Id*. at 140. Argentina submitted a written statement to the Programme of Action asserting:

a reservation on the same subject, expressing its understanding that the terms "reproductive health," "reproductive rights," "regulation of fertility," and "other terms" exclude the concept of abortion. According to the statement, this reservation should also apply to all regional and international agreements referring to these concepts.[37]

The delegations of these states were, however, not persuasive enough, inasmuch as "fertility regulation" was not cut out in the text. In the final version of the ICPD Programme of Action "fertility regulation" was altered only to "regulation of fertility" (section 7.2), which does not change its content.

Therefore, the inclusion of this provision, implying that safe and legal abortion has been recognized as a means of fertility control and that individuals shall have access to it, is but one of the hard-won gains of the Cairo Conference. Several of the above-mentioned states maintained the same reservations to the Beijing Declaration and Platform for Action.[38] Argentina, for example, declared that it continues to condemn abortion as a method of birth control. The Holy See emphasized that the language used in the Beijing Declaration in regard to fertility regulation "could be interpreted as including societal endorsement of abortion."[39] As a matter of fact, a recent U.N. report declared that abortion is indeed one of "the most widely used" methods of fertility regulation.[40]

The Impact of the Final Documents

The differing viewpoints among states on fertility regulation are indeed of practical importance, since it is still to a great extent up to the individual state to imple-

"The Argentine Republic cannot accept the inclusion of abortion in the concept of 'reproductive health' either as a service or as a method of regulating fertility." *Id*. at 142.

37.   *Id*. at 143, 148. Regarding the terms "sexual health," "reproductive rights" and "reproductive health," the Holy See did not consider abortion or access to abortion as a dimension of these terms. Moreover, a concern has been expressed that the final document, as opposed to the earlier documents of the Bucharest and Mexico City Conferences, recognizes abortion as a dimension of population policy and, indeed of primary health care, i.e., abortion services belong within primary health care as a method of choice.

With reference to the terms "contraception," "family planning," and "regulation of fertility," the Holy See did not change its well-known position concerning those family planning methods which the Catholic Church considers morally unacceptable.

The delegation of Ecuador entered a similar reservation on the meaning of the above concepts pointing out that as they are used within the context of the ICPD's Programme of Action, "could involve abortion." The government of Guatemala made a reservation on the whole Chapter VII and relevant parts of Chapter VIII with the motivation that the GA's mandate to the Cairo Conference did not extend to the creation and formulation of rights such as, e.g., "reproductive rights," "reproductive health" and "fertility regulation." *Id*. at 144–45.

38.   *See* Beijing Declaration, U.N. Doc. A/CONF.177/20, 157–76, Oct. 17, 1995. Para. 17 of the Beijing Declaration stipulates that states are convinced that "the explicit recognition and reaffirmation of the right of all women to control all aspects of their health, in particular their own fertility, is basic to their empowerment."

39.   *Id*. at 162.

40.   U.N. Doc. E/CN.9/1996/2, § 54 (1996).

ment the ICPD Programme of Action and the Beijing Platform for Action.[41] The impact of both world conferences will be measured by the concrete actions undertaken by states and international organizations to fulfill the goals of the final documents. Thus, persistent objection influences the applicability of customary international law but not its very existence. In other words, if one country's government refuses to recognize a rule as one of law, nothing prevents other states from accepting it *inter se*. (This is not to imply that the right to fertility regulation has acquired the status of a customary rule.) Nevertheless, it should be mentioned that the Main Committee of the ICPD succeeded in adopting *ad referendum* the entire Programme of Action on September 12, 1994. The above-mentioned reservations were noted. Entering reservations to selected portions of the document (as well as to the Beijing final document) essentially provided dissenters with a mechanism for accepting the document even though they found portions disagreeable. The large number of reservations on health and sexuality reflects abiding political and cultural differences that the Cairo and Beijing Conferences exposed, but could not realistically be expected to resolve. Both conferences adopted, without a vote, the final documents on September 13, 1994, and September 15, 1995, respectively. The documents were later endorsed by the U.N. General Assembly.[42]

It seems that there is agreement in contemporary international law that GA resolutions may generate new legal norms or trends. Thus, declarations resulting from the mentioned conferences are considered "signposts of the direction in which international human rights law is developing."[43] Their significance consists of their influ-

---

41.   Implementation and follow-up did not receive sufficient attention in Cairo. Since governments will have to determine what is relevant for their countries it may lead to uneven levels of implementation. However, Chapter XVI calls on the GA to organize a regular review of the implementation of the Programme of Action. The Beijing Conference was a conference of international as well as of national commitment and action. The inclusion of requirement of commitments from governments and the international community was an Australian initiative from 1994, which was supported by major NGOs. It implies an invitation to participating states to use their plenary speeches to announce undertakings consistent with the objectives of the Platform for Action. Many delegations did so. This is but a push-forward implementation as well as a rallying point for new and existing constituencies around the world. The Commitments furthermore increase the NGOs ability to propose specific examples of initiatives to their governments when defining national strategies for implementation. As noted in § 297 of the Platform for Action, states should, as soon as possible and preferably by the end of 1995, begin to develop strategies to implement it. They should be developed together with plans of actions preferably by the end of 1996. With regard to the reference to commitments in § 293 (commitments on national level), states have the primary responsibility for implementing the Platform of Action. Notably, only the U.S. delegation declared explicitly that it would not interpret the Platform of Action as legally binding.

42.   *See* GA Res. 49/128, Dec. 19, 1994; GA Res. 50/124, Dec. 20, 1995; and GA Res. 50/203, Feb. 23, 1996. Paras. 4 and 6 of the latter resolution establish that governments have the primary responsibility for implementing the Platform for Action and that commitment at the highest level is essential for its implementation. Moreover, governments should as soon as possible, and not later than 1996, develop comprehensive implementation strategies or plans of action. The GA, ECOSOC, and the CSW will play the primary role in the overall policy-making and follow-up of the documents.

43.   Cook, *supra* note 18, at 29.

ence on the international conduct and domestic law of states and participants in the conferences, but not parties to the Women's Convention and other human rights treaties of relevance.[44] Thus, the conferences must not be viewed in isolation. Their results will have far-reaching impact on future meetings within the U.N., such as subsequent conferences linked to similar issues. Consequently, new, weaker language cannot be permitted.

More importantly, these documents should be taken into consideration by the international supervisory bodies charged with interpreting the relevant rules in existing human rights treaties.[45] The potential of the final documents produced by previous U.N. conferences has been underexploited.

Fertility Regulation in Relation to Family Planning

Abortion should be distinguished generally from family planning, since it cannot be considered as a desirable method of family planning. Rather, family planning should be viewed as a means to reduce the number of abortions.[46] In other words, this

---

44.   At the CSW's session in Mar. 1996, which was aimed at general discussion on the follow-up of the Beijing Conference, the representative of Brazil stated that the Platform for Action had inspired innovative policies within the country. For that purpose special measures were included in the Programme for the Integral Assistance to Women's Health.

45.   Para. 36 of GA Res. 50/202 (1996) requests CEDAW within its mandate, to take into account the Platform for Action, when considering reports submitted by states parties. CEDAW recommended, after the consideration of Ukraine's report under the Women's Convention, that the government should in subsequent reports provide information on the status of implementation of commitments made at the Beijing Conference. U.N. Doc. CEDAW/C/SR.302, § 25 (1996).

46.   MAJA K. ERIKSSON, THE RIGHT TO MARRY AND TO FOUND A FAMILY 141 (1990). Some of the recommendations (e.g., Recommendation No. 18, subpara. (e)) adopted by the International Conference on Population, held in Mexico City in 1984, include a passage that refers to the need to help women avoid abortion and stating that abortion should in no case be promoted as a method of family planning. The referred recommendation was the subject of a heated debate and was one of the few instances where a governmental delegation requested a separate statement; while joining the consensus reached on that issue Sweden wanted to express its understanding that one step toward the elimination of illegal abortion was the provision of access to abortions that were legal and safe. U.N. Doc. A/CONF.171/4, § 124. The U.S. delegation denounced abortion and declared that it would not give aid to family-planning programs that offered it. In consequence, the final document spurned abortion. In the years following the Mexico City conference, the WHO took the official position that abortion must not be considered a method of family planning. In 1990, at an international conference in Tbilisi, representatives of WHO declared that the organization does not hold any position with regard to abortion, but is, of course, concerned with its health implications. At the same conference, the UNFPA stated that it does not regard abortion as means of family planning. SUNDSTRÖM, *supra* note 10, at 65. Another example is Sweden, which takes a liberal approach to the abortion issue. The *travaux préparatoires* to the Swedish Abortion Act (SOU 1983:31,15), emphasize that abortion is to be regarded as an emergency measure and only a part of the wider issue of fertility regulation. It is not to be made a deliberate alternative to family planning by preventive methods. In addition, the Regional Programme of Action for the Women of Latin America and the Caribbean, 1995–2001, presented at Beijing, noted that while governments of that region recognized the importance of abortion as a public health problem, abortion should in no case be considered a method of family planning. U.N. Doc. E/CN.6/1995/5/Add.3, § 88 (1995).

chapter subscribes to the view that the term "family planning" is narrower in scope than "fertility regulation" or "regulation of fertility." At the same time it must be acknowledged that some scholars, such as Kajsa Sundström, have shown preference for the term "family planning," giving it a broader meaning, i.e., understanding it to cover methods, services, and programs for "fertility regulation." According to Sundström, the main methods for fertility regulation include: social control of sexuality and reproduction; contraception; and abortion, safe or unsafe.[47] Sundström consequently considers abortion to be a method for fertility regulation, and since she regards "family planning" to contain "fertility regulation," both concepts include abortion within them.

Some support for this position may be found in statements made in international fora. At the third U.N. Conference on Women in 1985, representatives for the organization Third World Women demanded their right to "all methods of family planning, including abortion as a back-up method, and to choose ourselves what is best for us in our situation." The Committee on Elimination of All Forms of Discrimination Against Women (CEDAW), in its report to the same conference, included information on abortion laws under the title "Family Planning and Counseling." Many states indicated that abortion was legal and free of charge. Only two states—the Philippines and Rwanda—reported that abortion was forbidden.[48]

CEDAW seemed, on one occasion, to have subsumed regulation of fertility into family planning. Its General Recommendation No. 21 (section 23), dealing with Article 16(1)(e) of the Women's Convention (family planning issues), contains the following illustrative clarification: "Where there are freely available appropriate measures for the voluntary regulation of fertility," the health of the members of the family improves. Still, an argument can be made that the examples above provide an insufficient basis for a conclusion that CEDAW interprets the above provision of the Women's Convention as comprising a right to fertility regulation including abortion. The view in this chapter is that such a right is not yet part of the convention and therefore not *lex lata*, that is, enforceable as part of international human rights law.

FAMILY PLANNING

The Emergence of the Concept

The acceptance of the concept "family planning" as a basic human right is relatively recent. The term was introduced after World War II, and it was first used in a U.N. resolution adopted in 1965 by the U.N. Commission on the Status of Women (CSW), which stated that married couples should have access to all relevant information concerning family planning. It was, however, not until the first U.N. Conference

---

47.   SUNDSTRÖM, *supra* note 10, at 17.

48.   U.N. Doc. A/CONF.116/13, § 249 (1985). Also in the legal doctrine are references to abortion as a family planning method. *See, e.g.*, Elba Mercado, *Consequences of Unwanted Pregnancies in Bolivia: An Overview, in* UNWANTED PREGNANCIES AND PUBLIC POLICY: AN INTERNATIONAL PERSPECTIVE 179 (Hector Correa ed., 1994) [hereinafter UNWANTED PREGNANCIES]; A. B. Marcelino, *Combating Opposition in the Philippines*, 1 IPPF 30 (1996).

on Human Rights held in Teheran in 1968 that matters of procreation and family planning were specifically linked to human rights. Article 16 of the Proclamation adopted at that conference states: "Parents have a basic right to determine freely and responsibly the number and spacing of their children."[49]

The right to family planning has been restated repeatedly and further elaborated in international documents since 1968. Family planning was defined as a human right in Article 14(f) of the concluding document adopted at the World Population Conference in Bucharest in 1974, which provides: "All couples and individuals have the basic right to decide freely and responsibly the number and spacing of their children and to have the information, education and means to do so." The right of couples and individuals to decide the number, spacing, and timing of their children was endorsed in sections 7.2. and 7.3 of the IPCD final document and in section 95 of the Beijing Declaration. In addition, section 223 of the Beijing Platform for Action establishes that reproductive rights "rest on the recognition of the basic right of all couples and individuals to decide freely and responsibly the number, spacing and timing of their children."

Even though the importance of these documents should not be underestimated, because resolutions of the GA may have a crucial role in the norm-creating process of international law, of greater significance for our discussion is whether and, if so, how the principles reflected in them are specified in treaty law. The first universal treaty to proclaim family planning as a human right was the Convention on Elimination of All Forms of Discrimination Against Women.[50] This treaty creates legal obligations for the majority of states in the world and requires them to take all appropriate measures to ensure that women have the same right as men to decide "freely and responsibly on the number and spacing of their children and to have means to enable them to exercise this right."

The Substantive Content of the Right to Family Planning

CEDAW's Interpretation

The ultimate challenge for the twenty-first century is to give greater substance to existing human rights. The lack of specific content in the term "family planning" in international law documents, as well as other factors, seems to have given rise to some skepticism as to whether there *is* a universally accepted right to family planning. While doubt may be justified with regard to the vague character of the norm, it should not be exaggerated. There exists considerable difficulty in reaching consensus worldwide on its exact content. But abstract or ambiguous wording does not necessarily deprive a rule of its legal character. Such a rule permits a scale several degrees of implementation.

Therefore, it might be wise to explore whether there are any statements by international quasijudicial organs which might cast some light on the content of the right

---

49.   Final Act of the International Conference on Human Rights, Teheran, Apr. 22–May 13, 1968, U.N. Doc. A/CONF.32/41 (1968).

50.   GA Res. 34/180, Dec. 18, 1979, art. 16(1)(e).

mentioned above. Thus far, only CEDAW, established under the Women's Convention, adopted Recommendation No. 21 on equality in marriage and in family relations.[51] The Committee reached the conclusion that the responsibilities of bearing and raising children both affect women's personal development and impose inequitable workloads on them. The impact on their physical and mental health carries with it the right to decide the number and spacing of their children. Therefore, women have the right to decide the number and spacing of their children.[52] This is a rather new approach to the Convention's requirements. Moreover, recommendations create criteria by which the Committee may measure the state party's compliance with the provisions of the Convention.

The main components of the right to "family planning," though the term is not explicitly mentioned, have been identified by CEDAW as guaranteed sex education and the availability of family planning services, namely, the availability of safe and reliable methods of contraception. The Committee further emphasized the importance of freely available and appropriate measures for the voluntary regulation of fertility to the health and well-being of all members of the family. In other words, family planning and regulation of fertility are considered interrelated issues in the broader context of health. And yet, the avoidance of the term "family planning" indicates that it has become outmoded or too restrictive and that it ought to be replaced by the more comprehensive umbrella term "reproductive health." Since this is the only existing authoritative interpretation of the right to family planning, it will serve as the basis for our analysis.

Religious Resistance to an Expansive Interpretation

Religious norms are often invoked against an extensive interpretation of the right to family planning. Whereas in certain religions, like Judaism, the fetus is not seen as a person before birth and "abortion is not only permissible, but indeed required if the life of the mother is threatened by continuing the pregnancy,"[53] Catholicism and Islam limit the application of human rights in this area.[54] Ensuring compatibility of religious norms with human rights law has become one of the main controversies in the area of reproductive health.

---

51.   CEDAW, General Recommendation No. 21 on equality in marriage and in family relations, U.N. Doc. E/CN.6/1993/CRP.2 (1993); *see also* CSW, Res. 38/6, Gender equality in population programmes, Commission on the Status of Women, U.N. Doc. E/CN.6/1994/14, 18–21 (1994).

52.   General Recommendation No. 21, *id*. at § 21.

53.   S. Jenkins, *Abortion Rights, Poor Women, and Religious Diversity, in* FROM ABORTION TO REPRODUCTIVE FREEDOM, TRANSFORMING A MOVEMENT 152 (Marlene Gerber Fried ed., 1990).

54.   Human rights documents emanating from Islamic organizations follow an approach different in many respects from human rights standards. In the preamble of the Cairo Declaration on Human Rights in Islam, adopted by the 19th Islamic Conference of Foreign Ministers in 1990, it is explained that for reasons that lie in the nature of the Shari'a "the highest Islamic state and religious law," Islamic nations in parts of the African, Asian, and Arab land masses, have difficulties bringing internationally recognized human rights standards into conformity with Shari'a. Article

The attitude of the Catholic Church toward the right to family planning is expressed in the 1983 Charter of the Rights of the Family, which states:

> The spouses have an inalienable right to found a family and to decide on the spacing of births and the number of children to be born, taking into full consideration their duties towards themselves, their children already born, the family and society, in a just hierarchy of values and in accordance with the objective moral order which excludes recourse to contraception, sterilization and abortion.

The Church has not moderated its view on this subject. On the contrary, at a meeting between Mrs. N. Sadik (the Secretary-General of the Cairo Conference) and Pope John Paul II on March 18, 1994, the Pope repeated his previous opposition to modern contraception, sterilization, and abortion. The Pope said that anything other than periodic abstinence in marriage is contrary to the moral law inscribed in the human heart and is an assault on the sacredness of life. The Vatican became one of the most active participants at the Cairo Conference, objecting to all references to abortion and contraceptives in the final document and specifically declaring abortion evil. In the Pope's "Letter to Women,"[55] the Church reaf-

---

7 stipulates that "both the foetus and the mother must be protected and accorded special care." Access to family planing is obviously not envisaged as a right. U.N. Doc. A/45/421/5/21797, 199. *See also* INTERNATIONAL HUMAN RIGHTS, DOCUMENTS AND INTRODUCTORY NOTES 324–327 (Felix Ermacora et al., 1993). The above-cited text is much more restrictive compared with Article XIX (a) of the Universal Islamic Declaration of Human Rights adopted earlier by the Islamic Council on Sept. 19, 1981, which envisages every person's right to marry and to found a family. *See* discussion in Tomaševski, *supra* note 25, at 54. The Arab Plan of Action for the Advancement of Women to the Year 2000, which was presented at Beijing states that governments in the region should review all legislation related to women in order to bring it into line with the rapidly changing conditions in Arab societies in such a way that it does not contradict original religious values. U.N. Doc. E/CN.6/1995/5/Add.5, § 25 (1995).

At the same time, we cannot ignore the fact that Muslim countries have very different policies regarding reproductive rights even though political leaders pretend to act in conformity with Islam. The Qur'an is not explicit on the issue of family planning. Interpretations vary depending on whether the community is Shia or Sunni. Thus, Islam like other religions is relatively open, containing the seeds of both liberal and conservative approaches to reproduction. There are four main schools of thought within the Sunni sect. The following examples may be illustrative of the diversity in the Muslim world. Tunisia offers both contraception and free abortion services to women, whereas women in Bangladesh may be subjected to forcible contraception and abortion. Turkey has enforced a law that permits abortion for a variety of reasons during the first 120 days of pregnancy. Most Islamic schools of law agree that abortion is acceptable before ensoulment and unacceptable afterwards. The Malikis school of jurisprudence considers that ensoulment happens near the end of the first trimester. Therefore, abortions are allowed until that point. However, in Oman, Yemen, and the United Arab Emirates, abortion is prohibited unless it is necessary to save the woman's life. *See* World Abortion Policies 1994, U.N. Department for Economic and Social Information and Policy Analysis, Population Division (1994).

55.   The Vatican text of the papal letter to women issued in preparation for the Beijing Conference is dated June 29, 1195, and was released on July 10, 1995, at the Vatican. The prolific Pope John Paul II has published ten papal letters. Also in the Encyclical *"Evangelium Vitae"*— *"Gospel of Life,"* signed on Mar. 30, 1995, he addresses the issue of abortion, which, according to him is but an encroaching "culture of death" that threatens human dignity. He pleads for the creation of an alternative "culture of life" that respects human dignity from conception to the moment of death. Of relevance on this issue is also his latest book, CROSSING THE THRESHOLD OF

firmed its teaching[56] on this matter. On November 14, 1995, the representative of the Holy See, presenting a report before the Committee on the Rights of the Child,[57] reaffirmed that the Charter of the Rights of the Family, makes "explicit the sense of the right to life in all dimensions, being the protection and absolute respect of the life of a child from its conception, excluding abortion." In other words, the Charter reflects the Catholic position of ethics.

Peru's delegation to the Cairo Conference made an oral interpretative statement regarding the concept of "family planning" in connection with its approval of the final document, which was thereafter attached to it as an interpretative reservation of section 8.25.[58] The Constitution's recognition of the fundamental role of the family and the role of parents in responsible parenthood and maternity was emphasized, implying everyone's right to use the methods of family planning they wish, "provided that it does not place life at risk." In this context, the Peruvian government referred to Article 2 of its Constitution, "which accords to everyone the right to life from the moment of conception; abortion is rightly classified as a crime in the Criminal Code of Peru, with the sole exception of therapeutic abortion." In addition, the reservation implies a restrictive interpretation of the terms "reproductive health," "reproductive rights," and "fertility regulation;" that is, a total exclusion of abortion on the previous grounds. It should be noted, however, that the majority of Catholic countries did not make any reservations at all. Countries such as Bolivia, Colombia, and El Salvador expressly supported the Beijing Declaration; and Spain even expressed special satisfaction with the chapter on reproductive health.

Provisions embracing the right to family planning intend to guarantee freedom of reproductive choice and access to services for family planning. The first element of the core of the human right to family planning,[59] as well as the right to found a family[60] as

---

HOPE (1994), especially at 12, 65, 204–11. Much of his message is concerned with human rights. In this regard, the Pope emphasizes that "the legalization of the termination of pregnancy is none other than the authorization given to an adult, with the approval of an established law, to take the lives of children yet unborn and thus incapable of defending themselves." *Id.* at 205. For the Pope, abortion is a form of "murder," a violation of the Biblical commandment against killing. But abortion is not mentioned as such in the Bible.

56.   The Church's teaching authority is binding on all Roman Catholics, and it is irreversible. At the same time many Catholic theologians and Church members believe that when there is doubt (e.g., there is no definitive doctrine on personhood), there should be a freedom to make an individual choice. Jenkins, *supra* note 53, at 152.

57.   U.N. Doc. CRC/C/3/Add.27, (1994). Article 4(a) of the Charter says that "Abortion is a direct violation of the fundamental right to life of the human being."

58.   Cairo Programme of Action, *supra* note 15, at 150.

59.   For a more detailed analysis of the scope of the right, *see* Maja K. Eriksson, *Family Planning as a Human Rights Issue, in* PARENTHOOD IN MODERN SOCIETY 191 (John Eekelaar & Petar Sarcevic eds., 1993); and UNFPA and Human Rights Issues, U.N. Doc. A/CONF.157/PC/61/Add.9, 4 (1993).

60.   This right is stipulated in art. 23 of the International Covenant on Civil and Political Rights, art. 12 of the European Convention, and art. 17(2) of the American Convention on Human Rights. The African Convention does not contain a corresponding provision. The right to found a family

established in international law concerns the right to "informed consent," i.e., making knowledge available and respecting the views of the individual. Personal autonomy is consequently highly valued. The rights are not at all identical, although they partially overlap.

FREEDOM OF CHOICE—A BASIC VALUE

Access to Information—Shaping Universal Consensus

Information and education are crucial aspects of reproductive health—they make informed consent and responsible, voluntary, deliberate choices about childbearing and parenting possible. Knowledge of human rights is indispensable to their exercise, since its absence allows easy violation. In other words, possessing information on the rights that women should enjoy enables women to demand them, giving them power and providing them with the ability to master their own destiny. The need to provide women with information on their rights is crucial. Access to family planning information and quality family planning services was specifically referred to as a "long recognized basic right for all individuals"[61] at the 1993 World Conference on Human Rights in Vienna.[62] Mentioned among the main objectives of the Cairo Programme of Action is the improvement of the "quality of family planning advice, information, education, communication, counseling and services," as described in section 7.14(d).

The Beijing Platform for Action section107(e) makes counseling and accessible information, especially on sexuality and reproduction, an obligation of governments. In addition, one of the U.N.'s critical areas of concern in the Medium-Term Plan for the Advancement of Women (1996–2001) is reproductive health. This part of the document is based on a pragmatic and participatory approach with the goal of providing individuals and couples with access to information and services to prevent unwanted pregnancies "that are too early, too closely spaced or too late."[63]

A woman's right to information and counseling on family planning is explicitly expressed in Articles 14(b) and 16(e) of the Women's Convention. In addition, several universal[64] as well as regional treaties[65] on human rights contain specific provi-

---

is more narrowly formulated than the right to family planning in the relevant U.N. resolutions and the Women's Convention. Thus, the latter presupposes not only the right to decide on the size of the family but, in addition, demands access to education for the parents to be in order to prepare them for the responsibilities of a planned parenthood. Otherwise, as Cook has observed, the right to found a family does not merely comprise a right to conceive, gestate and deliver a child. It also involves "the right of a woman positively to plan, time, and space the births of children to maximize their health and her own." Cook, *supra* note 18, at 38.

61. The right to information on family planning was stipulated in art. 14(f) of the World Population Plan of Action, 1974 and in Recommendation No. 25 of the World Population Plan of Action, 1984.

62. U.N. Doc. A/CONF.157/6, 3 (1993).

63. U.N. Doc. E/CN.6/1996/CRP.2, § 71 (1996).

64. *See, e.g.,* art. 19(1) of the ICCPR.

65. *See, e.g.,* art. 10(1) of the European Convention and art. 13(1) of the American Convention on Human Rights.

sions regarding freedom of information as a right on its own merits (the right to seek, receive, and impart information).

So what relevance do these provisions have to the abortion issue? To begin, only when women have full knowledge about the ramifications of accepting or rejecting a particular health option, including explanations of medical procedures and their risks and benefits, can decisions be informed and voluntary. Thus, states must not prohibit the dissemination of information on methods of fertility regulation, including information about abortion facilities. Such a prohibition infringes on the freedom of expression set out in the human rights conventions, which includes among other things the freedom to receive information. Denying women this right will seriously limit their ability to control their health or their educational and social status.

The recent inclusion of reproductive health as a central component of women's human rights would infer an emerging right to non-directive counseling to enable women to make free, fully informed choices among various methods of fertility regulation as well as other health services. The international texts of a declarative nature also mean that women require information and services not just during the reproductive ages, but prior to and after these stages as well.

The European Experience

The case law of the European judicial organs indicates that the right to receive information should be paramount. At the same time, the right can be limited (as is the case in other conventions) on the grounds of public health and morals. The European Court of Human Rights has often allowed a wide margin of appreciation; that is, national authorities are given the power to decide that when a common European understanding is lacking, certain information should not be imparted because of its immoral nature. This has, however, not prevented the Court from scrutinizing and materially reconsidering decisions made by domestic authorities in a particular case, as in Ireland's justification of the prohibition on giving information on abortion on moral grounds.[66]

Despite the absence of any uniform policy in the member states of the European Communities and the Council of Europe today, in view of the cases we will refer to, there is a clear tendency towards a greater uniformity of domestic legislation, even on controversial issues.[67] The existing case law of the European Court of Justice (ECJ) and the European Court of Human Rights concerns companies engaged in non-directive counseling of pregnant women in Ireland, including advice on obtaining abortions in clinics in the United Kingdom. The Supreme Court of Ireland has found such activities unconstitutional. The international judicial organs are of the view, however,

---

66. *Open Door Counselling Ltd and Dublin Well Women v. Ireland*, ECHR Judgement of Mar. 24, 1992, ser. A, No. 246–A, § 61 (1992).

67. To achieve a harmonization of the legal regimes of the twelve members of the EC as far as the abortion issue is concerned is not an easy task. On one side, there are countries with a very conservative approach to abortion, like Belgium and Germany, and on the other there are societies with more liberal views, such as the Netherlands and the United Kingdom.

that a ban on information about lawful services related to pregnancy and its termination constitutes a violation of the freedom of expression. Ireland is the only member country of the European Community (EC) and the Council of Europe opposing legalized abortion. The EC law and the European Convention on Human Rights might, by decree, introduce legal abortion services in Ireland, since the binding decisions of the European organs do promote a uniform interpretation and application of the human rights guaranteed. This has not been the case yet.

Two cases against Ireland highlight some of the relevant aspects of the freedom of information in relation to family planning. Both decisions uphold the right of women to receive information about abortion services without interference by the public authorities. The first of these was the *Grogan* case,[68] decided by the Court of Justice of the European Communities. During the 1980s many women with unwanted pregnancies went to England for abortions, and information concerning abortion was available from a number of organizations. The Society for the Protection of Unborn Children (SPUC), an entity devoted to prevention of the decriminalization of abortion, sought to restrain the activities of two such organizations. Therefore, it filed suit against a number of persons who published an annual guidebook with names and addresses of abortion clinics in the United Kingdom. The SPUC claimed that any publication of the aforementioned information was contrary to Article 40.3.3 of the Irish Constitution, which guaranteed the right to life of the unborn child from the moment of conception. It also argued that Irish common and criminal law made it an offense to procure or attempt to procure an abortion, to administer an abortion or to assist in an abortion by supplying any noxious thing or instrument.[69]

The ECJ, after considering the merits of the case, delivered its judgement on October 4, 1991, holding that termination of pregnancy in the member states of the EC constituted a medical activity covered by the term (cross-border) "service" within the meaning of Article 60 of the Treaty of the European Economic Community. The Court rejected SPUC's argument that abortion is immoral and that it cannot come within the definition of service. In SPUC's view, since the information initiative was not connected with the promotion of the economic interests of abortion clinics, the factual situation had to be seen merely as a manifestation of the freedom of expression. Implicitly, the ECJ acknowledged a corollary right to receive information about a service. At the same time, the emphasis was put on the drafter's intention to guarantee the fundamental freedom of consumers to receive services found in a member state. Therefore, persons receiving medical treatment are recipients of services and are entitled to the benefit of the free movement provisions of the EEC treaty. Nevertheless, a right for women residing in Ireland can be derived from the right in European Community law—the provisions of the Treaty of Rome dealing with the freedom to provide services—to obtain information as to abortion clinics in member states of the European Community and even to use the medical facilities in those

---

68.   Case C–159/90, *The Society for the Protection of Unborn Children Ireland Ltd v. S. Grogan and Others*, 3 CMLR 849 (1991).

69.   For instance, *see* Sections 58 and 59 of the Offences against Person Act 1861.

countries in order to terminate their pregnancies. This interpretation of the Community law is very much consistent with the meaning of Article 10 of the European Convention on Human Rights,[70] according to which everyone has the right "to receive and to impart information and ideas without interference by public authority and regardless of frontiers."

The European Convention is an important source of the European Community legal order, even though the ECJ does not consider itself bound by the European Convention. Of particular note as regards the case referred to above is Advocate-General Van Gerven's inclination against restricting a pregnant woman's right to travel abroad to have abortion. In his view, "[m]easures which would be disproportionate—in as much as they would excessively impede the freedom to supply services—would include for example a ban on pregnant women going abroad."[71] It has been asserted that his warning influenced the adoption of the secret Protocol No. 17 to the Maastricht Treaty.[72] However, later developments compelled the Irish Government to launch the following Solemn Declaration: "This Protocol shall not limit the freedom to travel between member states or to obtain or make available in Ireland, in accordance with conditions which may be laid by Irish legislation, information relating to services lawfully available in Member States." In consequence of the injunction,[73] which the Supreme Court of Ireland granted to the plaintiffs mentioned above, the defendants brought the case to the European Commission on Human Rights on August 19 and September 22, 1988,[74] asking for determination as to whether the injunction amounted to an infringement of Article 10 of the European Convention. Both the European Commission and the Court reached the conclusion that the injunction constituted a breach of the right to freedom of expression. The European Court of Human Rights ruled in a decision of October 29, 1992, that the existing ban in Ireland on counseling women on the availability of abortion services abroad violated Article 10(1) of the European Convention.[75] Thus, the applications concerned the

---

70. Human rights treaties of which member states are part supply guidelines within the framework of the European Community law. *See, e.g.*, ECJ Judgement of May 14, 1974, in Case 4/73, Nold v. Commission 1974, ECR 491, § 13.

71. *Id.* at 1991, 3 CMLR 849, 875, § 29.

72. The protocol states: "Nothing in the Treaty of the European Union or in the Treaties establishing the European Communities or in the Treaties or Acts modifying or supplementing those Treaties shall affect the application in Ireland of Article 40.3.3. of the Constitution of Ireland." *See* Paul Ward, *Ireland: Abortion: "X" + "Y" ' ?!*, 33 U. Lou. J. Fam. L. 401 (1994–95); Janet Hadley, Abortion, Between Freedom and Necessity 20 (1996).

73. The Supreme Court ruled: "It is ordered that the defendants and each of them, their servants or agents be perpetually restrained from assisting pregnant women within the jurisdiction to travel abroad to obtain abortions by referral to a clinic, by the making for them of travel arrangement, or by informing them of the identity and location of the method of communication with a specified clinic or clinics or otherwise." I. R. (1988), 593, 627.

74. Applications Nos. 14234 and 14235/88, respectively.

75. *Open Door and Dublin Well Women v. Ireland* case, *supra* note 66, §§ 387–88. This case dealt with the right of women to travel outside the Irish jurisdiction to obtain an abortion not lawfully available in Ireland, and provisions in Ireland relating to information and assistance in respect to abortion abroad. *Id.*

restrictions placed on the applicant clinics (Dublin Well Women Centre Ltd. and Open Door Counsellng) by Irish authorities in order to prevent them from providing non-directive pregnancy counseling to pregnant women as to the location or identity of, or method of communication with, abortion clinics in Great Britain.

In the view of the European Court, recognition of the right to life of the unborn in the Irish Constitution does not exclude a right to receive information on how to procure an abortion abroad. The European Court did not, however, rule whether the European Convention guarantees a right to abortion. It stated that "it is not called upon to examine whether a right to abortion is guaranteed under the Convention"[76] in this particular case, since the applicants had not claimed that the Convention contained such a right. By applying the test of "proportionality," the majority of the Court arrived at the conclusion that Ireland's policy of protecting the life of the unborn was not a compelling justification to abridge the freedom of speech as protected by the Convention. However, several dissenting judges, a few of them from cultures influenced by the Catholic Church, took the view that the imposed restriction was not disproportionate and that there was a reasonable margin of states' discretion in the field of the protection of morals. Of further interest to our study is the evidence presented by the applicants as to the adverse implications of the health of Irish women arising from the injunction in the present case, namely:

(1) an increase in the birth of unwanted and rejected children;

(2) an increase in illegal and unsafe abortions;

(3) a lack of adequate preparation of Irish women obtaining abortions;

(4) an increased delay in obtaining abortions with ensuing increased complication rates; and

(5) poor postcare with a failure to deal adequately with medical complications and a failure to provide adequate contraceptive advice.

The Impact of International Decisions on Domestic Law

The Irish Example

The above case law achieved favorable, albeit limited, results. The impact of the decisions of international organs on the domestic application of Article 40.3.3 of the Irish Constitution can be demonstrated by reference to the Supreme Court of Ireland's decision in the *Attorney General v. X and Others* case on March 5, 1992.[77] The Supreme Court held unanimously that abortion within the state could be lawful in certain circumstances and that the right to life of the unborn expressed in the Irish Constitution is not absolute, but relative, when the mother's life is in danger. In the light of the circumstances of the case it ruled that balancing the right to life of the

---

76. *Id.*, § 66.

77. Supreme Court of Ireland, Dublin, Judgement of Mar. 5, 1992, The Attorney General v. X and Others, *reprinted in* 13 Hum. Rts. L.J. 210 (1992).

fourteen-year-old girl against the right to life of the unborn was necessary. The Court found that the substantial risk to the life of the mother in this case could only be avoided by the termination of her pregnancy and that termination of that kind is permissible with regard to a true interpretation of Article 40.3.3. of the Irish Constitution.

The effect of the Supreme Court decision was that legislative and/or constitutional changes were found to be necessary. Therefore, on November 25, 1992, a referendum took place in Ireland in which people were asked to vote on an amendment of Article 40.3.3 of the Constitution as to the right to life, travel, and information. The right to life amendment was turned down by the majority of the population, obviously since it would have left undisturbed the existing affirmation in Article 40.3.3 of the Constitution of the right to life of the unborn. The current constitutional position is as set out in the decision of the Supreme Court in the *"X"* case, making the rules concerning abortion more permissive. The Government has committed itself to introduce legislation to regulate this position. The other two proposals received the majority's support in the referendum with the consequence that the government in 1995 introduced new legislation (referred to as the "Abortion Information Law") in order to regulate the availability of information on abortion services obtainable outside Ireland.

This development of the national law of Ireland is fully in conformity with the judgements of the European Court of Human Rights in the *Open Door* case and in the Court of the European Communities in the *Grogan* case. In such a framework, Europe is a modernizing influence. Thus, Ireland cannot uphold restrictions as to the dissemination of information concerning the identity and location of abortion facilities in other states. Neither can women's right to travel abroad for an abortion be restricted. There is no pressing social need for restrictions of that kind. Neither would such measures be proportionate. In other words, the EC law and the European Convention have a tremendous role to play in reconciling domestic abortion law with international human rights standards. The case law of the international organs consequently provides for greater uniformity in Europe, having a concrete impact on national law of the member states of the Council of Europe and the European Union. In order to ensure enforcement of international law, national law should be coordinated with international law. Countries with restrictive law can be forced to introduce more liberal rules on the subject matters of concern. Thus, in a suitable case in the future the European Court of Human Rights might, by using the comparative method of interpretation, rule that abortion must be legalized. The effect of international case law and/or the *"X"* case on the domestic jurisdiction of Ireland has not been the introduction of a right to abortion *per se*. However, under the *"X"* case test (based on the existence of a real and substantive threat to the life of the mother) a limited class of persons are now entitled to a legal right to abortion.[78] Moreover, impeding legislation ought not restrict the right to obtain and provide information (the international organs did not apply interpretative methods that would have extended the right to expression

---

78.   In his address to the Cairo Conference on Sept. 6, 1994, the Irish representative, Mr. B. Howlin acknowledged that "policy and legislation in relation to the circumstances in which the termination of pregnancy may be permitted is a matter for each country to determine for itself."

to comprise *counseling*, which involves a higher degree of societal performance) on abortion services available within the member states of the EU and the Council of Europe.

Other Parts of the World

In contrast to the European discussion, other parts of the world, especially Asia, feature examples of expansive information campaigns on family planning services including abortion in other parts of the world. In the province of Quang-Ninh (Vietnam), for example, there is a one-minute television program every day, a tele-vised play every month, and a page in the newspapers which address these issues. In the mountainous, coastal and minority areas, where it is not common for most peo-ple to have access to TV, information is spread by loudspeakers in the rice fields. Moreover, a magazine, *Happy Family*, which focuses on family planning services, is distributed by the NCPFP (the National Committee on Population and Family Planning) to every family in Vietnam.

Freedom from Interference in Decisionmaking

Freedom from Governmental Interference

The right to choose on matters related to procreation is an inherent human right. It is an activity that falls within the private domain, and since it affects a person's entire life it must be considered a fundamental civil right. The common denominator for the right to family planning as well as the right to found a family is that they are regarded primarily as a "negative right." In other words, the individual ought to decide matters of procreation voluntarily and free of arbitrary governmental interference. The choice factor raises the question as to what value systems, and what desired out-come, should lie behind these decisions. In this respect, international human rights law gives us some useful guidance.

Forced Pregnancy, Forced Abortion, and Sterilization

CEDAW commented in its General Recommendation No. 21 that some coun-try reports reviewing the domestic implementation of the Women's Convention dis-closed coercive practices such as forced pregnancies, abortions, or sterilization. CEDAW considers such practices to affect women's physical and mental health adversely and infringe the rights under Article 16(1)(e) of the Convention. Consequently, the Committee concluded that "[d]ecisions to have children or not, while preferably made in consultation with spouse or partner, must not nevertheless be limited by spouse, parent, partner or government." It was ascertained that where there are freely available appropriate measures for the voluntary regulation of fertil-ity, the health and well-being of all members of the family improves. On that basis, CEDAW called upon states to ensure that measures are taken by states parties to the Women's Convention to prevent coercion in regard to fertility and reproduction.[79] Coercion in reproductive matters was banned at the Cairo Conference in 1994. Article

---

79.   U.N. Doc. CEDAW/C/1995/7, § 465, at 28 (1995).

7(12) in the ICPD Programme of Action states: "The principle of informed free choice is essential to the long term success of family planning programs. Any form of coercion has no part to play." It is, however, acknowledged that while demographic goals legitimately are the subject of government development strategies, they "should not be imposed on family planning providers in the form of targets or quotas for the recruitment of clients." Also the Beijing Declaration stresses in section 97 that the human rights of women "include their right to have control over and decide freely and responsibly on matters related to their sexuality," including reproductive health and freedom from coercion. Furthermore, Article 115 defines forced sterilization and forced abortion, coercive/forced use of contraceptives, female infanticide, and prenatal sex selection as acts of violence against women.[80]

On the regional level, the European Commission on Human Rights has in its case law[81] considered the right to found a family as defined in Article 12 of the European Convention as an "absolute right;" that is, one not allowing any state interference whatsoever. In addition, a resolution on a Charter on the Rights of Women in Childbirth adopted by the European Parliament/EEC in 1988 underlines as a basic principle that maternity should be entered into freely.[82]

On the basis of several frequently made international statements, the following examples of an unjustified state interference can be named: compulsory non-procreation measures such as forced sterilization, forced abortion,[83] or compulsion to use contraceptives or other limitations regarding the maximum number of children, such as the single-child family planning policy in China,[84] and the maximum of two children policy in the Socialist Republic of Vietnam.[85] In addition, limitations regarding the maximum number of children may lead, as seen in Asia, to widespread son-preference

---

80. Several delegates to the Beijing Conference condemned such practices in their speeches. U.S. First Lady Hillary Rodham Clinton expressed the view on Sept. 5, 1995, that it is a violation of human rights to deny women the right to plan their own families, and that "includes being forced to have abortions or being sterilised against their will." Mrs. Madeleine Albright, the representative of the U.S. to the Conference said categorically on Sept. 6, 1995, that "[N]o woman, whether in Birmingham, Bombay, Beirut or Beijing, should be forcibly sterilized or forced to have an abortion." In addition the Chief of the Federal Department of the Interior of Switzerland declared on Sept. 8, 1995, that forced abortion, forced sterilization, and prenatal sex selection are particularly grave violations of women's human rights. Press Release, WOM/857, September 8, 1995.

81. *X v. UK*, Application No. 6564/74, 2 D&R, 106.

82. Official Journal of the European Communities, C 187, 173, July 18, 1988.

83. Such practices have occurred in China in accordance with the implementation of Article 14 of the Sichuan Family Planning Regulation of 1987. Couples who have serious hereditary diseases are forced to remain childless and those who are already pregnant must terminate the pregnancy. Reed Boland et al., *Honoring Human Rights in Population Policies: From Declaration to Action, in* POPULATION POLICIES RECONSIDERED: HEALTH, EMPOWERMENT AND RIGHTS 98 (Gita Sen, Adrienne Germain, & Lincoln C. Chen eds., 1994).

84. *How China Implements its Family Planning Programs*, CHINA INTERCONTINENTAL PRESS, Sept. 1, 1995.

85. Vietnam, Population and Family Planning Policies 1988, Council of Ministers Decision No. 162 Concerning a Number of Population and Family Planning Policies, art. 2, § 1.

and female infanticide. The World Bank has made the following observation in this regard: "In China the one-child policy has been challenged by an apparent preference for sons. The same bias in favor of sons exists in Korea."[86] Another phenomenon connected with the "one birth per couple" policy is that when a family has a baby girl, the girl is often not registered as the hope for a son lives with the parents. It has been suggested that there are over a million unregistered women in China today. The negative effects of non-registration on the person's legal status are obvious.[87]

The great attention given internationally in mass media to the coercive measures and the sanctions for non-compliance with the one-child policy in China resulted in not only condemnation by the international community but also withdrawals of financial support to the country.[88] China responded by arguing that these external measures are an intervention in matters essentially within the domestic jurisdiction of a state. The Chinese government strongly opposed the extensive critique of its family planning program and population control as contrary to respect of human freedom by stating that "[a]ny such practice of interfering in China's internal affairs has not only deviated from the basic principle set up in the field of population by the international community, but it has also violated the established principles of international law."[89] The term "interference" as used in this context is vague; it can include such measures as international criticism or negative media coverage, which is not comprised by any prohibitive rule of international law. Besides, the practical significance of the doctrine of national sovereignty versus human rights has been minimized through the latest developments in international human rights law.

Coercion, furthermore, is not only a violation of the principle of free choice but also includes brutal methods of physical violence. Manipulation and withholding of information about side-effects and alternative contraceptive measures may be regarded as an element of "coercion," if it prevents the free choice of the individuals. In addition, we should mention that some societies emphasize the *moral* obligation of spouses to procreate. Although it cannot be denied that societal interest in reproduction to a certain extent is legitimate, coercive methods to make individuals beget children cannot be justified within the realm of international human rights law. On the contrary, the referred practices, including forced pregnancies, have serious consequences for

---

86. The World Bank, World Development Report 1984, 178 (1985).

87. The Committee on the Rights of the Child's concluding observations in connection with the consideration of China's report under the Convention on the Rights of the Child, in May 1996, are illustrative. The Committee expressed first of all its concern in regard of the deficiencies in the registration system in China, which had lead to children being deprived of basic safeguards for the promotion and protection of their rights, "including in the areas of child trafficking, abduction, sale and maltreatment, abuse or neglect." In the Committee's view family planning policy must be designed to avoid any "threat to the life of children, particularly girls." China's government was urged to take further action for the maintenance of strong and comprehensive measures to combat the abandonment and infanticide of girls. U.N. Doc. CRC/C/SR.298–300, §§ 16, 36 (1996).

88. Tomaševski, *supra* note 27, at 27.

89. Information Office of the State Council of the People's Republic of China, Family Planning in China 34 (1995) (hereinafter Family Planning in China).

women. They affect women's physical and mental health adversely and infringe on their right to choose "the number and spacing of their children" as guaranteed in Article 16 (1)(e) of the Women's Convention.[90]

Coercion in Relation to HIV/AIDS

Another important question of current interest is whether states may, compatibly with human rights, introduce restrictions in their domestic law and/or administrative practice on the right to family planning by explicitly referring to the risks and consequences of HIV infection. Some biological, social, and physiological features predispose women to greater vulnerability to most sexually transmitted diseases, including AIDS.[91] It may of course be argued that the protection of the health of the mother and the unborn child constitutes a legitimate aim for governmental intervention. At the same time there seems to be an international consensus, manifested during the International Consultation on AIDS and Human Rights held at Geneva in July 1989, that it is not of "sufficient weight"[92] to justify measures against the mothers' wishes. Even though the rapid spread of HIV is a cause for great concern, non-discrimination in regard to free decisionmaking is also vital in cases of pregnant women with HIV/AIDS. Thus, mandatory abortions or sterilizations for HIV-infected women would be a violation of the human right to found a family and the right to family planning, as protected by international law, and cannot in the author's view be justified on any legal grounds. Despite the fact that six to eight out of every ten children born to HIV-positive mothers will be unaffected, in several countries pregnant women with HIV have experienced pressure, most often from doctors, to terminate their pregnancies.[93]

Closely related to that issue is the on-going discussion on the legitimacy of selective abortions. Eugenic movements in various countries have periodically argued for the necessity of compulsory control of family planning in order to protect society from the offspring of certain groups. So the coercive sterilization law targeting Roma as well as persons considered unfit to beget children—such as mentally ill persons or criminals in the former Czech and Slovak Republic—was based on such motives.[94] However, it is apparent that there is no justification under current human rights law for rules that are selective in this manner.

---

90.   *See also* CEDAW, General Recommendation No.18, 10th Sess., 1991, U.N. Doc. HRI/GEN/1/Rev.1, § 22.

91.   The Secretary-General of the International Federation of the Red Cross referred in his speech to the Beijing Conference to estimates according to which by the year 2000 over 13 million women will have been infected with HIV. Press Release, WOM/BEI/861, Sept. 12, 1995.

92.   United Nations, Report of an International Consultation on AIDS and Human Rights 49 (1991); *see also* Paul Sieghart, Aids and Human Rights, A UK Perspective (1989).

93.   Proposals concerning involuntary sterilization of infected women has been discussed in the legal literature by H. Amaro, *Women's Reproductive Rights in the Age of AIDS, New Threats to Informed Choice, in* From Abortion to Reproductive Freedom, Transforming a Movement 253 (Marlene Gerber Fried ed., 1990).

94.   Tomaševski, *supra* note 27, at 26.

The Use of Incentives and Disincentives

The state should not intervene in the sphere of family planning, whether by use of reward or punishment, in order to influence people who have "too many" or "too few" children. Such an approach will result in social inequality—the financial situation of the family is in most societies dependent on the number of children. Sanctions against large families, like the loss of tax benefits, for example, may infringe upon the rights not only of the parents but also of the child/ren. Besides, such measures have not been very effective in modifying fertility levels. The use of substantial material incentives, which has been practiced frequently in some countries, especially in Asia,[95] may indirectly prevent the free choice of the spouses. For people living under the incessant threat of starvation, the scope of free choice on family size is very narrow. If, as in China in recent years, it is legally established that a family allowance will not be paid if the number of children in a family exceeds the limit set by the state, this, too, will constitute a violation of the right concerned. The Representative of China told the U.N. Commission on Population and Development that families who prefer fewer children are better-off, because the state offers them preferential treatment, like access to low-interest loans and to means and techniques of production. Further, single-child insurance and an old-age security system have been established, thus reducing rural people's need for more children.[96]

Another human rights issue is the fact that quite severe disincentives, some of which can be deemed penalties, are imposed on the citizens in the Republic of Vietnam by a political institution, the People's Committee. Families with more than two children must contribute to a social support fund, which includes funds for education and health care and increased contribution of socially beneficial labor.

Families with more than the allowed number of children must pay a housing or land rent calculated at a high price for the extra space they request.[97] According to Decision No. 1664 (section 4b), in force since 1992 in the Quang Ninh province, couples in agricultural areas with more than two children must pay fines equaling 80–200 kg of raw rice every year for five years; government or military employees with more than two children can have their salary reduced and can even be discharged. In addition, families with three children or more are not be permitted to move into the urban centers of municipalities, cities, and industrial zones. Therefore, the society has different disincentives for different groups. As a consequence there is an obvious risk for discrimination and for difficulties to uphold the principle of equality before the law, which should be the primary consideration in a state governed by the rule of law.

---

95. The countries that can be mentioned in this regard are first and foremost India, Korea, Pakistan, Taiwan, Sri Lanka, Turkey, and China. L. GORDON, BIRTH CONTROL IN AMERICA 339 (1977).

96. Peng Yu, Representative of China at the 29th Session of the U.N. Commission on Population and Development, General Debate on National Experience in Population Matters, New York, Feb. 26, 1996.

97. Council of Ministers Decision No. 162, *supra* note 85, § 6.

The spacing of pregnancies is important for maternal and child health. However, an example of governmental interference inconsistent with human rights norms is the prescription of a specific space between the births of the children as established in the domestic law of Vietnam. The earlier mentioned decision of 1988 (section 3) defines the intervals between births of the children. Each couple is allowed to have two children with a space of three to five years between them. The recommended childbearing age is twenty-two years of age or older for women and twenty-four years of age or older for men. People are also advised not to have children after the age of thirty-five.

Finally, it would appear that financial burdens influence reproductive decision-making. Therefore the right to family planning would also be violated if care facilities, health subsidies, maternity leave, and access to land in rural areas are conditioned on compliance with state-imposed restrictions on the number of children.

Coercion in the Private Sphere

Interpersonal Relations

Human rights are, as earlier pointed out, primarily designed to protect individuals against the abuse of power by a state, but through the application of the *"Drittwirkung"* doctrine, they may place obligations upon states to render unlawful acts of private individuals, that is, to include prohibition of coercion by other individuals, that infringe the guaranteed rights. The U.N. Commission on Human Rights adopted a resolution on the elimination of violence against women at its session in April 1996, obligating governments to refrain from engaging in violence against women and to take appropriate and effective action concerning acts of violence against women, "whether those acts were perpetrated by the State or by private persons."[98] One scholar summarized this development in international law, stating: "The emergence of gender discrimination on the human rights agenda broadened the reach of human rights from 'vertical' relations between individuals and governments, to 'horizontal' relations, namely between private individuals, within families and communities, and ultimately within couples."[99]

Recent developments in the case law of the Inter-American and the European Court on Human Rights indicate that these international organs have taken a step towards the recognition of the applicability of the regional conventions on behavior in the private sphere, a fact which is of great significance.[100] In consequence, freedom of choice as the core element of the right to found a family as well as of the right

---

98. U.N. Doc. E/CN.4/1996/L.83 (1996). *See also* art. 2 of the 1994 Inter-American Convention on the Prevention, Punishment and Eradication of Violence Against Women, "Convention of Belém do Pará," in force since Mar. 3, 1995. Violence against women is defined as acts that occur within the family or domestic unit and that occur in the community. *See also* THOMAS BUERGENTHAL & DINAH SHELTON, PROTECTING HUMAN RIGHTS IN THE AMERICAS 645 (1995).

99. TOMAŠEVSKI, *supra* note 27, at 40; *see also* Andrew Clapham, *The Drittwirkung of the Convention, in* THE EUROPEAN SYSTEM FOR THE PROTECTION OF HUMAN RIGHTS 163 (R. St. Macdonald et al. eds., 1993).

100. The regional developments have influenced also the work on human rights standards within

to family planning means that a person does not have a right to beget a child with a particular person, so that even for persons living in marriage there is no obligation for the wife to become pregnant, nor for the husband to impregnate her. Thus, neither of the spouses may compel the other spouse to reproduce. Marital rape and forced impregnation are included in the U.N. definition of violence.[101] Moreover, rape by the husband is considered a violation of Article 16 of the Women's Convention.[102] Nevertheless, in many parts of the world, coercion amounting to violence against women, including rape, is a frequent occurrence within the family. In societies where there is no real partnership between the spouses, and the man is considered to have absolute authority within the family unit (including matters of procreation) gender is the sole basis of discrimination. Practices of this kind are in obvious contradiction to human rights rules, according to which decisions on procreation should rest equally on both spouses.[103] Violence against women in the form of rape affects women's ability to protect themselves from unwanted pregnancies as well as sexually transmitted diseases, including AIDS/HIV. Clearly, in addition to other trauma, rape can have serious consequences for women's reproductive health.

Another phenomenon, though not falling within the term "violence" but still contradictory to the above-mentioned Convention's demand that human rights be enjoyed on equal footing among the family members, is the legal empowerment of the husband to veto his wife's access to family planning services, including abortion.[104]

Resolving Conflicting Interests

Sometimes a difference of opinion and interest may exist between a pregnant woman and the father-to-be regarding the continuation or interruption of pregnancy. A pregnancy may be unwanted by the woman, who is pregnant, by the man who has impregnated her, or by both.[105] Voluntary abortion clearly impacts the interests of the

---

the U.N. The Vienna Declaration and Programme of Action of 1993 calls for governments and the U.N. to eliminate violence against women in public and private life as a human rights obligation.

101. A clear and very comprehensive definition of the notion "violence against women" is contained in § 1 of the U.N. Declaration on the Elimination of Violence against Women, adopted by GA Res. 48/104 on Dec. 20, 1993. *See* THE UNITED NATIONS AND THE ADVANCEMENT OF WOMEN, 1945–1995 459 (1995); *see also* CEDAW, General Recommendation No. 19, Violence Against Women, adopted in 1992, U.N. Doc. CEDAW/C/1992/L.1/Add.15.

The term violation has been broadened to include female infanticide and prenatal sex selection in the Beijing Declaration and Platform for Action, *supra* note 38, at Strategic Objective L. 7, § 283 (d).

102. U.N. Doc. CEDAW/C/1993/4 § 60 (1993).

103. *See* Women's Convention, *supra* note 50, at art. 16(1)(e).

104. Indonesian authorities introduced recently rules for spousal veto in regard of family planning services on the island Lombok with the deprecatory motivation that home-alone wives should not be tempted to wrongful acts while their husbands are away. JAKARTA POST, Oct. 8, 1996.

105. A recent country study shows that in Bolivia in the majority of the cases (about 64 percent)

male partner, but does he have a right to prevent or to insist on the birth of his child? It has been argued that since the fetus is as much part genetically of the man who conceived it as of the woman, putative fathers have a moral stake in the decision concerning woman's access to abortion. The UDHR and other human rights documents recognize that one person's human rights may conflict with those of another person. Still, there are no principles for determining priority among conflicting rights.[106] CEDAW has, however, in its analysis of the content of Article 16 of the Women's Convention, concluded: "The rights allocated to both spouses as individuals should not depend on the one receiving permission from the other, thereby placing one spouse in an inferior position."[107]

In early Roman society the right to decide upon abortion belonged to the *pater familias* rather than the mother.[108] Men enjoyed a very powerful position in the family and children were treated as if they were the possession of the father. He had, for example, the right to leave unwanted children in the wilderness to die if he wished to reject them. Exposure was totally prohibited in the late Empire, but such practices continued and were not outlawed in other societies, as for example until the 13th century in Sweden.[109] Over time, women were ensured stronger guarantees for their right to private life, and nowadays a father has no possibility of taking action on behalf of the unborn child against the mother's will to undergo abortion.

In the case of *Paton v. United Kingdom*,[110] the European Commission on Human Rights dealt with the question of whether a national regulation protecting a pregnant woman from being compelled to continue an unwanted pregnancy by her husband's veto of an abortion is compatible with the European Convention. One of the issues was whether a prohibition on the termination of pregnancy after the twelfth week under the 1967 Abortion Act could constitute interference with the husband's right to private life. The European Commission expressed the opinion that the European Convention was not breached in the particular case. So the right of the husband to respect for private life (having an interest in the birth of his child) had to give way to the woman's right to privacy. Consequently, abortion is primarily a matter for the pregnant woman to decide. The Commission held, moreover, that the applicant's right to

---

the decision for abortion was taken jointly by the couple. In 25 percent of the cases, it was the woman's decision and in 4 percent it was solely the husband's decision. Mercado, *supra* note 48, at 184.

106. LOUIS HENKIN, INTERNATIONAL LAW: POLITICS AND VALUES (1995).

107. U.N. Doc. CEDAW/C/1993/4, § 161 (1993). The representative of Tunisia referred during the review of the country report by CEDAW at its meeting on Jan. 23, 1995, to the fact that in regard to abortion the husband's agreement is not required and that the decision to continue or interrupt a pregnancy "is the wife's prerogative."

108. MICHAIL ANDREEV, RIMSKO CASTNO PRAVO 170 (1971). *See also* A. DOBLER, *DER VÖLKERRECHTLICHE SCHUTZ DES KINDES* 13 (1959).

109. BARNETS RÄTTIGHETER OCH SAMHÄLLETS SKYLDIGHETER, LAGAR OCH REGLER 35 (1991).

110. Application No.1416/78, The Report of the European Commission, *adopted on* Mar. 13, 1980.

privacy could not be interpreted as including a legal right to be consulted on his wife's decision.

The question of a man's legal interest in abortion in general and the compatibility of national law of Norway with the standards of the European Convention was raised before the European Commission in *Knudsen v. Norway*.[111] The Commission ruled that the applicant was not affected differently by the domestic legislation than other citizens and declared the application incompatible *ratione personae* with the provisions of the European Convention on March 8, 1985. The applicant insisted that an amendment to the Norwegian Abortion Act, authorizing the woman herself to make the final decision as to whether to terminate a pregnancy before the end of the twelfth week of pregnancy, implied "abandonment of every legal protection of the budding human life and involved in principle a denial of the foetus's human worth."[112] The applicant claimed, moreover, that the said Act was in conflict with basic Christian values and Article 2 of the European Convention and that it therefore should be declared void. Mr. Knudsen was, furthermore, of the opinion that he had a direct legal interest in the examination of the acceptability of the Norwegian Abortion Act in relation to the European Convention because he had risked and lost his office as vicar of Balsfjord within the Norwegian State Church on account of his views on the abortion issue. The European Commission stressed, however, that a priest who could not be deemed a potential father could not be considered to be the victim[113] of the violation he alleged. Therefore, he had no right to petition.

The consequences of the case law described above may briefly be established as follows: abortion cannot be subject to the consent of the husband, and he cannot oppose it on the grounds of existing provisions in the European Convention on Human Rights.

This position is justifiable for several reasons. Forced sexual intercourse, also in the form of marital rape, sometimes occurs for the purpose of securing the conception of a child in the family, a situation in which the woman's right to choose to become a parent or not is clearly violated. Women with low legal status, with no education, and no financial independence are in no position to negotiate issues like the planning and spacing of their children. They are often at risk of violence from uncooperative spouses. Within a great number of domestic jurisdictions rape or physical force within marriage does not constitute a crime.[114] Under such circumstances the

---

111. Application No.11045/84, D&R 42, 247 *et seq*.

112. *Id.* at 250.

113. The ECHR interpreted a "victim of a violation" in the sense of the European Convention to mean that the person has to be *actually* affected by the violation of a human right. *See* Klass and Others v. Germany, ECHR Judgement of Sept. 6, ser. A, No.28, (1978).

114. L. J. MACFARLINE, THE THEORY AND PRACTICE OF HUMAN RIGHTS 58 (1985); Cook, *supra* note 18, at 12. On the other hand there is also a tendency within the domestic legal systems of several states to recognise rape between spouses as an offence. The German Parliament for example passed through a draft law making rape within marriage a criminal offence by the votes 318 in favor and 306 against, on May 9, 1996. *See* U.N. Doc. Suppl. No. 38, A/44/38, § 309.

innocent partner with the weaker position has to be protected and requiring the husband's permission for abortion cannot be justifiable.

The case law of other national jurisdictions supports the right of the pregnant woman to choose abortion without regard to her partner's preferences.[115] The Supreme Court of the United States has, for example, based its decisions in two important cases on arguments related to two important interests of the pregnant woman, namely: rearing burdens and gestational burdens.[116] Thus, the different legal position of a man and a woman with respect to family planning is regarded as justifiable.

Women have been guaranteed a freedom of choice with respect to the continuation of a pregnancy, in accordance with international human rights law as well as domestic jurisprudence. A man simply does not have the same position. He can neither compel nor prevent abortion. As the right to family planning is formulated in international law he has a right to participate in the decisionmaking process and nothing else. This position has, however, been questioned on the basis of its compatibility with the principle of equality before the law. Professor Meron has advanced the argument that "[b]ecause men have equal rights with women in matters of family planning, abortion . . . [w]ould be not a woman's individual right, which she might exercise independently of consent of the father."[117]

On the other hand, the national legislation of some countries in Asia and in Africa require a husband's authorization for a woman's abortion.[118] Even though the HRC's General Comment No. 16, dealing with privacy did not explicitly mention this issue, provisions providing the husband with veto power in procreation matters are unquestionably incompatible with contemporary human rights law. CEDAW underlined in its comment on Article 16(1)(e): "Women's right to full and free exercise of their reproductive functions, including the right to decide whether to have children or not, must not be limited by spouse or government."[119]

Finally, it is clear that a man cannot find justification on the basis of existing human rights law for the use of force in order to compel a woman to have an abortion against her will. In such a case, he had the opportunity to make a choice, when deciding to use contraceptives or not in order to prevent an unwanted pregnancy, before he had sexual intercourse.

---

115. *See* M. N. Coleman, *Embryo Transplant, Parental Conflict, and Reproductive Freedom: A Prospective Analysis of Issues and Arguments Created by Forthcoming Technology*, 15 HOFSTRA L. REV. 611 (1987).

116. *Id.* at 613.

117. THEODOR MERON, HUMAN RIGHTS LAW-MAKING IN THE UNITED NATIONS: A CRITIQUE OF INSTRUMENTS AND PROCESSES 72 (1986).

118. Rebecca J. Cook & Jeanne M. Haws, *The United Nations Convention on the Rights of Women: Opportunities for Family Planning Providers*, 12 INT'L FAM. PLAN. PERSP. 51 (1986). In Islamic law spousal consultation for access to family planning services, including abortion, is required in general. Rebecca J. Cook & Deborah Maine, *Spousal Veto over Family Planning Services*, 77 AM. J. PUB. HEALTH 340, 340–43 (1987).

119. U.N. Doc. E/CN.6/1993/CRP.2, § 46 (1993).

Women's Freedom of Choice in Special Situations and During Armed Conflicts

Women in Detention

Women in detention frequently suffer abuse, most often of a sexual nature, by prison officers, the police, and the military. ECOSOC has adopted several resolutions relating to sex-specific violence against detained women.[120] Still, very few countries mentioned concern for improving the situation of women in prison in their reports on the implementation of the Nairobi strategies in 1990. Also CEDAW has on several occasions called attention to the need for special laws and/or administrative measures to protect pregnant women prisoners.[121]

A pregnant woman is particularly vulnerable to torture and/or to detention in cruel and degrading conditions. She risks miscarriage and severe injury from untreated medical complications of her pregnancy. A body of principles in international law is directed at safeguarding the physical safety of detainees and prisoners.[122] Notwithstanding their existence, several governments still ignore the special needs for protection of pregnant women. For example, the number of pregnant women detained in South America is still very high. Many of them are held under intolerable conditions and are subject to treatment that contravenes contemporary human rights law. They have been kicked and beaten frequently, and they have, with malicious aforethought, been assigned to heavy labor in order to induce a miscarriage. Such acts fall within the prohibition of forced abortion. States should pursue without delay by all appropriate measures and in accordance with Article 4 of the U.N. Declaration on Violence against Women a policy eliminating this kind of violence against women.

The 1993 Vienna Declaration condemned forced pregnancy,[123] which has been interpreted to include legally forced continuation of a pregnancy. Although the referred paragraph deals with violence against women, it is maintained that forced continuation of pregnancy constitutes a form of violence against women, a major emphasis of the Cairo and Beijing Conferences,[124] and is therefore contrary to reproductive

---

120. *See, e.g.*, ECOSOC Res. 1986/29 of May 23, 1986, and Res. 1990/5 of May 24, 1990.

121. GA Res. A/48/38, § 399 (1993); *see also* AMNESTY INTERNATIONAL, RAPE AND SEXUAL ABUSE: TORTURE AND ILL-TREATMENT OF WOMEN IN DETENTION (1991).

122. *See, e.g.*, The U.N. Standard Minimum Rules for the Treatment of Persons in Detention and Imprisonment, the ICCPR, the European and American Convention on Human Rights, the Convention Against Torture and the European Convention against Torture, and the U.N. Declaration on Violence against Women. *See also* Karen Parker, *Human Rights of Women During Armed Conflict*, in section II this volume.

123 Vienna Declaration, *supra* note 2, at Part II, § 38.

124. Also during the World Summit for Social Development which was held in March 1995, states committed themselves to take effective measures to combat and eliminate all forms of violence against women in accordance with international instruments and declarations (commitment 5(h)). Violence against women was considered as a growing threat to the security of individuals, families, and communities everywhere.

health.[125] Inhuman and degrading acts against women have been declared incompatible with the dignity and worth of the human person, and elimination of this treatment must be given high priority.

Women in War and in Armed Conflicts

Sexual and gender-based violence place women at high risk of physical and mental trauma, disease, and unwanted pregnancy. Armed conflicts often lead to increased sexual violence and other forms of gender-based violence against women, a fact which requires specific protective and punitive measures. If victims of wartime rape are denied abortion and are forced to bear children resulting from rape, it constitutes coercion and is therefore, among other things, a violation of the freedom of choice. Such an act can even be regarded as a central element of genocide, for example, in the case of systematic rape of Bosnian women during the armed conflicts in the territory of the former Yugoslavia. In this author's view, the fact that a great number of impregnated women have actually been held captive beyond the legal period for termination of a pregnancy in Croatia and Bosnia-Herzegovina[126] is to be regarded as an attempt to block procreation of Bosnian Muslims. There can be little doubt that the captivity is carried out deliberately to make termination of the pregnancies impossible.[127] One can also expect that raped women may meet considerable psychological barriers to future pregnancy. In other words, acts of rape may indirectly lead to the prevention of births within the target group. Genocide, as defined in Article II(d) of the U.N. Convention on the Prevention and Punishment of the Crime of Genocide, comprises measures intended to prevent births within a national, ethnic, racial, or religious group with the intention of destroying the group as such.

Forced pregnancy, forced maternity, and other forms of sexual violence fit within the acts that may constitute genocide. Forced pregnancy and forced maternity may, furthermore, be considered implicitly covered by the prohibition of any "form of indecent assault" contained in Article 27 of the Fourth Geneva Convention of 1949. There is international consensus that rape crimes are "an extremely grave violation of international humanitarian law."[128] This is a very encouraging development, since acts of violence against women during armed conflict have historically been "the least condemned crimes" and the least prosecuted crimes.[129] The establishment of the *ad hoc* International Criminal Tribunals for the former Yugoslavia and for Rwanda, and the

---

125. *See* Rebecca J. Cook & Mahmoud F. Fathalla, *Advancing Reproductive Rights Beyond Cairo and Beijing*, in this volume.

126. *See* HUMAN RIGHTS WATCH, WORLD REPORT 1995 337, 342 (1995). Where abortion following rape is legally denied or practically obstructed, as in the above referred cases, woman's reproductive choice is clearly "imperiled." Rebecca J. Cook, *Human Rights and Reproductive Self-Determination*, 44 AM. U. L. REV. 997 (1995).

127. *See, e.g.,* ELENOR RICHTER-LYONETTE, MISSION ON GENDER-BASED WAR CRIMES AGAINST WOMEN AND GIRLS DURING THE GENOCIDE IN RWANDA 8–10 (1995).

128. U.N. Doc. E/CN.4/1994/5, § 16 (1994).

129. *See, e.g.,* KELLY DAWN ASKIN, WAR CRIMES AGAINST WOMEN: PROSECUTION IN INTERNATIONAL WAR CRIMES TRIBUNALS (1997); U.N. Doc. E/CN.4/1995/42 (1995).

jurisprudence emerging from these bodies, bears witness to the fact that the international community has reached a turning point in its willingness to prosecute perpetrators of gender-specific crimes against women.[130]

The Quest for Sons and Sex-Selective Abortions

The freedom of choice compatible with international norms on human rights does not allow freedom of the spouses to decide on their child's sex if that would result in total devaluation of one of the sexes. The great number of selective abortions of female fetuses in India and China is a manifestation of devaluing women. Nevertheless, it has been argued that since there is a demand for sex selection, freedom of choice includes freedom to have a child of one's own choice. Proponents of this view try to justify the preference for sons over daughters, a worldwide problem, though it is most marked in South Asia and the Middle East, by alleging that choosing the sex of a child is a logical extension of the right to family planning. Such practices not only curtail girl children's access to food, health services, and education, but may prevent them from being born. The majority of families living in India, Pakistan, Nepal, Bangladesh, South Korea, Syria, Jordan, and China are known for their strong preference for male children. In those societies, the family lineage is carried through the male line.[131] Sons are seen as potential earners as well as sources of future support. Another reason for this practice is the social and cultural stigma attached to having a girl child—considerable costs (dowry) are attached to marrying off a daughter.[132] It is presupposed that if the daughter does not marry she will remain dependent upon her family. Therefore, prenatal tests designed to discover fetal abnormalities are widely used in China,[133] India, and the Republic of Korea to determine the gender of the child,

---

130. *See, e.g.*, Kelly D. Askin, *Sexual Violence in Decisions and Indictments of the Yugoslav and Rwandan Tribunals: Current Status*, 93 AM. J. INT'L L. 97 (1999).

131. GERALDINE VAN BUEREN, THE INTERNATIONAL LAW ON THE RIGHTS OF THE CHILD 309 (1995). The practice of son preference is considered to be outlawed by the first universal treaty to prohibit harmful traditional practices, *i.e.*, the Convention of the Rights of the Child (art. 24(3)). Such practices were previously outlined in the 1986 Report of the Working Group on Traditional Practices affecting the Health of Women and Children, U.N. Doc. E/CN.4/1986/42 (1986). At the same time one of the most well-known maxims of Hindu religion concerns the significance of *kanya dan* (the gift of a daughter), which implies that a father must give a daughter away in marriage in order to guarantee his salvation. Barbara D. Miller, *Unwanted Daughters in Northwest India, in* UNWANTED PREGNANCIES, *supra* note 48, at 194.

132. The practice of dowry and bride-price not only leads to young women becoming objects of speculation for their parents, but it certainly contributes to the low status of women. A woman may even lose her life if she has brought an insufficient dowry as in the many reported cases from India. *See* ELISABETH BUMILLER, MAY YOU BE THE MOTHER OF A HUNDRED SONS 46–49, 111–112 (1990); Indira Jaising, *Violence Against Women: The Indian Perspective, in* WOMEN'S RIGHTS HUMAN RIGHTS, *supra* note 7, at 53.

133. The government has, however, recently initiated legal reforms strictly forbidding fetus sex appraisal with modern medical means for non-medical purposes. Authorities were in addition urged to "seriously investigate and deal accordingly with such criminal acts as killing, trading and cruelly injuring new-born baby girls." THE PROGRAMME FOR THE DEVELOPMENT OF CHINESE WOMEN 1995–2000, 22 (1995).

resulting in abortion or female infanticide if it is a girl. This conduct is contrary to the prohibition of discrimination on the grounds of sex found in central documents of international law[134] and is a form of violence within the family.[135] First and foremost, discrimination based on sex is wrong when it is based on false and invidious beliefs about persons of one sex or the other; that is, when the worth of a human being is limited by its sex. Second, the desire to preselect sex, except for certain medical reasons, such as to avoid a birth of a child with a sex-linked disease such as Duchenne's muscular dystrophy, may cause additional harm to those discriminated against.

Nevertheless, even the use of sex preselection on medical grounds has been morally questioned. Academic commentators have argued that such circumstances would result in the abortion of perfectly normal fetuses of the one sex, such as male fetuses suffering from hemophilia, while they allow the birth of female children who might be carriers of the genetic disease.[136] One may also wonder whether the argument that sex-selective abortions must be regarded as an injustice against an individual person is very strong at all, bearing in mind that the case law of the European organs for the protection of human rights shows that the fetus, under the European Convention, does not have an absolute right to continued existence. Thus, abortion in the first trimester of pregnancy has not been held contrary to this human rights treaty.

Another proposal made in the scientific debate suggests that sex-selective abortions should be rejected because they might lead to other forms of positive eugenics that are morally objectionable—namely, preselection of desired traits, such as a certain intelligence quotient. A distinction must be upheld between possible legal toleration for selecting for *desirable* traits and against *undesirable* traits. Each of the procedures must be discussed separately. Obviously, some of the preselective abortions belonging to the first group would have lesser social significance than sex-selective ones. The long-term social consequences of sex preselection would probably be detrimental to women and society as a whole. It would lead to the institutionalization of the perception that males should continue to be more highly valued, remaining in possession of the structural power, comprising among other things the control of economic, legal, and other key social institutions. It would lead to the confinement of women to subordinated "female" roles. An individual's freedom of choice in terms of international law implies only a choice of the number of children that one wishes to have and when to have them, but not to have a child of the sex of one's choice.

It is often argued that it is better for the spouses to choose the sex of the baby by technical means rather than forcing them to have several daughters before pro-

---

134. The HRC, during the examination of the governmental report of India under the ICCPR, included abortion of female fetuses for example in its questions on non-discrimination and equality between sexes. KATARINA TOMAŠEVSKI, WOMEN AND HUMAN RIGHTS 87 (1993). The Nepalese delegation at the Beijing Conference expressed on Sept. 5, 1995 serious concern for these practices in developing countries.

135. U.N. Doc. E/CN.6/1995/3, § 6 (1995).

136. Mary Anne Warren, *The Ethics of Sex Preselection, in* THE ETHICS OF REPRODUCTIVE TECHNOLOGY 234 (Kenneth D. Alpern ed., 1992).

ducing a son. This is said to increase the probability of the couple having a child of their own choice. The usage of such techniques would also help reduce population growth in developing countries. However, such reasoning is contrary to human rights law. The cultural and social perceptions perpetuated and generated by this reasoning are clearly contrary to the prohibition of discrimination on the ground of sex. An approach of this kind is, moreover, counterproductive to the international community's aspiration to enhance the social and legal status of women. Several provisions embodied in recent[137] universal human rights documents rest upon this strong consequentialist argument for banning sex preselection.

One of the objectives of the ICPD Programme of Action as mentioned in section 4(16) is to eliminate the root causes of son preference, "which result in harmful and unethical practices regarding female infanticide and prenatal sex selection." Governments are urged on the basis of section 4(23) to take the necessary measures to prevent such practices. National leaders are encouraged to "speak out and act forcefully against patterns of gender discrimination within the family, based on preference for sons." The need for equitable inheritance rights is emphasized. Other long-term measures of importance in this context are the enactment of legislation which enables women to maintain their maiden name and to pass it to their children so that the desire, where it exists, to continue the family name is fulfilled;[138] and guarantees social security for elderly people in order to free them from dependence upon economic support. It follows that the practice of dowry must also be eradicated to serve this end.

Furthermore, the Fourth World Conference on Women singled out the problem of son preference.[139] Governments as well as international organizations were urged to give priority to the elimination of harmful practices such as son preference and early marriage.[140] It was stressed that one of the important actions to be taken by states in this regard is to enact and enforce legislation against prenatal sex selection.[141]

Finally, sex selection may have unpredictable results, including a sharp imbalance in the sex ratio. Disturbing this balance may have grave consequences. One of the results could be increased violence and civil unrest. Recent data presented by the CSW show that for every 100 females delivered into the world, there are 105 males born.[142] Since

---

137. On the regional level however, government members of the Council of Europe, in 1986, prohibited the preselection of sex through genetic manipulation on the basis of Recommendation No. 1046.

138. Mrs. B. Bhutto said in her address to the Beijing Conference on Sept. 4, 1995 that boys are wanted in her part of the world to satisfy the ego: "they carry on the father's name." The Japanese delegation reported at the same occasion that the government will review the legal system pertaining to marriage by introducing a legal measure that permits a couple to retain their respective surnames after their marriage.

139. Beijing Declaration, *supra* note 38, at §§ 39 and 259.

140. *Id.* at § 107(a).

141. *Id.* at § 124(i).

142. U.N. Doc. E/CN.6/1995/3/Add.3, § 26 (1995). In India there are 957 females aged four years or under for every 1,000 males in the population. U.N. Doc. E/CN.6/1995/3/Add.3, § 27 (1995).

female human beings are generally biologically more resistant, the surplus of male infants is nature's way of balancing the sex ratio in the population. However, in parts of the world this male-to-female imbalance is never overcome, probably because of sex-selective abortions as well as the practice of infanticide. In India, where scientific selection technology is frequently used and the birth of a daughter is considered a serious calamity, only one out of 1,000 aborted fetuses are male.[143] In addition, female children still have a higher death rate than males, due mainly to neglect or mistreatment. At the Women's Conference in Beijing the striking discrepancy in the sex ratio was observed once again and emphasized as a cause for concern.[144] For instance, there are 50 million less women than men in India. In China, the average sex ratio is 125 boys for every 100 girls (in some provinces the ratio is 164 newborn boys for every 100 girls).[145] Still, there is no indication that scarcity would raise women's value. Therefore, one of the strategic objectives as defined in the final document is the encouragement of governmental actions as well as actions by international and nongovernmental organizations to eliminate the root causes of son preference.[146] Social acculturation processes over generations are not easy to break down, but the task is not impossible.

Responsible Choice

Most of the international documents containing provisions on the right to family planning mention the individuals' or couples' right to make decisions on procreation freely in conjunction with the adjective "responsibly." Since the late 1960s, the concept of responsibility in this context has been elaborated in a number of documents. Article 4 of the Declaration on Social Progress and Development adopted by the GA in 1969 states: "Parents have the exclusive right to determine freely and responsibly the number and spacing of their children." There was consensus among state's delegations that this right should take priority over all other considerations, but at the same time the right to have children was tied to the responsibility of the couple not to have more children than they can support. Parents were expected to guarantee their children a life in dignity, that is, to ensure them food and clothing, to take care of them, and to give them a good upbringing. The concept of responsible parenthood was further particularized in paragraph 14(f) of the World Population Plan of Action of 1974, which stresses the importance for couples and individuals, as regards family planning, to take consideration of their own situation as well as the implications of their decisions for the balanced development of their children and of the community and the society in which they live. In other words, a limitation on the freedom of reproductive choice was introduced, since the right-bearers were expected to take

---

143. W. Harcourt, *Bio-Medical Interventions: Young Women's Future Choice or Control?*, 1 DEVELOPMENT 63 (1990).

144. The Beijing Declaration, *supra* note 38, § 259; *see also* U.N. Doc. E/CN.6/1995/Add.1, § 52 (1995).

145. Miller, *supra* note 131; HADLEY, *supra* note 72, at 97. In industrialized countries the sex ratio was ninety-four males to one hundred females at the beginning of the 1990s.

146. Beijing Declaration, *supra* note 38, at Part L.2.

decisions on procreation after considerations as to their own situation, the impact of the decision on their (living and future)[147] children, and considerations of the community and society in which they live.

A decision to become a parent is indeed one of the most complex lifetime decisions that individuals and couples are called upon to make. Becoming a *responsible* parent involves a sustained commitment to economic, social, and psychological support of the child for many years. Thus, the choice to enter parenthood involves the assessment of current and likely future circumstances of several matters. The private life and the wishes of the individual/couples will necessarily encroach upon the life of the community as a whole. A government can therefore determine how much it may interfere with a certain right in the interest of societal control as well as in order to protect rights and freedoms of others. Ergo, it seems that human rights law justifies the government in determining whether a decision on family planning matters is responsible or not. Both the 1974 and 1984 World Population Plans of Action state that population policies should, among other things, be consistent with "national goals and values." The IPCD Plan of Action section 7(3) recognizes that "the formulation and implementation of population-related policies is the responsibility of each country." Moreover, the promotion of the responsible exercise of reproductive rights should be the fundamental basis for governmental and community-supported policies and programs.

An interesting feature in recently adopted consensual documents, for example, section 7(3) in the IPCD Programme of Action and section 95 of the Beijing Declaration, is that they no longer uphold a request for the consideration of one's own needs in decisionmaking on procreation. The emphasis in family planning today, consequently, embraces not only individual, personal choices but choices about relationships with others. Thus, the current interpretation of the term family planning involves a higher degree of individual responsibility toward coming generations and toward our planet as a whole. China has captured these changes and has sought justification for its family planning program for the years 1995–2000 on this basis, stressing that if unlimited population growth is allowed "the interests of the majority of the people, including those of new-born infants, will be seriously harmed."[148] Moreover, an effective solution to China's population problems (the country is the home of more than one-fifth of the world's population) is seen not just as responsibility toward the well-being of the Chinese people and future generations, but "a duty owed to maintaining the stability of the world's population."[149] It is for the common interests of all humanity. Such a policy could be considered compatible with the latest developments in responsible parenthood, provided that it is based on voluntariness. One should bear

---

147. Ten years later after the adoption of the above mentioned document this phrase was added to the above definition in Recommendation No. 30 of the International Conference on Population held at Mexico City in 1984.

148. FAMILY PLANNING IN CHINA, *supra* note 89, at 37.

149. *Id.* at 39.

in mind that not only is coercion contrary to human rights but "people cannot be held responsible when denied choice."[150]

Finally, we should mention that during the Cairo Conference, the Beijing Conferences, and the Copenhagen World Summit for Social Development, states agreed that changes in both men's and women's attitudes are necessary in order to achieve a harmonious partnership between men and women and to promote equal responsibility, including responsible reproductive behavior.[151] Male responsibility in family life, the Cairo Conference declared, must be included in the education of children from the earliest ages. Indeed, family planning is not just a "woman's issue;" rather, it affects both men and women. However, women are clearly most affected by reproduction and its consequences. Encouragement of joint decisionmaking in the family and male support for the partners' choices related to reproduction are vital for a participatory orientation to reproductive health.[152]

DENIAL OF ABORTION AND THE QUEST FOR ITS LEGALIZATION

Universal Trends

The Efforts of CEDAW

The increasing concern for maternal health and the legal and social position of women in society,[153] as expressed in contemporary international law, legitimize the demands for an expansion of women's reproductive freedom to include legal abortion,[154] if necessary. Forcing a woman to bear the burden of an unwanted preg-

---

150. TOMAŠEVSKI, *supra* note 27, at 22.

151. *See* §§ 4(24), (27) of the ICPD's Plan of Action and § 96 of the Beijing Declaration; Commitment 5(g) of the Copenhagen final document.

152. UNFPA, THE STATE OF WORLD POPULATION 36 (1995).

153. Already in 1974 the World Population Conference recognized that the right to family planning had immediate benefits for the health, well-being, and economic independence of women. Thereafter, both CEDAW and the CSW have produced comments of relevance. At its eighth session (1989), members of CEDAW asked government representatives from Ireland during the consideration of its report under the Women's Convention, whether "the fact that abortion was illegal was not considered by the Government to be contrary to the objectives of equality of opportunity and self-determination enshrined in the Convention." The Committee requested data on deaths resulting from illegal abortions and it also wished to know if anything was being done to change the law. U.N. Doc. Supp. No. 38, GA, A/44/38, § 89 (1990). In 1993, CEDAW requested representatives from among others Iraq and Kenya to present more information on legislation and statistics on abortion under art. 12 of the Women's Convention. U.N. Doc. GA, A/48/38, §§ 70, 128, 352 (France), 438 (Republic of Korea), 582 (England) (1993). In 1995, the CSW stressed the fact that the ability of women to control their own fertility was one important basis for the enjoyment of other human rights and it enables them to achieve their personal objectives. In consequence, all women should be in a position to plan and to organise their lives. U.N. Doc. E/CN.6/1995/3/Add.3, §§ 5 & 16 (1995).

154. The term is sometimes used by the public to refer to induced abortions. Within the scholarly literature on that issue, *see* RONALD DWORKIN, LIFE'S DOMINION, AN ARGUMENT ABOUT ABORTION AND EUTHANASIA 3 (1993) ("Abortion, . . . [m]eans deliberately killing a developing human

nancy by upholding prohibitive rules on abortion would have a discriminating effect. Thus, pregnancy imposes a heavy burden on women that is not placed on men.[155] Additionally, legal denial of abortion can be considered a violation of women's freedom of reproductive choice. On this basis, the possibilities of justifying a right to abortion as a component of the right to family planning will be explored.

The negative element of the right to family planning, as stipulated in Article 16(1)(e) of the Women's Convention,[156] infers a freedom for the individual to decide *not* to have a child.[157] Such an interpretation of the relevant provision was given by CEDAW at its session in 1993 in a comment on the content of Article 16(1)(e):

> Women's right to full and free exercise of their reproductive functions, including the right to decide whether to have children or *not*, must not be limited by spouse or government, and women must also be guaranteed access to information about safe contraceptive methods, sex education and family planning services.[158]

CEDAW has, moreover, encouraged states in the recommendations adopted at the same session to "provide information on the incidence of interruption of pregnancy and what legislative measures are in place to regulate it."[159]

A question may be asked whether this view provides sufficient ground for an assumption that CEDAW, by applying a dynamic method of interpretation of the concept of family planning, supports the (not necessarily unconditional) right to legal abortion and access to abortion services, and that the right as such can be interpreted into the Women's Convention.[160] The reservation made by the government of Malta, when

---

embryo.") Within the context of international law, abortion was defined by WHO in 1950 as "all foetal deaths in the early period up to nineteen weeks and intermediate period up to twenty eight weeks of gestation, whereas the term stillbirth should apply to the latest period." B. W. HARRISON, OUR RIGHT TO CHOOSE, TOWARDS A NEW ETHIC OF ABORTION 193–94 (1983).

155. Apart from the argument based on lack of total control of the circumstances, in which women become pregnant, *i.e.*, in the case when men forcibly impregnate women, there is a need for a right to abortion as long as mothers live in a social situation of relative disadvantage. A freedom of choice about abortion will remain consequently necessary. Legal abortion is required in a context of women's cumulative inequality. In other words, the argument for freedom of choice as regards abortion is strengthened when it is based on the demand in international law to improve gender equality. S. Martin, *A Women-Centered Approach to Laws on Human Reproduction, in* HUMAN RIGHTS IN THE TWENTY-FIRST CENTURY 913 (K. E. Mahoney & P. Mahoney eds., 1993).

156. The text of the article reads as follows: "States parties shall take all appropriate measures to eliminate discrimination against women in all matters relating to marriage and family relations and in particular shall ensure, on a basis of equality of men and women: the same rights to decide freely and responsibly on the number and spacing of their children and to have access to the information, education and means to enable them to exercise these rights."

157. As regards the right not to procreate, it is significant to make the distinction between non-abortifacient procedures (such as contraception), contragestion, and abortion.

158. U.N. Doc. E/CN.6/1993/CRP.2, § 46 (1993) (emphasis added).

159. *Id.* § 47.

160. Members of CEDAW interpreted the Women's Convention as requiring access to all methods of fertility control, including abortion already in 1983 when reviewing the country report from

ratifying the treaty in regard to the content of Article 16(1)(e), is indicative and supportive of this presumption to some extent.[161] It implies that Malta considered itself not bound by the article because of the fear of a probable interpretation of the right to family planning as imposing an obligation for states parties to legalize abortion.

If that is the case, it might also influence the interpretation and the implementation of other international documents containing similar provisions. The contemporary approach towards human rights law is to regard it as a coherent set of rules. Moreover, it is agreed that priority should be given to a rule affording the best protection or status to the individual. In other words, human rights treaties should be interpreted in favor of the individual, who after all is the object of international protection.[162]

Legal Abortion—A Key Issue During the Cairo and the Beijing Conferences

Adopted international documents also give some support for an extensive interpretation of the right to family planning as indicated above. At the Cairo Conference, the reference to "legal abortion" in the draft section 8.25 (dealing with family planning) was the one that gave rise to the most heated debate during the whole conference. Decriminalization of abortion and eradication of existing repressive practices related to that issue was a proposal put forward by the Norwegian delegation.[163] It brought about criticism that this international gathering had become a conference on the abortion issue instead of population matters. Malta's delegation took the position in this regard that a state cannot be expected to legalize something it considers illegal. In addition, Afghanistan, Guam, and Honduras required that the reference to legal abortion in the final document be deleted. The Holy See asserted that it attaches great importance to the question of maternal death and endorses those aims of the relevant paragraph that address women's health, but for moral reasons it does not approve legal abortion.[164] In other words, these delegations perceived the proposed provision as

---

Ecuador. *See* Cook, *supra* note 126. *See also* U.N. Doc. Supp. No. 45 (A/39/45) Vol. I, §§ 72, 169 and Vol. II, §§ 84, 257; Supp. No. 38 (A/42/38), §§ 97, 416 and Supp. No. 38 (A/43/38), §§ 154, 321 for additional support. In addition, CEDAW, in its analysis of art. 16, referred to the U.N. Expert Group Meeting on Family Planning which took place in 1992 and which rejected any attempt on the part of Governments or international organisations "to prohibit abortion entirely." U.N. Doc. CEDAW/C/1993/4, § 115 (1993).

161. Lars A. Rehof, Guide to the *Travaux Préparatoires* of the United Nations Convention on the Elimination of All Forms of Discrimination Against Women 265 (1993); *see also* U.N. Doc. CEDAW/C/1995/6, § 30 & Annex 3 (1994).

162. *See* Inter-American Court of Human Rights, *In the Matter of Viviana Gallardo et al. v. Costa Rica*, No. G/101/81, Decision of November 1981, Ser. A, Judgements and Opinions, § 16.

163. The Norwegian Prime Minister Mrs. Gro Harlem Brundtland emphasized in her speech on Sept. 5, 1994, that: "Morality becomes hypocrisy if it means accepting mothers suffering or dying in connection with unwanted pregnancies and illegal abortions, and unwanted children living in misery."

164. Speaking before the adoption of the Programme of Action, the observer for the Holy See said that "[T]he Holy See affirms that human rights begin at the moment of conception. Thus, it

favoring legal abortion and in the view of the Holy See its approval might elevate it to "the level of a right."[165] Reservations similar to the ones cited above were indicated by the delegations from Argentina, Peru, and the Dominican Republic. The representative of Jordan, supported by Libya, said that his country would interpret the discussed paragraph in accordance with Islamic law. On the other hand, Zambia's delegation affirmed that keeping the reference to legal abortion in the Cairo Programme of Action was their rock bottom position. It seems that the latter position was also the majority's.

However, consensus on that article was not reached until the very last day of the conference and its formulation became weaker than proposed. Thus, it just refers to "circumstances in which abortion is not against the law;" it does not require the legalization of abortion *per se*. U.N. conferences are processes of interstate negotiations between different parties and are to some extent based on documents adopted on a regional level by governments and international organizations. Several decisions made nationally and internationally in preparation for the Cairo Conference reflect the existing tensions between demographic goals, democratic values, interventionist anti-natalist or pro-natalist policies, and reproductive and sexual health programs; they all contributed to the very complicated negotiations in Cairo. The major obstacle to the adoption of a progressive provision was a handful of countries, the so-called "hardliners," among them the Holy See, Honduras, Nicaragua, Malta, Benin, Morocco, Guatemala, and Argentina, with obstructive anti-contraception/abortion positions. Still, women's advocates succeeded in weakening the position of this group and, as a

---

could never accept population programmes that condone abortion." U.N. Doc. Press Release POP/572, 2, 14, Sept. 14, 1994. The Vatican's Permanent Observer Mission enjoys U.N. status identical to Switzerland's (i.e., as a non-member state permanent observer). This status places restrictions upon an entity's role at the U.N. But because the U.N. treats the Holy See as a state, the Roman Catholic Church is able to participate fully and to vote in most U.N. conferences. In some of the latest conferences on various human rights issues the Holy See has taken a high profile position that has sparked world-wide attention and raised questions regarding its status at the U.N. The viewpoint is held that it does not meet the criteria for statehood and that it is in reality governing arm of a religious and not a civil institution. In fact the Vatican has never made a formal membership (U.N.) application. The credibility of its report to the Beijing Conference was moreover challenged on several grounds. It was argued among other things that, taking into account the structure of the Holy See, there are no women in policy making, neither is there any indication that women have been voluntarily consulted in the development of the Vatican's relevant documents. In other words, the position reflected in this document was said to be one-sided—that of men. *Women-Church Convergence, Equal Is as Equal Does: Challenging Vatican Views on Women*, 2 IPPF 10–13 (1995). While the Holy See is a party to a few human rights treaties, it is not a party to the Women's Convention. It might be of some interest to mention that several NGOs presented a petition to withdraw U.N. observer status from the Holy See during the NGO Forum at the Beijing Conference. *See, e.g.*, a publication of the Centre for Research on Population and Security, North Carolina and the mailed petitions to CFFC, Washington. The petition of the Holy See was considered by many delegates as overreaching its observer status and obstructing with increasing frequency action and development of consensus among member states. The Holy See had publicly opposed the credentials of certain women's NGOs seeking accreditation to the Beijing Conference at the 1995 CSW meeting. Cook, *supra* note 18, at 10.

165. Statement delivered by H. E. R. R. Martino on Sept. 7, 1994.

consequence, increasing women's opportunities for decisionmaking on their fertility, sexuality, and childbearing options was recognized as a fundamental premise for women's empowerment. On that basis, it was maintained that women should have access to safe contraception and legal abortion under the rubric of broader health care. Thus, a major achievement of the Cairo Conference is that unsafe abortions[166] were declared to be a threat to the health of women, as noted in Article 12.17. It was pointed out that unsafe abortions threaten the health of women of reproductive age more than anything else worldwide.[167] Reality shows indeed that unsafe, illegal abortions are a major contributing factor to maternal mortality in many countries. According to estimates, some 70,000–200,000 women die needlessly each year as a result of undergoing avoidable, unsafe abortions.[168] Most of the deaths could be prevented if women had access to decent health care. Recent figures show that approximately 30 to 60 million abortions occur each year, in both societies where abortion is absolutely prohibited[169] and in those where it is not. At least half of these abortions are illegal and performed under unsafe conditions.[170] The incidence of unsafe abortion is highest in South America, despite the Catholic Church's influence in the countries of this region. Among developing regions, the estimated rate of unsafe abortion is lowest in Asia.[171]

In addition, unsafe abortions cause long-term bad health for at least one million other women. Between 125,000 and 200,000 women die every year from complications resulting from an abortion, of which the majority occur in developing countries such as Ethiopia, Colombia, and Bangladesh. The term "unsafe abortion" has been given a broad meaning, comprising not only illegal abortions, but also situations where there is a doubt that the legislated right to abortion actually provides women with access to safe abortions. Lack of legal restrictions on abortion, for example, has not assured access to safe abortions as evidenced by the relatively high incidence of unsafe

---

166. The term "unsafe abortion" is defined in a footnote to §§ 7.44 and 8.25 of the ICPD's Programme of Action, *supra* note 15, as follows: "Unsafe abortion is defined as a procedure for terminating an unwanted pregnancy either by persons lacking necessary skills or in an environment lacking the minimal medical standards or both."

167. J. L. Jacobson, *Women's Reproductive Health, The Silent Emergency, in* WORLD WATCH INSTITUTE 5 (1991); *see also* U.N. Doc. A/171/4, § 167.

168. UNICEF & UNIFEM, CONVENTION ON THE ELIMINATION OF ALL FORMS OF DISCRIMINATION (1995); WHO, COMPLICATIONS OF ABORTION (1995).

169. For example, the Brazilian Penal Code classifies induced abortion among crimes against life. Nevertheless, induced abortions are widely carried out. Estimates vary from 1 million up to 6 million abortions per year. Moreover, abortion was at the beginning of the 1990s the fifth leading cause for hospitalisation in the country. Ellen Hardy *et al., Illegal Induced Abortion Among Female Employees of a Brazilian University, in* UNWANTED PREGNANCIES AND PUBLIC POLICY: AN INTERNATIONAL PERSPECTIVE 110 (Hector Correa ed., 1994); J. Pitanguy, *Feminist Politics and Reproductive Rights: The Case of Brazil, in* POWER AND DECISION, THE SOCIAL CONTROL OF REPRODUCTION 117 (H. H. Pyne, G. Sen & R. C. Snow eds., 1994).

170. SUNDSTRÖM, *supra* note 10, at 12; Swedish Government Official Reports, SOU 1994:37, Marc Bygdeman & Katarina Lindahl, *Sex Education and Reproductive Health in Sweden in the 20th Century, in* REPORT FOR THE INTERNATIONAL CONFERENCE ON POPULATION AND DEVELOPMENT IN CAIRO 1994 35 (1994).

171. THE UNITED NATIONS, THE WORLD'S WOMEN 1995, TRENDS AND STATISTICS 43 (1995).

abortions (estimated by WHO at thirty unsafe abortions per 1,000 women aged 15–49 years) in the former USSR, despite the availability of abortion on request since 1956.[172] The Cairo Conference document broadens considerably the document adopted at the end of the Mexico City Population Conference in 1984; family planning has expanded to include, among other important issues, women's reproductive health and the promotion of women's equality. The blueprint provided by the Programme of Action emerging from the Cairo Conference will serve as a guide for international population activities and national actions in the new millennium.

This legal development was reaffirmed and further elaborated at the Conference in Beijing, where the abortion issue was only one of the major advances over previous conferences. Paragraph 106(k) of the Beijing Declaration and Platform for Action contains a commitment for states to consider reviewing laws containing punitive measures against women who have undergone illegal abortions. During the Cairo and Beijing Conferences about twenty states out of 181—a small but determined group of states from Latin America, the Southeast Asian regions, and several Arab states—indicated that they did not condone abortion and expressed reservation to that specific provision.[173] Some of them referred to traditional values and cultural principles as justification for the reservation (the Maldives, the Dominican Republic, Iraq, Nigeria, and others) to domestic legislation[174] and religious practices[175] (e.g., Benin,

---

172. U.N. Doc. E/CN.9/1996/2, § 55 (1996).

173. U.N. Doc. A/CONF.177/20, 157–77. It is noteworthy, however, that only the delegations of the Dominican Republic, Ecuador, Nicaragua, and Peru entered reservations to § 220 of the Regional Programme of Action 1995–2001, which was adopted in preparation for the Beijing Conference in 1994. This document endorsed § 8.25 of the ICPD. U.N. Doc. E/CN.6/1995/5/Add.3, (1995).

174. The Argentine delegation took a position based, as it said, on the legal tradition of the country and the practice of its courts, that Article 106(k) does not constitute "a proposal to decriminalise abortion or exempt from criminal responsibility those who may be accomplices or participants in this offences." U.N. Doc. A/CONF.177/20, 158. Argentina submitted the same reservations concerning the Regional Programme of Action for the Women of Latin America and the Caribbean, adopted in Santiago, Chile, in June 1995.

175. The Peruvian President A. Fujimori criticized in his speech at the closing plenary of the Beijing Conference on Sept. 15, 1995, the Catholic hierarchy in Peru for opposing the country's comprehensive family planning policy. A striking feature from the Beijing Conference is that representatives from about twenty Islamic states who took the floor to comment on the Declaration and Platform for Action, noted reservations to the final text in regard to the demand to review punitive domestic laws for illegal abortion since, they maintained, it was not in conformity with Islamic law. On the other hand the prime Minister of Pakistan Mrs. M. B. Bhutto representing a Moslem country, stressed in her speech at the opening Plenary on Sept. 4, 1995, that it is not the religion itself but social prejudices that are denying women's rights. This is in contrast to the assertion made by three male professors representing the Al-Azhar University at the Cairo Conference who said that Islam was not against family planning generally, but it allowed abortion only to save the mother's life or health. Although the *fatwas* or religious proclamations by this university carry much weight amongst Muslims, these statements were heavily challenged as not authentic message of Islam by several Muslim NGOs and Muslim feminists participating in the Cairo Conference. Riffat Hassan, *Women in Islam: Qur'anic Ideals Versus Muslim Realities*, 2 IPPF 8 (1995). This is but a clear hardening of the Islamic position according to which abortion is allowed

the Philippines, Ecuador, Kuwait, Libya, and Morocco). At the same time it is noteworthy that a great number of countries from various geographical regions of the world and with populations linked to one or several of the major religions of the world (e.g., India, Bolivia, Colombia, El Salvador, South Africa, Tanzania, and Spain on behalf of the EU) declared that they had no reservations whatsoever to the final document. On the contrary, they were very satisfied with its wording and expressly supported it.

There is a clear tendency in the international community to recognize the negative effects of unsafe abortions on women's health,[176] and the need to decriminalize inducive abortion has been stressed. Several arguments were presented at the Beijing Conference against the opponents of legalized abortion, including that legalization would not, as feared, increase abortion rates. Statistics indicate that this fear lacks factual grounds. On the contrary, statistics from countries with liberal legislation on abortion show that the rate of abortions stabilizes a short time after the progressive reforms and even declines. Principally, existing legislation prescribes where and under which medical circumstances women can undergo surgery. Several indications likewise support the assertion that illegal abortions are commonly resorted to in countries with a restrictive nature of legislation.[177] Illegal abortions are generally unsafe, inasmuch as they are often performed by an unskilled provider. The risk of death from such an abortion is 100 to 1,000 times greater than from an abortion performed by a qualified provider.[178] Therefore, the requirement contained in the above-mentioned recent U.N. documents implying that "abortion shall be safe" and that women shall "have access to quality services for the management of complications arising from abortion" is a small but important step forward in establishing an obligation for states to provide women with *safe* abortion services (regardless of legality).

---

until ensoulement, which is believed to take place after the first trimester. Some Muslim scholars consider that ensoulement occurs after 120 days, others that it occurs after eighty or even forty days. Until these days had passed, the fetus did not count as a human life. *Algeria, in* THE RIGHT TO KNOW: HUMAN RIGHTS AND ACCESS TO REPRODUCTIVE HEALTH INFORMATION, ARTICLE 19, 114 (Sandra Coliver ed., 2d ed. 1995) [hereinafter THE RIGHT TO KNOW]; Carla M. Obermeyer, *A Cross-Cultural Perspective on Reproductive Rights*, 17 HUM. RTS. Q. 378 (1995). Within the scholarly literature Aristotle wrote in one of his biological treatises (History of Animals, Book VII, Ch. 3, 583 b) that the male embryo develops a human soul about forty days after conception, whereas a female fetus acquires its soul at about ninety days. For much of its history, the Christian Church believed in the delayed-ensoulement principle and allowed first trimester abortions. It was first in 1869 that Pope Pius IX forbade all abortions and declared that the soul was present from the instant of conception. *See* RONALD DWORKIN, LIFE'S DOMINION, AN ARGUMENT ABOUT ABORTION AND EUTHANASIA 40–44 (1993); JANET HADLEY, ABORTION, BETWEEN FREEDOM AND NECESSITY 31 (1996). The medical profession today appears to follow the viability criteria.

176. The Minister for Foreign Affairs of Finland argued on Sept. 6, 1995, at the Beijing Conference that the right to health includes sexual and reproductive rights and that safe abortion is essential to those rights. U.N. Press Release, WOM/BEI/21 (1995).

177. SOU 1983:31, 30; U.N. Doc. E/CN.9/1996/2, § 55 (1996). The incidence of unsafe abortions varies from a high of thirty or more unsafe abortions per 1,000 women aged fifteen to forty-nine years in Eastern and Western Africa, Latin America, and the Caribbean to fewer than two unsafe abortions per 1,000 women aged fifteen to forty-nine years in Northern Europe and Northern America.

178. UNFPA, *supra* note 152, at 48.

Both U.N. Conferences stressed that states must make attempts to eliminate the need for abortion. Safe and effective means of contraception and sterilization as well as the elimination of certain types of violence against women, like rape, would guarantee freedom of choice without resort to abortion for women. Women resort to abortion predominantly under duress. Therefore restrictive and punitive laws on abortion are not very effective in preventing abortion as such, but expose women who must have a clandestine abortion to risk of health and life. So, today the controversy emphasizes not so much the question of whether or not to accept abortion, but merely *what* kind of abortion we will have and how to legitimize it.[179]

European Actions

The Committee of Ministers within the Council of Europe recommended that the regional member governments "take all necessary steps to eliminate the practice of illegal abortion with its attendant dangers."[180] This document sets out guidelines for, among other things, the achievement of greater unity among the member states of the Council of Europe on this subject matter. Principle D(3) requires that abortion, when permitted by domestic law, be available as a medical service to all women, regardless of social or economic position. In Principle D(4), states are, furthermore, requested to eliminate the practice of illegal abortion with its accompanying dangers.[181] The resolution is perfectly clear in its position that abortions should not be made *illegal*. On the other hand, a resolution of the Committee of Ministers is still considered by the majority as a category of "soft law" instruments.[182] It has been maintained that such a document prescribes important international principles, although not yet as binding law.

However, non-legal instruments may have regulatory effects, as Professor J. Sztucki has observed, "by influencing national legislation and judicial decisions, or

---

179. Hardy et al., *supra* note 169, at 109.

180. Council of Europe, Res. (75) 29 of Nov. 14, 1975, of the Committee of Ministers on Legislation relating to Fertility and Family Planning, § D *in* COLLECTION OF THE COUNCIL OF EUROPE'S WORK RELATING TO EQUALITY BETWEEN WOMEN AND MEN (1950–1988), EUROPEAN COMMITTEE FOR EQUALITY BETWEEN WOMEN AND MEN, COUNCIL OF EUROPE 129 (1989).

181. The delegations from Belgium and the Federal Republic of Germany reserved, however, their governments' right not to comply with the text of Principle D, paragraph 4. The representative of Ireland expressed his government's view that it did not consider itself obliged to comply with the text of the resolution as a whole.

182. P. Weil has presented the following definition of "soft law:" "The term 'soft law' is not used solely to express the vague and therefore, in practice, non-compelling character of a legal norm but is also used at times to convey the sub-legal value of some non-normative acts, such as certain resolutions of international organisations." P. Weil, *Towards Relative Normativity in International Law*, 77 AM. J. INT'L L. 414 (1983). For a critical and thorough analysis of the concept in the international law doctrine, *see* Jerzy Sztucki, *Reflections on International "Soft Law,"* *in* FESTSKRIFT TILL LARS HJERNER, STUDIES IN INTERNATIONAL LAW 499–575 (1990). Professor Sztucki considers the term "soft law" as "counterproductive, inadequate, misleading and even dangerous," since it leads to relativisation of normative values in international law in the sense that certain rules are being considered as more binding than others. *Id.*

by constituting directly *ratio decidendi* in disputes on the international level."[183] It could be argued that the term "soft law" presupposes different phases in the law-making process in international law. Neither does such a view necessarily exclude the possible compelling role that non-legal norms can play in international law. In that way, even provisions of a non-legal character, on the pre-normative stage (embryonic norm), may have significant juridical relevance. Moreover, the above-mentioned resolution reflects the prevailing opinion concerning the quest for the legalization of abortion and making it safe, within a regional international organization.

Several years later, in 1990, the European Parliament adopted a resolution dealing with the abortion issue, in which it expressed its conviction that "judicial prosecution is not an acceptable way to reduce its incidence."[184] The emphasis here was instead put on the right to the self-determination of women with regard to their fertility and their own lives.

The current developments within international organizations, mapped out in the review above, are very much in line with recently presented theories in the human rights law doctrine. Coercion has, for example, been defined broadly to include also the denial of safe and legal abortion.[185] From another perspective, abortion is an important means of assuring women's right not to be forced into unwanted motherhood. It is, instead, a means to support a voluntary and responsible motherhood.

In addition to the sources discussed above of relevance for a right to legal abortion and/or access to abortion services, the following sections shall explore whether there is any support for the current approaches to abortion in international law on the domestic level.

Societal Attitudes Toward Abortion and Domestic Laws

Interruption of unwanted pregnancies is a phenomenon with an ancient history. Early-term abortion has been practiced in all times and places. Ideas about and attitudes toward abortion have, however, to a great extent depended on what legal status has been attached to the fetus and the influence of religious norms in a certain society. Views about abortions are as diverse among nations as among individuals. Consequently, opinions on the abortion issue have varied from serious condemnation to acceptance and to regulating it by law or even prescribing it.[186] This diversity of

---

183. Sztucki, *supra* note 182, at 568.

184. Sharon Detrick, *The Irish Case*, 9 INT'L CHILDREN'S RTS. MONITOR 6 (1992).

185. Boland et al., *supra* note 83, at 100; Cook, *supra* note 126, at 997.

186. A common rationale for desirable abortion in some traditional societies is the so-called "improper" paternity. In East Africa, the Masai mandate abortion if the father is an "old, weak, or infirm man." *See* LAURENCE H. TRIBE, ABORTION, THE CLASH OF ABSOLUTES 54 (1990). Abortion was widely approved and was a common practice in ancient Greece. Philosophers as Plato and Aristotle saw the use of abortion as a means of family planning. R. H. Fleen, *Abortion and Exposure in Ancient Greece: Assessing the Status of the Foetus and "New-Born,"* in ABORTION AND THE STATUS OF THE FETUS 290 (William B. Bondeson et al. eds., 1983).

views about the legal status of abortion may to a certain extent explain the hesitancy of the international organs dealing with human rights issues to take a clear stand on this important legal issue.

Categorization of Domestic Laws

Contemporary global approaches[187] to abortion, as reflected in national laws, can be described with the help of the following distinctive features, which to some extent are typical of the great variety of legal solutions to the issue. Within the first category fall jurisdictions, about fifty states, in which abortion is completely banned or allowed only when the woman's life would be endangered if the pregnancy is carried to term. For example, this is the law in countries such as Afghanistan, Ecuador, the Philippines, Saudi Arabia, and the Democratic Republic of Congo.[188] In some of these countries abortion is regulated within the realm of criminal law and is punishable. In Nepal, for instance, women risk lengthy terms of imprisonment for self-induced abortion.[189] Regulations of that kind often contain reference to the right to life of the fetus. Still, prohibitive law and religion have been powerless to stem the tide of up to four million illegal abortions every year in Latin America.[190]

Within the second category fall some eighty-one countries having statutes authorizing abortion on broad medical grounds and for juridical reasons (incest or rape) but not for social (including economic) reasons alone or on request. It seems, however, that in reality these restrictions on a woman's freedom of procreative choice are rarely upheld strictly,[191] because each day as many as 150,000 unwanted pregnancies are terminated through induced abortions.[192] Still, interpreting abortion data is difficult, since surveys in many countries indicate that abortion is grossly underreported, and the availability of reliable statistics is very limited. Abortion is often a secret business. Most jurisdictions that have liberalized their abortion laws have also extended abortion eligibility from traditional indications to new indications, such as family cir-

---

187. Most examples of prohibitive and restrictive laws on abortion are to be found in Latin America, parts of the francophone Africa and partly North Africa. *See* Rebecca J. Cook, *International Protection of Women's Reproductive Rights*, 24 N.Y.U. J. INT'L L. & POL. 667 (1992); RAIMO LAHTI, LAW AND MORAL DILEMMAS AFFECTING LIFE AND DEATH; Council of Europe, CJ-DE/XX (90) 5, 18 (1990).

188. *See* WORLD ABORTION POLICIES 1994, U.N. DEPARTMENT FOR ECONOMIC AND SOCIAL INFORMATION AND POLICY ANALYSIS (1994). In 173 of the world's 190 countries, abortion is permitted to save the life of a woman. N. SADIK, THE STATE OF WORLD POPULATION 43 (1995).

189. TOMAŠEVSKI, *supra* note 27, at 74.

190. ALLAN GUTMACHER INSTITUTE, CLANDESTINE ABORTION: A LATIN AMERICAN REALITY (1994).

191. Cook, *supra* note 187, at 669. According to statistics about 30–40 million legal abortions are performed in the world each year. Given the clandestine nature of unsafe abortion, its incidence is very difficult to gauge. WHO has estimated that some 20 million unsafe abortions are performed each year. U.N. Doc. E/CN.9/1996/2, § 51 (1996).

192. WHO, Reproductive Health: A Key to a Brighter Future, Biennial Report 1990–1991, Special 20th Anniversary Issue 2 (1992); *see also* U.N. Doc. A/CONF.171/4, § 125 (1994).

cumstances, AIDS, or HIV infection. Fifty-six countries belonging to this category allow abortion on social and medical grounds.[193]

The third category comprises the national laws of forty-one countries, which allow abortion on a woman's demand. Thus, an unconditional right to abortion on a woman's request is guaranteed. Even in these jurisdictions, however, women do not have a right to obtain abortion during the entire length of the pregnancy. The vast majority of legislatures distinguish between early and late stages of gestation. Thus, the right to abortion implies that women are in a position to decide whether or not to obtain an abortion only during the early stages of pregnancy. In other words, they are not obliged to give any reasons and need not specify any grounds for having an abortion during the first three months of pregnancy.

An interesting feature of countries with a permissive abortion system is that the rate of abortions is kept relatively low, as in the Netherlands and Japan.[194] Contrastingly, Romania, with a strict abortion law in force, has one of the highest abortion rates.[195] Statistics show that the number of abortions has even decreased after the liberalization of the abortion regulations in Hungary,[196] Denmark,[197] and Finland.[198] In the district of Stockholm (Sweden), abortions declined 13.5 percent during 1993.[199] Consequently, several countries with a liberal approach to abortion have not shown that the legislation itself is counterproductive to the legal protection afforded to the fetus since abortion occurs less than in many countries where it is considered a crime.[200] Thus, law has an impact on the safety of abortion but not on the numbers. There is no sufficient factual basis for the argument that legal abortion promotes promiscuity. Moreover, these countries have a very high total fertility level. Also in countries belonging to the former communist block, like Russia, Albania, and Romania, the number of abortions has fallen as much as 23 percent in 1993 in comparison to the number of abortions performed in 1989. Increased poverty is the perceived reason for this development.

---

193. Mahmoud F. Fathalla, *Fertility Control Technology: A Women-Centered Approach to Research, in* POWER AND DECISION, THE SOCIAL CONTROL OF REPRODUCTION 227 (H. H. Pyne, G. Sen & R. C. Snow eds., 1994); *see also* U.N. Doc. A/CONF.171/4, § 126.

194. H. P. Kee, *Abortion in Singapore: A Legal Perspective*, 42 ICLQ 392 (1993); *see also* K. Shiota, *Induced Abortion and Unwanted Pregnancies in Japan, in* UNWANTED PREGNANCIES, *supra* note 48, at 145; HADLEY, *supra* note 72, at 137.

195. MARY ANN GLENDON, ABORTION AND DIVORCE IN WESTERN LAW 60 (1987); *see also* UNFPA, *supra* note 152, at 156.

196. U.N. Doc. CEDAW/C/13/Add.1, Amend. 1, 6.

197. U.N. Doc. CEDAW/C/13/Add.14, 20.

198. U.N. Doc. CEDAW/C/5/Add.56, 24.

199. F. Mellgren, *Aborterna minskar i länet*, SvD, Feb. 11, 1993, at 8; *see also* SOU 1994:37, 33–35 (1994). The legal right to abortion in Sweden has resulted in an improved health situation, fewer unwanted pregnancies, and a decreasing number of abortions in the whole country. STATISTICAL YEARBOOK 320 (1995).

200. Per Westman, *Protection of the Unborn Child and the Rights of Parents*, 78 SvJT 479 *et seq* (1993).

The Current Abortion Climate

The international picture of abortion laws reflects a great deal of contrast. Along with the attitudinal changes, which have lead to increased legalization of induced abortion, there is also a tendency towards a more restrictive approach to abortion in some European countries with a previously liberal attitude. In Germany, for example, the Federal Constitutional Court (*Bundesverfassungsgericht*) in Karlsruhe declared on May 28, 1993[201] (by a six-to-two ruling in a 183-page decision) that substantial parts of the liberal law regulating abortion previously adopted in 1992 with a clear majority as a compromise for the reunified Germany,[202] was incompatible with the Basic Law of Germany, which in Article I, section 1 and Article 2, section 2 establishes an unlimited duty upon the state to protect unborn life. According to this decision, abortion is unlawful, but it is not penalized.[203]

The judgement has mainly practical implications, since if abortion is considered unlawful, no state-supported compulsory public health insurance program can cover the costs of an abortion. Moreover, abortions will as a rule not be performed in state-funded clinics. The creation of a two-class medical system, where performance of abortion is dependent upon the financial power of a woman, is difficult to defend.

At the same time we cannot ignore the fact that action towards a greater liberalization of laws on abortion has been growing steadily in many countries, most notably in Belgium, Romania, Albania,[204] Spain,[205] Bulgaria, and Italy.[206] In these

---

201. Bundesverfassungsgericht, Zweiter Senat, Urteil vom 28. Mai 1993, 2 BVFG 2/90; 2 BVFG 4/92; 2 BVFG 5/92; NJW, Heft 26, 1751 (1993).

202. Before the reunification of West and East Germany in 1989 the national laws regulating abortion in both countries differed greatly. In the German Democratic Republic abortion was permitted on demand, while in West Germany a doctor's certificate was required justifying the necessity of the abortion (on medical, genetic, or ethical grounds, or because of social hardship) in each case. Counseling was mandatory. The so-called *Indikationslösung* has been in force since May 18, 1976 (BGBl 1976, I, 1213) making the termination of pregnancy within the first twelve weeks of pregnancy punishable under the criminal code. Therefore it was believed that the Pregnancy and Family Assistance Law of July 27, 1992 (BGBl 1992, I, 1398) had adequately balanced these varying concerns. A termination of pregnancy within the first twelve weeks remained non-punishable if the pregnant woman consulted a recognized office. However, this law did not take effect.

203. "Schwangerschaftsabbrüche, die ohne Feststellung einer Indikation nach der Beratungsregelung vorgenommen werden, dürfen nicht für gerechtfertigt (nicht rechtswidrig) erklärt werden. Es entspricht unverzichtbaren rechtsstaatlichen Grundsätzen, daß einem Ausnahmetatbestand rechtfertigende Wirkung nur dann zukommen kann, wenn das Vorliegen seiner Voraussetzungen unter staatlicher Verantwortung festgestellt werden muß." Die Entscheidung des Bundesverfassungsgerichts zum Schwangerschaftsabbruch vom 28. Mai 1993, Juristen Zeitung, 2 Sonderausgabe 7. Juni 1993.

204. Whereas abortion was thoroughly suppressed by the former Albanian regime, in June 1991 the Albanian Ministry of Health authorized abortion on request. Eva Sahatci, *Albania: Discovering the Human Right to Family Planning*, 2 IPPF 25 (1995).

205. GLENDON, *supra* note 195, at 11.

206. DWORKIN, *supra* note 154, at 5. Between 1967 and 1987 abortion laws were liberalized in about sixty-five countries. Sandra Coliver, *The Right to Information Necessary for Reproductive*

countries, access to legal abortions has been made easier by recent legislation, although abortion is far from being available on request. In other European countries, like Ireland, such efforts have been less successful. Thus, procuring an abortion in Ireland still remains a criminal offense. Because of international law, impeding legislation ought not restrict the right to obtain and provide information on abortion.

In conclusion, it appears that about 48 percent of the world's population live in countries (22 percent of the member states of the U.N.) with a very liberal attitude towards abortion, where abortion is considered an unconditional right upon a woman's request.[207]

Access to Abortion Services

Women's ability to exercise the right to their own choice in procreation matters is the second element of the right to family planning, that is, the right to implement such decisions, because "the abstract right to make a decision is meaningless if the conditions needed to carry it out do not exist." The relevant provision of the Women's Convention reflects this line of reasoning, since it entitles women to demand means necessary for the exercise of their right to family planning, such as access to contraception methods and not merely to information on fertility. Furthermore, Articles 12(1) and 14(2)(b) of the same Convention place states parties under a duty to take appropriate measures to ensure access to "family planning" services. Such an obligation has been restated in Article 24(2)(f) of the Convention on the Rights of the Child, where states parties undertake to develop, in addition to preventive health care, guidance for parents family planning education and services.

The self-evident interpretation of this right promotes equal access to family planning services, in the sense that women would have the right to obtain contraceptives without spousal authorization. However, the *travaux préparatoires* of these provisions are silent on the question of whether access to (safe) abortion services is also included therein. Neither did CEDAW mention it in the text of its General Recommendation No. 21. Paragraph 21 strongly states that women are entitled to be "guaranteed access to sex education and family planning services." The understanding of the right to family planning as including access to abortion services has, however, been confirmed earlier, at the World Conference with the aim to review and appraise the achievements of the U.N. Decade for Women, which took place in Nairobi in 1985. In the recommendations adopted at the Conference it was stated that "[l]egal, good-quality abortion services should be made easily accessible to all women."[208]

Health and Choice under International Law, in THE RIGHT TO KNOW, *supra* note 175, at 64.

207. At the same time one should remember that many of the reforms leading to liberal abortion laws in the countries of Central and Eastern Europe were primarily motivated by the goal to protect women from the negative impact of unsafe and illegal abortion on their health rather than a conviction that a woman had a legal right to terminate her pregnancy. Sandra Coliver & Wanda Nowicka, *Poland, in* THE RIGHT TO KNOW, *id.* at 270.

208. U.N. Doc. A/CONF.116/5/ Add. 6.

The 1993 Vienna World Conference on Human Rights recognized the importance of the enjoyment by women of the highest standard of physical and mental health and reaffirmed women's right to "accessible and adequate health care and the widest range of family planning services."[209] Access to abortion services was not mentioned in the final document. But only one year thereafter, in 1994, some 181 states agreed that one of the important goals of the ICPD Programme of Action, as defined in section 7.16, is to provide "universal access to a full range of safe and reliable family planning methods and to related health services which are not against the law" by the year 2015. In section 7.20, Governments are especially urged to remove unnecessary legal, medical, clinical, and regulatory barriers to information and to access to family planning services and methods in order to make it easier for couples and individuals to take responsibility for their own reproductive health. Abortion services are mentioned in section 7.6, according to which all countries shall strive to make them available through the primary health-care system (with reference to section 8.25). Thus, state action is required to minimize the negative health impact of unsafe abortions. This is one of the areas where substantial progress was later achieved at the Beijing Conference as earlier mentioned, since the Beijing Platform for Action expanded beyond the earlier texts in adding that abortions in section 106(k), where they are not against the law, "should be safe."

Unfortunately, firm conclusions cannot be drawn regarding whether safe abortion services exist and are affordable to all who need them on the national level, since no large-scale studies have been undertaken on the issue.[210] The UNFPA referred in a report from 1995 only to the fact that "120 million women would be using family planning if [a]ffordable services were easily available," and that most women in developing countries do not have access to safe abortion services.[211] An inquiry carried out in late 1995 based on the response of seventy-eight developing countries identifies that 38 percent of them did not have any abortion services available as required in section 8.25 of the ICPD Programme of Action.[212] One explanation for this undesirable state of affairs can be found in the poor allocation of governmental resources to such activities. Family planning services account for less than .5 percent of governmental budgets of developing countries and "less than 1.5 percent of all foreign aid" to these countries.[213] It is apparent that in order to be able to implement the Cairo and the Beijing documents the donor governments, the international donors, and the developing countries themselves have to increase expenditures in order to meet the requirement for increasing the safety of abortion services to all. Safe abortion should not be an option only for high-income and rich women. Governments should provide some funding at least for those who are in need but who cannot afford such services. Yet

---

209. U.N. Doc. A/CONF.157/6, Part II, June 12, 1993, § 41.

210. Jennifer Zeitlin et al., *Financing Reproductive and Sexual Health Services, in* POWER AND DECISION, THE SOCIAL CONTROL OF REPRODUCTION 246 (H. H. Pyne, G. Sen & R. C. Snow eds., 1994).

211. UNFPA, *supra* note 152, at 31, 47.

212. U.N. Doc. E/CN.9/1996/3, § 27 (1996).

213. Sandra Coliver & Sofia Gruskin, *Global Overview, in* THE RIGHT TO KNOW, *supra* note 175, at 85.

another problem for women living in rural areas in developing countries is that even if abortion services are free, it can be expensive to get to them because of transportation costs. Loss of income also can be an additional burden. Health centers and clinics are often located too far away from the women seeking abortion. In Kenya about 23 percent of the women of fertile age live more than eight kilometers from health facilities.[214]

These circumstances lead to the conclusion that a legal right to abortion might in reality be of lesser importance if abortion services are not accessible. Abortion may be legal and yet unsafe. And contrastingly, safe abortion services may be available despite legal constraints. Abortion services are available, for example, in Bangladesh as well as in some areas in Malaysia and Indonesia despite restrictive legal rules on abortion.[215] Another example is Belgium, where abortion was illegal until 1990, but was available, safe, and inexpensive. The ideal solution would be if abortion is legal, safe, affordable, and rare since neither the law nor religious norms will stop a woman who desperately wants an abortion. Still the scope of state's obligations in regard to the right to access to family planning services has to be articulated by international supervisory organs.

LEGAL ABORTION—AN EMERGING HUMAN RIGHT IN INTERNATIONAL LAW?

Developments on the Universal Level

The Women's Convention

The fifth part (Articles 17–22) of the Women's Convention contains provisions for a supervisory system. A committee, CEDAW, consisting of twenty-three experts in the field of women's rights, reviews individual country reports of the states parties to the Convention on the measures adopted to implement it and on the progress made.

CEDAW has interpreted the Woman's Convention during the course of its work.[216] The interpretation of some of the provisions contained therein is reflected in the questions of CEDAW members to the representatives of states parties during consideration of their periodic reports. These questions identify CEDAW's collective perception[217] of, among other things, the meaning of Article 16 (the right to family planning) as guaranteed by the Convention. When a great number of similar questions are frequently raised by experts during CEDAW's sessions dealing with a specific substantial issue under the Convention and there is no dissent among the experts,

---

214. Janet W. Kabeberi-Macharia, *Kenya, in* THE RIGHT TO KNOW, *id.* at 190.

215. UNFPA, *supra* note 152, at 43.

216. Andrew Byrnes, *The 'Other' Human Rights Treaty Body: The Work of the Committee on the Elimination of Discrimination Against Women*, 14 YALE J. INT'L L. 46 (1989).

217. CEDAW has suggested that "by looking at the questions asked and issued raised over time by the Committee under the various articles during the constructive dialogue, its views about the nature of the States Parties' obligations under the Convention will emerge." U.N. Doc. CEDAW/C/1995/7, § 305 (1995).

the questions are to be considered a shared view and as an expression of a high degree of consensus among CEDAW experts. There is, furthermore, a new practice evolving in the work of CEDAW implying that individual members act as coordinators of questions in relation to specific articles. Moreover, a pre-session Working Group has been established, since the ninth session, which meets before each subsequent session to prepare a list of issues and questions relating to the country reports to be considered at the CEDAW session to come. Many questions relating to abortion have frequently been asked in relation to a number of periodic country reports.[218]

Members of CEDAW have on different occasions interpreted the Women's Convention as requiring access to all methods of fertility control, including abortion. In other words, an abortion choice must be legally available and, furthermore, could place an obligation on the state to provide such services.[219] CEDAW has consequently indicated that it does not consider the issue of legal abortion as being outside the state parties treaty obligations. The issue of women's access to abortion counseling and to safe abortion services has also been of major concern to expert members of CEDAW. Several members of CEDAW advocated, in their discussion of women's health issues during the 284th meeting (February 3, 1995), access to safe and legal abortions. It was noted that in countries with widely available contraception—and abortion—the incidence of abortion was often quite low. In its consideration of states parties reports in regard to Article 12(2), which is considered to impose a limited duty on states to provide free health care, the Committee has required information about any family planning policy in place in the state party in question.[220] CEDAW habitually also determines whether abortion is legal and if so, whether, and what kind of, legal restrictions there are, and whether illegal abortions are performed. The interplay of several provisions, for example Articles 12 and 16 of the Conventions, constitutes a part of the context, which might prove significant in the process of interpretation.

Nonetheless, CEDAW has not yet mentioned what specific requirements the Women's Convention may impose on the substance of domestic abortion laws. It is

---

218. Some illustrative examples can be found in the following documents: U.N. Doc. CEDAW/C/5/Add.23 (1983); U.N. Doc. CEDAW/C/CRP.15/Add.1 (1990); U.N. Doc. CEDAW/C/CRP.15 (1990); U.N. Doc. CEDAW/C/1995/4, § 87 (1995).

219. Art. 12 of the Women's Convention has been interpreted by CEDAW in the sense that family planning services including abortion should be assured to women in the states parties to the Convention. *See* B. G. Elder, *Human Rights and the United Nations*, 25 CRIME AND SOCIAL JUSTICE 21 (1986); *see also* U.N. Doc. CEDAW/C/1995/7, §§ 422, 428, 430 (1995). The drafting history of this provision reveals that some countries were opposed to the mention of "family planning services" in § 1, since these did not exist everywhere and it was feared that it could lead to refusal to ratify the Convention. Several other delegations felt, however, that the Convention should reflect the desired state of affairs and it should serve as a guideline for the future. U.N. Doc. A/C.3/33/L.47, §§ 114, 116; *see also* REHOF, *supra* note 161, at 144–46.

220. Art. 12(2) reads as follows: "Notwithstanding the provisions of paragraph 1 of this article, States Parties shall ensure to women appropriate services in connection with pregnancy, confinement and the post-natal period, granting free services where necessary, as well as adequate nutrition during pregnancy and lactation." *See also* Commentary, HENRY J. STEINER & PHILIP ALSTON, INTERNATIONAL HUMAN RIGHTS IN CONTEXT 909 (1996).

obvious that the existence of tremendous differences in the national legislation as regards the grounds for the lawful performance of abortion, and which reflect different degrees of permissiveness in the judicial systems worldwide, make such a standpoint a very sensitive issue.

Of further importance for the clarification of the content of the established rights in the Women's Convention is the recently developed CEDAW practice of preparing and adopting general recommendations of a detailed nature dealing with various substantive issues. These recommendations are to be considered collective pronouncements of an international human rights monitoring body. CEDAW itself regards the general recommendations as an "important source of jurisprudence of the Convention" since they contribute to the understanding of the normative content of the rights contained therein.[221] In regard to this activity the timing of certain international events seems to have been decisive for the selection of specific issues for the preparation of general comments. The pronouncement of the U.N. International Year of the Family (1994) contributed, for example, to the choice of "The Family" as the theme to be examined by CEDAW. It resulted in CEDAW's Recommendation No. 21, in which the meaning of Articles 9, 15, and 16 of the Women's Convention were explored[222] and which has served as a starting point to this study. It appears that CEDAW, when issuing this recommendation, relied on the teleological approach, *i.e.*, the provisions in question were interpreted in the light of the Convention's object and purpose. This theory is especially suitable in the field of general multilateral conventions, particularly those of the social, humanitarian, and lawmaking type.[223] Human rights conventions have lawmaking character. They permit interpretation of rights in accordance with progressive developments.

Legal Abortion—A Prerequisite for Gender Equality

The Vienna Convention on the Law of the Treaties,[224] which depicts generally accepted principles of law on the interpretation of treaties, gives a prominent position to the teleological method. According to Article 31, paragraph 1 of the Convention: "A treaty shall be interpreted in good faith in accordance with the ordinary meaning to be given to the terms of the treaty in their context and in the light of its object and purpose."

In general terms, the promotion of equality between men and women and the elimination of all forms of discrimination against women, which "violates the respect

---

221. U.N. Doc. CEDAW/C/1995/7, § 490 (1994).

222. General Recommendation 21(thirteenth session): Equality in marriage and family relations, U.N. Doc. HRI/GEN/1/Rev. 1, 90–100 (1994).

223. D. J. Harris, Cases and Materials on International Law 767 (1991). CEDAW has recently emphasized that it has assumed an important role in the international arena, not only in monitoring the implementation of the Women's Convention but beyond, through its contribution to the "progressive development of international human rights law." U.N. Doc. CEDAW/C/1995/7, § 165 (1995).

224. Vienna Convention on the Law of Treaties, 331 U.N.T.S. 1155 (1969).

for human dignity,"[225] can be identified as the object and purpose of the Women's Convention. This principle has found expression in its Preamble. The aims of that treaty include the protection of the basic respect for women's dignity and well-being and the attainment of substantial equality between women and men. Each provision in the Women's Convention is aimed at achieving this goal. Closely linked with human dignity is control over reproduction and sexuality, which are considered essential elements of achieving equality.

Such an approach would also imply that one of the most important grounds for justification of the adoption of permissible rules on abortion would be the respect for human dignity of women.[226] Justification of legal rules relates primarily to explanations why they ought to be respected. Human dignity has implications as to how human beings ought to be treated. The essence of human rights comprises, according to Marsha Freeman, respect for human dignity and for the capacity "to make responsible choices, regardless of gender or geography."[227] The principle of the dignity of a person as understood in contemporary human rights law enables individuals to realize a chosen life plan (namely, to be free to make decisions about one's reproductive destiny without coercion from the government or outside factors) and relinquish access to certain goods or acquire access to others.[228] With this background, access to legal abortion has been considered to be of particular importance to women because "how reproduction is managed and controlled is inseparable from how women are managed and controlled."[229] Abortion is an issue that fundamentally affects the life and the

---

225. Most of the human rights instruments stress the worth of the individual. The Preambles of both the U.N. Charter and the Women's Convention refer to the "dignity and worth of the human person." The Preambles of the UDHR and the CCPR speak of the "inherent dignity" of the human person. In § 8 of the Beijing Declaration, governments reaffirm their commitment to "the equal rights and inherent dignity of women and men."

226. Criticism has been put forward with regard to argumentation that connects woman's freedom to decide in procreative matters and the concept of human dignity. Indeed, it is argued that: "[s]uch actions are clearly not celebrations or vindications of human dignity and freedom, but a confession of our failure to push back the walls of necessity to find more human solutions to our problems." James P. Hanigan, *Unwanted Pregnancies and the Common Good, in* UNWANTED PREGNANCIES AND PUBLIC POLICY: AN INTERNATIONAL PERSPECTIVE 13 (Hector Correa ed., 1994).

227. Marsha A. Freeman, *The Human Rights of Women in the Family: Issues and Recommendations for Implementation of the Women's Convention, in* WOMEN'S RIGHTS HUMAN RIGHTS 149 (Julie Peters & Andrea Wolper eds., 1995).

228. CARLOS SANTIAGO NINO, THE ETHICS OF HUMAN RIGHTS 129 (1991). Justice Blackmun in Thornburgh v. American College of Obstetricians and Gynecologists, 476 U.S. 747 (1986) made a very forceful assertion of the right to abortion as follows: "Few decisions are more personal and intimate, more properly private, or more basic to individual dignity and autonomy, than a woman's decision [w]hether to end her pregnancy." *Id.* at 2185.

229. S. ATKINS & B. HOGGET, WOMEN AND THE LAW 83 (1984). Davis also emphasizes that birth control, including abortions when necessary, is a fundamental prerequisite for the emancipation of women. According to the same author it was not a coincident that women's consciousness of their reproductive rights was born within the organised movement for women's political equality. A. Davis, *Racism, Birth Control, and Reproductive Rights, in* FROM ABORTION TO REPRODUCTIVE FREEDOM, *supra* note 93, at 15–18; L.L. Heise, *Freedom Close to Home, in* WOMEN'S RIGHTS HUMAN RIGHTS, *supra* note 7, at 250.

well-being of a woman and conditions her social status. This has been emphasized also in national court decisions.[230] If women are unable to decide on procreation matters, they will be deprived of benefits regarding "their health, education or employment and their roles in family and public life,"[231] and there will be very few and limited social options. Limitation of fertility has been a definite factor in the increasing levels of female participation in public spheres.

As was clearly stated at the Beijing Conference in 1995, empowering women to make informed decisions about their sexuality and their fertility also empowers them in other domains.[232] In other words, the status of women is inextricably linked with fertility. A woman's educational level, employment status, and position in the family influences decisions concerning the size of her family.[233] An abortion right in the context of gender equality would necessarily focus on an assurance of a woman's autonomy, requiring affirmative needs-oriented initiatives on the part of the state which can guarantee preconditions for self-realization. This means an expansion of the doctrine based on privacy rights[234] which employs merely the notion of non-interference by the state. Protection of dignity should mean not only respect for a person's humanity but also creation of the necessary conditions for self-fulfillment. The U.N. Secretary General emphasized as early as 1949 that "human dignity implies that human beings are to be treated as ends in themselves and not as mere means to an end."[235]

Within the privacy doctrine, Andrew Clapham advocates that dignity and democracy, which are but the two basic values aimed to be protected by the European Convention on Human Rights, ought to be used as "the tools with which to analyze

---

230. *See, e.g.*, the U.S. Supreme Court decision in *Roe v. Wade*, 410 U.S. 113 (1973). Of special interest is Justice Harry Blackmun's opinion.

231. McDougal, Lasswell, & Chen, *Human Rights for Women and World Public Order: The Outlawing of Sex-Based Discrimination*, 69 Am. J. Int'l L. 497, 504 (1975). The 1994 African Platform for Action stresses in § 15 that women's ability to exercise "control over their fertility is a major step in enabling them to make the necessary choices in other areas." U.N. Doc. E/CN.6/1995/Add.2 (1995).

232. U.N. Doc. CEDAW/C/1996/3/Add.1, § 13 (1995).

233. Arvonne S. Fraser, The U.N. Decade for Women, Documents and Dialogue 46 (1987).

234. In the United States, abortion has been for example legally justified as part of a constitutional right to privacy. Rhonda Copelon has argued that the privacy doctrine is inadequate as a theory for reproduction and sexual self-determination "because it perpetuates the myth that the right to choose is inherent in the individual" instead of acknowledging that choices are shaped, facilitated, or denied by social conditions. Rhonda Copelon, *From Privacy to Autonomy: The Conditions for Sexual and Reproductive Freedom, in* From Abortion to Reproductive Freedom, *supra* note 93, at 38. Privacy must be in other words transformed into the affirmative right to self-determination and grounded in the broader principle of equality. Within the jurisdiction of the United States in the litigation in *Webster v. Reproductive Health Services* one amicus curiae brief forwarded the argument that the denial of legal abortion constitutes sex discrimination. *See* Catharine A.MacKinnon, *Reflections on Sex Equality Under Law*, 100 Yale L.J. 1288 (1991); Robin West, *Jurisprudence and Gender, in* Feminist Legal Theory 214–15 (Katharine B. Bartlett & Rosanne Kennedy eds., 1991).

235. U.N. Commission on Human Rights, The Main Types and Causes of Discrimination, Memorandum submitted by the Secretary General, 4 (1949).

human rights in the private sphere."[236] This approach could be applied without difficulty with regard to universal treaties dealing with women's rights too since, in the words of Professor Rosalyn Higgins, human rights are understood as "part and parcel of the integrity and dignity of the human being."[237]

Consideration of the context of a treaty may include a review of related agreements among the states parties as well as other documents adopted by the international community. Seen in a historical perspective, it was not until the announcement of the U.N. Decade for Women (1975–1985) that planned parenthood in international law (in the sense of a right to procreative freedom) was coupled with the advancement of women's status in society.[238] The link between women's position and their ability to make decisions as regards their fertility was further reaffirmed during the 1984 International Conference on Population in Mexico:

> The ability of women to control their own fertility forms an important basis for the enjoyment of other rights: likewise the assurance of socio-economic opportunities on an equal basis with men and the provision of the necessary services and facilities enable women to take greater responsibility for their reproductive lives.[239]

The right of a woman to determine whether to have children was confirmed at the World Conference in Nairobi in 1985,[240] and thereafter it was endorsed in principle 4 and Chapter 7 of the ICPD Programme of Action. Several of the provisions on reproductive health in the Beijing Declaration and Platform for Action are interrelated with gender equality and empowerment of women. Therefore, a woman's right to reproductive freedom has gained prominence, and indeed, "invoking the prohibition of all forms of discrimination against women may be considered a fundamental key that opens up women's capacity to enjoy other human rights."[241]

---

236. Andrew Clapham, *The 'Drittwirkung' of the Convention, in* THE EUROPEAN SYSTEM FOR THE PROTECTION OF HUMAN RIGHTS 203 (R. St. J. MacDonald et al. eds., 1993).

237. ROSALYN HIGGINS, PROBLEMS AND PROCESSES: INTERNATIONAL LAW AND HOW TO USE IT 96 (1995). The concept of human dignity is, however, problematic. Some academic commentators claim that with reference to traditional African societies, human dignity and human rights are two distinct notions. Thus, safeguards to human dignity in these societies are based on duties and not on human rights. Jack Donnelly, *Human Rights and Human Dignity: An Analytical Critique of Non-Western Conceptions of Human Rights*, 76 AM. POL. SCIENCE REV. 312 (1982). Others tend to consider human rights and human dignity as synonyms. Khushalani emphatically argues, *e.g.*, that the right of women to their dignity "is a fundamental, substantive, legal and inalienable right." YOUGINDRA KHUSHALANI, DIGNITY AND HONOUR OF WOMEN AS BASIC AND FUNDAMENTAL HUMAN RIGHTS 153 (1982). As to the practical effects of the linkage of human rights to human dignity as a justification, Professor Henkin gives a balanced picture. In his view this has "encouraged a tone and mood" as well as "discouraged definitions." HENKIN, *supra* note 106, at 185.

238. Increased concern regarding the abortion issue was given during the Copenhagen World Conference in 1980 thanks to the activities and pressure of the Copenhagen NGO Forum (Forum 80); *see also* Rebecca J.Cook, *International Human Rights and Women's Reproductive Health, in* WOMEN'S RIGHTS HUMAN RIGHTS, *supra* note 7, at 261.

239. Pramilla Senanayake, *Family Planning*, U.N. Doc.EGM/SSMAW/1988/WP. 2 (1988).

240. U.N. Doc. A/CONF.116/5/Add.6, 2.

241. Cook, *supra* note 238, at 261.

Fear of the economic and social burdens of unwanted parenthood and social inequality may be eliminated by advancing the freedom to choose safe abortion when needed and so facilitating a woman's ability to combine motherhood and family life with equal opportunities to personal fulfillment and a professional career. This would also have a positive impact on the children to be born. Indeed, studies dealing with situations in developing countries have shown that the health and survival of infants rise in direct relation to the education of the mother. Yet, only about 40 percent of the women in Africa and in parts of Asia are literate. In some countries illiteracy rates among women are as high as 97 percent.[242] Often, condoms or other pregancy prevention aids are unavailable. Access to legal and safe abortion should be available for women to enable them to plan their lives rationally, without unwanted random interruption. Unwanted pregnancies create future risks, psychological as well as physical, and are obstacles in achieving *de facto* equality among men and women. The right to family planning, as afforded in Article 16(1)(e) of the Women's Convention, is crucial to women and their status. CEDAW has indicated during discussions with governmental representatives when reviewing reports on the implementation of the Convention, that it considers Article 16 as a provision essential to the object and purpose of the Women's Convention and that it constitutes its *raison d'être*.[243] Article 16 is a core obligation.[244]

Having the aforesaid in mind and taking into consideration several international studies,[245] official pronouncements of international organs, and state practice, the objectives of family planning may be summarized as follows:

(1) Enhancing both the status of women and the exercise of their human rights;

(2) Improving their opportunity for attaining self-determination;

(3) Enabling the voluntary efforts of individuals to postpone, prevent, or encourage conception as well as to continue or interrupt pregnancy;

---

242. CONVENTION ON THE RIGHTS OF THE CHILD, UNITED NATIONS CENTRE FOR HUMAN RIGHTS Note No. 6 (1991).

243. On the other hand the Human Rights Committee, in its controversial general comment (GC No. 24/52 of 2 November 1994, U.N. Doc. CCPR/C/21/Rev.1/Add.6, § 8), on issues relating to reservations to multilateral treaties, referred in its very comprehensive list solely to reservations on the right of a person of marriageable age to marry, excluding the right to found a family, as incompatible with the object and purpose of the Covenant. The enumeration of provisions that may not be the subject of reservations is based on the Committee's understanding of Covenant provisions "that represent customary international law (and *a fortiori* when they have the character of peremptory norms)." Thus, the HRC rejected the opinion that all the rights of the Universal Declaration of Human Rights (which includes also the right to found a family) have achieved the status of customary international law.

244. LIESBETH LIJNZAAD, RESERVATIONS TO U.N. HUMAN RIGHTS TREATIES, RATIFY AND RUIN? 303–304 (1995).

245. *See, e.g.*, U.N., SOCIAL WELFARE AND FAMILY PLANNING, DEPARTMENT OF ECONOMIC AND SOCIAL AFFAIRS (1976).

(4) Protecting the rights of the child to be wanted and understanding the importance of substitute families for those children living without their natural parents;

(5) Promoting the concept of responsible parenthood, within which parents have the right and the duty to secure the best conditions for the physical and emotional development of their children.

Focusing on and applying the object and purpose test to the Women's Convention leads to the conclusion that interpreting "family planning" as including legal and safe abortion is important, and this interpretation is warranted, especially with reference to the results from the Cairo and Beijing conferences. One of the strengths of the final documents adopted at these conferences is that they link family planning and reproductive health with empowerment of women and the enhancement of their status. From the emphasis placed upon the teleological method of interpretation it follows that human rights instruments must be given a dynamic interpretation, that is, taking into account present day conditions and developments. Another argument supporting an expansive interpretation of the Women's Convention would be the attempt in international human rights law to choose an interpretation which leads to an effective[246] and progressive protection of the individual rights to be safeguarded. Thus, human rights treaties are for the benefit of persons within a state's jurisdiction.[247]

On the other hand, a convention cannot be interpreted so broadly as to introduce into it a new right that was not intended to be included when the document was drafted.[248] After all, by the adoption of its Recommendation No. 21, CEDAW did not, as in the case of General Recommendation No. 19, express the view that prohibition of abortion and/or unsafe abortion *per se* should be regarded as a breach of the Women's Convention. In Recommendation No. 19, CEDAW firmly placed gender-based violence within the conventional obligations even though it is not explicitly mentioned in the treaty text. The Committee stressed furthermore that states parties should take measures to eliminate violence against women.

Within the doctrine, Professor Meron has shown some caution as to the possible inclusion of a right to abortion within the family planning activities addressed in Article 16(1)(e) of the Women's Convention.[249] Rebecca Cook has, on the other hand, convincingly argued that Article 12 of the same Convention is offended by restrictive abortion laws since such rules do "have a significant impact in perpetuating women's oppression."[250] Thus, gender inequality results from the fact that women's health is affected by contraceptive failure.

---

246. F. Matscher, *Methods of Interpretation of the Convention, in* THE EUROPEAN SYSTEM FOR THE PROTECTION OF HUMAN RIGHTS 67 (R. St. J. MacDonald et al. eds., 1993).

247. HRC, GC No. 24, U.N. Doc. CCPR/C/21/Rev.1/Add.6, § 8 (1994).

248. D. J. HARRIS ET AL., LAW OF THE EUROPEAN CONVENTION ON HUMAN RIGHTS 8 (1995).

249. MERON, *supra* note 117, at 72.

250. Cook, *supra* note 238, at 261.

Other Universal Instruments

The International Covenant on Civil and Political Rights (ICCPR)

International human rights law should be seen as a coherent system, implying that the obligations under one human rights treaty will have to be consistent with the obligations under another treaty. Therefore a short overview of other international treaty provisions is necessary, since they might be of support for a right to abortion.

The supervisory functions for the implementation of the ICCPR are carried out by the Human Rights Committee (HRC). However, no case dealing with the issue of abortion has been considered by the HRC under the First Optional Protocol to the ICCPR. On the other hand, under Article 40 of the Covenant, which directs a very important implementation mechanism, the HRC has elaborated a large number of general comments comprising authoritative interpretations of the rights embodied in the ICCPR. Several states have officially declared that they do not consider the General Comments (GC) adopted by the HRC legally binding, though they consider them as commanding "great respect given the eminence of the Committee" and the status of the Covenant.[251] They are also intended to assist states parties in their implementation of the Covenant. Regarding clarification of the content of the right to found a family in accordance with Article 23, the Committee avoided express mention of abortion in its GC No.19 of 1990, only indicating that states, when deciding family planning policies, should act in accordance with the provisions of the Covenant. Neither did the Committee in its GC No. 6 (on the right to life) and in GC No. 16 (on the right to privacy) address the possible implications of the relevant provisions on the reproductive rights of women and their access to abortion services.[252] Article 6 of the Covenant, which guarantees the right to life, is of special importance to the abortion issue. An examination of the *travaux préparatoires* reveals that a prospective life was not intended to be protected from the moment of conception. The proposal made by Belgium, Brazil, Mexico, and Morocco to amend this provision and which was designed to make it clear that the article would apply "from the moment of conception" was rejected by vote of thirty-one to twenty, with seventeen abstentions,[253] on the grounds, among other things, that domestic laws differ on this matter.

---

251. *See Observation by the United Kingdom on General Comment No. 24*, 16 Hum. Rts. L.J. 424 (1995). *See also* the Observation by the United States of America on General Comment No. 24(52), *id.* at 422, where it is declared that the Covenant "does not impose on States Parties an obligation to give effect to the Committee's interpretations or confer on the Committee the power to render definitive or binding interpretations of the Covenant." This part of the argument might be formally correct but one should emphasize that the interpretation of international legal instruments should be left to international institutions and not to each state party in order to ensure the coherence of the human rights law system.

252. The texts of the mentioned general comments have been reprinted in U.N. Doc. HRI/GEN/1/Rev.1 (1994).

253. U.N. Doc. A/C.3/SR.820. A similar debate on art. 3 of the Universal Declaration of Human Rights resulted in the adoption of a general formula, which does not *verbatim* articulate any prohibition of abortion. However, several delegations have expressed doubts as to whether art. 3 should be considered as comprising the legality of (all) provoked abortions. Lars A. Rehof, *Article*

The HRC has also expressed its view on the meaning of several provisions during its consideration of periodic reports. A great number of questions have been asked by individual expert members of the HRC to representatives of governments during the review of their country reports indicating strong support for the interpretation of Article 6 in the sense that it provides for a developmental protection for the fetus and the existence of a woman's right freely to decide on an interruption of her pregnancy during its first stages.[254] During the consideration of a number of periodic reports,[255] members of the HRC have also asked under what circumstances abortions were authorized in the respective jurisdictions. Thus, there is a clearly recognizable presumption that abortion is lawful in the domestic jurisdictions subject to consideration. It is, however, still unclear whether all members of the HRC agree with a question or a comment on a particular issue under the Covenant brought forward by an individual expert. Therefore there is still some uncertainty as to whether the interpretation of each provision of the Covenant is based on consensus within the entire HRC.

On the other hand, the HRC presents the issues as a rule in its annual reports to the GA in a summarized form, which all members have found to be of great importance. This can be used as evidence for existing consensus on the substantial issues at hand. Moreover, an academic commentator, McGoldrick, has argued that the common position of all members of the HRC becomes apparent in the final observations presented at the end of the consideration of each state's report.[256]

In conclusion we may note that there are some indications, albeit not always unequivocal, that a limited right to abortion might be comprised within the provisions of the ICCPR, since the HRC has not opposed the view that abortion does not constitute any violation of human rights obligations. On the contrary, the Committee has abstained from declaring that the unborn child's right to life is included within the realm of Article 6. At the same time, Rebecca Cook has rightly criticized the contemporary interpretation of this provision as "essentially male oriented" since it ignores the deaths of women from pregnancy-related causes. She suggests moreover that woman's right to life under Article 6 should "entitle her to have access to basic reproductive health services."[257]

3, *in* THE UNIVERSAL DECLARATION OF HUMAN RIGHTS, A COMMENTARY 76 (A. Eide et al. eds., 1992); U.N. Doc. A/C.3/L.654.

254. Dinah Shelton, *International Law on Protection of the Fetus, in* ABORTION AND PROTECTION OF THE HUMAN FOETUS 12 (Stanislav Frankowski et al. eds, 1987).

255. William A. Schabas, *Substantive and Procedural Hurdles to Canada's Ratification of the American Convention on Human Rights*, 12 HUM. RTS. L.J. 408 (1991). When considering the country report of Italy, one of the members of the HRC stated that he "thought the abortion laws so strict that they infringed perhaps on religious grounds the woman's freedom in that respect." DOMINIC MCGOLDRICK, THE HUMAN RIGHTS COMMITTEE, ITS ROLE IN THE DEVELOPMENT OF THE INTERNATIONAL COVENANT ON CIVIL AND POLITICAL RIGHTS 330 (1991).

256. MCGOLDRICK, *id.* at 83.

257. Cook, *supra* note 238, at 262.

The Convention on the Rights of the Child

A few number of the reservations entered by states parties with respect to Articles 1 and 6 of the Convention on the Rights of the Child are of some relevance to the abortion issue. First of all, of the states parties to the Convention,[258] only two, Argentina and Guatemala, have stated in their declarations to Article 1 that they shall interpret the term "child" as a human being from conception to eighteen years of age. In consequence, the unborn child's right to life is protected in these jurisdictions and abortion is illegal.[259] Other countries, like China, France, and Tunisia, have at the same time referred in their reservation or declarations to the Convention to their national legislation, which allow voluntary interruption of pregnancy. In their view, the Convention should not be interpreted to impede the application of the rules already in force.[260] No government has objected to this view. Moreover, the Swedish member of the Committee on the Rights of the Child, Mr. T. Hammarberg, stated at the Committee's first session in October 1991:

> The Committee should not take up the issue of the rights of the child before birth, since States parties had not assumed any such obligations under the Convention. If the Committee had doubts on the subject, it should begin by requesting a special study on that important and sensitive issue, which would retrace the history of the negotiations that had led to the Convention and bring out the divergent views expressed at the time.[261]

This has not yet been the case. It seems therefore that the prevailing opinion remains that the child's "inherent right to life" contained in Article 6(1) of the Convention as well as in other international treaties does not apply from the moment of conception. In practice, this means that voluntary, early interruption of an unwanted pregnancy would be judged as compatible with these provisions of international treaties.

Developments on the Regional Level

Within Europe

Within the Council of Europe, the Strasbourg organs for the protection of human rights have so far left open the question whether, if at all and if so, to what extent, access to legal and safe abortion is guaranteed by the European Convention on Human Rights. The first case considered by the European Commission, which directly confronts access to abortion as a privacy right (Article 8), was the *Brüggemann and*

---

258. Bea Verschraegen, Die Kinderrechtekonvention 112–13 (1996).

259. Abortion is defined in domestic law as offence against life; it is considered as criminal conduct in which the death of the fetus is caused deliberately, "within the mothers womb or by its premature expulsion." U.N. Doc. CEDAW/C/Gua/1–2, § 210 (1991).

260. Also the Swedish legislator argued in the preparatory work for the ratification of the Convention that the Swedish Abortion Act is not incompatible with arts. 1 and 6 of the Convention. Prop. 1989/90:107, Godkännande av FN-konventionen om barnens rättigheter, 29 (1990).

261. U.N. Doc.CRC/C/1991/SR.11/, 6, § 27 (1991).

Scheuten v. FRG case.[262] The majority of the European Commission concluded that not every termination of pregnancy was a matter solely of the mother's right to private life, since pregnancy creates a close connection between her life and that of the developing fetus.[263] Professor Opsahl stated, however, in a dissenting separate opinion, that "punishment of unlawful abortion, or the threat of it, cannot be justified on any of the grounds set out in Article 8(2)" of the European Convention. The European Commission did note in this case that when the European Convention entered into force there was no "evidence that it was the intention of the Parties to the Convention to bind themselves in favor of any particular solution" in regards to a time limit vis-à-vis interruption of pregnancy.[264]

At the same time, in a separate opinion Opsahl, Norgaard, and Kellberg persuasively argued that "laws regulating abortion ought to leave the decision to have it performed in the early stage of pregnancy to the women concerned." The Nordic members of the European Commission continued their reasoning by saying that the "Fristenlösung, based on self-determination, is the most consistent with what we think a right to respect for private life in this context ought to mean in our time."[265] This view was upheld by the European Commission in a later case involving abortion, *H v. Norway*,[266] in which the lawful abortion of a fourteen-week-old fetus on social ground was held not to be contrary to the Convention. Such a pregnancy could place a woman in a "difficult situation of life" according to the Commission's majority.

It may be concluded from the above examples of the case law under the European Convention that abortion for health and social reasons in the first weeks (twelve to fourteen weeks) of the pregnancy has been regarded as compatible with the Convention. In consequence, Article 2 (the right to life) does not impose any far-reaching restrictions on the domestic legislator's right to set conditions for abortion. The abortion cases have consisted of complaints that restriction on abortion has limited the private rights guaranteed in Article 8 of the Convention, impinging upon the right to self-determination in regard to procreation matters.

Within the Inter-American System

The Inter-American Commission on Human Rights, in the *White & Poter v. USA* (Baby Boy) case,[267] adopted arguments similar to those made in the European Commission on Human Rights. According to the claimants, the intentional interruption of pregnancy constitutes an offense against the right to life and is a violation of

---

262. Brüggemann and Scheuten v. Federal Republic of Germany, App. No. 6959/75, 10 Eur. Comm'n H.R. Dec. & Rep. 100 (1978).

263. *Id.* at 116.

264. *Id.* § 64, at 117.

265. *Id.* at 120.

266. Application No. 17004/90 (unreported) (1992).

267. Resolution 23/81, Case No. 2141 Inter-Am. C.H.R. (Mar. 6, 1981), OAS/Ser. L/V/II.54 doc. 9 rev.,16, 25–33 (Oct.1981).

the American Declaration of the Rights and Duties of Man. The Commission concluded that none of the rights in the American Declaration had been violated, finding that the right to life of the fetus as outlined in that document is not absolute. The Commission referred to a number of states that permitted abortion. Thus, a ban of abortion from the moment of conception was rejected because it would have invalidated the laws in force at that time in eleven member states of the Organization for the American States. The Commission based several of its arguments on an examination of the legislative history of the relevant articles in the American Declaration as well as in the American Convention on Human Rights.[268]

The above-referred cases, general comments, and general recommendations permit reciprocal influence and impact, which will help achieve normative uniformity.[269]

From the legal situation in the majority of countries and the concern by the international community to accord, albeit limited, protection to the unborn child,[270] at present, a woman's right to abortion is generally accepted only at the early stages of pregnancy. It has been held that national legislations may impose limits upon post-viability abortion without contravening the human rights of the mother.[271]

EVALUATION

This study has addressed the abortion issue in the context of existing and evolving human rights law. It has demonstrated that international law has become more responsive to women's needs. However, women's perspectives have still not been sufficiently included in legal considerations by international organs regarding several human rights provisions. Recent statistics show furthermore that women's reproductive aspirations are seldom fulfilled and that they still have inadequate control over their reproduction.[272] This author has argued that the recent endorsement of the new concept "reproductive health" requires, among others, a holistic and comprehensive approach to existing law, linking several human rights provisions with the right to family planning and the right to found a family. In other words, the notion "family

---

268. *See* THOMAS BUERGENTHAL & DINAH SHELTON, PROTECTING HUMAN RIGHTS IN THE AMERICAS 77–84 (1995).

269. Professor Kiss has emphasized in this regard the importance that no system for the protection of human rights be "considered in isolation." All systems (universal, regional, and national) must be studied and applied. *See* discussion in *id.* at chapter VII.

270. Eriksson, *supra* note 6, at 95. The European Commission came to the conclusion in the *Paton v. UK* case that under certain circumstances, such as the late stage of pregnancy, the unborn child is protected under the European Convention. A similar argument has been advanced in regard to Article 6 of the ICCPR by Professor Henkin in LOUIS HENKIN, THE INTERNATIONAL BILL OF RIGHTS 122 (1981).

271. Bartha Maria Knoppers, *Modern Birth Technology and Human Rights*, 33 AM. J. INT'L L. 22 (1985).

272. The percentage of reportedly unwanted births ranges from two to twenty-six in Africa, six to twenty-one in Asia and five to thirty-five in Latin America and the Caribbean. The percentage of births reportedly mistimed ranges from six to fifty-two in Africa, eight to twenty-eight in Asia and thirteen to twenty-five in Latin America and the Caribbean. U.N. Doc. E/CN.9/1996/2, § 32 (1996).

planning" needs to be integrated into a wider framework that addresses women's over-all health, well-being, and status. Further, through application of the "disadvantage" test in determining whether discrimination on the basis of sex exists, one can con-clude that a total ban on abortion and other very prohibitive laws on abortion do not counter discrimination against women. On the contrary, they perpetuate oppression of women and are not compatible with one of the most fundamental principles in international human rights law—the principle of non-discrimination on the basis of sex—which has become a part of international customary law.[273]

Although this survey has shown that the discussed terms do not *de lege lata* include access to legal abortion, the scope and the content of human rights evolve continuously. Therefore, the increasing concern for maternal health and the legal and social position of women in society, as expressed in contemporary international law, legitimates the demands for an *de lege ferenda* expansion of the mentioned provisions so as to comprise legal abortion and access to safe abortion services if needed. Thus, through the legalization of abortion the detrimental effects of widespread illegal abor-tion on the health of women and adolescents girls can be diminished. Professor Cook has argued that a positive right to abortion could be based on a claim to preserve the woman's health.[274] Thus, an unwanted pregnancy may endanger a woman's health. Unsafe abortion has been referred to in the final documents as the most neglected underlying cause of reproductive ill-health, constituting a major public health issue adopted at the Cairo and at the Beijing conferences. The most recent developments in international law are consequently supportive to this theory.

Denying abortion often implies a long-lasting disadvantage for the unwanted children subsequently born. They may be abandoned, abused, or raised in detrimen-tal circumstances or conditions, such as being born into poverty. Many governments have tried to abolish abortion, but none have succeed. Instead, they have driven it underground and/or created a lucrative traveling industry. Women who can afford it travel elsewhere in order to obtain an abortion, and a heavy burden falls on the poor and disadvantaged. Therefore, decriminalizing abortion all over the world should be the minimal response of the international community to the existing reality. Most women, given the choice, would not seek the experience of abortion, but if they do, it should be available to them in a legal, safe, accessible, and affordable environment. A clear advantage of linking abortion to health issues is that it may be easier for women to argue for abortion services as a part of a public health service and there-fore payable out of public health funds. Anti-abortion strategy often denies abortion

---

273. *See* Lung-chu Chen, An Introduction to Contemporary International Law 179 (1989); Ian Brownlie, Principles of Public International Law 513 (1990); Henkin, *supra* note 106, at 190; Steiner & Alston, *supra* note 220, at 146, 906.

274. Rebecca Cook, *International Protection of Women's Reproductive Rights*, 24 N.Y.U. J. Int'l L. & Pol. 645, 720 (1992). Professor Cook has also claimed that the right to found a family includes "the right to maximise the survival prospects of a conceived or existing child" through, among other efforts, abortion. Cook, *supra* note 9, at 265. It should be mentioned that in Canada, abortion is justified as part of an entitlement to health.

as a health issue. It is accordingly about "killing babies."[275] One possible disadvantage of defining abortion solely as a health issue and disconnecting it from its human rights context is that it would place doctors in the position of arbiters of its necessity, which may curtail women's entitlement to decide themselves.

It remains to be seen whether the international supervisory bodies for human rights protection will willingly accept the challenge of applying a dynamic method of treaty interpretation to forward an evolution of existing human rights law to comprise access to legal abortion. At present, the very few reviewed international cases suggest that international human rights law does not oppose abortion at the early stage of pregnancy. However, there is still no strong support for the proposition that there is a formally recognized enforceable right to abortion under international law. Such a right is only at an embryonic stage, since only 22 percent of the member states of the U.N. guarantee an unconditional right to abortion upon woman's request. But such a right is in a process of evolving. The full potential of the international human rights framework in this respect is not exhausted.

---

275. The statement delivered by L. Galea, the representative of Malta to the Cairo Conference on Sept. 8, 1994, is illustrative as to that point. He stressed that "The national legislation of our country reflects our culture and our respect for human life in that it forbids the taking of human life, including abortion."

ADVANCING REPRODUCTIVE RIGHTS BEYOND CAIRO AND BEIJING

Rebecca J. Cook and Mahmoud F. Fathalla*

The International Federation of Gynecology and Obstetrics' 1994 World Report on Women's Health concluded that improvements in women's health need more than better science and health care—they require state action to correct injustices to women.[1] Women's health is often compromised, not by lack of medical knowledge, but by infringements on women's human rights. The use of human rights guarantees to advance reproductive health and self-determination has gained momentum through recent United Nations (U.N.) conferences, particularly the 1994 International Conference on Population and Development held in Cairo and the 1995 Fourth World Conference on Women held in Beijing.

The Programme of Action adopted by 184 U.N. member states in Cairo recognizes the importance of human rights in protecting and promoting reproductive health.[2] The Cairo Programme strongly endorses a new strategy for addressing population issues, focused on meeting the needs of individual women and men rather than on achieving demographic targets. A key to this approach is empowering women and protecting their human rights, particularly those relevant to reproductive health. Building on the World Health Organization's definition of health, the Cairo Programme explains that reproductive health is:

> a state of complete physical, mental and social well-being and . . . not merely the absence of disease or infirmity, in all matters relating to the reproductive system and to its functions and processes. Reproductive health therefore implies that people are able to have a satisfying and safe sex life and that they have the capability to reproduce and the freedom to decide if, when and how often to do so. Implicit in this last condition are the right of men and women to be informed [about] and to have access to safe, effective, affordable and acceptable methods of family planning of their choice, as well as other methods of their choice for regulation of fertility which are not against the law, and the right of access to appropriate health-care services that will enable women to go safely through pregnancy and childbirth and provide couples with the best chance of having a healthy infant.[3]

---

* Reproduced with the permission of the Alan Guttmacher Institute from Rebecca J. Cook and Mahmoud F. Fathalla, *Advancing Reproductive Rights Beyond Cairo and Beijing,* Comment, 22(3) INTERNATIONAL FAMILY PLANNING AND PERSPECTIVES (Sept. 1996).

1. M.F. Fathalla, *Women's Health: An Overview,* 46 INT'L J. GYN. & OBS. 105, 105–118 (1994).

2. *Report of the International Conference on Population and Development,* U.N. Doc. A/CONF.171/13, at para. 7.3 (1994) [hereinafter Cairo Programme].

3. *Id.* at para. 7.2.

The Declaration and Platform for Action adopted by 187 U.N. member states in Beijing reaffirm the Cairo Programme's definition of reproductive health,[4] but advance women's wider interests:

> The human rights of women include their right to have control over and decide freely and responsibly on matters related to their sexuality, including sexual and reproductive health, free of coercion, discrimination and violence. Equal relationships between women and men in matters of sexual relations and reproduction, including full respect for the integrity of the person, require mutual respect, consent and shared responsibility for sexual behaviour and its consequences.[5]

The Cairo Programme and the Beijing Platform are points of advancement in identifying particular steps that countries have agreed to take to achieve reproductive rights within specified time periods. The Beijing Platform explains that "reproductive rights embrace certain human rights that are already recognized in national laws, international human rights documents and other consensus documents."[6] However, both documents lack mechanisms for holding governments legally accountable; such mechanisms generally exist in national laws and constitutions and in regional and international human rights treaties, though, which establish general legal obligations that can be applied to the quest for reproductive health and self-determination.[7] National and international human rights law has yet to be adequately applied to reproductive health matters.

In this article, we explain how national constitutions and international human rights law can be applied to hold governments accountable for neglecting or violating these rights, how the Cairo Programme and the Beijing Platform can be used to add specific detail to reproductive rights, and how programs have been developed to protect and promote reproductive rights beyond Cairo and Beijing.

HOLDING STATES ACCOUNTABLE

Most states commit themselves to promote and protect the human rights of women through national constitutions and by membership in regional and international human rights conventions. For example, as of July 1, 1996, 153 states had ratified the Convention on the Elimination of All Forms of Discrimination Against Women (the Women's Convention) and are thus obligated ". . . to ensure the full development and advancement of women, for the purpose of guaranteeing them the exercise and enjoyment of human rights and fundamental freedoms on a basis of equality with men."[8]

---

4.   *Beijing Declaration and Platform for Action*, adopted by the Fourth World Conference on Women, Sept. 15, 1995, U.N. Docs. A/CONF.177/20 (Oct. 17, 1995) and A/CONF.177/20/Add.1 (Oct. 27, 1995), at para. 94.

5.   *Id*. at para. 96.

6.   *Id*. at paras. 95, 223.

7.   *See* Table 1, below.

8.   Convention on the Elimination of All Forms of Discrimination Against Women, G.A. Res. 34/180, U.N. GAOR, 34th Sess., U.N. Doc. A/RES/34/180, art. 3 (1979) [hereinafter Women's Convention].

Ratifying countries are to report regularly on what they have done ". . . to ensure the full development and advancement of women." They report to the Committee on the Elimination of Discrimination Against Women (CEDAW), which was established under the Women's Convention to monitor its implementation. Countries that have ratified other human rights conventions (see Table 1) also accept reporting obligations. Mechanisms existing under some conventions (such as the European Convention on Human Rights and the International Covenant on Civil and Political Rights) enable individuals from consenting countries to bring complaints against them for violations of their rights.

Violations of reproductive rights can be categorized into three groups:

- Category 1 violations result from direct action on the part of a state (such as coercive sterilization); such actions are contrary to freedom from unwarranted state intrusion into reproductive health interests.

- Category 2 violations relate to a state's failure to meet the minimum core obligations of human rights, such as neglecting to reduce maternal mortality rates. These violations result when state action or inaction is contrary to the freedom to receive essential health services and the means of protecting one's reproductive health. For such violations to be demonstrated, standards showing that states are meeting their minimum core obligation of reproductive health protection and promotion have to have been formulated.

- Category 3 violations consist of patterns of discrimination, such as persistent and gross discrepancies in access to health services, that cumulatively disadvantage the reproductive health of groups such as adolescents. These violations breach the right to freedom from discrimination or the freedom to a positive allocation of resources as redress for past discrimination.

Meticulous documentation can show that human rights abuses represent systematic state policies rather than merely individual aberrations. Evidence in court cases can show that a government has failed to eliminate and remedy reproductive rights abuses, and such evidence can be used to analyze conscious patterns over time. Complaints before national, regional, and international legal tribunals and incidents publicized by non-governmental human rights organizations can also be used to direct attention beyond the facts to the underlying conditions of abuse of reproductive rights for which states are legally answerable.

If reproductive rights are to be effectively protected, committees created by conventions to monitor their observance need to develop systematic standards of performance for the states that have ratified them. Monitoring state compliance requires a clear conception of the specific components of each right and the concomitant obligations of states; the delineation of performance standards for each component, including the identification of violations; the collection of relevant data, appropriately disaggregated by sex and other significant variables; the development of information management systems to analyze these data and facilitate the examination of trends

Table 1. Provisions of international human rights documents concerning rights related to reproductive health and self-determination

International document	Right											
	Life & survival	Liberty & security	Highest standard of health	Benefits of scientific progress	Receive & impart information	Education	Marry & found a family	Private & family life	Sexual non-discrim.	Age non-discrim.	Nondiscrim. on grounds of disability
Universal Declaration of Human Rights	3	1, 3	25	27(2)	19	26	16	12	1, 2, 6	1, 2, 6	1, 2, 6
International Covenant on Civil and Political Rights	6	9	na	na	19	na	23	17	2(1), 3	2(1)	2(1)
International Covenant on Economic, Social and Cultural Rights	na	na	12	15(1)(b), 15(3)	na	13, 14	10	10	2(2), 3	2(2)	2(2)
International Convention on the Elimination of All Forms of Racial Discrimination	na	5(b)	5(e)(iv)	na	na	5(e)(v), 7	5(d)(iv)	na	na	na	na
Convention on the Elimination of All Forms of Discrimination Against Women	na	na	11(1)(f), 12, 14(2)(b)	na	10(e), 14(b) & 16(e)	10, 14(d)	16	16	1–5	na	na
Convention on the Rights of the Child	6	37(b)–(d)	24	na	12, 13, 17	28, 29	8, 9	16	2(1)	2(2)	2(2)

European Convention on Human Rights, Its Five Protocols, and Its Social Charter	2	5	Charter: 13	na	10	Protocol 1:2, Charter: 13	12	8	14	14	14
American Convention on Human Rights and Its Protocol	4	7	26; Protocol: 9, 10	26	13	26	17	11	1, 24	1, 24	1, 24
African Charter on Human and Peoples' Rights	4	6	16	22	9	17	18	4, 5	2, 3, 18(3), 28 (duty)	2, 3, 18(3), 28	2, 3, 18(4), 28
Cairo Programme of Action	Principle 1, 8.21, 8.25	4.10, 4.22, 5.5, 7.12, 7.40	7.2, 7.3, 7.5, 7.6, 7.16, 7.23, 7.27–7.33, 8.28–8.35	2.10 & 12.10–12.26	7.3, 7.20, 7.23	4.18, 7.47, 11.8	4.21	7.3, 7.12, 7.17–7.20	4.16, 4.25	7.41, 7.45, 7.46	7.34–7.40, 8.34
Beijing Declaration & Platform for Action	97, 106(i)–106(l)	97, 106(g), (h), (k), 107(e), (q), 124(l), 135, 269, 277(d), 283(d)	92, 94, 95, 98, 103, 106(c), (e), (g), 108	104, 106(g), (h), 108 (o), (p)	95, 103, 106(m), 107(e), 108(l), 223	74, 80, 81, 83(k), (l), 267, 277(a)	93, 274(e), 275(l)	103, 107(e), 108(m), 267	97, 277(l)	83(k), (l), 106–108, 281	99, 108

Note: Numbers show the relevant provisions of the international documents that relate to each named right.

over time and comparison of the reproductive rights of groups within a country; and the analysis of collected data.[9]

Treaty-monitoring committees develop performance standards through their general recommendations, which guide states in preparing reports. For example, at its 1995 meeting, CEDAW agreed to use the Cairo Programme in developing performance standards[10] to determine whether states are in compliance with their obligations to "take all appropriate measures to eliminate discrimination against women in the field of health care in order to ensure . . . access to health care services, including those related to family planning . . . pregnancy, confinement and the post-natal period, granting free services where necessary, as well as adequate nutrition during pregnancy and lactation."[11]

APPLYING HUMAN RIGHTS

Reproductive rights may be protected through specific legal rights. Which rights are invoked and how they are shown to have been violated depends on the particular facts of an alleged violation and on the underlying causes of reproductive ill-health. The rights addressed here are not exhaustive, but only suggest some of the approaches that may be developed to advance reproductive interests. Table 1 shows the relevant provisions of the respective international instruments relating to each right. Moreover, we indicate only certain ways in which specific rights may be applied to reproductive interests and how the Cairo Programme and Beijing Platform can be used to add meaning to them. As human rights laws are applied more vigorously to reproductive interests, a variety of ways of applying them will emerge to serve reproductive interests.

Life and Survival

The Cairo Programme reaffirms that "everyone has the right to life" [Principle 1]. A strong case can be made to apply this right to the lives of the estimated 500,000 women who die each year of pregnancy-related causes, in order to hold governments accountable for their failure to achieve significant reductions in national rates of maternal mortality.[12] Governments have agreed through the Cairo Programme[13] and the Beijing Platform[14] to reduce maternal mortality to one-half of their 1990 levels by the year 2000 and to cut levels by a further one-half between 2000 and 2015.

---

9. A. Chapman, *Monitoring Women's Right to Health Under the International Covenant on Economic, Social and Cultural Rights*, 44 Am. U.L. Rev. 1157, 1159 (1995).

10. *Report of the Committee on the Elimination of Discrimination Against Women*, U.N. Doc. A/50/38 (1995).

11. Women's Convention, *supra* note 8, at art. 12.

12. C. AbouZahr & E. Royston, Maternal Mortality: A Global Factbook 1 (1991).

13. Cairo Programme, *supra* note 2, at para. 8.21.

14. Beijing Platform, *supra* note 4, at para. 106(i).

The root causes of maternal mortality are complex, ranging from a lack of contraception or of trained birth attendants to women's unequal status in society, which results in poor schooling and early marriage.[15] In order to use human rights effectively to hold a government accountable for neglecting the high rate of maternal mortality in a community, the causes of maternal mortality in that community must be understood. If the causes are multifaceted (which is often the case), then the right to life may be invoked in addition to the rights discussed below. If, for instance, the predominant cause is a lack of trained birth attendants, the right to the highest attainable standard of health might be more appropriately invoked to require governments to provide services. This is so in developing countries, where WHO data indicate that only about 55 percent of women are attended at delivery by a health worker who has received at least the minimum of necessary training.[16]

A lack of effective means of birth spacing and fertility control also endangers women's survival and health. All pregnancies and births carry some health risks, but these are higher when pregnancies are too early, too late, too closely spaced, or unwanted. Without obstetric care, women who give birth before age eighteen are three times as likely to die in childbirth as are women aged twenty to twenty-nine under similar circumstances; among women aged thirty-five and older, the risk of maternal mortality is five times as high as among twenty to twenty-nine-year-olds.[17] Comprehensive reproductive health care, including contraceptive services[18] and requested terminations of ill-timed or high-risk pregnancies, would build toward safe motherhood. Further, evidence shows that if births could be spaced so that they came when women wanted them, overall child mortality in many countries might be reduced by more than 20 percent.[19]

Sexual abstinence is an obvious way to prevent unwanted pregnancy. However, sex is a natural part of life; furthermore, many women lack the power to determine when they will have intercourse. Thus, contraception is a necessary alternative.

Contraception is not proof against failure, however. For women who wish to terminate a pregnancy after contraceptive failure, safe abortion and contraceptive aftercare are necessary to reduce their risk of death.[20] Global estimates of maternal deaths arising from unsafe abortion number as many as 200,000 per year.[21] The Cairo Programme (for the first time at a U.N. Population Conference) calls on governments to recognize unsafe abortion as a leading cause of maternal mortality and as a "major

---

15. M.F. Fathalla, *The Long Maternal Road to Maternal Death*, 14(3) PEOPLE 8, 9 (1987).

16. WHO, COVERAGE OF MATERNITY CARE: A TABULATION OF AVAILABLE INFORMATION 12 (3d ed. 1993).

17. WORLD BANK, WORLD DEVELOPMENT REPORT 1993—INVESTING IN HEALTH 84 (1993).

18. J.A. ROSS & E. FRANKENBERG, FINDINGS FROM TWO DECADES OF FAMILY PLANNING RESEARCH 85–87 (1993).

19. WORLD BANK, *supra* note 10, at 83.

20. *Id.* at 84.

21. *Id.*

public health concern."[22] The call for safe abortion was underscored in the Beijing Platform.[23]

The Cairo Programme recognizes that increasing women's ability to survive pregnancy is an issue of their being "equal in dignity and rights" to men.[24] If women are to be equal, governments have at least the same obligation to prevent maternal death as to prevent death from disease. In fact, given that maternity, the sole means of natural human propagation, is not a disease, equity requires more protection against the risk of maternal mortality than against death from disease.

Disparities between rich and poor countries are greater for rates of maternal mortality than for any other public health indicator. Almost 99 percent of maternal deaths occur in developing countries, and the lifetime risk of maternal death is as high as one in twenty for women in parts of Africa (compared with one in 4,000 for women in North America).[25] The magnitude of this differential is a challenge to the universality application of human rights, even though the Cairo Programme and the Beijing Platform emphasize that "the human rights of women . . . are an inalienable, integral and indivisible part of universal human rights."[26]

Liberty and Security of Person

States apply the right to liberty and security to reproductive self-determination in a variety of ways. In the Beijing Platform, governments recognize women's liberty interest by agreeing, for instance, to consider "reviewing laws containing punitive measures against women who have undergone illegal abortions."[27] Courts have addressed abortion by finding restrictive criminal abortion provisions unconstitutional as violations of women's right to liberty and security. For example, the Supreme Court of Canada declared a restrictive criminal abortion provision to violate women's right to security of the person.[28] Several Constitutional Courts, including those of Austria,[29] France,[30] Italy,[31] and the Netherlands[32] have also found that liberal abortion laws are consistent with women's right to liberty.

---

22. Cairo Programme, *supra* note 2, at para. 8.25.

23. Beijing Platform, *supra* note 4, at paras. 97, 106(j), 106(k).

24. Cairo Programme, *supra* note 2, at Principle 1.

25. Fathalla, *supra* note 1.

26. Cairo Programme, *supra* note 2, at Principle 4 ; Beijing Platform, *supra* note 4, at para. 10.

27. Beijing Platform, *supra* note 4, at para. 106(k).

28. R. v. Morgantaler, [1988] 44 D.L.R.(4th) 385 (Can.).

29. Judgement of Oct. 11, 1974, [1974] Erklanrungen des VfGH 221,

30. Judgement of Jan. 15, 1975, Cons. const., [1975] D.S. Jur. 529, J.O., Jan. 16, 1975.

31. June 25, 1981, Judgement No. 108/81, 57 Racc. uff. corte cost. 823.

32. Juristenvereiniging Pro Vita/De Staat der Nederlanden, Court, The Hague, Feb. 8, 1990 ND 413, 707, *as summarized in* 19(5) Eur. Law. D. 179–80 (1991).

Government regulation of population size may violate the liberty and security of the person if it results in compelled sterilization and abortion[33]—or, at the other extreme, in criminal sanctions against contraception, voluntary sterilization, and abortion.[34] The potential for abuse of rights is often greater among women from minority and low-income communities, indicating that great care must be applied in delivering family planning services in such communities. In the United States, for example, some attempts have been made to exert subtle means of control over the reproduction of poor and minority women, such as when courts have offered low-income female offenders release on probation if they will use long-acting contraceptive implants.[35]

In other places, barriers to the removal of hormonal implants that were originally inserted without coercion or inducement have been reported. One study in Bangladesh, for example, reported that 15 percent of women with contraceptive implants had had to make at least three requests for removal.[36] The Cairo Programme affirms that "the principle of informed free choice is essential to the long-term success of family planning programmes [and that] any form of coercion has no part to play,"[37] a principle reaffirmed in the Beijing Platform.[38]

The right to liberty and security of the person has not yet been effectively applied to hold governments accountable over their failure to enforce existing laws against female genital mutilation. This practice, also known as "female circumcision," is supposed to attenuate sexual desire, thus "saving" young girls from temptation and preserving chastity and marital fidelity.[39] Female genital mutilation occurs in one form or another in about forty countries, mostly in East and West Africa and in areas of the Arabian Peninsula. However, as emigration from these regions has increased, the practice is now reported occasionally in Europe and North America. The prevalence of female genital mutilation ranges by country from 5 percent to almost 98 percent;[40] worldwide, about 6,000 girls are circumcised every day.

Governments agreed to enforce the prohibition of female genital mutilation under the Cairo Programme[41] and the Beijing Platform.[42] The Cairo Programme urges

---

33.   R. Boland et al., *Honoring Human Rights in Population Policies: From Declaration to Action, in* POPULATION POLICIES RECONSIDERED: HEALTH, EMPOWERMENT AND RIGHTS 89–106 (1994).

34.   C. Hord et al., *Reproductive Health in Roumania: Reversing the Ceausescu Legacy*, 22 STUDIES IN FAMILY PLANNING 231–40 (1991).

35.   T. Lewin, *Implanted Birth Control Device Renews Debate Over Forced Conception*, N.Y. TIMES, Jan. 10, 1991, at A20.

36.   K. Hardee et al., *Contraceptive Implant Users and Their Access to Removal Services in Bangladesh*, 20 INT'L FAMILY PLANNING PERSPECTIVES 59–63 (1994).

37.   Cairo Programme, *supra* note 2, at para. 7.12.

38.   Beijing Platform, *supra* note 4, at paras. 106(g), 106(h), 107(e).

39.   Fathalla, *supra* note 1.

40.   *Id.*

41.   Cairo Programme, *supra* note 2, at paras. 4.22, 5.5, 7.40.

42.   Beijing Platform, *supra* note 4, at paras. 124(i), 283(d).

governments "to prohibit [female genital mutilation] wherever it exists and to give vigorous support to efforts among non-governmental and community organizations and religious organizations to eliminate such practices."[43] The Beijing Platform underscores the importance of education, particularly of parents, to aid understanding of the health consequences of the practice.[44]

Related to the right to liberty and security is the right to freedom from torture and from inhuman and degrading treatment. The Beijing Platform recognizes that women are tortured, sexually and otherwise, because of their low status in society and their sexual vulnerability[45] and calls on governments to prevent it.[46] Globally, the physical consequences of rape and sexual violence account for about 5 percent of disease burden among women.[47]

The Beijing Platform condemns "torture, involuntary disappearance, sexual slavery, rape, sexual abuse and forced pregnancy."[48] The Cairo Programme urges governments "to identify and condemn the systematic practice of rape and other forms of inhuman and degrading treatment of women as a deliberate instrument of war and ethnic cleansing and take steps to assure that full assistance is provided to the victims of such abuse for their physical and mental rehabilitation."[49] The Inter-American Commission on Human Rights' Report on the Situation of Human Rights in Haiti under the Raoul Cedras Administration determined that the rape and abuse of Haitian women were violations of their right to be free from torture and inhuman and degrading treatment and of their right to liberty and security of the person.[50]

Highest Attainable Standard of Health

The Cairo Programme and the Beijing Platform identify components of the right to the highest attainable standard of reproductive health from a woman's perspective. Both stress the importance of affordable, accessible, and acceptable services throughout the life cycle;[51] "acceptable" services include gender-sensitive standards for the delivery of quality services.[52] Concerning the scope of reproductive health services, the Cairo Programme and the Beijing Platform state:

---

43. Cairo Programme, *supra* note 2, at para. 422,

44. Beijing Platform, *supra* note 4, at para. 277(d).

45. *Id.* at para. 135.

46. *Id.* at para. 107(q).

47. WORLD BANK, *supra* note 10, at 50.

48. Beijing Platform, *supra* note 4, at para. 135.

49. Cairo Programme, *supra* note 2, at para. 4.10.

50. OEA/Ser.L/V II.88, Feb. 9, 1955, at 12–13, 29–47, 93–97.

51. Beijing Platform, *supra* note 4, at paras. 92, 106(e); Cairo Programme, *supra* note 2, at paras. 7.5, 7.23.

52. Beijing Platform, *supra* note 4, at paras. 93, 103, 106(c), 106(g); Cairo Programme, *supra* note 2, at para. 7.23.

Reproductive health care is defined as the constellation of methods, techniques and services that contribute to reproductive health and well-being by preventing and solving reproductive health problems. It also includes sexual health, the purpose of which is the enhancement of life and personal relations, and not merely counseling and care related to reproduction and sexually transmitted diseases.[53]

The Cairo Programme sets targets whereby states agree to:

make accessible through the primary health care system, reproductive health to all individuals of appropriate ages as soon as possible and no later than the year 2015;[54] [and] take steps to meet family planning needs of their populations as soon as possible and should, in all cases by the year 2015, seek to provide universal access to a full range of safe and reliable family planning methods and to related reproductive health services which are not against the law.[55]

The unmet need for family planning services is immense. In developing countries, an estimated 350 million of the 747 million married women of reproductive age are not using contraceptives. Of these, 100 million would prefer to space their next birth or not have more children. Worldwide, women would prefer to delay or avoid about 25 percent of all pregnancies that occur.[56]

In addition, through the Cairo Programme and the Beijing Platform, governments have committed themselves to act on the prevention of sexually transmitted diseases (STDs)—including the human immunodeficiency virus (HIV) and AIDS— and to provide services to treat and counsel those who are infected.[57]

Treaty-monitoring bodies will build on commitments made in consequence of the Cairo and Beijing texts to develop performance standards to determine whether states have met their minimum core obligations to respect individuals' right to the highest attainable standard of reproductive health throughout the life cycle.[58]

The Benefits of Scientific Progress

The Cairo Programme and Beijing Platform require governments to promote women's health research to ensure that women enjoy the benefits of scientific progress.[59] For example, the Beijing Platform calls on governments to "support and initiate research which addresses women's needs and situations, including research on HIV infection and other sexually transmitted diseases in women, on women-

---

53. Beijing Platform, *supra* note 4, at para. 94; Cairo Programme, *supra* note 2, at para.7.2.

54. Cairo Programme, *supra* note 2, at para. 7.6.

55. *Id.* at para. 7.16.

56. M. Catley-Carlson, *The Challenges of Population: Reflections on the Eve of Cairo*, NEW WORLD 1–3 (1994).

57. Beijing Platform, *supra* note 4, at paras. 98, 108; Cairo Programme, *supra* note 2, at paras. 7.27–7.33.

58. A. Rahman & R. Pine, *An International Human Right to Reproductive Health Care: Toward Definition and Accountability*, 1 HEALTH & HUM. RTS. 400, 426 (1995).

59. Beijing Platform, *supra* note 4, at paras. 104, 108(o), 108(p); Cairo Programme, *supra* note 2, at paras. 12.10–12.26.

controlled methods of protection, such as non-spermicidal microbicides, and on male and female attitudes and practices."[60] It similarly requires "action-oriented research on affordable methods, controlled by women, to prevent HIV and other sexually transmitted diseases, on strategies empowering women to protect themselves from sexually transmitted diseases, including HIV/AIDS, and on methods of care, support and treatment of women, ensuring their involvement in all aspects of such research."[61]

The right described above is to the benefits of scientific progress. As a result, the Cairo and Beijing texts recognize that any compromise of women's liberty and security through the inappropriate use or the abuse of medical research or technology frustrates scientific progress.[62]

The right to enjoy the benefits of scientific progress has yet to be effectively applied to requiring governments to give a high priority to reproductive health research. This right could be applied, for instance, where women are denied access to antiprogestins for nonsurgical abortion or to emergency contraception or where women are denied oral contraceptives (as is the case in Japan[63]). Both women and men are entitled to this human right. Thus, the Cairo Programme specifically notes that men too should enjoy the right to the benefits of scientific progress, by calling on governments to give high priority to developing new male contraceptives to serve as alternatives to such methods as condoms, withdrawal and vasectomy.[64]

Receiving and Imparting Information

The texts from Cairo and Beijing call on governments to remove legal, medical, clinical, and regulatory barriers to reproductive health information[65] and to improve its quality.[66] The significance of information to reproductive health is reinforced by the Women's Convention, which requires that women have "specific educational information to help to ensure the health and well-being of families, including information and advice on family planning."[67]

Nonetheless, in a number of countries it remains a criminal offense, sometimes described as a crime against morality, to spread information about contraceptive methods or to publicize where women can obtain pregnancy termination

---

60. Beijing Platform, *supra* note 4, at para. 108(p).

61. *Id.* at para. 108(o).

62. Beijing Platform, *supra* note 4, at paras. 106(g) and 106(h); Cairo Programme, *supra* note 2, at para. 2.10.

63. M. Jitsukawa & C. Djerassi, *Birth Control in Japan: Realities and Prognosis*, 265 SCI. 1048 (1994).

64. Cairo Programme, *supra* note 2, at para. 12.14.

65. Beijing Platform, *supra* note 4, at paras. 95, 103, 106(m); Cairo Programme, *supra* note 2, at paras. 7.3, 7.20.

66. Beijing Platform, *supra* note 4, at para. 103; Cairo Programme, *supra* note 2, at para. 723.

67. Women's Convention, *supra* note 8, at art. 10(h).

services.[68] The European Court of Human Rights recently held Ireland in violation of individuals' right to receive and impart information because the government tried to prevent the circulation of information about abortion services legally available in Britain.[69]

Education

The right to education is particularly important for the promotion and protection of health. Research has consistently shown that women's education strongly influences improved reproductive health, including infant survival and healthy growth of children.[70] Despite broad progress toward literacy, a huge gap still exists worldwide between men and women. According to U.N. estimates, illiterate girls and women in the world in 1985 numbered 597 million, an increase from 543 million in 1970. Illiteracy in men increased from 348 million to 352 million in the same period,[71] showing that women are still disproportionately disadvantaged. The Cairo Programme and the Beijing Platform call for instituting universal primary education by the year 2015 and for closing the gender gap in levels of secondary, vocational and higher education.[72]

The Cairo and Beijing documents encourage an educational setting designed to eliminate all barriers that impede the schooling of married or pregnant young women and young mothers.[73] Such a barrier was removed in 1995, for instance, when the Botswana Court of Appeal ruled as unconstitutional a college regulation that discriminated against female students by requiring that they inform the college director of their pregnancy, and thus become liable to suspension or expulsion.[74]

These documents also urge governments to address adolescent sexuality through educational programs in sexual and reproductive health made available to and understandable by the young and through the provision of contraceptive counseling and

---

68. THE RIGHT TO KNOW: HUMAN RIGHTS AND ACCESS TO REPRODUCTIVE HEALTH INFORMATION (S. Coliver ed., 1995).

69. Open Door Counselling and Dublin Well Women Centre v. Ireland, 16 Eur. H.R. Rep. 244 (1992).

70. J.N. HOBCRAFT, *Woman's Education, Child welfare and Child Survival: A Review of the Evidence*, 3 HEALTH TRANSITION REV. 150 (1993).

71. UNITED NATIONS, THE WORLD'S WOMEN, 1970–1990, 15 (1991).

72. Beijing Platform, *supra* note 4, at paras. 80–81; Cairo Programme, *supra* note 2, at para. 4.18.

73. Beijing Platform, *supra* note 4, at para. 277(a); Cairo Programme, *supra* note 2, at para. 11.8.

74. *Student Representative Council, Molepolole College of Education v. Attorney General of Botswana (for and on behalf of the Principal of Molepolole College of Education and Permanent Secretary of Ministry of Education)*, unreported, Civil Appeal No. 13 of 1994, Misca No. 396 of 1993; judgement delivered on Jan. 31, 1955; as reported in E.K. Quansah, *Is the Right to Get Pregnant a Fundamental Human Right in Botswana?*, 39 J. AFR. L. 97 (1995).

services, including services related to STDs.[75] The inclusion of reproductive health information in school curricula can be controversial, because sexual biology and behavior may be explained in ways that parents oppose, at a time they consider premature, or with the effect of causing children to ask questions at home with which parents are uncomfortable. The European Court of Human Rights has respected sensitivity to parents' views, but has upheld a compulsory sex education course in a state's schools because "the curriculum is conveyed in an objective, critical and pluralistic manner [and does not] pursue an aim of indoctrination that might be considered as not respecting parents' religious and philosophical convictions."[76]

Family and Private Life

In some regions, infertility due to reproductive tract infection jeopardizes the right to form a family and the right to the highest attainable standard of health. In some parts of Africa, this is the cause of up to 50 percent of infertility.[77] Because such infections are generally identifiable, curable, and preventable, governments appear to have a positive obligation to provide relevant information, education, and services to protect the formation of families.

At times, rights may be in conflict. Laws concerning the minimum age at marriage prevent early family formation, but they might well be justified as a way of promoting maternal survival and the formation of families later in the reproductive life span. Both the Cairo and Beijing texts require that governments and non-governmental organizations generate social support for compliance with laws on the minimum age of marriage, in particular by providing women with educational and employment alternatives to entering marriage prematurely.[78]

To ensure women's autonomous and confidential choice in reproductive matters, the Cairo Programme and the Beijing Platform invoke the right to private life against public officials' intrusions.[79] Claims by women to autonomous choices against their partners' attempted vetoes have been consistently upheld by courts in countries of all regions of the world[80] and by the European Commission of Human Rights.[81] Moreover, national laws allowing resort to abortion on privacy

---

75.   Beijing Platform, *supra* note 4, at paras. 74, 83(k), 83(l), 267; Cairo Programme, *supra* note 2, at para. 7.47.

76.   Kjeldsen v. Denmark, 1 Eur. H.R. Rep. 711, at para. 53 (1976).

77.   J. Wasserheit, *The Significance and the Scope of Reproductive Tract Infections Among Third World Women*, INT'L J. GYN. & OBS. 145, Supp. 3 (1989).

78.   Beijing Platform, *supra* note 4, at paras. 93, 274(e), 275(b); Cairo Programme, *supra* note 2, at para. 4.21.

79.   Beijing Platform, *supra* note 4, at paras. 103, 107(e), 108(m), 267; Cairo Programme, *supra* note 2, at paras. 7.3, 7.12, 7.17–7.20.

80.   R. Boland, *Population Policies, Human Rights and Legal Change*, 44 AM. U. L. REV. 1275, 1276 (1995). *See also* R.J. Cook & D. Maine, *Spousal Veto over Family Planning Services*, 77 AM. J. OF PUB. HEALTH 339 (1987).

81.   Paton v. United Kingdom, 3 Eur. H.R. Rep. 408 (1980).

grounds, including U.S. law,[82] have been approved under international human rights instruments.[83]

Nondiscrimination

Sex. The Women's Convention identifies the need to confront the social causes of women's inequality by addressing "all forms" of discrimination suffered by women, including discrimination on grounds of both biological characteristics and of social, cultural, and psychological constructs. The need to eliminate all forms of discrimination against women is a unifying and pervasive theme in the Cairo and Beijing texts. A particular contribution of these texts to sexual equality is that they urge states "to eliminate all forms of discrimination against the girl child and the root causes of son preference, which results in harmful and unethical practices regarding female infanticide and prenatal sex selection"[84] and "to encourage and enable men to take responsibility for their sexual and reproductive behaviour and their social and family roles."[85]

Age. Discrimination on the grounds of young age is comprehensively addressed through the Convention on the Rights of the Child, whereby states agree "to ensure that no child is deprived of his or her right of access to . . . health care services."[86] However, the Cairo Programme recognizes that the "reproductive health needs of adolescents as a group have been largely ignored to date by existing reproductive health services."[87] In many countries, high rates of adolescent unmarried pregnancy are epidemic, and in others appear endemic.[88]

The Cairo and Beijing texts call for the removal of regulatory and social barriers to reproductive health information and care for adolescents.[89] These documents urge countries to ensure that the programs and attitudes of health care providers do not restrict adolescents' access to appropriate services,[90] and that to reduce the number of adolescent pregnancies, they protect and promote the rights of adolescents to reproductive health education, information and care.[91]

---

82. Roe v. Wade, 410 U.S. 113 (1973).

83. Case No. 2141, Inter-Am. C.H.R. 25, OEA/ser.L./V/1154, Doc.9, rev. 1 (1981).

84. Beijing Platform, *supra* note 4, at para. 277(c); Cairo Programme, *supra* note 2, at para. 4.16.

85. Beijing Platform, *supra* note 4, at para. 97; Cairo Programme, *supra* note 2, at para. 4.25.

86. Convention on the Rights of the Child, art. 24(1).

87. Cairo Programme, *supra* note 2, at para. 7.41.

88. P. Senanayake and M. Ladjali, *Adolescent Health: Changing Needs*, 46 INT'L J. GYN. & OBS. 137 (1994).

89. Beijing Platform, *supra* note 4, at paras. 106–108, 281; Cairo Programme, *supra* note 2, at para. 7.45.

90. Beijing Platform, *supra* note 4, at paras. 106–108; Cairo Programme, *supra* note 2, at para. 7.45.

91. Beijing Platform, *supra* note 4, at paras. 83(k) and (l), 107(g), 281; Cairo Programme, *supra* note 2, at para. 7.46.

Adolescents suffer unjust discrimination when they are not free to seek reproductive health counseling and services with the same confidentiality as adults. Courts have rejected laws and interpretations of laws that, on the grounds of age, deny competent adolescents reproductive health services without parental consent. When minors are intellectually mature or emancipated, many courts will recognize their equal rights with adults to health care and to confidentiality.[92] A sign of maturity in minors is their understanding of the need to protect their reproductive health, and their requesting contraceptive services when they are or are about to be sexually active.

Disability. Human rights conventions prohibit discrimination not only on specified grounds, such as sex and age, but also on general grounds. The general prohibition includes discrimination on grounds of disability (such as HIV infection). The Cairo and Beijing texts require governments to eliminate discrimination against persons infected with HIV and their families; strengthen services to detect HIV infection, making sure that they ensure confidentiality; and devise special programs to provide care and the necessary emotional support to men and women affected by AIDS and to counsel their families and near relations.[93]

The Cairo and Beijing texts also recognize that HIV infection in women often reflects women's "preconditioning disability": that, as women, they lack social and legal power to control whether, when, and with what protections they have sexual relations.[94]

MOVING BEYOND CAIRO AND BEIJING

The Cairo and Beijing texts suggest a variety of strategies for effectively protecting and promoting reproductive rights at every government level, from local government to international agencies. The Beijing Platform recognizes that legal literacy and legal service programs are required to ensure that women understand their human rights, how to use them, and how to gain access to courts to enforce then.[95] Moreover, the Beijing text recommends support of those who try to uphold human rights, sometimes against great odds.[96]

Important efforts toward this end include hearings held at the Cairo and Beijing non-governmental forums, where women testified about violations of their reproductive rights.[97] At the national level, for instance, Profamilia, the largest provider of reproductive health services in Colombia, has integrated legal programs into its orga-

---

92.   Gillick v. West Norfolk and Wisbech Area Health Authority and the DHSS, [1986] App. Cas. 112 (H.L. Eng.).

93.   Beijing Platform, *supra* note 4, at para. 108; Cairo Programme, *supra* note 2, at para. 8.34.

94.   Beijing Platform, *supra* note 4, at para. 99; Cairo Programme, *supra* note 2, at paras. 7.34–7.40.

95.   Beijing Platform, *supra* note 4, at paras. 232–33.

96.   *Id*. at para. 232.

97.   CENTER FOR WOMEN'S GLOBAL LEADERSHIP, FROM VIENNA TO CAIRO: THE CAIRO HEARING ON REPRODUCTIVE HEALTH AND HUMAN RIGHTS (1995).

nization.[98] Women who come for reproductive health services thereby have access to advocates who can educate them about their rights and counsel them if these have been violated. Legal services advocates can recommend individual and collective remedies for such violations, as well as preventive actions that governments can take in anticipation of rights violations.

The Cairo and Beijing texts also indicate a variety of mechanisms with which to determine whether states are in compliance or violation. The Beijing Platform recommends creating independent ombudspersons, rights advocates, or defenders with the power to investigate alleged violations of reproductive rights, issue periodic reports, advise governmental and other agencies, and make recommendations for reforms.[99]

An alliance of the health and legal professions could encourage governments, for instance, to enact reproductive health laws that give force to the human rights that serve reproductive health and self-determination. A law could require that social, economic, political, or other relevant policies, developed by either public or private agencies, be accompanied by reproductive rights impact assessments.[100] Since the Cairo Conference, Argentina is considering enactment of a reproductive health law[101] and Guyana has enacted components of one.[102] State policies that protect and promote reproductive health within a wider program of women's health have been enacted in Colombia[103] and Brazil.[104]

The Cairo and Beijing documents recommend that the health professions develop, disseminate, and implement ethics codes to ensure practitioners' conformity with human rights, ethical, and professional standards.[105] Promising signs are the development of ethical guidance by medical associations such as the International Federation of Gynecology and Obstetrics[106] and the Commonwealth Medical Association.[107]

---

98. M.I. Plata, *Reproductive Rights as Human Rights: The Colombian Case, in* HUMAN RIGHTS OF WOMEN: NATIONAL AND INTERNATIONAL PERSPECTIVES (R.J. Cook ed., 1994).

99. Beijing Platform, *supra* note 4, at para. 232(c).

100. K. TOMAŠEVSKI, HUMAN RIGHTS IN POPULATION POLICIES (1994).

101. La Ley de Procreatión Responsable (Law of Responsible Parenthood), 251–D–948, Buenos Aires, Argentina, July 1995.

102. Medical Termination of Pregnancy Act 1995, Guyana Act No. 7 of 1995.

103. Plata, *supra* note 98.

104. J. Pitanguy, *From Mexico to Beijing: A New Paradigm*, 1 HEALTH AND HUM. RTS. 454, 458 (1995).

105. Beijing Platform, *supra* note 4, at para. 106(g); Cairo Programme, *supra* note 2, at para. 7.17.

106. COMMITTEE FOR THE STUDY OF ETHICAL ASPECTS OF HUMAN REPRODUCTION, RECOMMENDATIONS ON ETHICAL ISSUES IN OBSTETRICS AND GYNECOLOGY (1994).

107. COMMONWEALTH MEDICAL ASSOCIATION, MEDICAL ETHICS AND HUMAN RIGHTS: GUIDING PRINCIPLES (1994).

Overall, the Cairo and Beijing documents develop the content and meaning of reproductive rights. These rights will mean very little to the well-being of women and men, however, if national, regional, and international human rights instruments are not used to ensure governments' compliance with their Cairo and Beijing commitments. Moreover, where violations exist, these instruments have to be used to hold governments accountable, legally and politically, for such violations if reproductive rights are to be advanced beyond Cairo and Beijing.

SEXUAL RIGHTS: FROM CONCEPT TO STRATEGY

Susana T. Fried and Ilana Landsberg-Lewis*

A DEFINITION IN FORMATION

For many years, women's movements and lesbian and gay rights advocates have been pushing at the boundaries and definitions of human rights, so that violations targeted at them can be more adequately recognized and protected by the international human rights community. These efforts have primarily focused on two areas. First, they seek to show where women's rights and lesbian/gay/transgender rights are already protected within the existing human rights framework, but have been ignored or rendered invisible (for example, rape as torture, forced medical treatment as degrading treatment, and sexual violence in armed conflict as a war crime). Second, these efforts endeavor to expand the boundaries of the human rights framework to better incorporate the reality of women's (both lesbian and heterosexual), gay men's, and transgendered people's experiences of human rights violations (for example, by challenging the public/private distinction, advancing the discussion of government inaction and due diligence, etc.), and by giving name to amalgams of rights, like sexual rights.

"Sexual rights" recently emerged as a term used in the international women's human rights agenda. However, the issues considered under the rubric of sexual rights have a long history in women's (and men's) resistance to the regulation of sexuality. This chapter investigates the significance of the coalitions that have formed to advance sexual rights as a human rights concept. The authors contend that sexuality is a fundamental aspect of the human personality. Its protection is therefore a key aspect of the defense of human dignity.

Sexuality, as we understand it, is composed of gender identity, sexual identity and orientation, sexual desire, and sexual practices, which together constitute an individual's sexual subjectivity in society. Sexuality is, of course, mediated by social location and, in particular, an individual's experiences of race, class, culture, and understanding of their body within a specific cultural and material context.[1] In this

---

* The authors wish to thank Deborah Liebowitz for her critical and valuable editing, analytic assistance, and review.

1.   For a discussion about the components defining sexuality, *see* Evelynn M. Hammonds, *Toward a Genealogy of Black Female Sexuality: The Problematic of Silence, in* FEMINIST GENEALOGIES, COLONIAL LEGACIES, DEMOCRATIC FUTURE (M. Jacqui Alexander & Chandra Talpede Mohanty eds., 1997) [hereinafter FEMINIST GENEOLOGIES]; Ayesha Imam, *The Muslim Religious Right ("Fundamentalists") and Sexuality, in* WOMEN LIVING UNDER MUSLIM LAWS 7–23 (Dossier, June 17, 1997); JANICE IRVINE, DISORDERS OF DESIRE: SEX AND GENDER IN MODERN AMERICAN SEXOLOGY (1990);

chapter, a distinction is made between sexual identity and orientation and their expression, and sexual behavior. From a rights perspective, one can argue that sexual identity and orientation as fundamental aspects of the human personality must be protected as inalienable human rights. There are, on the other hand, cases in which sexual behavior may be legitimately regulated without violating human rights (e.g., rape, incest, and other forms of non-consensual and coercive behavior).

While a great deal of conceptual and activist work has already been done to develop these ideas, the goal here is not to produce a genealogy (however useful that might be), but to reflect on the import of the emergence of intense interest in sexual rights, to discuss the wide public attention it has recently received, and to suggest some implications for future organizing.

The concept of sexual rights is a powerful organizing tool because of its ability to spark the imagination of a diverse group of women's rights advocates and the term's potential to encompass a wide range of rights. Work in the area of sexual rights offers the opportunity to form global alliances founded on a diversity of situations, culture, race, class, and sexual identity, rather than the possible divisiveness of identity politics. It is fashioned on conceptual and activist work that has been done in a variety of fields, including reproductive health and rights, women's health, women's human rights, and lesbian and gay rights. Thus, work on sexual rights draws on the strength of these experiences, while providing a new locus for organizing.

Sexual rights are embedded in the ideal of women's enjoyment of their human rights, as well as their right to live free from violations. Women's capacity to control their reproductive and sexual lives is inextricable from their sexual autonomy, their health, their bodily integrity, and their economic well-being. As we develop a better understanding of sexual rights, the linkages between sexual rights, women's health, women's human rights, and sexual orientation are thus brought to the foreground of debate. This underscores that a spectrum of issues affect women as sexual agents—or, as is often the case, sexual outlaws—within the context of the construction of and resistance to gender norms.

The prohibition of women's sexual autonomy is bound up with traditional and contemporary precepts about female gender identity and prescribed gender roles, perpetuated within the context of cultural, religious, and ideological beliefs in all societies. Indeed, discrimination and the fear of violence based on the attribution of sexual behavior, sexual identity, and sexual orientation affect all aspects of all women's lives and often present obstacles to their political participation. As Radhika Coomaraswamy, the U.N. Special Rapporteur on Violence Against Women noted in her 1997 report on Violence Against Women in the Community:

> Women who choose options which are disapproved of by the community, whether to have a sexual relationship with a man in a non-marital relationship, to have such a relationship outside of ethnic, religious or class communities, or to live out their sex-

CINDY PATTON, SEX AND GERMS (1985); and Yasmin Tambiah, *Sexuality and Human Rights, in* FROM BASIC NEEDS TO BASIC RIGHTS: WOMEN'S CLAIM TO HUMAN RIGHTS (Margaret A. Schuler ed., 1995).

uality in ways other than heterosexuality, are often subjected to violence and degrading treatment. . . . To strive to live and work outside the watchful gaze of the family and community is to risk becoming a target for male violent behavior.[2]

Indeed, both discrimination and the fear of violence based on the attribution of an "unacceptable" sexual orientation and/or lifestyle (i.e., living as a single woman) affect all aspects of all women's lives. The capacity of women who resist gender norms to participate in the political, social, and cultural life of their communities is obstructed by pervasive hostility and the fear of being the object of discrimination or violence because of this perceived transgression of the norms of appropriate female sexuality.

The fact that women's lives (and the construction of their gender-roles in societies) are curbed both by the abuses they face, and by the ideological/religious constrictions placed on their freedom to exercise their rights, underscores the imperative that recognition of the right to bodily integrity and autonomy will not be achieved on an individual basis, but only as social rights. Indeed, as Petchesky and Correa have noted, "the body exists in a socially mediated universe."[3] A positive right entails facing squarely the idea of the body as an essential component of the self, and the self as socially embedded. In other words, sexual rights are incomprehensible outside of the context of women's "social needs that erode the reproductive and sexual choice for the majority of the world's women, who are poor."[4] While reproductive rights and sexual orientation are both part of the sexual rights "package," they only comprise a portion of those rights. The right to be free from discrimination and violence as a result of one's sexual choices, along with the rights to bodily integrity and fertility regulation, comprises yet another aspect of sexual rights. These combine to help shape a definition-in-formation that emphasizes both women's right to protection from violations as well as to the affirmation and enjoyment of their rights.

The conceptual foundations of sexual rights lie in at least three distinct but related histories. One is the development of concepts and jurisprudence in women's human rights, and in particular, of violence against women. Work on violence against women as a human rights violation highlighted the way in which women's sexualized bodies are so often the target of human rights abuse, thus emphasizing the inadequacy of a too-limited application of concepts such as freedom from violence, the right to privacy, and bodily integrity.

A second foundation for the notion of sexual rights is the work that has taken place on women's right to health, and in particular, women's reproductive health rights. Reproductive rights advocates have long used the language of rights to frame their concerns, but the development of women's human rights discourse has allowed for an expansion of the reproductive rights framework. This expansion resulted from the

---

2.   *Report of the Special Rapporteur on Violence Against Women, Its Causes and Consequences*, at paras. 8 and 9, U.N. Doc. E/CN.4/1997/47 (1997).

3.   Sonia Correa & Rosaline Petchesky, *Reproductive and Sexual Rights: A Feminist Perspective*, *in* POPULATION POLICIES RECONSIDERED: HEALTH, EMPOWERMENT, AND RIGHTS 107–126 (G. Sen, A. Germain & L.C. Chen eds., 1994).

4.   *Id.* at 107.

work that had been done on violence and extended the concept of legitimate women's human rights to include issues of reproductive and sexual health.

Finally, a third foundation of sexual rights builds on work done in the area of sexual orientation and human rights.[5] Legal argument concerning the right to privacy and the right to equal treatment have been given the most attention. The European Court of Human Rights cases date to 1981 (*Dudgeon v. the UK*), and advocacy efforts pre-existed these. For instance, Amnesty International first began publicly discussing the inclusion of human rights violations on the basis of sexual orientation in 1974. These three human rights discourses comprise the building blocks of the sexual rights concept.

Women's human rights advocates have highlighted the importance of a holistic understanding of human rights, including an examination of violations of rights, the enjoyment of rights, and the conditions that enable the exercise of rights. The demand for sexual rights facilitates a clearer and deeper critique of the existing human rights framework while constructing new visions of human rights based on women's everyday experiences. It facilitates the deconstruction of traditional categories of sexual orientation and the identification of these categories as dualistic oppositions (e.g., heterosexual/homosexual). Further, feminist human rights theorists have argued that women's experiences of human rights abuse challenge the traditional boundaries of human rights discourse and international law and typify the significance of the "indivisibility of human rights." By indivisibility, it is meant that women's civil and political rights, like freedom of speech, association, or expression, are inseparable from women's cultural, social, and economic rights, such as the right to health, food, and shelter. In such a paradigm, women's experience of violence is, for example, inextricable from the feminization of poverty and to governments' policies of cutting back on reproductive and sexual health care services.

Gender norms, and their implications for women's sexual lives, are both intensely held and fractious, acceded to and resisted. Many governments are reluctant to step overtly into the arena of sexuality, so they label it a private issue and refrain from interference, thus denying their complicity in regulating women's "private" lives. Nonetheless, governments are often complicit in maintaining the conditions that restrict and control women's lives. In other cases, governments see the regulation of women's sexuality as a central aspect of their raison d'être—to maintain the values and welfare of their citizens and to reaffirm their culture. Thus, private acts and public goals regarding women's sexual autonomy frequently intersect and clash.[6]

---

5.   *See, e.g.*, MARK BLASIUS, GAY AND LESBIAN POLITICS: SEXUALITY AND THE EMERGENCE OF A NEW ETHIC (1994); Hagland, Paul EeNam Park, "International Theory and LGBT Politics: Testing the Limits of a Human Rights-Based Strategy," conference paper delivered at the American Political Science Association, 1996; THE PINK BOOK: A GLOBAL VIEW OF LESBIAN AND GAY LIBERATION AND OPPRESSION (Aart Hendriks, Rob Tielman, & Evert van der Veen eds., 1993); Nicole LaViolette & Sandra Whitworth, *No Safe Haven: Sexuality as a Universal Human Right and Gay and Lesbian Activism in International Politics*, 23 (3) MILLENNIUM: J. OF INT'L STUD. 563–88 (1994); James D. Wilets, *International Human Rights Law and Sexual Orientation*, 18(1) HASTINGS INT'L & COMP. L. REV. 1–119 (1994).

6.   *See, e.g.*, M. Jacqui Alexander, *Erotic Autonomy as a Politics of Decolonization: An*

It is at this nexus of women's "public" and "private" lives (their rights and limitations as citizens and members of communities, and the responsibility of governments to their citizens or others within their borders), that the potential of international organizing around sexual rights rests. In providing women's rights advocates with a common agenda, organizing around sexual rights provides a locus for challenging prevailing and enduring ideologies, practices, and policies that abrogate women's rights and freedoms. Moreover, as noted earlier, it necessitates a focus on the "enabling" conditions that make the exercise of rights possible. As Copelon and Petchesky have argued:

> The realization of these [sexual and reproductive] rights is, in turn, dependent upon larger structural changes. . . . In other words, reproductive and sexual rights ultimately require a radical shifting of priorities toward expenditures that serve social welfare and the quality of life and away from market incentives, private profit and militarism.[7]

As such, the claim for sexual rights is both an affirmative claim of women's right to exercise citizenship in all its manifestations as self-determining agents and a demand for protection against the use of women's bodies as sites of human rights violations. The discussion of sexual rights pushes the analytical boundaries of rights as individually held and socially constituted, and highlights the importance of acknowledging the multiplicity of identities of those pursuing their rights in a public/societal context. This propels us to untangle the relationship between gender and other identity categories (such as race, ethnicity, and religion), out of which a rights-bearing, socially embedded individual emerges. As Rhode warns, while "gender is an important part of what constructs and constrains human identity, its influence is heavily dependent on other cultural institutions, ideologies, and ideals."[8] In other words, such factors as sexual orientation, nationality, immigration status, occupation, physical ability, age, race, ethnicity, religion, and social status also are essential components to be considered when defining, discussing, debating, or seeking to protect sexual rights.

The organizing of women's rights advocates out of which the discussion of sexual rights has emerged (for instance, at U.N. world conferences) represents a shift in analysis. It moves beyond single-issue politics, and identity/geographically based organizing, and illustrates the possibility of constructing global alliances based upon collective political goals and common agendas without glossing over obvious and important differences. Indeed, women's organizations have constructed concrete strategies and coalitions around the language of rights, most visibly during the World Conference on Human Rights (Vienna, 1993), the International Conference on Population and Development (Cairo, 1994), and the Fourth World Conference on Women (Beijing, 1995). Meetings held during the Fourth World Conference on

---

Anatomy of Feminist and State Practice in the Bahamas Tourist Economy, in FEMINIST GENEALOGIES, *supra* note 1.

7.   Rhonda Copelon & Rosalind Petchesky, *Toward an Interdependent Approach to Reproductive and Sexual Rights as Human Rights: Reflections on the ICPD and Beyond, in* FROM BASIC NEEDS TO BASIC RIGHTS: WOMEN'S CLAIM TO HUMAN RIGHTS 343–68 (Margaret A. Schuler ed., 1995.)

8.   Deborah L. Rhode, *Theoretical Perspectives on Sexual Difference, in* THEORETICAL PERSPECTIVES ON SEXUAL DIFFERENCE (Deborah L. Rhode ed., 1990).

Women, and later during the meeting of the U.N. Commission on the Status of Women, emphasized the necessity of building a broad coalition, with a wide range of regional representation and perspectives, in order to adequately negotiate a definition of sexual rights and sexual autonomy.

The current struggle for "sexual rights" presents international women's movements with an organizing tool that can facilitate coalition-building between those working on reproductive rights, women's health, human rights, and the rights of lesbians, gay men, and transgendered people. It gives a name to women's efforts to understand their sexual and reproductive lives within a human rights framework, thus underscoring, as Jacqueline Pitanguy comments, that the "discourse on health, sexuality, and reproduction is ultimately a discourse on social relations, power, and citizenship. Mediated by social class, race, and gender, health and disease reflect the structural linkages between the body and society."[9]

This brief conceptual overview sets out the major components of defining and organizing around sexual rights. It is referred to as a "definition-in-formation" to illustrate the dynamic process of conversation, strategy, and action through which sexual rights is taking on a variety of meanings. The remainder of this chapter continues to illustrate this dynamic process through a discussion of several arenas in which sexual rights emerge as a concept and a strategy.

The next two sections look at parallel and interrelated arenas: testimonies from two global tribunals on violations of women's human rights that were held in the nongovernmental forums at the World Conference on Human Rights (WCHR) and the Fourth World Conference on Women (FWCW), and the formal debates among governmental delegates at the International Conference on Population and Development (ICPD) and the FWCW. It is instructive to note both the similarities and differences in how women's sexual rights are perceived, defined, and constrained in these venues. The final section moves beyond the world conferences to explore how the concept of sexual rights is being used by women as a strategy to organize their efforts and to advance their human rights.

ARTICULATING SEXUAL RIGHTS THROUGH WOMEN'S EXPERIENCES

> [A]wareness and articulation must always be a precursor to assertion. . . . Women have begun to write their own histories and communicate their own ideas. The monopoly over language has been broken and the silence is slowly evaporating.[10]

This section explores what it means to define sexual rights through women's own descriptions of violations of their human rights. Testimonies from a series of

---

9. Jacqueline Pitanguy, *From Mexico to Beijing: A New Paradigm*, 1(4) HEALTH & HUM. RTS. 454–60 (1995).

10. Radhika Coomaraswamy, *Report of the Special Rapporteur on Violence Against Women, Its Causes and Consequences, supra* note 2.

global tribunals and hearings[11] illustrate how women's human rights activists have used the language of rights to bring what has been historically regarded as private phenomena into the public realm. These tribunals and hearings were coordinated by the Center for Women's Global Leadership, in collaboration with partners in the Global Campaign for Women's Human Rights, in order to bring women's voices, and their everyday experiences of human rights violations, onto the global public stage. Human rights as defined from the perspective of women's experiences requires moving beyond narrowly defined individual rights or demands constrained by existing local, national, or international laws and gives women the opportunity to participate in the development of the meaning and application of human rights norms and standards at all levels.

These stories illuminate the ways in which coercion and violence impinge on women's reproductive and sexual lives. The nexus between economic, social, cultural, and political factors, and the ways in which these function together to regulate women's sexuality, is dramatically highlighted by the experiences of the testifiers. Indeed, sexual rights both highlights and is predicated upon the complexity of the construction and regulation of women's sexuality. Sexual rights is the thread which runs through these disparate experiences; it offers the affirmative vision of a life lived with human dignity, including bodily integrity, sexual autonomy, political expression, and economic well-being.

As women testify publicly about violations of their human rights, they engage in an act of resistance. In this moment they begin to affirm their rights. Envisaging sexual rights along a spectrum from violation to sexual autonomy places these experiences within women's ongoing efforts to identify, articulate, and enjoy their human rights.

Mary McGoldrick, Ireland

Mary met and fell in love with the man who was to become her husband when she was fourteen years old. She became pregnant and married him at the age of seventeen. Between 1977 and 1989, she lived with him and they had three children. During those years, she was repeatedly subjected to violence and intimidation by her husband. Every effort she made to seek help, including from medical practitioners and civil servants, was unsuccessful. Mary finally won a barring order against her husband, but was unable to get the police to enforce it. As divorce was not yet legal in Ireland, she tried to obtain a legal separation, but was put on a waiting list. At the time of her testimony in 1995, she was still on this waiting list, and her protection order had expired and could not be renewed without fresh evidence. She currently volunteers with an anti-violence organization in Ireland. She tells her story:

---

11.   Center for Women's Global Leadership, "Testimonies of the Global Tribunal on Violations of Women's Human Rights," Center for Women's Global Leadership, Douglass College, Rutgers University, New Brunswick, N.J. (1993); WITHOUT RESERVATION: THE BEIJING TRIBUNAL ON ACCOUNTABILITY FOR WOMEN'S HUMAN RIGHTS 45 (Niamh Reilly ed., 1996); DAPHNE SCHOLINSKI, THE LAST TIME I WORE A DRESS (1997).

In 1978, while pregnant on [sic] my second child, his brother-in-law left me his baby to take care of and went out with my husband. They were gone for hours, and I couldn't cope with the two babies. I was annoyed when they returned, so my husband started to beat me. I begged his brother-in-law not to leave, but he just took his baby and went, saying it was none of his business. I tried to leave that night, but he made me go to bed with him. My mouth was bleeding and my body ached. I was afraid for the child I was carrying. . . .

I had my third child in April 1989. During my pregnancy he made me feel ugly and stayed out as much as he could. I was constantly worried that he would lose his temper and that he would beat me. The memories of my previous pregnancy were very vivid, so I tried to do everything right, like keeping the house clean and cooking nice meals to keep him in a good mood. I never argued or spoke my mind for fear he would beat me. The following August, he left to live with a woman he said he was in love with because, according to him, I was no longer sexually attractive. I was both relieved and terrified. Because I had been brought up as a Catholic, I believed that marriage was for life. I had taken vows which I believed on my wedding day: "For better or worse, till death do us part."

The majority of people would say, "you made your bed, now lie in it." I felt that I was a failure. I was ashamed of admitting that I was a deserted wife with three children to bring up on my own. . . .

Because of the beatings I received over the years, I had to have a damaged disc removed from my spine. I will never be able to return to manual work without risking further surgery, and I have never been compensated by either my husband or the State for injuries received. . . . I have to depend on Social Welfare for my income, which would be stopped immediately if I were to co-habit in a new relationship with a man. Again I would become, in the eyes of the State, totally dependant on a man to support me and my children. . . .

I feel that I have been sentenced to a life of hardship and isolation for the crimes that my husband committed on me and my children. His only punishment was being ordered not to live in the family home for twelve months. He can re-enter my home at any time. The Irish government have never treated his actions as a serious crime. Their failure to prosecute men in cases of domestic violence and rape clearly gives the message that these crimes are not serious. Since then, my husband has been free to enter into a relationship with another woman who has since had two children with him. He has never been asked if he is a Miss, Mrs., or Ms. He is always Mr. in the eyes of the world.

Mary's story vividly illustrates how violence and women's subordinate and often dependent economic status can make sexual autonomy and independence arduous and dangerous for women. Women are consistently discouraged and punished for demanding that they be treated with respect. In Mary's case, the threat of shame of censure to which women are subjected was reinforced every time she sought assistance. Moreover, the state appears complicit in creating and reinforcing women's subordination—by failing to protect women (e.g., not enforcing restraining orders) and by maintaining laws, such as those which deem divorce to be illegal, that reaffirm social, cultural, and political sanctions against women's autonomy.

Violence against women remains a pervasive obstacle to women's autonomy, well-being, and capacity to engage fully and equally in the development of their societies. The insistence by an international coalition of women's human rights activists that violence against women is a human rights violation has been an effective strategy, gaining attention and access to new tools and mechanisms in this ongoing strug-gle. However, the danger of using the human rights framework is that we may fail to highlight and address the sexualized nature of much violence against women. The concept of sexual rights, then, allows us to use the concepts of human rights, while paying close attention to the interplay of gender-based violence and the regulation of female sexuality.

Lidia Casas for "Maria," Chile

Lidia Casas works with the *Foro Abierto de Salud y Derechos Reproductivos*, a network of women's organizations promoting and defending women's health and reproductive rights. Lidia told the story of Maria. Maria is a forty-year-old woman who moved from southern Chile to Santiago when she was fourteen, and was mar-ried two years later. At seventeen, she had her first child. Her husband began beating her after her second child was born and continued to abuse her with increasing inten-sity. Eventually, she separated from him.

In 1990, Maria was treated at a public hospital, where her IUD was wrongfully removed, due to a misdiagnosis—she actually had a burst appendix. (This procedure resulted in further intrusive surgery.) The hospital staff did not provide her with any contraceptives after they removed her IUD, although they did tell her not to get preg-nant for medical reasons. When Maria found herself pregnant eight months later, she procured an illegal abortion. She went back to the same hospital for treatment due to complications from the abortion and was reported to the police by the hospital staff:

> I was brought to the capital, Santiago, when I was fourteen to work as a live-in maid. I got married two years later. My husband did not allow me to work. By the time I was seventeen, I had my first child. Every year, I had a child. After my second child, my husband began beating me really badly, at any time of the day or night, for no reason at all. . . . When I became pregnant again, my husband thought the child was not his, so he kept beating me more and more. Sometimes he would chase me with a knife, and I had to take refuge with the neighbors. I would go to the police to report him, but they would not get involved in domestic fights.

> My life was not easy with my husband's beatings, taking care of my three children, and working at two jobs to feed them. . . . I separated and met another man, a good man, but my health was no longer good. At the beginning of 1990, I went to the local clinic, because I felt something in my lower stomach. . . . At the clinic they said I had a tumor. . . . A few days later I talked to my boss, and she said I should go to the hos-pital emergency room after work. I was taken to . . . San Juan de Luis hospital, which was publicly run. A doctor there thought that my IUD was making me sick, so he removed (it). While at the hospital, I began to feel worse, and all of a sudden I could barely walk to the bathroom. I was taken to surgery right away. The hospital had mis-diagnosed my condition; my appendix had burst. When I woke up I had a hole in my belly—a colostomy. I was in hospital for a month and was told not to get pregnant, or I would be risking my life. But they didn't give me contraceptives, or put in a new IUD, or anything else. But they kept telling me not to get pregnant. . . .

> After I left hospital I did not have sex for a long time, but later I did, and I got preg-nant. . . . I was sad, I was scared, I wanted to have the baby, but I couldn't. So I talked to my children and my whole family, and we decided that it was better to have an abortion. . . . Later, after the abortion, I was feeling very sick. I was taken to the same

hospital, where they had removed my IUD. . . . The minute I was taken into the emergency room, the woman began to insult me. She told me that it hurt, but that I had done it to myself. A nurse ordered me to get into a stretcher, but I couldn't. I waited until a doctor came. He made a slight cut in my arm and I lost consciousness. . .

Things began to happen really fast. They took me on a stretcher to another room, and I felt blood running through my legs. First, I think they completed the abortion. I was awake and felt all the pain during the procedure. Then my arm was amputated—it was gangrened because of an infection caused by the illegal abortion. The pain was so great, I don't wish this pain on anybody. Later they opened me up again, I didn't know why, but I later found out they had done a full hysterectomy. When I woke up my mind was clear, thank God I was alive. But then, a court officer came to my room, and she said to me with a stiff face that I was under arrest. . . . Later I was placed in an isolation room. . . .While I was in isolation, two armed plainclothes policemen came in. Displaying their arms, they asked me why and where I had the abortion. I told them I was not well, and that I was already in detention. They said in a threatening way that they were going to pick me up at home the moment I got out of jail. . . .

On Christmas Eve, I asked to go home. The janitor told the prison guard that I was being discharged under my own responsibility. The prison guard called the "paddy-wagon," and I was taken to jail in my night-gown even though I pleaded to get some clothes. In April 1992, I was found guilty and given a suspended sentence of three years and one day in prison.

Maria's experience demonstrates the role the state plays in punishing women who deviate from a particular ideology of acceptable sexuality and reproductive decision-making. The fact that women are not provided with information about the full range of options for reproductive issues results in violence and constitutes a human rights violation. Sexual rights cannot be realized if women do not have the capacity to control their reproductive and sexual lives. When abortions are not legal and women are denied adequate medical information and deprived of proper medical care, their right to sexual autonomy, bodily integrity and security of the person, freedom of choice, and the right to live free from torture or cruel, inhuman, or degrading treatment or punishment will remain elusive.

The concept of sexual rights puts the question of autonomy at the center of the violations Maria experienced. In contrast to her experience, sexual rights requires access to information, the highest standard of medical care, and the provision of conditions that allow a woman to fully exercise reproductive and sexual rights.

Gertrude Fester, South Africa

Gertrude was an executive member of the United Women's Organization, which supported repealing the ban on the African National Congress. In May 1988, she was detained, interrogated for about seven hours, and imprisoned under the Internal Security Act:

It was 4 a.m., and the house I was living in at that time with two other women, my mother and a friend, was surrounded by about twenty security policemen, all armed. . . . [T]hen at 4:30 a.m., they banged on the door. . . . After they searched the house and ransacked everything, they took me outside to the cars. . . .

I became very, very frightened. Then, all the stories of other women friends and feminists who had been imprisoned before confronted me. Stories of rape, threats to rape you if you do not co-operate, electrodes put on your nipples, things shoved up your vagina. Shaheeda was told that if she did not cooperate, they would rape her five-year old daughter. . . .

For about seven hours I was interrogated. It would change, sometimes it was friendly, other times it was aggressive and harsh, sometimes they pushed me around, making all kinds of sexual allusions. When they find you are a feminist, they use their sexuality and their male power as a weapon over you. I was asked to be a police spy for them. When I refused to become an informer, they converged on me. . . .

I was charged under Section 29—the Internal Security Act. Under Section 29, you have no rights; you are not allowed to see a lawyer or doctors of your own choice—only the State ones. You cannot receive any visitors. . . .

The first thing that I noticed about the cell was that the bed was opposite the cell door. Behind the bed was the toilet. Because the bed was of a small type, the toilet was fully visible to anyone from the corridor. . . .

The cream gloss-painted walls were filled with phallocentric graffiti. I wanted to use the toilet, but I felt too awkward with the open door, the guard sitting there and watching me, and worst of all, the men, either police or prisoners, passing the door. But I had to use the toilet. . . . Because all the other doors in this long hallway were closed except mine, everyone who passed would peer in curiously, and jeer and comment, and there I was on the toilet open to all these comments. . . .

That first night, as I opened the blankets to get into the bed, I was confronted with a drawing of an enormous erect penis on the sheet. I threw it off and asked for another sheet but this was denied. I then made up the bed so that I could not see this penis, nor touch it with any part of my body. . . . I had to be stripped when I returned from interrogation, but I soon realized that it was to humiliate me rather than search me. . . .

After my release, I had to spend three months in a hospital for nervous disorders. I want to emphasize that what happened to me was easy compared to what others have suffered.

In Gertrude's case, it is clear that the state utilized the regulation of her sexuality and her vulnerability to sexual violence to achieve political ends. The situation was all the more threatening for Gertrude because shame is linked to power and was integral to the form of abuse being perpetrated (i.e., being stripped in front of the Captain, forced to use the toilet in public view, etc.). She was arrested for clear political reasons—she was an ANC supporter—yet the form of abuse she experienced was highly sexualized.

Gertrude's human right to live free from cruel, inhuman, or degrading punishment or treatment was violated in this case. However, adding the analytic lens of sexual rights brings to the foreground the particular aspects of the sexually charged atmosphere of her imprisonment. As she was being arrested, Gertrude recalled the experiences of sexual violation to which other women had been subjected while in custody. The fact of fear of having her sexuality questioned, maligned, or targeted for violation, functioned to limit Gertrude's political work, and more generally, served to threaten all women's activism for fear of reprisal.

Daphne Scholinski, USA[12]

At the time of her testimony, Daphne was twenty-nine years old, an artist-writer living in San Francisco, California. At the age of fourteen, Daphne was confined for four years to a mental hospital in Chicago. Her primary diagnosis was "gender-identity disorder." She was released five days after her eighteenth birthday:

> Most of my childhood I was mistaken for a boy. Constantly in need of defense, for my self-expression, I spent a lot of time hiding. I would be asked, "why don't you try to look more like a girl?" I couldn't even if I tried. . . . I was continually abused verbally and physically by my family, teachers, and peers for being too masculine. . . . I became angry and rebellious. . . . I eventually gave in to the depression caused by these circumstances, and at the urging of doctors and teachers, my parents had me institutionalized. . . .

> I was admitted for reasons of: depression, not adjusting well to adolescence, not attending school, exhibiting suicidal thoughts and gestures, but more specifically, as they put it, for lacking signs of being a "sexual female.". . .

> My primary diagnosis was "gender identity disorder" . . . . The doctors attempted to "cure" me of "pre-homosexuality" and of any wish they thought I had of being a boy. . . . Much of my so-called treatment consisted of pressure to conform to norms of heterosexuality and femininity. . . . [T]he goals set for me were to "learn about make-up, dress more like a girl, curl and style my hair, and spend quality time learning about girl-things with female peers, such as what boys like, etc.". . .

> Stretches of solitary confinement, heavy medication, physical restraint, and horrific treatment from staff became routine. . . . The woman who lived next door to me screamed, over and over again, "I want to die, let me die!" And I was supposed to be maintaining my sanity? I was growing up in a mental hospital. . . .

> A staff person once held his foot on top of my head while he said, "shut up you fucking crazy ass queer," and then yelled for help to calm me down because he felt I was out of control. . . .

> They described my relationship with my best friend as "an expression of a fixated level of sexuality that was being acted out." Nothing about our friendship was out of the ordinary. But because of my "masculine" manner, we became suspected of "acting gay" and presumed to be sexual, which we never were. They never believed us. . . . [W]e were not allowed to speak about each other or to each other. . . .

> I had been sentenced to an adolescence spent surrounded by white walls and lab coats. . . . Quite a punishment for a fourteen-year-old, who was really showing the typical signs of growing up gay in a heterosexual society. . . .

> I was finally released, five days after my eighteenth birthday, when they were unable to legally keep me, and conveniently, just as my insurance ran out. . . .

Daphne's non-conformity with stereotypical notions of "appropriate" femininity exposed her to abrogations of her bodily integrity, freedom of expression, and dignity. In this instance, deviation from the heterosexual "norm" and imputed homosexuality was seen as just cause for her institutionalization and persistent harassment or even violence.

---

12. *See also* SCHOLINSKI, *supra* note 11; Laurence R. Helfer & Alice M. Miller, *Sexual Orientation and Human Rights: Toward a United States and Transnational Jurisprudence*, 9 HARV. HUM. RTS. J. 61 (1996).

The notion of sexual rights links Daphne's experience to the other ways in which women's sexuality is regulated, including through the denial of adequate medical care, reproductive decision-making, or compulsory heterosexuality.

A key aspect of sexual rights is the ability of all people to enjoy and express their sexuality in a myriad of ways without action by state or non-state actors that constitutes a human rights violation. The development of an analysis of sexual rights affords the opportunity to broaden and enrich human rights discourse and practice, rather than limiting it to a set of preconceived notions of acceptable sexuality. As Daphne's story illustrates, violence and discrimination based on real or imputed sexual orientation constitutes a human rights violation.

Khalida Messaoudi for "Oum Ali," Algeria

Oum Ali is a thirty-four-year-old woman, recently divorced, and living alone with seven children. Accused of immorality, she was pressured to leave town, and further harassed and intimidated by fundamentalists. She sought police protection, but the request was rejected. In June 1989, her house was set on fire while her children were at home. Her three-year-old son, who was handicapped, was not able to escape. While twelve accomplices were arrested, the heaviest sentence imposed was fifteen years:

> In June 1989, the Muslim army burned down her house. Her only "crime" was to be living alone. . . . What did they accuse Oum Ali of? They accused her of prostitution, they accused her of making the neighborhood impure, of affecting the morality, the religiousness of the Muslims, and the spiritual health of the town. Even if it were the case, even if she were a prostitute, they should know that if she went that route, it was because there were men willing to exploit her. . . .

> Because, in the eyes of the fundamentalists, a woman living without a husband is a menace to the good morality of the town, Oum Ali was pressured to leave. They organized, and made nightly visits to her home, in order to intimidate her. She asked for the protection of the police, but they did not take her seriously. . . .

> The day the criminals were arrested, there was a demonstration by Islamic militants of Ouargla; they marched toward the police headquarters, chanting and asking for the immediate release of the arsonists. By their logic, they need not deny the crime. They believed they have the right to ensure that the religious precepts are properly followed by all. In their minds, and by their convictions, they have the right to persecute any person—particularly women who are alone, who they believe are representatives of Satan, representatives of danger and immorality—and the right to persecute any person who goes against their ideas actively or simply through their existence.

> Oum Ali . . . is still terrorized.

As with Daphne, in Oum Ali's situation, allegations alone exposed her (and her children) to violence. Often, women who make a positive assertion, like the choice to live alone, are met with extreme resistance and punishment. Clearly, however, even if evidence existed that Oum Ali was "promiscuous," her human rights were still grossly violated by an intolerant group determined to impose their "values" on another through violence.

The spectrum of women's experience can be seen on a continuum, at one end compulsory heterosexuality, on the other, women's right to determine their sexuality free from discrimination, violence, or coercion. The conceptual analysis afforded by sexual rights incorporates the full range of women's experiences of their sexuality along that continuum—from violations to positive expressions. The continuum must always be contextualized in women's social and cultural realities. In Oum Ali's case, compulsory heterosexuality takes the form of charging her with immorality simply because she chooses to live with her children without a man or because she has male visitors to whom she is not married.

While the explicit focus of these testimonies is on human rights violations, they simultaneously suggest the necessary conditions for the enjoyment of rights. Sexual autonomy, and therefore sexual rights, are central. Without sexual rights, women cannot achieve reproductive and sexual health, let alone the enjoyment of the right to freely choose and exercise their sexuality.

Women's testimonies, such as those above, shape and challenge the theories of human rights. They cross the boundaries, but at the same time they powerfully illustrate the indivisibility of human rights. For example, in Mary's case, it is impossible to extricate her economic dependence and the unequal access to economic opportunity from her vulnerability to physical and sexual violence from her husband. In Oum Ali's situation, one cannot talk about the brutality she and her children suffered without exploring the complicated nexus of religious and traditional practices, cultural dictates, and gender norms. The denial of one's freedom to determine how and with whom one seeks adult and consensual sexual intimacy is inseparable from the enforcement of coercive traditional values, as demonstrated by Daphne's testimony.

Therefore, it must be argued that sexual rights are founded upon the notion of indivisibility of human rights. This means not only the indivisibility of economic, social, cultural, civil, and political rights, but also the inseparability of rights from the capacity to enjoy those rights. The above testimonies illuminate how women's lack of sexual autonomy and sexual rights are built into all cultural norms and gender roles. While human rights address the violations these women have experienced, the notion of sexual rights leads to a deeper analysis of social conditions. Indeed, it becomes clear that the status quo itself constitutes a limitation on women's human rights to sexuality free from coercion, violence, and discrimination. Therefore, the freedom of women to enjoy these rights requires governments and private actors to actively engage in creating conditions that make the enjoyment of these rights possible.

The next section of this chapter focuses on formal discussions by governments in international fora about women's human rights and sexuality. A gap is evident between women's own articulation of sexualized human rights abuses and the much narrower parameters of government discussions. Despite the narrowness of these parameters, a series of U.N. world conferences analyzed below provided the backdrop for NGO organizing, which helped to galvanize a broader discussion of sexuality and women's human rights.

ENTERING THE PUBLIC STAGE: SEXUAL RIGHTS IN CAIRO AND BEIJING

Feminist scholars have long argued and recognized the power of language to shape and reflect society's understanding of the gendered nature of the role ascribed to women in a particular community. This can be seen in haute relief in the context of United Nations conferences. Language—the terms and words used in U.N. conference documents—is the arena in which governments and non-governmental organizations contest government policies and commitments and struggle for recognition of particular issues.

As is so often the case, conservative backlash to advances made by historically disadvantaged and marginalized groups often defines the terms and locus of debate. In U.N. conferences, the often subtle (sometimes legalistic) political negotiations around language to be used in final documents reveals the progress women's groups have made in advancing the international community's understanding and acceptance of women's perspective of, analysis of, and solutions for the issues affecting their lives. It also reflects the areas in which the women's movement has yet to convince the public and the international community of the veracity of the arguments they advance regarding women's human rights and socially constructed gender roles.

This section explores the emergence of sexual rights as a human rights concept, examining the beginnings while simultaneously recognizing that the concept is still being formulated. While many "advocacy communities" can lay claim to the concept, it has entered the public stage primarily in two U.N. World Conferences: the International Conference on Population and Development and the Fourth World Conference on Women. The origins of sexual rights as a human rights concept are briefly traced, and then the outcomes of the ICPD and the FWCW are extensively analyzed.

At the ICPD and later at the FWCW, governments were unwilling to acknowledge sexual rights per se. Still, what emerged out of these conferences was a major step forward: the beginning of a definition of sexual rights, even though the phrase itself was not included in the final conference agreements. The hard-fought paragraph 96 of the Beijing Platform for Action acknowledges that:

> The human rights of women include their right to have control over and decide freely and responsibly on matters related to their sexuality, including sexual and reproductive health, free of coercion, discrimination and violence.[13]

While the conference delegates took care not to give a name to the concept as it was stated in the Platform, the media, NGOs, and even U.N. agencies have been more

---

13. Beijing Platform for Action adopted by the Fourth World Conference on Women, Beijing, 1995, para. 96, U.N. Doc. A.CONF.177/20/Add.1 27 (1995). For a discussion of sexual rights in certain other contexts, *see generally* George W. Lee, *The Sexual Rights of the Retarded—An International Point of View, in* SEXUAL RIGHTS AND RESPONSIBILITIES OF THE MENTALLY RETARDED 58 (Medora S. Bass et al. eds., 1973); H. RODMAN, S. LEWIS & S. GRIFFITH, THE SEXUAL RIGHTS OF ADOLESCENTS: COMPETENCE, VULNERABILITY, AND PARENTAL CONTROL (1984).

forthcoming. Indeed, this language is now being interpreted in a variety of ways, sometimes using the terminology of sexual rights explicitly.[14]

Prior to 1993, no international human rights document referred explicitly to women's sexuality. This resulted from, among other factors, a rigid split between the public and private spheres in the understanding and implementation of human rights doctrine, which itself was the result of a theory and practice of human rights considering men to be the primary actors in a human rights complex. As Correa and Petchesky assert, "the construction of a legal and normative boundary between 'public' and 'private' insulates the daily, routine practices of gender subordination."[15] This historical construction of "human rights" has contributed to the exemption of women's reproductive and sexual health and rights from the traditional sphere of promotion and protection of human rights. Various forms of violations against women, including gender-based violence, have only recently received serious attention by the international human rights community. For decades, human rights doctrine tended to emphasize the overarching concern of male citizens about a realm of protection and privacy from their government, codified as civil and political rights.

One of the most significant implications of this construction, from the perspective of defining and protecting women's sexual rights, is the need to illustrate how the free expression of sexuality (reproduction/sexual expression/orientation) has been relegated to the "private" arena of the individual sphere/home. Such a definitional move obscures the role and responsibility of the state in regulating and promoting women's sexual autonomy. Women's human rights advocates insist that civil or political rights cannot be understood separately from women's social, cultural, and economic rights.[16] The notion of sexual rights challenges the traditional hierarchy of "generations" of rights (civil and political as "first generation," social, cultural, and economic rights seen as "second generation") because it cuts across the categories— it is, inter alia, a social right, a cultural right, an equality right, and a citizenship right.

For the most part, women's sexual lives are not considered as part of the appropriate realm of human rights promotion or protection, or they are considered to be

---

14. For instance, even before the delegates in Beijing had reached a final agreement on the Platform for Action, a New York Times headline read: *Women's Meeting Agrees on Right to Say No to Sex*, N.Y. Times, Sept. 11, 1995. *See also* Rone Tempest & Maggie Farley, *Beijing Meeting Affirms Sexual Rights of Women*, L.A. Times, Sept. 16, 1995, at A1 (the Beijing Plan of Action "strongly affirms a woman's sexual rights, including her right to defend herself against violence and sexually transmitted disease"); Mario Osava, *Women: Health Successes Threatened by Fundamentalism*, Inter Press Service, Mar. 21, 1997 (at the International Women and Health Conference, Rio).

15. Correa & Petchesky, *supra* note 3, at 107.

16. Rebecca Cook, *Introduction, Women's International Human Rights Law: The Way Forward*, Human Rights of Women, National and International Perspectives (Rebecca Cook ed., 1994); Georgina Ashworth, Changing the Discourse: A Guide to Women and Human Rights (1993); Florence Butegwa, *International Human Rights Law and Practice: Implications for Women, in* From Basic Needs to Basic Rights 27 (1995); Celina Romany, *State Responsibility Goes Private: A Feminist Critique of the Public/Private Distinction in International Human Rights Law, in* Cook, *supra*.

"private" and therefore outside the sphere of public protection or debate. For instance, while women's reproductive lives have been listed as part of the international human rights agenda, this has occurred only minimally, rooted either in the context of heterosexual marriage or in women's reproductive "function," and not as a broader concept of sexual autonomy or self-determination. For instance, the 1974 World Population Plan of Action (Bucharest) declares that "[a]ll couples and individuals have the basic right to decide freely and responsibly the number and spacing of their children and to have the information, education and means to do so."

The Nairobi Forward Looking Strategies[17] and the Convention on the Elimination of All Forms of Discrimination Against Women[18] both refer to women's rights to control their fertility and sexual equality free from discrimination, but neither assert a positive right to sexual autonomy or identity. Indeed, the articulation of a person's rights with regard to marriage, family, or religion, or to respect for the privacy of home life, have each been explored, albeit not exhaustively, within the framework of international human rights documents in a narrow manner. These rights concern the most intimate and private spheres of an individual's personal life, unlike the common notion of rights as comprising only public sector activities. Sexuality, though, as a central and integral component of one's life, and particularly to women's experiences of domination and control, is neither acknowledged nor even mentioned in human rights instruments or agreements prior to 1993.

Discussion of a woman's "sexual being" has begun to emerge in human rights discourse, although this discussion has been either in veiled terms or in reference to violations. For instance, the 1993 Declaration on the Elimination of Violence Against Women includes a denunciation of "physical, sexual and psychological violence against women."[19] These rights are derived from pre-existing human rights norms as articulated in international instruments such as the Universal Declaration of Human Rights (UDHR).[20] For instance, Article 3 of the UDHR articulates the right to life, liberty, and security of the person; regional instruments such as the African Charter articulate the inviolability of the person and physical and mental integrity, freedom from torture, and cruel and inhuman punishment.[21] The extension of human rights

17. The Nairobi Forward-Looking Strategies for the Advancement of Women adopted by the Third World Conference on Women to Review and Appraise the Achievements of the United Nations Decade for Women: Equality, Development and Peace, held in Nairobi, Kenya, July 15–26, 1985.

18. Convention on the Elimination of All Forms of Discrimination against Women, G.A. Res. 34/180, U.N. GAOR, 34th Sess., Agenda Item 75, U.N. Doc. A/RES/34/180 (1979), *entered into force* Sept. 3, 1981.

19. Declaration on the Elimination of Violence against Women, G.A. Res. 48/104, U.N. GAOR, 48th Sess., 85th plen. mtg., at art. 2(a), U.N. Doc. A/RES/48/104 (1993).

20. Universal Declaration of Human Rights, at art. 3, adopted and proclaimed by G.A. Res. 217A (III), U.N. GAOR, 1st Sess. (1948).

21. African Charter on Human and Peoples' Rights, at arts. 4 and 6, Organization of African Unity, *adopted* June 17, 1981, *entered into force* Oct. 21, 1986, OAU Doc. CAB/LEG/67/3 Rev. 5 (1982).

protection to women's sexuality is based upon these already articulated human rights norms.

The clearest challenge to the historical absence of women from the international human rights agenda, and to the public/private distinction that has dominated this discourse in international policy making, was articulated in the Vienna Declaration and Programme of Action of the World Conference on Human Rights (WCHR). This document declares that "[t]he human rights of women and of the girl-child are an inalienable, integral and indivisible part of universal human rights" and that "[g]ender-based violence and all forms of sexual harassment and exploitation, including those resulting from cultural prejudice and international trafficking, are incompatible with the dignity and worth of the human person, and must be eliminated."[22] It further insists that both public and private actors should be held accountable for human rights violations.

In recognizing that "violence against women is a violation of their human rights," the Vienna Declaration charted new territory that expands the boundaries of state accountability.[23] Such an affirmation rested upon an understanding of the indivisibility of human rights supported by women's human rights advocates. This insistence on indivisibility, including the right to development and the positive duty of states to ensure, promote, and protect these indivisible rights, allows for a broader examination of human rights and development issues, including autonomy and identity. The proscription against sexual violence as a human rights abuse opened the door to a broader understanding of bodily integrity, which might be seen to include "the protection of sexual identity and/or expression."[24]

International Conference on Population and Development (Cairo, 1994)

The gains from the International Conference on Population and Development (ICPD) reflected persistent efforts on the part of reproductive rights, women's health, and women's human rights advocates to ensure that a broad definition of reproductive rights as human rights would be incorporated into the ICPD Programme of Action.[25] Some feminist organizations were reluctant to engage in this process because they were wary about the efficacy of engaging the international system. Others directed significant resources toward this advocacy effort, arguing that changes in international policy could have a significant impact, forming the basis for further advocacy and the potential to become a factor in national policymaking.

---

22.   Vienna Declaration and Programme of Action, World Conference on Human Rights, at para. 18, U.N. Doc. A/CONF.157/23 (1993).

23.   *Id.*

24.   Alice M. Miller, AnnJanette Rosga & Meg Satterthwaite, *Health, Human Rights and Lesbian Existence*, HEALTH & HUM. RTS. 428 (1995).

25.   International Conference on Population and Development, Program of Action, at para. 7.3, U.N. Doc. A/CONF.171/13 (1994).

Success was by no means a foregone conclusion at this conference. Population control programs and male-centered development models had variously victimized, targeted, and excluded women. The coalition of reproductive health and human rights advocates succeeded, albeit only partially, in their demand that reproductive rights be viewed as part of the "package" of indivisible human rights in the ICPD Programme. After a protracted struggle, governments at the Cairo Conference agreed that reproductive rights were indeed human rights, embracing "certain human rights that are already recognized in national laws, international human rights documents and other relevant United Nations consensus documents." Reproductive rights as human rights were based upon:

> the recognition of the basic right of all couples and individuals to decide freely and responsibly the number, spacing and timing of their children and to have the information and means to do so, and the rights to attain the highest standard of sexual and reproductive health. It also includes the right of all to make decisions concerning reproduction free of discrimination, coercion and violence as expressed in human rights documents.[26]

Framing reproductive rights as essential components of human rights, while affirming the right to reproductive and sexual health, was crucial as an alternative to the perspective that reproductive rights are subordinate to population control and fertility. Further, this perspective clearly articulated a critical component to an understanding of women's human rights as indivisible and interrelated—in other words, the enjoyment of any right depends upon the attainment and protection of all other rights.

Thus, in Cairo, issues surrounding women's reproductive and sexual health were situated squarely within the human rights framework, creating the potential to advance the understanding of the indivisibility principle. Recognizing these rights as within the human rights framework begins the process of seeking state accountability for actions that inhibit or hinder women's expression or practice of these rights. It also suggests a substantive notion of equality as essential for the elimination of poverty, gender-based inequities, discrimination, and other adverse conditions which constrain women's freedom to shape their own lives.

The ICPD Programme, then, asserts women's right to bodily integrity, ability to control their fertility, and the importance of male respect for women and male responsibility in reproduction. While there is no explicit recognition of sexual rights or sexual orientation—a blatant omission discussed in more detail below—the document does embrace the concept that women's sexual life is their own to determine. For instance, the ICPD adopts the World Health Organization's definition of "sexual health," its purpose being defined as the enhancement of life and personal relations, and not merely counseling or care related to reproduction and sexually transmitted disease.[27]

---

26. *Id.*

27. Constitution of the World Health Organization, *signed* July 22, 1946, and *entered into force* on Apr. 7, 1948, *reprinted in* WHO, BASIC DOCUMENTS (39th ed. 1993).

Sexual and reproductive health are considered interdependent, requiring that "people are able to have a 'satisfying and safe sex life'" (not explicitly limiting this mandate in the text to heterosexual sex). It establishes a basis for asserting that women's right to determine, exercise, and control their sexuality and live free from gender-based violations is an integral part of security of the person and bodily integrity, and supports women's empowerment to participate fully and equally in the development of their societies.

Feminist advocacy efforts targeting the Cairo Programme strongly affirmed the power of the coalition between women's human rights and reproductive rights advocates. The strength of this coalition should not be underestimated, as the gains articulated above prevailed in spite of the fundamentalist, Vatican-led opposition, which battled mightily to thwart these gains. This opposition argued (and ultimately prevailed) for a traditional understanding of the family—limiting it to a heterosexual model, "the basic unit of society." Indeed, they were ultimately successful in deleting any reference to sexual rights whatsoever. In spite of these limitations, however, it can be argued that the Cairo Programme of Action urges states to be proactive in promoting social, cultural, and economic rights for women, and providing them with sexual and health services. The call to "enable them [women] to deal in a positive and responsible way with their sexuality" does not specify a heterosexual content to such education and leaves open the interpretation that girls and women must be educated in all choices of sexuality, in order to become a healthy, informed, and positive sexual being. The Cairo Programme affirms women's sexual autonomy and ability to make informed and unfettered decisions when protected from private and state transgressions against them and their bodies. This sets the crucial groundwork for the recognition of the role of women's sexuality as a component of their reproductive and sexual health.

As mentioned above, however, governments fell short of explicitly acknowledging a right to determine one's own sexual orientation. The concept of women's human rights was not expanded to encompass a woman's right to freely decide and express her sexuality. The rights of lesbians, gay men, and transgendered people, then, continued to be invisible in the mandates emerging from the U.N. international conferences. The absence of any mention of alternative models of the family, to lesbians, gay men, and transgendered people in no small measure has its locus in the homophobia and conservative traditionalism surrounding women's sexuality (seen as confined within the strict context of procreation) propagated by the Vatican and fundamentalists and supported by many states in varying degrees. The debate about women's sexual and reproductive health and rights in Cairo must also be seen within the context of the discomfort of states in considering women's sexuality (and freedom to exercise it as they will) as a part of the "package" of rights regarded as worthy of protection and promotion, and to which states are committed to fostering and enabling.

The Final Preparatory Committee Meeting for the Fourth World Conference on Women (The "Beijing PrepCom")

Before women's NGOs had advanced a consensus on the meaning, importance, and implications of sexual rights, a resounding backlash to Cairo was launched at the last Preparatory Committee meeting (held in New York) for the Fourth World Conference on Women. Many were surprised at the final PrepCom when the debate on language focused on the use of the term "gender" in the Draft Platform for Action. This struggle was initially perplexing in the context of a meeting to prepare for an international conference on women. Furthermore, the word "gender" had already appeared in countless U.N. documents.

While many highly contentious issues were up for consideration during this final preparatory meeting, few were prepared when the Vatican, a handful of U.N. member states, and some religious fundamentalist groups vociferously objected to the use of the term gender.[28] These parties argued that they could only accept the term "gender" if it was explicitly framed to refer only to the "natural" roles of men and women predicated on their biology. The rhetoric and strategy of these groups is key to understanding how threatening the term sexual rights is and why a well-organized and sophisticated lobby of women's NGOs were unable to get the term incorporated into the Beijing Platform for Action.[29]

The women's coalition in Cairo was considered dangerous by those who promote adherence to traditional notions of femininity and masculinity and traditional concepts of family. Thus, the Vatican's contentions at the Beijing PrepCom sought to undermine this global coalition, insisting that the use of the word "gender" emerged from Western, North-American-style feminists and feminist-lesbians. The Vatican and its supporters sought to overturn the gains made at Cairo in a campaign appealing to homophobia, fears of "imperialistic/foreign ideas," a resistance to freedom of female sexual expression, and a North-South divide. The virulent attacks on lesbians and feminists (and the conflation of feminism with lesbianism) mounted by the Vatican and its cohorts were clearly designed to thwart any attempt to repeat the Cairo gains and to prevent any expansion of sexual rights, including lesbian rights, or an affirmation of women's sexual autonomy.[30]

---

28. Vatican representatives obtained materials being used in a U.S. women's studies course that discussed the socially constructed nature of gender and contrasted it with biological determinism. The Vatican claimed that the word "gender" was in fact being used as a feminist/lesbian codeword, denoting the acceptance of lesbian, gay, bisexual, heterosexual, and transgendered sexual orientations. They therefore insisted that the language in the Platform should refer to "sex" rather than "gender," in order to maintain adherence to the idea that gender-assigned roles are determined by biology.

29. As noted above, success in including more progressive and expansive language in the Cairo Programme for Action was in no small measure due to the tireless lobbying of an internationally composed coalition of women's human rights and health groups. These groups were, significantly, comprised of women from every region of the world, with different political agendas, foci, regional experiences and realities. Together they forged a unified front, presenting a vision and political platform rich in diversity (unified in its insistence of the universality of women's experiences of oppression), and demanding that these violations were issues of global human rights for women.

30. The campaign was overt in its agenda to subvert the successes of Cairo, decrying language on diverse family forms and reproductive rights and promoting the concept of parental rights as a guise for the advancement of the heterosexual nuclear family. The Vatican even succeeded at one juncture in having the word gender bracketed throughout the entire Draft Platform for Action.

This strategy was both a success and a failure. It created a general nervousness about the existence of a "feminist/lesbian" agenda and therefore constrained the efficacy of openly advocating for lesbian or sexual rights. Ultimately, the Holy See and like-minded representatives succeeded in excluding any explicit mention of sexual rights in the Platform. However, their strategy failed to divide the women's NGO community along a North/South line and did not quell support for sexual rights, including reproductive and health rights.

Beijing: The Conference

At the government conference in Beijing, debates about the human rights of women continued to express the tensions that emerged in the PrepCom around women's role in society and the construction of gender. Different theories of women's subordination led to widely divergent proposals, often manifested in opposing positions between religious and secular states, and resulting in difficult negotiations. Thus, the subtext of the negotiations over the Platform continued to be the on-going controversy about feminism and gender roles.

Further, a small group of governmental representatives was mandated to seek agreement on the use and meaning of the word "gender." After consultations, this group reaffirmed that the terminology "gender," as used in the Platform, "[was] intended to be interpreted and understood as it is in ordinary, generally accepted usage." Having failed in its effort, the Vatican noted in their final statement of the conference, that they understood the term "gender" to be "grounded in biological sexual identity, male or female. . . . The Holy See [the Vatican] thus excludes dubious interpretations based on world views which assert that sexual identity can be adapted indefinitely to suit new and different purposes."[31]

The prevalence of the women's human rights agenda strengthened efforts to use a human rights framework to address violence, health, reproductive rights, sexuality, education, and girls' and adolescents' issues in the Platform. The expanded understanding of human rights was evident in the debate about sexual rights. The Platform took incremental steps towards a broader definition of women's sexual autonomy. This, and the use of human rights to frame an ever-widening set of concerns, reflects the success of an international coalition of women who organized at all levels.

Two of the most contentious issues at the official government conference in Beijing illustrate differing theories on the construction of gender and women's human rights. One relevant issue concerned whether or not to include language explicitly proscribing discrimination on the basis of sexual orientation. A second issue concerned whether or not to include a footnote in the health section of the Platform (the section which would include references to women's human rights and sexuality) which would qualify governments' commitments to implementation of the section based on

---

These brackets meant that the concept was too contentious to include without qualification in the document and would be debated and resolved at the official government conference.

31.   *United Nations Report of the Fourth World Conference on Women* 164 (1995).

issues of sovereignty and religious and cultural values. These two issues were not resolved until the final hour of the negotiations when the chairperson of an informal government working group made a ruling on the "majority sentiment," deciding not to include "sexual orientation" in the Platform for Action, and not to include the footnote.

Sexual Orientation

In the draft Platform for Action, sexual orientation was included in four paragraphs in square brackets.[32] Initial opposition over its use included a demand for a definition of the term (which was never officially given). There was also a concern that use of the term sexual orientation would create a "new human right," something which many governments clearly opposed. The bracketed language cited discrimination on the basis of sexual orientation as one of the forms of discrimination that prevents women from fully exercising their human rights. The final debate over inclusion of "sexual orientation" took place with reference to Paragraph 48 of the Platform. Ultimately, while the committee reviewing this section decided not to include "sexual orientation" in the Platform, the debate was useful. Sixteen states supported inclusion of the language on "sexual orientation" in the Platform. This support for prohibiting discrimination and violence on the basis of sexual orientation came from representatives of all regions of the world. They argued that references to prohibiting discrimination based on "other status" prevalent throughout the document, and human rights instruments generally, should be interpreted as inclusive of prohibiting discrimination based on sexual orientation.

Sexual Rights

The key phrase alluding to sexual rights can be found in the health section of the Platform. Paragraph 96 is a broad statement about sexuality framed as a human rights issue. In the draft version of the Platform, the paragraph explicitly referred to women's sexual rights. The compromise, and final language, replaced "sexual rights" with "human rights." The final version reads: "the human rights of women include their right to have control over and decide freely and responsibly on matters related to their sexuality, including sexual and reproductive health, free of coercion, discrimination and violence."[33] The agreement in this paragraph is reinforced in the human rights section of the Platform, which calls upon governments to ensure that the human rights of women related to sexuality, sexual health, and reproductive health and rights, are fully respected and protected.[34]

The absence of any explicit reference to sexual rights or sexual orientation revealed a certain cynicism in the way that reaching consensus was given priority over affirming basic principles. Thus, in the Platform, as in many international agreements,

---

32. Phrases and sentences around which a consensus cannot be reached in preparatory negotiations are placed in square brackets for further negotiation.

33. Beijing Platform for Action, at Ch. IV, para. 96, U.N. Doc. A/CONF.177/20/Add.1 (1995).

34. *Id.* at para. 232(f).

the compromise language is vague rather than explicit and debates center around seemingly minute but significant differences in the description of the issue (e.g., the "equal right to inheritance" rather than the "right to equal inheritance"). The incomplete language not only represents a compromise but a tacit agreement amongst women's NGOs that the substance of sexual rights (and the language in the Platform alluding to it), will be expanded in future application both in theory and in practice. This is important because, as Rosalind Petchesky notes:

> In many countries and communities, still, to speak openly of women's right to varied sexual pleasures is to invite the closing down of your organization, ostracization of its members, verbal and physical attack, and even death. The spiral of resistance is still, as always, constrained by power; and these power dynamics are reproduced in the souls of all of us, however radical our vision. In this political context, to begin to speak of sexual rights, even tentatively, is a big step.

Given this, it is significant that, when read together, Paragraphs 96 and 48 provide women's human rights advocates with the basis for arguing that a concept of sexual autonomy and self-determination are present in the Platform.

DEVELOPING THE CONCEPT BEYOND BEIJING

As we move towards defining the concept of sexual rights more clearly, it is important not to impose rigid or narrow definitional parameters. The term can be as fluid and expansive as the spectrum of women's sexuality. The challenge is to sustain the fluidity of the concept and its ability to include an ever-growing understanding of the range of experiences heterosexual, lesbian, bisexual, and transgendered women have as sexual beings and to expand the boundaries of what sexual rights mean, rather than limiting its application and meaning with over-definition.

This section re-examines conceptual and strategic debates about the meaning and use of sexual rights for purposes of local, national, and international organizing. There continues to be excitement and interest among women's rights advocates in elaborating the concept of sexual rights. Conversations continue at the international level, as well as in national and local settings, about how this concept can strengthen existing advocacy efforts. Establishing a clearer understanding of sexual rights must begin with the claim that sexual rights is a fundamental aspect of women's human rights and their human dignity. As Lynn Freedman comments:

> [C]ontrol over reproduction and sexuality is an essential element of human dignity. It therefore has intrinsic—and not merely instrumental—value. Although control over reproduction and sexuality is certainly an essential precondition for women's ability to exercise other rights and to fulfil other basic needs, it is also a worthy and valuable end in its own right, and not merely a means to reach other ends.[35]

The discussion of sexual rights demands that we give greater clarity to the meaning of human rights as indivisible, interrelated, and integral, since women's sexual rights are intimately connected to the realization of their economic rights, as well as their

---

35. Lynn P. Freedman, *Censorship and Manipulation of Reproductive Health Information: An Issue of Human Rights and Women's Health, in* THE RIGHT TO KNOW: HUMAN RIGHTS AND ACCESS TO REPRODUCTIVE HEALTH INFORMATION (1994).

right to information, right to dignity, right to privacy, and to the highest standard of sexual health, and to physical, mental, and moral integrity while realizing sexual choice. The challenge for those engaged in this definitional process is that it requires a multi-issue, multi-level approach which integrates social justice, economic rights, reproductive rights, sexual health, and lesbian rights into international human rights discourse and practice. The affirmation of sexual autonomy includes a woman's right to choose freely how to exercise her reproductive and sexual capacity, whether or not this conforms to norms of compulsory heterosexuality.

The concept of sexual rights helps to highlight state responsibility for violations of women's sexual autonomy. At times, states actually promote policies which are discriminatory and may encourage or participate in violence against women. However, the state is also culpable when it passively acquiesces to community or family violence against sexual minorities or those transgressing gender norms. It is therefore important to stress that in order to facilitate women's exercise of their human rights, the state must ensure the conditions within which women can exercise these rights "free of coercion, discrimination and violence."[36]

The struggle to incorporate recognition of sexual rights into the international agreements of Cairo and Beijing indicates how strategic efforts to use the law to promote women's human rights are constrained by the political and legal contexts. Feminist theorists and activists have struggled with the question of how to insert women's issues into a male-biased and/or purportedly neutral body of law. Where equality is conceptualized as "sameness," the law imposes a regime of formal equality, which guarantees facially neutral treatment to both men and women. However, there is a hidden male bias in this model. According to the sameness model, women who do not (and any woman to the extent that she does not) or cannot conform to the male standard, are denied the fruits of equality.

In international law, the formal equality perspective has dominated. One of the by-products of this formal equality approach has been a desexualization of women's experiences of inequality and human rights violations. This is particularly troubling since so much of women's experience of inequality relates to aspects of their sexual selves. In emphasizing the sameness of women and men, the "body," and particularly a sexual body, is erased. The concept of sexual rights helps highlight why an alternative conceptualization of equality is necessary.

The focus must be placed on equality of results instead of formal equality. It is only such a substantive theory of equality that can guarantee women's ability to exercise their sexual autonomy free of violence and coercion. This model of equality concentrates on the effect of the state's intervention, rather than the form that the intervention takes. The question is not whether the state has chosen to treat women identically to or differently from men, but whether the state has taken the necessary action to provide the conditions which would enable women to realize and enjoy their rights. As Amartya Sen explains, what the state must guarantee is "equality of capa-

---

36.   ICPD, at para. 96, *supra* note 25.

bility and well-being for women."[37] This understanding is at the heart of the sexual rights concept.

Indeed, one of the compelling aspects of sexual rights as a concept is the realization that sexual rights requires a number of enabling conditions. Sexual rights and civil, political, economic, social, and cultural rights are integrally connected and interdependent. Sexual rights cannot be realized simply by requiring states to treat women the same as men are treated or by giving them special treatment. What is necessary is that a state take full responsibility for creating conditions that make women's sexual autonomy/agency possible. A wide range of responses must be envisioned and undertaken—economic empowerment, reproductive and health rights, and others.

This definition of sexual rights focuses not on the content of women's choices, but on the relationship between a woman's ability to make and effectuate those choices, and her ability to maintain a sense of control over what happens in her life—both to her physical body and her spiritual/emotional person. Stated in the negative, human dignity implies a right not to be alienated from one's own reproductive and sexual capacity; a right not to have one's reproductive and sexual capacity used as an instrument to serve the interests of other individuals, collectives, or states without one's consent and without the opportunity to participate in the political processes by which such interests are defined.

It is one thing to maintain that rights are indivisible, but if the state is responsible for guaranteeing women's exercise of their sexual rights in real terms, other rights that support, inform, and enable sexual rights must be realized. In other words, the concept of sexual rights promotes substantive equality.

SEXUAL RIGHTS POST-BEIJING: DIRECTIONS IN ORGANIZING

This section highlights some of the implications of organizing to affirm and protect sexual rights. In doing so, the directions of a definition and practice of sexual rights as a part of women's human rights take clearer shape. Organizing around sexual rights poses a strong challenge to the human rights framework, forcing the articulation of the "other side" of human rights: that is, the positive assertion of the full exercise and enjoyment of rights, including free expression of sexual identity. A palpable excitement and intensity has permeated discussions about sexual rights. These conversations have explored the fashioning of a whole picture of women's human rights, comprised of both the prohibitions on discrimination and violations (such as violence, systemic rape, sexual exploitation, etc.), and the positive affirmation of women's right to sexual autonomy (e.g., rights to sexual autonomy, to lesbian identity, and to gender transgression).

The notion of a continuum situating and connecting all women's experiences has emerged in the discussions, integrating a challenge to the norms and enforcement

---

37. Amartya Sen, "Inequality Re-Examined: Capability and Well-Being," paper delivered at the Conference on the Quality of Life, organized by the World Institute of Development Economics Research (WIDER), Helsinki, Finland, July, 1988.

of institutionalized and compulsory heterosexuality. Debates about sexual rights continue to be founded on the indivisibility of rights and the conditions necessary to realize them, and the connections between the different agendas promoted by women's rights advocates. Defining and exploring sexual rights has reinforced the recognition of the multiple and varied ways in which patriarchy and compulsory heterosexuality shape, constrict, and regulate women's lives around the globe. It has also highlighted the necessity of discussing female sexuality in all its complexity and diversity.

Restrictions on women's sexual freedom, whether in the form of homophobia or other traditional conceptions of appropriate female behavior, are often situated within a broad set of assumptions about familial and social responsibilities. This was powerfully illustrated in the tribunal testimonies reported above. Time and again, women's sexuality forms a visceral and central element of the violations of their rights—whether on the basis of marital status, their sexual orientation, reproductive choices, or other status. Examining these violations through the lens of sexual rights takes one through an analysis of rights already enshrined in international human rights instruments, such as: the right to bodily integrity and security of every person (the UDHR and the International Covenant on Civil and Political Rights (ICCPR)); the right to freedom from sexual exploitation (the Women's Convention and the Convention on the Rights of the Child (CRC)); the right to be free from torture or cruel, inhuman or degrading treatment or punishment (the UDHR and the ICCPR); the right to the highest standard of physical and mental health (the UDHR, International Covenant on Economic, Social, and Cultural Rights, and the Women's Convention); the right to privacy, equality, and equal protection before the law (the UDHR, ICCPR, and the Women's Convention); and to non-discrimination (the UDHR, ICCPR, CRC, and Women's Convention).

The concept of sexual rights, which includes reproductive rights, women's right to health, women's human rights, and the rights of lesbians, gay men, and transgendered people, is expanding as more communities demand that their experiences be represented. Women of color from the north, women from the global south, and sexual minorities are engaging the issues and concepts, and adapting them to fit diverse contexts. Thus a discussion has ensued about how sexual autonomy and sexual rights are inextricable from other struggles for social change—the rights to health, self-determined sexual lives, and elimination of poverty. These endeavors to abrade the conditions that disempower and impoverish women require the dissolution of boundaries between human rights, sexuality, and development.

The flexibility of the concept, and its resonance, is evident in the wide range of activities that are now taking place in the name of sexual rights. This work is not only taking place outside of the mainstream of human rights. Indeed, several major human rights organizations have taken up various aspects of this emerging notion. For instance, the Women's Rights Project of Human Rights Watch has underscored repeatedly the violation of women's sexual autonomy among the human rights abuses occurring in particular cases. For example, a recent report of Human Rights Watch focused upon forced virginity testing in Turkey.[38] Women and girls in Turkey have been compelled to undergo forced virginity tests by school authorities (in conjunction with family members) as well as by police and other state actors. In discussing such abuses in the context of international law, Ralph and Lai assert:

> Such regulation of women's sexual behavior is offensive to the notion of sexual autonomy, but to what extent can the state be held responsible under international law for virginity exams? By focusing on the role of the Turkish government in both conducting and tolerating forced virginity exams, a human rights approach challenges the notion that female virginity is of legitimate interest to the family, community and state, and exposes the social and legal context that the state's regulation of female virginity reflects and perpetuates.[39]

Amnesty International/USA has also initiated work that falls within the general rubric of sexual rights. In 1991, Amnesty International (AI) expanded its mandate to include advocacy on behalf of those imprisoned for the private, consensual, adult practice of homosexuality, as well as those imprisoned for advocating gay rights. AI found the basis of this work in fundamental human rights guarantees of equality and dignity. This interpretation was substantiated by the Human Rights Committee (which monitors states parties compliance with the International Covenant on Civil and Political Rights) in a 1994 decision in which a Tasmanian sodomy statute was found to violate Australia's obligations under ICCPR articles establishing the right to privacy when read in conjunction with the guarantee of non-discrimination. In 1994, AIUSA initiated the "Breaking the Silence" campaign, which included a report documenting human rights violations internationally against lesbians and gay men along with other typical campaign activities—letter writing to authorities, outreach and education to local, national, and international organizations, and advocacy with governments. Since then, AIUSA has integrated efforts to protect lesbians and gay men from torture, imprisonment, and killing into their ongoing county and prisoner work.

At the same time, lesbian and gay organizations have initiated efforts to address the human rights of sexual minorities. For instance, the International Lesbian and Gay Association (ILGA) engaged in monitoring the United Nations and even received consultative status, later revoked due to the efforts of conservative members of the U.S. Congress. The International Gay and Lesbian Human Rights Commission (IGLHRC) was established specifically to address these issues and has actively participated in several U.N. world conferences as well as in monitoring conference agreements. For instance, IGLHRC coordinated a petition drive directed toward the Fourth World Conference on Women to "put sexuality on the agenda." The petition called upon member states:

> to recognize the right to determine one's sexual identity; the right to control one's body, particularly in establishing intimate relationships; and the right to choose if,

---

38. HUMAN RIGHTS WATCH WOMEN'S RIGHTS PROJECT, STATE CONTROL OF WOMEN'S VIRGINITY IN TURKEY (1994).

39. Sarah Lai & Regan Ralph, *Female Sexual Autonomy and Human Rights*, 8 HARV. HUM. RTS. J. 201 (1995).

when, and with whom to bear or raise children as fundamental components of the human rights of all women regardless of sexual orientation.[40]

As discussed above, these endeavors were ultimately unsuccessful in incorporating such language into the Platform for Action. However, the petition, supported by lesbian organizing at the NGO Forum, was impressive in the geographical and cultural diversity of the women and organizations that signed the petition and advocated on behalf of the human rights of lesbians. Groups from over sixty countries as disparate as Romania, Mexico, Turkey, Suriname, Austria, Philippines, Norway, Pakistan, Sri Lanka, and Ireland signed the petition, which was presented to the Secretary-General of the Beijing Women's Conference in March 1995 at the final preparatory committee session.

Women's organizations are also incorporating claims to sexual rights into broader agendas. Among the more pressing claims, feminist groups working in situations of armed conflict have illustrated the particular way that women's sexuality is used to excuse systematic and brutal abuse. For instance, organizations combating rape and sexual violence in the countries of the former Yugoslavia have pointed out how women's bodies are used literally and symbolically as territorial markers, thus making rape a weapon of war. Julie Mostov notes that, "Mothers, wives, and daughters designate the space of the nation and are, at the same time, the property of the nation."[41] The genocide propaganda in Rwanda also illustrates such sensationalist rhetoric: "Tutsi women were targeted on the basis of the genocide propaganda which had portrayed them as calculated seductress-spies bent on dominating and undermining the Hutu."[42] As these cases indicate, women's supposed purity or promiscuity comes to symbolize that which must be protected or destroyed.

Local women's organizations have also found a rallying call or programmatic purpose in sexual rights. The Yokohama Association for Communication and Networking (YWACN) in Japan used the demand for sexual rights to address women's right to determine their fertility as well as their sexuality as an informed choice. The claim to sexual rights, for the YWACN, expresses the capacity of women to be empowered and to take control of their bodies, sexuality, and lives.[43]

The Fundacion Dialogo Mujer in Bogota, Colombia, has incorporated the claim to sexual rights into their sexual education curriculum for adolescent girls. The pamphlet, "Talking Amongst Ourselves: Non-Sexist Education for Adolescent Women" asks: "What are women's sexual rights?" The answer emphasizes the "freedom women

---

40. *Put Sexuality on the Agenda at the World Conference on Women*, Petition Campaign, International Gay and Lesbian Human Rights Commission, Beijing, China, 1995.

41. Julie Mostov, *Our Women/Their Women: Symbolic Boundaries, Territorial Markers, and Violence in the Balkans*, 20(4) PEACE & CHANGE 515 (1995).

42. HUMAN RIGHTS WATCH/AFRICA AND HUMAN RIGHTS WATCH/WOMEN'S RIGHTS WATCH AND FEDERATION INTERNTAIONALE DES LIGUES DES DROITS DE L'HOMME, SHATTERED LIVES: SEXUAL VIOLENCE DURING THE RWANDAN GENOCIDE AND ITS AFTERMATH (1996).

43. Newsletter of the Yokahama Women's Association for Communication and Networking, 8 YOKAHAMA WOMEN'S FORUM (1996).

must have to express their sexuality with dignity, under pleasant circumstances, free of violence or abuse."[44]

Other international women's and family planning organizations also actively include women's sexual rights in their mandates. The International Women's Health Coalition actively advocated for the inclusion of sexual rights in both the Cairo and Beijing conference agreements and it continues sexual rights advocacy in its programming. The new International Planned Parenthood Federation Charter, adopted in November 1995, is entitled "IPPF Charter on Sexual and Reproductive Rights." The Charter enumerates the fundamental principles that guide the work of the federation and includes twelve rights:

> The right to life; the right to liberty and security of the person; the right to equality, and to be free from all forms of discrimination; the right to privacy; the right to freedom of thought; the right to information and education; the right to choose whether or not to marry and to found and plan a family; the right to decide whether or when to have children; the right to health care and health protection; the right to the benefits of scientific progress; the right to freedom of assembly and political participation; and the right to be free from torture and ill-treatment.[45]

Since the IPPF has member family planning associations in over 140 countries, the connections it illustrates between human rights, family planning, and sexual and reproductive health services may have significant programmatic consequences.

At the 1996 session of the Commission on the Status of Women (CSW) (now mandated with reviewing implementation of the Beijing Platform for Action), women's rights advocates representing diverse organizations met to discuss sexual rights. Another group met at the annual conference sponsored by the Association for Women in Development in Washington in 1996. A group of primarily U.S.-based women's health and human rights activists met to discuss the possibility of having a resolution passed in support of sexual rights at the CSW and began to talk about the kind of language that they would like to see in such a document. As these examples illustrate, women's human rights advocates persevere in capitalizing on every fora available to meet, define, expand, and strategize around the implementation of sexual rights.

CONCLUSION

The unifying and coalition-building possibilities of a concept like sexual rights have a dynamism that continues to compel women activists around the globe to engage in discussions exploring its meaning and potential. Women's human rights advocates are bridging differences, and finding theoretical and concrete commonalties. Women's health, reproductive rights, and human rights advocates are now more than ever able to creatively engage in the language of women's human rights and expand its purview to meaningfully include the diversity of women's lives and experiences.

---

44. *What are Women's Sexual Rights?*, WOMEN'S GLOBAL NETWORK FOR REPRODUCTIVE RIGHTS 50 (Jan.–Mar. 1996).

45. International Planned Parenthood Federation Charter, Factcard #2 (Sept. 1996).

Perhaps sexual rights provide a "next step" for women's NGOs—the challenge to envision and articulate an affirmative vision of women's right to enjoy their human rights, to draw together the threads of those rights that are now accepted as indivisible, and to demand that the conditions established truly enable all women to freely exercise all rights in concert. The rhetoric and moral persuasion of the international human rights framework provides much of the groundwork for sexual rights, but it is the commitment and need illustrated by women's groups from around the world that will make sexual rights a potent and meaningful element of the imperative realization of all aspects of women's human rights.

SELECTED PERSONAL RIGHTS AND FREEDOMS: RIGHTS TO WEAR CLOTHING OF ONE'S CHOICE, TO DRIVE, AND TO TRAVEL UNATTENDED AND WITHOUT PERMISSION

Barbara Roblin Mirza

INTRODUCTION

What constitutes a "personal" right within the array of claims that may be characterized as rights? At first glance, all rights—even those tied to a group claim—appear in some way to be personal since the claim must be generated by and the remedy directed toward protection of the individual human being. Some rights, however, are tied in an especially intimate manner to a woman's daily, personal choices as she pursues her life with dignity and some degree of autonomy. The rights and violations thereof that will be canvassed in this chapter—the right to wear clothing of one's choice, the right to drive, and the right to travel unattended and without permission—are examples of such rights having a uniquely personal quality.[1] The personal rights and freedoms included in this chapter surely are not the only personal rights and freedoms of concern to the world's women. However, each has been violated so explicitly and with such increasing intensity that they deserve special attention.

These topics raise of their own accord certain common themes. For example, it will become clear that each of these rights has a close association with either Muslim women, Muslim states, or both. While this chapter intends to focus exclusively on certain specific rights (and to explore the common themes linking them), it also alludes to a wider, ongoing dialogue about politics, religion, culture, and human rights and will, where appropriate, discuss particular facets of that dialogue.

The right to wear clothing of one's choice, the right to drive, and the right to travel unattended and without permission are examined in turn: in each case, pertinent background information is provided, along with a summary report of violations of the right. Once all three issues are reviewed, the intersection of religion, culture, and politics within the human rights discourse is examined in order to lay the groundwork for the final section, which presents recommendations for future action.

---

1. It is problematic to refer to any claim (short of, for example, specifically enumerated rights such as the right to be free from torture) as a "right." Later in this chapter, certain claims will be analyzed in order to demonstrate that they do fall within the scope of protections outlined in various international human rights documents. It should also be noted that these rights will at times be referred to as "freedoms" for linguistic variety and to demonstrate their complex character.

CHOICE IN CLOTHES

Introduction

For two reasons this section is the longest of the three discussing specific rights. First, this right has a dual aspect: in some countries, women are forced to wear certain forms of dress; in other countries, women are forbidden from wearing the very same forms of dress. (As the latter issue has been to a large degree ignored, more space is devoted to its analysis; however, any such difference in coverage here does not infer a difference in importance.) Second, a separate subsection is required in order to describe and analyze issues raised by the more extensive media coverage that has surrounded this issue.

The discussion here will focus primarily on Muslim women, because Muslim rules of dress have given rise to some of the most flagrant violations of the right to wear clothing of one's choice (both by states that force women to wear a certain form of clothing against their will and by other states that force women not to wear that form of clothing). These rules—along with some explanations as to why a woman might choose to or not to wear some form of Muslim dress—are explored at some length. The importance of understanding this context cannot be overestimated, as even sympathetic writers have approached the issue of the clothing choices of Muslim women with a surprising degree of ignorance regarding the variety and diversity of both the clothing and the women, frequently with unfortunate analytical results.

Explanation of Muslim Rules of Dress

Muslin Rules of Dress

The Holy Book of Islam is the Koran, which serves for Muslims not only as a spiritual guide, but also as a practical manual for living: "[I]t tells us everything we need to know about God and human nature, how to treat each other, how to create a humane society, where we came from, what life's meaning is, and what our ultimate destiny will be."[2] It is for this reason that many Muslims turn to the Koran for guidance regarding such varied issues as family life, diet, lending policies, charitable works, and dress. In order to understand Muslim rules of dress, it is crucial to consult the Koran.

One verse in the Koran regarding veiling states: "Prophet, enjoin your wives, your daughters and the wives of true believers to draw their veils close around them. That is more proper so that they may be recognized and not molested."[3] Another passage states: "[S]peak to the believing women that they display not their ornaments, except those which are external; and that they throw their veils over their bosoms."[4]

---

2.   IRA G. ZEPP, A MUSLIM PRIMER 59 (1992).

3.   *Id.* at 176, *citing* THE KORAN, sura 33:59.

4.   THE KORAN, sura 24 (J.M. Rodwell trans., 1994). For a detailed analysis and interpretation of the passages of the Koran relating to Muslim dress, *see* Fatima Mernissi, *The Hijab, the Veil, in* THE VEIL AND THE MALE ELITE (Mary Jo Lakeland trans., 1991).

Some have interpreted the passage as meaning that a woman should cover her chest in order to conform with Koranic dictates; they point to the fact that before Islam, many Arabian women wore topless garb. Others have interpreted it to mean that a woman should cover her hair; or her hair and face; or her entire body, from head to toe. These guidelines are typically intended to apply at all times, except perhaps when a woman is with her close family or in the sole company of other women.

Widespread confusion surrounds the terms that may be used to describe these various options. *Hijab* commonly refers to a scarf that covers the head. Depending on the beliefs of the wearer (or her society), it might be tied loosely behind the head or tightly beneath the chin, exposing none of her hair. The term *hijab* is also sometimes used (usually by non-Muslims) to denote the Islamic dress code more generally. The *niqab* is a veil that covers a woman's face completely. The *chador* is a covering that cloaks a woman from head to toe. Terms less commonly known are the *abaya*, a head-to-toe cloak with arm slits (usually black); and the *burka*, a stiff face mask.[5] Each is most commonly worn in the Gulf States. Other types of Islamic dress include the *jalabiyya*, a buttoned, ankle-length coat; the *magneh*, a cowl-like covering for the head;[6] and the *milaya-laff*, a sari-like black garment worn by certain classes of Egyptian women.[7] A further complication is raised by the fact that in different regions of the world, different words are used to refer to similar garments. For example, a head scarf might be called a *shayla* in some predominantly Arabic-speaking countries, a *roosarie* in Iran,[8] or a *ghata* in Egypt. In Kuwait, a face covering might be called a *boshia*,[9] while, as noted earlier, women in other regions might call a similar item of clothing a *niqab* or a *burka*.[10] Thus there are numerous variants of Islamic dress, and the clothes a woman wears may be determined by both her personal beliefs and preferences and by her community affiliations.

Why A Woman Might or Might Not Choose to Wear Muslim Dress

For some people, it is difficult to understand what might inspire a woman to wear *hijab, niqab, chador*, or any other form of Muslim dress. After all, particularly to the "outsider," such dress would seem to carry with it a measure of physical and social discomfort. Indeed, many Muslim women themselves choose not to wear Muslim dress because they sincerely believe that it is not a requirement of Islam, but rather a product of community-imposed coercion. In the most extreme case—where a state forcibly imposes the requirement that a woman wear strict Islamic dress—the feelings of some Muslim women are especially intense:

---

5.   GERALDINE BROOKS, NINE PARTS OF DESIRE: THE HIDDEN WORLD OF ISLAMIC WOMEN 240 (1995).

6.   *Id.* at 242.

7.   LOIS BECK & NIKKI KEDDIE, WOMEN IN THE MUSLIM WORLD 522 (1978).

8.   BROOKS, *supra* note 5, at 242–3.

9.   BECK & KEDDIE, *supra* note 7, at 175.

10.   In Afghanistan, the term "burka" might also be used to refer to a robe that covers the head, face and body. Gayle Kirshenbaum, *A Fundamentalist Regime Cracks Down on Women*, Ms., May/June, 1997, at 12.

For them, the veil symbolizes social deprivation and oppression; it is an anachronism antithetical to progress. With anger, they oppose it and view all previous steps taken toward liberation as being eclipsed by this forced return to the Dark Ages, with which in their mind the veil is associated. Paralyzing inertia, they argue, inevitably results from being engulfed by this wall shrunk to a portable size. Sousan Azadi, after her escape from Iran, explains the sensation of being forcibly veiled in her autobiography, *Out of Iran:* "As I pulled the *chador* over me, I felt a heaviness descending over me. I was hidden and in hiding. There was nothing visible left of Sousan Azadi. I felt like an animal of light suddenly trapped in a cave. I was just another faceless Moslem woman carrying a whole inner world hidden inside the *chador*."[11]

While the reasons a woman might not want to wear Muslim dress have been canvassed thoroughly in the mainstream media and are generally well understood, there is little understanding outside the Muslim world of the various reasons why many Muslim women make an informed choice to wear Muslim dress. This section will attempt to articulate, in the words of Muslim women themselves, some of these reasons. The descriptions of the reasons will be brief, as they are intended only to provide a sense of the diversity of the reasons behind the choices that some women make.

As an Act of Worship

This reason has been placed first deliberately, as it is part of the contention of this section that the importance of the believers' religious convictions has been increasingly discounted and even ignored. Even supportive writers tend to stress the community and political aspects of choosing to wear *hijab*[12] while neglecting to explore and understand the deep religious devotion that often motivates such a decision.

Latifa Weinman, an American Muslim convert, states: "As I often explain it to children and non-Muslims, 'If *you* sincerely believed that God was telling you to do something—for example, to cover your head—wouldn't you *do* it?'"[13] Sandra Harhash echoes this deep-seated conviction when she says: "I dress like this because this is what God ordered me to do. . . . [W]earing a *hijab* comes so naturally now that I feel almost naked without it. When people ask if my clothes are hot in the summer, I say, 'It's hotter in hell.'"[14] For many women, then, the demands of secular authority and secular convention are subordinate to the demands of their religious beliefs.

To Publicly Identify Herself as a Muslim

It has been noted that "dress is a 'badge' identifying a man or woman as belonging to a particular community."[15] It can be a source of identity and pride for a woman

---

11. Farzaneh Milani, Veils and Words: The Emerging Voices of Iranian Women Writers 44 (1992).

12. *See, e.g.*, A.E. Galeotti, *Citizenship and Equality: The Place for Toleration*, 21 Political Theory 585 (1993).

13. L. Weinman, *Peace and Freedom for Women*, 62 Utne Reader 93, 94 (1994) [emphasis in original].

14. J.E. Schiffer, *Dixie Islam*, 62 Utne Reader 89, 91–92 (1994).

15. Beck & Keddie, *supra* note 7, at 402.

to proclaim her identity through her dress. Her clothing can identify her not only as a Muslim, but sometimes also as a Muslim from a specific geographic region or class. For a woman who has moved from a predominantly Muslim country to a predominantly non-Muslim country, her clothing can help her to retain a sense of her identity in an unfamiliar world as well.

To Publicly Disassociate Herself from the Perceived Immodesty of the "West"[16]

In Geraldine Brooks' *Nine Parts of Desire: The Hidden World of Islamic Women*, she describes the taking on of *hijab* by her young upper-class interpreter Sahar, who is from Cairo. Sahar states:

> I would sit there and read in the holy Koran that women should be covered, and then walk out into the street with bare arms. It just seemed to me that I was dressing that way because it was Western. Why imitate everything Western? Why not try something of our own?[17]

Disassociation from perceived immodesty in the West can also be a motive for Western women to convert to Islam and to wear Muslim dress; no sharp distinctions need be drawn between Western and non-Western Muslim women here. Just as some women may desire and choose to dress in a non-conservative manner, other women may desire and choose to dress in a conservative manner.

To Feel a Greater Sense of Security in Public Space

Women living in major urban areas who have dressed less conservatively may find themselves drawn to more conservative clothes as the political climate of a country changes. For example, urban Algerian women in the 1970s found the social climate of their cities transformed as more conservative, rural Algerians began to move to the cities. Indeed, "an unveiled and hence 'immodest' young woman became the object of continual verbal and other attacks, especially in the capital city, and many preferred to return to traditional dress and appearances to avoid being molested in the streets."[18] This sentiment is echoed by Lama Abu-Odeh, who notes that Muslim dress can decrease a woman's sense of ambiguity, particularly (but not exclusively) in places that are predominantly Muslim:

> A woman's willingness to raise objections to . . . male intrusions is notably different when she is veiled. Her sense of the untouchability of her body is usually very strong, in contrast to the woman who is not veiled. . . . The veiled woman . . . is more likely to confront the man with self-righteousness: "Have you no fear of Allah treating his believers in such shameless fashion?"[19]

---

16.   The term "West" is used in its colloquial sense to include (for example) Canada, the United States, Australia, New Zealand, and much of Europe. Although it will not be placed within quotation marks throughout this chapter, the reader should assume that those quotation marks are present implicitly, as this term, while convenient, is complex and multifaceted.

17.   BROOKS, *supra* note 5, at 8.

18.   BECK & KEDDIE, *supra* note 7, at 168.

19.   Lama Abu-Odeh, *Post-Colonial Feminism and the Veil*, 26 NEW ENG. L. REV. 1527, 1530 (1992).

Clearly, dressing in conservative clothing to curtail molestation and harassment does not serve to quash or confront the discriminatory norms or practices which Muslim dress may be used to prevent. Nonetheless, since gender-based discrimination, abuse, and violence persists, women should not be prevented from dressing in a manner that they feel affords them increased protection, respect, or security.

To Network

In some cultures and communities, the wearing of Islamic dress can serve as a means of accessing certain "networks" or receiving assistance from an associated group. Sahar, the interpreter from Cairo, found:

> Prying permits and appointments out of government departments became easier if she sought out other veiled women among the bureaucrats working there. Wanting to see an Islamic sister succeed in her job, they'd give her requests a preferential push.[20]

In a broader sense, the wearing of Islamic dress can give a woman an immediate sense of community and solidarity with other Muslim women, particularly in public space.

To Improve Relationships with Men by Increasing Respect

For many women, one major benefit of wearing Islamic dress is that men may treat them with increased respect: "They have to deal with my mind," Sahar says, "not my body."[21] As noted above, a woman wearing Muslim clothes is looked upon in most Muslim societies as inviolable; for Muslim men, she is a "sister." Thus when he encounters her on a bus, in a government office, or at work, he is compelled to treat her with dignity and respect. While wearing Muslim or conservative dress does not address underlying derogatory stereotypes implying that women who do not conform to prevailing Islamic norms do not deserve respect, it may nevertheless afford women respect or improved standing that they would not receive without the dress.

For Family Status and Honor

In some cases, the adoption of full *chador* by the women of a family—often in combination with their increased seclusion—can increase the status of the family. It is seen as "a sign that the family's women did not have to work or expose themselves to circumstances that would threaten their honor."[22] Frequently, it has been noted that women "are regarded by their societies as major repositories of the honor of the family or basic social unit."[23] Therefore, dressing in accordance with their beliefs about the Koran can serve purposes not only for them, but also for their families. This observation is merely an explanation, not intended to condone practices requiring women to maintain family "honor." It should not be inferred as supporting seclusion, and it

---

20. BROOKS, *supra* note 5, at 9.

21. *Id.* at 10.

22. BECK & KEDDIE, *supra* note 7, at 6 and 9.

23. *Id.* at 403.

is not intended to address complex issues surrounding elitism or social status. Nonetheless, women who make informed decisions to increase personal or family status and honor by wearing certain forms of dress, including Muslim dress, should not be prevented from doing so, particularly through comparisons with Western norms or standards.

Women Being Forced to Wear Certain Dress

While some women choose to wear a certain form of dress, others are forced to follow state-imposed rules of dress that may or may not correspond to the choices each individual woman would otherwise have made. This issue is explored next. The headings used in the following subsections correspond to those used in the U.S. State Department's annual Country Reports on Human Rights Practices.

Africa

In Sudan, government directives require female students and teachers, as well as women in government offices, to conform to what it deems an Islamic dress code entailing, at minimum, the wearing of a head covering. Additionally, the Passport Office refuses to issue a passport to a woman of any faith whose head is uncovered in her passport photo. Furthermore, government employees often will refuse to wait on any woman whose head is not covered. Enforcement of dress code regulations is uneven.[24]

East Asia and the Pacific

Religious authorities in Brunei strongly encourage Muslim women to wear the *tudong*, a traditional head covering. While many women comply, some Muslim women do not, and there is no official pressure on non-Muslim women to do so. However, all female students in government-operated schools are required, and students in non-government schools are officially encouraged, to wear the *tudong*.[25]

In Malaysia's opposition-controlled state of Kelantan, the state government has imposed restrictions on women's attire in the workplace. This restriction is justified by the state government as reflective of Islamic values. The federal structure of government in Malaysia allows for no legal means, short of amending the Constitution, by which the central government can overturn such state laws.[26]

Near East and North Africa

In Iran, the enforcement of conservative Islamic dress codes has flagged since the death of Ayatollah Khomeini in 1989. Nevertheless, such dress codes persist and

---

24. UNITED STATES DEPARTMENT OF STATE, COUNTRY REPORTS ON HUMAN RIGHTS PRACTICES FOR 1995, 257 (1996) [hereinafter COUNTRY REPORTS ON HUMAN RIGHTS].

25. *Id.* at 556.

26. *Id.* at 668–69.

are enforced arbitrarily.[27] Indeed, "[r]efusal to conform to strict dress codes and norms of behaviour often leads to degrading and humiliating punishment for women, such as public reproach and even flogging, sexual abuse and deprivation of all public and civil services."[28] Iran's Prosecutor General issued a warning that "Iranian women failing to cover themselves from head to foot in Islamic fashion could face death under the Islamic Republic's religious laws."[29]

In Kuwait, sexual harassment is experienced more frequently by women wearing Western attire and by foreign women than by women wearing traditional Islamic garb.[30]

In Saudi Arabia, a woman is required to wear the *abaya*, a black garment covering the entire body, while in public. Her head and face are also required to be covered. Women from Arab countries, Asia, and Africa are generally expected to comply more fully with Saudi customs than are Western women; nonetheless, in recent years the Mutawwa'in (religious police) have also attempted to force Western women to wear the *abaya* and to cover their hair.[31]

South Asia

In Taliban-controlled areas of Afghanistan, women may appear in public only if wearing an all-encompassing head-to-toe garment with a mesh veil for the face. In April of 1995, the U.N. Office for Coordination of Humanitarian Assistance to Afghanistan (UNOCHA) cancelled a donor visit to Kandahar province because the Taliban-controlled Shura (Governing Council) refused to meet with female diplomats and insisted that they wear full Islamic dress to visit project sites. The Shura eventually relented, allowing female diplomats to visit Kandahar and meet with local authorities on the condition that they wear a head covering. Increasingly in the last few years, the Taliban has implemented extremely prohibitive laws that violate women's basic rights and freedoms.

Women Being Prevented from Wearing Certain Forms of Dress

Summary of Violations

While there have been incidents in the West of women being forced to wear a skirt rather than pants in the context of their employment,[32] these cases have typically been resolved through domestic legislation and litigation[33] and will not be the focus

---

27.   *Id*. at 1158.

28.   PARLIAMENTARY HUMAN RIGHTS GROUP (U.K.), IRAN: THE SUBJECTION OF WOMEN 2 (1994).

29.   THE DAILY TELEGRAPH, Aug. 16, 1991, *as cited in id*. at 8.

30.   COUNTRY REPORTS ON HUMAN RIGHTS, *supra* note 24, at 1210.

32.   For example, in Spain, in Sept. 1995, inspectors from the Ministry of Labor fined a hospital in Bilbao for requiring its female nurses to wear skirts instead of pants while at work.

31.   COUNTRY REPORTS ON HUMAN RIGHTS, *supra* note 24, at 1256.

33.   *See, e.g.*, EEOC Case No. 81–20 (Apr. 8, 1981), 27 Fair Empl. Prac. Cas. (BNA) 1809 (1981).

here. Rather, restrictions on women's freedom to wear clothing of religious significance to them—in particular, the right of female Muslim students to wear a head covering while attending school—will be analyzed.

Since 1989, and particularly since 1993, an increasing number of reports from countries as diverse as Egypt, France, and Canada tell of female students being warned that they must either refrain from wearing the *hijab* or be expelled from school.

In France, three young women of North African origin were suspended from school in the autumn of 1989 and were readmitted only upon the intervention of the Socialist National Minister of Education.[34] The highest administrative court ruled in that year that the "ostentatious" wearing of these headscarves violated a law prohibiting proselytizing in schools. Similar incidents were reported in 1993[35] and 1994.[36] In 1994, the French government announced the creation of a policy that would ban the wearing of headscarves in public schools; this policy overrides any school's local decision to permit the wearing of headscarves.[37] The Ministry of Education issued a broad directive prohibiting the wearing of "ostentatious political and religious symbols" in schools, without specifying the symbols in question, thus leaving school authorities considerable discretionary authority. In 1995, France's highest administrative court confirmed that the simple wearing of a headscarf does not in itself provide grounds for exclusion from school, and several hundred students continue to wear *hijab*.[38]

In Egypt, tensions between the Mubarek government and conservative Muslims have increased in recent years and, "as the battle lines have become increasingly drawn, they have most symbolically been expressed in a growing tussle over whether female students and teachers could attend classes veiled."[39] In 1993, the government banned the *niqab*, and in 1994 it attempted to ban the *hijab*, but was overruled by Egypt's Supreme Court.

In Montreal, Canada, in the autumn of 1994, a thirteen-year-old female student was sent home from school for wearing *hijab*, while a fifteen-year-old was told that she "would have to transfer to another school if she wanted to observe *hijab*."[40] The Quebec Human Rights Commission responded by issuing a legal opinion ruling the *hijab* ban illegal.[41] The ban, the Commission said, is a violation of the students' right

---

34.   N.C. Moruzzi, *A Problem With Headscarves: Contemporary Complexities of Political and Social Identity*, 22 POLITICAL THEORY 653, 653 (1994).

35.   LE MONDE, Nov. 6, 1993, at 14.

36.   LA REPUBBLICA, Apr. 15, 1994, at 14.

37.   N.Y. TIMES, Sept. 11, 1994, at 4.

38.   COUNTRY REPORTS ON HUMAN RIGHTS, *supra* note 24, at 859–60.

39.   M.A. Weaver, *The Novelist and the Sheikh*, THE NEW YORKER, Jan. 30, 1995, at 52, 63.

40.   Amber Nasrulla, *Educators Outside Quebec Mystified by Hijab Ban: Events in France Suggested as Link to Schools' Actions*, TORONTO GLOBE AND MAIL, Dec. 13, 1994, at A1.

41.   A. Picard, *Hijab in Schools Supported*, TORONTO GLOBE AND MAIL, Feb.15, 1995, at A1.

to public education and to freedom of religion, and a school should intervene only if a student is being forced to wear the *hijab*. The judgment, however, leaves school boards and individual schools "free to regulate its use according to local conditions."[42]

Thus, a ban on *hijab* has been attempted, and sometimes effectively implemented, in countries on at least three continents. A note on terminology is appropriate here. For the rest of this section, the word *hijab* will generally be used since this is the item of clothing that has typically been banned. As the *hijab* is the least "extreme" form of Muslim dress (from the perspective of most non-Muslims), the assumption here is that if a state bans *hijab*, it also implicitly intends to ban other forms of Muslim dress.

Media Coverage of the Violations

Western media reports of these alleged violations are briefly reviewed here, since such reports sometimes reflect public opinion and frequently shape it. The debate has been distorted through misperceptions created by a stereotypical depiction of Islam and by "the three images to which the media are addicted: the Terrorist, the Veiled Woman, and the Demon Demagogue."[43]

In France, where media coverage has been largely critical of the wearing of *hijab*,[44] five prominent intellectuals of the Left published an open letter[45] that vigorously supported the *hijab* ban:

> They held that only the absolute rule of a national policy of secularism, by which the young women students from North African families must abide—and if they did not, they must not be allowed to enter the classroom—could save these women from the tyranny of their fathers.[46]

This attitude is demeaning, ignoring the diverse and complicated reasons that a woman or girl might choose to wear *hijab*. Rather than being subjects participating in a complex discussion, they become instead objects in a falsely dichotomized debate. Ignoring an opportunity to create and strengthen bridges between communities, many feminists chose not to reach out to the students and instead judged them from the other side of the barricades. One writer "made it clear that for her, the [1989 French incident] could be reduced to (Islamic) fundamentalist threats to the (French) Republic."[47] Even a supposedly sympathetic commentator intentionally mischaracterized the *hijab* by terming the students' clothing *"chador,"* which, as noted above, is a completely different form of dress. She justified this mislabelling by stating that the use of the term "might . . . be the easiest symbolic way to label the general attitude of the three

---

42. Daniel Latouche, *What Everyone's Talking, and Talking, About*, Toronto Globe and Mail, Mar. 3, 1995, at A25.

43. Eric Utne, *Islam (Introduction)*, 62 Utne Reader 75 (1994).

44. Country Reports on Human Rights, *supra* note 24, at 859.

45. Le Nouvel Observateur, Nov. 2–8, 1989, at 58.

46. Moruzzi, *supra* note 34, at 659.

47. *Id.* at 661.

students."[48]

In Canada, some commentary has criticized the *hijab* ban as a rights violation.[49] However, there has also been commentary in support of the *hijab* ban. One author, writing generally about women's rights, stated that women who choose to wear the "shroud-like *chador* . . . willingly embrace their own oppression."[50] Daniel Latouche, a columnist for *Le Devoir*, asserted: "[T]he *hijab* is indeed a reminder of the 'proper' place of women in society and has become a symbol of the violation of the most basic human right: that of dressing and walking on the street in the attire of your desire."[51] He mentions with approval the Parti Québécois Minister of International Affairs who, "made it clear that a sovereign Québec would not subsidize ethnic ghettos and multicultural entrapment."[52] Finally, in the opinion pages of a major Canadian newspaper, a woman[53] wrote: "I say that people who want to promenade in this country as slaves should not be allowed to do so. It is an affront to the rest of us; to human dignity and self-respect."[54] In response, Rahat Kurd, a Muslim woman who wears *hijab*, wrote: "I don't cover to please any man, and I'm not going to uncover to please any woman."[55]

Clearly, the *hijab* ban has inspired vigorous debate in the press of those countries in which it has been enacted, as well as in other countries around the world. While there have been some spirited defenses of the right to wear Islamic dress, the strongly negative sentiments about the wearing of Muslim dress expressed by both the Left and the Right in support of the ban have most marked the debate.

State Justifications for the Hijab Ban

There are a number of justifications advanced by states for banning the *hijab*. Arguably, however, in considering all surrounding circumstances and in balancing the interests of the parties, none of the potential justifications are persuasive enough to defeat the students' claims that they should be allowed to wear the *hijab*.

---

48. Galeotti, *supra* note 12, at 585.

49. *See, e.g.*, S. Fine, *When the law comes to a head*, TORONTO GLOBE AND MAIL, Mar. 11, 1995, at D2.

50. Margaret Wente, *Counting Your Problems? Count Your Blessings*, TORONTO GLOBE AND MAIL, Mar. 11, 1995, at A2.

51. Latouche, *supra* note 42. His characterization of choice of dress as the most basic human right is rather questionable.

52. *Id.*

53. With an M.A. in Islamic Studies, no less.

54. M. Lemon, *Understanding Does Not Always Lead to Tolerance*, TORONTO GLOBE AND MAIL, Jan. 31, 1995, at A20.

55. R. Kurd, *My Hijab Is an Act of Worship—And None of Your Business*, TORONTO GLOBE AND MAIL, Feb. 15, 1995, at A20. Defenses of wearing *hijab* have also appeared in the Egyptian media. Weaver, *supra* note 39, at 64.

Islamic Dress Offends the Equality of Women, Which We as a State Have to Protect

A state could claim it illogical and incoherent to force it to guarantee the rights discussed above in a manner that violates the rights of other individuals. In particular, the state could point to its obligations under the various equal protection clauses found in international human rights documents, and its obligations under the Convention on the Elimination of All Forms of Discrimination Against Women, to guarantee the equality of women. Two provisions of the Women's Convention to which the state might point are Articles 2(f) and 5, both of which require the state to alter those customary practices that are incompatible with the equality of men and women. Article 5(a) states:

> States Parties shall take all appropriate measures:
>
> (a) To modify the social and cultural patterns of conduct of men and women, with a view to achieving the elimination of prejudices and customary and all other practices which are based on the idea of the inferiority of either of the sexes or on stereotyped roles for men and women.

The state might thus claim that the *hijab* constitutes a customary practice based on the idea of women as inferior or as perpetrating stereotyped gender roles. What this reasoning ignores is that a state's promotion of the equality of men and women does not mean that the state should force all women to be the same. To properly ensure the protection of women's rights requires, above all, preserving a woman's right to make choices about how she wants to live her life. To take away this right of choice would be the truly subjugating act.

It is interesting that the concern expressed about Muslim women has not also been directed at Orthodox Jewish men, Sikh men, or Catholic nuns who choose to wear the traditional head covering and/or clothing that indicates their religion. Presumably men are allowed the individual dignity to make this choice without it being assumed that they are oppressed by their faith. Presumably Catholic nuns have escaped scrutiny in the West by virtue of the fact that they cannot be placed under the umbrella of "oppressive" Islam. It has been noted that:

> [C]olonial authorities often seem to preoccupy themselves with the oppression of colonized women, a situation that devolves into White men saving Brown women from Brown men. It seems something similar can apply in post-colonial situations as well.[56]

Muslim women, then, should be allowed the same dignity to choose to wear the clothing of their faith that men and women of other religions are allowed.

Islamic Dress Endangers the National Security, Public Order, Public Health, or Morals of the Country

As noted *infra*, the exercise of a number of rights may be legitimately restricted if their full exercise would endanger the national security, public order, public health, or morals of the country. France has claimed that it must limit the wearing of Muslim

---

56. Moruzzi, *supra* note 34, at 670 n. 28.

clothing because it is, allegedly, a symbol of alliance with Islamic causes in Algeria and elsewhere. Additionally, French school officials have expressed concern that the wearing of *hijab* could lead to social unrest: "[T]he principal feared that if he allowed the three to wear their headscarves, he next would have thirty wearing them, and then twenty Jewish students again refusing to attend on Fridays and Saturdays, and then community chaos."[57] The Mubarek government in Egypt has banned the *niqab* and attempted to ban the *hijab* in order to battle "Islamic fundamentalism in the schools,"[58] and more generally, Islamic fundamentalism in Egypt. Implicit in this is a concern that the fundamentalist movement is a threat to the stability of Egypt's government.

It is neither obvious nor likely that the wearing of *hijab* could cause such instability, that the banning of *hijab* could decrease such instability, or that the alleged instability is of such nature and magnitude as to trigger permissible limitations on human rights. Each of these assertions would have to be proven by a state before the limitation would be legal. Beyond this, moreover, the right to freedom of religion, the right perhaps most obviously violated here, is non-derogable even in a state of emergency under the ICCPR and the American Convention, thus weakening the ability of states to limit the right to freedom of religion by using arguments analogous to that of a public emergency, such as those arguments described above.

Islamic Dress Offends Our State Policy of Secularism

In France, the major officially articulated reason for banning *hijab* is that it conflicts with France's state policy of secularism. Secularism in France is:

> one of the most cherished legacies of the Revolution. . . . Secularism was to be the antidote to the religious control of education, and specifically to the Christian, Roman Catholic influence. . . . For the established intellectual Left, secularism may be the most defining tenet of French national identity.[59]

However, as one author has noted, the policy is not truly secular, insofar as it is compatible only with Christianity (e.g., a Sunday holiday and uncovered head are considered "secular," and there is no ban in France on the wearing of crosses).[60] Thus the policy serves to allow most outward expressions Christian in nature or consistent with Christianity, but bans external manifestations of other religions. By relying on the secularism excuse, France is in effect justifying its discriminatory treatment of Muslim women by pointing to a policy that legitimizes discrimination.

As a State, We Should Be Allowed a Margin of Appreciation

The last refuge for any state is to plead that it must be accorded a margin of appreciation; that is, an "area of discretion"[61] within which to determine what "free-

---

57.   *Id*. at 658.

58.   Weaver, *supra* note 39, at 63.

59.   Moruzzi, *supra* note 34, at 663.

60.   *Id*. at 664–65.

61.   J.G. MERRILLS, THE DEVELOPMENT OF INTERNATIONAL LAW BY THE EUROPEAN COURT OF HUMAN

dom of religion" or "freedom of expression" will mean. While it is true that states are generally given some leeway within which to interpret a given right, the limitation that is placed on the rights here is discriminatory.

Consider these questions: How meaningful is freedom of religion if one must worship in a manner in accordance with the practices of the dominant faith? How meaningful is freedom of expression if one can only express that which the majority accepts? How meaningful is freedom of education if one must deny one's most fundamental convictions in order to receive that education? And how meaningful are the rights of minority groups if they must conform to the behaviors of the majority in order to be protected?

If all previous attempts at justification have failed in the manner described above, then a plea for a margin of appreciation on the part of the state must fail as well. If the margin of appreciation is this broad, then there is very little room left for the right itself.

THE RIGHT TO DRIVE

> [T]he meaning and use of the automobile have become powerfully inscribed through law. . . . [T]he car has sustained and enhanced traditional understandings about women's abilities and roles in areas both public (the road) and private (the driveway). Specifically, the car has reinforced women's subordinated status in ways that make the subordination seem ordinary, even logical.[62]

Introduction

The automobile promises its driver "solitude and independence"[63]—things which those who violate women's personal rights seek to control. Furthermore, the ability to drive allows for the exercise of many other rights: for example, the automobile helped women to organize the suffragist movement in the United States. In discussing the ramifications of potentially allowing Saudi Arabian women to drive, one commentator stated:

> Allowing women to drive would radically redefine their role and status in Saudi society. . . . [A] driver's license is a powerful instrument of physical and social mobility. It would allow women to escape the house. It would give them access to more job opportunities. It could even make them financially independent of male relatives or husbands.[64]

It is little wonder, then, that states seeking to restrict women's freedoms sometimes focus on women's right to drive motor vehicles.

RIGHTS 136 (1988). This doctrine has been developed primarily in the European system, but it could be applied more widely.

62.   Carol Sanger, *Girls and the Getaway: Cars, Culture and the Predicament of Gendered Space*, 144 U. PA. L. REV. 705 (1995).

63.   *Id.*

64.   Tom Hundley, *Road Rally May Help Give Saudi Women New Role*, CHI. TRIB., Nov. 13, 1990, at 5.

Summary of Violations

Until recently, Saudi Arabia was the only country that banned its female citizens from driving.[65] By custom—and now by law—no woman, including a foreign civilian, may legally drive motor vehicles or ride bicycles. Women are further restricted in their use of public transportation; they must enter city buses by a separate rear entrance and are required to sit in specially designated sections. Even while merely riding in a motor vehicle, women are subject to regulation, since they are forbidden from riding in a vehicle driven by a male who is neither an employee nor a close male relative.[66]

In 1990, forty-seven Saudi Arabian women "gathered in a supermarket parking lot, dismissed their chauffeurs and drove themselves in an orderly procession through downtown Riyadh."[67] The women were subsequently detained by the police, fired from their jobs, and denied the papers necessary for travel. Their names were broadcast from the mosques with a call for their beheading[68] and they were termed "portents of evil" by the Saudi government.[69]

King Fahd declared that a committee of religious scholars be formed to determine the illegality of the act under Muslim law. This committee found:

> there was no specific prohibition in the Koran on driving. In fact, during the time of the Prophet, women regularly led camels across the desert. Even now, Bedouin women have regularly been permitted to drive cars and trucks in isolated parts of the kingdom. The committee nevertheless gently advised against repeating the experiment.[70]

Thus the act contravened only custom, not religious law. Nevertheless, the Saudi Interior Ministry issued a decree formalizing the ban on women driving:

> [W]omen are not permitted to drive motor vehicles and any of them who does so [sic] will be given appropriate punishment through which deterrence may be accomplished, and this is in order to protect sanctities and prevent unforeseen signs of evil as clear from shari'ah evidence which necessitates preventing anything that leads to making women cheap or exposes them to sedition.[71]

The Interior Minister further stated that all protests and demonstrations by women were forbidden.[72] The fundamental meaning of the ban was captured by one profes-

---

65.   Caryle Murphy, *Saudis Pulled Between Past and Present*, WASH. POST, Nov. 20, 1990, at A1; William Dowell, *Life in the Slow Lane*, TIME, Nov. 26, 1990, at 46, as cited in Sanger, *supra* note 62.

66.   COUNTRY REPORTS ON HUMAN RIGHTS, *supra* note 24, at 1256.

67.   Dowell, *supra* note 65.

68.   *Saudi Arabia: Update on Women at the Wheel*, MS., Nov.–Dec. 1991, at 17, *cited in* Sanger, *supra* note 62.

69.   Paul Dean, *Driving a Wedge in Saudi Sand*, L.A. TIMES, Nov. 19, 1990, at E1.

70.   Dowell, *supra* note 65, at 46.

71.   BBC Summary of World Broadcasts, Nov. 13, 1990, at Part 4, AI.

72.   James LeMoyne, *Saudi Interior Minister Prohibits All Protest for Change by Women*, N.Y. TIMES, Nov. 18, 1990, at 16.

sional Saudi woman, who stated: "What this means is that I have to remain dependent on men."[73]

Restrictions on a woman's right to direct her own transportation is not limited to Saudi Arabia. For example, in Qatar, a woman may apply for a driver's license only if she has permission from a male guardian. Non-Qatari women are not subject to this restriction.[74] In Afghanistan, the Taliban is one of the most powerful factions, carrying out a campaign of repression against women that includes, among other things, a ban on driving by local and foreign women alike.[75] In Iran, some scholars have advocated banning women from riding bicycles, and some members of the state-run volunteer militia have attacked cyclists and ransacked the Chitgar sports complex, the only place where women and men can both ride bicycles. They have also attacked the administrators of the center.[76] The ban has been supported by hard-line publications such as the *Jomhuri Islami* and the speaker of the parliament, Ali Akbar Nateq-Nouri, but has been opposed by Fa'ezeh Hashemi, a member of the Majlis (parliament) and daughter of President Hashemi Rafsanjani.

FREEDOM TO TRAVEL UNATTENDED AND WITHOUT PERMISSION

Introduction

Along with restrictions on a woman's freedom to use an automobile or bicycle, more general restrictions on her freedom to travel can curtail her ability to have a whole variety of experiences. Depending upon the severity of the restriction, a woman may be unable to leave her country, her region, or indeed even her home without a male escort from her family. Should those male relatives not be amenable to or available for accompanying her, she may in fact face an absolute prohibition on movement. Even if the male relatives do agree, a woman will be forced to request them to accompany her, thus increasing the degree to which she is beholden to them and giving them leverage which they may use to control her in other ways.

Summary of Violations

Africa

In the northern provinces of Cameroon, traditional leaders (Lamibe) keep their wives confined to their palaces.[77] Muslim women in Djibouti are frequently forbidden from travelling unless they are accompanied by a spouse or an adult male.[78] In

---

73. *Id.*

74. COUNTRY REPORTS ON HUMAN RIGHTS, *supra* note 24, at 1247.

75. Kathy Gannon, *Women Anxious About Future: Taliban Faction Threat to Role*, ROCKY MOUNTAIN NEWS, Mar. 10, 1996, at 44A; available in Westlaw at 1996 WL 7560072.

76. The women cyclists observe the Islamic dress code, wearing a head scarf and loose smock while cycling. A.P., May 2, 1996, available in Westlaw at 1996 WL 4422755.

77. COUNTRY REPORTS ON HUMAN RIGHTS, *supra* note 24, at 39.

78. *Id.* at 75.

Gabon, married women are required under an unevenly enforced law to receive their husband's permission in order to travel abroad.[79] A woman in Kenya must receive consent from her husband or father in order to obtain a passport.[80]

Among the Hausa and Fulani peoples of eastern Niger, some women are cloistered and permitted to leave their homes only if escorted by a male and typically only after dark.[81] In Nigeria, women are typically required to obtain permission from a male family member in order to receive a passport, and in part of Nigeria's far north, girls and women are kept in *purdah*, secluded from men outside the family.[82]

In Sudan, women are forbidden from travelling abroad without the permission of their husbands or male guardians. The Passport Office refuses to grant a passport to a woman of any religion who does not have her head covered in her passport picture.[83]

Under traditional law in Swaziland, a married woman is required to receive her husband's permission in order to apply for a passport, while unmarried single women must receive the permission of a close male relative. In order to leave the country, a woman generally needs her husband's permission.[84]

In Uganda, a married woman is required to have her husband's signature on her passport application in order to travel with her children on her passport,[85] while a woman in the Democratic Republic of Congo is required by law to obtain her spouse's permission before applying for a passport.[86]

East Asia and the Pacific

In Thailand, several regulations intended and used to reduce trafficking in women and children for the purposes of prostitution could be used as well to infringe on the right of women and children to travel freely. One statute (rarely used and dating to the last century) states that a woman must obtain her husband's permission in order to travel outside of Thailand. Female passport applicants under the age of thirty-six are required to submit to a series of interviews regarding their employment records and finances. Passport applications by single Thai women and children under the age of 14 must also be approved by the Department of Public Welfare.[87]

---

79. *Id.* at 98.

80. *Id.* at 132.

81. *Id.* at 194–95.

82. *Id.* at 207.

83. *Id.* at 255, 257.

84. *Id.* at 262, 264.

85. *Id.* at 284.

86. *Id.* at 293.

87. *Id.* at 725.

Near East and North Africa

Under the Family Code in Algeria, women under nineteen years of age are required to obtain their husband's or father's permission to obtain a passport or to travel abroad.[88] In Egypt, an unmarried woman under the age of twenty-one is required to obtain permission from her father in order to obtain a passport or to travel; a married woman must obtain the same permission from her husband. In August of 1995, Egypt's highest religious figure endorsed a proposed new marriage contract, thus freeing the Egyptian government to adopt it. The contract applies only to Muslims and would replace the current version, which was drafted in 1931. It stipulates negotiations regarding the terms of the marriage, including the woman's right to work, study, and travel abroad.[89]

In Iraq, women are forbidden from travelling abroad without a male relative. Furthermore, the Iraqi government frequently prevents citizens who hold dual citizenship—principally, the children of Iraqi fathers and foreign-born mothers—from visiting the country of their other nationality.[90]

Jordanian women, and foreign women who are married to Jordanians, must obtain written permission from a male guardian in order to apply for a passport or leave Jordan to travel abroad. This requirement is typically enforced only when a married woman plans to travel abroad with children. Thus fathers can prevent their children from leaving the country, even when they are travelling with their mothers.[91] Fathers are not similarly prevented from taking children abroad without the mother's permission.

In Kuwait, unmarried women age twenty-one and over may obtain a passport and travel abroad, but a married woman is required to obtain her husband's written permission in order to apply for a passport. A woman is not required to obtain her husband's permission in order to travel, though he may prevent her from travelling abroad by contacting the immigration authorities and placing a twenty-four-hour travel ban on her. After this period, the husband may not prevent his wife from leaving the country without a court order.[92]

In Libya, a woman may not travel abroad without her husband's permission,[93] while in Oman, a woman must obtain the permission of her husband, father, or nearest male relative in order to obtain a passport.[94]

---

88.   *Id.* at 1125.

89.   *Id.* at 1147, 1149.

90.   *Id.* at 1167, 1170.

91.   *Id.* at 1200, 1202.

92.   *Id.* at 1208.

93.   *Id.* at 1225.

94.   *Id.* at 1241.

In Qatar, a woman is not generally forced to obtain permission from a male guardian to travel, though traditional and social pressures cause most to travel with a male escort. A man may, however, prevent a female relative from travelling abroad by placing her name with immigration officers at ports of departure. Female government employees are technically required to obtain official permission to travel abroad when requesting leave, though it is unclear to what extent this regulation is enforced.[95]

Women in Saudi Arabia are required to obtain written permission from their closest male relative before authorities will permit them to travel abroad or to board public transportation between different parts of the country. Furthermore, women are forbidden from accepting jobs in rural areas of Saudi Arabia if the job would require them to live apart from their families.[96] Additionally, a businesswoman entering Saudi Arabia without a husband, father, brother, or son must present a letter from her company that has been signed by a Saudi official in order to enter the country or to stay at a hotel by herself.[97] It should be noted that these restrictions are lessened during the hajj, or annual pilgrimage, when a woman may supersede her husband's authority in order to attend, so long as she is accompanied by another close male relative (such as her uncle, son, or brother).[98]

In Syria, a husband may file a request with the Ministry of the Interior to prohibit his wife's departure; however, in practice, a wife may file the same type of request with regard to her husband. In addition, a father may request that the Ministry prohibit travel abroad by unmarried daughters, even if they are over eighteen years of age.[99]

In the United Arab Emirates, a husband may bar his wife and children from leaving the country,[100] while in Yemen, women must obtain permission from a male relative before applying for a passport and must be accompanied by a male relative when travelling abroad.[101]

South Asia

In Afghanistan, the Taliban has kept girls from attending school and threatened girls and women "with harsh punishment if they leave their homes unaccompanied by a man."[102] The fundamentalist Taliban has violated women's fundamental human

---

95. *Id.* at 1246, 1247.

96. *Id.* at 1254, 1256, 1257.

97. Lynn Woods, *Women's Travel Challenge: Many Restrictions Mark Cultural Gap*, USA Today, May 7, 1996, at 4E.

98. Suleiman Nimer, *Women Pilgrims Enjoy Rare Freedoms in Saudi Arabia*, Agence France-Presse, Apr. 27, 1996; available in Westlaw at 1996 WL 3845446.

99. Country Reports on Human Rights, *supra* note 24, at 1263.

100. *Id.* at 1277, 1278.

101. *Id.* at 1283, 1285.

102. Gannon, *supra* note 75.

rights and freedoms. Not only are women not allowed to travel domestically or abroad, but even their right to travel and movement in their own community is severely restricted.

RELIGION, CULTURE, POLITICS, AND HUMAN RIGHTS

Introduction

The violations described in this chapter raise complex questions about the intersection of gender with religion, politics, and culture. In order to more fully understand these violations and to propose viable solutions, certain subtleties of this intersection are briefly explored in the following sections.

Religion

As discussed, the violations of a woman's freedom to drive, travel unattended, or wear clothing of her choice have been justified primarily by reference to religion (in particular, Islam) or, in the case of the *hijab* ban, to a rejection of Islam. A fundamental question presents itself: what is it about Islam that has placed it at the crux of these particular debates about human rights?

First, in the case of the *hijab* ban, a decrease in respect for overt religiosity, especially in connection with minority religions, has played some role in the conflict. Overt religiosity was at one time relatively common in the West. While private religious belief (including such practices as prayer) is still quite strong, in most geographical regions overt expressions of faith have arguably become a new "unmentionable." Indeed, "[o]ne way to end a conversation," notes one author, "—or start an argument—is to tell a group of well-educated professionals that you hold a political position . . . because it is required by your understanding of God's will."[103]

For devoutly religious people, occasions of conflict between what their religion orders them to do and what the broader culture requires arise with relative frequency. This is exacerbated in the case of individuals who are not Christian, as many "secular" countries tend to have customs (e.g., Sunday holidays) consistent with Christianity. The choice that is expected of such conflicted individuals is frequently all too clear: "[T]he consistent message of modern American society is that whenever the demands of one's religion conflict with what one has to do to get ahead, one is expected to ignore the religious demands and act . . . rationally."[104]

It is not difficult to see how this theory plays itself out in the present context. By wearing *hijab*, the students are making a public proclamation of their religious faith, and thus violating the unwritten "rules" of an increasingly secular world. (In France, it is viewed as a violation of an actual policy of secularism.) By following the authority of what they believe to be divine will, and not the secular authority of

---

103. Steven L. Carter, The Culture of Disbelief: How American Law and Politics Trivialize Religious Devotion 15 (1993).

104. *Id.* at 13.

the school authorities, they are deemed to be acting "irrationally." It is almost as if this is embarrassing for some people to witness. While only a few decades ago it was expected among Christians that women would cover their heads when entering a sacred place, today only certain groups of nuns wear head coverings, and they are typically seen as women who have removed themselves, in many respects, from everyday society. To see a woman who covers her head but who also participates in the everyday world—who is, in effect, both "sacred" and "secular" at the same time—is confounding for many people.

In Islam, the Koran serves as a comprehensive guide for living, rather than solely a set of abstract theological principles unconnected to the seemingly mundane choices of daily living; as noted earlier, the very nature of personal rights and freedoms connects them to just these "mundane" choices. Furthermore, the rules set forth in the Koran are not absolutely gender blind; they *do* explicitly make reference to the role of women, and depending on interpretation, these references can serve as obstacles or avenues of progress. As such, there are textual "hooks" on which to hang interpretations of the "proper" role of women in the ideal Islamic society, and thus a general means by which to justify restrictions on women's personal rights in furtherance of this role.

Perhaps most importantly, the elites in every country attempt to maintain power using whatever tools are available. Since Islam is the official religion of a number of states, it is perhaps inevitable that the elites of those states, predominantly male, use Islam to consolidate and perpetuate their power. As noted by "Nada," a Saudi woman who sought political asylum in Canada, "[t]he status of women in the Middle East is deteriorating, not because of Islam as some claim, but because of political oppression. . . . In the Middle East, as everywhere else, men would do anything to preserve their power and authority."[105] Prominent Islamic scholar Fatima Mernissi echoes this when she states: "[I]f women's rights are a problem for some modern Muslim men, it is neither because of the Koran nor the Prophet, nor the Islamic tradition, but simply because those rights conflict with the interest of a male elite."[106] Indeed, politics enter into this debate in other ways, as demonstrated in the following section.

Politics

Hijab Ban

Although a lack of respect for and understanding of religiosity helps to partially explain the support for the *hijab* ban, it is an incomplete explanation. In particular, it is not very helpful in explaining the discrimination that occurs in countries where public religiosity is not in such sharp decline. One possible explanation may be found

---

105. Ann Elizabeth Mayer, *Universal Versus Islamic Human Rights: A Clash of Cultures or a Clash With a Construct?* 15 MICH J. INT'L L. 307, 397 (1994).

106. *Id., citing* FATIMA MERNISSI, *supra* note 4. For a detailed exposition of Mernissi's views, see FATIMA MERNISSI, BEYOND THE VEIL: MALE-FEMALE DYNAMICS IN MODERN MUSLIM SOCIETY (1987).

in Huntington's controversial article, *The Clash of Civilizations.*[107] His basic premise is that the new pattern of conflict in the world will occur on the fault lines between civilizations; that is, that conflict will be based primarily on cultural differences rather than ideology (as in the Cold War) or economics. His formulation is problematic and has been challenged on some grounds by other scholars.[108] But the notion that there is a simmering conflict—or at least a popularly perceived conflict—between "Islam" and "the West" (each as characterized and too often caricatured by the other) is indisputable.[109] Huntington notes that "conflict along the fault line between Western and Islamic civilizations has been going on for 1300 years" and asserts that "the Velvet curtain of culture has replaced the Iron Curtain of ideology."[110]

While immigration, intermarriage, and conversion have blurred the lines between Islam and the West somewhat, the *hijab* conflict can be construed as an instance of such a clash of civilizations, the site of which is women's bodies. A fear of Islam and what it is perceived to stand for is perhaps at the heart of both the *hijab* ban and the xenophobic commentary supporting it.

This clash can be seen also in violations that take place in Islamic states. Restrictions on women's right to drive unattended or to wear clothing of their choice has been justified by reference to Islam and particularly as a reaction to perceived immorality in the West. However, this clash is not between the West and Islam *qua* Islam, but rather between the West as perceived and Islam as interpreted by a particular state.[111]

Culture

Intermingled with the influence of religion and politics is the influence of culture. Islam is an international religion with adherents in countries throughout the world. However, from the discussion above about those restrictions on women's personal freedoms purportedly based on Islam, it is clear that these violations are concentrated in the Middle East and parts of Africa. By contrast, many areas of South and Southeast Asia that are predominantly (or at least to a significant degree) populated by Muslims are not marked by sweeping, explicit restrictions on women's free-

---

107. Samuel P. Huntington, *The Clash of Civilizations*, 72 FOREIGN AFFAIRS 22 (1993).

108. *See, e.g.*, R.E. Rubenstein & J. Crocker, *Challenging Huntington* 96 FOREIGN POLICY 113 (1994); Robert W. Cox, *Civilizations: Encounters and Transformations* (The Occasional Papers Series, Department of Political Science, York University, Canada).

109. A day's worth of the mainstream Western print and television media makes it all too clear. For example, consider the reports on Apr. 19 and 20, 1995, on United States network and cable television which reported that "Middle Easterners" or "Muslim extremists" were the immediate suspects in the Oklahoma City bombing. This was based partially on the still-echoing emotional reverberations of the World Trade Center bombing. That Muslims were immediately suspected suggests that Islam has replaced Communism in some quarters as the new primary (perceived) enemy of the "West."

110. Huntington, *supra* note 107, at 31.

111. Mayer, *supra* note 105, at 308–20, highlights this distinction well.

dom to drive, travel unattended and without permission, or wear clothing of their choice.

Too often, Westerners make the mistake of equating Islam with the form of its practice in countries such as Saudi Arabia, which has imposed among the most severe restrictions in the Muslim world. This can lead even sympathetic observers to the conclusion that these restrictions are somehow inherent in Islam, and that to criticize the policies is to criticize Islam itself, but this neglects the importance of the underlying culture in shaping the manner in which Islam is practiced. For example, Islam as practiced by the Arab peoples of the Middle East is based to a significant degree on "a view of the relations between men and women which was deeply rooted in the culture of the Middle East, which had existed long before the coming of Islam, and [which] was preserved in the countryside by immemorial custom."[112] It is perhaps not surprising, then, that Islam as practiced in these countries is extremely conservative.

Furthermore, states purporting to be Islamic are often not recognized as such by other such states. For example:

> Neither Iran's clerics nor the Saudi royal family recognize each other's claims to constitute an Islamic government even though each regime is by self-designation Islamic; indeed, Iran's and Saudi Arabia's rulers routinely anathematize each other in the name of their respective Islams.[113]

Therefore, while many Islamic countries impose restrictions on women's personal freedoms, these restrictions may be based more on commonly shared cultural assumptions than on the tenets of Islam.

In this context, "culture" is not self-perpetuating, but rather is reinforced by the domestic political framework in which it is situated. "Nada" notes: "When governments impose a certain set of beliefs on individuals, through propaganda, violence or torture, we are dealing not with culture but rather with political expediency."[114] Thus, the elements of this chapter—religion, politics, culture, and human rights—are constantly interacting in complex ways.

Culture enters into this debate with regard to violations which may not be connected with Islam. In particular, violations occurring in some African countries may have more to do with traditional African customs than with Islamic teachings.[115] Finally, Western culture is not in some way "neutral," with other cultures defined as such insofar as they deviate from the Western "standard." Rather, since Western culture contributes much of the language of modern human rights discourse, and in particular the

---

112. ALBERT HOURANI, A HISTORY OF THE ARAB PEOPLES 120 (1991).

113. Mayer, *supra* note 105, at 321.

114. *Id.* at 397.

115. *See, e.g.*, *supra* for descriptions of restrictions on women's freedoms in Cameroon, Gabon, Kenya, Nigeria, Swaziland, and Uganda. The same principles discussed in this section regarding the complexities of improving human rights conditions in countries imposing Islamic law are pertinent to those countries that impose traditional law.

documents of international human rights law, Western culture itself often serves as a factor in this complex debate. It is this set of concepts which is explored below.

Human Rights

International human rights law sets a standard by which the actions of states can be measured and judged. This body of law must be understood through reference to the interweaving of politics, religion, and culture. In order to understand the place of international human rights law standards in this debate, it is first necessary to describe how these standards could potentially be applied to restrictions on women's personal freedoms. Once these legal standards are articulated and applied, the interrelationship between the standards and the complicating factors of politics, religion, and culture are examined.

Provisions relating to women's freedom to drive, travel unattended and without consent, and wear clothing of their choice can be found in various international human rights instruments.[116] These specific protections work in tandem with general provisions designed to guarantee that the protections of these human rights instruments are enforced on an equal basis. An equal protection clause is contained in the United Nations Charter (art. 55(c)), the Universal Declaration of Human Rights (UDHR, art. 2), the International Covenant on Civil and Political Rights (ICCPR, arts. 2 and 3), the International Covenant on Economic, Social and Cultural Rights (ICESCR, arts. 2 and 3), the European Convention on Human Rights (art. 14), the American Convention on Human Rights (art. 1), the American Declaration on the Rights and Duties of Man (art. 2), and the African Charter on Human and Peoples' Rights (art. 2). The nondiscrimination clause functions to guarantee the rights in the document to all people without discrimination, including discrimination based on gender/sex or religion. In the present context, this guarantee requires that each of the following rights be afforded not only in the abstract on its own terms, but also on an equal basis among individuals in the state.

Travel / Drive

Since the freedom to drive can be conceptualized as a specific example of the freedom to travel unattended, provisions in international conventions relating to restrictions on movement can be applied to both. The Women's Convention states explicitly in Articles 1 and 2 that states parties have an obligation to modify or abolish all existing laws, regulations, customs, and practices that constitute discrimination against women, regardless of their marital status. Thus, the differences in laws relating to the ability of married and single women to travel are in violation of the Women's Convention.

Furthermore, the UDHR states: "Everyone has the right to freedom of movement . . . within the borders of each state" and "Everyone has the right to leave every

---

116. The 1990 Cairo Declaration on Human Rights in Islam will not be discussed here, since it does not serve to protect any of the discussed freedoms. For a thorough discussion of the treatment of women in this document, *see* Mayer *supra* note 105, at 327–33.

country, including his [or her] own" (art. 13). This is echoed in the ICCPR (art. 12), the American Convention (art. 22), and the African Charter (art. 12). However, each of these documents allows restrictions on the right to freedom of movement in order to protect "morals." Therefore, while the violations described above clearly trigger these provisions, a state might claim that restrictions on women's freedom of movement, whether via passport restrictions, a driving ban, or an outright travel ban, are necessary in order to preserve and promote the traditional values of the state. However, the morals clause cannot be used to severely restrict the freedom of movement of at least half of a country's population, nor to violate competing human rights and fundamental freedoms.[117]

Hijab Ban

In order to demonstrate that the *hijab* ban, particularly as implemented in educational facilities, is contrary to international human rights instruments, various forms of pertinent provisions in these documents are examined below.

Freedom of Religion

A clause protecting freedom of religion is contained in the UDHR (art. 18), the ICCPR (art. 18), the European Convention (art. 9), the American Convention (art. 12), the American Declaration (art. III), and the African Charter (art. 8). There are some restrictions placed on this right. Article 18 of the ICCPR states that, "freedom to manifest one's religion or beliefs may be subject only to such restrictions as are prescribed by law and are necessary to protect public safety, order, health or morals or the fundamental rights and freedoms of others," and the right is specified in Article 4(2) as one that is non-derogable in a state of emergency. Article 9 of the European Convention echoes the limitations in Article 18 of the ICCPR, as does Article 12 of the American Convention, which also denotes the right as non-derogable. All of the rights of the American Declaration are limited "by the rights of others, by the security of all, and by the just demands of the general welfare and the advancement of democracy."[118] The African Charter states that the right is subject to "law and order."

No state discussed in this section has explicitly said that women cannot practice their religion; that is, there has been no ordinance outlawing Islam *per se*. However, by outlawing what some people sincerely believe to be an essential practice of Islam (i.e., the wearing of Islamic clothing), the state is undermining the true exercise of the religion.

Some cases under the European Convention can provide guidance here. It was noted by one commentator in 1987 that "there has been no successful application

---

117. The presence of such a clause highlights a weakness of using international agreements to force domestic change in the area of personal rights. This theme will be discussed in more detail below.

118. American Declaration, Article XXVIII, *reprinted in* T. BUERGANTHAL, R. NORRIS, & D. SHELTON, PROTECTING HUMAN RIGHTS IN THE AMERICAS: SELECTED PROBLEMS 288 (1982) [hereinafter PROTECTING HUMAN RIGHTS].

brought before the European Commission or Court of Human Rights which was based primarily on Article 9."[119] It is instructive to examine two such decisions in order to determine the basis for their lack of success.

In *Chappell v. United Kingdom*,[120] the applicant complained that the decision to temporarily close Stonehenge—thus preventing the Druids from practicing their mid-summer solstice ceremony—infringed upon freedom of religion under Article 9. The application failed because the Commission determined that the decision to close Stonehenge during the solstice:

> was a necessary public safety measure, and that any implied interference with the applicant's rights . . . was in accordance with the law and necessary in a democratic society in the interests of public safety, for the protection of public order or for the protection of the rights and freedoms of others, within the meaning of Art. 9(2).[121]

In *Ahmad v. United Kingdom*,[122] a teacher complained that he had been forced to resign from his full-time position because he had been refused permission to attend mosque on Friday afternoons. This would have required a forty-five minute absence from general school duties. The Commission discussed the various positions put forth by the parties regarding whether such attendance was really an Islamic requirement, but then stated that it did not need to resolve the issue in order to reach a decision on the case. It noted that freedom of religion is subject to the limitations set out in Article 9(2), and that furthermore, "it may, as regards the modality of a particular religious manifestation, be influenced by the situation of the person claiming that freedom."[123] It was stressed by the Commission that Mr. Ahmad had knowingly entered into this contractual relationship without disclosing that he would need the time off, and it was noted that, "in most countries, only the religious holidays of the majority of the population are celebrated as public holidays."[124]

The situation of female Muslim students who choose to wear Islamic dress (and other Muslim women who choose to do so, for that matter) is not analogous to either of these scenarios. Leaving aside for the moment the issue of whether the decisions in these cases were correct, it should be clear that there is no counter-balancing factor in the present case that is as weighty as those described above. There is no concern about the protection of property as in *Chappell*, and the students have not voluntarily entered into contractual arrangements as in *Ahmad* that would preclude their wearing *hijab*. There is no significant interest asserted which weighs against their right to choose a mode of Islamic dress in keeping with their religious beliefs.

---

119. D. M. Clarke, *Freedom of Thought and Education Rights in the European Convention*, THE IRISH JUROR 28 (1987).

120. App. No. 12587/86 (1987), 10 E.H.R.R. 503.

121. *Id*. at 511.

122. App. No. 8160/78 (1981), 4 E.H.R.R. 126.

123. *Id*. at 134.

124. *Id*. at 138.

Turning to a different region, a Resolution adopted by the Inter-American Commission on Human Rights[125] declared that the Government of Argentina had violated the right to freedom of religion under the American Declaration[126] by, among other things, prohibiting the public exercise of the religion of Jehovah's Witnesses and expelling children who, on religious grounds, refused to salute national emblems and sing the national anthem.

This is more closely analogous to the present case, since in the Argentinean situation the children were accused—as are the Muslim students—of attempting to upset a dominant ideology. The Jehovah's Witness children were targeted because they refused to honor the authority of the state over the authority of what they believed to be religious truth. The concern seemed to be that the children were showing a lack of respect to the symbols of their state.[127] In the present case, the students are also being targeted because they refuse to honor the demands of a secular authority (the state, as represented by the secular education system) over the demands of their religious beliefs. The demand by the state that they show this respect does not carry the same weight that the competing concerns (protection of property, contractual obligations) did in the European cases. It is for this reason that the Commission sided with the children in the Argentinean case and that the Muslim students should prevail in the case of the *hijab* ban. Indeed, this reasoning has been vindicated in the above-discussed decision by the Quebec Human Rights Commission, which stated that the *hijab* ban is an infringement of a student's right to freedom of religion.[128]

The violation of the guarantee of freedom of religion violates not only the specific sections mentioned above, but also the equal protection clauses. The right of Muslim boys to attend school without violating their religious beliefs has not been interfered with; thus the right to freedom of religion has been afforded on a basis that is discriminatory on the basis of sex. The violation also breaches the Convention on the Rights of the Child (Child's Convention), which requires states to "respect the right of the child to freedom of thought, conscience and religion" (art. 14(1)).[129]

---

125. Resolution 02/79, *as discussed in* PROTECTING HUMAN RIGHTS, *supra* note 118, at 78.

126. The American Declaration is relevant because those OAS states that are not evaluated against the standards of the American Convention are evaluated against the standards set out in the Declaration. Cecilia Medina notes that although the Declaration was adopted as a non-binding set of standards, "it is almost impossible to maintain that the Declaration is not a source of legal obligations for the member states of the OAS." Cecilia Medina, *Toward a More Effective Guarantee of the Enjoyment of Human Rights by Women in the Inter-American System, in* HUMAN RIGHTS OF WOMEN: NATIONAL AND INTERNATIONAL PERSPECTIVES 257, 263, 282 (Rebecca Cook ed., 1994).

127. PROTECTING HUMAN RIGHTS, *supra* note 118, at 78.

128. Picard, *supra* note 41.

129. Art. 14(2) requires states to respect the rights and duties of parents or guardians to provide direction to the child "in the exercise of his or her right in a manner consistent with the evolving capacities of the child." Art. 14(3) limits the freedom to manifest one's religion or beliefs as "prescribed by law" and as "necessary to protect public safety, order, health or morals, or the fundamental rights and freedoms of others."

Freedom of Expression

A clause protecting freedom of expression is contained in the UDHR (art. 19), the ICCPR (art. 19), the European Convention (art. 10), the American Convention (art. 13), the American Declaration (art. IV), and the African Charter (art. 9, freedom to express opinions).

The ICCPR states that this right is subject to limits such as are provided by law and necessary for the respect of the rights or reputations of others, and for the protection of national security, public order, public health, or morals. The European Convention largely mirrors this. The American Convention does as well, adding to the list the moral protection of childhood and adolescence. The African Charter states that the right may only be exercised "within the law."

The right to freedom of expression is implicated here because by wearing the *hijab* these students are not only exercising their freedom of religion, but are also expressing those religious beliefs. Thus the *hijab* ban is a violation not only of their right to freedom of religion, but also of their right to freedom of expression: a violation of their right to religious expression.

Two cases under the European Convention demonstrate how the right to religious expression has been analyzed. In *Yanasik v. Turkey*,[130] a student complained that he had been dismissed from a military academy because of Islamic fundamentalist activities, thus (amongst other alleged violations) violating his freedom of religion. In resolving the complaint, the Commission analyzed what freedom of religion might imply with regard to public expression, stating: "[T]he Article specifically protected the practice and teaching of a religion or belief. It did not always guarantee the right to behave in public in accordance with that belief. Thus 'practices' in Article 9(1) does not cover any act motivated or inspired by a religion or belief."[131] The Commission stressed that life in a military academy by necessity imposed controls on its members, and noted that the applicant had not alleged that he was unable to fulfill his religious obligations within those constraints.

In *App. No. 9820/82 v. Sweden*,[132] a man who had been convicted of disorderly behavior—after repeatedly and loudly proclaiming in public the dangers of pornography, fornication, and alcohol—complained that his freedom of religion had been violated. The Commission disagreed, stating:

> [T]he applicant was not prevented from conveying his religious messages to the public, neither by word of mouth or by showing placards. It is true that the applicant wished to shout out his messages "like a trumpet" in obedience to Isaiah, and that he also did that. The Commission is of the opinion that under the Convention a State is permitted to put limits on the manner in which individuals can behave in public places.[133]

---

130. App. No. 14524/89 (1993), 16 E.H.R.R. CD5.

131. *Id.*

132. App. No. 9820/82 (1982), 5 E.H.R.R. 297.

133. *Id.*

The situation of the Muslim students is not analogous to these cases. The students have not given up the freedom to control many aspects of their everyday life by entering the rigid control of a military academy, as in *Yanasik*. By wearing *hijab*, they are not engaging in "disorderly behavior," as was the applicant in the Swedish case. While their *hijab* does proclaim their religion clearly—as does, for example, a Christian's cross, a priest's white collar, a nun's habit, or a Jewish male's yarmulke—it can be distinguished from the sartorial equivalent of "shouting like a trumpet."[134]

A child's right to freedom of expression is guaranteed in the Child's Convention (art. 13), subject only to certain limited circumstances in which it is necessary to restrict freedom of expression to "respect the rights or reputations of others" or for the protection of national security, public order, public health, or morals.

Right to Education

A clause protecting the right to education is contained in the UDHR (art. 26), the ICESCR (art. 13), the American Convention (art. 26),[135] the American Declaration (art. XII), the African Charter (art. 17), the First Protocol to the European Convention (art. 2), and the Women's Convention (art. 10).

The right to education is typically not subject to specific limitation within the context of these documents because it is inherently subject to limitation by virtue of the fact that it is a "social right." The phraseology of the documents in which this right embedded typically requires the state only to "take steps" or "adopt measures" "to the maximum of its available resources" in order to achieve the rights contained within them "progressively." In this way, rights such as the right to education are limited by the very context in which they are articulated.

Beyond this concern with limitation provisions, it is important to analyze the guarantees in order to determine whether they contain phrases that might prove useful in dealing with the *hijab* ban. Article 13 of the ICESCR emphasizes that the state must respect the rights of parents to "ensure the religious and moral education of their children in conformity with their own convictions." Protocol 1(2) of the European Convention requires that "the State shall respect the right of parents to ensure such education and teaching in conformity with their own religious and philosophical convictions." Finally, Article 10(a) of the Women's Convention requires states to provide equal conditions for access to studies for males and females.

The right to education has been violated with regard to hijab bans because the state has made the students' right to attend school contingent upon their acquiescing

---

134. While wearing a scarf-like head covering is relatively innocuous, full covering is clearly more obvious than the wearing of a cross or a yarmulke. Yet, minority religious rights are drained of much of their meaning if "acceptable" religious practices are defined by reference to majority religious traditions.

135. The right is protected by implication, since art. 26 incorporates the standards set out in the Charter of the OAS (relevant here: arts. 31(h), 47, 48) as amended by the Protocol of Buenos Aires.

to violations of their right to freedom of religion and freedom of expression. That is, the guarantee of freedom of education presupposes that the conditions under which that education will be given will not themselves violate other rights.

Thus far this section has referred to the students' religious beliefs, but the provisions above require that, in the context of children's education, the parents' religious beliefs be respected.[136] Two cases decided under the European Convention are relevant here. In *Kjeldsen, Busk, Madsen and Pedersen v. Denmark*[137] (the Danish Sex Education Case), the European Court of Human Rights interpreted Protocol 1(2) as asserting: "[P]arents may require the State to respect their religious and philosophical convictions. Their right . . . corresponds to a responsibility closely linked to the enjoyment and exercise of the right to education."[138] While noting that the state cannot "indoctrinate" children in a manner that disrespects these convictions, the court stated that the policy of neutral sex education legislated by Denmark in that case did not offend the convictions of those parents.

In a subsequent case, the reasoning in the Danish Sex Education Case was followed by the Commission, which stated explicitly: "[T]he essence of Prot. No. 1, Art. 2, is the safeguarding of pluralism and tolerance in public education."[139] However, the Commission held that the denial of a space in a single sex school to their children did not violate the parents' convictions in the requisite manner.

It might be suggested that so long as parents have the option of enrolling their children in a private school or educating them at home, their rights have not been violated. However, the better interpretation of the judgements under the European Convention is that "as soon as states assume any functions in education . . . they are legally obliged to respect the religious and philosophical convictions of parents."[140] In this case, a state party to the European Convention may not claim that it is permissible to ban *hijab* so long as private educational options are available for those students who choose to wear *hijab*.

The reasoning in the cases under the European Convention has been echoed in a decision under the ICCPR, in which the Human Rights Committee held that an alternative course on the history of religions could be taught to the children of committed atheists, "if such alternative course of instruction is given in a neutral way and respects the convictions of parents and guardians who do not believe in any religion."[141]

---

136. *But see* Child's Convention, especially arts. 28, 29, and 30. The Child's Convention focuses on the "evolving capacities" of a child and corresponding rights to make her or his own decisions.

137. Series A, No. 23 (7 Dec. 1976), 1 E.H.R.R. 711.

138. *Id.* at 730.

139. Apps. Nos. 10228 and 10229/82 v. United Kingdom, 7 E.H.R.R. 141, 143.

140. Clarke, *supra* note 119, at 49.

141. *Erkki Hartikainen v. Finland*, Communication No. 40/1978, *as reproduced in* UNITED NATIONS, SELECTED DECISIONS UNDER THE OPTIONAL PROTOCOL 74, 76 (Vol. 1, 1985).

Thus, human rights decision-making bodies have had a propensity to affirm the rights of parents to have their convictions respected in the schooling of their children, while also finding that certain circumstances do not constitute a violation of that right. However, the facts of the *hijab* ban are sufficiently distinct to indicate that a different result should be reached in that case. To hold that neutral sex education, mixed-sex schooling, or teaching the history of religion do not conflict with parents' convictions requires balancing the strength and nature of the convictions vis-à-vis the difficulty faced by the school in attempting to accommodate those convictions. In the present case, the rebuttable presumption is that the conviction is strong, since it is unambiguously of a religious character and deals with an explicit manifestation of what many believe to be a central tenet of Islamic faith. Furthermore, the school faces little or no difficulty in complying with the students' choice to wear *hijab*; for example, it does not have to construct a separate course of study.

Recall also Resolution 02/79 adopted by the Inter-American Commission on Human Rights, in which it was found to be a violation of not only the right to freedom of religion, but also a violation of the right to education under the American Declaration to expel children who refused, on religious grounds, to salute national emblems and sing the national anthem. This is more closely analogous to the *hijab* case, since allowing the children to express their religious beliefs in this manner is not onerous for the school, and its reasoning has been vindicated in the above-cited opinion published by the Quebec Human Rights Commission.[142]

The violation of the guarantee of freedom of education violates not only the specific sections mentioned above but also the equal protection provisions described earlier. Since there is typically no dress code for Muslim boys conflicting with non-Muslim dress, the right of Muslim boys to attend school without violation of their religious beliefs has not been infringed; thus the right to freedom of education has been afforded in a manner discriminatory on the basis of sex.

Group Rights

Clauses protecting the rights of peoples are contained in the African Charter (art. 20, 22), and in the ICCPR (art. 27), which states:

> In those States in which ethnic, religious or linguistic minorities exist, persons belonging to such minorities shall not be denied the right, in community with other members of their group, to enjoy their own culture, to profess and practice their own religion, or to use their own language.

---

142. Picard, *supra* note 41. One interesting element of this ruling was its statement that "a school should intervene only if a student was wearing the scarf against her will." *Id.* Given that the right to education, as articulated in most international human rights instruments, stresses that it is the beliefs of the *parents* that should be respected (within bounds of reasonableness), it seems incongruous to take this right away from Muslim parents only unless some overriding legal authority can be cited. However, others agree, as supported by the Child's Convention, that a student should not have to wear Muslim dress (or religious attire of any religion) against their informed will, depending on their evolving capacities.

The ICCPR makes no reference to what limitations on this right are permissible; neither does the African Charter, except to state in Article 20 that colonized or oppressed peoples "shall have the right to free themselves from the bonds of domination by resorting to any means recognized by the international community." Since Article 2 of the ICCPR guarantees all rights contained therein (including Article 27) to all people without distinction, including distinction on the basis of sex, the right to culture must not only be guaranteed on its own terms: it must also be guaranteed to women and men without discrimination.

In *Lovelace v. Canada*,[143] Sandra Lovelace complained that a section of Canada's Indian Act violated Article 27. This section stated that an "Indian" woman who marries a "non-Indian" man loses her Indian status, while an Indian man who marries a non-Indian woman does not lose his Indian status. Lovelace, an Indian woman, had married a non-Indian man (whom she subsequently divorced), thus losing her Indian status. While she made several complaints regarding the effects of the law, in agreeing with her the Committee emphasized one in particular:

> [T]he significant matter is her last claim, that the major loss to a person ceasing to be an Indian is the loss of the cultural benefits of living in an Indian community, the emotional ties to home, family friends and neighbors, and the loss of identity.[144]

Therefore, the key aspect of the violation was the disruption of her right to enjoy her culture and to maintain her identity.

In an individual opinion appended to the Committee's views, Mr. Néjib Bouziri stated that not only had Lovelace's Article 27 rights been violated, but so had her rights to family life and to equal protection under Articles 2, 3, 23, and 26, because "some of the provisions of the Indian Act are discriminatory, particularly as between men and women."[145]

The *hijab* ban situation is closely analogous to the *Lovelace* case since, as noted above, among the many reasons that a woman might choose to wear *hijab* or any other form of Muslim dress is to publicly identify herself as a Muslim and to feel a sense of community. Here the students are being forced to forego a form of religious expression that make them feel that they are a part of their community and serves to communicate that community affiliation. Indeed, if the students are forced to remove the *hijab* while at school, they could be ostracized from some segments of their community. Part of the purpose of guaranteeing rights for minority groups is that by allowing members of those groups to express their cultural and religious identity, the group's survival is aided. If the students are forbidden to wear *hijab*, their community allegiances might weaken and they could become more assimilated to the dominant culture than they would have otherwise. The guarantee of minority group rights is thus weakened if the right to wear Muslim dress is restricted in this manner.

---

143. Communication No. 24/1977, July 30, 1981, at 83.

144. *Id.* at 86.

145. *Id.* at 87.

Freedom Not to Wear Certain Clothing

No explicit provision exists in an international human rights document guaranteeing the freedom of women to not be forced to wear a certain form of clothing. The closest approximation of such a provision may be found in the provisions guaranteeing freedom of expression, as set forth in the UDHR (art. 19), the ICCPR (art. 19), the European Convention (art. 9), the American Convention (art. 13), and the African Charter (art. 9). As in the case of provisions guaranteeing freedom of movement, freedom of expression may be restricted in the interest of "morals," except under the African Charter, which allows such restriction on the basis of "the law." Thus, as with freedom of movement, the protections afforded by these documents may be difficult to obtain where a state insists that it considers the imposition of an Islamic dress code to be an essential component of public morality.

Limitations of the International Human Rights Regime

While human rights documents together represent an elegant and powerful statement about the equal dignity of human beings, and while they have on occasion served to protect women's personal rights, "recourse to international procedures is likely to have a very limited direct impact in redressing violations of human rights in many of the cases that might be brought before international bodies under one procedure or another."[146] Although a provision may seem explicitly tailored to the violation at hand, locating a procedure that may be used in connection with the state concerned, even where such state has ratified the relevant document (which, in the case of many of the countries described above, is unlikely) can be difficult. As well, a complainant is usually required to exhaust domestic remedies before embarking on an international procedure, which may itself take years. Furthermore, international decision-making bodies are overwhelmingly male in composition, thus rendering a sympathetic hearing of a woman's complaint less likely.[147]

It might be suggested that the usefulness of these provisions in protecting a woman's right to drive, travel unattended, or wear clothing of her choice can at least be found in their capacity to define norms of internationally accepted behavior. However, as noted in the earlier discussion of the religious, political, and cultural complexities surrounding restrictions on women's freedoms, the use of these documents to impose standards explicitly denominated as representing an international (or, in some cases, regional) consensus can be fraught with difficulties. For example, the sensitivity to ideas perceived as Western in some non-Western countries was demonstrated by the reaction in Saudi Arabia to the 1990 driving protest by nearly fifty female members of the country's elite, as detailed above. The harsh government crackdown on these women, while deplored by some members of the intelligentsia,

---

146. Andrew Byrnes, *Enforcement Through International Law and Procedures, in* Cook, *supra* note 126, at 192.

147. For a thorough discussion of the weaknesses of the international system in addressing women's issues, as well as suggestions for reform, *see* Byrnes, *id.*

was reported to have been supported by the majority of Saudi Arabians.[148] Although the women maintained that they were influenced most strongly by the sight of Kuwaiti women fleeing with their families by car during the Gulf War, religious conservatives distributed pamphlets which described the protestors as "immoral, Non-Islamic and tainted with 'secular Americanist' ideals." Prince Naif Abdul bin Aziz, the Interior Minister, emphasized that some of the women had been brought up outside Saudi Arabia and were "not brought up in an Islamic home."[149] If an action taken by citizens of Saudi Arabia themselves can provoke such reflexive anti-Western sentiments, an attempt by non-Saudis to impose those same human rights standards as articulated in international human rights documents would likely produce an even stronger negative reaction.

It is for these reasons that the international human rights regime will probably not, in the context of violations of some human rights of women, serve as a primary engine of change. Rather, it "must form part of a broader political strategy."[150] The following recommendations for future action represent an attempt to outline some of the possible tactics that such a strategy might encompass.

RECOMMENDATIONS FOR FUTURE ACTION

Journalism

Part of the challenge in confronting the issues discussed in this chapter is that there is no clear consensus regarding what solutions women subjected to these violations might view as appropriate. In order for a solution to have credibility and effectiveness, it must be based on a sensitive understanding of the perceptions and feelings of affected women—perceptions and feelings which may vary considerably from region to region, religion to religion, and culture to culture, and will likely even vary within the same region, religion, and culture.

Telling the stories of women subjected to restrictions on their freedom to drive, travel unattended and without permission, and/or wear clothing of their choice is a crucial part of this task. This function could potentially be performed not only by professional journalists, but also by individuals who, by virtue of their personal and professional contacts, have access to women affected by these restrictions. Those with translation skills could prove particularly valuable in this effort. It is only once these stories have been told in a spirit of partnership with affected women that solutions based on a legitimate understanding of what the women affected by these violations truly want may be developed.

---

148. *See*, for example, Michael Field, *Slow Road to Social Reform*, FINANCIAL TIMES, Dec. 12, 1990, at VII; James Le Moyne, *Ban on Driving Reaffirmed by Saudis*, N.Y. TIMES, Nov. 15, 1990, at 19.

149. James LeMoyne, *Saudi Interior Minister Prohibits All Protests for Change by Women*, N.Y. TIMES, Nov. 18, 1990, at 16.

150. Byrnes, *supra* note 146, at 192.

Education

One theme which emerges from this discussion is the degree to which interpretations of the Koran by elite groups of men can result in the imposition of broad restrictions on women's personal freedoms:

> [T]raditionally, only men have interpreted the sources on which the practice of Islam is based. . . . Unarmed with masculinity and its concomitants (authority, money, legality, and especially the power of the written word), women have rarely been given a chance to challenge publicly the androcentric "Muslim" ideology that pervades Islamic institutions. Neither have they had the power to emphasize the Qor'anic passages that would support their struggle for the equal treatment of men and women.[151]

The acquisition of knowledge of the Koran by a broader cross-section of the population could serve to increase the diversity of interpretations of the Koran. One way to encourage this is to support improvements in education for female students, with religious education a part of the curriculum. The tools provided by this education could allow each woman to formulate her own beliefs about her faith, her country's laws, and the relationship between the two, without forcing her to accept interpretations made by a tiny elite, by society, by males attempting to retain their power base, or by outsiders.

Funding Indigenous Groups

As noted earlier, citizens of countries that place restrictions on women's personal rights tend to be sensitive to the imposition of redress by outsiders, particularly Western outsiders. One way for individuals who are not victims of these violations to provide assistance to women who are so affected is to channel money to indigenous groups implementing solutions tailored to their particular regions. Very often such indigenous groups have the most sensitive grasp of the local situation and have greater domestic support than any outsider ever could receive, yet they frequently lack funding. By uniting these groups with international sources of financial support, assistance could be provided with less chance of creating a counterproductive backlash.

Refugee Law

Individuals in countries which are largely free of a particular violation could pressure their governments to adopt policies granting political asylum to women affected by restrictions on their personal rights. The success of such an endeavor is, however, far from assured—a lesson learned by "Nada," a Saudi Arabian woman in her twenties. Nada sought political asylum in Canada in 1991 on the grounds that she had been persecuted for refusing to adhere strictly to the Saudi dress code and for disagreeing with the country's restrictions on women's freedoms. Nada was in fact denied all three rights considered in this chapter—the right to drive, to travel unattended and without permission, and to wear clothing of her choice—and she was stoned and harassed in the street. She told the Canadian government that "for her,

---

151. *See* MILANI, *supra* note 11, at 43.

being trapped in Saudi Arabia was like death, and she indicated that she wanted to regain her dignity and personal integrity. However, her belief in gender equality was not deemed by Canadian officials to rank as a "political opinion" that would qualify her for refugee status."[152] As previously mentioned, Nada was eventually given permission to remain in Canada after protests by women's groups, but only on humanitarian grounds. Given this sort of resistance, it would be strategically useful for supporters of women's personal freedoms to begin a campaign for gender-sensitive, liberally worded refugee guidelines in their home countries in order to prepare for future political asylum claims of this kind.

Cross-Religious Education

The power of the interpretive elites in Islamic countries is such that many people outside those countries assume that Islam as interpreted by those elites corresponds literally to the Islam of the Koran. This can lead to an inappropriate level of tolerance for violations based on an idiosyncratic interpretation of the Koran. In order to counteract this tendency, non-Muslims should be educated about the basic tenets of Islam (and vice versa). Many Christians and Jews are, for example, unaware of the theological connections between Islam, Judaism, and Christianity. Individuals who have converted to Islam from another faith, those involved in a Muslim/non-Muslim mixed marriage, clergy with an interest in interfaith dialogue, and religious educators would be particularly valuable in this effort.

Litigation

In the case of the *hijab* ban in Western nations, often the primary solution is to bring a legal challenge. As noted above, this has sometimes been a successful strategy. This solution should be implemented in tandem with other strategies in order to understand, address, and remedy the underlying prejudices which have created the violations in the first place.

---

152. Mayer, *supra* note 105, at 395.

Section II

Issues Affecting Specific Groups

DEVELOPING RIGHTS OF THE GIRL CHILD IN INTERNATIONAL LAW

Cynthia Price Cohen

INTRODUCTION

The world is beginning to realize that implementation and recognition of women's rights have their foundation in childhood. As a consequence, the rights of the girl child are an increasingly important focal point of international law. It is to be expected that a child who understands her rights as a girl will be much more prepared to demand recognition of her rights when she becomes a woman.[1] It is the purpose of this chapter to survey the growing body of international human rights law and practice that is expressly applicable to the girl child. The discussion will not be confined to treaties and treaty analysis, but will also include various acts on the part of the world community that exemplify the growing respect for the girl child's human rights. In other words, in addition to treaty law, declarations, and resolutions from a variety of international bodies, the chapter will discuss international events that provide examples of developing support for the rights of the girl child.

This chapter will make no direct attempt to analyze or to discuss international law relating to the rights of women[2]—except to the extent that such mention may be required in order to clarify the rights of the girl child and her position in international law. The goal of the chapter is to acquaint the reader with the developing international legal status of the child, the situation of the girl child, the impact that the Convention on the Rights of the Child[3] has had on the girl child's international legal position—including linguistic recognition—and the multiplicity of actions and activities that are currently taking place to support recognition of the girl child's human rights. As part of this discussion, it is important to bear in mind that the girl child is not to be thought of as a "pre-woman." This would not be in keeping with evolving international child rights norms which assert that the child is not to be a "pre-human" being, but rather that childhood is simply part of every human being's continuum of development.

---

1.   *See infra* notes 165–175 and accompanying text.

2.   *See, for example*, Convention on the Elimination of All Forms of Discrimination Against Women, *adopted* Dec. 18, 1979, G.A. Res. 180, U.N. GAOR, 34th Sess., Supp. No. 46, at 193. U.N. Doc A/34/36 (1980), *reprinted in* 19 I.L.M. 33 (1980) (entered into force Sept. 3, 1981) [hereinafter *Women's Convention*].

3.   *Adopted* Nov. 20, 1989, G.A. Res. 44/25 (Annex), U.N. GAOR 44th Sess., Supp. No. 49, at 166, U.N. Doc. A/44/49 (entered into force Sept. 2, 1990) [hereinafter *Convention*].

RIGHTS OF THE CHILD IN INTERNATIONAL LAW

The history of international recognition of the rights of the girl child is understandably linked to developments recognizing human rights in general, including the notion that the child—as a human being—can also be a holder of rights. Some historians have noted that until the sixteenth or seventeenth centuries, there was a general indifference to children. Unwanted children—girls in particular—were simply left to die. Children were commonly considered to be simply part of the family work force and for economic reasons, they were often sold into indentured servitude. Children were beaten, harshly disciplined and generally treated as sub-human.[4] According to one author, "The young child was a sort of pet, a little monkey without shame, to entertain people. . . . The general rule of that time must have been: 'a child can *do* nothing and therefore *is* nothing.'"[5]

Questioning of these attitudes started in the eighteenth and nineteenth centuries, when the developing trend was to consider children as "tomorrow's prosperity." They were given a special status that focused entirely on the child's "care and protection."[6] Children were relegated to a social position that Professor Eugeen Verhellen of the Children's Rights Centre refers to as "not yets." They were "not yet" ready to make decisions; not yet ready to have economic freedom; not yet ready to vote or take part in society on an equal basis with adults.[7] A study of the evolving history of childhood concepts leads to a single conclusion: the child was viewed as an "object," not as a "person." In this view the child was a "being" that must have things done "to" and

---

4.   *See, e.g.*, Lloyd deMause, *The Evolution of Childhood, in* THE HISTORY OF CHILDHOOD (L. deMause ed., 1974).

5.   Marc Depaepe, *The History of Childhood and Youth: From Brutalization to Pedagogization?, in* UNDERSTANDING CHILDREN'S RIGHTS 46 (Eugeen Verhellen ed., 1996) (referring to the work of PHILLIPE ARIES, L'ENFANT ET LA VIE FAMILIALE SOUS L'ANCIEN REGIME). [Emphasis added.]

6.   This emphasis on "care and protection" is important, because it makes the distinction between rights of nurturance and rights of self-assertion. The author refers to these latter rights as rights of "individual personality." The words "individual personality" describe rights that are personal to the "individual," in comparison to rights that belong to the group or society in general. This has been done to bring attention to the fact that the Convention on the Rights of the Child recognizes that each child has an "individual personality" of his or her own and that there are corresponding rights which attach to this recognition. *See* Cynthia Price Cohen, *The Developing Jurisprudence of the Rights of the Child*, 6 ST. THOM. L. REV. 1 (1993).

The term "individual personality" incorporates two of the many descriptive terms that have been applied to rights that are generally thought of in international law as civil-political rights. Such rights as freedom of speech, religion, association, assembly, and the right to privacy are sometimes called "individual" rights. They are also referred to as "personal" rights, "rights of personality," or "basic rights." *See,* H. LAUTERPACHT, INTERNATIONAL LAW AND HUMAN RIGHTS 280–86 (1950). *See also* GUY S. GOODWIN-GILL, THE REFUGEE IN INTERNATIONAL LAW 39–40 (1985); MYRES McDOUGAL, ET AL., HUMAN RIGHTS AND WORLD PUBLIC ORDER 854–56 (1980).

7.   *See* EUGEEN VERHELLEN, CONVENTION ON THE RIGHTS OF THE CHILD 14 (1994). Professor Verhellen is the director of the Children's Rights Center at the University of Gent, Belgium. The Centre undertakes child rights studies and sponsors an annual one-week child rights course at the university.

"for" "it," as contrasted with an idea of the child as a "person" that things are done "by" and "with."

As the nineteenth century progressed, this "caretaking" notion prompted many nations to enact legal provisions that lead to special care for disabled or orphaned children. Simultaneously, a movement developed that urged the creation of special procedures for handling juvenile delinquency cases.[8] The "caretaking" approach to children persisted after the turn of the century, when the child became a subject of international law. The first child-focused multinational treaties were of two types: those that sought to prevent trafficking[9] and those that sought to control child labor.[10] The child labor treaties were the product of the International Labour Organisation (ILO), a body originally established under the auspices of the League of Nations. The first ILO conventions, adopted in 1919,[11] were merely the beginning of a continuing series of treaties that seek to prevent exploitative child labor practices.[12]

During this same period, concern about World War I's effects on children prompted an English woman named Eglantyne Jebb to found Save the Children International Union.[13] That organization drafted the first international declaration of

---

8.   *See, among others*, ANTHONY M. PLATT, THE CHILD SAVERS (1969).

9.   International Convention for the Suppression of Traffic in Women and Children, League of Nations Geneva, Sept. 30, 1921, *reprinted in* RIGHTS OF THE CHILD (Rita Maria Saulle ed., 1996).

10.   The first two child labor treaties to be adopted by the International Labour Organisation were: Convention No. 5 Fixing the Minimum Age for Admission of Children to Industrial Employment (Oct. 29, 1919); and Convention No. 6 Concerning the Night Work of Young Persons Employed in Industry (Oct. 29, 1919).

11.   *Id.*

12.   Other ILO treaties applicable to children include: Convention No. 7 Fixing the Minimum Age for Admission of Children to Employment at Sea (June 15, 1920); Convention No. 10 Concerning the Age for Admission of Children to Employment in Agriculture (Oct. 25, 1921); Convention No. 15 Fixing the Minimum Age for the Admission of Young Persons to Employment as Trimmers or Stokers (Oct. 25, 1921); Convention No. 33 Concerning the Age for Admission of Children to Non-Industrial Employment (Apr. 30, 1932); Convention No. 2 Fixing the Minimum Age for Admission of Children to Employment at Sea (Oct. 24, 1936); Convention No. 59 Fixing the Minimum Age for Admission of Children to Industrial Employment (June 22, 1937); Convention No. 60 Concerning the Age for Admission of Children to Non-Industrial Employment (June 22, 1937); Convention No. 79 Concerning the Restriction of Night Work on Children and Young Persons in Non-Industrial Occupations (Oct. 9, 1946); Convention No. 90 Concerning the Night Work of Young Persons Employed in Industry (July 10, 1948); Convention No. 112 Concerning the Minimum Age for Admission to Employment as Fishermen (July 19, 1959); Convention No. 115 Concerning the Protection of Workers Against Ionizing Radiations (June 22, 1960); Convention No. 123 Concerning the Minimum Age for Admission to Employment Underground in Mines (June 22, 1965); and Convention No. 138 Concerning Minimum Age for Admission to Employment (June 26, 1973). *Also see* Recommendation No. 146 Concerning Age for Admission to Employment (June 26, 1973). The latest ILO child labor treaty was adopted in 1999. It is Convention No. 182 Concerning the Worst Forms of Child Labour. As of Apr. 2000, it was not yet in force.

13.   The Save the Children International Union went through several reincarnations. In its final form it was known as the International Union for Child Welfare (IUCW), which was disbanded in the early 1980s due to rumored financial misdeeds by the director. It is interesting to note that Ms.

the rights of the child—the "Declaration of Geneva"[14]—which was adopted by the League of Nations in 1924. The Declaration of Geneva had five paragraphs and although it is now considered to be an international children's rights instrument, none of its paragraphs actually made mention of the word "right." The 1924 Declaration solidified the prevailing view of childhood by focusing on the "care" and "protection" of children and listed things that must be done "to" and "for" the child. For example: the child was to be "given the means for normal development;" the child was to be "helped," "fed," "sheltered," "reclaimed," and "protected against exploitation." In other words, the Declaration perpetuated the prevailing view of the child as "object"—not "person." This objectification of the child is especially notable in paragraphs I and V, which refers to the child not as "he" or "she," but instead uses the word "it"—a word that denotes a "non-person."[15] While World War I made children visible, World War II awakened even greater international concern for the condition of children and prompted the drafting of new legal instruments to protect the child. First, children were specifically recognized in the 1949 Geneva Convention relative to the Protection of Civilian Persons in Time of War,[16] which contains several sections that instruct occupying forces about how children should be treated.[17] This was

---

Jebb's work inspired numerous other child rights organizations, in particular it supplied the foundation for the present worldwide network of Save the Children organizations which are coordinated through the International Save the Children Alliance in Geneva. To a certain extent, Defence for Children International was also a spin-off of the IUCW, because it was established by a frustrated IUCW staff member (Nigel Cantwell), who felt that the IUCW should take a more activist role in defending children's rights.

14.   "Declaration of Geneva," adopted by the League of Nations, Mar. 1924, *reprinted in* RIGHTS OF THE CHILD (Maria Rita Saulle ed., 1996) [hereinafter *Geneva Declaration*] [emphasis added]:

Declaration of Geneva

By the present Declaration of the Rights of the Child, commonly known as the "Declaration of Geneva," men and women of all nations, recognizing that mankind owes to the child the best that it has to give, declare and accept it as their duty that, beyond and above all considerations of race, nationality or creed:

I.   The child must be given the means requisite for *its* normal development, both materially and spiritually;

II.   The child that is hungry must be fed; the child that is sick must be helped; the child that is backward must be helped; the delinquent child must be reclaimed; and the orphan and the waif must be sheltered and succored;

III.   The child must be the first to receive relief in times of distress;

IV.   The child must be put in a position to earn a livelihood and must be protected from every form of exploitation;

V.   The child must be brought up in the consciousness that its talents must be devoted to the service of *its* fellow men.

15.   *Id.*

16.   Geneva Convention Relative to the Protection of Civilian Persons in Time of War (1949), *reprinted in* HUMAN RIGHTS, A COMPILATION OF INTERNATIONAL INSTRUMENTS, UNITED NATIONS (1993).

17.   *For example, see id.* arts. 24, 60, and 68. It is in this treaty that one can find the first enunciation of the international norm prohibiting execution of young persons for crimes committed when they were under the age of eighteen.

followed by the drafting and U.N. General Assembly's adoption in 1959 of a new Declaration of the Rights of the Child.[18] The 1959 Declaration was made up of ten principles. Although the word "right" does appear in few places in this instrument, like the "Declaration of Geneva" the 1959 Declaration places its emphasis on the child's "care" and "protection." Nevertheless, there are three innovations in the 1959 Declaration that clearly distinguish it from the 1924 "Declaration of Geneva." The new Declaration proclaimed the child's right to a name and nationality,[19] the child's right to protection against discrimination,[20] and it introduced the concept of the "best interests" of the child.[21] While the 1959 Declaration did not follow the Declaration of Geneva's practice of referring to the child as "it," it did follow the then-accepted human rights treaty practice of using only the masculine personal possessive pronoun when describing the child's rights.[22] In other words, the rights of all children were expressed as in terms of "him" or "his."

CONVENTION ON THE RIGHTS OF THE CHILD

During the half-century since the adoption of the "Declaration of Geneva," the international law of children's rights has undergone a significant evolution. The most obvious changes have had to do with the way in which the child is now portrayed. As discussed above, until 1989, and adoption of the Convention on the Rights of the Child by the U.N. General Assembly,[23] international legal instruments tended to depict children solely as "objects" requiring "care" and "protection." By contrast, the Convention on the Rights of the Child gives legally binding recognition to the child's "human dignity" by also recognizing the child's rights of "individual personality,"[24] including such rights as the "right to be heard."[25] In addition, because it has rejected

---

18. Declaration of the Rights of the Child, G.A. Res. 1386, U.N. GAOR, 14th Sess., Supp. No. 16, at 19, U.N. Doc. A/4354 (1959) [hereinafter *1959 Declaration*], *reprinted in* THE UNITED NATIONS CONVENTION ON THE RIGHTS OF THE CHILD: A GUIDE TO THE "TRAVAUX PRÉPARATOIRES" APP. (Sharon Detrick ed., 1992).

19. *Id.* at principle 3.

20. *Id.* at principle 1.

21. *Id.* at principle 7.

22. For example, principle 3 of the *1959 Declaration* states that: "The child shall be entitled from *his* birth to a name and nationality." [Emphasis added.]

23. *Convention, supra* note 3.

24. For a discussion of the concept of "individual personality" rights, *see supra* note 5. For an overview of the background of the Convention on the Rights of the Child *see* Cynthia Price Cohen, *The Human Rights of Children*, 12 CAP. UN. L. REV. 369 (1983). *Also see*, Cynthia Price Cohen, *United Nations Convention on the Rights of the Child Introductory Note*, 44 THE REV. 36 (1990); and Cynthia Price Cohen, *Drafting of the United Nations Convention on the Rights of the Child: Challenges and Achievements, in* UNDERSTANDING CHILDREN'S RIGHTS (Eugeen Verhellen ed., Gent, Belgium: Children's Rights Centre, 1997).

25. *See Convention, supra* note 3, at art.12. For an explanation of the drafting history of art. 12, *see* Cynthia Price Cohen, *Role of the United States in Drafting the Convention on the Rights of the Child: Creating a New World for Children*, 9 LOYOLA POVERTY L.J. 4 (1998) *Also see* Guidelines, *infra* notes 104 to 118 and accompanying text.

the standard accepted practice of using masculine singular possessive pronouns to mean both male and female persons—using both "him" and "her" instead—the Convention on the Rights of the Child has put an end to a long human rights treaty history that subtly discriminated against women and girls.

Drafting Process

The 1979 International Year of the Child (IYC) can be viewed as the turning point in the evolution of children's rights and the rights of the girl child as well.[26] It was as a part of the celebration of IYC—commemorating the twentieth anniversary of the 1959 Declaration—that the government of Poland proposed that IYC be celebrated by the drafting of a treaty that would make the rights of the child legally enforceable. To facilitate the drafting process, Poland submitted a model convention to the Commission on Human Rights for its approval.[27] That first model was rejected and a second, more detailed model, became the framework used by the U.N. Working Group that had been delegated the task of drafting the Convention on the Rights of the Child.[28] This second Polish draft contained the seeds that would change the world view of the child, by adding an article recognizing the child's "individual personality" right to freedom of expression to the already internationally accepted rights of "care" and "protection." During the ten-year drafting process, this second Polish model of the Convention was expanded from its original twenty substantive articles into a treaty affirming the full range of the rights of the child. In addition to recognizing the child's right to education, health and a standard of living, the Convention's forty-one substantive articles ensure the child's right to freedom of expression and information, freedom of religion, freedom of association and assembly and the right to privacy. In other words, the Convention not only protects the child's economic-social-cultural rights, it also protects the child's civil-political rights.[29] The end result is that the

---

26. International Year of the Child, G.A. Res. 169, U.N. GAOR, 31st Sess., Supp. No. 39 at 74, U.N. Doc. A/31/169 (1976).

27. The first model was basically a replication of the *1959 Declaration*, with an implementation mechanism added. This model was rejected by the Commission on Human Rights. See E/CN.4/1292 (1978).

28. *See* E/CN.4/1324 (1979).

29. In principle, civil-political rights are those rights that protect the individual's freedom from governmental intrusion, while economic-social-cultural rights imply governmental responsibility to care for the general well-being of citizens. Other types of rights include the rights of refugees and the law of armed conflict. For an example of the various types of human rights, *see* Universal Declaration of Human Rights, G.A. Res. 217A (III) U.N. Doc. A/810 (1948) [hereinafter *Universal Declaration*]; the International Covenant on Civil and Political Rights, *adopted* Dec. 16, 1966, 999 U.N.T.S. 171 (entered into force Mar. 23, 1976) [hereinafter *CCPR*]; the International Covenant on Economic, Social and Cultural Rights [hereinafter *ESCR*]; the Geneva Convention Relative to the Protection of Civilian Persons in Time of War (1949) [hereinafter *Geneva IV*]; Protocol Additional to the Geneva Conventions of Aug. 12, 1949 and Relating to the Protection of Victims of International Armed Conflicts [hereinafter *Protocol I*]; Protocol Additional to the Geneva Conventions of Aug. 12, 1949, and Relating to the Victims of Non-International Armed Conflicts [hereinafter *Protocol II*]; and Convention relating to the Status of Refugees (1951) [hereinafter *Refugee Convention*].

Convention on the Rights of the Child demands respect for the total child—not just the small defenseless child—but the assertive, thinking child, as well. It also makes a clear statement that these rights apply equally to girls and boys.

Substantive Rights

The Convention on the Rights of the Child supports the child's right to a nurturing family and recognizes the responsibility of parents to provide "in a manner consistent with the evolving capacities of the child, appropriate direction and guidance in the exercise" of the Convention's rights.[30] The Convention protects the child from discrimination,[31] as well as ensuring the child's survival and development,[32] the child's best interests,[33] and the child's right to be heard.[34] It protects the child from neglect and abuse,[35] from economic[36] and sexual exploitation,[37] from trafficking[38] and drug abuse,[39] and provides for foster care[40] and adoption[41] when a nurturing home is not a possibility. The Convention has provisions for the child's education,[42] standard of living,[43] and health care,[44] as well as regulations for participation in armed conflicts[45] and the treatment of refugee children.[46] In other words, it can be said that the Convention draws together the established human rights norms—economic-social-cultural, civil-political, and humanitarian—in a form that is applicable to children while also adding new rights not previously protected under international law.

Drafting of the Convention on the Rights of the Child took place during a series of sessions that were held one week each year between 1979 to 1989.[47] The first draft,

---

30. *Convention, supra* note 3, at art. 5.

31. *Id.* at art. 2.

32. *Id.* at art. 6.

33. *Id.* at art. 3.

34. *Id.* at art. 12.

35. *Id.* at art. 19.

36. *Id.* at art. 32.

37. *Id.* at arts. 34 and 36.

38. *Id.* at art. 35.

39. *Id.* at art. 33.

40. *Id.* at art. 20.

41. *Id.* at art. 21.

42. *Id.* at art. 28.

43. *Id.* at art. 27.

44. *Id.* at art. 24.

45. *Id.* at art. 38.

46. *Id.* at art. 22.

47. These meetings generally took place just before the regular meetings of the Commission on Human Rights. However, to facilitate completion of the Convention by 1989 (the thirtieth anniversary of the Declaration of the Rights of the Child), the Working Group was granted two two-week

in which the rights of the child were defined (known as a "first reading") was completed in January 1988. The "second reading," in which the text was reviewed and modified, took place in the fall of 1988.[48] The final text was adopted by the General Assembly on November 20, 1989.[49] It should be noted that the singular possessive pronouns in the first reading draft were mixed: some exclusively masculine, some both masculine and feminine and some were the non-human objectifying word "it." During the "second reading," as it sought to correct and clarify the language of the Convention, the U.N. Working Group systematically eliminated the exclusive use of masculine singular possessive pronouns, thus impacting the style of all human rights treaty making processes for the future.[50]

CONVENTION ON THE RIGHTS OF THE CHILD AND THE PROTECTION OF GIRLS AND YOUNG WOMEN

While the Convention on the Rights of the Child cannot be expected to totally eradicate years of discrimination against girls, it can and is providing the framework for worldwide change. This is taking place for four reasons. First, the Convention on the Rights of the Child has given worldwide affirmation to the child's right to have his or her dignity respected. Second, the Convention has altered the way in which human rights are stated, because it enumerates the rights of girls in terms that are clearly equal to those of boys.[51] Third, as the Convention is implemented, it is having a major impact on the way the world views the girl child, because it demands that her situation be given special attention.[52] Finally, the speedy and near-universal ratification of the Convention on the Rights of the Child is causing its standards to be implemented in all parts of the world, simultaneously.[53]

---

sessions in 1988: one in January to complete the first reading text and the other in November/December, to complete the second reading.

48.   Technically, the second reading was held under the auspices of the 1989 Commission on Human Rights, even though the actual meetings took place in November/December 1989 in order to be ready for the 1989 meeting of the Commission.

49.   The signing ceremony for the Convention on the Rights of the Child, held in New York in January 1990, broke all previous records, with sixty-three nations signing on that day. The Convention also broke records for speed of entry into force on Sept. 2, 1990.

50.   For the report of the Working Group's second reading, *see Question of a Convention on the Rights of the Child: Report of the Working Group*, U.N. Commission on Human Rights, 45th Sess., Agenda Item 13, at 1; U.N. Doc. E/CN.4/1989/48 (1989) Note, for example, the dual use of male and female singular possessive pronouns in the Hague Convention on the Protection of Children and Cooperation in Respect of Intercountry Adoption (1997). The African Charter of the Rights and Duties of the African Child (1990), which was adopted immediately after the Convention on the Rights of the Child, did not make its language gender neutral. But all other new treaties have.

51.   *See infra* notes 53 to 70 and accompanying text.

52.   National efforts to ensure implementation of the Convention have led to many international initiatives on behalf of the girl child. *See* discussion *infra*.

53.   The Convention on the Rights of the Child has been ratified by every country in the world, except for the United States and Somalia.

Linguistic Factors

The change in the use of singular possessive pronouns from exclusively masculine to both masculine and feminine is far from trivial. From the earliest declarations of rights—for example, the French Declaration of the Rights of Man and Citizen or the American Declaration of Independence—rights holders were always portrayed as masculine. In the beginning this was factually true. Women had no recognized rights. It was not until this masculine language was "interpreted" to include them that women were recognized a having rights. This single gender linguistic practice continued to be replicated in twentieth century human rights instruments—even as the text itself was proclaiming non-discrimination. Beginning with the Universal Declaration of Human Rights,[54] whenever a singular possessive pronoun has been used in the enumeration of rights, it has always been in the masculine form.[55] For the sake of simplicity, and to illustrate how differently the matter of gender has been handled in the Convention on the Rights of the Child, one only need look at the right to privacy as it appears in the five international human rights instruments below:

Universal Declaration of Human Rights:

No one shall be subjected to arbitrary interference with *his* privacy, family, home or correspondence, nor to attacks on *his* honour and reputation.[56]

International Covenant on Civil and Political Rights:

No one shall be subjected to arbitrary or unlawful interference with *his* privacy, family, home or correspondence, nor to unlawful attacks on *his* honour and reputation.[57]

European Convention for the Protection of Human Rights and Fundamental Freedoms:

Everyone has the right to respect for *his* private and family life, *his* home and *his* correspondence.[58]

American Convention on Human Rights:

No one may be the object of arbitrary or abusive interference with *his* private life, *his* family, *his* home or *his* correspondence, or of unlawful attacks on *his* honor or reputation.[59]

---

54.   *Supra* note 28.

55.   All of the comparisons made here will be among English versions of the treaties. This is especially important since the original version of all treaties is usually in English and it is the language of international treaty-drafting.

56.   *Universal Declaration, supra* note 28, at art. 12.

57.   *CCPR, supra* note 28, at art. 17, § 1.

58.   European Convention for the Protection of Human Rights and Fundamental Freedoms, Nov. 4, 1950, 213 U.N.T.S. 221 at art. 8, § 1 (entered into force Nov. 3, 1953).

59.   American Convention on Human Rights, done at San Jose, Nov. 22, 1969 (entered into force, July 18, 1978), O.A.S. Treaty Ser. L/V/II.23 doc. 21 rev. 6, at art. 11, § 2 (1979), *reprinted* in 9 I.L.M. 673 (1970).

Convention on the Rights of the Child:

> No child shall be subjected to arbitrary or unlawful interference with *his or her* privacy, family, home or correspondence, nor to unlawful attacks on *his or her* honour and reputation.[60]

Note that in the Convention on the Rights of the Child, the article protecting the child's right to privacy duplicates the wording of the International Covenant on Civil and Political Rights, except that it replaces the word "one" with the word "child" and adds "or her" whenever the word "his" is used. In other words, despite the fact that all human rights treaties contain the principle of non-discrimination, it was not until the Convention on the Rights of the Child that both genders were given explicit linguistic equality in the exercise of their rights.[61]

In its break with the entrenched international human rights treaty practice of exclusively using masculine singular possessive pronouns, the Convention on the Rights of the Child has created a new treaty drafting model: treating genders equally in language as well as in theory. In reality, drafters of the Convention attempted to avoid the mention of gender entirely, preferring instead to simply use the word "child." For example, the Convention requires states parties to "respect the right of the *child* to freedom of thought conscience and religion."[62] Nevertheless, whenever it became impossible to avoid using a singular possessive pronoun, both masculine and feminine versions were incorporated into the text.[63] This model has been followed by subsequently drafted rights related treaties.[64]

Interestingly, the Convention on the Rights of the Child did not start out to be a "gender neutral" treaty.[65] The first Polish model Convention was based on the text of the 1959 Declaration and, consequently, repeated the masculine singular possessive pronoun formulation and such language as "The child shall be entitled from *his* birth to a name and a nationality."[66] When this draft was rejected by the Commission on Human Rights as inadequate, because it was not in language that was legally enforce-

---

60.   *See Convention, supra* note 3, at art. 16 § 1 (emphasis added).

61.   *See supra* note 50 for a discussion of the changing use of personal possessive pronouns.

62.   *See Convention, supra* note 3, at art. 14, § 1 (emphasis added).

63.   Of the forty-two substantive articles in the Convention on the Rights of the Child, the double singular pronoun can be found in nineteen. The formulation is usually "his or her," but in art. 3 it is "him or her" and in art. 26 it is "he or she." Overall, the double singular pronoun appears in forty different places in the Convention. Most frequently, it is before the word "parents." In other formulations, it often precedes the word "family" or the phrase "well-being."

   For a survey of these articles, *see Convention, supra* note 3, at arts. 2(1); 3(2); 7(1); 8(1), (2); 9(1); 10(1), (2); 12(1); 14(1); 16(1); 17(e); 20(1); 22(1), (2); 22(2), (3); 24(1); 25; 29(c); 30; 37(b), (c), (d); and 40(2)(ii), (iii), (iv), (vii).

64.   *See supra* note 50.

65.   The expression "gender neutral" was the term applied by members of the Working Group to explain their efforts to eliminate gender exclusivity.

66.   Draft Convention on the Rights of the Child, at art. 3 *reprinted in* THE UNITED NATIONS CONVENTION ON THE RIGHTS OF THE CHILD: A GUIDE TO THE "TRAVAUX PRÉPARATOIRES" 33, 34 (Sharon Detrick ed., 1992).

able, the Polish government submitted a second draft. It too was written in the singular masculine possessive pronoun formulation.[67]

The Convention on the Rights of the Child was drafted over a period of ten years,[68] but it was not until a female delegate from Canada objected to the exclusive use of the masculine gender that the word "her" was added to the text.[69] Even though this incident took place about halfway through the drafting process, it did not become an automatic practice to add the word "her" to subsequently drafted articles. In fact, at one point in the deliberations, the effort to avoid preferential gender language resulted in the child being referred to once again as an "it."[70] This gender inconsistency in the text was not totally resolved until after the first draft of the text was completed in 1988. During the "second reading," in which the first reading text was submitted to careful scrutiny by governmental delegations, the drafters diligently undertook to make the Convention, as they put it, "gender neutral." In fact, what they accomplished was to make the Convention on the Rights of the Child truly "gender-equal."[71]

Relevant Rights

The text of the Convention on the Rights of the Child is written in the language of a constitutive instrument. It is purposefully general in its terminology in order to allow for variations in national interpretation. That is not to say that the Convention is relativistic. On the contrary, the Convention's protection of the child is quite clear. However, accommodation of a wide range of legal and economic systems requires a text that allows for elasticity of interpretation. The Article 1 definition of the child is an excellent example of this type of accommodation.

Defining childhood presented two problems for the Convention's drafters: childhood's beginning and its end. The questions involved whether the fetus was a child and, considering the various cultural differences, whether there could be a single age at which a child becomes an adult. In order to avoid clashes of opinion over whether the Convention should be applicable to the unborn child, the Convention's drafters agreed that no direct mention should be made of the beginning of childhood. Instead, by using the words "human being," it was left to the discretion of ratifying nations to interpret the text according to their own laws and customs. While age eighteen was agreed upon as a general end to childhood, Article 1 allows for national variations for when the child can assume adult responsibilities. The final text reads:

---

67. For the text of this draft, as well as the Declaration of the Rights of the Child and U.N. documents relating to the drafting of the Convention on the Rights of the Child, *see id.*

68. Drafting began during the International Year of the Child in 1979 and ended in 1989.

69. Coleen Swords from the Canadian Department of External Affairs raised the objection.

70. *See Geneva Declaration, supra* note 17.

71. Judith Ramirez of the Canadian Immigration and Refugee Board prefers the phrase "gender-inclusive."

> For the purposes of the present Convention, a child means every human being below the age of eighteen years unless, under the law applicable to the child, majority is attained earlier.[72]

However, because of the drafter's choice of pronouns—even without turning to the anti-discrimination passages of Article 2—it is evident that all of the rights in the Convention are applicable to the girl child. In fact, certain articles stand out as being particularly relevant to the girl child's situation: Articles 6 (right to survival and development);[73] 24 (right to health and health services);[74] 28 (right to education);[75] 32

---

72. *See Convention, supra* note 3, at art. 1.

73. *Id.* at art. 6 (right to survival and development):

    1. States Parties recognize that every child has the inherent right to life.

    2. States Parties shall ensure to the maximum extent possible the survival and development of the child.

74. *Id.* at art. 24 (health and health services):

    1. States Parties recognize the right of the child to the enjoyment of the highest attainable standard of health and to facilities for the treatment of illness and rehabilitation of health. The States Parties shall strive to ensure that no child is deprived of his or her right of access to such health care services.

    2. States Parties shall pursue full implementation of this right and, in particular, shall take appropriate measures:

       (a) To diminish infant and child mortality;

       (b) To ensure the provision of necessary medical assistance and health care to all children with emphasis on the development of primary health care;

       (c) To combat disease and malnutrition, including with the framework of primary health care, though *inter alia* the application of readily available technology and through the provision of adequate nutritious foods and clean drinking water, taking into consideration the dangers and risks of environmental pollution;

       (d) To ensure appropriate pre- and post-natal health care for expectant mothers;

       (e) To ensure that all segments of society, in particular parents and children, are informed, have access to education and are supported in the use of, basic knowledge of child health and nutrition, the advantages of breast-feeding, hygiene and environmental sanitation and the prevention of accidents;

       (f) To develop preventive health care, guidance for parents, and family planning education and services.

    3. States Parties shall take all effective and appropriate measures with a view to abolishing traditional practices prejudicial to the health of children.

    4. States Parties undertake to promote and encourage international co-operation with a view to achieving progressively the full realization of the right recognized in this article. In this regard, particular account shall be taken of the needs of developing countries.

75. *Id.* at art. 28 (right to education):

    1. States Parties recognize the right of the child to education, and with a view to achieving this right progressively and on the basis of equal opportunity, they shall, in particular:

       (a) Make primary education compulsory and available free to all;

       (b) Encourage the development of different forms of secondary education, including general and vocational education, make them available and accessible to every child,

(protection from economic exploitation);[76] 33 (protection from drug abuse);[77] 34 (protection from sexual exploitation);[78] and 35 (protection from trafficking).[79]

---

and take appropriate measures such as the introduction of free education and offering financial assistance in case of need;

(c) Make higher education accessible to all on the basis of capacity by every appropriate means;

(d) Make educational and vocational information and guidance available and accessible to all children;

(e) Take measures to encourage regular attendance at schools and the reduction of drop-out rates.

2. States Parties shall take all appropriate measures to ensure that school discipline is administered in a manner consistent with the child s human dignity and in conformity with the present Convention.

3. States Parties shall promote and encourage international co-operation in matters relating to education, in particular with a view to contributing to the elimination of ignorance and illiteracy throughout the world and facilitating access to scientific and technical knowledge and modern teaching methods. In this regard, particular account shall be taken of the needs of developing countries.

76. *Id*. at art. 32 (protection from economic exploitation):

1. States Parties recognize the right of the child to be protected from economic exploitation and from performing any work that is likely to be hazardous or to interfere with the child s education, or to be harmful to the child s health or physical, mental, spiritual, moral or social development.

2. States Parties shall take legislative, administrative, social and educational measures to ensure the implementation of the present article. To this end, and having regard to the relevant provisions of other international instruments, States Parties shall in particular:

(a) Provide for a minimum age or minimum ages for admission to employment;

(b) Provide for appropriate regulation of the hours and conditions of employment;

(c) Provide for appropriate penalties or other sanctions to ensure the effective enforcement of the present article.

77. *Id*. at art. 33 (protection from drug abuse):

States Parties shall take all appropriate measures, including legislative, administrative, social and educational measures, to protect children from the illicit use of narcotic drugs and psychotropic substances as defined in the relevant international treaties, and to prevent the use of children in the illicit production and trafficking of such substances.

78. *Id*. at art. 34 (protection from sexual exploitation):

States Parties undertake to protect the child from all forms of sexual exploitation and sexual abuse. For these purposes, States Parties shall in particular take all appropriate national, bilateral and multilateral measures to prevent:

(a) The inducement or coercion of a child to engage in any unlawful sexual activity;

(b) The exploitative use of children in prostitution or other unlawful sexual practices;

(c) The exploitative use of children in pornographic performances and materials.

79. *Id*. at art. 35 (protection from sale, trafficking and abduction):

States Parties shall take all appropriate national, bilateral and multilateral measures to prevent the abduction of, the sale of or traffic in children for any purpose or in any form.

One article that is of special significance for the girl child is the protection against intrafamilial violence, a proscription which, considering the worldwide problem of domestic violence, was somehow omitted in the Women's Convention.[80] Article 19 of the Convention on the Rights of the Child calls on states parties to take measures to:

> protect the child from all forms of physical or mental violence, injury or abuse, neglect or negligent treatment, maltreatment or exploitation, including sexual abuse, while in the care of parent(s), legal guardian(s) or any other person who has the care of the child.[81]

A related, innovative article requires states parties to remedy the effects of traumatic events. States parties are obligated to take measures to:

> promote physical and psychological recovery and social reintegration of a child victim of: any form of neglect, exploitation, or abuse; torture or any other form of cruel, inhuman or degrading treatment or punishment; or armed conflicts.[82]

Such rehabilitation from trauma can do much to ameliorate the previously described problems that are faced by girls on a daily basis. While it may not immediately stamp out these harmful practices, at least the girl child may be given a second chance to lead a safe, normal life.

Finally, of special importance to the girl child is paragraph 3 of the article on health, requiring states parties to "take all effective and appropriate measures with a view to abolishing traditional practices prejudicial to the health of children."[83] By use of the words "traditional practices," drafters of the Convention on the Rights of the Child meant for this paragraph to put an end to female genital mutilation.[84] The

---

80. *See Women's Convention, supra* note 2.

81. *Id.* at art. 19 (protection from abuse and neglect):

1.   States Parties shall take all appropriate legislative, administrative, social and educational measures to protect the child from all forms of physical or mental violence, injury or abuse, neglect or negligent treatment, maltreatment or exploitation, including sexual abuse, while in the care of parent(s), legal guardian(s) or any other person who has the care of the child.

2.   Such protective measures should, as appropriate, include effective procedures for the establishment of social programmes to provide necessary support for the child and for those who have the care of the child, as well as for other forms of prevention and for identification, reporting, referral, investigation, treatment, and follow-up of instances of child maltreatment described heretofore, and, as appropriate, for judicial involvement.

82. *Id.* at art. 39 (recovery and reintegration):

States Parties shall take all appropriate measures to promote physical and psychological recovery and social reintegration of a child victim of: any form of neglect, exploitation, or abuse; torture or any other form of cruel, inhuman or degrading treatment or punishment; or armed conflicts. Such recovery and reintegration shall take place in an environment which fosters the health, self-respect and dignity of the child.

83. *Id.* at art. 24, § 3. The Working Group originally considered using the words "female genital mutilation." However, some delegations objected to this formulation on the ground that the language was too narrow. As a result the more general "traditional practices" language was substituted.

84. *See infra* notes 163 to 165 and accompanying text.

Convention on the Rights of the Child is the only human rights treaty that explicitly discourages this practice.

CONVENTION ON THE RIGHTS OF THE CHILD: IMPLEMENTATION

Implementation of the Convention on the Rights of the Child follows the model of other United Nations human rights treaties: States parties—nations that have ratified the treaty—are required to submit to a committee of experts, periodic reports describing the measures they have taken to implement the treaty.[85] The frequency and content of these reports may vary from treaty to treaty, as may the number of experts and the frequency of their meetings, but the monitoring body format is a constant. The implementation process of the Convention on the Rights of the Child is laid out in Articles 43 through 45.

Committee on the Rights of the Child (Article 43)

The monitoring body for the Convention on the Rights of the Child is known as the Committee on the Rights of the Child.[86] It is made up of "ten experts of high moral standing and recognized competence,"[87] chosen by states parties from among their nationals, with a goal of geographic diversity.[88] While Committee members are elected by states parties, they serve their four-year terms on the Committee in their "personal capacities," with elections being held every two years.[89] The first elections for Committee membership took place at a January 1991 meeting of the states parties. Of the ten Committee members elected at that time, six were women.[90] Subsequent elections have not altered the Committee significantly—and the gender makeup of the Committee as this chapter is being written has remained more or less constant with a few more women than men.[91] As might be expected, considering the

---

85.   The timing of these reports varies from treaty to treaty, as does the number of members of the committees.

86.   *See Convention, supra* note 3, at 43, § 1.

87.   *Id.* at art. 43, § 2.

88.   There is a pending amendment to the Convention that would enlarge the Committee's size from ten to eighteen members.

89.   *See Convention, supra* note 3, at art. 43, § 4.

90.   The first members elected to the Committee included: *Ms. Hoda Badran (Egypt); Mgr. Luis A. Bambaren Gastelumendi (Peru); Ms. Akila Belembaogo (Burkina Faso); *Ms. Marie de Fatima Borges de Omena (Brazil); *Ms. Flora Euphemio (Philippines); Mr. Thomas Hammarberg (Sweden); Mr. Youri Kolosov (Russian Federation (former U.S.S.R.)); Ms. Sandra Prunella Mason (Barbados); *Mr. Swithun Mombeshora (Zimbabwe); and *Ms. Marta Santos Pais (Portugal). (Asterisk denotes a two-year term). The two-year delegates were reelected in 1993 to four-year terms that expired in 1997. *See Report of the Committee on the Rights of the Child*, U.N. GAOR, 47th Sess., Supp. No. 41, Annex II, at 13, U.N. Doc A/47/41 (1993).

91.   As the states parties prepared to elect or re-elect the five Committee members whose terms expired in 1997, Committee membership had remained unchanged from the initial 1991 election—with the exception of the replacement of Ms. Marie de Fatima Borges de Omena (Brazil) by Dr. Marilia Sardenberg (Brazil) and Mgr. Luis A. Bambaren Gastelumendi (Peru) by Ms.

preponderance of female members of the Committee, the rights of the girl child are always given careful scrutiny in Committee's analysis of states parties' reports.

Article 43 also gives the Committee the freedom to "establish its own rules of procedure."[92] This means that the Committee not only controls the manner in which it reviews states parties' reports, but as will be explained below, the Committee has interpreted this power in a way that adds innovations, such as its Pre-Sessional meetings and a special day of General Discussion.[93]

State Party Reporting Obligations (Article 44)

States parties are required to submit an initial report to the Committee on the Rights of the Child two years after the Convention has been ratified and entered into force.[94] This first report is the most extensive in that it should also contain detailed demographic information that will not be necessary to repeat in the periodic reports that are to follow every five years.

Reports are to be comprehensive, explaining measures that have been taken to implement the Convention as well as any difficulties that may impede implementation. The Committee is empowered to request further information from the state party if the report is deemed insufficient. At the end of every session, the Committee drafts Concluding Observations for each state party's report examined at that session. The results of its deliberations are subsequently submitted to the General Assembly (via the Economic and Social Council).

Judith Karp (Israel). However, at the 1997 meeting of states parties, Committee membership underwent a major change. Ms. Marta Santos Pais (Portugal)—the Committee's rapporteur—decided not to run for reelection. At the same time, Ms. Akila Belembaogo (Burkina Faso) and Mr. Thomas Hammarberg (Sweden) withdrew mid-term and were replaced by Awa N. Ouedraogo and Lizabeth Palme, respectively. Of those members running for re-election, only Dr. Marilia Sardenberg (Brazil) retained her membership. Replacement members were: Elizabeth Mary Queen Mokhuane (South Africa); G. S. Rabah (Lebanon); Francisco Carlo Fulci (Italy); Nafsiah Mboi (Indonesia).

The 1999 election of Committee members resulted in a new group of members that had none of the original members remaining and only three members who had served for more than four years (Karp, Sardenberg and Ouedraogo). As of 1999, membership in the Committee on the Rights of the Child was made up of the following persons: Jacob Egbert Doek (Netherlands); Amina Hamza El Guidi (Egypt); Francesco Paolo Fulci (Italy); Judith Karp (Israel); Esther Margaret Queen Mokhuane (South Africa); Awa N'Deye Ouedraogo (Burkina Faso); Ghassan Salim Rabah (Lebanon); Marilia Sardenberg (Brazil); Elisabeth Tigerstedt-Tähtelä (Finland); with Dr. Nafsiah Mboi (Indonesia) withdrawing to take a position at the World Health Organization.

92.　*See Convention, supra* note 3, at art. 43, § 8.

93.　*See infra* notes 102–127 and accompanying text.

94.　*See Convention, supra* note 3, art. 44. In accordance with the requirements of Article 49 of the Convention on the Rights of the Child, the Convention went into force on Sept. 4, 1990, one month after the deposit of the twentieth instrument of ratification with the Secretary-General of the United Nations. All subsequent ratifications enter into force one month after they are deposited. *See infra* notes 102–120 and accompanying text.

Perhaps the most innovative element of Article 44 is that it requires states parties to "make their reports widely available to the public in their own countries."[95] This paragraph, coupled with the Convention's Article 42 requirement that states parties must make the "principles and provisions of the Convention widely known"[96] establishes a formula for ensuring that the public can participate in ensuring the implementation of the Convention.

Additional Components (Article 45)

Since a treaty is only as effective as its implementation mechanism, all of the fine standards of the Convention on the Rights of the Child would be meaningless if countries did not adhere to them. Consequently, in order to support the work of the Committee on the Rights of the Child, drafters of the Convention saw fit to include a special article aimed at facilitating treaty implementation. Article 45 adds a component to the implementation mechanism of the Convention on the Rights of the Child that is lacking in other human rights treaties.[97] It gives the Committee on the Rights of the Child the power to:

(1) obtain information from sources other than the states parties themselves;[98]

(2) provide aid to countries that need technical assistance in order to adequately implement the Convention;[99] and

(3) request that studies of general interest to states parties be undertaken on specific child rights issues.[100]

Central participants in the Convention's Article 45 processes are: UNICEF; the U.N. specialized agencies; other U.N. organs; and non-governmental organizations (NGOs), which are referred to in the Convention as "other competent bodies."[101]

---

95. *See Convention, supra* note 3, at art. 44, § 6.

96. *Id.* at art. 42, which reads: "States Parties undertake to make the principles and provisions of the Convention widely known, by appropriate and active means, to adults and children alike."

97. While no other human rights treaty explicitly outlines the processes as clearly as the Convention on the Rights of the Child, other treaty bodies have either included such information-gathering possibilities in their Rules of Procedure or have made arrangements for informal consultations with nongovernmental organizations.

98. *See Convention, supra* note 3, at art. 45, § a.

99. *Id.* at art. 45, § b.

100. *Id.* at art. 45, § c.

101. The words "other competent bodies" were used by the Convention's drafters to create a role for non-governmental organizations (NGOs). For a history of how NGOs participated in the drafting of the Convention, *see* Cynthia Price Cohen, *Role of Non-Governmental Organizations in the Drafting of the Convention on the Rights of the Child*, 12 HUM. RTS. Q. 137 (1990). *Also see,* Cynthia Price Cohen, *The Role of Nongovernmental Organizations in the Drafting and Implementation of the United Nations Convention on the Rights of the Child, in* CONFERENCE PROCEEDINGS—THE LEGITIMACY OF THE UNITED NATIONS: TOWARDS AN ENHANCED STATUS OF NON-STATE ACTORS? (1996).

The Committee has given a generous interpretation of the Convention's Article 45 language regarding the role of "other competent bodies" in the Convention's implementation process. As a result, the Committee is able to obtain information on the status of children from any credible source. NGOs, both national and international, regularly communicate with the Committee regarding the reports of individual states parties, with some NGOs submitting complete reports paralleling those of states parties. Special reports are also submitted to the Committee by independent scholars and other experts.

The reason for the unique, cooperative relationship between the NGOs and the Committee on the Rights of the Child can be traced to the drafting of the Convention. During this process, a group of about thirty NGOs, known as the NGO Ad Hoc Group on the Drafting of the Convention on the Rights of the Child met twice each year to collaborate with one another regarding development of the text of the Convention and to draft recommendations for changes in the draft Convention's text. Their efforts were very successful and greatly influenced the deliberations of the U.N. Working Group in charge of drafting the Convention. As a result, the Working Group gave NGOs a role to play in the Convention's implementation process.

After the Convention was adopted by the General Assembly in 1989, the original group of NGOs reorganized as the NGO Group for the Convention on the Rights of the Child (NGO Group). In their new configuration they are undertaking many projects aimed at maximizing their Article 45 role of facilitating the Convention's implementation. To this end they have been encouraging and assisting with the establishment of national coalitions of NGOs to monitor state party compliance with the Convention at the local level. As part of this project, they try to ensure that national NGOs are present when the Committee on the Rights of the Child holds its Pre-Sessional preparatory meetings to review the states parties reports from their countries.

Processes of the Committee on the Rights of the Child

Originally slated to meet for two weeks once a year, the overwhelming number of ratifications of the Convention on the Rights of the Child gradually forced an increase in the number and length of the Committee's sessions, so that the Committee now meets three times a year for sessions of four weeks each.[102] These are usually held during January, May/June, and September/October.

The first meetings of the Committee on the Rights of the Child where given over to the election officers,[103] and to the drafting the Committee's *Provisional Rules*

102. A session consists of three weeks of public oral examinations of states parties' reports, plus a one-week closed session to prepare for the next session's reports. *See id.* at 43, § 2. The original meeting schedule of two weeks, once a year was quickly increased to three weeks twice a year. Subsequently, because of the overwhelming workload of the Committee resulting from the Convention's enormous worldwide popularity, the General Assembly added a third session each year. A session consists of three weeks of public oral examinations of states parties' reports, plus a one-week closed session to prepare for the next session.

103. Officers of the Committee are the Chairperson; three alternate Chairpersons, and a Rapporteur. They are elected for terms of two years.

of Procedure[104] and their *General Guidelines Regarding the Form and Content of Initial Reports to be Submitted by States Parties Under Article 44, Paragraph (a) of the Convention (Guidelines).*[105] Although the first reports were due in Fall 1992, formal examination of the reports did not commence until the Committee's January 1993 session. Once a report is received by the United Nations it is first translated into the Committee's three languages (English, French, and Spanish) and then given a document number that reflects the session at which the Committee will examine the report.

State Party Report Examination

The Committee devotes the first three weeks of each session to the oral examination of states parties' reports. The fourth and final week of each session is spent in preparation for the following session. Reports scheduled for the up-coming session are reviewed by the Committee at a closed "Pre-Sessional" preparatory meeting. It is during this Pre-Sessional meeting that the Committee studies the reports, gathers outside information from UNICEF, other U.N. bodies, and NGOs, and formulates questions for the state party to answer in writing prior to the subsequent oral examination. Questions asked at this formal, public examination are based, in part, on the written replies to the earlier written questions and answers.

Because the Convention is so comprehensive, the Committee felt it necessary to draft a set of guidelines that would simplify and systematize the report drafting process. The result was what are commonly referred to as the Committee's *Guidelines.*[106] They request that states parties divide their reports into sections that cluster articles under appropriate headings. In sections I and II of the *Guidelines*, states parties are asked to provide information on their general measures of implementation and on their definition of the child. Section III lists four "general principles"—articles that the Committee considers to impinge on all other articles of the Convention. These four overarching principles are: Article 2 (non-discrimination),[107] Article 3 (the best interests of the child),[108] Article 6 (survival and development),[109]

---

104. *See* Committee on the Rights of the Child: Provisional Rules of Procedure, 1st Sess., 22d mtg., U.N. Doc. CRC/C/4 (1991); *see also* U.N. Doc. CRC/C4 (1992); *also see* U.N. Doc. A/47/41 (1992) at Annex IV [hereinafter *Rules of Procedure*].

105. *See Committee on the Rights of the Child: General Guidelines Regarding the Form and Content of Initial Reports to be Submitted by States Parties Under Article 44, Paragraph (a) of the Convention,* U.N. Doc. CRC/C.5 (30 Oct. 30, 1991) [hereinafter *Guidelines on Reporting*]; U.N. Doc. A/47/41 (1992) at Annex III.

106. *Id.* It should be noted that Article 44 requires states parties to submit their initial reports two years after the Convention goes into effect for that country, with periodic reports every five years thereafter. The Committee has also issued a comprehensive set of *Guidelines* for the upcoming periodic reports. *See General Guidelines for Periodic Reports*, Comm. on the Rights of the Child, 13th sess., 343rd mtg., U.N. Doc. CRC/C/58 (1996) [hereinafter *Periodic Guidelines*].

107. *Convention, supra* note 3, at art. 2.

108. *Id.* at art. 3.

109. *Id.* at art. 6.

and Article 12 (respect for the views of the child).[110] The remaining articles of the Convention are clustered into sections covering: the child's civil rights and freedoms;[111] family and alternative care;[112] basic health and welfare;[113] education, leisure and cultural activities;[114] special protection measures—children in situations of emergency;[115] children in conflict with the law,[116] children in situations of exploitation, including physical and psychological recovery and social reintegration;[117] and children belonging to a minority or indigenous group.[118] The Committee not only requests that states parties follow these *Guidelines*, but NGOs and other child advocates and scholars submitting information to the Committee are also encouraged to follow this same pattern. While the *Guidelines* were originally developed for the initial states parties' reports, the Committee has drafted similar, more elaborate *Guidelines* for the subsequent periodic reports that follow this same basic format.[119]

At the end of each session, the Committee drafts a set of "Concluding Observations" for each state party's report. This document includes: a review of the report's "Positive Aspects;" "Factors and Difficulties Impeding Implementation of the Convention;" "Principle Areas of Concern;" and "Suggestions and Recommendations."[120]

Rules of Procedure (General Discussion Days)

Interpreting its powers broadly, the Committee has instituted a practice at its fall session of holding a General Discussion Day on a topic of general interest to states parties. Thus far, topics have included children and war, economic exploitation, children and families, juvenile justice, the child and the media, and a special additional day of discussion on the girl child during its January 1995 session prior to the Beijing Fourth World Conference on Women.[121] The purpose of the General Discussion Day is to bring together experts who can augment the knowledge of Committee members with regard to a particular topic.

---

110. *Id.* at art. 12.

111. VI. Civil rights: arts. 7, 8, 13, 17, 14, 15, 16, 37(a).

112. V. Family and alternative care: arts. 5, 18(1), 18(2), 9, 10, 27(4), 20, 21, 11, 19, 39, 25.

113. VI. Basic health and welfare: arts. 6(2), 23, 24, 26, 18(3), 27(1), 27(2), and 27(3).

114. VII. Education, leisure, and cultural activities: arts. 28, 29, and 31.

115. VIII. Special protection measures—children in situations of emergency: arts. 22, 38, and 39.

116. IX. Children in conflict with the law: arts. 40, 37(a), 37(b),. 37(c), 37(d), and 39.

117. X. Children in situations of exploitation: arts. 32, 33, 34, 35, 36, and 39.

118. XI. Children belonging to a minority or indigenous group: art. 30.

119. *See Periodic Guidelines, supra* note 106.

120. For examples of the Committee's treatment of girl child issues in its *Concluding Observations, see infra* notes 128–140 and accompanying text.

121. The Committee's general discussion on the girl child, held Jan. 23, 1995, can be found in *Report Adopted by the Committee at Its 209th Meeting on Jan. 17, 1995*, Committee on the Rights of the Child, 8th Sess., U.N. Doc. CRC/C/38 (1995).

In advance of the general discussion on the girl child, the Chair of the Committee prepared an outline for distribution to all possible participants: United Nations bodies, specialized agencies, and "other competent bodies."[122] It emphasized "the principle of non-discrimination, the need for the girl child to enjoy all her fundamental rights, including the right to make free and informed decisions concerning her life."[123] The Committee's report of its General Discussion Day speaks of "the place in society of girls" as raising "serious and unresolved questions of inequality and indifference, manifested by discrimination, neglect, exploitation and violence."[124] The General Discussion report, citing information taken from states parties' reports, listed a full range of deprivations faced by girls, deprivation that is usually based on custom: household responsibilities at an early age, responsibilities for younger siblings, refused access to education, son preference, neglect, less food, little health care, inferiority leading to violence and sexual abuse, early marriage and pregnancy, female circumcision (FGM) and forced marriage.[125] The report mentions a variety of steps to be taken to correct this situation. However, in one of the report's most significant statements the Committee urged that girls need not be seen as a "special group entitled to special rights."[126] Rather, the Committee said:

> [G]irls are simply human beings who should be seen as individuals and not just as daughters, sisters, wives or mothers, and who should fully enjoy the fundamental rights inherent to their human dignity.[127]

The Committee's Inquiry into Status of the Girl Child

The Twelfth Session in June 1996 provides a good example of how the Committee approaches the issue of the girl child. At that session,[128] the Committee examined the reports from five states parties: China, Guatemala, Lebanon, Nepal, and Zimbabwe.[129] A survey of the "Principle Areas of Concern" of the *Concluding Observations* for this session shows that not one of these countries was without fault with regard to the girl child. In its observations on the Chinese report, the Committee remarked that:

> inadequate measures taken in the field of social security may have led to an over-reliance on children providing future care and support to their parents. This may have contributed to the perpetuation of harmful traditional practices and attitudes such as

---

122. The Committee on the Rights of the Child has given the broadest interpretation to the Article 45 phrase "other competent bodies," extending the phrase to include scholars and other individual experts. *See supra* note 101 and accompanying text.

123. *See Report Adopted by the Committee at Its 209th Meeting, supra* note 121, at ¶ 276.

124. *Id.* at ¶ 282.

125. *Id.* at ¶ 286.

126. *Id.* at ¶ 283.

127. *Id.*

128. The Twelfth Session was held May 20–June 7, 1996.

129. The Committee also examined the report of Cyprus, but this information was not readily available for analysis.

a preference for boys, to the detriment of the protection and promotion of the rights of girls. . . .[130]

The Committee also pointed out that Chinese laxity in the registration of children had ramifications in regard to the government's ability to protect children against "trafficking abduction, sale, mistreatment or neglect."[131] It went on to say that "the situation of 'unregistered girls' as regards their entitlement to health care and education is a matter of concern to the Committee."[132]

The Committee consistently inquires about the minimum age for marriage, since it is known to have negative effects on the development of the girl child. Often this practice is linked to a range of local customs. The Committee noted that in Nepal there were "persistent discriminatory attitudes towards girls, as reflected in the prevailing son preference, the persistence of early marriages, the notably lower school attendance of girls and their higher drop-out rate."[133] Similarly, the Committee's response to Lebanon's report stresses:

> The Committee is worried by the widespread practice of early marriage and the related consequence of high child mortality rates and the negative impact on the health of girls bearing children at an early age.[134]

The Committee pointed out that there was also a discrepancy between boys and girls in the minimum age for marriage.[135] In commenting on the report from Guatemala, the Committee observed that "the low age of marriage for girls, which is different than the one for boys, is, in the Committee's view, also incompatible with the principles and provisions of the Convention."[136] The Committee's *Concluding Observations* on the Zimbabwe report cited concern over "the persistence of behavioral attitudes" and of cultural and religious practices that interfered with the implementation of the children's rights.[137] In particular the Committee was concerned about:

> the situation of female victim of practices such as *ngozi* (girl child pledging), *lobola* (bride price), and early marriage. . . .[138]

The Committee observed that local law prevented girls from having inheritance rights, that there was "discrimination on the basis of race in relation to the minimum age for

---

130. *See Concluding Observations of the Committee on the Rights of the Child: China*, Committee on the Rights of the Child, 12th Sess. ¶ 12., U.N. Doc. CRC/C/15/ADD.56 (1996).

131. *See id.* ¶ 16.

132. *Id.*

133. *See Concluding Observations of the Committee on the Rights of the Child: Nepal*, Committee on the Rights of the Child, 12th Sess. ¶ 12., U.N. Doc. CRC/C/15/ADD.57 (1996).

134. *See Concluding Observations of the Committee on the Rights of the Child: Lebanon*, Committee on the Rights of the Child, 12th Sess. ¶ 16., U.N. Doc. CRC/C/15/ADD.54 (1996).

135. *Id.*

136. *See Concluding Observations of the Committee on the Rights of the Child: Guatemala*, Committee on the Rights of the Child, 12th Sess. ¶ 15., U.N. Doc. CRC/C/15/ADD.58 (1996).

137. *See Concluding Observations of the Committee on the Rights of the Child: Zimbabwe*, Committee on the Rights of the Child, 12th Sess. ¶ 13., U.N. Doc. CRC/C/15/ADD.55 (1996).

138. *See id.*

marriage, inheritance and children born out of wedlock," and that there were different minimum marriage ages for girls and boys.[139] The Committee also pointed out that in Zimbabwe the "costs of secondary education are leading to an increasing dropout rate for girls."[140]

The Committee's Twelfth Session was not unique. These inquiries and commentaries have been replicated in the *Concluding Observations* for subsequent sessions.[141]

WORLD SITUATION OF THE GIRL CHILD

In the world social order—whether they live in rich, developed countries or nations that are poor and underdeveloped—girl children are the lowest of the low. In almost every country girls face major obstacles, solely by virtue of the fact that they are female. As might be expected, the situation of girls is worst in the poorest countries.[142]

Beginning in the 1990s, after the Convention on the Rights of the Child went into force, the world began to take notice of the situation of the girl child. Early studies showed that discrimination against the girl child begins before birth. Although the bases for "son preference" may differ, countries such as the Republic of Korea, India, and China share in the practice of using ultrasound techniques to determine the sex of the fetus in order to allow for selective abortion.[143] Ultrasound-inspired abortions are not the only method used to diminish the number of female children. Infanticide is also widespread. According to a UNICEF/UNIFEM fact sheet, in one section of India 58 percent of the deaths among female infants were due to infanticide.[144]

Provided that she is carried to term, survival of the girl child is threatened from the moment she is born. According to the World Health Organization, girls in many poorer countries are breast-fed for shorter periods of time, receive fewer calories, and are more likely to suffer from malnutrition than boys.[145] Girls are usually the last to eat—the better food goes to the boys, and girls get what is left over. Studies show that girls have less access to health care than boys. They are taken to treatment centers less often and are sicker when they finally receive treatment. This results in a higher rate of illness and stunted growth.[146]

---

139. *See id.* at ¶ 12.

140. *See id.* at ¶ 19.

141. All of the documents relating to the Committee's state party report examination procedures, including all submitted state party reports, summary records of the oral examinations and the Committee's *Concluding Observations* can be found on the web site of the United Nations High Commissioner for Human Rights: <www.unhchr.ch>.

142. *See, e.g., infra* notes 145–153 and accompanying text.

143. *See* MAGGIE BLACK, GIRLS AND WOMEN: A UNICEF DEVELOPMENT PRIORITY 8 (1993).

144. *See* Girls' Rights, UNICEF/UNIFEM Fact Sheet.

145. *See* UNICEF/UNIFEM, *id.*

146. *See* BLACK, *supra* note 143.

A study by UNICEF points out that by the time that they are six, girls are expected to take on adult household duties: caring for siblings, cooking, cleaning, and other heavy domestic chores.[147] These tasks make it difficult for a girl to get an education. As a result, girls are seen as a burden on their families and are "married off" at an early age. Such marriages are often arranged by the families and frequently for money.[148] This abbreviated childhood is then followed by teenage pregnancy, which further diminishes the girl child's health and can lead to premature death.[149] The UNICEF survey points out that "Girls who marry so young spend up to 80 percent of their lives pregnant, nursing and caring for children, and serving husbands and in-laws."[150]

Substantiating UNICEF studies, the World Health Organization (WHO) describes widespread "nurture discrimination"[151] against girls, including less food and less access to health care, that leads to malnutrition and death. Early marriage and early childbirth have also been examined by WHO. Cited as a major element in this constellation of events is the minimum age for marriage, which in underdeveloped countries often ranges from low to even lower. For example, while some countries have the comparatively low minimum age for marriage of fifteen, others, such as Chile, Ecuador, Panama, Paraguay, Sri Lanka, and Venezuela have an even lower minimum age of twelve.[152] The outcome of these early marriages is early childbirth which WHO reports results in high maternal mortality.[153]

The UNICEF/UNIFEM fact sheet reiterates the child domestic labor observations of other studies and adds that in countries, such as Bangladesh, girls as young as six or seven are sent away to be domestic servants living in the most difficult circumstances.[154] It is estimated that in New Delhi, India, alone there are approximately 400,000 girls who are working as domestic servants.[155] An additional factor that com-

---

147. *Id.*

148. In some cases the reasons for these abortion and infanticide are based on a tradition of "son preference," in others they are purely economic. There are cultures in which girl children are considered to be expensive, especially when there are costs attached to arranging for her marriage.

149. *See* BLACK, *supra* note 143, at 8. Children of teenage mothers are usually born too small and too early. Because the girl's body is still growing it cannot adequately support both the health requirements of a growing mother and those of her child. According to UNICEF, one quarter of the 500,000 women who die annually from childbirth are teenage girls.

150. *Id* at 9.

151. *See* UNICEF/UNIFEM, *supra* note 144.

152. All of these countries have been states parties to the Convention on the Elimination of All Forms of Discrimination Against Women for more than ten years. The fact that the Women's Convention failed to cite a definite standard for the minimum age for marriage would seem to be a factor in the continuing inadequacy of their marriage legislation.

153. *Id.* According to WHO the maternal mortality rate for girls ten to fourteen is five times higher than that for young women twenty to twenty-four years of age. It should be noted that the infant mortality rate is also higher for child mothers.

154. *See* UNICEF/UNIFEM, *supra* note 144.

155. *Id.*

promises the quality of life for the girl child is her lack of education. A 1990 survey concluded that of the 130 million children in the world that do not have access to primary education, 81 million were girls.[156] This is especially tragic when one considers that educated young women have been found to have fewer and healthier children.[157] In 147 of the 150 countries listed in UNICEF's statistics on education—found in its 1995 *State of the World's Children*—more boys than girls attended primary school.[158] During the years 1983–1990 only sixty-seven countries had primary school attendance ratios in which the gap between boys and girls was less than ten points (others were much greater).[159] Interestingly, statistics for secondary school were somewhat better. Forty-nine countries had higher ratios for girl students and ten of these were at least ten points higher.[160] There were sixteen countries in which the ratios on education for girls were greater than that for boys at both the primary and secondary school levels. In other words, despite improvements, there are still 134 countries in which girl students are disproportionately outnumbered by boys.[161]

The general quality of life picture for girls is even more distressing when one takes into account the various ways in which a girl's sexuality makes her a target for abuse. Youth is no protection from sexual exploitation and assault. As the AIDS virus has spread, the demand for younger and younger sex partners has grown. The 1994 Human Development Report estimated that there were over half a million child prostitutes in the Philippines, Sri Lanka, and Thailand alone.[162] The UNICEF/UNIFEM fact sheet cites—as proof of the extent to which very young girl children are sex targets—a 1988 study conducted in Nigeria in which 16 percent of the patients treated for sexually transmitted diseases were found to be *under the age of five*.[163]

---

156. *See* BLACK, *supra* note 143, at 23.

157. *See* 1991 World Bank statistics cited in *id*. at 25.

158. UNICEF, STATE OF THE WORLD'S CHILDREN, app. tbl. IV: Education (1995).

159. On the positive side, however, is the fact that primary school ratios were higher for girls than boys in twenty-six countries and that many of these were countries that are underdeveloped. Countries where primary education statistics for girls exceeded those for boys were: Singapore, Germany, Switzerland, the United Kingdom, the Netherlands, Italy, the Republic of Korea, Greece, Belgium, Jamaica, Kuwait, Malaysia, Colombia, Mauritius, Venezuela, Argentina, Paraguay, Lebanon, Albania, Dominican Republic, Botswana, Mongolia, and Lesotho. Primary education statistics were equal for boys and girls in Sweden, Japan, Denmark, Ireland, Austria, Norway, Australia, Israel, Spain, Hungary, Trinidad and Tobago, Estonia, Jordan, Latvia, and South Africa. *See id*.

160. The countries having secondary education ratios of ten points or more for girls were: Finland, Cuba, Portugal, Colombia, United Arab Emirates, Mauritius, Estonia, Dominican Republic, South Africa and Lesotho. *Id*.

161. Countries where both primary and secondary education statistics for girls exceeded those for boys were: Singapore, Germany, Switzerland, the United Kingdom, the Republic of Korea, Belgium, Jamaica, Malaysia, Colombia, Mauritius, Paraguay, Lebanon, Dominican Republic, Botswana, Mongolia, and Lesotho. *Id*.

162. *See* UNICEF/UNIFEM, *supra* note 144.

163. *Id*.

Perhaps the most horrible outcome of the fixation on a girl's sexuality is the practice of infibulation, otherwise known as "female circumcision" or "female genital mutilation" (FGM).[164] In cultures where FGM is an acceptable practice, an uncircumcised girl is perceived to be promiscuous and threatening.[165] The purpose of FGM is allegedly to ensure female fidelity. In reality, the practice is terrifying, life threatening, and destructive. It completely destroys the young woman's ability to enjoy intercourse and can cause dangerous complications during childbirth.[166] As the world moves into the twenty-first century, the situation of the girl child as outlined in the early studies remain essentially the same. Girl children are still second class citizens in most countries. However, although change may be slow, it is inevitable. International action is slowly breaking down stereotypes, while international law is enforcing equality.

INTERNATIONAL ACTION ON BEHALF OF THE GIRL CHILD

Current international interest in the girl child can be directly linked to the Convention on the Rights of the Child. Although the world movement for women's rights brought female issues onto the international agenda, it is the Convention on the Rights of the Child that is changing the agenda from exclusive concern for the rights of women to one that embraces the rights of the girl child, as well. It is the Convention on the Rights of the Child that has been the primary catalyst in creating the international dialogue on the rights of the girl child and has brought about the non-treaty actions undertaken by the international community to recognize and remedy problems faced by the girl child. The discussion below illustrates the various ways in which the girl child is being taken into consideration in resolutions of the United Nations General Assembly and the Commission on Human Rights, in the work of the Special Rapporteur on the Sale of Children and in deliberations at international conferences.

United Nations General Assembly and Commission on Human Rights

The mid-1990s, influenced by the 1993 World Conference on Human Rights, the 1995 Fourth World Conference on Women and implementation of the Convention on the Rights of the Child, saw the institution by both the General Assembly and the Commission on Human Rights of a practice of drafting annual resolutions on the rights of the girl child. While both bodies' resolutions address the status of the girl child, so far they have done it in different ways. The General Assembly has chosen to

---

164. Female genital mutilation varies among cultures from practices that remove only the tip of the clitoris to practices that remove the entire clitoris and labia minora and sew the labia majora together leaving only a small opening for urination and menstruation. All of these procedures are usually carried out in less than sanitary conditions and may lead to infections resulting in death.

165. *See* Cecelia W. Dugger, *Genital Ritual Is Unyielding in Africa*, N.Y. TIMES, Oct. 5, 1991 at A1.

166. For a graphic description of the results of FGM, *see Woman Betrayed by Loved Ones Mourns a Double Loss*, N.Y. TIMES, Sept. 11, 1996, at B7.

draft and adopt a separate, extensive resolution on the Girl Child, while the Commission on Human Rights has included the girl child as one of the separate segments of its omnibus resolution on the Rights of the Child. The General Assembly adopted its first Girl Child resolution in 1995,[167] and the Commission followed its example in by including the girl child in its 1996 child rights resolution.[168]

Most striking about the General Assembly's first Girl Child resolution was its reiteration in preambular paragraph two that "the advancement and empowerment of women throughout their life-cycle must begin with the girl child."[169] In addition, the resolution called on states to "increase awareness of the potential of the girl child;"[170] take into account the girl child's nutritional needs;[171] and "eliminate all forms of violence against children, in particular the girl child."[172] It is interesting to note the continuing growth and extensiveness of the General Assembly's Girl Child resolutions. The first resolution in 1995 had four preambular paragraphs and eight substantive paragraphs. The 1996 Girl Child resolution increased in size to seven comprehensive preambular paragraphs and thirteen substantive paragraphs—including one with six subsections. With each successive year, the General Assembly's Girl Child resolutions have been expanded. They have called for legal reforms and legislation, elimination of negative cultural attitudes, protection from rape and other forms of violence, free consent in marriage and support for the girl child with disabilities, with the number of preambular paragraphs and substantive paragraphs increasing each year.[173] One rather striking addition in the 1998 resolution was preambular paragraph 6:

> *Stressing* that discrimination and neglect of the girl child can initiate a lifelong downward spiral of deprivation and exclusion from the social mainstream.[174]

The history of the Girl Child resolutions adopted by the Commission on Human Rights has followed a similar pattern of gradual enlargement. As mentioned above, the Commission's resolutions are about the Rights of the Child in general and have numerous sub-sections, one of which is the Girl Child. In its 1996 resolution, the Commission placed the Girl Child in sixth place, just before refugee and internally displaced children, but after all of the other sections, such as the Convention on the Rights of the Child and its implementation; children affected by armed conflicts; sale of children, child prostitution and child pornography; exploitation of child labor; and the plight of street children. In that resolution, the girl child's basic concerns were

---

167. *See* The Girl Child, U.N. Doc. A/RES/50/154 (Dec. 21, 1995)

168. *See* The Rights of the Child, Reservation 1999/80.

169. *See supra* note 167, at preamble ¶ 2.

170. *Id.* at ¶ 3.

171. *Id.* at ¶ 4.

172. *Id.* at ¶ 5.

173. *See* U.N. Docs. A/RES/52/76 (Dec. 12, 1996); A/RES/52/106 (Dec. 12, 1997) and A/RES/53/127 (Dec. 9, 1998).

174. *See* U.N. Doc. A/RES/53/127 (Dec. 9, 1998) at preamble ¶ 5.

covered in two paragraphs. One paragraph called for the elimination of discrimination against the girl child.[175] The other encouraged states to:

> enact and enforce legislation protecting girls from all forms of violence, including female infanticide and pre-natal sex selection, genital mutilation, incest, sexual abuse, sexual exploitation, child prostitution, child pornography and to develop age-appropriate, safe and confidential programmes and medical, social and psychological support services to support girls who are subjected to violence.[176]

Beginning in 1997, the Commission's resolutions moved the Girl Child's section to second place, immediately following the Convention on the Rights of the Child. The Girl Child sections have also gotten longer and more comprehensive—as has the entire annual resolution. What was originally an eight-page resolution with two paragraphs devoted to the Girl Child, had become by 1999 an eighteen-page document devoting eight paragraphs with numerous subsections to the rights of the Girl Child.[177] To a certain extent, the concerns voiced in the Commission's resolutions mirror the General Assembly's resolutions. They include elaborated versions of problems cited in the Commission's paragraph quoted above, in addition to which they have added recommendations for full and equal enjoyment of rights, gender-sensitive strategies in education, legal reforms, and public awareness campaigns. What is particularly interesting about the Commission's 1999 Rights of the Child resolution is that it added new categories not covered by previous resolutions, including juvenile justice, children with disabilities, child health, and education. This augmentation of the resolution reflects a growing appreciation of the full extent of the rights of the child and removes the narrow perception of children's rights as only being relevant for children in difficult circumstances.

Special Rapporteur on the Sale of Children

The Vienna Declaration of the 1993 World Conference on Human Rights covered most human rights subjects that are regularly on the agenda of the United Nations Commission on Human Rights, but with one exception. That was the work of the Special Rapporteur on the Sale of Children, Child Prostitution and Child Pornography. The first Special Rapporteur, Professor Vitit Muntharbhorn, was appointed in the fall of 1990.[178] His office was established as the result of Resolution 1989/42 of the Sub-Commission on the Prevention of Discrimination and the Protection of Minorities entitled "Sale of Children" in which it requested the appointment of the Special Rapporteur by the Commission. The request was subsequently adopted by both the Commission and the Economic and Social Council. Upon appointment, the Special Rapporteur's first act was to ask for assistance from governments and non-governmental organizations in carrying out his mandate. Professor Muntharbhorn's initial report in 1991 was devoted to laying out the framework for further investigation.

---

175. *Id.* at ¶ 44.

176. *Id.* at ¶ 45.

177. *See* Commission on Human Rights resolutions: 1996/85; 1997/78; 1998/76; and 1999/80.

178. Professor Vitit Muntharbhorn was the Special Rapporteur from 1991–1994. He was replaced in 1995 by Ms. Ofelia Calcetas-Santos.

Beginning in 1992, the results of the Special Rapporteur's investigations were itemized in annual reports to the Commission on Human Rights. Although the mandate of the Special Rapporteur covers the sale of all children, within each of his reports there were sections that singled out the special problems of the girl child. In the 1992 report, citing specific cases, the Special Rapporteur looked at the incidence of forced marriage and concluded that it was not limited to developing countries.[179] In addition, Professor Muntharbhorn pointed out that cultural influences can be a factor in child prostitution.[180]

> In some settings, there is a class system that perpetuates the use of young girls in prostitution. There also exists the practice of handing over young girls as "sex goddesses" in certain regions of the world.[181]

The Special Rapporteur noted that once young girls have become enmeshed in a life of prostitution, societal taboos make it very difficult for them to change occupations.[182]

Professor Muntharbhorn's 1993 report was much larger in scope than that of 1992. In regard to the girl child, the Special Rapporteur explained that "[F]emale foeticide has been banned by law, but socio-cultural prejudices remain."[183] He noted that in developing countries girls have "fewer educational and occupational opportunities than boys" and that many end up as prostitutes and domestics.[184] Child prostitution is both national and international. In Sri Lanka there have been allegations of "a large number of girl prostitutes in the free trade zone in the country, who are coerced into rendering sexual services."[185] The report continued, describing girls trafficked from Nepal and Bangladesh into India, stating: "The girls being trafficked into India are mostly fair skinned girls from the Mongol community, mostly of the Tamag ethnic group who are scattered into the country."[186]

The 1993 report on Sale of Children was also expanded to look at other forms of "sale," such as sale for adoption, kidnaping for various purposes, including adoption, sale of organs, bonded labor and, in the case of girls, rape.[187] Building on his

---

179. *See Sale of Children*, Commission on Human Rights 48th Sess. Agenda Item 22, ¶ 87, U.N. Doc. E/CN.4/1992/55 (1992) at ¶ 87. One cited case was that of a Saudi national who was arrested for "buying a young Indian girl for marriage." *Id*. In another case, an immigrant to Britain tricked his daughter into marrying a Yemeni citizen when they were on holiday in Yemen. *Id*.

180. The topic of child prostitution appeared in all three of Professor Muntharbhorn's reports. *See, e.g., id*. ¶¶ 220–238.

181. *Id*. ¶ 144.

182. *Id*.

183. *See Sale of Children*, U.N. Commission on Human Rights 49th Sess. Agenda Item 24, ¶ 83, U.N. Doc. E/CN.4/1993/67 (1993).

184. *Id*. The Special Rapporteur is referring to Bangladesh, Nepal, India, and Pakistan.

185. *Id*. ¶ 175.

186. *Id*. ¶ 176.

187. *See id*. ¶¶ 128–133.

1992 report, the Special Rapporteur observed that the problem of arranged child marriages could be found in numerous countries, especially India, Pakistan, Nepal and Bangladesh.[188] He also concluded that child labor involving girls is a problem everywhere: from the United States, where children can be found in sweat shops, to the Philippines, where girl laborers are exploited in the garment industry.[189]

The final report by Professor Muntharbhorn in 1994 once again addressed the problems of child labor, child marriage, prostitution, and trafficking. Pointing out that in Bangladesh and Pakistan girls six to fourteen are the preferred ages for domestic labor, he stated, "The girls are discharged at puberty and may end up in a brothel."[190] As for child marriages, the Special Rapporteur painted a bleak picture.

> Poor girls without a trade or dowry are often taken as second wives by older men and kept in near slavery. If the first wife does not recognize the second marriage, it is not registered, and when the girl becomes pregnant, she can be abandoned without a legal remedy.[191]

Trafficking also has unexpected hazards. Girls trafficked from Bangladesh into Pakistan often end up being detained in jail as illegal immigrants.[192] Moreover, although Pakistan has laws against bonded labor, they are not enforced.[193] In addition, there are reports that children employed as domestic servants in Sri Lanka are often sexually abused.[194] Interestingly, it appears that the demand for South Asian women is transnational, with customers coming from "a variety of Gulf States and Middle Eastern countries."[195]

The Special Rapporteur found that sexual exploitation of girls was widespread, especially in Eastern Europe. The 1994 report spoke of children being sold for prostitution in Russia and of Romany girl prostitutes in Czechoslovakia.[196] It also noted that numerous Western countries gave information to the Special Rapporteur about their efforts to stamp out sexual exploitation and sex tourism, in particular.[197] The well-known problems of child prostitution in Eastern countries was cited once again.[198]

---

188. *See id.* ¶ 85.

189. *See id.* ¶¶ 86–91.

190. *Sale of Children, Child Prostitution and Child Pornography*, U.N. Commission on Human Rights 50th Sess., Agenda Item 22, ¶ 82, U.N. Doc. E/CN.4/1994/84 (1994).

191. *Id.* ¶ 83.

192. *See id.* ¶ 84.

193. *See id.* ¶ 85.

194. *See id.* ¶ 86.

195. *See id.* ¶ 87.

196. *See id.* ¶ 144.

197. *See id.* ¶ 145. The Western countries mentioned in the report are Belgium, France, the United Kingdom, Sweden, Germany, Australia, and Japan. *See id.* at 33–38.

198. The countries known to be the biggest sources of child prostitution are: Cambodia, Malaysia, Sri Lanka, Philippines, Burma, Thailand, Laos, China, Viet Nam, India, Nepal, and Pakistan.

Professor Muntharbhorn withdrew from the post of Special Rapporteur in 1994 and was replaced by Ms. Ofelia Calcetas-Santos, who submitted her first report in 1995. That report and her subsequent reports have built on the work begun by Professor Muntharbhorn. The typical report has covered information about the Rapporteur's activities, relevant international developments regarding the sale of children, child prostitution and pornography, trafficking, and significant regional and national developments, including short, specific country reports and details of regional conferences on sexual exploitation.[199] Some of Ms. Calcetas-Santos' reports have focused on child labor and most recently she has begun to examine the problem of family violence.

While the work of the Special Rapporteur concentrates on children in general, it is clear that most of the problems addressed are those of the girl child. Currently being debated by the Commission on Human Rights is a draft Optional Protocol to the Convention on the Rights of the Child that directly addresses the areas being studied by Ms. Calcetas-Santos.[200] Although the girl child is not specifically mentioned in the draft Optional Protocol, it is obvious that girls make up the majority of victims of the rights violations that it seeks to end.

International Meetings and Conferences

World Summit for Children (1990)

Shortly after the Convention on the Rights of the Child was adopted by the United Nations General Assembly on November 20, 1989, UNICEF put forward a plan to hold a world summit that would focus on children's issues.[201] This idea was supported by a number of governments which worked with UNICEF to bring the idea to fruition.[202] On September 29–30, 1990, more than eighty Heads of State met at the United Nations in New York to participate in the World Summit for Children. One of the World Summit's outcomes was the drafting of the World Declaration on the Survival, Protection and Development of Children (World Declaration).[203]

---

199. For an example of a typical report from Mrs. Calcetas-Santos, *see* U.N. Doc. A/53/311 (Aug. 26, 1998).

200. The text of the draft Optional Protocol to the Convention on the Rights of the Child on the Sale of Children, Child Prostitution and Child Pornography appears in the Annex to U.N. Doc. E/CN.4/2000/75.

201. The purpose of the World Summit for Children was to ensure that children's concerns did not disappear from the international agenda after the Convention on the Rights of the Child was adopted by the General Assembly. At that time no one could foresee the fact that the Convention would be so welcomed by the international community that it would already be in force by the time that the Summit was held. Nor would it have been predicted that, five years after the Convention was opened for signature, there would be 187 states parties to the Convention.

202. Cynthia Price Cohen & Per Miljeteig-Olssen, *Status Report: United Nations Convention on the Rights of the Child*, 8 N.Y. L. Sch. J. Hum. Rts. 367, 369 (1991).

203. *See World Declaration on the Survival, Protection and Development of Children, in* UNICEF, First Call for Children 1 (1990) [hereinafter *World Declaration*].

The World Declaration gives special attention to the girl child, stating: "*Girls* must be given equal treatment and opportunities from the beginning."[204] It further notes that of the "over 100 million children who are without basic schooling . . . two-thirds of them are *girls*."[205] As part of their commitment to children, participating governments pledged to "provide educational opportunities for all children, irrespective of their background and gender."[206] To actualize these goals the World Declaration called for the creation of the Plan of Action for Implementing the World Declaration on the Survival, Protection and Development of Children in the 1990s (World Summit Plan of Action).

Section II of the World Summit Plan of Action, "Specific Actions for Child Survival, Protection and Development," lists two actions particularly aimed at improving the condition of the girl child.[207] The first action has to do with ensuring the availability of clean water and safe sanitation, which are "not only essential for human health and well-being, but also contribute greatly to the emancipation of women from the drudgery that has a pernicious impact on children, *especially girls*."[208] The second action places an emphasis on education, urging that "primary education or equivalent learning achievement by at least 80 percent of the relevant school age children with emphasis on reducing the disparities between boys and *girls*."[209] The Appendix's goals support the above actions by calling for "Special attention to the health and nutrition of the female child" and "Universal access to primary education with *special emphasis for girls*. . . ."[210]

World Conference on Human Rights (1993)

The World Conference on Human Rights, sponsored by the United Nations and held in Vienna June 14–25, 1993, concluded with the adoption of a document known as the Vienna Declaration and Programme of Action (Vienna Declaration).[211] The

---

204. *Id.* at 3 (emphasis added).

205. *Id.* (emphasis added).

206. *Id.* at 5. The *World Declaration* is divided into five sections: *The Challenge, The Opportunity, The Task, The Commitment,* and *The Next Steps.* Although the *World Declaration* focuses on children in general, in the section on *The Commitment* it gives special attention to the girl child.

The World Declaration is accompanied by a *Plan of Action for Implementing the World Declaration on the Survival, protection and Development of Children in the 1990s* and an Appendix entitled *Goals for Children and Development in the 1990s. Id.* at 6–39.

207. *See Plan of Action for Implementing the World Declaration on the Survival, Protection and Development of Children in the 1990s* in UNICEF, First Call for Children 9 (1990). It is divided into three sections: I. Introduction; II. Specific Actions for Child Survival, Protection and Development; and III. Follow-Up Actions and Monitoring. It is followed by an Appendix outlining "Goals for Children and Development in the 1990s."

208. *Id.* at 14 (emphasis added).

209. *See id.* at 14, 18 (emphasis added).

210. *See id.* at 32 (emphasis added).

211. *See* Vienna Declaration and Programme of Action, U.N. Doc. A/CONF.157/23 (July 19, 1993), 32 I.L.M. 1661.

Vienna Declaration presents a comprehensive view of aspirations based on the current status of human rights. The girl child is specifically mentioned in two paragraphs of the Vienna Declaration's General Principles. The first asserts that "The human rights of women and of the *girl-child* are an inalienable, integral and indivisible part of universal human rights."[212] The second paragraph, while speaking of the need for early ratification of the Convention on the Rights of the Child and children's rights in general, states that "[N]ational and international mechanisms and programmes should be strengthened for the defence and protection of children, in particular, the girl-child."[213]

The Vienna Declaration also contains a special section on Equality, Dignity and Tolerance.[214] Within this section are subsections that discuss racism, minorities, the disabled, torture, women and, most importantly, the rights of the child.[215] The nine-paragraph subsection on children's rights has two paragraphs that refer to matters relative to the girl child. The first paragraph asserts that effective measures are required to protect against female infanticide.[216] The second paragraph states:

> The World Conference on Human Rights supports all measures by the United Nations and its specialized agencies to ensure the effective protection and promotion of human rights of the girl child. The World Conference on Human Rights urges States to repeal existing laws and regulations and remove customs and practices which discriminate against and cause harm to the *girl child*.[217]

Fourth World Conference on Women, Beijing (1995)

The Beijing Declaration and Plan of Action of the Fourth World Conference on Women[218] devoted approximately nine pages to a survey of the situation of girl child. It echoed the findings in the UNICEF/UNIFEM Fact Sheet, discussed above.[219] The Beijing Declaration and Plan of Action restated the fact that the girl child faces discrimination "from the earliest stages of life, through her childhood and into her adulthood."[220] In addition, it supported other research and stated that "in some parts of the world, men outnumber women by 5 in every 100."[221] The reason given for this discrepancy was:

---

212. *Id.* pt. I, ¶ 18 (emphasis added).

213. *Id.* pt. I, ¶ 21 (emphasis added).

214. *Id.* pt. II, ¶¶ 19–65.

215. *Id.*

216. *Id.* ¶ 48.

217. *Id.* ¶ 49 (author's emphasis). While this language does not incorporate any of the usual terms for female genital mutilation, such as "traditional practices" or FGM, it is sufficiently broad to indicate that FGM is encompassed, along with other practices such as gender preference and child marriage.

218. *See Report of the Fourth World Conference on Women, Beijing, China, Sept. 4–15, 1995* [hereinafter *Beijing Report*], U.N. Doc. A/CONF/177/20 (1995). Ch. I, Res. I, Annex I & II.

219. *Platform for Action*, Annex 2, Ch. 4 *in Beijing Report, supra* note 218 at ¶¶ 259–285.

220. *Id.* ¶ 259.

221. *Id.*

among other things, harmful attitudes and practices, such as female genital mutilation, son preference—which results in female infanticide and prenatal sex selection—early marriage, including child marriage, violence against women, sexual exploitation, sexual abuse, discrimination against girls in food allocation and other practices related to health and well-being.[222]

The Declaration and Plan of Action also reported that "more than 15 million girls aged 15–19 give birth each year"[223] and that "sexual violence and sexually transmitted diseases, including HIV/AIDS are among the sex-related dangers to girls.[224]

The Declaration and Plan of Action included a list of "strategic objectives" to improve the situation of the girl child. For each of these objectives, the Declaration and Plan of Action included outlines of specific actions that should be taken by governments in cooperation with international and non-governmental organizations in order to implement these objectives. The following nine strategic objectives were designated as areas in which the need for action was most urgent:

(1) Eliminate all forms of discrimination against the girl child;

(2) Eliminate negative cultural attitudes and practices against girls;

(3) Promote and protect the rights of the girl child and increase awareness of her needs and potential;

(4) Eliminate discrimination against girls in education, skills development and training;

(5) Eliminate discrimination against girls in health and nutrition;

(6) Eliminate the economic exploitation of child labor and protect young girls at work;

(7) Eradicate violence against the girl child;

(8) Promote the girl child's awareness of and participation in social, economic and political life;

(9) Strengthen the role of the family in improving the status of the girl child.[225]

FUTURE PROSPECTS FOR THE GIRL CHILD

The twentieth century laid the framework for supporting the human dignity of the girl child and worldwide recognition that girls are entitled to respect for their human rights. At the beginning of the Twenty-first Century the world seems poised to carry this initiative forward. During the first two years of the new century, follow-

---

222. *Id.*

223. *Id.* ¶ 268.

224. *Id.* ¶ 269.

225. *Id.* ¶¶ 274 –285 (strategic objectives L.1–L.9).

up conferences have been planned for both the World Summit for Children and the Fourth World Conference on Women.[226]

There will be a similar follow-up conference to the World Congress on Commercial Sexual Exploitation of Children (World Congress) which, because it was primarily an NGO initiative and not a United Nations sponsored conference, was omitted from the list of conferences above, although its impact on child prostitution has been considerable.[227] The World Congress was held in Stockholm in late August 1996 and was jointly sponsored by the Swedish Government; ECPAT—an NGO that works to end sex tourism;[228] the International Catholic Child Bureau; Defence for Children International and the NGO Group.[229] Typically, the World Congress concluded with the adoption of the World Congress Declaration and Agenda for Action. Interestingly, this document makes only two references to "girls" or "girls and boys." The main body of the document refers only to "the child' or to "children." Just as in the Convention on the Rights of the Child, which it cites repeatedly. It appears that the World Congress Declaration made the attempt to be gender-equal.

As might be expected, all contemporary international legal instruments (including declarations and resolutions) that impinge upon the situation of the child make reference to the Convention on the Rights of the Child. The Convention is at the base of all movements to protect the girl child and it is providing a solid foundation for protecting her rights in the future. New child rights treaties continue to be developed, but they all refer back to the Convention. There are two new Optional Protocols to the Convention on the Rights of the Child: the draft Optional Protocol to the Convention on the Rights of the Child on Involvement of Children in Armed Conflict and the draft Optional Protocol to the Convention on the Rights of the Child on the Sale of Children, Child Prostitution and Child Pornography.[230] While neither of these treaties specifically mentions the *girl child*, their relationship to the Convention on the Rights of the Child makes all of its protections applicable and, significantly, three new treaties avoid the use of masculine singular possessive pronouns by confining the text to gender neutral words like "the child," "children," or the plural possessive pronoun "they." On the other hand, the International Labour Organization's most recent child labor treaty, the Worst Forms of Child Labour Convention (C182), does single out the girl child for special protection. In Article

---

226. A follow-up World Summit for Children is to be convened in 2001 and "Women 2000: Gender Equality, Development and Peace for the Twenty-First Century" was held June 5–9, 2000, in New York. *See* U.N. Doc. E/CN.4/2000/L.62 (Apr. 17, 2000).

227. It has spawned a number of national child sex exploitation conferences, as well as adding support to the work of the Special Rapporteur and drafters of the new Optional Protocol. *See infra* note 230 at Annex B.

228. The letters ECPAT stand for End Child Prostitution in Asian Tourism.

229. Both Rädda Barnen and the International Catholic Child Bureau are members of the NGO Group. For further information about the activities of the NGO Group for the Convention on the Rights of the Child and their actions regarding sexual exploitation of children, the NGO Group may be contacted at:<dci-hq@pingnet.ch>.

230. *See* U.N. Doc. E/CN.4/2000/L.62 (Apr. 17, 2000), Annexes I and II.

7 (dealing with implementation and enforcement), ILO ratifying Members are required to "take account of the special situation of girls."[231]

There appears to be no retreat in the worldwide movement to support and implement the rights of the child, and indeed there is express action to improve the lot of the girl child. Given the current state of world affairs, prospects for the future of the girl child have never been better.

---

231. *See* International Labour Organization, Worst Forms of Child Labour Convention (C182) (1999) at art. 7 ¶ (e).

THE PROTECTION OF WOMEN REFUGEES

Carolyn Patty Blum & Nancy Kelly

I never realized how strong I am. My life has not been how I thought it would be. Things I could never have imagined I have survived. . . . After everything I have been through, I know I can face anything, I can do anything. . . .

Woman Refugee[1]

INTRODUCTION

As the development of standards for the protection of the human rights of women has progressed, so has the recognition of the need to address seriously the protection of women refugees.[2] With increasing pressure from women's rights, human rights, and refugee advocacy groups, the United Nations High Commissioner for Refugees (UNHCR), the European Parliament, and the governments of several countries, including Australia, Canada, the United Kingdom, Germany, the United States, and New Zealand, have begun to recognize that women who face gender-specific forms of persecution or persecution inflicted because of gender should be granted protection under the United Nations Convention on the Status of Refugees.[3] Thus, the growing recognition, in the refugee context, of violence directed specifically against women mirrors a similar movement, within the human rights framework, to protect women from the same forms of persecution.

These developments seek to remedy long-standing problems in both asylum and human rights law. Both of these areas of law traditionally have privileged male-dominated public activities over the activities of women which take place, to a large extent, in the private sphere.[4]

---

1. DEPARTMENT OF LABOUR, NEW ZEALAND IMMIGRATION SERVICE, REFUGEE WOMEN: THE NEW ZEALAND REFUGEE QUOTA PROGRAMME 38 (1994) [hereinafter NEW ZEALAND IMMIGRATION SERVICE].

2. A rich literature on women refugees exists. For a good bibliographic reference, *see* WOMEN REFUGEES IN INTERNATIONAL PERSPECTIVES, 1980–1990, AN ANNOTATED BIBLIOGRAPHY (Gertrud Neuwirth & Christine Vincent eds., 1997). *See also Select Bibliography*, 14 REFUGEE SURVEY Q. (1995) (Special Issue on Refugee Women) [hereinafter REFUGEE Q. SPECIAL ISSUE]. For a good introductory overview, *see* SUSAN FORBES MARTIN, REFUGEE WOMEN (1991).

3. *See infra* notes 11–15 and accompanying text.

4. For example, persecution in retaliation for overt expression of political opinion through traditional methods, such as involvement in political parties and organizations or participation in military actions, has universally been regarded as a basis for political asylum, while less traditional means of political expression, such as refusal to abide by discriminatory laws or to follow gender-based rules of conduct dictated by culture or religious interpretation, have often been categorized as personal preference. *See* UNHCR Division of International Protection, *Gender-*

Women throughout the world are subjected to violence at the hands of their governments, their communities, and their families. They are beaten for speaking out, for failing to conform to their assigned roles, or simply for being female. They are subjected to rape and other forms of sexual violence by government officials or soldiers because of their political activity, because of their relationships to male family members, or because officials want to undermine their role in their societies. They are subjected to harmful cultural or traditional practices with no recourse to government protection. Yet until relatively recently, such harms to women were largely dismissed as personal or private, not as matters that should be the subject of international refugee protection.[5] But it is precisely these conditions—as well as the wars, ethnic conflicts, and violations of human rights that affect both men and women—that have forced women from their homelands and which account for their comprising, with their children, 80 percent of the world's refugee population.[6]

In the refugee context, one finds a consistent lack of attention to the particular experiences of refugee women and their special needs in refugee camps and in obtaining permanent resettlement. Further, in the context of protection of women seeking permanent asylum,[7] three primary problems have arisen. First, the definition of refugee

---

Related Persecution: An Analysis of Recent Trends, INT'L J. REFUGEE L. 79–113 (1997) (Special Issue) [hereinafter REFUGEE J. SPECIAL ISSUE]; Nasreen Mahmud, *Crimes Against Honour: Women in International Refugee Law*, 9 J. REFUGEE STUD. 367 (1996); Nancy Kelly, *Gender-Related Persecution: Assessing the Asylum Claims of Women*, 26 CORNELL INT'L L.J. 625, 625–29 (1993). This same public/private distinction has served as one of the major obstacles to the achievement of women's human rights. *See* Noreen Burrows, *International Law and Human Rights: The Case of Women's Rights, in* HUMAN RIGHTS: FROM RHETORIC TO REALITY 80, 86–96 (Tom Campbell et al. eds., 1986); Riane Eisle, *Human Rights: Toward an Integrated Theory for Action*, 9 HUM. RTS. Q. 287 (1987); Charlotte Bunch, *Women's Rights as Human Rights: Towards a Re-vision of Human Rights*, 12 HUM. RTS. Q. 486 (1990); Hilary Charlesworth et al., *Feminist Approaches to International Law*, 85 AM. J. INT'L L. 613 (1991). *See also* discussion of this issue elsewhere in these volumes.

5. These volumes analyze, from a human rights perspective, these forms of violations (as well as many others) of the rights of women. This chapter will not duplicate the in-depth treatment found elsewhere in these volumes.

6. *See* Executive Committee of the High Commissioner's Programme, Sub-committee of the Whole on International Protection, *Report of the Working Group on Refugee Women and Refugee Children*, 24th mtg., U.N. Doc. EC/SCP/85, at para. 3 (1994) [hereinafter *1994 Working Group Report*]; Deborah Anker et al., *Women Whose Governments Are Unable or Unwilling to Provide Reasonable Protection From Domestic Violence May Qualify as Refugees Under United States Asylum Law*, 11 GEO. IMM. L.J. 709, 716 n.28 (citing a variety of sources). The proportion of women or children may rise to ninety percent in some situations, where fathers, sons, and husbands have been killed, taken prisoner, or forcibly recruited as combatants. *See* DEPARTMENT OF PUBLIC INFORMATION, FOCUS ON WOMEN, REFUGEE WOMEN, U.N. Doc. DPI/1691/Wom–95–13598 (1995) (prepared for the Fourth World Conference on Women in Beijing) [hereinafter FOCUS ON WOMEN].

7. This chapter uses both the terminology "refugee" as well as the terminology "asylum-seeker." For purposes of the discussion here, the term "refugee" will be used, in the broadest sense, to refer to women uprooted forcibly from their countries of origin due to war, civil conflict, human rights abuses, or other abusive circumstances. "Refugee" also may be used more narrowly to define a refugee within the meaning of the Refugee Convention. *See infra* notes 11–15 and

contained in the Refugee Convention[8] does not provide specifically for protection from harm inflicted because of gender. Second, interpretations of the international refugee definition have developed principally through the adjudication of male claims and, therefore, primarily incorporate the realities faced by male applicants; to a large degree, then, these decisions are not relevant to the situations faced by female applicants. Third, the procedures traditionally applied in adjudicating asylum claims have not taken into account the particular circumstances and difficulties faced by female applicants in presenting their claims. As a result, assessments of the situation of the individual female applicant often are inaccurate.

This chapter first presents a survey of international efforts to acknowledge and address the special concerns of women refugees and to re-interpret the scope of international refugee protections. Next, the chapter analyzes domestic application of protections for women asylum-seekers in the United States and Canada.[9] This chapter is intended to catalog and analyze essential international and domestic law on the protection of women refugees.

INTERNATIONAL PROTECTION

> Obtaining adequate protection in international law [for women refugees] has been a slow and difficult process.
>
> Sadako Ogata, United Nations High Commissioner for Refugees[10]

Basic Standards: The International Definition of Refugee

The international standards for protection of refugees generally are derived, in large part, from the 1951 United Nations Convention Relating to the Status of

---

accompanying text. The term "asylum-seeker" will be used, in a narrower sense, to refer to a woman who is seeking permanent asylum in a receiving country and presents herself for a formal adjudication of that status. This is sometimes referred to as "asylum procedures" or as "refugee status determination procedures" in the literature. This chapter will address the international law norms affecting both sets of women. The domestic law discussion focuses on the claims of asylum-seekers.

8.   *See infra* text accompanying notes 11–15.

9.   The authors have chosen to focus on Canada and the United States for a number of reasons. First, these are the countries with which we are most conversant and therefore which we feel we could offer the most useful analysis. Second, they are the first two countries to directly address the situation of women asylum-seekers by adopting formal guidelines for the adjudication of women's claims. Third, each country now has an emerging body of jurisprudence of significant interpretive value. This choice in no way reflects any judgement about the progress of other nations around the world to develop mechanisms to protect women refugees and asylum-seekers. For an excellent overview of developments in other countries, *see* REFUGEE J. SPECIAL ISSUE, *supra* note 4, at 33–75, and EUROPE AND REFUGEES: A CHALLENGE? (Jean-Yves Carlier & Dirk Vanheule eds., 1997). For developments in New Zealand, *see* Rodger Haines, *Gender-Based Persecution: New Zealand Jurisprudence*, REFUGEE J. SPECIAL ISSUE, *supra* note 4, at 129–58, and NEW ZEALAND IMMIGRATION SERVICE, *supra* note 1. For developments in Australia, *see* DEPARTMENT OF IMMIGRATION AND MULTICULTURAL AFFAIRS, GUIDELINES ON GENDER ISSUES FOR DECISION MAKERS (1996), *reprinted in* REFUGEE J. SPECIAL ISSUE, *supra* note 4, at 195–212.

10.   Sadako Ogata, *Foreword* to REFUGEE J. SPECIAL ISSUE, *supra* note 4, at 2.

Refugees (Refugee Convention)[11] and the 1967 Protocol Relating to the Status of Refugees (Refugee Protocol).[12] One of the principal purposes of the Refugee Convention and the Refugee Protocol is to define who will be considered a refugee under international law and to "define the legal status of refugees and their rights and duties in their country of refuge."[13] Under the Refugee Convention, a refugee is defined, in male-based language, as a person who:

> [a]s a result of events occurring before 1 January 1951 and owing to a well-founded fear of being persecuted for reasons of race, religion, nationality, membership in a particular social group or political opinion, is outside the country of his nationality and is unable or, owing to such fear, is unwilling to avail himself of the protection of that country; or who, not having a nationality and being outside the country of his former habitual residence as a result of such events, is unable or, owing to such fear, is unwilling to return to it.[14]

The Refugee Protocol eliminated the temporal and geographic limitations of the Refugee Convention, thus making the definition universally applicable.[15]

United Nations High Commissioner for Refugees: International Protection Agency

The Office of the United Nations High Commissioner for Refugees (UNHCR) was established in 1951.[16] Its mandate, outlined in the Statute of the Office of the High Commissioner for Refugees, states that the High Commissioner will "assume the function of providing international protection, under the auspices of the United Nations, to refugees who fall within the scope of the present Statute and of seeking permanent solutions for the problem of refugees."[17]

---

11.   Convention Relating to the Status of Refugees, *opened for signature* July 28, 1951, 19 U.S.T. 6259, 189 U.N.T.S. 150 (1954) [hereinafter Refugee Convention].

12.   Protocol Relating to the Status of Refugees, Jan. 31, 1967, 19 U.S.T. 6223, 606 U.N.T.S. 267 (1967) [hereinafter Refugee Protocol].

13.   UNITED NATIONS HIGH COMMISSIONER FOR REFUGEES, HANDBOOK ON PROCEDURES AND CRITERIA FOR DETERMINING REFUGEE STATUS UNDER THE 1951 CONVENTION AND THE 1967 PROTOCOL ON THE STATUS OF REFUGEES (1979) [hereinafter UNHCR HANDBOOK]. Over 130 states are party to either or both of these instruments. *See* U.S. COMMITTEE FOR REFUGEES, 1997 WORLD REFUGEE SURVEY 9 (1997). Individual states parties have incorporated their obligations under the Convention and the Protocol through domestic legislation. For example, the United States, which acceded to the Protocol in 1968, incorporated many of its international obligations by passing the Refugee Act of 1980, Pub. L. No. 96–212, 94 Stat. 102 (1980) (codified at 8 U.S.C. § 1101 et seq.). The refugee definition, which mirrors that of the Protocol, can be found at Immigration and Nationality Act (INA) § 101(a)(42), 8 U.S.C. § 1101(a)(42).

14.   Refugee Convention, *supra* note 11, at art. 1(A).

15.   The 1967 Protocol deleted the words "As a result of events occurring before 1 January 1951 and . . ." and the words "as a result of such events" from the definition, thus extending protection to cover new refugees whose situations result from events occurring after 1951. *See* Refugee Protocol, *supra* note 12, at art. 1(a).

16.   *See* G.A. Res. 428(V), U.N. GAOR, 5th Sess., Supp. No. 20, U.N. Doc. A/1775, Annex (1950).

17.   *The Activities and Programme of the UNHCR on Behalf of Refugee Women: Report of the Secretary-General*, World Conference to Review and Appraise the Achievements of the UN

Since its creation, the mandate has been expanded through General Assembly resolutions, and it now includes people in "refugee like situations."[18] The UNHCR has a variety of functions. It is responsible for providing material assistance to and health services, education, and employment training opportunities for refugees in emergent situations within its mandate. In this capacity, it must establish and negotiate with governments for refugee camp sites and equip these sites with makeshift shelters, food, medical supplies, and water facilities.[19] UNHCR also encourages accession by governments to the international legal instruments pertaining to refugees, encourages states to grant permanent resettlement, as needed, and establishes safeguards against the forcible return of refugees to their home countries where they fear persecution. Increasingly, UNHCR emphasizes voluntary repatriation of refugees where possible.[20]

Further, the UNHCR is recognized domestically (by courts and administrative bodies) and internationally as an authoritative source of guidance in refugee status determinations.[21] In all these endeavors, UNHCR is dependent on the voluntary contributions of governments and non-governmental organizations (NGOs) as well as private individuals.[22]

Executive Committee Conclusions Concerning Women

In exile, we women became very united, of necessity, because we did not know each other. We were 11,000 refugees all together, most of us women. It was up to us to organize and promote our needs.

Salvadoran woman refugee[23]

Decade for Women: Equality, Development and Peace, Nairobi, Kenya, July 15–26, 1985, A/Conf.116/11 (1985) (citing G.A. Res. 428(V), *supra* note 16) [hereinafter *1985 Secretary-General Report*].

18. *See generally* JAMES C. HATHAWAY, THE LAW OF REFUGEE STATUS (citing P. Maynard, *The Legal Competence of the United Nations High Commissioner for Refugees*, 31 INT'L COMP. L.Q. 415 (1982), and GERVAIS COLES, PROBLEMS ARISING FROM LARGE NUMBERS OF ASYLUM-SEEKERS: A STUDY OF PROTECTION ASPECTS 15 (1981)).

19. *See 1985 Secretary-General Report, supra* note 17, at 3.

20. *See id.*

21. The UNHCR HANDBOOK is seen as the authoritative guide to UNHCR's interpretation of the Convention and Protocol requirements. It does not have a section devoted to gender-based claims, but many of its general principles are relevant to women asylum-seekers. A number of courts and other authorities have cited the HANDBOOK as authoritative. *See, e.g,* INS v. Cardoza-Fonseca, 480 U.S. 407, 436–37 (1987); ASYLUM BRANCH, IMMIGRATION AND NATURALIZATION SERVICE, U.S. DEPART-MENT OF JUSTICE, BASIC LAW MANUAL: ASYLUM, SUMMARY AND OVERVIEW CONCERNING ASYLUM LAW (1991); IMMIGRATION AND REFUGEE BOARD, GUIDELINES ISSUED BY THE CHAIRPERSON PURSUANT TO SECTION 65(3) OF THE IMMIGRATION ACT: WOMEN REFUGEE CLAIMANTS FEARING GENDER-RELATED PERSECUTION (1993) [hereinafter CANADIAN GENDER GUIDELINES].

22. *See 1985 Secretary-General Report, supra* note 17.

23. FOCUS ON WOMEN, *supra* note 6, at 4.

Throughout the 1980s, the UNHCR Executive Committee,[24] in an atmosphere of increasing awareness of the special circumstances of refugee women, adopted a series of conclusions aimed at affording more meaningful protection to women fleeing from persecution in their home countries. Some of the Executive Committee conclusions have been aimed at addressing the need of women for protection in refugee camps and equal participation in relief programs. In addition, some of the conclusions have focused on the substantive interpretation of the Refugee Convention's definition as it relates to the refugee claims of women. This body of "conclusions" forms an important precedent, at the inter-governmental level, for setting standards and raising awareness of the special nature of refugee women's concerns. This section of the chapter will review both aspects of the Executive Committee's work.

Women Refugees

Beginning in 1985, the Executive Committee recognized the need for UNHCR and receiving governments to focus specific attention on the international protection of refugee women.[25] Subsequently, the Executive Committee continued to recognize that women occupy a particularly precarious and vulnerable situation as refugees,[26] that the participation of women refugees in programs affecting them would help ensure greater responsiveness to their needs, and that "an active senior level Steering Committee" on refugee women was needed to facilitate and strengthen existing policies and programs helping refugee women while ensuring that the various cultures of refugee women are respected.[27] In its next session, the Executive Committee, for the first time, called for the resettlement of women at risk.[28] In this effort, the Committee

---

24. The function of the Executive Committee, established in 1957 and composed of representatives of fifty governments, is to advise the High Commissioner "in the exercise of the statutory functions; and advising on the appropriateness of providing international assistance through UNHCR in order to solve such specific problems as may arise." GUY GOODWIN-GILL, THE REFUGEE IN INTERNATIONAL LAW 9 (1996) (*citing* U.N. G.A. Res. 1166 (XII) (1957) and U.N.G.A. Res. 49/171 (1994)).

25. *See* Executive Committee of the High Commissioner's Programme, *Refugee Women and International Protection*, 36th Sess., Conclusion No. 39 (XXXVI) (1985) [hereinafter Conclusion No. 39]; *see also* Executive Committee of the High Commissioner's Programme, Sub-committee of the Whole on International Protection, *Note on Refugee Women and International Protection*, U.N. Doc. EC/SCP/39 (1985). Most of the documents of the Executive Committee of the High Commissioner's Programme are reprinted in REFUGEE Q. SPECIAL ISSUE, *supra* note 2, at 181–258.

26. Executive Committee of the High Commissioner's Programme, *General Conclusions on International Protection*, 38th Sess. (1987).

27. *See* Executive Committee of the High Commissioner's Programme, *Refugee Women*, 39th Sess., Conclusion No. 54 (XXXIX) (1988); *see also* Executive Committee of the High Commissioner's Programme, Sub-committee of the Whole on International Protection, *Note on Refugee Women and International Protection*, U.N. Doc. No. EC/SCP/59, para. 1 (1990) [hereinafter *1990 Note on Refugee Women*].

28. *See* Executive Committee of the High Commissioner's Programme, *Refugee Women*, 40th Sess., Conclusion No. 60, para. (c)(XL) (1988). The Executive Committee further

"urged the High Commissioner to develop a methodology for systematically addressing gender issues in refugee programmes and, as a basis for this, requested the High

specifically sought the support of other NGOs to exchange information and to expand their own understanding of the gender implications of their work.[29]

The Executive Committee's 1990 session saw an attempt at a more comprehensive approach to women refugees. The Committee urged states and the UNHCR to undertake a number of measures to promote the safety of refugee women, including: integrating considerations specific to the protection of refugee women into assistance activities from their inception (including in planning refugee camps and settlements to deter, detect, and redress instances of physical and sexual abuse, as well as other protection concerns at the earliest possible moment); providing all refugee women and girls with effective and equitable access to basic services, including food, water, relief supplies, health, sanitation, education, and skills training; making wage-earning opportunities available to women; and providing for informed and active consent and participation of refugee women in individual decisions about long-lasting solutions.[30]

The Executive Committee also published a policy framework for future action which outlines, in substantial detail, an organizational work plan for integrating refugee women into programming and project activities.[31] The paper recognized that refugee men and women face different problems and therefore require different forms of assistance. It also advocated the integration of the resources and needs of refugee women into all aspects of programming, rather than creating special women's projects, as a means to ensure that the special needs of women are fulfilled.[32]

In its forty-first session, the Sub-committee of the Whole on International Protection[33] of the Executive Committee recommended, along with the United Nations Commission of the Status of Women,[34] the elaboration of revised internal guidelines for refugee women. After the guidelines were revised and published,[35] the Executive Committee focused increasingly on sexual exploitation and violence against refugee women. In addition, the Executive Committee emphasized that women heads of households must be protected and actively involved in decision making impacting

---

Commissioner to collect and analyze demographic, anthropological and socioeconomic information on refugee populations, in particular, data on gender roles and responsibilities to ensure that such information is used in planning UNHCR programmes."

Id.

29. *See id.* at para. (m).

30. *See* Executive Committee of the High Commissioner's Programme, *Refugee Women and International Protection*, 41st Sess., Conclusion No. 64 (XLI) (1990).

31. *See* Executive Committee of the High Commissioner's Programme, *UNHCR Policy on Refugee Women*, 41st Sess., U.N. Doc. A/AC 96/754 (1990).

32. *See id.*

33. *See 1990 Note on Refugee Women, supra* note 27.

34. *See id.* at para. 4.

35. *See generally* text accompanying notes 45–56.

their lives.[36] Again, in 1993, the Executive Committee stressed the need "to deter and redress instances of sexual violence to effectively protect asylum-seekers and refugees."[37] The Executive Committee also recommended that victims of sexual violence and their families be provided with quality medical and psychological care in culturally appropriate counseling facilities. They further reiterated the necessity of including women field staff in refugee programs.[38]

The focus now has turned to the successful implementation of the policies articulated over the years.[39] In 1994, for example, the chair's opening remarks stated that there was a gap between the UNHCR policy regarding refugee women and children and the actual practice.[40] He noted that women and children make up some 80 percent of the refugee population worldwide and emphasized that the implementation of the report's recommendations should include: that the number of female staff in the field and in protection posts be increased; that UNHCR should put women in charge of food distribution on an experimental basis and evaluate the result; that programming should address both refugee women and children's problems and needs; that the Training Section and the Division of International Protection should ensure that all UNHCR staff are educated about human rights and humanitarian laws; and that they should be trained to understand the specific ways in which these doctrines can be utilized to improve protection for refugee women and children.

Evaluating Claims of Asylum-Seekers

The Executive Committee also has focused on the substantive interpretation of the Refugee Convention's definition as applied to women asylum-seekers. For exam-

---

36.   *See generally* Executive Committee of the High Commissioner's Programme, *Note on Certain Aspects of Sexual Violence Against Refugee Women*, Doc. No. A/AC.96/822 (1993) [hereinafter *1993 Note on Sexual Violence*]; REFUGEE Q. SPECIAL ISSUE, *supra* note 2, at 202 n.2 (citing numerous Executive Committee publications dealing with sexual violence, including the 1985 Note on Refugee Women and International Protection, U.N. Doc. EC/SCP/39); the 1988 Note on Refugee Women, U.N. Doc. A/AC.96/XXXIX/CRP.1; the 1989 Report on Refugee Women U.N. Doc. A/AC.96/727; the Office's Policy on Refugee Women, U.N. Doc. A/AC.96/754; the 1991 Guidelines commended by the Executive Committee the same year; and the 1992 Progress Report on the Implementation of the Guidelines, U.N. Doc. EC/SCP/74). *See also infra* text accompanying notes 79–121.

37.   Executive Committee of the High Commissioner's Programme, *Refugee Protection and Sexual Violence*, Conclusion No. 73 (XLIV) (1993) [hereinafter Conclusion No. 73].

38.   *See id.* at para. (h).

39.   *See* Executive Committee of the High Commissioner's Programme, Sub-committee on Administrative and Financial Matters, *Refugee Women: Achievements and Challenges*, 46th Sess., 35th mtg., U.N. Doc. EC/SC.2/77 (1995); Executive Committee of the High Commissioner's Programme, Sub-committee of the Whole on International Protection, *Report of the Working Group on Refugee Women and Refugee Children*, U.N. Doc. No. EC/SCP/85 (1994) [hereinafter *1994 Report on Women and Children*].

40.   *See 1994 Report on Women and Children*, *supra* note 39, at para. 2. Similar concerns have been raised by non-governmental organizations as well. *See, e.g*, AFRICA WATCH & WOMEN'S RIGHTS WATCH, HUMAN RIGHTS WATCH, SEEKING REFUGE, FINDING TERROR: THE WIDESPREAD RAPE OF SOMALI WOMEN REFUGEES IN NORTH EASTERN KENYA 3, 19–21 (1993).

ple, in 1985, the Executive Committee recognized that "[s]tates, in the exercise of their sovereignty, are free to adopt the interpretation that women asylum-seekers who face harsh or inhumane treatment due to their having transgressed the social mores of the society in which they live may be considered as a 'particular social group' within the meaning of Article 1 A(2) of the 1951 United Nations Refugee Convention."[41]

The Executive Committee has expressed its support for "the recognition of persons whose claim to refugee status is based upon a well-founded fear of persecution, through sexual violence, for reasons of race, religion, nationality, membership in a particular social group or political opinion."[42] The Executive Committee called upon states and the UNHCR to ensure that women have equal access to the refugee status determination process. They also recommended that victims of sexual violence and their families be provided with good medical and psychological care in culturally appropriate counseling facilities.[43]

Guidelines on Refugee Women

> I thought for a long time about whether I should talk to you about all the bad things that happened to me—the attacks, the rapes, seeing my husband die, and my children suffering. It is difficult. . . . In the end, I decided to tell what happened. That is because, although it is terrible to talk of such experiences, I think, in some ways, it is more terrible for people not to know that these things are happening.
>
> Woman Refugee[44]

In 1991, the UNHCR published its *Guidelines on the Protection of Refugee Women* in order to help UNHCR staff respond to issues, problems, and risks refugee women face.[45] These *Guidelines* outline responses to refugee women who were victims of physical and sexual attacks during their flight or in the receiving country.[46]

---

41. Conclusion No. 39, *supra* note 25, at para. (k). *See generally* Anders Johnsson, *The International Protection of Women Refugees: A Summary of Principal Problems and Issues*, 1 INT'L. J. REFUGEE L. 221 (1989). A similar resolution was adopted by the European Parliament in 1984. *See* Felicite Stairs & Lori Pope, *No Place Like Home: Assaulted Migrant Women's Claims to Refugee Status and Landings on Humanitarian and Compassionate Grounds*, 6 J. L. & SOC. POLICY 148, 167 (1990).

42. Conclusion No. 73, *supra* note 37, at para. (d). Noting the need for particular sensitivity in dealing with asylum-seekers who have suffered sexual violence, the Executive Committee also recommended the establishment by states of training programs designed to ensure that those involved in the refugee status determination process are adequately sensitized to issues of gender and culture, *see id.* at para. (j), and the development by states of "appropriate guidelines on women asylum-seekers, in recognition of the fact that women refugees often experience persecution differently from refugee men." *Id.* at para. (e).

43. *See id.* at para. (f). *See generally 1993 Note on Sexual Violence, supra* note 36.

44. NEW ZEALAND IMMIGRATION SERVICE, *supra* note 1, at 60.

45. *See* UNHCR, GUIDELINES ON PROTECTION OF REFUGEE WOMEN (1991) [hereinafter UNHCR GUIDELINES ON REFUGEE WOMEN] ("International protection goes beyond adherence to legal principles. Equally important, the protection of refugee women requires planning . . . and enforcing priorities that support their well-being.").

46. *See id.* at paras. 30–52.

The *Guidelines* urge that the physical design and location of refugee camps be altered in order to increase security. They suggest using security patrols and diminishing the use of closed detention centers.[47] In addition, they support employing women staff to work with refugee women and to help identify issues of concern to women. They also suggest that refugee women be educated about their rights[48] and priority be given to assess the protection needs of unaccompanied refugee women. Finally, the *Guidelines* recommend that women have direct access to food and any other services that are offered.[49]

The *UNHCR Guidelines* also contain a number of important provisions regarding a gender-sensitive interpretation of the standard for determining refugee status. First, they address situations in which persecution inflicted because of gender or a factor related to gender may constitute persecution on account of one of the five grounds enumerated in the Refugee Convention's definition. They reiterate the Executive Committee's 1985 Conclusion that women who face harsh or inhumane treatment because of having transgressed their society's laws or customs regarding the role of women may be granted refugee protection as part of a particular social group.[50] They also note that many women flee their countries because of severe discrimination by governmental bodies or by their communities, and that, under certain circumstances, such discrimination may constitute persecution under the Refugee Convention.[51] In addition, the *UNHCR Guidelines* address the difficulty faced by many women who have been subjected to rape by military personnel in establishing that they are victims of political persecution rather than random violence, particularly when they have been victimized because of the political activities of a male relative.[52]

Next, the *UNHCR Guidelines* address gender-specific types of persecution inflicted on women:

> Persecution of women often takes the form of sexual assault. The methods of torture can consist of rape, the use of electric currents upon the sexual organs; mechanical stimulation of the erogenous zones; the insertion of objects into the body-openings (with objects made of metal or other material to which an electrical current is later connected); the forced witnessing of unnatural sexual relations; forced masturbation or to be masturbated by others; fellatio and oral coitus; and finally, a general atmosphere of sexual aggression and threats of the loss of the ability to reproduce and enjoyment of sexual relations in the future.[53]

The *Guidelines* then detail numerous problems faced by women in the asylum adjudication process which interfere with the ability to obtain a meaningful deter-

---

47.   *See id.* at paras. 79–81.

48.   *See id.* at paras. 103–110

49.   *See id.* at paras. 82–102.

50.   *See id.* at para. 54.

51.   *See id.* at para. 55.

52.   *See id.* at para. 56.

53.   *Id.* at para. 59.

mination of claims. These problems include: consideration of a woman's application as part of a family unit rather than giving independent consideration to a woman's individual claim; requiring a woman to provide testimony concerning emotionally painful issues such as sexual torture, particularly when discussing such experiences can cause further isolation of the women from her family or her community; requiring a woman to provide testimony concerning the experiences and activities of male family members when she may not be privy to such information; and granting less than full refugee status to a woman who is considered a derivative beneficiary under a claim presented by her spouse.[54]

Finally, the UNHCR Guidelines make recommendations to increase the likelihood of a fair adjudication of women's claims. These recommendations include a number of procedural considerations, such as recruitment of female interpreters and training of interviewers on gender-sensitive interviewing techniques.[55] They also include a substantive analysis which incorporates "the principle that women fearing persecution or severe discrimination on the basis of their gender should be considered a member of a social group for the purposes of determining refugee status" and that "others may be seen as having made a religious or political statement in transgressing the social norms of their society."[56]

Special Issues

Refugee Camps

> While I stayed in the refugee camp for years, they gave not enough food for my four children and for me. Always it was the men who got the best of everything. If someone gave me anything, because the men were stronger, they would push and fight me and take it from me, so I was afraid to take anything, even for my children. That is how it is for a woman who has no husband.
>
> Woman Refugee[57]

Women and girls are among the most vulnerable in refugee camps. They not only must contend with carrying out their traditional roles as food preparers, water and wood gatherers, and child care providers, but they must attempt to maintain the family's sense of cohesion, well-being, and cultural values in what is usually an alien environment.[58] Women and children face a myriad of risks in the refugee camp environment.[59] UNHCR states:

---

54.   *See id.* at paras. 60–62.

55.   *See id.* at para. 72.

56.   *Id.* at para. 71.

57.   New Zealand Immigration Service, *supra* note 1, at 60.

58.   *See 1985 Secretary-General Report, supra* note 17, at 7; Genevieve Camus-Jacques, *Refugee Women: The Forgotten Majority, in* Refugees and International Relations 151 (Gil Loescher & Laila Monahan eds., 1989); Martin, *supra* note 2, at 33.

59.   For an excellent case study, see Dodo Thandiwe Motsisi, *Elderly Mozambican Women Refugees in The Tongogara Refugee Camp in Zimbabwe: A Case Study*, 14 Refuge 7 (1995).

> Social justice would require that women and children had first access to the limited resources; yet in many cases, assistance tends to reach them last. Thus, while some problems are common to all refugees, the social and physical vulnerability of women makes them more likely to bear the brunt of deprivation, discrimination and abuse in situations of hardship.[60]

One major deterrent to change is that many women refugees simply do not have the time in their daily lives, consumed as they are with subsistence, to obtain instruction, receive medical attention (if it is available), or to be trained to receive skills that would decrease health and other risks of camp life.[61]

Women and girl refugees are more susceptible than men to hunger and hunger-related illnesses. Inequity in food distribution still prevails. These inequities lead to high death rates in infants and mothers in refugee populations.[62] Rarely is provision made for recognizing that many refugee women are the heads of households.[63] For example, during the Afghani war, widows in Pakistani refugee camps were starving for weeks due to a food distribution system that favored men, at the expense of the women.[64] In general, refugee women alone are responsible for caring for children. Consequently, if they are ill or undernourished, their children suffer.[65] In addition, if a woman is malnourished, the chances of her dying during childbirth are very high.[66] Most pressing is the need for access to safe drinking water and sanitary facilities.[67] In refugee camps, because refugee women are responsible for collecting the water, they are more likely to get water-borne diseases. Dirty water leads to typhoid, cholera, dysentery, and infectious hepatitis. Further, women refugees can become contami-

---

60. NEW ZEALAND IMMIGRATION SERVICE, *supra* note 1, at 10.

61. *See 1985 Secretary-General Report, supra* note 17, at 7. Diana Quick notes that women in camps in Goma, Zaire had to walk up to seventeen miles, without water, food, or shoes, to food distribution points and then had to wait in line for hours, or even overnight, for food, water, or shelter materials. *See* Diana Quick, *Refugee Women: In Special Need of Protection*, ISSUE 22, REFUGEE PARTICIPATION NETWORK 15 (1996).

62. *See* MARTIN, *supra* note 2, at 35 ("the predominance of male-dominated food distribution [in refugee camps] is clearly at odds with traditional patterns in which women play a lead role in food production"); *see also* J. Olaka-Onyango, *The Plight of the Larger Half: Human Rights Gender Violence and the Legal Status of Refugee and Internally Displaced Women in Africa*, 24 DENV. J. INT'L L. & POL'Y 349, 383 (citing Tina Wallace, *Taking the Lion by the Whiskers: Building on the Strengths of Refugee Women*, *in* CHANGING PERCEPTIONS: WRITINGS ON GENDER AND DEVELOPMENT 62 (T. Wallace & C. March eds., 1991)); Keiko Osaki, *When Refugees Are Women: Emergence of the Issue on the International Agenda*, 16 REFUGE 9, 15 (1997); Quick, *supra* note 61, at 15.

63. *See* MARTIN, *supra* note 2, at 35–37.

64. *See* Sima Wali, *Human Rights for Refugee and Displaced Women*, *in* WOMEN'S RIGHTS, HUMAN RIGHTS: INTERNATIONAL FEMINIST PERSPECTIVES 339 (Julie Peters & Andrea Wolper eds., 1995).

65. *See* MARTIN, *supra* note 2, at 38. Martin notes that poor nutrition leads to lack of lactation; thus, women with babies are dependent on the use of distributed milk powder. However, the milk powder is mixed with the only available water, which is usually unclean, adding to the risk of illness for the baby. *Id.* at 37–38.

66. *See id.* at 38.

67. *See 1990 Note on Refugee Women, supra* note 27, at para. 36.

nated with sleeping sickness, malaria, yellow fever, and river blindness through insects breeding in nearby water.[68] In addition, refugee women are last to obtain medical attention, and are usually the first to starve to death. Women are supposed to forgo their own needs for the political and religious requirements of the male hierarchy. Western aid workers may perpetuate this problem by granting assistance and protection to male refugees, justifying their actions by claiming that it is "culturally appropriate."[69]

Women refugees often assume, for the first time, full economic responsibility for their families. Stress is increased because of such factors as inability to provide guidance to children in a new cultural environment, lack of marketable skills, and marital conflict owing to role changes.[70]

While women refugees require education and vocational training in order to become independent,[71] most of the projects established in the camps tend to be in the health field or are labeled "women's projects."[72] Often these projects are marginal economic activities, or they have excessive administrative costs or inadequate funding. Refugee women rarely are participants in the bigger projects that focus on infrastructure development or agricultural activities. Further, few of these projects lead to long-term self-sufficiency for women.[73] For example, in refugee camps in Southeast Asia, women were offered little training or education. The majority of the women were illiterate, and more men than women had jobs with NGOs in the camps and were recipients of training and education.[74]

Understanding the cultural and economic background of women in refugee camps assists in developing skills and training activities geared to the background of those particular women. Training projects that can correspond to women refugee's needs and the demands of the local host economy also tend to facilitate economic integration post-repatriation.[75] UNHCR and other organizations increasingly have recognized the necessity of inclusion of women in all stages of planning and implementation of skills training and projects for self-sufficiency.[76] The active involvement

---

68. *See id.* at paras. 35, 38; MARTIN, *supra* note 2, at 38; Osaki, *supra* note 62, at 15.

69. Wali, *supra* note 64, at 337. Many women also have health problems as the result of female genital mutilation. *See* MARTIN, *supra* note 2, at 38–39. Additionally, mental health services, to deal with depression or post-traumatic stress disorder, likely outcomes of torture, sexual abuse, or the many dislocations of women refugees' lives, are severely lacking. *See id.* at 39–40.

70. *See 1985 Secretary-General Report supra* note 17, at 10.

71. *See* MARTIN, *supra* note 2, at 51; *1990 Note on Refugee Women, supra* note 27, at paras. 47–53.

72. *1990 Note on Refugee Women, supra* note 27, at para. 50.

73. *See id.* at paras. 51–53; Quick, *supra* note 61, at 16; Osaki, *supra* note 62, at 15.

74. *See* Kate Haovresen, *Refugee Women and Repatriation: Perspectives from Southeast Asia,* 14 REFUGE 4 (1995).

75. *See* Motsisi, *supra* note 59, at 11.

76. *See 1990 Note on Refugee Women, supra* note 27, at para. 52; MARTIN, *supra* note 2, at 57–63.

of women refugees in all aspects of implementing humanitarian assistance within the camps is crucial, both to achieve aid objectives and as a means of empowering women.[77]

Sexual Violence

> In my culture when a woman is raped, it is almost like she is dead. She no longer has a life. She is "dirty," like "damaged goods," and no man will want her for a wife. And it is not only her shame, but the shame and dishonour of her family and her community.
>
> Woman Refugee[78]

In 1995, the UNHCR issued its *Guidelines on Sexual Violence Against Refugees.*[79] These *Guidelines* contain valuable information concerning the nature of sexual violence,[80] its effect on refugee women and the measures that can be taken to protect refugee women from sexual violence and exploitation.

The *UNHCR Guidelines on Sexual Violence* contextualize the reality of sexual violence against refugees.[81] Women refugees are raped for a number of reasons.[82] The motivation for sexual violence most frequently is a desire for power and domination. The objective is to control and humiliate the victim, violating her innermost physical and mental integrity.[83] During internal conflict, violence can occur prior to flight. Male leaders sometimes barter women or girls for ammunition or

---

77.　*See* Camus-Jacques, *supra* note 58, at 155. Camus-Jacques delineates an approach that "not only ensures equal access to facilities but also . . . increase[s] participation in community-level organizations." *Id.* at 153. *See also id.* at 152–55; Quick, *supra* note 61, at 16 ("Women should not be thought of solely as the beneficiaries of humanitarian assistance programmes. They must also fully participate in their design and implementation.").

78.　New Zealand Immigration Service, *supra* note 1, at 60.

79.　UNHCR, Sexual Violence Against Refugees: Guidelines on Prevention and Response (1995) [hereinafter UNHCR Guidelines on Sexual Violence]. *See also* Executive Committee of the High Commissioner's Programme, *Note on Certain Aspects of Sexual Violence Against Refugee Women*, 44th Sess. (1993) [hereinafter *Note on Sexual Violence*] (investigating sexual abuse of refugee women and girls in light of UNHCR's background in the subject, the implications for prevention and remedial action along with durable solutions and suggestions for specific measures upon which states and the UNHCR could embark to eliminate this problem, including enforcing relevant national laws, state compliance with international human rights and humanitarian law, and implementation of Executive Committee Conclusion, General Assembly resolution, and the *UNHCR Guidelines on the Protection of Refugee Women*).

80.　The *UNHCR Guidelines on Sexual Violence* define sexual violence as including, but not limited to, rape, insertions of objections into the genital or anal openings, oral and anal sex, attempted rape, threat of force in order to have sexual acts performed by a third person, molestation. *See id.* at 1.

81.　*See id.* at 4–10.

82.　*See* Human Rights Watch, The Human Rights Watch Global Report on Women's Human Rights 101, 102 (1995) ("Rape and other forms of sexual assault are frequently gender-specific not only in their form but also in their motivation. Thus, refugee and displaced women and girls are raped because of their gender, irrespective of their age, ethnicity or political beliefs.").

83.　*See* UNHCR Guidelines on Sexual Violence, *supra* note 79, at 1.

other necessities.[84] Women are particularly vulnerable as refugees during flight or in their country of asylum.[85]

Sometimes, the reasons for the rape of refugee women are political in character: for example, rape may be intended to degrade an entire ethnic or political group.[86] Indeed, "[r]ape is directed not only toward women, but toward the ethnic group to which a particular woman belongs. Ethnic affiliation determines who will be victimized, while gender determines the kind of violence that will be perpetrated."[87] Women are frequently used as tools in political bargaining or in resolving issues with enemies in their home countries.[88] It has even been reported that refugee women may be required to bear children in order to replenish male populations killed during war.[89]

Women in Refugee Camps

Women who are victims of sexual violence are often violated by those assigned to protect them, such as border and military guards and camp administrators.[90] Women who are alone or who are heads of households are most vulnerable to sexual violence.[91] Women in refugee camps who are relatively economically successful or materially privileged are often targeted. Local populations may participate in the sexual violence in response to the consequences of the refugee presence in their home country, such as fear of crime or degradation of the environment and depletion of natural resources.[92]

Women and girls in refugee camps may be accosted for sexual favors in exchange for assistance.[93] For example, men are often responsible for distributing food or goods in refugee camps, thereby potentially exposing women to the risk of sexual coercion to obtain necessities.[94] Attacks also can occur while women are working in daily activities in isolated areas, such as when washing or cleaning in rivers or streams, when gathering wood, or when traveling to and from remote areas. They frequently occur at night in women's homes in front of their family members.[95] Women and girl refugees

---

84. *See id.* at 3.

85. *See* MARTIN, *supra* note 2, at 16. See examples described in Camus-Jacques, *supra* note 58, 145–46.

86. *See* Oloka-Onyango, *supra* note 62, at 384; Jadranka Cacic-Kumpes, *War, Ethnicity, and Violence Against Women*, 14 REFUGE 12 (1995); Catherine A. MacKinnon, *Rape, Genocide, and Women's Human Rights*, 17 HARV. WOMEN'S L.J. 5 (1994).

87. Cacic-Kumpes, *supra* note 86, at 12.

88. *See* Wali, *supra* note 64, at 337.

89. *See id. See also* Cacic-Kumpes, *supra* note 86.

90. *See* Wali, *supra* note 64, at 338; Quick, *supra* note 61, at 15.

91. *See* UNHCR GUIDELINES ON SEXUAL VIOLENCE, *supra* note 79, at 2, 8.

92. *See id.* at 7.

93. *See* Quick, *supra* note 61, at 15; Johnsson, *supra* note 41, at 226.

94. *See* UNHCR GUIDELINES ON SEXUAL VIOLENCE, *supra* note 79, at 9.

95. *See id.* at 3; Wali, *supra* note 64, at 338.

may experience sexual violence during repatriation operations or during reintegration phases.[96]

Refugee women lacking proper personal documentation are also prone to sexual violence. Often the male members of the family are designated as the heads of the household and therefore, they are given the identification documents.[97] Prevailing male attitudes of disrespect toward or contempt of single women may incite sexual violence towards refugee women in refugee camps, as they view the women as common sexual property.[98] Other refugees may also commit rapes against refugee women. The uprooting from their homes and culture often means leaving behind norms or taboos that would have inhibited sexual violence against women. Often men feel powerless upon becoming refugees and express this feeling through sexual violence towards those more vulnerable—women and girls.[99] Male refugees also are in a situation in which they cannot assume normal cultural, social and economic roles and therefore feel worthless and dejected. In response, they may behave in a sexually violent manner towards the women in their homes.[100]

Some of the injuries refugee women suffer as a result of sexual violence include HIV infection, sexually transmitted disease, miscarriages by women raped when pregnant, abortion, hemorrhaging for long periods, inability to control urination, sleeplessness, nightmares, chest and back pains, and painful menstruation.[101] In addition, when women and girls have been subject to extreme forms of female genital mutilation, they can suffer severe injuries if their genitalia are reopened by a knife or by the force of penetration itself.[102]

Psychological trauma often occurs regardless of the degree of physical injury.[103] Women regularly feel paralyzed with fear and experience both physical and emotional pain. Common symptoms include self-hatred, powerlessness, worthlessness, apathy, and inability to perform daily functions. Some women experience deep depression leading to "chronic mental disorders, suicide, self-termination of pregnancy, endangering their lives, or abandonment of their babies."[104]

Refugee women seldom report their sexual victimization. Therefore, accurate statistics on the frequency of sexual violence perpetrated on women refugees are

---

96. *See* UNHCR GUIDELINES ON SEXUAL VIOLENCE, *supra* note 79, at 4.

97. *See id.* at 8–9.

98. *See id.* at 8.

99. *See* HUMAN RIGHTS WATCH, *supra* note 82, at 102.

100. *See* UNHCR GUIDELINES ON SEXUAL VIOLENCE, *supra* note 79; MARTIN, *supra* note 2, at 21.

101. *See* HUMAN RIGHTS WATCH, *supra* note 82, at 102; UNHCR GUIDELINES ON SEXUAL VIOLENCE, *supra* note 79, at 6.

102. *See* UNHCR GUIDELINES ON SEXUAL VIOLENCE, *supra* note 79, at 6.

103. *See id.* at 6, 45–46.

104. *Id.* at 6.

largely unavailable.[105] One main reason for underreporting is that in most cultures, sexual attacks are viewed as embarrassing and shameful for the victim and her family, and survivors become wrongfully stigmatized. Loss of virginity may bring shame to the entire family. Consequently, female victims of sexual violence are often ostracized by their communities and unable to marry or stay married. Some cultures consider the woman responsible for the sexual violence inflicted upon her, and she may be subject to severe punishment. Therefore, not only are women the victims of devastating physical, emotional, intellectual, and psychological violence, but they also face stigmatization and alienation by their own families and communities.[106] As a result, refugee women survivors of sexual abuse are unlikely to seek medical help or to contact the authorities.[107] Relief workers too often focus on the traumatic experience rather than on the discriminatory social and cultural norms that allow the practices to continue.[108]

Camp design and location may increase the likelihood of sexual violence, particularly if the camp is isolated from the local population. Overcrowding can lead to enemies being placed adjacent to one another within the same refugee camp, increasing the risk of sexual violence.[109] In addition, security problems can arise if gathering areas, latrines, and washing facilities are at a distance from the living quarters.[110] Poorly lit camps also increase the danger for women at night, particularly when refugees must travel far to reach food, water, and fuel distribution points. There are also usually no locks on sleeping quarters and washing areas.[111] The absence or lack of access to the UNHCR or other NGOs also can lead to greater insecurity in a refugee camp.[112]

The *UNHCR Guidelines on Sexual Violence* recommend a number of ways to diminish the risk of sexual violence. The emphasis of the *Guidelines* is on preventive measures.[113] These include: increasing law enforcement officials in border areas; training military units; enhancing the awareness of the refugee community itself; establishing security patrols in camps; improving lighting and other camp design elements; and acting quickly to resettle women particularly exposed to physical violence and abuse.[114]

---

105. *See id.* at 4; Osaki, *supra* note 62, at 15.

106. *See* UNHCR GUIDELINES ON SEXUAL VIOLENCE, *supra* note 79, at 4–5; Wali, *supra* note 64, at 338.

107. *See* HUMAN RIGHTS WATCH, *supra* note 82, at 103.

108. *See* Wali, *supra* note 64, at 338.

109. *See* UNHCR GUIDELINES ON SEXUAL VIOLENCE, *supra* note 79, at 9.

110. *See* MARTIN, *supra* note 2, at 21; Quick, *supra* note 61, at 15.

111. *See* UNHCR GUIDELINES ON SEXUAL VIOLENCE, *supra* note 79, at 9.

112. *See id.*

113. *See id.* at 11–27.

114. *See id.; see also* Johnsson, *supra* note 41, at 228. Johnsson points out that measures to protect refugee women can only really succeed in a generally more hospitable climate for refugees. *Id.*

Although these *Guidelines* improve refugee protection, they have been inconsistently implemented. Further, protection for refugee women is contingent on the degree of equality accorded to women in a receiving country. More equitable treatment from the authorities and better treatment from other members of the refugee community can be expected in those countries with greater women's rights.[115]

Legal Analysis Relevant to Asylum Claims of Women Subject to Sexual Violence

The *UNHCR Guidelines on Sexual Violence* also contain legal analyses for evaluating a claim to refugee status based on sexual violence and procedural considerations that might facilitate an interview of a woman who had been subjected to sexual violence.

With regard to refugee status determination, the *UNHCR Guidelines on Sexual Violence* provide that "when rape or other forms of sexual violence are committed for reasons of race, religion, nationality or membership in a particular social group or political opinion, it may be considered persecution if it is 'knowingly tolerated' by the authorities, or if the authorities refuse, or prove unable, to offer effective protection."[116] A claim to refugee status may be based on a well-founded fear of sexual violence in such circumstances.[117] Even when an applicant does not have a well-founded fear of future sexual abuse, a past experience of rape or sexual abuse may be so severe that it nonetheless constitutes a compelling reason for not applying the cessation clauses of the Convention.[118] In addition, in some circumstances, a survivor of rape or other forms of sexual violence may face additional human rights violations if she returns to her country. For example, she may be banished from her family or her community, or she may be forced to marry her attacker or to become a prostitute. In such cases, the *Guidelines* indicate that the applicant may be considered a refugee *sur place*.[119]

The *UNHCR Guidelines on Sexual Violence* also contain detailed instructions concerning interviewing a woman who has been the victim of sexual violence.[120] They stress the importance of honoring a woman's desire for confidentiality, guarding against actions during the interview which would re-traumatize the victim, properly

---

115. *See* Johnsson, *supra* note 41, at 228.

116. UNHCR GUIDELINES ON SEXUAL VIOLENCE, *supra* note 79, at 67.

117. *See id.* at 68.

118. *See id.* Ordinarily, once the conditions giving rise to the fear of persecution have ceased, a refugee should avail herself of the protection of her home country. However, if there are "compelling reasons arising out of previous persecution" for the refugee to refuse to return, she may continue to be afforded protection outside her country of nationality. Art. 1(C)(5), Refugee Convention, *supra* note 11.

119. *See id.; see also* UNHCR HANDBOOK, *supra* note 13, at paras. 94–96 ("A person who was not a refugee when he left his country, but who becomes a refugee at a later date, is called a refugee 'sur place.'").

120. *See* UNHCR GUIDELINES ON SEXUAL VIOLENCE, *supra* note 79, at 38–41.

using an interpreter, and conducting the interview in a setting that is appropriate and sensitive.[121]

International Human Rights

It is now widely recognized that a determination of which harms constitute persecution—the legal basis for refugee protection[122]—must take place within the framework provided by international human rights instruments.[123] This framework encompasses core human rights principles embodied in the Universal Declaration of Human Rights[124] and the International Covenant on Civil and Political Rights,[125] which include equal rights as to marriage (before marriage, during marriage, and at its dissolution);[126] the right to life, liberty, and security of person;[127] the right not to be subjected to torture or to cruel, inhuman, or degrading treatment or punishment;[128] the right not to be subjected to slavery;[129] and the right not to be subjected to arbitrary arrest, detention, or exile.[130] The international human rights framework also includes human rights instruments that elaborate on these core principles with specific reference to the circumstances of women. Several international human rights instruments and recent interpretations of those instruments address fundamental human rights as they relate to gender.[131] These international documents recognize that violence, including rape and other sexual abuse, domestic violence, and harmful practices reinforced by culture and tradition, whether occurring in the public or private sphere, constitute violations of internationally protected human rights.[132] They impose an affirmative duty on states to provide protection from such treatment and to remedy the conditions through which such treatment is perpetuated.[133]

---

121. *See id.*

122. *See supra* text accompanying notes 11–15.

123. *See* UNHCR HANDBOOK, *supra* note 13, at para. 51 stating:

There is no universally accepted definition of "persecution," and various attempts to formulate such a definition have met with little success. From Article 33 of the 1951 Convention, it may be inferred that a threat to life or freedom on account of race, religion, nationality, political opinion or membership of a particular social group is always persecution. Other serious violations of human rights, for the same reasons, would also constitute persecution.

124. Universal Declaration of Human Rights, G.A. Res. 217, 3rd sess., U.N. Doc. A/811 (Dec. 10, 1948) [hereinafter Universal Declaration].

125. 999 U.N.T.S. 171, 6 I.L.M. 368 (entered into force Mar. 23, 1976) [hereinafter ICCPR].

126. *See* Universal Declaration, *supra* note 124, at art. 16; ICCPR, *supra* note 125, at art. 23.

127. *See* Universal Declaration, *supra* note 124, at art. 3; ICCPR, *supra* note 125, at arts. 6 & 9.

128. *See* Universal Declaration, *supra* note 124, at art. 5; ICCPR, *supra* note 125, at art. 7.

129. *See* Universal Declaration, *supra* note 124, at art. 4; ICCPR, *supra* note 125, at art. 8.

130. *See* Universal Declaration, *supra* note 124, at art. 9; ICCPR, *supra* note 125, at art. 9.

131. These volumes treat the interpretation of these international legal instruments in greater depth elsewhere.

132. Each of these issues is discussed separately elsewhere in these volumes.

133. In addition to the formal conventions and declarations, attention has been focused on the

Convention on the Elimination of All Forms of Discrimination Against Women

The Convention on the Elimination of All Forms of Discrimination Against Women (Women's Convention)[134] is the most comprehensive human rights instrument to address the particular situation of women. The Women's Convention not only prohibits overt discrimination against women,[135] but it also requires states to take affirmative steps to eliminate discriminatory treatment by both state and private actors.[136] The Women's Convention does not directly address the issue of violence against women. However, the Committee on the Elimination of Discrimination Against Women (CEDAW), the body charged with the task of overseeing the implementation of the Women's Convention, has adopted the position that gender-based violence is a "form of discrimination which seriously inhibits women's ability to enjoy rights and freedoms on a basis of equality with men."[137] Referring to Article 1 of the Women's Convention, Recommendation 19 states:

> This definition of discrimination includes gender-based violence—that is violence which is directed against a woman because she is a woman or which affects women disproportionately. It includes acts which inflict physical, mental or sexual harm or suffering, threats of such acts, coercion and other deprivations of liberty. Gender-

---

protection of women refugees in a number of international fora. *See, e.g.*, Report of the International Conference on Population and Development, U.N. Doc. A/Conf.171/13,18 (1994) (urging governments to ensure that asylum-seekers have access to fair hearings and expeditious processing of asylum requests; that guidelines and procedures for the determination of refugee status be sensitive to the particular situation of women and that effective protection of and assistance to refugee populations, with particular attention to the needs and physical security of refugee women and refugee children—especially against exploitation, abuse and all forms of violence— is provided). *See also id.* at 76–77, paras. 10.22(c), 10.24, and 10.27. The Beijing Platform of Action also noted the needs of refugee women. *See* BEIJING PLATFORM OF ACTION, FOURTH WORLD CONFERENCE ON WOMEN 113–119 (Sept. 4–15, 1995) ("The factors that cause the flight of refugee women, other displaced women in need of international protection and internally displaced women may be different from those affecting men; these women continue to be vulnerable to abuses of their human rights during and after their flight.").

134. Convention on the Elimination of All Forms of Discrimination against Women, Dec. 18, 1979, G.A. Res. 34/180, U.N. GAOR, 34th Sess., Supp. No. 46, at 194, U.N. Doc. A/RES/34/46 (1980) [hereinafter Women's Convention].

135. Article 1 of the Women's Convention, *id.*, defines discrimination broadly:

For the purposes of the present convention, the term "discrimination against women" shall mean any distinction, exclusion or restriction made on the basis of sex which has the effect of, or the purpose of impairing or nullifying the recognition, enjoyment or exercise by women, irrespective of their marital status, on a basis of equality of men and women, or human rights and fundamental freedoms in the political, economic, social, cultural, civil or any other field.

136. *See* Pamela Goldberg & Nancy Kelly, *Recent Developments: International Human Rights and Violence Against Women*, 6 HARV. HUM. RTS. J. 195 (1993).

137. U.N. Committee on the Elimination of Discrimination against Women, *Violence Against Women*, 11th Sess., General Recommendation No. 19, at 1, U.N. Doc. CEDAW/C.1992/L.1/ Add.15 (1992).

based violence may breach specific provisions of the Convention, regardless of whether those provisions mention violence.[138]

The UNHCR Executive Committee also has found that severe discrimination experienced by women in violation of the Women's Convention can form the basis for a grant of refugee status.[139]

Declaration on the Elimination of Violence Against Women

In June 1993, the World Conference on Human Rights was held in Vienna. A major focus of the conference was the recognition of women's rights as human rights and the importance of ensuring full and equal enjoyment by women of all human rights. The Vienna Conference stressed "the importance of working towards the elimination of violence against women in public and private life, the elimination of all forms of sexual harassment, exploitation and trafficking in women, the elimination of gender bias in the administration of justice and the eradication of any conflicts which may arise between the rights of women and the harmful effects of certain traditional or customary practices, cultural prejudices, and religious extremism."[140] The Vienna Conference also called upon the General Assembly to adopt the draft Declaration on Violence Against Women,[141] and consequently, on December 20, 1993, the General Assembly adopted the Declaration,[142] which recognizes violence against women, whether occurring in public or private life, as both a *per se* violation of human rights and as an impediment to the enjoyment by women of other human rights and fundamental freedoms.[143] The Declaration defines violence against women as: "any act of gender-based violence that results in, or is likely to result in, physical, sexual, or psychological harm or suffering to women, including threats of such acts, coercion or arbitrary deprivation of liberty, whether occurring in public or in private life."[144] The Declaration enumerates certain forms of harm which are encompassed by the definition, including violence occurring in the family, such as battering, sexual abuse of female children, dowry-related violence, marital rape, female genital mutilation and other traditional practices harmful to women, non-spousal violence, and violence

---

138. *Id.* at 2.

139. *See* CANADIAN GENDER GUIDELINES, *supra* note 21 (citing *1990 Note on Refugee Women, supra* note 27, at 5).

140. *Adoption of the Final Documents and Report of the Conference: Report of the Drafting Committee, Addendum, Final Outcome of the World Conference on Human Rights*, U.N. GAOR, U.N. Doc. A/Conf.157/DC/1/Add.1, at 22–23 (1993) [hereinafter *Vienna Final Document*]. *See also* THE WORLD CONFERENCE ON HUMAN RIGHTS, WOMEN ON THE MOVE, PROCEEDINGS OF THE WORKSHOP ON HUMAN RIGHTS ABUSES AGAINST IMMIGRANT AND REFUGEE WOMEN (Leni Marin & Blandina Lansang-De Mesa eds., 1993).

141. *See Vienna Final Document, supra* note 140.

142. Declaration on the Elimination of Violence Against Women, G.A. Res. 2/8/104, Supp. No. 49, U.N. Doc. A/48/49 (1994).

143. *Id.* at arts. 1 & 2.

144. *Id.* at art. 1.

related to exploitation,[145] as well as violence occurring within the general community[146] and violence perpetrated or condoned by the state.[147]

The Declaration reiterates numerous core human rights contained in the Universal Declaration and the International Covenant on Civil and Political Rights, stresses that "women are entitled to the equal enjoyment and protection of all human rights and fundamental freedoms in the political, economic, social, cultural, civil or any other field,"[148] places an affirmative duty on states to condemn violence against women, to refrain from invoking custom, tradition, or religious considerations as a means of avoiding their obligations, and requires states to "pursue by all appropriate means and without delay a policy of eliminating violence against women."[149]

Inter-American Convention on the Prevention, Punishment and Eradication of Violence Against Women

On a regional level, the Inter-American Convention on the Prevention, Punishment and Eradication of Violence Against Women (Convention of Belem do Para),[150] adopted by the Organization of American States in June 1994, places an affirmative duty on states to protect women from violence in both the public and the private sphere. The Convention of Belem do Para adopts a broad definition of violence that recognizes actions by state and non-state actors, and incorporates physical, sexual, and psychological violence[151] occurring within the family or domestic unit, any other interpersonal relationship, or the community as well as violence perpetrated or condoned by the state or its agents, regardless of where it occurs.[152] The convention reiterates that "[e]very woman has the right to the recognition, enjoyment, exercise and protection of all human rights and freedoms embodied in regional and international human rights instruments,"[153] and recognizes that violence against women, in

---

145. *See id.* at art. 2(a).

146. *See id.* at art. 2(b).

147. *See id.* at art. 2(c).

148. *Id.* at art. 3.

149. *Id.* at art. 4.

150. Inter-American Convention on the Prevention, Punishment and Eradication of Violence Against Women, June 9, 1994, 33 I.L.M. 1534 (1994) [hereinafter Convention of Belem do Para].

151. The Convention of Belem do Para specifically enumerates the following types of violence: rape, battery, sexual abuse, torture, trafficking in persons, forced prostitution, kidnaping, and sexual harassment. *See id.* at art 2.

152. *See id.*

153. *Id.* at art. 4. The rights enumerated include: the right to life, the rights to have her physical, marital and moral integrity respected, the right to personal liberty and security, the right not to be subjected to torture, the right to have the inherent dignity of her person respected and her family protected, the right to equal protection before the law and of the law, the right to simple and prompt recourse to a competent court for the protection against acts that violate her rights, the right to associate freely, the right of freedom to profess her religion and beliefs within the law, and the right to have equal access to the public service of her country and to take part in the conduct of public affairs, including decision-making. *See id.* at art. 4.

the private and public spheres, prevents and nullifies the exercise of those rights.[154] The Convention of Belem do Para specifically recognizes that certain legal or customary practices may "sustain the persistence and tolerance of violence against women" and places an affirmative duty on states parties to "pursue by all appropriate means and without delay, policies to prevent, punish and eradicate such violence."[155] Specifically, states parties agree to refrain from engaging in any act or practice of violence, to apply due diligence to prevent, investigate, and impose penalties for violence, to include preventive and punitive measures in domestic legislation, to adopt legal measures to restrain perpetrators from harassing, intimidating, or threatening women, and to provide effective remedies for victims.[156]

These mechanisms are just a part of a complex set of norms evolving at the intergovernmental, regional, and governmental levels to ensure that women's rights are acknowledged and protected as human rights.[157] To that extent, then, these normative developments contribute, in concrete and crucial ways, to the evolution of international law protections directed towards refugee women.

PROTECTION WITHIN THE DOMESTIC CONTEXT

Only recently have governments begun to pay attention to the unique aspects of the asylum claims of women. Asylum advocates increasingly have become aware of the relevance and usefulness of the international human rights framework to the claims of female asylum-seekers. As a result, they have pressed asylum-receiving countries to rethink and reform their analysis of the asylum claims of women. This section will focus on the evolution of that process in Canada and the United States, two Western countries that have issued guidelines to guide adjudicators in their consideration of the asylum claims of women.

Canada

> The 1951 Convention Relating to the Status of Refugees has affirmed the principles set out in the Universal Declaration of Human Rights, "that human beings shall enjoy fundamental rights and freedoms without discrimination." Violence and discrimination against women are anathema to the objectives of these international instruments. Governments that tolerate a culture of violence and abuse against women should reflect on the harm and suffering they are causing by turning a blind eye to the greater part of their society.
>
> Canadian Immigration and Refugee Board[158]

---

154. *See id.* at art. 5.

155. *Id.* at art. 7.

156. *See id.* at art. 8(b).

157. These mechanisms are discussed in much greater depth elsewhere in these volumes.

158. Immigration and Refugee Board (Ref. Div.) Decision No. U92–08714 (1993) (quoting the Preamble to the 1951 Convention, *supra* note 11).

For several years, Canada has been at the forefront of the movement to provide protection to women refugees.[159] One of the earliest cases to raise the issue of gender-related persecution was a Canadian Immigration Appeals Board decision, issued in 1987, granting asylum to a woman seeking to avoid deportation to Turkey.[160] Although the claimant based her application on her religion and her nationality,[161] the Board expanded her claim to include membership in the particular social group of "single women living in a Moslem country without the protection of a male relative."[162] The claimant was a widow and mother who was subjected to harassment on a daily basis by young Moslem men. When she sought the protection of the police, she was refused. Her daughter also was sexually assaulted. The Board granted refugee status to the claimant and her daughter, recounting their mistreatment and finding that "the [Turkish] State does not wish to protect the applicant and her daughter, two Armenian women who were Christians and who lived alone in a Moslem country where, according to Islamic tradition, they should have had the protection of a male relative."[163] During the late 1980s, the Immigration and Refugee Board (IRB) of Canada[164] reaffirmed gender-related social group classifications in a handful of cases

159. Even in such a short time, a fairly extensive and rich literature analyzing Canadian law, policy, and procedure affecting women refugees exists. *See, e.g.*, Stephanie Kuttner, *Gender-Related Persecution as a Basis for Refugee Status: The Emergence of an International Norm*, 16 REFUGE 17 (1997); Chantal Bernier, *The IRB Guidelines on Women Refugee Claimants Fearing Gender-Related Persecution*, REFUGEE J. SPECIAL ISSUE, *supra* note 4, at 167; Anker, *supra* note 6; Deborah Anker, *Rape in the Community As a Basis for Asylum: The Treatment of Women Refugee Claims to Protection in Canada and the United States (Part I)*, 2 BENDER'S IMM. BULL. 476 (1997); Valerie L. Oosterveld, *The Canadian Guidelines on Gender-Related Persecution: An Evaluation*, 8 INT'L J. REFUGEE L. 569 (1996); Audrey Macklin, *Refugee Women and the Imperative of Categories*, 17 HUM. RTS. Q. 213 (1995); Judith Ramirez, *The Canadian Guidelines on Women Refugee Claimants Fearing Gender-Related Persecution*, 14 REFUGE 3 (1994).

160. Incirciyan v. Minister of Employment and Immigration, Immigration Appeal Board Decision No. M8701541X (1987).

161. *See id.* at 1.

162. *Id.*

163. *Id.* at 3. The Board offered no instruction on the standard to be applied in evaluating a social group claim. However, certain principles are evident in its characterization of the case. First, the claimant belonged to a social group comprised of women who have violated the mores of society—by living alone when they were expected to have the protection of a male relative. Second, since the persecution she feared did not directly emanate from the government, it was necessary to address the power or willingness of the government to provide protection to the claimant and her daughter.

164. The Immigration and Refugee Board (IRB), created in 1989, is an independent administrative tribunal. The IRB reports through the Minister of Citizenship and Immigration to the Canadian Parliament and is composed of three divisions: the Convention Refugee Determination Division, the Immigration Appeal Division and the Adjudication Division. *See* Nurjehan Mawani, Remarks by the Chairperson, Immigration and Refugee Board: Canada's Refugee Determination System: Due Process in a Non-Adversarial Context, Address before the Open Society Institute, New York, Feb. 19, 1998, at 2. Refugee determination proceedings are conducted before the Refugee Division of the IRB using a non-adversarial, inquisitorial model. Hearings are normally conducted before two Board members, and the burden of proof is shared between the applicant and the Board. A positive decision by one of the Board members results in a grant of status to the

involving Lebanese Moslem women[165] and Sri Lankan Tamil women.[166] These cases did not receive widespread attention, however, and the Canadian government never applied a uniform policy.

The issue of gender-related persecution was first brought to public attention in Canada in 1991 with the case of "Nada," a young women from Saudi Arabia who sought asylum to escape the severe restrictions placed on women in her country and the punishment imposed on women who step outside the bounds of so-called "accept-able" behavior. Nada refused to wear a veil in public. As a result, men threw rocks at her, spit at her, and called her obscene names. At school, she studied nursing because it was one of the few subjects open to women. On the basis of being female, she was prohibited from driving a car or traveling without the permission of a male relative. Upon arriving in Canada, she applied for refugee status. She argued that, if returned to Saudi Arabia, she faced arrest and possible torture by the religious police for her failure to follow the laws regarding women. After her application was denied by the IRB and she was ordered deported, she decided to make her case public. She gained widespread support, largely because of the position taken by the Immigration and Refugee Board—that she should simply learn to obey the laws applied to all women in Saudi Arabia. In its original decision, the Board said:

> Like all Saudi Arabian women, the claimant would have to obey the laws of general application that she denounces, in all circumstances and not only as she did to attend school, work or accommodate the feelings of her father who, like the other members of his large family, was opposed to the liberalism of his daughter.[167]

---

applicant. *See id.* at 3. Panels are assisted in case preparation and in the hearing room by Refugee Claim Officers who are employees of the Board. *See id.* Both the refugee claimant and the Minister of Citizenship and Immigration have the right to seek judicial review of a decision from the Refugee Division. The claimant must obtain leave to seek judicial review before the trial division of the Federal Court of Canada. The Federal Court can quash the decision and return it to be heard by a different panel of the Board. *See id.* at 12. The claimant can appeal the decision of the Federal Court Trial Division to the Federal Court of Appeal "provided the Federal court Trial Division certifies that the case raises a 'serious question of general importance.'" *Id.*

165. *See* Immigration and Refugee Board (Ref. Div.) Decision No. T89–00260 (1989) (endorsing the "particular social group" theory presented in *Inciriyan*, but finding that the claimant had not established that the harms she faced were a result of her membership in a particular social group).

166. *See* Immigration and Refugee Board (Ref. Div.) Decision No. T89–00587, T89–00588, T89–00589 (1989). In this decision, the Board found the applicant had a well-founded fear of persecution on account of her perceived political opinion and her membership in the particular social group of "young Tamil women." *Id.* The applicant and her family had been subjected to sustained persecution by the Sri Lankan military and the Indian Peace-Keeping Force. On one occasion, she had been taken from her home and stripped by the soldiers. Her aunt had been raped and killed by the Indian Peace-Keeping Forces. The Board did not discuss the requirement for establishing eligibility through membership in a particular social group but noted in its decision the particular vulnerability of young Tamil women in Sri Lanka. *See also* Immigration and Refugee Board (Ref. Div.) Decision No. M89–01213 (1989) (finding, with no analysis of the social group standard, applicant was part of the group of young Tamil females and also part of a family perceived to be opposed to the government of Sri Lanka).

167. [1991] C.R.D.D. M91–04822(T) n.1096.

The situation was compounded when the Immigration Minister refused to intervene, making public comments to the effect that granting status to women fleeing gender-based persecution would amount to cultural imperialism and would open the floodgates to vast numbers of women.

Advocates took issue with what they saw as a paternalistic and discriminatory ruling, and women's groups waged a campaign to flood the minister with telephone calls, letters, and faxes. In January of 1993, the minister recanted and granted Nada permanent resident status for "humanitarian" reasons.[168]

In March of 1993, Canada became the first country to issue guidelines for the evaluation of refugee claims of women.[169] The IRB's *Gender Guidelines* were not intended to reflect a change in the law of asylum. Rather, they set out a legal framework, consistent with evolving standards of asylum law, for the evaluation of women's cases and defined procedures to be followed to ensure that women have the right to present claims independent of male family members in a setting that takes into account the particular circumstances of female applicants.

The *Canadian Gender Guidelines* recognize that "[a]lthough gender is not specifically enumerated as one of the grounds for establishing Convention refugee status, the definition of Convention refugee may properly be interpreted as providing protection to women who demonstrate a well-founded fear of gender-related persecution by reason of any one, or a combination of, the enumerated grounds."[170] The *Canadian Guidelines* establish four broad categories of women who may have claims to refugee status: women who fear persecution under the Refugee Convention on the same grounds, and in similar circumstances, as men;[171] women who fear persecution for reasons related solely pertaining to kinship;[172] women who fear persecution due to severe discrimination on grounds of gender;[173] women who fear persecution as the consequence of failing to conform to, or for transgressing, certain gender-discriminating religious or customary laws and practices in their country of origin.[174] The *Canadian Gender Guidelines* explore the analysis to be used in determining whether the feared persecution is based on particular social group membership or any of the other four grounds enumerated in the refugee definition.[175] In determining whether the feared harm constitutes persecution within the Refugee Convention's definition, the *Canadian Gender Guidelines* instruct that "[t]he social cultural, traditional and religious norms and the laws affecting women in the claimant's country of origin

---

168. *See* Allan Thompson, *Saudi Woman Allowed to Stay as Minister Intervenes in Case,* TORONTO STAR, Jan. 30, 1993, at A10.

169. *See* CANADIAN GENDER GUIDELINES, *supra* note 21.

170. *Id.* at 2.

171. *See id.*

172. *See id.* at 3.

173. *See id.*

174. *See id.*

175. *See id.* at 4–7.

ought to be assessed by reference to human rights instruments which provide a framework for recognizing the protection needs of women."[176]

The Canadian Gender Guidelines note certain evidentiary matters that may adversely affect a woman's ability to establish her claim to refugee status, and instruct that, to alleviate these problems, adjudicators should take particular steps, including not requiring particularized evidence setting out a specific set of facts when a woman comes from a situation of generalized violence against women, not requiring statistical data on the incidence of sexual violence in the applicant's country, and requiring the consideration of evidence that the government may have condoned violence if it had been aware of incidents of such violence.[177] They also note factors that may impede a woman's ability to establish that her testimony is trustworthy, namely that women from certain societies may be reluctant to disclose experiences of sexual violence in order to keep their "shame" to themselves and not dishonor their family or community, that women in certain cultures are not privy to the details of the political, military, or social activities of their spouses or other male relatives, and that women who have suffered sexual or domestic violence may exhibit a pattern of symptoms referred to as Rape Trauma Syndrome that may severely affect their ability to present credible testimony.[178]

Finally, the *Canadian Gender Guidelines* set out a framework which instructs adjudicators to:

(1) assess the particular circumstances which give rise to the claimant's fear or persecution;

(2) assess the general conditions in the claimant's country of origin;

(3) determine the seriousness of the treatment which the claimant fears;

(4) ascertain whether the claimant's fear is based on any of the enumerated grounds;

(5) determine whether there is adequate state protection available to the claimant; and

(6) determine whether, in considering all the circumstances, including any internal flight alternatives, the claimant's fear is well-founded.

With the *Canadian Gender Guidelines* came a series of groundbreaking decisions from the IRB. One of the first, issued in February 1993, a month prior to the

---

176. *Id.* at 7. The *Canadian Gender Guidelines* enumerate the following human rights instruments as defining what constitute permissible conduct by a state towards women: the Universal Declaration of Human Rights, the International Covenant on Civil and Political Rights, the International Covenant on Economic, Social and Cultural Rights, the Convention on the Elimination of all Forms of Discrimination Against Women, the Convention on the Political Rights of Women, and the Convention on the Nationality of Married Women.

177. *See id.* at 8.

178. *See id.* at 9.

release of the *Guidelines*, involved a woman from Zimbabwe who sought protection from a polygamous, arranged marriage to an abusive man.[179] The woman in that case raised a claim based on her religion, which forbade polygamy, and on her membership in two social groups of women subjected to the traditional practices of bride price and arranged marriage. Specifically, the claimant advanced as a basis for her claim the particular social groups of "[u]nprotected Zimbabwean women or girls subject to wife abuse" and "Zimbabwean women or girls forced to marry according to customary laws of kuzvarira [bride price] and lobola [arranged marriage]."[180] The IRB relied on Articles 3, 5, and 16 of the Universal Declaration and Articles 7, 9, and 23 of the ICCPR. It found that the claimant had no reasonable expectation of effective state protection given that: it had been denied her in the past; women, particularly from rural areas, generally experience serious discrimination at the hands of Zimbabwean male society; physical abuse, rape, and killings are integral parts of this abuse; the authorities are not yet able to provide adequate safeguards to control the situation; and the government is unable to protect her from her influential husband.

In a second case, the IRB granted protection to a woman from Ecuador who sought protection from domestic abuse as a member of a particular social group.[181] The claimant in that case was subjected to several years of domestic abuse, including beatings (in one instance, so severe that she suffered a miscarriage) and rape. On one occasion when she attempted to report the abuse to the police, they laughed at her and "said she must have done something wrong to be beaten."[182] In reaching its decision, the IRB examined the social structure of Ecuador, in which domestic abuse is the norm, and concluded that "violence is the result of structural relations of power, dominance and privilege established among men and women in society."[183] The Board concluded that the law in Ecuador protects the male aggressor and that female victims have no access to protection under the law or within a system of women's centers and organizations, finding that the "documentary evidence makes it abundantly clear that the government of Ecuador is unwilling to protect the rights of women who are subject to domestic abuse."[184] In finding that the abuse endured by the claimant was severe enough to rise to the level of persecution, the Board compared domestic violence to torture:

> There is a vast difference between a matrimonial home and a torture chamber. If a wife is subjected to violence repeatedly then in our assessment, she stands in no different situation than a person who has been arrested, detained and beaten on a number of occasions because of his political opinion. As a matter of fact, such a person suffers to a lesser degree over a period of time, because, after each detention he is released and enjoys his freedom. The wife, on the other hand, has no respite from her agony of torture and grief. She must endure these misfortunes continuously. The law

179. *See* Immigration and Refugee Board (Ref. Div.) Decision No. U92–06668 (1993).

180. *Id.* at 16.

181. *See* Immigration and Refugee Board (Ref. Div.) Decision No. U92–08714 (1993).

182. *Id.* at 2–3.

183. *Id.* at 5.

184. *Id.* at 6.

should not sit idly by while those who seek relief lose hope, and those who abuse it are emboldened by its failure to provide sanctions.[185]

Since the implementation of the *Canadian Gender Guidelines*, the Canadian federal courts and the Immigration and Refugee Board have granted refugee status under the particular social group category to women fleeing domestic abuse, cultural practices such as arranged marriage, and government policies discriminating against women based on gender.[186] In one case, the Board granted protection to a young woman from Pakistan who had become pregnant as the result of a rape.[187] The applicant in that case had been raped in retaliation for her political activities on behalf of the Pakistan People's Party. She did not divulge the rape to her father because she feared that her father would kill her to the protect the family honor. The Board noted that, under the law of Pakistan, in order to prove that she had been raped, the claimant would have to produce a confession from the rapist or the testimony of four male witnesses to the rape. If she were not able to produce the witnesses, she was vulnerable to prosecution for illicit sex. The Board granted the claimant refugee status based on her membership in the particular social group of "single raped Pakistani female[s] with a child born out of wedlock."[188]

In another case, the Board granted asylum to protect a girl from the forcible imposition of female genital mutilation.[189] The claimants in that case were a Somali woman and her son and daughter. They raised a claim based on the potential infliction of FGM on the daughter and mandatory loss of custody of the children by the mother under the laws of Somalia. The Board found that the mother would lose her internationally protected rights as a parent because she would automatically lose custody of her children to her husband under the divorce laws of her country. The Board stated:

> Women are harshly subordinated in Somali society. Somali culture is overwhelmingly restrictive and patriarchal. Because Somalia is a patrilineal society, . . . children belong to the clan of their father and for this reason a divorced woman would not be given the custody of her children, either male or female.[190]

With regard to the daughter, the Board found that the practice of FGM, widespread in Somalia, is a gross violation of her right to personal security in contravention of Article 3 of the Universal Declaration as well as the United Nations Convention on

---

185. *Id.* at 7.

186. Between Mar. 1993 and Sept. 30, 1996, the Immigration and Refugee Board finalized 1134 gender-related claims. Of those, 624 claims were accepted and 347 were rejected. During the same period, a further 163 claims were either withdrawn, abandoned, discontinued, or otherwise finalized and 238 were pending. *See* Immigration and Refugee Board, News Release 96–03 (Nov. 25, 1996).

187. Immigration and Refugee Board (Ref. Div.) Decision No. U93–06373 (1993).

188. *Id.* at 4.

189. *See* Immigration and Refugee Board (Ref. Div.) Decision No. T93–12198, T93–12199, T93–12197 (1994).

190. *Id.* at 4–5.

the Rights of the Child.[191] Finding that the government of Somalia would not protect her from the practice, the Board found that she had established eligibility for refugee status as a member of two particular social groups: women and minors.

In a number of cases, the Board has granted protection to women from domestic violence when the government of their countries have failed in their duty to provide protection.[192]

---

191. Convention on the Rights of the Child, U.N. GAOR, *adopted* Nov. 20, 1989, G.A. Res. 44/25 (Annex), U.N. GAOR 44th Sess., Supp. No. 49, U.N. Doc. A/44/49 (*entered into force* Sept. 2, 1990).

192. *See, e.g.*, Immigration and Refugee Board (Ref. Div.) Decision No. U93–07988/89 (1994) (granting refugee status to a Pakistani woman seeking protection from domestic abuse as a member of the particular social group of Pakistani women subject to wife abuse by relying on a finding that the "social ethos in Pakistan militates against a wife seeking the protection of the state if she has been physically abused by the husband"); Immigration and Refugee Board (Ref. Div.) Decision U93–08203/05/06/07/08 (1994) (granting refugee status to a Korean woman and her daughters by noting the objective unreasonableness of approaching the state for protection, in spite of recently implemented legislation, by relying on the U.N. Convention Against Torture and Other Cruel, Inhumane and Degrading Treatment or Punishment, 39 U.N. GAOR Supp., No. 51, U.N. Doc. A/39/51 (1984); the ICCPR, *supra* note 125, at art. 3; and the Women's Convention, *supra* note 134, as well as on testimony and documentation establishing the "widespread nature of domestic abuse," and "the inadequacy of facilities to assist these victims" in Korea); Immigration and Refugee Board (Ref. Div.) Decision No. U93–08028 and Decision No. U93–10558 (1994) (granting refugee status to an Ecuadoran woman and her daughter because documentary evidence established that "[a]lthough violence against women, including within marriage, is prohibited by law, it is common practice" in Ecuador, and thus claimants had no reasonable expectation of effective state protection); Immigration and Refugee Board (Ref. Div.) Decision No. T93–12477 (1994) (granting refugee status to a Bulgarian woman by relying on the claimant's testimony and evidence of "similarly situated individuals" whom the state had failed to protect, namely an editorial from a Bulgarian newspaper); Immigration and Refugee Board (Ref. Div.) Decision No. V93–01772 (1994) (granting refugee status to a Chilean woman by finding that the domestic abuse the claimant had suffered cumulatively amounted to persecution, and finding it objectively unreasonable for the claimant to approach the state for protection given the abuse she "endured" in Chile from which neither her family nor the state was able to protect her, even though "there [had since] been some changes in the law to reduce domestic violence against women, [because it not had] been matched by a change in attitude in society, police or the courts"); Immigration and Refugee Board (Ref. Div.) Decision No. T93–07375 (1994) (granting refugee status to a woman from Barbados because the "claimant in her particular circumstances, because of her specific vulnerability, [could not] receive timely and adequate protection from the state from her abusive husband [in spite of the fact] that Barbados is not a country in which domestic violence is condoned or that there is no recourse for victims of domestic violence, generally"); Immigration and Refugee Board (Ref. Div.) Decision No., U93–09791 (1994) (granting refugee status to an Ecuadoran indigenous woman by relying on the Universal Declaration *supra* note 126, at arts. 3 & 5, to find that the harm the claimant had been subjected to constituted a violation of the security of person and amounted to cruel, inhuman and degrading treatment, and that it was not reasonable to expect the claimant to seek an internal flight alternative given the general climate of discrimination and lack of protection regarding indigenous women and the fact that the claimant would be denied her ability to earn a living by making and selling artifacts since she could not economically transport materials to the capital city and other areas due to her husband); Immigration and Refugee Board (Ref. Div.) Decision No. T93–08296 (1993) (granting refugee status to an Argentinean woman by basing its decision on an evaluation of the values and cultural norms of Argentina society and concluding that testimony clearly indicated that "the notion that

In evaluating gender-related claims, the primary focus of the IRB has been on the severity of the harm and on the availability of state protection. Generally, when the abuse seriously violates a human right and the claimant is able to demonstrate that she was denied state protection, or that it would have been futile for her to seek state protection, refugee status will be given. In contrast, when the claimant cannot demonstrate that the government has failed to protect her, the claim will fail.[193]

In 1993, the Supreme Court of Canada decided *Canada (Attorney General) v. Ward*,[194] which set forth the standard for evaluating a refugee claim based on membership in a particular social group. In *Ward*, the Supreme Court elaborated three possible categories of particular social groups: (1) groups defined by an innate or unchangeable characteristic; (2) groups whose members voluntarily associate for reasons so fundamental to their human dignity that they should not be forced to forsake the association; and (3) groups associated by a former voluntary status, unalterable due to its historical permanence. As examples of particular social groups which would fit these requirements the court offered the following:

> [T]he first category would embrace individuals fearing persecution on such basis as gender, linguistic background and sexual orientation, while the second would encompass, for example, human rights activists. The third branch is included more because of historical intentions, although it is also relevant to the anti-discrimination influences, in that one's past is an immutable part of the person.

The court's decision in *Ward* opened the door for consideration of a particular social group defined *solely* by gender.[195]

In November of 1996, the Board issued an update to the *Gender Guidelines* to incorporate the developing case law in the area, including the *Ward* decision, several federal court decisions recognizing the importance of the *Guidelines* and providing elaboration on issues regarding gender-related persecution,[196] and the *UNHCR's*

---

a man has a right to discipline his wife is deeply rooted in the history of Argentinean society"); Immigration and Refugee Board (Ref. Div.) Decision No. T93–07281, T93–07282 (1993) (granting refugee status to a Venezuelan woman by relying on the Torture Convention and basing its decision on the fact that the claimant had no reasonable expectation of effective state protection on an assessment of the Venezuelan state's obligations under the Women's Convention).

193. *See, e.g.*, Immigration and Refugee Board (Ref. Div.) Decision No. TN3–08122 (1994) (denying asylum to a Jamaican woman because she did not seek police protection from an abusive husband); Immigration and Refugee Board (Ref. Div.) Decision No. UN3–04148 (1994) (denying asylum to a Kenyan woman because she did not seek the intervention of the police).

194. [1993] 2 S.C.R. 689.

195. *See* Immigration and Refugee Board, Women Refugee Claimants Fearing Gender-Related Persecution: Guidelines Issued by the Chairperson Pursuant to Section 65(3) of the Immigration Act, Update 8 (Ottawa, Canada, Nov. 25, 1996) [hereinafter Canadian Gender Guidelines Update].

196. In a number of cases, the Federal Court of Canada has found "women subject to domestic abuse" to be a particular social group. *See* Navarez v. M.C.I. [1995] F.C.T.D. No. IMM–36660–94 (reversing denial by the IRB and granting refugee status to a woman from Ecuador based on membership in the particular social group of "women in Ecuador subject to domestic violence" where applicant had been subjected to violence, including rape, during and after the marriage, and where

Conclusions on Refugee Protection and Sexual Violence,[197] which emphasized that international instruments relating to refugees must be interpreted in a way that recognizes sexual violence as a form of persecution.[198]

The updated *Guidelines* maintain the original four broad categories of claims for women and reiterate the ways in which gender can intersect with race, religion, nationality, and political opinion in evaluating a claim to refugee status. They also reiterate considerations specific to gender that are imperative in determining the nature and the grounds of a woman's persecution. Taking into account principles elaborated through cases decided since the issuance of the original guidelines, they expand the original guidelines in several ways. First, they explicitly recognize, citing the *Ward* decision, that a particular social group can be based exclusively on gender.[199] Second, in assessing whether a particular harm constitutes persecution, the updated *Guidelines* direct adjudicators to a growing body of cases which recognize as persecution "female-specific experiences, such as infanticide, genital mutilation, bride-burning, forced marriage, domestic violence, forced abortion, or compulsory sterilization."[200]

The updated *Guidelines* also expand the evidentiary considerations to include situations in which it may be objectively unreasonable for a claimant to have sought the protection of the state[201] and the types of evidence that a woman might offer to establish that her government was unwilling or unable to provide her with

---

applicant was unable to obtain the protection of the police); Williams v. S.S.C. [1995] F.C.T.D. No. IMM 4244–94 (reversing denial by the IRB and granting refugee status to a woman from Grenada who was subjected to ongoing severe physical abuse by common law husband, a police officer, where applicant attempted to approach officers at the police station where her husband worked to ask them to persuade him to stop the abuse and they "just started laughing and they said that this is not a problem"); Diluna v. M.E.I. [1995] F.C.T.D., No. IMM–3201–94 (reversing denial by the IRB and granting refugee status to a woman from Brazil based on membership in particular social group of "women subject to domestic violence in Brazil" where applicant demonstrated continuous violence committed against her by her husband and the inability or unwillingness of state authorities to protect her). *But see* Fouchong v. S.S.C. [1994] F.C.T.D. No. IMM–7603–93 (dismissing appeal of decision of IRB denying application of woman from Grenada where evidence supported a finding that police protection was available to the applicant).

197. *See* Conclusion No. 73, *supra* note 37.

198. CANADIAN GENDER GUIDELINES UPDATE, *supra* note 195, at 2.

199. *See id* at 8 ("Gender is an innate characteristic and therefore, women may form a particular social group within the Convention refugee definition. The relevant assessment is whether the claimant, as a woman, has a well-founded fear of persecution in her country of nationality by reason of her membership in this group.") *See also* [1993] C.R.D.D. T93–055935/36; [1994] C.R.D.D. T93–12198/12199/12197.

200. CANADIAN GENDER GUIDELINES UPDATE, *supra* note 195, at 10.

201. *Id.* at 13 ("When considering whether it is objectively unreasonable for the claimant not to have sought the protection of the state, the decision-maker should consider, among other relevant factors, the social, cultural, religious, and economic context in which the claimant finds herself. If, for example, a woman has suffered gender-related persecution in the form of rape, she may be ostracized from her community for seeking protection from the state. Decision-makers should consider this type of information when determining if the claimant should reasonably have sought state protection.")

protection.[202] Further, they caution against assuming that a change in a country's circumstances may constitute a positive change for a woman and caution in assessing the reasonableness of an internal flight alternative.

Finally, the Board offers an amended framework for analyzing a gender-related claim:

(1) assess the harm feared by the claimant to determine, according to international human rights standards, whether it constitutes persecution;

(2) ascertain whether the claimant's fear of persecution is based on any one or a combination of grounds enumerated in the Refugee Convention;

(3) determine whether the claimant's fear of harm is well-founded, including whether the state is willing and able to provide protection; and

(4) determine whether there is an internal flight alternative which does not cause hardship to the claimant.[203]

The United States

In this case, I conclude that the applicant's fear is of imminent female genital mutilation, related to being forced to enter an arranged marriage, documented in the record as constituting a mandatory tribal custom. The harm or abuse amounting to persecution is the genital mutilation opposed by the applicant. The reason the persecution would be inflicted, the "on account of" element, is because of the persecutor's intent to overcome her state of being non-mutilated and accordingly, free from male-dominated tribal control, including an arranged marriage.

In re Kasinga[204]

Until relatively recently, the asylum system of the United States provided few protections for women refugees.[205] Prior to 1993, with the exception of one Federal

---

202. *Id.* at 13 ("In determining whether the state is willing or able to provide protection to a woman fearing gender-related persecution, decision-makers should consider the fact that the forms of evidence which the claimant might normally provide as "clear and convincing proof" of state inability to provide protection, will not always be either available or useful in cases of gender-related persecution.")

203. *Id.*

204. *In re* Kasinga, Interim Decision 3278 (BIA 1996) (Rosenberg, concurring).

205. For reference to controlling domestic law in the United States, *see supra* note 13. An important difference between the definition of a refugee in U.S. law and the Refugee Convention definition is that U.S. law expressly provides eligibility for asylum protection not only for those who can establish a well-founded fear of future persecution, but also for those who have been persecuted in the past. *See* 8 U.S.C. § 1101(a)(42)(A); 8 C.F.R. § 208.13(b)(a) (1997); Matter of Chen, 20 I & N Dec. 16 (BIA 1989).

An application for asylum under section 208, 8 U.S.C. § 1158, is also considered an application for withholding of deportation under 8 U.S.C. § 1231(b)(3)(A). Asylum is a discretionary form of relief, and withholding of deportation is mandatory for those who meet the eligibility requirements. *See id.* An applicant who is granted political asylum becomes eligible to apply for lawful permanent residence after one year. *See* 8 U.S.C. § 1159(b)). A grant of withholding of deportation does not carry this benefit.

Circuit Court case,[206] no published decisions of the Board of Immigration Appeals (BIA)[207] or the U.S. Federal Courts recognized rape or other forms of sexual violence as persecution or that a woman may be eligible for protection under U.S. asylum laws when she is harmed because of a factor related to her gender.

In December 1993, the Third Circuit Court of Appeals issued the first decision to provide a detailed analysis of gender-related persecution. In *Fatin v. INS*,[208] the court reviewed a denial by the BIA of a case of an Iranian woman who argued that she would be persecuted in Iran because of her political opinion and her membership in the particular social group of women who failed to conform to the Iranian government's gender-specific laws and social norms. The court made three important findings. First, the court found that, when a woman expresses her opinion concerning the treatment of women in her country or her culture, she is expressing a political opinion. Second, the court found that "women" and members of a subgroup

---

Jurisdiction to adjudicate an asylum application for an applicant already within the United States lies with either an Asylum Officer (AO) of the Asylum Office of the Immigration and Naturalization Service (INS) or an Immigration Judge (IJ) of the Executive Office for Immigration Review (EOIR). *See* 8 C.F.R. 208.2(a) & (b). An AO has jurisdiction over applicants who are not in deportation, exclusion or removal proceedings, whether the applicant is in lawful or unlawful immigration status. *See* 8 C.F.R. § 208.2(a). Claims presented before an AO are considered in an informal non-adversarial interview. *See* 8 C.F.R. § 208.9. AOs may grant a claim or refer the applicant for a removal hearing before an IJ. *See* 8 C.F.R. § 208.14(2). If an applicant is maintaining lawful immigration status, the AO may deny the claim without referral to an IJ. *See* 8 C.F.R. § 208.14 (3)). The IJ will reconsider the applicant's asylum claim in the removal proceeding through a formal adversarial hearing. An applicant denied at this stage may appeal the decision to the Board of Immigration Appeals (BIA), which will conduct a *de novo* review of the record before the IJ.

206. In one far-reaching case, the Ninth Circuit in 1987 granted asylum to a woman from El Salvador who had, among other things, been sexually assaulted over a prolonged period by a military officer who threatened to denounce her as a subversive if she tried to escape the abuse. *See* Lazo-Majano v. INS, 813 F.2d 1432 (9th Cir. 1987). The court found that, through his abuse of and threats to Olimpia Lazo-Majano, the military officer was "asserting the political opinion that a man has a right to dominate and he has persecuted Olimpia to force her to accept this opinion without rebellion." *Id.* at 1435. This decision stands in striking contrast to other decisions which dismissed gender-specific harm as a personal matter and therefore not a basis from asylum protection. *See, e.g.*, Campos-Guardado v. INS, 809 F.2d 285 (5th Cir. 1987) (upholding denial of asylum to a woman from El Salvador who had been raped after witnessing the politically motivated murder of family members and while companions of the rapist shouted political slogans, and finding that later threats from the rapist were personal rather than political); Klawitter v. INS, 970 F.2d 149, 152 (6th Cir. 1992) (upholding denial of asylum to a Polish woman who had been blacklisted for her refusal to join the communist Party and sexually abused by a colonel who was chief of security and internal affairs for the Polish government, and characterizing the harm she experienced as sexual harassment not rising to the level of persecution and not inflicted on account of any of the five bases enumerated in the refugee definition).

207. The Board of Immigration Appeals (BIA), part of the Executive Office for Immigration Review, is an administrative tribunal created by regulation. *See* 8 C.F.R. § 3.1(a)(1). Only a small number of BIA decisions are published. Published decisions serve as precedent, binding on immigration judges throughout the country, except in jurisdictions where there is a federal court ruling to the contrary. *See* DEBORAH E. ANKER, THE LAW OF ASYLUM IN THE UNITED STATES 14 (2d ed. 1991).

208. 12 F.3d 1233 (3rd Cir. 1993).

comprised of "women who refuse to conform to the Iranian government's gender-specific laws and social norms" could constitute a particular social group within the meaning of refugee as defined by the immigration laws and interpreted by the BIA.[209] Third, in the context of evaluating whether forcing a woman to adhere to strict codes of behavior, including veiling, would constitute persecution, the court recognized that forcing a person to engage in conduct abhorrent to their own beliefs might rise to the level of persecution.[210]

In May 1995, the U.S. Immigration and Naturalization Service (INS), following the lead of the Canadian Immigration and Refugee Board, issued a set of gender guidelines in the form of a memorandum addressed to all INS Asylum Officers from Phyllis Coven of the INS's Office of International Affairs.[211] Entitled *Considerations for Asylum Officers Adjudicating Asylum Claims from Women (INS Gender Guidelines)*,[212] this memorandum sets out both procedural and substantive guidelines

---

209. The Third Circuit cited the standard set forth by the Board of Immigration Appeals in *Matter of Acosta*, Interim Dec. No. 2986, at 25 (BIA 1985). In *Acosta*, the Board defined a particular social group as:

> a group of persons all of whom share a common, immutable characteristic. The shared characteristic might be an innate one such as sex, color, or kinship ties, or in some circumstances it might be a shared past experience such as military leadership or land ownership. . . . It must be one that the members of the group either cannot change, or should not be required to change because it is fundamental to their individual identities or consciences.

Id. at 233. The *Fatin* Court set out three criteria which must be met to establish asylum eligibility based on social group membership: (1) the group must constitute a particular social group within the meaning of the Immigration and Nationality Act; (2) the applicant must be a member of that group; and (3) the applicant has been persecuted in the past or has a well-founded fear that she will be persecuted in the future based on her group membership. *See* Fatin v. INS, 12 F.3d 1233, 1240 (3rd Cir. 1993). The court did not grant protection because it found that Fatin had not established that all women in Iran were subject to persecution or that she was a member of the particular subgroup of women who would fail to conform.

210. *Fatin*, 12 F.3d at 1242. The two examples the court cited were being forced to renounce one's own beliefs or desecrate a holy object. *Id.* But Fatin had not shown she would disobey the rules affecting women or that her obeyance of them would be "profoundly abhorrent" so as to amount to persecution. *Id.*

211. The *Guidelines* formally apply only to the "affirmative" asylum process, that is, the process through which an applicant can apply directly to the Asylum Office of the Immigration and Naturalization Service, and not to cases before the Executive Office for immigration review. However, because the *Guidelines* are an interpretation of existing law, the issues highlighted within them are equally relevant in a removal context.

212. Phyllis Coven, *Considerations for Asylum Officers Adjudicating Asylum Claims from Women* (May 26, 1995) (*INS Gender Guidelines*). In July 1996, Australia became the third country to issue guidelines for women's claims to refugee status. *See supra* note 9. In 1997, non-governmental groups in Denmark issued a call for gender guidelines in that country. The government of Sweden has passed a special law for the recognition of such claims, and the United Nations Human Rights Commission's Special Rapporteur on Violence against Women has urged that all parties who are signatories to the Refugee Convention broaden their asylum laws to include gender-based claims of persecution, including domestic violence. *See* United Nations Human Rights Commission, Report of the Special Rapporteur on Violence Against Women, Its Causes and

for evaluating asylum claims brought by women. The *Guidelines* offer an interpretation of existing law that takes into account the unique ways in which an applicant's gender affects the asylum process. The *Guidelines* highlight a number of factors which asylum officers should consider in conducting interviews of women applicants and evaluating evidence presented in support of a claim. Like those developed by the UNHCR and the Canadian Immigration and Refugee Board, the *INS Gender Guidelines* address issues tied to gender that may affect a woman's ability to accurately and completely present her claim to an asylum officer. For example, they discuss psychological[213] and cultural[214] considerations to be taken into account when evaluating a woman's testimony concerning sexual abuse or other persecution and the effect that a rape may have on a woman's ability to continue to live within her community.[215]

The *INS Gender Guidelines* recognize that while women often seek asylum on grounds similar to those asserted by men, their substantive claims are often directly related to their gender. Gender-related claims fall into two broad categories: claims in which the persecution consists of a type of harm that is gender-specific, and claims in which the persecution is inflicted because of the applicant's gender or a factor related to her gender. In evaluating whether a particular treatment rises to the level of persecution, the *Guidelines* encourage the use of an international human rights framework, including documents specific to women such as the Convention on the Elimination of Discrimination Against Women, the United Nations Declaration on the Elimination of Violence Against Women, and the UNHCR Guidelines on the Protection of Refugee Women.[216]

The *INS Gender Guidelines* recognize that certain types of persecution are unique to women or may befall women more commonly than men. Among the forms of gen-

---

Consequences, Ms. Radhika Coomaraswamy, submitted in accordance with Commission on Human Rights Resolution 1995/85, U.N. Doc. E/CN.4/1996/53 (Feb. 5, 1996). *See generally* Deborah Anker, Lauren Gilbert, & Nancy Kelly, *Women Whose Governments are Unable or Unwilling to Provide Reasonable Protection from Domestic Violence May Qualify as Refugees under United States Asylum Law*, 11 GEO. IMM. L.J. 709, 710 (1997).

213. The demeanor of traumatized applicants can vary. They may appear numb or show emotional passivity when recounting past events of mistreatment. Some applicants may give matter-of-fact recitations of serious instances of mistreatment. Trauma may also cause memory loss or distortion, and may cause other applicants to block experiences from their minds in order not to relive their horror by the retelling. (*INS Gender Guidelines, supra* note 212, at 7.

214. In Anglo-American cultures, people who avert their gaze when answering a question, or seem nervous are perceived as untruthful. In other cultures, however, body language does not convey the same message. In certain Asian cultures, for example, people will avert their eyes when speaking to an authority figure as a sign of respect. This is a product of culture, not necessarily of credibility. *Id.*

215. Women who have been raped or otherwise sexually abused may be seriously stigmatized and ostracized in their societies. They may also be subject to additional violence or discrimination because they are viewed as having brought shame and dishonor on themselves, their families, and their communities. *Id.* at 5.

216. *Id.* at 2–3.

der-specific persecution recognized within the *Guidelines* are sexual abuse, rape, infanticide, genital mutilation, forced marriage, slavery, domestic violence, and forced abortion.[217] The *Guidelines* recognize that rape and other forms of sexual violence are serious physical harms and that serious physical harm has consistently been held to constitute persecution.[218] They caution against treating harm as personal simply because it is sexual.[219] They also recognize that persecution is not limited to physical harms, but is "broad enough to include governmental measures that compel an individual to engage in conduct that is not physically painful or harmful but is abhorrent to that individual's deeply held beliefs."[220] For example, the imposition on a woman of a particular religious code or laws may constitute persecution if the laws or code are fundamentally abhorrent to that woman's deeply held religious convictions.[221]

To constitute a basis for asylum, the persecution must be "on account of" one of the five grounds enumerated in the Act: race, religion, nationality, membership in a particular social group, or political opinion. In evaluating the nexus between the harm and the persecution, the *Guidelines* instruct adjudicators to consider how gender affects each of the grounds enumerated within the refugee definition.[222] For example, when a woman is persecuted for expressing her views concerning the treatment of women by her government or her society, that persecution is inflicted on account of her political opinion.[223] Similarly, when a woman is harmed for refusing to conform to an interpretation of a religious requirement imposed specifically on women, that persecution is inflicted on account of religion.[224] If a woman is persecuted because she is a woman or because she is part of a sub-group of all women (e.g., women who refuse to conform to their country's strict behavioral mores for women), her case should be evaluated within the "particular social group" category of the refugee definition.[225] For example, when a woman is persecuted because she refuses to obey rules or norms regarding the behavior of women in her country or her society, she may face persecution because of her membership in the particular social group of "women who fail to conform." Finally, while the persecutor will usually be the government, the

---

217. Although women applicants frequently present asylum claims for reasons similar to male applicants, they may also have had experiences that are particular to their gender. A woman may present a claim that may be analyzed and approved under one or more grounds. For example, rape (including mass rape in, for example, Bosnia), sexual abuse and domestic violence, infanticides and genital mutilation are forms of mistreatment primarily directed at girls and women and they may serve as evidence of past persecution on account of one or more of the five grounds. *Id.* at 4.

218. *Id.* at 9.

219. *Id.*

220. *Id.* at 10 (citing *Fatin*, 12 F.3d at 1241).

221. *Id.* at 10 (citing Fisher v. INS, 37 F.3d 1371 (9th Cir. 1994), *rev'd on other grounds*, 79 F.3d 955 (9th Cir. 1996) (citing *Fatin*, 12 F.3d at 1381)).

222. *Id.* at 8.

223. *Id.* at 11.

224. *Id.* at 10.

225. *Id.* at 13.

guidelines recognize that, in gender-related cases, the persecutor is often a non-governmental actor or entity whom the government is unable or unwilling to control.[226] For example, in a case involving domestic violence or the forcible imposition of a harmful cultural practice, the persecutor will often be a member of the applicant's own family. In such cases, the applicant must demonstrate that the persecution is based on one of the five enumerated grounds and that she cannot obtain protection from her government.[227]

With the *INS Gender Guidelines* have come a number of groundbreaking decisions by Immigration Judges, the BIA, and federal courts that have begun to address both gender-specific persecution and persecution on account of gender. In 1995, the Board of Immigration Appeals, in *Matter of D—V—*,[228] designated as a precedent its first gender-related decision. Finding that rape constituted a form of grievous harm amounting to persecution, the Board overturned the decision of an immigration judge and granted asylum to a Haitian woman who had been brutally raped by soldiers in retaliation for her political opinions and activities and rendered permanently unable to bear children as a result.[229] *Matter of D—V—* opened the door to a number of decisions by immigration judges and unpublished decisions of the Board of Immigration Appeals granting asylum to women who have been subjected to rape or other forms of sexual violence.

Despite the growing recognition of the severity of sexual violence and its use as a tool of political persecution, however, applicants continue to face difficulties in obtaining recognition of the political nature of their harm. In a recent case, the Seventh Circuit overturned a decision of the BIA denying the claim of a woman from Bulgaria who had been subjected to sexual assault by a government official during an interrogation regarding her political activities.[230] In that case, the INS argued that the applicant should be denied asylum because she had failed to establish that her attacker was not motivated by sexual attraction. One justice on the Court of Appeals for the Seventh Circuit considered the Service's argument:

> Like Angoucheva, I was taken aback by the argument that a sexual assault like this one could be attributed to sexual attraction alone. Rape and sexual assault are generally understood today not as sexual acts borne of attraction, but as acts of violent aggression that stem from the perpetrator's power over and desire to harm his victim. I was therefore somewhat surprised that a division of the United States Department of Justice would take a different view.[231]

---

226. *Id.* at 17.

227. *Id.*

228. Interim Decision 3252 (BIA 1993). Although this decision was rendered in 1993, it was not designated as precedent until 1995, very close to the time when the *INS Gender Guidelines* were issued. *See INS Published Gender Persecution Guidelines* 72 Int. Rel. 772 (June 5, 1995); E. Hull, *At Long Last; Asylum Law is Beginning to Address Violence Against Women, in* XVIII In Defense of the Alien 186 (1996).

229. Interim Decision 3252 (BIA 1993).

230. *See* Angoucheva v. I.N.S., 106 F.3d 781 (7th Cir. 1997).

231. *Id.* at 793 (citations omitted).

In another recent case, the Ninth Circuit considered a decision by the BIA deny-ing asylum to a Nicaraguan woman who had been detained for fifteen days and sub-jected to repeated rape and sexual abuse in detention.[232] The Board had denied the woman's claim, finding that, although she had been persecuted in the past, she no longer had a well-founded fear of persecution because the government responsible for her detention was no longer in power and that no humanitarian or compelling bases could be found for providing asylum based on past persecution alone.[233] The Ninth Circuit reversed the decision of the Board, finding that rape at the hands of government authorities while imprisoned can constitute an atrocious form of past per-secution which would warrant a grant of asylum as a discretionary matter despite lit-tle likelihood of future persecution.[234] The court reviewed extensive literature regarding the severity of the effects of rape and noted that the suffering of rape survivors is "strikingly similar in intensity and duration to the suffering endured by torture sur-vivors."[235] The court specifically noted that the INS had recently taken official action, through the promulgation of the *Gender Guidelines*, to recognize rape and sexual abuse as potential forms of persecution.[236]

The BIA took a further step in 1996 when it issued its first precedential deci-sion granting asylum to a woman seeking to obtain protection from the forcible impo-sition by her family of a harmful cultural practice. In *Matter of Kasinga*,[237] the Board granted asylum to a young woman seeking to avoid female genital mutilation and forced marriage. The Board granted protection to her as a member of a particular social group, finding that the harm she feared was severe enough to rise to the level of persecution,[238] that it would be imposed on her because of her tribal membership,[239] and that the government would not protect her from its infliction.[240] The *Kasinga* case

---

232. Lopez-Galarza v. INS, 99 F.3d 954 (9th Cir. 1996).

233. *Id.* at 961–62.

234. *Id.* at 961–63.

235. *Id.* at 963.

236. *Id.*

237. Interim Decision 3278 (BIA 1996).

238. The Board described the practice of FGM as:

> [A] practice in which portions of the female genitalia are cut away. In some cases, the vagina is sutured partially closed. This practice clearly inflicts harm or suffering upon the girl or woman who undergoes it.

> FGM is extremely painful and at least temporarily incapacitates. It permanently disfigures the female genitalia. FGM exposes the girl or woman to the risk of serious, potentially life-threatening complications. These include, among others, bleeding, infection, urine reten-tion, stress, shock, psychological trauma, and damage to the urethra and anus. It can result in permanent loss of genital sensation and can adversely affect sexual and erotic functions.

Id. (citations omitted).

239. The applicant was a citizen of Togo and a member of the Tchamba-Kunsuntu Tribe.

240. The Board noted:

> The FGM Alert, compiled and distributed by the INS Resource Information Center,

is significant in several respects. It is the first precedential decision of the BIA to recognize that forcible imposition of a harmful cultural practice can constitute persecution. It is also one of the first to recognize that persecution may be inflicted not only by the government or a hostile force which the government is unable or unwilling to control, but may be inflicted by a member of the applicant's own family. The Board specifically noted that persecution does not require a malignant intent:

> As observed by the INS, many of our past cases involved actors who had a subjective intent to punish their victims. However, this subjective "punitive" or "malignant" intent is not required for harm to constitute persecution.[241]

Perhaps most significant, *Kasinga* is the first formal recognition by the BIA that asylum can be granted based solely on membership in a gender-based particular social group.[242] While *Kasinga* remains the only precedential decision of the BIA to address the practice of FGM, a number of immigration courts have now considered claims to asylum and other forms of relief based on FGM.[243]

As in Canada, women in the United States are beginning to raise claims for asylum to obtain protection from domestic violence in their home countries.[244] Neither the BIA nor the federal courts have yet to address a claim on this basis. However, a number of immigration courts have granted protection to women fleeing domestic abuse in situations where they have been unable to obtain the protection of their gov-

---

notes that "few African countries have officially condemned female genital mutilation and still fewer have enacted legislation against the practice." Further, according to the FGM Alert, even in those few African countries where legislative efforts have been made, they are usually ineffective to protect women against FGM. The FGM Alert notes that "it remains practically true that [African] women have little legal recourse and may face threats to their freedom, threats or acts of physical violence, or social ostracization for attempting to protect their female children." Togo is not listed in the FGM Alert as among the African countries that have made even minimal efforts to protect women from FGM.

Supra note 237, at 6 (citations omitted).

241. *Id.* at 12 (citation omitted).

242. Significantly, however, while the Board limited its legal analysis to the particular social group category of the refugee definition, the social group identified by the Board included the qualifying factor that members of the group not only belong to the tribal group which engages in the practice but that they as individuals hold a belief in opposition to the practice. The Board found that she was a member of a particular social group comprised of "young women of the Tchamba-Kunsuntu Tribe who have not had FGM, as practiced by that tribe, and who oppose the practice." *Id.* at 13.

243. *See, e.g.*, Matter of Oluloro, A72 147 491 (EOIR, Portland, OR, Mar. 23, 1994) (finding that the imposition of FGM on two U.S. citizen children constitutes extreme hardship and granting suspension of deportation); Matter of M—K—, A73 374 558 (EOIR, Arlington, VA, Aug. 9, 1995) (granting asylum to a woman from Sierra Leone based on past imposition of genital mutilation, physical abuse by her spouse, and physical violence to herself and her family inflicted because of her political opinion). *But see* Matter of H—O— (EOIR, Sept. 19, 1995) (denying asylum to a woman who had been subjected to FGM because she presented no medical corroboration of the procedure).

244. *See* Anker, *supra* note 6.

ernments. In one of the first cases to address this issue, an immigration judge granted political asylum and withholding of deportation to a woman from Jordan based on severe, sustained domestic abuse over many years at the hands of her husband.[245] The judge found, despite the Service's position that the harm she experienced was the result of a "personal marital dispute,"[246] that the beatings and other mistreatment she suffered constituted persecution within the meaning of the INA.[247] The judge analyzed the severity of the abuse to which the applicant was subjected and the motivation underlying the abuse. He found that the abuse constituted persecution and that it was inflicted on the applicant to punish her for her attempts to express her political opinion through asserting her autonomy as a woman and her membership in a gender-based particular social group:

> The respondent is among the group of women who are challenging the traditions of Jordanian society and government. The respondent's challenge of these traditions is threatening the core of Jordanian society, and because of this, the respondent is beaten to achieve her submission into the society's mores. The respondent should not be required to dispose of her beliefs. Indeed, the respondent has shown that she is willing to suffer the consequences of espousing her beliefs. The description of the respondent's social group is basic to her political opinion. I find that, in this case, the grounds of political opinion and membership in a particular social group are interchangeable.[248]

In another case, an immigration judge found that a woman from Sierra Leone who had been beaten repeatedly over a period of approximately two years because she was "mouthy" and attempted to assert her independence, and because she refused to accept a polygamous marriage, was eligible for political asylum based on past persecution and well-founded fear of future persecution.[249] The judge specifically found that domestic violence constituted persecution within the meaning of the Refugee Convention's definition:

> Respondent was previously persecuted by being punished with physical spousal abuse for attempting to assert her individual autonomy and resisting mandated female subservience. She sustained injuries on a number of occasions, including black and blue

---

245. Matter of A—and Z—, A72 190 893, A72 793 219 (EOIR, Arlington, VA, Dec. 20, 1994).

246. *Id.* at 15.

247. *Id.*

248. *Id.*

249. Matter of M—K—, A72 374 5580 (EOIR, Arlington, VA, Aug. 9, 1995). The respondent in that case also raised claims based on female genital mutilation and political party activism as well as domestic violence. *See also* Matter of R—P— (number withheld) (EOIR, York, PA, May 23, 1997) (granting asylum to a woman from India seeking to obtain protection from abuse, including attempted burning, at the hands of her mother-in-law, finding that the harms constituted persecution based on her membership in a particular social group defined as either "middle class women whose family would not meet dowry needs and disagreed with the demands and who made complaints to the police or caused embarrassment to the husband's family" or "married Indian women who did not bear a son"); Matter of Sharmin, 9A73 556 833 (EOIR, New York, N.Y., Sept. 27, 1996) (granting asylum to a woman from Bangladesh seeking protection against abuse at the hands of her husband based on her feminist political opinion and her membership in the particular social group, "young, Westernized, educated Muslim wives in Bangladesh.").

eyes, swollen neck and forehead, and bruises. She also faces persecution because of her husband's threat to kill her.[250]

A CONCLUDING EXAMPLE: THE INTERSECTION OF HUMAN RIGHTS AND ASYLUM LAW

The *UNHCR Guidelines on Sexual Violence*, the *Canadian Gender Guidelines*, the *INS Gender Guidelines*, and case law in the United States and Canada all recognize that claims by women for refugee protection must be viewed within the framework of existing international human rights instruments and the interpretation of these instruments by international organizations. The development of these instruments and their interpretations in a way which meaningfully addresses the circumstances of women is therefore crucial to the development of asylum protection for women. Further, cooperation and collaboration between asylum and human rights advocates is crucial to developing a strategy for the protection and advancement of women's human rights.

In 1994, in a strategy that brought together human rights and asylum law, a group of women's rights, human rights, and asylum advocates from throughout the United States and Haiti launched an effort to obtain recognition that rape under certain circumstances is torture, one of the most severe forms of human rights abuses, and a basis for political asylum. In response to growing reports of rape inflicted by supporters of the 1991 military coup in Haiti, asylum and human rights advocates collected testimonies documenting a pattern of politically motivated rape directed against women in Haiti who were viewed as supporters of the Aristide government. Advocates compiled several hundred pages of reports from government agencies, including the U.S. Department of State, intergovernmental bodies, and human rights organizations, confirming the use of rape and other sexual torture as a political weapon in Haiti; the reports also contained statements and affidavits by individuals, including victims, legal advocates, doctors, and therapists, documenting over 150 individual cases of government-sponsored rape. This documentation was submitted to the Inter-American Commission on Human Rights (IACHR) of the Organization of American States (OAS). At the same time, advocates made a public request to the BIA to publish and to designate as binding precedent *Matter of D—V—*,[251] issued the year before, but never publicly released, granting asylum to a Haitian woman who had been beaten and raped by military personnel in retaliation for her pro-democracy activities.

In early spring of 1995, the Inter-American Commission on Human Rights issued a report confirming the facts presented in a September hearing regarding the treatment of women in Haiti.[252] Specifically, the Commission found that rape as it had been applied in Haiti constituted torture within the meaning of the Inter-American

---

250. Matter of M—K—, *id*. at 13.

251. *See supra* notes 228–229 and accompanying text.

252. Inter-American Commission on Human Rights, Report on the Situation of Human Rights in Haiti, OEA/Ser.L/V.11.88 Doc. 10 rev. (Feb. 9, 1995), at 39–46.

Convention to Prevent, Punish and Eradicate Torture and the United Nations Convention Against Torture and Other Cruel, Inhuman or Degrading Treatment or Punishment as well as a violation of several other human rights instruments, including the American Convention on Human Rights, the American Declaration on the Rights and Duties of Man, the Convention on the Elimination of All Forms of Discrimination Against Women and the Inter-American Convention on the Prevention, Punishment, and Eradication of Violence Against Women.[253] Shortly after the issuance of the IACHR Report, the BIA decided to issue the previously unpublished Haitian rape case as a precedential decision.

The movement to incorporate the claims of women into mainstream asylum law has gone hand-in-hand with the movement to incorporate the circumstances of women into human rights law. Central to the development in both areas has been the recognition that harms women face often occur in situations previously considered private and outside the control of the government, that governments have a duty to provide their female citizens with protection from private as well as public harms, and that when a government fails in its duty to provide protection, a woman has the right to seek protection elsewhere.

---

253. This finding is consistent with findings made by the Special Rapporteur to the U.N. Human Rights Commission who described rape in detention as torture. *See Torture and Other Cruel, Inhuman or Degrading Punishment: Report by the Special Rapporteur*, U.N. ESCOR, Hum. Rts. Comm., para. 119, U.N. Doc. E/CN.4/1986. It is also consistent with the Statute of the International Criminal Tribunal for the former Yugoslavia which names rape a crime against humanity. *See* Report of the Secretary-General Pursuant to para. 8 of the Security Council Resolution 808, U.N. Doc. 5/25704 (1993), pursuant to S.C. Res. 827 (1993).

THE HUMAN RIGHTS OF WIDOWS IN DEVELOPING COUNTRIES

Margaret Owen

There is a saying that when a man dies, his widow can cry with only one eye, for the other one must keep watch over the in-laws (and others) who may strip the widow of her home, her household goods, and even her children.[1]

INTRODUCTION

The intention of this chapter is to create awareness of the principal human rights issues surrounding the status of widowhood and to draw attention to the need for more socio-legal research into the discrimination experienced by widows, particularly those living in traditional communities of developing countries. These topics have been profoundly neglected; indeed, the literature concerning widows is sparse and the jurisprudence is undeveloped. Further hindering efforts, the handful of successful or significant court decisions are rarely reported and legal training seldom covers the complex conflicts between the different systems of law that are crucial to widows' rights. The universal human rights of widows is an area in dire need of application, training, and enforcement.[2]

There is an astonishing ignorance about and lack of public concern for the suffering of widows and their children. This lacuna is particularly shocking because in many developing countries, widows are among the most oppressed, discriminated against, ignored, and abused of all women in their communities.[3] They are often the poorest and the least protected by the law.[4]

The following sections display the lack of domestic and international legislation that protect and promote the rights of widows, particularly in developing countries; the most specific discussion will be directed toward widows in Africa and Asia.

---

1. Based on communication with the author, a widow working globally to improve the plight of widows. While the saying is from Zambia, it is applicable to the situation of widows in numerous countries. For example, in 1994, the President of Zimbabwe stated: "I cannot have it that property that is family property be registered in two names. If the woman wants property in her own right, why did she get married in the first place?" In Kenya, a lawyer discussing inheritance law reform queried: "How can a chattel inherit a chattel?"

2. *See generally* M. CHEN & J. DREZE, WIDOWS AND WELL-BEING IN RURAL NORTH INDIA (LSE, London, 1992); WIDOWS IN AFRICAN SOCIETIES (B. Potash ed., 1986); MARGARET OWEN, A WORLD OF WIDOWS (1996).

3. OWEN, A WORLD OF WIDOWS, *id.*

4. See *Zambia Poverty Assessment*, World Bank Report No. 12985–ZA 1994, at 46–47.

Nonetheless, while most concentration has been focused upon African and Asian women, the situation can be applied to widows in developing countries throughout the world, and indeed, even to widows in so-called developed nations.[5] The following sections may occasionally portray widows as helpless, a depiction resulting from the harsh neglect and abuse heaped on these women by legal and social regimes. Widows have been egregiously victimized, deprived of all property, social standing, and legal rights solely because they are female. In patriarchal society, women are inherently undervalued and devalued and discriminated against in education and employment; any value attained is due largely to their work within the home, as wives and mothers. Their legal and social status is often intrinsicly tied to their husbands. With the death of their husbands, women, already suffering various extremes of marginalization, may be suddenly and ruthlessly stripped of all possessions, including homes, land, money, cattle, and other property. They may not even have a legal right to their own children.

It is important to clarify that when afforded equal treatment under the law, widows are able to provide essential, innovative, productive, and energetic contributions to society. Widows are only helpless when antiquated laws, customs, and practices render them helpless, and even under such debilitating circumstances, many have demonstrated a courageous and resouceful ability to survive despite the overwhelming obstacles.

BRIEF HISTORICAL BACKGROUND—WIDOW INHERITANCE AND DISINHERITANCE[6]

At one time, customary law and practice ensured that even when a widow could not inherit property, she was nonetheless protected by her husband's family, allowed to stay in her home, and given access to land. However, in recent decades,[7] as a consequence of a host of factors such as increased poverty, the effect of structural adjustment programs, migration, land shortage, urbanization, the fragmentation of social relationships, the AIDS pandemic, and invigorated patriarchal practices, that former protection has been replaced by callous neglect and exploitation; thus, the human rights of widows are regularly violated with impunity. In those countries where widows have no legal right to stay in their homes or use the land or other property, no

---

5.   For example, in Canada, "60 percent of all widows and single women over the age of 65 live below the official poverty line." Greta Hofmann Nemiroff, *Canada: The Empowerment of Women, in* SISTERHOOD IS GLOBAL 104, 105 (Robin Morgan ed., 1984).

6.   While the practice of having male heirs of the deceased husband marry ("inherit") the widow is sometimes referred to as widow inheritance, it should not be confused with the situation of widows as women being forbidden from owning property (which could be referred to as *non-*inheritance) or from losing their property on the death of their husband (*dis*inheritance). Inheritance laws apply to real and personal property inherited by heirs upon death, not the so-called "inheritance" of widows into a marriage arrangement upon the death of their husband.

7.   For discussion of land rights, see *Third World Legal Studies: Women's Legal Entitlements to Agricultural Development*, International Third World Legal Studies Association and the Valparaiso University School of Law, 1991.

corresponding legislation provides, or often even allows, these women alternative means of survival, livelihood, shelter, or food security.[8]

Historically, women were regarded and treated as property, as chattel, to be owned and controlled by man.[9] While legal and legislative improvements were made in the twentieth century,[10] patriarchal attitudes and practices still prevail. For instance, in China, traditional treatment of widows is still in evidence:

> Widows were not allowed to remarry, and girls who had been betrothed or married as children were considered widows if their husbands died before the girls reached maturity. Widows were expected to enter Buddhist convents, serve their parents-in-law, or commit suicide. Widows in poor families were often sold by their parents-in-law, who kept their children; marriage to a widow was inauspicious, so they were usually sold as concubines or slaves.[11]

While some demeaning and demoralizing practices are no longer the norm, various abuses against widows as widows still occur with alarming frequency.[12] Females have been universally considered the lesser sex and weaker gender,[13] and widows, a class comprised of women and even young girls, have been especially forgotten, ignored, or silenced. Globally, widows suffer the full gamut of abuses.

MYTHS AND ERRONEOUS ASSUMPTIONS

It is often assumed that there is no urgent need to be concerned with the human rights of widows because they either remarry or are looked after by extended or joint families, especially adult sons. In addition, there is a tendency to think of widows almost exclusively as old women who are protected, cared for, and objects of respect in their communities. This is a romantic, idealized notion, useful as an excuse for inaction, but it does not reflect reality. Indeed, many tend to view widows as disposable, not worthy of time, effort, and resources, as they are deemed to have outlived their usefulness, their ability to make a positive contribution to society, and thus the hardships or demise of widows are regarded as irrelevant, perhaps even necessary.[14]

---

8.   Adetoun O. Ilumoka, *African Women's Economic, Social, and Cultural Rights: Toward a Relevant Theory and Practice, in* HUMAN RIGHTS OF WOMEN: NATIONAL AND INTERNATIONAL PERSPECTIVES 307 (1994).

9.   *See generally* LEWIS OKUN, WOMAN ABUSE 3–4 (1986); WOMEN AND PROPERTY—WOMEN AS PROPERTY (Renee Hirschon ed., 1984).

10.   *See, e.g.*, WIDOWHOOD IN MEDIEVAL AND EARLY MODERN EUROPE (Sandra Carallo & Lyndan Warner eds., 1999).

11.   SISTERHOOD IS GLOBAL 143 (Robin Morgan ed., 1984).

12.   *See e.g.*, CATHERINE WINBERGER-THOMAS ET AL., ASHES OF IMMORTALITY: WIDOW-BURNING IN INDIA (1999); SAKUNTALA NARASIMHAN, SATI: WIDOW BURNING IN INDIA 2 (1990); JUDITH N. ZUR, VIOLENT MEMORIES: MAYAN WAR WIDOWS IN GUATEMALA (1998).

13.   *See generally* KATARINA TOMAŠEVSKI, WOMEN AND HUMAN RIGHTS (1993); WOMEN'S RIGHTS, HUMAN RIGHTS: INTERNATIONAL FEMINIST PERSPECTIVES (Julie Peters & Andrea Wolper eds., 1995); FROM BASIC NEEDS TO BASIC RIGHTS: WOMEN'S CLAIM TO HUMAN RIGHTS (Margaret A. Schuler ed., 1995); HUMAN RIGHTS OF WOMEN (Rebecca J. Cook ed., 1994).

14.   *See e.g.*, paper presented in 1995 at the Beijing Conference: Martha Alter Chen, *Why*

Widows remarry far less often than do widowers, and when they do remarry, the arrangements are often forced upon them, along with unwanted pregnancies. In some cultures widows are subject to a *levirate* arrangement in which they are forced to marry their brother-in-law or are subject to sexual harassment, physical abuse, or rape as a part of mourning ceremonies, as discussed *infra*. If the widows refuse such unions or oppose these practices, or if they insist on remarrying outside their family, caste, or clan and without its sanction, they may risk losing custody of their children, shelter, and sustenance.[15] Physical or sexual violence may be the consequence of resistance to so-called "customs." Further, they may end up in a brutal marriage simply because marriage offers the best option for survival.[16]

Contrary to popular belief, sons are often unwilling or unable to care for widowed mothers, perhaps due to poverty, migration, emigration, or dispersion. Married daughters, who may have moved away in marriage, are themselves discriminated against, being unable to inherit and subject to their own husbands. The males who inherit the estate may be unable financially and geographically to provide support, even though emotionally there may exist a close relationship. The widow's brothers and brothers' wives may not see it as their duty to offer shelter to the bereaved sister.

While millions of widows who are afforded legal rights and practices are self-sustaining, millions without these rights are not. Countless widows live in humiliating conditions, often on the streets or as unwelcome temporary residents moving between the homes of various relatives (which results in their absence in the census). Widows, as women, may have suffered extreme discrimination in education and employment; most sacrificed in these areas in order to maintain the family home. Upon the death of their husbands, if made homeless through eviction, many are forced to beg, become exploited workers in the informal sector, or, in desperation, resort to prostitution.

Widows' human rights are frequently violated systematically and on a daily basis: they often lose their basic rights (to shelter, food, clothing, health care, and protection from violence and degrading treatment) and their equal rights (such as those to inheritance, ownership of land, custody of children, freedom of residence, choice of remarriage or to resist a forced marriage, to training, fair employment, social security, and full participation in society). All of these rights are now guaranteed in international instruments, and, increasingly, in national Bills of Rights, Constitutions, and modern legislation; yet these rights are generally so inadequately enforced and implemented that they have little impact on the lives of the majority of widows, particularly in developing countries.

Widowhood Matters, available at http://www.un.org/esa/documents/conf/fwcw/pim/feature/2WIDOWS.TXT.

15.   Going *nata* in Hindu societies means marrying outside the allowed kinship group, or marriage when the widow is from a non-marrying caste. These problems were reported at the Bangalore Widows' Conference in Bangalore in 1995. *See also* discussion in J. Dreze, *Widows in Rural India*, No. 26 (The Development Economics Research Programme, London School of Economics, August 1990).

16.   *See* LINDA GREEN, FEAR AS A WAY OF LIFE: MAYAN WIDOWS IN RURAL GUATEMALA 83–124 (1999).

STATISTICS

Widows makes up a significant proportion of the female population in all societies, and the percentage increase in the numbers of widows is substantial.[17] The bloody wars which were waged during the twentieth century have likely contributed to this increase. The 1981 Indian Census revealed more than 25 million widows, comprising approximately 8 percent of the population, which is comparable to the percentage of agricultural laborers in the male population. In some African countries, more than 65 percent of all women are widowed. Anecdotal information suggests that in African countries stricken with AIDS, child marriage, and therefore child widowhood, may be increasing.[18]

In general, widows greatly outnumber widowers everywhere, due primarily to the longer life expectancy of women and the frequent age gap between spouses (men often prefer to marry younger women). In developing countries, widows may outnumber widowers five to one. However, not all countries have been able to organize the collection of information for the census so as to give an accurate count of this category of women, the nature of their life, or their economic contribution.[19] The majority of married women are likely to become widows at some stage of their lives. Widows predominate among the elderly. All widows deserve to be visible in their country's statistics, and to have their economic contribution, among others, acknowledged and recorded.[20]

In spite of the numbers involved, little research on widows' status exists. Despite a dearth of quantitative and qualitative information, public policies have not developed to protect widows' rights in accordance with state obligations under international human rights instruments or in any equality provisions existing in national Constitutions and domestic legislation.[21]

---

17.   *Aging in the Third World, in* EMPOWERING OLDER WOMEN: CROSS-CULTURAL VIEWS 66 (E.M. Chaney ed., American Association of Retired Persons, 1990).

18.   *IWRAW To CEDAW Country Report on Uganda* (International Women's Rights Action Watch, 1995); and OLOWO-FREERS & BARTON, IN PURSUIT OF FULFILMENT: STUDIES OF CULTURAL DIVERSITY AND SEXUAL BEHAVIOUR IN UGANDA (UNICEF Uganda, 1992).

19.   As mentioned *supra*, many widows have no fixed abode but move as unwanted visitors between several households, or survive by begging and living on the streets, or are forced to become migrant workers overseas in, for example, domestic service.

20.   For instance, in Nigeria, widows are known to function as farmers, although "[s]tatistics are not available with respect to the number of widows residing in rural areas. Past and current censuses categorized population figures based on sex and age, thereby ignoring the vital statistics on widowhood." Noble J. Nweze, *Women in the Mobilization and Allocation of Household Savings in Developing Countries, in* THE FEMINIZATION OF DEVELOPMENT PROCESSES IN AFRICA 181, 184 (Valentine Udoh James & James S. Etim eds., 1999).

21.   Exceptions are the work of Dreze & Chen, *supra* note 2, and WILDAF and WLSA in southern Africa.

INTERNATIONAL NEGLECT

Although millions of widowed women and their children are subject to grave human rights infringements, the mainstream human rights machineries and even the women's movement have taken little notice of this group.[22] Further, widows do not feature prominently or sufficiently in literature on such issues as poverty, development, or war.

An illustration of the international neglect of widows is the fact that in the 1995 Beijing Platform for Action,[23] a document resulting from the largest international women's conference ever held, not only is there no separate section on widows, but the egregious infringements of human rights that widows experience are not specifically referenced. The obligation of governments to reform gender discriminatory inheritance laws appears instead under the heading of the Girl Child.[24] Nor is there any mention of degrading burial and mourning rights (discussed *infra*), even in the section where traditional rites harmful to women are discussed. In addition, the special type of domestic violence meted out to widows within the family is not mentioned.[25] Correspondingly, in the Forward Looking Strategies (FLS), the document resulting from the 1985 World Conference on Women held in Nairobi, Kenya, the only reference to widows appears in paragraph 286, concerning elderly women. Inclusion in this passage gives the distinct impression that widowhood is mainly an experience of elderly women. Thus, even when finally referenced in international documents, the treatment of widows is insufficient and misleading.

The neglect of widows by the international community, governments, and NGOs is especially serious given that many of the deprivations experienced by widows are not only widespread, but also extremely severe. Widow abuse and disregard occurs in all cultures, religions, and geographical locations. In addition, these human rights violations and omissions are passed on to and suffered by widows' children; daughters in particular are critically disadvantaged by their widowed mothers' precarious and unprotected existence.[26] The low status and marginalization of widows therefore has implications for the whole of society, not just women, and for progressive development in general.

---

22. *See, e.g.*, Andrew Byrnes, *The "Other" Human Rights Treaty Body: The Work of the CEDAW*, 14(1) YALE J. INT'L L. (1989).

23. Beijing Declaration and Platform for Action, U.N. Fourth World Conference on Women, U.N. Doc. A/CONF.177/20 (1995).

24. Beijing Declaration and Platform for Action, *id.* at para. 61.

25. *Id.* at paras. 113 and 117.

26. *See* OWEN, A WORLD OF WIDOWS, *supra* note 2, at Chapter 7, *Child Widows and Children of Widows*.

USE OF CUSTOM, TRADITION, AND RELIGION AS JUSTIFICA-
TIONS FOR OPPRESSING WIDOWS

In some societies, tradition or custom are commonly advanced by the husband's family as justification for driving widows from their homes, seizing their property, and/or forcing them into marriage, widow inheritance, or a *levirate* arrangement;[27] and for subjecting them to degrading burial and mourning rituals, to physical and sexual abuse, and/or to negative social stereotypes.

In some African cultures, death does not end a marriage, and a widow is expected to move into a *levirate* arrangement with her brother-in-law (the *levir*) or other male relative, whereby the widow continues to produce children in the name of the dead man; in other societies, she is "inherited" by the heir.

Many widows resist these practices for a myriad of reasons. However, their inability to seek legal advice, their fear of violence should they protest, and the inaccessibility of the justice systems make it easy for male relatives to take advantage of widows sexually and economically under the guise of custom. So widespread is the harassment of widows that the household descriptions of two of the most common violations have been adopted into the formal language in several African countries—chasing-off and property-grabbing—phenomena which are particularly pervasive in Africa, as discussed *infra*.

Legal systems operate both locally and nationally; enforcement of laws intended to protect widows' rights is inconsistent and neglected. Amid this plurality of laws—customary and religious on the one hand, and the modern law and received law of the former colonial power on the other hand—it is the former that determine disputes concerning the family, land, and the rights and wrongs of traditional ritual practices, such as those accompanying funerals and burials of a husband. All of these matters are of crucial significance to the widow.[28] Whether or not such laws are applied in the state courts, it is the interpretation of religious, traditional, or customary law at the local level that is most relevant to widows' lives. Interpretations by local officials, by patriarchal power groups in the community, by the male relatives of the widow, and by less than independent male judges are a source of oppression to widows and serve to perpetuate women's dependence on men.[29] Local legal and protective systems tend to operate without the monitoring necessary to ensure enforcement and compliance.

27.　In Israel, for example, the Levirate Law stipulates that a widow without children becomes the property of her deceased husband's brother. The brother-in-law may use a *halitza* (an ancient custom in which the widow kneels by the brother-in-law to remove one of his shoes) to release him from his obligation, thereby freeing the widow. *See* SISTERHOOD IS GLOBAL 357, 362–63 (Robin Morgan ed., 1984).

28.　*See* WLSA, *Uncovering Reality: Excavating Women's Rights in African Family Law* (Women and Law in Southern Africa, Working Paper No.7, 1994, Zimbabwe). *See also* WLSA, PICKING UP THE PIECES: WIDOWHOOD IN SOUTHERN AFRICA (1995).

29.　*See* statement by Dr. Nafis Sadik, Executive Director of UNFPA to the Harvard Islamic Law Forum on Reproductive Health and Islam, Apr. 1996.

There are basically two types of so-called domestic customary law: official customary law and living law. Official customary law is a product of the social and economic transformation that many countries experienced through exposure to capitalism and colonialism, codified by colonial administrators into something rigid.[30] It is used by governments as an excuse to resist their obligations under the Convention on Elimination of all Forms of Discrimination Against Women (Women's Convention) and other human rights instruments intended to protect human rights, including widows' rights; it is also used by states as a reason for their reservations to these instruments. Indeed, Article 16 of the Women's Convention, which requires states parties to take all appropriate measures to eliminate discrimination against women in family matters, has attracted more reservations than any other provision in the Convention, on the grounds that it interferes with custom.

The second version of customary law is referred to as "living law": that which reflects the true situation and aspirations of people in their daily lives. Living law is dynamic, uncodified, and untrapped by precedent or case law; it makes *ad hoc* decisions to resolve disputes, is capable of flexibility, and able to respond to new situations as they arise. If one takes this version of customary and religious law (for example, gender-positive interpretations of the Koran could be included here), its very flexibility is a potential force for improving the human rights of women.[31] Some progressive judges have attempted to interpret custom in a pioneering way, using concepts of equality and human rights laid down in Constitutions and in international treaties, and reminding governments of their obligations under the Women's Convention concerning equality and freedom from discrimination on the basis of sex, but they are still a rare breed. And because very few widows are empowered and sufficiently aware of their rights to bring cases to courts, judges have had few opportunities to create case law and precedent that would protect widows from discrimination.[32]

LEGAL DETERMINATION OF A MARRIAGE

Another complex problem for widows caught in the mixture of laws and practices is the nature or legal status of a marital arrangement, i.e., whether it is regarded as a statutory marriage, a registered customary marriage, an unregistered customary or common-law marriage, or no legal marriage at all. Determination of this issue defines whether the survivor of a union is indeed a "widow," and therefore entitled to inheritance under progressive laws. On the other hand, if a woman is married under

---

30. For example, according to Rule 19, Order No.4 of 1963, General Notice 436/63, which codifies Tanzanian customary law, the eldest son in the deceased's first marriage has the right to family land.

31. WLSA, *Uncovering Reality, supra* note 28.

32. For example, in 1995 the Supreme Court of Nepal ordered the government to consult with women's organizations on reform of the Ancestral Inheritance Laws that denied women rights to land. Other examples are given in Florence Butegwa, *Using the African Charter to Secure Women's Access to Land, in* HUMAN RIGHTS OF WOMEN 498 (Rebecca Cook ed., 1994).

customary law, her relatives might claim that the full bride-price (*lobolo*) had not been paid, in which case the widow has no legal rights to anything.

Some governments, for instance in Botswana and Zimbabwe, have taken various approaches to regulating customary marriages because confusion over a widow's matrimonial status has implications for not only inheritance and custody matters but also for widows' rights to insurance policies, accident compensation, and pension funds. Thus, women who have lived with a man for many years, borne and raised their children, cared for him in his final illness, or made personal sacrifices in order to maintain the family home, may find themselves thrown out of the home without any legal redress, either because the relatives deny they are legally widows or because widows have no legal rights or have lesser legal rights than male heirs.

AFRICAN CHARTER OF HUMAN AND PEOPLES' RIGHTS

In Africa, the African Charter of Human and Peoples' Rights and petition to the African Commission have been used to promote the dominance of human rights law over traditional and religious laws and to protect the widows' basic survival rights and her equality rights. The African Charter makes clear that regardless of tradition, discrimination against women, regardless of marital status, is prohibited.

The human rights of widows could be promoted and protected through this regional system. Legal rights awareness campaigns might include information on regional human rights systems, and NGOs and innovative lawyers could base their arguments on behalf of widows resisting rigid and degrading customs on both regional and international human rights instruments. Ironically, the trend to abuse tradition and custom so as to deprive widows of the support they would originally have enjoyed runs its pernicious course in many communities precisely at a time when the majority of governments have ratified human rights instruments.

STATE CONSTITUTIONS AND CASE LAW

Many Constitutions and Bills of Rights contain provisions guaranteeing equality between the sexes and prohibiting discrimination. Judiciaries could play a leading role in the elimination of discrimination and harassment of widows if they would invoke these provisions. For instance, in *Ephraim v. Pastory*[33] the High Court of Tanzania held that the Tanzanian Constitutions and Bill of Rights forbade discrimination on the grounds of sex and that these instruments took precedence over Haya (Tanzanian) customary law. The judge stated: "From now on females all over Tanzania can . . . hold their heads high and claim to be equal to men as far as inheritance of clan is concerned."[34] In *Asha Mbulayambele v. William Shibungi*, the High Court of Tanzania held that despite Islamic law entitling a widow to inherit only one eighth of

---

33. Ephraim v. Pastory (PC) Civil Appeal No. 70 of 1989 (unreported).

34. Ephraim v. Pastory, High Court of Tanzania, Feb. 22, 1990, 87 I.L.R.106.

her late husband's estate, due to equity and hardship considerations, the widow should receive half of the estate.[35]

In the *Unity Dow* case, a Botswana judge concluded that if the Constitutions had intended to preserve the patrilineal structure of the society, it would have expressly exempted customary law gender discrimination from its general equality provisions. As it did not do so, the judge took the position that principles of international human rights norms contained in the Constitutions negated customary law that subordinated women.[36]

In 1992, a judge in Zambia held that discrimination on the grounds of sex was unlawful since it was prohibited in the Zambia Constitution and in the Women's Convention.[37] In 1994, a widow in Ghana cited the equality provisions of her country's Constitution in her legal action against a forced *leviratic* marriage, and won the case.[38]

Much work remains to be done, however, in educating court officials on gender issues and reversing traditional notions devaluing women. In Malawi and in Uganda, for example, officials charged with the responsibility of managing probate are reported to have disregarded a dead husband's will, and permitted, in the name of custom, male relatives of the deceased to seize the estate.[39]

Equality and sex non-discrimination provisions in Constitutions could be used to support widows' claims to equal inheritance rights, custody of children, return of seized property, freedom to remarry or not, and protection from degrading customs associated with burial and mourning (widowers are not subject to such practices). These provisions could also provide equal access to economic resources such as credit, technology, appropriate training, equal wages, and bargaining power in employment.

Widows could use, and occassionally have used, these Constitutional guarantees to challenge in their national and local courts a whole range of legal and executive decisions made against their interest. Enormous potential exists in this area of the law to protect widows against blatant infringement of their personal and property rights. Nonetheless, some Constitutions exclude from the general anti-discrimination provision all matters regarding marriage, divorce, and inheritance.

---

35. Asha Mbulayambele v. William Shibungi, High Court Civil Appeal No. 56 (1986). The couple had no children and no close relatives, and applying Islamic law of succession would result in a distant relative receiving a sizable share of the estate, while the widow would receive a small share on which to live. *See* discussion in Bart Rwezaura, *Tanzania: Building a New Family Law Out of a Plural Legal System*, 33 U. LOUISVILLE J. FAM. L. 523 (1995).

36. Attorney-General of Botswana v. Unity Dow, (1991) L.R.C. 574; Unity Dow v. Attorney-General of Botswana, (1992) L.R.C. 623 (Ct. App.) (Bots.).

37. Longwe v. Lusaka Intercontinental Hotels, [1993] 4 L.R.C. 221 (High Court of Zambia).

38. For this and other cases globally upholding, advancing, or denying rights of widows, see a website devoted to the human rights of widows at: www.oneworld.org/empoweringwidows/.

39. Personal communication to author during research visits in 1994 (on file with author).

WIDOWS IN WAR-TORN SOCIETIES AND REFUGEE WIDOWS

While widows in peacetime often have to endure blatant inequity, widows in armed conflict, civil strife, and political unrest are confronted with virtually insurmountable obstacles. Widows who have survived the horrific genocide in Rwanda also have to struggle to protest the discriminatory customary laws and practices that debar them from access to their husbands' land for shelter, subsistence farming, and food security. War widows have to confront this discrimination in addition to the other traumas endemic in war, such as death of family and friends, various forms of sexual violence, destruction of homes and other property, and loss of income structures. Indeed:

> The violence against women took many forms during the counterinsurgency war. Not only were they witness/survivors of the brutal repression; at times they were its [more direct] victims. Stories from *aldeas* (villages) relate unimaginable brutalities: pregnant women eviscerated, their unborn babies used as balls to play with; women forced to cook for the soldiers after having watched their husbands tortured and killed. And, of course, rape. . . . Widows in particular are forced to confront multidimensional problems as they struggle to survive: not only the loss of family members but in some cases the rupture of family ties and outright hostilities within families, in some cases leading to domestic violence; not only the crisis of taking on the dual economic and social role of head of household but the prolonged psychological impact of their own intimate suffering.[40]

Refugee women face continued and widespread hardship. Returning refugee widows in Mozambique have been confronted with customary rules which prevent them from inheriting land. In Kabul, Afghanistan, the Taliban have subjected to *purdah* and house confinement 40,000 impoverished war widows, who are prohibited from working outside their homes in order to feed and sustain their children or themselves.[41] In the reconstruction process, when the peace comes, widows often find they are the *de facto* heads of households but without any legal rights to make themselves economically independent and capable of providing for their dependants or themselves.

This lack of rights forces them into dependence on men who then are likely to exploit them. In the aftermath of war, women, including the many widows, should have a right to be involved in the decisionmaking process, including the establishment of new institutions and structures that will shape the future of their war-torn country. In discussing the aftermath of the conflict in the context of Guatemala, Green states:

> Many of the widows have suffered doubly, as both victims and survivors. As victims they not only witnessed the unimaginable atrocities of the disappearances or brutal

---

40. LINDA GREEN: FEAR AS A WAY OF LIFE: MAYAN WIDOWS IN RURAL GUATEMALA 31–32 (1999). Zur provides a similar analysis, stating: "War widows, that is, widows of men whose deaths are attributed to *La Violencia* . . . are the most vulnerable to intimidation and abuse: many have experienced economic and sexual exploitation, rape or gang rape; some have been murdered." Judith Zur, *Reconstructing the Self through Memories of Violence among Mayan Indian War Widows, in* GENDER & CATASTROPHE 65 (Ronit Lentin ed., 1997).

41. SHATTERED LIVES: SEXUAL VIOLENCE DURING THE RWANDAN GENOCIDE AND ITS AFTERMATH (Human Rights Watch and The Federation International des leagues de Droits de l'Homme (FIDH), Sept. 1996).

deaths of family members and neighbors, but in some cases they themselves were violated and raped. As survivors they live on the economic and social margins of their
impoverished communities; more, they continue to experience the trauma engendered
by the violence to both their bodies and memories.[42]

In addition, refugee widows suffer particular gender-related disadvantages in
camps, on resettlement, and on their eventual return. They often have onerous responsibilities as surviving heads of households and families, caring for other elderly widows and child dependants when the male adult members have died.[43] Widows' human
rights are breached when they are refused political asylum or immigration visas
because of the difficulties they have in providing documentation and proof that the
marital connection endangers their freedom should they return to their country of origin. Widows fleeing personal violence, such as a forced marriage to a male relative,
or coercion into a degrading mourning rite, should be granted political asylum.[44]

CHILD WIDOWS

Clearly, all widows are not elderly women. Indeed, many widows may still be
children. Age of Marriage Acts enacted in the majority of countries govern marriages
without the consent of parents; however, marriages of minors that occur through the
arrangement or consent of parents are not covered by the Acts. Child marriage
inevitably results in some children becoming widows.[45] Second marriages of these
young girls (if allowed by the religion or culture) are often problematic. Almost no
research of child widowhood exists; nevertheless, their tragedies—deprivation of the
enjoyment of childhood and of education, being forced into health-threatening situations or exploited economically and sexually, etc.—are issues that the Children's
Convention seeks to eliminate. Ratified by most countries around the world, this international treaty should be used to draw attention to and offer redress for the plight of
widowed children.

ELDERLY WIDOWS

Only a few developing countries have been able to afford a system of social security or a pension scheme for old and destitute people. In some Indian states, destitute
widows are entitled to some financial support, but the bureaucratic process is so slow,
corruption so widespread, and the sums so small that poverty remains a virtual
inevitable accompaniment to old age. The criteria of "destitution" may also have
encouraged impoverished family members to abandon the elderly widow so as to

---

42. GREEN, *supra* note 40, at 111.

43. *See* MARTIN S. FORBES, REFUGEE WOMEN (1992), and OWEN, A WORLD OF WIDOWS, *supra* note
2, at Chapter 9, *Refugee Widows*.

44. Violence is finally beginning to be recognized as a legitimate reason for women to be
granted asylum. For instance, France and Canada have granted political asylum to women based
on a well-supported fear of female genital mutilation. *See* Patty Blum & Nancy Kelly, *Human
Rights of Refugee Women*, *supra* this volume.

45. OWEN, A WORLD OF WIDOWS, *supra* note 2, at Chapter 7, *Child Widows and the Children of
Widows*.

make her eligible for the charitable handouts. The Vienna International Plan of Action on Aging, the UN Declaration of Rights for Older Persons, and the relevant sections in the Women's Convention provide some leverage for the NGOs working with governments to protect older widows.

WIDOWS IN THE CONTEXT OF AIDS

In several African countries, for example, Uganda, Malawi, Kenya, Zambia, and Zimbabwe, widows whose husbands have died of AIDS are doubly disadvantaged for they risk being accused themselves of promiscuity, or witchcraft, and possibly murder since they have survived and their husbands have died.[46] There is anecdotal evidence of stoning to death of AIDS widows in some rural communities.[47] All women have an equal human right to receive appropriate health care, but AIDS widows, often themselves HIV infected, rarely access the health services available to men with AIDS, due in part to extreme poverty and stigma. As noted earlier, widows may be forced into new unions with men already HIV infected or suffering from AIDS and into a polygamous union with a man with multiple wives where they are even more likely to be infected. Or, aware that they are infected, women may attempt to resist any sexual relationship, thus subjecting themselves to physical and sexual violence. In response, women are seeking means and venues in which to fight for their rights. For example, in Uganda, there are powerful groups of AIDS widows who have come together to help each other live and work independently of men.[48]

MOURNING AND BURIAL RITES DEGRADING AND HARMFUL TO WIDOWS

In many ethnic groups, widows are considered "inauspicious" and bringers of bad luck; local customs reinforce this negative stereotype. In some cultures and religions there are restrictive rules relating to lifestyle, residence, hygiene, sex, remarriage, dress, work, and even personal habits of women. The nicknames for widows are often synonymous with words describing witches, prostitutes, or misfortune.[49] In higher castes in India, a widow must wear a white sari and remove her *kum-kum* (the mark of the married woman); she is forbidden to wear jewelry or oil her hair. Her hair must be shaved (a common practice in several cultures) and she must remain indoors. Her diet might be restricted to bland food without relish. A Hindu widow is often

---

46. *See e.g.*, Peter Margulies, *Asylum, Intersectionality, and AIDS: Women with HIV as a Persecuted Social Group*, 8 GEO. IMMIGR. L.J. 521 (1994).

47. Personal communication to author during the Widows' Rights workshop at the Huairou NGO Forum, 1995. The informant came from Zambia.

48. *See* OWEN, A WORLD OF WIDOWS, *supra* note 2, at Chapter 5, *Widowhood in the Context of AIDS*.

49. For example, in Ibo, Nigeria, a widow is called *nwanyi ajadu*, a term implying that the widow's deceased husband might still be alive if she brought good luck instead of misfortune. *See* Ifeyinwa E. Umerah-Udezulu, *The State and Integration of Women in Ibo: Patriarchy and Gender Advancement, in* THE FEMINIZATION OF DEVELOPMENT PROCESSES IN AFRICA 131, 135 (Valentine Udoh James & James S. Etim eds., 1999).

considered so inauspicious that it is bad luck to walk in her shadow. She must never dance or sing or attend social functions.[50] Her status is so low that she is unlikely to obtain legal protection if she is subjected to assault and other abuse, or to be believed if she makes a complaint to the police.[51] Some Hindu castes do not allow remarriage, so that even a very young widow may have to spend all her life in a sort of *purdah*, the practice of female seclusion, confined to the house, vulnerable to ill-treatment and sexual abuse as an unpaid family domestic servant.

In various ethnic groups in different regions of Africa, Francophone and Anglophone, there are customs relating to burial and mourning which are positively harmful. For example, sexual acts are sometimes required as part of the rituals surrounding death and inheritance. "Ritual Cleansing" is, in some cultures, believed needed in order to exorcise the evil spirits from the widow and to protect the dead man's children.[52] Among the Sebei of sub-Saharan Africa, the legal heir has to have sex with the widow to clean out the ashes ("*erendet*") three days after the death. In many ethnic groups in Africa,[53] a widow might be inherited by the heir, or taken in *levirate* to continue to produce children in the name of the dead man; the *levir* could be a brother of the husband or another male relative, such as his son by another woman.

Practices such as ritual group sex during funeral gatherings are life-threatening as well as degrading to widows, and can spread STDs and the AIDS virus;[54] acceptance of this ritual could be tantamount to state-sanctioned rape. The extreme powerlessness of women in these situations makes it impossible for many of them to resist these traditions, since the rites may be intricately linked with questions of property, land, and custody of the children. Failing to comply with these practices may result in allegations that the widow was not a "proper" wife, causing stigma and rejection, or may result in more serious accusations, such as witchcraft or murder.

In addition to sexual rites, there are various degrading customs such as scarification, shaving of the head, body piercing, tattooing, drinking the water in which the dead husband's body has been washed, being forced to sit naked, or denial of basic hygiene that threatens a widow's physical and mental health. Many widows are reported to have committed suicide due to these practices.[55]

---

50. Stories told by Indian widows attending a conference in Bangalore in 1994.

51. Personal testimonies to this author from widows in Bangladesh, India, and various countries in Africa.

52. OLOWER-FREERS & BARTON, IN PURSUIT OF FULFILMENT: STUDIES OF CULTURAL DIVERSITY AND SEXUAL BEHAVIOUR IN UGANDA (UNICEF Uganda, 1992) (gives many examples of mourning and burial rites which are degrading and harmful to women, in the context of STDs and AIDS).

53. For example, among the Luo in rural Western Kenya, failure to go through the ritual might result in the widow being deprived of her children or accused of using witchcraft to kill her husband.

54. *See* OWEN, A WORLD OF WIDOWS, *supra* note 2, at Chapter 4, *Sex and Sexuality*.

55. Personal communication between the author and the Widows' Ministry, an NGO in Bolga, Northern Ghana.

In Asia, particularly India, an exceptionally egregious rite is widow burning, known as *sati*. In general, *sati* is the practice in which a widow is voluntarily, coercively, or forcibly burned alive, purportedly to "further the progress of the dead husband's soul."[56] In essence, a widow casts herself into the burning flames of the funeral pyre of her dead husband and joins him in death. Officially prohibited, the practice still occurs, primarily because of the social deification of the widow. The act of *sati* is considered one of extreme loyalty or virtue, the ultimate sacrifice a woman can make.[57] Evidence suggests, however, that widows may not always commit *sati* voluntarily. For coercion or force plays a role if the need arises, and "the need invariably . . . arise[s] if the deceased husband left any considerable estate."[58] However, financial considerations are assuredly not the only reason women commit *sati*, for one study revealed that poor women were most apt to burn themselves alive:

> [A]n analysis of the details pertaining to the economic status of each case of sati shows that those in poor and middling circumstances were in fact in the majority. . . . [T]he plight of widows in Bengal was (and continues to be) particularly wretched; and given the ethos that looked upon widows as ill-starred, inauspicious and deserving of only privations, impoverished widows had precious little to look forward to, if they outlived their husbands, except acute distress, both physical and emotional. Thus a widow would have been damned if she was well off, and damned if she was poor.[59]

Indeed, is was the denigration of widows, the fate of a life worse than death that has caused women to subject themselves to an excruciatingly painful death on their husband's pyre. For widowhood was "the worst calamity that could befall a woman; it became the ultimate degradation because it practically invalidated her continued existence. . . . [A widow was doomed to] a miserable existence at best, with social, economic and religious injunctions against her."[60] Aberrant treatment of widows by such customs and practices demeans not only widows, but all of society, and perpetuates the continued degradation of women and girls.

Article 5 of the Women's Convention obliges governments to "modify the social and cultural patterns of conduct of men and women" that might be derogatory to women. In addition, negative treatment of widows is contrary to the non-discrimination requirements guaranteed in Article 1 of the Women's Convention, since widowers are not subjected to such customs. A few governments are beginning to take steps towards redressing this discriminatory treatment. For example, Ghana has a penal code amendment which expressly criminalizes harmful and degrading practices, and

---

56. SISTERHOOD IS GLOBAL, *supra* note 11, at 765.

57. NARASIMHAN, *supra* note 12, at 1–8. The event is glorified, monuments may be erected in the widows' honor, tens of thousands may turn out to witness the event, and the family of the *sati* may get rich from the immolation. *Id.* Not surprisingly, "[i]nstances of *sata*—men ending their lives on the death of their wives—are not unknown, though the number is exceedingly small. But no temples have ever been raised to their conjugal devotion, nor is a man deified for such fealty or even love." *Id.*, at 112.

58. Manjula Giri, *Nepal: Women as a Caste, in* SISTERHOOD IS GLOBAL 460 (Robin Morgan ed., 1984).

59. NARASIMHAN, *supra* note 12, at 116.

60. *Id.* at 36.

volunteered widows' mourning rites as an illustration of violence to women when responding to a CEDAW committee questionnaire in 1992. Nigeria also has amended its penal code to outlaw degrading customs. Section 498 of the Indian Penal Code,[61] raising the penalty for cruelty to a woman when committed "by a husband or relative of a husband" was enacted to combat the prevalence of dowry deaths.[62] This provision could also be used to protect Hindu widows from *sati* and harassment or physical assault by their in-laws relating to unlawful demands for property.

INHERITANCE LAWS AND PRACTICES

While in some regions women are legally excluded from inheritance rights or property ownership, in the majority of countries or societies, the widow is *not* completely excluded from inheritance by law. She may be allowed full inheritance, or more likely, granted a designated portion of her deceased husband's estate. For instance, Muslim widows are entitled to one-fourth of their husband's estate if he had no children; if there are children, she receives one-eighth of the estate. When the law does not designate discriminatory yet definitive inheritance percentages for the widow, various methods, such as wills, intestate laws, and custom may prevail. Even when a husband designates the wife as sole beneficiary in his will the widow still rarely receives the full inheritance, due to the devaluation of women in society or due to other discriminatory norms, such as laws or practices prohibiting women from owning land or having bank accounts. (The Zimbabwean film *Nuria*[63] entertainingly but pointedly depicts the familiar story of the educated urban widow robbed by her envious brother-in-law. The film ends with an unfamiliar story, with the widow's sewing group helping her to find a law and go to court, where a benign judge decides in her favor and orders the return of her car, her house, and her children.)

As discussed above, in some traditional societies, women cannot inherit. On the contrary, the woman herself might be inherited as a chattel. The husband's estate goes to the heir (who is usually the eldest son), and if there is no son, to another male relative. But the equal right to inheritance is spelled out in Article 16 of the Women's Convention, and given added weight in paragraph 61 of the Beijing Platform for Action, in which governments commit to undertake administrative and legal reforms

---

61.   K. Singh, *Obstacles to Women's Rights in India, in* HUMAN RIGHTS OF WOMEN (Rebecca Cook ed., 1994).

62.   Essentially, a dowry is material items, including money, livestock, etc., paid in consideration of marriage. In Gujarat alone, one state in India, estimations are that 1,000 women a year are burned alive (bride burning) in dowry-related incidents. Joanna Kerr, *The Context and the Goal, in* OURS BY RIGHTS, WOMEN'S RIGHTS AS HUMAN RIGHTS 3, 4 (Joanna Kerr ed., 1993). *See also* Yasmeen Hassan, *Stove Burning, Acid Throwing, and Honor Killings*, in volume 2 of this treatise, and Christina M. Cerna and Jennifer C. Wallace, *Women and Culture*, in volume 1 of this treatise.

63.   This film was funded by the Swedish International Development Agency (SIDA) and shot in Zimbabwe, with Zimbabwean actors. It is an effective tool for educating widows and women's organizations on the effectiveness of widows banding together and daring to take disputes over property-grabbing to court.

to ensure that women can enjoy the right to inheritance, land and property ownership, credit, and other essential rights and resources.

PROPERTY-GRABBING

"Property-grabbing" is commonly experienced by widows upon the death of their husbands, especially among ethnic groups in Africa, although it also occurs in Asia, particularly in India and Bangladesh. Widows are often victims of physical and sexual violence and robbery at the hands of their husbands' relatives, even while they are still in a state of grief and shock. These acts of violence and theft may accompany attempts to seize the homestead, the household goods, or the children of the marriage. In addition, widows, in the trauma of coping with bereavement, and because of illiteracy or taboos against dealing with male officials (widows in *purdah* or under mourning seclusion), are regularly tricked or coerced into allowing male relatives or strangers to manage their affairs and ultimately take control of assets. The result of forced displacement of women can have extremely harsh consequences for widows:

> To die in Benares [a town in India] is believed to bring special merit, therefore widows driven out of their homes or with no means of support congregate here in their thousands, to eke out a miserable existence, poorly fed, poorly clad, unwanted, uncared for and unloved. They beg or subsist on the crumbs doled out to them as charity, live in inhuman conditions, and die unlamented. Given no choice, they consider this wretchedness as punishment for the offence of having outlived the men they were married to.[64]

Clearly, these widows are not afforded even the most basic, fundamental rights. Undoubtedly, there are widows in virtually every region and country in the world, developed or developing, living in similar appalling conditions.

ATTITUDES OF PUBLIC OFFICIALS

Widows are prone to be tricked, coerced, threatened, or assaulted by male relatives or strangers seeking control of their material or real property upon the death of their husbands, often with impunity from the predominantly male police or justice system. Even if the widow seeks help and protection from those robbing and abusing her, she is unlikely to find it, for it is shamefully common for police, village heads, administrator-generals, court officials, and magistrates to turn a blind eye to such infringement of widows' human rights. When widows seek assistance from the appropriate authorities, their complaints tend to be treated as "domestic matters" to be resolved by male family members. Clearly, not only inheritance laws affect widows, however, most matters concerning women, particularly domestic violence or sexual assault, are considered outside the public domain, to be resolved as private issues.

An NGO in Northern Ghana disclosed in a report received by the author that when widows attempted to file sexual assault complaints with the police department, the police refused to listen to them and took no action. In some Muslim communities, a raped widow is considered guilty of "*zina*," for she has brought dishonor to her

---

64.   Narasimhan, *supra* note 12, at 54–55.

kin. In Pakistan, women who have been raped may find themselves imprisoned.[65] In the Somali refugee camps in Northern Kenya, brothers have killed their raped widowed sisters because of the disgrace the sexual violence brought upon the family. For these reasons many widows, whilst survivors of rape or other such grave violations, are fearful to report the violence, realizing that an official complaint could attract additional abuse, including social rejection, imprisonment, or death.

POVERTY AND URBAN MIGRATION

Deprived of home, land, and other property, millions of widows become destitute beggars. Many are forced to move into the most exploited forms of informal sector work, such as domestic service or prostitution. Without land, widows possess no collateral for loans and their food security through subsistence agriculture is destroyed. Many find a shred of refuge in city slums, shanty towns, and barrios where their economic exploitation is severe, since the informal sector work that is their last resort keeps them hidden from any regulatory scrutiny.[66] The situation of women in Bangladesh has been described thus:

> Many women, such as those who were widowed or divorced, or those who had been abandoned by men who had gone to urban centres in search of employment, found themselves in a terrible predicament, especially if they also had children to care for. The traditional support system for such people within rural society had gradually fallen apart, and they found themselves with nowhere to turn.[67]

Widows in Guatemala endure a similar situation, using their skills to survive while combating mass production and lower prices:

> Many Mayan widows can now no longer spare the time and money to weave only for themselves and their families or the local market. Without ready access or alternatives for earning much needed cash, they are forced by the exigencies of survival to invest their time in weaving cloth to sell to development projects. . . . The widows need cash, and there are very few ways for them to earn it while remaining in their rural communities.[68]

WIDOWS UNDER MUSLIM LAW

Under Muslim personal laws, widows inherit either a quarter or one eighth of their husband's estate (depending on whether the decedent had children), and the hus-

---

65. *Zina* means "disgrace" or "dishonor" to the family, especially through so-called sexual misconduct, such as adultery or rape. A woman is guilty of *zina* if she is the victim of rape or if she consented to adultery or fornication. For discussion on how this has been applied in Pakistan, see Radhika Coomeraswamy, *To Bellow Like a Cow: Women, Ethnicity, and the Discourse of Rights, in* HUMAN RIGHTS OF WOMEN 50 (Rebecca J. Cook ed., 1994).

66. Governmental or non-governmental organizations can favorably impact upon these women. For example, SEWA, the Self-Employed Women's Association of Ahmedabad, India, has achieved spectacular results in empowering such informal sector women workers and fighting for their human rights in fair employment, just wages, health, and safety precautions.

67. Santi Rozario, *"Disasters" and Bangladeshi Women, in* GENDER & CATASTROPHE 260 (Ronit Lentin ed., 1997).

68. GREEN, *supra* note 40, at 130.

band cannot change this proportion in his will.[69] The discriminatory implications and erroneous applications evidenced by the fact that the widow (not to mention daughters) never receives greater than a quarter of her husband's (or father's) estate are rarely addressed. Nonetheless, the fact that a portion of the estate cannot be legally denied to the widow has been praised.

However, studies in Bangladesh and among Muslim widows in India have shown that, in practice, widows are commonly persuaded by their in-laws to renounce the right to this inheritance.[70] In Bangladesh, for example, widows who moved away or remarry are frequently counseled to give up their share to their brothers, and the widows do so in the hope that should their marriage end, they may return to their natal family. Later they frequently find that they have been deceived and no sibling support is provided. What Islam appears to have given, the local male-dominated society has taken away, at least in many rural areas. Thus, neither daughters nor widows can be sure they will receive their designated shares. Bangladeshi widows rarely initiate litigation for fear of further offending their families.[71] In one Bangladesh village, widows were threatened with physical violence when they attempted to attend a legal literacy workshop.[72] As elsewhere, it is the local, religious, or customary practices that decide a widow's future, and not the official Shari'a law, the modern Constitutions, or human rights norms guaranteed in such instruments as the Women's Convention.

Widows' inheritance rights in Asia and other developing countries are covered by traditional law (custom), religious law, modern law, and actual practice. In India, since the passing of the modern succession law in 1956, a Hindu widow can officially inherit. In practice, however, land is rarely inherited by women. Or if it is, for example, because she is to be the temporary owner whilst her sons grow up, it is common for her husband's relatives to use various devices, coercions, or pressures to deprive her of it. Certain states in India have gone further than others in protecting widows' property rights through inheritance. For example, land rights of widows are more extensive in West Bengal than in Uttar Pradesh or Gujerat. Family relationships and the composition and leadership of the local village councils are crucial in determining how much respect is given to the letter of the modern law at the local level, and therefore to the notion that women too should be allowed some basic, fundamental rights.

WIDOWS WORKING TOGETHER

A major problem with laws protecting or affording rights to widows is enforcement. The powerlessness of widows individually to make complaints and secure legal

---

69. For an example, however, of how judicial creativity has redressed this problem, see note 35 *supra*, citing the *Mbulayambele* case.

70. I. SHAMIM & K. SALAHUDDIN, WIDOWS IN RURAL BANGLADESH: ISSUES AND CONCERNS (Centre for Women and Children's' Studies, Dhaka, 1995).

71. SHAMIM & SALAHUDDIN, *id.*

72. Information received by the author from a paralegal trainer working for BRAC (Bangladesh Rural Advancement Committee) in 1994.

remedies given their low status, the isolation of local courts from mainstream central law reforms and the influence of human rights laws, and the ambiguity about the criteria that might be used to distinguish harmful customs from benign or harmless ones often paralyzes attempts to protect women's rights. An answer may lie in support for widows working together, forming non-governmental grassroots organizations, taking collective actions,[73] and using national and international networks so as to exchange ideas on how to implement new legislation and human rights treaties.

There are some good examples of how widows banding together in solidarity have taken collective action, marched, protested, spoken publicly, and educated their community and national leaders on the treatment and the wrongs they endure. According to reports received by the author, widows in Kampala, Uganda, organized themselves to march, protest, and deliver personal testimonies describing what had happened to them before an audience which included judges, magistrates, and police. Likewise in India, in North Gujerat, 500 widows from the villages, unaccustomed to public demonstrations or public speaking, marched to deliver to local officials a list of their grievances at a public meeting. Widows themselves, and the paralegals and voluntary lawyers' associations that advise them, village leaders, officials, traditional and religious court magistrates, and state court judges require basic training in the status and application of international human rights law, in particular gender issues, including specific attention to issues affecting widows.[74] In Guatemala, CONAVIGUA (National Coordination of Guatemalan Widows), founded in 1988 by Mayan widows, demanded increases in the human rights of widows, staged protests, and sought state compensation for women whose husbands had been killed during the conflict. The organization was so successful in bringing issues to the forefront that the military took action to suppress the organization.[75]

The driving force behind the changes has to be the widows themselves and the women's movement generally. The means of action must include legal battles, test cases, social criticism, use of media, lobbying of political parties and local power groups, and various kinds of collective action to provide support to specific demands.[76]

---

73. Grassroots organizations taking collective action on behalf of widows have been established in India, Nigeria, Ghana, Uganda, Zimbabwe, and Zambia. For information, *see* Margaret Owen, *Organizing for Change, in* A WORLD OF WIDOWS (1996). *See also* WIDOWS BANDING TOGETHER, PEOPLE AND PLANET (1995).

74. At a Widows' Conference held in Bangalore in March 1994, various presenters drew attention to the ignorance and confusion among officials and lawyers' groups over the relationship between the modern Hindu Law of Succession (1956) and local laws and traditions. Similarly, voluntary lawyers' groups in Bangladesh, and in several countries in Anglophone Africa, in discussions with this author, have admitted confusion as to the status of the CEDAW. Legal training and judicial administration courses organized through British institutions or funded by Western donors barely address the issues concerned with human rights, customary law, religion, traditional and local courts.

75. *See* discussion in GREEN, *supra* note 40, at 106–07.

76. In India, deserted and divorced women (parityakta) have formed a movement. In Gujerat, India, and in Kampala, Uganda, widows organized themselves into a protest march, and presented testimonials about their ill-treatment before members of the judiciary and other officials. Communication with author.

The dichotomy to be overcome is that widows (women) must have basic empowerment before they can effectively seek equal or comparable empowerment rights afforded to widowers (men).

THE WOMEN'S CONVENTION AND WIDOWS

The Convention on the Elimination of All Forms of Discrimination against Women is the most comprehensive international legal instrument concerning the human rights of women. The Women's Convention sets forth a minimum standard of treatment. While the Women's Convention regretfully does not specifically mention widows, many of its articles are relevant to various aspects of widowhood. It does, therefore, provide a framework for advocacy and action on behalf of promoting and protecting the human rights of widows.

The Women's Convention particular importance lies in its imposition of legal obligations on ratifying governments to act to eliminate discrimination. Therefore, to conform, governments *inter alia* should outlaw (by properly enforced penal legislation) all actions that deprive widows of their property. This would entail a great deal more than simply passing a law prohibiting such offenses as "property-grabbing" or "chasing-off." Widows should not be afforded fewer rights than widowers. Thus, appropriate legislation would require, at a minimum, enforcement provisions and severe penalties for any person (including government officials) who perpetrates, aids, or abets discriminatory actions, or implicitly condones the crime by refusing assistance to widows when under an obligation to protect them.

Under Article 5 of the Women's Convention, states parties should take all appropriate measures to "modify the social and cultural patterns of conduct of men and women, with a view to achieving the elimination of prejudices and customary and all other practices which are based on the idea of the inferiority or the superiority of either of the sexes." Governments who have ratified the Women's Convention are obliged to study how widows are treated under traditional law, and to prohibit, by penal law, any actions that are degrading, harmful, or humiliating to widows. For instance, since widowers are not bound to follow degrading mourning customs, such practices must be deemed unequal treatment proscribed by the Women's Convention.[77]

As previously mentioned, the government of Ghana, responding to a 1990 enquiry from the Committee on the Elimination of all Forms of Discrimination against Women (CEDAW) on what governments were doing to reduce violence to women, cited a 1963 penal law and its amendments that made criminal any mourning rite "degrading and harmful to widows." However, many developing countries, when ratifying the Women's Convention, reserved on those parts of the Convention which they considered to be in conflict with their culture, customs, and traditions. The most contentious reservations—the reservations which appear most threatening to women (and

---

77.   The intent here is simply to illustrate a clear discrepancy in gender treatment. Please note that even if widowers were required to follow degrading mourning customs, the author would not then find the degrading treatment acceptable, since neither gender should be subjected to demeaning practices.

widows)—are the broad reservations that indicate that the major articles of the Convention are accepted only to the extent that they are consistent with, for example, the Islamic *Shari'a* or with traditional customs and practice. Since many of the traditional customs and practices consistently and pervasively deny women basic rights, if women are granted rights only when they are not in conflict with traditional/religious/customary laws and practices, women are in fact granted nothing. Clearly, reliance on patriarchal customs and rigid conceptions of privacy as justification for the oppression and subordination of women must be rejected.

Compliance with Article 16 of the Women's Convention (concerning marriage and the family), implicitly requires governments to work towards legislation that allows widows to refuse or choose to marry, to inherit property, and own land. Article 16 asserts, in pertinent part:

> 1. State Parties shall take all appropriate measures to eliminate discrimination against women in all matters relating to marriage and family relations and in particular shall ensure, on a basis of equality of men and women:
>
> a) the same right to enter marriage;
>
> b) the same right to choose a spouse and to enter into marriage with their full and free consent;
>
> d) the same rights and responsibilities as parents, irrespective of their marital status . . .
>
> h) the same rights for both spouses in respect of the ownership, acquisition, enjoyment and disposition of property.
>
> 2. The betrothal and marriage of a child shall have no legal effect, and all necessary action, including legislation, shall be taken to specify a minimum age for marriage and to make registration of a marriage in an official registry compulsory.

Restrictions on a widow's right to inherit property, including the entire estate, are among the most widespread discriminatory aspects of customary legal systems. Property assures additional security, power, and respect, and a lack of property begets reduced security, power, and respect; promoting or restricting its ownership is a weapon of patriarchy. Even where law reform has taken place to give women partial or full rights in inheritance, widows still are unlikely to enjoy the benefits of such legislation because of their ignorance of the legal changes, inability to access the justice system, or due to threats, intimidation, coercion, or force, all constraints cultivated by a system of marginalization and discrimination.

Since Article 16 of the Women's Convention emphasizes the human right of women to the same right as men to free choice of a spouse and to enter marriage only with their free and full consent, this provision might be successfully used by widows opposing a *levirate* arrangement or other forced cohabitation or marriage to the dead husband's brother. Likewise, a widow who resists pressure to bear children in the name of the dead husband through impregnation by his brother should be able to obtain protection through the judicial system.

Article 16 states that the welfare of children shall be paramount in deciding all questions on the dissolution of marriage (implicitly this must include dissolution by death); dependence on this subparagraph should ensure that a widow retains custody of young children. The practical problem for a widow is how to shelter, feed, clothe, and educate young children when not granted full inheritance rights and is also discriminated against in education and employment. Further, rural widows seldom receive land or usufructuary rights for even subsistence farming.

To ensure that the children are not automatically taken from their widowed mother, governments need to take positive action on behalf of the children, particularly the discriminated against daughters. This action may be in the form of educational scholarships and grants to allow daughters to attend secondary as well as primary schools. Changes in administrative measures are needed so that school arrangements take account of the girl-child's domestic chores of assisting her widowed mother, such as sibling care.[78]

THE WOMEN'S CONVENTION AND HEALTH CARE FOR WIDOWS

Article 12 of the Women's Convention requires governments to eliminate discrimination in the field of health care. To ensure the protection of health care rights for widows, collective action could be taken, for example, against health care facilities that discriminate (in attitude as well as action) against and between women and widows, denying the latter family planning and reproductive health services. Most reproductive health services address married women or young women, as only these women are deemed to be sexually active; widows frequently are not considered. Yet widows, just like other women, may need treatment for sexually transmitted diseases, cancer, gynecological problems, or other ailments that affect women. Widows may have sexual relations, become pregnant, be sexually assaulted, or contract AIDS or venereal diseases. Article 12 of the Women's Convention requires state parties to ensure that "health care services, including those relating to family planning" are available to women. This right pertains to all women, including widowed women, so failing to provide these services to widows is a breach of obligations under the Women's Convention.

Surveys have shown that Indian widows face a death rate nearly twice that of married women of similar age. Widows predominate among elderly populations, and elderly women have particular health care needs. Poverty brings ill health due to many factors, including poor nutrition, stress, neglect, and vulnerability to disease.[79]

---

78. The human right to education is hard to realize when parents in many developing countries, especially in Africa, must pay up to 100 percent of the school fees, and where widows are among the poorest of the poor. Other measures should also be taken, such as crèches at school for younger siblings and free hostels in town for secondary school girl students, to make this human right for widows' children an actuality. *See generally* World Bank, *Letting Girls Learn: Promising Approaches in Primary and Secondary Education* 133 (World Bank Discussion Paper, 1991) (describing some interesting approaches to increasing and lengthening girls' school attendance).

79. For the linkages, *see* M. T. Feurstein, Poverty and Health (1997). Further, widows are often traditional birth care attendants (TBAs), and health care providers for their communities, and this role too needs to be acknowledged so that they can be trained to protect their own health while dealing with the sickness of others.

Considering the higher mortality of widows compared to married women of the same age, reliance on Article 12 of the Women's Convention could conceivably be used to oblige governments to improve health care for widows of all ages.

EMPOWERING WIDOWS IN DEVELOPMENT (EWD)[80]

Following a Widows' Rights workshop at the 1995 Huairou NGO Forum, held during the Fourth World Conference on Women, a new international NGO for widows was established. This organization, EWD, was developed as an information clearinghouse, an advocacy force, a training resource, and a networking center for promoting the human rights of widows. At its core are the principles that widows' voices must be heard internationally, nationally, regionally, and locally, and gender sensitivity training and awareness must be given adequate attention in the agendas of all human rights bodies and organizations and by all state and local governments.

RECOMMENDATIONS FOR IMPROVING THE STATUS OF WIDOWS

Numerous steps could be taken both domestically and internationally to improve the rights of widows, including:

(1) Analyzing, from the perspective of widowhood, policies and programs relating to structural adjustment, external debt, education and health services for widows and their children, training, agricultural extension services, employment income-generating, and credit facilities.

(2) Developing rural agricultural and fishing sectors especially for widows and their children.

(3) Analyzing the interrelations between poverty and ill-health among widows, through comparative studies.

(4) Researching and regulating the informal sector employment field, especially domestic service.

(5) Distinguishing widow-headed from other female-headed households, and looking specifically at the conditions of widows who are homeless or who are forced to move, for example, as exploited domestic workers, between various households.

(6) Developing anti-poverty programs targeting rural widows to allow them to remain in their villages and cultivate gardens as subsistence farmers.

(7) Supporting organizations providing refuge for elderly widows and those with young children who cannot work.

(8) Ensuring access to free or low-cost legal services for widows, and supporting training of all those involved in the justice system (including traditional

---

80. Empowering Widows in Development, 36 Faroe Rd., London W14 OEP, U.K., ph/fax 44 (0) 171–603–9733; margaretowen@compuserve.com; http://www.oneworld.org/empoweringwidows/.

and religious courts) in international human rights laws, in particular the Women's Convention.

There are also strategic objectives that can be achieved, including revising laws and administrative practices. Actions needed to be taken in these regards include:

(1) Legal literacy on all aspects of widowhood, including inheritance rights, land ownership, custody of children, protection from property-grabbing and violence.

(2) Legislative and administrative reforms to give widows full and equal access to economic resources including the rights to inheritance and ownership of land and other property, credit, natural resources and appropriate technology.

(3) Enforcing the international laws against trafficking and prostitution of women.

(4) Enacting laws to safeguard the employment rights of widows working in the informal sector, such as domestic service.

(5) Enacting penal laws, with heavy sentences, to prohibit property-grabbing and chasing off. Making it a criminal offense for police, magistrates, judges, village headmen, and state officials to condone such actions, or to fail to respond to requests from widows for assistance.

(6) Making it a crime for anyone to remove property from a widow except with an order from a court.

(7) Encouraging special credit facilities for widows without land collateral.

(8) Granting a widow's daughter full and complete access to education; organizing free and safe hostels for widows' daughters attending secondary schools; supporting crèches in all schools where daughters can bring younger siblings.

(9) Informing all relevant organizations and individual officials of the existence of the U.N. Special Rapporteur against Violence to Women.

Actions needed regarding gender-based methodologies and research to address widowhood include:

(1) Collecting gender and age-desegregated data on widowhood, poverty, health, employment, residence, and violence; developing qualitative and quantitative statistical indicators on widowhood.

(2) Collecting qualitative and quantitative information on remarriage, child marriage, and child widowhood.

Actions to be taken regarding child widowhood include:

(1) Researching, monitoring and regulating child marriage and child widowhood.

(2) Ensuring the disaggregation by sex and age of all data relating to the children of widows and child widows.

(3) Setting up special educational program for the daughters of widows to reduce the incidence of early marriage. Endow special scholarships for such children and for child widows.

(4) Developing and implementing comprehensive programs to protect the children of widows from violence and abuse.

(5) Researching the linkages between the children of widows and child prostitution, street children, debt bondage, and other forms of exploited child labor.

(6) Encouraging studies on the development and welfare of widows' daughters, comparing them with other categories of children.

CONCLUSION

Widows are among the most discriminated against, disempowered, and disadvantaged women throughout the world. The plight of widows has been ignored by national and international bodies, including human rights organizations, and indeed, even by the women's community. This silence and injustice must be confronted and redressed.

Governments and the international community must no longer ignore the claims of widows to enjoy their fundamental human rights to life, home, resources, employment, and dignity, nor the fate of so many millions of children dependent on widowed mothers.

One important step towards progress on the issue of widow's human rights might be initiated through the CEDAW. Understanding of the many complex issues and how to deal with them would be greatly enhanced if the CEDAW could select widow discrimination as a subject for reporting by states parties. Further, the status of widows must be placed on the CEDAW agenda, with steps taken to resolve the blatant discrimination and violence facing widows. Ideally, a Special Rapporteur on Widows would be appointed to intensively review the status of widows, and make recommendations to improve the situation of widows throughout the world.

DISABLED WOMEN AND INTERNATIONAL HUMAN RIGHTS

Theresia M. Degener

HUMAN RIGHTS VIOLATIONS AND DISABLED WOMEN

Disabled women face a multitude of physical or mental circumstances that may seriously impair their full enjoyment of, or participation in, all levels of public or private life. The disabilities come in various forms, including visual, auditory, and mobility challenges. Despite the fact that disability affects women of all nationalities and ethnic groups,[1] of all ages, religions, social classes, or other status, disabled women have long been ignored in disability as well as state or nongovernmental gender policy.

Traditional pre-natal maternal health and family planning programs have never included disabled women as a specific category of beneficiary, despite their special needs. Women with disabilities are often not considered to be fit mothers or fit for motherhood. Maternal health programs, which prepare pregnant women for motherhood, generally exclude disabled mothers. Like most mothers, disabled mothers feel insecure with their first newborn. But unlike non-disabled mothers, they must solve many technical problems for which neither the private market nor the health care system offers advice or assistance. If disabled mothers fail as caretakers for their child, they face the danger of losing custody. The law is replete with blind, deaf, physically challenged, or other disabled mothers having to fight for custody of their child or children and often losing. Guardianship laws commonly provide that the child be separated from an unfit mother, and disabled mothers are at high risk to be considered as such, or other relatives, viewed as more capable, are given custody. For instance, in Greece, a blind woman was denied custody of her children because of her impairment.[2] In Germany, disabled women are rarely allowed to adopt a child.[3] In Spain, the Constitutional Court decided in 1994 that disabled women may be sterilized against their will.[4] In 1995, a court in

---

1.   In Germany, there is a growing concern about use of the term "race," which is seen as a socially constructed distinction with no scientific background. Considering the special role the terminology of "race" played in the genocide and eugenic policies of National Socialism, the term is increasingly excluded from modern German language and replaced by the term "ethnic group."

2.   *Invisible Citizens, Disabled Person's Status in the European Treaties*, Report for the European Day of Disabled Persons, European Parliament (D/1995/7560/2) (1995).

3.   Theresia Degener, *Benachteiligung behinderter Frauen, in* FEMINISTISCHER JURISTINNENTAG, Passau 31.3.–2.4.95, Dokumentation 35–46 (1996).

4.   S. Arnade, *Zur rechtlichen Situation von Frauen mit Behinderungen, in* NETZWERK VON FRAUEN UND MÄDCHEN MIT BEHINDERUNGEN NORDRHEIN WESTFALEN 27 (1995).

Northern Ireland ordered a seventeen-year-old intellectually disabled woman to undergo a compulsory abortion.[5]

Guardianship laws usually do not recognize the social circumstances under which disabled women may become unfit parents. Even if technical solutions have been developed to assist mothers with disabilities,[6] they do not fall within the services of general family programs, but rather are delivered under what is called a medical rehabilitation program that has not been developed to assist mothers with disabilities. Medical policy and law are typically male-oriented. Most countries developed medical rehabilitation programs during and after war to provide services for a great number of injured servicemen.[7] War injuries to civilians, especially women, were not given appropriate attention. For example, after the First and Second World Wars, medical and vocational rehabilitation programs for injured belligerents took priority in the governmental policies of most European countries and the United States. Similar developments took place in Zimbabwe after its war of independence.[8] These programs were designed to rehabilitate war-disabled men.

Apart from disability benefits based on military status, the other main category in rehabilitation law is employment injury disability. The laws which regulate eligibility, benefits, and services provided by these programs are based on the assumption that an injured or disabled worker is male. Disabled women slip through the cracks. Often they are not eligible for rehabilitation benefits because they have not served as soldiers or they did not become disabled through a work accident. Many rehabilitation schemes do not cover those disabled women who became disabled through an accident, such as while working in the home. Similarly, as stated, neither family programs nor any other combined programs are available to assist disabled women.

Neglect of disabled women's interests can also be detected in the history of the women's movements all over the world. When (white) feminists claimed their right to privacy and reproductive autonomy in the 1960s and 1970s, they usually meant free choice to have an abortion. However, disabled women more often find that they are expected to undergo abortion rather than to bring their pregnancy to term. Deemed "unfit" mothers, or unfit to become mothers, they are often the target of anti-natal eugenic population policies and practices. Many disabled women have experienced compulsory sterilization at a young age.[9] Disabled women living in institutions are often forced to have hysterectomies to "solve hygienic problems" associated with

---

5.   *Id.*

6.   The U.S., the Netherlands, and some of the Scandinavian countries have taken steps in this direction.

7.   *See* Theresia Degener, Personal Assistant Service Programs in Germany, Sweden and the USA: Differences and Similarities (1992); B. Duncan & D. Woods, Social Security Disability Programs: An International Perspective (1987).

8.   S. Lonsdale, Women and Disability 46, 47 (1990).

9.   Theresia Degener, *Sterile Without Consent, in* Imprinting Our Image 114–123 (D. Driedger & S. Gray eds., 1992).

menstruation.[10] Many women with disabilities have no access to birth control because disabled persons are expected not to have any sexual life. As a consequence, disabled women receive no information on where to get and how to use birth control methods. Some doctors even refuse to prescribe the birth control pill to disabled women because they consider it a waste of medication.[11]

SEX, VIOLENCE, AND EXPLOITATION

Because of the false but widely held belief that disabled women are asexual, they frequently are not taken seriously when reporting instances of sexual violence and/or exploitation. For a long time, this subject was a taboo within the taboo of sexual violence against women. While non-disabled feminists established the first crisis centers for rape victims and networks of feminist lawyers specializing in representing rape victims in court, disabled women did not benefit from these social developments, even though isolation in overprotective families or institutions for disabled persons makes it impossible to escape a perpetrator, who is more often a relative or staff member than a complete stranger. Police stations or women's crisis centers are usually inaccessible to women using wheelchairs, sign language, or who are blind or intellectually disabled. Often, disabled rape victims do not even have access to conveniences most people take for granted, such as transportation or a telephone. Insufficient education about sexuality and the right to intimacy contributes to these barriers, and disabled women often have extremely low self-esteem. Analogous domestic criminal laws fail to protect disabled women from sexual violence for several reasons. For one, the standard concept of violence applied in courts does not recognize the special vulnerability of disabled women. Additionally, the applied definition of "incapacity to resist" used in some countries is so narrow that most disabled women are excluded: they are too disabled to fight back but deemed able-bodied enough to "resist."

Procedural laws in some countries also discriminate against disabled victims of physical or sexual assault. According to these laws, intellectually disabled persons are legally incapable of giving testimony in court or of filing a complaint. Even if the disabled woman is able to tell her story or use some other form of communication, her testimony will not count as evidence in some common law countries.[12] In addition, some countries do not accept actions taken by the legal representative as a substitute. The European Court on Human Rights ruled in 1985 that these procedural shortcomings may violate the European Convention for the Protection of Human

---

10.   Regarding Japan, *see* Nakanishi, *Independence from Spoiling Parents: The Struggle of Women with Disabilities in Japan, in* IMPRINTING OUR IMAGE 25–30 (D. Driedger & S. Gray eds., 1992). Regarding Germany, *see* S. KÖBSELL, EINGRIFFE: ZWANGSSTERILISATION GEISTIG BEHINDERTER FRAUEN (1987).

11.   KRÜPPEL-TRIBUNAL: MENSCHENRECHTSVERLETZUNGEN IM SOZIALSTAAT (S. Daniels & Theresia Degener et al. eds., 1983).

12.   DICK SOBSEY, VIOLENCE AND ABUSE IN THE LIVES OF PEOPLE WITH DISABILITIES: THE END OF SILENT ACCEPTANCE? (1994).

Rights and Fundamental Freedoms (ECHR).[13] The case concerned a Dutch woman with intellectual disabilities who had been sexually exploited in a sheltered institution by a male relative of a staff member. The perpetrator could not be criminally charged according to Dutch criminal law because the complaint had not been filed in due time by the victim herself. The father's complaint was not accepted as a substitute. The Dutch woman slipped into a gap of the law. The European Court on Human Rights considered this as a violation of Article 8, the right to respect of private life.

While evidence establishes that sexual exploitation of disabled women most often occurs behind the walls of "sheltered" institutions[14] or within the family, most of these cases are kept from the public eye. Ironically, sterilization of disabled women has long been viewed as a method of preventing sexual exploitation.[15]

These are only some examples of systematic human rights violations against disabled women. No legal recourse at all is available for most human rights violations in the field of economic and social rights of disabled women. Disabled girls have less access to educational services than disabled boys and non-disabled girls. In higher education, disabled women are still an exotic exception. Consequently, disabled women have fewer vocational opportunities and are more often unemployed or underpaid. In the labor force they experience double or multiple discrimination: as women, as female disabled, and other forms of discrimination, such as race, poverty, etc; additional discrimination because of membership in other disadvantaged groups compounds these problems.[16]

THE RIGHTS OF DISABLED WOMEN AS A DISTINCT ISSUE

Until recently, women with disabilities had no lobby group and their interests were neglected in both the disability movement and in the women's movement. As a result, there was no awareness about human rights violations against disabled women at the national and international level. The first changes happened during the 1980s, when disabled women started to organize their own caucuses.

DAWN (Disabled Women's Network) of Canada was one of the first organizations of disabled women and remains one of the most successful groups. Today there are numerous networks of disabled women in both wealthier countries, such as Finland, the U.S., the U.K., Germany, the Netherlands, Denmark, Japan, and Australia, and also in poorer countries, such as Congo, Zimbabwe, India, and Pakistan. Projects and studies on sexual violence and abuse against disabled women have been initiated and

---

13.   X and Y v. the Netherlands, 91 Eur. Ct. H.R. (ser. A) (1985).

14.   C. NOACK & H. J. SCHMID, SEXUELLE GEWALT GEGEN MENSCHEN MIT GEISTIGER BEHINDERUNG (1994); C. SENN, GEGEN JEDES RECHT: SEXUELLER MISSBRAUCH UND GEISTIGE BEHINDERUNG (1993); A. VOSS & M. HALLSTEIN, MENSCHEN MIT BEHINDERUNG (1993).

15.   Theresia Degener, *Opfer wehrlos in jeder Hinsicht*, PRO FAMILIA MAGAZINE, Jan. 1990, at 3–5; M. FINE & A. ASCH, WOMEN WITH DISABILITIES 22 (1988).

16.   E. BOYLAN, WOMEN AND DISABILITY (1991).

undertaken by these networks.[17] The first international leadership seminar for disabled women was held in 1988 in Jamaica. With the help of Johanna Dohnal, then Minister of Women's Affairs of Austria, the first international conference on sexual abuse and domestic violence against disabled women took place in Vienna at the end of 1992. In the 1990s, sheltered houses for abused and battered disabled women were set up, such as the "Power House," established in London in 1995. Self-defense courses for disabled women were taught in the Netherlands, the U.S., and the U.K. Most importantly, disabled women have started to publish their life experiences, along with political views on disability and gender issues.[18] Among the issues being raised has been the relationship between disabled women and the feminist movement.[19]

The United Nations Decade of Disabled Persons (1983–1992) supported these developments. Networks of disabled women, like the European organization DIS-WEB (European Network of Disabled Women), came to life during this decade. This was not only revolutionary from the gender perspective, it also marked a major policy change—disabled persons themselves taking control of disability organizations. Earlier, disability organizations based on rehabilitation, education, or other disability groups were run by non-disabled experts. Non-disabled functionaries were used to "speak" for "the disabled." Disability policies were typically viewed in terms of charity and welfare work. With the rise of the independent living movement,[20] disabled people came to see their disability as a human rights issue and their relation to non-disabled rehabilitation experts generally as one of domination and subordination.

Disabled Persons' Organization on the Rise

Based on the firm belief that disabled persons themselves are the best experts on disability policy, organizations *of* persons with disabilities were established as an alternative to organizations *for* the disabled. When the first international non-governmental organization (NGO) *of* the disability movement was founded in 1980, Disabled Peoples' International (DPI), disabled women were among the founders.[21]

---

17.   *See, e.g.*, L. SIMPSON & M. BEST, COURAGE ABOVE ALL (1991); S. MASUDA & J. RIDINGTON, MEETING OUR NEEDS (1992); SOBSEY, *supra* note 12; SENN, *supra* note 14; VOSS & HALLSTEIN, *supra* note 14.

18.   *See generally* FINE & ASCH, *supra* note 15; LONSDALE, *supra* note 8; S.E. BROWNE, D. CONNORS, & N. STERN, WITH THE POWER OF EACH BREATH (1985); C. EWINKEL & G. HERMES, GESCHLECHT BHEHINDERT BESONDERES MERKMAL FRAU (1985); G. MATTHEWS, VOICES FROM THE SHADOWS (1983); I ALWAYS WANTED TO BE A TAP DANCER (A. Lawrence ed., 1989); J. MORRIS, PRIDE AGAINST PREJUDICE: TRANSFORMING ATTITUDES TO DISABILITY (1991); IMPRINTING OUR IMAGE (D. Driedger & S. Gray eds., 1992).

19.   FINE & ASCH, *supra* note 15; MORRIS, *supra* note 18; Theresia Degener, *Female Self—Determination Between Feminist Claims and "Voluntary" Eugenics, Between "Rights" and "Ethics,"* 3 (2) ISSUES IN REPROD. HEALTH & GENETIC ENGINEERING 87–99 (1990); ENCOUNTERS WITH STRANGERS: FEMINISM AND DISABILITY (Jenny Morris, ed. 1996).

20.   N. CREWE & K. ZOLA, INDEPENDENT LIVING FOR PHYSICALLY DISABLED PEOPLE (1983); R.K. SCOTT, FROM GOOD WILL TO CIVIL RIGHTS (1984).

21.   For a comprehensive history of DPI, *see* D. DRIEDGER, THE LAST CIVIL RIGHTS MOVEMENT (1989).

Nonetheless, women within DPI had to fight to be equally represented within the organization. At DPI's second World Congress in the Bahamas in 1985, disabled women protested and threatened to leave the organization unless they were heard.[22] As a result, a women's committee was established within DPI, and gender has been on the agenda ever since.[23] One focus of the DPI women's committee has been advocacy and awareness-raising inside the organization through leadership training seminars and workshops on women's issues. Seminars at the regional level—with special focus on disabled women—were organized in Korea in 1986, Pakistan in 1987, Bangok in 1988, Jamaica in 1989, Fijii in 1990, Germany in 1995, and the U.K. in 1996. In Africa, leadership training seminars were organized in Mauritius in 1987, Zimbabwe in 1989, and Mauritania in 1990.[24] Another focus has been lobbying on disabled women's issues at the United Nations. In cooperation with another functional committee of the DPI, the human rights committee, the DPI women's committee has initiated, participated in, or otherwise been involved in virtually all activities of the United Nations which concern disabled women.

The United Nations and Disabled Women

Although 1983–1992 was declared the U.N. Decade for Disabled Persons, within the United Nations system, disabled women were not substantially recognized as a vulnerable group with respect to human rights violations until the Nairobi World Conference on Women in 1985. As an "area of special concern," disabled women were recognized in the final document.[25] Other U.N. agencies or organizations, notably the ILO and UNESCO, followed this example and initiated publications and projects on women with disabilities.[26] At a U.N. seminar on disabled women in Vienna, Austria, in 1990, disabled women from twenty member states had the chance to officially raise their voices on disabled women's human rights violations. As a result of the seminar, recommendations were made in a wide range of subjects.[27] In the field of ethics and human rights, it was recommended:

---

22.   Id.

23.   In addition, women are now equally represented on the board of DPI. Three of the six world officers elected at the Fourth World Congress in Sydney, Australia, were women.

24.   Equalization of Opportunities, Proceedings of the Third World Congress of Disabled Peoples' International, Vancouver, B.C., Canada, Apr. 21–26, 1992.

25.   Report of the World Conference to Review and Appraise the Achievement of the United Nations Decade for Women; Equality, Development, and Peace, Nairobi, July 15–26, 1985, at para. 296, U.N. Sales No. E.85.iv.10. An exceptional publication prepared by the Junic/NGO subgroup on women and development in cooperation with several U.N. organizations before Nairobi is the Resource Kit, E. Z. CSEKME, WOMEN AND DISABILITY (1981).

26.   S. STACE, VOCATIONAL REHABILITATION FOR WOMEN WITH DISABILITIES (1986); DISPELLING THE SHADOW OF NEGLECT: A SURVEY ON WOMEN WITH DISABILITIES IN SIX ASIAN AND PACIFIC COUNTRIES (1989); N. NOSSEIR, WOMEN AND DISABILITY (1989); United Nations Economic and Social Council, Economic and Social Commission for Western Asia, Conference on the Capabilities and Needs of Disabled Persons in the Escwa Region, Amman, Nov. 20–28, 1989; BOYLAN, supra note 16.

Appropriate legislation that guarantees the full exercise of the rights of women to decide on sexuality, pregnancy, new reproductive technology, adoption, motherhood and any other relevant issue in this respect should be adopted and implemented. No medical decisions concerning a disabled woman should be made without her informed consent.[28]

Under the subheading of marriage and parenthood, it was recommended:

Disabled women should have access to family planning methods as well as to information about the sexual functioning of their bodies. That information should be provided on cassette, in large print, in Braille and in sign language or by counselors in public social services on a local basis.[29]

The participants broke through the taboo against discussing sexual violence against disabled women and acknowledged that the issue "is a major problem and statistics show that disabled girls and women are more likely to be victims of violence because of their vulnerability."[30] They condemned "discrimination against disabled women with regard to the availability of health care services"[31] as well as "sexual bias" in "rehabilitation services."[32]

Considering the wide scope of the Vienna recommendations, it was disappointing to see disabled women's issues marginalized again in the first comprehensive U.N. Report on Human Rights and Disability (Despouy Report), which was presented in 1991 to the Sub-Commission on Prevention of Discrimination and Protection of Minorities and was later adopted and published.[33] Although disabled women were explicitly mentioned as a vulnerable group, only a limited number of disabled women's human rights problems were specified, notably appropriate access to health care and the right to receive and refuse medical treatment.[34] Significantly, however, forced sterilization and female circumcision were condemned as human rights violations.[35] Indirectly, the report also addressed sexual violence and eugenic population control when it stated:

---

27. Themes included: Statistical Information, Ethics and Human Rights, National Legislation, Legal Instruments, National Focal Points on Women, Leadership Development, Education, Vocational Training and Employment, Marriage and Parenthood, Violence, Sexual Abuse and Safety, Mass Media, Counselling, Social Security, Health, Rehabilitation, Public Building, Transportation, Technical Needs, and Assistance and Research.

28. Report from the Seminar on Disabled Women (unedited), Vienna, Aug. 20–24, 1990, at paras. 17 and 18. *See also* WOMEN AND DISABILITY, SOME ISSUES; SEMINAR ON DISABLED WOMEN (Vienna, Aug. 20–24, 1990), U.N. Doc. SDW/1990/wp.1 (1990).

29. SEMINAR ON DISABLED WOMEN, *supra* note 28, at para. 51.

30. *Id.* at para. 52.

31. *Id.* at para. 70.

32. *Id.* at para. 71.

33. *Human Rights and Disabled Persons, Report of the Special Rapporteur of the Sub-Commission on Prevention of Discrimination and Protection of Minorities,* U.N. Centre for Human Rights, U.N. Sales No. E.92.xiv.4 (1993).

34. *Id.* at paras. 140, 144.

35. *Id.* at para. 174.

Several non-governmental organizations have pointed out that forced sterilization is more often used on disabled women than men in order to prevent them from having children. Often, disabled women are sterilized for eugenic reasons or simply because they are often victims of rape. Indeed, sterilization is sometimes a prerequisite for entry into an institution.[36]

While disabled women could only meet informally at Nairobi, they became more visible at other U.N. conferences. They took an active part in the 1994 Cairo Conference on Population and Development[37] and managed to influence the wording of the Programme of Action, which calls upon governments to "eliminate specific forms of discrimination that persons with disability may face with regard to reproductive rights."[38] At the Fourth World Conference on Women at Beijing in 1995, disabled women became even more visible.

Women's International Linkage on Disability (W.I.L.D.), a network of disabled women from various NGOs active in the disability field,[39] organized an international symposium on issues of women with disabilities at the NGO forum. The symposium took place on August 29, 1995 and was attended by more than 200 disabled women. DPI Program Officer Justine Kiwanuka, an organizer of the symposium, later reflected: "To many women, the Beijing Conference was just another United Nations conference. To women with disabilities, it was a major historical event, marking the integration of disabled women into the mainstream women's movement."[40] Furthermore, disabled women successfully lobbied for the inclusion of disabled women's interests in the final declaration and action platform of the Beijing Conference.[41] Among the major issues raised at Beijing were human rights violations affecting reproductive rights and the right to personal integrity of disabled women, economic rights, and the right to non-discrimination.

Human Rights and Disability—A Shift in Paradigm

Disabled persons have long been disregarded and mistreated. As with women and children, legal systems have tended to exclude disabled persons as "non-persons." Eugenic population policies have been carried out through sterilization and killing programs to eliminate those deemed disabled. What occurred during German National-Socialism during WWII was the most cruel and far-reaching policy of this kind, but its ideology and goals were neither new nor exceptional.[42]

---

36. *Id.* at para. 175.

37. Y. Fricke, *DPI Representatives Attend Population Conference*, 1(4) Disability Int'l 22–24, 32 (1994).

38. *Report of the International Conference on Population and Development*, at para. 6.31, U.N. Doc. A./Conf.171/13 (1994).

39. Mobility International, DPI, and the World Blind Union also belong to the network.

40. J. Kiwanuka, *Beijing: Disabled Women Finally on the Agenda*, 2(3) Disability Int'l 15–16 (1995).

41. *Report of the Fourth World Conference on Women*, U.N. Doc. A/Conf.177/20 (1995).

42. Gerald W. Fleming, Hitler, The Final Solution (1982) (over 80,000 mental patients exter-

Modern disability policies are much more benign, but they are also based on the assumption that disabled people are not real citizens. Labelled non-productive members of society, disabled persons are often still excluded from mainstream society, frequently locked in large institutions, and deprived of all that non-disabled people take for granted: liberty, social and political life, work, education, and privacy, to name but a few areas. Disability policy has been based on welfare and charity concepts and has not allowed disabled persons to escape object status and experience full self-determination. Thus, to estimate and evaluate the dimension of human rights violations, the general perception of disability itself has to be examined. Activists of the disability movement have concluded that the rehabilitation concept of disability is a one-dimensional perception of a complex phenomenon.[43]

Perceiving disability as a condition similar to illness and exclusively as a functional limitation means that disability is considered an individual rather than a societal problem, and solutions are sought in the individual sphere through therapy and technical or personal support. According to this approach, neither society nor the environment needs to be changed. The awareness that individual abilities and problems of disabled persons often relate to attitudinal, architectural, and structural barriers of the environment, and to the willingness of society to include or exclude the needs of disabled persons in every designing process, was a crucial factor in turning the disability movement into a civil rights movement. The international disability movement rejects the medical approach because of the subjectivity of the defining process and the power relations in which it takes place. What is regarded as a disability depends to a great extent on individual, societal, cultural, and medical perceptions of what is "normal." This in turn depends on the point of comparison. In addition, the person who is considered "normal" has the right to feel superior, while disabled people are frequently described as "different" without having the right to be different.

Developing Approaches Regarding Disabled Women

While the development of the social theory of disability marked a revolutionary shift in disability awareness, women with disabilities felt only marginally included. The experience of synchronic discrimination as females and as disabled[44] was not reflected in the social theory of disability. In recent years, feminist disabled persons have begun to consider the social versus medical concept of disability from a gender

---

minated by Nazis); Jost Dülffer, Nazi Germany, 1933–1945: Faith and Annihilation 219 (1996) (handicapped persons sterilized or killed by Nazis during WWII).

43. P. Abberly, *The Concept of Oppression and the Development of a Social Theory of Disability*, 2(1) Disability, Handicap & Society 5–19 (1987); H. Hahn, *Toward a Politics of Disability: Definitions, Disciplines and Policies*, 22(4) Social Science J. 87–105 (1985); M. Oliver, The Politics of Disablement (1990); C. Barnes, Disabled People in Britain and Discrimination (1991).

44. Certainly, other grounds of discrimination may also be relevant.

perspective.[45] Three aspects seem to be essential in the development of a feminist analysis of disabled women's lives. The first aspect relates to the male-oriented structure of rehabilitation systems. The male-oriented development of (technical) rehabilitation aids and social services neglects disabled women's needs and interests. The needs of disabled mothers or pregnant disabled women, for example, are far from being met by the "market" of rehabilitation technology.

Another example is found in personal assistant service programs (PAS),[46] which are designed to enable disabled persons to be able to live within community-based settings. However, those states which provide public- or private-funded PAS programs do not provide, on request, female assistants for disabled women.[47] Indeed, in a German case it was decided that forcing a disabled woman to accept being washed by a male assistant does not constitute a human rights violation. This form of neglect of female's needs in the rehabilitation system may be called "neutralization of gender issues" within the medical concept of disability. It is part of the medical concept of disability because the focus is on functional limitations, without seeing the person behind it.

The second aspect of structural discrimination against disabled women within the medical concept may be called "medicalization of gender issues." It relates to human rights violations disabled women experience with respect to marriage and family planning. Laws and practices prohibiting disabled persons from marrying affect both disabled men and disabled women. However, many more disabled women are sterilized against their will or without their informed consent than disabled men.[48] Other methods of eugenic population control, such as forced abortion, only affect women. While these methods of population control also have been applied to non-disabled women, they become forms of "medical therapy" when used on disabled women, who tend to be regarded as "unfit mothers" because of their disabilities, which—in addition to causing functional limitations—raises the alarm that the disability might be of a hereditary nature.

Problems in child raising associated with disability are entirely viewed as an individual, rather than a social, problem. The disability serves as an excuse to apply eugenic population control under the pretext of medical therapy. But methods of

---

45.　Morris, *supra* note 18; Fine & Asch, *supra* note 18; B. Hillyer, Feminism and Disability (1993).

46.　Old-fashioned names for these services are "attendant care" or "nursing care" services. The disability movement rejects this terminology as paternalist. *See* Degener, Personal Assistant Service Programs, *supra* note 7, at 4.

47.　The agency offering PAS services works with conscientious objectors who serve in social service instead of military service. They are much less expensive to employ than employees in the open labor market. Because only men are obliged to do military service, most assistants are men. The case is discussed in Theresia Degener, *Personal Assistance Services and Laws: A Commentary, in* Personal Assistance Services in Europe and North America 15–20 (B. Duncan & S. Brown eds., 1993).

48.　Degener, *Sterile Without Consent, supra* note 9.

eugenic population control are not means of medical therapy because nothing is cured. What is regulated in effect is a gender issue, the procreational behavior of disabled women. This is the core criticism of the medicalization of gender issues.

The third aspect relates to sexual violence against disabled women and may be called the "depersonalization aspect." According to feminist theory, sexual violence has nothing to do with the act of sex itself, but rather with power and oppression. The widespread use of sexual violence against women throughout history has been analyzed as a key weapon of patriarchal domination. As a means of humilating and degrading women, sexual violence against disabled women aggravates the object status of disabled persons. No disabled person is expected to have a right to sexual self-determination because disability is associated with an asexual life-style. This stereotype of disability deprives disabled persons of personhood in that a disabled individual is not seen as a person with private desires and wishes. Sexual violence and exploitation must be seen as another form of depersonalization. It is a severe violation of human rights and human dignity and contributes to the object status of disabled women.

These three aspects demonstrate that violations of the human rights of disabled women have both a gender and a disability component. The (minimum) double discrimination against disabled women must be addressed by a two-fold approach. In addition to raising gender awareness with respect to disability-based discrimination, the construction of disability as a medical issue has to be dismantled and substituted by a social model of disability. In a nutshell, this means that most problems associated with disability are not of medical cause, but rather result from socially constructed barriers, attitudes, exclusions, and devaluations. These debilitating factors are not gender neutral. From this perspective, the present U.N. human rights instruments for disabled women have to be examined and improved.

International Human Rights Instruments for Disabled Women

Despite the fact that disabled persons constitute an extremely large minority afflicted with serious human rights violations, disabled persons are not covered by the United Nations concept of minority. For example, a recent study of the Sub-Commission on Prevention of Discrimination and Protection of Minorities states that only ethnic, linguistic, or religious groups constitute a minority.[49] Notwithstanding the fact that at least hearing-impaired persons who use sign language could qualify as a linguistic minority, disabled persons have always been excluded from the United Nations concept of minorities.[50]

Disabled persons also find themselves at a disadvantage to other vulnerable groups in that there is currently no binding human rights instrument explicitly

---

49.   *Second Progress Report*, U.N. ESCOR Commission on Human Rights, Sub-commission on Prevention of Discrimination and Protection of Minorities, U.N. Doc. E/CN.4/Sub.2/1993/34 (1993).

50.   A. LERNER, GROUP RIGHTS AND DISCRIMINATION IN INTERNATIONAL LAW 8–19 (1991).

protecting their human rights. While the proposed adoption of a draft Convention on the Elimination of all Forms of Discrimination against Disabled Persons was rejected by the General Assembly,[51] the U.N. Decade resulted in a new instrument of a different kind that is supposed to be the basic international legal standard for programs, laws, and policies on disability in future years. The Standard Rules on the Equalization of Opportunities for Persons with Disabilities (StRE) were adopted by the General Assembly on December 20, 1993[52] with the purpose of achieving "positive and full inclusion of persons with disabilities in all aspects of society" under the "leadership role of the United Nations therein."[53] The StRE firmly builds on the principles and concepts enshrined in the World Programme of Action concerning Disabled Persons (WPA), which was the guideline for the U.N. Decade of Disabled Persons and which has been readopted as the guideline for the future.[54]

While the WPA has been a useful first tool for directing disability policies internationally, the StRE marks real progress in the development of human rights instruments for disabled women. In the WPA, disabled women were not even mentioned, and human rights issues such as the right to marry and have a family were dealt with as isolated problems of some disabled persons.[55] Furthermore, the WPA has been criticized for its primarily medical approach to social problems, especially with respect to the WPA's prevention component.[56]

Prevention of disability is portrayed as one of the three major elements of disability policy. The WPA does not clarify whether eugenic methods of population control are covered by its concept of prevention of disability. Thus, vagueness allows countries like the People's Republic of China, which adopted eugenic legislation in 1994 that banned some (intellectually) disabled persons from having children, to use the WPA as a defense.[57] In contrast, the StRE clearly promote disabled persons' rights to personal integrity and condemns disability-based discrimination with respect to "sexual relationship, marriage and parenthood" (Rule 9). It is the first time that a human rights instrument addresses this area as a distinct topic of discrimination against disabled persons.

With the historical background of eugenics and prejudices against procreation of disabled persons in many member states of the U.N. under consideration, the StRE has been analyzed as a groundbreaking instrument.[58] In addition to being based on

---

51. Draft Convention on the Elimination of All Forms of Discrimination Against Disabled Persons, U.N. Doc. A/C.3./42/SR.13 (1987).

52. Standard Rules on the Equalization of Opportunities for Persons with Disabilities, U.N. Doc. A/48/96 (1993) [hereinafter StRE].

53. U.N. Doc. A/48/95 (1993).

54. U.N. Doc. A/48/99 (1993).

55. *Id.* at paras. 74 and 140.

56. O. Nagase, Difference, Equality and Disabled People: Disability Rights and Disability Culture 36 (1995) (manuscript); DRIEDGER, *supra* note 21, at 97–99.

57. DRIEDGER, *supra* note 21, at 36.

58. *Id.* at 42; Theresia Degener, *Disabled Persons and Human Rights: The Legal Framework, in*

the social theory of disability, the StRE also displays gender-awareness. This may be regarded as a shift from gender-neutral instruments to gender-awareness of human rights instruments for disabled persons.[59] Equal opportunities and full participation for disabled girls and women are primary aims of the instrument.[60] In other provisions, states are asked to give special attention in the field of education to disabled women.[61] The preamble of the StRE also recalls the Convention on the Elimination of All Forms of Discrimination Against Women (Women's Convention).

This most important human rights treaty for women does not mention disabled women explicitly. However, the definition of gender-based discrimination in Article 1 of the Women's Convention is open-ended since it covers gender-based discrimination in "the political, economic, social, cultural, civil *or any other field*."[62] This interpretation is shared by the monitoring body of the treaty, the Committee on the Elimination of All Forms of Discrimination Against Women (CEDAW). Recognizing that disabled women are not explicitly mentioned in the Women's Convention, CEDAW passed a general recommendation on disabled women to ensure that states parties understand that this instrument also covers the human rights of disabled women.

General Recommendation 18 of 1991 requests states parties to provide information on disabled women in their periodic reports and on measures taken to deal with their particular situation, including special measures to ensure that women have equal access to education, employment, health services, and social security, and to ensure that they can participate in all areas of social life and culture.[63] The first country to follow this recommendation was Finland, in its second periodic report.[64] While the Women's Convention is silent on sexual violence against women, it does contain a number of provisions that are important to disabled women. For instance, Article 16 concerning marriage and children calls on states parties to:

> ensure, on a basis of equality of men and women . . . (e) The same rights to decide freely and responsibly on the number and spacing of their children and to have access to the information, education and means to enable them to exercise these rights; (f) The same rights and responsibilities with regard to guardianship, wardship, trustee-

---

HUMAN RIGHTS AND DISABLED PERSONS: ESSAYS AND RELEVANT INSTRUMENTS 9–39 (Theresia Degener & Y. Koster-Dreese eds., 1995).

59.   The Declaration on the Rights of Mentally Retarded Persons (DRM) of 1971 and the Declaration on the Rights of Disabled Persons (DDP) of 1975 were both particularly gender-neutral instruments. Both instruments, at para. 7 of the DRM, and para. 10 of the DDP, deal with "abuse" and "exploitation" as severe forms of human rights violations from a gender-neutral perspective.

60.   StRE, *supra* note 52, at para. 15, Introduction.

61.   *Id*. at Rule 6(5)(c).

62.   Convention on the Elimination of All Forms of Discrimination Against Women, G.A. Res. 34/180, U.N. GAOR, 34th Sess.(1979), at art. 1 [emphasis added].

63.   General Recommendation 18, CEDAW, C/L.8/Add.18.

64.   Ministry of Foreign Affairs (1993).

ship and adoption of children, or similar institutions where these concepts exist in national legislation; in all cases the interests of the children shall be paramount.[65]

Given that many disabled women are denied the right to procreate and raise children, and that most adoption laws regard disabled women as inadequate social mothers, Article 16 may provide much support to disabled women. However, the question of with whom disabled women are to be compared remains. As in many other provisions, Article 16 speaks of the "same rights" as men. Is the standard of sameness the non-disabled man or the disabled man?

If it is the latter case, Article 16 does not provide much protection. While in practice, it is more often the disabled mother who is discriminated against by eugenic laws and guardianship laws, disabled men are not treated as legally different than disabled women. Legislation and practices in this area do not discriminate on grounds of gender, but rather on grounds of disability. Thus, if the comparative standard is the disabled man, Article 16 of the Women's Convention does not provide sufficient protection for disabled women. The same holds true for other provisions of the treaty. Thus, the Women's Convention can only be read as protecting human rights of disabled women if it is interpreted in conjunction with the StRE; then it becomes clear that disabled women shall be protected against discrimination in the field of marriage and family planning. The legal basis for this integrative interpretation of the Women's Convention can be seen in the preamble of the StRE, which refers to the convention. This finds support in General Recommendation 18(x) of CEDAW,[66] which is an authoritative statement that disabled women are covered by the Women's Convention.

Another important source of protection for intellectually disabled women who are institutionalized is found in the Principles for the Protection of Persons with Mental Illness (PMI), which were adopted by the United Nations General Assembly in 1991.[67] It is one of the most important international human rights instruments addressing human rights violations carried out by medical personnel. In 1983, a special report by Sub-Commission member Erica Daes on human rights violations within psychiatric institutions gave evidence that this is a rampant problem which also affects women.[68] Disability Awareness in Action (DAA), a U.K.-based newsletter, frequently reports about abuses of disabled persons in institutions.[69] Despite their non-binding character, the PMIs are gaining recognition as a useful and authoritative tool for international and national human rights advocacy with respect to disabled persons.[70] The

---

65. Convention on the Elimination of All Forms of Discrimination Against Women, G.A. Res. 34/180, U.N. GAOR, 34th Sess., Art. 16 (1979).

66. *See supra* note 63.

67. *Principles for the Protection of Persons with Mental Illness and for the Improvement of Mental Health Care*, G.A. Res. 119, U.N. GAOR, 46th Sess., Supp. No. 49, Annex, U.N. Doc. A/46/49 (1991) [hereinafter PMI Principles].

68. *Principles, Guidelines and Guarantees for the Protection of Persons Detained on Grounds of Mental Ill Health or Suffering from Mental Disorder*, U.N. Doc: E/CN.4/Sub.2/1983/17 (1983).

69. DAA Newsletter 22, Nov./Dec. 1994, at 3; DAA Newsletter 25, Mar. 1995, at 7; DAA Newsletter 40, July/Aug. 1996, at 4.

70. For a comprehensive guide on such instruments for international human rights advocacy,

Principles reflect fundamental human rights values, such as the principle of dignity and autonomy of all human beings, the right to freedom, the right to be different, the right to due process of law, and the right to be protected against discrimination and harm. Few national laws contain similar prohibitions that are as clear as the PMI on such topics as sterilization as a means of treatment[71] or on the patient's right to reject treatment.[72]

The PMI offer comprehensive procedural safeguards against abuse of professional power in mental health institutions; however, they are weak on substantive limitations on coercion in deciding upon the best interest of the patient. In this field, vast discretion is left to the health professionals. Another shortcoming might be seen in the fact that disabled women are not explicitly covered, and as a result, the issue of sexual violence against, and exploitation of, institutionalized disabled women is not addressed. This aspect is also left out in the Declaration on the Elimination of Violence against Women (Declaration Against Violence), adopted by the General Assembly in 1993.[73] While disabled women are mentioned in the preamble as "especially vulnerable to violence," they are not recognized any further in the Declaration Against Violence.

The only binding human rights instrument which mentions disabled women is the International Labour Organization (ILO) Convention Concerning Vocational Rehabilitation and Employment (Disabled Persons), (Convention No. 159) of 1983.[74] Convention No. 159, and its supplementary Recommendation No. 168, were both adopted in 1983 and updated earlier instruments in the field of vocational rehabilitation.[75] They emphasize the need to formulate, implement, and periodically review national policies on vocational rehabilitation, which should provide appropriate services to all categories of disabled persons and focus on the equalization of opportunities for disabled persons compared to non-disabled workers. The model of equality adopted by Convention No. 159 includes different treatment measures that aim at effective equality between disabled and non-disabled workers.

Similar to the definition of discrimination found in Article 1 of the Women's Convention, Article 4 of ILO Convention No. 159 clarifies that positive actions undertaken to equalize opportunities for disabled workers cannot be regarded as (wrongful) discrimination against non-disabled workers. Disabled women are explicitly mentioned in the equality clause of the instrument (art. 4). Thus, the convention also addresses disabled women's experiences of, at a minimum, the double discrimination

---

see Eric Rosenthal & Leonard S. Rubinstein, *International Human Rights Advocacy Under the "Principles for the Protection of Persons with Mental Illness,"* 16 INT'L J. L. & PSYCHIATRY 257–300 (1993).

71. PMI Principles, *supra* note 67, at 11(12).

72. *Id.* at 11(4).

73. Declaration on the Elimination of Violence Against Women, U.N. Doc. GA 48/104 (1993).

74. *Reprinted in* International Labour Office, *International Labour Standards on Vocational Rehabilitation* (1984).

75. *Id.* at 23.

faced as a result of being disabled as well as being women. In this regard, the first binding ILO instrument on disabled persons[76] can be called a ground-breaking instrument. Two other key issues of Convention No. 159 and Recommendation No. 168 are community participation (art. 5) and vocational rehabilitation in rural areas (art. 8), which reflect the outcome of former projects of the ILO in this field.

Without active involvement of the community, vocational rehabilitation efforts will have limited effects, and without outreach to rural areas, 80 percent of disabled persons living in developing countries (most of whom are female) will be excluded from vocational rehabilitation systems. Finally, it needs to be emphasized that Recommendation No. 168 is one of the few international instruments that openly addresses the fact that abuse and exploitation of disabled persons takes place in institutions even though these are sometimes called "sheltered employment" locations (para. 11(m)). Because disabled women are more likely to be victimized by these forms of human rights violations, ILO Convention No. 159 and Recommendation No. 168 can be regarded as gender-sensitive human rights instruments. It is not surprising that the clearest human rights instruments for disabled women have been developed and adopted under the auspices of the ILO. During the U.N. Decade of Disabled Persons, the ILO organized and initiated more projects on women and disability than any other U.N. organization.

CONCLUSION

International human rights instruments on disability have evolved from the medical concept of disability to the social approach. This development has taken place within two decades culminating in the StRE. Despite its non-binding character, the StRE presently is the most significant human rights instrument with respect to disability.

Disabled women have long been neglected in disability as well as women's human rights instruments. This is a reflection of the longtime invisibility of disabled women in both policy fields. Vast endeavors for change have been undertaken by organizations and networks of disabled women during the last decade, resulting in the integration of disabled women into the mainstream women's movement at the Fourth World Conference on Women in Beijing in 1995. Increasingly, these developments are also reflected in recent human rights instruments. The StRE marks a shift from gender-neutrality to gender-awareness in the standard-setting process concerning human rights of disabled persons. Likewise, human rights instruments relating to women show a growing concern for the inclusion of disabled women. This may be regarded as a first step toward the analysis of disabled women's human rights issues from the perspective of the feminist social theory of disability.

---

76. It should be noted, however, that disabled persons were explicitly included in earlier ILO instruments, such as Convention No.142 (Human Resources Development).

HUMAN RIGHTS OF WOMEN DURING ARMED CONFLICT

Karen Parker

This chapter presents the human rights and humanitarian law applicable to women during periods of armed conflict. It begins with a general discussion of violations of the rights of women in wartime. Because war invokes humanitarian law (the law of armed conflict), this chapter gives a brief presentation of humanitarian law, setting out its historical development and present treaty-based and customary standards relating to women. It discusses the interrelationship between human rights law and humanitarian law, with an emphasis on women's rights. This chapter pays particular attention to the rights and duties of women combatants; it presents the situation of women in contemporary wars; it describes initiatives to improve the situation of women in war, including action in international human rights forums and the International Tribunals; it concludes with an overall assessment of women's rights in war and recommendations for the future.

INTRODUCTION

Women have been portrayed in history, story, and myth as great warriors—the Amazons, the Valkyries—and war has often been portrayed as noble and just. The emulation of heroines, heros, and noble deeds, however, failed to mask the grim reality of war and particularly the treatment of women in war. People sought scapegoats, and in many early cultures women were blamed for war. For example, Homer identifies Helen as the cause of the Trojan War: the Trojan Paris steals Helen from Greek Menelaos, whose brother Agamemnon then pursues with his army to Troy. Virgil lays the blame for the war in his *Aeneid* on the wrath of Juno.[1] Ishtar and Aphrodite were goddesses of both love and war. In myth from India, Kali the terrible mother ruled war and destruction, as did Coatlique in Aztec lore.[2]

The *Iliad* also illustrates another aspect of the grim reality of women in war—women as victims of atrocities. In the *Iliad*, the atrocities are war-rape and slavery: Agamemnon steals Chryses from Apollo's priest to be his concubine; Agamemnon must give her back but then steals Achilles' concubine Briseis; Achilles refuses to fight until Briseis is returned. War-rape and slavery of conquered women have been features of war since time immemorial, and other examples in history, story, and myth abound.

---

1. Virgil, *Aeneid*. "Of arms and man I sing . . . of which Juno's hate and rage [is] the cause."

2. *See, e.g.*, ERICH NEUMANN, THE GREAT MOTHER 149, 153 (2d ed. 1963) (discussing Kali and Coatlique); RIANE EISLER, THE CHALICE AND THE BLADE 42–59 (1988) (discussing the role of women in war in ancient cultures).

In contemporary wars, women continue to be raped and inflicted with other forms of torture, held hostage and forced into a variety of slave-labor situations, including systematic war-rape schemes. As wars become increasingly indiscriminate, they are killed in larger numbers. Women have had their children taken from them, to serve as soldiers, to be killed, or to prevent them from being soldiers. They have lost husbands and fathers. They have starved to death because of destruction of their homes, livelihoods, properties, and means of subsistence. They have been employed, frequently at low wages, in factories and other enterprises supporting war efforts through manufacture of munitions, uniforms, and other war *materiel*.

In modern times, women combatants have been denied their rights as prisoners of war. They have also been victims of discrimination in the military and as combatants. In some situations women are not allowed to serve in the military at all; in others women are treated unequally in comparison to men in the military. Throughout the world, women have not been fully integrated into all aspects of the military.

OVERVIEW OF HUMANITARIAN LAW

The law of armed conflict—also referred to as the laws and customs of war, humanitarian law, or *jus in bello*—has two branches: (1) the law governing the conduct of combat, and (2) the law governing treatment of persons affected by war. In the modern age, the law governing the conduct of combat is frequently referred to as "Hague law" because the most important multilateral treaties relating to combat were drafted at conferences held in The Hague, the Netherlands. Humanitarian law, governing treatment of persons affected by war, is now referred to as "Geneva law" because of the important multilateral treaties drafted at similar conferences held in Geneva, Switzerland.[3] Humanitarian law is both customary and treaty-based.[4]

The historical prominence of armed conflict made humanitarian law a fundamental motivator of the development of international law (the law of nations) and

---

3.   *See, e.g.*, Mohammed Bedjaoui, *Humanitarian Law at the Time of Failing National and International Consensus, in* MODERN WARS: THE HUMANITARIAN CHALLENGE 9 (M. Bedjaoui ed., 1986) (distinguishing the law of the Hague from the law of Geneva). Some definitions of armed conflict law emphasize the Hague law and some Geneva law. For example, International Court of Justice Judge Mohammed Bedjaoui favors Geneva law: "[H]umanitarian law . . . is a set of legal rules intended to protect and aid victims of all situations of armed violence." *Id.* at 8. The International Committee of the Red Cross invokes both branches of humanitarian law in its definition: Humanitarian law is comprised of "international rules, established by treaties or custom, which are specifically intended to solve humanitarian problems directly arising from international or non-international armed conflicts and which, for humanitarian reasons, limit the right of parties to a conflict to use weapons and means of warfare of their choice or protect persons and property that are, or may be, affected by conflict." *The Efforts of the ICRC in the Case of Violations of International Humanitarian Law, in* THE INTERNATIONAL REVIEW OF THE RED CROSS, Mar.–Apr. 1981, at 1.

4.   For compilations of humanitarian law instruments, *see* THE LAWS OF ARMED CONFLICT: A COLLECTION OF CONVENTIONS, RESOLUTIONS, AND OTHER DOCUMENTS (Dietrich Schlinder & Jiri Toman eds., 1973); THE LAW OF WAR: A DOCUMENTARY HISTORY (Leon Friedman ed., 1971–72).

may have been its source:[5] the laws and customs of war were the earliest international laws. Most of the early laws and customs of war were unwritten, and this led to prominence of the commentators. Underscoring again the importance of war on the development of international law, most of the international law treatises from the Renaissance were exclusively devoted to the laws and customs of war. Some of the most influential of the early commentaries include Bartolo de Sassoferrato, whose *Tractatus represaliarium* was issued in 1354, and Giovanni de Lagnano, whose *De Bello* was issued in 1360. The first commentator to indicate a major concern for victims of war was Francisco de Vitoria.[6] This concern was also raised by Pierino Belli in his *De Re Militari et Bello Tractatus*,[7] first issued in 1563. Alberico Gentili's influential text on the law of war was published in 1612.[8] Grotius, considered by many the most important of the early legal commentators, was the first to publish a treatise on international law that included extensive discussion of peacetime law.[9] Vattel's later instrumental treatise on international law also included peacetime law, but gave major prominence to war.[10]

The power of the commentators of humanitarian law to define its scope is clearly evident in the enactment of the Lieber Code during the Civil War in the United States[11] and in the fact that most of the relatively few cases in the United States involving humanitarian law rely heavily on expert opinion.[12] The commentators continue to be cited in judicial or legal forums in situations where treaty-based humanitarian law fails to fully address a particular point or for interpretation of a treaty provision.[13] As

---

5.   One commentator states: "It has been said that war is the well from which the science of the law of nations was drawn." STANISLAW NAHLIK, A BRIEF OUTLINE OF INTERNATIONAL HUMANITARIAN LAW 8 (1984).

6.   His major work is FRANCISCO DE VITORIA, DE JURE BELLI HISPANOORUM IN BARBAROS (trans., 1917) (1557).

7.   PIERINO BELLI, DE RE MILITARI ET BELLO TRACTATUS (Herbert Nutting trans., 1936) (1563).

8.   ALBERICO GENTILI, DE IURE BELLI (John Rolph trans., 1935) (1612).

9.   *See* HUGO GROTIUS, DE JURE BELLI AC PACIS LIBRI TRES (Francis Kelsey trans., 1949) (1625).

10.   EMERIC DE VATTEL, THE LAW OF NATIONS (J. Chitty trans., 1870) (1758).

11.   The Lieber Code (General Orders 100), War Dept. Classification No. 1.12, Oct. 8, 1863, *reprinted in* THE LAW OF WAR: A DOCUMENTARY HISTORY 158 (L. Friedman ed., 1971). Lieber was a leading scholar of international law, and in this code that he prepared and which bears his name, he sought to codify for the United States the laws and customs of war. The Lieber Code, never promulgated as a treaty, was also adopted by Prussia, the Netherlands, France, Russia, Spain and Great Britain, and was clearly a starting point for the Hague Conventions of 1899 and 1907.

12.   *See, e.g., Ex Parte* Quirin, 317 U.S. 1, 13 (1942) in which petitioner argues "[t]he law of war, like civil law, has a great *lex non scripta*, its own common law. This 'common law of war' (*Ex Parte* Vallandigham, 1 Wall. 243, 249) is a centuries old body of largely unwritten rules and principles of international law. . . ." The Court and both petitioner and respondent heavily cited expert authority. Another case illustrating the weight of the commentators is *The Paquete Habana*, 175 U.S. 677 (1900).

13.   This author has cited the early commentators (Gentili, Vitoria, Grotius, and Vattel, among others) in numerous courts to defend persons assisting Salvadoran and Guatemalan victims of war seeking haven in the United States (the "sanctuary" defendants); to defend Salvadoran,

in the formation of customary international law, war played a major role in the development of treaty-based law, and most of the earliest treaties were peace treaties.[14] Treaties regulating armed conflict were initially bilateral: two warring parties would enter into agreements governing the armed conflict between them. Post-war peace treaties began to include substantive humanitarian law issues.

Modern humanitarian law dates from the first Geneva Convention, promulgated in 1864.[15] Since the first Geneva Convention, there has been substantial development of treaty law protecting victims of armed conflict, illustrated by the promulgation of the Geneva Convention of 1906,[16] Geneva Convention (Wounded and Sick) of 1929[17] and Geneva Convention (Prisoners of War) of 1929,[18] the Geneva Conventions I–IV of 1949,[19] and Protocols Additional I and II of 1977.[20]

Guatemalan, Sri Lankan and Kashmiri victims of war; to argue that war-rape was a violation of international law during World War II and that victims of war-rape have a right to compensation (the "comfort women" cases, in courts in Japan). *See* In Re Santos-Gomez, Immigration Court for Washington, D.C., Case #A29564–781, 785 & 801 (1990) (opinion cites Grotius and Vattel, presented by author who testified as expert); Opinion of Karen Parker, The Jugun ianfu cases, Kakyu saibansho minji saiban reshu (Tokyo) (1995) (on file with author) (cites Grotius). *See also* Committee of U.S. Citizens Living in Nicaragua v. Reagan, 859 F.2d 929 (D.C. Cir. 1988) (involves issues of humanitarian law and *jus cogens* and shows heavy reliance on commentators).

14. The earliest known treaty appears on a stone tablet dating from about 3000 B.C. in Sumaria. It sets out terms for ending a conflict between two cities.

15. Convention for the Amelioration of the Condition of the Wounded in Armies in the Field, *signed* Aug. 22, 1864, 1 Bevans 7, 1 Am. J. Int'l L. (Supp.) 90 (1907). This convention was urged by Swiss doctor Henri Jean Dunant following his visit to the battlefield of the 1859 battle of Solferino; it sets out basic protections for wounded combatants and medical personnel. Dunant, whose book A Memory of Solferino was published in 1862, was instrumental in founding the Red Cross and in the calling of the conference that drafted the first Geneva Convention. This convention, though limited in scope, was the first general multilateral treaty to begin to codify the laws and customs of war. For his work in urging the Geneva Convention and for founding the Red Cross, Henri Dunant shared the first Nobel Prize in 1901 with Frederic Passy. One earlier document (not a treaty), the Declaration of Paris, recognized the neutrality of the enemy's merchant goods and ships. Declaration of Paris, *dated* Apr. 16, 1856, 1 Am. J. Int'l L. (Supp.) 89 (1907). This declaration arose from the peace conference called to end the Crimean War.

16. Geneva Convention of 1906, *signed* July 6, 1906, 35 Stat. 1885, 1 Bevans 506, 1 Am. J. Int'l L. (Supp.) 201 (1907).

17. Geneva Convention (Wounded and Sick) of 1929, *signed* July 27, 1929, 47 Stat. 2974, 118 L.N.T.S. 305.

18. Geneva Convention (Prisoners of War) of 1919, *signed* July 27, 1929, 47 Stat. 2021, 118 L.N.T.S. 343.

19. Geneva Conventions I–IV of 1949: Geneva Convention I, *in force* Oct. 21, 1950, 6 U.S.T. 1114, 75 U.N.T.S. 31 (armed forces in the field); Geneva Convention II, *in force* Oct. 21, 1950, 6 U.S.T. 3217, 75 U.N.T.S. 85 (armed forces at sea); Geneva Convention III, *in force* Oct. 21, 1950, 6 U.S.T. 3315, 75 U.N.T.S. 135 (prisoners of war); Geneva Convention IV, *in force* Oct. 21, 1950, 6 U.S.T. 3516, 75 U.N.T.S. 267 (civilians).

20. Protocol Additional I to the Geneva Conventions of 1949, *in force* Dec. 7, 1978, 1125 U.N.T.S. 3, *reprinted in* 16 I.L.M. 1391 (1977); Protocol Additional II to the Geneva Conventions of 1949, *in force* Dec. 7, 1978, 1125 U.N.T.S. 609, *reprinted in* 16 I.L.M. 1442 (1977).

The law of protections for persons affected by war (Geneva law) has one over-riding principle: combatants *hors de combat* and civilians not directly engaged in armed combat may not be the target of military operations and must be treated humanely.[21] This body of humanitarian law addresses the right of combatants to medical care if sick or wounded; the duty of medical personnel to treat sick or wounded combatants even if the combatants belong to the enemy forces; the obligation to protect medical personnel, equipment, and facilities from military attacks; rules for the treatment of prisoners of war (POWs); and protection of the civilian population from the hazards of war and their right to medical care, subsistence needs, and services. Geneva law outlaws torture, slavery, wilful killing (killing outside of legal combat), and other inhumane acts at all times.

The Hague Conventions of 1899[22] and 1907,[23] multilateral treaties resulting from the peace conferences held in the Hague in 1899 and 1907, developed the law of combat.[24] Subsequent treaties and declarations have focused on prohibitions against certain weapons (i.e. napalm, chemical, and biological weapons) and against modification of the environment for hostile purposes:[25] there have been no major revisions of the treaty law of combat since the Hague Conventions of 1899 and 1907.[26] Customary

---

21. Pictet words this principle thus: "Persons placed *hors de combat* and those not directly participating in hostilities shall be respected, protected and treated humanely." JEAN PICTET, THE PRINCIPLES OF INTERNATIONAL HUMANITARIAN LAW 32 (1966).

22. The Hague Convention (II) of 1899, *signed* July 29, 1899, 32 Stat. 1803, 187 Parry's T.S. 429. *See also* The Hague Peace Conference of 1899, Final Act of the International Peace Conference, July 29, 1899, 7 J.B. MOORE, DIGEST OF INTERNATIONAL LAW 78 (1906). There were two other conventions and three declarations from the 1899 conference, the only one still arguably relevant (others were largely superseded by the Hague Convention of 1907) prohibits expanding (dum-dum) bullets, named for the factory near Calcutta where they were first made.

23. The Hague Convention (IV) of 1907 and Regulations, *signed* Oct. 18, 1907, 36 Stat. 2277, 1 Bevans 631. The full name of this convention is The Laws and Customs of War on Land. *See also* The Hague Peace Conference of 1907, Final Act and Conventions of the Second International Peace Conference (Oct. 8, 1907), *reprinted in* THE HAGUE PEACE CONFERENCES OF 1899 AND 1907 (J. Scott ed., 2d ed. 1972) (1909); PROCEEDINGS OF THE HAGUE PEACE CONFERENCE OF 1907 (J. Scott ed. & trans., 1920–21). The Hague Convention (V) of 1907, *signed* Oct. 18, 1907, 36 Stat. 2310, 1 Bevans 654 (the full name is Convention Respecting the Rights and Duties of Neutral Powers and Persons in Case of War on Land), has become substantially superseded by post-World War II attention to collective security apparent in the Charter of the United Nations and in numerous regional arrangements established under authority of Articles 52–54 of the United Nations Charter.

24. The first international instrument to limit weapons was the Declaration Renouncing the Use, in Time of War, of Explosive Projectiles under 400 Grammes Weight, *signed* Dec. 11, 1868, 1 AM. J. INT'L L. (SUPP.) 95 (1907).

25. *See, e.g.*, Convention on the Prohibition of Military or Any Other Hostile Use of Environmental Modification Techniques, *in force* Oct. 5, 1978, 31 U.S.T. 333, 1108 U.N.T.S. 151; Convention on the Prohibition of the Development, Production and Stockpiling of Bacteriological (Biological) and Toxin Weapons and on their Destruction, *in force* Mar. 26, 1975, 26 U.S.T. 583, 1015 U.N.T.S. 163 *reprinted in* 11 I.L.M. 310 (1972).

26. One exception is the Hague Convention for the Protection of Cultural Property in the Event of Armed Conflict, *signed* May 14, 1954, 249 U.N.T.S. 240. This convention expands protections

humanitarian law (including customary humanitarian law discerned by expert opinion) is therefore especially important.

The law of military operations (Hague law) also has one overriding principle: any military operation necessary to defeat the enemy forces is legal unless specifically prohibited or limited.[27] Prohibitions or limitations may be found in any source of international law: treaties, customary law, principles of law of civilized nations, decisions of tribunals, expert opinion, the laws of humanity, and the dictates of the public conscience.[28] Prohibitions may also be included in agreements between the parties to a conflict. Because of the extensive prohibitions and limitations found in these sources of humanitarian law, this principle of humanitarian law is now frequently stated by its corollary rule: the means of warfare are not unlimited. This formula first appeared in the Hague Convention (IV) of 1907 (Regulations, Article XXII), explicitly stating: "The right of belligerents to adopt means of injuring the enemy is not unlimited."

The Hague body of humanitarian law defines combatants (belligerents) and addresses the rights of combatants to engage in combat. It limits or forbids certain combat activities such as use of poison; killing a person who has surrendered; military operations against towns, villages, or buildings that are undefended; and pillage. It establishes rules for administration over seized enemy territory and provides for compensation for violations. It provides rules for proper use of uniforms and insignia, including insignia (red cross, red crescent) of humanitarian or medical relief providers.

---

set out in the Hague Convention of 1907, *supra* note 23, Regulations, art. XXVII which provides that "all necessary steps must be taken to spare, as far as possible, buildings dedicated to religion, art, science, or charitable purposes, historic monuments . . . not being used at the time for military purposes." A standard explanation of why the international community has not significantly augmented treaty-based humanitarian law in this area is that first the League of Nations Covenant and subsequently the United Nations Charter seeks to abolish war. *See, e.g.* NAHLIK, *supra* note 5. The United Nations Charter provisions abolishing aggressive war include Article 1.1 (sets out purpose of UN to maintain peace), Article 2.3 (mandates peaceful settlement of disputes), and Article 2.4 (prohibits threat or use of force). These principles are now *jus cogens*. Military and Paramilitary Activities in and Against Nicaragua (Nicar. v. U.S.) 1986 I.C.J. 14, 100–01, 113–15 (opinion of Court); 151–53 (Singh, J., separate opinion), 199–200 (Sette-Camara, J., separate opinion).

27. This principle also invokes the concept of "necessity": the customary principle that military operations must not inflict more injury to the enemy than necessary to gain the only legal objective of war—to defeat the enemy forces. Thus humanitarian law seeks to balance necessity with the requirement of humanity. *See* PICTET, *supra* note 21, at 30–32. In the words of one prominent early commentator: "No use of force is lawful, except so far as it is necessary. A belligerent has, therefore, no right to take away the lives of those subjects of the enemy that he can subdue by any other means." HENRY WHEATON, ELEMENTS OF INTERNATIONAL LAW (photo. reprint 1936) (1866). Thus even if a particular means of warfare has not been specifically prohibited, if it is not necessary or if there would be undue loss of life compared to the realized military gain, it may not be used in that situation without violating the laws and customs of war. The author has been amazed by the frequency of situations in contemporary wars that call up this principle, including the "human wave" combat used by Iran against Iraq and numerous military actions in the Gulf War.

28. All except the last two of these sources are set out in the Statute of the International Court of Justice. Stat. I.C.J. art. 38. The last two sources are taken from the Hague Convention of 1907, *supra* note 23, 8th preamble. para., included in each Geneva Convention and in Protocol Additional I.

Hague and Geneva law are becoming unified: both 1977 Protocols Additional to the 1949 Geneva Conventions contain provisions historically considered part of Hague law.[29] For example, Protocol Additional I has a section called "methods and means of warfare"[30] that restates the basic rule of Hague law,[31] and prohibits certain weapons and means of warfare.[32] Geneva law originally did not address civilian objects other than hospitals. The Protocols each address a wide range of civilian objects that may not be subjected to military action. For example, Protocol Additional I expands upon the provision of the Hague Convention of 1907 prohibiting attacks on undefended towns, villages, or civilian buildings.[33] The Protocol also provides for duties and protections for civil defense[34] and establishes new regulations concerning aircraft signals and other electronic identification.[35] Both Protocols severely restrict attacks on public works of installations containing dangerous forces: dams, dikes, and nuclear installations.[36] This modern blending of the two branches of humanitarian law is in part due to the fact that there has been no effort to revise and update the Hague Conventions themselves. There has also been substantial development of human rights law impacting on humanitarian law, as discussed later in this chapter.

Modern humanitarian law applies in three main types of war: international wars, civil wars, and wars of national liberation.[37] Each is governed by different provisions in humanitarian law, although the basic principles are applicable to all armed conflicts.[38]

---

29.   *See, e.g.*, Erickson, *Protocol I: A Merging of the Hague and Geneva Law of Armed Conflict*, 19 VA. J. INT'L L. 557 (1979).

30.   Protocol Additional I, *supra* note 20, at pt. III, § I, arts. 35–42.

31.   *Id.* art. 35.1.

32.   *Id.* arts. 35.2 and 35.3. Article 35.3 prohibits methods or means of warfare that damage the environment.

33.   The Hague Convention of 1907, *supra* note 23, Regulations, art. XXV. The Protocol provides a detailed scheme for declaration of non-defended locations (Protocol Additional I, *supra* note 20, art. 59), and provides for demilitarized zones, art. 60.

34.   *Id.* arts. 61–67.

35.   *Id.* annex I, arts. 5–13.

36.   *Id.* art. 56; Protocol Additional II, *supra* note 20, art. 15.

37.   Most commentary on contemporary wars includes "internationalized civil war" because many of the current armed conflicts beginning as civil wars involve extensive military and political action from third parties. *See, e.g.*, Karen Parker & Anne Heindel, Armed Conflict in the World Today: A Country by Country Review (Humanitarian Law Project/International Educational Development 1996) (unpublished manuscript, on file with the Notre Dame Law School Library) (discussing the wars in Afghanistan, Bosnia, Croatia, El Salvador, Liberia, Mozambique, Rwanda, and Somalia as internationalized); Hans-Peter Gasser, *Internationalized Non-international Armed Conflicts: Case Studies of Afghanistan, Kampuchea and Lebanon*, 33 AM. U. L. REV. 145 (1983). The definition of war or armed conflict itself is part of the laws and customs of war and does not appear in humanitarian law instruments. Under customary usage, a war exists when there is armed action carried out by military forces (as distinguishable from police action carried out by civilian police forces) utilizing the methods (whether conventional or guerilla) and *materiel* (combat arms, tanks, other military vehicles) of war.

38.   For example, the International Court of Justice has identified principles from both custom-

In general, a war is considered international in character when military action or hostilities take place between two or more separate states. The treaty-based and customary international law relating to international war applies to these conflicts.

Traditionally, a war is considered internal in nature when armed conflict takes place in one state between government armed forces and opposition armed forces or groups who have identifiable and responsible military commanders, who control enough territory to carry out armed conflict, who distinguish themselves from the civilian population by means of distinct uniforms or other readily identifiable physical features, and who have the means to comply with humanitarian law obligations relating to civil wars. However, as a result of recent jurisprudence, the distinction between characterization of a conflict as internal or international, and the body of law applicable to each, is narrowing.[39]

An armed conflict is a war of national liberation when a group having a claim to self-determination carries out armed actions against a colonial or alien power or against a racist regime.[40]

WOMEN'S RIGHTS IN HUMANITARIAN LAW PRIOR TO 1949

Rights of women were not a prominent feature of international law until the twentieth century; women were barely mentioned at all in peacetime contexts.

---

ary and treaty-based humanitarian law that are applicable in all conflicts. *See* Corfu Channel (U.K. v. Alb.), 1949 I.C.J. 4 (Apr. 9). The Court determined that the failure to warn of sea mines was a violation of principles "underlying" its expression in treaties and is a violation of "certain general and well recognized principles, namely: elementary considerations of humanity, even more exacting in peace than in war." *Id*. at 22. *See also Military and Paramilitary Activities in and Against Nicaragua* (Nicar. v. U.S.) 1986 I.C.J. 14, 114 (June 28) in which the Court declared that Common Articles 1 and 3 of the Geneva Conventions I–IV of 1949 "constitute a minimum yardstick, in addition to the more elaborate rules which also apply in international armed conflicts; and they are rules which reflect what the Court in 1949 [in the Corfu Channel case] called 'elementary considerations of humanity.'" Regarding Common Article 1 the Court held: "There is an obligation on the United States government, in the term of Art. 1 of the Geneva Conventions, to 'respect' the Conventions and to 'ensure respect' for them 'in all circumstances,' since such an obligation does not derive only from the Conventions themselves, but from the general principles of humanitarian law to which the Conventions merely give specific expression." *Id*.

39.   *See* Prosecutor v. Duško Tadić, Judgement, App. Ch., IT–94–1–A, July 15, 1999.

40.   Self-determination is the collective right of a people to freely determine their own political status and to pursue economic, social and cultural development. Enshrined in the United Nations Charter as one of the fundamental purposes of the United Nations (U.N. CHARTER, art. 1.2), the right to self-determination is the first article in each of the two human rights treaties, the International Covenant on Civil and Political Rights, *in force* Mar. 23, 1976, 999 U.N.T.S. 171 and the International Covenant on Economic, Social and Cultural Rights, *in force* Jan. 3, 1979, 999 U.N.T.S. 3. *See* Karen Parker & Lyn Beth Neylon, *Jus Cogens: Compelling the Law of Human Rights*, 12 HASTINGS INT'L & COMP. L. REV. 411, 440 (1989), drawing on A. CRITESCU, THE RIGHT TO SELF-DETERMINATION, U.N. Doc. E/CN.4/Sub.2/404/Rev.1, U.N. Sales No. E.80.XIV.3 (1980) and H. GROS ESPIELL, THE RIGHT TO SELF-DETERMINATION, U.N. Doc. E/CN.4/Sub.2/405/Rev.1, U.N. Sales No. E.79.XIV.5 (1980), and Western Sahara Case, 1975 I.C.J. 12. People claiming self-determination must show a history of independence or self-rule in an identifiable territory, a distinct culture, and a will and capability to regain self-governance.

However, protection for women in war existed in many early texts[41] and was addressed fairly consistently by all the early international law commentators.[42] For example, in his treatise,[43] originally issued in 1563, Belli indicates that the crime of rape during wartime was traditionally punished by death.[44]

Specific protections for women, directly or indirectly related to war, were included in bilateral and multilateral treaties promulgated from as early as the sixteenth century. These treaties, generally incorporating the opinions of the commentators, also served to advance the evolution of customary humanitarian law. For example, the Treaty of Amity and Commerce between the United States and Prussia provided: "If war should arise between the two contracting parties . . . all women and children . . . shall not be molested in their persons."[45] There was no other mention of women in that treaty. Individual countries began to incorporate protections for women into their internal military statutes. In the United States, general orders were issued by General Winfield Scott in 1847 identifying rape as a military offense that should be severely punished.[46] The Lieber Code[47] also provided protection for women:

> The United States acknowledge and protect, in hostile countries occupied by them, religion and morality; . . . and the persons of the inhabitants especially those of women; and the sacredness of domestic relations. Offenses to the contrary shall be vigorously punished.[48]

At the same time that serious progress was being made to codify the basics of the laws and customs of war, the international community began addressing slavery. The prohibitions against slavery constitute the first international action in what is now known as human rights, and while not specifically addressed in terms of armed conflict, these early prohibitions applied equally to times of war as well as peacetime.[49] Of particular importance to women in war, prohibitions against the practice

---

41.   *See, e.g.,* Deuteronomy 20:15, which allows warriors discretion to kill or not kill conquered women and children. The preceding verse requires that all conquered males be killed. An early ninth century text on Islamic law forbids killing women during war. ISLAMIC LAW OF NATIONS §§ 29–31 (Khadduri trans., 1966) (9th cent.).

42.   *See generally* YOUGINDRA KHUSHALANI, DIGNITY AND HONOUR OF WOMEN AS BASIC AND FUNDAMENTAL HUMAN RIGHTS (1982).

43.   BELLI, *supra* note 7.

44.   *Id.* at 177–78. Fourquevaux, in his LA DISCIPLINE MILITAIRE (1592) concurred: violations against the modesty of women incurred a death sentence. L. C. GREEN, THE CONTEMPORARY LAW OF ARMED CONFLICT (1993).

45.   Treaty on Amity and Commerce, July 9–Sept. 10, 1785, U.S.–Prussia, 8 Stat. 84.

46.   General Orders 20 (Winfield Scott 1847), *reprinted in* WILLIAM E. BIRKHEIMER, MILITARY GOVERNMENT AND MARTIAL LAW 581 (2d ed. 1904).

47.   The Lieber Code, *supra* note 11.

48.   *Id.* art. XXXVII.

49.   *See generally* BENJAMIN WHITAKER, SLAVERY, U.N. Doc. E/CN.4/Sub.2/1984/20/Rev.1, U.N. Sales No. E.84.XIV.1 (1984); Ved Nanda & M. Cherif Bassiouni, *Slavery and the Slave Trade: Steps Toward Eradication*, 12 SANTA CLARA L. REV. 424 (1972); M. Cherif Bassiouni, *Enslavement as an International Crime*, 23 N.Y.U. J. INT'L L. & POL. 445 (1991).

of forced prostitution ("white slavery"), a common feature of war-rape and slavery of women in war, was first prohibited by the international community in 1904.[50] With the adoption of the Hague Conventions of 1899 and 1907, the development of international prohibitions against slavery, and other principles of the laws and customs of war, the concept that women had rights in war was clearly established at the time of World War I.

The Hague Conventions of 1899 and 1907, which seek to codify "the laws and customs of war on land" and to "serve as a general rule of conduct for the belligerents and their mutual relations and in their relations with the inhabitants"[51] do not contain many provisions directly granting rights to women. Women's issues are only specifically addressed in the Regulations (Article XLVI in each), which provide that "family honour and rights . . . must be respected." Although relatively vague (humanitarian law provisions are frequently very precise and specific), this provision does provide a framework to address some concerns of women in armed conflicts, such as separation from their children and war-rape or other abuse. However, the general protections of civilians and civilian sites, regulations governing administration of occupied territories, and similar provisions provide a wide range of protections from the hazards of war as they have been suffered by women during periods of armed conflict.

Added to specific rights and provisions in the Hague Conventions of 1899 and 1907 is the famous Martens Clause that brings into treaty law the foundation of the customs of war: in situations not specifically addressed, civilians and combatants are always protected by "the principles of the law of nations, as they result from the usages established among civilized peoples, from the laws of humanity and the dictates of the public conscience."[52] The Martens Clause is considered a binding legal provision,[53] and both on its own and in conjunction with Common Article XLVI, should be construed to prohibit most intolerable practices affecting women in armed conflict: capture, slavery, war-rape, separation from children, torture, and other such harm.[54]

---

50.   International Agreement for the Suppression of the White Slave Traffic, *signed* Mar. 18, 1904, 1 L.N.T.S. 83. This agreement was followed by the Convention for the Suppression of the White Slave Traffic, *signed* May 4, 1910, 211 Consol. T.S. No. 45.

51.   The Hague Convention of 1907, *supra* note 23, pmbl. ¶ 5.

52.   This citation is from the Hague Convention of 1907, *supra* note 23, pmbl. ¶ 8. Martens also drafted the nearly identical paragraph in the preamble to the Hague Convention of 1899. Martens, a Russian soldier, was a member of his country's delegation to both conferences in The Hague. *See* Stanislaw E. Nahlik, *The Role of the 1977 Geneva Protocols in the Progress of Armed Conflict Law, in* EUROPEAN CONFERENCE ON HUMANITARIAN LAW ii, 17 (1979) (citing THE LAWS OF ARMED CONFLICT (Dietrich Schlinder & Jiri Toman eds., 1973)).

53.   *See, e.g., Ex parte* Quirin, 317 U.S. 1, 14 (1942). The *Quirin* Court had earlier stated: "From the very beginning of its history this Court has recognized and applied the law of war as . . . part of the law of nations." *Id.* at 10. In words echoing the Martens Clause, the International Court of Justice has referred to the binding nature of "elementary considerations of humanity." *See, e.g.,* Corfu Channel case, 1949 I.C.J. 4, 22 (Apr. 9, 1949).

54.   Prohibitions against all these practices are specifically set out in subsequent humanitarian law and human rights instruments promulgated after World War II. However, even absent these later instruments, the Hague Convention of 1907 contains the basic provision of women's rights

If there had been any doubt as to the meaning of the provision addressing women in the 1907 Hague Convention, or the content of protection for women in the then-existing customs of war, the peace instruments ending World War I provided more certainty. As part of the process, the parties established a special commission to investigate violations of the laws and customs of war.[55] In its work investigating treatment of women, the commission identified violations of the rights of women, especially rape, as a violations of "explicit regulations [of] established customs [and the] clear dictates of humanity."[56] This post-war process also saw the development of the concept of war crimes and crimes against humanity, as the Treaty of Versailles imposed individual responsibility on the Emperor and war criminals.[57]

During and immediately following World War II, the rights of women and other civilians were even more explicitly set out in the peace talks ending that war. For example, during the occupation of Germany, the allied powers established military authority and promulgated basic laws, called Control Council Laws,[58] for the area. Control Council Law No. 10 listed some inhumane acts:

> (b) war crimes [are] atrocities of offenses against persons or property constituting violations of the laws or customs of war, including, but not limited to , murder, ill treatment or deportation to slave labour or for any other purpose, of the civilian population from occupied territory, murder or ill treatment of prisoners of war . . .

> (c) crimes against humanity [are] atrocities and offenses, including but not limited to murder, extermination, enslavement, deportation, imprisonment, torture, rape, or other inhumane acts committed against any civilian populations . . . .[59]

The Charter of the International Military Tribunal[60] and the Charter of the International Military Tribunal for the Far East[61] incorporate directly or by inference

---

through operation of Regulations Article XLVI and the Martens Clause. This issue has been very relevant in the past several years as women seek compensation for war-rape carried out by Japan during World War II. *See* Karen Parker & Jennifer Chew, *Compensation for Japan's World War II War-rape Victims*, 17 HASTINGS INT'L & COMP. L. REV. 497 (1994).

55.   The Commission on the Responsibilities of the Authors of the War and the Enforcement of Penalties (Versailles Commission).

56.   *Report of the Commission of the Authors of War and the Enforcement of Penalties, reprinted in* 14 AM. J. INT'L L. 95 (SUPP. 1920). *See also Violations of the Laws and Customs of War: Report of the Majority and Dissenting Reports of American and Japanese Members of the Commission on Responsibilities, Conference of Paris, 1919, reprinted in* 14 AM. J. INT'L L. 95 (SUPP. 1920).

57.   Treaty of Peace Between the Allied and Associated Powers and Germany, June 28, 1919, 11 MARTENS NOUVEAU RECUEIL (Ser. 3) 323, art. 227, 228. The Covenant of the League of Nations formed Part I of this treaty.

58.   Control Council Law, Official Gazette of the Control Council for Germany, No. 3, 1946, *reprinted in* 1 THE LAW OF WAR, *supra* note 4.

59.   Control Council Law, *supra* note 58, art. II(b) & (c).

60.   The Charter was annexed to the Agreement for the Prosecution and Punishment of the Major War Criminals of the European Axis, *signed* Aug. 8, 1945, 59 Stat. 1544, 3 Bevans 1238, 1240 (hereinafter *Nuremberg Charter*). The Nuremberg Charter is also reprinted in 1 THE LAW OF WAR, *supra* note 4, at 885.

61.   The Charter for the International Military Tribunal for the Far East, T.I.A.S. No. 1589, 4

the same listing of acts affecting women and the civilian populations as a whole that represent serious violations of the laws and customs of war.[62]

While the pre-World War II laws and customs of war provided women basic protections from serious violations of their rights, the post-war period from 1949 to the present has greatly expanded women's rights in armed conflict, including protection from acts not grave enough to be considered crimes against humanity or war crimes but that nonetheless have tremendous impact on women in war. With the promulgation of the Geneva Conventions of 1949 and the Protocols Additional of 1977 women's rights in treaty-based armed conflict law was greatly advanced. The development of human rights law provided a wide range of protections applicable in peacetime as well as in war. Further, the United Nations General Assembly and other bodies began addressing human rights concerns in war on a regular basis, enhancing customary rights. Finally, the International Criminal Tribunals for the former Yugoslavia and for Rwanda have made enormous progress in interpreting treaties progressively for protecting gender-based crimes and in providing criminal sanction for violations.[63]

WOMEN AND THE GENEVA CONVENTIONS OF 1949 AND PROTOCOL ADDITIONAL I[64]

The Right to Non-Discrimination

Each Geneva Convention of 1949 addresses non-discrimination based on sex (i.e., gender) within the context of its field of application: Geneva Convention I pro-

---

Bevans 20 (hereinafter *Tokyo Charter*). The Tokyo Charter is actually not a treaty but a proclamation made by the Supreme Commander for the Allied Powers, General Douglas MacArthur, on Jan. 19, 1945. The full text of the Tokyo Charter is reprinted in 1 THE LAW OF WAR, *supra* note 4, at 894.

62.   The Tokyo Charter omits the listing of particular crimes in its definition of war crimes, the established lists from Control Council Law No. 10 and the Nuremberg Charter having already done so.

63.   Please note, however, that because most of the Tribunal jurisprudence is contained in judgements rendered after this chapter was written, it will not be addressed in much detail here. For information, *see especially* Prosecutor v. Anto Furundžija, Judgement, IT–95–17/1–T, 10 Dec. 1998; Prosecutor v. Zejnil Delalić et al., Judgement, IT–96–21–T, 16 Nov. 1998; Prosecutor v. Jean-Paul Akayesu, Judgement, ICTR–96–4–T, 2 Sept. 1998. For articles detailing this jurisprudence, *see, e.g.*, Kelly D. Askin, *Sexual Violence in Decisions and Indictments of the Yugoslav and Rwandan Tribunals: Current Status*, 93 AM. J. INT'L L. 97 (1999); Dorean Koenig & Kelly Askin, *International Criminal Law and the International Criminal Court Statute: Crimes Against Women, in* WOMEN AND INTERNATIONAL HUMAN RIGHTS LAW (Kelly D. Askin & Dorean M. Koenig eds., vol. 2, 2000).

64.   The Geneva Conventions of 1949 contain extensive treatment of the concept of "Protecting Power," a state not party to the conflict that undertakes responsibility for protecting Geneva Convention rights. This discussion ignores those provisions for several reasons: first of all, these provisions have been almost totally ignored by the international community and second, the rights set out here are rights regardless of who is responsible for their provision. Regarding the first point, protecting powers have only been invoked in four wars since World War II: Suez, 1956; Goa, 1961; the Indo-Pakistani war, 1971; and the Malvinas/Falklands war, 1982. *See* Georges Abi-

hibits adverse distinction of sick and wounded combatants based on sex;[65] Geneva Convention II prohibits adverse distinction of sick and wounded or ship-wrecked at sea combatants based on sex;[66] Geneva Convention III prohibits adverse distinction of prisoners of war based on sex;[67] and Geneva Convention IV prohibits adverse distinction of civilians based on sex.[68]

Military Women[69]—Rights of Wounded, Sick, or Shipwrecked[70]

Wounded, sick, or shipwrecked combatants and military personnel must be treated humanely; Geneva Conventions I and II specifically prohibit murder, torture, medical experimentation, or wilful denial of medical care or wilful exposure to adverse medical situations.[71] Medical care must be given based on urgency of sickness or injury.[72] Both conventions specify that women "shall be treated with all consideration due to their sex."[73] An important protection of sick, wounded, or shipwrecked

---

Saab, *Respect of Humanitarian Norms in International Conflicts, in* MODERN WARS: THE HUMANITARIAN CHALLENGE 67 (M. Bedjaoui ed., 1986). Abi-Saab presents the usual explanations for this: one party does not recognize the other (the Middle East problem); the parties continue to maintain diplomatic relations in spite of the war; because the UN Charter prohibits war, the parties are reluctant to admit a war exists; the Protecting Powers system is cumbersome; most States are not sufficiently neutral (the Cold War problem); the responsibility is enormous and expensive, given the specifics of the Geneva Conventions and diplomatic necessities. *Id.* at 68.

65.   Geneva Convention I, *supra* note 19, art. 12.

66.   Geneva Convention II, *supra* note 19, art. 12.

67.   Geneva Convention III, *supra* note 19, arts. 14, 16. Geneva Convention III provides special rights for women POWs, as is discussed *infra*.

68.   Geneva Convention IV, *supra* note 19, art. 27.

69.   The actual term used in the Hague and Geneva Conventions is "members of the armed forces," which can include women who are both combatant and non-combatant. There are other categories of persons who are also covered by these provisions: supply contractors, war correspondents, and even civilians who spontaneously and openly take up arms. *See* The Hague Conventions of 1899, *supra* note 22, and 1907, *supra* note 23, Regulations, Common Articles II and III; Geneva Convention I, *supra* note 19, art. 13. The author's term "military women" is meant to include all women covered.

70.   Geneva Convention I, art. 13, defines combatants for purposes of its application. Geneva Convention II, Article 13, defines combatants for purposes of its application. Protocol Additional I enlarges the definition of combatant to include combatants of a Party not recognized by an adverse Party. Protocol Additional I, *supra* note 20, art. 43. This addition was necessary because in many wars of national liberation, occupying powers do not recognize the legitimacy of a self-determination claim and attempt to deny application of humanitarian law in its entirety. Wounded, sick and shipwrecked combatants are owed these rights by both their own forces and enemy forces. Neutral powers must apply these rights by analogy. Geneva Convention I, *supra* note 19, art. 4. Geneva Convention II, *supra* note 19, art. 5. The civilian population is prohibited from carrying out acts of violence against sick or wounded. Geneva Convention I. *Id.* art. 18.

71.   Geneva Convention I, *supra* note 19, art. 12; Geneva Convention II, *supra* note 19, art. 12.

72.   *Id.*

73.   *Id.*

combatants is that they are not allowed to renounce their rights.[74] The remaining articles of these two Conventions set out in considerable detail the protections of medical personnel, medical facilities, and supplies and requirements for identifying medical units, hospital ships, and medical convoys.

Military Women—Rights of Women Prisoners of War

Women prisoners of war (POWs) in international armed conflicts, including wars of national liberation, are granted all the rights of men POWs of equal rank and also have special rights granted only to them.[75] Women and men POWs must be treated humanely and are entitled to care, including necessary medical care, at no cost and on a non-discriminatory basis.[76] If interrogated, POWs need only give name, rank, serial number, and date of birth.[77] Geneva Convention III provides extensive detail on minimum standards for POW facilities,[78] food,[79] clothing,[80] medical care,[81] and prison labor.[82] POWs have the right to send and receive communications and relief parcels.[83] POWs have the right to freedom of religion and practice of religion.[84] POWs charged with offenses (disciplinary or penal) have a right to procedural safeguards.[85] Severely wounded POWs have the right to be repatriated or accommodated in a neutral country, depending on the gravity of the condition.[86]

Women POWs have the right to separate quarters under supervision of women during disciplinary punishment.[87] Women POWs awaiting trial for criminal offenses or already sentenced also have the right to separate quarters under the supervision of women.[88] Protocol Additional I provides that pregnant women or mothers with dependent children detained for "an offense related to the armed conflict" may not be executed.[89]

---

74. Geneva Convention I, *id.* art. 8; Geneva Convention II, *id.* art. 7.

75. Geneva Convention III, *supra* note 19, arts. 14, 16. Article 14 requires women to be treated "with all the regard due their sex." *Id.*

76. *Id.* arts. 14–16.

77. *Id.* art. 17.

78. *Id.* arts. 21–25.

79. *Id.* art. 26.

80. *Id.* art. 27.

81. *Id.* arts. 29–32.

82. *Id.* arts. 49–68.

83. *Id.* arts. 71–75.

84. *Id.* art. 34. This article also requires that facilities for religious services be provided.

85. *Id.* arts. 95–108.

86. *Id.* arts. 109–117.

87. *Id.* art. 97.

88. *Id.* arts. 103, 108.

89. Protocol Additional I, *supra* note 20, art. 76. This article also provides that parties "should avoid the pronouncement of the death penalty" in these circumstances. *Id.*

The Model Agreement Concerning Direct Repatriation and Accommodation in Neutral Counties of Wounded and Sick Prisoners of War[90] recommends that POWs who are pregnant or mothers with children should be eligible for accommodation in a neutral country.[91]

Civilian Women—Humane Treatment

Article 27 of Geneva Convention IV provides the basic right to humane treatment to women and other civilians when in the hands of an opposing party or under the authority of an occupying power. This article also states that women and other civilians have a right to "respect for their persons, their honour, their family rights, their religious convictions and practices, and their manners and customs."[92] It also forbids acts or threats of violence, "insults and public curiosity."[93] Targeting the abuse or war-rape and other forms of frequent mistreatment of women, Article 27 mandates that women be protected against "any attack on their honour, in particular against rape, enforced prostitution, or any form of indecent assault."[94]

Civilian Women—Medical Rights

Regardless of under whose authority they may be,[95] women and other civilians are entitled to medical care[96] and are entitled to the security of medical facilities.[97]

---

90. Geneva Convention III, *supra* note 19, annex I.

91. *Id.* § B(7). The model agreement describes medical conditions warranting either direct repatriation or accommodation in a neutral country. This author has invoked the model agreement in several civil war situations, and in efforts joined by others was successful in obtaining the release and accommodation in Cuba of severely war-wounded combatants of the opposition forces of El Salvador.

92. Geneva Convention IV, *supra* note 19, art. 27.

93. *Id.* The protection against public curiosity is clearly meant to address such acts as forcing defeated populations to be paraded in public display or to be subjected to hairshaving or other marks of abasement or humiliation.

94. *Id.* This provision is also included with similar language in Protocol Additional I. Protocol Additional I, *supra* note 20, art. 76.1 ("Women shall be the object of special respect and shall be protected in particular against rape, forced prostitution and any other form of indecent assault.")

95. Most provisions of Geneva Convention IV govern the rights of civilian women and others who are in the hands of opposition forces. The section relating to medical rights and the protection of medical facilities and supplies applies to all persons of the countries at war. Women could accordingly bring actions against their own government for breach of these rights. While some have considered that the limitation of many rights by their application only against opposition forces leaves a major *lacuna* in rights, this author is convinced that the enlarged scope of application regarding civilians in Protocol Additional I and the evolution of human rights standards go a long way to protecting all civilians affected by war, regardless of in whose power they may be. For example, this author considers that a woman affected by the war in Rwanda would have an action for war-rape if she were raped by a member of her own forces, by a member of the opposition forces, or by a person from another country who might be attached to a relief or monitoring organization.

96. *Id.* art. 16.

97. *Id.* arts. 18–23.

Medical care must be in conformity with sound medical practice;[98] it is forbidden to carry out medical experimentation,[99] mutilation,[100] or removal of organs or tissue for transplants even with consent.[101] All civilian women who are pregnant are entitled to "particular protection and respect."[102] Women who are "maternity cases"[103] may be taken out of areas under siege.[104]

Civilian Women—Rights as Internees

The rights of civilian internees held by occupying forces comprise Articles 79–141 of Geneva Convention IV and numerous articles of Protocol Additional I. Except for detention of persons accused or convicted of crimes, detention of protected civilians may only occur for "imperative reasons of security"[105] and must take place in separate facilities from those for POWs or persons detained for criminal offenses.[106] All internees have a right to minimum standards of accommodation and

98.   The term "generally accepted medical practice" was included in Geneva law for the first time in Protocol Additional I (art. 11.1), but because of the nature of medical rights and the strong prohibition throughout the four Geneva Conventions to medical experimentation (each of the "grave breach" provisions sanction medical or biological experimentation), the term must be viewed as part of the laws and customs of war, even for states, such as the United States, that have not ratified Protocol Additional I.

99.   Geneva Convention IV, *supra* note 19, art. 32; Protocol Additional I, *supra* note 20, art. 11.2 (b).

100.   Geneva Convention IV, *supra* note 19, art. 32; Protocol Additional I, *supra* note 20, art. 11.2 (a). This provision prohibits, *inter alia*, female genital mutilation. *See generally Report of the Special Working Group on Traditional Practices Affecting the Health of Women and Children*, U.N. Doc. E/CN.4/1986/42. *See also* Isabelle R. Gunning, *Women and Traditional Practices: Female Genital Surgery, in* WOMEN AND INTERNATIONAL HUMAN RIGHTS LAW 651 (Kelly Askin & Dorean Koenig eds., vol. 1, 1999).

101.   Protocol Additional I, *supra* note 20, art. 11.2 (c).

102.   Geneva Convention IV, *supra* note 19, art. 16.

103.   This presumably means both pregnant women and women with infants.

104.   Geneva Convention IV, *supra* note 19, art. 17. Article 22 provides that aircraft used to evacuate "maternity cases" and other civilian sick or wounded may not be attacked. *Id.* art. 22.

105.   *Id.* art. 78 (relating to civilians in the hands of an occupying power). Articles 41, 42, 43, and 68 also address civilian detainees. Article 42 relates to civilians in the hands of a "detaining power," and allows for confinement "only if the security of the Detaining Power makes it absolutely necessary." These provisions were added to the 1949 Geneva Convention following the internment of both German nationals and persons in occupied German territories as well as the internment of Americans and citizens of countries with whom the United States was not at war, but the wording of these provisions appears to exclude some of above-cited situations from coverage. While persons detained by Germany from conquered territories would be covered, Peruvians of Japanese descent seized in Peru and interned by the United States in camps in Texas and elsewhere would not because Peru was not at war with the United States and was not even a party to the conflict at all. Internment of Americans of Japanese ancestry on a mass scale would also not be prohibited by these provisions. However, humanitarian law as now informed by evolving standards of human rights law clearly prohibits internment of any person unless for compelling reasons of absolute necessity. *See* discussion *infra* section on human rights and humanitarian law.

106.   Geneva Convention IV, *supra* note 19, art. 84. Protocol Additional I adds that families that

hygiene,[107] food and water,[108] clothing,[109] medical attention,[110] practice of religion, recreational or educational activities,[111] and working conditions.[112] Women must be interned in separate facilities unless placed with family units.[113] Pregnant and nursing women must be provided with extra food;[114] "maternity cases" must be given adequate treatment.[115]

There are many provisions relating to personal property, administration, and discipline of civilian internment camps, including mail, relief shipments, and transport of internees.[116] Only a few of these provisions specially address women: Article 97 prohibits male officials from searching women internees, and Article 124 provides that women internees given punishment must be confined apart from men and must be under the supervision of women.

Civilian Women—Procedural Rights and Rights as Detainees

Geneva Convention IV provides only a minimum of procedural guarantees and rights of persons detained for criminal offenses: Article 71 requires adequate notice; Article 72 provides the right to counsel, the right to present evidence, and the right to prepare a defense; and Article 73 provides for the right to appeal. Similar to Article 124 above applicable to the treatment of internees, Article 76 requires that civilian women in occupied territories who are detained for offenses must be given separate quarters under the supervision of women.[117]

Article 75 of Protocol Additional I greatly expands on these rights, providing the rights to speedy trial, individual penal liability, freedom from ex post facto laws, presumption of innocence, presence at trial, freedom from self-incrimination, examination of witnesses, freedom from double jeopardy, public announcement, and provision of post-conviction remedies.

---

are interned must, "whenever possible, be held in the same place and accommodated as family units." *Id.*

107. *Id.* art. 85.

108. *Id.* art. 89.

109. *Id.* art. 90.

110. *Id.* arts. 91–92.

111. *Id.* arts. 93–94.

112. *Id.* arts. 95–96.

113. *Id.* art. 85. As an "exceptional and temporary" measure, women internees may be in the same camp as men internees, but they must be given separate sleeping and sanitary facilities. *Id.*

114. *Id.* art. 89.

115. *Id.* art. 91.

116. *Id.* arts. 97–128.

117. *Id.* art. 76.

Civilian Women—The Right to Family Information/Reunification

Civilian women, men, and children have the right to send and receive news and information to/from family members regardless of where they are.[118] Families separated by the war have the right to unification.[119]

War Refugees

The right of war refugees centers on the right of *non-refoulement*.[120] Geneva Convention IV provides a general right of safety to refugees of war by forbidding their transfer to any country not willing and able to protect their Geneva Convention rights, including their right to protection from the dangers of war.[121] This provision does allow war refugees to be returned "after cessation of hostilities."[122] War refugees may also not be transferred to any country where there is reason to fear persecution.[123] Assuming war refugees have sought shelter in another country, that country would not be able to send them back to their country of origin until the war is over or unless there is clear protection from the dangers of war.[124]

Article 45 provides that a country that returns or sends a war refugee elsewhere continues to have legal responsibility for that refugee until hostilities cease. The rights of war refugees are reinforced by the prohibition of forced transfers of civilians from occupied territories.[125] While evacuation for safety reasons or for "imperative military reasons" is allowed, an occupying power must provide basic necessities and family unity.[126] Both Article 45 and Article 49 rights are reinforced by the identification of unlawful deportations or transfers of civilians as a grave breach.[127]

---

118. *Id.* art. 25.

119. *Id.* art. 26.

120. The principle of *non-refoulement*, from the French *refouler* (to return) provides that persons may not be sent back to their countries of origin under certain circumstances indicating threats to personal security. While usually arising from fear of persecution and hence addressed by refugee law, threats to personal security can arise because of the dangers of war and war crimes. *See* Karen Parker, *Geneva Convention Protection of Salvadoran Refugees*, 13 IMM. NEWS 1 (1984); Karen Parker, *Human Rights and Humanitarian Law*, 7 WHITTIER L. REV. 675 (1985).

121. Geneva Convention IV, *supra* note 19, art. 45.

122. *Id.*

123. *Id.*

124. *Id.*

125. *Id.* art. 49.

126. *Id.*

127. *Id.* art. 147. For a discussion of breaches, see *infra* section on grave breaches.

WOMEN AND COMMON ARTICLE 3 AND PROTOCOL ADDITIONAL II

The Right to Non-Discrimination

Women affected by civil war are granted the same protection against discrimination as women in international wars: both Common Article 3 and Protocol Additional II prohibit adverse distinction based on sex.[128]

The Right to Humane Treatment

Common Article 3 requires humane treatment of civilian women and men and women and men combatants who have "laid down their arms [or] are *hors de combat* by sickness, wounds, detention, or any other cause."[129] Humane treatment includes freedom from "violence to life and person, in particular murder of all kinds, mutilation, cruel treatment and torture."[130] Women may not be used as hostages,[131] they must not be degraded or humiliated,[132] and they must be given all procedural rights "recognized as indispensable by civilized peoples."[133]

Protocol Additional II reiterates the right to humane treatment on a non-discriminatory basis[134] and enumerates further examples of inhumane treatment: violence to mental well-being, corporal punishment, acts of terrorism, rape, enforced prostitution, indecent assault, slavery, pillage, and threats to commit any of these acts.[135]

The Right to Religious Freedom

Common Article 3 provides for non-discrimination based on religion or faith,[136] but does not otherwise address religious practices. Protocol Additional II provides for the right to "respect for . . . religious practices."[137] It also provides for the respect and protection of religious personnel, requiring that their work receive "all available help"[138] and specifying that they may not be "compelled to carry out tasks incompatible with their humanitarian mission."[139] Women and men detainees are entitled to

---

128. Common Article 3(1); Protocol Additional II, *supra* note 20, art. 2.1.

129. Geneva Conventions I–IV, *supra* note 19, art. 3(1).

130. *Id.* art. 3 (1)(a).

131. *Id.* art. 3(1)(b).

132. *Id.* art. 3(1)(c).

133. *Id.* art. 3(1)(d).

134. Protocol Additional II, *supra* note 20, art. 4.

135. *Id.* art. 4.2(a)–(h).

136. Geneva Conventions I–IV, *supra* note 19, art. 3(1).

137. Protocol Additional II, *supra* note 20, art. 4.1.

138. *Id.* art. 9(1).

139. *Id.* This provision has become especially meaningful in the civil wars in both El Salvador and Guatemala, where women religious have been murdered, raped and severely abused by the

practice their religion and may request and receive the assistance of clergy.[140] Protocol Additional II also protects religious sites and artwork.[141]

The Right to Freedom of Opinion/Convictions

Common Article 3 does not specify protection for freedom of belief or opinion. Protocol Additional II includes belief, political, or other opinion in the specific enumeration of bases for adverse distinction.[142] It adds the right to respect for one's convictions as a fundamental guarantee.[143]

Rights as POWs or Civilian Detainees

Common Article 3 itself provides no standards for detention other than humane treatment and only refers to detention as a reason that some members of the armed forces are *hors de combat*. This wording implies that some detainees could be prisoners of war (POWs). Thus, women detained as POWs in civil wars governed only by Common Article 3 are entitled to the rights of prisoners of war as they exist in the laws and customs of war, which would require minimum standards of "humane treatment."[144] Civilian women detained should be afforded the right to humane treatment in conformity with Common Article 3 in Geneva Convention IV (civilians), taking into account the rule of analogy.

Protocol Additional II sets out the specifics of rights of detainees in some detail, thus partially avoiding the legal exercise of construing Common Article 3 in conformity with the relevant Geneva Convention and invoking the rule of analogy. Article

---

military forces of both governments. At the time of these abuses, both countries had ratified this Protocol, El Salvador being the third country to ratify. El Salvador ratified Protocol Additional I and II on Nov. 23, 1978. Guatemala ratified both on Oct. 19, 1987.

140. *Id.* art. 5.1(d).

141. Protocol Additional II, *supra* note 20, art. 16. This article invokes and complements the Hague Convention for the Protections of Cultural Property in the Event of Armed Conflict, *supra* note 26.

142. Protocol Additional II, *supra* note 20, art. 2.1.

143. *Id.* art. 4.1.

144. Common Article 3 is a part of each Geneva Convention of 1949, and should be interpreted in conformity with each Convention. For example, the whole of Geneva Convention III (Prisoners of War) should be consulted to determine humane treatment of women or men combatants held by the opposing side in civil wars of states that have not ratified Protocol Additional II. While not all its provisions would be binding in civil wars, those essential to humane treatment would. Additionally, those provisions of Geneva Convention III considered customary law may also be applicable in civil wars, even if not essential for humane treatment of POWs. For example, the duty to provide public information regarding POWs is applicable in civil wars as customary law. *See* Geneva Convention III, *supra* note 19, arts. 122–125. The whole of Geneva Convention IV (civilians) should be consulted to determine humane treatment for civilian detainees in civil wars. Additionally, the Geneva Conventions require parties to conflicts to provide for circumstances not specifically addressed "in conformity with the general principles." *See, e.g.*, Geneva Convention I, *supra* note 19, art. 45. This principle, called the "rule of analogy," is useful to enumerate rights affording minimum standards of humane treatment of detainees.

5 of Protocol Additional II, the longest article and practically a convention in miniature, applies to "persons whose liberty has been restricted"[145] or to "persons deprived of their liberty for reasons related to the armed conflict, whether they are interned or detained."[146] Women and men interned or detained have the right to treatment if sick or wounded, to food and drinking water equal to that of the locality, to health and hygiene safeguards, and to protection from the climate and the armed conflict. Women have a right to separate quarters and must be supervised by women.[147] Women and men detainees have a right to receive individual and collective assistance (humanitarian aid), the right to send and receive correspondence, the right to practice their religion and receive assistance from clergy or spiritual advisors, and the right to medical examinations. Their health may not be jeopardized by any act or omission. They may not be subjected to medical procedures that are not "generally accepted." They may not be detained in places near combat zones and must be evacuated if they are "exposed to danger arising out of armed conflict."[148] They have the right to these protections after armed conflict ceases until they are freed.[149]

Procedural Rights

Procedural rights are addressed as part of the humane treatment provision in Common Article 3, requiring judicial guarantees "recognized as indispensable by civilized peoples."[150] The same legal exercise discussed above relating to detention rights can be used to create procedural rights out of judicial guarantees "recognized as indispensable." Protocol Additional II, however, makes that exercise also somewhat unnecessary because it provides a comprehensive scheme for procedural rights of women and men applicable "to the prosecution and punishment of criminal offenses related to the armed conflict."[151] Protocol Additional II frames judicial rights under the mandate for a court that is independent and impartial.[152] Whether tried in a military or

---

145. Protocol Additional II, *supra* note 20, art. 5 (caption).

146. *Id.* art. 5.1. The distinction between "interned" and "detained" seems to relate to differentiation between combatants held as captives (POWs) and civilian detainees, although the rights themselves are not limited to one group or the other.

147. *Id.* art. 5.2(a). Women may be accommodated with their male family members, but this is not a right. *Id.* Because Article 4.3(b) requires that children must be united with family members if possible when they have become separated, it is logical to assume that women detainees have a right to be housed with their children even though it is not so stated.

148. *Id.* art. 5.2(c).

149. *Id.* art. 2.2.

150. Geneva Conventions, *supra* note 19, Common Article 3.

151. Protocol Additional II, *supra* note 20, art. 6.1.

152. *Id.* art. 6.1. Since the time of this Protocol's adoption, the international community has addressed the issue of whether military courts may be used to try civilians. While there is acceptance of military courts being used to try civilians for military offenses (Protocol II addresses "offenses related to the conflict" which are not necessarily military but could be civilian offenses), the preference is for civilian courts even for "military-like" offenses. Because of the impact of human rights law on all international law, use of military courts to try civilians for non-military offenses is strongly condemned. (*See, e.g.*, Montreal Declaration on the Independence of the Judiciary.)

civilian court, women and men defendants can only be tried for offenses on the basis of "individual penal responsibility."[153] Defendants are entitled to prompt notice of the charges and all necessary means of defense before and during trial. They have the right to be present during trial.[154] Defendants have the right to the presumption of innocence and freedom from self-incrimination.[155] If convicted, they have the right to notice of all judicial or other remedies.[156] Pregnant women and women with young children may not be executed.[157]

Refugees of Civil War

Neither Common Article 3 nor Protocol Additional I address the situation of refugees. The obligation to interpret Common Article 3 in conformity with Geneva Convention IV and utilizing the rule of analogy is therefore imperative to protect refugees of civil wars. As discussed above, Geneva Convention IV provides certain protections, including the protection of *non-refoulement*, in international wars. The needs of refugees of civil wars are equal to those in international wars: protection from the dangers of war and protection from the enemy.[158] Humane treatment of a refugee of civil war must reflect the rights set out in Geneva Convention IV. The rule of analogy is particularly useful because unlawful deportation of a civilian in an international war is severely condemned as a grave breach.[159]

GRAVE BREACHES

Each Geneva Convention of 1949 and Protocol Additional I identifies violations within the contexts of its field of application that constitute grave breaches (the Geneva Convention term for war crimes).[160] The grave breach article in Geneva Conventions

---

153. *Id.* art. 6.2(b).

154. *Id.* art. 6.2(e).

155. *Id.* art. 6.2(f).

156. *Id.* art. 3.

157. *Id.* art. 6.4.

158. *See* Karen Parker, *Human Rights and Humanitarian Law*, 7 WHITTIER L. REV. 675 (1985) (discussing situation of refugees from civil wars).

159. This author also considers the International Court of Justice's interpretation of Common Article I in the 1986 Nicaragua case and its 1949 Corfu Channel useful in this regard. *See supra* note 38 and accompanying text. This author has successfully presented this analysis in cases in U.S. courts. *See* In Re Santos-Gomez, Immigration Court for Washington, D.C., Case #A29564–781 (1990).

160. The enumeration of grave breaches in the Geneva Conventions differs somewhat from the enumeration of war crimes and crimes against humanity set out in the Nuremberg and Tokyo Charters. It is important to consult at least the Geneva Conventions, the post-World War II tribunals and the statutes of the two current international tribunals for the former Yugoslavia and Rwanda for a comprehensive listing of these crimes. The rule of analogy is also useful in this context. The Convention on the Non-Applicability of Statutory Limitations to War Crimes and Crimes Against Humanity, *in force* Nov. 11, 1970, 754 U.N.T.S. 73, *reprinted in* 8 I.L.M. 68 (1969) (hereinafter *War Crimes Convention*) incorporates the definition of war crimes in the Nuremberg Charter and the "grave breaches" enumerated in the Geneva Conventions of 1949 as war crimes.

I and II are identical and list wilful killing, torture, inhumane treatment or biological experimentation, wilfully causing great suffering to sick or wounded combatants.[161] These articles also identify destructive military acts not justified by military necessity as grave breaches.[162] The grave breach article in Geneva Convention III contains the list of acts against the person, deletes the military necessity clause, and adds forced service of a POW in the armed forces of the enemy and denying a POW fair trial rights as grave breaches.[163] Geneva Convention IV identifies wilful killing, torture, or inhumane treatment of civilians and the rest of the enumeration of acts against the persons and adds unlawful deportation, transfer, or detention of civilians and taking civilian hostages.[164]

Protocol Additional I greatly expands the enumeration of grave breaches, especially in an extensive listing of military acts against civilian and civilian property: targeting the civilian population, indiscriminate attacks on the civilian population, attacks against installations containing dangerous forces, and excessive damage to civilian locales or cultural, religious works, or property.[165] The Protocol also provides clarification of medical and scientific experimentation and lists a variety of acts as grave breaches.[166] Finally, the Protocol adds transfer of its own population into occupied territory, *apartheid* or other racially motivated practices, and delay in repatriation of POWs as grave breaches.[167]

HUMAN RIGHTS AND HUMANITARIAN LAW[168]

Contemporary humanitarian law is informed by contemporary human rights law, a field of international law that was incorporated into the Charter of the United

---

Id. art. I. Crimes against humanity include the enumeration in the Nuremberg Charter and the Convention on the Prevention and Punishment on the Crime of Genocide. *Id.*

161. Geneva Convention I, *supra* note 19, art. 50; Geneva Convention II, *supra* note 19, art. 51.

162. *Id.* This provision relates more closely to the Hague law.

163. Geneva Convention III, *supra* note 19, art. 130.

164. Geneva Convention IV, *supra* note 19, art. 147. This article contains the provision about extensive destruction "not justified by military necessity and carried out unlawfully and wantonly," as is also included in Geneva Conventions I and II.

165. Protocol Additional I, *supra* note 20, art. 85.

166. *Id.* (incorporating Article 11 which discusses, *inter alia*, tissue or organ transplants, and the right to refuse medical treatment).

167. *Id.*

168. For general discussions of the interrelationship between human rights and humanitarian law see Dietrich Schlinder, *Human Rights and Humanitarian Law: Interrelationship of the Laws*, 31 AM. U. L. REV. 935 (1982); A. H. Robertson, *Humanitarian Law and Human Rights, in* STUDIES AND ESSAYS ON INTERNATIONAL HUMANITARIAN LAW AND RED CROSS PRINCIPLES (International Committee of the Red Cross ed., 1984); Cesar Sepulveda, *Interrelationships in the Implementation and Enforcement of International Humanitarian Law and Human Rights Law*, 33 AM. U. L. REV. 117 (1983); Louise Doswald Beck & Sylvain Vite, *International Humanitarian Law and Human Rights Law*, 33 INT'L REV. RED CROSS 94 (Mar.–Apr. 1993). A number of older but useful articles are listed in Diana Vincent-Daviss, *Human Rights Law: A Research Guide to*

Nations.[169] To establish what is meant by human rights, in 1948 the General Assembly promulgated the Universal Declaration of Human Rights,[170] which in its thirty articles provides a full array of civil, political, economic, social and cultural rights granted to all people.[171] The Universal Declaration of Human Rights is considered binding customary international law.[172] Since promulgation of the Universal Declaration, a number of international and regional human rights treaties have been enacted that further advance human rights law.[173]

Certain human rights provisions are non-derogable: they may not be abrogated or suspended under any circumstances.[174] These human rights protections are there-

---

the Literature (Part II: International Protection of Refugees and Humanitarian Law), 14 N.Y.U. J. INT'L L. & POL. 487, 517, 561–73 (1982).

169. The United Nations was founded to "reaffirm faith in fundamental human rights," U.N. CHARTER pmbl., and to "promot[e] and encourag[e] respect for human rights," *id.* art. 1; *see also* arts. 55–56.

170. G.A.Res. 217(III)A, U.N. Doc. A/810 (1948).

171. The United Nations considers these rights enjoyed by persons in countries that are not members of the United Nations. For example, before either the Republic of Korea or the People's Democratic Republic of Korea were members, petitions were lodged and discussion took place regarding violations of human rights in both countries. Non-member Switzerland was criticized for its policies regarding persons seeking political asylum. Some human rights norms, such as those prohibiting slavery, were already a part of international law. However, until the post-World War II period, there had been no general codification of human rights. The American Declaration of the Rights and Duties of Man, Ninth Int'l Conf. Am. States Res. XXX (1948), *reprinted in* ORGANIZATION OF AMERICAN STATES INTER-AMERICAN COMMISSION ON HUMAN RIGHTS, HANDBOOK OF EXISTING RULES PERTAINING TO HUMAN RIGHTS IN THE INTER-AMERICAN SYSTEM (1985) was the first regional human rights instrument.

172. Proclamation of Teheran, U.N. Doc. A/CONF.32/41, U.N. Sales No. E.68.XIV.2 (1968), *endorsed in* G.A. Res. 2442 (XXIII), U.N. GAOR, 23d Sess., Supp. No. 18 at 49, U.N. Doc. A/7218 (1969). In 1993, the United Nations called the universal nature of these rights "beyond question." *Vienna Declaration and Programme of Action*, U.N. Doc. A/CONF.157/23 (1993).

173. *See, e.g.*, International Covenant on Civil and Political Rights, *signed* Dec. 6, 1966, 999 U.N.T.S. 171; International Covenant on Economic, Social and Cultural Rights, *signed* Dec. 16, 1966, 993 U.N.T.S. 3; American Convention on Human Rights, *in force* July 18, 1978, O.A.S. T.S. No. 36, *reprinted in* 9 I.L.M. 673 (1970); European Convention for the Protection of Human Rights and Fundamental Freedoms, *in force* Sept. 3, 1953, Europ. T.S. No 5; African Charter on Human and Peoples' Rights, O.A.U. Doc. CAB/LEG67/3 rev.5, *reprinted in* 21 I.L.M. 58 (1982). There are also a number of human rights instruments addressing narrower issues such as women's rights, children's rights, prohibitions against torture, and racial discrimination. For the text of many of these instruments, see U.N. HUMAN RIGHTS: A COMPILATION OF INTERNATIONAL INSTRUMENTS, U.N. Doc. ST/HR/1/Rev.4, U.N. Sales No. E.93.XIV.1 (1993).

174. The International Covenant on Civil and Political Rights, *supra* note 173, Article 4, prohibits derogations from the right to life, the right to freedom from torture, the right to freedom from slavery and forced labor (it allows, however, labor as a sentence and military service or other normal civil obligation as set out in Article 8(b) & (c)); the right to freedom from jail for debt; the right to freedom from *ex post facto* laws, the right to be recognized as a person before the law, and the right to freedom of religion. Measures taken in derogation may involve discrimination based on sex or other basis. The American Convention on Human Rights, *supra* note 173, adds the rights

fore *jus cogens*.[175] Because war is a circumstance that allows for some suspension of human rights, these non-derogable or *jus cogens* rights are particularly useful to augment areas where humanitarian law treaties fall short.[176] In this way, human rights standards have become part of customary humanitarian law, just as binding as if they were included in humanitarian law treaties.

Humanitarian law standards have also informed human rights norms. For example, humanitarian law provides that even in civil wars, there is a right to judicial guarantees "recognized as indispensable by civilized peoples."[177] Human rights law provides extensive enumeration of judicial or procedural rights but United Nations and Council of Europe human rights instruments allow for their derogation in war.[178] However, the Council of Europe's European Court of Human Rights and the United Nations Human Rights Committee have subsequently assimilated the Geneva Convention (and American Convention) approach by declaring a right to judicial guarantees necessary to protect the non-derogable rights.[179] The interplay of the two bod-

---

of the family, the right to a name, the right to participate in government, and the right to judicial guarantees "essential for the protection of such rights." *Id*. art. 27.

175. While scholars may differ as to whether at the time of drafting of the International Covenants the inclusion of certain human rights as non-derogable was a recognition that they were *jus cogens*, these non-derogable rights have long been accepted as *jus cogens*. *See, e.g*., Parker & Neylon, *Jus Cogens, supra* note 40; *see also* RESTATEMENT (THIRD) OF FOREIGN RELATIONS LAW § 702 (1987) ("Not all human rights norms are peremptory norms [*jus cogens*], but those in clauses (a) to (f) of this section are"). Clauses (a) to (f) lists the non-derogable rights. Some rights, such as the right to freedom from torture, are clearly set out in both humanitarian and human rights law. The fact that certain prohibitions are set out in each body of law reinforces their *jus cogens* nature, especially because grave breaches are universally viewed as violations of *jus cogens*. *See* Parker & Neylon, *id*. at 432–35.

176. One area where the Geneva Conventions are viewed as inadequate is in the field of application discussed above. Many provisions, including the provisions for humane treatment set out in Article 27 of Geneva Convention IV apply only to persons in international armed conflicts in enemy hands or in the hands of a party of which they are not national. Thus, this Convention has been viewed as not applicable when a warring party violates the rights of its own citizens. Because most of these rights are *jus cogens* and are accordingly applicable at all times and regarding any person or government, a government could be held in breach of customary humanitarian law for acts committed against its own citizens. The identification of *non-refoulement* as *jus cogens* reinforces its application in civil wars as well as in international wars. *See* Parker & Neylon, *supra* note 40 (asserting that rights norms, such as those prohibiting slavery, were already a part of international law). However, until the post-World War II period, there had been no general codification of human rights.

177. Geneva Conventions, *supra* note 19, art. 3 (common).

178. *See* European Convention for the Protection of Human Rights and Fundamental Freedoms, *supra* note 173. The American Convention on Human Rights does not allow derogation from judicial guarantees necessary to protect the non-derogable rights. American Convention on Human Rights, *id*., art. 27. This provision of the American Convention reflects the directive of Common Article 3 of the Geneva Conventions. The African Charter on Human and Peoples' Rights, *id*., does not contain a derogation clause.

179. *See* Lanza de Netto, *Weisman and Perdomo*, Hum. Rts. Comm. No. R2/8, U.N. Doc. A/35/40, Annex IV; Camargo v. Colombia, Hum. Rts. Comm. No. R.11/45, Annex XI; Ireland v. United Kingdom, 25 Eur. Ct. H.R. (Ser. A) (1978). For cases interpreting the provision for mini-

ies of law has created a *jus cogens* right to certain judicial guarantees whether in peacetime or war.

One significant contribution of human rights law to humanitarian law has been in the area of prohibitions against gender discrimination.[180] While the Geneva Conventions amply provide for non-discrimination based on sex for victims of armed conflicts, neither the Hague Conventions nor any other aspect of the Hague humanitarian law addresses equal rights of women in the military. However, many provisions of human rights instruments mandate equality for women in all circumstances and can be invoked to address gender discrimination in the military. For example, the Universal Declaration of Human Rights recalls that a purpose of the United Nations is equal rights of men and women[181] and provides for both the right to equality in public service[182] and the right to equal pay for equal work.[183] These provisions are especially useful in situations arising in countries (such as the United States) where there is no Constitutional provision requiring equality of women and men.

The Convention on the Elimination of All Forms of Discrimination Against Women[184] is also important to the issue of women and armed conflict: it recognizes the impact of war on women's rights,[185] sets out the right to gender equality in all aspects of employment (including equal pay and pay based on "equal value"),[186] and specifies the right to participate in the formulation and implementation of government policy.[187]

---

mal judicial guarantees in the Inter-American Court of Human Rights, see Habeas Corpus in Emergency Situations, Inter-Am. C.H.R. Ad. Op. OC-8/87 (1987); Judicial Guarantees in States of Emergency, Inter-Am. C.H.R. Ad. Op. OC-9/87 (1987). The provisions for judicial guarantees in the Geneva Conventions of 1949 and the Protocols Additional reflects a growing regime of rights in both treaty-based and customary humanitarian law: the old customary rule was that a belligerent could hold enemy aliens, even civilians, with no habeas rights. *See, e.g., Ex Parte Quirin,* 317 U.S. 1, 12 (1942) in which the respondent U.S. government cited a variety of pre-World War II cases declaring that rule. In *Ex Parte Quirin,* the Supreme Court did not itself pronounce on that rule, finding that the aliens in question fell under the category of spies or unlawful belligerents. According to treaty and customs unchanged by the Protocols Additional, spies are not entitled to POW status and may be tried for violations of the rules of war by military tribunals. This author expects that evolving standards will require that spies be considered combatants for purposes of POW status.

180. The international standards of human rights law relating to discrimination based on gender provides a legal framework to address discrimination faced by women in the military.

181. Universal Declaration of Human Rights, pmbl., *reprinted in* Basic Documents on Human Rights (Ian Brownlie ed., 3d ed. 1992).

182. *Id.* art. 21.

183. *Id.* art. 23.

184. The Convention on the Elimination of All Forms of Discrimination Against Women, U.N. GA Res. 34/180, Dec. 18., 1979, *in force* Sept. 3, 1981, *reprinted in* 19 I.L.M. 33 (1980).

185. *Id.* pmbl.

186. *Id.* art. 11.

187. *Id.* art. 7.

WOMEN'S ISSUES IN CONTEMPORARY ARMED CONFLICTS

The need for gender equality in the military is particularly acute at the present time because of the increased participation of women in armed conflict. In past military conflicts, women participated in a more auxiliary fashion, principally as nurses or office personnel.[188] In many contemporary armed conflicts, women have had an increasing combat role and are beginning to carry over a more equal military participation in civilian life. For example, women participated actively in military operations of the Frente Sandinista de Liberacion Nacional (FSLN) during the recent civil war in Nicaragua. Military participants became civilian members of the national legislature and cabinet members of both administrations since the conclusion of that civil war.[189] A civilian opposition member, Violeta Chamorro, became president.

In El Salvador, women have also played a large part in military operations as well as in opposition political leadership during the recent civil war in that country. A number of women commanders from that conflict were killed in combat or assassinated by the government forces.[190] Nidia Diaz, the commander of one of the groups of the Frente Marti de Liberacion Nacional (FMLN), was severely wounded and captured, on April 18, 1985. She was the first captured combatant recognized as a prisoner of war in that conflict[191] and later became Chairperson of the Committee of the

---

188. During World War II women actively participated in the resistance movements in France and Norway. Women also participated dramatically in the Algerian independence movement, and in the "long march" period in China. According to one woman eyewitness, during the victory celebrations in Norway, "women were not allowed to participate in the parades but had to work in silence and to sew soldiers' distinctions and epaulets on their male comrades jackets and caps." Address by Berit Aas, Professor at University of Oslo, International Women's Day Conference, in Paris (Mar. 9, 1996) (on file with author). This same historian pointed out that following the conclusion of the various conflicts mentioned above, women did not carry forward gains made during armed struggles into civilian political or social power. *Id.*

189. One former military leader of the FSLN, Leticia Herrera, was one of a number of women elected to the Nicaraguan legislature. She was subsequently denied visas by the United States because of her participation in the Nicaraguan civil war, which the United States Department of State has erroneously characterized as "terrorist." On July 24, 1994, she was arrested by the United States on a transit stop in Miami while she was on a mission of Nicaraguan parliamentarians to Venezuela, and this author presented her case at the 1994 session of the United Nations Sub-Commission on Prevention of Discrimination and Protection of Minorities. *See* Letter from Vilma Nunez de Escoria, President of the Nicaraguan Center for Human Rights, to Karen Parker (Aug. 3, 1994); *Statement of Karen Parker*, United Nations Sub-Comm'n on Prevention of Discrimination and Protection of Minorities, U.N. Doc. E/CN.4/Sub.2/1994/SR. 29 (1994).

190. For example, Clara Elizabeth, a founder of the Fuerzas Popular de Liberacion (FPL) and one of its directors, was killed in combat in 1976. Claudia Calderon (Comandante Sonia), second in command of FPL, was assassinated in 1983. Comandante Arlen Siu died in combat, June 26, 1985. *See* NIDIA DIAZ (Marta Valladares M. de Lemus), NUNCA ESTUVE SOLA 74, 138 (San Salvador, 1988).

191. This author visited Comandante Nidia on May 4, 1985, and again on May 20, 1985, and successfully sought her recognition by the El Salvadoran government authorities of her status. *See* NIDIA DIAZ (Marta Valladares M. de Lemus), NUNCA ESTUVE SOLA 98 (1988) ("Desde Estados Unidos ... vino a verme gente que ni me imagine. Una tarde, cuando me llevaron a la sala de registro, aparecieron Karen Parker, doctora en derecho humanitario, el doctor Kimball y el doctor

Judiciary and Human Rights of the Salvadoran National Congress. In 1984, she had represented the FMLN in the first peace talks held in La Palma. Women have also played an important political role in opposition in El Salvador. Marianella Garcia Villa, a political figure, was a founder of the non-governmental El Salvador Commission on Human Rights.[192] In Guatemala, women have played a similar role both in military activity and in military-political leadership. For example, Luz Mendez Gutierrez has represented the opposition at United Nations sessions and at direct negotiations[193] and there have been several internationally known cases of women prisoners of war.[194] Nobel laureate Rigoberta Menchu Tum organized rural indigenous peoples and represented humanitarian law and human rights concerns at numerous sessions of the United Nations human rights bodies.

Women have played an even larger role in some contemporary conflicts in Asia. For example, in the war in Sri Lanka, the Tamil forces (Liberation Tigers of Tamil Eelam or LTTE) have a major division of women combatants called the Women's Military Unit. This unit uses all weapons used by men combatants, including surface to air missiles (SAMs) and other heavy artillery. The Women's Military Unit first fought in combat in Mannar in 1989. Since that time, they have carried out many successful large-scale military operations against government (Sinhala) military bases and against military vessels and aircraft.[195] In July 1996, the Women's Military Unit

---

Gossi [sic]. . . . Todos me dieron animos. . . . Me regalaron . . . los convenios de Ginebra y sus protocolos addicionales. No lo podia creer. Me senti contenta. Estaba experimentando personalmente la solidaridad de los pueblos." [From the United States people who I never would have imagined came to visit me. One afternoon, when they took me to the registration room, Karen Parker, humanitarian law lawyer, Dr. Kimball and Dr. Gossi [sic, actually Dr. Goosby] appeared. They gave me courage. They gave me the Geneva Conventions and the Protocols Additional. I couldn't believe it. I was happy. I was directly experiencing the solidarity of peoples.] (trans. by author). Actually, we visited Comandante Diaz in the morning, but she had been severely wounded and interrogated practically round the clock for nearly two weeks and had no clear concept of time. Up to that date, opposition combatants captured by the El Salvadoran government were killed in captivity, and there was no compliance with any of the Geneva Convention rules regarding treatment of captured combatants.

192. Marianella Garcia Villa, a colleague of this writer, was murdered by the Salvadoran forces in March 1983.

193. Ms. Mendez Gutierrez is a co-signer of the March 1995 Peace Agreement, U.N. Doc. S/1995/256 and A/49/882 (1995).

194. For example, Commander Veronica Ortiz of the Unidad Revolucionaria Nacional Guatemalteca (URNG) was captured in October 1991. At first, the government forces denied her capture, but Ramiro de Leon Carpio, the government's Human Rights officer and subsequent President, was notified a month after her capture that Comandante Veronica was being held in a military hospital. Subsequently released after two more months into de Leon's custody, she apparently renounced her allies, perhaps to protect her then four-year-old daughter. Interview with Jorge Rosal, Representative of URNG to the United Nations, in Geneva (Mar. 5, 1992). This author also met with President de Leon Carpio regarding this and other issues relating to the armed conflict in Guatemala.

195. Five interviews with S. Krishnakumar ("Commander Kittu"), in London and Geneva (1990–1992). *See* ADELE ANN, WOMEN FIGHTERS OF LIBERATION TIGERS (London, 1993); Margaret Trawick, *Combatants' Positions: An Account from the East, in* AUSTRALIAN HUMAN RIGHTS FOUN-

was part of the military effort that successfully overran the Mullaitivu Army Camp. Over 1,200 Sri Lankan troops were killed and the entire military arsenal was seized. Many of the 250 casualties of the LTTE were women.[196] In Tamil-controlled areas, women play a significant role in civil administration.[197]

In Burma, women have fought as part of the war of the ethnic nationalities, especially the Karen and the Karenni,[198] against successive Burman-military dominated governments. Resistance efforts have been directed against the State Law and Order Restoration Committee (SLORC).[199] Women continue to play combat roles in the armed opposition and in the political opposition: the major political opposition party, the National League for Democracy, is currently headed by Nobel Peace Prize laureate Daw Aung San Suu Kyi.

In the former Dutch and Portuguese East Indies territories consolidated into Indonesia by treaty and seizure by Indonesian armies, women also play key roles in the opposition military and political leadership. For example, the president of the Republik Maluku (the Moluccas) (in exile) is Mrs. J. Bernard-Tamaela.[200]

DATION, PEACE WITH JUSTICE: INTERNATIONAL CONFERENCE ON THE CONFLICT IN SRI LANKA (Canberra 1996) (includes accounts of and personal interviews with women combatants).

196. LTTE, Press Communique, July 27, 1996.

197. *Id.* The President and Prime Minister of Sri Lanka are both women: Chandrika Bandaranaike Kumaratunga is President and her mother Sirimavo R.D. Bandaranaike is Prime Minister. In spite of these two women in key leadership positions, the rest of the civilian Sinhala government is nearly all male, and the government military forces have no women in leadership or combat positions.

198. Interviews with Abel Tweed and See Sein, Foreign Minister and Deputy Foreign Ministers of Karenni State, in New York and San Francisco (1992–1994). The author has also met with leaders of the Karen National Union, the Democratic Alliance of Burma, and the National Coalition Government of the Union of Burma who all verify the small but increasing role of women in military and political efforts against the SLORC regime in Burma. The author has also met with women involved in military and political activity whose names are not given here for reasons of their personal safety.

199. See *Human Rights in Burma: Hearings on Burma Before the Subcomm'n on Asian and Pacific Affairs of the House Comm. on Foreign Affairs*, 103d Cong., 1st Sess. 120 (1993) (statement of Karen Parker).

200. For a discussion of the Maluku question, see Karen Parker, Republik Maluku: The Case for Self-determination (Humanitarian Law Project/International Educational Development 1996) (report prepared for the 1996 session of the U.N. Comm'n on Human Rights, on file at University of Notre Dame Law School). Wars are also occurring in Acheh between the Indonesian forces and the Acheh/Sumatra Liberation Front and in East Timor between the Indonesian forces and the National Council of Maubere Resistance (incorporating the Fretilin). *See* Parker & Heindel, Armed Conflict, *supra* note 37, at 6, 29, 51. The participation of women is more limited in these wars. Of note is that the Acheh liberation movement waned during the post-World War II period until 1976 because by 1911, the Dutch had killed every male survivor (except small children) of the ruling di Tiro family. In 1976, Tengku Hasan M. di Tiro became head of state of Acheh Sumatra and renewed the Acheh's long resistance to foreign domination. Memorandum [on Acheh/Sumatra] from Tengku Hasan M. di Tiro to the Parliamentary Human Rights Group (United Kingdom) (Apr. 23, 1993) (copy on file with author).

Severe human rights abuses in Iran have generated political and military opposition. The situation in Iran offers the starkest contrast of war and politics and women in the contemporary world as each side has radically different practices and policies. The government severely oppresses women and allows almost no meaningful participation of women in the armed forces or in the civilian government: it appears to use oppression of women as a major strategy for maintaining control in Iran.[201] The opposition military and political leadership is more heavily controlled and dominated by women than any other current government or opposition group in contemporary society: its president is a woman, more than 50 percent of its civilian government are women, nearly 70 percent of its military commanders are women, and women (30 percent of the army) have equal combat positions and authority in all phases of military activity.[202] Women military units have won impressive military victories such as the capture of the city of Mehran by an all-woman brigade.[203]

Women have played a lesser military and political role in current conflicts in other parts of the world. For example, women have not been major military participants in the recent conflicts in the former Yugoslavia or in the Middle East. In Africa, women combatants participated in the recent Eritrean war of national liberation[204] but have not played a major role in other contemporary African wars. And while there is some political participation of women in the Kashmiri war, the combatants on both sides are overwhelmingly men.

WOMEN VICTIMS IN CONTEMPORARY ARMED CONFLICTS

Regardless of whether the wars have female military or political participants, women continue to be primary victims of serious breaches of humanitarian law. Modern wars are exceptionally hard on women. To compound the problem, women's issues have not been considered as important as other issues arising from war. Finally, remedies for wartime violations of women's rights, far from being integrated into regular legal processes as required by law, are practically non-existent.[205]

---

201. *See, e.g.*, Jonathan Wright, *Women Take Charge of Iran's Opposition Army*, WASH. TIMES, Nov. 22, 1995, at 8 (quoting Farid Suleimani: "Everything about the Khomeini regime depends to some extent on the oppression of women. Whenever they feel threatened, they choose women as scapegoats").

202. Interview with Maryam Rajavi, President of the National Council of Resistance (Iran), in Paris (Mar. 9, 1996); Interview with Mohammad Mohaddessin, Chair, Foreign Affairs Committee, National Council of Resistance (Iran), in Geneva (Apr. 18, 1996). *See also* Wright, *supra* note 201; Georgie Anne Geyer, *Women Excel in Combat Against Mullahs*, THE DENV. POST, Aug. 28, 1994, at G4.

203. Geyer, *supra* note 202, at G4.

204. Interview with Michael Ghebrenegus, Foreign Relations spokesperson for the Eritrean People's Liberation Front, in Geneva (Aug. 15, 1992); *see also* Geyer, *supra* note 202, at G4 ("Eritrean women distinguished themselves in battles against Ethiopia").

205. Until the 1994 appointment of Radhika Coomaraswamy as United Nations Special Rapporteur on violence against women, there was little or no attention to serious violations of women's rights at the United Nations Commission on Human Rights or its Sub-Commission on Prevention of Discrimination and Protection of Minorities. In the resolutions and reports on coun-

In part because of the traditional silence of the international community regarding women's rights in war, war-rape continues to be a major violation of the rights of women (as well as a vehicle for repression) in contemporary wars.[206] A war-rape scheme similar to that of Japan in World War II was part of the war in the former Yugoslavia.[207] The war in the former Yugoslavia has also affected women in numerous other ways: forced relocation, arbitrary detention or killing, loss of children and infants, and overall extreme hardship.[208] Because of the serious breaches of humanitarian law in this war, the United Nations established the first international war crimes tribunal since the Nuremberg and Tokyo trials following World War II.[209]

One of the worst current armed conflict situations from the perspective of humanitarian law in general and rights of women in particular occurred during the Rwanda conflict.[210] This war has told a horror story of genocide, slaughter of civilians on a massive scale, rape and other forms of sexual violence, wholesale destruction, and unspeakable human misery.[211] Rape has been a feature of the atrocities of this conflict.[212] More

---

tries with armed conflicts or serious human rights problems, the situation of women as a separate topic was not included. The United States Country Reports, an annual review of human rights around the world gave no regular analysis on the situation of women. Mention of the situation of women in the resolutions and reports on Burma, the former Yugoslavia and Rwanda as discussed *infra*, are "firsts."

206. *See, e.g.*, Madeline Morris, *By Force of Arms: Rape, War and Military Culture*, 45 DUKE L.J. 651 (1996); KELLY DAWN ASKIN, WAR CRIMES AGAINST WOMEN: PROSECUTION IN INTERNATIONAL WAR CRIMES TRIBUNALS (1997); Kelly D. Askin, *Women and International Humanitarian Law*, vol. 1 of this treatise.

207. The United Nations Security Council referred to war-rape in Yugoslavia as "massive, organized and systematic detention and rape of women." S.C. Res. 827 (1993). *See Final Report of the Commission of Experts*, U.N. Doc. S/1994/674 (1994). *See also* Radhika Coomaraswamy, *Preliminary Report on Violence Against Women*, U.N. Doc. E/CN.4/1995/42 (1995) at 65 (hereinafter *Preliminary Report*); Elizabeth Kohn, *Rape as a Weapon of War: Women's Human Rights During the Dissolution of Yugoslavia*, 24 GOLDEN GATE U. L. REV. 199 (1994); Catherine Niarchos, *Women, War and Rape: Challenges Facing the International Tribunal for the Former Yugoslavia*, 17 HUM. RTS. Q. 619 (1995). There are a number of other articles in law journals on sexual violence committed in the former Yugoslavia and this conflict has clearly generated the most attention among U.S.-based women's groups. This is not the only example of contemporary war-rape and may not be the worst contemporary war from the perspective of violence against women.

208. *See* Parker & Heindel, Armed Conflict, *supra* note 37, at 13, 15, 25–26 (listing all major U.N. documents relating to conflict in the former Yugoslavia).

209. S.C. Res. 827 (May 25, 1993). The Statute of the International Criminal Tribunal for the former Yugoslavia is found in U.N. Doc. S/25704 (1993).

210. For a list of U.N. documents relating to this war, *see* Parker & Heindel, Armed Conflict, *supra* note 37, at 54–56.

211. Even casual review of the reports of the United Nations Special Rapporteur for Rwanda shows the unique horror of the Rwandan situation. For his 1995 reports see Rene Degni-Segui, *Report on the Situation of Human Rights in Rwanda*, U.N. Docs. E/CN.4/1995/7; E/CN.4/1995/12; E/CN.4/1995/70; E/CN.4/1995/71.

212. *See, e.g.*, Rene Degni-Segui, *Report on the Situation of Human Rights in Rwanda*, U.N. Doc. E/CN.4/1996/7, at 10; Kelly Dawn Askin, *The Rwanda Tribunal and Its Treatment of Crimes Against Women*, *in* INTERNATIONAL HUMANITARIAN LAW: ORIGINS, CHALLENGES & PROSPECTS (John Carey & R. John Pritchard eds., vol. II, 2000).

than 2.5 million people, many of them women, were crammed into refugee camps, where many people died, trampled in the sea of people. Lack of food, water, and medicine resulted in thousands of deaths of war refugee women, men and children from starvation, exhaustion, dehydration, cholera and dysentery.[213] The Special Rapporteur commented that rebuilding national life will have to begin from nothing.[214] As a reflection of the level of violations in this war, the United Nations established its second war crimes tribunal, the International Criminal Tribunal for Rwanda.[215] Prosecution for war-rape and other atrocities against women has been a key part of the work of the Tribunal.[216]

Rape is also commonplace in other contemporary armed conflicts. In Somalia, war-rape and other abuse of women was so commonplace that one woman survivor described the war as "a war on women."[217] According to this witness, no woman or girl was safe from capture, rape, and violence, even from her own husband.[218] In the Kashmiri war, Indian occupation forces[219] have routinely used rape on a large scale to intimidate or silence Kashmiri opposition.[220] One human rights group reported on the incidents of February 23, 199,1 in Kunan Poshpura when the Indian army surrounded the whole town and attacked women, a large number of whom were raped.[221]

---

213. Rene Degni Segui, *Report on the Situation of Human Rights in Rwanda*, U.N. Doc. E/CN.4/1995/12, at 4–5.

214. *Id.* at 4.

215. S.C. Res. 955 and annexed Statute (1994).

216. *See* Prosecutor v. Jean-Paul Akayesu, Judgement, ICTR–96–4–T, Sept. 2, 1998 (accused found guilty of genocide and crimes against humanity for acts including sexual violence); Askin, *supra* note 212.

217. Susan Martin, Refugee Women 24 (1991).

218. *Id.* The witness stated that if a husband found out his wife was raped, he was likely to kill her for shame. If the armed forces knew a husband knew his wife was raped, the husband would himself be killed or would go into hiding. Women who tried to protect their husbands from capture were killed.

219. This author refers to Indian occupation forces because the political status of Kashmir has not yet been decided. In 1948, the United Nations Commission for India and Pakistan and the Security Council mandated a plebiscite of the people of Kashmir to decide their political future. S.C. Res. 47 (1948). This resolution, which authorized India to set up the plebiscite, was superseded by the resolution of Jan. 5, 1949, of the Security Council's Commission for India and Pakistan which placed the authority of the plebiscite to the U.N. Secretary-General. This was approved by the Security Council as a whole in its subsequent resolutions on this issue. The UN has maintained a military observer group (United Nations Military Observer Group for India and Pakistan, UNMOIP) in Kashmir since 1949. For a list of these resolutions and analysis of the political situation in Kashmir, see Karen Parker, The Kashmiri War: Human Rights and Humanitarian Law (International Educational Development/Humanitarian Law Project 1996) (hereinafter *Kashmiri War*) (copy on file with author).

220. *See* Coomaraswamy, *Preliminary Report, supra* note 207, at 65 (noting reports of 822 women gang raped by Indian security forces in 1992 alone). *See also* Parker, *Kashmiri War, supra* note 219, at 26; Asia Watch, Rape in Kashmir: A Crime of War (1993); Jammu and Kashmir High Court Bar Association, Report of Violations of Human Rights in Kashmir (1994); Jammu and Kashmir Council for Human Rights, Women and Children: Rape and Torture (1993).

221. Etienne Jaudel et al., Kashmir: Human Rights Violations Committed by the Indian Security Forces in Jammu and Kashmir 16 (International Federation of Human Rights 1993).

The group also interviewed Kashmiri refugees of India-occupied Kashmir about other incidents of rape and abuse.[222]

Women have been targeted victims in the armed conflicts in Burma, where rape and other serious violence is a major feature of the SLORC military of Burma against the women of ethnic nationalities in the area.[223] Much abuse takes the form of slave porterage, a serious violation of humanitarian law in which women and men are seized and made to carry the military supplies of the SLORC forces.[224] War-rape has been a feature of the civil war in Sri Lanka, and in the 1987–1990 war in Sri Lanka between Tamil forces and the Indian Peace Keeping Force (IPKF). As another example, rape of women, especially religious women—national or foreign—played a major role in the government forces efforts against their own people in Central American conflicts.

Women have also been victims of loss of life and war injuries because of the tendency in modern conflicts to attack by the air, thus resulting in high overall numbers of civilian casualties. Fortunately, there has been some condemnation of this tactic at the international level. For example, the United Nations Commission on Human Rights condemned the indiscriminate bombings of the civilian populations in the war in El Salvador.[225] Indiscriminate bombing of civilian areas, including refugee shelters with large numbers of women and children, by the Sri Lankan military forces has also received international condemnation.[226]

Women and the civilian population in general are also victims of the sheer brutality of war. The 1995 attacks in the Ganyiel area of Sudan were especially bad: 210 villagers (53 women, 30 men and 127 children) were slaughtered with spears and

---

222. *Id.* at 17.

223. *See* Yozo Yokota, *Report on the Situation of Human Rights in Myanmar*, U.N. Doc. E/CN.4/1995/65 (1995) at 27; Yozo Yokota, *Report on the Situation of Human Rights in Myanmar*, U.N. Doc. E/CN.4/1996/65 (1996) at 224 (hereinafter *Yokota 1996*); *U.N. Comm'n on H.R., Statement of Yozo Yokota, Special Rapporteur for Myanmar*, U.N. Doc. E/CN.4/1995/SR.49 ¶ 33; U.N. Comm'n on H.R. Res. 1996/80, U.N. Doc. E/CN.4/1996/L.91; U.N. Comm'n on H.R. Res. 1995/72, U.N. Doc. E/1995/23 at 207. *See also* ASIA WATCH, MYANMAR: RAPE, FORCED LABOUR AND RELIGIOUS PERSECUTION IN NORTHERN ARAKEN (Human Rights Watch 1992).

224. *Yokota 1996, supra* note 223, at 34. Because women cannot pay bribes to release them from slave-porterage, they are increasing as victims. This author has had many meetings with Special Rapporteur Yokota to present this and the issues of humanitarian law violations in Burma. In addition to his own observations and investigations, the Special Rapporteur has been presented with voluminous evidence from other sources as well indicating rape, sexual assault, forced porterage, targeting of the civilian population (especially women and children) and other grave breaches of the Geneva Conventions and the laws and customs of war. His recent proposals to the United Nations Commission on Human Rights for a team of human rights field officers was turned down by the Commission. *Id.* at 39.

225. U.N. Comm'n on Human Rights Res. 1984/52, U.N. Doc. E/1994/14 at 87, 88 ("[The Commission] expresses its deep concern at the reports that prove that government military forces regularly resort to bombarding urban areas which are not military objectives in El Salvador").

226. *See, e.g.*, International Committee of the Red Cross, Sri Lanka: Displaced Civilians Killed in Air Strikes, ICRC Communication to the Press No. 95/30 (July 11, 1995). On July 12, 1995, Pope John Paul II issued a statement regarding bombing of a refugee-packed Catholic Church.

knives.[227] Nearly 2,000 households were destroyed and 3,500 head of cattle taken.[228] The United Nations Special Rapporteur also comments on the special targeting of women by the government and government forces in Sudan (though perhaps not all strictly related to the civil war there) including the abduction of women for slavery and atrocities committed against women of ethnic or religious minorities.[229]

Women who become human rights activists, or political or military leaders in opposition to repressive regimes, have been assassinated or imprisoned in almost every conflict. Regrettably, except for sporadic international attention to certain cases, such as that of Nidia Diaz and a few others in the Central American conflicts, there has been almost no attention paid in the international community to women combatants or activists, which is made even more serious because of the almost total non-compliance of humanitarian law obligations or human rights norms.

TAKING ENFORCEMENT OF HUMANITARIAN LAW SERIOUSLY

Humanitarian law is like any other body of international law and is judicially enforceable as treaty, custom, or humane principle. States may bring actions against others state in their own courts for breaches. States may also seek international arbitration or may present allegations to international tribunals[230] or bring criminal actions against individual violators.[231] With the entry into force of Protocol Additional I, there

---

227. Gaspar Biro, *The Situation of Human Rights in Sudan*, U.N. Doc. E/CN.4//1996/62 (1996), at 20.

228. *Id.*

229. *Id.* at 24. The Rapporteur also calls for the cessation of "indiscriminate aerial bombardments of civilian targets." *Id.* at 30.

230. *See, e.g.*, Military and Paramilitary Activities in and Against Nicaragua (Nicar. v. U.S.) 1986 I.C.J. 14. In this action Nicaragua sought a finding of violations and monetary compensation for damages. Bosnia-Herzegovina brought an action at the International Court of Justice against Yugoslavia for genocide. While the Court did not find Yugoslavia guilty of genocide, it did order Yugoslavia to take all measures within its power to prevent the crime of genocide. Case Concerning Application of the Convention on the Prevention and Punishment of the Crime of Genocide (Bosnia and Herzegovina v. Yugoslavia (Serbia and Montenegro), 1993 I.C.J. 325 (Sept. 13, 1993)).

231. Each Geneva Convention of 1949 and both Protocols Additional addresses separate and joint action to prosecute violators. In a common provision of the Geneva Conventions of 1949, parties to the conventions "shall be under an obligation to search for persons committing, or ordering to be committed, . . . [any] grave breaches, and shall bring such persons, regardless of their nationality, before its own courts. It may also . . . hand over such persons for trial to another High Contracting Party concerned, provided such High Contracting Party has made out a prima facie case." Geneva Convention I of 1949, *supra* note 19, art. 49; Geneva Convention II of 1949, *supra* note 19, art. 50; Geneva Convention III of 1949, *supra* note 19, art. 129; Geneva Convention IV of 1949, *supra* note 19, art. 146. The same article requires states to assure necessary internal criminal laws for these cases. *Id.* Protocol Additional I expands on the duty of states to cooperate in any legal actions brought against violators. Protocol Additional I, *supra* note 20, art. 88. Such cooperation could include production of evidence and witnesses, service of process and handing over the accused, and legal consultation. Some cases of domestic tribunals for violators include the cases of *Lt.Calley, Adoph Eichmann* and *Claus Barbie*.

is now an international commission with authority to evaluate allegations of grave breaches and to act through good offices.[232] Direct enforcement is also possible through the establishment of specialized tribunals, such as the tribunals for the former Yugoslavia and Rwanda. The International Criminal Court will also be a tool for prosecuting war crimes, crimes against humanity, and genocide.

Enforcement of humanitarian law may also be indirect. In its case Military and Paramilitary Activities in and Against Nicaragua, the International Court of Justice ruled that Common Article 1 of the Geneva Conventions of 1949, which requires states to "respect and ensure respect for . . . [humanitarian law] in all circumstances is universally binding as customary law," even when such state is not directly involved in armed conflict.[233] Thus, not only must a state comply with provisions regarding prosecution of violators, but states must conform all aspects of their dealings with a state involved in war to humanitarian law, such as: provision of arms or military advice, other monetary assistance, recognition of diplomats or other political figures, and other interactions must all be evaluated for their effect on compliance with humanitarian law.

Enforcement of humanitarian law may also occur through international findings and condemnation of human rights bodies. For example, the United Nations human rights bodies have increasingly invoked humanitarian law in recent years.[234] Violations have been noted in resolutions on such countries as Angola, Cyprus, El Salvador, Guatemala, Burma, Somalia, Sri Lanka, Rwanda, Afghanistan, and the former Yugoslavia. Although some of these resolutions mention the civilian population, violations of women's rights in war have been singled out only in resolutions addressing the former Yugoslavia, Rwanda, and Burma.[235] Violations have also been noted in the reports of special rapporteurs or working groups of the human rights bodies.

The Organization of American States' Inter-American Commission on Human Rights has also raised humanitarian law issues in its work and has been a major supporter and advocate of enforcement of humanitarian norms as they relate to human rights during wars in member countries. For example, during the civil war in El Salvador, the Inter-American Commission commented on violations of the right to

---

232. Protocol Additional I, *supra* note 20, art. 90 The Commission may look into lesser violations at the request of a party to the conflict only if the party concerned consents. *Id.*

233. Military and Paramilitary Activities in and Against Nicaragua (Nicar. v. U.S.) 1986 I.C.J. 14, 114.

234. For citation to United Nations resolutions and reports on countries at war, see Parker & Heindel, Armed Conflict, *supra* note 37.

235. *See, e.g.*, U.N. Comm'n on Human Rights Res. 1995/89, 1995 U.N. ESCOR, Supp. No. 4. at 262, U.N. Doc. E/1995/23 (expressing concern of rape and degrading treatment of women as "deliberate instrument of war" and recommends rehabilitation of women traumatized by the war); U.N. Comm'n on Human Rights Res. 1995/72: *Situation of Human Rights in Myanmar*, 1995 U.N. ESCOR, Supp. No. 4, at 207, U.N. Doc. E/1995/23 (urging Myanmar to end abuse of women). Resolutions in prior years relating to these conflicts have also mentioned abuse of women in the context of war.

life resulting from military operations in which civilians were killed.[236] Because of its authority to carry out on-site investigations, the Inter-American Commission on Human Rights has played a critical role in verifying facts relating to violations of humanitarian law in the Central American conflicts and in situations of military *coups-d'etat.*[237]

Victims may seek compensation and other remedies in national courts, or in relevant regional or international forums. The right to compensation or other remedy for wrongs in general is one of the basic principles of law, without which the rule of law is not possible.[238] The right to compensation has been understood to exist both in peacetime and in war for at least several hundred years. For example, recognition of the duty to compensate and the right of victims to redress was recognized in international law early in American history by the United States Supreme Court, which ruled that individuals could be entitled to compensation, especially in claims arising from the laws of war.[239] Private compensation was granted in an action against Confederate soldiers for burning a courthouse—an act identified as a violation of the "laws of nations."[240] Authors of treatises on international law also emphasize compensation.[241] This principle was codified in Article III of the Hague Convention of 1907,[242] reflective of the international understanding of the right to compensation for violations of the laws and customs of war. The United Nations Security Council recently spoke out on the right of individuals to receive compensation when it stated:

---

236. *See, e.g.*, Inter-Am. C.H.R. 152, OEA/Ser.L./V/II.68, doc. 8 rev.1 (1986).

237. The Inter-American Commission has issued reports of fact-finding investigations in, for example, El Salvador, Guatemala, Nicaragua, and Suriname during civil wars or military coups or crises.

238. Hugo Grotius listed the obligation to make restitution for wrongful acts fourth in his five basic elements of law. Grotius, *supra* note 9, at 12. Former Calcutta High Court Judge Roy states: It is "a timeless axiom of justice without which social life is unthinkable, that a wrong done to an individual must be redressed by the offender himself or by someone else against whom the sanction of the community may be directed." Guha Roy, *Is the Law of Responsibility of States for Injuries to Aliens a Part of Universal International Law?*, 55 Am. J. Int'l L. 863 (1961); *see also* Benjamin Ferencz, *Compensating Victims of Crimes of War*, 12 Va. J. Int'l L. 343 (1972).

239. Ware v. Hylton, 3 U.S. (3 Dall.) 199, 279 (1796) ("[These] rights [are] fully acquired by private persons during war, more especially if derived from the laws of war . . . [and] against the enemy, and in that case the individual might be entitled to compensation.").

240. Christian County Court v. Rankin, 63 Ky. (2 Duv.) 502, 505 (1866). In 1926, a U.S claims court awarded compensation to parents of a girl killed by an American soldier. Decision of the General Claims Commission, United States and Mexico, Garcia v. United States 1926 (Docket No. 292) Dec. 3, *reprinted in* 21 Am. J. Int'l L. 581 (1927).

241. *See, e.g.*, Theodore D. Woosley, Introduction to the Study of Law 17–18 (1892) ("The right of redress exists in the case of individuals . . . . Redress consists of compensation for injury inflicted and for its consequences.").

242. The Hague Convention of 1907, *supra* note 23, art. III ("[violators of the regulations] shall, if the case demands, be liable to pay compensation").

[T]he work of the International Tribunal [for the former Yugoslavia] shall be carried out without prejudice to the right of the victims to seek, through appropriate means, compensation for damages incurred as a result of violations of international law.[243]

Actions for prosecution of violators or compensation for victims involving grave breaches of the Geneva Conventions (war crimes) and crimes against humanity should be free from time bar limitations. Some cases of prosecution and deportation of former participants in the Nazi atrocities have received international acclaim, even involving countries, such as the United States, that have not yet ratified the War Crimes Convention.[244]

In spite of the clear directives of the international law regarding punishment of violators and compensation for victims, contemporary legal actions in these areas are extremely rare given the large number of armed conflicts since World War II. The late California Supreme Court Judge Frank C. Newman has commented that no serious violators of humanitarian law were brought to international tribunals from 1950 to 1990.[245] National military forces have brought few alleged violators to military court-martials. Compensation for violations of humanitarian law lags far behind compensation for other types of wrongs.[246]

Several hopeful signs have emerged in recent years for victims seeking remedies for humanitarian law violations and remedies at the Organization of American States. In one case, the Organization of American States' Inter-American Commission

---

243. S.C. Res. 827 (May 25, 1993).

244. The War Crimes Convention states: "it is necessary and timely to affirm in international law, through this Convention, the principle that there is no period of limitation for war crimes and crimes against humanity, and to secure its universal application." *War Crimes Convention, supra* note 160, pmbl. The Preamble also indicated war crimes as the gravest of international crimes and stressed that punishment of violators is an "important element of prevention." *Id*. This language evokes *jus cogens*: war crimes and crimes against humanity violate *jus cogens*, therefore punishment and the right to redress for violations should also be viewed as *jus cogens*.

245. Frank. C. Newman, *Redress for Gulf War Violations of Human Rights*, 20 DENV. J. INT'L L. & POL'Y 213, 218 (1991).

246. This author is frequently asked why contemporary enforcement of humanitarian law is practically non-existent. The reasons she generally gives are: (1) lawyers and judges assume humanitarian law is somehow different from other law, and may only be invoked by the military or maybe the International Committee of the Red Cross (education in humanitarian law in law schools or for practicing attorneys or judges does not exist in the United States); (2) wars are highly political—the "my freedom fighter is your terrorist"/"I'm 100% right, you are a war criminal" syndromes—, and attorneys and victims may face volatile and hostile public condemnation; (3) states wish to carry out domestic or foreign policy, including wars, with no restraints—press are barred, documents are restricted or classified, reliable information is difficult or impossible to obtain; (4) the "cold war" created an even more hostile environment for humanitarian law adjudication. *See* Karen Parker, *International Human Rights and Humanitarian Law*, 22 S.F. ATT'Y (April/May 1996), at 17. This author frequently comments on the near silence of the United States bar associations when the United States government refused to accept the binding judgement of the International Court of Justice in the Nicaragua action against the United States (a case invoking humanitarian law) and the fact that there have been no military court actions for violations of the United States forces in Grenada, Panama, or the Gulf War, in spite of information indicating extremely serious breaches of the Geneva Conventions.

on Human Rights admitted a petition brought by victims of the United States bomb-ing of a hospital for mentally ill and mentally challenged persons.[247] In another case, the Inter-American Commission admitted a petition brought by survivors and other victims of the United States military action in Panama who sought recognition of vio-lations of human rights and humanitarian law and compensation from the United States for injury resulting from these violations.[248]

The difficulties faced by individuals seeking compensation for war crimes is perhaps best illustrated by the long ordeal for compensation of Japan's surviving World War II war-rape victims. Women who were victims of Japan's *jugun ianfu* scheme (the "comfort women") have yet to be adequately compensated.[249] Recently, the government of Japan encouraged the establishment of the Asian Women's Fund to provide redress to Japan's war-rape victims and also to address issues affecting Asian women as a whole.[250] Many persons associated with redress efforts, including this author, have challenged the Japanese government's attempts to avoid direct com-pensation for its victims, and consequently have been unsatisfied with the use of the Asian Women's Fund as the sole vehicle for redress.[251] At the time of this writing, the Japanese government has announced it will pay about $20,000 to the Asian Women's Fund for compensation to the *jugun ianfu*.[252] Each victim will receive a personal let-ter from the Japanese Prime Minister expressing "apology and remorse."[253] It is unclear

---

247. Case 9213, Inter-Am. C.H.R. 184, OEA/Ser/L/V/II.74, doc.9 rev.1 (1987) (admissibility). This author was the attorney in this case, which was the first case against the United States accepted by the Inter-American Commission on Human Rights. *See also*, Case 9213, Inter-Am. C.H.R., OEA/Ser/L/V/II.91, doc.16 (1996) (conclusion of case: petitioners granted conclusion of case because United States had completed a new facility for the surviving residents, and had pro-vided "satisfactory compensation," including food, clothing, and care).

248. Case 10.573, Inter-Am. C.H.R. 312, OEA/Ser.L/V/II.85, doc. 9 rev. (1993).

249. *See* Karen Parker & Jennifer Chew, *Compensation for Japan's World War II War-Rape Victims*, 17 HASTINGS INT'L & COMP. L. REV. 497 (1994); Radhika Coomaraswamy, *Report on the Mission to the Democratic People's Republic of Korea, the Republic of Korea and Japan on the Issues of Military Sexual Slavery in Wartime*, U.N. Doc.E/CN.4/1996/53/Add.1 (1996). The *jugun ianfu* scheme involved the abduction of perhaps as many as 200,000 girls as young as twelve and women from China, Korea, Burma, Netherlands East Indies, Philippines, Malaysia, and Taiwan. During captivity, these girls and women were raped daily and subjected to other forms of torture and extremely harsh conditions. Only about 25 percent survived this treatment by the end of the war. Parker & Chew, *id*. at 498–510. This author was invited by the attorneys presenting many of the *jugun ianfu* cases in Japanese courts to submit an expert opinion to the courts regarding the violations of then-existing international law and the right to compensation. *See* Opinion of Karen Parker, The Jugun ianfu cases, Kakyu saibansho minji saiban reshu (Tokyo) (1995) (copy on file with author).

250. U.N. Comm'n on Human Rights, *Note verbale of Japan*, U.N. Doc. E/CN.4/1996/137 (1996), at 4. This note verbale also presents an overview of Japan's current policies, *id*. at 3–6, and criticizes the reports of Special Rapporteur Coomaraswamy, *id*. at 8–9.

251. *See, e.g.*, U.N. Comm'n on Human Rights, *Statement of Karen Parker for International Educational Development/Humanitarian Law Project*, U.N. Doc. E/CN.4/1996/SR.[ ] (1996) (original text on file with author).

252. *Japan's Wartime Sex Slavery*, S.F. CHRON., June 6, 1996, at A22, col. 1.

253. *Id*.

what effect this plan will have on the current lawsuits in Japan for redress. Even Prime Minister Hashimoto admits his letter "must be something that will not be used against us in lawsuits."[254]

RECOMMENDATIONS

For Governments

(1) All employees of governments in the areas of foreign and military affairs, including all members of the military forces, should have meaningful training in human rights and humanitarian law.

(2) Governments should greatly increase the numbers of women working in foreign affairs and in the military. Employment should be at all levels, including the highest levels of decisionmaking.

(3) Issues relating specifically to women in armed conflict should be given due attention.

(4) Women who experience discrimination or any other unequal treatment in the military should have meaningful recourse to grievance procedures and effective legal remedies.

(5) Governments should establish a women's military task force to monitor the situation of women in wars, the education of all personnel in foreign affairs and the military, and the implementation of employment parity in the military.

(6) Governments should fund programs providing aid for victims of violations of the laws and customs of war, including aid to victims seeking domestic or international legal or other remedies.

(7) Governments should identify alleged violators of the laws and customs of war, whether nationals or foreign, and should alone, or in concert with other governments or international forums, bring such persons to trial.

Human Rights Work

(1) Women should be included in on-site investigations in war situations.

(2) On-site investigation in war situations should review all aspects of humanitarian law rights, including women's rights.

(3) Women's groups should consider an urgent action network to mobilize attention to grave problems of women in war.

(4) Groups should seek to establish special funds for care and rehabilitation of women war victims and to enable women victims to pursue effective remedies, including legal remedies, for violations.

---

254. *Id.*

Education

(1) Beginning in elementary school, humanitarian law should be taught along with human rights law and general international law. Graduate schools in law and government should include human rights and humanitarian law in the curriculum.

(2) Students should be encouraged to write on humanitarian law topics for courses or for publication in academic or popular journals.

(3) Schools should seek out internship placements and job opportunities with governmental, intergovernmental, and non-governmental national and international groups working on the problems of war.

Legal Community

(1) Legal education should include course work in human rights and humanitarian law, internship possibilities, and placement services for human rights and humanitarian law careers.

(2) The law bars should include sessions on humanitarian law in training sessions, conferences, and conventions.

(3) The legal community should speak up when its government or other entities in war violate humanitarian, human rights, or other related international law issues.

(4) Legal work on behalf of war victims, wherever they may be, should be funded or sponsored by bar associations or other associations in the legal community. Legal work can include on-site investigations, reporting, and pursuing legal actions at domestic and international levels.

(5) Bar associations or other legal associations should sponsor or fund legal work relating to the identification of violators of the laws and customs of war and should assist in any way reasonable with the work of tribunals or other forums by which such persons are judged.

CONCLUSION

In spite of the increase in treaty-based protection and the evolving customary rules of war, the contemporary period has seen no abatement of the age-old sufferings of women in war. Violations of the rights of woman in war will continue as long as wars continue—there has yet to be a war fought completely free of both human rights and humanitarian law violations. Women in the military will experience discrimination for many years to come and probably for many years after discrimination in civilian affairs subsides. This is in part because the military has been more exclusively male-dominated than any other organ of society.

In spite of the poor prognosis for the near future, women have made and will continue to make dramatic advances in protecting themselves from the worst horrors of war, in seeking and obtaining meaningful action to halt and redress these horrors, and in achieving at least some parity in the military.

Most of these advances have been because of the concerted attention and action by women themselves. While this has been useful in mobilizing women to promote and defend their own rights, it clearly illustrates that men have not treated the rights of women in war and women in the military as issues of priority.

Humanitarian law is probably the least understood area of law, even less understood than human rights law: except for a handful of persons in the military, few people in government, in human rights organizations, or in society as a whole even know the basics. Little can be done to achieve lasting improvement of the rights of women in war until the law of war is far more widely known.

Obviously, given the nearly total control of men in the military and political/military arena, giant steps for improvements cannot be made until men treat the issues seriously. This author believes that the rights of women in armed conflict will not reach parity with those of men in armed conflict until women gain substantial power in the military itself.

CONCERNS OF WOMEN IN ARMED CONFLICT SITUATIONS IN LATIN AMERICA

Dinorah La Luz*

INTRODUCTION

Latin America is a diverse and rich region, and one that experienced tremendous upheaval, conflict, and transition in the twentieth century.[1] The violence to which

*   The author thanks the following individuals and organizations who provided complementary documents, suggestions, referrals, and support to make this work possible: Dr. Jiri Toman, Director, Henry Dunant Institute and the personnel at the Institute; Prof. Cynthia A. Mertens, Santa Clara University School of Law; Prof. Dinah Shelton; Tim Eicke, Esq.; Ms. Burga Metzer, International Committee of the Red Cross, Geneva; Dr. Alfred DeZayas, Centre for Human Rights, Geneva; Dr. Ursula-Maria Ruser, Chief Archivist, U.N. Library, Geneva; Dr. Werner Simon, Chief, Specialized Reference Unit, U.N. Library, Geneva; Mr. Peter Wilborn, Assistant Legal Officer and staff at the International Commission of Jurists, Geneva; Ms. Barbara Lochbihler, former Secretary-General and staff, Women's International League for Peace and Freedom (WILPF), Geneva; Ms. Laura J. Gross, Resources Div., WILPF Philadelphia branch; Netherlands Institute of Human Rights, Utrecht University; U.N. Secretariat of the Fourth World Conference on Women, and the U.N. Non-Governmental Liaison Service, New York; Judge Antonio Cancado Trinidade and visiting professor, International Institute of Human Rights, Strasbourg; librarian and staff, International Institute of Human Rights, Strasbourg; Ms. Jennifer M. Green, Esq. and the Center for Constitutional Rights, New York; Ms. Cosette Thompson, Amnesty International, San Francisco Branch; Prof. Irwin M. Abrams, Antioch University; Dr. Peter van den Dungen, University of Bradford, United Kingdom; Ms. Cindy Arnold, National Commission for Democracy in Mexico, Texas; Mr. Ariel Dulitzky, Center for Justice and International Law (CEJIL), Washington, D.C.; Jan Susler, Esq.; Ofensiva '92, Puerto Rico; Dr. Maria Elena Moreira, Ecuador; Legal Research Center librarians, University of San Diego School of Law; Maria Paula Poggio, Esq.; Markus Feldman, Esq.; Susana Sanchez-Gallego, Esq.; Lilia Velasquez, Esq.; Mrs. Danielle Bridel, Esq., Geneva; Jaime J. Rizo Pereira, Esq., Nicaragua; Ambassador Jose El Taiana, Executive Secretary and staff, OAS, Washington, DC.; Tracy Thompson, Foreign & International Law librarian and Keneth Rudolf, Yale Law School; Annia Feliciano, President, Organizacion de Mujeres Estudiantes de Derecho; Maria Dolores Fernos, Esq., CODEM, Puerto Rico.

I also thank some colleagues and friends for their support: Dr. John Poole and family; Emily Millar, Esq.; Mrs. Vureyka Catanzaro; Ms. Luz N. Lizarribar; Blanche Vahle, Esq. and family; and, especially Joy Kent, Esq., for her excellent editorial work, suggestions, and patience.

This chapter is an updated, excerpted, and edited version of: Dinorah La Luz, Concerns of Latin-American Women in Armed Conflicts (unpublished LL.M. thesis, University of San Diego School of Law, 1996).

1.   *See* THE (UN)RULE OF LAW & THE UNDERPRIVILEGED IN LATIN AMERICA (Juan Mendez, Guillermo O'Donnell, & Paulo Sergio Pinheiro eds., 1999).

women and girls have been regularly subjected is relentless and unrepentant.[2] Women in many countries in Latin America have been intimidated continuously by such means as threats to kill them or their relatives, threats of rape or other forms of sexual violence, or by beatings and torture. Many of these violations disproportionately affect women; indigenous women and women activists are especially targeted for abuse. Gender-based crimes are presented in this chapter within the framework of instability as it continues to exist in some countries. Particular emphasis will be placed on El Salvador, Guatemala, and Honduras.[3] While violations of women's human rights are the result of patriarchal structures in society that exist not only in wartime but also during peacetime, the purpose of this chapter is primarily to expose the violations of human rights and humanitarian laws that women suffer in armed conflict situations in Latin America. It will include a discussion about accountability of individuals or groups, particularly the military, quasi-military groups, death squads, and guerrillas (mostly in the Peruvian situation), and will examine the accountability of states for actions or omissions of individual actors.

Women's response to gross violations such as illegal detention, torture, rape, and disappearances, and to an ineffective state system of redress has been twofold: through violent means, such as active involvement in guerilla movements (e.g., Sandinistas in Nicaragua, and in Puerto Rico); and through non-violent means, such as through work in non-governmental organizations (NGOs).

International and local NGOs are instrumental in addressing state disregard of international and regional obligations. This is particularly true in cases where NGOs have represented women and minorities in the Inter-American system. Other contributions by NGOs include efforts to create public awareness and exert pressure against states to bring perpetrators to justice and to ensure states comply with their obligations.

---

2.   *See, e.g.*, CIRCLE OF LOVE OVER DEATH: TESTIMONIES OF THE MOTHERS OF THE PLAZA DE MAYO (Matilde Mellibovsky et al. eds., 1997); ASCUNCION LAVRIN, WOMEN, FEMINISM AND SOCIAL CHANGE IN ARGENTINA, CHILE, & URUGUAY, 1980–1940 (1995); DIANA TAYLOR, DISAPPEARING ACTS: SPECTACLES OF GENDER & NATIONALISM IN ARGENTINA'S 'DIRTY WAR' (1997); THE FACES OF HONOR: SEX, SHAME, AND VIOLENCE IN COLONIAL LATIN AMERICA (Lyman L. Johnson & Sonya Lipsett-Rivera eds., 1998).

3.   The cases that will be discussed in this chapter deal mostly with indigenous women in Latin America. Cases like Haiti, where women have been tortured, raped, and murdered for political reasons (e.g., accused by the authorities of being Aristide's supporters in times of the military regime) have other characteristics (like the refugee crisis) that are not a subject in this discussion, although reference will be made to the conclusions in the Report on Haiti issued by the Inter-American Commission on Human Rights (IACHR). The IACHR concluded during its on-site visit to Haiti on May 1994 that "rape represents not only inhumane treatment that infringes upon physical and moral integrity under Article 5 of the [American] Convention, but also a form of torture in the sense of Article 5(2) of that instrument." IACHR, Report on the Situation of Human Rights in Haiti, OEA/Ser.L/V/II.88, Doc. 10 Rev., Feb. 9, 1995, at 43.

WOMEN AS VICTIMS OF ARMED CONFLICTS IN LATIN AMERICA

Women's Rights Violations by Country

El Salvador

Latin American history is characterized by economic and ethnic discrimination against a large segment of the population (usually the indigenous peoples) and by the corruption of those in power. In El Salvador, civil war—a result of economic and social conditions (75 percent of the population had little education, land, and food[4])—began with the destruction of the communal landownership of the peasants. When new laws on private property were implemented by the government, the dispossessed were left with very few ways to earn a living. The economy and the government are now controlled by the wealthy who have the support of foreign governments, investors, and multinational corporations.

Between 1980 and 1991, the Farabundo Marti National Liberation Front (Frente Farabundo Marti para la Liberacion Nacional-FMLN)[5] and the United States-backed government fought a war that resulted in approximately 75,000 deaths.[6] Political killings, disappearances, tortures, and bombings of civilian neighborhoods by the Security Forces were common. Fraudulent elections, corruption, and violent repression of protests during the 1970s culminated in the March 1980 assassination of Archbishop Romero by a death squad. In 1981, as a response to the escalating problems, the United Nations began to monitor El Salvador's situation. The U.N. Commission on Human Rights named a special representative to oversee El Salvador, however, the United Nation's efforts and General Assembly resolutions were largely ineffective. The political climate changed with the murder of six U.S. Jesuits (the Lawyers Committee for Human Rights reports that eighteen priests and lay workers were killed in the 1970s and 1980s, and that during this period, five Catholic nuns were also raped and assassinated by government forces).[7] International outrage followed and U.S. support for the government that was held responsible for those deaths was eventually withdrawn. Finally, some progress in alleviating the unrest was realized, resulting in the Peace Accords of January 16, 1992. The government negotiated with the FMLN for the dissolution of the military and the guarantees of respect for human rights.[8] While this agreement did not actually achieve the dissolution of the military, it diluted the power of the military and their ability to engage in more repressive tactics under the guise of maintaining "public order." A National Civil Police

---

4.   SHELLEY SAYWELL, WOMEN IN WAR: FIRST HAND ACCOUNTS FROM WORLD WAR II TO EL SALVADOR 282 (1985).

5.   By 1981, the FMLN controlled a large part of the country's territory. *See* Reed Brody, *The United Nations and Human Rights in El Salvador's "Negotiated Revolution,"* 8 HARV. HUM. RTS. J. 155 (Spr. 1995).

6.   U.N. Observer Mission in El Salvador (ONUSAL), El Salvador Agreements: The Path to Peace, at i, U.N. Doc. DPI/1208–92614 (1992).

7.   *See* MARTHA DOGGETT, DEATH FORETOLD, THE JESUIT MURDERS IN EL SALVADOR vii (1993).

8.   Brody, *supra* note 5, at 156.

(PNC) was created.[9] The government also proposed reforms in the judiciary and eventually created a human rights ombudsman, whose mandate included the investigation of human rights violations and the initiation of administrative and judicial remedies.

The El Salvadorian government agreed, under FMLN pressure, to investigate the massacres of civilians, although there was no mention of prosecuting the perpetrators. The U.N. proposed the creation of a "Truth Commission" composed of three members selected by the U.N. Secretary-General, to investigate the acts of violence and issue binding recommendations.[10]

When this Commission issued their report and presented it to the U.N. and the Salvadoran President, it created a crisis in the peace process. The government, still under pressure from the military, reacted negatively, rejecting the Truth Commission's report. It delayed but later partially complied with the recommendations to discharge 103 officers, including officers at the top of the hierarchy, such as the Minister of Defense.

Subsequently, in 1993, President Cristiani called for a general amnesty. The ombudsman, condemned by the non-governmental organizations as being slow to take any initiative and perceived as being submissive to other state institutions, remained silent about the general amnesty.[11]

After the peace agreement between the Salvadoran government and the FMLN, the Inter-American Commission on Human Rights (IACHR) reported that although some progress had been made, the government had the same problems of implementation. Interestingly, while the IACHR mentions that some progress was made in dismantling the illegal armed groups or "peace squads," it acknowledges that other groups with similar characteristics were created in 1993.[12] Furthermore, security for citizens deteriorated, and the IACHR reported that there was a "resurgence of arbitrary executions by the illegal groups known as death

---

9. Agreement on Human Rights, U.N. GAOR, 44th Sess., Annex, Agenda Item 34; U.N. SCOR, 45th sess., U.N. Doc. A/44/971; and, U.N. Doc. S/21541 (1990).

10. ONUSAL, El Salvador Agreements: The Paths to Peace, at i, U.N. Doc. DPI/1208–92614 (1992).

11. Brody, *supra* note 5, at 172.

12. *See* Report of the Joint Group for Investigating Politically Motivated Illegal Armed Groups in El Salvador, July 28, 1994, in IACHR Annual Report 1994, OEA/Ser.L/V/II.88, Doc. 9 Rev., Feb. 17, 1995, at 172–73. The Joint Group defined "death squadrons" (and the Truth Commission used the following definition when drafting its report) as: "organizations of groups of persons usually dressed in civilian clothes, heavily armed, who act clandestinely and hide their affiliation or identity. . . , [who are] linked to government structures by active participation or by tolerance and that ceased to be a marginal phenomenon and became an instrument of terror and systematic elimination of political opponents." Report of the Truth Commission on El Salvador, at 139, in IACHR Annual Report 1994, at 173 n.39.

A report was issued on July 28, 1994, by the Joint Group, and endorsed by the U.N. Security Council, concluding that such groups "appear to be pursung the destablization of the peace process." U.N. Doc. S/1994/989, Oct. 22, 1994.

squads."[13] Another inconsistency noted in the report was that "since October 1992 no forced disappearances have occurred in El Salvador when, in fact, such disappearances had occurred."[14]

El Salvador's Legislative Assembly approved a General Amnesty Law for the Consolidation of Peace of March 20, 1993. However, the amnesty violates the American Convention of Human Rights (to which El Salvador is a party), the case law of the Inter-American Court of Human Rights,[15] and the recommendations of the IACHR's Report on the Situation of Human Rights in El Salvador in 1994,[16] which specifically mentions that the reciprocal amnesty of El Salvador constitutes a violation of international obligations in the American Convention on Human Rights, since the government does not acknowledge responsibility regarding compensation for victims.[17]

El Salvador ratified the four 1949 Geneva Conventions without reservations and the two 1977 Protocols Additional to the Geneva Conventions, also without any reservations. Even though the government of El Salvador did not qualify the conflict as an internal conflict as defined by the Geneva Conventions and Protocols, Protocol II and Common Article 3 apply.[18]

During 1983 and 1993, the IACHR issued reports on individual complaints against the government of El Salvador. The government has not responded to any of the recommended actions or requests made by the IACHR, nor has it recognized the jurisdiction of the Inter-American Court of Human Rights.

Still unresolved is Case No. 7,571 of June 30, 1983, alleging the rape and murder of four U.S. nuns by the Salvadoran Armed Forces. The IACHR declared that the material facts in the petition constituted "extremely grave violations to the right to life (Article 4), the right to humane treatment (Article 5), the right to privacy (Article 11) and the obligation of state parties to respect and enforce the American Convention on Human Rights (Article 1.1)."[19]

In addition, the IACHR reported six cases of rape in which no satisfactory reply has been received from the government of El Salvador. On January 21, 1988, the Salvadoran Air Force (FAS) landed in the villages within the jurisdiction of Agua

---

13.   IACHR Annual Report 1994, *id.* at 169–73; Human Rights Watch/Americas, *El Salvador— Darkening Horizons: Human Rights on the Eve of the March 1994 Elections*, VI HUM. RTS. WATCH/AMERICAS RPT., No. 4 (Mar. 1994).

14.   IACHR Annual Report 1994, *supra* note 12, at 171. As of 1998, El Salvador had not signed the Inter-American Convention on the Forced Disappearance of Persons.

15.   *See* Advisory Opinion OC–14/94 of Dec. 9, 1994, and Advisory Opinion OC–13/93, in IACHR Annual Report, *supra*, at 181.

16.   IACHR Special Report 1994, *supra* note 12, at 77 (1994).

17.   *Id.*

18.   *See* CHRISTOPHE SWINARSKI, INTRODUCCION AL DERECHO INTERNACIONAL HUMANITARIO 53 (CICR & IIDH, 1984).

19.   IACHR's Report on the Situation of Human Rights in El Salvador, OEA/Ser.L/V/II.85, Doc. 28 Rev., Feb. 11, 1994, at 22 [hereinafter, IACHR's Report on El Salvador].

Caliente, department of Chalatenango. The Air Force fired on people's homes and captured, raped, and arbitrarily executed five minor girls (ages twelve to eighteen). The bodies were buried in Quezera only after the FAS soldiers gave the families permission to do so. After repeated requests, the government replied to IACHR, asserting a different set of facts and requesting filing of the case.[20]

On November 11, 1989, another girl, age thirteen, was illegally detained near Metapan Market by a member of the Salvadoran Treasury Police in civilian clothes.[21] He blindfolded her, tied her up, and took her to the headquarters of the Treasury Police. The girl-child was taken to a cell, where she was kept for several days, bound and blindfolded, until she was transferred to a dark cell, where she was kept for twenty-two days; it is alleged that a man entered her cell, chained her, and raped her on two different occasions, threatening to kill her if she reported the incident. The IACHR requested the government of El Salvador to reply to the charges, but no reply has been issued.

These cases illustrate the criticism that the ability of the IACHR to redress injustices perpetrated during civil upheaval is largely ineffective without full government cooperation.

On January 26, 1996, El Salvador ratified the Inter-American Convention on the Prevention, Punishment and Eradication of Violence Against Women (Convention of Belém do Pará of 1995). It remains to be seen whether El Salvador will comply with its obligations under the convention. Article 7 lists measures that states parties must adopt to restraint agents from discriminatory practices or acts against women and urges states parties to exercise due diligence when investigating and sanctioning violence against women.

Guatemala

Indigenous women in Guatemala have also suffered ethnic related violence,[22] which continues despite "democratization." One of the first steps required to achieve full democratization is bringing to justice the persons who perpetrated genocide, crimes against humanity, and war crimes, and compensating the victims. The military still has substantial power and influence in the Guatemalan government.[23]

---

20.   Case No. 10,367, IACHR's Report on El Salvador, *id*. at 59–60.

21.   Case No. 10,773, *id*. at 63.

22.   During 1981 and 1982 more that 400 villages were demolished and "between 377,000 to 407,000 Guatemalans suffered destruction of their homes, villages and economic activities." Thousands were assassinated. Survivors were forced to flee or placed themselves under army control, which meant that they were forced to take part in self-defense patrols or to be moved to "'model village' contraction centers." *See* IACHR's Special Report on the Human Rights Situation on the So-Called "Communities of People in Resistance in Guatemala," OEA/Ser.L/V/II.86, Doc. 5 Rev. 1, June 16, 1994, at 3 *et seq. See also* I, RIGOBERTA MENCHU, AN INDIAN WOMAN IN GUATEMALA (Elizabeth Burgos-Debray ed. & Ann Wright trans., 7th reprint 1994). Rigoberta Menchu's mother was kidnapped, raped, and tortured by army officers. After she was disfigured and left almost starving, the doctors revived her so she could be tortured and raped again. *Id*. at 198.

23.   *See* Daniel Wilkinson, *"Democracy" Comes to Guatemala*, 12 (4) WORLD POL'Y J. 71 (Winter 1995–96.)

Civilians have been murdered, raped, and otherwise tortured supposedly for being subversives and bandits. Mechanisms used to silence victims range from threats to further violence by government sponsored patrols. Living with violence has affected everyone, especially women who are continuously intimidated by threats to kill them or their relatives[24] or by threats of rape. Women who help organize groups, irrespective of whether the groups are for human rights or just for survival,[25] have also been victims of violence.

The Inter-American Commission on Human Rights reports that, in spite of government efforts to redress problems, results are "incipient and unsatisfactory." The IACHR made recommendations that are basically geared toward achieving democratic process without addressing the human rights violations and impunity of violators. During the IACHR investigations, some government officials conceded that the police or civil officers abuse their authority with minimal risk of being punished.[26]

This report does not mention the applicability of the new regional instruments. However, the Inter-American Convention to Prevent and Punish Torture (Inter-American Convention on Torture)[27] would apply, since Guatemala signed it in 1987.

On February 25, 1999, Guatemala's Historical Clarification Commission (CEH) issued its report, concluding that Guatemala had been responsible for acts of genocide and other human rights violations against indigenous Mayan communities. The CEH determined that over 2,000 Guatemalans disappeared or were killed by government forces. Eighty percent of these victims were Mayans. Women and children were subject to arbitrary execution, forced disappearance, torture, rape, and "forced union." Indeed, sexual violence was determined to be part of the genocidal regime. The Commission did not name those responsible, but urged the Guatemalan government to bring those perpetrators in the military forces and its collaborators to justice.[28]

Mexico: The Chiapas Conflict

Recognized NGOs, including Amnesty International and Human Rights Watch,

---

24. *See* Judith Zur, *The Psychosocial Effects of "La Violencia" on Widows of El Quiche, Guatemala, in* WOMEN AND CONFLICT (Helen O'Connell ed., 1993.)

25. Amnesty International has reported that trade, political, and human right activists are suffering threats, murders, tortures, and disappearances for their work-related activities in almost every country. They are also singled out as potential witnesses to killings in the communities. *See* HUMAN RIGHTS ARE WOMEN'S RIGHTS, AMNESTY INTERNATIONAL (1995).

26. IACHR Annual Report 1994, *supra* note 12, at 186. In 1997, the IACHR reported that violations continue. *See* IACHR, Annual Report 1997, at 993–94 (1997).

27. OAS Treaty Series No. 67, OEA/Ser. A/42 (SEPF) (1985).

28. *See* Guatemala—Memory of Silence, Report of the Commission for Historical Clarification, Conclusions and Recommendation (CEH), at http://www.hrdata.aaas.org/ceh. For a detailed discussion on the gender based crimes committed in Guatemala during the conflict, see Jan Perlin, *The Domestic Application of International Human Rights Law: The Case of the Guatamalan Historical Clarification Commission, in* INTERNATIONAL HUMANITARIAN LAW: ORIGINS, CHALLENGES & PROSPECTS (John Carey & R. John Pritchard eds., forthcoming 2000).

have expressed concern about the continuing human rights violations in Latin America. In their country reports they have pointed to Mexico's violations, which include the arbitrary imprisonment, torture, forced disappearance, and extrajudicial executions of indigenous peoples in the state of Chiapas.[29] The International Commission of Jurists (ICJ) also reported, even before the 1994 conflict, that civilian victims, especially indigenous peoples, suffered evictions, illegal detentions, abuses of power, and murder in the hands of the "guardias blancas."[30]

On January 1, 1994, when NAFTA was supposed to be in force and Mexico had ratified many of the international and regional instruments applicable to this situation,[31] the Ejercito Zapatista de Liberacion Nacional (EZLN) occupied a large portion of the southern state of Chiapas in Mexico. Under the command of Subcommander Marcos, the EZLN rebels or "Zapatistas" occupied Ocosingo, Las Margaritas, and Altamirano.[32] Ten thousand government soldiers were mobilized to the area and an intense five-day conflict began. Periods of sporadic violence have followed, interrupted by negotiations and talks that have not led to a definitive solution to the Chiapas conflict. As of February 2000, the military continues to maintain the populations under siege in the emergency zones.

Approximately three dozen civilians died during the 1994 conflict. However, due to authorities' handling of the cases, this number is not precise.[33] Instances of abuses such as forced displacement, arbitrary detentions, torture, and inhumane treatment have also been reported as having been perpetrated by the military.[34] The International

---

29.   *See* AMNESTY INTERNATIONAL REPORT 1994 at 210–11 (1995). *See also* HUMAN RIGHTS WATCH WORLD REPORT 1996: EVENTS OF 1995 at 110 *et seq.* (1996); HUMAN RIGHTS WATCH WORLD REPORT 1999 132 (1999); AMNESTY INTERNATIONAL REPORT 1999 248 (1999).

30.   ICJ, *Mexico, rebelion indigena en Chiapas* (1994) [hereinafter, ICJ, *Mexico Report*]. Landowners have paramilitary groups who have harassed and murdered the indigenous peoples with impunity. *Id.* at 45–46.

31.   It has ratified the four Geneva Conventions and Additional Protocol I, but not Protocol II, which applies to internal conflict. In addition, Mexico has ratified the International Convention on the Elimination of All Forms of Racial Discrimination, the International Covenant on Economic, Social and Cultural Rights, the International Covenant on Civil and Political Rights (Political Covenant or ICCPR), the Convention Against Torture and Other Cruel, Inhuman or Degrading Treatment or Punishment, the Convention on the Rights of the Child, and the Convention on the Elimination of All Discrimination Against Women, and the following regional instruments: American Declaration of the Rights and Duties of Man, the American Convention on Human Rights, and the Inter-American Convention to Prevent and Punish Torture. Mexico ratified the Women's Convention in 1981 and made it the supreme law of the land by integrating the principles of non-discrimination contained in the Convention. *See* IACHR, Situation of Human Rights of Women in the Hemisphere, Annual Report of the Inter-American Commission on Human Rights 1992–1993, OEA/Ser.L/V/II.83, doc. 14 corr. 1, Mar. 12, 1993, 251–263, *in* THOMAS BUERGENTHAL & DINAH SHELTON, PROTECTING HUMAN RIGHTS IN THE AMERICAS, CASES AND MATERIALS 338 (4th rev. ed. 1995).

32.   PHILIP L. RUSSELL, THE CHIAPAS REBELLION (1995).

33.   *See* ICJ, *Mexico Report, supra* note 30, at 51.

34.   *See* HUMAN RIGHTS WATCH, SYSTEMIC INJUSTICE: TORTURE, "DISAPPEARANCE," AND EXTRAJUDICIAL EXECUTION IN MEXICO (1999); PHYSICIANS FOR HUMAN RIGHTS AND HUMAN RIGHTS WATCH/AMERICAS REPORT, MEXICO: WAITING FOR JUSTICE IN CHIAPAS 100 (1994).

Commission of Jurists did not report any cases of abuses against civilians by the EZLN.[35] However, human rights organizations have reported war crimes committed by the EZLN.[36]

Three situations of armed conflict resulted mostly in civilian losses in Ocosingo,

---

35.   What appears to be an interesting variable between the EZLN and other guerilla groups, most significantly the Shining Path in Peru, is that the EZLN not only respects civilians, but helps to rebuild and provide basic human needs for the indigenous communities under its control. It is estimated that thousands are under the Zapatistas. Interview with woman from the township of "La Realidad" in Chiapas, by Jorge Ramos, Noticiero Univision (Mar. 11, 1996) (transcript on file with author). The government claims that because the EZLN does not want to receive government assistance, conditions are worse than ever. *See* IACHR's Report on the Situation of Human Rights in Mexico, at 35 (1998).

In an interview on Mar. 5, 1996, Sub-Commander Marcos described the Zapatistas as a regular organized army. Marcos appears to understand fully the role of the Zapatistas in this conflict. The Zapatistas have issued a Declaration urging the international bodies and the ICRC to regulate combat and protect civilians. *See Declaracion de la Selva Lacandona, in* ICJ, *Mexico report, supra* note 30, at 17 *et seq. See also* 1 EZLN—DOCUMENTOS Y COMUNICADOS 34 (reprint 1995). The EZLN has also declared its intention to be subject to the laws of war of the Geneva Conventions and Protocols, and claiming that they are belligerents in their struggle for liberation. Their public expressions and their actions point to this knowledge of the characteristics necessary to attain a belligerency status. Art. 1, para. 1 of Additional Protocol II to the 1949 Geneva Conventions requires that the dissident groups: (a) act under responsible command; (b) control part of the territory to be able to carry out military operations in a sustained and concerted manner; and (c) implement Protocol II. *See* Protocol [II] Additional to the Geneva Conventions of Aug. 12, 1949, and Relating to the Protection of Victims of Non-International Armed Conflicts, June 8, 1977, 1125 UNTS 609; Dec. 12, 1977, U.N. Doc. A/32/144 annex II. Specifically, the Zapatistas have a distinguishable uniform, they exhibit their arms openly, and they have part of the Mexican territory under control. However, whether they have sufficient part of the territory under their control to be able to be recognized as a belligerent force or not and their classification of a struggle for liberation are some of the points in controversy. In addition, the EZLN declared that they would respect the life of prisoners of war and would see that such wounded enemy prisoners will receive medical attention under the ICRC. The International Commission of Jurists reported that the EZLN has complied with humanitarian requirements. *See* ICJ, *Mexico Report, supra* note 30, at 58.

The Mexican government has not recognized the belligerency status of the Zapatistas, but qualifies them instead as a group of transgressors. The "recognition of belligerency" is unilateral and discretionary and can be issued explicitly or tacitly by the government of the state. *See* J. Siotis, *Le droit de la guerre et les conflicts armes d'un caractere non international* (Paris, 1958), *in* COMMENTARY ON THE ADDITIONAL PROTOCOLS OF JUNE 8, 1977, TO THE GENEVA CONVENTIONS OF AUG. 12, 1949 at 1320 (Yves Sandoz, Christophe Swinarski, Bruno Zimmermann eds., ICRC, 1987) [hereinafter ICRC Commentaries]. Tacit recognition can be deduced from the government's behavior (measures and attitudes) when dealing with the conflict. Recognition grants insurgents "a sort of legal personality as subjects of rights and duties within the confines of the laws of war." ICRC Commentaries, *id.* at 1320–1. Nevertheless, in an official communique of Jan. 7, 1994, the military recognized that the EZLN is a "violent, professional and well-trained organization." *See* ICJ, *Mexico report, supra* note 30, at 19.

In their efforts to destroy the insurgents, the military have also killed many civilians. The response of the National Defense Secretary (SEDENA) to the national and international exposure of these human rights violations was denial. *See Comunicado Num. 18 de la Secretaria de Defensa Nacional, in id.*

36.   *See* PHYSICIANS FOR HUMAN RIGHTS AND HUMAN RIGHTS WATCH/AMERICAS REPORT, MEXICO: WAITING FOR JUSTICE IN CHIAPAS 33 (1994).

Rancho Nuevo, and Altamirano. At the Social Security Clinic (Clinica del Seguro Social) in Ocosingo, ten Zapatistas were executed along with civilians; five Zapatistas were summarily executed while their hands and feet were tied. Even after the combat ended, government troops executed two bound and blindfolded Zapatistas. In the Rancho Nuevo incident, not all of the fourteen Zapatistas who died were engaged in combat. An additional victim was a girl who was killed by indiscriminate attacks by the military.

Members of the military troops have committed abuses at the military checkpoints, especially against the indigenous women in Chiapas. In June 1994, three Tzeltal sisters ages sixteen, eighteen, and twenty, who were on their way to San Cristobal de las Casas, were abused at the Altamirano checkpoint. The girls were accused of being Zapatistas and were locked in a room near the military camp, where they were beaten and raped by soldiers. Due to NGO pressure, the military was forced to investigate.[37] However, the investigation was later suspended. After the exhaustion of local remedies proved to be ineffective, two NGOs, The Center for Justice and International Law (CEJIL) and Grupo de Mujeres, filed a case on behalf of the three sisters in the IACHR on January 16, 1996.[38] According to Mr. Ariel Dulitzky of CEJIL, in the investigation phase they submitted their first communication to the IACHR with the findings of facts. As of this writing, proceedings are continuing according to the regulations of the IACHR.[39]

Different international and regional instruments can be applied to this situation. The main instrument in the Inter-American system is the American Convention, whereby Article 1.1 (parties undertake to respect and ensure rights and freedoms without discrimination), Article 5 (right to humane treatment), Article 7 (right to personal liberty), Article 8 (right to a fair trial), Article 11 (right to privacy: honor and dignity), and Article 25 (right to judicial protection) can be applied. Another applicable source is the Inter-American Convention on Torture, which Mexico has also ratified.[40] In addition, the following international instruments can be used: the U.N. Declaration

---

37. One of the groups was CONPAZ (Paz para Chiapas). Interview with Roger Maldonado, director of CONPAZ at the time (California, Nov. 2, 1994). Amnesty International has also reported this case indicating that the soldiers responsible for these crimes had not been brought to justice. AMNESTY INTERNATIONAL, THE 1996 REPORT ON HUMAN RIGHTS AROUND THE WORLD 224–25 (1996).

38. There is an unfortunate lack of communication among different NGOs, which makes it more difficult to exert pressure to the pertinent fora and governments. In Sept. 1995, at the NGO Forum, in Huairou, China as part of the Fourth World Conference on Women, various NGOs were represented, including Grupo de Mujeres, among others. This author asked attorney Marta Figueroa from Grupo de Mujeres if they had decided to file the case of the three sisters with the IACHR, to which she responded affirmatively. The case was filed with the IACHR on Jan. 16, 1996, under Case No. 11,565.

39. Telephone interview with Ariel Dulitzky (May 13, 1997) (transcript on file with author).

40. This Convention does not apply to the cases previously mentioned, since, even though Mexico signed the Inter-American Convention on the Prevention, Punishment and Eradication of Violence Against Women during the 25th OAS Assembly, the Mexican Senate ratified this Convention on Nov. 26, 1996, and it still needs President Zedillo's signature. (The information about the dates was provided by the Mexican Consulate in Puerto Rico, May 14, 1997).

on the Elimination of Violence Against Women and the Convention Against Torture and Other Cruel, Inhuman or Degrading Treatment or Punishment.[41]

The Women's Organization of San Cristobal de las Casas compiled at least fifty documented cases during 1995 and part of 1996 related to attacks on women. On October 4, 1995, three nurses from the Secretary of Health and Assistance were sexually attacked by twenty-five armed men in the community of San Cristobalito. A complaint was filed with the state Police Department for the Highland region of Chiapas. Rights advocate Cecilia Rodriguez, Coordinator of the U.S.-based National Commission for Democracy in Mexico, was raped on October 26, 1995, by several heavily armed men in the Lakes of Montebello in Chiapas. The assault occurred while negotiations were under way between the EZLN and the Mexican government. The National Commission for Democracy in Mexico agrees that the rape of Cecilia Rodriguez was perpetrated as a means of political retaliation and as an intimidation for those who are in favor of the peace process and human rights in Chiapas.[42]

A member of the State Convention of Women in Chiapas, Sebastiana Martinez, reports that women are defenseless, living in communities where there are "no roads, no hospitals, nothing, except illness and hunger," adding "we can no longer leave to get money or food [because] the soldiers continue patrolling the communities."[43] Women in these communities have denounced the fact that the youngest women are being used as prostitutes. In a meeting held October 19–21, 1995, by the Central American Work Group Against Domestic and Sexual Violence, fifty women delegates from various organizations urged Mexico, the United States,[44] and other member states of the U.N. to stop and prevent the use of rape as a weapon of war. They also urged that authorities continue investigations regarding the attacks on the nurses. The High Commissioner for Human Rights has expressed concern for the impunity still existing in Mexico.[45]

International Procedures and Remedies

---

41. Telephone interview with Ariel Dulitzky (Apr. 5, 1996) (transcript on file with author).

42. Press Release, "Stop Sexual Violence Against the Women of Chiapas!," National and Chiapas Mexican Women's Organizations, Mexico City, Nov. 2, 1995. Letter from Cindy Arnold, National Commission for Democracy in Mexico, USA, of Dec. 1, 1995. *See* Cecilia Rodriguez, *Human Rights Worker in Chiapas: "I Was Raped,"* S.F. Examiner, Nov. 24, 1995, at A–23. *See also The EZLN will look for the aggressors against women*, La Jornada, Nov. 13, 1995, at back cover page (Communique from the Indigenous Revolutionary Clandestine Committee, General Command of the Zapatista Army for National Liberation, Mexico). This Communique refers to the attacks as "cowardly," and asserts that the Mexican government is "incapable of guaranteeing the security of any person in Chiapas."

43. Information provided by the National Commission for Democracy in Mexico, USA.

44. For an account of the U.S. involvement in Mexico, *see* Peter Lumsdaine, *Lighting at the End of the Tunnel: U. S. Military Involvement in Mexico's Quagmire Deepens*, Global Exchange, Sept. 1995, provided by the National Commission for Democracy in Mexico, USA.

45. Salvador Corro, *Sostiene la PGR que fue un viejo antagonismo entre dos grupos*, Proseso, Dec. 20, 1998.

Military Investigations

One of the characteristics of military investigations in most of the Latin American countries is the lack of governmental will to effectively investigate and punish perpetrators of human rights violations. This occurs because most of the so-called democracies are under pressure by the military. The situation in El Salvador is an example of this failure.

El Salvador

In El Salvador the military has a strong presence; the police and military investigations are also expected to be partial and subjective. After the murders of the Jesuits, the "auxiliary organs"[46] of the court provided that the Security Forces (National Police, National Guard, and Treasury Police) would investigate the killings, identify the suspects, and hand them to the court along with the evidence.[47] Since the Security Forces were under the jurisdiction of the Armed Forces, a clear conflict of interest arose when those suspected of the crimes, members of the Armed Forces, were investigating the case. The National Guard and Treasury Police were supposed to be dissolved pursuant to the 1992 Peace Accord. However, the newly created police force transferred some members of the militarized unit to the National Police. This organ was eventually but slowly replaced by the National Civilian Police. Even though the Special Investigative Unit (SIU) was not one of the auxiliary organs for the administration of justice, the investigators of SIU, who were active duty members of the Security Forces, were the unit in charge of the investigation of the Jesuits murders. In a situation where the SIU investigates a case, no other auxiliary organ may intervene and all the investigative files must be turned over to the SIU.[48]

Internal Investigations in Mexico

While there is no overt pressure of the military in Mexico, investigations are still ineffective.[49] In an internal military investigation of the Ocosingo Massacre in Chiapas, the only officer under investigation was Lt. Arturo Jimenez Morales. When Lt. Jimenez Morales purportedly committed suicide, the case was closed. The Army recognized that civilians were murdered extra-officially in the Ocosingo Hospital, but no other military personnel was accused. Human Rights Watch/Americas reported that the suicide note allegedly written by Jimenez Morales states that he was follow-

---

46.   Martha Doggett, Death Foretold: The Jesuits Murders in El Salvador 237 (1993), citing art. 11, Salvadoran Criminal Procedure Code.

47.   Doggett, *id.*, citing art. 137, Salvadoran Criminal Procedure Code.

48.   *Id.* at 239, citing Ley de la Creacion de la Comision de Investigacion de Hechos Delictivos, art. 10.

49.   Human Rights Watch has reported that in the case of Maria Gloria Benavides (alleged Commander Elisa), a judge acquitted her since the evidence gathered was the product of an illegal search of her home, and the confession made was obtained in violation of her constitutional rights. *See* Human Rights Watch/Americas, *Mexico—Torture and Other Abuses during the 1995 Crackdown on Alleged Zapatistas*, 8 Hum. Rts. Watch/Americas Rpt. 9–10, No. 3(B) (Feb. 1996).

ing orders when the incident happened. Human Rights Watch questions the exclusive responsibility of the officer and the circumstances surrounding his death. Even some members of the military question the inconsistencies found in the investigation performed by the special military prosecutor.[50]

Even if a state party to a conflict does not recognize the internal conflict, it can be accountable for the actions or omissions of private actors. A state can be responsible for systematically failing to provide protection to private actors. The concepts of "respect and ensure"[51] and "due diligence"[52] included in international and regional instruments are important mechanisms for holding the state accountable for human rights abuses.

Anyone who gave an illegal order, carried it out, knew or should have known a crime was being committed and had the authority and ability to prevent and punish the crime[53] may be held liable for their acts or omissions.[54] The reasoning behind this is that commanders are responsible for the behavior of their troops. Articles 82 and 87 of Additional Protocol I to the Geneva Conventions impose the duty on High Contracting Parties to be informed and instruct their armed forces to "prevent and, where necessary, to suppress and report to competent authorities breaches of the Conventions and this Protocol."[55]

The Inter-American Convention to Prevent and Punish Torture provides in Article 4 that no exemption from criminal liability will be provided if the person committing the crime acted under superior orders. The same is provided expressly in Article VIII

---

50. *See* Rocio Ortega, *Chiapas: Otra Version*, EL NORTE, July 4, 1995, at 11.

51. Several human rights conventions include "respect and ensure" clauses. Art. 2(1) of ICCPR and art. 1(1) of the American Convention on Human Rights require state parties to undertake the obligation to respect rights and freedoms in the conventions and to ensure that not only individuals under their territory and under their jurisdiction respect those rights and freedoms; a state party is also obliged to make other states respect those principles. For a more detailed discussion of this, *see* Theodor Meron, *Obligations of States to Respect and Ensure Human Rights*, RECUEIL DES COURS, 26th Study Session, International Institute of Human Rights (Strasbourg, July 1995).

52. According to the Special Rapporteur on Violence Against Women, states are legally responsible for acts and omissions of individuals when: (a) they are agents of the state; (b) their acts are provided in a treaty; (c) the state is an accomplice; or, (d) the state fails to exercise due diligence. *See* Preliminary report submitted by the Special Rapporteur on Violence Against Women, its causes and consequences, Ms. Radhika Coomaraswamy, in accordance with Commission on Human Rights Resolution 1994/45, E/CN.4/1995/42, 22 Nov. 1994, at 24.

An example of a regional convention that has included the due diligence standard in its wording is the Inter-American Convention on the Prevention, Punishment and Eradication of Violence Against Women. Art. 7(b) of this Convention imposes the duty on states to apply due diligence "to investigate and impose penalties for violence against women."

53. *See In Re Yamashita*, 4 WAR CRIMES RPT. 1, 327 U.S. 1 (1945–6). *See also* L.C. GREEN, THE CONTEMPORARY LAW OF ARMED CONFLICT 292 (1993).

54. *Id.* at 292.

55. *See* Protocol [I] Additional to the Geneva Conventions of Aug. 12, 1949, and Relating to the Protection of Victims of International Armed Conflicts, June 8, 1977, 1125 UNTS 3, U.N. Doc. A.32/144 annex I, at arts. 62, 65.

of the Inter-American Convention on the Forced Disappearances of Persons.[56] The latter also provides for the state's duty to train public law enforcement personnel or officials to avoid the offense of forced disappearance. Article IX of the Inter-American Convention on Disappearances also provides that this offense "shall not be deemed to have been committed in the course of military duties."

JUDICIAL PROCEDURES

Perpetrators on Trial

Military and State Representatives, and Death Squads

Honduran Cases

The Ombudsman Office was created in 1992 to investigate the pattern of disappearances in Honduras from 1980 to 1993. Commissioner Leo Valladares was selected by President Callejas from a list provided by the National Reconciliation Commission, and he was influenced by the Inter-American Commission and the Inter-American Court cases when he began to investigate and sanction those responsible for the forced disappearances.[57] Various cases played a significant role in changing the record of violations on forced disappearances, particularly the *Velasquez Rodriguez, Fairen Garbi, Solis Corales,* and *Godinez Cruz* cases, which were submitted by the Inter-American Commission to the Inter-American Court of Human Rights on April 24, 1986.[58] The Court subsequently ordered Honduras to compensate the victims on finding that Honduras did not protect the rights of its inhabitants by failing to investigate and prosecute abuses.

Commissioner Valladares found that the armed forces were responsible for 179 disappearances, and that the amnesty proclaimed had to be interpreted according to international law. In spite of these findings, Honduran courts have not convicted anyone based on the Commissioner's first report.[59]

Human rights organizations claim that the military is reactivating the death squads. The death of two teenagers after the police arrested them has been attributed to these death squads. In addition, four soldiers were killed in order to prevent them from testifying against the criminal acts committed by their military superiors. The Chief of National Police, Col. Julio C. Chavez, said that they would investigate the

---

56. Resolution adopted at the Seventh Plenary Session, June 9, 1994. OEA/Ser.P AG/doc. 3114/94 Rev. 1; June 8, 1994.

57. NAOMI ROHT-ARRIAZA, IMPUNITY AND HUMAN RIGHTS IN INTERNATIONAL LAW AND PRACTICE 154, 155 (Naomi Roht-Arriaza ed., 1995).

58. *See* IACHR Annual Report 1985–1986, Resolution No. 22/86, Case No. 7929 at 40; Res. No. 23/86; Case No. 7951 at 47; Res. No. 24/86; Case No. 8097 at 49. *See also* Christina M. Cerna, *The Inter-American Court of Human Rights, in* INTERNATIONAL COURTS FOR THE TWENTY-FIRST CENTURY 131 (1992).

59. ROHT-ARRIAZA, *supra* note 57, at 154–5.

killings, but the military has traditionally denied links to the death squads.[60]

Investigations and judicial proceedings of the human rights violations commit-ted in the 1980s continued during 1998 to no avail. In 1998, the First Criminal Court in Tegucigalpa ruled in favor of applying the 1991 Amnesty Laws to an officer of the armed forces who was guilty of murder, torture, and unlawful detention of six stu-dents. Nine other offices were charged for the same violations but no penalties were imposed.[61]

Peru's Military and the Shining Path

A report issued by Human Rights Watch/Americas has documented more than forty cases of rape of women during interrogation,[62] while in police custody, in the emergency zones,[63] or during the massacres of civilians by the security forces. Rape has been used as a weapon of war throughout Peru's internal war.[64] Rapes have been perpetrated by both sides: the military[65] and the guerillas, especially the Shining Path.[66] The reason, according to the witnesses, has been mostly political; each side accuses women of taking sides with the enemy. Each side also uses violence against women to punish or intimidate relatives suspected of belonging to either group or simply because women find themselves in certain risk areas.[67] Rape has been used as a weapon of power to humiliate and degrade these women and girls. This stigma is increased for indigenous women, called "cholas" (which is in itself a racial epithet). Others who have been singled out are the students and teachers unions because they supposedly belong to subversive groups.[68] It has been reported that paramilitary death squads are responsible for the torture and disappearance of women activists regis-

---

60. *Honduras Military Faces New Death Squad Accusations*, Dow Jones Int'l News, Feb. 21, 1996.

61. Amnesty International Report 1999 (1999).

62. Women arrested are mostly "mestizas" suspected of subversion. *See* Human Rights Watch, Untold Terror: Violence Against Women in Peru's Armed Conflict 26 *et seq*. (Human Rights Watch/Americas, 1992).

63. Rapes of indigenous women is common in the emergency zones. *Id*. at 34 *et seq*. During 1998, 16 percent of Peru's territory was in the emergency zones. *See* Human Rights Watch World Report 1999, 139 (1999).

64. *See* Report of the Special Rapporteur on Violence against Women, Its Causes and Consequences, Ms. Radhika Coomaraswamy, submitted in accordance with Commission resolu-tion 1997/44, E/CN.4/1998/54, at 13, 26 (Jan. 1998).

65. *See* IACHR Annual Report 1995, OEA/Ser.L/V/II.91.

66. There is another group called Movimiento Revolucionario Tupac Amaru (MRTA), that apparently is less involved in human rights violations of the indigenous peoples.

67. This information was published by the International Women's Rights Action Watch (IWRAW). Non-governmental organizations assist the CEDAW Committee in the monitoring process through country reports like this one. *See* Sharon Ladin, *IWRAW 1995—Informe por paises de IWRAW a CEDAW* (IWRAW, Dec. 1994).

68. As an example, a law student (Mirtha Ira Bueno Hidalgo), while waiting for transportation, was arrested on suspicion of hanging posters for the Shining Path. Even though there was no evi-

tered in the University of the Center in Huancayo during 1992.[69] In a case taken to the IACHR by CEJIL, a woman was illegally detained, accused of acts of terrorism, and sentenced by a faceless civil tribunal after being acquitted by a military court. She was raped and tortured while detained.[70] CEJIL argued violations of the American Convention, specifically, violations of due process, violations of physical integrity and dignity, and torture.

Rape by security forces and by the guerillas has been condoned or at least ignored by Peru's authorities. Women are intimidated in order to discourage them from reporting the violations. When women do report the cases, instead of punishing the rapist, the police and the army condone the crimes by easily dismissing the matter with excuses or by inaction. As an example, officers were found guilty of murdering and raping sixty-nine peasants in Accomarca in 1985. One junior officer was charged for these crimes. However, even though a military court found him guilty of disobeying orders, instead of serving time in prison he was promoted.[71] Where the military controls certain regions under the "state of emergency" legislation, human rights cases are tried in military courts. However, soldiers accused of violations are not taken to civilian courts for prosecution.[72]

Both the Shining Path and the military continue to use sexual violence as a weapon of war but the incidence is lower in the Shining Path, perhaps due to the high number of female militants in that group. In the Shining Path's ideology, sex discrimination is prohibited and their "code of conduct" forbids "men to sexually molest women and women should also avoid sexually molesting men." However, these guidelines are neither distributed nor enforced.[73]

---

dence against her and in spite of being acquitted at first by the High Court of Lima, the Supreme Court ordered a retrial, and on Mar. 26, 1996, the Special Chamber of the Higher Court of Lima sentenced her to twelve years of imprisonment for terrorism. There were no new grounds nor evidence to justify the change of verdict. *See* Human Rights Watch/Americas, *Peru—Presumption of Guilt, Human Rights Violations and the Faceless Courts in Peru*, 8 Hum. Rts. Watch/Americas Rpt 24–25, No. 5(B) (Aug. 1996).

69.   *See* Untold Terror, *supra* note 62, at 16.

70.   CEJIL argued violations of the American Convention; specifically, violations of due process, physical integrity, dignity, and torture. Telephone interview with Ariel Dulitzky, CEJIL (Apr. 5, 1996). Loayza Tamayo Case, Inter-American Court of Human Rights, Preliminary Exceptions, Judgement of Jan. 31, 1996. (Original in Spanish, provided by CEJIL.) The IACHR dismissed the Preliminary Exception made by Peru.

See also Question of the Human Rights of All Persons Subjected to Any Form of Detention or Imprisonment in Particular Torture and Other Cruel, Inhuman or Degrading Treatment or Punishment, Report of the Special Rapporteur, Mr. Nigel S. Rodley, Submitted pursuant to Commission on Human Rights Resolution 1995/37, Addendum, Summary of Communications Transmitted to Governments and Replies Received, U.N. Doc. E/CN.4/1996/35/Add. 1, Jan. 16, 1996, at 101 *et seq.* (Provided by the U.N., Geneva.)

71.   Untold Terror, *supra* note 62, at 3.

72.   For a more detailed analysis of the emergency legislation, *see id.*, at 4, 19.

73.   Juan Lazaro, *Women and Political Violence in Peru*, 15 Dialectical Anthropology 233–47 (1990).

This guerilla group intimidates and attacks women involved in human rights organizations who are alleged to be collaborating with the government, or if they refuse to join the group's ranks, or simply because human rights organizations are perceived as competition. Women's groups, such as Flora Tristan Women's Center, Manuela Ramos Movement, Women's Center-Arequipa, Association for the Development and Integration of Women, and Peru-Mujer are considered by the Shining Path as an instrument of oppression of women.[74] Twenty-four female community leaders were killed by the guerillas during the first two months of 1992.[75]

Peru has ratified the Geneva Conventions and Additional Protocols,[76] and is bound by them. Although arguments can be made about the applicability of Protocol II, the Shining Path cannot claim the protection of Protocol II, since the group does not respect civilians, acts arbitrarily, and carries out executions, including executions of women activists. Nevertheless, Article 3 Common to the Geneva Conventions applies to both parties in the conflict, regardless of whether the Shining Path recognizes the Geneva laws or not, since Common Article 3 is applicable to internal conflicts and prohibits murder, torture, outrages upon personal dignity, and sentencing and punishment without a judgement from a regularly constituted court. All of these are fundamental principles applicable to all parties to the conflict.

Peru has also ratified the Convention Against Torture and Other Cruel, Inhuman or Degrading Treatment or Punishment and the Inter-American Convention to Prevent and Punish Torture. The state would also be responsible for these acts even though it did not commit the atrocities directly, because it is bound to exercise due diligence in protecting its citizens, and in punishing those responsible for the violations. This is notwithstanding its duty to provide protection under its domestic criminal laws.

EXECUTIVE AND LEGISLATIVE REMEDIES

Impunity in Chile

Under the Constitution in Chile, former President General Augusto Pinochet, who appointed himself a senator-for-life in 1998, also appointed eight senators,[77] ensuring him some control of the Senate. Pinochet continued to be the commander-in-chief of the Chilean Army until 1998.

Before President Patricio Aylwin took office, the Constitutional Tribunal, which consisted of seven members appointed by the military, ratified the appointment of senators made by General Pinochet. It restricted the investigation of the acts com-

---

74.   The Shining Path believes that these women's groups oppress other women because these groups impose their Western-style ideas on peasant women. For additional information, *see Mas hambre y desocupacion sobre la Mujer*, EL DIARIO, Feb. 21, 1992.

75.   *Sendero: Informe de Lima*, QUEHACER, Mar.–Apr. 1992, at 34–55.

76.   Jean-Bernard Marie, *International Instruments Relating to Human Rights, Classification and Status of Ratification as of 1 January 1995*, offprint from 16 HUM. RTS. L.J. 1–3 (1995).

77.   BUERGENTHAL & SHELTON, *supra* note 32, at 570.

mitted by public officials to those acts committed after March 11, 1990, the date upon which President Aylwin would assume power. The result was that the atrocities committed before that date would go unpunished. In addition, the military decreed an Amnesty Law, so the military courts dismissed actions against 130 detainees.[78]

Pressured by public opinion, President Aylwin's government issued a decree establishing the National Committee for Truth and Reconciliation on April 24, 1990. This Committee was charged with investigating serious violations of human rights, such as forced disappearances, executions, torture, abductions and physical assaults, for which the state "seems to bear some moral responsibility because of acts of its agents or people working for it." The Committee would also identify the victims and recommend measures "it considers just for relief or recovery,"[79] and would "recommend legal and administrative measures that, in its opinion, should be adopted to obstruct or prevent the commission of similar acts."[80] The proceedings of the Committee were private, supposedly to "pave the way to reconciliation."[81] In March 1991, President Aylwin published a report on human rights violations that helped to establish reparation and compensation measures for victims and their families.[82]

After the government coalition and the new President, Eduardo Frei Ruiz-Tagle, won the presidential elections on December 11, 1993, little changed in terms of the Senate, armed forces, and the police.[83] The impunity of the perpetrators of human rights violations in Chile will remain as long as Gen. Pinochet and those responsible for these crimes are not brought to justice.

In October 1998, Judge Baltazar Garzon of Spain attempted to bring Pinochet to justice. General Pinochet was arrested in the United Kingdom (where he was undergoing medical treatment) after an extradition request from Spain. Other extradition requests have been filed from Belgium, France, and Switzerland. The extradition request from Spain deals with accusations of murder, conspiracy to commit murder, torture, and illegal detention, and ill-treatment of hostages who were Spanish citizens in Chile.

Pinochet claimed immunity as a former head of state.[84] A decision from the Court in the United Kingdom granting immunity was appealed to the House of Lords,

---

78. *Id.* at 571. The Chilean Supreme Court determined that the Amnesty Law would no longer be in force (CNN Espanol, Sept. 10, 1998). This information has not been confirmed nor denied by the Chilean Supreme Court nor the Chilean Consulate in Puerto Rico (communication of Oct. 17, 1998).

79. President Aylwin's Inaugural Address of Mar. 12, 1990.

80. *Id.* at 573.

81. *Id.*

82. Four thousand relatives of victims are receiving benefits provided under the 1992 Reparations Law. For additional information, *see* Human Rights Watch/Americas, *Chile— Unsettled Business: Human Rights in Chile at the Start of the Frei Presidency*, VI HUM. RTS. WATCH/AMERICAS RPT. 1 *et seq.*, No. 6 (May 1994).

83. *Id.*

84. *See* House of Lords, Pinochet (No. 1), 19 HJLJ No. 8–12 (1998).

which ruled that Pinchet was not entitled to immunity for acts taking place after Chile ratified the Convention Against Torture.[85] Legal maneuvering is continuing in the case, and regardless of the outcome, it has already set an important precedent for the progressive development of international law.

Amnesty Laws

El Salvador

The U.N. Secretary-General's Special Envoy for El Salvador stated that the recommendations of the Truth Commission were binding "regardless of the Amnesty Law, since the latter did not affect the Commission's recommendations that certain persons mentioned in its Report be either removed from office or declared ineligible for public office."[86] El Salvador cannot claim that Amnesty Laws or any political agreements among the parties in conflict exempt the state from its obligations under the American Convention on Human Rights or any other international instrument to which El Salvador is a party. El Salvador is bound by the 1949 Geneva Conventions and the 1977 Additional Protocols. Moreover, under Articles 27 and 46 of the Vienna Convention on the Law of Treaties, states parties cannot invoke domestic law as a justification for not complying with international obligations. El Salvador is also bound by the Inter-American Convention to Prevent and Punish Torture, which was ratified in 1994. The IACHR has stated that each state has a legal duty to undertake "a serious investigation of violations committed within its jurisdiction, to identify those responsible, to impose the appropriate punishment and to ensure the victim adequate compensation," otherwise the state has failed to comply with its duties.[87]

Recently, four guards reportedly admitted that the slayings of three U.S. nuns and a layworker in 1980 were ordered by their superiors. Salvadoran and U.S. officials had continuously maintained that the killers acted on their own. The guards had been convicted in May 1984 and sentenced to thirty years in prison.[88]

As a result of Amnesty Laws, members of the armed forces who were sentenced for the killing of eight representatives of the Catholic Church were released. Although this release was challenged in court by human rights groups, the Salvadoran Supreme Court ruled that it did not have jurisdiction "over purely political questions."[89]

---

85.   *See* Alejandro Teitelbaum, *Caso Pinochet, Declara la Asociacion Americana de Juristas,* CLARIDAD, 21al 27, 2000.

86.   IACHR's Report on the Situation on Human Rights in El Salvador, *supra* note 19, at 72.

87.   IACHR's Report on the Situation on Human Rights in El Salvador, *id.* at 71.

88.   *See* THE SAN JUAN STAR (Assoc. Press), Apr. 4, 1998, at 30.

89.   Amnesty International Report, *Latin America—Crime Without Punishment: Impunity in Latin America* (Nov. 1996), at 16.

State Compensation and Reparations[90] to Victims[91]

Compensation and reparations by states at the international level has generally been considered to be a domestic issue. The fear of embarrassing governments and causing continued divisions within a country that has gone through civil war has almost invariably led to the unwillingness of states to compensate victims of gross violations of human rights. These violations are contrary to fundamental principles of international law, and the situation is exacerbated when governmental inaction renders reparations to victims useless.[92] Non-governmental organizations and interest groups are focusing attention on victims in an effort to relieve the suffering, begin the healing process, and provide justice to those victims.[93] Compensation and reparations may take different forms. Compensation can include monetary compensation, rehabilitation, reinstatement, or reimbursement of expenses. Reparations can include the issuance of public apologies, mechanisms to deter future violations, and programs to ensure accountability for violations of human rights.[94] These programs should include full disclosure of the violations committed by the state. Considering the psychological trauma of victims and the difficulties encountered in convincing governments to release evidence, implementation of an effective remedy seems to require the suspension of any statute of limitations. At least, the statute of limitations should be geared to the victim's needs. The burden of proof should be on the government.

90.　A distinction is made between compensation, i.e., pecuniary damages; and reparations, i.e., non-pecuniary. Reparations would include the promotion and protection of human rights, and prevention of violations of those rights. *See* Theo van Boven *et al.* eds., *Seminar on the Right to Restitution, Compensation and Rehabilitation for Victims of Human Rights and Fundamental Freedoms*, 12 SIM Special at 6 (Maastricht, Mar. 11–15, 1992).

　　Acknowledgement is also made that corporations can be held accountable for human rights violations. This chapter will only consider state accountability. This includes the direct participation of agents of the state (individuals or groups) or indirect participation for acts that can be attributed to states.

91.　A definition of victim is provided in the Declaration of Basic Principles of Justice for Victims of Crime and Abuse of Power: "Victim not only means a person who has suffered human rights violations himself or herself, now or in the past, but also relatives and dependants, loved ones, people who have suffered because they tried to help a victim, communities to which victims belong etc." G.A. Res. 40/34 of Nov. 29, 1985.

92.　This would be the case of the former so-called "comfort women." *See* USTINA DOLGOPOL & SNEHAL PARANJAPE, COMFORT WOMEN—AN UNFINISHED ORDEAL—REPORT OF A MISSION 172 (ICJ, 1994).

93.　For the implementation of human rights standards, governments should establish national institutions and structures that are authorized to receive individual or group complaints that provide for independent fact-finding mechanisms for investigation (for example, by appointing an ombudsman), and appropriate remedies through conciliation and other means of redress for victims. *See* R. Wieruszeski, *Application of International Humanitarian Law and Human Rights Law: Individual Complaints, in* IMPLEMENTATION OF INTERNATIONAL HUMANITARIAN LAW 442–43 (Frits Kalshoven & Yves Sandoz, eds., 1989).

94.　Mechanisms like administrative processes, whereby the state establishes effective compensation programs, or judicial (criminal trials), or civil actions against individual perpetrators must be created or strengthened.

However, neither this statute of limitations argument[95] nor considerations to eliminate state immunities[96] are fully accepted by the international community of states.[97]

Many governments refuse to take responsibility for their actions and invoke the principles of foreign sovereign immunity as an impediment for filing individual suits against them. In these situations, victims might consider seeking redress from intergovernmental bodies like the U.N. and its agencies, international criminal tribunals, or regional bodies. The U.N. Human Rights Committee has called on all governments to pay compensation when required, but difficulties arise in monitoring and determining states compliance. One possibility is a program of compensation to foreign nationals, like that established by the U.N. Security Council in the case of Iraq's invasion of Kuwait. This program is administered by the U.N. Claims Commission.[98] The compensation provided is for pecuniary and non-pecuniary losses resulting from mental pain and anguish of a series of violations like death, torture, serious personal injury, "sexual assault or aggravated assault or torture."[99] The Commission, consequently, recognizes that sexual assault can constitute torture, although the compensation is not limited to rapes that are an instrument of torture.[100] In addition, the U.N. has established an international financial assistance program with the Monetary Fund for Victims of Torture to meet the immediate needs of the victims of such crimes.[101] International law (conventions and

---

95. Pursuant to the Convention on the Non-Applicability of Statutory Limitations to War Crimes and Crimes Against Humanity, the statute of limitations does not apply for the punishment of war crimes and crimes against humanity. *See* Convention on the Non-Applicability of Statutory Limitations to War Crimes and Crimes Against Humanity, Adopted by Resolution 2391 (XXIII) of the United Nations General Assembly on Nov. 26, 1968, *in* SCHINDLER, DIETRICH & JIRI TOMAN, THE LAWS OF ARMED CONFLICTS—A COLLECTION OF CONVENTIONS, RESOLUTIONS AND OTHER DOCUMENTS 83 *et seq.* (3rd rev. ed. 1988).

96. For a description of the theories of sovereign immunities in the U.S., *see* ANDREAS F. LOWENFELD, INTERNATIONAL LITIGATION AND ARBITRATION 589 *et seq.* (1993).

97. *See* Theo van Boven, Study Concerning the Right to Restitution, Compensation and Rehabilitation of Victims of Gross Violations of Human Rights and Fundamental Freedoms: Final Report, Sub-Commission on Prevention of Discrimination and Protection of Minorities, E/CN.4/Sub.2/1993/8. *See also* E. Lutz, *Course on Reparations*, International Institute of Human Rights, 26th Study Session (Strasbourg, July 1995).

98. The U.N. Compensation Commission was established by Security Council Resolution 687 (1991) on Aug. 2, 1991 for the creation of a fund to pay compensation for claims "under international law for any direct loss, damage, including environmental damage and the depletion of natural resources, or injury to foreign governments, nationals or corporations as a result of Iraq's unlawful invasion and occupation of Kuwait." *See also* Resolution 674 (1990); and Report on the Situation of Human Rights in Kuwait under Iraqi Occupation, by Special Rapporteur Dr. Walter Kalin, U.N. Doc. E/CN.4/1992/26, Chapters 2 and 3; Larisa Gabriel, *Victims of Gross Violations of Human Rights and Fundamental Freedoms Arising from the Illegal Invasion and Occupation of Kuwait by Iraq, in* van Boven *et al., Seminar, supra* note 90, at 29–39.

99. *Id.*

100. Gabriel, *supra* note 98, at 35–36.

101. *See* Lutz, *supra* note 97, at 4.

custom) requires that states enact legislation to provide effective penal sanctions and punish or extradite the offender.[102]

Article 8 of the Universal Declaration of Human Rights (UDHR) establishes that every person should have the right to an effective remedy.[103] Other international instruments, for example, Articles 2(3)(a) and 9(5) of the ICCPR[104] and Article 14(1) of the Convention Against Torture[105] provide for similar wording on remedies. Regional instruments afford basically the same right, for example, Article 10 of the American Convention asserts: "Every person has the right to be compensated in accordance with the law in the event he has been sentenced by a final judgement through a miscarriage of justice." The Inter-American Convention on Torture provides that "[t]he State Parties undertake to incorporate into their national laws regulations guaranteeing adequate compensation for victims of torture." Article 7(g) of the Inter-American Convention on Violence Against Women provides also for compensation when it says that states parties undertake to "establish the necessary legal and administrative mechanisms to ensure that women subjected to violence have effective access to restitution, reparations or other just and effective remedies."

Another source of redress has been case law attacking human rights violations through different domestic courts. As an example, United States courts have applied the Alien Tort Claims Act[106] in procedures against perpetrators of human rights vio-

---

102. *See* Ameur Zemmali, *Reparations for Victims of Violations of International Humanitarian Law, in* van Boven, *et al., Seminar, supra* note 90, at 61. The 1949 Geneva Conventions require governments to enact legislation, search for persons alleged to have committed or ordered the commission of grave breaches, or fail to stop them. Also, states must prevent such actions and bring perpetrators to trial whether under criminal jurisdiction domestically or before an international tribunal. Extradition is also required due to the universality of such sanctions. In addition, Art. 91, Protocol I, states the responsibility of the Parties to the conflict: "A Party to the conflict which violates the provisions of the Conventions or of this Protocol shall, if the case demands, be liable to pay compensation. It shall be responsible for all acts committed by persons forming part of its armed forces." Protocol I, *supra* note 55.

103. The UDHR states: "Everyone has the right to an effective remedy by the competent national tribunals for acts violating the fundamental rights granted him by the constitution or by law." Universal Declaration of Human Rights, art. 8.

104. Art. 2(3)(a) of the International Covenant on Civil and Political Rights states that Parties shall ensure that rights and freedoms included in the ICCPR "shall have an effective remedy," and Art. 9(5), that a victim of unlawful arrest or detention "shall have an enforceable right to compensation."

105. Art. 14(1) of the Convention Against Torture and Other Cruel, Inhuman or Degrading Treatment or Punishment provides:

> Each State Party shall ensure in its legal system that the victim of an act of torture obtains redress and has an enforceable right to fair and adequate compensation, including the means for as full rehabilitation as possible. In the event of the death of the victim as a result of an act of torture, his dependants shall be entitled to compensation.

106. Alien Tort Statute, 28 U.S.C. § 1350 (1988), provides that: "The district courts shall have original jurisdiction of any civil action by an alien for a tort only, committed in violation of the law of nations or a treaty of the United States." *See also* Filartiga v. Pena-Irala, 630 F.2d 876 (2d Cir. 1980).

lations. Illustrative cases include *Filartiga*[107] (against Paraguay for torture and death); the *Suarez-Mason* cases[108] (against Argentina for murder, torture, and disappearances); *Xuncax v. Gramajo and Ortiz v. Gramajo*[109] (against the former Defense Minister of Guatemala for murder, torture, and forced exile); and *Paul v. Avril,*[110] (against the former dictator of Haiti for torture).

Compensation Laws in Argentina

Prosecution of the members of the military juntas for crimes against humanity after the internal conflict in Argentina that lasted from 1976 to 1983 was decreed by the former President of Argentina, Raul Alfonsin. Military tribunals had competency over such cases, with appeal to civil courts or adjudication by a civil appellate court in case of inactivity by the military tribunal.[111] The Supreme Council of the Armed Forces refused to prosecute; the proceedings were then conducted at the Federal Chamber of Appeals in Federal Criminal and Reformatory Matters of the Federal Capital. This court convicted seven of the accused high-ranking military officers.[112] Two thousand members of the armed forces were involved in criminal proceedings, and as a result, there were two military uprisings. The President was pressured, and Congress approved Act No. 23.492 (Ley del Punto Final) of December 24, 1986,[113] which gave those members of the military who had not been summoned sixty days to testify (the statute of limitations for the criminal action). Criminal tribunals called hundreds of officers and policemen to make their statements. This resulted in a third uprising. The President and the Congress then passed Act No. 23.521 (Ley de Obediencia Debida) of June 8, 1987, which exempted from prosecution members of

---

107. *Id.* For a short discussion on the Alien Tort Claims Act and non-state and state actors, *see* Theodore R. Posner, *Kadic v. Karadzic—Second Circuit Decision on Federal Court Jurisdiction over Alleged Genocide and Certain War Crimes Under Alien Tort Claims Act,* 90(4) Am. J. Int'l L. 658 (1996).

108. Alfredo Forti v. Suarez-Mason, 672 F. Supp. 1531 (NDCA 1987); 694 F. Supp. 707 (1988), and the other four cases, in Human Rights and Peace Law Docket 30.6 (5th ed. 1995).

109. Gramajo Cases (DMA Civ 91–11564, Civ 91–11612), *id.*, at 34.9.

110. Paul v. Avril, 901 F. Supp. 330 (S.D. Fla. 1994).

111. Emilio F. Mignone, *The Experience of Argentina, in* van Boven *et al. eds., Seminar, supra* note 90, at 125 *et seq.*

112. Mignone, *id.* at 125. *See also Argentina: National Appellate Court (Criminal Division) Judgement on Human Rights Violations by Former Military Leaders (Excerpts),* 26 I.L.M. 317, No. 2 (Mar. 1987).

113. Article 1 of this law states in its original version:

> Se extinguira la accion penal respecto de toda persona por su presunta participacion en cualquier grado, en los delitos del art. 10 de la Ley 23.049, que no estuviere profugo, o declarado en rebeldia, o que no haya sido ordenada su citacion a prestar Declaracion indagatoria, por tribunal competente, antes de los sesenta dias corridos a partir de la fecha de promulgacion de la presente Ley.

Extincion de la accion penal por presunta participacion en cualquier grado en los delitos del art. 10 de la Ley 23.049 y por aquellos vinculados a la instauracion de formas violentas de accion politica hasta el 10/12/83," Ley 23.492, 24 diciembre 1986, B.O. 29/12/86, ADLA XLVII–A, p. 192).

the military and the police who had committed crimes by virtue of due obedience. Only commanders in chief who had already been tried were held responsible. The next President, Carlos Saul Menem, issued a pardon to those officers convicted in 1985.[114]

Ex-prisoners who had been detained for political reasons between 1976 to 1983 obtained compensating judgements against the state from civil courts for the damage suffered. By Decree No. 70 of January 10, 1991,[115] persons who were detained and those who died while detained by the National Executive during the state of siege were eligible for compensation, provided they initiated proceedings prior to December 10, 1985. Another Act (No. 24.043) confirming the Act of January 10, 1991, was promulgated on December 23, 1991.[116] This legislation provided for an administrative procedure in which the state indemnifies, in six installments, those victims detained during the state of siege or those who had suffered detention by virtue of judgements by military tribunals, provided they had not received a judgement in their favor. The measures adopted compensate for damages and injuries suffered by unlawfully detained persons, but neither cover torture nor deal adequately with cases regarding abductions and forced disappearances.[117] Still, the IACHR recognized it as an accomplishment.[118] The Human Rights Committee reported that the Law of Due Obedience (Act 23.521) and the Law of Punto Final (Act 23.492) deny effective remedies to victims of violations of Articles 2(2)(3), and 9(5) of the ICCPR. The Human Rights Committee also pointed out that it welcomes the accomplishments made by Act 24.043 and Act 24.411 (which grants benefits to relatives of disappeared persons), but "regrets" that the state does not provide for compensation for victims of torture.[119]

WOMEN'S RESPONSE TO CONFLICT IN LATIN AMERICA THROUGH NON-VIOLENT AND VIOLENT MEANS

Women's Movements and Women in Combat

Latin American women have survived countless abuses, including illegal detention and imprisonment, torture, rape, combat, and the disappearance of loved ones. The responses to these crimes range from influencing lawmaking at the interna-

---

114. Mignone, *supra* note 111, at 127.

115. *See* HUMAN RIGHTS AND PEACE LAW DOCKET 70.5 (5th ed. 1995); and Mignone, *supra* note 111, at 127. *See also* IACHR Report 1/93, Friendly Settlement Procedure in Cases 10.299, 10.310, 10.496, 10.631 and 19.771 (Argentina), Annual Report of the Inter-American Commission on Human Rights 1992–1993, OEA/Ser.L/V/II.83, doc.14, corr.1 Mar. 12, 1993, pp. 3540.

116. *See* BUERGENTHAL & SHELTON, *supra* note 32, at 128.

117. *See* Mignone, *supra* note 111, at 128.

118. For the details on the friendly settlement in several detention cases submitted to the IACHR, *see* BUERGENTHAL & SHELTON, *supra* note 32, at 128–29.

119. Nineteenth Annual Report of the Human Rights Committee, U.N. Doc. A/50/40 (1995), at 36–37.

tional level[120] and forming representative groups to address their situation,[121] to actively fighting to improve their lives.[122]

Women have entered the guerilla movements, hoping that revolution will bring change to their situation and the situation in their countries. Women have taken up

---

120. Latin-American women who have influenced lawmaking at the international level and have struggled in favor of women's issues include: Gabriela Mistral, Margarida Maria Alves, Bertha Lutz, and Rigoberta Menchu Tum.

Gabriela Mistral (1889–1957), a Chilean poet, was an advocate of Inter-American and world peace, social justice for women and children, and the indigenous peoples. The Chilean government appointed her to international bodies like the League of Nations and later to the United Nations. *See Bertha von Suttner and Other Women in Pursuit of Peace* at 23 (Exhibition Catalog, U.N. Library, Geneva, 1993).

Margarida Maria Alves, president of the Union of Rural Workers of Alagon Grande in Paraiba, Brazil, was (and still is) a symbol to many in her country representing their struggle for justice. In 1988 she was posthumously honored with the Pax Christi International Peace Award. *Id.* at 26.

Bertha Lutz, also from Brazil, was a member of the delegation of Brazil to the U.N. and had the opportunity of addressing the General Assembly in San Francisco in 1945. Lutz pressed for the recognition of women's issues and her influence, together with that exerted by other women, bore fruit: the United Nations ECOSOC established a Sub-Commission (to the Commission on Human Rights) on the Status of Women. *See* Division for the Advancement of Women, Secretariat Fourth World Conference on Women, *Women on the Move*, No. 7, "A Long Road to Equality," at 5 (U.N. Pub., 1995).

Rigoberta Menchu Tum of Guatemala has committed her life to the struggle for human rights and the dignity of her people: the indigenous people of Quiche, Guatemala. In 1992 she was awarded the Nobel Prize for Peace.

For the accounts of other women, *see also* Michael Henderson, All Her Paths Are Peace—Women Pioneers in Peacemaking (1994).

121. Salvadoran women whose family members had disappeared or were political prisoners, together with other women, formed an organization called Association of Women in El Salvador (AMES) to represent the "needs and concerns of women." *See* Saywell, *supra* note 4, at 291–92.

Argentinean women formed a group called "Mothers of the Plaza de Mayo" to protest the disappearance of their loved ones. Similar organizations were formed in Chile and other countries under dictatorial regimes. Marta Zabaleta, Women in Argentina—Myths, Realities and Dreams 36 *et seq.* (Change Report 19, 1993).

For the history of one of the most influential NGOs, the Women's International League for Peace and Freedom (WILPF), see Gertrude Bussey & Margaret Tims, Pioneers for Peace—Women's International League for Peace and Freedom, 1915–1965 (reprint 1980). The WILPF continues to be very active and involved in women's rights and the peace process. This organization has helped shape government policies through public awareness campaigns. In their long experience as observers in the United Nations, they have been able to influence international policy-makers. They formed also a section with "Liga Internacional de Mujeres por la Paz y la Libertad" (LIMPAL) for dealing with the problems in Latin America like the embargo against Cuba, NAFTA, and U.S. interventionist policies in Latin America. For additional information on women activists, *see* Amnesty International, Human Rights Are Women's Rights 57 (1995).

122. *See* Companeras, Voices from the Latin American Women's Movement (Gaby Kuppers ed., 1994); and Margaret Randall, Our Voices, Our Lives, Stories of Women from Central America and the Caribbean (1995).

arms in many Latin American countries,[123] including Guatemala,[124] Mexico,[125] Peru,[126] El Salvador,[127] and Nicaragua.[128]

Nicaragua's Sandinista Women

After the Batista dictatorship in Cuba was defeated by the Cuban revolution in 1959, the Latin American left expected a new movement for a more egalitarian society that would both include and benefit women. However, the patriarchal structures remained almost unaltered. From 1970 to 1973 during the Allende government, Chile experimented with a socialist form of government, but this was cut short by the U.S.-backed Pinochet dictatorship. The question of how much the Allende government would have respected women's rights remains unanswered. Subsequently, Nicaragua's Sandinistas in the National Liberation Front (Frente Sandinista de Liberacion Nacional-FSLN) became the new hope in Latin America.

The FSLN organized the Association of Women Facing the Nation's Problem (Asociacion de Mujeres Ante la Problematica Nacional-AMPRONAC), which included women of different classes, ages, and occupations. This association had to respond to the Party's leadership. Nevertheless, Anastacio Somoza's regime was so oppressive that women united with the Christian-based communities to denounce Somoza's government nationally and internationally.[129] AMPRONAC later became AMNLAE (Asociacion de Mujeres Nicaraguenses Luisa Amanda Espinosa) and remained under the FSLN leadership. The AMNLAE program has been criticized for limiting women to activities on behalf of mothers of those killed or housewives participating in neigh-

---

123. *See, e.g.*, ANGELA WOOLLACOTT, ON HER THEIR LIVES DEPEND: MUNITION WORKERS IN THE GREAT WAR (1994); JEANNE VICKERS, WOMEN AND WAR 18 (1993).

124. Most women are members of the revolutionary movement called URNG (Guatemalan National Revolutionary Unity). *See* RANDALL, *supra* note 122, at 37–38.

125. One third of the Zapatistas are women. Lyn-li Torres Pugh, Delegate for "Encuesta Contra el Neoliberalismo y por Humanidad, Chiapas"; Conference sponsored by San Diegans for Dignity, Democracy and Peace in Mexico and Support Committee for Maquiladora Workers (June 12, 1996). One of the most prominent of the Zapatista women is Commander Ramona.

126. Unfortunately, as noted *supra*, women participating in the Shining Path in Peru are also part of indiscriminate killings of indigenous peoples and women activists.

127. When the murders of priests and nuns escalated in El Salvador, more women joined the revolutionary movement. In the 1980s, the revolutionary forces expanded; 40 percent of Salvadoran guerilla leaders were women. Young women were trained militarily and all-women battalions were formed in El Salvador's countryside. *See* SAYWELL, *supra* note 4, at 297.

128. Women have also been in the battlefield in World War I and II, as members of the armed forces. They have been active as doctors, nurses, journalists, clerical workers, and spies. Women also joined the revolutionary and guerilla movements during World War II (mostly Italian and Polish women). *See* ANGELA WOOLLACOTT, ON HER THEIR LIVES DEPEND–MUNITION WORKERS IN THE GREAT WAR (1994); SAYWELL, *supra* note 4, at 2, 12. For a brief account of women in guerilla movements, see JEANNE VICKERS, WOMEN AND WAR 18 (1993).

129. *See* MARGARET RANDALL, SANDINO'S DAUGHTERS REVISITED—FEMINISM IN NICARAGUA 25 (1994).

borhood committees.[130] The emphasis was on the main goals of the Party, and as a consequence women's issues were accorded little weight. The feminist movement per se was seen as divisive and foreign.[131] Nevertheless, AMNLAE was the training ground for the current women's movements. Even though the FSLN has not yet attained real equality between men and women in Nicaragua, women gained more power and leadership positions through it than in any of the other Latin American movements.[132]

Thirty percent of the FSLN combatants during the civil war were women.[133] Women also became commanders and were thus part of the leadership of the Party. After Somoza's defeat in 1979, women combatants were actively involved in the reconstruction of the country. In particular, the experiences of two women, Doris Tijerino and Dora Maria Tellez, are of interest. Doris Tijerino was tortured and imprisoned under the Somoza regime in 1969 and participated in the struggle throughout her life. She became full commander in the Sandinista Army. Doris describes herself and the women in the FSLN as revolutionaries who happened to be women.[134]

Many other women took on what were traditional men's roles in the armed conflict. Dora Maria Tellez was known as Commander Two. She participated in the 1978 takeover of the National Palace. In June 1979, five women, including Tellez, and two men occupied Leon, the second largest city in Nicaragua. Somoza fled the country a month after that conflict. Subsequently, Dora Maria Tellez held key posts within the Party, but she was not promoted to the FSLN governing body in spite of her excellent work and continued activism. Dora Maria was Minister of Public Health until the electoral defeat in 1990, and then managed to retain a senatorial seat in the Nicaraguan National Assembly.[135]

The Sandinistas' defeat in the 1990 elections[136] has been attributed to the exhaustion of the population from the war, their ongoing fight to defend themselves against outside armed forces, and continuing U.S. pressure.[137] However, Nicaraguan women have not abandoned their struggle. In 1992, women from different ideologies and sectors met in Managua. The slogan of the conference was "Unity in Diversity." For the first time, women were united and mobilized into specific issues that affected them.[138]

---

130. Maria Teresa Blandon, *The impact of the Sandinista Defeat on Nicaraguan Feminism, in* COMPAÑERAS, VOICES FROM THE LATIN AMERICAN WOMEN'S MOVEMENT 97 (G. Kuppers ed., 1994).

131. *Id.* at 99.

132. RANDALL, *supra* note 129, at 135.

133. *Id.* at 5.

134. *Id.* at 210.

135. *Id.* at 231 *et seq.*

136. For an account of the political violence from both sides after the inauguration of President Violeta Chamorro in April 1990, *see* Human Rights Watch/Americas, *Nicaragua—Separating Facts from Fiction—The Work of the Tripartite Commission in Nicaragua,* VI HUM. RTS. WATCH/AMERICAS RPT., No. 13 (Oct. 1994).

137. RANDALL, *supra* note 129, at 249.

138. Blandon, *supra* note 130, at 100–1.

National Liberation Groups

Puerto Rican Women as Political Prisoners

Since the latter part of the 1700s, independence groups in Puerto Rico have fought against Spanish colonialism. Prior to the Spanish-American War, Puerto Rico enjoyed a brief period of autonomy under Spain due to the "Carta Autonomica." At the end of the Spanish-American War in 1898, pursuant to the Treaty of Paris, control was transferred to the United States. At this time, a military regime was established, which lasted for two years until the U.S. Congress created a civil government. The current system in Puerto Rico still maintains some provisions imposed by the U.S. Congress from that period.[139]

The Nationalist Party (Partido Nacionalista), created in 1930, objected to the way the U.S. took control of Puerto Rico. This party refused to recognize the jurisdiction of the U.S. over Puerto Rico and advocated the use of violence to obtain independence for the island.[140] In 1954, members of the Nationalist Party were involved in an attack on the U.S. Congress. This incident attracted international attention. One of the four members of the Nationalist Party attacking the U.S. Congress was a woman, Lolita Lebron.[141] Since then a series of armed groups have been formed.[142]

---

139. The situation of Puerto Rico and the legislation regarding the current political status is much more complex than what will be presented in this chapter. Two of the main acts applicable are the Foraker Act of 1900, Ch. 191, 31 Stat. 77 (1990), amended by Ch. 145, 39 Stat. 951 (1917); and the Jones Act of 1917, Ch. 145, 39 Stat. 951 (1917), amended in part by Ch. 490, 61 Stat. 770 (1947) and Ch. 446, 64 Stat. 319 (1950). For a more thorough discussion, see RAUL SERRANO GEYLS, 1 DERECHO CONSTITUCIONAL DE ESTADOS UNIDOS Y PUERTO RICO 427 et seq. (1986); JOSE TRIAS MONGE, 1 HISTORIA CONSTITUCIONAL DE PUERTO RICO 135 et seq. (1980); VICENTE GEIGEL POLANCO, LA FARSA DEL ESTADO LIBRE ASOCIADO (2d ed. 1981); and MANUEL MALDONADO DENIS, PUERTO RICO: UNA INTERPRETACION HISTORICO-SOCIAL (1974).

140. Due to government repression and an incident known as the Ponce Massacre in 1937, the "nacionalistas" decided to retaliate. Another event that influenced this group into action was the referendum held in 1951. The referendum was held so Puerto Ricans could decide between two options: the Commonwealth (Estado Libre Asociado or ELA) status or the status quo at the time. The Commonwealth won the referendum, and this option was established in 1952. Puerto Rico was allowed to have its constitution under the ELA, but under the parameters imposed by the U.S. Constitution. As an example, art. 20 was deleted from the Bill of Rights (social and economic rights) of Puerto Rico's Constitution because it was perceived as too leftist. Even today, the ELA has not attained the autonomy that Puerto Rico had under the Carta Autonomica under Spain. See SERRANO GEYLS, supra note 139, at 493 et seq.

141. After serving almost all her life in prison, Lolita Lebron was released for humanitarian reasons. She was elected President of the Nationalist Party on Feb. 16, 1997. On a local radio (Notiuno) interview on Feb. 19th, she expressed her intentions of still struggling for independence, but this time through peaceful means. Nevertheless, Lolita could not disregard the possibility of sacrificing herself again in order to obtain the independence for Puerto Rico.

142. These groups have marginal support in the population and are perceived as "independentistas" who fight for independence through violent means.

Two of the most prominent groups are Fuerzas Armadas de Liberacion Nacional (FALN), and the Ejercito Popular Boricua or "Macheteros,"[143] which were formed in the 1970s. In April 1980, eleven Puerto Ricans alleged members of FALN were arrested in Illinois and were accused of seditious conspiracy. Traditionally, independence groups fighting through violent means claim that they are not fighting against the American people, but against the U.S. military and multinational corporations. They assert that the military and the multinationals are destroying the people and the environment of the island.[144] FALN and the Macheteros consider themselves commandos fighting for the final goal of obtaining national liberation and sovereignty for Puerto Rico. As a consequence, when captured they ask to be treated as prisoners of war and political prisoners.

Six of the sixteen persons arrested and accused so far (linked to the FALN) are women.[145] These women were accused of seditious conspiracy[146] to overthrow the government of the United States in Puerto Rico and of related offenses to building and placing explosives in twenty-eight locations in Chicago and New York.[147]

Most of these prisoners have been interned from ten to sixteen years or more in harsh prison conditions. The severity of the sentences can be illustrated by compar-

---

143. The name "Macheteros" comes from the symbol they use, the Puerto Rican flag and a "machete," which is a long knife mostly used by the peasants who used it to work in the fields.

144. The women are Alejandrina Torres, Carmen Valentin, Ida Luz Rodriguez, Dylcia Pagan, Alicia Rodriguez, and Haydee Beltran Torres. For many years now, the U.S. armed forces have conducted military operations in the islands of Vieques and Culebra (which are part of Puerto Rico) in spite of the danger this poses to the population and to the ecosystem. For a more detailed description *see* RONALD FERNANDEZ, PRISONERS OF COLONIALISM: THE STRUGGLE FOR JUSTICE IN PUERTO RICO 116 *et seq.* (1994).

145. These women were teachers, organizers, and counselors in the community of Puerto Ricans living in the U.S. The Puerto Rican women prisoners have spoken on women's equality as within the context of national liberation and not as an individual struggle. Nevertheless, they acknowledge the strength that comes from unity of women, especially during adversity, and the importance of gaining control of their lives. *See* Alejandrina Torres, LIBERTAD, Mar. 1989, at 7; Alicia Rodriguez, LIBERTAD, Nov.–Dec. 1989, at 6; Ida Luz Rodriguez, LIBERTAD, Mar. 1989, at 5–8; JAN SUSLER, PALOMAS VOLADORAS POR CIELOS DE LIBERTAD 20 (1995).

146. Representatives of Ofensiva '92, a human rights organization in Puerto Rico that works on behalf of these political prisoners, argue that since the charge of "seditious conspiracy requires opposition to a legitimate authority, and since United States authority over Puerto Rico is not legitimate, there is no offense." Luis Nieves Falcon, Jan Susler & Michael E. Deutsch, *The International Covenant on Civil and Political Rights: The United States Failure to Comply with respect to Puerto Rico, the Puerto Rican Independence Movement, and the Puerto Rican Political Prisoners in Prison in the United States*, at 11–12 (Apr. 14, 1994).

147. U.S. v. Maria Haydee Torres, no. 77 CR 680 (S.D.N.Y.); U.S. v. Alejandrina Torres, et al., no. 83 CR 494 (ND 11), transcript at 2360–2367.

Attorney Jan Susler stated in a telephone conversation on May 30, 1996, that some courts have accepted their status as political prisoners and prisoners of war. For a more detailed analysis, *see* Jan Susler, *The Women's High Security Unit in Lexington, KY*, 1 YALE J. L. & LIB. 31, 39–40 (1989).

ing those imposed upon them with those meted out to common felons.[148] The average term for a felony such as murder and similar offenses is ten years. The average sentence imposed on the FALN women prisoners is 72.8 years.[149] Not only are the sentences comparatively higher,[150] but prison conditions are also harsher, amounting to cruel or inhuman treatment.[151]

Human Rights Watch has reported that illegal bodily searches of women in custody by male guards is frequent in U.S. prisons.[152] Women detainees should be covered under various international instruments, including: Article 5 of the Universal Declaration of Human Rights (UDHR); Articles 2(1), 7, and 10(1) of the ICCPR; Articles 1 and 16, Convention against Torture and Other Cruel, Inhuman or Degrading Treatment or Punishment;[153] and, Article 5, American Convention on Human Rights

---

148. The argument that they are common criminals as opposed to political prisoners cannot stand when one compares the sentences imposed. Telephone interview with Jan Susler, Esq. (May 30, 1996).

149. Information provided by Ofensiva '92 (mimeo "NO ES JUSTO!") (on file with author).

150. Compare the sentences imposed by U.S. courts on groups like the Ku Klux Klan for having an arsenal of arms in their possession (an average of five years), with one of the women that had a pistol and was sentenced to thirty-five years. *See* Luis Nieves Falcon, *in* Rodolfo Casals, *Granma Internacional*, 30th yr., No. 6, Feb. 8, 1995, at 16. (Provided by Ofensiva '92).

151. *See* Question of the Human Rights of All Persons Subjected to Any Form of Detention or Imprisonment in Particular Torture and Other Cruel, Inhuman or Degrading Treatment or Punishment, Report of the Special Rapporteur, Mr. Nigel S. Rodley, Submitted pursuant to Commission on Human Rights resolution 1995/37, Addendum, Summary of Communications Transmitted to Governments and Replies Received, U.N. Doc. E/CN.4/1996/35/Add.1, Jan. 16, 1996. *See also* PAUL WILLIAMS, TREATMENT OF DETAINEES–EXAMINATION OF ISSUES RELEVANT TO DETENTION BY THE UNITED NATIONS HUMAN RIGHTS COMMITTEE 69–70, 159, 162, 218 *et seq.* (1990), in particular General Comments on art. 10 of ICCPR and the General Comments on Article 7 of ICCPR; and the Declaration on the Protection of All Persons from Being Subjected to Torture and Other Cruel, Inhuman or Degrading Treatment or Punishment, Adopted by General Assembly Resolution 3452 (XXX) of Dec. 9, 1975 (and Annex). *See also* THE PROTECTION OF HUMAN RIGHTS IN THE ADMINISTRATION OF CRIMINAL JUSTICE—A COMPENDIUM OF UNITED NATIONS NORMS AND STANDARDS 61 *et seq.* (Cherif Bassiouni ed., 1994).

152. HUMAN RIGHTS WATCH GLOBAL REPORT ON WOMEN'S HUMAN RIGHTS 142 *et seq.* (1995); Human Rights Watch/Women's Right Project, *All Too Familiar Sexual Abuse of Women in U.S. State Prisons* (Dec. 1996).

153. Art. 5 of UDHR prohibits torture and cruel, inhuman or degrading treatment or punishment. Art. 2(1) of ICCPR deals with non-discrimination and equal protection; Art. 7 of the ICCPR prohibits torture and subjection to medical or scientific experimentation without consent. Art. 10(1) of ICCPR states that "[a]ll persons deprived of their liberty shall be treated with humanity and with respect for the inherent dignity of the human person." Arts. 1 and 16 of the Torture Convention are also relevant. Art. 1 includes the definition of torture: "any act by which severe pain or suffering, whether physical or mental, is intentionally inflicted on a person for such purposes as obtaining from him or a third person information or a confession, punishing him for an act he or a third person has committed or is suspected of having committed, or intimidating or coercing him or a third person, or for any reason based on discrimination of any kind. . . ." Art. 16 specifies that the acts that do not amount to torture as defined in Art. 1, but to cruel, inhuman or degrading treatment or punishment include those acts committed by or at the instigation, consent, or acquiescence of a public official or someone acting in an official capacity.

("Pact of San Jose").[154] Also applicable are the U.N. Standard Minimum Rules for the Treatment of Prisoners (especially Rule 31),[155] the Basic Principles for the Treatment of Prisoners (Annex),[156] and the Body of Principles for the Protection of All Persons Under Any Form of Detention or Imprisonment.[157] In addition, Economic and Social Council (ECOSOC) Resolution 1986/29 deals specifically with detained women and the continuing pattern of physical violence, rapes, and other forms of sexual violence.[158] The latter four, although not legally binding, are authoritative and generally accepted guidelines for the treatment of prisoners.[159]

These instruments can be applied to the situation of the Puerto Rican women prisoners. In 1982, Haydee Beltran was beaten by two federal guards while in custody at the Metropolitan Correctional Center (MCC) in San Diego. Before her trial, she was interned in a cell without access to fresh air or sunlight. She was denied access to any of the programs offered to other women prisoners and her visitors were restricted. This treatment lasted for two and a half years and was only modified when she became sick.[160] Haydee was then transferred to West Virginia, and she was put in

---

The European Commission on Human Rights defined "degrading treatment" as that which "grossly humiliates one before others or drives him to act against his will or conscience." Greek Case, 1969 Y.B. Eur. Conv. on H.R. (Eur. Comm'n on H.R.) 186.

154. Art. 5, para. 2, of the American Convention establishes that persons in custody or deprived of their liberty shall be treated with dignity.

155. The Standard Minimum Rules for the Treatment of Prisoners adopted by the First United Nations Congress on the Prevention of Crime and the Treatment of Offenders held in Geneva in 1955, and approved by the Economic and Social Council by its Resolutions 663 C (XXIV) of July 31, 1957, 24 U.N. ESCOR Supp. (No. 1) 11, U.N. Doc. E/3048 (1957), and 2076 (LXII) of May 13, 1977. Rule 31 states that: "corporal punishment, punishment by placing in a dark cell, and all cruel, inhuman or degrading punishment shall be completely prohibited as punishments for disciplinary offences."

156. Basic Principles for the Treatment of Prisoners [adopted by the Eighth Congress on the Prevention of Crime and the Treatment of Offenders (Annex), Havana, Cuba, Aug. 27–Sept. 7, 1990, U.N. Doc. A/Conf. 144/28/Rev. 1, I.A.S.] G.A. Res. 45/111, Dec. 14, 1990, 45 U.N. GAOR Supp. (No. 49A), 1990, U.N. Doc. A/Res/45/111. The first paragraph states that all prisoners shall be treated with respect "due to their inherent dignity and value as human beings." The second paragraph declares that there shall be no discrimination on the grounds of sex, political or other opinion, nationality, etc.

157. The Body of Principles for the Protection of All Persons under Any Form of Detention or Imprisonment, G.A. Res. 43/173, Dec. 9, 1988, 43 U.N. GAOR Supp. (No. 49) 297, U.N. Doc. A/43/49. For an analysis of the Body of Principles, *see* Tulio Treves, *U.N. Body of Principles for the Protection of Detained or Imprisoned Persons*, 84 Am. J. Int'l L. 578 (1990). Principle 1 states that all imprisoned or detained persons shall be treated humanely and with dignity. Principle 6 prohibits torture or cruel, inhuman or degrading treatment or punishment. Cruel, inhuman or degrading treatment shall be interpreted liberally to extend the widest possible protection.

158. Physical Violence Against Detained Women that Is Specific to Their Sex, ECOSOC Res. 1986/29 of May 23, 1986, U.N. Doc. E/RES/1986/29 and E/1986/INF/1. *See also* Katarina Tomaševski, Women and Human Rights 73 (1993).

159. Human Rights Watch Global Report on Women 143–145 (1995). *See also* Treves, *supra* note 157, at 584.

160. *See* Susler, *supra* note 145, at 58.

a cell with a triple door to isolate the noise. Every movement was monitored, her mail was intercepted, and political literature denied. Ida Luz Rodriguez was also subjected to this type of treatment.[161] These two inmates were kept in isolation for six years. There were no incidents of violence reported on their part; on the contrary, they had a record of good behavior. When Haydee's health deteriorated, the nurse advised her that she could not get out of her cell no matter how sick she was, nor could she go to the hospital. Intervention by her lawyers and different organizations resulted in her being taken to the hospital in Lexington penitentiary in Kentucky.[162]

The other women were also subjected to isolation and restrictions on their activities. There were intrusive body searches by the prison authorities, including body cavity examinations.[163] Male guards watched the inmates while they were bathing and entered the cells when the women were undressing or using the toilet.[164]

The Amnesty International observer sent to the maximum security unit in Lexington concluded that conditions there were deliberately and unjustly oppressive, and that due to the conditions in the unit, it should be closed immediately.[165] Amnesty determined that the fact that these women suffered these conditions was due to their political beliefs, and the treatment constituted cruel, inhuman, and degrading treatment, a violation of the Universal Declaration of Human Rights.[166]

The defense of these Puerto Rican woman prisoners finds its legal basis in the U.N. Charter and subsequent General Assembly resolutions. Specifically, based on Article 73 of the U.N. Charter, Resolution 1514 (XV) was approved by the General Assembly (G.A.) on December 14, 1960.[167] There are other resolutions used, such as G.A. Resolution 2852 (XXVI) of December 20, 1971, and G.A. Resolution 3103 (XXVIII) of December 12, 1973.[168] Resolutions 2852 (XXVI) and 3103 (XXVIII) are applicable to cases dealing with combatants and prisoners of war according to the Geneva Conventions and Protocols. Resolutions 1514 (XV) and 3103 (XXVIII) have become precedents for subsequent documents now in force, i.e., for the Additional

---

161. Deposition for the "Special International Tribunal" in New York, Nov. 1990, reported in *id.* at 59.

162. Interview with Haydee Beltran Torres, Dec. 7, 1989, in *id.* at 60–61.

163. U.S. Federal law authorizes these body searches, but authorities must have reasonable doubt that inmates are illegally hiding something inside their bodies. Warden William Perrill admitted that the authorities did not have any indication of smuggling. Baraldini v. Meese, deposition of William Perrill, May 24, 1988, pp. 36–41; in SUSLER, *id.* at 74.

164. *Id.* at 63.

165. Amnesty International, *The High Security Unit, Lexington Federal Prison, Kentucky*, Aug. 15, 1988. *See also* Susler, *supra* note 147.

166. Amnesty International, *Allegations of Ill Treatment in Marion Prison*, May 1987; *see also* Susler, *The Women's High Security Unit in Lexington, KY*, 1 YALE J. L. & LIB. 31, 38 (1989).

167. Declaration on the Granting of Independence to Colonial Countries and Peoples, U.N. G.A. Res. 1514, U.N. GAOR 15th Sess. Supp. No. 16, Dec. 14, 1960, U.N. Doc. A/L.323 and Add. 1–6 (1960).

168. *See* Alejandro Torres, *Los prisioneros politicos y de guerra*, CLARIDAD, Dec. 2–8, 1994, at 34–5.

Protocols to the Geneva Conventions, specifically for Article 1(4) of Protocol I. Article 1(4), Protocol I, refers to the "peoples"[169] who are fighting against colonial domination and alien occupation.[170] In relation to Article 1(4) of Protocol I, Articles 43 and 44, and 96 of Protocol I[171] have to be examined as well. In addition, General Assembly Resolution 35/118 of December 11, 1980, reaffirms the right to fight by all means available against colonial and racist regimes.[172]

According to some commentators, there are alternative bases for establishing the validity of national liberation movements. For example, under Article 51 of the U.N. Charter, the peoples fighting in national liberation movements may defend themselves against armed attacks from the colonial power. Professor Abi-Saab argues that "armed resistance to forcible denial of self-determination by imposing or maintaining by force colonial or alien domination is legitimate according to the Declaration" on Principles of International Law.[173] However, this view is not generally accepted.

---

169. The Geneva law does not provide the definition of "peoples." Some theorists have interpreted the term as meaning "nations," which could encompass indigenous populations as well as those geographically separate and ethnically or culturally distinct, although this is not generally accepted. Others limit the "self" to the territorial self not necessarily meaning ethnic or religious self. Higgins provides the following definition of self-determination: "Self-determination refers to the right of the majority within a generally accepted political unit to the exercise of power. In other words, it is necessary to start with stable boundaries and to permit political change within them." *See* Higgins, *The Attitude of Western States Towards Legal Aspects of the Use of Force* 104, cited in JUDITH G. GARDAM, NON-COMBATANT IMMUNITY AS A NORM OF INTERNATIONAL HUMANITARIAN LAW 50 (1993).

170. According to the ICRC Commentary on the Protocols, the main General Assembly resolutions on this subject are 1514 (XV), 2625 (XXV) and 3103 (XXVIII). In addition, there are other General Assembly resolutions applicable to persons fighting against racist or colonial regimes when detained. All of these resolutions deal with the treatment of prisoners of war and political prisoners according to international law. They were adopted after the International Conference on Human Rights (No. XXIII) held in Teheran on May 12, 1968, under the auspices of the U.N. That same conference had adopted resolution VIII establishing that captured "freedom fighters" should be treated as POWS in the sense of the Third Geneva Conventions of 1949. The objectives of resolution XXIII were affirmed in G.A. resolution 2444 (XXIII), titled "Respect for Human Rights in Armed Conflict." The resolutions that followed had the same title with the following numbers: 2597 (XXIV) of Dec. 16, 1969; 2674 (XXV) of Dec. 9, 1970; 2676 (XXV) of Dec. 9, 1970; 2677 (XXV) of Dec. 9, 1970; 2853 (XXVI) of Dec. 20, 1971; 3032 (XXVII) of Dec. 18, 1972; 3102 (XXVIII) of Dec. 12, 1973; 3319 (XXIX) of Dec. 14, 1974; 3500 (XXX) of Dec. 15, 1975; 31/19 of Nov. 24, 1976; 32/44 of Dec. 8, 1977. *See* ICRC Commentary, *supra* note 35, at 44, 51, 1573–76.

171. Arts. 43 and 44 of Protocol I deal with combatants and POWS; art. 96(3) deals with the "authority representing a people." For more discussion, *see* Antonio Cassese, *Wars of National Liberation and Humanitarian Law, in* ETUDES ET ESSAIS SUR LE DROIT INTERNATIONAL HUMANITAIRE ET SUR LES PRINCIPES DE LA CROIX-ROUGE EN L'HONNEUR DE JEAN PICTET 324 (Christophe Swinarski ed., ICRC 1984). Art. 44(3) applies to wars of national liberation if, first, the colonial, racist or occupying power is a party to Protocol I, and second, if the national liberation movement complies with Art. 96(3), Protocol I, i.e., if the national liberation movement makes a declaration that it undertakes to apply the Geneva Conventions and Protocols, and addresses this declaration to the depositary. *See also* FRITZ KALSHOVEN, CONSTRAINTS ON THE WAGING OF WAR 74 (ICRC 1987).

172. *See* discussion in Torres, *supra* note 168, at 34–35.

173. Abi-Saab, *Wars of National Liberation in the Geneva Conventions and Protocols*, IV

A more accepted view is that of self-defense when a territory is attacked by the armed forces of the colonial power or when the peoples are defending themselves against human rights abuses and annihilation (as preservation.)[174] Article 1 of the ICCPR, and Article 5 of the American Convention (which deals with dignity of the human person) are more specific. These sources of conventional law could in fact have more impact than U.N. resolutions upon the actions of state parties.

One of the main arguments advanced by the Puerto Rican dissident groups is that, notwithstanding the fact that the U.S. has not signed Protocol I, it is still bound by customary international law. In order to maintain that a non-party to a treaty is bound by custom, it is necessary that the requirements establishing custom are satisfied.[175] The statements and the general practice of a state cannot be considered in isolation. The statements and general practice of both parties in a conflict[176] must be considered together with those of states in the international community[177] in relation to the specific norm that is to be applied as a customary rule of law. What is required is careful analysis of a specific rule of law in conjunction with the *travaux preparatoires* and related provisions in the multilateral treaty in question (i.e., the Geneva Conventions and Protocols). Other criteria to be considered are whether this particular provision was adopted without controversy during the negotiating stages, and the authorities or commentators' interpretation of which provisions are established as custom.

The *opinio juris* of the parties in the conflict consists of statements made, military manuals, and judicial decisions.[178] When dealing with the United States' mili-

---

RECUEIL DES COURS 165, 371–2 (1979); HEATHER A. WILSON, INTERNATIONAL LAW AND THE USE OF FORCE BY NATIONAL LIBERATION MOVEMENTS 133 (1988).

174. *See* ELIZABETH CHADWICK, SELF-DETERMINATION, TERRORISM AND THE INTERNATIONAL HUMANITARIAN LAW OF ARMED CONFLICT 3 (1996).

175. Custom consists of *opinio juris cive necessitatis* (mostly, statements) and general practice (usage or habit) of states. *See* Nicaragua Judgement (Nicar. v. U.S.), 1986 I.C.J., in Theodor Meron, *The Continuing Role of Custom in the Formation of International Humanitarian Law*, 90 AM. J. INT'L L. 238, 239–240 (Apr. 1996). *See also* Rosas Eide & Theodor Meron, *Combating Lawlessness in Gray Zone Conflicts Through Humanitarian Standards*, 89 AM. J. INT'L L. 215, 218 (1995). Most theorists agree in emphasizing not the consent of each state to submit to customary international law, but rather the collective *opinio juris* and evidence of state practice in the international community. *See* L. R. Penna, *Customary International Law and Protocol I: An Analysis of Some Provisions, in* ETUDES ET ESSAIS SUR LE DROIT INTERNATIONAL HUMANITAIRE ET SUR LE PRINCIPES DE LA CROIX-ROUGE EN L'HONNEUR DE JEAN PICTET, STUDIES AND ESSAYS ON INTERNATIONAL HUMANITARIAN LAW AND RED CROSS PRINCIPLES 206 (Christophe Swinarski ed., ICRC 1984).

176. For the application of custom to both Parties in conflict, *see* Meron, *The Continuing Role of Custom in the Formation of International Humanitarian Law, supra* note 175, at 239–40.

177. It is necessary to consider statements and practice of third states since the recognition of a peoples fighting for self-determination of art. 1(4) depends or is strengthened by outside recognition. Although opinions are divided regarding intervention (directly or indirectly) of third states intended to further self-determination of another state. Even though the right of peoples to self-determination is an established principle, the right to non-intervention of other countries is also well-established customary international law.

178. Judicial decisions on the political status of the island or on the political prisoners will not

tary manuals and official statements, the U.S. has expressed that the general principles of the Geneva Convention referring to POWS are "declaratory of the customary
law of war, to which all States are subject."[179] This statement about the recognition of
custom in the Third Geneva Convention is compatible with the practice of the United
States. The U.S. prefers to accept custom in these cases covered by the Third Geneva
Convention because of reciprocity. Nevertheless, the U.S. takes exception to Protocol
I in certain provisions. It refuses to treat the wars of national liberation as interna-
tional conflicts and does not grant combatant status to "irregular forces."[180] When
Protocol I was adopted, the majority of states accepted the rule in Article 1(4) of
Protocol I as having a general character in the international community. As the delegations of Egypt, Greece, and Australia phrased it, Article 1(4) echoed what had
already been established in general international law, particularly in Resolution 3103
(XXVIII). Apart from Israel, no other delegation challenged Article 1(4) during the
approval phase, and national liberation movements became thus international armed
conflicts.[181]

The FALN and Macheteros statements show that they accept Protocol I. However,
it is not clear that they have submitted the unilateral declaration to the depositary nor
that they intend to comply with the laws and customs of war as specified in the Geneva
Conventions and Additional Protocols.[182] Due to the covert nature of national liberation movements in the occupied territory, these groups have always had difficulty
in distinguishing themselves from civilians. By definition urban guerillas must to
some extent blend in, otherwise their effectiveness would be short lived. Since it is
difficult for them to distinguish themselves, Article 44(3) provides for POW status if

---

be examined here. For information, *see* Lisa Napoli, *The Puerto Rican Independentistas:
Combatants in the Fight for Self-Determination and the Right to Prisoner of War Status*, 4 (1) CAR-
DOZO J. OF INT'L & COMP. L. 131, 133 (1996). Regarding political status, see SERRANO GEYLS, *supra*
note 139, at 432; TRIAS MONGE, *id*. at 135.

179. *See* U.S. Dept. of the Army, The Law of Land Warfare 6 (Field Manual No. 27–10, 1956);
2 U.S. Dept. of the Army, International Law 249 (Pamphlet No. 27–161–2, 1962), in Theodor
Meron, *The Geneva Conventions as Customary Law*, 81 AM. J. INT'L L. 348, 358 (Apr. 1987).

180. *See* EDWARD KWAKWA, THE INTERNATIONAL LAW OF ARMED CONFLICT: PERSONAL AND MATERIAL
FIELDS OF APPLICATION 26 (1992).

181. CDDH/SR.36, paras. 62, 70–71, and 122.

182. According to an author who has documented the attacks by these groups, the Macheteros
have issued various communiques saying that they intend to "respect the lives of all innocent people that [they] understand are victims of the oppressive system." RONALD FERNANDEZ, PRISONERS OF
COLONIALISM: THE STRUGGLE FOR JUSTICE IN PUERTO RICO 227, 232 (1994). The problem with this
statement is the interpretation of who will be considered a civilian (victim) or a combatant.

The national liberation groups have supposedly only targeted symbols of colonialism. When
they choose military targets, there would be no problem with the principle of distinction, but if
they choose to attack other targets there may be problems with respecting civilian lives. If federal
buildings are considered symbols of colonialism, it would be in compatible with Geneva law when
non-combatants who work there are injured. Government officials and blue collar workers with
no combat mission are non-combatants. *See* Knut Ipsen, *Combatants and Non-Combatants, in* THE
HANDBOOK OF HUMANITARIAN LAW IN ARMED CONFLICTS 84 (Dieter Fleck ed., 1995).

they comply with the requirements of carrying their arms openly during military engagement and preceding the launching of an attack. This requirement seems to be a contradiction in itself. Either they are exempt from distinguishing themselves (which is also incompatible with protecting civilians) or they distinguish themselves by the mere fact of carrying their arms and insignias openly, in which case they would certainly be discovered before launching any attack. In any case, if the combatants fail to meet the requirements, they still have some protections equivalent to other POWS. They are entitled to due process, a fair trial, and the conditions of capture and imprisonment should conform to the same conditions as the armed forces of the detaining power "in terms of health and humanity."[183]

The international community seemed to agree when adopting Article 1(4) that a struggle for self-determination was an international conflict, and that this is an established principle of customary international law.[184] But an analysis of Article 1(4), Protocol I is problematic. The *travaux preparatoires* of this article reflect the intention of the parties participating in the Diplomatic Conference to apply this provision to a large scale armed conflict.[185] This type of conflict would seem to involve an authority representing the *majority* of the peoples fighting for self-determination.

There are other hurdles to overcome in relation to Article 1(4), specifically in relation to Articles 44(3) and 96(3) of Protocol I, which are an integral part of the interpretation. Articles 44(3) and 96(3) are not part of custom, and most of the principles embodied within them are not yet custom. One commentator argues that the distinction principle in Article 44(3) is part of an existing rule of customary law.[186] The bearing of the particular insignia and carrying arms openly are part of the distinction principle, or "crystallised customary law in process of formation."[187] However,

---

183. *See* arts. 99–108, Third Geneva Convention. Geneva Convention Relative to the Treatment of Prisoners of War, Aug. 12, 1949, 75 UNTS 135. Art. 108, paras. 2 and 3 are specially pertinent when they specify that:

> A woman prisoner of war on whom such a sentence has been pronounced shall be confined in separate quarters and shall be under the supervision of women. In any case, prisoners of war sentenced to a penalty depriving them of their liberty shall retain the benefit of the provisions of Articles 78 [Complaints and Requests] and 126 [Supervision of Protecting Powers or of the ICRC] of the present Convention. Furthermore, they shall be entitled to receive and despatch correspondence, to receive at least one relief parcel monthly, to take regular exercise in the open air, to have the medical care required by their state of health and the spiritual assistance they may desire. Penalties to which they may be subjected shall be in accordance with the provisions of Article 87, third paragraph [Collective punishment for individual acts, corporal punishments, imprisonment in premises without daylight and, in general, any form of torture or cruelty, are forbidden].

184. Gardam argues that the *right* is accepted but not the *application*. GARDAM, *supra* note 169, at 158.

185. *Id.* at 158–59.

186. *See* Penna, *supra* note 175, at 215 *et seq.*

187. Treaty rules may become customary law (binding on all states) when the treaty rule: (1) is declaratory of pre-existing custom; (2) has crystallised customary law in process of formation; and,

being under responsible command and observing the laws and customs of war is not part of an existing rule of customary law.[188] For these provisions to be applicable, the colonial power has to be a party to Protocol I, and the national liberation movement has to make a declaration to the depositary, pursuant Article 96(3), as an authority representing the people, that it undertakes to apply the Geneva Conventions and Protocols.[189] This is due to the contractual character of Articles 44 and 96 of Protocol I.

Nevertheless, the majority of theorists agree that the non-state party is bound by customary international law to accept Protocol I (when dealing with POW status) on an equal footing with the Third Geneva Convention. The Third Geneva Convention, in particular Article 4(2),[190] if interpreted broadly, is similar to Protocol I in referring to POWS as members of "resistance movements."

In the case of the Puerto Rican women prisoners, Article 130 of the Third Geneva Convention could be applied to allege inhumane treatment. Article 130 lists as grave breaches of the Geneva Conventions, *inter alia*, the willful killing and torture or inhumane treatment of prisoners of war.[191]

The provisions of the international instruments dealing with international humanitarian law and human rights are difficult to apply to the states and, in particular, to the United States, when the problems of enforcement and implementation are considered. A non-state party to Additional Protocol I—such as the United States—could argue also that the conflict taking place is not one of self-determination and, therefore, could treat POWS as common criminals.[192] In this scenario, the

---

(3) is found to have generated new customary law subsequent to its adoption. *See* North Sea Shelf Cases, 1969 I.C.J. Rep. 3; and Nicaragua Case (Nicar. v. U.S.), 1986 I.C.J. 14. *See also* Jeremy McBride, *Seminar in Public International Law*, RECUEIL DES COURS 58 (Geneva, June 1995).

188. *See* Penna, *supra* note 175, at 215–16.

189. *See* FRITS KALSHOVEN, CONSTRAINTS ON THE WAGING OF WAR 74 (ICRC 1987).

190. Art. 4(1) and (2) of the Third Geneva Convention, *supra* note 183, defines prisoner of war as:

(1) Members of the armed forces of a Party to the conflict as well as members of militias or volunteer corps forming part of such armed forces.

(2) Members of other militias and members of other volunteer corps, including those of organized resistance movements, belonging to a Party to the conflict and operating in or outside their own territory, even if this territory is occupied, provided that such militias or volunteer corps, including such organized resistance movements fulfil the following conditions:

(a) that of being commanded by a person responsible for his subordinates;

(b) that of having a fixed distinctive sign recognizable at a distance;

(c) that of carrying arms openly;

(d) that of conducting their operations in accordance with the laws and customs of war.

191. *See* Horst Fisher, *Protection of Prisoners of War, in* THE HANDBOOK OF HUMANITARIAN LAW IN ARMED CONFLICTS 321, 325–26 (Dieter Fleck ed., 1995).

192. An alternative argument about terrorism and the applicable laws will not be examined in this study.

United States would have to impose sentences consistent with felonies. Prisoners should consequently be incarcerated in proportion to their crimes. It remains to be seen if the United States can argue successfully that seditious conspiracy is compatible with a common crime.

Whether or not one agrees with the applicability of the Geneva Conventions, the Additional Protocols, or other sources, or whether the prisoners are terrorists or patriots or common criminals, or even in disagreement with the political status of Puerto Rico, international humanitarian law and domestic law requires that the Puerto Rican prisoners be accorded humane treatment while in custody.

On September 10, 1999, five of the six female political prisoners were given a conditional pardon by President Clinton. Haydee Torres Beltran is still incarcerated. One of the fourteen conditions imposed for the release of the five women was that they renounce or agree not to instigate the use of violence, including when related to the struggle for the political status of Puerto Rico.

RECOMMENDATIONS

States have a moral and a legal duty to comply with international and regional obligations. Prompt ratification of international and regional instruments, and withdrawal of reservations that conflict with the object and purpose of such instruments, is imperative. In particular, ratification of new conventions in the regional system is important, especially in the case of the Inter-American Convention on the Prevention, Punishment and Eradication of Violence against Women.

Effective sanctions for violations and non-compliance with the protection of women's human rights should be implemented by different means. Collective international sanctions, both economic and political, and public condemnation should be vigorous in the international community.

To prevent future abuses and protect women's rights, states must take measures to implement effective systems of domestic criminal legislation to prevent these crimes and punish perpetrators. Above all, states should conduct fair and impartial internal investigations. Amnesty laws and pardons should conform to what international and regional instruments declare, i.e., that they are incompatible with the object and purpose of human rights conventions, when their intention is to protect perpetrators of war crimes, crimes against humanity, or genocide.

States must create and implement effective judicial systems with trained personnel who do not dismiss crimes like rape as something inherent or normal during armed conflict. In addition, they should follow and strictly enforce court decisions, in particular those of the Inter-American Court of Human Rights. Also, extradition measures in cases where other states have tried and convicted an offender of these types of crimes must be followed. States should also provide for a fair and effective system of compensation and reparations to address the needs of women who have been victims of rape, torture, and other violations not only during peacetime but also during wartime.

Other measures that states should take include the submission of periodic and accurate reports to Special Rapporteurs and Commissions, in particular to the Inter-American Commission of Human Rights, besides promptly adopting the recommendations made by these organs and representatives.

Due to the increasing recognition of the importance of individual access to the international and regional systems, women who are victims of human rights violations and the organizations protecting such victims have more choices today than ever before. In order to have effective regional and international measures for prevention and protection of the human rights of women, bodies such as the Inter-American Commission and Court should make investigations and hearings more accessible, impartial, fair, and expeditious.

A priority for NGOs and international and regional bodies should be to create public awareness by exposing violators in investigations and country reports, educating the public, and joining forces when exerting pressure for effective compliance.

Section III

Religious Issues

ISSUES AFFECTING THE HUMAN RIGHTS
OF MUSLIM WOMEN

Ann Elizabeth Mayer

GENERAL INTRODUCTION[1]

The work of feminists proves that Islam can be interpreted to embrace equality for women and that it can be compatible with women's human rights, but this entails dramatic revisions of traditional ways of understanding what Islam requires.

In Muslim environments, international human rights law has gained influence and won adherents, but it has the disadvantage of being identified with Western culture. The bitter experience of European colonialism, when Muslims were subjugated by Europeans and their culture was denigrated, as well as current political tensions between the West and Muslim countries, have exacerbated anti-Western feelings. This historical baggage has often made advocacy of human rights seem tantamount to cultural treason.

Islamic law may be identified with indigenous values and cultural authenticity. Conversely, international law may be associated with European civilization or—

---

1. Material in this section was compiled from the following works: Faith and Freedom, Women's Human Rights in the Muslim World (Mahnaz Afkhami ed., 1995); Women in the Middle East, Perceptions, Realities, and Struggles for Liberation (Haleh Afshar ed., 1993); Leila Ahmed, Women and Gender in Islam (1992); Reza Afshari, Egalitarian Islam and Misogynist Islamic Tradition: A Critique of the Feminist Reinterpretation of Islamic History and Heritage, J. Crit. Stud. Iran & Mid. East 4, 13–34 (1994); Margot Badran, Feminists, Islam, and Nation (1995); Abdelwahab Bouhdiba, Sexuality in Islam (A. Sheridan trans., 1995); Kevin Dwyer, Arab Voices, The Human Rights Debate in the Middle East (1991); Nilufer Gole, Modern Mahrem (1994); Women, Islam and the State (Deniz Kandiyoti ed., 1991); Gendering the Middle East (1996); Michelle Kimball & Barbara R. von Schlegell, Muslim Women in the World: A Bibliography, with Selected Annotations (1996); Ann Elizabeth Mayer, Islam and Human Rights: Tradition and Politics (2nd ed. 1995); Islam and Democracy, Fear of the Modern World (Mary Jo Lakeland trans., 1991); The Veil and the Male Elite, A Feminist Interpretation of Women's Rights in Islam (1991); John Makdisi & Marianne Makdisi, Islamic Law Bibliography, Law Lib. J. 69–192 (Winter 1995); Naila Minai, Women in Islam, Tradition and Transition in the Middle East (1981); Ziba Mir-Hosseini, Marriage on Trial: A Study of Islamic Family Law (1993); Gender and National Identity: Women and Change in Muslim Societies (1994); Bouthaina Shaaban, Both Right and Left Handed: Arab Women Talk About Their Lives (1988); Hisham Sharabi, Neopatriarchy: A Theory of Distorted Change in Arab Society (1988); Women and Revolution in Africa, Asia and the New World (Mary Ann Tetreault ed., 1994); Old Boundaries, New Frontiers: Women in the Arab World (Judith Tucker ed., 1993); Susan E. Waltz, Human Rights and Reform, Changing the Face of North African Politics (1995); Feminism and Islam: Legal and Literary Perspectives (Mai Yamani ed., 1996).

equally bad—a godless and immoral modernity. Thus, some of the resistance to international human rights principles results not from a rejection of the substantive principles but from reactions based on cultural nationalism. The insistence that Muslims should respect local cultural traditions may be accompanied by attacks on any Muslims calling for adopting women's human rights, labeling them agents of hostile Western forces bent on the corruption of Muslim societies. In actuality, Muslims have had considerable input into the formulation of human rights principles affecting women's rights, but Muslims who are aware of this may have trouble convincing their coreligionists that conventions like the Convention on the Elimination of Discrimination Against Women are not simply products of Western feminism.

While Muslim advocates of women's human rights seek to demonstrate the compatibility of Islam and human rights, they must contend with a variety of supposedly "Islamic" human rights schemes that have been put forward in recent years as alternatives to the international human rights standards by various conservative institutions and reactionary regimes. To date, such Islamic rights schemes have been designed to dilute human rights guarantees and to strip women of the rights afforded them under international law. These schemes have placed vague Islamic criteria above human rights so that, in case of a conflict, it is the Islamic principle that prevails over the rights principle. That is, these schemes envisage conflicts between Islamic criteria and human rights and aim to uphold the primacy of Islam. However, the authors of Islamic human rights frameworks have tended to try to minimize the discrepancies between their formulations of women's rights and provisions in international human rights law, as if they were anxious to avoid accusations that following Islamic rights schemes means sex discrimination.

Male bias in traditional interpretations of the Islamic sources can be seen as the major problem in reconciling the Islamic tradition and human rights. Regrettably, even today very few of the males who rank as leading figures in Islamic law possess a grasp of human rights principles affecting women, and the rare ones who are familiar with women's human rights may reject them. As a whole, members of the Islamic religious establishment have tended to be conservative, if not reactionary, in their attitudes towards women's rights. Moreover, religious authorities, who do sympathize with Muslim women's aspirations to enhanced rights, may be deterred by an intimidating intellectual climate from openly registering their support for women's rights.

To date, men have exercised a monopoly over the advanced study of Islamic law and all the positions in the religious hierarchy. Not surprisingly, with all the interpreters and authorities being male, the juristic formulations of Islamic law have tended to ratify male privilege. Now, progressive Muslims are seeking to produce feminist interpretations of the Islamic sources. Muslim women, many of whom show mastery of modern human rights instruments, are increasingly claiming the right to participate in interpreting the Islamic sources and are starting to press claims that women have a human right to be trained in the religious sciences.

Although the rules affecting women's rights have until recently been elaborated exclusively by men, it is hard to find Islamic authority for the practice of barring women from studies that would allow them to become credentialed in the Islamic religious sciences. Thus, whereas the male monopoly on interpretations has been a reality, it is not necessarily a monopoly approved by the religion itself.

One task facing Muslim feminists is to disaggregate what is properly Islamic from patriarchal attitudes and customs and to highlight the elements in the Islamic heritage that are favorable to women's claims to freedom and equality. In the past Islam has been identified with the values of the patriarchal systems prevailing in most Muslim societies, but there are reasons to challenge the linkage of Islam and patriarchy. Many elements in the Islamic tradition are serviceable for feminist projects. Among other things, the reforms originally introduced by the *Qur'anic* Revelation tended to advance women's rights. There are passages in the *Qur'an* that address women believers as if they stood on a footing of parity with male believers, with the same religious obligations and subject to judgement according to the same standards in terms of piety and religious observance. Women played significant and respected roles in the early period of Islam, when they often interacted with men as peers. Moreover, many aspects of the life and sayings of the Prophet Muhammad accord with an enlightened feminist consciousness.

Feminist perspectives could counterbalance the sex-stereotyping that has been traditionally incorporated into the interpretations of Islamic requirements. Like sex-stereotyping elsewhere, this entails images of women as tender, fragile, emotional, unstable, less mature and less intellectually capable than males. Ideas to the effect that women should not vote, should not occupy political office, should not serve as judges, and should not head governments are presented as being grounded in Islam. However, these ideas, which are embodied in laws and policies in some Muslim countries, turn out upon examination merely to reflect sex-stereotyping.

Difficulties in challenging patriarchal attitudes are exacerbated by the activities of powerful fundamentalist movements in many societies. Fundamentalists have tried to have Muslim women who endorse feminist positions declared apostates from Islam and have issued death threats to women who dared to question whether male privileges and superior rights had any genuine warrant in the Islamic sources. Fundamentalists typically decry even modest reforms enacted to enhance women's rights and call for strengthening the patriarchal order. They may promote measures such as restricting women's opportunities in employment and education in the interest of keeping them cloistered in the home, imposing veiling and sex segregation, and strengthening a stringent sexual morality that accords protecting women's chastity as the highest priority. How readily Muslims will be persuaded to discount fundamentalists' claims that Islam upholds ingrained patterns of patriarchy remains to be seen.

As noted, campaigns for women's rights can be conducted within the confines of Islamic law. However, after the exploitation of Islamic criteria by fundamentalist groups, traditionalist forces, and reactionary regimes in Muslim countries, one finds substantial disillusionment in some quarters regarding the prospects for making sufficient adjustments in Islamic doctrine to accommodate women's equality. Some Muslims are persuaded that the elements in the Islamic tradition standing in the way of accepting international norms amount to insurmountable problems and are therefore prepared to dismiss Islamic approaches to rights issues as inherently deficient. These Muslims may prefer to work instead for women's equality on the basis of secular international law principles.

In relying on secular principles, such Muslims may feel that they are breaking merely with legal rules that are no longer serviceable in present circumstances, rather than with the mandates of their Islamic faith. Although the tendency has been to treat law as a central element of the Islamic tradition, there are strains in Islamic thought that de-emphasize the legal dimensions of Islam and stress instead mystical experience of the divine or the duties of the individual believer to follow the ethical precepts that pave the way for salvation. Muslims who disagree with fundamentalists' insistence that contemporary nations are duty bound to implement Islamic law often point to the prevalent pattern of displacing Islamic law with modern laws of European derivation in almost all areas—with an exception in areas affecting women's rights.

The general pattern of importing Western-inspired laws can be cited to argue that codified European laws have shown that they are better suited to the needs of contemporary societies. Given the overall prevalence of borrowed Western laws, the determination to retain Islamic law in personal status codes and other laws where this means perpetuation of discrimination against women can be attacked as being motivated by men's desire to hold on to their privileges.

In sum, Muslims differ as to whether Islamic law should or should not be seen as an obstacle to women enjoying full human rights. Similarly, they also differ on whether the Western origins of human rights should make them inapplicable in Muslim milieus.

DIVERSITY IN LEGISLATION BASED ON ISLAMIC PRINCIPLES[2]

One cannot discuss the conflicts between women's human rights and laws in force in contemporary Muslim countries without first acknowledging a major caveat. There has never been a single, authoritative Islamic standard on questions affecting the rights of Muslim women, and over the last century Islamic thought has exhibited ever greater variety. The rethinking of Islamic principles affecting women began in some milieus in the nineteenth century, but the most dramatic re-evaluations have occurred in the last few decades. To the traditional variety in interpretations by jurists belonging to different sects and schools of law, one must now add diverging national laws that reflect more or less enlightened views of Islamic requirements. What one country insists is legislation derived from Islamic principles will be dismissed as an incorrect understanding of Islam in another. Contemporary legislation ranges from rules in Tunisia that effectively give women equality in most areas (aside from inheritance) to rules in Saudi Arabia that leave Muslim women in much the same vulner-

---

2.   The material in this section was compiled from the following works: AFSHAR, *id.*; BOUHDIBA, *id*; SHAHLA HAERI, LAW OF DESIRE: TEMPORARY MARRIAGE IN SHI'I IRAN (1989); Valerie Hoffman-Ladd, *Polemics on the Modesty and Segregation of Women in Egypt*, INT'L J. MID. EAST STUD. 19, 23–50 (1987); KIMBALL & VON SCHLEGELL, *id.*; KHAWAR MUMTAZ & FARIDA SHAHEED, WOMEN OF PAKISTAN, TWO STEPS FORWARD, ONE STEP BACK? (1987); NORANI OTHMAN, SHARI'A LAW AND THE MODERN NATION-STATE: A MALAYSIAN SYMPOSIUM (1994).

able, subjugated condition that they have endured for centuries. In some Muslim countries the reforms have been extensive, and the residue of traditional Islamic rules is now minimal. In a rare case of radical secularization, in the 1920s Turkey elected to completely replace Islamic law with laws of European inspiration.

Not only does one encounter wide variations in the degree to which Islamic principles dictate the laws in force in Muslim countries but, to make matters even more complicated, many "Islamic" rules assigning women second-class status have only the most tenuous connections with Islam. Frequently, traditions and customs have become associated in the popular mind with Islam when they actually have little or no connection to the Islamic sources. In addition, discriminatory features in laws affecting women are often found in legislation borrowed from European models, because European laws were imported by Muslim countries in an era before Europeans reformed their laws in accordance with modern rights norms. For example, nationality laws in Muslim countries frequently assign nationality to children of mixed marriages based on the nationality of the father, precluding mothers from passing on their nationality to their children. Muslim countries have clung tenaciously to such discriminatory nationality rules even though they have no warrant whatsoever in the Islamic heritage, where the modern concept of nationality was unknown.

INHERITANCE[3]

Under Islamic law, women can only claim one half the share of males inheriting in the same capacity. Widows receive especially small shares of their husband's estates by contemporary standards—one quarter if there are no children, and one eighth if there are children. The widow's portion must be reduced even further when the deceased husband leaves more than one wife to claim shares in his estate.

The rules of Islamic inheritance law would seem to present great difficulties for those seeking to end sex discrimination. The *Qur'an* treats rules of inheritance in more detail than any other legal topic; the discriminatory features in contemporary laws on inheritance are strongly based on the central Islamic source. Although inheritance has remained the area most resistant to reform, the old rules are now being contested by reformers—often on the grounds of changed economic circumstances that have made what might have seemed equitable provisions for women in the past now seem discriminatory. However, attempted reforms in national legislation have rarely progressed beyond modest adjustments to the traditional doctrines.

ISLAMIC CRIMINAL AND TORT LAW[4]

By and large, the standards of criminal law and tort law in force in Muslim countries are inspired by Western models. However, recent Islamization programs have

---

3.   The material in this section was compiled from the following works: JAMES NORMAN ANDERSON, LAW REFORM IN THE MUSLIM WORLD (1976); Makdisi & Makdisi, *supra* note 1.

4.   The material in this section was compiled from IN THE EYE OF THE STORM: WOMEN IN POST-REVOLUTIONARY IRAN (Mahnaz Afkhami & Erika Friedl eds., 1994); ANDERSON, *supra* note 3; BOUHDIBA, *supra* note 1; MUMTAZ & SHAHEED, *supra* note 2.

led to a reinstatement of aspects of Islamic criminal and tort law in several countries. In rare instances (e.g., Saudi Arabia), Islamic criminal and tort law has never been abandoned.

In Islamic law women have been valued at one half that of men for purposes of assessing compensation after a killing, whether deliberate or accidental, a clear sign of their lower status. However, women have full criminal and tort responsibility.

Muslim women who find this and other rules unfair cannot escape Islamic strictures by converting to another religion. According to the traditional understanding of the law of apostasy, a Muslim woman who repudiates Islam can be imprisoned for her apostasy until she repents and returns to Islam. Islamic law is thereby conceived of as a kind of scheme of control to which a Muslim woman is condemned, even if she rejects Islam. Furthermore, although a Muslim woman's apostasy should mean civil death for her and thereby terminate her marriage to her Muslim husband, this rule may be ignored in cases where it has been decided that Muslim women are seeking to exploit the rules mandating civil death for apostates as an easy way to terminate unhappy marriages.

ENFORCEMENT OF SEXUAL MORALITY[5]

Islamic law treats sexual intercourse outside of marriage as one of the most heinous crimes. The penalties range from floggings of one hundred lashes to stoning to death and are difficult to reconcile with international standards barring the imposition of cruel, inhuman, or degrading punishments. The penalties of Islamic criminal law should apply equally to men and to women; both sexes are commanded to reserve sexual intercourse exclusively for marriage. The penalties for *Qur'anic* crime of *zina*, consensual sexual intercourse outside of marriage, are in theory only applicable where the guilty party has confessed or where there are four respectable Muslim male eyewitnesses to the actual act of illicit copulation. In practice, in their eagerness to punish people for *zina*, courts or police may waive the proof requirements set forth in the *Qur'an*. The penalties for *zina* in practice tend to be imposed in a discriminatory fashion, penalizing women more often than men. The plight of women accused of *zina* is aggravated by the Islamic rules of evidence. In the past, the adoption of secular rules of evidence meant that Muslim women's testimony was treated as equivalent to that of men, but the recent trend to revive Islamic rules of evidence has worked significantly to women's disadvantage. Generally, in Islamic law men's testimony is weighted as twice the value of women's testimony, but women's testimony is altogether barred for proof of crimes like *zina*. Recent legislation reviving the crime of *zina* and the old evidentiary standards of Islamic law has led to situations where a woman's testimony can be barred in cases where she has been raped—meaning that a woman who should have a complete legal defense to a charge of *zina* may be pre-

---

5. The material in this section was compiled from the following works: IN THE EYE OF THE STORM: WOMEN IN POST-REVOLUTIONARY IRAN, *id.*; BOUHDIBA, *supra* note 1; GOLE, *supra* note 1; Hoffman-Ladd, *supra* note 2; MINAI, *supra* note 1; NAWAL EL-SAADAWI, MEMOIRS FROM THE WOMEN'S PRISON (Marilyn Booth trans. 1994); SHARABI, *supra* note 1.

cluded from testifying to prove that she did not voluntarily engage in extramarital intercourse. Thus, in practice, *zina* laws may be applied in a discriminatory fashion, so that women who are victims of sexual assault are punished, whereas male rapists may escape punishment for want of formal proof.

In defiance of the principles of the *Qur'anic* model, which dictates that men's sexual transgressions are as serious as women's, mores in many Muslim communities mandate that it is women's honor that must be upheld; there is little concern for punishing men's immorality, but terrible punishments for minor breaches of taboos by women. Extrajudicial executions of women for so-called honor crimes are common in some regions, and governments have done little to curb such customary practices. National legislation may even affirm the right of male relations to murder women for sexual transgressions. As part of policing women's morality, governments may also support or mandate forced virginity examinations of unmarried girls and women. Although such virginity exams violate basic Islamic norms of modesty, they may be associated with preservation of Islamic morality.

A major question facing contemporary Muslims is determining the implications of the emphasis in Islamic law on the preservation of chastity and deterrence of sexual immorality. Muslim conservatives have traditionally tended to assume that these concerns imply that society should impose extensive curbs on women's freedoms. The underlying notion is that women are sexual temptresses and that the sight of women (other than family members) or contact with them inevitably stirs up sexual desire in men that can lead to infringements of the code of morality. Thus, the interests of morality may be understood as requiring a long list of rules to protect men from contact with unrelated women and consequent sexual temptation. Whether such rules actually possess an Islamic warrant remains hotly debated.

In the effort to forestall any possible sexual transgressions, women may be pressed into early marriages—often at the moment when they reach puberty. Women may be required to don full veils—ones that fully enshroud them or leave only the face and hands uncovered—when leaving home. Women may be denied medical attention if female doctors and nurses are unavailable. Women may be subjected to genital mutilations of greater or lesser severity.

Related rules may prevent women from traveling or even moving about outside their domiciles without male chaperons. Women may be barred from driving cars. Women may have to be segregated from men in educational institutions and in the workplace. Women may be denied opportunities to obtain educations or to work outside the home. Women may be prevented from participating in organized sports or forced to compete only when no men can see them or while wearing tent-like garments. They may be barred from jobs in radio and television, on the basis that the sight of women or the sound of women's voices is sexually stimulating. They may be excluded from praying in mosques or be segregated when they do come to mosques to pray.

Sometimes the rules requiring sex segregation can work to women's advantage, in that men may be excluded from certain jobs that can then be monopolized by women. In order to ensure that women receiving professional services will not have to deal with male strangers, qualified women may be given easy access to certain positions in fields like teaching, banking, or medicine—especially in gynecology and obstetrics.

FAMILY LAW[6]

In the *Qur'an* men are established as the managers of women's affairs (4:34) and as existing a degree above women (2:228). The implications of these verses for relations between men and women are being vigorously debated. Traditionally, the jurists have interpreted these as buttressing patriarchal authority in the family. Among other things, feminists have argued that the verses address the situation as it was before economic changes and enhanced educational opportunities meant that wives effectively became their husband's partners.

Many Muslim countries have entered "Islamic" reservations to the Women's Convention regarding provisions affecting marriage and divorce, as if convinced that upholding Islamic law stood in the way of accepting women's human rights in this area. These reveal that governments conceive of the international standard of equal rights for women as incompatible with their family law. By and large, Muslim countries preserve elements of Islamic law in their personal status laws, although reforms since the nineteenth century have generally been in the direction of secularization. Over the second half of the twentieth century, reforms tended to make the rights and duties of spouses more equal than they were in the past.

Following is a discussion of some of the problematic elements in Islamic family law that may affect the laws in force in Muslim countries.

Muslim women cannot marry outside the faith, whereas Muslim men are allowed to marry women who belong to the people of the book: Christians and Jews. Muslim women, regardless of their age, may be unable to marry without the consent of a marriage guardian—typically a father. Traditional interpretations of Islamic law allowed marriage guardians to force a female ward into marriage, especially when a woman was a virgin or under the age of adulthood. Today forced marriages still take place, but more often by reference to local custom rather than by reference to the laws in force in Muslim countries. To curb the practice of compelling girls to marry in early adolescence, most Muslim countries have tended to increase the minimum age of marriage to levels approximating those found in Western countries.

A Muslim marriage requires the groom's commitment to pay a dower to the bride, a rule that feminists deprecate because it can indicate that a woman is a purchasable commodity. In order to deter divorce or establish the bride's high social standing, the dower amount required may be exorbitant, making it difficult for women to

---

6. The material in this section was compiled from the following works: IN THE EYE OF THE STORM, *supra* note 4; AHMED, *supra* note 1; ANDERSON, *supra* note 3; BOUHDIBA, *supra* note 1; HAERI, *supra* note 2; Makdisi & Makdisi, *supra* note 1; THE VEIL AND THE MALE ELITE, *supra* note 1; MINAI, *supra* note 1; MIR-HOSSEINI, *supra* note 1; and MUMTAZ & SHAHEED, *supra* note 2.

marry men of their own choosing and of their own ages. However, because alimony provisions for divorced women tend to be weak or nonexistent, a woman may have to rely on such dower payments for subsistence after a divorce.

In the medieval treatises, marriage was known as *nikah*, referring to licit sexual intercourse, and the marriage contract was understood as an agreement permitting the husband sexual access to the wife in return for his commitment to pay her a dower and maintain her. Islamic law imposes an obligation on the husband to support his wife and to meet all the expenses of the household; the wife is assumed to be dependent. Thus, stereotyped sex roles are incorporated into the law in the form of maintenance rules. Even under traditional juristic versions of Islamic law, there was reciprocity in the obligations of husband and wife. The wife's duty to submit to her husband and cohabit with him ceased when the husband was derelict in his financial obligations to her.

Progressive Muslims have argued that because economic circumstances have changed greatly and women often share in the burden of supporting the family and meeting household expenses, the husband's rights should be modified accordingly. The trend in contemporary legislation has been to reform the definition of the marital relationship to emphasize mutual affection and support and to de-emphasize the aspects that make it look like an exchange of the wife's sexual services for the husband's financial support.

According to Islamic law, wives owe obedience to their husbands, and the *Qur'an* stipulates that wives may be beaten if they persist in disobedience (4:34). This has been a particularly problematic verse for Muslims who are seeking to establish that Islam upholds the principle of equal rights of men and women in marriage and abhors spousal violence. As part of their right to demand obedience, husbands are typically allowed to veto their wives' wish to work outside the home. Moreover, husbands may still retain the right to call on law enforcement to compel wives to return home when they are absent without permission.

Men may have up to four wives, although the tendency has increasingly been to enact reforms that require the husband to first persuade a judge that he has a justification for taking an extra wife. Women have been agitating for, and in some countries have obtained, the right to terminate their marriages if their husbands marry other wives or if they marry them without the first wives' consent.

Men may have unlimited temporary wives according to the rules of the Shi'i sect of Islam. Temporary marriages thus can be used as a means of marrying many wives simultaneously or indulging in numerous brief sexual liaisons. Women who contract temporary marriages tend to be of low social status, which makes this institution look exploitative. Muslim feminists, many of whom would analogize this institution to prostitution, have tended to condemn temporary marriage. However, temporary marriages can also be used in ways that serve women's interests, such as by creating fictive "marriages" that establish artificial family ties, which can allow women to associate freely with the male relations of their supposed "husbands." In

Muslim societies where there were slaves, masters were allowed to take unlimited numbers of their women slaves as concubines. In rare regions where slavery has survived, women may still be enslaved and treated like concubines.

Women need to prove grounds for divorce, but the rules in this area vary greatly. Some versions of Islamic divorce require stringent minimal grounds that make it virtually impossible for wives to sever their marital ties if their husbands object. Others provide lenient standards, which may include marital breakdown on a no-fault basis. Men are generally still allowed to divorce their wives without grounds, and in some countries they are still allowed to do so simply by uttering a "divorce formula," without ever going to court. Increasingly, however, the rule is that divorces must be supervised by courts. The ease with which husbands can sever the marriage bond turns out to be one of the most contentious issues today. Islamic law traditionally did not provide for alimony payments; the husband's duty to maintain his wife ceased after either three menstrual cycles following the divorce, or after the divorced wife had given birth to a child conceived during the marriage. In the absence of alimony requirements, women can be divorced without cause and then left bereft of sustenance. The financial hardships to which divorced women are exposed have been exacerbated by economic changes and the crumbling of the old support network provided by the traditional extended family. Reforms in many countries have been adopted to expand the divorcing husband's financial obligations to his former wife and to place hurdles in the way of unilateral divorces by husbands.

After divorce, child custody rules favor women as long as the children are still in infancy but give custody to husbands after certain ages, which vary considerably. Guardianship rules favor the husband even when the mother has custody of a child.

Notwithstanding these discriminatory features, from the outset Islamic law has contained elements that were more favorable to women's rights in marriage than were laws in many Western settings until very recently. Therefore, there are some battles that women in the West have had to fight that Muslim women do not face in their campaigns for enhanced rights. For example, in Islamic law women have always enjoyed full legal personality, including the capacity to sue and to be sued, which is not affected by their entering into marriage. They may retain their family names. Islamic women have also always been legally entitled to own and manage their own property.

In the past, when it was assumed that all women wanted children, Islamic rules on contraception worked out by the jurists were concerned with regulating the husband's use of coitus interruptus. Islamic law traditionally had liberal attitudes regarding birth control, and most schools of law also espoused liberal positions on abortion during the early months of pregnancy. Now that Muslim women are tending to want fewer children and potentially dispose of mechanisms like birth control pills to limit conception, the tendency has been to adopt new interpretations saying that Islam discourages contraception and even that it bans abortion absolutely.

CONCLUSION

In sum, there is such diversity in interpreting Islamic requirements affecting women's human rights that it is perilous to attempt to generalize about whether Islam presents real obstacles to women's human rights. What hinders the acceptance of women's human rights in Muslim countries varies. In a given situation it may be Islamic law, a particular feature of Islamic law upheld by a faction, male biases in the interpretations of the Islamic sources, patriarchal norms enshrined in imported European laws, or local customs and traditions that may be wrongly associated with Islam.

What is not in doubt is that many Muslims—and especially Muslim women—are now prepared to present arguments that Islam, properly understood, can be rethought to accommodate women's human rights. Many of the current debates over women's human rights take modern international human rights into account, and familiarity with international human rights standards like those embodied in the Women's Convention seems to have spurred fresh interest in re-interpreting Islam. In this process, it seems that the values of international human rights are being assimilated in Islamic thought regarding the status of women, leading to the possibility that in the twenty-first century human rights concepts may become successfully interwoven in the fabric of an updated Islamic tradition.

ISLAM, LAW, AND CUSTOM:
REDEFINING MUSLIM WOMEN'S RIGHTS

Azizah al-Hibri*

INTRODUCTION

Muslim women's rights have been the subject of a great deal of debate, most recently in Beijing and Huairou.[1] While many secular feminists have criticized patriarchal religiously justified laws in Muslim countries, many Muslim women have defended Islam as the guarantor *par excellence* of women's rights. This broad perceptual gap among women is partly explained by some as the result of miscommunication.[2] Secular feminists tend to blame Islam for laws that are oppressive to women

*   Research for this chapter was partially supported by a summer research grant from the University of Richmond Law School, 1996. The chapter is partly based on a paper written by this author for the Arab Regional Preparatory Meeting for the Fourth World Conference on Women, held in Amman, Jordan, in Sept. 1995, entitled *"Mashru' Bahth Naqdi li Qawanin al-Ahwal al-Shakhsiyah fi Buldan Arabiyah Mukhtarah,"* (Draft Critique of Personal Status Codes in Select Muslim Countries), published by ESCWA, United Nations (Doc. No. 94–054, Arabic, Nov. 1994), final version (Arabic and English) (1997). The paper was also presented at the ESCWA Expert Group Meeting on the Arab Family in a Changing Society, Abu Dhabi, United Arab Emirates, Dec. 10–14, 1994. This chapter is also partly based on an unpublished manuscript presented by the author at a seminar about the three Abrahamic religions entitled *Teach a Woman, Teach a Nation*, held at Auburn Theological Seminary, New York, Winter 1994. The author thanks participants in the above meetings for their comments and help, particularly, Dr. Farida Bennani, Professor of Law, University of Qadhi 'Iyadh, Marrakesh, Morocco; and Nabila Hamza, formerly of the Center of Arab Women for Training and Research, Tunisia. The author also thanks Professor Adrien Wing, College of Law, University of Iowa; Professor Gary Leedes, University of Richmond Law School; Drs. Fathi Osman and Maher Hathout, Islamic Center of Southern California; and Dr. Taha al-Jaber al-Alwani, School of Islamic and Social Sciences, Leesburg, Virginia, for their valuable comments. Most of all the author acknowledges her debt to and deep appreciation of the late Dr. Yorgy Hakim, Near Eastern and African Law Division, Library of Congress, for his enthusiastic help and support. Last but not least, the author thanks Ms. Patricia Collins, her student assistant. Without the diligent assistance of Ms. Collins, this chapter would not have been completed on time.

This chapter contains citations to Arabic Islamic sources which are not available in English. For these sources, the editors relied entirely on Professor al-Hibri's translation and interpretation.

This chapter first appeared in 12 AM. U. J. INT'L L. & POL'Y 1 (1997).

1.   Meetings of the U.N. Fourth Conference on Women and the NGO Forum, held in Huairou, China, Aug. 1995. Some participants in the NGO Forum observed the rise of spirituality among women as indicated by the sharp rise in the number of sessions addressing matters relating to religion or spirituality.

2.   Faulty reasoning, in particular the fallacy of *non-sequitur*, is often involved in arguments of some secular feminists. A defective law does not necessarily imply that the premises from which

in Muslim countries. Muslim women tend to defend Islam in light of their familiarity with the "ideals of Islam."[3] In this chapter, attemps were made to close this communication gap by studying two types of problems that have been of significant concern to Muslim women and others in the international community. The first is that of the personal status codes, which address matters of family law, in Muslim countries; the second is that of the education of women.

The reason for selecting these two problems for this chapter is that each problem represents a different level of complexity in Islamic jurisprudence. This means that different approaches may be adopted to resolve them. Yet, they are not jurisprudentially or practically unrelated. Understanding this fact will help us in the development of the best and fastest strategy for change in Muslim countries. It provides us criteria for prioritizing certain demands in order to lay the proper foundation for others.

In discussing personal status codes, the chapter focuses on three specific issues: the right of a woman to contract her own marriage, the duty of the wife to obey her husband, and the right of the wife to initiate divorce. There are several good reasons for focusing on these issues. Foremost among them is the fact that they have been and continue to be of great concern to Muslim women. Another reason is that despite their diverse subject matter, these three issues are based on the same jurisprudential foundation. Hence, discussion and critical analysis of that foundation will have similar implications for all three.

In discussing the three issues, an internal critique of the jurisprudence that led to their adoption is provided. In the process, some light is shed on the logic of Islamic jurisprudence and its historical relation to existing personal status codes in Muslim countries. Finally, a Muslim feminist solution to the advancement of women's rights in Muslim countries is proposed.

For reasons of space, this chapter focuses on the personal status codes of select Muslim countries: Egypt, Algeria, Morocco, Tunisia, Syria, Jordan, and Kuwait (collectively, their codes will be referred to as the "Codes"). For the same reason, the scope of the discussion in the section on Muslim women's rights and personal status codes is limited to Qur'anic sources only. Ideally, a critique which also takes into

---

it was derived suffer a similar defect. In fact, the defect may be the result of a faulty derivation or even a misunderstanding of the proper scope or significance of the premise. A later part of this chapter illustrates such problems of derivation and interpretation.

3. *Sisters in Islam*, a Malaysian women's organization, issued a press release in Huairou in Aug. 1995 stating that "two dominant and opposing views on Islam" emerged in the NGO Forum at Huairou. The release characterizes the first view as focused on "comparing the ideals of Islam with the reality and ills of the Western world." The second view, it adds, "rejects religion as a reaction against Islamic conservatism and abuses committed in the name of Islam." *Sisters in Islam* rejects both positions and "advocates a reconstruction of Islamic principles, procedures and practices in light of the basic Qur'anic principles of equality and justice." Dr. Laila Al-Marayati, a member of the official U.S. delegation to the U.N. Fourth World Conference on Women, held in Beijing during Sept. 1995, issued a statement echoing similar views on Islam and the need for alternative jurisprudential interpretations.

account the *hadith* (the words of the Prophet Muhammad) would be preferable. But that task shall remain for another day. In any case, it is important to remember that, traditionally, a *hadith* which appears to contradict a Qur'anic passage is usually viewed as based on a false report or is reinterpreted in a fashion consistent with the Qur'an.

Incidentally, the Codes apply only to Muslims. Non-Muslims are subject to their own religious laws. Therefore, the problems reflected in these Codes primarily affect Muslim women. The problems experienced by non-Muslim women, who live in these countries under their own religious personal status codes, will not be addressed here.

The Importance of Internal Critiques

It is important to keep in mind that most Muslim women tend to be highly religious and would not want to act in contradiction to their faith. As an example, consider the following experience. A couple of years ago, this author met some "modern" Muslim women behind closed doors in a certain Muslim country. The object was to have frank discussions about Islam and the rights of women. The women reflected a high degree of conflict and frustration. They wanted to be good Muslims, but they wanted to have their rights as well. When focusing on the issue of greatest concern to them, the Qur'anic view of gender relations, and providing a non-patriarchal Qur'anic interpretation on the subject, sighs of relief filled the room. The conflict created by patriarchal interpretations for Muslim women who do not have the benefit of a religious education is frightening.

The majority of Muslim women who hold strictly to their religion will not be liberated by a secular approach imposed from the outside by international bodies or from above by undemocratic governments. The only way to resolve the conflicts of these women and remove their fear of pursuing rich and fruitful lives is to build a solid Muslim feminist jurisprudential basis which clearly shows that Islam not only does not deprive them of their rights, but in fact demands these rights for them.

The last statement is of course quite controversial, and many knowledgeable readers may be ready to recount various counter-examples to the claim that Islam provides a liberating world view. Indeed, it has been "established" for quite a while in the international community that Islam is oppressive to women. It is this author's view that such a position is based either on mistaken belief or secular bias. In the first case, the international community appears to have readily embraced the patriarchal interpretations of Islam as authoritative. In the second case, individuals may have reached their conclusions based on an *a priori* view of religion as such.

In either case, Muslim women have been quite suspicious and resentful of Western feminist concern about "their plight." For one, they note that Western culture has not exactly improved the status of women. It created "super moms," who are eternally exhausted, and turned female sexuality into a commodity. For another, they detect an Orientalist perspective which has its roots in colonialist periods when some occupiers, such as the French in Algeria, attempted to "liberate" Muslim women by tearing their veils. In fact some of these "liberators" were more anxious to "liberate" colonized women than their own compatriots.[4] The lessons Muslims were quick to draw from such experiences is that the so-called liberators were pursuing a well-studied policy to destabilize Muslim societies and tear apart their familial structures. This view has received added support by the attitude that Western governments have taken recently towards democracy in Muslim countries. They advocate it, they praise it, but their deeds belie their words. They lend unconditional support to regimes that consistently violate human rights, so long as these regimes continue to protect Western economic and geopolitical interests.[5]

Given this sad state of affairs, it is imperative that Muslim women find their own way in the thickets of patriarchal religious reasoning, just as Christian and Jewish women have been doing. To deny them equal opportunity in this regard would be nothing short of discriminatory. This position does not mean that Western women, secular or religious, will have no role in the struggle for Muslim women's rights. Rather, it means that their role will be supportive and thus secondary to that of Muslim women, as it should be in this matter.

AN OVERVIEW OF ISLAMIC JURISPRUDENCE

General Observations

Many aspects of the life of Muslims in Muslim countries, including their views on the education of women and their family laws, rest in substantial part on medieval Islamic jurisprudence. Scholars based this jurisprudence on two components: religion and culture. The cultural component gave rise to certain fundamental social and political assumptions. These assumptions have become so deeply rooted in Islamic jurisprudence that many Muslims are no longer aware of their non-religious origins. The assumptions gave rise to a then common model of state and family relationships which are best described today as authoritarian/patriarchal. This model has not only been very detrimental to women, but it has also caused serious damage to society as a whole.

It is worth noting that the rise of patriarchy in the Muslim world was not historically an isolated event. Muslim Arab patriarchy was greatly influenced in its development by the neighboring Byzantine and Persian empires. In fact, during that period the whole world was in the firm grip of patriarchy. It took women endless centuries before they could even begin to successfully challenge it.

---

4.   *See* RANA KABBANI, IMPERIAL FICTIONS (Pandor rev. and exp. ed. 1994); MARNIA LAZREG, THE ELOQUENCE OF SILENCE, especially 136, 224 (Routledge ed. 1994).

5.   For a critique of the international human rights movement and its use by the West as a tool for spreading its hegemony, *see, e.g.*, HUMAN RIGHTS: MYTH OR REALITY—AN ASSESSMENT OF WESTERN AND ISLAMIC VIEWS (Islamic Political Programme Series Broadcast, London 1995). *See also* Richard Falk, *Cultural Foundations for the International Protection of Human Rights, in* HUMAN RIGHTS IN CROSS-CULTURAL PERSPECTIVES, 44–64, especially 55 (Abdullahi Ahmed An-Na'im ed., 1992) (stating "[m]ost states, even when avowedly concerned about human rights, often lack capability and credibility, having too much to hide themselves and generally subordinating their human rights concerns by according priority to geopolitics").

As patriarchal forces tightened their grip on Muslim countries, they attempted to reduce the status of women in society to that of inactive immature dependent beings who are neither full-fledged citizens of the state nor are capable of being in full control of their own destiny.[6] When this status is compared to that of Muslim women during the life of the Prophet, the contrast is shocking. Early Muslim women were actively involved in every aspect of the life of the nascent Muslim society. They included businesswomen, poets, jurists, religious leaders, and even warriors.[7] Yet, it is futile to attempt to establish the liberating influence of Islam on women by pointing to these ancient historical examples alone. So much patriarchal jurisprudence and practice has developed in the interim that we must also seriously examine these patriarchal developments.

One problem immediately presents itself at this point. To critically examine patriarchal Islamic jurisprudence from within the tradition, a woman must be familiar with the logic of *usul al-fiqh* (Islamic jurisprudence and its basic principles of reasoning). This requirement is difficult to satisfy because over the centuries patriarchy has drastically reduced women's access to the arena of Islamic jurisprudence despite the women's early involvement and contribution to it. Consequently, the demand for the education of women, particularly in the area of religious studies, is critical.

Basic Sources of Islamic Jurisprudence

The Qur'an is the foundation of Islamic Law. The *sunnah* (the *hadith* and example of the Prophet) is used as a secondary source for further clarification and guidance. Where the Qur'an and *sunnah* leave a question unanswered or unresolved, Muslim scholars resort to *ijtihad* (the science of interpretation and rulemaking). Under established principles of *ijtihad*, if the Qur'an and *sunnah* are silent on a matter, it is permissible (among other things) to resort to local custom, so long as that custom is consistent with the Qur'an and *sunnah*. In the legal arena, this meant that it was permissible to supplement religiously based law with customary law.[8]

As one may expect, scholars from different societies, and even from the same society, disagreed in their *ijtihad*. No doubt then that some of them were wrong at times. But so long as the *ijtihad* was based on (linguistic and religious) knowledge, and was conducted piously and in good faith, then the *mujtahids* (those who engage

---

6.   Azizah al-Hibri, *A Study of Islamic Herstory: Or How Did We Get Into This Mess, in* WOMEN AND ISLAM 207–19, especially 214–15 (Azizah al-Hibri ed., 1982).

7.   For a good book from a woman's perspective, *see* 1 ABD AL-HALIM ABU SHUQQAH, TAHRIR AL-MAR'AH FI 'ASR AL-RISALAH (5 vols.) *passim* (Kuwait 1990); OMAR KAHALAH, A'LAM AL-NISA' FI 'ALAMAY AL-'ARAB WA AL-ISLAM (5 vols.) *passim* (Beirut 1959); ABU JA'FAR AL-TABARI, TARIKH AL-TABARI: TARIKH AL-UMAM WA AL-MULUK (6 vols.) *passim* (9th cent. reprint, Beirut 1991).

8.   *See, e.g.,* SUBHI MAHMASSANI, MUQADDIMAH FI IHYA' 'ULUM AL-SHARI'AH 67–69 (Beirut 1962); *see also* MOHAMMAD SHALABI, USUL AL-FIQH AL-ISLAMI 325–28 (Beirut n.d.).

in *ijtihad*) did not have to fear retribution from God.[9] In fact, in a famous *hadith*, the Prophet stated that a *mujtahid* who erred in *ijtihad* would even be rewarded by God, presumably for exerting the effort to reach the correct answer.[10] Individual Muslims who were not *mujtahids* were free to select the school of jurisprudence they found most convincing and follow its guidance.[11] Islam guaranteed for each individual the freedom of choice in such matters because ultimately, each Muslim will have to account personally to God for that individual's own choices.

Early jurists viewed disagreements among them as a sign of God's mercy,[12] because these disagreements injected Islamic laws with the degree of flexibility necessary for a religion which proclaimed itself suitable for all times, all people and all societies.[13] Thus, hundreds of schools of *ijtihad* developed, each best suited to its own community and that community's culture, with its attendant customs and traditions.[14] Since all these ancient communities espoused patriarchal values of one form or another, *ijtihad* was itself often unwittingly affected by, and hence reflected, these values. Furthermore, since these later communities (unlike the Prophet) did not approve of the participation of women in public life, *ijtihad* became increasingly the male's preserve. In the end, *ijtihad*, and in fact the judiciary as a whole, became predominantly the domain of men. Thus, the woman's voice was ultimately reduced to a whisper in this arena.

At the same time, authoritarian/patriarchal political authorities were dissatisfied with the freedom of *ijtihad* practiced by scholars, even though that freedom was accessible primarily to males. For obvious reasons, these authorities preferred that *ijtihad* serve their own narrow political interests, especially on such critical issues as Islamic constitutionalism. Consequently, they made the life of dissident *mujtahids*, and there were many, difficult. Many famous *mujtahids*, such as Imam Malik Ibn Anas, suf-

---

9.   2 WIHBAH AL-ZUHAYLI, USUL AL-FIQH AL-ISLAMI (2 vols.) 1043–51,1066,1092–93 (Damascus 1986); *see also* MAHMASSANI, *supra* note 8, at 30; ABDEL QADER ABU AL-'ILA, BUHUTH FI AL-IJTIHAD 71–75 (Egypt 1987) (discussing conditions of *ijtihad*).

10.   4 ABU ABDALLAH AL-BUKHARI, SAHIH AL-BUKHARI BI HASHIAT AL-SINDI (4 vols.) 268 (9th cent. reprint, Beirut n.d.); 12 ABU AL-HUSSEIN MUSLIM, SAHIH MUSLIM BI SHARH AL-NAWAWI (18 vols.) 13–14 (9th cent. reprint, Beirut n.d.) (includes commentaries in the margin by the al-Nawawi, a well-known 13th century jurist); 2 AL-ZUHAYLI, *supra* note 9, at 1039; MAHMASSANI, *supra* note 8, at 30.

11.   For more on this point and on the deterioration of the Muslim citizen's right to freely choose a religious school of thought, *see* text accompanying notes 20–23.

12.   ABI ABDULLAH MUHAMMAD BIN ABD AL-RAHMAN AL-SHAFI'I, RAHMAT AL-UMMAH FI IKHTILAF AL-A'IMMAH *passim* (14th cent. reprint, Beirut 1994) (discussing this thesis in detail and including a bibliography on the subject).

13.   I discuss the significance of this approach to the development of Islamic jurisprudence in Azizah al-Hibri, *Islamic Constitutionalism and the Concept of Democracy*, 24 CASE W. RES. J. INT'L L. 1 (1992). *See also* MAHMASSANI, *supra* note 8, at 67–69; 2 AL-ZUHAYLI, *supra* note 9, at 1116–18.

14.   MAHMASSANI, *supra* note 8, at 67–69; *see also* 1 ABI HAMID AL-GHAZALI, 'IHYA' 'ULUM AL-DIN (4 vols.) 33 (11th cent. reprint, Egypt 1939) (discussing the tolerant nature of early *mujtahids* toward disagreements among them).

fered indignities at the hands of political authorities, and at times even torture, for exercising their right of free thought and speech on politically significant matters.[15] Given this political atmosphere and the fact that women had been gradually removed from public and jurisprudential life, women were in no position in those days to wage a successful fight for their rights.

For a number of reasons, very few major schools of thought remain viable today. These include the Hanafi, Maliki (established by Imam Malik referred to above), Shafi'i, Hanbali and Ja'fari schools. Almost all Muslim countries have formally adopted the *ijtihad* of one of these schools as the primary basis of their family laws. Syria, Egypt, and Jordan have adopted the Hanafi school of jurisprudence, while Morocco, Algeria, and Kuwait have adopted the Maliki school. Therefore, these two schools will be the focus of this paper. Tunisia has resorted in the formulation of its code to the doctrine of *Takhayur* (selection), which will be discussed below.

Basic Principles

The five schools of thought mentioned above generally agree that Islamic laws:

(1) change with the passage of time and with the change of place or circumstance;[16]

(2) must avoid harm;[17]

(3) may be discarded if they are based on a cause (*'Illah*) that itself has disappeared;[18] and

(4) must serve the commonweal ("public *maslaha*").[19]

Unfortunately, however, in applying these principles the all-male judges tended to define such notions as "harm" and "commonweal," and analyze concepts such as *'illah* and circumstantiality, in terms that not only reflected a purely male perspective, but often the perspective of the political authorities as well.

---

15. 1 AL-GHAZALI, *supra* note 14, at 33, 34, 48; *see also* MAHMASSANI, *supra* note 8, at 20 (noting that, at one point, even jurists discouraged *ijtihad* for fear of persecution). It must be noted that some rulers encouraged certain schools of thought.

16. 2 AL-ZUHAYLI, *supra* note 9, at 1116–18. *See also* SUBHI MAHMASSANI, AL-AWDA' AL-TASHRI'IYAH FI AL-DUWAL AL-ARABIYAH 478–79 (Beirut, 3d ed. 1965); YUSUF HAMID AL-'ALIM, AL-MAKASSID AL-'AMMAH 44–45 (1991) (quoting *Ibn Qayyim al-Jawziyah* on the limits of this principle). A derivative principle permits a change in the law whenever related customs change.

17. AL-'ALIM, *supra* note 16, at 89; MAHMASSANI, *supra* note 16, at 480. A related principle is that of choosing the lesser of two evils.

18. AL-'ALIM, *supra* note 16, at 123–25; *see also* MAHMASSANI, *supra* note 16, at 479. A story about Khalifah Omar is often mentioned in connection with this principle. In that story, the Khalifah stopped giving a certain group of people their share of *sadaqah (alms)*, despite a clear Qur'anic injunction to do so because, he reasoned, the *'Illah* or cause underlying that injunction had disappeared. Many jurists have followed in Khalifah Omar's footsteps.

19. MAHMASSANI, *supra* note 16, at 480; *see also* AL-'ALIM, *supra* note 16, at 124–25; 2 AL-ZUHAYLI, *supra* note 9, at 1017–29.

It is important to note certain differences between the role of traditional jurisprudence and that of the modern Codes. As mentioned earlier, originally, individuals were free to select and follow the school of *ijtihad* they preferred. They could even combine it with preferred parts of the jurisprudence of other schools. As the state grew more powerful, such choices were increasingly taken out of the hands of individuals. Ultimately, the state took choice away from Muslim citizens altogether in many areas of the law by selecting the jurisprudence of one of the schools as the law of the land.[20]

The selection by the state of a major school of thought denied individual Muslims the ability to practice Islam according to their own understanding and convictions in certain matters where the official state position differed from theirs.[21] While such selection was contemplated by an Islamic state as early as the eighth century, it was not successfully implemented until the sixteenth century by Sultan Salim I of the Ottoman empire.[22] Actual codification of the law, however, did not take place until the nineteenth century (the turn of this century, in the case of the personal status code) when the Ottoman Empire came increasingly under Western influences.[23]

One of the later stages in the codification process adopted the doctrine of *takhayur*.[24] This is a good doctrine which was unfortunately put to extensive patriarchal use in modern times by jurists charged with codifying Muslim family law. According to this doctrine, in drafting a Code for a certain country that adhered to the views of a major school of jurisprudence, a jurist is permitted to abandon the jurisprudence of that school on a particular matter and adopt a competing point of view offered by another major school, if he deemed the latter point of view superior for one reason or another. This approach is acceptable in light of the tradition of freedom of *ijtihad*, the Prophet's advice to Muslims to choose the easiest legitimate solution,[25] and the readiness of traditional jurisprudence to adapt to cultural, temporal and other circumstantial factors, so long as that adaptation does not conflict with the Qur'an. Additionally, where the Code is silent on a matter of family law, it is supplemented by the jurisprudence of the school to which the country officially adheres. I will name this latter rule the "doctrine of incorporation." As a result of the operation of this doctrine, the Codes tend to be incomplete. For example, a code may refer to a

---

20. A good discussion of the various historical stages that led to codification and the implications of each of these stages as to the individual religious liberties of the Muslim citizen and the freedom of *ijtihad* in society, can be found in MAHMASSANI, *supra* note 16, at 157–60; 170–202.

21. TAWFIQ AL-SHAWI, FIQH AL-SHURA 268–70 (Egypt 1992); *see also* MAHMASSANI, *supra* note 8, at 30 (stating that Imam Malik prohibited Khalifa Abu Ja'far al-Mansour and Khalifa al-Rashid from ordering their people to follow the Maliki school of thought).

22. MAHMASSANI, *supra* note 16, at 176–81.

23. *Id*. at 192–205.

24. *Id*. at 179.

25. 1 AL-BUKHARI, *supra* note 10, at 24; MAHMASSANI, *supra* note 16, at 479 (using a Qur'anic verse, *hadith* and other material to support the thesis that a Muslim is permitted to do even the prohibited out of necessity).

wali (guardian) without having ever properly introduced that term.[26] The most notable example of the utilization of this doctrine is the Egyptian Code itself which is quite fragmentary. It has no provisions governing marriage, and concentrates on such issues as maintenance and divorce.[27]

The doctrine of *takhayur* was used and continues to be used to this day to inject into Codes some of the most patriarchal contributions to Islamic jurisprudence. Even the proposed Uniform Personal Status Code, which is being considered for adoption by various Arab countries as a further step towards modernization, continues this unfortunate trend.[28]

MUSLIM WOMEN'S RIGHTS AND PERSONAL STATUS CODES

The three major issues to focus upon in the Codes are:

(1) the right of a woman to contract her own marriage;

(2) the duty of the wife to obey her husband; and

(3) the right of the wife to initiate a divorce.

The Right of a Woman to Contract Her Own Marriage

The general rule for six of the seven countries enumerated earlier (Tunisia being the exception), and for many other Muslim countries, is that women do not have the right to contract their own marriage.[29] In these countries, a Muslim woman needs a *wali* (guardian) to contract the marriage on her behalf.[30] The *wali* is usually the father.

---

26. *See, e.g.*, Decree No. 59 (1953) regarding Personal Status Law, *amended by* Law No. 34 (1975), Bk. 1, Tit. 2, Chs. 3, 4 [hereinafter Syrian Code]; Family Law No. 84–11 (1984), Bk. 1, Tit. 1, Ch. 1, Arts. 9, 11 [hereinafter Algerian Code]. The most fragmentary code is the Egyptian code, which addresses very few matters such as maintenance and divorce, leaving most other matters to be dealt with according to the incorporated school of thought.

27. Act No. 25 (1920) in respect of Maintenance and Some Questions of Personal Status and Act No. 25 (1929) regarding certain Personal Status Provisions, *as both are amended by* Act No. 100 (1985) [collectively, hereinafter Egyptian Code].

28. *See* Ahmad al-Khamlishi, *al-Tajdid Am al-Taghallub 'Ala 'Akabaat al-Tariq, in* Jadid al-Fikr al-Islami 79, 99–100 (Saudi Arabia 1989).

29. Royal Decree No. 343.57.1 (1957), *as amended by* Royal Decree No. 347.93.1, 1993, Bk. 1, Tit. 3, Ch. 12, Art. 2 [hereinafter Moroccan Code]. Algerian Code, *supra* note 26, at Bk. 1, Tit. 1, Ch 1, Arts. 9, 11. The Egyptian Code contains this provision indirectly as a result of the "doctrine of incorporation" mentioned earlier. *See* Art. No. 280, Act No. 78 (Egypt 1931). Syrian Code, *supra* note 26, at Bk. 1, Tit. 2, Ch. 3, Arts. 21–24. Personal Status Code, Provisional Law No. 61 (1976), Ch. 1, Art. 6, and Ch. 2, Arts. 9–13 [hereinafter Jordanian Code]. Personal Status Code Decree, dated Aug. 13, 1956, *as amended* 1993, Bk. 1, Art. 6 [hereinafter Tunisian Code] (specific provision applies only to minors; Tit. 9 allows adults to marry without a *wali*). Law No. 51 (1984) Regarding Personal Status, Part 1, Bk. 1, Tit. 2, Ch. 2, Arts. 29–30 [hereinafter Kuwaiti Code].

30. Royal Decree No. 343.57.1 (1957), *as amended by* Royal Decree No. 347.93.1, 1993, Bk. 1, Tit. 3, Ch. 12, Art. 2. Algerian Code, *supra* note 26, at Bk. 1, Tit. 1, Ch 1, Arts. 9, 11. The

This requirement is somewhat similar to the Western traditional approach under which the father "gives away" the bride, but in this case it is a legal requirement.

There are, however, significant exceptions to this general rule. The Moroccan Code makes an exception for the adult mature woman who is fatherless.[31] The Syrian Code permits a pubescent woman who is over seventeen years old to request a judge to perform the marriage.[32] Before the judge can do so, however, he must ask the *wali* (who is usually the father) for his opinion. In the absence of a non-frivolous objection from the *wali*, the judge may proceed with the marriage so long as the prospective husband is eligible.[33] This last condition is very important. If the husband is ineligible, the *wali* has the right to demand judicial annulment, unless the wife has conceived.[34]

The Jordanian Code permits a previously married woman who is rational and over eighteen years old to contract her own marriage.[35] Presumably, this means that the Jordanian Code continues to require a *wali* for the rational adult *bikr* (previously unmarried woman).[36]

The Kuwaiti Code permits a previously married woman or one who has reached the age of twenty-five to make her own decision about marriage, without reference to the views of her *wali*.[37] But the law continues to require that the *wali* execute the marriage contract on her behalf.[38]

The Algerian Code goes furthest in underlining the importance of this requirement. In that jurisdiction, the *wali* can prohibit his *bikr* daughter from entering into a marriage, if he deems the prohibition in her interest.[39]

It is worth noting that after the recent amendment to the Moroccan Code, it has become the rule in all the named jurisdictions that no woman, particularly a *bikr*, may

---

Egyptian Code contains this provision indirectly as a result of the "doctrine of incorporation" mentioned earlier. *See* Art. No. 280, Act No. 78 (Egypt 1931). Syrian Code, *supra* note 26, at Bk. 1, Tit. 2, Ch. 3, Arts. 21–24. Personal Status Code, Provisional Law No. 61 (1976), Ch. 1, Art. 6, and Ch. 2, Arts. 9–13. Personal Status Code Decree, dated Aug. 13, 1956, *as amended* 1993, Bk. 1, Art. 6 (specific provision applies only to minors; Tit. 9 allows adults to marry without a *wali*). Law No. 51 (1984) Regarding Personal Status, Part 1, Bk. 1, Tit. 2, Ch. 2, Arts. 29–30.

31.   Moroccan Code, *supra* note 29, Bk. 1, Tit. 1, Ch. 12, Art. 4.

32.   Syrian Code, *supra* note 26, Bk. 1, Tit. 1, Ch. 2, Art. 20.

33.   *Id.*

34.   *Id.*, Art. 27–30.

35.   Jordanian Code, *supra* note 29, Ch. 2, Art. 13.

36.   This is implied by the remaining requirements of the Jordanian Code, Ch. 2, Arts. 9–14.

37.   Kuwaiti Code, *supra* note 29, Pt. 1, Bk. 1, Tit. 2, Arts. 8, 29, 30.

38.   *Id.*

39.   Algerian Code, *supra* note 26, Bk. 1, Tit. 1, Ch. 1, Art. 12.

be forced into marriage against her will.[40] All these Codes have provisions providing the woman with a judicial venue in case the *wali* unfairly blocks her marriage.[41]

The Duty of the Wife to Obey Her Husband

Until a few years ago, all Codes listed or implied a duty of obedience (*ta'ah*) by the wife.[42] The present Tunisian Code no longer requires obedience, although it continues to describe the husband as the "head of the family."[43]

The duty of *ta'ah* is very important because it includes the duty not to leave the home without the husband's permission, and because violating the duty of *ta'ah* (*nushuz*) has financial repercussions. All Codes (other than the Tunisian Code) expressly recognize customary limits for *ta'ah*. For example, the wife may leave the home without her husband's consent for a "legitimate reason" (as such term is defined in Islamic law) such as visiting her family.[44] But the number of such permissible visits is limited by some Codes to what is customary.[45] More recently, some Codes have permitted the wife to leave her home for legitimate (moral, unobjectionable) work.[46] The Jordanian Code specifies domestic violence and maltreatment as legitimate causes for leaving the home.[47] The Kuwaiti Code regards the wife's departure from the marital home justifiable (and hence not *nushuz*) if the husband is not "trustworthy."[48]

40. Moroccan Code, *supra* note 29, Bk. 1, Tit. 2, Ch. 5, Art. 1.

41. Algerian Code, *supra* note 26, Bk. 1, Tit. 1, Ch. 1, Art. 12; Jordanian Code, *supra* note 29, Ch. 1, Art. 6; Kuwaiti Code, *supra* note 29, Pt. 1, Bk. 1, Tit. 3, Ch. 2, Art. 31; Moroccan Code, *supra* note 29, Bk. 1, Tit. 3, Ch. 13; Syrian Code, *supra* note 26, Bk. 1, Tit. 2, Ch. 2, Art. 20. Tunisian Code, *supra* note 29, Bk. 1, Art. 6 (applying to minors only).

42. Moroccan Code, *supra* note 29, Bk. 1, Tit. 6, Ch. 36, Art. 2; Algerian Code, *supra* note 26, Bk. 1, Tit. 1, Ch. 4, Art. 39; Egyptian Code, *supra* note 27, Law No. 25 (1929) (amended 1985), Ch. 2, Art. 11 Repeated Twice; Jordanian Code, *supra* note 29, Ch 7, Art. 39; Kuwaiti Law, Pt. 1, Bk. 1, Tit. 5, Ch 3, Arts. 84–91; Syrian Code, *supra* note 26, Bk. 1, Tit. 4, Ch. 3, Art. 75, by implication and generally as a result of the doctrine of incorporation. Tunisian Code, *supra* note 29, Bk. 1, Old Art. 23 (*superseded*). Some of these provisions only partially address the *ta'ah* requirement simply because the Codes make use of the doctrine of incorporation.

43. Tunisian Code, *supra* note 29, Bk 1, Art. 23 (amended 1993).

44. Algerian Code, *supra* note 26, Bk. 1, Tit. 1, Ch. 4, Art. 38; Egyptian Code, *supra* note 27, Law No. 25 (1920) (amended 1985) Bk. 1, Pt. 1, Art. 1; Jordanian Code, *supra* note 29, Ch. 9, Art. 69; Kuwaiti Code, *supra* note 29, Pt. 1, Bk. 1, Tit. 3, Art. 89 (*see also* comments on this provision in the related Explanatory Memorandum); Moroccan Code, *supra* note 29, Bk. 1, Tit. 6, Ch. 35; Syrian Code, *supra* note 26, Bk. 1, Tit. 4, Ch. 3, Art. 75. The Kuwaiti, Egyptian, Syrian, and Jordanian provisions derive their full impact from their use of the doctrine of incorporation or reference to customary law.

45. *See, e.g.*, Algerian Code, *supra* note 26, Bk. 1, Tit. 1, Ch. 4, Art. 38; Moroccan Code, *supra* note 29, Bk. 1, Tit. 6, Ch. 35.

46. *See, e.g.*, Egyptian Code, *supra* note 27, Law No. 25 (1920) (amended 1985), Bk. 1, Ch. 1, Art. 1; Kuwaiti Code, *supra* note 29, Part 1, Bk. 1, Tit. 3, Art 89. *Cf.* Syrian Code, *supra* note 26, Bk. 1, Tit. 4, Ch. 73 (amended 1975); Jordanian Code, *supra* note 29, Ch. 9, Art. 68.

47. Jordanian Code, *supra* note 29, Ch. 9, Art. 69.

48. Kuwaiti Code, *supra* note 29, Pt. 1, Bk. 1, Tit. 3, Art. 87, cl. 3.

The Explanatory Memorandum to the Kuwaiti Code quotes the Qur'an, arguing that a marriage union is intended to bring two souls together in tranquillity, affection, and mercy.[49] It explicitly rejects the view defining the wife as the "object of sexual enjoyment."[50] The section on *ta'ah* in the Kuwaiti Code is relatively short and contains many provisions protecting women.

Also, under the Kuwaiti Code, if the wife refuses unjustifiably to move in with her husband, then the court may order her to do so.[51] If the woman refuses to obey the court order, she becomes *nashiz* (disobedient).[52] The Kuwaiti court order cannot be used to force the woman to move to her husband's home (as used to be the case in Egypt).[53] It can only be used as the basis for forfeiture of the wife's maintenance by the husband.[54]

Most Codes permit the husband to cease his maintenance of a *nashiz* wife.[55] The Moroccan Code, however, does not permit such cessation, unless the wife has violated a court order requiring her to return home to her husband's house and bed, and unless a judge decides to penalize the wife for the violation.[56]

The Right of the Wife to Initiate Divorce

The general rule is that the primary right of divorce resides in the husband.[57] Unless that right is delegated to the wife in one form or another, the wife must seek either *khul'* (a form of divorce or annulment which will be discussed below) or judicial annulment, separation, or divorce. Justifications for granting the wife judicial

---

49. Explanatory Memorandum to Draft Personal Status Code, comment on Pt. 1, Bk. 1, Tit. 1, Art. 1. *See also* the Explanatory Memorandum, relating to Egyptian Act No. 100 (1985) which contains similar language. Moroccan Code, Bk. 1, Tit. 1, Ch. 1, is more explicit than either the Kuwaiti or Egyptian Code in describing the relationship between the spouses as one characterized by "peace, affection, and respect," but the rest of the code makes it clear that this relationship is also very hierarchical.

50. Explanatory Memorandum to Draft Personal Status Code, comment on Pt. 1, Bk. 1, Tit. 1, Art. 1.

51. Kuwaiti Code, *supra* note 29, Pt. 1, Bk. 1, Tit. 3, Art. 87.

52. *Id.*

53. *Id.* arts. 87, 88.

54. *Id.*

55. Algerian Code, *supra* note 26, Bk. 1, Tit.. 1, Ch. 4, Art. 37; Egyptian Code, *supra* note 27, Art. 1; Jordanian Code, *supra* note 29, Ch. 9, Art. 68–69; Kuwaiti Code, *supra* note 29, Pt. 1, Bk. 1, Tit. 5, Art. 87; Syrian Code, *supra* note 26, Bk. 1, Tit. 3, Art. 74.

56. Moroccan Code, *supra* note 29, Bk. 3, Tit. 5, Ch. 123.

57. Algerian Code, *supra* note 26, Bk. 1, Tit. 2, Ch. 1, Art. 48; Egyptian Code, Law No. 25 (1929) (amended 1985), by virtue of its adoption of the doctrine of incorporation, Art. 1; Jordanian Code, *supra* note 29, Ch. 10, Art. 83; Kuwaiti Code, *supra* note 29, Pt. 1, Bk. 2, Tit. 1, Art. 97; Moroccan Code, *supra* note 29, Bk. 2, Tit. 1, Ch. 44; Syrian Code, *supra* note 26, Bk. 2, Tit. 1, Ch. 85, 87, Art. 2. For the Tunisian Code approach, see *infra* note 60.

divorce include the presence of defects in the husband, insanity, harm,[58] prolonged absence, sexual abandonment, cessation of maintenance, and imprisonment of the husband.[59]

The Tunisian Code is the exception to this rule. It authorizes divorce requested by mutual agreement.[60] It also authorizes judicial divorces upon the request of either party.[61]

The Algerian Code permits the judge to decree divorce if either party exhibits *nushuz*.[62] (The notion of *nushuz* when applied to men has a different meaning.[63])

As stated earlier, all these Codes are based on the jurisprudence adopted by the country of the respective Code or adopted on the basis of the doctrine of *takhayur*. Thus, in search of a better understanding of the above laws, their jurisprudential underpinnings will be examined.

THE MALIKI AND HANAFI IJTIHAD ON THE THREE ISSUES

Because of the particular Codes being examined in this chapter, the Hanafi and Maliki schools of thought have been selected for study. It is worth noting that referring below to the "Hanafi view" or the "Maliki view" we are simplifying the jurisprudence of these school tremendously. Each school consists of the thought of many scholars who followed in the footsteps of the one after whom the school was named and who may have ultimately differed with him or other followers on certain matters. Nevertheless, it is acceptable in each case to identify the school with the predominant line of thought within it.

This too must be said: it would be ludicrous to suggest that the mounds of painstakingly careful jurisprudence developed across the ages by such jurisprudence

---

58. Certain Codes explicitly specify that verbal abuse is grounds for granting the wife judicial divorce. *See* Jordanian Code, *supra* note 29, Ch. 10, Art. 132; Kuwaiti Code, *supra* note 29, Pt. 1, Bk. 2, Tit. 3, Art. 126. The Moroccan Code speaks of "harm of any kind," Moroccan Code, *supra* note 29, Bk 2, Tit. 1, Ch. 56, Art. 1.

59. Algerian Code, *supra* note 26, Bk. 1, Tit. 2, Ch. 1, Art. 53; Moroccan Code, *supra* note 29, Bk. 2, Tit. 1, Ch. 53–58; Syrian Code, *supra* note 26, Bk. 2, Tit. 1, Art. 105–12; Jordanian Code, *supra* note 29, Ch. 10, Arts. 113–34; Egyptian Code, *supra* note 27, Law No. 25 (1929) (amended 1985), Arts. 2 and 3; Kuwaiti Code, *supra* note 29, Pt. 1, Bk. 2, Tit. 3, Arts. 120–42.

60. Tunisian Code, *supra* note 29, Bk. 2, Art. 31, cl. 1, *but* cl. 3 suggests that it is still easier for the husband to seek divorce.

61. *Id.*

62. Algerian Code, *supra* note 26, Bk. 1, Tit. 2, Ch. 1, Art. 55.

63. The notion of *nushuz* when applied to men has a narrower meaning, since men have no legal duty to obey women. The core meaning of the notion of *nushuz*, which applies to both male and female, is "acting superior to the other because of extreme dislike or some other reason." *See, e.g.*, the definition of "*nashiz*" in 4 ABU JA'FAR AL-TABARI, TAFSIR AL-TABARI (16 vols.) 64, 304 (9th century, Beirut 1992) (providing authority for the view that the word "*nushuz*" for men and women means "to act superior, to desire separation from the other;" but also providing other authority for the definition of a female *nashiz* as one who disobeys her husband).

giants as Abu Hanifah and Malik Ibn Anas can be properly evaluated or even addressed in this chapter. There is no doubt that these scholars did not only have vast knowledge of their subject matter, but also great minds and piety. To describe them as patriarchal jurists is, therefore, not to detract from their achievements. Rather, it is to suggest that despite their indisputable genius, these scholars were nevertheless the products of their times. As they themselves recognized, laws change with changes in time, place, and custom. We are no longer living in their times and some of what worked for their societies no longer works for ours.

The Woman's Right to Contract Her Own Marriage

The basic requirement which affects all jurisprudence on this matter is that of the *wali*. Traditional Muslim jurisprudence and the above-mentioned Codes generally concur in requiring a *wali* for a *bikr* if she had not reached maturity.[64] Her marriage cannot be concluded without such a *wali*, who is required to be male and is usually her father.[65] The requirement that a *wali* contract the marriage was historically defended as a protective measure for women who may be swept away by their emotions. It also protects the family's honor in cases where women may elect to marry ineligible males.[66] This rationale was found so appealing that even Hanafis, who recognized the right of the adult women to contract her own marriage without a *wali*, expressed their preference for the woman's delegation of that right to a *wali*.[67]

Jurists also generally concur, with the notable exception of the Malikis, that a *bikr*'s marriage cannot be concluded without her consent. Jurists also agree (with the exception of some Malikis) that it is not necessary to inform the *bikr* that her silence constitutes consent.[68] Schools differ as to the duration and nature of the *wilayah* (guardianship) of marriage.[69]

---

64. *See* 4 ABDUL RAHMAN AL-JAZIRI, KITAB AL-FIQH 'ALA AL-MATHAHIB AL-ARBA'AH (5 vols.) 51 (Beirut 1969); *see also* MUHAMMAD JAWAD MAGHNIYAH, AL-FIQH 'ALA AL-MATHAHIB AL-KHAMSAH 321(Beirut, 6th ed. 1969); AHMAD FARAJ, AL-ZAWAJ WA AHKAMUHU FI MATHHAB AHL AL-SUNNAH 126–34 (Egypt 1989).

65. AHMAD GHANDOUR, AL-AHWAL AL-SHAKHSIYAH FI AL-TASHRI' AL-ISLAMI 122, 135–36 (Kuwait 1972); FARAJ, *supra* note 64, at 126; 4 AL-JAZIRI, *supra* note 64, at 52–53; *see also* MUHAMMAD ABU ZAHRAH, MUHADARAT FI 'AQD AL-ZAWAJ WA ATHARUH 135, 139 (Egypt 1958); 7 MUWAFFAQ AL-DIN IBN QUDAMAH, AL-MUGHNI (12 vols.) 337, 346 (12th cent. reprint, Beirut n.d.).

66. 4 AL-JAZIRI, *supra* note 64, at 49–50. *See, e.g.*, ABU ZAHRA, *supra* note 65, at 135; 9 MUSLIM, *supra* note 10, at 205 (al-Nawawi's commentary in the margin providing divergent views on the need for a *wali*).

67. GHANDOUR, *supra* note 65, at 125–26. *See* ABU ZAHRAH, *supra* note 65, at 136 and related note 1, 154; *see also* 1 AHMAD AL-KHAMLISHI, AL-TA'LIQ 'ALA QANUN AL-AHWAL AL-SHAKHSIYAH (2 vols.) 194 (1987).

68. *See* 9 MUSLIM, *supra* note 10, at 205 (al-Nawawi's commentary in the margin); *see also* 6 MUHAMMAD IBN AL-SHAWKANI, NAYL AL-AWTAR (9 vols.) 254 (Beirut 1973).

69. *See, e.g.*, GHANDOUR, *supra* note 65, at 131–32; FARAJ, *supra* note 64, at 129–38.

Muslim jurists viewed the *wali* requirement as an expression of their protectiveness of innocent and naive Muslim women who may be victimized by designing men. This concern appears reasonable, but it makes sense legally only if we adopt a patriarchal view of women. A rational independent woman of sound judgement requires no protection (although she may seek advice); an emotional, dependent and impulsive woman does. This fact was pointed out by Abu Hanifah who recognized the mature woman's right to contract her own marriage. Hanafis and others holding this point of view noted that since Islam gave women the right to contract in financial matters without interference or guardianship from any one, women should be equally able to contract their own marriage without the need for a *wali*.[70]

The Hanafi View

Under this view, a *wali* has only advisory powers unless the ward chooses an "ineligible" husband.[71] At that point the *wali* acquires the power to void the marriage, so long as no child has been born.[72]

As stated earlier, "eligibility" is a term of art, endowed with a broad range of meanings. The Prophet defines "eligibility" in terms of faith and piety.[73] But the Hanafi school departs from this pristine definition. Instead, it defines it in accordance with classist customs so as to include, in addition to religion, lineage, financial condition, and skill or profession. Consequently, the definition reflects traditional patriarchal concerns that were so strong as to justify ignoring the woman's choice and voiding her marriage.[74]

---

70. GHANDOUR, *supra* note 65, at 126; ABU ZAHRAH, *supra* note 65, at 138; 4 AL-JAZIRI, *supra* note 64, at 46; FARAJ, *supra* note 64, at 134, 136; MUHAMMAD ZAKARIYA AL-BARDISI, AL-AHKAM AL-ISLAMIYAH FI AL-AHWAL AL-SHAKHSIYAH 199 (Egypt 1965).

71. GHANDOUR, *supra* note 65, at 126; AL-BARDISI, *supra* note 70 at 199; *see* 4 AL-JAZIRI, *supra* note 64, at 51; *see also* FARAJ, *supra* note 64, at 128; 1 MUHAMMAD AL-DIJWI, AL-AHWAL AL-SHAKHSIYAH LI AL-MISRIYIN AL-MUSLIMIN 48 (Cairo n.d.).

72. *See* 4 AL-JAZIRI, *supra* note 64, at 51, 56; AL-DIJWI, *supra* note 71, at 48; ABU ZAHRAH, *supra* note 65, at 173; AL-BARDISI, *supra* note 70, at 192.

73. *See* FARAJ, *supra* note 64, at 111; *see also* AL-DIJWI, *supra* note 71, at 55; ABU ZAHRAH, *supra* note 65, at 169, 171, n.1; 6 AL-SHAWKANI, *supra* note 68, at 262.

74. *See* 4 AL-JAZIRI, *supra* note 64, at 54–58; *see also* FARAJ, *supra* note 64, at 111–12; ABU ZAHRAH, *supra* note 65, at 163–67. The story of Sheikh Ali Yusuf, whose marriage to Safiyah al-Sadat was annulled (*faskh*), is one major example of the issue at hand. The case, which took place in 1904, sharply divided public opinion in Egypt. Sheikh Ali was born to a poor family in a distant Egyptian village. In time, however, he was able to build a highly successful career as an activist journalist, and accumulated substantial wealth. He asked for the hand of Safiyah Sadat, a beautiful woman from an aristocratic family. After princes, ministers and other leaders of the community interceded on his behalf, the father accepted and the engagement was announced. But, for years, the father refused to set a marriage date. Finally, Sheikh Ali took matters into his own hands. He agreed with Safiyah to marry, and the marriage took place without the father's knowledge. The father sued in family court for annulment on the basis that Sheikh Ali did not meet the "eligibility" requirement. He particularly noted that Sheikh Ali did not have a noble ancestry comparable to that of Safiyah. Furthermore, he added, Sheikh Ali's profession was a lowly one. The

Furthermore, the patriarchal stereotype of women as irrational, dependent, and impulsive (the "Stereotype") plays an important role in permitting the Hanafi *wali* to void an unsuitable marriage. It is based on the view that women, as a group, are vulnerable to designing men and need to be saved from their grip by the "other" men in their lives, namely *walis*.[75] One may view this argument as a cover for more serious economic and class concerns by *walis*. In either case, it enables a *wali* to stop his ward from making the "wrong" decision. Notice that young men can make "wrong" choices with no fear of interference. But part of the rationale is that the male's social status is not derived from that of his wife; the woman's status, however, is derived from that of her husband.[76] This means that these jurisprudential decisions were not reached in a vacuum. Rather, as they should, they took into account the kind of society in which these rules were formulated. Therefore, as society changes and women increasingly acquire their own independent social standing, the older rules must be reformulated to facilitate the change and reflect new realities.

The interaction of the various Codes' requirement that the woman delegate the right to contract her marriage to her *wali* with the *wali*'s right to object to the marriage if the husband is not eligible is particularly troublesome. If the powers conferred by these provisions are misused by the *wali*, a marriage may be blocked altogether and forever, unless the female is willing to sue her *wali*. While many Codes contain provisions that prevent the *wali* from unjustifiably preventing his ward from marrying, it is unlikely that the majority of wronged women would seriously consider availing themselves of these provisions and suing their *wali*.[77] Such course of action is not realistic in Muslim countries, even in extreme cases. Litigation causes negative social consequences for the female and for her relationship with the *wali*, who is probably her father and sole provider. To solve this problem, the legislature in Muslim countries must be relied on to devise more realistic ways to prevent and punish abuses by the *wali*.

Most importantly, the legislator must revisit certain fundamental issues. For example, despite the partially enlightened Hanafi view on the role of a *wali*, one must raise the question as to why a woman is required to have a *wali* at all today, especially since men are not subject to the same requirement. There are three answers to this

---

court then ordered Safiyah to return to her father's house until the case was decided. She vehemently refused to do so, but moved instead to a third location. In the meantime, the public was hotly debating the issue. Finally, the court ordered that the marriage be annulled, and the order was affirmed by the higher court. Later, after additional efforts by leading members of the community, the father relented and permitted a new marriage contract to take place. For more on this story, *see* 1 AL-DIJWI, *supra* note 71 at 539–53.

75.   *See* 4 AL-JAZIRI, *supra* note 64, at 49; *see also* 7 IBN QUDAMAH, *supra* note 65, at 339; AL-BARDISI, *supra* note 70, at 196 (evaluating the assumption).

76.   *See* 4 AL-JAZIRI, *supra* note 64, at 57, 60; *see also* ABU ZAHRAH, *supra* note 65, at 170.

77.   *See* 4 AL-JAZIRI, *supra* note 64, at 50 (discussing the importance of keeping a good relationship by the woman with her *wali*); *cf.* GHANDOUR, *supra* note 65, at 140–41 (noting the case of a Kuwaiti woman who sued her *wali* for blocking her marriage unfairly to an eligible male and won).

question. The first is claimed to derive from the Qur'an, and that claim shall be addressed in a separate section. The second is based on the Stereotype, while the third points to the nature of patriarchal society that shows no mercy toward women who are not protected by men. In the latter two cases, the argument in favor of a *wali* appears to proceed from the desire to protect women.

While such an attitude is laudable, the *wali* requirement must be restated as a voluntary option for the mature woman, which once exercised by her becomes binding upon the *wali*. The Stereotypical view of women, which is demonstrably false, must be abandoned along with its attendant compulsory protectionism. In making this demand, one must be mindful of the fact that many of the recent rulers in Muslim countries, and colonialist powers before them, have historically resorted to similar protectionist arguments to deny citizens their political liberties. While such attitudes served in some cases only to delay political independence or the emergence of democracy in some countries, more often they have resulted in a great deal of upheaval and social instability. Learning from that experience, one must conclude that an orderly change of outdated family laws is highly advisable.

The Maliki View

A Maliki father (acting as a *wali*) can force his *bikr* daughter, regardless of her age into marrying a man of his choice unless the father had previously declared his daughter mature.[78] Jurists justified this position by relying on the Stereotype. They argued that the virgin (who might be a thirty-five-year-old lawyer or physician) lacks experience in men and may be swayed by emotion in reaching her decision.[79] Malikis allowed such a *bikr* daughter to escape a forced marriage only if the prospective husband suffered from mental illness or from certain serious diseases like leprosy or sexual impotence.[80] The ability of the *wali* to force his ward into marriage does not extend to women who are not *bikr* or women whose *wali* has declared them mature.[81] The Maliki eligibility requirement is closer to the *sunnah*, requiring only piety and freedom from serious illnesses and diseases.[82]

A major indication that this part of the Maliki jurisprudence is no longer suitable for today's world is the fact that Morocco has recently amended its Code to delete the oppressive provision that permits a forced marriage by a *wali*. The rest of the *wilayah* jurisprudence remains intact and continues to complicate social relationships.

---

78. *See* 2 ABI AL-BARAKAT AHMAD AL-DARDIR, AL-SHARH AL-SAGHIR (4 vols.) 353–54 (18th cent. reprint, Cairo 1972); *see also* 4 AL-JAZIRI, *supra* note 64, at 33; FARAJ, *supra* note 64, at 130.

79. *See* ABU ZAHRAH, *supra* note 65, at 137–38; FARAJ, *supra* note 64, at 130, 136; 4 AL-JAZIRI, *supra* note 64, at 49.

80. *See* 4 AL-JAZIRI, *supra* note 64, at 33; *see also* FARAJ, *supra* note 64, at 130.

81. 2 AL-DARDIR, *supra* note 78, at 353–54; *see also* 4 AL-JAZIRI, *supra* note 64, at 33; FARAJ, *supra* note 64, at 131. These women can also escape such a marriage, usually, but through a different provision of the law.

82. 4 AL-JAZIRI, *supra* note 64, at 58; *see also* ABU ZAHRAH, *supra* note 65, at 167; FARAJ, *supra* note 64, at 115.

Ta'ah

As elaborated by traditional jurists of the various major schools, this concept is perhaps the most degrading to the Muslim woman. It diminishes her fundamental liberties as a human being worthy of equal status under the law. Ta'ah enables the husband to prohibit the wife from leaving her home, unless she is willing to risk loss of financial support and, in some cases, divorce. While many Codes contain a few carve-outs that permit legitimate exceptions to this rule, it shocks the conscience to have the rule in the first place. One wonders what Khadijah, the successful businesswoman and wife of the Prophet, would say to those medieval jurists who confined wives to their homes and permitted their unauthorized exit only in cases of extreme necessity.[83]

This power to confine the wife to her home was described by some traditional jurists as *ihtibas* and was viewed as the *quid pro quo* for her maintenance.[84] Under this point of view, the woman was allowed to visit and receive her family a limited number of times during the year without her husband's consent, although other jurists argued even against this modest carve-out.[85] This traditional jurisprudence is not obsolete. As pointed out earlier, unless a specific provision of traditional jurisprudence is explicitly ruled out by the Code, it is part of that Code by incorporation. Furthermore, every reference in the Code to "custom" is a reference to an anachronistic patriarchal custom on which much of this traditional jurisprudence is based.

The concept of *ta'ah* as now presented in the Codes is a patriarchal hierarchical construct which, as as argued below, contradicts the fundamental Islamic concept of *tawhid* (the unity of God). In fact, a critique of the *Ta'ah* concept would be very similar to a critique of the concept of *ta'ah* as used in the political arena. The notion of *ta'ah* to the ruler has also been rendered extremely hierarchical and oppressive. Strict forms of *Ta'ah* are due only to God, and not to a ruler or husband. Human-oriented *ta'ah* is a much more modest concept based on a variety of requirements, such as those of *shura* (consultation) and genuine consent whether in the public or private sphere. Furthermore, it is symmetrical in that the ruler is also required to obey the will of the people and serve them just as much as the people are required to obey the ruler.[86] The limits of the people's obedience are defined by God (as is the ruler's). The nature of that obedience is one that is more akin to self-discipline, collective organization, and mutual responsibility and advice than to hierarchy, oppression, and violence. The same is true of *ta'ah* in marriages.

---

83.   *See* ABU ZAHRAH, *supra* note 65, at 196; *see also* AL-BARDISI, *supra* note 70, at 330–32 (providing reasons for restricting the wife's mobility); 2 AL-GHAZALI, *supra* note 14, at 58–59; 8 IBN QUDAMAH, *supra* note 65, at 129.

84.   *See, e.g.,* AL-BARDISI, *supra* note 70, at 292–93; 4 KAMAL AL-DIN AL-SIWASSI, SHARH FATH AL-QADIR 378–80 (13th cent. reprint, Egypt n.d.) (text and commentary).

85.   *See* ABU ZAHRAH, *supra* note 65, at 196; *see also* 2 AL-GHAZALI, *supra* note 14, at 58–59; 8 IBN QUDAMAH, *supra* note 65, at 129.

86.   *See* AL-HIBRI, *supra* note 13, at 11–26.

There are too many decent frightened women whose lives have been frittered away because their husbands did not "permit" them to go out or have a reasonable measure of autonomy. There are too many stories about divorces "caused" by the wife's disobedience. This unbelievable oppression is an intolerable violation of Qur'anic and international standards of human dignity. Men would never tolerate confinement by their spouses for a split second, yet Muslim women one century after another have been denied the basic human right of freedom of movement. All of this was done in the name of Islam and under the twin doctrines of ta'ah and "al-Qarar fi al-bayt" (staying put at home). The latter doctrine is also claimed to be based on the Qur'an. Later in this section, focus will be placed on one major argument (involving the concept of *qiwamah*), based on a Qur'anic *ayah* and used by patriarchal jurists for the subjugation of Muslim women.

It is relevant to mention that Muslim jurists have always recognized the validity of including certain conditions in the marriage contract.[87] These conditions tend to be protective of the woman, and some of them, such as the right of the woman to divorce her husband at will or the right to refuse to move with him away from her town, clearly limit the husband's right to ta'ah within the family. Clearly, therefore, even within traditional jurisprudence, the husband's right to ta'ah can be negotiated away. It is interesting in this regard to mention the marriage contract for the third marriage of Sukaynah, the granddaughter of the Prophet who was known for her piety and independence. Supposedly, it included conditions that would be defined by most of the Codes today as *nushuz*. For example, Sukaynah included in the contract the condition that her husband could not prohibit her from doing what she wanted.[88] She also required him not to contradict her wishes.[89] A third condition was that he may not touch another woman while married to her.[90] If such reports were accurate, then it would appear that Sukaynah transferred contractually to her husband (at least partially) the duty of obedience.

The Prophet's *sunnah* itself indicates a lack of commitment to a gender-based division of labor and hence to *ihtibas*. His wife Khadijah was a prominent business-woman. After her death, the Prophet married A'isha who became a distinguished political and religious leader. Both enjoyed the full freedom of locomotion, a fact which at several points caused A'isha problems. The Prophet himself mended his own clothes, cut meat, and performed other household chores.[91] In short, as a husband, the Prophet

---

87. ABU ZAHRAH, *supra* note 65, at 186; 4 AL-JAZIRI, *supra* note 64, at 85–89 (text and notes); MAGHNIYAH, *supra* note 64, at 301–02.

88. 16 ABU AL-FARAJ AL-ISBAHANI, KITAB AL-AGHANI 102 (9th cent. reprint, Beirut 1959). *See* 'A'ISHAH ABD AL-RAHMAN (BINT AL-SHATI'), SUKAYNAH BINT AL-HUSSAIN 106 (Egypt 1965) (listing reported conditions in Sukaynah's marriage contracts).

89. AL-ISBAHANI, *supra* note 88, at 102.

90. ABD AL-RAHMAN, *supra* note 88, at 106. Al-Mansur, the famous Abbaside statesman also entered a marriage contract which prevented him from additional marriages. KAHALAH, OMAR, AL-ZAWAJ 57 (Beirut 1977).

91. 2 AL-GHAZALI, *supra* note 14, at 354; *see also* ABU AL-HASSAN AL-NADAWI, AL-SIRAH AL-NABAWIYAH 370 (1977).

did not demand "obedience" at home. Instead, his private life was characterized by cooperation and consultation, all to the amazement of some of the men who knew about it.[92] This egalitarian model is not the basis of the Codes which have departed from this *sunnah*.

The present situation cannot be corrected by merely revising the Codes discussed in this chapter. Revision would be a good start. But much more is needed, for example, religious re-education of Muslims. Muslims need to know what is the proper Islamic position with respect to the status of women. Muslims should be informed about the corruption of Islam by authoritarian/patriarchal cultural influences. Re-education should be introduced in a well-conceived manner and synchronized with a plan to raise popular consciousness and create a new consensus.

As a first step towards righting this monumental wrong against Muslim women, women and their parents must be educated about the necessity of including in the marriage contract conditions that would protect the wife. But first, discussion will turn to the right of the woman to initiate divorce, which raises similar problems and solutions.

The Right of the Woman to Initiate Divorce

Jurists disagree on whether to give the right to initiate divorce to the wife, and those who gave her that right disagree on the form in which she may have it. But all jurists agree that it is not a right that she is entitled to automatically. In places where the right is recognized, the woman has to bargain for it at the outset. Otherwise, she has only standard traditional solutions; namely, seeking judicial action or buying her freedom from her husband through *khul'*.

The position of jurists on this issue derives to a large extent from their position on two more basic issues: (1) the Stereotype; and (2) the validity of conditions in the marriage contract. Jurists use the Stereotype to argue against giving women the right to divorce. They argue that women are by nature emotional, and hence if given that right, they might use it unadvisedly in an angry moment.[93] On the second issue, patriarchal assumptions were deeply embedded in the reasoning of jurists.

Since the marriage contract is a contract, it stands to reason that the parties should be able to negotiate its terms to reflect the kind of marital relation they would like to have. But jurists placed important limitations on agreements resulting from these negotiations. All Codes and jurisprudence permit only those conditions in the

---

92. 2 Abu Shuqqah, *supra* note 7, at 147–49, 153.

93. 4 al-Jaziri, *supra* note 64, at 370; *see also* Muhammad Abu Zahrah, al-Ahwal al-Shakhsiyah 283 (Egypt, 3d ed. 1957); al-Bardisi, *supra* note 70, at 356. Actually, one could argue that the opposite is true, namely that the male is the emotional partner who acts rashly in anger. As proof, the male is given by divine law a period of time (*'iddah*) during which he may revoke the divorce he sought and obtained. The woman has no such opportunity for retracting a *khul'* divorce once it is granted. *See* Ghandour, *supra* note 65, at 292 (discussing the importance of the husband's right to revoke a divorce that he may have initiated during a fit of anger).

contract which do not contradict the contract's goal and purposes.[94] The limitation sounds quite reasonable until one realizes that these goals and purposes were defined from an archaic patriarchal perspective that damaged the rights of women. Consequently, some perfectly legitimate conditions were declared by some jurists as unacceptable.

For example, for Malikis (and many others) a condition in the marriage contract which eliminates the husband's duty to support the wife is invalid.[95] One arguably noble reason for this position is the protection of economically dependent women who may be unable to defend their basic rights, such as the right to maintenance. Yet, an unfortunate consequence of this position is that, given the rest of the Maliki jurisprudence on this matter, the position also operates to preserve the traditional patriarchal model in which the husband supports the wife in exchange for her housework, sexual availability, and/or confinement.[96]

In today's world, the Maliki position runs afoul of the fact that regardless of their marriage contracts, many Muslim women in Maliki jurisdictions are the main (if not sole) income earners of their families.[97] To deal with this new situation, new arrangements which take into account new economic realities must be contemplated by jurists. Simply permitting the wife to work without explicit permission from her husband does not suffice. The Code cannot turn a blind eye to these new economic realities and continue to regard the male as the "boss" in his family, simply by virtue of his being male and regardless of his contributions or the lack thereof to his family.

The patriarchal treatment of conditions in the marriage contract creates legal problems in at least two different ways. Problems may arise when a party inadvertently includes in its contract a void condition. They may also arise from a willful violation of a perfectly valid condition. In addition to the wife's right to divorce, among the most commonly discussed conditions are those that prohibit the husband from taking a second wife and from moving the wife away from her hometown.

Hanafis recognize the validity of a condition in the marriage contract that gives the wife the right to divorce the husband at will.[98] While Hanafis, like other jurists, regard the right to divorce as residing initially with the husband, they recognize the

---

94. ABU ZAHRAH, *supra* note 93, at 159; 6 AL-SHAWKANI, *supra* note 68, at 281.

95. 4 AL-JAZIRI, *supra* note 64, at 88. KAWTHAR KAMEL 'ALI, SHURUT 'AQD AL-ZAWAJ FI AL-SHAR-I'AH AL-ISLAMIYAH 71 (Cairo 1979).

96. It is important to note here that several major jurists do not consider housework as a wifely duty. Their view is that marriage is about companionship not service. ABU ZAHRAH, *supra* note 65, at 197 (reporting that Abu Hanifah, Malik and al-Shafi'i espouse the view that wives have no duty to perform housework). He also mentions other jurists, including himself, who disagree with this view. *Id.*

97. MA'ADI ZAINAB, AL-'USRAH AL-MAGHRIBIYAH BAYN AL-KHITAB AL-SHAR'I WA AL-KHITAB AL-SHA'BI 124–37 (1988).

98. 1 AL-KHAMLISHI, *supra* note 67, at 322. 4 AL-JAZIRI, *supra* note 64, at 85. GHANDOUR, *supra* note 65, at 344–50; 2 AL-DARDIR, *supra* note 78, at 593–603; 8 IBN QUDAMAH, *supra* note 65, at 287–303.

valid transfer of that right (*tafwid*) to the wife as a result of contract negotiations.[99] Consequently, they readily honor such a condition to the fullest and do not permit the husband to withdraw the transfer after marriage.[100]

Hanafis consider the condition prohibiting the husband from taking another wife null and void because it is viewed as encroaching upon a legitimate right of the husband.[101] Hanafis have reached this conclusion despite the various historical precedents to the contrary, such as that of Prophet's refusal to allow his son-in-law to take a second wife. Therefore, a wife who includes this condition in her marriage contract must make sure that she is not in a Hanafi jurisdiction. Otherwise, the condition is void, the husband may violate it with impunity, the marriage contract remains valid, and she has no recourse other than *khul'* or judicial divorce. Fortunately, several Codes in Hanafi jurisdictions have parted company with Hanafi jurisprudence on this point.[102]

Where the violation relates to a valid condition (other than a valid right to divorce), the Hanafi remedy is a modest monetary one equaling the reduction in the wife's dowry resulting from the inclusion of the violated condition.[103] This remedy, as well as the Hanafi treatment of marriage contract conditions in general, leads one to conclude that Hanafis did not seriously consider all of the needs and rights of women in this area. Recognizing that conditions are usually introduced into a standard marriage contract in order to protect the wife's rights, the Hanafi attitude towards such conditions appears highly patriarchal. The Hanafi view is also contrary to the Prophet's position ranking promises (conditions) in the marriage contract highest among all types of promises and urged their fulfillment.[104] Only the Hanbali school follows carefully the Prophet's pronouncement on this matter.[105]

Hanafis disagree on whether a prohibition against relocating the wife is binding, but they do accept the condition giving the wife the right to divorce. Their justification is that women must be provided with an inducement to marry. It appears therefore that many Hanafi women were hesitant to marry if they were not given a valid right to divorce. In response, jurists recognized the related condition as valid, but not without introducing into the situation an element of complication. They accepted the condition as valid only in cases where it was negotiated as part of the marriage contract or after its execution upon a request initiated by the prospective wife.[106]

---

99.   1 AL-KHAMLISHI, *supra* note 67, at 322; GHANDOUR, *supra* note 65, at 349.

100.   1 AL-KHAMLISHI, *supra* note 67, at 322.

101.   *See* 7 IBN QUDAMAH, *supra* note 65, at 448–49; K. 'Ali, *supra* note 95, at 71–72.

102.   *See, e.g.*, The Egyptian Code, *supra* note 27, Law No. 25 (1929) (amended 1985), Art. 2 cl. 11 (repeated); *see also* The Jordanian Code, *supra* note 29, Ch. 3, Art. 19 (1).

103.   AL-BARDISI, *supra* note 70, at 270. *See also* 1 MUHAMMAD IBN YAHYA IBN AL-MUTAHHAR, AHKAM AL-AHWAL AL-SHAKHSIYAH MIN FIQH AL-SHARI'AH AL-ISLAMIYAH (2 vols.)157 (Beirut 1985); 6 AL-SHAWKANI, *supra* note 68, at 280–81.

104.   ABU ZAHRAH, *supra* note 65, at 187.

105.   *See id.* at 186–87; *see also* 7 IBN QUDAMAH, *supra* note 65, at 448–49.

106.   4 AL-JAZIRI, *supra* note 64, at 85 n.1; 1 AL-KHAMLISHI, *supra* note 67, at 322.

Malikis also recognize the validity of a condition giving the wife the right to divorce, but they complicate that right. Among other things, the validity of the right appears to depend upon the form through which it was transferred.[107] Furthermore, the wife may lose that right inadvertently, if she willingly engages in sexual intercourse with her husband or fails to utilize her right to divorce in a timely fashion.[108] She may also lose it as a result of unilateral unsolicited judicial action.[109] Malikis recognize the validity of other conditions, such as the condition prohibiting the husband from taking a second wife and from relocating the wife.[110]

In short, under traditional jurisprudence which relies on the Stereotype, Muslim women do not have an unfettered right to divorce, similar to that of their husbands. Furthermore, even in jurisdictions that recognize the validity of a negotiated right to divorce, social pressures make it almost impossible for a proud patriarchal male to accept this condition in his marriage contract. Finally, when some women successfully acquire the right to divorce, it can be inadvertently lost in some jurisdictions. In the absence of a valid right to divorce, the wife has to resort to courts or to the method of *khul'* to exit her marriage. Under this method as practiced today, the wife obtains the consent of the husband to the divorce by paying him a sum of money. The husband may refuse to grant his consent at any price or demand a very high price for his consent. As a result, the wife may be unable to regain her liberty even through *khul'*.

Originally, *khul'* was meant to be an equitable solution. According to Prophetic precedent, a woman who does not like her husband through no fault of his own has the option of leaving him, so long as she returns to him the *mahr* (usually translated as dowry) he gave her. The actual story goes as follows: a woman developed great dislike for her husband, through no fault of his own. She went to the Prophet seeking a way out of the marriage. The Prophet instructed her to return to the man his *mahr* (in this case, a garden). She was so pleased by the prospect of ending the marriage that she offered to give the husband other things as well. The Prophet said: "As for the garden, yes. As for more, no."[111]

The idea was that it would be unfair for the wife who decides to leave her husband through no fault of his own to do so and take the *mahr* as well without having fulfilled her part of the contract. Yet, today, as a result of centuries of patriarchal jurisprudence, women are expected to pay more than their *mahr* in order to obtain divorce by *khul'*. The situation has become so serious that at times it has resembled

---

107. This issue is discussed in great detail in Azizah al-Hibri, *Marriage Laws in Muslim Countries*, 4 INT'L REV. COMP. PUB. POL'Y 227, 235 (1992). *Also see* 1 AL-KHAMLISHI, *supra* note 67, at 323–28.

108. 1 AL-KHAMLISHI, *supra* note 67, at 323–24.

109. al-Hibri, *supra* note 107, at 235; 1 AL-KHAMLISHI, *supra* note 67, at 323–24.

110. 4 AL-JAZIRI, *supra* note 64, at 88; al-Hibri, *supra* note 107, at 236; *cf.* MUHAMMAD BIN JUZAYY, QAWANIN AL-AHKAM AL-SHAR'IYAH 243 (14th cent. reprint, Beirut 1979) (distinguishing among the different ways by which the condition is introduced into the marriage contract and the related consequences).

111. 8 IBN QUDAMAH, *supra* note 65, at 173–75, 182–83.

blackmail.[112] This state of affairs is the direct result of the fact that jurists made the husband's consent necessary to the *khul'* process. Obviously, this condition does not have strong jurisprudential support and is ignored in some jurisdictions, such as Pakistan.[113] All these facts point to the corruption of Islamic values and women's rights by Patriarchy. To further bolster this thesis, one major traditional claim, namely that all these laws and the Stereotype are rooted in the Qur'an and not in patriarchal tradition, is addressed.

THE QUR'ANIC VIEW OF GENDER RELATIONS

Many good Muslim women and men will disagree in good faith with arguments presented in this chapter. This disagreement is not surprising; even the views of the best Muslim jurists were contested by some of their contemporaries. But there is also the possibility of diminishing or eliminating some areas of disagreement; otherwise, the science of logical argumentation would be futile. The best method for resolving disagreements among Muslims is the one suggested by the Qur'an itself. The Qur'an clearly states that if believers disagree among themselves on a matter, they should seek the answer in the Qur'an and the *sunnah* of the prophet.[114] This Qur'anic advice is followed here. Because of space limitations, however, concentration will be placed on only part of one *ayah*, leaving the treatment of the remaining parts of the *ayah*, other *ayahs* and related *hadith* for the future. This means that any systematic disagreements will not be settled by this chapter, but hopefully some progress towards a proper resolution will occur.

All Muslims agree that the Qur'an is rich with meaning. Furthermore, the structure of Qur'anic truth is at once both absolute and dialectical. It is absolute in so far as it is the Word of God. It is dialectical because our developing human consciousness grasps that absolute truth in a dialectical manner which grows as we grow in our understanding. The Qur'an itself recognizes this human limitation in its methodology. It was revealed gradually, and some of its prohibitions (such as drinking alcohol) were also imposed gradually. Other prohibitions and fundamental changes (like those relating to women and slaves) were introduced so as to achieve their final results over a period of time. This part of Qur'anic philosophy is not only based on the principle of gradualism in social change but also on the divine wisdom of fostering human democracy, i.e., the society's collective ability to make its own choices.[115] Otherwise, God would have initially denied us all freedom of choice and imposed all truths upon

---

112. *See* 2 MUHAMAD RASHID RIDHA, TAFSIR AL-QUR'AN AL-HAKIM (TAFSIR AL-MANAR) (12 vols.) 435 (Beirut 1947) (describing abuses of the Khul' process by husbands).

113. *See* KEITH HODKINSON, MUSLIM FAMILY LAW: A SOURCEBOOK 285–287 (London 1984) (relating criticism of the consent requirement by a Pakistani court). *See also* AL-KHAMLISHI, *supra* note 67, at 335 (describing this point).

114. QUR'AN 4:59. Where English Qur'anic translations were used in this chapter, the author relied primarily on the translation of A. YUSUF ALI, THE HOLY QUR'AN: TEXT, TRANSLATION AND COMMENTARY (1983). The author has modified this translation at times to make it more precise.

115. al-Hibri, *supra* note 13, at 9–10.

us. This result, however, would be contrary to the Qur'anic assertion that there is no compulsion in matters of religion.[116]

For example, the Qur'an did not prohibit slavery outright in a world in which slavery was rampant and economically very significant. Instead, it provided rules and principles which if followed by pious Muslims carefully, would have totally eliminated slavery in a generation or two. The fact that it took the world in general, and Muslims in particular, many centuries to achieve the Islamic ideal of eliminating slavery only illustrates how deeply rooted that idea was in the world community, and how extensive the changes necessary for achieving it were.

Therefore, it is important to understand the Qur'anic worldview in order to try and capture those absolute truths in it that we need to approximate in our present world. The central concept in the Qur'an is that of *Tawhid*, i.e., that there is only *one* supreme being and that being is God. This concept permeates the whole Qur'an. For our present purposes, it is instructive to approach it from the perspective provided by the story of the fall of Iblis (Satan).[117] According to the Qur'an, Iblis's fall from grace was the result of his vanity. He was the only one who refused to obey God's order to bow to Adam. Iblis objected to God, saying: "I am better than him; you created me from fire and created him from clay."[118] This statement captured the essence of Satanic logic which is based on feelings of such vanity and superiority that it posits (in the minds of the vain) a layer of demi-gods between God and his creatures. These demigods are so arrogant and self-centered that they disobey God in order to impose their will and preserve their vanity. In one stroke they commit both *shirk* (denial of *tawhid*) and disobedience.[119]

Muslims who are vain and arrogant, whether for individual, racial, economic or gender-related reasons, engage in Satanic logic. The Qur'an states clearly and repeatedly that we were all created from the same *nafs* (soul).[120] In particular, the very first *ayah* in *surat al-Nisa'* states:

> "O people! reverence God (show piety towards God) who created you from one *nafs* and created from her (the *nafs*) her mate and spread from them many men and women; and reverence God, through whom you demand your mutual rights, and the wombs (that bore you), (for) God watches you."[121]

The question presented by this *ayah* is this: if all humans are made of the same *nafs*, why did God create so many differences among us? The Qur'an again provides us with answers. On the question of race and ethnicity, it tells us that we were created as different tribes and nations, so that we may become acquainted with each other

---

116. QUR'AN 2:256.

117. The significance of this story was first brought to the author's attention by Sheikh Hassan Khalid, the late Mufti of Lebanon, may God rest his soul in peace.

118. QUR'AN 7:12.

119. *See* 3 AL-GHAZALI, *supra* note 14, at 326–43.

120. QUR'AN 4:1, 6:98, 7:189.

121. *Id.* 4:1.

(i.e., to enjoy each other's differences and company, or to put it differently, variety is the spice of life).[122] On the question of gender, the Qur'an informs us in *surat al-Rum* that God created for us from our *anfus* (plural of *nafs*) mates *so that we may find tranquillity with them*, and God put affection and mercy between us.[123] "That," the Qur'an adds, "is a sign for those who ponder."[124] (This *ayah* will be referred to as the Equality Principle.) This *ayah* on gender relations is repeated in various forms in the Qur'an.[125] Consequently, one may justifiably conclude that it articulates a basic general principle about proper gender relations; namely, that they are relations between mates created from the same *nafs*, which are intended to provide these mates with tranquillity and are to be characterized by affection and mercy. Such relations leave no room for Satanic hierarchies which result only in strife, subordination, and oppression.[126]

One *ayah* appears to conflict with the Equality Principle. It is a highly controversial *ayah* which is often cited by some secular feminists as proof that Islam is structurally patriarchal. Because of this challenge, the first (and most cited) part of this *ayah* is addressed here. Again, the treatment can only be rudimentary because of space limitations. But hopefully this treatment would suffice to indicate the line of thought that needs to be adopted in explaining the rest of the *ayah* and other similar *ayahs* that are often cited in discussing this issue.

The first part of the 34th *ayah* of *surat al-Nisa'* (which will be referred to as the Complex Phrase) starts with the following statement, which has often been used to justify male dominance:

> (i) Men are *qawwamun* over women *bima* God *faddala* some of them over others, and *bima* they spend of their own money. . . .

A modern translation of this phrase is the following:

> (ii) Men are the *protectors and maintainers* of women, because God has *given the one more (strength) than the other*, and because they support them from their means.[127]

Translation (i) was intentionally left partial, because a full translation would unilaterally resolve important issues left open by the original Arabic language. For this reason, where the original Arabic meaning was critical but undetermined, the Arabic

---

122. *Id.* 49:13.

123. *Id.* 30:21.

124. *Id.* 30:21

125. *See, e.g., id.* 35:11, 39:6; *see also supra* note 111. FARIDA BENNANI, TAQSIM AL-'AMAL BAYN AL-ZAWJAYN 27–28 (Marakesh 1992). Bennani, a Moroccan Muslim, who is also a law professor, argues in this award winning book that the Qur'an clearly states in several places that men and women are equal intellectually as well as physically. She also relates *hadiths* to the same effect, and cites other evidence.

126. BENNANI, *supra* note 125, at 13–14 (noting that Muslim patriarchal societies used the concept of *qiwama* to create a hierarchical structure within the family, headed by the husband). She also argues that such hierarchy contradicts the basic principle of gender equality revealed in the Qur'an. *Id.* at 27–28.

127. ALI, *supra* note 114, at 190.

word was retained. Because Translation (ii) settles all open issues, it is problematic. The Arabic words in (i) will now be examined.

The word *qawwam* (singular of *qawwamun*) has been interpreted variously to mean "head," "boss," "leader," "protector," or even "manager," "guide," and "advisor." Meanings with strict hierarchical significance tend to be found in older commentaries. Part of the reason for this discrepancy is rooted in the relational meaning of the word. One old Arabic dictionary defines the related word "*qiyam*," specifically in the context of the ayah, as "having the meaning of preservation and betterment."[128] Another old dictionary defines the related word "*qayyim*" as: "one who manages the people's affairs, leads, and straightens them out."[129] Both meanings, while not necessarily hierarchical, are open to hierarchical authoritarian interpretations. So, where a society was authoritarian, it made sense that interpreters colored these meanings with their own authoritarian perspective.[130] As the world changed, modern interpreters tried to regain for the word its original meaning. Given my bias in favor of democracy, the less hierarchical interpretations of the word have been used.

The verb "*faddala*" in the Complex Phrase is usually translated as meaning "being superior."[131] Linguistically, "*faddala*" is explained as having a distinction, a preferred difference over another, i.e., a feature or ability the other lacks.[132] At this point, the reader should resist concluding prematurely that the Qur'an therefore states that men and women are essentially different, and that the man is superior. That is in fact the patriarchal conclusion. Later discussion will place the word "*faddala*" in the Complex Phrase in its proper context and provide its full accurate meaning.

The word "*bima*" is the most complex in this passage. Linguistically, it is composed of two parts: "*bi*" and "*ma.*" The first is a connector with more than one meaning. Among the most prevalent meanings of "*bi*" are: (a) one that conveys a relation

---

128. 11 MUHAMMAD IBN MANTHUR, LISAN AL-'ARAB (18 vols.) 355 (12th cent. reprint, Beirut 1992).

129. 5 ABI ABDUL RAHMAN AL-FARAHIDI, KITAB AL-AYN (8 vols.) 232 (8th cent. reprint, Beirut 1988).

130. *See, e.g.*, 2 RIDHA, *supra* note 112, at 380; 5 RIDHA, *supra* note 112, at 67–70; *see also* MUHAMMAD ABDUL HAMID, AL-AHWAL AL-SHAKHSIYAH FI AL-SHARI'AH AL-ISLAMIYAH 122 (Cairo 1966); 4 AL-TABARI, *supra* note 63, at 60 (calling men "princes" over women).

131. *See, e.g.*, 5 RIDHA, *supra* note 112, at 67; GHANDOUR, *supra* note 65, at 235–36.

132. 10 IBN MANTHUR, *supra* note 128, at 280. Linguistically, the root verb "*fadl*" refers to "the opposite of deficiency," and "*fudalah*" means remnant. *See* 7 AL-FARAHIDI, *supra* note 129, at 43; IBN MANTHUR, *supra* note 128, at 281. Consequently, a secondary meaning of the word reduces "*faddala*" to mere difference, without ascribing any value to that difference. As a result of this secondary meaning, the science of differential equations is called in many Arab universities "'*ilm al-tafadul,*" i.e., the science of difference. This meaning is not linguistically appropriate in the context under discussion. The appropriate meaning here is the primary one of having some distinction, quality or attribute the other does not have. But as we shall see later, this is not a reference to male superiority over women. Rather it is one of two requisite characteristics that a male must satisfy before he can even attempt to advise a woman.

of causality (*sababiyah* or *'illiyah*), (b) one which conveys circumstantiality (*tharfiyah*), and (c) one which conveys a quantity which is less than all (*tab'idh*).[133] "*Ma*" acts here as a pure connector (*mawsuliyah*) but may have at times a more enhanced meaning (indicating a *masdar*).[134] It is used to refer to inanimate objects only.[135]

The critical meaning then of "*bima*" revolves mostly around the "*bi*" segment. As a result, "*bima*" could mean: (a) "because," (b) "in circumstances where," and (c) "in that which," a meaning that indicates *tab'idh*, i.e., a portion or a part of, but not the whole.

The above translation can now be revised to read:

(iii) Men are [advisors/ providers of guidance] to women [because/ in circumstances where/ in that which] God made some of them different from some others and [because/in circumstances where/ in that which] they spend of their own money. . . .

Discussion will now turn to the apparent conflict between the Equality Principle and the Complex Phrase. A basic rule of Islamic jurisprudence is the following: where *ayahs* appear to conflict, they must be carefully studied in search of a meaning that makes them consistent with each other.[136] Another basic rule states that one way to resolve apparent conflict between *ayahs* is to check the scope of each.[137] If one is general and the other is particular, then the second may be an exception to or a carve-out from the first.

Here, the Qur'anic phrase which articulates the Equality Principle is clearly general. It has no qualifiers, provisos, or carve-outs. It is also repeated in similar forms several other times in the Qur'an.[138] The *ayah* which articulates the Complex Phrase is totally different in structure. In stating what appears to be a general statement, namely that "men are *qawwamun* over women," the phrase immediately provides an explanation. The explanation acts as a limitation upon the apparently general statement (*takhsis* of the *'aam*), by specifying the reasons (*'illahs*) or circumstances (as indicated by the various meanings of "*bima*") that would entitle a male to be *qawwam*.[139] These include differences between some males and some females.[140]

---

133. These meanings can be found in a regular Arabic dictionary. *See, e.g.,* MUHAMMAD ISBIR AND BILAL JUNAIDI, AL-SHAMIL 235–36 (Beirut 1981). *See also* 1 FAKHR AL-DIN AL-RAZI, AL-MAHSUL FI 'ILM USUL AL-FIQH (6 VOLS.) 379, 381, n.3 (12th cent., Beirut 1992) (for the meaning of "*tab'idh*").

134. ISBIR AND JUNAIDI, *supra* note 133, at 764. *See also infra* note 132 and accompanying text.

135. *See, e.g.,* 2 AL-RAZI, *supra* note 133, at 333–34.

136. 2 AL-ZUHAYLI, *supra* note 9, at 1177, 1182–83.

137. *Id.*

138. *See supra* note 120.

139. SHALABI, *supra* note 8, at 428–29, 432–64.

140. BENNANI, *supra* note 125, at 35–36. Bennani and others point out that the structure of the phrase permits the interpretation that the differences referred to there are not differences between men and women, but rather between men and other men. She argues that such differences are based on the man's ability to maintain his family.

The elements of this limitation are two. The first part of (iii), namely that men are *qawwamun* over women, is a general statement. But it is operative only where God has endowed a male (in a certain circumstance or at a certain time) with a feature, ability, or characteristic that a particular woman lacks (and presumably needs in that circumstance or at that time) *and* where that male is maintaining that particular woman. Only under *both* of these conditions may the man presume to offer guidance or advice to the woman. The first element is important for explaining why the advisory role of the male is acceptable at all, the second element is important for limiting the advisory role to the man who is already taking care of the woman as her provider (if the woman is indeed being provided for). Otherwise, she may be faced with droves of men who want to provide unsolicited advice (*fudhuliyun*).

The Qur'an clearly indicates that not all men satisfy both conditions. For one, as the above-mentioned meaning of "*bima*" indicates, the reference in the *ayah* is to a part of a group, but not the whole. The remaining text of the *ayah* reinforces this fact when it explicitly uses the word "*ba'dhuhum*," which means "some." More precisely, the remainder of the phrase speaks of "some" whom God *faddala* over "some" others.[141] (Note that the broad linguistic Qur'anic construction bears also the interpretation that God "*faddala*" some men over some other men and women and "*faddalah*" some women over some men and other women.) This explicit use of "*ba'dhuhum*" in the second part of the phrase establishes the *tab'idhi* meaning of the whole phrase, since *tab'idh* was indicated at least once and perhaps twice in the Complex Phrase.

In other words, the Qur'an was describing (and not recommending) in this *ayah* a situation akin to the traditional one existing at the time, where some women were financially dependent. In those circumstances, the *ayah* informs us, God gave the man supporting her the responsibility (*taklif*, not privilege) of offering the woman guidance and advice in those areas in which he happens to be more qualified or experienced.[142] The woman, however, is entitled to reject both (otherwise the advisory role is no longer advisory).

Although this author's interpretation differs from that offered by traditional jurists, it is based on traditional religious and linguistic sources. In that sense, it does not constitute a departure from tradition. It *is* a traditional interpretation.[143] As proof,

---

141. It is interesting in this regard to examine the interpretation of RIDHA, 5 RIDHA, *supra* note 112, at 68, in which he argues that, in this case, "some" means "all."

142. BENNANI, *supra* note 125, at 35, makes a similar point.

143. A recent article referred to this author as a "progressive purist" legal scholar. Lino J. Lauro and Peter A. Samuelson, 37 HARV. INT'L L.J. 65, at 127, 131(1996). The article defined a "purist" methodology as one which "seeks to overcome defects in an existing system through wholesale change or replacement." *Id.* at 66. As this and other articles illustrate, my work is solidly based on traditional Islamic jurisprudence. It engages in careful analysis of this jurisprudence in order to separate its cultural dimension from the religious one. In using this approach, I am careful to seek change only to the extent it is religiously justifiable and necessary for safeguarding the rights of Muslim women. I reject a wholesale change partly for the reasons mentioned herein in the section entitled "The Importance of an Internal Critique." Lauro and Samuelson appear to concur with

a similar (but not identical) interpretation of *"bima"* offered by the famous thirteenth century jurist al-Razi is offered.[144]

Al-Razi focused on the meaning of *"bima"* in another Qur'anic phrase directly following the Complex Phrase in the same *ayah*. The other phrase states that: "righteous women are *qanitat* and guard *al-gaib bima* God guarded."[145]

The noun *"Qunut,"* from which the adjective *"qanitat"* is derived, refers usually to the act of being devoutly obedient to God. Because *"qanitat"* means "women who exhibit *'qunut,'"* al-Razi, among other jurists, concluded that the obedience of righteous women referred to here must be obedience to their husbands as well as to God.[146]

Similarly, the word *"al-gaib"* usually refers to the unknown, i.e., the future which only God knows. But again, because the phrase spoke exclusively of women, the word *"al-gaib"* was interpreted as referring to absent husbands, and the relevant part of the above phrase was interpreted as referring to the wife's duty to guard her chastity and her husband's property in his absence.[147]

Al-Razi argued that *"bima"* in the phrase *"bima"* God guarded" had one of the following two meanings:

(1) *"Bima"* may mean "that which," where *"ma"* acts as a pure connector.

Al-Razi then explained that given this meaning of *"bima,"* the phrase means that women are to guard the husband's rights *in exchange for that which* God guarded of women's rights against their husbands.[148]

Notice that al-Razi's interpretation of *"bima"* does more than merely connect the two parts of the phrase. As he himself observes, it expresses also causality (*sababiyah*) between them through the use of the locution "in exchange for."

(2) *"Bima"* may be *masdariyah*.

Under this category of Arabic grammar, the phrase means either "women guard their husband's rights *because* (*sababiyah*) God helps women succeed in their effort (*bi tawfiq il-lah*)" or "women guard their husband's rights *because* (circumstantial)

---

my reasoning in this section when they point out that many progressive purists "have presented a false dilemma to many devout Muslims, who feel they must choose between God and modernization." *Id.* at 127. My analysis in this article presents no such dilemma. Hence, I do not satisfy the definition of "progressive purist."

144. Those familiar with Arabic and the exact nature of the words used in the Qur'an should reflect on how the meaning of the phrase would have changed had the word *"lima"* been used instead of *"bima."* It is significant that it was not.

145. QUR'AN 4:34.

146. *See, e.g.,* 10 AL-RAZI, *supra* note 133, at 92.

147. *Id.*

148. *Id.*

they guard (i.e., obey) God's orders by obeying their husbands.[149] Thus al-Razi too provides at least two meanings of *"bima"* in this context, one of causality and another of circumstantiality.

In addition to al-Razi, analysis here is supported by several standard dictionaries.[150] In other words, there is nothing extraordinary about the linguistic analysis provided here for *"bima"* in the Complex Phrase. The problem arises only when this analysis is taken seriously and an interpretation is based on it. At that point, the fundamentally limiting scope of the Complex Phrase (whether causal, circumstantial or *tab'idhi*) becomes apparent, a matter which traditional jurists ignored or dismissed.[151]

Our linguistic analysis shows that the Complex Phrase makes perfect sense. Indeed, if our conclusion is correct, the phrase about the *qiwamah* (state of being *qawwam*) of certain women over certain men under similarly specified conditions would also make sense from the theoretical point of view. Such a phrase, however, would not have addressed any existing conditions in need of limitation at the time of revelation. Nevertheless, when at one point it became necessary to speak of a symmetrical responsibility for guidance and protection between men and women, the Qur'an did not hesitate. It said, of male and female believers, that some of them are *wali*'s of some of the other male and female believers.[152] Thus, it is important to emphasize this *ayah* as a suitable foundation for gender relations in today's Muslim societies.

The Complex Phrase was revealed in an authoritarian/patriarchal society that the Prophet was attempting to civilize and democratize. Consequently, it should be viewed for what it really is. It is a *limitation* on men preventing them from assuming automatically (as many did then) oppressive authoritarian roles with respect to women.[153] At most, the Complex Phrase tells them that they can guide and advise only these women they support financially and then only when certain conditions obtain. The rest of the *ayah* does not change this analysis if one takes a fresh non-patriarchal look at it.[154]

This result is also consistent with the Hanafi and Maliki views that a woman may include in her marriage contract conditions that would give her greater rights

---

149. *Id.*; 4 AL-TABARI, *supra* note 63, at 61–63, has a somewhat similar explanation.

150. *See supra* notes 133–134.

151. *See supra* notes 126, 141.

152. QUR'AN 9:71.

153. *See supra* note 130 and accompanying text.

154. The author hopes to analyze the rest of the *ayah* and related concepts, such as *wilayat al-ta'dib*, in a series of subsequent articles. It is also hoped that the *hadiths* usually quoted in support of the subordination of women will also be addressed. For the purposes of the arguments made in this chapter, it is important to keep in mind that the traditional approach is to discard or reinterpret *hadiths* that appear to contradict an *ayah* in the Qur'an.

and freedoms within the marriage, including the right to divorce.[155] Such conditions usually modify the traditional balance within the family in favor of the wife, thus detracting from the male's "superiority" or authority. For this reason, they are widely resisted, and when accepted are kept secret. Thus, when a female member of the Jordanian parliament recently divorced her husband, many Jordanians were shocked and some were even scandalized.[156] The woman, Tujan al-Faisal, had included in her marriage contract a condition which gave her the right to divorce. When she finally exercised that condition, many (including women) argued that the condition was either invalid, "unnatural," or acceptable only to inferior men.[157]

Despite its limiting structure, the Complex Phrase has been misused by traditional jurists to build an edifice of patriarchal oppression within the family.[158] This structure has destroyed for many women all tranquillity and imposed upon them obedience and loss of basic liberties of such a nature and to such an extent as to make them wards, virtual slaves, and prisoners in their own homes and marriages.[159] Traditional jurisprudence ignored totally the limitation aspect of the phrase and instead generalized it as a right and a distinction belonging to *all* men, even in cases where God clearly favored some women over some men with brains, skills, wealth, and other gifts.[160]

This analysis sheds new light on the traditional insistence that the husband *must* maintain the wife (so that any condition in the marriage contract to the contrary would be void). It reveals that a husband who does not maintain his wife would lack one of the two prerequisites necessary for *qiwamah* (regardless of the meaning of that word), and hence would not be *qawwam*.[161] The traditional prohibition against women entering the workforce can also be viewed in the same light, as perpetuating their financial dependence on men.

In other words, the traditional approach of jurists towards the issue of *qiwamah* of men was two-pronged. One prong was based on the argument that God had favored all men over all women by endowing them with more brains and brawn. This sexist argument allowed the jurists to view the first part of the two conditions in the Complex

---

155. *See supra* notes 98–100, 107–110 and related text.

156. *See* Sᴀʏɪᴅᴀᴛʏ Mᴀɢᴀᴢɪɴᴇ, June 29–July 5, 1996, at 90–92 (reporting this incident).

157. *Id.*

158. Bᴇɴɴᴀɴɪ, *supra* note 125, at 14–17 (pointing out that the basis of that edifice was the division of labor within the family). The division of labor was in turn justified by the Stereotype.

159. *See, e.g.*, ᴀʟ-Bᴀʀᴅɪsɪ, *supra* note 70, at 327–37. *See also* 8 Iʙɴ Quᴅᴀᴍᴀʜ, *supra* note 65, at 129.

160. *See, e.g.*, 5 Aʙu Sʜuǫǫᴀʜ, *supra* note 7, at 100; *supra* notes 129–130 and related text. *See also* the discussion by 2 Rɪᴅʜᴀ, *supra* note 112, at 380 (arguing that men are more deserving of the position of "head of the family" than women, because men are better at recognizing the interest of the family, and more capable of pursuing such interest with their influence and money); Bᴇɴɴᴀɴɪ, *supra* note 125, at 12–42 (debunking these claims as inconsistent with the Qur'an).

161. For the significance of this point, *see* discussion of 1 ᴀʟ-Kʜᴀᴍʟɪsʜɪ, *supra* note 67, at 231–32.

Phrase as automatically satisfied.[162] The other prong sought to secure the woman's financial dependence. So jurists confined the woman to her home, thus banning her from public life and from any real possibility of providing for herself (unless she was already independently wealthy). All this was done despite the fact that all jurists recognized that Islam preserved for the woman her financial independence and that early Muslim women were business leaders in their society.[163]

Traditional jurists not only espoused the patriarchal model, but they actively worked at making it a universal reality by passing restrictive laws which were highly detrimental to women. They utilized the Stereotype and their legal power to assert the automatic *qiwamah* of all men.[164] This unjust approach defeated the limiting purpose of the Complex Phrase. Their interpretation of the Complex Phrase was based on a patriarchally biased interpretation of that *ayah*, an oppressive behavior toward women, and the supplementation of Qur'anic law with a stereotype that harbored a deep contradiction with the Qur'anic Equality Principle as stated in several *ayahs*. Consequently, thoughtful Muslims should no longer accept that interpretation; Muslim women must rediscover the truth of the Qur'anic Equality Principle in order to achieve liberation and freedom without guilt.

To be able to reach this challenging goal, Muslim women must formulate a strategy for change. In this strategy, the dramatic increase in the number of women seeking legal and religious education must rank very high. Therefore, the discussion will turn now to an assessment of such a demand from an Islamic point of view.

THE RIGHT TO EQUAL EDUCATION

Introduction

The Platform for Action, adopted by the Fourth World Conference on Women, on September 15, 1995, contains a special section on education and the training of women in the chapter entitled "Strategic Objectives and Actions."[165] The section declares that "[e]ducation is a human right." It also lists several specific strategic objectives, including the following:

---

162. *See, e.g.,* 2 MUHAMMAD AKLAH, NITHAM AL-USRAH FI AL-ISLAM (3 vols.) 17–20 (Amman 1983); GHANDOUR, *supra* note 65, at 235; AL-BARDISI, *supra* note 70, at 327 *See also supra* notes 129–130 and related text.

163. MAHMASSANI, *supra* note 16, at 495; ABD AL-HAMID, *supra* note 130, at 127.

164. BENNANI, *supra* note 125, at 25 (alluding to this point when she wonders whether present gender differences were not artificially produced by patriarchal manipulation of the rules and laws of society and the family). *See* FATIMAH NASIF, HUQUQ QL-MAR'AH WA WAJIBATUHA FI DAW' AL-KITAB WA AL-SUNNAH 238–40 (Jeddah 1992) where the Saudi author argues that the husband is entitled to head his family by virtue of the natural capabilities that God endowed all men with. Among her reasons for giving men the leadership status are the following two: each organizational structure must have a head, and the husband is better suited to be that head, because of his physical strength and his role as maintainer and protector.

165. UNITED NATIONS, PLATFORM FOR ACTION AND THE BEIJING DECLARATION 46–56 (1996).

(1) ensuring equal access to education;

(2) eradicating illiteracy among women; and

(3) improving women's access to vocational training, science and technology, and continuing education.[166]

A report prepared by UNICEF notes that "the Arab World has recently witnessed a substantial decrease in the educational gender gap."[167] It also states that "the most dramatic improvements in [the primary level of] female education have been achieved in Jordan, Kuwait and Bahrain . . ." and that "the gender gap has completely been closed in the U.A.E."[168] All the countries named consist of traditional Islamic societies which follow Islamic law. It would thus appear that the Platform strategic objectives on the education of women and those of Islamic societies are mutually consistent.

The report, however, points out that a gender gap does exist in Arab countries at higher levels of education due to variety of reasons, including poverty, political unrest and patriarchal attitudes. Some of these attitudes appear to be influenced by traditional religious justifications which require women to be confined to the home and the segregation of the sexes.[169] They also appear to be a rejection of Western secular education in Muslim countries and the morality it engenders.[170]

Recently, the French paper *Le Monde* reported that since a certain Islamic group of fighters in Afghanistan has taken a city, women there no longer had the right to work or attend school. In defense of the new policy, the following explanation was provided by the group: "We want to set up a government based on the precepts of the holy Koran and the Prophet's recommendations."[171] Whether the report is accurate or not, it is a fact that some Muslim male jurists have argued in the past that women should not be accorded the same education as men.[172] Their views continue to influence the decisions of some Muslim families, especially in case of scarce resources. Consequently, this chapter will next discuss the Muslim woman's right to education.

---

166. *Id.*

167. RAEDA AL-ZOUBI, ENDING GENDER DISPARITIES IN THE ARAB WORLD 16 (UNICEF 1995).

168. *Id.* at 17.

169. *See supra* notes 84–85 ; *infra* notes 210–211 and accompanying text.

170. Note for example the recent Kuwaiti decision to segregate higher education. Those who opposed the decision were branded as secularists and Western lackeys. *See, e.g., Editorial*, AL-MAJTAMA, June 25–July 1, 1996, at 9.

171. LE MONDE, Oct. 29, 1995, at 20.

172. For more on this, *see infra* notes 207–209 and accompanying text.

The Islamic Position on Education

Prophet Muhammad was illiterate. The first divine word revealed to him was the imperative: "Read."[173] The rest of the Qur'an is replete with verses that emphasize the importance of the pursuit of knowledge. For example, the Qur'an exhorts Muslims to ask God to increase their knowledge.[174] It underscores the importance of knowledge: "God elevates by several degrees the ranks of those of you who believe and those who have knowledge."[175] The Qur'an even asks rhetorically in one passage, "Say, are those two equal: those who know and those who do not know?"[176]

The Prophet himself emphasized the importance of knowledge and education. Among his most famous statements on the subject are the following: "Scholars are the heirs of prophets";[177] "all that is in heaven and earth asks God's forgiveness for a scholar";[178] "pursuit of knowledge is the duty of every Muslim";[179] and "pursue knowledge even if you have to go as far as China."[180]

Many Muslim jurists viewed education as either completely or practically compulsory, based on an *ayah* that states: "[T]hose who conceal [from people] the clear Signs which we revealed and the Guidance, after we have made it clear to people in the Book [the Qur'an], shall be cursed by God and others who [are entitled to] curse."[181]

---

173. The first part of the *surah* says in full: "Read in the name of God who Created; Created the human being from a [mere] clinging clot. Read and God is the most noble, who taught with the pen. He taught the human being what that being did not know." QUR'AN 96:1–5.

174. QUR'AN 20:114.

175. *Id.* 58:11.

176. *Id.* 39:9.

177. 1 AL-BUKHARI, *supra* note 10, at 23. 1 MUHAMMAD IBN MAJAH, SUNAN IBN MAJAH 81 (9th cent. reprint, Cairo n.d.).

178. 1 IBN MAJAH, *supra* note 177, at 81.

179. *Id.*; MUHAMMAD AL-IBRASHI, AL-TARBIYAH AL-ISLAMIYAH WA-FALSAFATUHA 53 (Cairo, 3d ed.1975). The latter reference confirms the traditional understanding of the generic word "Muslim" in the *hadith* as referring to both males and females.

180. 1 MUHAMMAD NASIR AL-DIN AL-ALBANI, SILSILAT AL-AHADITH AL-DA'IFAH WA AL-MAWDU'AH 413 *et seq.* (Beirut, 4th ed. 1977). This *hadith* is viewed by major scholars as weak, i.e., its attribution to the Prophet has not been satisfactorily established. It is, nevertheless, important to include here, if only because of the popularity of this *hadith* among the Muslim masses. Indeed, it is the first *hadith* that Muslims are likely to quote on the subject. Thus, the impact of this *hadith*, despite its weakness, has been quite significant on the consciousness of Muslims throughout the Ages. This fact makes it specially deserving of mention in this paragraph, especially because it is consistent with the Qur'an and the authenticated *hadith*.

181. QUR'AN 2:159. Many modern scholars have discussed this topic and concluded that education in Islam is compulsory. *See, e.g.*, 1 'ABD ALLAH 'ALWAN, TARBIYAT AL-AWLAD FI AL-ISLAM (2 vols.) 262 (Beirut, 6th ed. 1983); AL-IBRASHI, *supra* note 179, 53–59 (arguing that education of the public is practically compulsory in Islam); MAJID AL-KILANI, TATAWWUR MAFHUM AL-NAZARIYAH AL-TARBAWIYAH AL-ISLAMIYAH 64, 93 (Beirut, 2d ed. 1985). For an overview of the Islamic position on education and learning, *see generally* AHMAD BIN SHU'AYB AL-NASA'I, KITAB AL-'ILM (9th cent. reprint, 1993).

Imam al-Shafi'i, an important fourteenth century jurist, went so far as to argue that if the inhabitants of a province of a Muslim state unanimously agree to abandon learning, it is the duty of the ruler to force them to pursue it.[182] Al-Qabisi, a prominent tenth century jurist, noted that, if parents are financially unable to educate their children, the community must pay to educate them instead.[183]

There was more significant disagreement among Muslim jurists, however, on what scope of knowledge was required of or desirable for Muslims. Some wanted to limit the type and scope of knowledge to those prevalent during the time of the Prophet and his Companions.[184] Others found this rigid view unacceptable. For example, Abu Hanifah, a major figure in Islamic jurisprudence whose views on family law were examined above, argued that a Muslim must receive a broad education.[185] He noted that unless Muslims studied the main currents of thought in their historical epoch, they will be unable to properly distinguish truth from falsehood. For, Abu Hanifah argues, the basis for such distinction can only be knowledge and not ignorance. When criticized for advocating the learning of matters not attended to by the Companions of the Prophet, Abu Hanifah noted that the Companions lived in a different time and a different society.[186]

Ibn Taymiyah, another prominent thirteenth century scholar, also denounced narrow-mindedness and advocated openness towards learning the views of non-Muslims as well as those of other Muslims. This was especially true, he argued, in fields such as medicine and mathematics which serve the interests of the Muslim community. He defended his position by recounting a statement by the Khalifah Omar who said that Islam would be gradually undone, if a [generation of] Muslims grew up ignorant of *jahiliyah* (The Age of Ignorance which preceded Islam).[187]

Al-Ghazali, a major scholar of the eleventh century, divided knowledge into two categories: *fardh ayn* and *fardh kifayah*.[188] The first category contained the kinds of knowledge that every Muslim must acquire. Al-Ghazali noted that Muslims disagreed on what to include in this category. Some wanted to include only knowledge of the Qur'an and *sunnah*. Others wanted to include Islamic jurisprudence as well. Still others wanted to include other topics that they judged important. His solution was flexible. Al-Ghazali included in the first category (*fardh ayn*) whatever knowledge Muslims need to properly discharge all their duties in the particular society in which they live and in light of their own relevant circumstances.[189] Knowledge in the category of *fardh kifayah* is that which a community needs for its well-being, but such

---

182. AL-KILANI, *supra* note 181, at 93 (quoting al-Bayhaqi on the matter).

183. AHMAD AL-AHWANI, AL-TARBIYAH FI AL-ISLAM 101 (Cairo 1980).

184. AL-KILANI, *supra* note 181, at 88.

185. *Id.* at 89.

186. *Id.* at 88.

187. *Id.* at 205.

188. 1 AL-GHAZALI, *supra* note 14, at 20–21.

189. *Id.* at 21–22.

that the need can be satisfied by some (but not necessarily) all of the members acquiring it. Examples of such knowledge include medicine, agriculture and engineering.

The relativization of compulsory knowledge to one's social and individual context is eminently reasonable. But unfortunately, like all reasonable arguments, this argument becomes full of pitfalls when combined with patriarchal assumptions. As demonstrated later, a variant of this logic was used by al-Qabisi and others to deny women full education.

Educating Muslim Women

The Status of Muslim Women

The Islamic position on the education of women is derived from both the Islamic view of women and that of education. As mentioned earlier, the Qur'an states that all humans were created from one *nafs* and that God made from that *nafs* her mate so that he (the mate) may find tranquillity with her.[190] The Qur'an adds that God put love and mercy between the two mates.[191]

Absent from the Qur'an is the view that God created Eve from Adam's rib.[192] Also absent is the notion that Adam's fall to earth was caused by Eve and the pursuit of (carnal) knowledge. Rather, the Qur'an tells us, the fall of Adam and Eve occurred when they both succumbed to Satan's offer of immortality and disobeyed God in its pursuit.[193]

Furthermore, in Islam men and women have similar religious duties and obligations. This fact is emphasized by the Qur'an in content as well as in form. As to content, the *ayah* mentioned above says it all: "male believers and female believers, some of them are the *wali*'s (moral guides, supporters, protectors) of others."[194] As to form, the Qur'an specifically uses on numerous occasions female as well as male-gendered words in addressing women and men simultaneously. From a linguistic point of view, such dual address is unnecessary since the Arabic language, like the English language, permits the use of the male pronoun in addressing both genders collectively. So, why did the Qur'an use this dual form of address?

According to commentators, the dual form of address in the Qur'an followed a discussion between Muslim women and the Prophet.[195] The women complained that Qur'anic *ayahs* (up to that point) appeared to address men only, while Muslim women

---

190. QUR'AN 30:21.

191. *Id.*

192. Such statements do appear, however, in Islamic literature, including *hadith*. This literature must be critically reviewed in light of Qur'anic statements as well as the general spirit of the Qur'an. So far, patriarchal schools of thought have tended to accept it uncritically. *See, e.g.,* 1 ABU SHUQQAH, *supra* note 7, at 288–90.

193. QUR'AN 20:117–121.

194. *Id.* 9: 71.

195. 10 AL-TABARI, *supra* note 63, at 299–300.

were performing religious and other duties similar to those of men. Of course the women were not oblivious to the patriarchal linguistic convention. Many of these women were accomplished poets. Instead, they were making a feminist critique of language, similar to that made by the feminist movement in the United States over 1,400 years later. God responded to that critique positively and immediately. Hence the dual form of address.

An incident which further illustrates the equal and active status of women in Islam is mentioned in the Qur'an. When the Prophet was selected to lead the Muslims, women participated in that selection. They came to the Prophet as a delegation of the women of Arabia and extended to him their *bay'ah* (vote of confidence). The Qur'an refers to this event as well as to the words of the Prophet on that occasion.[196] Thus, the event is eternally recorded by divine revelation as evidence of the Muslim woman's right to participate in the electoral process.

Even more surprising is another incident in the Qur'an, which is recounted in the *surah* entitled "The Woman Who Argued."[197] Generally, translators tend to translate the title inaccurately as "The Woman Who Pleaded." In fact, the concerned woman did argue with the Prophet. She had come to him with a complaint against her husband. The Prophet's answer to her complaint did not satisfy her because it was not responsive to her needs. She therefore asked him to ask for God's revelation instead. After some insistence on her part, a revelation came to the Prophet. It was sympathetic to her plight, and the woman was thankful. So should be the Muslim women of today for whom this incident provides direct Qur'anic evidence of their standing to participate in religious dialogue even with the Prophet.

In the exciting atmosphere of building a new and equitable society, A'isha, the wife of the Prophet, became a major religious figure. After the death of the Prophet, she became a major source of *hadith*. She also became involved in the political life of the community and, on one occasion, led a group of Muslims into battle over the issue of political succession. There were also hundreds of women who were among the Companions of the Prophet. These women exhibited a real interest in the pursuit of an education.

History makes clear that the religious education of women in early Islam proceeded hand in hand with that of the men. Consequently, women would enter into debates with men about the proper interpretation of a certain verse in the Qur'an, or of a *hadith*, or the significance of a certain event. A famous incident took place in the mosque between the Khalifah (Caliph) Omar and an unknown woman.

The Khalifah wanted to place an upper limit on the amount of *mahr* a woman may demand from a man. But *mahr* was not intended as consideration for the woman's entry into a monogamous sexual relation with a man, but rather to provide the woman with a precautionary safety net which she may decide to exploit during the life of the

---

196. Qur'an 60:12.

197. *Id.* 58 (improperly translated by Ali as "The Woman Who Pleaded").

marriage or later, either by investing it or by using it to start her own business.[198] That money is to be her personal property, one to which the husband may have no access even if he were in need. Thus, the importance of this safety net cannot be over-emphasized. By arguing for placing a ceiling on the amount of the *mahr*, in order to facilitate the marriage of young men, the Khalifah was taking away from women their right to determine the size of the safety net that makes them comfortable. A woman understood the significance of this proposal and stood up in the mosque taking issue with the Khalifah. She said: "you shall not take away from us what God has given us." She then cited a passage from the Qur'an which supported her argument. The Khalifah realized his error, saying: "A woman is right and the Khalifah is wrong."[199]

This story is remarkable not only because it is an illustration of the participation of women in the religious activity of interpretation (*ijtihad*), but also because it reveals the degree of democracy in the early days of the Islamic state. The woman was unknown, but through her Qur'anic knowledge, she successfully made the Khalifah withdraw his proposal.

The literature abounds with stories of women who dialogued with men about proper Islamic practices, or the preferred interpretation of an Islamic text.[200] Women also were major reporters of *hadith*.[201] As a result, many prominent men came to them for religious education and guidance.[202] This trend continued for several centuries after the death of the Prophet. As the concept of education expanded, many women leaders appeared in the various disciplines. There were prominent female literary figures, religious leaders, doctors, judges, politicians, and teachers to name a few.

It might be useful at this point to mention some of these women. Among the outstanding literary figures are Sukaynah bint al-Hussayn, the granddaughter of the Prophet, A'isha bint Talha, and Walladah Bint al-Mustakfi. Among the physicians are Zainab, the physician of the tribe of bani Awd and Um al-Hassan, daughter of Judge Abu Ja'far al-Tanjali. Among those who actively participated in politics are Hind bint Yazid al-Ansariyah and 'Akrashah bint al-Utroush. Among the heads of state were Shajarat al-Durr of Egypt and Queen Arwa of Yemen. There were, of course, many other accomplished Muslim women in many diverse fields. Some of them have been mentioned in books but remained nameless.[203]

---

198. Jamal Nasir, The Status of Women Under Islamic Law and Under Modern Islamic Legislation 43 (1990) (arguing that *mahr* is neither a bride-price nor consideration for the marriage and quoting codes which stress this view). Ghandour, *supra* note 65, at 188–89 (arguing that *mahr* is solely the woman's property).

199. 1 al-Ghazali, *supra* note 14, at 50.

200. Ahmad Shalabi, *Al-Tarbiyah wa al-Ta'lim*, in 5 Mawsu'at al-Hadarah al-Islamiyah 342–44 (Cairo, 8th ed. 1987).

201. *Id.* at 343–44. *See also* 12 Muhammad al-Sakhawi, al-Daw' al-Lami' (12 vols.) *passim* (15th cent. reprint, Beirut n.d.).

202. Shalabi, *supra* note 200, at 343–44; 12 al-Sakhawi, *supra* note 201, *passim*.

203. al-Ibrashi, *supra* note 179, at 127–31. For a good work on Muslim women, *see* Kahalah, *supra* note 7.

Furthermore, many great male Islamic scholars were taught by great female Islamic scholars. However, unfortunately the latter's contributions were not as quickly recognized by their contemporaries or as meticulously preserved by male historians. Among the male scholars who studied under female scholars are al-Shafi'i, Ibn Khillikan, and Abu Hayyan.[204] Ibn 'Asaker, a prominent *hadith* scholar, mentioned that his female mentors and teachers numbered more than eighty.[205] Today, Muslim women are conducting research to rediscover and expand their knowledge of these once prominent Muslim female scholars.

On Education

There is general agreement among Muslim scholars that educating women is a duty, not just an option or a luxury. This view is based upon the Qur'anic statements on education mentioned above, as well as the clear words of the Prophet who stated that education is a duty (*fardh*) upon all Muslims (whether male or female).[206] It is also a consequence of the equality in religious duties and obligations incumbent upon male and female. Since understanding one's religion is *fardh ayn*, as al-Ghazali put it, Muslim women, just like men, must have full access to religious education.

Historically, the clarity of the Islamic position on the education of women served only to shift the debate from *whether* women have a right to an education to the *scope* and *mode* of a woman's rightful education. One group argued that women have the right to a full education, including higher education.[207] Others, such as al-Qabisi were not so sure. Al-Qabisi agreed that education is generally good for women, but he also wanted women to be taught only those subjects which were good and beneficial to them. He advised the females' guardians that they had a duty to steer their daughters away from subjects which may lead them "to what we fear."[208]

The issue discussed above reveals precisely the juncture at which patriarchal views of a hierarchical societal order, and the role and status of women therein, intersect. It also reveals how patriarchy presents its highly damaging conclusions in the guise of a standard application of neutral jurisprudential principles. In this instance, al-Qabisi argued that it would be "safer" not to teach girls how to write, and advocated that their curriculum be free of poetry, literature, and writing.[209] This position is sadly ironic in light of the fact that some of the most famous poets in early Islam were women.

---

204. AL-IBRASHI, *supra* note 179, at 131.

205. *Id.* at 126.

206. 1 AL-GHAZALI, *supra* note 14, at 15; 2 ABU SHUQQAH, *supra* note 7, at 41; AMINAH AHMAD HASAN, NATHARIYAT AL-TARBIYAH FI AL-QUR'AN WA TATBIQATUHA FI 'AHD AL-RASUL 'ALAYHI AL-SALAT WA AL-SALAM 188 (Cairo 1985); AL-KILANI, *supra* note 181, at 64.

207. AL-IBRASHI, *supra* note 179, at 127, 131.

208. AL-AHWANI, *supra* note 183, at 289.

209. *Id.*

The argument to restrict the female's education offered by al-Qabisi and many others, however, became popular with some Muslim fathers. Given these fathers' patriarchal attitudes, the argument provided them with a satisfactory reconciliation between their duty (discussed earlier) to educate their children, whether male or female, and their patriarchal *cultural* bias. The proposal to restrict the female's education was especially attractive because it created, during a period of entrenched patriarchy, the illusion of discharging the fathers' religious responsibilities towards their daughters. The woman's voice, as citizen and daughter, was effectively muted during this debate.

Al-Qabisi's view, however, must be placed within the context of the totality of his views on education. For example, he also listed poetry (non-romantic), arithmetic and grammar as a merely optional part of the boys' curriculum, but again, at the option of the parents. This fact illustrates how far al-Qabisi had strayed from the tradition of education in the Arabian Peninsula whose backbone was poetry, the social glue of the community.

Furthermore, al-Qabisi argued that young girls may be educated so long as they did not attend classes with older boys. Others went further, arguing that while women were entitled to an education, they should be educated at home.[210] In both cases, the arguments superimposed patriarchal cultural values on traditional jurisprudential principles. Two of the jurisprudential principles involved in advocating the separation of sexes in the classroom were those of barring pretexts and promoting public interest.[211] The latter principle is usually implied in arguments which call for the protection of the morality of Muslim women or, alternatively, for the protection of the morality of Muslim men from *the fitnah* (temptation, seduction) of women.

Therefore, looking at these arguments from a woman's perspective, the debate among the various groups of men is not really about the proper education of women in Islam. Rather, it is a *cultural* debate on the status and role of the circumstances and function of women in society.

CONCLUSION

Patriarchal reasoning and culture have influenced Islamic jurisprudence for centuries. That state of affairs is not surprising given that the interpreters were, like every one else, the products of their milieu. Furthermore, the fact that *ijtihad* was permitted to adjust to the needs of the society in which it was conducted injected that *ijtihad* with desirable features, such as flexibility and diversity, but simultaneously opened it to patriarchal influences.

Given the basic jurisprudential principle that laws change with the change of time and place, it is now time to review that jurisprudence in light of less patriarchal conditions. For example, it should be possible today to develop a jurisprudence which

---

210. AL-AHWANI, *supra* note 183, at 105; AL-IBRASHI, *supra* note 179, at 131.

211. ABU ZAHRAH, USUL AL-FIQH 268–76, 341–43 (Cairo n.d.); 2 AL-ZUHAYLI, *supra* note 9, at 873–74.

takes into account the fact that the patriarchal Stereotype of women is false and that the international community has made a commitment to women's rights. The new jurisprudence should therefore reexamine all traditional jurisprudence in light of these developments and purge it from all patriarchal cultural biases that are foreign to our lives today. The result would be truer to the Qur'anic Principle of Equality.

This argument is being made from the point of view of an American Muslim woman. A non-American Muslim woman may point out that her culture is still heavily patriarchal, regardless of any international pressures. This is true. However, for Muslims, it is God and not the international community who gave women their rights, and a good Muslim must strive to achieve the ideals of Islam which include the Principle of Equality. Muslim women can advance this point of view through a critique of jurisprudence similar to the one undertaken in this chapter. Their work will reshape the discussion in many of these countries by showing that Islam does not require, in fact is diametrically opposed to, the oppressive laws adopted there. This fact places gender issues on a new plane. Religion will no longer be accepted for justifying oppressive arguments. The real basis of such arguments, namely patriarchal culture, will be exposed. In a land where religion is of primary importance, separating Islam from the web of patriarchal culture is a major step forward.

It is important to note that some Muslim women are already busy writing on these issues in these countries.[212] Very often, however, the expressed views are timid because of the nature of the situation. American Muslim women have the advantage of addressing matters more aggressively because they are not as much at risk as their non-American sisters are for expressing these views. Non-Muslim Western women could also help in this delicate equation by respecting this Muslim feminist approach and resisting the temptation to label Islam itself as patriarchal, an act that can only make the feminist project suspect in Islamic societies.

Finally, it should be crystal clear at this point that no real progress in human rights is achievable without true democracy. Indeed, it ought to be an important part of our American feminist project to hold our government accountable for its support of dictatorial regimes in Muslim countries. It is often argued that such support is necessary to protect American interests. Samuel Huntington not withstanding, the true interest of the American people lies in long term friendships with the rest of the *people* of the world.[213]

---

212. *See* Azizah al-Hibri, *A Survey of Womanist Islamic Thought, in* THE BLACKWELL COMPANION TO FEMINIST PHILOSOPHY (1997).

213. Samuel P. Huntington, *The Clash of Civilization*, FOREIGN AFF. 22–49 (Summer 1993).

ISSUES AFFECTING MOSLEM WOMEN IN IRAN

Parvin Darabi

They differed with me over what times we are living in. It is not democracy when a man can talk about politics without anyone threatening him. Democracy is when a woman can talk of her lover without anyone killing her.

Dr. Sauad M. Al-Sabah

THE VALUE OF A WOMAN

I am a Moslem woman. I have no face, I have no identity. At age nine, based on the lunar year (a lunar year is twelve months of twenty-eight days each or 336 days) or when I am actually eight years and eight months old, I am considered an adult. Being an adult means that I have to adhere with the Islamic laws of Iran as stated below.

I have to pray five times a day, fast one month out of the year and cover myself from head to toe in yards of black fabric. I am eligible to be married and can be punished for any wrong doing. I can be incarcerated and, if needed, executed for my crimes, even political ones.

Islam's law—that Allah sent down to his messenger Muhammad—came to announce that women (exactly like men) are full human beings. Women (like men) are therefore required to follow the way appointed by Allah.

A woman (like a man) is therefore obligated with all three degrees of this religion: Islam (outward submission to Allah), *iman* (inward faith in Allah), and *ihsan* (perfection of worship of Allah).

Women have such honorable rights as obligations, but men have a (single) degree above them.

The Koran 2:228

Men are the managers of the affairs of women because Allah has preferred men over women and women were expended of their Rights.

The Koran 4:34

Islam believes and promotes only one relationship between male and female and that is the relation of lust:

If a man and a woman are alone in one place, the third person present is the devil.

Prophet Mohammed

A Moslem woman in Iran is not allowed to swim, ski, ride a bike, dance, learn to play musical instruments, play gymnastics, or any other sport. It is not even permitted to watch men play sports either in the stadium or on television. And women are not permitted to participate in Olympic games.

421

From age seven, a girl is segregated from all males within and outside of her extended family. Her father, grandfather, uncles, brothers, or male cousins are not allowed to be present at any ceremonies for her accomplishments. They will not be allowed to participate in her birthday parties.

She must study under female teachers and professors. However, since women of prior generations were not allowed to go to school, there are not that many qualified women teachers and professors. Male professors must teach a girl-child from behind a wall.

Women and girls must be treated by female doctors and female dentists. And if there are none then she must go without or must be examined through some sort of divider.

She is not allowed to practice birth control or have abortions, even if carrying or having a child means her death.

A woman's worth, based on the Islamic Laws of Retribution, is half that of a man.[1] It doesn't matter who she is, how educated she is, or what earning potential she may have. Her worth is half of a man—any man.

Article 1, regarding *diyeh* or blood money paid to the victim or next of kin as compensation for bodily injury or murder of a relative states in Clause 6, regarding the *Dieh* (cash value of the fine), that the cash fine for murdering a woman intentionally or unintentionally is half as much as for a man. The same clause adds that if a man intentionally murders a woman and the guardian of the woman himself is not able to pay half of the *Dieh* (the value of 50 camels or 100 cows) to the murderer, the murderer will be exempted from retribution.

Pursuant to Article 85 of the Constitution, the Islamic penal code was implemented in December 1981. According to Article 300, blood money or *diyeh*, a sum paid to the next of kin as compensation for the murder of a relative, is twice as much in the case of a murdered man as in the case of a woman. The number of witnesses required to prove a crime is higher if the witnesses are female. For example, Article 237 of the penal code states that first degree murder must be proven by testimony of two just men and evidence for second-degree murder or manslaughter requires the testimony of two just men, or one just man and two just women, or of one just man and the accuser. A woman's testimony in a court of law is equal to half of that of a man.

A woman cannot get custody of her children, even if their father dies. In the case of divorce or death she must surrender her children to their father and/or his family.

A woman cannot travel, work, go to college, join organizations, even visit her friends and relatives without the permission of her father or husband. She must live where her husband desires. She is banned from studying such topics as engineering, agriculture, archaeology, restoration of historic monuments and handicrafts, and many other fields. She is not allowed to become a judge.

---

1.   Islamic Laws of Retribution, Clauses 33 and 91, Qasas, 24th ed., Dec. 1982.

Under the terms of Koranic law, any judge fulfilling the seven requirements is qualified to dispense justice in any type of case. The seven requirements are that he has reached puberty, is a believer, knows the Koranic laws perfectly, is just, and is not affected by amnesia, is not a bastard, or of the female sex.

A woman has no right to choose the clothing she wears in public. This is done by the Office of the Islamic Guidance, which sets the color, the style, and the accessories for women and girls as young as six years of age. She may be arrested, beaten, and sometimes even executed if she wears makeup, nylons, or bright colors (especially the color of red).

A woman cannot choose her own mate and is not permitted to divorce him if things do not work out. According to Khomeini, the Iranian Islamic Imam, "The most suitable time for a girl to get married is the time when the girl can have her first menstrual period in her husband's house rather than her father's."[2] She must meet all her husband's desires including the sexual ones. And if she refuses, he has the right to deny her food, shelter, and all life's necessities. She must say yes every time he wants to have sex.

According to Hojatoleslam Imani, Religious Leader in Iran: "A woman should endure any violence or torture imposed on her by her husband for she is fully at his disposal. Without his permission she may not leave her house even for a good action (such as charitable work). Otherwise her prayers and devotions will not be accepted by God and curses of heaven and earth will fall upon her."[3]

A husband can divorce his wife without her knowledge and by the Islamic law he is required to support her for only 100 days. And if he dies she is entitled to 1/8 of his estate. She can only ask for divorce if her husband is impotent, does not have sex with her at least one night in every forty nights, or refuses to provide her with a minimum standard of living.

A husband can have four permanent wives, and if he is from the Shi'i sect, he can have as many temporary wives as he wants.

The Koran says, "Men, your wives are your tillage. Go into your tillage anyway you want." This means that a man is allowed to sodomize his wife and she cannot complain.

In some countries they even mutilate, cut and sew a woman or girl's female sexual parts in order to control and regulate her sexual desire.

According to the Islamic Laws, a woman is supposed to be seen outside of her home three times in her life. When she is born, when she gets married, and when she dies.

---

2.   THE LITTLE GREEN BOOK, SAYINGS OF THE AYATOLLAH KHOMEINI, POLITICAL, PHILOSOPHICAL, SOCIAL AND RELIGIOUS, with a Special Introduction by Clive Irving 109 (1979).

3.   League of Iranian Women, *Women's Conditions in the Islamic Republic of Iran* 22 (Paris, June 1992) (Hereinafter L.I.W.) (citing to religious leader's views expressed in Poldokhtar, Keyhan newspaper May 26, 1985).

In Islam, the age of majority for a girl is nine years and for a boy is fifteen years. This means that a nine-year-old girl and a fifteen-year-old boy are considered to have the same level of maturity. Now if girls reach maturity six years earlier than boys then why did God place men in charge of women? Was there something wrong with God's judgement?

In some Islamic countries such as Iran, if a woman is arrested for wearing make-up, the guards will force her to clean her face with cotton balls rubbed in pieces of glass. This cuts her face. The barbaric revolutionary guard, while watching the blood run out of her flesh, will tell her, "next time you think about this and will not wear it."[4]

As a political prisoner a woman will be used as a concubine for the revolutionary guards. In case she is condemned to death she will not undergo the sentence as long as she is a virgin. Thus she will be systematically raped before the sentence is executed. Mullahs believe that virgin girls who die go to heaven but politically inclined girls are ungodly creatures and they do not deserve to go to heaven. Therefore, they are raped so that the Mullahs can be sure that they indeed will be sent to hell.

In Islam if a six or seven year old girl is raped by an adult man, she will be the one that gets punished. It is her fault, because she provoked it. The parents then will burn or kill her because she has dishonored the family.

It has been said that the Moslem Prophet got very upset one day noticing his wives flirting with men who visited him and ordered the women to stay behind a dividing curtain when speaking with men. The idea of *hijab*, the covering up of women, became a law in Islamic countries from that day.

In 1991, the Prosecutor-General of Iran, Abolfazl Musavi-Tabrizi, declared that "anyone who rejects the principle of *hijab* is an apostate and the punishment for an apostate under Islamic law is death."[5]

There is no reasonable explanation of why God denied a female everything and made males in charge of them, if there is a God. Perhaps there never was one.

Homa Darabi

A beloved member of the author's family, her only sister, Dr. Homa Darabi's brief life and death scenario may serve as an example for the impact these laws have on women in Iran and other Islamic countries:

Homa was a medical doctor specializing in pediatrics, neuro-psychiatry and child and adolescent psychiatry, and was licensed to practice medicine in New Jersey, New York, and California. In addition to being a doctor of medicine, Homa was an outspoken feminist and a political activist. She also was a naturalized citizen of the United States.

---

4. *Id.*, citing Dr. Homa Darabi's description of a patient devastated by the experience.

5. L.I.W., *supra* note 3, at 28, citing statement made on Aug. 15, 1991.

To help the deprived and poverty-stricken Iranian children, she returned to Iran in 1976 and was appointed as a professor at the University of Tehran School of Medicine. She opened her private practice at the same time and very quickly became known all across Iran. She established the first children's psychiatric clinic in Tehran.

In 1990 she was ordered to comply with the strict rules of *hijab*. She refused. So she was considered an apostate. The government, however, did not kill her directly. This would not have been a good move, because of its international implications. So they made her life so miserable that she did it on their behalf. She self-immolated.

She was one of the strong supporters of the revolution. However, when the democratic revolution turned Islamic, Homa became devastated and totally broke away from all politics. She then devoted her time to her profession as a medical doctor and continued her struggles as a women's human rights activist.

To shut her up in retaliation, she was first fired from her position as a professor of medicine at the University of Tehran and later harassed in her private practice. At age fifty-two, she finally had to close down her practice, and be confined to her home for the first time in her life.

As a prominent psychiatrist, her services were requested by devastated and helpless parents whose daughters were subjected to floggings and beatings for such violations as wearing make up and nylons. They would beg her to go to the courts and declare their daughters insane to suspend their punishment.

To label a perfectly healthy, sane young woman as insane was not a big issue with the parents. They wanted their daughters unharmed, but it was a moral issue with Homa. She felt she was ruining a young girl's life forever. A month prior to her death, a sixteen-year-old girl was shot to death in Northern Tehran for wearing lipstick. Homa could no longer stand this brutality. She protested the oppression of women by setting herself on fire in Northern Tehran, on February 21, 1994. Her last cries were:

Death to Tyranny

Long Live Liberty

Long Live Iran.

Where Do These Ideas Come From? Quotes From Islamic Leaders

Following are quotes from some of the top Islamic Leaders within the Islamic Republic of Iran:

Hashemi Rafsanjani, President of the Islamic Republic of Iran:

Men's brains are bigger so men are more inclined to fight and women are more excitable. Men are inclined to reasoning and rationalism, while women have a fundamental tendency to be emotional. The tendency to protect is stronger in men, whereas most women like to be protected. Such differences affect the delegation of responsi-bilities, duties, and rights.[6]

Sadegh Khalkhali, the most notorious revolutionary tribunal judge of the Iranian Islamic Revolution:

Human Rights mean that unsuitable individuals should be liquidated so that others can live free.[7]

From one of the principal ideologues of the Islamic Republic of Iran:

The specific task of women in a society is to marry and bear children. They will be discouraged from entering legislative, judicial, or what-ever careers which may require decision making, as women lack the intellectual ability and discerning judge-ment required for these careers."[8]

Hashemi Rafsanjani, President of the Islamic Republic of Iran, recently dis-covered the difference between men and women. He states:

Equality does not take precedence over justice. Justice does not mean that all laws must be the same for men and women. One of the mistakes the Westerners make is to forget this. The difference in the stature, vitality, voice, development, muscular qual-ity and physical strength of men and women show that men are stronger and more capable in all fields.[9]

Polygamy is legal in Islam. A man may marry "four permanent" and as many "provisional" or temporary wives as he desires:

Marry such women as seem good to you, two, three, four; but if you fear you will not be equitable, then only one, or what your right hand owns; so it is likelier you will not be partial.[10]

Most Europeans have mistresses. Why should we suppress human instincts? A rooster satisfies several hens, a stallion several mares. A woman is unavailable during certain periods whereas a man is always active. . . .[11]

SEXUAL APARTHEID

The Koran

It is forbidden for a man to look upon the body of a woman who is not his wife, under any pretext whatsoever. It is equally forbidden for a woman to look upon the body of a man who is not her husband. To look upon the face and hair of a girl who has not reached puberty, if it is done without intention of enjoyment thereof, and if one is not afraid of succumbing to temptation, may be tolerated. It is however rec-ommended that one not look upon her belly or thighs, which must remain covered.

---

6. Statement made at a Friday Public Prayer in the early 1990's.

7. Robin White, In the Name of God, The Khomeini Decade 68 (1989).

8. L.I.W., *supra* note 3.

9. *Supra* note 6.

10. The Koran 4:3.

11. Ayatollah Ghomi, Le Monde, Jan. 20, 1979.

To look upon the faces and hands of Jewish or Christian women, if this is not done with intention of enjoyment thereof, and if one does not fear temptation, is tolerated. A woman must hide her body and her hair from the eyes of men. It is highly recommended that she also hide them from those of pre-pubic boys, if she suspects that they may look upon her with lust.

It is forbidden to look upon the genitals of another person, even from behind a glass, or in a mirror, or in standing water. It is even expressly recommended to abstain from looking at the genitals of a child who knows the difference between good and evil. But it is permitted for husband and wife to look upon each other in all parts of their bodies.

A man must not look upon the body of another man with lustful intent. Likewise, a woman may not look upon another woman with such intent.

It is not forbidden for a man to photograph a woman other than his wife, but if, in order to do so he must touch her, then he must not photograph her.

If a woman is called upon to give an enema to a woman or to a man other than her husband, or to wash their genitals, then she must cover her hand so as not to come into direct contact with the genital organs; the same precautions must be taken by a man where another man or a woman other than his wife are concerned.

If a man is called upon, for medical reasons, to look upon a woman other than his wife and to touch her body, he is permitted to do so, but if he can give such care by only looking at the body, he must not touch it, and if he can give it by only touching, he must not look at it. If a man or woman be forced, in order to administer medical care, to look upon the genitals of another person, he or she must do so indirectly, in a mirror, except in case of absolute necessity.

Segregation

Women are segregated from men on buses, where women must sit in the rear. Government office buildings have separate entrances for men and women. Women are not allowed to engage in public sports activities where they may be seen by men. Curtains separate men and women in the sea or they can swim during certain hours designated for women only.

Any form of friendship or association between the sexes outside the marriage contract is punishable by flogging, imprisonment, forced marriage, and stoning to death.

Dress Code

Based on the writings of the Koran, the Sura of Lights, God apparently told Prophet Mohammed: "Prophet, tell your wives [he had somewhere between sixteen to twenty-five wives—most of them forty-plus years his junior], daughters, and other women who believe in me to conceal their eyes and their treasures from the sight of strangers."[12]

---

12. World Organization of Iranian Women Solidarity, *Women Struggle in Iran* 18 (Paris 1990).

The problem in the Islamic world, however, is to know how far a woman should be dressed to conceal her treasures. According to the Mullahs, "[T]he limit has also been set by God. Therefore, the *Litham* should rise to the chin and only the outline of the face may be seen. The body should be covered to the wrists. Thus *Chador* is a perfect outfit."[13] For most women, especially the professional ones, however, this kind of "treasure-concealing" is quite cumbersome and uncomfortable. Women who do not conceal their hair or expose their feet and those who seem to be wearing a veil, but actually do so negligently, should be severely punished, per order of the government.

The government of clergy believes that, "women who do not comply with the strict rules of *hijab* promote a contemptuous attitude towards themselves becoming mere objects for men's pleasure. Moreover, such conduct causes a drop in the marriage rate. A woman with a pleasant appearance hinders other girls from finding a husband. It also makes the selection difficult for men. They will constantly think of a model who is beyond everybody."[14]

The Ministry of Education specifies the color and the style of the suited clothing for the girl students (black, straight, and covered from head to toe for children as young as six years of age). And the Ministry of Guidance sets the rules of clothing for older women (only black, brown, and dark blue—Islamic colors—are allowed; bright colors, especially red, are prohibited).

It has been reported that on August 15, 1991, the Prosecutor-General, Abolfazl Musavi-Tabrizi, said that "anyone who rejects the principle of *hijab* in Iran is an apostate and the punishment for an apostate under Islamic law is death."[15]

To suppress the refractory women, the government set up special units. Revolutionary Guards patrol the streets and arrest any woman not observing the Islamic *hijab*.

In 1980, in the Islamic Republic of Iran, the dress code, *hijab*, became mandatory in all public places for all women, regardless of citizenship or religion. Women must cover their hair and body, except for face and hands, and they may not use cosmetics. Those in contravention of the dress code are subject to punishment that may range from a verbal reprimand, to a fine, to seventy-four strokes of the lash, to a prison term of one month to a year. Women are regularly harassed and arrested or detained under legal pretexts for wearing make-up or being improperly veiled. Arrests and harassment have been carried out by the morality police (such as Komitehs, Revolutionary Guards, and Baseej), who verify that women's dress meets Islamic

---

12. WORLD ORGANIZATION OF IRANIAN WOMEN SOLIDARITY, WOMEN STRUGGLE IN IRAN 18 (Paris 1990).

13. *Id.*

14. Statement by Maryam Behrouz, Representative of the Iranian Women Mp's Keyhan Newspaper, Sept. 26,1984.

15. L.I.W., *supra* note 3, at 28. (Statement made Aug. 15, 1991).

standards. Government offices, hospitals, cinemas, and other public places have been asked to prevent women not fully complying with the dress code from entering their premises.

Education of Women and Girls

> The specific task of women in this society is to marry and bear children. They will be discouraged from entering legislative, judicial, or what ever careers which may require decision making, as women lack the intellectual ability and discerning judgement required for these careers.[16]

Islamic law bans women from becoming judges. In Article 163 of the Islamic Constitution, the qualifications for becoming a judge is stated to be decided according to religious measures and women have been specified as unqualified for the job. Women are banned from studies such as engineering, agriculture, archaeology, restoration of the historic monuments and handicrafts, and many other fields.

Khomeini has stressed that, "All our society's miseries come from universities." He also has said, "Economy is a matter of donkeys" and "War is a blessing."[17]

Marriage

A woman may legally belong to a man in one of two ways: by continuing marriage or temporary marriage. In the former, the duration of the marriage need not be specified; in the latter, it must be stipulated.

In accordance with Article 1075 of the civil code, a temporary marriage may be undertaken for a specified period of time from one hour to a maximum of ninety-nine years. A temporary marriage is a contract for sexual services for a predetermined sum to be paid to the woman. Men are allowed to have an unlimited number of temporary wives. While the husband may terminate the marriage at any time, the woman may not do so under any condition. At no time is he required to make support payments.

Marriage, whether continuing or temporary, must be sealed by a religious formula spoken either by the woman or by the man, or by one of their representatives. As long as the woman and man have not contracted a religious marriage, they are not entitled to look upon one another. To allow that, it is not enough to assume that the marriage formula has been spoken, but if the person representing them states that it has been spoken, then that is enough to validate the marriage. If a woman authorizes someone to marry her to a man for a period of ten days, for example, without specifying the exact date, the man may contract the marriage at his pleasure, but if the woman has specified a precise day and hour, the formula must be spoken at that specified time. The legal marriage formula must be read in Arabic, but if one cannot speak that language correctly, it may be spoken in a different language.

---

16.   *Id.* (Quoting Ayatollah Mutahari, one of the principal ideologues of the Islamic Republic of Iran.)

17.   Reported by the Iranian Media, stated after his return to Iran, when the students complained about the poor economic conditions in Iran and during the Iran/Iraq war.

A father or a paternal grandfather has the right to marry off a child who is insane or has not reached puberty by acting as its representative. The child may not annul such a marriage after reaching puberty or regaining his sanity, unless the marriage is to his manifest disadvantage.

Any girl who is a virgin and wishes to get married and is of age, that is, capable of understanding what is in her own best interest, must procure the authorization of her father or paternal grandfather. The permission of her mother or sister or brother is not required. If a father or paternal grandfather marries off a pre-pubic son or grandson, the latter will be responsible, once he has reached puberty, for taking care of his wife's material needs.

A marriage is annulled if a man finds that his wife is afflicted with one of the seven following disabilities: madness, leprosy, eczema, blindness, paralysis with after-effects, malformation of the urinary and genital tracts or of the genital-tract and rectum through conjoining thereof, or vaginal malformation making coitus impossible. On the other hand, leprosy, eczema, blindness, or paralysis with after-effects suffered by a husband are not grounds for divorce or annulment of marriage if the woman desires a divorce. However if a wife finds out after marriage that her husband is suffering from mental illness, that he is castrated, impotent, or has had his testicles excised, she may apply for annulment of her marriage.

If a wife has her marriage annulled because her husband is unable to have sexual relations with her either vaginally or anally, he must pay her, as damages, one-half of the dowry specified in the marriage contract. If the husband or wife annuls the marriage for any of the above-mentioned reasons, the man owes nothing to the woman, if they have had sexual relations together; if they have not, he must pay her the full amount of the dowry.

It is forbidden to marry one's mother, sister, or stepmother. It is forbidden to marry one's mother-in-law, or one's wife's maternal or paternal grandmothers or any of her great-grandmothers, even though one's marriage to her may never have been consummated. A man who marries a woman and has sexual relations with her may not marry her daughter or granddaughter, even if these be by a different marriage. A man may not marry his wife's daughter, even if their marriage has not been consummated.

Aunts of the bride's father and the aunts of her grandparents need not wear the veil in the presence of the groom; the father, grandfather, and great-grandfather of the groom, as well as his sons, grandsons, and all his male descendants, may freely look upon the bride. A man may not marry the nieces of his wife without the latter's consent; if he should nevertheless do so without getting consent, but his wife raises no objection, then there is no problem.

A man who has committed adultery with his aunt must not marry her daughters, that is to say, his first cousins. If a man who has married his first cousin commits adultery with her mother, the marriage is not thereby annulled. If a man commits adultery with a woman other than his aunt, it is highly recommended that he not marry the daughter of that woman. If he marries a woman, consummates the marriage, and then commits adultery with her mother, the marriage is not thereby annulled. Nor is it automatically annulled in the case of his having committed such adultery before the marriage was consummated, but in that case it is better if the husband voluntarily annuls the marriage.

A Moslem woman may not marry a non-Moslem man; nor may a Moslem man marry a non-Moslem woman in continuing marriage, but he may take a Jewish or Christian woman in temporary marriage.

A man who marries an already-married woman must break off his marriage with her and refrain from ever marrying her again.

A married woman remains legally married after having committed adultery. However, should she not repent and should she continue to be unfaithful to her husband, it is preferable for the latter to repudiate her, but with full payment to her of her dowry.

The mother, sister, or daughter of a man who has been sodomized by another man may not marry the latter, even if both men or one of them had not yet reached puberty at the time; but if the one who was the victim of the act cannot prove it, his mother, sister, or daughter is allowed to marry the other man.

If a man who has married a girl who has not reached puberty possesses her sexually before her ninth birthday, inflicting trauma upon her, he has no right to repeat such an act with her.

If a man sodomizes the son, brother, or father of his wife after their marriage, the marriage remains valid.

A woman who has contracted a continuing marriage does not have the right to go out of the house without her husband's permission. She must remain at his disposal for the fulfillment of any one of his desires, and may not refuse herself to him except for a religiously valid reason. If she is totally submissive to him, the husband must provide her with food, clothing, and lodging, whether or not he has the means to do so.

A woman who refuses herself to her husband is guilty, and may not demand from him food, clothing, lodging, or any later sexual relations; however, she retains the right to be paid damages if she is repudiated.

A husband is not obligated to pay travel expenses incurred by his wife that exceed what her expenses would have been at home. But if the travel was undertaken at his own suggestion, then he must take care of the expenses.

A wife who scrupulously obeys her husband has the right to be paid the daily household expenses from any of the husband's assets, in the case the latter refuses voluntarily to pay for them. But if she is forced to meet such expenses out of her own pocket, she is not obligated to obey her husband.

A man who has contracted a continuing marriage may not leave his wife for so long a time as to allow her to question the validity of the marriage. However he is not obligated to spend one night out of every four with her. A husband must have sexual relations with his wife at least once in every four months.

If, at the time of contracting the marriage, no specific time was indicated at which the husband was to pay the dowry to his wife, the wife may refuse herself to her husband for so long as that amount of money has not been paid her. But once she has agreed to have sexual relations with her husband, she can no longer later refuse to, except for religiously valid reasons.

A temporary marriage, even though only one of convenience, is nevertheless legal. A man must not abstain from having sexual relations with his temporary wife for more than four months. If the temporary marriage contract includes a clause specifying that the husband is not entitled to have normal sexual relations with his wife, such a clause must be respected. He must then be satisfied with giving her pleasures in other ways. But as soon as the wife consents to it, he may perform the natural sex act with her.

A woman who has been temporarily married in exchange for a previously established dowry has no right to demand that her daily expenses be paid by her husband, even when she becomes pregnant. A temporarily married wife may not inherit from her husband; nor may he inherit from her. A temporarily married woman is entitled to go out of the house without asking her husband's permission, unless the fact of her so going out harms him in one way or another.

If a father (or paternal grandfather) marries off his daughter (or granddaughter) in her absence without knowing for a certainty that she is alive, the marriage becomes null and void as soon as it is established that she was dead at the time of the marriage.

If the husband has included in the marriage contract a clause guaranteeing his wife's virginity, he may annul the marriage if it turns out that she was not a virgin.

If a woman abjures her faith before her marriage is consummated, the marriage is annulled. The same is true after conclusion of the marriage, if she is menopausal. But if she is not menopausal and returns to her Moslem beliefs within a hundred days after the breaking off of the marriage, it again becomes valid.

A man whose father or mother was a Moslem at the time of his conception, and who himself embraced the Moslem faith after reaching puberty, will have his marriage automatically abolished if he becomes an apostate.

The marriage of a man born of non-Moslem parents but who himself became a convert to Islam is automatically annulled if he renounces his faith before consummating the marriage. If he renounces his faith after having sexual relations with his wife, she must wait one hundred days after the annulment of the marriage before marrying again, if she is of an age to have menstrual periods. Thus, the marriage remains valid if during those one hundred days the husband returns to the Moslem fold; otherwise, the annulment is irreversible.

The husband of a woman who has had a daughter by a previous marriage may marry that daughter to a son of his by a previous marriage. He himself has the right to marry the mother of a girl married to his son.

A woman who becomes pregnant as a result of adultery must not have an abortion. A child born of an adulterous father is legitimate. If a man commits adultery with an unmarried woman, and subsequently marries her, the child born of that marriage will be a bastard unless the parents can be sure it was conceived after they were married.

One need not believe a woman who claims to have entered menopause. On the one hand, she must be believed if she asserts that she is not married.

It is highly recommended that a girl be married off as soon as she reaches the age of puberty. One of the blessings of man is to have his daughter experience her first period not in her father's house, but in that of her husband. It is a sin to have sexual relations with one's wife during the fast of Ramadan or while she is having her menses, but the child born of such relations is legitimate.

If a man marries a woman and possesses her sexually, he may no longer marry any girl whom this woman has breast-fed. A man may not marry a wet nurse who has breast-fed his wife. A man may not marry a girl who was ever breast-fed by his mother or his grandmother.

Iranian women are prevented from marrying foreigners unless they obtain a written permission from the Ministry of Interior. The Ministry of Interior's Director General for the Affairs of Foreign Citizens and Immigrants, Ahmad Hosseini, stated on March 30, 1991:

> Marriages between Iranian women and foreign men will create many problems for these women and their children in future, because the marriages are not legally recognized. Religious registrations of such marriages will not be considered as sufficient documentation to provide legal services to these families.[18]

The legal age for girls to marry was reduced from eighteen to thirteen after 1979, and was later further reduced to nine. A virgin female of any age must obtain the permission of her father or paternal grandfather to marry. According to Article 1060 of the civil code, a Muslim female is forbidden to marry a non-Muslim. There is no such limitation on a Muslim man. Men are allowed to have up to four permanent wives. Although Islamic law requires that a husband treat all his wives in an "equally fair" manner, the civil code has designated the husband himself as the sole judge of whether he can be equally fair to two or more wives. In return for her submission to the "head" of the family, the wife is entitled to receive financial support. Article 1108 of the civil code specifies: "If the wife refuses to fulfill her nuptial obligations without justifiable cause she shall not be entitled to financial support."

---

18.   L.I.W., *supra* note 3, at 9.

Divorce

According to the Islamic Republic's Canon Law, divorce is an indisputable right of men, unless otherwise stated in the marriage contract. A husband may divorce his wife without her knowledge. It is absolutely lawful for a woman to receive her divorce deed with no prior consultation. Article 1133 of the civil code stipulates that a man can divorce as he pleases while a woman must prove that the marriage is in violation of one of twelve enumerated grounds. Article 1130 states that the wife may sue for divorce if the continuation of the marriage causes undue hardship. Determination of such instances has been left to the judgement of the court.

A man who repudiates his wife must be of sound mind and past the age of puberty. He must do so of his own free will and without any constraint; therefore, if the formula for divorce is spoken in jest the marriage is not annulled.

The woman must not be having her period at the time of the divorce, and the husband must not have had sexual relations with her since her last period. In three cases, a man may repudiate his wife while she is having her period: if he has had no sexual relations with her since their marriage; if she is pregnant while the husband believes she is having her period, and it is learned only later that she was pregnant at the time of the repudiation; if he is not certain, because of the distance that separates them, whether his wife is then having her period.

A man who has had sexual relations with his wife after her last menstrual period must wait for her to have her next one before he may divorce her. But he may divorce his wife if she has not yet reached her ninth birthday, or is pregnant, or is menopausal. If a husband who has had sexual relations with his wife between menstrual periods, divorces her during this time and learns later that she was pregnant when the divorce took place, the latter remains valid.

A woman temporarily married, say, for a month or a year, has her marriage automatically annulled at the end of that time, or at any other time when the husband releases her from the balance of her engagement. It is not necessary for this that there be any witnesses, or that the woman have had her period.

A woman who has not yet reached the age of nine or a menopausal woman may remarry immediately after divorce, without waiting the hundred days that are otherwise required. A woman who has had her ninth birthday, or who has not yet entered menopause, must wait for three menstrual periods after her divorce before being allowed to remarry. If a woman who has not reached her ninth birthday or who has not entered menopause gets temporarily married, she must, at the end of the contract or when the husband has released her from part of it, wait two menstrual periods or forty-five days before marrying again.

If a man commits adultery with a woman he knows is not his wife, while the woman is unaware that the man is not her husband, she must wait one hundred days before remarrying. If a man encourages a married woman to leave her husband so as to marry him, they are both committing a great sin, but the divorce and their marriage remain in force.

If the father or paternal grandfather of a boy has him marry a woman for a temporary marriage, he may prematurely cancel it in the boy's interest, even if the marriage was contracted before the boy reached the age of puberty. If, for example, a fourteen-year-old boy has been married off to a woman for a period of two years, they may return her freedom to the woman before this time has run its course; but a continuing marriage cannot be broken in this way.

If a man repudiates his wife without informing her of it, and continues to meet her expenses for a period of, say, a year, and at the end of that time informs her that he got a divorce a year earlier and shows her proof of it, he may require that she return to him anything he has bought or given her during that time, provided that she has not used it up or consumed it, in which case he cannot demand its return.

Children and Custody

The best person to breast-feed a newborn baby is its own mother. It is preferable that she not ask to be paid for such service, but that her husband pay her for it of his own free will. If the sum the mother asks for is greater than that charged by a wet nurse, the husband is free to take the child from its mother and turn it over to the wet nurse.

It is recommended that the wet nurse be a faithful Shi'ite, intelligent, modest, and pretty. On the other hand, it is most inadvisable that she be feebleminded, a nonbeliever in the Twelve Imams, ugly, a bastard, or of bad character. It is equally inadvisable to select as a wet nurse a woman who has an illegitimate child. It is recommended that every child be breast-fed for two years.

According to Article 1169, in the event of divorce, the father has legal custody of boys after the age of two and girls after the age of seven. The mother loses this minimal right of custody over her children as soon as she remarries. Survivors of domestic violence have no recourse in the courts. At the end of this "legal" period the child should be returned to the father with no visitation rights for the mother. If the father is dead, the children must be handed over to the father's family. Women cannot have the custody of their children unless the children have no known fathers—mostly children born from temporary marriages.

No social support is provided to a woman who leaves her husband. Even the possibility of leaving the country is precluded, since her husband's permission is required.

Inheritance

Under Article 907 of the civil code, upon the death of the parent, "each son's share of the inheritance will be twice that of the daughter's." The widow of a man who has left children or grandchildren behind is entitled to only one-eighth of her husband's inheritance; if he has left no children, she is entitled to one-quarter (the rest is deemed property of the state). If the man had more than one wife, the one-eighth is shared among the wives. If the woman dies, the rights of her surviving husband are double those she would get if he died. While the husband's share of the inheritance covers all the wife's property, the wife's share of the estate, according to Article 946, will only be from movable property, buildings and trees. With regard to the parents' inheritance from their daughter, if the deceased has no surviving children, the mother's share is one-sixth and the father's share is five-sixths of the estate.

ON PERSONAL RIGHTS

Obstacles to Leaving the Country

In accordance with a draft resolution presented to the Majlis (The Islamic Parliament) in May 1991, unmarried women and girls will not be allowed to leave the country. Although at present there is no law forbidding girls from leaving the country, authorities, in practice, create many obstacles for those who wish to leave. The authorities are allegedly particularly severe with those unmarried women and girls who have won scholarships to study abroad.

A Husband's Permission

A married woman cannot travel, work, join organizations, go to college, or even visit her friends and relatives without her husband's permission. Married women are not allowed to travel abroad without presenting written permission from their husbands to the authorities.

A woman should dwell where her husband desires. However, if the woman inserts into the marriage contract a clause binding her husband not to move her away from the city, and the husband accepts such a clause, then he must abide by it.

Citizenship

Citizenship is granted on the basis of one's paternal status. Article 976 of the civil code specifies that those born in and outside Iran and whose fathers are Iranian will be considered Iranian citizens. If a man becomes a naturalized Iranian citizen, his minor children will also become Iranian; for a naturalized Iranian woman, her children will not be considered Iranians. Article 976 grants Iranian nationality to any woman of foreign nationality who marries an Iranian man. However, if an Iranian woman marries a man of foreign nationality, her husband will not be accorded Iranian citizenship and she may be compelled to acquire her husband's nationality, thereby losing her Iranian citizenship.

Stoning, Prison Rape, Executions, and Other Punishments of Women

Stoning

According to Article 115 of the penal laws of the Islamic Republic on stoning, if the person condemned to stoning flees from the hole where he or she has been buried, down to the waist, he or she should be returned and the punishment should be carried out. But if the person confesses to the fornication and the escape takes place after the first stone was thrown, the person must be left unharmed. Article 116 of the penal laws on stoning says that the stones used in stoning should neither be big enough so as to kill the person at the first or second blow, nor as small as a pebble.

A couple of weeks following Dr. Homa Darabi's self-immolation, a young woman was stoned to death in the city of Qom in front of her husband and her two small children. Her guilt was adultery, even though no man was found to have had sexual relations with her. She did not receive any trial and was not allowed to have an attorney. A Mullah convicted her in less than sixty seconds and the stoning took place the next day. Her head was shaven and she was buried in mud up to her shoulders.[19]

Female Political and Other Prisoners

Under the Islamic Republic, most of the female political prisoners are charged with waging war against God. Thus, according to the Islamic Officials they are war prisoners and may be considered as the slaves of the Islamic Warriors. Consequently, the guardians of the revolution, namely the Pasdars, may treat them as they like. Each woman in the prison belongs to one guard. He may lawfully consider his slave as his concubine and force her into sexual intercourse or inflict other tortures on her.

Despite the fact that all Conventions and agreed covenants of the United Nations, including the Universal Declaration of Human Rights, have to be strictly observed by the member states, the Islamic Republic of Iran's Constitution mentions nothing about the equality of men and women. Article 19 of the Islamic Constitution concerning the equality of people is silent on this.

Amnesty International has documented a number of cases where women associated with political opposition parties have been subjected to lengthy pre-trial detention without judicial supervision during which they faced torture or other forms of coercion, following which they were then convicted at summary trials. Amnesty International reports that because in Islam virgins are believed to go to heaven, they are raped before they are executed.

Thousands of women have been imprisoned, raped, flogged, shot, hanged, or stoned to death, mostly under false accusations and all has been done under the name of God and apparently in accordance with the Islamic judicial system.

Female Executions

Recent reports published by various international organizations such as Amnesty International and the United Nation's Human Rights Commission give a clear picture of the circumstances faced by Iranian women. They are denied the most basic human rights. According to a report published by the Organization of Women Against Execution in Iran, the number of women executed from 1981 through 1990 exceeds

---

19.   Reported by Iranian Radio News.

a few thousand. The Organization has been able to prepare a list containing 1,428 names. Some of the data were gathered through official channels and some from the relatives of the victims. According to this report, out of 1,428 women executed, 187 were under the age of eighteen, with nine girls under the age of thirteen. Thirty-two women were pregnant, and fourteen were between the ages of forty-five to seventy-two at the time of their execution. The youngest girl executed was ten years and the oldest was seventy-two years of age.

On his last visit to Iran in 1991, Professor Reynaldo Galinde Pohl, Special Representative of the United Nation's Human Rights Commission, interviewed the Islamic Republic's Minister of Justice, Mr. Hojatolislam Esmail Shoushtari, and according to a report referring to the penalties of amputation and stoning indicated that Iran's system of government was Islamic, thus Islamic laws were enforced and some penalties could not be changed. Murder, for example, was punished by the death penalty, and that rule could not be changed; however, judges were empowered to negotiate with the victims' relatives to replace the death penalty by another, and that did happen in 95 percent of cases. Theft was punished by amputation, and adultery by stoning (to death). Those penalties could not be changed, because they were punishments especially established under Islam.

Political Aspirations

Women are also denied any political, spiritual or leadership aspirations in many Islamic countries. Article 115 of the Islamic Republic of Iran's Constitution clearly states that the president of the country should be elected a Man out of all God-fearing and dedicated men. This brings the perception that a woman can neither be president nor possess the rank of Valiat-e-Faghih (the religious spiritual leader) or the position of leader of a Shi'i-Muslim nation.

The Sexual Code

Adultery

Under *hodud*, punishment prescribed under religious law, the penal code accords the death penalty, stoning, or flogging to the adulterer or adulteress depending on whether s/he is married or unmarried. Article 102 states: "The stoning of an adulterer or adulteress shall be carried out while each is placed in a hole and covered in soil, he up to his waist and she up to a line above her breasts." The law stipulates the size of stone that must be used in stoning to ensure maximum suffering of the accused.

Adultery is a crime mostly committed by women (men can have as many women as they want) and is punished by stoning (to death). Even the prophet himself had some nineteen to twenty-six wives after his first wife Khadijeh died. Prophet Mohammed married a seven-year-old girl, named Ayeshe, when he was fifty-four. And according to his revelations, he could have all his female cousins without dowry, all the slaves and all the women he ever wanted. God even told the prophet Mohammed to tell his followers that if they wanted to go to heaven they should make their daughters marry the prophet.

Sodomy and Homosexuality

In case of sodomy, both the active and the passive persons will be condemned to punishment. Punishment for sodomy is death if both the active and passive persons are mature, of sound mind and have free will; the Sharia Judge decides on how to carry out the execution. If a mature man of sound mind commits sexual intercourse with an immature person, the doer will be killed and the passive one will be subject to *Ta'azir* of seventy-four lashes if not under duress. If an immature person commits sexual intercourse with another immature person, both of them will be subject to *Ta'azir* of seventy-four lashes unless one of them was under duress.[20]

Ways of Proving Sodomy in Court

Confessing four times to having committed sodomy establishes punishment against the one making the confession. A confession made less than four times to having committed sodomy does not involve punishment of "*Had*" but the confessor will be subject to *Ta'azir* (lesser punishments). A confession is valid only if the confessor is mature, of sound mind, and has free will and intention.[21]

Sodomy is proved by the testimony of four righteous men who might have observed it. If less than four righteous men testify, sodomy is not proved, and the witnesses shall be condemned to punishment for *Qazf* (malicious accusation).[22]

Testimony of women alone or together with a man does not prove sodomy. The Sharia judge may act according to his own knowledge which is derived through customary methods.[23]

Punishment for *Tafhiz* (the rubbing of the thighs or buttocks) and the like committed by two men without entry, shall be one hundred lashes for each of them. However, if the doer is a non-Muslim and the subject is a Muslim, the doer will be condemned to death. If *Tafhiz* and the like are repeated three times without entry and punishment is enforced after each time, the punishment for the fourth time would be death.[24]

If two men not related by blood stand naked under one cover without any necessity, both of them will be subject to *Ta'azir* of up to ninety-nine lashes. If someone kisses another with lust, he will be subject to *Ta'azir* of sixty lashes.[25]

---

20. Arts. 108–113.
21. Arts. 114–116.
22. Arts. 117–118.
23. Arts. 119–120.
24. Arts. 121–122.
25. Arts. 123–124.

If the one committing *Tafhiz* and the like, or a homosexual man, repents before the giving of testimony by the witnesses, his punishment will be quashed; if he repents after the giving of testimony, the punishment will not be quashed. If sodomy or *Tafhiz* is proved by confession and thereafter repented, the Sharia judge may request the leader (Valie Amr) to pardon him.[26]

Lesbianism

Mosaheqeh (lesbianism) is homosexuality of women by stimulation of the genitals. The ways of proving lesbianism in court are the same by which homosexuality of men is proven.[27]

Punishment for lesbianism is one hundred lashes for each party. Punishment for lesbianism will be established vis-a-vis someone who is mature, of sound mind, and has free will and intention. In the punishment for lesbianism, there is be no distinction between the doer and the subject, nor between a Muslim or non-Muslim. If the act of lesbianism is repeated three times, and punishment is enforced each time, a death sentence will be issued the fourth time.[28]

If a lesbian repents before the giving of testimony by the witnesses, the punishment will be quashed; if she does so after the giving of testimony, the punishment will not be quashed. If the act of lesbianism is proved by the confession of the doer, and she repents accordingly, the Sharia judge may request the leader (Valie Amr) to pardon her.[29]

If two women, who are not related by blood stand naked under one cover without necessity, they will be punished with up to one hundred lashes (*Ta'azir*). In case of repetition as well as the repetition of punishment, one hundred lashes will be issued the third time.[30]

Pimping

Pimping occurs when someone brings two individuals together, or puts them in contact with each other, for fornication or homosexuality. Pimping is proven by two confessions, if the confessor is mature, of sound mind, has free will and intention, or by the testimony of two righteous men.[31]

Punishment of a man for pimping is seventy lashes and exile from the place of his domicile for a period of three months to one year. Punishment of pimping by a woman is seventy-five lashes only.[32]

---

26. Arts. 125–126.
27. Arts. 127–128.
28. Arts. 129–131.
29. Arts. 132–133.
30. Art. 134.
31. Arts. 135–137.
32. Art. 138.

Qazf (malicious accusation) means that someone associates fornication or sodomy with a certain person. Punishment for *Qazf* (malicious accusation) is eighty lashes for a man or woman.[33]

CONCLUSION

All the authoritative international documentation and testimony gathered in the last seventeen years of the life of the Islamic Regime in Iran is full of unceasing, systematic brutality, and oppression of masses, especially women.

---

33.   Arts. 139–140.

ISSUES AFFECTING CHRISTIAN WOMEN

Janice Love

Christianity, the largest religion in the world, represents almost as much diversity as humanity itself. Similarly, Christian women, more than half of all Christian adherents, demonstrate substantial differences among themselves. Therefore, many of the issues that affect women all over the world also affect Christian women, just as the concerns, perspectives, and gifts Christian women bring to the practice of their religion share much in common with those of women in other religions.

Seizing on their diversity as a strength, many women actively engage their churches, seeking to change them and help them better respond to women's religious and secular needs and aspirations. This engagement represents one of the most far-reaching challenges the Christian family faces, a challenge perhaps as profound in its implications as that of the Protestant Reformation, which shook the very foundations of the faith as it was known at the time.

This chapter seeks to document a range of issues affecting Christian women. Two larger contexts, however, first provide necessary background material for the discussion on women: some characteristics of the world of Christians as a whole, and some Christian perspectives on broader issues of human rights.

THE WORLD OF CHRISTIANITY

Estimates of the number of Christians range from one billion to two billion;[1] one billion represent the number of more active adherents, and two billion account for those with a loose attachment. Although historically associated with the Middle East and Europe, Christians now live in all regions of the world; the fastest growing populations are in Africa and Latin America.[2]

Doctrinal and ecclesial differences separate Christians into a number of denominations. The Roman Catholic Church (RCC) and various Orthodox Churches are the oldest. The RCC is also the largest, claiming more than half of all adherents. The Anglican family of churches and various Protestant denominations together represent about one-quarter of the Christian population. Denominations with no historic ties to Europe—the so-called independent or indigenous churches—are growing in

---

1. *See* 3 THE WORLD BOOK ENCYCLOPEDIA 523–27 (1996); ACADEMIC AMERICA ENCYCLOPEDIA 412–14 (1996); and John Taylor, *The Future of Christianity, in* THE OXFORD ILLUSTRATED HISTORY OF CHRISTIANITY 628–65 (John McManners ed., 1990).

2. *See* Taylor, *id.* at 633–37.

numbers and significance. Churches, especially in small countries, often unite across denominational lines, and seek to lessen the doctrinal distinctions among their congregations.[3]

Yet substantial theological differences reach across many denominations and cause divisions within churches as significant as the division among churches. For example, liberation theology from Latin America, Africa, and Asia can be found among both Catholics and Protestants.[4] Likewise, expressions of fundamentalism range across denominations.[5] Churches and governments choose a variety of relationships to each other, such that some churches get instituted as state churches and others do not (e.g., Anglicans in England but not in Kenya; Lutherans in Norway but not in the United States). Church responses to the concerns, perspectives, and contributions of women also cut across traditional divisions.

In an attempt to reconcile some of the differences among Christians, to increase practical cooperation among churches, and to celebrate diversity within the faith, church leaders organized a number of ecumenical organizations in the early to late twentieth century. Some of these organizations gather denominations according to a common confession. For instance, Methodists belong to the World Methodist Council and Presbyterians or Reformed Churches belong to the World Alliance of Reformed Churches. The World Council of Churches (WCC), founded in 1948, brings churches together across denominational and confessional lines. Its constituency of about 340 different denominations contains Protestant, Anglican, Orthodox, Old Catholic, and independent or indigenous churches from more than 100 countries.[6] It cooperates with the Roman Catholic Church, which as a whole remains separate organizationally from all other churches.[7]

CHRISTIANITY AND HUMAN RIGHTS

At best, churches and Christians can claim a very mixed historical record with regard to promoting and protecting human rights, as well as to confronting situations

---

3.   *See* METHODIOS FOUYAS, ORTHODOXY ROMAN CATHOLICISM AND ANGLICANISM (1973); MARTIN E. MARTY, PROTESTANTISM (1972); John Taylor, *supra* note 1.

4.   *See* N. S. ATEEK, JUSTICE AND ONLY JUSTICE: A PALESTINIAN THEOLOGY OF LIBERATION (1989); J. COMBLIN, THE HOLY SPIRIT AND LIBERATION (1989); THE FUTURE OF LIBERATION THEOLOGY: ESSAYS IN HONOUR OF GUSTAVO GUTIERREZ (M. H. Ellis & O. Maduro eds., 1989); A.T. HENNELLY, LIBERATION THEOLOGY: A DOCUMENTARY HISTORY (1990); J. PIXLEY & C. BOFF, THE BIBLE, THE CHURCH AND THE POOR: BIBLICAL THEOLOGICAL AND PASTORAL ASPECTS OF THE OPTION FOR THE POOR (1989); V. WAN-TATAH, EMANCIPATION IN AFRICAN THEOLOGY: AN INQUIRY ON THE RELEVANCE OF LATIN AMERICAN LIBERATION THEOLOGY TO AFRICA (1989).

5.   *See generally* THE FUNDAMENTALISM PROJECT (Martin E. Marty & R. Scott Appleby eds., vols. 1–2 1991, 1993).

6.   *See* HANDBOOK OF MEMBER CHURCHES: WORLD COUNCIL OF CHURCHES (Ans. J. Van der Bent ed., 1982).

7.   Some RCC dioceses in some parts of the world join in ecumenical organizations, such as the RCC membership in the Council of Churches for Britain and Ireland. The Vatican, however, does not belong to ecumenical bodies.

and structures of injustice. For example, over the last 2,000 years, some churches helped to create, or were complicit in maintaining, conditions of oppression. Some witnessed the loyalties of their constituents mobilized or manipulated for perverse political, social, or economic ends. Some churches found themselves mired in complex circumstances of injustice without a clear way out. Yet, in contrast, some Christians and churches chose to side with victims of oppression, often at great cost.

In the twentieth century, the considerable practical work of Christians from many denominations to protect people threatened by human rights violations during both world wars lead in part to the future establishment of ecumenical organizations. Explicit discussions and declarations within churches and ecumenical bodies about international norms and standards of human rights, however, parallel similar debates within the United Nations after World War II. Together with other non-governmental organizations, church representatives from North America played a crucial role in pressing for and drafting references to human rights in the United Nations Charter as well as the Universal Declaration on Human Rights. Although a number of Christian women and women's organizations participated in these proceedings, little attention was focused on the need for protection of women's rights. Protestant churches, in particular, gave priority to religious liberty, as evidenced in 1948 by the WCC first assembly's statement on religious freedom.[8]

Official Catholic declarations on human rights came under the leadership of Pope John XXIII, particularly in the encyclical *Pacem in Terris* (1962) and in the Second Vatican Council's pastoral piece *Gaudium et Spes* (1965). A considerably broadened agenda for many churches and ecumenical organizations on human rights began developing the late 1960s in the wake of newly emerging liberation theology and the United States' civil rights movements. In 1969, the WCC established its controversial Program to Combat Racism designed to provide moral and material support to both secular and religious movements for racial justice, particularly in southern Africa.[9] A WCC consultation on human rights in 1974 set the stage for further engagement on human rights in many parts of the world,[10] while alarm within the Christian community over the massive human rights violations accompanying a number of *coups de etat* in Latin America gave new urgency to cooperation among Protestants and Catholics in the region on these issues.[11]

---

8.   *See* CLARK M. EICHELBERGER, ORGANIZING FOR PEACE: A PERSONAL HISTORY OF THE FOUNDING OF THE UNITED NATIONS (1977); NINAN KOSHY, CHURCHES IN THE WORLD OF NATIONS: INTERNATIONAL POLITICS AND THE MISSION AND MINISTRY OF CHURCHES (1994); Erich Weingartner, *Human Rights, in* DICTIONARY OF THE ECUMENICAL MOVEMENT 484–88 (Nicholas Lossky et al. eds., 1991); and ANS J. VAN DER BENT, COMMITMENT TO GOD'S WORLD: A CONCISE CRITICAL SURVEY OF ECUMENICAL SOCIAL THOUGHT 89–90 (1995).

9.   *See* ELISABETH ADLER, A SMALL BEGINNING: AN ASSESSMENT OF THE FIRST FIVE YEARS OF THE PROGRAMME TO COMBAT RACISM (1974).

10.   *See* Ans van der Bent, *Human Rights, in* VITAL ECUMENICAL CONCERNS: SIXTEEN DOCUMENTARY SURVEYS 243–60 (WCC, 1986); World Council of Churches, *Human Rights and Christian Responsibility, in* REPORT OF THE CONSULTATION IN ST. POLTEN, AUSTRIA 21–26 (WCC, 1974).

11.   *See* ERICH WEINGARTNER, BEHIND THE MASK: HUMAN RIGHTS IN ASIA AND LATIN AMERICA (1988); LAWRENCE WESCHLER, A MIRACLE UNIVERSE: SETTLING ACCOUNTS WITH TORTURERS (1990).

In the twentieth century, Christian women played significant roles in the active defense of human rights within movements in Europe, North America, Southern Africa, Latin America, and elsewhere. Yet in all this work, little attention focused on the human rights of women. Historically, individual female Christians fought for basic rights for women in the various revolutions and movements for social justice since the American Revolution.[12] Women also provided leadership in a variety of ways throughout the history of Christianity.[13] Only in the late twentieth century, however, did churches themselves come to confront persistent and unrelenting pressure to address issues important to women.

WOMEN'S CONCERNS, PERSPECTIVES, AND CONTRIBUTIONS

Christian women articulate a range of issues related to women's rights from a variety of perspectives. For purposes of discussion here, these issues will be grouped into five categories: participation, theology, bodily functions and sexuality, social justice, and relations among women.

Participation

Controversy over women's role and authority in the church dates back to the early church. Well aware of the interpretation put on Paul's various admonitions to women in his New Testament letters (which may have been added later by another author[14]), women have nonetheless always carved out creative niches in which to work and serve.[15] The world wars in the early twentieth century created a shortage of male labor in the church with the consequence that women took over a number of roles previously held only by men. Following similar trends in the secular world, such practicality and necessity gave a boost to efforts by women in subsequent decades to assert new possibilities for their work in the church. Adding legitimacy to women's work

---

12. *See* GEORGIA HARKNESS, WOMEN IN CHURCH AND SOCIETY: A HISTORICAL AND THEOLOGICAL INQUIRY (1972).

13. *See* WOMEN OF SPIRIT: FEMALE LEADERSHIP IN THE JEWISH AND CHRISTIAN TRADITIONS (Rosemary Ruether & Eleanor McLaughlin eds., 1979) [hereinafter WOMEN OF SPIRIT].

14. Robin Scroggs, *Men and Women in the Early Church, in* WE BELONG TOGETHER: CHURCHES IN SOLIDARITY WITH WOMEN 49–51 (Sarah Cunningham ed., 1992).

15. *See* WADE C. BARCLAY, METHODIST EPISCOPAL CHURCH 1845–1939, VOL. III: WIDENING HORIZONS 1845–95 (1957); Alice L. Hageman, *Introduction: No More Silence, in* SEXIST RELIGION AND WOMEN IN THE CHURCH: NO MORE SILENCE 17–28 (Hageman ed., 1974); Rosemary Radford Ruether, *Mothers of the Church: Ascetic Women in the Late Patristic Age, in* WOMEN OF SPIRIT, *supra* note 13, at 71–98; Eleanor McLaughlin, *Women, Power and the Pursuit of Holiness in Medieval Christianity, in* WOMEN OF SPIRIT, *id.* at 99–130; Ruth Liebowitz, *Virgins in the Service of Christ: The Dispute over an Active Apostolate for Women During the Counter-Reformation, in* WOMEN OF SPIRIT, *id.* at 131–52; Barbara Brown Zikmund, *The Feminist Thrust of Sectarian Christianity, in* WOMEN OF SPIRIT, *id.* at 205–24; Nancy Hardesty et al., *Women in the Holiness Movement: Feminism in the Evangelical Tradition, in* WOMEN OF SPIRIT, *id.* at 225–54; Mary Ewens O.P., *Removing the Veil: The Liberated American Nun, in* WOMEN OF SPIRIT, *id.* at 255–78; *Introducing the Ecumenical Decade for Churches in Solidarity with Women*, 40 ECUMENICAL REVIEW (1988).

for change, the WCC launched "The Ecumenical Decade of the Churches in Solidarity with Women, 1988–98," to highlight issues of women's participation as a matter for churches all over the world. Such issues revolve around two interrelated concerns: women's ordination and women's decision-making roles in the life of the church.

To ordain is to invest with ministerial or priestly authority. Most Christian churches do not ordain women, most notably, the oldest among them—the RCC and the Orthodox. This means that the vast majority of Christians do not experience women as priests or ministers, the most formal authoritative role in any congregation.

Historically, radical movements of the Protestant Reformation, such as the Anabaptists, accepted women as ministers. Only in the nineteenth century, however, did movements to ordain women develop out of the context of the changing roles of women in industrial societies of the West. Protestant churches in the United States began ordaining women in 1853 when a small congregational church in New York ordained Antionette Brown. Very few churches in Europe or the United States followed suit until a century later when Methodists and Presbyterians in the United States agreed to ordain women in 1956. Lutherans in the United States took up the practice in 1970, and Episcopalians followed in 1976.[16] The Church of England, the birthplace of Anglicanism, agreed by a small margin of votes to ordain women in 1992. Even at that late date, the Church of England subsequently promised to pay three million pounds to compensate about 200 of its male clergy who resigned rather than serve in a church that ordains women.[17]

A 1976 declaration, *Inter Insigniores*, states the official Roman Catholic objection to changing the unbroken tradition of a male priesthood. Pope John Paul II reaffirmed the RCC position in May 1994 in an apostolic letter entitled, "On reserving priestly ordination to men alone," in which he stated: "I declare that the church has no authority whatsoever to confer priestly ordination on women and that this judgement is to be definitively held by all the church's faithful." He also called into question ecumenical relations between the RCC and those churches which do ordain women, a matter of concern primarily to the latecomers to women's ordination, the

---

16.   *See* Barbara Zikmund, *The Struggle for the Right to Preach, in* WOMEN AND RELIGION IN AMERICA, VOL. 1: THE NINETEENTH CENTURY 191–241 (Rosemary Radford Ruether & Rosemary Skinner Keller eds., 1981); Barbara Zikmund, *Winning Ordination in Mainstream Protestantism: 1900–1965, in* WOMEN AND RELIGION IN AMERICA, VOL. 3: THE TWENTIETH CENTURY (Rosemary Radford Ruether & Rosemary Skinner Keller eds., 1981); FREDERICK W. SCHMIDT, A STILL SMALL VOICE: WOMEN, ORDINATION AND THE CHURCH (1996); Virginia Lieson Brereton et al., *American Women in Ministry: A History of Protestant Beginning Points, in* WOMEN OF SPIRIT, *supra* note 13, at 301–32; Mary Tanner, *Ordination of Women, in* DICTIONARY OF THE ECUMENICAL MOVEMENT 752–55 (Nicholas Lossky et al. eds., 1991).

17.   *UK: Church of England votes to ordain women*, ECUMENICAL PRESS SERVICE, Nov. 1992, at 1; *Church of England agrees to pay departing priests*, ECUMENICAL PRESS SERVICE, June 1994, at 4. An Anglican bishop in Hong Kong ordained a woman in 1944 because of the shortage of priests. The Church of England rejected the ordination, however, and she resigned her orders. Norene Carter, *Entering the Sanctuary: The Struggle for Priesthood in Contemporary Episcopalian and Roman Catholic Experience, in* WOMEN OF SPIRIT, *supra* note 13, at 71–98.

Anglicans and Lutherans. Orthodox churches together articulated their opposition to women's ordination in 1989.[18]

Churches' disputes over issues related to the ministry of the church are long-standing.[19] Those who oppose women's ordination argue that the issue is not one of human rights, or in secular terms, equal access to authoritative positions within an institution. Instead, they assert, theology lies at the heart of the issue. Most women and men who study the issue and advocate ordination would agree.

Most simply put, opponents state that Jesus was a man and that he had no women disciples. Advocates reply that Jesus was a Jew, and that many of the disciples were also Jewish—some of them were even husbands and fathers—thus, should churches consider the possibility that all priests be Jewish? Why select maleness, rather than Jewishness, as the defining characteristic of Jesus and the early disciples? Furthermore, Jesus surrounded himself with women, and women exercised vital functions in the early church.[20] Women who encountered Jesus were the first to proclaim the most profound messages Jesus gave regarding his own ministry: that a messiah would be born; that Jesus is that messiah; and, in the face of the male disciples' deep doubt, that Jesus is resurrected. Advocates assert that if Jesus selected and trusted women to be the first to hear these messages essential to the faith, then why not trust them to be ordained?

Once ordination became possible, women began flocking to seminaries. In Protestant faiths, women often make up at least half the seminary students. Yet limits exist on the career prospects for these female ordinands; most serve outside of local congregations in specialized ministries, such as university or hospital chaplaincies or other social services. Even though they may not be ordained, Orthodox and Roman Catholic women can receive theological training, which prepares them for a number of lay orders or particular leadership functions in worship liturgies.

Protestant and Anglican churches in the United States and Europe that rely on the office of bishop have begun to elect ordained women as bishops, a matter which raises larger issues of women's full participation in the church.

Lay women make up more than half of church members and Christian adherents and play vital roles in each congregation. They rarely, however, get equal access to decision-making positions on local church councils or throughout the hierarchies. On the whole, women, ordained or lay, do not head churches or ecumenical organizations. Most women consider such exclusion a denial of human rights, and it draws four types of response, which sometimes overlap.

---

18.   *Pope's "no" to women priests*, ECUMENICAL PRESS SERVICE, June 1994, at 1; *Despite one big obstacle, Pope and Carey aim for eventual unity*, ECUMENICAL PRESS SERVICE, Dec. 1996, at 6; Tanner, *Ordination of Women, supra* note 16, at 752–55.

19.   *See* WORLD COUNCIL OF CHURCHES, BAPTISM, EUCHARIST AND MINISTRY (1982).

20.   *See* Elisabeth Schussler Fiorenza, *Word, Spirit, and Power: Women in Early Christian Communities, in* WOMEN OF SPIRIT, *supra* note 13, at 29–70.

One response is simply to continue their presence in the church, at times persistently pushing for greater leadership opportunities but remaining faithful when such possibilities are denied. Other responses present more of a challenge to the institution.

Historically, when denied an opportunity to participate fully in the church itself, women often responded by forming their own monastic orders, organizations, and even denominations, in order to develop spiritually and to serve others and carry out mission. Examples include: women in aesthetic communities begun in the early centuries of Christendom; other female orders either separated in monasteries or more actively connected to secular communities; women's leadership in sectarian communities such as the Shakers; women's missionary societies founded in the nineteenth century; and the movement of women-church among primarily Catholic women in recent decades.[21]

Normally these organizations limited their purpose to finding spaces where women might exercise their own lay ministries and leadership. With rare exceptions, they did not actively challenge the prevailing theology or organizational base of the church. Women usually maintained control of their own groups, but they exercised such control only with the permission and (sometimes distant) oversight of male church authorities. While in many respects these groups provided extraordinary freedom for women within the confines of the organization, they also served the purpose of channeling women's energy and creative expressions away from demanding change in the church. This women's space was and is separate from and institutionally unequal to the church, but it often provides the only option available for women determined to live out their faith through active ministries over which they could have some control. Such separation cost the institution the numerous and sometimes remarkable gifts and talents of women that could have been exercised together with men for the whole life of the church.

The third response women demonstrate when denied access to decision making in the hierarchy is to question the hierarchy itself as unfaithful to basic Christian principles. Throughout the history of Christianity, dissident male and female theologians alike have argued that institutional arrangements whereby a privileged few rule over the subordinate many denies basic tenants of the faith. Such criticism grew in the late

---

21.   *See* Ruether, *Mothers of the Church, supra* note 15; McLaughlin, *Women, Power and the Pursuit of Holiness in Medieval Christianity, supra* note 15; Liebowitz, *Virgins in the Service of Christ, supra* note 15, at 131–52; Zikmund, *The Feminist Thrust of Sectarian Christianity, supra* note 15; Ewens O.P., *Removing the Veil, supra* note 15; Virginia Lieson Brereton & Christa Ressmeyer Klein, *American Women in Ministry: A History of Protestant Beginning Points, in* WOMEN OF SPIRIT, *supra* note 13, at 301–32; DIANN L. NEU & MARY E. HUNT, WOMEN-CHURCH SOURCEBOOK (1993); BARBARA E. CAMPBELL, IN THE MIDDLE OF TOMORROW (1975); SPIRITUALITY AND SOCIAL RESPONSIBILITY: VOCATIONAL VISION OF WOMEN IN THE UNITED METHODIST TRADITION (Rosemary Skinner Keller ed., 1993); PENNY LERNOUX, HEART ON FIRE: THE STORY OF THE MARYKNOLL SISTERS (1993); LORA ANN QUINONEZ, ET AL., THE TRANSFORMATION OF AMERICAN CATHOLIC SISTERS (1992); JANE REDMONT, GENEROUS LIVES: AMERICAN CATHOLIC WOMEN TODAY (1992); THELMA STEVENS, LEGACY FOR THE FUTURE: THE HISTORY OF CHRISTIAN SOCIAL RELATIONS IN THE WOMEN'S DIVISION OF CHRISTIAN SERVICE 1940–1968 (1978).

twentieth century as women increasingly articulated alternative theological expressions and used some of their own organizations to nurture such theologies, a challenge which is discussed below.

Disgusted by the inability of the institutional church to practice what it preaches, to embrace women as full and equal participants, and to disavow patriarchy and any theological justification for it, some women exercise a fourth response: simply leaving to find a religious home elsewhere. Some of these women call themselves "post-Christian."[22]

Theology

The theology of the "church fathers" often overtly justified women's subordination. In 1974, Mary Daly sarcastically summarized a now clear and common understanding:

> The long history of legitimation of sexism by Christianity is by now too well known to require detailed repetition here. I need not allude to the misogynism of the Church Fathers—for example, Tertullian, or Augustine, who opined that women are not made in the image of God. I omit reference to Thomas Aquinas and his numerous commentators and disciples who defined women as misbegotten males. I pass over Karl Barth's proclamation that woman is ontologically subordinate to man and Dietrich Bonhoeffer's insistence that women should be subordinate to their husbands. All of this is well known. The point has been made: patriarchal religion supports and perpetuates patriarchy.[23]

A critical mass of women theologians and liturgists has found its voice in recent decades, and a few men have joined the ranks of those who proclaim feminist articulations of the faith. Women probably contributed significant theological insights in earlier centuries, and some previous contributions are now being recovered.[24] Rarely, however, has the church witnessed such powerful attempts at reinterpretation and

---

22. *See* Mary Daly, Beyond God the Father: Toward a Philosophy of Women's Liberation (1973); and Gyn/Ecology: The Metaethics of Radical Feminism (1990).

23. Mary Daly, *Theology After the Demise of God the Father: A Call for the Castration of Sexist Religion, in* Sexist Religion and Women in the Church: No More Silence 125–42 (Hageman ed., 1974); *See also* Mary Daly, The Church and the Second Sex (1968).

24. *See* Valerie A. Abrahamsen, Women and Worship at Philippi: Diana/Artemis and other Cults in the Early Christian Era (1995); Sisters of the Spirit: Three Black Women's Autobiographies of the Nineteenth Century (William L. Andrews ed., 1986); Electa Arenal & Stacey Schlau, Untold Sisters: Hispanic Nuns in their Own Words (1989); Carollyn D. Blevins, Women in Church History: A Bibliography (1995); Witness for Change: Quaker Women over Three Centuries (Elisabeth P. Brown & Susan M. Stuard eds., 1989); Elizabeth Dreyer, Passionate Women: Two Medieval Mystics (1989); Birgetta of Sweden (Marguerite T. Harris ed., 1990); Evelyn Higginbotham, Righteous Discontent: The Women's Movement in the Black Baptist Church 1880–1920 (1993); Andre Jaques, Madeleine Barot (1991); Joan M. Nuth, Wisdom's Daughter: The Theology of Julian of Norwich (1991); Patricia Ranft, Women and the Religious Life in Premodern Europe (1996); In Our Own Voice: Four Centuries of American Women's Religious Writing (Rosemary Radford Ruether & Rosemary Skinner Keller eds., 1995); Alison Weber, Theresa of Avila and the Rhetoric of Femininity (1990).

reorientation of long-held beliefs and traditions as those that presented now by women and by other forms of liberation theology and theologies of creation.

One early fundamental theological issue simply was that of the inclusion of women throughout the various expressions of the faith. Sacred texts, liturgies, and hymns came under new scrutiny. Without altering the intention of the original Hebrew and Greek texts, new translations of the Bible were written to employ more gender-neutral terminology in passages where previous translations preferred male images, references, and pronouns.[25] Other translations went farther in "re-imaging of the holy scriptures and our relationship to them."[26] To help churches provide worship that alienates fewer women and reflects a wider spiritual discipline, many Protestant denominations in the United States revised their hymnals to include more songs with female imagery and more inclusive language.[27] Women also began creating a wide range of worship materials.[28]

Yet soon feminist theologians moved considerably beyond simple issues of inclusion to matters of reconstructing and re-imagining new understandings of women and women's stories in the Bible, new male and female as well as non-anthropomorphic concepts and pictures of God, and new interpretations of Jesus Christ, including "Christa," to broaden the traditional understanding of Christ. Women are reading church history and sacred texts again to garner more traces of female presence and imagery. Fundamental questions are being raised about doctrines, practices, and institutions held dear by tradition, because they are now seen to be expressions of patriarchical cultures rather than matters central to the faith. Women are articulating new visions of a new Christianity based on new insights about the past.[29]

---

25. *See* National Council of Churches of Christ in the United States of America, Division of Christian Education, The Holy Bible (1989).

26. *See* Priests for Equality, The Inclusive New Testament (1994).

27. For example, *see* The United Methodist Publishing House, The United Methodist Hymnal (1989).

28. For example, *see* World Council of Churches, Ecumenical Decade 1988–1998: Churches in Solidarity with Women: Prayers and Poems, Songs and Stories (1992); I Will Pour Out My Spirit: Ecumenical Decade of Churches in Solidarity with Women (1992); Ruth C. Duck, Bread for the Journey: Resources for Worship Based on the New Ecumenical Lectionary (1981); Flames of the Spirit: Resources for Worship (1985); and Touch Holiness (Ruth C. Duck & Maren C. Tirabassi eds., 1990).

29. *See* Sherry R. Anderson & Patricia Hopkins, The Feminine Face of God: The Unfolding of the Sacred in Women (1991); Sheila Collins, A Different Heaven and Earth (1974); Shelley D. Finson, Women and Religion: A Bibliographic Guide to Christian Feminist Liberation Theology (1991); Elisabeth Schussler Fiorenza, In Memory of Her: A Feminist Theological Reconstruction of Christian Origins (1984); But She Said: Feminist Practices of Biblical Interpretation (1992); Discipleship of Equals: A Critical Feminist Ekklesia/logy of Liberation (1993); Searching the Scriptures: A Feminist Introduction (1993); Jesus: Miriam's Child, Sophia's Prophet: Critical Issues in Feminist Christology (1994); Maurice Hammington, Hail Mary? The Struggle for Ultimate Womanhood in Catholicism (1995); Mary E. Hunt, Fierce Tenderness: A Feminist Theology of Friendship (1991); Sallie McFague, Models of God: Theology for an Ecological, Nuclear Age (1987); Virginia Ramey Mollenkott, Sensuous Spirituality: Out from Fundamentalism (1992); Carol A. Newsome & Sharon H. Ringe, The Women's Bible Commen-

Women's theology has flourished so much in the last three decades that many new voices have developed around the world, and these voices from different races, classes, cultures, and nationality do not always sing in unison[30]—a matter of women's relations among themselves that will be discussed below.

TARY (1992); SALLY B. PURVIS, THE POWER OF THE CROSS: FOUNDATIONS FOR A CHRISTIAN FEMINIST ETHIC OF COMMUNITY (1993); IVONI RICHTER REIMER, WOMEN IN THE ACTS OF THE APOSTLES: A FEMINIST LIBERATION PERSPECTIVE (1995); ROSEMARY RADFORD RUETHER, LIBERATION THEOLOGY: HUMAN HOPE CONFRONTS CHRISTIAN HISTORY AND AMERICAN POWER (1972); RELIGION AND SEXISM: IMAGES OF WOMAN IN THE JEWISH AND CHRISTIAN TRADITION (Rosemary Radford Ruether ed., 1974); ROSEMARY RADFORD RUETHER, NEW WOMAN NEW EARTH: SEXIST IDEOLOGIES AND HUMAN LIBERATION (1975); SEXISM AND GOD-TALK: TOWARD A FEMINIST THEOLOGY (1983); GAIA AND GOD: AN ECOFEMINIST THEOLOGY OF EARTH HEALING (1992); LETTY M. RUSSELL, HUMAN LIBERATION IN A FEMINIST PERSPECTIVE—A THEOLOGY (1974); DICTIONARY OF FEMINIST THEOLOGIES (Letty M. Russell & J. Shannon Clarkson eds., 1996); SANDRA M. SCHNEIDERS, BEYOND PATCHING: FAITH AND FEMINISM IN THE CATHOLIC CHURCH (1991); ELIZABETH CADY STANTON, THE WOMAN'S BIBLE (1974); RECONSTRUCTING THE CHRIST SYMBOL: ESSAYS IN FEMINIST CHRISTOLOGY (Maryanne Steven ed., 1993); SAVINA J. TEUBAL, HAGAR THE EGYPTIAN: THE LOST TRADITION OF THE MATRIARCHS (1990); PHYLLIS TRIBLE, GOD AND THE RHETORIC OF SEXUALITY (1978); and MARY JO WEAVER, SPRINGS OF WATER IN A DRY LAND (1993).

30.   See MARIA PILAR AQUINO, OUR CRY FOR LIFE: FEMINIST THEOLOGY FROM LATIN AMERICA (1993); MARGA BUEHRIG, WOMEN INVISIBLE: A PERSONAL ODYSSEY IN CHRISTIAN FEMINISM (1993); KATIE G. CANNON, BLACK WOMANIST ETHICS (1988); INHERITING OUR MOTHERS' GARDENS: FEMINIST THEOLOGY IN THIRD WORLD PERSPECTIVE (Katie G. Cannon et al. eds., 1988); HYUN KYUNG CHUNG, STRUGGLE TO BE THE SUN AGAIN: INTRODUCING ASIAN WOMEN'S THEOLOGY (1990); KELLY B. DOUGLAS, THE BLACK CHRIST (1994); WE DARE TO DREAM: DOING THEOLOGY AS ASIAN WOMEN (Virginia Fabella & Sun Ai Lee Park eds., 1990); STONY THE ROAD WE TROD: AFRICAN AMERICAN BIBLICAL INTERPRETATION (Cain Hope Felder ed., 1991); JACQUELYN GRANT, WHITE WOMAN'S JESUS AND BLACK WOMAN'S JESUS: FEMINIST CHRISTOLOGY AND WOMANIST RESPONSE (1989); ADA MARIA ISASI-DIAZ, EN LA LUCHA/IN THE STRUGGLE: A HISPANIC WOMAN'S LIBERATION THEOLOGY (1993); HISPANIC/LATINO THEOLOGY: CHALLENGE AND PROMISE (Ada Maria Isasi-Diaz & Fernando F. Segovia eds., 1996); THE POWER WE CELEBRATE: WOMEN'S STORIES OF FAITH AND POWER (Musimbi R.A. Kanyoro & Wendy S. Robins eds., 1992); JANE KATZ, MESSENGERS OF THE WIND: NATIVE AMERICAN WOMEN TELL THEIR LIFE STORIES (1995); HISAKO KINUKAWA, WOMEN AND JESUS IN MARK: A JAPANESE FEMINIST PERSPECTIVE (1994); MELANIE MAY, BONDS OF UNITY: WOMEN, THEOLOGY AND THE WORLDWIDE CHURCH (1989); WOMEN AND CHURCH: THE CHALLENGE OF ECUMENICAL SOLIDARITY IN AN AGE OF ALIENATION (Melanie May ed., 1991); MERCY ODUYOYE, WHO WILL ROLL THE STONE AWAY? THE ECUMENICAL DECADE OF THE CHURCHES IN SOLIDARITY WITH WOMEN (1990); THE WILL TO ARISE: WOMEN, TRADITION AND THE CHURCH IN AFRICA (Mercy Oduyoye & Musimbi R. A. Kanyoro eds., 1992); THE COMMUNITY OF WOMEN AND MEN IN THE CHURCH: THE SHEFFIELD REPORT (Constance F. Parvey ed., 1983); SEXISM IN THE 1970S: DISCRIMINATION AGAINST WOMEN, A REPORT OF A WORLD COUNCIL OF CHURCHES CONSULTATION WEST BERLIN (1974); DOROTHEE SOELLE, ON EARTH AS IN HEAVEN: A LIBERATION SPIRITUALITY OF SHARING (1993); LIFT EVERY VOICE AND SING: CONSTRUCTING CHRISTIAN THEOLOGIES FROM THE UNDERSIDE (Susan Brooks Thistlethwaite & Mary Potter Engel eds., 1990); A TROUBLING IN MY SOUL: WOMANIST PERSPECTIVES ON EVIL AND SUFFERING (Emilie M. Townes ed., 1993); EMILIE M. TOWNES, IN A BLAZE OF GLORY: WOMANIST SPIRITUALITY AS SOCIAL WITNESS (1995); GLORIA WADE-GAYLES, PUSHED BACK TO STRENGTH: A BLACK WOMAN'S JOURNEY HOME (1993); BARBEL VON WARTENBERG-POTTER, WE WILL NOT HANG OUR HARPS ON THE WILLOWS: ENGAGEMENT AND SPIRITUALITY (1987); PAULINE WEBB, SHE FLIES BEYOND: MEMORIES AND HOPE OF WOMEN IN THE ECUMENICAL MOVEMENT (1993); RENITY J. WEEMS, JUST A SISTER AWAY: A WOMANIST VISION OF WOMEN'S RELATIONSHIPS IN THE BIBLE (1988); DELORES S. WILLIAMS, SISTERS IN THE WILDERNESS: THE CHALLENGE OF WOMANIST GOD-TALK (1993); LOIS MIRIAM WILSON, TELLING HER STORY: THEOLOGY OUT OF WOMEN'S STRUGGLES (1992).

The strength of women doing theology can be judged in part by the backlash fomented by those who cherish traditional doctrines. The American Catholic bishops refused to issue a more inclusive text of the Bible. The Vatican silenced or excommunicated a number of liberation theologians, including women and feminist men. Protestant conservatives have called for heresy trials for women and men who, on the basis of feminist theology, deviate from traditional doctrine, and denominations have fired women who stepped too far out of line. Such threats may drive women out of the institutional church, but they will not suppress this powerful movement which has gained increasing momentum in recent decades.[31]

Bodily Functions and Sexuality

Few issues evoke the heated and polarized debates that those related to women's bodily functions and sexuality generate. Much of Christian theology through the ages has presumed that women bear the God-given burden of being dirty and tainted because of menstruation and childbirth. Similarly, on the whole, sex has been considered evil. Therefore, this category contains a wide range of questions related to theology, doctrine, social policies, and institutional practices which have stirred controversy throughout the history of Christianity. In this section, however, the discussion will be limited to two of the more provocative issues currently significant to women's bodies and sexuality in churches across the world: abortion and homosexuality. Both also are significant in women's human rights discussions.

Deep divisions characterize the debate over abortion among Christian women and among the churches. With the exception of the Roman Catholic Church, most of the churches that hold formal positions on abortion are located in the United States and Europe. Therefore, the opinions of Christians and their churches in other parts of the world may not be represented in such articulations.

The Roman Catholic Church officially holds a very well-known position of opposition to abortion under any circumstance. A 1968 encyclical issued by Pope Paul VI entitled *Humanae Vitae* asserts an inextricable link between marriage and procreation. The duty of married couples is to transmit life, to have children. Therefore, any effort to prevent conception is against the will of God and the natural order and is unacceptable. The one exception to this proscription against birth control is the so-called rhythm method, which is considered to be in keeping with natural law. The church's stand on abortion follows this reasoning. Any attempt to obstruct the development of a fetus after conception occurs also meets with condemnation. Some national councils of Catholic bishops pressed further on the issue by expressly declaring that abortion is murder.[32] The RCC position, articulated at the U.N. Fourth World

---

31. For example, *see* Janice Love, *Commentary: Finding Space to Reimagine God*, SOJOURNERS 8 (May 1994); *Silencing of nun sparks protest*, THE CHRISTIAN CENTURY, Sept. 27–Oct. 4, 1995, at 881; Pamela Schaeffer, *Vatican Excommunicates Balasuriya*, NATIONAL CATHOLIC REPORTER, Jan. 17, 1997, at 3.

32. *See* Mark Ellingsen, *Abortion, in* THE CUTTING EDGE: HOW CHURCHES SPEAK ON SOCIAL ISSUES 87–102 (Mark Ellingsen ed., 1993).

Conference on Women in Beijing in 1995, reiterated the official policy and called on couples to meet the high standard of "self-discipline and self-restraint" in sexuality as the appropriate way of "ensuring deep respect for human life and its transmission."[33]

Some Protestant churches agree with the RCC position; others express more sympathy with women who may face difficult choices when the life of the fetus is pitted against the health, well-being or even life of the woman carrying it. They acknowledge that abortion might be the less evil option of those available in certain circumstances. No churches, however, affirm abortion as a normal means of birth control.[34]

Following the U.N. Conference on Population and Development in Cairo in 1994, the WCC issued a briefing paper for discussion among its approximately 340 member churches, both Protestant and Orthodox. Women in the Council made significant contributions to the text, which focuses broadly on matters of population, including the issue of abortion. Although not an official policy statement, unlike most documents issued by churches, the paper points to some of the difficult issues women face in these matters. For this reason, the text deserves extensive quotation:

> While women and men are together responsible for dealing with the multiplicity of issues that emerge in the debate on population and development, women need to be recognised as central to the discussion because they are the ones most deeply and intimately affected. Women have called for a fundamental reform of the concept, structures and implementation of population policies that are often imposed on them and have treated them as targets for fertility control. Examples of such coercion include the use of new and dangerous contraceptives, and of abortion as a family planning method in some countries. Women have identified how patriarchal structures have kept them out of decision-making on issues such as family planning, and insisted on the crucial importance of reproductive health and rights as intrinsically linked to women's human rights, with significant impact both on general health, and national and international family planning programmes.
>
> The sincerity with which women and men struggle with those issues as a matter of conscience should not be underestimated. Moral and ethical decisions around these issues are more often than not taken after careful and serious soul searching.
>
> The special responsibility of men in this context is often overlooked. Frequently, family planning programmes have proved to be unsuccessful primarily because of male antagonism. Widespread son preference is a case in point: women are generally unable to voice their opinions or advocate family planning in the face of their husband's, family's and society's overwhelming desire for sons.
>
> Reproductive rights include women's right to decide if, when, how, and under what circumstances to have children. In general reproductive rights are understood to encompass the right to safe, effective contraception, safe legal abortion, safe, women-controlled pregnancy and childbirth, and access to infertility treatment and health services that meet women's reproductive needs from puberty and menstruation through menopause and beyond. . . .

---

33.   *See* Head of the Delegation of the Holy See Professor Mary Ann Glendon, Address at the Fourth World Conference on Women, Beijing, China (Sept. 4–15, 1995) (transcript available at gopher://gopher.undp.org/1/unconfs/women/conf/gov) [hereinafter Glendon Address].

34.   *See* Ellingsen, *Abortion, supra* note 32.

This context of sexual and reproductive rights actively challenges the churches to develop holistic approaches to teaching sexual ethics and family planning. . . .

In the greater society, churches could help provide for public fora to encourage dialogue on reproductive rights and gender relations. Obviously, women must be involved as equal partners in such discussions. Since unsafe abortions are a major public health concern, this issue cannot be avoided in such dialogues. It is important that public awareness is raised concerning the concrete realities that shape the contexts in which women chose abortion, for example when pregnancy is the result of rape, incest or violation. Dogmatic assertions affirming the sanctity of life in isolation from the circumstances under which conception takes place fail to bring that assertion to bear on women's lives. Equally dogmatic assertions that women have a right to bodily integrity fail to recognize the social, cultural and historical contexts that shape the capacity for responsible "choice." While contraception is certainly the morally preferred means of birth control, many women feel that unjust treatment and systemic exploitation makes legal recourse to safe, voluntary abortion a moral imperative.[35]

Regardless of whether most Christian women would agree with such a statement, its significance lies in how it contrasts with typical institutional church pronouncements, most of which are written by men. Its tone, substance, and insistence that women be at the center of discussions and decisions on these matters differentiates it and clearly demonstrates the key roles women played in shaping it.

Christian debates on homosexuality prove to be at least as contentious as those on abortion. Although on rare occasion a prominent leader like now retired Archbishop Desmond Tutu of South Africa will advocate the civil rights of gays and lesbians as well as church acceptance of them,[36] most church officials presume that they need say nothing about the issue. Their assumptions might be characterized by the following: marriage between a man and woman is normative for Christians; therefore, sexual relations between members of the same sex are prohibited, and those who practice such relations have no civil and political rights. With such attitudes prevalent in most churches, homosexuals, as homosexuals, generally are not welcome.

Although most churches reject gays and lesbians, many gays and lesbians do not reject Christianity and the church. For example, the Metropolitan Community Church (MCC) was organized specifically to provide an accepting and nurturing Christian community for homosexuals. Though its largest membership is in the United States, the MCC now has congregations in a number of countries. Within larger Protestant churches and among Catholics, gays and lesbians increasingly make their presence and demands for acceptance known. Considerable literature now exists on their struggles with the church and with the faith.[37]

---

35.   WORLD COUNCIL OF CHURCHES, CHURCHES, POPULATION AND DEVELOPMENT: CAIRO AND BEYOND 18–21 (1996).

36.   *Tutu speaks out in defence of Norway's gay Christians*, ECUMENICAL NEWS INT'L, Jan. 30, 1996, at 1.

37.   For example, *see* MARILYN B. ALEXANDER & JAMES PRESTON, WE WERE BAPTIZED TOO: CLAIMING GOD'S GRACE FOR LESBIANS AND GAYS (1996); VIRGINIA L. BRERETON, FROM SIN TO SALVATION: STORIES OF WOMEN'S CONVERSIONS, 1800 TO THE PRESENT (1991); BARBARA FERRARO & PATRICIA HUSSEY, NO TURNING BACK (1990); BRUCE HILTON, CAN HOMOPHOBIA BE CURED? (1992); RAYMOND

One of the tensions among women who seek change in the church is the relationship between lesbians and heterosexual women, an issue which leads to the next category under consideration.

Relations Among Women

Tension between lesbian and "straight" women focuses on two issues: homophobia and strategies for change. Some Christian women involved in movements for change remain unconvinced about and uncomfortable with sexual expressions of love between people of the same sex. Therefore, they place little priority on pushing for acceptance of gays and lesbians in church or society. Others may be convinced that homosexual relationships and lifestyles can be as wholesome as that of the best heterosexual models, but they may not agree with their lesbian sisters about when and where to press for change in the church. Not only do women risk setbacks for other issues and greater backlash against their movements when they dare to express solidarity on matters of homosexuality, they also risk their positions in the church. As lesbians know too well, most churches' condemnatory attitudes and policies about homosexuality mean that churches are often not safe places to work, worship, or build a community.

Yet lesbians, whether known publicly as such or not, have played prominent leadership roles among Christian women seeking change in the church in the last few decades (and perhaps for much longer). These movements benefit substantially by lesbian talent and commitment, but often do not live up to the highest expectations of creating churches where all will be welcome.

Tension among women seeking change in the church also occurs between Western women and those from other parts of the world. As was the case in secular women's movements of the twentieth century, leadership among church women in early decades came primarily from the United States and Europe. Better access to education, more mobility in highly urbanized and industrialized societies, and enough wealth to underwrite women's active involvement explains in large part why Western women took the lead in the beginning.

These leaders often articulated their own issues as though they were universally understood and agreed upon by women all over the world, but such was not the case. Christian women from the West expressed particular interest in women's ordination, inclusive language for God and humanity, reproductive freedom, and women's participation in all aspects of the church's life. Western women paid little attention in the early years to those matters of economic justice, racism, and neocolonialism which lay at the heart of the concerns and contributions of women from Africa, Asia, and Latin America. Women from Eastern Europe and the West often allowed Cold War

C. HOLTZ, LISTEN TO THE STORIES: GAY AND LESBIAN CATHOLICS TALK ABOUT THEIR LIVES AND THE CHURCH (1991); MELANIE MORRISON, THE GRACE OF COMING HOME: SPIRITUALITY, SEXUALITY AND THE STRUGGLE FOR JUSTICE (1995); ELIZABETH STUART, JUST GOOD FRIENDS: TOWARDS A LESBIAN AND GAY THEOLOGY OF RELATIONSHIPS (1995); LEANNE MCCALL TIGERT, COMING OUT WHILE STAYING IN: STRUGGLES AND CELEBRATIONS OF LESBIANS, GAYS, AND BISEXUALS IN THE CHURCH (1996).

issues to intrude between them. By the 1980s, however, the following factors helped to ease this tension, particularly in global organizations of Christian women: increasing numbers of women from the so-called "third world" in leadership, greater commitment by everyone to strong representation from all parts of the world, and heightened recognition that, despite their diversity, women everywhere share a wide range of common struggles.[38]

A third source of tension among women is that between Protestant and Catholic women and Orthodox women. In this situation, Protestant and Catholic women took the lead in early years in part because of very limited access to women in Orthodox churches. Only in recent years have Orthodox church leaders been open to discussions about changing some of their practices in response to the concerns and contributions of women, with the consequence that more Orthodox women are given permission to participate in larger women's movements in the church. The hierarchy in most Orthodox churches, however, exercises greater control over the institution and over the faithful than many of their counterparts in other churches, leaving Orthodox women to take greater risks in making their demands.

Despite these differences and tensions, with several decades of experience in working across denominations, cultures, races, and countries, Christian women have forged substantial agreement on some areas of common work, particularly issues of participation by lay women and social justice.

Social Justice

Throughout the history of the church, women took the lead in charitable work as well as in efforts to achieve social justice. Much of the literature already discussed on women's theology and the history of women in the church stresses social justice issues as central to women's concerns and theological understandings.

Although these bodies represent constituencies with fairly stark differences, the separate contributions of the delegations from the RCC and the WCC to the 1995 U.N. Fourth World Conference on Women demonstrate remarkable agreement on a range of justice concerns related to women, and provide illustration of a growing consensus among Christian women and churches on some of these matters. Among the range of concerns surveyed, both focused substantial attention on violence against women and economic justice for women.

Through research done and visits made to virtually all of its member churches, the WCC statement asserted:

> [W]e have documented evidence of the various forms of violence women experience and the extent of this violence. It has been painful for us to acknowledge that institutions which should stand in solidarity with women, including governments and the churches, have not often responded with resolute action. . . . Our particular concern

---

38. *See* SUSANNAH HERZEL, A VOICE FOR WOMEN: THE WOMEN'S DEPARTMENT OF THE WORLD COUNCIL OF CHURCHES (1981); BETTY THOMPSON, A CHANCE TO CHANGE: WOMEN AND MEN IN THE CHURCH (1982).

is focused on the rights of migrant and refugee women, of women living under the yoke of racism and on the situation of Indigenous women who are often the targets of vicious violence.[39]

Echoing a similar sentiment, the RCC contribution specifically highlighted the issues of rape in war, female genital mutilation, child prostitution, trafficking in children and their organs, and child marriages.[40] Both statements pointed out that cultural and religious traditions often exacerbate violence; the WCC specifically expressed concern about religious extremism and "the deleterious consequences this has on women's legal, political and social rights."[41]

Emphasizing the need to eliminate poverty, both statements invoked and applauded work already accomplished at the 1995 U.N. World Summit on Social Development in Copenhagen. The RCC stressed the importance of finding "new ways of recognizing the economic and social value of women's unremunerated work."[42] Similarly, the WCC pointed to the need to "recognize, count and value unwaged work—still typically women's labour, in the home and in the community."[43]

The RCC gave prominence to education and public health as intimately related to the elimination of poverty, while also stressing the "priority of human over economic values;"[44] the WCC highlighted the global political economy, stating that:

> Many in the member churches of the WCC will testify that the effects of foreign debts and structural adjustment programmes erode the traditional occupations and livelihood of women and result in increasing poverty and marginalization of women both in rural and urban settings. . . . [W]e emphasize that structural adjustment programmes should be restructured to include social development goals, that they should include gender-sensitive social impact assessments. It should be ensured that women do not have to bear a disproportionate share of the burden of the transition costs.[45]

An issue that receives little attention in the RCC statement and some mention in the WCC statement is that of women and racism, yet it, too, represents a social justice priority with substantial consensus among women working for change in the churches. Many churches, as well as the WCC, have placed considerable emphasis on women participating in struggles against racism and attempts by women of color to cope with the deleterious effects of racism in their lives.

Another matter of social justice where as yet considerably less consensus exists, but where women often take the lead in articulating the issue, is that of ecology. Not

---

39. World Council of Churches, Statement at the Fourth World Conference on Women, Beijing, China Sept. (4–15, 1995) [hereinafter WCC Statement].

40. *See* Glendon Address, *supra* note 33.

41. WCC Statement, *supra* note 39.

42. Glendon Address, *supra* note 33.

43. WCC Statement, *supra* note 39.

44. Glendon Address, *supra* note 33.

45. WCC Statement, *supra* note 39.

only do Christian women often form the basis for some of the environmental movements, they also make substantial contributions to shaping discourse on the issue.[46]

CONCLUSION

A quick survey of church history and an hour spent in worship or work in many local congregations immediately raises serious questions for women as well as for all those interested more generally in issues of human rights. Why bother with an institution so deeply mired in obstructing women's full potential? Why devote time and energy to a religion whose adherents often fail so badly to uphold basic principles of human dignity? The great paradox of Christian churches is that they remain responsible for some of humanity's worst offenses at the same time that they have inspired some of humanity's greatest achievements in social justice.

Many women love their churches as they are and will remain devoted to them because they play a crucial role in women's lives, even if judged negatively by current international norms and standards of human rights or even by Biblical principles of love and justice. Increasing numbers of women all over the world, however, challenge the churches in ways previously unimagined. Drawing on the depths of their Christian faith and spirituality, the experiences of their social engagement, and the wisdom of women across the ages, these women seek to reconstruct churches to be communities where women, men, and children flourish and draw strength to serve a God of all humanity.

---

46. *See* ANNE PRIMAVESI, FROM APOCALYPSE TO GENESIS: ECOLOGY, FEMINISM AND CHRISTIANITY (1991); ECOFEMINISM AND THE SACRED (Carol J. Adams ed., 1993).

WOMEN'S RIGHTS IN THE BAHÁ'Í COMMUNITY: THE CONCEPT OF ORGANIC EQUALITY IN PRINCIPLE, LAW, AND EXPERIENCE

Martha L. Schweitz

Women and men have been and will always be equal in the sight of God.[1]

To accept and observe a distinction which God has not intended in creation is ignorance and superstition. . . .[2]

INTRODUCTION

The membership of the global Bahá'í community is highly diverse. As of April 1997, annually elected national Bahá'í institutions, called national spiritual assemblies, were functioning in 175 countries and territories,[3] a few of the most recently formed being those of Cambodia, Mongolia, and the republics of the former Soviet Union.[4] The worldwide Bahá'í population of about five million represents a wide range of social and economic classes within their own societies and some 2,112 races, tribes and ethnic groups,[5] rendering it likely "the most diverse organized body of people on the planet today."[6] In terms of the number of locations in which it is established, the Bahá'í Faith is the second most widespread religion in the world, after Christianity.[7]

This far-flung group may nevertheless be accurately referred to as a "community" because of its shared commitment to certain laws, beliefs, and universal principles. Among these principles is the equality of women and men, a concept strongly

---

1. *Tablet of Bahá'u'lláh, in* WOMEN: EXTRACTS FROM THE WRITINGS OF BAHÁ'U'LLÁH, 'ABDU'L-BAHÁ, SHOGHI EFFENDI, AND THE UNIVERSAL HOUSE OF JUSTICE, no. 54 (Research Dep't, Universal House of Justice ed., 1986) [hereinafter WOMEN].

2. 'ABDU'L-BAHÁ, Address to the Federation of Women's Clubs, Chicago (May 2, 1912), *in* THE PROMULGATION OF UNIVERSAL PEACE 74, 76 (1982), *reprinted in* WOMEN, *supra* note 1, no. 14.

3. *Ridván Message from Universal House of Justice*, AM. BAHÁ'Í (Nat'l Spiritual Assembly of the Bahá'ís of the U.S., Evanston, IL), May 17, 1997, at 2.

4. As of May 1994, Local Spiritual Assemblies had been established in 17,780 localities worldwide. BAHÁ'Í WORLD CENTRE, THE BAHÁ'Í WORLD 1994–95, at 317 (1996) [hereinafter BAHÁ'Í WORLD 1994–95].

5. *Id.*

6. BAHÁ'Í WORLD CENTRE, THE BAHÁ'Í WORLD 1993–94, at 24 (1994) [hereinafter BAHÁ'Í WORLD 1993–94].

7. *World Religious Statistics*, 1988 BRITANNICA BOOK OF THE YEAR (1988).

461

emphasized in the Bahá'í writings and gradually finding increased expression in Bahá'í life. The Bahá'í community is also unified through an organizational structure consisting of elected local, national and international institutions. The degree of autonomy held by locally elected Bahá'í institutions enables Bahá'ís to promote universal principles in ways that also value differences and reflect local priorities and conditions. Because of its human diversity but common moral foundation and organizational structure, the Bahá'í community presents an unusual model, though one still in the early stages of its development, of how gender equality may be promoted in a wide variety of cultural and legal contexts.

Bahá'ís are found in many parts of the world; both societies relatively advanced and those still highly traditional with respect to women's human rights increasingly appreciate and articulate both the uniqueness of the Bahá'í approaches to equality and the magnitude of change required to live up to the Bahá'í standard. Within the Bahá'í community, a strongly felt need to elevate the quality of the discourse on gender is emerging and serves to increase the level of activity needed to promote equality. The purpose of this chapter is to set forth one understanding of the Bahá'í teachings relevant to gender and to give a preliminary indication of how these teachings are being promoted in various cultural settings. While these concepts and approaches to gender equality are integrally related to the body of Bahá'í teachings as a whole, and a deliberate effort is made here to present them within their contextual framework, they are nevertheless proposed on their own merits as principles that can both enrich the current debate on gender issues worldwide and inform highly effective efforts to bring about equality.

Since the Bahá'í teachings are generally consistent with contemporary and evolving international standards of women's human rights, emphasis is placed instead on what is distinctive about Bahá'í approaches and the ways in which they arguably move beyond current rights discourse. The concept of *organic equality* is developed in an attempt to locate the essence of what is distinctive about the Bahá'í contribution. A paradigm of *complementarity* and *interdependence* is proposed as the most accurate and effective context for learning how to apply equality principles to everyday decisionmaking at all levels. A few aspects of Bahá'í marriage and certain laws drawing gender distinctions are selected for further explanation.

While the present discussion is appropriately situated in this work with other chapters on issues facing women in various religious groups, any description of the beliefs and practices regarding gender equality within the Bahá'í community will necessarily be of a very different character than one concerning, for example, Christianity or Islam. This is inevitable in light of the age, size, and nature of the Bahá'í community, as well as the nature of the sources considered to be authoritative within the given religion. In some ways these differences simplify the analysis in the Bahá'í context, but they also present additional challenges.

The Bahá'í Faith is young, having been founded in 1844 and introduced to the West at the end of the nineteenth century.[8] It is a transnational religious community,

---

8.   *See infra* Appendix to this chapter: Note on the History of the Bahá'í Faith.

but it is not the faith of the majority of the population of any nation, nor has it become a state religion. It is not and, according to its teachings, can never be affiliated with any political party. Bahá'ís are spread throughout the world's societies and cultures, and are still relatively unknown in some places, widely familiar in others, and actively persecuted elsewhere. Thus, it is considerably easier to identify Bahá'í beliefs and practices as such, without the difficulty of trying to disentangle religion from centuries of intricate historical intertwining with culture and government.[9] Nonetheless, in the Bahá'í analysis one must still make a deliberate effort to distance oneself from one's own culture (an effort that can never be wholly successful), in order to try to see the significance of various teachings on gender from different social perspectives.

Of course, Bahá'í scholarship is in its infancy. There are not centuries of theology and doctrine either to rely upon or to contend with. The analysis is further simplified by the fact that there are no denominations, sects or competing schools of theology within the Bahá'í community. A splintering of the Bahá'í membership into disunified groups would be a fundamental contradiction of the core Bahá'í purpose of promoting unity. Nor is there a clergy. Thus, while there is active discussion within the community of diverse opinions, this occurs, ideally, in the spirit of truth-seeking, or at worst as a personal dispute. The Bahá'í governance structure obviates competition for leadership. This has profound implications for the overall framework for dialogue within the Bahá'í community.

The sources considered to be authoritative within the Bahá'í Faith are clearly defined but voluminous. The teachings of Bahá'u'lláh, the Founder, were written during his lifetime and have been preserved. The right of authoritative interpretation is expressly limited to his son ('Abdu'l-Bahá) and great grandson (Shoghi Effendi),[10] whose writings elaborate those of Bahá'u'lláh. The right of enacting (and repealing) supplemental legislation is limited to the elected Universal House of Justice acting as a body. There is no credibility in oral traditions nor is any weight given to the interpretations of other individuals, regardless of how closely related they may be to the family of Bahá'u'lláh or how eminent in their own right. Within this body of writings are substantial portions bearing explicitly on gender issues. Beyond these, many of the Bahá'í writings on other subjects, such as conflict resolution, economics, and justice, are also pertinent to shaping an overall approach to promoting gender equality.

The Bahá'ís of Iran have given their lives for their faith. In the twentieth century, thousands of Bahá'ís were killed. Persecutions continued intermittently in this

---

9. As the Bahá'í Faith originated in mid-nineteenth century Persia (now Iran), the question sometimes arises whether Persian culture has had a disproportionate impact on how Bahá'ís presently understand and apply Bahá'í teachings on gender. In any case, this impact is diminishing as the Bahá'í Faith grows worldwide.

10. Shoghi Effendi was the son of 'Abdu'l-Bahá's eldest daughter. *See infra* note 211, and accompanying text. Bahá'u'lláh's daughter, Bahíyyih Khánum, did not have a position of formal authority but played an extraordinary role in the early development of the faith. She is regarded in the Bahá'í Faith as having a rank similar to that of the Virgin Mary in Christianity or Fátimih in Islam. SHOGHI EFFENDI, GOD PASSES BY 347 (rev. ed. 1974) [hereinafter GOD PASSES BY].

century, but became systematized following the revolution in Iran of 1979.[11] Since then, over 200 Bahá'ís have been executed, and hundreds more imprisoned and tortured. All nine members of the National Spiritual Assembly of the Bahá'ís of Iran disappeared in 1980, and eight of the members who replaced them were executed the following year.[12] Bahá'ís in Iran are denied both public and private employment, barred from universities, expelled from primary and secondary schools, and denied passports. Bahá'ís' homes, businesses and crops have been destroyed. This persecution is carried out as official government policy to destroy the Bahá'í religious minority of Iran, as stated in a confidential Iranian government document of 1991 later made public by the United Nations.[13] Iranian Bahá'í women and men have faced these threats with immense courage and faith, as documented in firsthand accounts.[14]

Since 1980, human rights organs of the United Nations have passed numerous resolutions concerning the treatment of Bahá'ís in Iran.[15] The Commission on Human Rights has appointed a Special Representative for Iran who continues to investigate and report on the situation there. Between 1982 and 1996, the U.S. Congress held hearings and issued concurrent resolutions six times condemning the actions of the Iranian authorities against the Bahá'ís.[16] The European Parliament and German Bundestag have likewise condemned the persecution. This international response has helped to moderate some of the most violent treatment since the early 1990s, but Bahá'ís remain deprived of fundamental human rights.

---

11.   The Bahá'í community of Iran, with about 350,000 members, is the largest religious minority in the country. However, unlike the Jewish, Christian, and Zoroastrian minorities, it is not recognized under the current national constitution and laws. BAHÁ'Í INT'L COMMUNITY, PERSECUTION OF THE BAHÁ'ÍS IN IRAN 1979–1986, 5 (1986) [hereinafter PERSECUTION].

12.   *Id.* at 9.

13.   Memorandum from Seyyed Mohammad Golpaygani, Sect'y of the Supreme Revolutionary Cultural Council, to Ayatollah Ali Khamenei (Feb. 25, 1991), *reprinted in Iran's Blueprint to Destroy the Bahá'í Community*, WORLD ORDER, Fall 1993, at 44, 46–49 (facsimile and English translation). This document was summarized in *Final Report on the Situation of Human Rights in the Islamic Republic of Iran by the Special Representative of the Commission on Human Rights, Mr. Reynaldo Galindo Pohl, pursuant to Commission Resolution 1992/67 of 4 Mar. 1992*, Commission on Human Rights, 49th Sess., Agenda item 12, at 55, U.N. Doc. E/CN.4/1993/41 (1993).

14.   *See, e.g.*, OLYA ROOHIZADEGAN, OLYA'S STORY (1993), written by a woman who was imprisoned with others who were later executed and who herself eventually escaped from Iran. She later testified about the treatment of Bahá'ís in Iran before the European Parliament and the U.N. Commission on Human Rights. *Id.* at 231–32.

15.   *See, e.g.*, G.A. Res. 142, U.N. Doc. A/52/PV.70 (1997) (press release GA/9380); Commission on Human Rights Res. 54, 64th mtg. (1997) citing the "grave breaches of the human rights of the Bahá'ís in the Islamic Republic of Iran . . . ." The references to the Bahá'ís were based on the *Report on the Situation of Human Rights in the Islamic Republic of Iran, prepared by the Special Representative of the Commission on Human Rights, Mr. Maurice Copithorne, pursuant to Commission Resolution 1996/84 and Economic and Social Council decision 1996/287*, Commission on Human Rights, 53rd Sess., Agenda item 10, at paras. 50–57, U.N. Doc. E/CN.4/1997/63 (1997).

16.   *See, e.g.*, H. Con. Res. 102 (1996), *reprinted in A Concurrent Resolution: The Emancipation of the Iranian Bahá'í Community*, WORLD ORDER, Fall 1996, at 7, 7–8, followed by the texts of the debates in the Senate and the House of Representatives.

The threats and difficulties faced by Bahá'í women in Iran are of a different order than those in most other nations. In 1983, ten Bahá'í women and teenaged girls were arrested and subjected to intense physical and mental abuse in order to coerce them to recant their faith. They refused and were subsequently executed.[17] Among the aspects of the Bahá'í Faith particularly offensive to Muslim clerics are its progressive stands on women's rights, independent investigation of truth, and education. Bahá'í women are frequently charged with prostitution in Iran, because the Bahá'í wedding ceremony enjoys no legal recognition, and no civil (non-religious) marriage ceremony is available under Iranian law. Bahá'ís are also charged with adultery and immorality, due to the fact that there is no segregation of the sexes at Bahá'í gatherings.[18]

Worldwide, the actual practices and day-to-day experience within the Bahá'í community on gender issues are, as one would expect at this formative stage, highly uneven and hindered by deeply entrenched social norms.[19] Bahá'ís from all regions recount stories of enormous change and progress at the personal, family, and community level; others complain of communities where members have yet to appreciate the scope of the problem. Anecdotal data is plentiful, but little empirical research has been done to date on the range of local community experience. Information is more readily available on national and international initiatives, including certain highly successful development projects with gender focus, but it is far from complete. Within these limitations, a section of this chapter attempts to describe Bahá'í efforts to promote gender equality at the local, national and international levels, and to venture some tentative conclusions as to the most effective processes at work and the greatest obstacles faced.

The major portion of this chapter, however, describes and analyzes Bahá'í principles and teachings relevant to gender. This emphasis on concept over practice is due only in part to the present lack of systematically collected data. Even if data were plentiful, it would be important at this stage in the growth of the Bahá'í Faith to dwell on teachings and theory. Bahá'ís are enjoined to create a new model of personal, social, and institutional relationships founded on the equality and complementarity of male and female. Those seeking specific instructions on creating new roles for men and women that would be appropriate for all people in all places and times will be disappointed. The Bahá'í teachings set out firm standards, principles, and processes for decisionmaking. The rest must be created on a daily basis by those seeking to apply them. Such an open-ended process of change is a rather frightening prospect for those comfortable with traditional roles and patterns. People can only be expected to let go of old habits as they develop a practical vision of the new. This in turn requires a considerably higher degree of understanding of the Bahá'í teachings on gender than is now prevalent in the Bahá'í community.

---

17.   BAHÁ'í INT'L COMMUNITY, THE BAHÁ'íS: A PROFILE OF THE BAHÁ'í FAITH AND ITS WORLDWIDE COMMUNITY 58–59 (1994).

18.   PERSECUTION, *supra* note 11, at 18.

19.   For example, only 13 percent of the members of Bahá'í national spiritual assemblies elected in Western Africa are women. *See infra* text accompanying note 158.

The present generation the world over is so steeped in male gendered patterns of law, relationships and institutional structures that it would seem impossible to imagine fully the nature of an "equal" society founded on the principles described below. To achieve gender equality is not analogous to simply changing one constant in a familiar equation and predicting the new location or slope of a line. It is changing the equation. The new "line" may prove instead to be a sphere. The full meaning of organic gender equality, within a paradigm of complementarity and interdependence, can only be discovered through experience and over time. Thus, the present effort to analyze the Bahá'í teachings on equality and to foresee their implications for society must be regarded as only a preliminary attempt.[20]

A BAHÁ'Í VISION OF GENDER EQUALITY

According to the Bahá'í writings, men and women are and always have been equal in the sight of God. "To accept and observe a distinction which God has not intended in creation is ignorance and superstition. . . ."[21] They are equal not only in spiritual but also all other human capacities. The present state of gender inequality is symbolized by a bird with two wings of unequal strength.[22] The Bahá'í writings teach that until the equality of women and men is fully realized, so that the two wings become equally developed, humankind will remain crippled and incomplete. Inequality is regarded as a severe form of injustice that not only inflicts suffering on individual women and prevents them from attaining their highest possibilities, but also diminishes societies as a whole. Injustice against women also prevents men from achieving "the greatness which might be theirs."[23] It perpetuates in men spiritually harmful attitudes of superiority,[24] and defers yet further the possibilities for attaining a just world peace.

For a Bahá'í, one's primary identity is as a soul, a spiritual creation, not as a gender. While multiple secondary identities such as gender also determine much of daily experience, this essential vision of reality at the level of the individual has profound implications for how one views not only oneself but others, for understanding

---

20. A further disclaimer is also required. It is fundamental to the Bahá'í belief system that each individual must investigate truth independently and free of prejudice, and that faith and reason are entirely compatible. Bahá'ís study the teachings and endeavor to reach increasingly productive understandings of their application to specific contemporary issues. However, no such individual explanations or understandings, such as those included in this chapter, may be considered to represent an official or conclusive position of the Bahá'í Faith, its institutions, or the Bahá'í community as a whole.

21. 'ABDU'L-BAHÁ, *supra* note 2.

22. 'ABDU'L-BAHÁ, SELECTIONS FROM THE WRITINGS OF 'ABDU'L-BAHÁ 302 (1978), *reprinted in* WOMEN, *supra* note 1, no. 13.

23. 'ABDU'L-BAHÁ, Address to the Theosophical Society, Paris (1911), *in* PARIS TALKS 127, 133 (1961), *reprinted in* WOMEN, *supra* note 1, no. 20.

24. Michael Rogell, The Role of Men in the Quest for Equality: Identify the Hidden Dynamics of Power (address at the Conference on Women in Bahá'í Perspective, U.S. Bahá'í National Center, Jan. 27–29, 1995) (unpublished manuscript, on file with author).

the purpose of relationships and the possibilities for social transformation. Equality of women and men is regarded as a spiritual fact that must be reflected in the world of human civilization, on which relationships must be grounded and social systems constructed.

Human Unity as the Context

The teachings of the Bahá'í Faith revolve around its proclamation of the spiritual truth of the oneness of humanity. The Faith's most basic social tenet is that the unity of humankind is the only basis on which peace can be built and civilization further advanced. This requires "abandonment of prejudice—prejudice of every kind—race, class, color, creed, nation, sex, degree of material civilization, everything that enables people to consider themselves superior to others."[25] Bahá'ís are enjoined to overcome these barriers and to promote unity while also valuing diversity and the rich differences among peoples and individuals. Efforts for gender equality reflect both of these aspects, the struggle for unity and the discovery of difference.

The essential spirit of Bahá'u'lláh's teachings on unity is conveyed in the following passage from the work of Shoghi Effendi:[26]

> Let there be no mistake. The principle of the Oneness of Mankind—the pivot round which all the teachings of Bahá'u'lláh revolve—is no mere outburst of ignorant emotionalism or an expression of vague and pious hope. Its appeal is not to be merely identified with a reawakening of the spirit of brotherhood and good-will among men, nor does it aim solely at the fostering of harmonious cooperation among individual peoples and nations. . . . Its message is applicable not only to the individual, but concerns itself primarily with the nature of those essential relationships that must bind all the states and nations as members of one human family. It does not constitute merely the enunciation of an ideal, but stands inseparably associated with an institution adequate to embody its truth, demonstrate its validity, and perpetuate its influence. It implies an organic change in the structure of present-day society, a change such as the world has not yet experienced. . . . It calls for no less than the reconstruction and the demilitarization of the whole civilized world—a world organically unified in all the essential aspects of its life. . . .[27]
>
> . . . It insists upon the subordination of national impulses and interests to the imperative claims of a unified world. It repudiates excessive centralization on one hand, and disclaims all attempts at uniformity on the other. Its watchword is unity in diversity. . . .[28]

---

25. Universal House of Justice, The Promise of World Peace 29 (U.S. Bahá'í Publishing Trust ed., 1985).

26. Shoghi Effendi was Guardian of the Bahá'í Faith and great grandson of Bahá'u'lláh. *See infra* note 211 and accompanying text.

27. Shoghi Effendi, *The Goal of a New World Order* (1931), *in* The World Order of Bahá'u'lláh 27, 42–43 (2d rev. ed. 1974). In quotations from the Bahá'í writings herein, the terms "men," "man" or "mankind" are non-gendered references to humanity, unless the context indicates otherwise. The original writings of Bahá'u'lláh and 'Abdu'l-Bahá are in Arabic and Persian, both of which languages, unlike English, have gender-neutral pronouns and therefore do not use male terms to include the female.

28. *Id.* at 42.

This faith in the fundamental reality and ultimate goal of the oneness of humanity is the context in which Bahá'í teachings on gender must be understood.

There is a very close connection in the Bahá'í writings between the concepts of unity and of justice. Justice is described as the "best beloved of all things in [God's] sight. . . ."[29] and also as the means to achieving unity.[30] As such, a Bahá'í concept of justice "does not focus on the preservation of the rights of autonomous, unconnected human beings."[31] Unity, in the Bahá'í sense, preserves individual rights and prerogatives while weaving connections among people.[32] Thus, human rights are not in themselves the ultimate end but are rather a critical aspect of justice and a means to promote organic unity of families, communities, and societies. Such unity requires eliminating oppression in all its forms and enabling individuals and societies to achieve, progressively, their capacity for virtue and spiritually oriented development. For these reasons, the Bahá'í teachings on equality often combine visions in a way that may at first seem unlikely from a Western-oriented individual human rights perspective.

The allusion in the quotation above to an "institution adequate to embody . . . , demonstrate . . . , and perpetuate" the oneness of humanity is a reference to the administrative structure now being established in accordance with the Bahá'í writings. Personal, individual transformation, however extensive, is considered insufficient alone to bring about the transformation required in society and human institutions. Elected local institutions and the principles guiding the functioning of a local Bahá'í community form the foundation of a governance system intended to both preserve rights and create unity.[33]

The term "Bahá'í community," in its narrowest sense, refers to all of the Bahá'ís living in a certain town, village, city, or area.[34] When the number of adult Bahá'ís in any such locality reaches nine, they elect annually nine members to form the Local Spiritual Assembly. When a person becomes a Bahá'í, she or he is automatically iden-

---

29. BAHÁ'U'LLÁH, THE HIDDEN WORDS OF BAHÁ'U'LLÁH pt. I, no. 2 (Shoghi Effendi trans., 1939).

30. "The light of men is justice. Quench it not with the contrary winds of oppression and tyranny. The purpose of justice is the appearance of unity among men." BAHÁ'U'LLÁH, *Kalimát-i-Firdawsíyyih [Words of Paradise], in* TABLETS OF BAHÁ'U'LLÁH REVEALED AFTER THE KITÁB-I-AQDAS 66–67 (Habib Taherzadeh trans., 1978). The concept of justice in the Bahá'í writings has many facets and a literature in English on the subject is developing. *See, e.g.,* TOWARD THE MOST GREAT JUSTICE—ELEMENTS OF JUSTICE IN THE NEW WORLD ORDER (Charles O. Lerche ed., 1996); JOHN HUDDLESTON, THE SEARCH FOR A JUST SOCIETY (1989).

31. Holly Hanson, *The Process of Creating Social Justice, in* TOWARD THE MOST GREAT JUSTICE, *supra* note 30, at 29, 31 (1996).

32. *See generally* Martha L. Schweitz, *Of Webs and Ladders: Gender Equality in Bahá'í Law,* WORLD ORDER 21 (Fall 1995).

33. All of the Bahá'ís living in a country also elect annually a national spiritual assembly, whose members elect every five years the Universal House of Justice. For further description of the Bahá'í electoral process and institutions, see *infra* notes 133–34 and 137.

34. The expression "Bahá'í community" can also be used more generally to refer to the worldwide membership or to the Bahá'ís living in a certain country or region, depending on the context. It will be used in all of these ways in this chapter.

tified with the local Bahá'í community of her or his geographical residence; there is no parallel to choosing one's local church affiliation. As a result, each Bahá'í community is potentially as diverse as the local population. People who otherwise would be unlikely to encounter each other or to form a personal relationship, due to traditional race, class or gender barriers or simple personality differences, find themselves joined in a Bahá'í community. In order to fulfill the functions of the Local Spiritual Assembly and conduct other aspects of community life, they must work together. Bahá'í writers have claimed that this elementary structure may be the single most essential method for progressively achieving unity, eradicating prejudice, and promoting collective human development.[35] It is within such communities that activities to promote gender equality are carried out and differences of opinion among members are confronted.

Equal Rights and Opportunities as the Foundation

The Bahá'í writings expressly maintain the "principle of equal opportunity, rights and privileges for both sexes. . . ."[36] "Women have equal rights with men upon earth. . . ."[37] Woman's diminished progress is due mainly to the denial of education:

> The sex distinction which exists in the human world is due to the lack of education for woman, who has been denied equal opportunity for development and advancement. Equality of the sexes will be established in proportion to the increased opportunities afforded woman in this age, for man and woman are equally the recipients of powers and endowments from God, the Creator.[38]

The Bahá'í writings promote universal compulsory education and heavily emphasize education for both sexes. Education is regarded as essential both to developing good character and spiritual perception in the individual and to advancing civilization as a whole.[39] It is a fundamental duty of parents to educate their children,[40] and the writings state that the curriculum for boys and girls must be the same.[41] Even so, if it is not possible for a family to educate all the children, preference is to be given to daughters, since the benefits of knowledge can be most effectively diffused throughout society by educated mothers.[42] Thus, education of women so that they may enjoy "equal opportunity for development and advancement" is a first step.

---

35. *See* HOLLY HANSON VICK, SOCIAL AND ECONOMIC DEVELOPMENT: A BAHÁ'Í APPROACH 75–86 (1989).

36. SHOGHI EFFENDI, THE WORLD ORDER OF BAHÁ'U'LLÁH xi–xii (1938 ed.).

37. 'ABDU'L-BAHÁ, *supra* note 23.

38. 'ABDU'L-BAHÁ, Address at the Church of the Messiah, Montreal (Sept. 1, 1912), *in* THE PROMULGATION OF UNIVERSAL PEACE, *supra* note 2, at 297, 300, *reprinted in* WOMEN, *supra* note 1, no. 46.

39. Education encompasses the physical, intellectual, and spiritual. *See generally* NATIONAL BAHÁ'Í EDUCATION TASK FORCE, NATIONAL SPIRITUAL ASSEMBLY OF THE BAHÁ'ÍS OF THE UNITED STATES, FOUNDATIONS FOR A SPIRITUAL EDUCATION—RESEARCH OF THE BAHÁ'Í WRITINGS (1995).

40. If parents are unable to educate their children, "the body politic must provide the means for their education. . . ." 'ABDU'L-BAHÁ, *supra* note 38.

41. 'ABDU'L-BAHÁ, Address at the Unitarian Church, Philadelphia (June 9, 1912) *in* THE PROMULGATION OF UNIVERSAL PEACE, *supra* note 2, at 172, 175, *reprinted in* WOMEN, *supra* note 1, no. 44.

42. UNIVERSAL HOUSE OF JUSTICE, *supra* note 25, at 27, *reprinted in* WOMEN, *supra* note 1, no. 50.

Another essential requirement of equality is that women participate fully and equally with men in all spheres of endeavor in public life. According to the Bahá'í teachings, *de facto* equality in world affairs is essential to bringing about international peace:

> So it will come to pass that when women participate fully and equally in the affairs of the world, when they enter confidently and capably the great arena of laws and politics, war will cease; . . .[43]

The dual role of women, as influential actors in all aspects of public life and as mothers, is repeatedly emphasized in the Bahá'í writings, and the two are expressly related to each other in service of peace:

> War and its ravages have blighted the world; the education of woman will be a mighty step toward its abolition and ending, for she will use her whole influence against war. Woman rears the child and educates the youth to maturity. She will refuse to give her sons for sacrifice upon the field of battle. In truth, she will be the greatest factor in establishing universal peace and international arbitration.[44]

What is new in the preceding passage is not the idea that mothers will oppose war, but that through education women will acquire sufficient influence in government policy to make this opposition effective long term.

In addition, full gender equality is regarded as essential in order to create the "moral and psychological climate" necessary for peace. Thus, the empowerment of women is also the hope for humanity:

> The emancipation of women, the achievement of full equality between the sexes, is one of the most important, though less acknowledged prerequisites of peace. The denial of such equality perpetrates an injustice against one half of the world's population and promotes in men harmful attitudes and habits that are carried from the family to the workplace, to political life, and ultimately to international relations. There are no grounds, moral, practical, or biological, upon which such denial can be justified. Only as women are welcomed into full partnership in all fields of human endeavor will the moral and psychological climate be created in which international peace can emerge.[45]

Complementarity: Equality in an Organic System as the Goal

It is well-recognized that providing women with the same rights and opportunities as men in civil and political life, education, and employment is not sufficient to bring about a condition in society that most (women) would regard as "equal." Even in those legal systems where considerable progress has been made in the struggle for legal equality, a structure of subordination remains.[46] What is it, then, that we are striving for, that is beyond rights and that we call "equality?"

---

43. 'ABDU'L-BAHÁ, Address at Women's Suffrage Meeting, Metropolitan Temple, New York (May 20, 1912), *in* THE PROMULGATION OF UNIVERSAL PEACE, *supra* note 2, at 133, 135, *reprinted in* WOMEN, *supra* note 1, no. 91.

44. 'ABDU'L-BAHÁ, Address at Hotel Schenley, Pittsburgh (May 7, 1912), *in* THE PROMULGATION OF UNIVERSAL PEACE, *supra* note 2, at 105, 108, *reprinted in* WOMEN, *supra* note 1, no. 79.

45. UNIVERSAL HOUSE OF JUSTICE, *supra* note 25, at 26–27, *reprinted in* WOMEN, *supra* note 1, no. 90.

46. One most devastating example is the feminization of poverty, a problem far transcending the capacity of an individual human rights approach to solve. While allocation of resources at the

Gender equality has long been regarded by many in the West as freedom to be treated without regard to sex. In practical terms, this means that women have essentially demanded the right to be treated the same as men. The struggle so defined has produced enormous progress in a great many societies worldwide. Nevertheless, it has become increasingly apparent that this approach is not complete, as it leaves untouched and unchallenged social structures of hierarchy and power, as well as the societal assumption of the male as the norm. Moreover, it debases women (and ultimately impoverishes society) by depriving them of the opportunity to discover what is different about their individual and/or collective contribution to work, family, and community from that of the men around them. The increasingly active participation in the global human rights dialogue of women from non-Western backgrounds, and of women from a wider range of social strata in the West itself, seems to have accelerated the shift in search of new paradigms of equality and equity. Not only do these voices focus on issues far different from those of personal independence, career, and reproductive/sexual freedom that animated the early days of the contemporary Western women's movement, such newer voices have also been willing to express their distaste for what they often perceive in the West to be the masculinization of women.

The Bahá'í vision of equality is not limited to the notion of equality as freedom to be treated without regard to sex. The latter approach goes far as an implementing principle of equality in a vast number of cases, but it does not do justice to the full range of relevant Bahá'í teachings. "Equal" does not always mean "identical"; nor does "equal treatment" necessarily imply "same treatment" if the circumstances of two given people are substantially different.[47] The Bahá'í teachings would seem to be fully consistent, however, with the concept of equality as "freedom from systematic subordination because of sex."[48] Bahá'í laws and principles undermine and replace embedded structures of subordination in all areas, including economics, politics, business, education, and family relations.

If gender equality does not mean sameness, and "equality of status does not mean identity of function,"[49] then it becomes necessary to consider what form of rela-

---

level of the family will be touched upon in this chapter, the body of Bahá'í teachings most broadly relevant to the question are those concerned with principles of economic justice and the means to eliminate the extremes of wealth and poverty. The intersection between Bahá'í principles on gender equality and on economic justice would be a productive area for research. *See generally* A BAHÁ'Í PERSPECTIVE ON ECONOMICS OF THE FUTURE: A COMPILATION FROM THE BAHÁ'Í WRITINGS (Badi Shams ed., 2d ed. 1991); Gregory C. Dahl, *Evolving toward a Bahá'í Economic System*, 4 J. BAHÁ'Í STUD. 1, 1 (Sept.–Dec. 1991); Farhad Sabetan, *An Exploration into the Political Economy of Global Prosperity*, 7 J. BAHÁ'Í STUD. 43 (June–Sept. 1997).

47. For the provisions in Bahá'í law that draw distinctions based on gender, see *infra* text accompanying notes 116–39.

48. Hilary Charlesworth et al., *Feminist Approaches to International Law*, 85 AM. J. INT'L L. 613, 632 (1991).

49. Letter from the Universal House of Justice (June 23, 1974), *in* WOMEN, *supra* note 1, no. 68. Different functions can be deemed equal or unequal on several different levels, some of which are relevant in determining whether they perpetuate the subordination of women. On the dangers of a "separate but equal" approach, *see infra* note 76 and accompanying text.

tionship between men and women can replace structures of domination/subordination and meet the demands of the equality sought. Drawing on observations in the world of nature, two possible types of relationships come to mind: mutualism, a symbiotic relationship between two species from which both benefit, or synergism, in which the combined action of two or more substances has a greater total effect than the sum of the individual parts.

The Bahá'í writings suggest a relationship between male and female that is mutualistic or synergistic, and arguably go further by identifying the relationship as one of complementarity: "The happiness of mankind will be realized when women and men coordinate and advance equally, for each is the complement and helpmeet [sic] of the other."[50] Although it is difficult in the present social context to describe comprehensively a vision of a transformed "equal" society, its fundamental nature is portrayed metaphorically in the Bahá'í writings as the perfecting of the social body. The human world has become so irretrievably interdependent that it may be likened to an organic system, a single biological entity composed of distinct parts. When the parts are put together and properly coordinated, they produce capacities, capabilities and qualities far beyond those inherent in any of the parts alone. Organic unity of male and female is described as follows:

> There is a right hand and a left hand in the human body, functionally equal in service and administration. If either proves defective, the defect will naturally extend to the other by involving the completeness of the whole; for accomplishment is not normal unless both are perfect. If we say one hand is deficient, we prove the inability and incapacity of the other; for single-handed there is no full accomplishment. Just as physical accomplishment is complete with two hands, so man and woman, the two parts of the social body, must be perfect.[51]

Thus, female and male not only provide mutual benefit and create together a distinct system, but each completes and makes perfect the other. Inequality, and the related "harmful attitudes and habits" of men,[52] have always deprived women of achieving their highest potential. Less recognized is the fact that they have also limited men. "As long as women are prevented from attaining their highest possibilities, so long will men be unable to achieve the greatness which might be theirs."[53] Men and women must each become strong and fully developed for the sake of themselves, the other, and the whole. Another symbol used in the Bahá'í writings to represent the need for equality is the bird. The "two wings" of the world of humanity must become "equally developed"[54] and "equal in strength"[55] in order that the bird may fly, i.e., in order to bring about human prosperity and happiness.

---

50. 'ABDU'L-BAHÁ, Address at the Baptist Temple, Philadelphia (June 9, 1912), *in* THE PROMULGATION OF UNIVERSAL PEACE, *supra* note 2, at 176, 182, *reprinted in* WOMEN, *supra* note 1, no. 18.

51. 'ABDU'L-BAHÁ, *supra* note 43, at 134, *reprinted in* WOMEN, *supra* note 1, no. 16.

52. *See supra* text accompanying note 45.

53. 'ABDU'L-BAHÁ, *supra* note 23.

54. 'ABDU'L-BAHÁ, *supra* note 22.

55. 'ABDU'L-BAHÁ, *supra* note 2, at 77.

Complementarity in the Bahá'í writings describes not only human relationships between male and female persons but also the connection between "the male" and "the female" as idealized abstractions of human qualities, all potentially present in both men and women:

> The world of the past has been ruled by force, and man has dominated over woman by reason of his more forceful and aggressive qualities both of body and mind. But the balance is already shifting—force is losing its weight and mental alertness, intuition, and the spiritual qualities of love and service, in which woman is strong, are gaining ascendancy. Hence the new age will be less masculine, and more permeated with the feminine ideals—or, to speak more exactly, will be an age in which the masculine and feminine elements of civilization will be more evenly balanced.[56]

The Bahá'í teachings do not ascribe different sets of qualities to women and men on the basis of inherent, biological determination, since "human virtues belong equally to all."[57] Nevertheless, such stereotypical masculine and feminine virtues are identified as resources and latent potential which are not presently being used to their full advantage, due to the imbalance between them both within individuals and in society and its institutions. The goal is to shift this balance, not just through the equal participation of women but through equal assignation of value, as defined in an ongoing consultative process. The so-called "feminine ideals" need to become better integrated into the character of men; "masculine ideals" need to become better integrated into the character of women; and the institutions and structures of state and economy that have been long dominated not just by men but by masculine character need to combine the two in order to promote progress in an organically unified world.[58]

When a system has arrived at such a condition of organic interdependence, it would seem hopelessly self-destructive to cling to models based on zero-sum competitiveness. Competition in some of its forms should still have an important role in such a world, but as an over-arching model for relationships and decisionmaking it is not only short-sighted but dangerous to the well-being of the system as a whole. Gender equality in a competitive model can be characterized simply as a transfer of power from one group to another, with power understood as the ability to control and dominate. In an organic model, equality demands a transfer of power, but it also redefines power itself. In so doing it renders some issues considerably more nuanced and complex, as suggested in the following two sections on family decisionmaking and parenthood.

SPECIFIC TEACHINGS BEARING ON EQUALITY

Family Decisionmaking Through Consultation

The vision of the Bahá'í family demonstrates in very practical terms the meaning of complementarity. The family is neither a purely rights-based structure nor is it

---

56. 'Abdu'l-Bahá, *quoted in* JOHN E. ESSLEMONT, BAHÁ'U'LLÁH AND THE NEW ERA 156 (3d rev. ed. 1970), *reprinted in* WOMEN, *supra* note 1, no. 25.

57. 'ABDU'L-BAHÁ, Address in Paris (Nov. 14, 1911), *in* PARIS TALKS, *supra* note 23, at 160, 162.

58. *See generally* Marilyn J. Ray, *Women and Men: Toward Achieving Complementarity*, WORLD ORDER 9 (Fall 1995).

the satrapy of the eldest male. Rights correlate with duties and the overall emphasis is on the family bond:

> The integrity of the family bond must be constantly considered, and the rights of the individual members must not be transgressed. The rights of the son, the father, the mother—none of them must be transgressed, none of them must be arbitrary. Just as the son has certain obligations to his father, the father, likewise, has certain obligations to his son. The mother, the sister and other members of the household have their certain prerogatives. All these rights and prerogatives must be conserved, yet the unity of the family must be sustained. The injury of one shall be considered the injury of all; the comfort of each, the comfort of all; the honour of one, the honour of all.[59]

In addition to being a group of individuals with personal rights and obligations, a family is also an entity in itself, in which injury, comfort, honor, etc., are experienced in common. The individual is not subsumed in the group, but nor is the family entity demolished in favor of a radical individualism.[60] The characteristics of such a "unity-based" family are different from other types of family systems, such as those that might be described as power-based or indulgence-based. Both the processes and outcomes differ in all basic aspects of family experience, including how love is expressed, how learning takes place, and how choices are made.[61]

Decisions in a Bahá'í family are to be made through consultation, the process prescribed in the Bahá'í writings for solving problems, making decisions, and maintaining unity in all contexts.[62] Consultation is fundamental to the operation of elected Bahá'í institutions at all levels. This is a consultative process founded on candor and mutual respect, in which each individual participates on an equal basis, frankly expressing her or his own opinion and seriously considering the views of others. Once an idea is spoken, it belongs not to the individual who voiced it but to the group:

> [T]he individual participants strive to transcend their respective points of view, in order to function as members of a body with its own interests and goals. In such an atmosphere, characterized by both candor and courtesy, ideas belong not to the individual to whom they occur during the discussion but to the group as a whole, to take up, discard, or revise as seems to best serve the goal pursued. Consultation succeeds to the extent that all participants support the decisions arrived at, regardless of the individual opinions with which they entered the discussion. Under such circumstances an earlier decision can be readily reconsidered if experience exposes any shortcomings.[63]

---

59. 'ABDU'L-BAHÁ, Address at Church of the Ascension (June 2, 1912), *in* THE PROMULGATION OF UNIVERSAL PEACE, *supra* note 2, at 163, 168, *reprinted in* WOMEN, *supra* note 1, no. 61.

60. Given the emphasis in the Bahá'í teachings on the spiritual importance of individual choice and will, the individual as an organic piece of a family and other social groups must nevertheless retain full responsibility for her or his own actions.

61. For a more thorough development of these concepts, *see* H.B. DANESH, THE VIOLENCE-FREE FAMILY: BUILDING BLOCK OF A PEACEFUL CIVILIZATION (1995).

62. "Say: no man can attain his true station except through his justice. No power can exist except through unity. No welfare and no well-being can be attained except through consultation." Tablet of Bahá'u'lláh, *in* CONSULTATION: A COMPILATION, no. 2 (Research Dep't, Universal House of Justice ed., 2d ed. 1995) [hereinafter CONSULTATION].

63. BAHÁ'Í INTERNATIONAL COMMUNITY, THE PROSPERITY OF HUMANKIND 15–16 (U.K. Bahá'í

Such a consultative process does not resemble certain forms of so-called consensus, which in fact give the most powerful voices an unspoken veto or prevent action unless unanimity is achieved. Nor does it resemble most contemporary styles of negotiation, compromise, or debate, much less the adversarial method. The object of consultation is the "investigation of truth"[64] and not the vindication of one's position. It requires purity of motive and sincerity of intent to succeed.

Between marriage partners, consultation is the optimal method for resolving conflicts and making decisions, as well as communicating aspirations and mutual support.[65] The unique problem regarding consultation in the marriage context is the question of what to do when, even after thoughtful and loving consultation, the wife and husband cannot agree on any proposed solution (including, perhaps, the option of postponing the decision).[66] The Bahá'í writings state that "[t]here are, therefore, times when a wife should defer to her husband, and times when a husband should defer to his wife, but neither should ever unjustly dominate the other."[67] Further, "[e]xactly under what circumstances such deference should take place, is a matter for each couple to determine."[68]

How a couple deals with the issue of one partner deferring to the other depends on whether they assume that they are operating within a competitive system or an organically unified one. If it is felt to be competitive, deferring to one's partner on any significant decision is likely to be experienced negatively as "I lose, you win. And you owe me." If the family system is felt to be organically unified, who should defer to whom in a given case may be determined on some rational, relevant, and equal basis free of gender-based bias. Such rational bases might include, for example, consideration of who will be most affected by the decision, who has greater experience with the subject matter, or who should be encouraged to make the decision in order to gain experience and responsibility in the given area. Deferring in this way can be experienced positively as a successful effort seeking the good of the family as a whole.

Another fundamental benefit of the consultative approach is that it necessarily takes into full account the circumstances of the particular family at the time and allows

---

Publishing Trust/Bahá'í Publications Australia ed. 1995), *reprinted in* WORLD ORDER 7, 15 (Spring 1995).

64.   'ABDU'L-BAHÁ, Address at Hotel Plaza, Chicago (May 2, 1912), *in* THE PROMULGATION OF UNIVERSAL PEACE, *supra* note 2, at 72, *reprinted in* CONSULTATION, *supra* note 62, no. 21. "The shining spark of truth cometh forth only after the clash of differing opinions." 'ABDU'L-BAHÁ, *id.* no. 9.

65.   For practical guidance on consultation within marriage, *see* A FORTRESS FOR WELL-BEING: BAHÁ'Í TEACHINGS ON MARRIAGE 67–70 (Daniel C. Jordan ed., 1973).

66.   In a local spiritual assembly or other elected Bahá'í institution, if unanimity cannot be reached a vote is taken and the majority prevails.

67.   Letter from the Universal House of Justice to a national spiritual assembly (Dec. 23, 1980), *in* WOMEN, *supra* note 1, no. 71.

68.   Letter from the Universal House of Justice (May 6, 1982), *in* WOMEN, *supra* note 1, no. 72.

for flexibility as conditions change and understanding matures. It is contextual deci-sionmaking, incompatible with the maintenance of inflexible roles and responsibilities.

Responsibilities of Mothers and Fathers

In the Bahá'í writings great honor and nobility are conferred on motherhood, yet the implications of this in the context of other teachings on the role of women are highly non-traditional.

Certain passages in the writings are consistent with a stereotypical view of women as mothers, and the utmost importance is attributed to this role. For example, mothers are described as the "first educators, the first mentors" of their children, and are enjoined to "suckle [their] children from their infancy with the milk of a univer-sal education."[69] Motherhood is most highly praised: "O ye loving mothers, know ye that in God's sight, the best of all ways to worship Him is to educate the children and train them in all the perfections of humankind; and no nobler deed than this can be imagined."[70] The writings state further that "[t]he task of bringing up a Bahá'í child . . . is the chief responsibility of the mother . . ."[71] and that a "corollary of this respon-sibility of the mother is her right to be supported by her husband. . . ."[72] However, "[t]his by no means implies that these functions are inflexibly fixed and cannot be changed and adjusted to suit particular family situations, nor does it mean that the place of the woman is confined to the home."[73] These primary (not sole) parental responsibilities not only can but must be changed within any family where such is the result of the consultative process. The father also has the responsibility to edu-cate his children, and "this responsibility is so weighty that Bahá'u'lláh has stated that a father who fails to exercise it forfeits his rights of fatherhood."[74]

Designating child-rearing and financial support to be the respective primary responsibilities of mothers and fathers has typically condemned women to suffer the classic patriarchal family structure. In fact, any expression of reverence for mother-hood has implied relegating women to second-class status, keeping them severely dis-advantaged both socially and economically. One need only recall the U.S. Supreme Court's references in 1873 (in construing the equal protection clause of the Fourteenth Amendment to permit excluding women from the legal profession) to the "natural and proper timidity and delicacy which belongs to the female sex," and to the "law of the Creator" that the "paramount destiny and mission of woman are to fulfil the

---

69. 'Abdu'l-Bahá, *supra* note 22, at 126, *reprinted in* Women, *supra* note 1, no. 56.

70. 'Abdu'l-Bahá, *supra* note 22, at 139, *reprinted in* Women, *supra* note 1, no. 58.

71. Shoghi Effendi, *quoted in* Letter from the Universal House of Justice, *supra* note 67.

72. Letter from the Universal House of Justice, *id.*

73. Letter from the Universal House of Justice (Aug. 9, 1984), *in* Women, *supra* note 1, no. 74. On the importance of consultation in developing an egalitarian environment among family mem-bers, see Hoda Mahmoudi & Richard DaBell, *Rights and Responsibilities in the Bahá'í Family System*, 5 J. Bahá'í Stud. 1, 6–8 (June–Sept. 1992).

74. Letter from the Universal House of Justice, *supra* note 67.

noble and benign offices of wife and mother."[75] It is equally discriminatory to simply proclaim the traditional functions of women in the home and men in the workplace to be "different but equal." This is just as dishonest, transparent, and illegitimate as it was in the days of *de jure* racial segregation when the U.S. Supreme Court upheld the doctrine of "separate but equal" facilities for the white and black races.[76]

Honoring motherhood is equivalent to marginalizing women if and only if it is set in the context of a social system that deliberately or in effect excludes women from full participation in business, economics, government, etc. The references in the Bahá'í teachings to the primary responsibilities of mothers and fathers must be understood within the context of other teachings in which they are embedded. The Bahá'í teachings insist that women are also to enter into full partnership with men in all fields of human endeavor.[77] How women collectively and individually can be both actively involved as mothers and equal to men in public life presents a serious challenge, a challenge that can lead to creative new patterns in both family and economic life.

Under present conditions, motherhood tends to exclude women permanently from significant participation in public affairs. Although there is no logical incompatibility, given an average life span, between women both being mothers and participating "fully and equally in the affairs of the world," it is more often than not a practical impossibility. The incompatibility of motherhood (or involved fatherhood, for that matter) and full civil participation flows rather from the nature of present economic and social systems, laws, and business practices. However different these systems, laws, and practices may be in various societies, they nearly all seem tailor-made to enforce a permanent division of labor between those who care for children and tend to homes and those who produce income in the formal economy and have a voice in public affairs.

Achieving equality and ending the systematic subordination of women would seem to be possible only in conjunction with (as both cause and effect of) the transformation of economic and social systems. Laws and practices founded on Bahá'í principles regarding economics and society may be anticipated to be radically different from those now considered the norm. It is an area calling for imaginative thinking and for learning from the best models and experiments that can be found in any

---

75.   Bradwell v. Illinois, 83 U.S. 130, 139 (1873).

76.   Plessy v. Ferguson, 163 U.S. 537 (1896). This analogy is made by Peggy Caton, *Introduction* to EQUAL CIRCLES: WOMEN AND MEN IN THE BAHÁ'Í COMMUNITY ix, xii–xvi (Peggy Caton ed., 1987). The Bahá'í teachings state that any work, however humble or magnificent, performed in the spirit of service, is a form of worship. Such "spiritual" equality between the lowly and the great, however, must not be permitted to distract attention from, let alone replace, the necessity for actual social equality in gender relations also strongly emphasized in the teachings:

Concepts of "spiritual" or "essential" equality can be abstractly applied to conditions of the greatest practical inequality without any seeming contradiction to those who do so. . . .

. . . On some spiritual level, yes, the cleaning lady is equal to the bank president. But is she fully equal? Does she have equal choices, opportunities, status, and freedom? Does she have equal opportunity to become bank president? *Id.* at xv–xvi.

77.   *See supra* text accompanying note 45.

society. In a context of transformed social values, it would be entirely possible for business, government, and community to take steps (steps they now regard as unbearable inconveniences or simply unreasonable) to promote the well-being of children and families by widely expanding the work choices open to women and men.[78]

Given the insistence in the Bahá'í writings on women's participation in public life and the consultative basis for all family decisionmaking, one may question why the writings also identify respective primary responsibilities of mothers and fathers. This default allocation of responsibilities suggests the likelihood that, along with the deep personal and social transformations that will occur in bringing about gender equality, it will be the mothers and not the fathers, in the majority of cases, who will remain most closely associated with and responsible for children in their earliest years. This is neither cause for alarm nor incompatible with full equality as described. Specifying these responsibilities places emphasis on the *accountability of parents* and ensures the *welfare of children*. When governments have decided that it is the state's responsibility to care for children in state-owned institutions while women are required to work long days, the results for children have ranged from unfortunate to disastrous. (Women in such societies have struggled for the right *not* to work.) Children suffer when they do not receive personal "motherly" care from some loving person(s), male or female, however it may be provided. Children also suffer when fathers who are capable of supporting their children and families choose not to, effectively abandoning them. The lack of accountability of fathers is a cause of great harm to both children and women the world over. In a Bahá'í system, parents may arrange their family responsibilities however they choose, but in the end the mother and the father bear personal responsibility for ensuring that their children are cared for and educated to the best of their combined abilities.

Violence and Force Condemned

The use of violence by individuals for any purpose other than self-defense[79] is entirely prohibited in the Bahá'í writings:

> The use of force by the physically strong against the weak, as a means of imposing one's will and fulfilling one's desires, is a flagrant transgression of the Bahá'í Teachings. There can be no justification for anyone compelling another, through the use of force or through the threat of violence, to do that to which the other person is not inclined. 'Abdu'l-Bahá has written, "O ye lovers of God! In this, the cycle of Almighty God, violence and force, constraint and oppression, are one and all condemned."[80]

---

78. Such transformation in social values requires substantially elevating the status associated with child-rearing and broadening the sense of responsibility for this vital work beyond the nuclear family. The Core Curriculum for Spiritual Education, for example, produced by the U.S. National Bahá'í Education Task Force, develops the concept of the "child-development centered community."

79. BAHÁ'U'LLÁH, THE KITÁB-I-AQDAS [THE MOST HOLY BOOK] 240–41 n.173 (Bahá'í World Centre trans., 1992) (1873) [hereinafter KITÁB-I-AQDAS].

80. Letter from the Universal House of Justice to an individual (Jan. 24, 1993) (on file with the National Spiritual Assembly of the Bahá'ís of the United States) [hereinafter Letter on Violence].

Emphasizing the responsibility of men to prevent cruelty to women, Bahá'u'lláh has written: "[Men] must be adorned with the ornament of justice, equity, kindness and love. As they do not allow themselves to be the object of cruelty and transgression, in like manner they should not allow such tyranny to visit [women]."[81] Bahá'í men are encouraged to play a particular role in this regard: "Bahá'í men have the opportunity to demonstrate to the world around them a new approach to the relationship between the sexes, where aggression and the use of force are eliminated and replaced by cooperation and consultation."[82]

Based on these teachings, it may be anticipated with certainty that Bahá'í law will treat domestic violence as a crime at least as serious as other assault and battery.[83] The Universal House of Justice has written that "[i]f a Bahá'í woman suffers abuse or is subjected to rape by her husband, she has the right to turn to the Spiritual Assembly for assistance and counsel, or to seek legal protection."[84] One role of the local spiritual assembly generally is to assist Bahá'ís with family or other problems, through consultation and/or referring them to competent professionals who can provide advice or counselling. On a more general, preventive level, another role of the Bahá'í community is to help promote learning, through study classes and institutes, of how to create healthy families, and to provide a forum for members to discuss issues of concern.

In cases of incest or sexual abuse of children, Bahá'í institutions are enjoined to be "uncompromising and vigilant in their commitment to the protection of the children entrusted to their care."[85] "A parent who is aware that the marriage partner is subjecting a child to such sexual abuse . . . must take all necessary measures, with the assistance of the Spiritual Assembly or civil authorities if necessary" to bring a stop to the behavior and to promote healing.[86] Parental rights should be called into question not only when a parent has committed incest but also when a parent "consciously fails to protect the child from flagrant sexual abuse."[87]

Sexual Morality and Reproduction

It is the Bahá'í view that, in modern society generally, sexual relations have become so over-emphasized as to become a major obstacle to appreciating and pursuing the more fundamental concerns of human life and relationships. The Bahá'í teachings do not advocate the suppression of the sex impulse but prescribe that, like

---

81.   *Tablet of Bahá'u'lláh, supra* note 1.

82.   Letter on Violence, *supra* note 80, at 3. For specific observations and suggestions on the role of men in eliminating violence against women, see Michael L. Penn, *Violence Against Women and Girls*, WORLD ORDER 43 (Spring 1995).

83.   Striking one another is prohibited in Bahá'í law. KITÁB-I-AQDAS, *supra* note 79, para. 148.

84.   Letter on Violence, *supra* note 80, at 4.

85.   *Id.* at 5.

86.   *Id.*

87.   *Id.*

other human instincts highly valuable but dangerous in excess, it be controlled and made to serve one's chosen purpose in life. The Bahá'í standard of sexual morality applies equally to men and women. It requires chastity before marriage and faithfulness within marriage,[88] where sexual relations find their spiritually oriented expression both for procreation and for the unity of the couple in the physical world.[89] Monasticism is prohibited. Marriage is not compulsory and may only be contracted with the free consent of each individual.

Any form of sexual relations outside of the marriage between a woman and a man are contrary to Bahá'í law.[90] Adhering to Bahá'í law is a duty freely accepted by a person when he or she chooses to become a Bahá'í.[91] While the Bahá'í community does not endorse homosexual conduct, this position cannot be associated with approval, tacit or otherwise, of the fear, hatred, and prejudice that are directed at gays and lesbians by many segments of society. The attitudes that should characterize individual Bahá'ís in their relationships with all people, within or outside the Bahá'í community, are those of loving kindness, freedom from prejudice, and absence of judgement of others' personal lives.[92]

---

88.   Letters from Shoghi Effendi (Sept. 5, 1938 & Sept. 28, 1941), *in* LIGHTS OF GUIDANCE: A BAHÁ'Í REFERENCE FILE nos. 681 & 708 (Helen Hornby ed., 1983).

> [T]he maintenance of such a high standard of moral conduct is not to be associated or confused with any form of asceticism, or of excessive and bigoted puritanism. The standard inculcated by Bahá'u'lláh, seeks, under no circumstances, to deny any one the legitimate right and privilege to derive the fullest advantage and benefit from the manifold joys, beauties, and pleasures with which the world has been so plentifully enriched by an All-Loving Creator.

SHOGHI EFFENDI, THE ADVENT OF DIVINE JUSTICE 28 (1969) (message written to the North American Bahá'í community in 1938).

89.   'Abdu'l-Bahá wrote as follows:

> But the marriage of the people of Bahá must consist of both physical and spiritual relationship for both of them are intoxicated with the wine of one cup, are attracted by one Peerless Countenance, are quickened with one Life and are illumined with one Light. This is the spiritual relationship and everlasting union. Likewise in the physical world they are bound together with strong and unbreakable ties.

'Abdu'l-Bahá, *in* BAHÁ'Í WORLD FAITH 373 (1956 ed.)

90.   Letter from Shoghi Effendi (Mar. 26, 1950), *in* LIGHTS OF GUIDANCE, *supra* note 88, no. 726.

91.   One becomes a Bahá'í because she or he has both recognized Bahá'u'lláh and understood that this belief is inseparable from the duty to adhere to his laws and standards. *See* KITÁB-I-AQDAS, *supra* note 79, para. 1. One does not become a member of the Bahá'í Faith solely on the basis of one's familial heritage. While administrative practices of different national spiritual assemblies vary slightly, it is generally the case that at the age of fifteen or any time thereafter the child of Bahá'í parents must expressly avow Bahá'í belief in order to be considered a member with the concomitant rights (at age twenty-one) to vote for and serve on elected Bahá'í institutions. Bringing pressure to bear on someone to become or continue as a member of the Bahá'í faith would be incompatible with the principle of the independent investigation of truth.

92.   Letter from the Universal House of Justice (Feb. 6, 1973), *in* LIGHTS OF GUIDANCE, *supra* note 88, no. 728.

With respect to reproductive rights, the Bahá'í teachings state that it is for the husband and wife to decide how many children they will have.[93] Like other decisions to be made by marriage partners, this decision should be made through frank consultation, neither partner unjustly dominating the other.[94] Likewise, the decision whether to use birth control methods is left to the judgement of the couple.[95] However, since the teachings state that the soul comes into being at the time of conception, any method of abortion after conception has taken place is to be avoided by Bahá'ís, unless there are circumstances justifying it on medical or other grounds.[96]

While homosexual conduct is contrary to Bahá'í law and abortion generally incompatible with Bahá'í teachings, it should be emphasized that the foregoing laws and guidelines are accepted now by Bahá'ís as integral to their own belief system and as binding on themselves. Bahá'ís have not participated in the public debates within the United States, for example, on abortion law and funding or on gay and lesbian rights issues.

Means to Achieve Equality

The principles described above have necessary and important implications for the methods through which the Bahá'í community promotes equality and how it responds to violations of women's human rights. As these methods should be generally apparent from the foregoing discussion, they will be treated only briefly here.[97] Nevertheless, it is important that they be stated explicitly, since they are distinct from and even contrary to some methods currently employed for promoting the rights of women.

Participation of Men

Men must be actively involved in the work of promoting gender equality and must be consciously engaged in the subjective transformation of values that this

---

93. Shoghi Effendi, *quoted in* Letter from the Universal House of Justice (July 31, 1970), *in* LIGHTS OF GUIDANCE, *supra* note 88, no. 698.

94. *See supra* text accompanying note 67.

95. Shoghi Effendi, *quoted in enclosure to* Letter from the Universal House of Justice (July 31, 1970), *in* LIGHTS OF GUIDANCE, *supra* note 88, no. 699. Since the primary (but not sole) purpose of marriage is the rearing and spiritual training of children, the use of birth control to prevent the procreation of *any* children would *generally* be against the spirit of Bahá'í law, absent particular reasons. Letter from the Universal House of Justice (Jan. 28, 1977), *in* LIGHTS OF GUIDANCE, *supra* note 88, no. 700. Such personal decisions are left to the consciences of the individuals concerned.

96. Letter from the Universal House of Justice (May 23, 1975), *in* LIGHTS OF GUIDANCE, *supra* note 88, no. 703. In cases of possible medical justifications for an abortion, the decision "is left to the consciences of those concerned," to weigh medical advice in light of the guidance in the Bahá'í teachings. *Id.* To date the other possible ground for abortion addressed by the Universal House of Justice is the case of pregnancy resulting from a rape. It has stated that in this situation the decision whether to continue or terminate the pregnancy is for the woman to make. Letter on Violence, *supra* note 80, at 5.

97. For examples of how these methods are put into practice, *see infra* text accompanying notes 141–205.

process requires. The essential need for the participation of men flows directly from the nature of the goals to be achieved. The goal is not only for women to become awakened to the nature of their oppression and to become inspired with the determination and courage to insist on their rights. The female wing of humanity is growing stronger through the tireless efforts of women the world over to become educated and to enter fields of work hitherto closed to them and through their dedication at all levels to promote international human rights norms and their effective implementation. This struggle has necessarily been defined to some extent as a struggle against men, since men generally have held the power to grant or deny women their rights.[98] Other aspects of the work to improve the well-being of women have simply proceeded on the assumption that men can be ignored. It is extremely difficult to transcend these approaches and often appears fruitless even to try to involve men constructively in the process, given the intransigence with which such efforts are often met. Yet, for the same reasons that the simple shifting of traditional power from men to women will not bring about full equality, it is ultimately self-defeating for women to proceed without the engagement of men as partners in the process.

Women must own the process of their own transformation, both individually and collectively, without male interference. Women's groups and men's groups of every variety can contribute greatly to this process. But at the same time, if complementarity is the goal for equality, what is also critical is changing how men and women relate to each other, individually and collectively, in all public and private fora. This is a distinct transformative process that requires on-going consultative work between women and men, and will not simply come about as the result of the strengthening of women. For example, empowering women economically while ignoring the role of husbands can further marginalize men from their families and ultimately increase the burden on women, an unintended and unsustainable outcome.[99] What is required is a collective effort to discover new patterns for family and community life and practical methods of harmonizing the public and private lives of both women and men. Achieving complementarity requires that both be actively engaged in a consultative and creative process of constructing new models of social and economic interaction.

"The required shifting of balance away from behavior traditionally prevalent among men and the increasing permeation of society by 'feminine ideals' cannot occur if half the world's population continues to cultivate maladaptive behavior that has created the current state of imbalance."[100] Bahá'í men are to demonstrate a new

---

98. For an interesting exploration of whether the exhortations in the Bahá'í writings to the white race on its role in abolishing racism can be applied to men in the case of gender inequality, see Tannaz Grant, The Role of American Bahá'í Youth in Establishing the Equality of Men and Women (address at the 19th Annual Conference, Association for Bahá'í Studies—North America, San Francisco, Oct. 13, 1995) (unpublished manuscript, on file with author).

99. This perspective is the basis for the alternative approaches used by the Bahá'í community in the Traditional Media as Change Agent Project in Malaysia, Bolivia, and Cameroon. *See infra* text accompanying notes 176–84.

100. Hoda Mahmoudi, *The Role of Men in Establishing the Equality of Women*, WORLD ORDER 27, 34 (Spring 1995).

approach to relationships that replaces aggression and force with cooperation and consultation.[101] They are also to assume active responsibility for promoting the rights of women,[102] and thus cannot claim that women's rights are only a woman's issue. The seeming inability of many men to truly hear women's voices will be improved generally in a Bahá'í community as women and men consult on other subjects, practicing the skills and gradually developing the qualities conducive to successful consultation.

Consultation as Attitude and Method

As discussed earlier in the context of family decisionmaking, consultation carried out in the manner described can be a most effective means to solve problems, improve understanding, and make decisions in any group, formal or informal. It is a procedure but it is also an attitude and a perspective on relationships within a group. Through a consultative approach, the struggle for gender equality can become part of a unifying process rather than a perpetually divisive one. It requires maturity to consult effectively, and a rare combination of audacity and patience, but it can also promote change at levels that otherwise seem inaccessible:

> Let us also bear in mind that the keynote of the Cause of God is not dictatorial authority but humble fellowship, not arbitrary power, but the spirit of frank and loving consultation. Nothing short of the spirit of a true Bahá'í can hope to reconcile the principles of mercy and justice, of freedom and submission, of the sanctity of the right of the individual and of self-surrender, of vigilance, discretion and prudence on the one hand, and fellowship, candor, and courage on the other.[103]

Injustice against women has produced such a degree of legitimate anger and rebellion in many of its victims that this in itself must be addressed directly and on a continuing basis in order for effective consultation to take place. Nevertheless, it is possible for a group committed to the consultative process to address even the most contentious of issues and ultimately preserve or build relationships.

One possible way, among others, to characterize Bahá'í consultation is to see in it a combination of the prototypical female and male styles of moral decisionmaking identified by Carol Gilligan.[104] It joins the "female" approach of making decisions that are suitable to the context and that aim to preserve relationships to the "male" approach of relying on abstract notions of right and wrong, in that any consultation among Bahá'ís proceeds within the framework of Bahá'í laws and principles.[105] Gilligan identifies such a combination of styles with the achievement of moral maturity.

---

101. *See supra* text accompanying note 82.

102. 'ABDU'L-BAHÁ, *supra* note 57, at 163, *reprinted in* WOMEN, *supra* note 1, no. 108.

103. Letter from Shoghi Effendi to the American Bahá'í community (Feb. 23, 1924), *in* BAHÁ'Í ADMINISTRATION—SELECTED MESSAGES 1922–1932, at 63–64 (1974 ed.), *reprinted in* CONSULTATION, *supra* note 62, no. 23.

104. *See* CAROL GILLIGAN, IN A DIFFERENT VOICE: PSYCHOLOGICAL THEORY AND WOMEN'S DEVELOPMENT (1982).

105. For further explanation, *see* Schweitz, *supra* note 32, at 21, 32.

Unity in Diversity

The social principles promoted by Bahá'ís (such as gender equality) are universal, that is, they are believed to apply generally to all people under all conditions. However, as the Bahá'í concept of unity embraces the value of diversity, the method of promoting a universal principle must be responsive to the needs and conditions of time and place. This will generally mean that the method must be locally determined. It is indispensable to share learning and experience across cultures and communities, but Bahá'ís generally understand that it is wrong and ineffective to dictate a solution or methods from a faraway place without regard to local conditions. Within the Bahá'í community, the key to progressively implementing universal principles on a local basis is the local spiritual assembly and the regular meeting of all community members held on the first day of each Bahá'í month. In addition to devotional and social portions, this meeting includes a time dedicated to general consultation, a report of the assembly's work, and recommendations from community members to the assembly. Through such consultations between the community and its assembly, as well as in the assembly's own consultations, local priorities can be identified and community plans can be made.

Another aspect of valuing diversity is to recognize it within a local community. The additional barriers that women face due to their race, age, language, religious background, ethnicity, disability, or other factors must be explicitly addressed. Within a diverse Bahá'í community people have the opportunity to learn from each other, in ways that can productively shape their approaches to solving social problems. The promotion of gender equality within a Bahá'í community is closely linked with work to eliminate racism and all of the other deeply ingrained prejudices of class, ethnicity, and other distinctions.

SELECTED ISSUES IN BAHÁ'Í LAW: EQUALITY AND DISTINCTION

Integrally related to the spiritual teachings and social principles of the Bahá'í Faith is a body of law, given by Bahá'u'lláh and further elucidated by his son as his authorized interpreter. One portion of Bahá'í law concerns devotional practices and the condition of the individual, such as laws on prayer and fasting, holy days, cleanliness, and prohibiting the establishment of a priesthood. These laws apply to Bahá'ís everywhere. Other laws generally in effect include those relating to marriage and divorce, the prohibition on using habit-forming drugs and alcohol (other than for medical reasons), the Bahá'í electoral process, and the functions of the Universal House of Justice and national and local spiritual assemblies. Another portion of Bahá'í law is intended for a future condition of society and is not presently in effect.[106]

---

106. Universal House of Justice, *Introduction* to KITÁB-I-AQDAS, *supra* note 79, at 4–7. The Bahá'í writings anticipate a time in the future when the process of human civilization, having evolved through the successive stages of tribe, city, and nation-state, matures into a worldwide system of governance, centralized only to the extent necessary to protect the rights and serve the needs of its constituent parts and individual members. The social laws Bahá'u'lláh has given for such future society, combined with the laws, principles, and law-making provisions already governing the nascent system of local, national and international elected Bahá'í institutions, may be

The laws concerning marriage and the few other laws that make distinctions based on gender are selected for discussion here. These laws seem to present the greatest challenge to Bahá'ís themselves now in their efforts, scholarly and/or personal, to form a comprehensive understanding of the concept of equality. Because some aspects of these laws depart in striking ways from contemporary Western and non-Western thinking, they can also serve as an invitation to question and possibly transcend culturally induced assumptions about equality. While Western rights advocates may pay tribute in general terms to the notion that individuals have duties to others as well as rights, and that the human need for belonging should be balanced with the virtues of individualism, it is unusual to engage in discussion on concrete measures to combine these visions. Certain aspects of the following laws would seem to be measures of this sort, and as such provide an opportunity to think seriously about practical application of this theoretical balance.

Aspects of Marriage Law

The essential legal requirement of a Bahá'í marriage ceremony is that the woman and man, before two witnesses, each state the following vow: "We will all, verily, abide by the Will of God."[107] These are two individual vows to God, not vows to each other. The marital union is to be an "eternal bond" but marriage partners are not subsumed in one another; they remain accountable before God and responsible for their own course. Marriage does not diminish the legal status of either partner, neither does it confer power on one over the other. Marriage is not obligatory and there is no stigma attached to remaining unmarried. Divorce is strongly discouraged but is possible at the initiative of either party in cases of irreparable disunity.[108]

Bahá'í marriage is consensual, dependent on the consent of both parties, freely given.[109] For a Bahá'í woman living in a society where arranged marriages are the norm, the requirement that she herself choose her husband has radical consequences for the development of her sense of and capacity for independence and responsibility. Bahá'í marriage is dependent also, after the two have chosen each other, on the consent of the living natural parents of each.[110] For Bahá'ís living in a society where

---

understood collectively as the constitutional foundation for future civilization and the kernel of a full legal system. *See generally* WILLIAM S. HATCHER & J. DOUGLAS MARTIN, THE BAHÁ'Í FAITH: THE EMERGING GLOBAL RELIGION 143–65 (1984) (describing Bahá'í administration and laws); James F. Nelson, *Obedience and the Universal Law*, WORLD ORDER 20 (Spring 1973); EMERGENCE: DIMENSIONS OF A NEW WORLD ORDER (Charles Lerche ed., 1991); Martha L. Schweitz, *The Kitáb-i-Aqdas: Bahá'í Law, Legitimacy, and World Order*, 6 J. BAHÁ'Í STUD. 35 (Mar.–June 1994).

107. KITÁB-I-AQDAS, *supra* note 79, at 105, question 3.

108. A FORTRESS FOR WELL-BEING, *supra* note 65, at 75–76. Bahá'í divorce becomes final by action of the local spiritual assembly if, despite assistance from the assembly and others, the relationship is not reestablished during a one-year period of waiting.

109. KITÁB-I-AQDAS, *supra* note 79, para. 65. Under Bahá'í law, one has legal capacity to enter into marriage from the age of fifteen years. However, in addition to the requirements of Bahá'í law, Bahá'ís must comply with applicable national law governing marriage (and divorce).

110. *Id.* There are certain narrow exceptions, such as in cases where a parent is incompetent or has lost his or her parental rights.

individuals believe that their choice of marriage partner is their exclusive prerogative, this requirement that parents consent has radical consequences for the development of their sense of and capacity for connection to family.[111]

The dowry is an aspect of marriage practices in many parts of the world that has led to abhorrent treatment of women. "Dowry deaths," though often prohibited by law, are still common. These are associated with the form of dowry in which the bride's family gives property to the groom. In another form known as a "bride price," the dowry is a payment from the groom to the bride's parents, implying that the wife becomes the husband's purchased property. Bahá'í law eliminates the potential for abuse in the custom of dowry, by providing for a dowry that is a gift from the groom to the bride herself. This law is not now in effect on a universal basis, and is not now applied in the West where there is no such traditional custom.[112] The Bahá'í dowry cannot be an obstacle to marriage, since it can be deferred if financially necessary. It is also protected from turning into a status symbol by provisions establishing its minimum and maximum amounts.[113]

A serious commitment to organic equality requires altering marriage practices in all cultures to a greater or lesser extent.[114] The Bahá'í marriage laws and the standards governing the marital relationship preserve the rights of each partner, eliminating the abuse of women that so often inheres in the institution of marriage, and aiming to create lasting unity at the level of the family. The family has been described as the "workshop of civilization," where human character and spiritual development are most strongly shaped.[115] Protecting and exercising individual rights need not be incompatible with achieving a selfless commitment to family.

Gender-Based Distinctions

The provisions of Bahá'í law that draw distinctions based on gender are very few in number and each is quite different in character. They must be considered very carefully because they may appear to be incompatible with a commitment to full gender equality. Making any gender-based distinction at all is anathema if one adheres to the view that equality requires identical treatment of men and women under all

---

111. On the requirement of parental consent, both its spirit and implementation, *see generally* A FORTRESS FOR WELL-BEING, *supra* note 65, at 41–45.

112. As a gift from the groom to the bride, however, the Bahá'í dowry is not unlike the Western practice of engagement rings.

113. The range in value is from a little over two troy ounces of silver to about eleven troy ounces of gold. KITÁB-I-AQDAS, *supra* note 79, para. 66. Since many societies in which traditional forms of dowry are practiced also severely limit women's rights to own property, one observer has noted that converting to the Bahá'í dowry in those places gives evidence of the right the wife should have to own property herself.

114. As another example, Shoghi Effendi was once asked to clarify whether the Bahá'í teachings alter the traditional practice whereby the man proposes marriage to the woman. He replied that "there is absolute equality between the two, and . . . no distinction or preference is permitted." Letter on Violence, *supra* note 80, at 2.

115. Danesh, *supra* note 61, at vii.

conditions. The alternative view presented here, however, is that the more fundamental test of equality is whether women are free from systematic subordination in all respects and in all fora, public and private. Within this view, a few gender-based distinctions may be beneficial or even necessary. Equality demands, however, that any such distinction withstand close examination on its merits to determine its observable or likely effect on the status, experience, and welfare of women.

The approach to provisions of Bahá'í law that draw gender-based distinctions will differ depending on whether one is examining them from within or from outside the perspective of Bahá'í belief. Since Bahá'ís accept their body of teachings as divinely given, they will understandably assume that the writings contain no inherent contradictions and are capable of being rationally understood.[116] Those who have not accepted or who expressly reject Bahá'í religious belief will understandably assume that provisions which do not accord with their own beliefs or view of the imperatives of equality are at best inconsistencies and at worst evidence of hypocrisy. Skepticism is justified, and so is belief based on rational investigation. The purpose of this section is not to advocate certain Bahá'í perspectives on these provisions of Bahá'í law nor to prove them compatible with gender equality, but simply to present the provisions in context.

One gender-based distinction that seems relatively easy to understand is giving preference to daughters over sons in education if it is impossible to educate both.[117] Since the Bahá'í writings make it incumbent on parents to educate all of their children, and this responsibility is so weighty that it is even tied to retaining parental rights,[118] it is hard to estimate the practical significance of this female preference. At a minimum, this preference serves to reverse the current pervasive bias in favor of educating boys over girls.

The gender distinctions relating to devotional matters grant certain exemptions to women. Since these exemptions are permissive rather than mandatory in nature, a Bahá'í woman may choose whether or not to avail herself of them in light of her own circumstances.[119] For example, women are not required to make the pilgrimage that is obligatory for men "if one can afford it and is able to do so, and if no obstacle stands in one's way."[120] With respect to the Bahá'í fasting period (nineteen consecutive days

---

116. Bahá'ís believe that faith and reason are compatible, that science and religion are both avenues of truth. "[Humanity] cannot fly with one wing alone. If it tries to fly with the wing of religion alone it will land in the slough of superstition, and if it tries to fly with the wing of science alone it will end in the dreary bog of materialism." 'Abdu'l-Bahá, *quoted in* ESSLEMONT, *supra* note 56, at 214.

117. *See supra* text accompanying note 42.

118. *See supra* text accompanying note 74.

119. KITÁB-I-AQDAS, *supra* note 79, at 173 n.20.

120. *Id.* para. 32, and pp. 191–92, notes 54–55. As two of the three specified sites of pilgrimage lie in Shiraz, Iran and Baghdad, Iraq and have been confiscated by the Iranian and Iraqi governments, respectively, Bahá'ís presently visit the third site, the resting place of Bahá'u'lláh near the Bahá'í World Centre in Israel. The law of pilgrimage is not yet in effect.

each year of refraining from eating and drinking from sunrise to sunset), women who are pregnant, nursing, or menstruating are exempt.[121] In addition, menstruating women may use another particular prayer in lieu of the usual daily obligatory prayers.[122] While this latter provision of Bahá'í devotional law seems highly peculiar from a Western perspective, it addresses a serious issue in those societies and religious traditions in which women, during their menstrual periods, are considered "ritually unclean" and are forbidden to pray and fast. Bahá'í law expressly abolishes this, concept of ritual uncleanness, along with such prohibitions.[123]

Intestacy Law and Universal House of Justice Membership

Economic dependency and political disempowerment have been the defining characteristics of women's subordination. Because the remaining two gender distinctions to be discussed touch on property rights and governance, respectively, they are considerably more difficult to understand in the context of equality.

There is no gender distinction in Bahá'í law with respect to rights to own or transfer property, and both men and women are obligated to write a will.[124] In writing a will, the individual Bahá'í has full jurisdiction over his or her property and may allocate it in whatever manner he or she may desire, after the payment of debts, funeral and burial expenses, and Huqúqu'lláh.[125] The Bahá'í writings further specify that in writing a will one is "morally and conscientiously bound to always bear in mind . . . the necessity of . . . upholding the principle of Bahá'u'lláh regarding the social function of wealth, and the consequent necessity of avoiding its over-accumulation and concentration in a few individuals or groups of individuals."[126] In addition to these provisions mandating a will, Bahá'í law includes detailed rules of intestacy (not now in effect) providing for the distribution of property among family members. These rules would appear to give certain preferences to male over female heirs,[127] although individuals have identified possible textual analyses that would severely minimize the effect of these gender-based preferences.[128] The complexity of the intestacy pro-

---

121. *Id.* at paras. 13 and 16. Other permissive exemptions from the fast apply to men or women who are traveling, ill, or engaged in heavy labor. The duty to fast begins when one reaches the age of fifteen years.

122. *Id.* at para. 13.

123. *Id.* at 173 n.20, 212 n.106. Some Western Bahá'í women, having considered how this provision for a special prayer during the time of menstruation applies in their own cultures, have come to appreciate it as a regular affirmation of what it means to be biologically female.

124. *Id.* at para. 109.

125. *Id.* at 127, question 69. On Huqúqu'lláh, see Hanson, *supra* note 31.

126. Shoghi Effendi, *quoted in* KITÁB-I-AQDAS, *supra* note 79, at 182, n.38.

127. These preferences by no means disinherit women, but the most significant distinction would leave the family residence to the eldest son, at least if it had been held in the name of a deceased father. For the intestacy provisions and further explanation, see *id.* paras. 20–28, pp. 182–88 notes 38–47, and related portions of the Questions and Answers section therein.

128. *See, e.g.,* Sen McGlinn, Some Considerations Relating to the Inheritance Laws of the Aqdas (address at the Colloquium on the Kitáb-i-Aqdas, sponsored by the Institute for Bahá'í Studies

visions renders them susceptible to various understandings. How and when to apply them will ultimately have to be decided by the Universal House of Justice.

Bahá'ís have devoted considerable thought to discovering how, assuming there is in fact some degree of male preference in the intestacy rules, this can be compatible with gender equality. Any effort to estimate the practical significance of such preferences and their impact on women remains highly speculative, both because they are default provisions applicable only if a will is found to be non-existent, invalid, or unenforceable,[129] and because they are not intended to apply under present social conditions.

Some Bahá'ís understand the possible male preferences in intestacy as a default correlation of resources with responsibilities, consistent with the father's primary responsibility, in the absence of other arrangements, to support his family financially.[130] Others see it as closely tied to, and in fact dependent on, a profound shift in perspective on the social function of wealth and on the rights and duties associated with property ownership. Under present conditions, the control of property is a means of acquiring power over others and of gaining independence from those who could do one harm. Economic dependency of women has always condemned them to suffering, be it deprivation of basic needs or the inability to escape abusive relationships. Behind these problems lies the belief and current reality that wealth confers privileges that the owner is free to use in an entirely self-serving manner. Alternatively, possession of property or resources may be understood to carry responsibilities, to impose on the owner duties to others. This is part of the Bahá'í vision of economic justice and is fundamental to the process through which the extremes of wealth and poverty are to be eliminated.[131] One who is entrusted with family property would bear the concomitant duty to use it for the benefit of the family as a whole,[132] thus converting property ownership from an opportunity to oppress others into a duty to provide for others.

As these intestacy rules are among the provisions of Bahá'í law to be applied to a future condition of society, it is necessary to assume—given the priority accorded in the Bahá'í writings to the advancement of the status of women—that they will be put into effect when and where economic and social conditions are such that they would not be oppressive to women. The essential social principles of Bahá'u'lláh, such as the advancement of women and elimination of racism, may be understood as constitutional principles, or higher law, in the Bahá'í legal system. As such, they guide and inform all decision-making processes of Bahá'í institutions. Therefore, when the

---

and the Haj Mehdi Arjmand Memorial Fund, Evanston, IL., Ma. 31–Apr.l 2, 1995) (unpublished manuscript, on file with author).

129. Bahá'u'lláh specifically stated that there is no duty to conform to the intestacy rules in writing a will. KITÁB-I-AQDAS, *supra* note 79, at 127, question 69.

130. *See supra* text accompanying notes 72–74.

131. *See supra* note 46.

132. On the moral responsibility of the eldest son to consider the needs of the other heirs, *see* KITÁB-I-AQDAS, *supra* note 79, at 186, note 44.

Universal House of Justice must resolve some ambiguity in the application of a law of Bahá'u'lláh, legislate on a matter not addressed in the Bahá'í writings, or exercise discretion in when to progressively implement a law, its avowed responsibility is to do so in a way consistent with such relevant constitutional principles.

The gender distinction in Bahá'í law that relates to governance concerns the composition of the Universal House of Justice.[133] While adult women and men alike are eligible for election to all local and national spiritual assemblies, and for selection to all levels of the appointed Bahá'í institutions, the nine elected members of the Universal House of Justice must all be men.[134] This is the one legal gender distinction that is not a permissive or default provision but is mandatory. As such, it has puzzled many Bahá'ís and provoked a lively dialogue that reveals a wide array of perspectives on gender-related issues. The Bahá'í writings state that the reason for this distinction will become clearly understood in the future.[135] Given what is stated

---

133. The Universal House of Justice is elected every five years by all members of all national spiritual assemblies voting as individuals. Members are eligible for re-election. (For a description of the Bahá'í electoral process generally, *see infra* note 137.) Within the Bahá'í administrative order, this is the institution that has the authority to deliberate on problems that have caused difference and to take decisions on matters not expressly addressed in the writings of Bahá'u'lláh (as further interpreted by his son and great grandson); it also may amend and repeal its own enactments. The Universal House of Justice explicitly does not have the function of making authoritative interpretations of Bahá'í texts, but must often "elucidate" matters in order to carry out its responsibilities. The practical difference between "interpreting" and "elucidating" is expected to become clearer over time, as the number of letters and decisions of the institution grows. Letter from the Universal House of Justice to an individual (June 3, 1997) (on file with Bahá'í World Centre).

The constitutional limitation on the authority of the Universal House of Justice is that its decisions must be consistent with the laws and principles of Bahá'u'lláh. However, there is no provision for judicial review of Universal House of Justice enactments, and its decisions are final and binding on the Bahá'í community. (For background on the formation of the Universal House of Justice, *see infra* Appendix, to this chapter: Note on the History of the Bahá'í Faith.)

134. In the Bahá'í administrative order, members of the *elected* institutions (local and national assemblies and the Universal House of Justice) exercise collective (not individual) decision-making authority within their respective areas of jurisdiction. There are also *appointed* institutions from the local through international levels, "institutions of the learned," whose members exercise no authority but fulfill an advisory role as individuals (not collectively). Those appointed at the international level (by the Universal House of Justice) compose the Continental Boards of Counsellors. They in turn appoint auxiliary board members, who may name assistants. Members of these appointed institutions exert significant moral influence in the Bahá'í community through their activities such as holding workshops, giving talks, and through personal discussions. Their input and consultative advice is sought by national and local assemblies and by individuals. On Bahá'í governance generally, *see* HATCHER & MARTIN, *supra* note 106, at 143–51.

Although women are excluded from Universal House of Justice membership, they serve actively on all other elected and appointed Bahá'í institutions at all levels. (For statistics on the percentages of members of these institutions who are women, *see infra* text accompanying notes 158, 160–66.) Other elected international bodies are anticipated in the Bahá'í writings, such as a Supreme Tribunal, for which women and men will both be eligible. Letter from the Universal House of Justice to a national spiritual assembly (May 31, 1988) (on file with Bahá'í World Centre).

135. 'Abdu'l-Bahá has explained that the Universal House of Justice is confined to men "for a

in the Bahá'í writings about the great capacity of women, the reasons must be presumed to rest on some ground other than a deficit on the part of women; any assumption to the contrary would be insupportable in the Bahá'í context.[136] Whatever the reasons for it, this provision has caused Bahá'ís to reflect more deeply both on their assumptions about gender equality and on how the Bahá'í governance system differs from contemporary political institutions.[137]

The Universal House of Justice is directly charged with promoting equal rights for women as one of the fundamental principles of Bahá'u'lláh. In the course of its work, the institution as a body, and its members individually, consult extensively with women (and men) as members of other Bahá'í institutions and in their individual capacities, on all issues including those relating to the status of women. But the absence of women as members of the House of Justice means that the men elected are themselves responsible for consulting, making decisions, and taking action to promote the advancement of women, since it cannot be relegated to female members to deal with as a "woman's issue." To date the Universal House of Justice has put itself at the forefront of promoting equality within the Bahá'í community, through its numerous and unqualified statements and letters on the importance of the issue,[138] by establishing and supporting the work of the Office for the Advancement of Women at the Bahá'í International Community offices at the United Nations,[139] and by designating

---

wisdom of the Lord God's, which will ere long be made manifest as clearly as the sun at high noon." 'ABDU'L-BAHÁ, *supra* note 22, at 79–80, *reprinted in* WOMEN, *supra* note 1, no. 12.

136. For example, '[t]he woman has greater moral courage than the man; she has also special gifts which enable her to govern in moments of danger and crisis." 'ABDU'L-BAHÁ, 'ABDU'L-BAHÁ IN LONDON 103 (1982), *reprinted in* WOMEN, *supra* note 1, no. 87.

137. From the point of view of an individual, election to a Bahá'í institution at any level is regarded as a form of service rather than a means to personal recognition or aggrandizement. Since all elected institutions (national and local assemblies and the Universal House of Justice) make decisions collectively as a body only, their individual members have no separate or individual authority. In all Bahá'í elections there is no nominating and no campaigning; individuals are elected by secret ballot on the basis of their personal qualifications of "unquestioned loyalty, of selfless devotion, of a well-trained mind, of recognized ability and mature experience." Letter from Shoghi Effendi to the American Bahá'í Conventiion (June 3, 1925), *in* BAHÁ'Í ADMINISTRATION, *supra* note 103, at 88. In the event of a tie for the ninth position on any elected Bahá'í institution between a member of an ethnic or other minority group and someone of the majority, the position must go to the minority member. Bahá'ís take their electoral process, established by Bahá'u'lláh, very seriously, as the basis of their confidence in the institutions themselves. The notion of a Bahá'í having an "ambition" to serve on any Bahá'í institution would be a contradiction of the spirit of selfless devotion that best qualifies a person for membership.

This is not to say that there is not a high degree of honor associated with service on the Universal House of Justice, nor that it would be selfish for women to wish to so serve. The point is simply that, unlike most political institutions, election to the Universal House of Justice is not an avenue to personal power and influence.

138. *See, e.g., supra* text accompanying note 45, and other statements of the Universal House of Justice quoted herein.

139. *See infra* text accompanying notes 167–71.

the status of women as one of the four areas for concentrated effort in external affairs work of the Bahá'í community.[140]

ACTION, EXPERIENCE AND LEARNING

Given the geographic breadth of the Bahá'í community, it is impossible to summarize in any comprehensive fashion the array of activities relating to the promotion of gender equality, much less to give a definitive estimate of their results. It must suffice to present the limited statistics currently available, together with a sampling of the types of activities, the patterns of experience, and the learning emerging over time.[141]

Some communities and Bahá'í institutions have been crucibles for an unusual degree of individual and collective transformation, the effects of which have spread beyond the Bahá'í community. Many individual Bahá'ís, men and women, when asked to comment on their experience, will say that they are actively engaged in realigning their personal, business, and community relationships as they come to more deeply understand equality. On the other hand, some communities reflect a persistent tendency toward complacency. Some also report a wide divergence of opinions among members as to how radical a change in gender roles is called for in the Bahá'í writings. In places where very little progress has been made, it appears to be either because the Bahá'ís themselves have not yet addressed the issue seriously or because Bahá'í women have been unable to escape the rigid, traditional restrictions placed on their activities by male family members.

At the local level, the scarcity of empirical research to date makes it risky to venture generalizations, but some tentative conclusions will be suggested as to the most effective processes at work and the greatest obstacles faced. Considerably more information is available on national and international initiatives, although it is far from complete. Some of the most vivid examples come from a few internationally acclaimed Bahá'í-sponsored development projects focusing on women, since they represent structured and intense efforts to implement the principles described and to evaluate the results. The work of the Bahá'í International Community's Office for the Advancement of Women at the United Nations also provides clear examples of current thinking on gender issues and of directions in which the community is moving.

A topic that is increasingly attracting the attention of Bahá'í writers and historians is the role of women in the development of the Bahá'í Faith.[142] While beyond

---

140. The other three priority areas are human rights generally, global prosperity, and moral development. Universal House of Justice, External Affairs Strategy (Sept. 19, 1994) (on file with Bahá'í World Centre).

141. In addition to consulting published sources, the author has contacted international and national Bahá'í institutions and offices, as well as a few dozen individuals in many countries. While this process was admittedly less than scientific, it nevertheless offered an opportunity to sample a diversity of current efforts and opinions within the Bahá'í community. Correspondence and records of conversations are on file with the author.

142. *See, e.g.*, Robert H. Stockman, *Women in the American Bahá'í Community, 1900–1912*,

the scope of this chapter, it should be mentioned that the subject of notable women in Bahá'í history is one of frequent study at Bahá'í classes and summer schools. This study generally begins with the story of the first heroine of the faith, Táhirih, a Persian poetess martyred for her beliefs and for daring to speak publicly of the advent of a new era for men and women. She is also known for both testing and inspiring the faith of her male fellow-believers, reportedly appearing unveiled at the Conference of Badasht in Persia in 1848, deeply shocking those assembled.[143] Bahá'ís view her proclamation of the emancipation of women as the beginning of the age in which women will finally achieve equality. Other Bahá'í women frequently studied and honored include Bahíyyih Khánum (1846–1932), daughter of Bahá'u'lláh; Martha Root (1872–1939), an American journalist who travelled extensively worldwide in her Bahá'í teaching work; Laura Dreyfus-Barney (1879–1974), who worked for women's rights through the League of Nations and the United Nations; and Muná Mahmúdnizhád (1966–1983), a seventeen-year-old teacher of Bahá'í children's classes who was hanged in Iran for refusing to recant her faith.[144] Biographies, collections of writings, and articles about such Bahá'í women and a number of others are widely read.[145] It is significant that the lifestyles and fields of endeavor of these outstanding role models vary widely. Some remained unmarried and childless, others combined an active family life with public service; some are known primarily for their individual activities, others for their work with Bahá'í or public institutions. As the literature on Bahá'í women grows, it is becoming an important source of inspiration, particularly for young women in the community and for those brought up with a highly circumscribed view of the potential of women.

Survey Results

The Bahá'í International Community offices at the United Nations[146] have conducted three surveys on the status of women in the Bahá'í community. They provide a start in understanding the three factors examined in each: the participation of women on elected assemblies, ways Bahá'í institutions encourage women's participation in community life, and strategies used to change discriminatory attitudes toward women.[147]

WORLD ORDER, Winter 1993–94, at 17; Gwendolyn Etter-Lewis, *African American Women in the Bahá'í Faith*, WORLD ORDER, Winter 1993–94, at 41; R. Jackson Armstrong-Ingram, *Recovering a Lost Horizon: Women's Contributions to North American Bahá'í History, in* EQUAL CIRCLES, *supra* note 76, at 33; Baharieh Rouhani Ma'ani, *Religion and the Myth of Male Superiority, in* EQUAL CIRCLES, *supra* note 76, at 3 (including discussion of the role and treatment of Iranian women in Bahá'í history).

143. NABÍL-I-A'ZAM [MUHAMMAD-I-ZARANDÍ], THE DAWN-BREAKERS: NABÍL'S NARRATIVE OF THE EARLY DAYS OF THE BAHÁ'Í REVELATION 293–97 (Shoghi Effendi trans. & ed., 1932) (circa 1890).

144. Muná Mahmúdnizhád was among the ten women executed in 1983. *See supra* text accompanying note 17.

145. Examples include DOROTHY FREEMAN, FROM COPPER TO GOLD—THE LIFE OF DOROTHY BAKER (1984); M.R. GARIS, MARTHA ROOT (1983).

146. *See infra* text accompanying notes 167–71.

147. Office for the Advancement of Women, Bahá'í Int'l Community, *The Status of Women in the Bahá'í Community, in* THE GREATNESS WHICH MIGHT BE THEIRS—REFLECTIONS ON THE AGENDA

These surveys consisted of sending questionnaires to all national spiritual assemblies and also, for the 1994 survey, to the appointed auxiliary board members.

The first survey, conducted in 1972 in preparation for International Women's Year (1975), reported that in all but one of the eighteen national Bahá'í communities responding (out of 113 then in existence), women participated actively in voting in Bahá'í elections. In remote village areas and other locations where women, due to the constraints of social tradition, generally had not yet become as active in Bahá'í community life as men, they nevertheless were "active" as voters.[148] Women also were elected to national assemblies; although the percentage of women members varied widely by region,[149] the world average was about 30 percent.[150] Unfortunately, no statistics have been compiled on the percentage of women elected to local assemblies at that time, but survey responses indicated that women were often elected even in places where only men served on the traditional village councils and where, "by tradition, women seldom speak when men are present."[151]

Apart from the statistical data, the rest of the results of this first survey consisted of subjective evaluations by those responding, but their comments are nonetheless informative. National responses reported progress in varying degrees in the level of women's participation in assembly consultation, generally increasing as the women became more educated in the Bahá'í way of life. Replies also indicated that many Bahá'í men encouraged the active participation of their wives in Bahá'í community life. Literacy programs and encouraging girls and women in their education were cited as typical widespread trends. It also appeared that teaching children about gender equality had taken strong root in many Bahá'í communities. The report on the survey concluded that the "influence of the Bahá'í communities on the societies within which they exist varies," but within the worldwide Bahá'í community "great advances have already been made towards equality of the sexes, and the advancement of women is constantly pursued."[152]

The report submitted by the Bahá'í International Community based on its second survey in 1984 observed that the "most frequently mentioned positive influence

AND PLATFORM FOR ACTION FOR THE UNITED NATIONS FOURTH WORLD CONFERENCE ON WOMEN: EQUALITY, DEVELOPMENT AND PEACE 81, 83 (Bahá'í Int'l Community ed., 1995) [hereinafter REFLECTIONS ON THE BEIJING AGENDA]. The results of the 1994 survey, other than an overview of the statistical data, have not yet been published.

148. Bahá'í Int'l Community, Preliminary Enquiry into the Status of Women in the Bahá'í World Community 2 (1974) [hereinafter Preliminary Enquiry]. "Active" is not defined; unfortunately, no statistics are given. What is interesting about the results is that they showed that elections are often the first point of entry for women in traditional societies to become involved in Bahá'í community life.

149. At that time, ten of the twenty-five national assemblies in Asia, and seven of the twenty-four in Africa, had no women members. In Europe, the Americas, and Australasia, all but four of a total of fifty-eight had women members. *Id.* at 6.

150. REFLECTIONS ON THE BEIJING AGENDA, *supra* note 147, at 84.

151. Preliminary Enquiry, *supra* note 148, at 3.

152. *Id.* at 6.

for the integration of women in community life" was the Bahá'í administrative order, i.e., the system and working process of elected assemblies and appointed auxiliary boards.[153] It quoted the following from the report of the National Assembly of India:

> The very act of becoming a Bahá'í is the first major personal decision for most women in rural areas. Then, as they are deepened in the Bahá'í teachings and the role they are expected to play in Bahá'í administrative activity, they are changed from being passive members of an existing social order into dynamic members of a new order. Because of their functions in serving on Bahá'í administrative bodies and in voting and in being voted for and elected, women have made great strides in a largely male dominated society.[154]

The report of the 1984 survey stated that "conferences, institutes, seminars, school programmes and study classes have played a prominent part in the education of men as well as women in Bahá'í families and communities."[155] It cited further the benefits of tutorial schools, literacy training projects, publication of information in local languages, cross-cultural experience, and activities to promote good nutrition and hygiene. Also included were samples from each region of specific national plans for future activities, from which could be gleaned the particular priority issues for each national community. The report of the 1984 survey concluded that, "Bahá'í communities, while realistic in their assessment of obstacles to be overcome, are dedicated to a change in attitudes, and are working systematically and in a practical way to win the goal of equality of the sexes."[156]

In the years between the first survey (1972) and 1995, the number of national assemblies had increased from 113 to 173, but the overall percentage of women elected to national assemblies remained constant at about 30 percent.[157] Regional variation was and is still deep. The highest percentages of women national assembly members are in Australia/New Zealand, Northern Europe and Eastern Europe (50 percent, 46 percent, and 43 percent, respectively); the lowest in Central Africa, Northern Africa, and Western Africa (15 percent, 15 percent, and 13 percent, respectively).[158] While the 30-percent average greatly exceeds the present world average for national legislatures,[159] it shows that the Bahá'í community is still far from its own goals. The for-

---

153. This survey was based on questionnaires sent to the 143 national assemblies then in existence, requesting information on activities conducted and obstacles faced during the U.N. Decade for Women (1976–1985). Bahá'í Int'l Community, Activities in the Bahá'í World Community to Improve the Status of Women during the United Nations Decade for Women, and Future Programmes for the Development of Women (report submitted to the World Conference to Review and Appraise the Achievements of the United Nations Decade for Women: Equality, Development and Peace, Nairobi, Kenya, July 15–26, 1985).

154. *Id.* at 3–4.

155. *Id.* at 5.

156. *Id.* at 1.

157. Fax letter from Dep't of Statistics, Bahá'í World Centre, to Office for the Advancement of Women, Bahá'í Int'l Community (Oct. 13, 1995) (on file with Bahá'í Int'l Community, New York, N.Y.) (reporting statistics as of Sept. 1995).

158. *Id.*

159. Globally, 10 percent of the members of national legislative bodies are women. Dep't of Pub-

mation of sixty new national assemblies in the twenty-three-year period indicates that there was significant growth in those countries in terms of both Bahá'í membership and level of activity, presumably implying that many new Bahá'ís and young local communities will require time to build practices consistent with the Bahá'í way of life. Further statistical work would be needed, however, to show the degree of correlation between age or institutional maturity of a national Bahá'í community and the election of women to national assemblies.

Complete statistics on all local assemblies worldwide have not been compiled, but the most recent survey (1994) of the Bahá'í International Community reported that 40 percent of local assembly members were women.[160] The same survey reported that of the appointed auxiliary board members responding, 47 percent were women and 50 percent of their appointed local assistants were women.[161] Of the counsellors appointed at the international level, 36 percent were women.[162]

Statistics for the Bahá'í community of the United States show that as of 1995, while service on elected and appointed Bahá'í institutions is well balanced by gender, stereotyping is still somewhat evident in the disproportionate number of men elected as local chairpersons and of women elected as local secretaries. Women comprise 54 percent of the total U.S. Bahá'í membership and at least the same percentage (or possibly slightly higher) of members elected to local assemblies.[163] However, elected chairpersons, vice-chairpersons, and treasurers are, respectively, 61 percent, 58 percent, and 56 percent male. Elected secretaries are 75 percent female.[164] It should be noted also that since women comprise a slight majority of assembly membership, they are also casting a slight majority of the votes to elect these officers. The present National Assembly of the Bahá'ís of the United States, elected to serve from April 1997 to April 1998, consisted of four women and five men. The last chair was a man.[165]

LIC INFORMATION, UNITED NATIONS, THE BEIJING DECLARATION AND THE PLATFORM FOR ACTION—FOURTH WORLD CONFERENCE ON WOMEN 109–10 (1996). The Economic and Social Council had endorsed a target of 30 percent women in decision-making positions by 1995. *Id.* at 109.

160. This reflected data available on 4,680 local communities, approximately one-fourth of the total. REFLECTIONS ON THE BEIJING AGENDA, *supra* note 147, at 85.

161. These figures are based on receiving responses from 65 percent (254 out of 389) of auxiliary board members serving worldwide. *Id.* at 83–84.

162. Out of a total of ninety counsellors, thirty-two are women. BAHÁ'Í WORLD CENTRE, THE BAHÁ'Í WORLD 1995–96, at 38 (1997) [hereinafter BAHÁ'Í WORLD 1995–96]. On the role of counsellors, auxiliary board members, and their assistants, *see supra* note 134.

163. Jane J. Russell, *Spiritual Vertigo at the Edge of Gender Equality*, WORLD ORDER, Fall 1995, at 41, 42–43 (based on data provided by the Research Office, Bahá'í National Center, Wilmette, IL).

164. *Id.* at 43. At the local level the position of assembly secretary entails substantial responsibility for proper community functioning but also includes considerable clerical duties.

165. The first woman chair of the combined National Assembly of the Bahá'ís of the United States and Canada, Dorothy Baker, was elected in 1946. As of 1997, no woman has been elected national secretary in the United States, a position of probably greater day-to-day influence than national administration than chairperson. Unlike the other U.S. National Spiritual Assembly members, those elected to serve as secretary and assistant secretary work full-time at the U.S. Bahá'í

Appointed positions in the United States appear to be well gender-balanced at all levels.[166]

Overall, the foregoing statistics suggest that the level of women's participation as elected members of Bahá'í institutions, while varying according to conditions in the national society at large, is also generally higher than the level of women's participation in political institutions in the same society. To determine how substantial these differences are, and how the level of women's participation changes over time as a local or national Bahá'í community matures, will require further research. It also appears that in the process of appointing individuals to the non-elected Bahá'í institutions, a serious effort is being made, fully successful in many locations, to achieve gender balance.

Bahá'í Office for the Advancement of Women at the United Nations

The Bahá'í community has been active with the United Nations since its founding, beginning with participation in the San Francisco Conference of 1945. The Bahá'í International Community has consultative status with the Economic and Social Council (category II, now known as "special consultative status") and also works with the United Nations Children's Fund and the World Health Organization. Its main office is located at U.N. Plaza in New York; its branch office is in Geneva. In 1989 the Bahá'í International Community established an Office of the Environment, and in 1992 an Office for the Advancement of Women (OAW). This Office coordinates Bahá'í interaction with international entities outside of the Bahá'í community concerned with the rights and well-being of women, and also advises national spiritual assemblies on participation in programs and projects to promote equality.[167]

The Bahá'í International Community has been extensively involved in all four U.N. World Conferences on Women, has participated actively for over twenty years in the work of the U.N. Commission on the Status of Women, and, beginning in 1988, served as convener of the organization Advocates for African Food Security: Lessening the Burden on Women.[168] Before the Fourth World Conference on Women in Beijing, Bahá'í delegations contributed to the work of the five Regional United Nations Preparatory Conferences as well as the Regional NGO Fora, and the director of OAW served on the global NGO Facilitating Committee to organize the NGO Forum on Women (Beijing, 1995).[169] In preparation for the conference, OAW published in 1995 *The Greatness Which Might be Theirs—Reflections on the Agenda and Platform for*

National Center and have considerable managerial responsibilities. A usual pattern has been a male secretary and female assistant secretary.

166. Half of the auxiliary board members serving in the United States and half of their local assistants are women. Russell, *supra* note 163, at 44.

167. BAHÁ'í WORLD 1993–94, *supra* note 6, at 83–84.

168. *Id.* at 84–85.

169. BAHÁ'í WORLD 1994–95, *supra* note 4, at 104, 146–47. For a description of the involvement of local and national Bahá'í women's groups in national preparations for the Beijing Conference, see *id.* at 105–06.

Action for the United Nations Fourth World Conference on Women: Equality, Development and Peace. The chapters in this collection each address one of the critical areas of concern in the Platform for Action.

The scope of the work of the Bahá'í International Community for women's human rights can be seen in the many statements it has submitted over the years to the Commission on the Status of Women and a number of other regional and global fora, both intergovernmental and non-governmental.[170] These statements bear on a wide range of topics, including violence against women, the girl child, the re-socialization of men, women's participation in sustainable development, motherhood and the family, political participation and decisionmaking, education, literacy, and health, and give examples of Bahá'í projects around the world.[171]

Development Projects with a Gender Focus

Bahá'ís have been engaged in social and economic development projects (although without applying that name to them) from the earliest days of the community, perhaps beginning with tutorial schools for girls established in Iran.[172] At the most basic level, of course, development is no more about "projects" than it is about economic growth. The heart of the development process lies in creating conditions under which heretofore marginalized people can learn to assume responsibility, work in groups, make decisions, and ultimately realize their own potential for the good of themselves, their families, their communities, and society as a whole. It is a gradual process of community and institution building, focused at the local level. It is a process in which Bahá'ís have always been engaged in their regular activities of consolidating their communities and learning to consult together, and by trying to apply Bahá'í principles of unity and equality in all of their efforts. Promoting gender equality has been a necessary aspect of these efforts, limited though it may have been by the extent to which it was as yet understood in a particular time and place. Thus, the Bahá'í development work that will prove to be the most significant in the long term and to affect the most people is that which goes on daily, largely unrecorded, as Bahá'ís go about exerting their personal best efforts to "live the life." While this work may not be consciously identified as "activity to uplift the status of women," it is in fact shifting the foundations of social relations and of attitudes toward gender among those whom it touches.

---

170. Copies of these statements are available from the Bahá'í International Community, 866 United Nations Plaza, Suite 120, New York, New York, 10017–1811.

171. Many of these statements are cited and used as the basis for explaining Bahá'í teachings and practices for equality in Loni Bramson-Lerche, *An Element of "Divine Justice": The Bahá'í Principle of the Equality of Women and Men, in* TOWARD THE MOST GREAT JUSTICE, *supra* note 30, at 75.

172. *See, e.g.,* the description of the Tarbíyat Girls' School in Tehran in Ann Boyles, *Towards the Goal of Full Partnership: One Hundred and Fifty Years of the Advancement of Women, in* BAHÁ'Í WORLD 1993–94, *supra* note 6, at 237, 253–54. The school opened in 1911 and was extremely progressive by contemporary Persian standards. Such Bahá'í schools trained the first generation of professional women in Iran, and the example set by the Bahá'í community is reported to have affected society as a whole. *Id.*

Building on the experience Bahá'ís have gained in such daily, community-based work, there have also been an array of projects carried out that aim specifically to benefit women, either within the Bahá'í community or extending to society at large. In addition to hundreds of non-formal education projects (including tutorial schools, literacy centers, and pre-schools), examples in Asia include the Personal and Family Development Program for Women in Malaysia, focused initially on health and child development, and the New Era Development Institute at Panchgani, India, engaged in health education, afforestation, adult literacy, rural technology, animal husbandry, and rural schools.[173] Another example is the Bahá'í Vocational Institute for Rural Women in Indore, India, a three-month residential program to train village women in literacy, health, and vocations such as sewing, weaving and agriculture, which has won recognition from the United Nations Environment Programme. Founded in 1983, the Institute's curriculum emphasizes Bahá'í principles of the dignity of the individual, the importance of work, equality of men and women, elimination of prejudice, and non-adversarial decisionmaking through consultation. An important goal is to strengthen the women's pride in their own culture, utilizing music, dance and tribal designs, and to help them develop confidence and leadership ability in order to share what they learn with their home communities.[174]

In Africa a wide range of activities have been initiated by Bahá'ís to enhance the status, involvement, and responsibility of women in development. They focus most often on education, primary health care and hygiene, and improving food production. In Swaziland, a training program for Bahá'í pre-school teachers was adopted by the government for nationwide use. Villagers have been trained in many countries to serve their communities as volunteer primary health educators. In Kenya, dozens of local Bahá'í women's groups and several regional women's committees have initiated agricultural projects.[175]

One effort that demonstrates certain unique aspects of the Bahá'í approach to gender equality was the Traditional Media as Change Agent Project, a two-year pilot project of the U.N. Development Fund for Women (UNIFEM) and the Bahá'í International Community, carried out in Bolivia, Cameroon, and Malaysia between 1991 and 1993.[176] Its principal aim was to stimulate improved social and economic

173. These projects are described in Bahá'í International Community, Report on Rural Poverty Alleviation Efforts in Asia and the Pacific, Focusing on Activities for Disadvantaged Women (submitted to the United Nations Regional Symposium on Cooperation between the Economic and Social Commission for Asia and the Pacific and Non-Governmental Organizations for Rural Poverty Alleviation, Bangkok, Dec. 16–19, 1991).

174. *Vocational Training for Rural Women in India Brings Unexpected Dividends*, ONE COUNTRY (Bahá'í Int'l Community, New York, N.Y.), Oct.–Dec. 1990, at 1, 8–10.

175. These projects are described in Bahá'í International Community, Statement to the Fourth Regional Conference on the Integration of Women in Development and on the Implementation of the Arusha Strategies for the Advancement of Women in Africa (Abuja, Nigeria, Nov. 6–10, 1989). For further examples of Bahá'í efforts to advance the status of women in all regions, see Boyles, *supra* note 172, at 251–59.

176. *UNIFEM/Bahá'í Project Strikes a Responsive Chord*, ONE COUNTRY (Bahá'í Int'l Community, New York, N.Y.) Oct.–Dec. 1993, at 1, *reprinted in UNIFEM/Bahá'í Project Raises*

development in the community by first uplifting the status of women through the use of traditional media presentations (such as theater, songs, and dances) created and performed by the local participants.[177] The ultimate goal of the project was to change attitudes, especially attitudes of men. It was based on the idea that improving the status of women requires changing attitudes of both men and women in ways that strengthen the family and the community. Unlike many women-in-development projects, this one involved men actively in the process of discovering how inequality between men and women related to local problems.

In this project, the core group of volunteers in each village was usually built around members of the local Bahá'í assembly, but the project was carried out by and for the village at large. Analyzing local problems required training in Bahá'í consultation (particularly important since many women felt that their opinion was not important), as well as in the use of tools such as focus groups, interviews, and community surveys. One of the most useful exercises was asking groups to list the typical daily tasks of a woman and a man, respectively, the men often becoming embarrassed that their list "was never even half as long as that of the women."[178] The results of the analysis were then presented through simple traditional media, known to be a non-threatening and highly effective form of communication in non-literate societies. At all three sites, the groups generally gave highest priority to the problems of illiteracy among women, mismanagement of funds by men, and the unfair burden of work on women. Issues such as domestic violence and alcohol abuse, while not often mentioned in focus group discussions, nevertheless emerged in skits created by participants.

While "success" in changing attitudes is hard to measure, statistical and anecdotal evidence points toward significant change.[179] It is reported that in the seven villages in Cameroon where the project operated, thereafter men more often worked with the women in the fields and consulted with them about family finances, resulting in increased spending on health, nutrition, education, and family farming. In the eight villages in Bolivia, women participated more in community decisionmaking. In Malaysia, the project stimulated spin-offs as the men and women in the village learned to consult with each other and women gained the opportunity and standing to bring up their problems. At all sites emphasis on female education resulted in programs on adult literacy for women and almost universal enrollment of girls in primary schools.[180]

Community Consciousness, in REFLECTIONS ON THE BEIJING AGENDA, *supra* note 147, at 51. UNIFEM provided funding of US $205,000; the Bahá'í communities provided local resources and a network of volunteers. Marjorie Thorpe, then Deputy Director of UNIFEM, in explaining why UNIFEM chose to fund the project, praised the Bahá'ís for their "very strong links with the grassroots" and for not being "elitist." *Id.* at 56.

177. *UNIFEM/Bahá'í Project, in* REFLECTIONS ON THE BEIJING AGENDA, *supra* note 147, at 52.

178. *Id.* at 58.

179. *Id.* at 53–55.

180. Mona Yazi Grieser, Women, Poverty and Income: A Systems Approach—Reflections on "Traditional Media as Change Agent" Project 4 (1994) (unpublished paper, on file with Bahá'í Int'l Community, New York, N.Y.)

Wives reported that drinking by men was substantially reduced and spouse abuse was reported to have all but disappeared among participating families.[181]

The systems approach underlying this project is unlike the current model of women-in-development programs focusing almost exclusively on women alone. Income-generating and credit schemes are acknowledged to be successful in increasing women's access to funds, thereby resulting in women's improved self-esteem, higher status, and increased decisionmaking. However, as analyzed by the international technical director of the Traditional Media Project, the current women-in-development model may prove in the long run to be as damaging to the social environment as early economic development projects were to the natural environment:[182]

> [E]xisting programs . . . can increase the already fragile ties linking men to families, they can reduce the productive role men have within the family, and they can further increase women's burden. Most significantly they can weaken the family structure itself by making men peripheral to the well-being of the family. The ultimate result is to pit men and women against each other for minimum resources. . . .[183]

Since the Traditional Media Project provided little or no material benefit, it eliminated the usual incentive for men to "hijack" projects in which they participate, thus also eliminating one reason women-in-development project organizers usually prefer to work with women only. It did not assume that men cannot or will not change. It focused on bringing men into the dialogue and presenting them with social incentives to change their behavior, including developing a social vision for their family and their community. It applied a partnership rather than a power model, a concept of organic equality rather than competition. The expectation (to be tested in future research) is that by first developing consultation skills and learning attitudes more consistent with gender equality, other projects with material benefits aimed at poverty reduction will be significantly more sustainable and healthful for families and local social systems.[184]

Scope of Activity at Local and National Levels

Conferences, seminars and workshops of every description seem to be the fora most widely used by Bahá'ís to explore equality, heighten awareness, share experiences, and propose practical solutions to problems. Such meetings are organized at the local, regional, and national levels, and have led to the creation of both broad-based and local networks of groups, very often including groups outside of the Bahá'í community. For example, *The Bahá'í World 1994–1995* reports on Bahá'ís invited to speak at and participate in major conferences and events on women organized by other groups in that year in Hungary, Sri Lanka, Korea, Hong Kong, Ireland, Guyana,

---

181. *Id.*

182. *Id.* at 6.

183. *Id.* at 2.

184. *Id.* at 7. The final report and evaluation of the project in Cameroon, as well as the manual written by an independent development communications consultant on the project, are available from Global Vision, Inc., 11802 Saddlerock Road, Silver Spring, MD 20902.

Saint Lucia, the Netherlands, Guinea-Bissau, India, Zaire, Tonga, the United Kingdom, and Nigeria.[185] The same volume reports on conferences and meetings organized by Bahá'í communities at the national/regional level for the public or primarily for Bahá'ís in France, Pakistan, Northern Ireland, Swaziland, Albania, the Netherlands, Germany, Malaysia, the Solomon Islands, Taiwan, Zambia, South Africa, Russia, Nigeria, the United States, India, and New Zealand.[186]

Frequently, the Associations for Bahá'í Studies have sponsored activities to promote equality, such as the 1989 annual conference of the North American Association for Bahá'í Studies entitled "Full Partnership."[187] A symposium held by the Australian Association for Bahá'í Studies in that same year resulted in the publication of a collection of papers in a volume entitled *The Role of Women in an Advancing Civilization*.[188] Another major conference was held in the United States in 1996, the "Wings of the Eagle Gender Equality Conference" in Louisville, KY.[189] Typically such conferences include small group workshops as well as plenary sessions, incorporate music, dance, and art presentations as well as talks and discussions, and actively encourage the participation of men. Some thirty national spiritual assemblies have established offices or committees for the advancement of women.[190] Such efforts at the national level have been strongly encouraged over the years by the Universal House of Justice, in its letters to national assemblies and to the Bahá'í world community generally.

Another example of a Bahá'í initiative was the conference on "Women and the Welfare of Humanity" held in 1996 at Landegg Academy, Switzerland. The participants were fifty Chinese women managers, judges, academics, and government officials and seventy European and North American men and women representing women's organizations and Bahá'í communities. Discussions focused on how women can improve the well-being of humankind both in their families and through their careers, emphasizing principles of equality and addressing the problems created by increasingly materialistic lifestyles in China and elsewhere.[191]

An example of Bahá'ís working with other groups to promote women's rights is collaboration in the United States to advocate for U.S. ratification of the Convention on the Elimination of All Forms of Discrimination Against Women. A Bahá'í representative currently serves as co-chair (along with a representative of Amnesty

---

185. Bahá'í World 1994–95, *supra* note 4, at 106–09.

186. *Id.* at 109–12. See earlier volumes for reports of activities in previous years.

187. Boyles, *supra* note 172, at 264.

188. Sitarih 'Ala'i & Colleen Dawes eds., 1989.

189. *Conference Puts Focus on Action Toward Equality*, Am. Bahá'í (Nat'l Spiritual Assembly of the Bahá'ís of the U.S., Evanston, IL), June 24, 1996, at 1.

190. *Around the World, Bahá'í Women's Groups Increase Their Activities*, One Country (Bahá'í Int'l Community, New York, N.Y.), Apr.–June 1997, at 12.

191. *Women from China and the West Find Common Challenges*, One Country (Bahá'í Int'l Community, New York, N.Y.), Apr.–June 1996, at 8.

International) of the Women's Convention Working Group, a coalition working nation-wide to solicit citizens' petitions, endorsements by community organizations, and city council resolutions supporting ratification, in addition to lobbying in Washington, D.C.[192]

Events organized at the local level to promote equality are largely unrecorded, though they may be reported in local newsletters or sometimes national publications. Such activities range from conferences and workshops to men's discussion groups to informal gatherings to study the relevant Bahá'í teachings. Gender equality is a common theme in local children's classes, summer school courses, and adult study groups. Individual Bahá'ís with related professional expertise often put their training to work within the Bahá'í community as well, for example, through race and gender counselling or holding management consultant style workshops on the problems in male/female communication.

National assemblies have made efforts to encourage and support change at the local level. For example, the National Spiritual Assembly of the Bahá'ís of Australia, in a 1988 letter announcing that it had established a National Bahá'í Women's Committee, asked the Bahá'ís to explore those attitudes and behaviors that conflict with equality.[193] It asked "each individual, each family, each Institution and all Bahá'í communities to bring equality to a state of functioning reality." It appealed "specially to Bahá'í men" to recognize that "[m]any women feel themselves cast in a role in which they are not listened to or respected as equals, in which their hopes to develop particular talents are crushed or a desire for service through activities outside the family is thwarted by a lack of understanding and support."[194] It addressed as well the most practical level of community functioning: "we cannot allow men or women to continue the slighting jokes, innuendoes and attitudes which reflect inequality; . . . we cannot continue to allow women to be the sole or frequent providers of food and child care at Bahá'í functions; we cannot continue to give men the more prominent positions at Bahá'í functions; . . ."[195] This frank and practical call to action has been highly appreciated by Bahá'ís both in Australia and elsewhere as an example of the sort of leadership from Bahá'í institutions that can effectively promote change and counter attitudes of complacency.[196] Likewise, the National Spiritual Assembly of the Bahá'ís of the United States has published a statement entitled, "Two Wings of a Bird: The Equality of Women and Men," concisely presenting the Bahá'í vision of equality and referring to the "damaging effects of gender prejudice" as a "fault line beneath the foundation of our national life."[197]

---

192. Information is available from the Women's Convention Working Group, e-mail: oea-washdc@usbnc.org.

193. Letter from the National Spiritual Assembly of the Bahá'ís of Australia to the Australian Bahá'í community (Aug. 1988), BAHÁ'Í BULLETIN (National Spiritual Assembly of the Bahá'ís of Australia), Aug. 1988, *reprinted in* WORLD ORDER, Winter 1993–94, at 12, 13.

194. *Id.* at 14.

195. *Id.*

196. *See, e.g.*, Russell, *supra* note 163, at 47.

197. *Two Wings of a Bird*, AM. BAHÁ'Í, *supra* note 3, at 3.

Patterns of Change

Ultimately, the success of all conferences, activities, and statements must be measured by the extent to which attitudes and behaviors of both individuals and groups change over time. In the absence of hard data on this question, a few writers have described conditions in the Bahá'í community based on their own experience. For example, frustration with a male-dominated Bahá'í study group led several Bahá'í women to publish a collection of essays entitled, *Equal Circles—Women and Men in the Bahá'í Community*.[198] Another writer, Jane Russell, describing conditions in the U.S. Bahá'í community, acknowledges the often "visibly conscious efforts" of Bahá'ís to live up to the standard of gender equality, but points out the persistence of patriarchal attitudes among many men and women.[199] Her examples focus primarily on ways that Bahá'í men effectively discount the contributions of women in consultation or seem to disapprove of women who exhibit traditional "male" strengths. She also observes Bahá'í women who choose to focus almost exclusively on the motherhood aspects of the Bahá'í writings, effectively ignoring injunctions for women to become the peers of men in public life. She feels that "until recently" such "anachronistic behaviors" have generally been "denied, deferred, and allowed to drift," at both the institutional and personal levels.[200] Russell attributes the resistance to change not to deliberate disobedience to the Bahá'í teachings or to ill will, but to unrecognized and deep fear. Citing Bahá'í writings referring to how the "world's equilibrium hath been upset" and "[m]ankind's ordered life hath been revolutionized" through the power of the Bahá'í revelation to transform world society, she concludes that "humanity may never have faced a psychological challenge of the magnitude of gender equality."[201] She recognizes as well that most people, "before surrendering their old identities, would like to have in hand clearly defined, specific, concrete definitions of masculinity and femininity with which to replace them,"[202] definitions which, for good reason, are not provided in the Bahá'í writings. Bahá'ís are nonetheless expected to move forward into this uncertainly, an experience that will necessarily produce severe anxiety for many.

Russell's analysis underscores the need for Bahá'í institutions at all levels to put and keep issues of gender equality at the forefront of community discussion and activity. Change does not occur spontaneously, but requires a process leading from conscious knowledge, to developing the will to change, and ultimately to action. A new Bahá'í most likely knows that the equality of men and women is a basic principle of the faith, but individuals will understand this principle initially on their own terms, based on their own sphere of prior cultural and personal experience. A new Bahá'í can claim to accept equality on some abstract level without understanding the extent to which this will require a change in his or her own actions and relationships. A

---

198. *See supra* note 76.

199. Russell, *supra* note 163, at 45.

200. *Id.*

201. *Id.* at 49.

202. *Id.*

superficial level of espousing equality can be a first step in opening channels of communication that can eventually lead to changes in behavior. Superficial acceptance can also, however, have the negative effect of sanctioning complacency. "Of course I believe in equality. What is there to talk about?" As one consultant on gender relations commented, religious communities are often the hardest to work with, because they have the attitude that "we are the good guys."[203]

The extent to which superficial acceptance of equality becomes understanding and actual change generally seems to depend on whether individuals in the community or the local assembly itself decide to take initiative on the matter. In societies where women are not accustomed to speaking out on their own behalf, or where they will be ostracized for standing out, it is far less likely that such initiatives will originate at the local level. In such places, the role of members of the appointed institutions is particularly critical, as they travel and work with local communities on all aspects of Bahá'í life. Likewise, conferences, workshops, and summer schools organized at the national or regional level may be essential to generate a serious look at equality issues locally.[204]

In Western societies with relatively advanced protection of women's rights, there is still a considerable divergence of opinion within the Bahá'í community as to the degree of change required by the teachings on equality. This may be due largely to the need to reconcile the emphasis in the Bahá'í teachings on both the value of motherhood and the essential necessity for women to be involved in the public sphere. Reconciling the two is admittedly a difficult task. It is easy to justify one's prior notions by emphasizing either of these aspects at the expense of the other, intentionally or otherwise. Doing so also, however, seriously retards progress. Only as Bahá'ís gain a deeper understanding of the teachings does a larger consensus and will to change seem to emerge.

It would appear that often much of what in fact promotes the advancement of women within a local Bahá'í community is not consciously identified by the participants as gender-directed activity. One of the most effective steps occurs when a woman is elected to the local spiritual assembly. It may be the first time she has been valued as a member of a decision-making group and her opinions sought. Since consultation requires that both domineering and withdrawn individuals change their ways, this often means that men must learn to listen and that women must find their voice. As women are elected to officers' positions on local assemblies, their responsibilities and capacities further increase. Since there is no clergy, Bahá'í community life depends in every aspect on the voluntary efforts of individual members. This, too, puts into motion a rather natural process within the community, whereby women can gradually assume roles and functions commensurate with their potential and less determined by gender stereotypes. In places where a woman's increasing involvement

---

203. Conversation with Mark Leach, specialist in intergroup relations and gender issues in the workplace (1996).

204. Stories recounted to the author by Bahá'ís in Southeast Asia, Liberia, and the South Pacific demonstrate this point.

in Bahá'í community life might bring objections from her husband, communities will often make deliberate efforts, direct or indirect, to educate husbands and to demonstrate new models of gender relations.

The Universal House of Justice has generally advised an integrated approach to advancing the status of women: "The principle of the equality between women and men . . . can be effectively and universally established . . . when it is pursued in conjunction with all the other aspects of Bahá'í life."[205] This underscores the importance in the Bahá'í community of promoting equality in ways that can also strengthen marriages and families and deepen the understanding that justice must be the foundation of all human relations. Establishing and maintaining a broad perspective on the significance of gender equality, while insisting on its application in matters large and small, can be both highly productive and ultimately unifying.

CONCLUSION: ORGANIC EQUALITY AS A TRANSFORMATIVE PROCESS

This chapter has explored the meaning of "equality" in the Bahá'í context, and concludes that more important than discovering a single all-encompassing definition is coming to understand the *process* of equality: a process to be pursued at both the personal and institutional levels and informed by the principles set forth. The Bahá'í writings would support defining equality as "freedom from systematic subordination because of sex,"[206] and such definition helps to shift attention from the symptoms to the root problem. But the continuous work that must follow is far more difficult, requiring principled consultation on how women are subordinated in a particular situation and how greater equality can be achieved, combined with sustained personal action and institutional innovation.

The personal transformation required calls for immense courage. Movement towards greater equality is a highly unsettling process, in that future steps may not be clearly visible until earlier ones are achieved. It is moreover an indeterminate process, in that the outcome will be more complex than simply replacing present stereotypes with new ones, and because results will not be uniform. Two families, or two businesses or communities, may each feel they have achieved a high level of gender equality based on the principles presented, although they function differently from each other. It is possible for them both to be right.

Gender inequality and the oppression of women are manifested in countless ways, extending even to such atrocities as systematic rape and wife burning. In combating extreme abuse of women in any form, it matters little what model of equality one espouses. But as one approaches more subtle issues of inequality, and can afford to think not in negative terms of stopping abuse but in positive terms of promoting desired models of conduct, the differences among approaches to equality become anything but subtle.

---

205. Letter from the Universal House of Justice (July 25, 1984), *in* WOMEN, *supra* note 1, no. 120.

206. *See supra* text accompanying note 48.

Competitive or power-based approaches will engender competitive and power-based methods and outcomes. This chapter has presented an alternative approach, described as *organic equality within a paradigm of complementarity*. This approach presents not only a different vision of the goal, but requires that different methods be used in order to move beyond present patriarchal systems. These methods require the participation of men, call for a consultative attitude and process, and insist on the value of diversity. The goal is not for women to share or assume the dominating role of men. This will only perpetuate oppression in new forms. Equality requires a profound appreciation for justice in all human relations.

The goal is "organic equality" in that it calls for the gradual perfecting of both female and male, not only for their own sakes but for the well-being of the body of humanity. The "individual finds fulfillment of his potential not merely in satisfying his own wants but in realizing his completeness in being at one with humanity and with the divinely ordained purpose of creation."[207] Complementarity and interdependence of male and female is a reality; principles guiding the struggle for equality must be consistent with this reality if they are to succeed.

It is well understood that however sound a set of principles and teachings may be, their ultimate test is in their ability to transform the lives of those who espouse them. Bahá'ís are actively engaged in a collective effort to eliminate the abuse of women, to discover new patterns for family and community life, and to find practical methods of harmonizing the public and private lives of both women and men. There is considerable evidence of transformation in attitudes, relationships, and institutional behavior in the Bahá'í community. The world will judge the extent to which the community lives up to its ideals over time.

APPENDIX: NOTE ON THE HISTORY OF THE BAHÁ'Í FAITH

As Judaism is the faith of Moses, Christianity the faith of Christ, and Islam the faith of Muhammad, the Bahá'í Faith is that of Bahá'u'lláh. Bahá'u'lláh was born in 1817 in Tehran, Persia and died an exile and prisoner on the outskirts of Akká in the Ottoman Empire (today Acre, Israel) in 1892.[208] His name at birth was Mírzá Husayn Alí. The title he assumed, Bahá'u'lláh, means the "Glory of God" in Arabic. He taught that religion is revealed progressively over the ages as humankind gradually matures and reaches new stages in its collective development.

According to Bahá'u'lláh, the founders of each of the major world religions[209] (including those mentioned above as well as Buddhism, Hinduism, and Zoroastrianism)

---

207. Universal House of Justice, Individual Rights and Freedoms in the World Order of Bahá'u'lláh 21 (1989).

208. Bahá'u'lláh was exiled from Persia to Baghdad in 1853, and from there to Constantinople and Adrianople. He was imprisoned in the 'Akká fortress in 1868 and remained under house arrest until the time of his death. For a comprehensive history of the Bahá'í Faith, *see* God Passes By, *supra* note 10.

209. Bahá'u'lláh wrote that, in addition to the major religions known today, God's messengers have been "sent down from time immemorial . . . to summon mankind to the one true God,"

have each had a two-fold mission. First, they revealed fundamentally similar spiritual truths in proportion to humanity's ability to comprehend the unfathomable realities of God, the Creator, by whatever name the Unknowable Essence may be called. Second, they revealed laws and social teachings that were intended for a period of history but were subject to change in subsequent ages by a new messenger or "manifestation" of God. Bahá'u'lláh taught further that all religions have been subject to decline and disunity as time passed, as the teachings of the founder became corrupted, lost, or laden with human-made dogma, interpretations, and unintended organizational structures. He explained that this is another reason why religion is revealed progressively and is renewed periodically, each messenger foretelling a time of another coming and subsequent revelation. The central beliefs of the Bahá'í Faith are the existence of one God, the essential oneness of His prophets, and the fundamental unity of humanity.

In his Will and Testament, Bahá'u'lláh appointed his eldest son, 'Abdu'l-Bahá[210] (1844–1921), to be the authoritative interpreter of his writings and head of the Faith. 'Abdu'l-Bahá travelled through Europe and North America from 1911 to 1913, his visits adding impetus to the growth of the Bahá'í Faith in the West. Upon his passing 'Abdu'l-Bahá designated as his successor Shoghi Effendi (1897–1957), his grandson, who, at that time, was a student at Oxford University.[211] Bahá'u'lláh's writings, as further elaborated by 'Abdu'l-Bahá, expressly provide for elected institutions at the local through international levels to guide and organize the collective life of the Bahá'í community. In 1963, after Shoghi Effendi died without heirs several years earlier and the establishment of a stable foundation of local and national Bahá'í institutions, the Universal House of Justice was first elected, pursuant to Bahá'u'lláh's mandate.[212] The seat of the Universal House of Justice and the Bahá'í World Centre are located in Haifa, Israel, on Mount Carmel, not far from the place of Bahá'u'lláh's last exile and death.

Bahá'u'lláh's writings range from highly mystical and poetic works to the prescription of detailed laws and appeals to the kings and rulers of his day.[213] Originally written in Persian and Arabic, they have been translated at least partially into over 800 languages.[214] In addition to the topics discussed herein, the Bahá'í teachings

---

though records of their lives may have been lost to history. BAHÁ'U'LLÁH, GLEANINGS FROM THE WRITINGS OF BAHÁ'U'LLÁH 174 (Shoghi Effendi trans. rev. ed. 1952).

210. His given name was 'Abbás. The name he assumed upon his father's passing, 'Abdu'l-Bahá, means in Arabic "Servant of Bahá [Glory]."

211. Shoghi Effendi is known as the Guardian of the Bahá'í Faith. He developed the Bahá'í World Centre, translated into English and interpreted through his letters the writings of Bahá'u'lláh and 'Abdu'l-Bahá, and promoted efforts to teach the Bahá'í Faith and build its local and national institutions around the world. BAHÁ'Í WORLD 1994–95, *supra* note 4, at 6–7.

212. For an explanation of the procedure for electing the Universal House of Justice and the responsibilities of this institution, *see supra* note 133.

213. The corpus of Bahá'u'lláh's writings consists of over one hundred volumes of letters, prayers, meditations, and long works.

214. BAHÁ'Í WORLD 1994–95, *supra* note 4, at 317.

address the spiritual foundation of life, the importance of prayer and meditation, over-coming racism, economic justice and elimination of the extremes of wealth and poverty, the unity of science and religion, global disarmament, the value of universal education, establishing a universal auxiliary language, and other subjects personal and public.[215]

---

215. Two comprehensive introductory works on the history and teachings of the Bahá'í Faith are HATCHER & MARTIN, *supra* note 106, and ESSLEMONT, *supra* note 56.

Section IV

Regional Issues

ISSUES AFFECTING MIDDLE EASTERN MUSLIM WOMEN: SELF-DETERMINATION AND DEVELOPMENT IN TURKEY, EGYPT, IRAN, IRAQ, AND SAUDI ARABIA

Anne H. Heindel

> Human rights are the fruit of a thought process that enables us to distance ourselves
> from our tradition and to learn how to understand others from their own viewpoint.[1]

INTRODUCTION

Women living in the Middle East have diverse concerns spanning the breadth of human rights instruments; their views and experiences vary by class and locality. The peoples and countries of the region vary in their ethnicity, religious beliefs, and economic and political systems. Because of the plethora of issues relevant to women of the region, this chapter does not attempt to be exhaustive, but instead addresses some general concerns of Muslim women living in a cross-section of countries including Turkey, Egypt, Iran, Iraq, and Saudi Arabia.[2] Although Egypt is not geographically a part of the Middle East, here it is included in a cultural definition as it has a shared history with its neighbors stemming from the Arab Muslim conquest of 641 A.D. The chapter's central theme is the impact on women of state development under conditions of unrealized self-determination.

The focus of this chapter is not women's rights within Islam, but rather contemporary manifestations of Muslim society in the Middle East. Nevertheless, a few historical points regarding the origin of Islamic law (*Shari'ah*) need to be mentioned to fully appreciate the legal development of these states. The modern history and laws of each country as they relate to women will then be discussed. Understanding patterns of experience is a crucial step in comprehending women's concerns as, all too often, women (and especially Muslim women) are viewed as ahistorical subjects. It is only by providing some context to the political, social, economic, and cultural life of the region that a complete image of women's role, and most importantly the potential for further development of that role, can be conceptualized. The chapter then reviews common factors that have affected the evolution of women's place in society: the growth of the modern Middle Eastern state under conditions of Western economic domination and the endurance of Islamic family law and the limited avenues

---

1. Interview with Jürgen Habermas by Markus Schwering in *Humbolt, cited in* U.N. Doc. E/CN.4/Sub. 2/1995/14.

2. *See* additional chapters in this work for discussion of non-Muslim women's concerns as well as Adrien Katherine Wing for coverage of Palestinian women's concerns.

for political participation. Domestic laws governing marriage and employment as well as the impact of cultural practices and armed conflict are discussed within the context of States' obligations under international law to promote equal rights. The chapter concludes by emphasizing the overarching influence of self-determination issues on the development of Middle Eastern society and women's place within it.

Women's Concerns

As expressed by regional preparatory documents and non-governmental organizations (NGOs) attending the 1995 World Conference on Women in Beijing, Middle Eastern women's concerns stem not only from historic attitudes toward women and states' domestic policies, but also from international economic, political, and cultural contexts. In the past few decades, women, as well as Middle Eastern society as a whole, have been experiencing rapid transformation caused by urbanization, industrialization, and the growing prevalence of the nuclear family. Recent drops in oil revenues have resulted in declining living standards throughout the region as migrant labor provides an increasingly limited outlet for the excess workforce of non-oil-producing states. The implementation of structural adjustment programs, growing foreign debt, and onerous debt servicing plans (plus a corresponding reduction in public services and government jobs) have led to increased socioeconomic inequality and a feminization of poverty. These changes are affecting the established foundation of society: the extended family and the state that replicates its patriarchal and hierarchical structure and values. War has been a constant feature of the region since the non-fulfillment of the General Assembly's 1947 resolution calling for the creation of a partitioned Palestinian State deprived the Palestinian people of their right to self-determination. Military expenditures have siphoned off states' development resources, and overriding defensive concerns have reduced attention to advancement in other areas of society. Together, these economic and political obstacles have contributed to a backlash against women's expanding integration into all aspects of society.

At the recent Women's Conference in Beijing, Arab and Muslim women rooted their priorities in these experiences. In the Arab Plan of Action, Arab women's concerns include: participation in power and decision making; alleviation of poverty; equality in education; equal access to health services; integration into labor markets; overcoming the impact of war, occupation, and armed conflict; elimination of violence against women; participation in environmental decision making; and improving media images of Arab women and Arab society in general.[3] In its statement of mission, the report grounds itself in religious values that "respect the rights of women as human beings," focuses on images and stereotypes of women, and emphasizes women's participation in sustainable development as a precondition to its success.[4] Similarly, the Islamabad Declaration, written at the first international conference of Muslim women legislators held in preparation for Beijing, calls for "special efforts

---

3.   Arab Plan of Action for the Advancement of Women to the Year 2000, *adopted* at the Arab Regional Preparatory Meeting (Nov. 9–10, 1994), U.N. Doc. E/CN.6/1995/5/Add.5 (1994) [hereinafter Arab Plan of Action].

4.   *Id*. at para. 4–5.

to abrogate discriminatory laws as well as cultural and customary practices so that our society can advance on an egalitarian and just basis."[5] It points to illiteracy, poverty, bias, and violence as priority issues. The Islamabad Declaration resolves to promote women's Islamic identity, values, and culture; discusses the impact of sanctions on Iraq; and calls for Israel's withdrawal from the occupied Arab territories. A declaration issued by the Arab NGO caucus attending Beijing expressed concern over some Islamic groups' statements suggesting that international human rights standards, and especially women's rights, were contrary to Islam. In it the caucus advocates that the realization of equality should be a priority for Arab nations and expressed concern with structural adjustment programs and the human rights of women in the Occupied Territories.[6]

Discrimination, poverty, violence, traditional attitudes toward women, and the occupation of Arab territories are all mentioned as core concerns. Significantly, in all three documents the authors assert that their views are grounded in the true spirit of Islam. These women acknowledge their acceptance of international human rights standards, including equality between men and women, but they make it clear that their values stem from Islam. The region's laws and policies, however, also claim to be rooted in Islam—an Islam that sanctions discrimination against women. Islamic doctrine cannot be addressed by international law, but the actions of the regions' governments are subject to its rules. Both the Middle Eastern states' right to choose their path of development and Middle Eastern women's right to choose their path of advancement are enshrined in the legal obligations of all states emanating from treaty obligations and customary international law standards.

International Law Standards

Equality is a basic principle underlying all human rights law.[7] Some assert that protecting human rights is a *jus cogens* obligation of all states.[8] From this is derived

---

5.   Beena Sarwar, *Women: Muslim Legislators Conference Sets the Tone for Beijing*, INTER PRESS SERVICE, Aug. 8, 1995.

6.   Ihsan Bouabid, *Women-Religion: What Arab Women Think*, INTER PRESS SERVICE, Sept. 15, 1995.

7.   *See* Universal Declaration of Human Rights, *adopted* Dec. 10, 1948, G.A. Res. 217A (III) at art. 2, U.N. Doc. A/810, at 71 (1948) [hereinafter Universal Declaration] ("Everyone is entitled to all the rights and freedoms set forth in this Declaration, without distinction of any kind, such as race, colour, sex, language, religion, political or other opinion, national or social origin, property, birth or other status.").

8.   *See generally* Karen Parker & Lyn Beth Neylon, *Jus Cogens: Compelling the Law of Human Rights,* 12 HASTINGS INT'L & COMP. L. REV. 411, 441–443 n.2 (1989) (arguing that the whole of human rights law is jus cogens); *See* Vienna Convention on the Law of Treaties, *in force* Jan. 27, 1980, art. 53, 1155 U.N.T.S 331, reprinted in 8 I.L.M. 679 (1969) (defining *jus cogens* as a "preemptory norm"). Rules of *jus cogens* have also been defined as "those rules which derive from principles that the legal conscience of mankind deem[s] absolutely essential to coexistence in the international community." U.N. Conference on the Law of Treaties, 1st and 2nd Sess. Vienna Mar. 26–May 24, 1968, at 294, U.N. Doc. A/CONF./39/11/Add.2 (1971) (statement of Mr. Suarez, Mexico).

the right to be free from discrimination in the exercise of economic, social, cultural, and political rights.[9] The Proclamation of Tehran states plainly that, "An inferior status for women is contrary to the Charter of the United Nations as well as the provisions of the Universal Declaration of Human Rights."[10] Equality is also integral to the right to development since development includes social justice—that is, advancement toward enjoyment by all people of their human rights.[11] Impediments to gender equality include traditional attitudes and national laws based on those attitudes that define women as primarily domestic and dependent, but women's ability to exercise their individual human rights without discrimination is also impacted by the ability of their society to exercise its collective right of self-determination.

Self-determination is "the prerequisite to the fulfillment of all other fundamental human rights,"[12] including the right to development.[13] It is defined in Common Article 1 of the Human Rights Covenants: "All peoples have the right of self-determination. By virtue of that right they freely determine their political status and freely pursue their economic, social and cultural development."[14] It is a right of peoples under colonial or alien domination, which has been defined by states to mean "any

9.   *See* International Covenant on Civil and Political Rights, *adopted* Dec. 16, 1966, *entered into force* Mar. 23, 1976, art. 2, 999 U.N.T.S. 171, *reprinted in* 6 I.L.M. 368 (1967) and International Covenant on Economic, Social and Cultural Rights, *adopted* Dec. 16, 1966, *entered into force* Jan. 3, 1976, art. 2, 993 U.N.T.S. 3, *reprinted in* 6 I.L.M. 360 (1967) [hereinafter Human Rights Covenants].

10.   PROCLAMATION OF TEHRAN at para. 15, U.N. Doc. A/CONF.32/41, U.N. Sales No. E.68XIV2 (1968).

11.   *See, e.g.*, Declaration on Social Progress and Development, G.A. Res. 2542 (XXIV) (1969), art. 1 ("All peoples and human beings, without distinction as to race, colour, sex, religion, nationality, ethnic origin, family or social status, or political or other conviction, shall have the right to live in dignity and freedom and to enjoy the fruits of social progress and should, on their part, contribute to it."); Aureliu Cristescu, The Right to Self-Determination: Historical and Current Developments on the Basis of United Nations Instruments at 71, U.N. Doc. E/CN.4/Sub.2/404/Rev.1, U.N. Sales No. E.80.XIV.3 (1981).

12.   The Right of Peoples and Nations to Self-Determination, G.A. Res. 637 (VII) (1952).

13.   *See* Declaration on the Right to Development, G.A. Res. 41/128 (1986), art. 1 ("The human right to development also implies the full realization of the right of peoples to self determination"); Declaration on Social Progress and Development, *supra* note 11, at art. 3.

The following are considered primary conditions of social progress and development:

    (a)   National independence based on the right of peoples to self-determination;

    (b)   The principle of non-interference in the internal affairs of States;

    (c)   Respect for the sovereignty and territorial integrity of States;

    (d)   Permanent sovereignty of each nation over its natural wealth and resources;

    (e)   The right and responsibility of each State . . . to determine freely its own objectives of social development, to set its own priorities and to decide in conformity with the principles of the Charter of the United Nations the means and methods of their achievement without any external interference;

    (f)   Peaceful coexistence, peace, friendly relations and co-operation among States . . .").

14.   *See* Human Rights Covenants, *supra* note 9, at common art. 1.

kind of domination, whatever form it may take, which the people concerned freely regard as such. It entails denial of the right to self-determination, to a people possessing that right, by an external, alien source."[15] It involves "not only the completion of the process of achieving independence . . . but also the recognition of their right to maintain, assure and perfect their full legal, political, economic, social and cultural sovereignty."[16]

Domination of one state by another leads to wars and other conflict, the loss of independent political decision making, the loss of ability to choose an individualized method of economic progress, and retardation of cultural development. Women are disproportionately affected by the loss of human rights attendant with these events when they face violence and lack autonomy within their own society. Such obstacles to national development most quickly and directly impact those without entrenched bases of power and act to reinforce their subordinance. However, the converse is also true—the inability of women to exercise their economic, social, and political rights is an obstruction to the sustainable development of states, which is based on the improved well-being of all its members and is now recognized to have the participation of women as an essential requirement.[17] Therefore, while the realization of the right to self-determination is indispensable for social development,[18] its attainment is dependent on the ability of women to achieve their full potential within society.

HISTORICAL AND LEGAL CONTEXT

Self-determination issues have been a core concern of the peoples of the Middle East at least since the invasion of Egypt by Napoleon in 1798 impressed upon the region Europe's growing military-technological superiority. As the region succumbed to political and economic domination by Europe and then the United States, the role of women in Muslim society became a focal point in the discourse about what path of development the area should take. For this reason, women's concerns became politicized to a rare degree. Imperialist powers, domestic advocates of "modernization," nationalists, and Islamists[19] have all employed the symbol of women's bodies to promote their vision of how Middle Eastern society should proceed. While the West has often used Muslim women to exemplify the backwardness, repressiveness, and exoticism of the region,[20] those seeking national liberation have often dismissed women's

---

15. Héctor Gros Espiell, Implementation of United Nations Resolutions Relating to the Right of Peoples under Colonial and Alien Domination to Self-Determination at 17, U.N. Doc. E/CN.4/Sub.2/405/Rev.1, U.N. Sales No. E.79.XIV.5 (1980).

16. *Id.* at 21.

17. *See, e.g.,* Report of the Secretary-General, Second Review and Appraisal of the Implementation of the Nairobi Forward-Looking Strategies for the Advancement of Women, U.N. Doc. E/CN.6/1995/3/Add.1 at para. 2.

18. Declaration on the Right to Development, *supra* note 13, at art. 1, §2.

19. This chapter uses the term "Islamists" to designate opposition groups whose activities and/or rhetoric are based on Islamic principles of morality.

20. *See generally* EDWARD SAID, ORIENTALISM (1979) (discussing "Orientalism" as the manufactured Western image of the Muslim world).

concerns as at best premature or (with a more devastating and pervasive effect) as an illegitimate product of cultural colonialism. From all sides, the debate has predominately focused on women's appearance, and efforts to "emancipate" them have been centered on either removing or returning to the veil. For this reason, reforms have failed to disturb traditional attitudes that view women's role within the family as essential to their identity.

Women in Islam[21]

In pre-Islamic Arabia, the tribe was the primary unit of social and political organization, and kinship was its binding force. Warfare between tribes over scarce resources was a way of life, and bravery and honor were the prized (masculine) values. The shortage of men due to constant warfare was one likely cause of the practice of polygamy.[22] Women were considered to be part of their husband's or guardian's estate and did not inherit. With the birth of Islam in 610 A.D., Islamic law became a unifying force throughout the region and its precepts governed all conduct between people, including both family and economic relations.

Quranic reforms gave Arab women economic rights, and thus legal status for the first time, and were perhaps the most advanced in the world at that time. A wife, instead of her father, was recognized as the principal party to the marriage contract with her husband. In addition, the practice of dowry was modified to give brides, instead of their family, the right to control the payment, as had been the custom. Women were guaranteed an independent legal status so that during marriage women could manage their property and upon divorce they would be able to retain ownership. Additionally, the Quran restricted polygamy by limiting men to four wives, and then only if they could treat them equally. As a curb on the unrestricted right of men to divorce their wives, a three-month period of separation was mandated to determine if the wife was pregnant, during which time the husband was to provide maintenance. If she was pregnant, he was bound to support her and the child for a period of time. Women also obtained the right to divorce, although this right was primarily limited to stipulations in the marriage contract. The "harmony" of rights and duties of the spouses was based on the husband's responsibility to provide maintenance and the wife's obligation to obey. Lastly, women gained inheritance rights, although not equal to those of men.

With the rapid Arab-Muslim conquests of neighboring lands came the defeat of the Sasanian Empire (Iran), the Byzantine Empire (including parts of Egypt, Palestine, Syria, Iraq, and Anatolia (Turkey)) and the exponential growth of Islam. Muslim society acquired traditions from the areas it controlled, most likely including the custom of veiling women: although the Quran requires that women dress modestly, the veil is not mandated. In the captured empires, however, middle- and upper-class women veiled as a sign of social status, and this practice was subsequently adopted by the Arabs.

---

21. *See generally* Ann Mayer, *Issues Affecting Muslim Women, supra* Section III, this volume.

22. NAZIH AYUBI, POLITICAL ISLAM: RELIGION AND POLITICS IN THE ARAB WORLD 36 (1991).

One of the customs most associated with Islamic culture as it developed is the link between women's bodies and family (male) honor. Women have been tradition- ally viewed as sexual creatures that lead men to lose control, and thus as the source of *fitna* (disorder). Because Islam is concerned with "public ethics and collective morals,"[23] and women are viewed as the moral center of the family, their behavior is circumscribed to protect the family name. The perceived need for control over women's bodies resulted in gender segregation including veiling and restrictions on move- ment.[24] Likewise, "crimes of honor," the murder of female relatives accused of *zina* (fornication and adultery), were considered justifiable and even necessary to reestab- lish the family's reputation.

The Modern Middle East[25]

The birth of the Ottoman Empire in the fourteenth century led to its domination of the region for over 400 years. Then, in the nineteenth century, European capital began to flood the area and previously self-sufficient economies were increasingly penetrated and made dependent on its continued flow. Raw materials were exported and manufactured goods were imported. Like the Ottomans, as Egypt and Iran embarked on technological modernization of their formerly superior armed forces to protect themselves from European imperial designs, they became indebted to European lenders. Further, the Capitulation agreements exempted resident Europeans from tax- ation and local jurisdiction and resulted in nearly autonomous power for European consuls. By 1874, about 60 percent of the Empire's expenditures went to servicing the debt and Europeans controlled the distribution of its revenues. The region's economies had been restructured by the influx of foreign capital and their integration into a European-dominated world economy. By the end of the century, the Ottomans and Egypt had both declared bankruptcy and Egypt was occupied by the British.

The importation of technical knowledge from Europe led to an unexpected result—the importation of Western ideas through the creation of a new European- educated elite. This extension of European influence into civil life led to the Tanzimat, or reorganization, in the Ottoman Empire. From 1839 to 1876 there was a period of intense reform, including recognition of the religious equality of all subjects, increased educational opportunities for all citizens, and new civil, penal, and commercial codes containing a blend of Western concepts and *Shari'ah*. At the end of the nineteenth century, with these new codes under the jurisdiction of European-dominated courts, the *Shari'ah* courts retained control only of personal status law.

The Young Turk movement of 1908 led to further secularization of the crum- bling Ottoman Empire, including curbs on the powers of the Sultan and the rein-

---

23.   *Id.* at 42.

24.   Of course this is generalized, as rural women, whose labor was always essential to the sur- vival of the household, never experienced gender segregation or veiling in the same way as elites.

25.   Unless otherwise noted, the historical content in this section has been derived from WILLIAM L. CLEVELAND, A HISTORY OF THE MODERN MIDDLE EAST (1994); ALBERT HOURANI, A HISTORY OF THE ARAB PEOPLES (1991).

statement of a constitution. Women began entering the civil service and other professions as a result of the mobilization of men into the military during World War I. A new family law in 1917 placed the *Shari'ah* courts under control of the state bureaucracy. Women gained broadened rights to initiate divorce, and polygamy was further restricted. At the end of the war the Ottoman Empire was dismantled and, with the sanction of the League of Nations, its Arab territories were divided into French and British mandates.

Turkey

With Istanbul and the Sultan under Allied control, Ottoman field commander Mustafa Kemal convened a national assembly in Ankara which adopted a constitution. Unlike its former Arab territories, Turkey was able to obtain full sovereignty in 1923. Kemal, given the surname Atatürk (father of the Turks) by the national assembly in 1935, embraced the European form of government, adopting codes based on foreign models for all areas of law. Most radically, family law as well was no longer based on *Shari'ah*.[26] Although the veil was not forbidden, Western dress for both women and men was encouraged. Polygamy was outlawed and women were given more grounds upon which they could initiate divorce. However, for rural women (and thus the majority of the population) these laws had only a limited impact. For example, to facilitate the elimination of polygamy, only children born from civilly registered marriages were recognized as legitimate and entitled to inherit. Nevertheless, the practice continued and, in 1950, the government needed to grant legal status to eight million children out of a total population of 21 million.[27]

Under Atatürk, universal education was adopted, and, in 1934, women were given the right to vote and to run for the national assembly. In the following years, small numbers of women became judges and were elected to public office. By the 1960s, women still had higher rates of illiteracy than men but continued to participate in education and government. Despite these reforms, Atatürk was intolerant of dissent and all oppositional views, especially those of the Kurds, were ruthlessly crushed.

The Turkish Constitution of 1982 provides for equality before the law, prohibits discrimination based on sex, and gives everyone the right to freedom of residence and movement.[28] The family is called the foundation of Turkish society, and mothers and children are given state protection.[29] Primary school is free and compulsory for all citizens and everyone has the right and duty to work.[30] Further, minors, women,

---

26. Despite his revolutionary views, Kemal's attitudes toward women were rooted in their role in the family. In 1923 he said, "I will not cease to repeat it, women's most important duty, apart from her social responsibilities, is to be a good mother," *quoted in* KUMARI JAYAWARDENA, FEMINISM AND NATIONALISM IN THE THIRD WORLD 36 (1986).

27. Leila Ahmed, *Feminism and Feminist Movements in the Middle East, A Preliminary Exploration,* 5 WOMEN'S STUDIES INT'L FORUM 153, 158 n.2 (1982).

28. CONSTITUTION OF THE REPUBLIC OF TURKEY, arts. 10 and 23, *reprinted in* CONSTITUTIONS OF THE COUNTRIES OF THE WORLD (A.P. Blaustein & G.H. Flanz eds.).

29. *Id.* at art. 41.

30. *Id.* at arts. 42, 48–49.

and the disabled are to receive special protection regarding working conditions.[31] The right to enter public service is to be based solely on qualifications.[32]

The Civil Code[33] was adopted from the Swiss in 1926 and, although progressive at the time, is now in conflict with the constitutional guarantee of equality. It bans polygamy and marriage by proxy, establishes the same grounds for divorce for men and women, provides for equal rights to child custody and inheritance and makes the court testimony of women equal to that of men. Despite these reforms, the patriarchal nature of the family remained intact. Thus, following the classic *Shari'ah* formulation, the husband is declared head of the family and is given the responsibility for its support while the wife is made responsible for running the home. The husband is given the power to represent his wife and children in legal cases and to choose their domicile, while the wife is required to bear her husband's surname and is made responsible for the day-to-day activities of the home. (The Code has recently been amended to allow women the right to choose their name.) If parents have a dispute regarding their children, the husband's decision is to be upheld. However, men and women are given the same grounds for divorce, and child custody is to be decided at the discretion of the judge. In 1990, the Code provision requiring a wife to obtain her husband's approval before engaging in paid employment was annulled as unconstitutional. The Criminal Code makes abortion a crime with a prison sentence, but because of recent population control policies by the government there is now an exception up to the tenth week of pregnancy under the Law on Population Planning.[34]

Law No. 1475 (1971), which governs employment standards for waged individuals, guarantees equal pay for equal work.[35] However, most women work in agriculture or the informal sector, which are exempt from this law. Although agricultural workers have been covered by minimum wage laws since 1989, most women are unpaid family workers. Maternity leave is covered by the Regulation on Conditions of Work for Pregnant or Nursing Workers, Nursing Rooms and Day Nurseries. Under it, working women are guaranteed maternity leave, yet they can be dismissed for being pregnant or for taking maternity leave. Nursing mothers are guaranteed time to nurse their babies at work, but in practice few employers provide facilities. Although the regulation requires employers of more than 150 female workers to provide nursing rooms and day-care centers at work, in practice the law is either not enforced or employers hire just below the minimum number of women. Restrictions on women's employment in night work and heavy or dangerous work act to confine women to lower-paying occupations.[36] The government has stated that the jobs most commonly

---

31.   *Id.* at art. 50.

32.   *Id.* at art. 70.

33.   *See generally* WORLD BANK, WOMEN IN DEVELOPMENT: TURKEY 88–91 (1993); Dr. Isik Urla Zeytinoglu, *Employment of Women and Labor Laws in Turkey,* 15 COMP. LAB. L.J. 177, 193–94 n.2 (1994).

34.   Law No. 2,827 (1983).

35.   *See generally* Zeytinoglu, *supra* note 33, at 194–98.

36.   WORLD BANK, *supra* note 33, at xix.

offered to women include baby-sitter, housemaid, secretary, and sales clerk.[37] Twenty-five percent of lawyers are women.[38] Turkey is currently the only Middle Eastern country with female judges.[39]

Since 1991, the Directorate General on the Status and Problems of Women has been affiliated to the Prime Ministry and a minister of state has had responsibility for women's concerns.[40] That same year, for the first time, two women in Parliament became government ministers. Subsequently, Tansu Çiller became the first woman Prime Minister and now holds the post of Foreign Minister and Deputy Prime Minister. However, the percentage of women members in parliament overall has decreased since the high of eighteen in 1935 (4.6 percent), to only eight (1.8 percent) after 1991.[41] The government has explained the attrition by stating, "This decline is an outcome of the fading away of the "symbolization of democracy" role played by women as a result of the initiation of the multi-party system."[42]

Egypt

With over 60 percent of Egypt's revenues going to payments on debt to European powers, Britain occupied the country in 1882 to prevent the ascendance of a nationalist government and remained until 1956. During the occupation, Egypt became increasingly dependent on the export of cotton. Between the World Wars, a constitution was adopted and the political elite espoused and emulated European culture. Women from the upper classes pressed for the right to vote, educational opportunities comparable to men, and family law reform. Prominent women began to remove their veils. However, as Ahmed writes: "[W]hile the issue of women and the improvement of their condition was thus as live among Egyptian intellectuals as it was among Turkish, no government, party, or male individual with access to power was to adopt it as a central issue, and this was to make a crucial difference to the evolution of the women's movement in Egypt."[43] Thus, while private education flourished, primary school became compulsory for both sexes in 1925, and women were allowed to attend the national university from that time, discriminatory family law remained intact.

In the 1930s, Islamic groups such as the Muslim Brotherhood advocated a return to *Shari'ah* in all areas of the law and pressed for economic reforms. Its ideas were popular with the urban poor, recent immigrants to the cities, and university students. After World War II and the first Arab-Israeli war, the Brotherhood attacked foreign businesses and officials regarded as complicitous with imperialist interests.

---

37. U.N. Doc. CEDAW/C/TUR/2 (1996) at 17.

38. *Id.* at 23.

39. Valentine M. Moghadam, Determinants of Female Labor Force Participation in the Middle East and North Africa 26 (May 1990), U.N. Doc. UNU/WIDER(05)/P2.

40. *Id.* at 2.

41. *Id.* at 19.

42. *Id.* at 18.

43. Ahmed, *supra* note 27, at 159.

After a coup d'état in 1952, Colonel Nasser began to dominate Egyptian and Arab politics and press for independence from the British. The government committed itself to the abolition of imperialism in the Constitution of 1956. It embarked on an Arab-socialist agenda including redistribution of land, nationalization of foreign-owned businesses, and the liberation of the Suez Canal from British control. A new bill of rights guaranteed citizens protection from discrimination on grounds including sex, but political parties were banned and Nasser's power was cemented by constitutional provisions giving strong powers to the president. Labor Law 91 of 1954 guaranteed equal rights and equal wages and contained special protection for married women and women with children. Its impact, however, was limited primarily to the public sector. In 1956, women were given the right to vote and run for the assembly, and the Charter of 1962 gave women legal equality with men. Educational opportunities for women greatly expanded and, with nationalization of the economy, a government job was guaranteed to every graduate. The result was massive numbers of public-sector jobs occupied by women. The traditional veil was increasingly abandoned, but there was no liberalization of family law regarding polygamy or women's right to initiate divorce.

With the loss of the Sinai peninsula in 1967 during the Six-Day War with Israel, Egypt and the other Arab powers' preoccupation with their military inferiority came to dominate all political issues. By the time Sadat became president in 1970, the country suffered from an enormous foreign debt from military purchases and a huge defense budget. He began an "open-door" policy that led to privatization of industry and increased foreign investment. Under advisement by the International Monetary Fund (IMF) that they would not provide further loans unless subsidies on basic commodities such as food were removed, Sadat complied. This opening up to foreign investment and foreign goods has been blamed for a deterioration of Egypt's industrial base and for increasing dependence on the West. Unemployment has grown, and job advertisements in Cairo often notify women that they need not apply despite legal prohibitions against gender discrimination.[44]

The Constitution of 1980 guarantees the equality of all citizens and prohibits discrimination based on sex.[45] Equality of opportunity is also guaranteed.[46] The family is deemed the basis of society and the state is "keen" to preserve its "genuine character" as well as its embodiment of values and traditions.[47] The state also guarantees the protection of motherhood, childhood, and women's role in the family.[48]

In 1979, Sadat issued Law No. 44 as a presidential decree. It required a man to inform both his present and future wives about each other's existence. If the first wife

---

44. NADIA HIJAB, WOMANPOWER: THE ARAB DEBATE ON WOMEN AT WORK 82 (1988).

45. THE AMENDMENT ISSUE OF THE CONSTITUTION OF THE ARAB REPUBLIC OF EGYPT, art. 40 [hereinafter EGYPTIAN CONST.], *reprinted in* CONSTITUTIONS OF THE COUNTRIES OF THE WORLD (A.P. Blaustein & G.H. Flanz eds.).

46. *Id.* at art. 8.

47. *Id.* at art. 9.

48. *Id.* at arts. 10–11.

was harmed by his second marriage, she had grounds to initiate divorce. The most significant reform was the requirement that the custodian of the children was to retain possession of the family home, as women are usually given custody of their young children with a possible judicial extension. Despite these reforms, women were still required to obtain permission from their husbands to work outside the home. In 1985, the method in which Law No. 44 was passed was challenged, and it was repealed. Feminists mobilized and a new personal code was passed, but it did not contain all the previous advancements. Regressive changes included requiring a judge to decide if a wife had been harmed by her husband's second marriage before she could have grounds for divorce.

Egyptian personal law includes the traditional agreement between spouses that, in return for maintenance, the wife will obey the husband. He may withhold maintenance if she becomes an apostate or leaves the house without her husband's permission.[49] After divorce, women are given custody of children of up to a maximum age of ten for boys and twelve for girls,[50] and both parents have visitation rights. Currently, women may work without their husbands' permission without losing their rights to maintenance, provided their employment does not conflict with the family's interests. Women have the same right as men to institute legal proceedings, but their testimony in court does not have the same weight. Women only inherit half as much as men.

Article 11 of the Constitution guarantees that the state will coordinate women's employment and family obligations. Labor law guarantees equal opportunity for women, but also prohibits employment of women in work harmful to their health or morals. Women who work for the public sector are entitled to two years unpaid maternity leave, women in the private sector are entitled to one year leave, and businesses employing 100 or more females are required to have a nursery close to the workplace. Although private-sector employers often do not comply with maternity leave and child care legislation or circumvent it by hiring just under 100 women, the government does not actively pursue compliance.[51]

Although thirty seats in the National Assembly and one or two seats on local councils were previously allotted to women with a right to compete for the rest, since 1987 these seats have no longer been set aside. The High Constitutional Court struck down the reserved seating on the grounds that it contravened the constitutional right to equality. While in 1984, thirty-six women were elected to the Assembly, by 1990 the number had decreased to seven.

Iran

Although on a smaller scale than the Ottomans or Egypt, Capitulation agreements also led to integration with the global economy in Iran. At the turn of the twen-

---

49. Law 25 of 1920 *as amended by* Law 100 of 1985.

50. Act. 25 of 1989.

51. Valentine M. Moghadam, *Economic Reform and Women's Employment in Egypt, in* Economic Reforms, Women's Employment and Social Policies 94, 105 (Valentine M. Moghadam ed.,
1995); U.N. Doc. UNU/WIDER(05)/W6 No.4.

tieth century there were several public protests against foreign domination in which women participated. In 1891, a revolt against economic exploitation was organized by the powerful Shi'a ulama with the aim of defending Islam against foreign influences. In 1901, the Shah gave a British subject the oil rights for the entire country and Britain became the major shareholder in the company holding the concession. The Shah obtained huge loans from Europe that he put to personal use as well as to pay the interest on old debts. These activities led to a "constitutional revolution" against his rule from 1905 to 1911. Eventually, he was forced to sign laws reducing his power and defining the rights of citizens and the Majlis (Assembly). As a result, Britain and Russia made an agreement to divide Iran into spheres of influence and, during the subsequent civil war, occupied their respective zones.

After World War I, British loans and military support maintained the Shah's control and led to anti-foreign and anti-government demonstrations. In 1921, Reza Khan, a military officer, took control and named himself Shah. A new civil code modeled on that of France was adopted in 1928, along with a modern penal code. Neither, however, questioned traditional patriarchal values or lessened men's dominant position in society since family law remained governed by *Shari'ah*. Moghissi asserts that "Reza Shah's main concern was to produce a Westernized image for Iran."[52] The Marriage Law of 1931 was the first to make marriage subject to secular law. In it, the grounds upon which a woman could initiate divorce were enlarged to include a husband's failure to provide maintenance and his ill-treatment of her. In 1936, Reza Shah banned the use of the veil and segregation in public places was abolished, but by the mid 1930s, all independent women's organizations had been suppressed.[53] Women could not vote until 1952, nor was polygamy abolished. It remained difficult for women, but easy for men, to initiate divorce.

During World War II, Britain and the Soviet Union re-occupied the country to protect their oil supplies. After the war, Muhammad Reza Shah (Reza Shah's son) came to power with the support of the British and subsequently the United States. Foreign economic and cultural domination was widely resented. The Anglo-Iranian Oil Company, dominated by Britain, had autonomy within the state and behaved like an independent government, including building infrastructure and negotiating with local tribes, while employing Iranians only as laborers. In 1953, after the Majlis nationalized the oil industry, the U.S. Central Intelligence Agency (CIA) organized a coup against the popular nationalist Prime Minister Muhammad Mosaddiq to maintain the Shah's fragile hold on the country. Subsequently, with the assistance of the United States and Israel, the Shah established SAVAK, a state security organization which was infamously brutal, torturing political prisoners and restricting political expression. Iran purchased extensive amounts of weapons from the United States and employed foreign military advisors (60,000 by 1977) who were given high salaries and privileged access to scarce resources.

---

52. HAIDEH MOGHISSI, POPULISM AND FEMINISM IN IRAN: WOMEN'S STRUGGLE IN A MALE-DEFINED REVOLUTIONARY MOVEMENT 39 (1994).

53. *Id.* at 40.

The Shah imposed a series of reforms known as the "White Revolution" during the late 1960s and early 1970s, but political representation was not included. Family protection laws in 1967 and 1975 allowed women to initiate divorce, gave women greater legal equality in marriage, required husbands to obtain consent from their wives before taking another wife, and increased women's child custody rights. Most reforms were incorporated as standard stipulations in all marriage contracts, thus maintaining the fiction that the parties were contracting for these provisions according to the accepted practice of Islamic law. The legal age of marriage was raised to eighteen for women and twenty for men. Overall, the reform's impact was limited: there was no right to alimony upon divorce, women could be prevented from engaging in employment that their husband thought was "incompatible with the family's best interests and his or his wife's respectability," women needed their husband's written approval to travel abroad, and crimes of honor remained legal. Further, the benefit of the reforms was confined to the privileged, as the majority of women continued to receive little education, few had economic independence, and most remained constrained by traditional attitudes.

Foreign investment and the encouragement of large-scale manufacturing destroyed many local economies and industries. Beginning in the 1960s, various rebel groups, including the People's Mojahedin mounted opposition against the Shah but were repressed through arrests, torture, and executions. Many women were active in these groups. The ulama also denounced the decadence of the Shah's regime, including the increase in consumption of consumer goods and the huge income discrepancies. The middle classes in the cities suffered from crippling inflation and recession leading to severe urban unemployment. Other sources of protest came from professionals, secular and theological students, and bazaar merchants. The Ayatollah Khomeini attracted wide support for his anti-imperialist message with its foundation in Islamic morality.

After the 1979 revolution, middle-class women became among the first to oppose Khomeini's Islamist policies. Although many had donned the veil to avoid the surveillance of SAVAK as well as to express their opposition to the Shah's domination by the United States, most never intended it to become obligatory. With the first order for mandatory veiling among public employees in 1979, there was a massive protest by women and the order had to be rescinded. However, once Khomeini had consolidated his authority, a female dress code was introduced.

The Preamble of the Constitution of 1979 focuses on the history of the struggle of the Iranian people against imperialist interests, and the reforms of the White Revolution are called an American conspiracy to reinforce the political, cultural, and economic dependence of Iran.[54] Women are given credit for their active role in overthrowing the Shah. They are singled out as having suffered greater oppression under his rule than men because of their having lost their true identity and human rights as a result of foreign exploitation. The Islamic view of the family as the fundamental

---

54. CONSTITUTION OF THE ISLAMIC REPUBLIC OF IRAN, *reprinted in* CONSTITUTIONS OF THE COUNTRIES OF THE WORLD (A.P. Blaustein & G.H. Flanz eds.).

unit of society and the "primary basis for man's development and growth," is said to liberate women from objectification and use as pawns in promoting consumerism and exploitation.

In the body of the Constitution, men and women are given equal protection by the law and enjoyment of "human, political, economic and cultural rights according to Islamic standards."[55] Equal rights are provided elsewhere, but not between the sexes.[56] The family is again said to be the fundamental unit of society, and laws "based on Islamic laws and moral concepts" exist for the purpose of protecting its sanctity.[57] Women's guaranteed rights "according to Islamic standards" include an environment favorable to personal growth; protection for mothers; the establishment of special insurance for widows, elderly, and destitute women; and guardianship rights to fit mothers whose children have no lawful male guardian.[58] "Everyone" is given the right to choose the profession "he" wishes, "provided it is not contrary to the principles of Islam," and free education through high school is guaranteed.[59] Women are precluded from becoming president because the position is only open to male religious and political dignitaries.

Under the Civil Code, inheritance laws give a widow one-quarter of her husband's estate; if there are children, she inherits one-eighth.[60] Men inherit half of their wives' estate and daughters receive an amount equal to one-half of their brother's share. Women are given ownership of the nuptial gift and the right to control its disposition, as well as the disposition of any of their other property.

The Code is made up of detailed information on the different rights and duties of females and males in the family: if a "virgin girl" marries, the permission of her father or paternal grandfather is required, "even if she has reached the age of puberty;" Muslim women and girls are not permitted to marry non-Muslim men; marriage can be permanent or temporary; and the husband is recognized as the head of the family. If a marriage is permanent, the husband must pay the wife's maintenance unless the wife refuses to "fulfill her matrimonial duties." Similarly, after divorce, the wife's right to maintenance depends on whether or not she was "attending to her duties" at the time. However, if a husband contracts a venereal disease after marriage, the wife can refuse to have intercourse without losing maintenance rights. *Mut'a* (temporary marriage) may be as short as an hour, can be terminated at any time, and does not allow for rights to maintenance.[61]

The marriage contract may include provisions setting up conditions under which the wife will be able to initiate divorce, such as upon a husband's taking of a second

---

55. *Id.* at art. 20.

56. *Id.* at art. 19.

57. *Id.* at art. 10.

58. *Id.* at art. 21.

59. *Id.* at arts. 28, 30.

60. CIVIL CODE OF IRAN (M.A.R. Taleghany trans. 1995).

61. *See infra* text accompanying notes 154–55 (discussing temporary marriage).

wife, but only those with both the husband's and wife's signatures are binding. Otherwise, she can rescind the marriage upon castration, impotency, or penal amputation prior to consummation. "Difficulty and hardship" in a marriage or the husband's refusal and/or inability to pay maintenance are grounds for a wife to request the *Shari'ah* court for a divorce. If the court rules in favor of the wife, it will compel the husband to divorce his wife. Men, however, can divorce their wives at any time by merely uttering a formula in the presence of two men. Women may not remarry for three months or three menstrual cycles after divorce, but men can remarry immediately. Men can have four wives at any time as well as unlimited temporary marriages, while women may only have one marriage at a time.

There are two kinds of divorce in the Civil Code, revocable *(rij'i)* and irrevocable *(ba'in)*. A husband may revoke his unilateral declaration of divorce and return to his wife during her period of withdrawal from the marriage *('Iddah)* by any deed combined with the intent to return. Men are only prohibited from returning to their wives in four situations, one of which is if the wife has reached the age of menopause.[62] Although a husband is obligated to support his wife during *'Iddah* (unless she was divorced while "not attending to her matrimonial duties"), a wife who is irrevocably divorced has no maintenance rights unless she is pregnant.

The Code dictates that the husband has the right to decide where the couple will live and can withhold his permission for his wife to work when it is "incompatible with the family interests or with the dignity of himself or of the wife." It also mandates that married women may only be employed in jobs that do not interfere with their duties to their marriage. Labor laws provide working women with maternity leave, protection from dismissal during leave, and, in a workplace with more than ten nursing mothers, require facilities for a creche.[63] While most waged and salaried female workers are employed by the government and are eligible for health insurance and pensions, a majority of women work in the private sector for themselves or as unpaid family workers and are not protected by labor laws.[64]

After coming to power, the Khomeini government dismissed all female judges. Women have been banned from studying law, accounting, commerce, engineering, and agriculture. The illiteracy rate among adolescent women has risen 30 percent since the revolution, and the number of employed women has declined from 14 percent of the labor force to 9 percent.[65] This is in spite of the increased need for female employment during the Iran-Iraq War (1980–1988).

---

62. Additional situations under which divorce is irrevocable by the husband include a divorce which takes place before consummation of the marriage, divorce initiated by the wife as long she has not asked for and received the return of her dowry ("the consideration which she has paid for the divorce") and a third divorce after three consecutive marriages by the same couple.

63. David Ziskind, Labor Laws in the Middle East: Tradition in Transit 229 (1990).

64. Valentine M. Moghadam, Modernizing Women: Gender and Social Change in the Middle East 59 (1993).

65. Parliamentary Human Rights Group, Iran: The Subjection of Women 13 (1994).

The effect of these laws is the almost total loss of rights for women both in public life and within marriage and the family. No consent is necessary for sex inside marriage, and women are supposed to obtain their husband's permission to leave the home. In practice, divorce is rarely permitted for women, and most financial claims must be forfeited for one to be obtained. Further limiting women's option for divorce is her loss of custody of sons over two years old and girls over seven. Rape outside the home commonly goes unreported because of fears of family reactions or prosecution by the state for adultery if the victim is unable to prove she has not given her consent. The government adopted a pronatalist policy in the 1980s that included the elimination of access to contraception and the lowering of the age of consent to marriage to thirteen. While girls as young as nine and sometimes seven have been given permission to marry with a physician's certificate attesting to their sexual maturity,[66] the age of marriage has actually risen since the Revolution. In rural areas, however, girls reportedly have been sold by their fathers to older husbands.[67] The suicide rate increased 17 percent from 1980 to 1990, with women making up two-thirds of the cases.[68]

The Criminal Code (Law of *Hodud* and *Qesas*) values a woman's court testimony at half that of a man's and considers it inadmissible in murder cases. Further, "[W]omen who appear in public areas and crossings without religious veil will be sentenced to punishment of up to 74 lashes." This dress code applies equally to non-Muslim women. Vice squads patrol for unveiling and "mal"-veiling—that is, showing hair from under the veil or wearing a colored veil. Government statistics show that 113,000 women were arrested for dissemination of moral corruption and mal-veiling in 1992.[69] Adultery carries a penalty of flogging for the unmarried and stoning to death for the married. Men who are to be stoned are buried to the waist while women are buried to the neck. In theory, the convicted person is allowed to go free if he or she can escape.[70]

Iran is currently fighting a civil war with the National Liberation Army of Iran (NLA). Beginning in 1987, the NLA has carried out sustained operations against the Iranian army and has held Iranian territory. Its political wing is the National Council of Resistance of Iran (NRC), a 235-member parliament-in-exile. The NRC was established in 1981 as an umbrella for the various groups opposing the Ayatollah's government, including the People's Mojahedin (long-time opponents of the Shah). Its strategy to liberate the country is based on its commitment to complete equality for women. It opposes the regime's restrictions on women (including mandatory veiling) and has initiated an internal policy of promoting women into leadership positions. Currently, more than half the parliament's members are women, as is the president-elect. The army is also integrated: women comprise seven of fifteen members of the General Command and one-third of the regular troops.

---

66. *Id.* at 6.

67. National Council of Resistance of Iran, Women, Islam & Equality 26 (1995).

68. *Id.* at 33.

69. *Id.* at 21.

70. Parliamentary Human Rights Group, *supra* note 65, at 10–11.

Iraq

After the breakup of the Ottoman Empire, the territory now known as Iraq remained occupied by the British. The areas that formed the new state in 1920 were ethnically and religiously diverse, including a population of about half Sunni and half Shi'a. Although Iraq began as a monarchy (1925–1958), military officers always had firm control over the government. Despite the country's formal independence in 1932, Britain maintained the right to provide its "security." Through the 1950s, 80 percent of Iraq's population lived in rural poverty under near feudal conditions. Successive military regimes adopted reformist policies but had difficulty obtaining support from the many divided interests within the country.

The first oil concession to the West occurred in 1925 in favor of the Iraqi Petroleum Company (IPC), a British consortium. In 1961, the government nationalized part of IPC's assets and took away most of its concession areas.[71] In retaliation, the company reduced production and, in 1972, the government nationalized its assets in the name of defending its sovereignty.[72] In 1973, Iraq also nationalized the interests of Exxon and Mobil in retaliation for the United States' financial and military backing of Israel.[73] By the 1970s, Iraq was the world's second largest producer of oil after Saudi Arabia.[74] However, during the Iran-Iraq War, exports at first ceased, then resumed at decreased levels until sanctions imposed at the behest of the United States in 1990 drastically reduced production.

In 1968, the Ba'ath Party assumed power, and decision making became dominated by the Revolutionary Command Council (RCC) and its president. The new regime was brutal with suspected opponents and engaged in public executions of political prisoners. Top positions in the government were dominated by individuals from the same town who were related through marriage. Iraq became a one-party state with the state controlling everything from labor unions to women's groups. With the growth of oil production, the government began to engage in public investments in heavy industries as well as social reform. Staple foods were subsidized, health care was made free, university tuition was abolished, and employment availability expanded.

The Constitution of 1970 announces the objective of creating a socialist state and makes Islam the official religion.[75] Education is associated with creating a populous that "struggles against capitalist ideology, exploitation, reaction, Zionism and imperialism for the purpose of realizing Arab unity, liberty and socialism."[76] Citizens are made equal before the law, discrimination on the basis of sex is forbidden, and

---

71. Law 80 of 1961.

72. S.H. Amin, Middle East Legal Systems 154 (1985).

73. *Id.*

74. *Id.*

75. The Interim Constitution of the Republic of Iraq, arts. 1, 4, *reprinted in* Constitutions of the Countries of the World (A.P. Blaustein & G.H. Flanz eds.).

76. *Id.* art. 28.

equal opportunities are guaranteed.[77] The family is called the "nucleus of society."[78] Free education is guaranteed at all levels for all citizens, and equality is guaranteed for appointment to public office.[79]

Personal status law,[80] though primarily based on the *Shari'ah*, was amended in 1978 to outlaw forced marriages, to increase the ability of women to initiate divorce, and to require judicial approval for polygamy. The minimum age for marriage is currently fifteen for girls or boys with parental permission and eighteen for both without permission. *Mut'a* is officially illegal in Iraq, but is practiced in predominantly Shi'a areas. Marriages between Muslim females and non-Muslim males are forbidden, while Muslim men can marry women who are "people of The Book" (Christians and Jews). Women have maintenance rights during marriage, provided they are available for their husbands and obey their lawful commands. The Civil Code gives guardianship of children to their father, with custody rights to the mother for boys of up to seven years old and for girls up to nine. Inheritance rights are equal for both sexes.

Husbands who seek a divorce are required to obtain a judgement in court. Both spouses may seek a divorce on the grounds of injury (including infidelity or the husband taking another wife without court permission) or discord. When the ground is discord, the court arbitrates to determine fault. If the court is convinced that there will be continued dissention, it will order a divorce if the husband does not do so. Iraq has stated to the Committee on the Elimination of All Forms of Discrimination against Women that women are not required to live with their husbands in the case of marital violence, lack of adequate financial support, when he breaks the law, or upon failure to pay the dowry.[81]

Under the Ba'ath party's rule, women's educational opportunities rapidly expanded and social services were provided to integrate them into the workforce. Education became free at all levels and has been encouraged in rural areas through the awarding of additional allowances to teachers serving in remote areas.[82] Both the 1976 law that made education compulsory and the literacy campaign of 1978 greatly benefitted women. However, as a result of the economic embargo in 1990, many families have stopped sending their children, especially girls, to school because of the high cost of clothing and school supplies.

The Labor Code guarantees the right to work under equal conditions and with equal opportunity without sex discrimination.[83] It mandates the creation of child care

---

77.   *Id.* art. 19.

78.   *Id.* art. 11.

79.   *Id.* arts. 27, 30.

80.   Law No. 188/1959. *See generally* S.H. AMIN, THE LEGAL SYSTEM OF IRAQ 427–459 (1989).

81.   U.N. Doc. CEDAW/C/SR.212, 213 and 216 (1993).

82.   Committee on Economic, Social and Cultural Rights, Concluding Observations on Iraq, U.N. Doc. E/C.12/1994/6.

83.   ZISKIND, *supra* note 63, at 89.

centers, equal pay for equal work, and full pay during maternity leave.[84] Leave can be extended up to nine months for a difficult birth or the birth of more than one child, but it is unpaid.[85] Facilities for a kindergarten on-site or by contract with an outside service are mandated for employers of women.[86] Unlike the rest of the region, no categories of workers are excluded from protection where one or more people are employed, and unemployment benefits are also provided. Iraqi women had been widely considered to have the highest legal and social status in the region until the Gulf War of 1991.[87]

Although Iraq has experienced massive growth with increasing oil revenues, the war with Iran (1980–1988) caused tremendous setbacks in its economic development plan. There was a great deal of physical damage, and the subsequent U.S. bombing in 1991 obliterated most of the state's infrastructure. Although health services are free to everyone, the government has been unable to continue providing adequate services since that time. The effect on women from economic sanctions has ranged from serious health problems including malnutrition and disease to unemployment and increased subjection to violence.[88]

Saudi Arabia[89]

From the late eighteenth century, Britain dominated the Western strip of Arabia, but otherwise, the area is unique in escaping a colonial experience. From 1902 to the end of World War I, Iban Sa'ud, a tribal chieftain, consolidated his power over the region's tribes. He obtained authority through his military victories, but also as the leader of the Wahhabi sect, a puritanical Islamic order. The King cemented his power through family alliances and ruled as a patriarch.

With the discovery of enormous oil reserves, Saudi Arabia went from being one of the poorest countries in the world to one of the richest. Because of a shortage of trained or willing workers, aliens from other Arab states and Asia soon became the resident majority. With rapid material advancement, a middle class was created that benefit from immense social services and well-paid employment, but remain excluded from political participation of all kinds. As the population becomes more educated, a strain is developing between phenomenal growth in technological modernization and the availability of consumer goods and restricted social and political development.

Despite recurring criticism about the extravagant and materialistic lifestyles of the royal family, the government maintains its legitimacy from its identification with

---

84. *Id.* at 229.

85. *Id.*

86. *Id.*

87. *See, e.g.,* AMIN *supra* note 80, at 458; HIJAB, *supra* note 44, at 80.

88. *See infra* text accompanying notes 178–89 (discussing economic sanctions against Iraq).

89. Unless otherwise noted, background material for this section comes from CLEVELAND, *supra* note 25, and SORAYA ALTORKI, WOMEN IN SAUDI ARABIA: IDEOLOGY AND BEHAVIOR AMONG THE ELITE (1986).

Islam. *Shari'ah* remains the basis of all traditional law. Exceptions to this are the laws governing business, investment, foreign trade, and immigration, which follow Western concepts but are justified with references to *Shari'ah*. Thus, modern Saudi society is a combination of rapid economic development and the enforced preservation of traditional social values.

While the rights of women are among the most unequal in the region, there have been marginal increments toward liberalization for some younger women. During courtship some families are permitting couples to meet at least once—a previously forbidden practice. Polygamy, while legal, is decreasing. To obtain a divorce, women must demonstrate one of a limited number of grounds, but men have no such requirement. However, with an increase in the number of divorced women, many of the educated now refuse to return to their father's home and instead live alone with their children. Despite these advances, a woman's testimony in court is worth half that of a man's, and daughters inherit less than sons.

Girl-children first received public education in the 1960s, with strict separation of the sexes observed after nursery school. At the university level, there have been difficulties finding female lecturers, so either women from other Arab countries are hired to fill the posts or the students watch lectures via closed-circuit television. Further, women's library facilities are inferior to men's. Fields of study for women are still usually limited to education, medicine, and liberal arts. There are restrictions on women traveling abroad for education, including the requirement that female graduate students on scholarship must be accompanied by their husbands. Despite these constraints, Saudi Arabia has the largest percentage of highly educated women in the region.[90]

Because all citizens are more or less subsidized by the state, in general, Saudi women have not felt the same financial compulsion to work as have other women in the region. Nevertheless, if they want or need to work outside of the home, they must obtain permission from their husband, or if unmarried, their father or brother. Although for the most part they are not formally limited to certain occupations, social attitudes function as effective barriers to many jobs. The Labor and Workmen's Regulation of 1969 prohibits women's employment in dangerous industries as well as mixing with men at work. It provides for maternity leave with payment for delivery by the employer and rest periods for nursing upon returning to work. Women may not be dismissed during their leave, and employers of fifty or more people are required to provide facilities with a nurse to care for children under the age of six.

Presently, approximately 5 percent of Saudi women work outside the home. They are generally limited to professions considered appropriate to their gender, such as teaching and health care, but there are also many female journalists. Women are being encouraged to work to reduce the country's reliance on foreign workers and also to enter professions such as medicine where they can retain a female-only clientele and

---

90.   Ihsan Bouabid, *Women-Mideast: No Easy Recipe for Change*, INTER PRESS SERVICE, Sept. 3, 1995.

maintain the state's policy of minimal male-female contact. Jobs such as nursing are seen by many as servile and demeaning, so non-citizens are still needed to provide these services. The government is currently promoting the training of women as medical secretaries, despite the traditional view that it is unacceptable work for women. This is significant because hospitals are the only place that unveiled women work with men.[91] Women own and run their own businesses, but must hire a man to handle day-to-day operations if they do not have an all-female clientele. In 1980, the first bank run by and catering solely to women opened. The directors are publicly admired, give radio and press interviews, and lecture to female students about their careers.[92] There are government plans to encourage more women-only businesses. Some women argue that Saudi women are in an advantageous position because they do not compete with men for jobs and therefore are taking over leadership positions with the confidence of people used to being in positions of authority, albeit solely among women. The role of working women is popularly debated in the press.

Women need the permission of their husbands to travel abroad, but when they do leave they become free of some of the restrictions of home. Abroad, many women dress in Western clothing and attend mixed parties with their husbands (although usually not with other Saudi men). Within the country, women are not allowed to drive their cars or to take public transportation without a male guardian. As a result, special female-only sections have been created on public buses, but they are confined to the major cities. The restriction on driving (thus mobility), and not the veil, is said to be the source of most resentment among women.[93] In 1990, a group of forty-seven women including many university professors drove their cars in Riyadh in protest of this custom, only to be sanctioned by losing their jobs.

In 1992, the Basic System of Rules was promulgated by the King after years of promises of its drafting, including a provision giving state protection to human rights "in accordance with the Islamic *Shari'ah*."[94] Various reasons have been suggested for its timing, including the growing frustrations of the middle class because of their lack of political participation as well as the desire to limit the activities of Islamist groups within the country. The rights provisions of the document are limited, but include protection from arbitrary arrest, punishment, and search. These legal protections are thought to be aimed at stemming the power of the *mutawwa'un*, or morality police, who regulate observance of Islamic principles and women's attire.[95] They are known to enter private homes at will, to imprison people for minor offenses, and harass peo-

---

91.   Nesta Ramazani, *Arab Women in the Gulf*, 39 MIDDLE EAST J. 258, 260 n.2 (1985). *See infra* text accompanying notes 159–60 (discussing veiling in Saudi Arabia).

92.   Louay Bahry, *The New Saudi Woman: Modernizing in an Islamic Framework*, 36 MIDDLE EAST J. 502, 506 n.4 (1982).

93.   Ramazani, *supra* note 91, at 264.

94.   *See generally* Rashed Aba-Namay, *The Recent Constitutional Reforms in Saudi Arabia*, 42 INT'L & COMP. L.Q. 295 (1993).

95.   *See, e.g., id.* at 326.

ple in public.[96] They are not officially a part of the government but are controlled by conservative ulama who fear corruption from foreign influences such as rampant consumerism and the large alien workforce.

With the massive numbers of foreign troops on Saudi Arabian soil during the Gulf War in 1991, Islamist groups gained moral ground against the regime—a particularly troublesome phenomenon for a family whose major source of legitimacy is derived from its Islamic credentials. The ruling family's notoriously materialistic and often decadent lifestyle has resulted in criticism from religious leaders as well as opposition groups who assert that its members' behavior goes against Islamic teachings. Islamist influence has been present within the country at least since the takeover of the Grand Mosque at Mecca in 1979 and its rhetoric forms the main avenue of protest for dissentious elements within society.[97] Declining living standards and growing social inequality have led to expanding activities by these groups in recent years. Some view the Gulf War as the catalyst for a surge of Islamist ardor because it highlighted the country's dependency on Western powers. Evidence for this may be seen in the recent attacks on American military forces as well as the government's increasing conservatism toward women since the war (including the issuance of a law prohibiting female drivers in the wake of the 1990 protest, and the government's failure to send any delegates to the Beijing women's conference). While demands by the Islamist groups have included the supremacy of the *Shari'ah* in all areas of law, including economic, they also have asked for legal equality and the redistribution of national wealth.

ISSUES CONCERNING MIDDLE EASTERN WOMEN

Common Factors

Despite the many differences in the history of the peoples of the Middle East, some common factors are apparent. For the countries discussed, with the exception of Saudi Arabia, Western economic domination is not a recent phenomenon but has been evolving for more than a century. Foreign control over resources and influence over domestic economic policies from constant debt have been an undeviating feature of the region's international relations. Similarly, defensive concerns have shaped national discourse. National liberation, the nonfulfillment of U.N. resolutions on Palestine, and the loss of three wars and consequent territory to Israel[98] have been the driving forces behind a majority of domestic, regional, and international policies. The effect of this history of Western encounters is that self-determination issues—political, economic, social, and cultural—have eclipsed other aspects of development.

---

96. *Id.*; Nabila Megalli, *"Enforcers" Step up Drive to Keep Saudis in Line,* L.A. TIMES, Jan. 19, 1992, at A27.

97. *See generally* R. Hrair Dekmejian, *The Rise of Political Islamism in Saudi Arabia,* 48 MIDDLE EAST J. 627 n.4 (1994).

98. Including the Golan Heights, West Bank, Gaza and the Sinai Peninsula (returned to Egypt in 1979).

One consequence is that human rights have not been the focus of drives for education and legal reform. Instead, reform was spawned from concerns about the ability of the state to progress on a model that could compete with the Western powers.[99] In many cases, movements for women's rights and the formation of women's organizations have been either introduced by men or ultimately co-opted by them for political reasons. This has impeded the ability of women to control their own issues and has resulted in women's concerns often being utilized in the service of some other power struggle. Atatürk encouraged women to give up the veil and outlawed the fez, mocking men who continued to wear it as appearing "uncivilized," in his pursuit of a modern identity for Turkey. Kadioglu writes that "all the major rights conferred on Turkish women during [the Atatürk years] were the result of the efforts of a male revolutionary elite, who had the goal of bringing Turkey to the level of contemporary Western civilization." She finds that "a State feminism instigated from above inhibited the evolution of a feminist consciousness on the part of these women."[100]

In Egypt, independent organization by women was prohibited by the government until 1987. Hatem says of early Egyptian women's groups, "They were created by the State, which defined their agendas and expected them to act as its auxiliaries."[101] In Iran in the 1930s, women's veils were forcibly removed by the police to improve the image of the country and to make it appear progressive, yet independent women's organizations were quashed. The Shah's creation of a single government-controlled women's organization led to a loss of legitimacy for feminist ideas, but also to a lack of mobilization among women of the middle class that could have sustained their spontaneous rejection of Khomeini's call for mandatory reveiling. Women's inability to define their own issues has prevented their voice from developing as an independent source of knowledge and power and has facilitated the limited nature and effect of legal reforms. An historic lack of political participation in the region is partially to blame, but the pattern of co-option of women's issues by domestic and foreign groups with ends of their own (or the belief that they know what Muslim women need) is also responsible. Unfortunately, this has also included some Western feminists, who have used their organizational experience to dominate the agenda at international conferences.

Another similarity is that the family law of all these states remains rooted in the *Shari'ah* (as interpreted to legitimize gender inequality). This is despite the absorption of "secular"—or perhaps more accurately, European—legal concepts and the adoption of constitutions proclaiming equality and non-discrimination between the

---

99.   *See* Valentine M. Moghadam, Development and Patriarchy: The Middle East and North Africa in Economic and Demographic Transition 6 (July 1992), U.N. Doc. UNU/WIDER(05)/P2, "Concepts of the emancipation of women came about in the context of nationalism and anti-colonialism, state-building, and self-conscious attempts toward modernity in the early part of the century." Ahmed, *supra* note 27, at 158–59.

100.   Ayse Kadioglu, *Women's Subordination in Turkey: Is Islam Really the Villain?*, 48 MIDDLE EAST J. 645, 652–53 n.4 (1994).

101.   Mervat Hatem, *Egyptian Discourses on Gender and Political Liberalization: Do Secularist and Islamist Views Really Differ?*, 48 MIDDLE EAST J. 661, 665 n.4 (1994).

sexes.[102] Family law in these countries is often the only remaining area based on traditional Islamic law. All these states consider the family, with women at its core, to be the basis of their society, and many limit provisions on equality to "equality within Islam." Where women are guaranteed the right to work outside the home, their primary loyalty is emphasized to be the family, and, in many cases, they need their husband's permission. Where this kind of discrimination is not explicitly stated, it nevertheless forms a part of the contractual duties of marriage: the wife's availability and obedience in return for maintenance from her husband. In both Egypt and Iraq, despite the primacy of secular law, the civil codes instruct judges to fill in legal gaps with the *Shari'ah*.

The Family[103]

The foundation of Middle Eastern society has been the extended family—a patriarchal and hierarchical construct that encourages polarized male and female roles and sanctions male dominance. Identity and community status have been linked to the family, as has social welfare protection. For this reason, the acts of an individual have been the concern and responsibility of the whole family and a reflection on family honor. The man has historically been responsible for the material needs of his wives and children as well as other relatives (depending on his position in the male hierarchy). A woman's place in the family has been based on obedience to the husband and as the transmitter of cultural values to younger generations. There has been a well-defined structure of power relations within the family: children show a great deference and respect to their elders, women to older women and men, and men to older men. Men have compelled unquestioning obedience to their authority, and women have been envisioned as behaving in a submissive and dependent manner.

A man's power in the family is formal and exclusive and thus, as Karmi points out, there is no direct outlet for dissent—it only can be expressed through rebellion, conspiracy, or mediation.[104] A woman's power is indirect, derived from her male relatives. At all times of her life she is defined by her relations to her male kin. Her power in the family increases with the birth of children, especially male. Morsy defines bearing and raising children as women's principal culturally defined function in the Middle East. She says that this, along with the loyalty she receives from her children, are "a woman's most significant and relatively durable power-base."[105] Women have

102. This is not to say that gender equality can be achieved by adopting a Western model. On the contrary, as has been shown by numerous authors, formal equality coexists with patriarchal relations in "liberal" societies.

103. *See generally* WOMEN AND THE FAMILY IN THE MIDDLE EAST: NEW VOICES OF CHANGE (Elizabeth Warnock Fernea ed., 1985).

104. Ghada Karmi, *The Saddam Hussein Phenomenon and Male-Female Relations in the Arab World, in* WOMEN IN THE MIDDLE EAST: PERCEPTIONS REALITIES AND STRUGGLES FOR LIBERATION 146, 151 (Haleh Afshar ed., 1993).

105. Soheir A. Morsy, *Rural Women, Work and Gender Ideology: A Study in Egyptian Political Economic Transformation, in* WOMEN IN ARAB SOCIETY: WORK PATTERNS AND GENDER RELATIONS IN EGYPT, JORDAN AND SUDAN 121 (Seteney Shami et al. eds., 1990).

also derived influence from maintaining social contacts with female relatives and neighbors. In rural areas, exchanges of visits between women have been critical for families wanting to strengthen political ties and acquire news. A woman's mediation between the father and her children is another source of her authority. While this behind-the-scenes activity is critical to maintaining the cohesiveness of the family unit and its social status, it remains under-appreciated and ultimately derivative. Because most women lack independent control of resources, they are obligated to obey social constraints and cater to the power dynamic of the family. Hegland states, "If a woman should lose her relationship with a man, she would also usually lose her financial and social standing."[106]

This "traditional" family is merely an ideal, although it remains firmly implanted in the expectations and aspirations of many people. The reality of family life has been undergoing increased modification with growing economic integration into world markets and the region's consequent industrialization and urbanization. Whereas previously the family worked together as an economic unit providing the major source of education, job access, and social support, the state's mounting encroachment into welfare areas has made it the largest employer in the Middle East. Further, as more people move to the cities to look for work, nuclear families have become increasingly common among the middle class with a resultant loss of support from the extended unit and a rise in power-sharing among family members. Children are less deferential as they find their family unable to guarantee their future status. Although rural women have always worked outside the home and were subject to only limited segregation, more and more urban families have been finding it necessary to have two incomes.

Power relations within the family are in a period of uncertainty because of these developments. Men's role as sole provider and protector of their families is being undermined, precipitating frustration and violence against women. As females and males become able to meet each other more freely in public places, arranged marriages following the custom of endogamy become less frequent, thus minimizing the ability of the family to use the institution as a tool to cement relationships and assist and control the family as a whole. These transformations have reduced a significant source of women's power: control of marriage alliances and maintenance of social bonds within the extended family unit. Women are unable to maintain social contacts to the same extent because they now need to work both inside and outside the home. Also, families transplanted to urban environments are often unable to find or afford housing in the same neighborhoods as other relatives and visits often require long bus trips. Further, the proliferation of television and video has reduced the necessity of social contacts for entertainment and information. At the same time, women often receive resentment instead of recognition for their outside employment. Thus women are experiencing a loss of status within the family without significant gain from their growing public roles and increased financial responsibility.

---

106. Mary E. Hegland, *"Traditional" Iranian Women: How They Cope,* 36 MIDDLE EAST J. 483, 488 n.4 (1982).

The State

The structure of familial relationships is reproduced at the state level. Further, "[w]hile kinship loyalties may conflict with national loyalty and undermine national consciousness, much of the legitimacy of political orders and of rulers derives from the family and its value orientations."[107] In this way hierarchical and patriarchal organization underlies all public relations, including those with teachers and employers, and is exemplified most blatantly in political authorities. The stereotypical Middle Eastern leader has been defined as a man who comes to power without popular consent, with promises of social justice, and who maintains his hold on power through repression and an intricate system of patronage.[108] Karmi says that this image evokes admiration as the ideal representation of Arab manhood.[109] The leader is viewed as father and calls his people his children. In Saudi Arabia, even the country is named after the ruling patriarchy.

Political expression is severely restricted by most governments in the region. Just as women and children are socialized with unquestioning dependency on men, citizens are excluded from participating in political life. As in the family, dissent cannot be expressed, but is limited to mediation through powerful patrons or to illegal action. Thus the majority of men and women are unable to participate in decisions about the development of their society.

Further, the lack of avenues for political participation or expression of dissent has, for the most part, resulted in the predominance of radicalized opposition groups for whom women's rights are, at best, secondary to national liberation.[110] This continues the pattern of anti-colonial movements in the region; while women have fought in wars of independence and revolutions and have participated in resistance activities, their contributions have not been rewarded with the right to participate in decisionmaking on an equal basis. Rather, during these times, women have been encouraged not to weaken the ranks of opposition by advocating gender-specific issues. When opposition groups have come to power, women have still not obtained equal rights in recognition of their contributions to national liberation—both because of the continuance of institutionalized patriarchy and because of the common perception in the region of a continuing struggle for self-determination from imperialist nations.

At the same time, the growth of the independent state has coincided with advances for women. Especially since its rapid expansion during the 1960s, women's educational opportunities have experienced dramatic growth and, along with this, employment opportunities in the public sector. The number of state institutions sup-

---

107. Halim Barakat, *The Arab Family and the Challenge of Social Transformation, in* WOMEN AND THE FAMILY IN THE MIDDLE EAST: NEW VOICES OF CHANGE, *supra* note 103, at 27, 44.

108. Karmi, *supra* note 104, at 148.

109. *Id.* at 149.

110. *See supra* at text following note 70 (discussing the National Council of Resistance of Iran as an exception to this).

porting the changing family arrangements, including services for the elderly and child welfare, are growing. The oil boom has been a factor, allowing governments, which spend a large percentage of their budget on national defense, to support social services at the same time. Although it has been compellingly argued that women have merely become the newest low-paid worker in the world economic order, many women have valued the opportunity for integration into public life beyond mere economic necessity.

During the 1980s however, the price of oil dropped and, by 1989, debt as a percentage of GNP reached 70 percent for the Middle East and North Africa.[111] Austerity measures led to "IMF riots" in Algeria, Jordan, Tunisia, and Turkey.[112] With the shrinking of the state, women's economic gains reversed. The decrease in the number of public jobs, as well as their status, disproportionately impacted women and increased female unemployment and underemployment. Moghadam finds that these economic policies, combined with social inequality and political repression, have led to a loss of confidence in the secular state and to a cultural re-evaluation, including questions about women's changing role in society.[113]

State promotion of women's rights has generally been limited to legal advancements for women in education and employment, because the state has ultimately remained a product of the family's gendered structure. Sharabi has argued that because the Arab states necessarily developed in a position of dependency (that is, as unequal members of the Western-dominated international economy), "modernization" never disturbed their basic patriarchal structure, but merely entrenched it in a modern form.[114] Thus, the state remains rooted in patriarchal values, including discrimination against women. Women's orthodox status in the family is protected by state policies, and family law often remains the last area still limited to traditional readings of *Shari'ah* because the family is the center of Islamic culture and women's place has been at its core. Efforts to expand women's participation in society have also been propagated under these conditions.

Advancement for women has been viewed by both liberals and Islamists as "Westernization," including national development through the adoption of Western cultural values. As a result, reform has remained confined within the context of an ongoing debate about the definition of independence and the quest to preserve a national and/or regional identity. Women's perceived role as guardians of cultural and religious tradition is safeguarded and glorified in a time of massive change and uncertainty. Thus, in spite of these states' vast differences, women in all these countries are considered to have "equivalent" rights, not equal rights, in the family; legal provisions guaranteeing the rights of women often immediately undercut their significance by associating women's relationship to the family and their right to participate in soci-

---

111. Moghadam, *supra* note 99, at 2.

112. *Id.*

113. *Id.*

114. H. Sharabi, Neopatriarchy (1988) (defining neopatriarchy as the product of the encounter between modernity and tradition in the context of dependent capitalism).

ety; and in domestic law as well as in treaty reservations to the Women's Convention, language placing women's rights within the context of traditional Islamic law qualifies otherwise apparently progressive statements.[115]

STATES' DUTIES TOWARD WOMEN UNDER INTERNATIONAL STANDARDS

All states are bound by international human rights law as it is embodied in the Universal Declaration of Human Rights.[116] This consists of equal application of its provisions without distinction based on sex, including equal rights under the law, freedom of movement, equal marriage rights (including at dissolution), the right of association, the right to participate in the political process and to hold public office, the right to work, the right to equal pay for equal work, and the right to education.[117] States are also obligated by the Human Rights Covenants to promote equality between women and men.[118]

Governments are therefore under a legal duty to ensure equality under the law for women. Further, states must act affirmatively to prevent private actors from discriminating against women under the due diligence standard.[119] Signatories of the Women's Convention are expressly obligated "to take all appropriate measures to eliminate discrimination against women by any person, organization, or enterprise."[120]

---

115. *See, e.g.,* EGYPTIAN CONST., *supra* note 45, at art. 11 (combining both types of language: "The State shall guarantee the proper coordination between the duties of women toward the family and her work in the society, considering her equal with man in the fields of political, social, cultural and economic life without violation of the rules of Islamic jurisprudence.").

116. Universal Declaration, *supra* note 7. The Universal Declaration of Human Rights is considered by most to be part of customary international law. *See, e.g.,* PROCLAMATION OF TEHRAN, *supra* note 10, at para. 2 ("The Universal Declaration of Human Rights states a common understanding of the peoples of the world concerning the inalienable and inviolable rights of all members of the human family and constitutes an obligation for the members of the international community."). Some view the Declaration as binding because of its incorporation into the U.N. Charter.

117. Universal Declaration, *supra* note 7, arts. 2, 7, 13, 16, 20, 21, 23, 26.

118. *See* Human Rights Covenants, *supra* note 9. Egypt, Iran, and Iraq are parties to the Covenants as well as Israel, Libya, Morocco, Syria, and Tunisia. Jordan is a party only to the International Covenant on Economic, Social and Cultural Rights.

119. *See generally* Radhika Coomaraswamy, *Violence Against Women, Its Causes and Consequences,* U.N. Doc. E/CN.4/1995/42 at 23–25; Committee on the Elimination of Discrimination Against Women, Eleventh session, General recommendation 19, at para. 9 (CEDAW/C/1992/L.1/Add.15) [hereinafter General recommendation 19] ("Under general international law and specific human rights covenants, States may also be responsible for private acts if they fail to act with due diligence to prevent violations of rights or to investigate and punish acts of violence, and for providing compensation."). Though not itself a binding document, it provides authoritative evidence of enforceable legal norms.

120. Convention on the Elimination of All Forms of Discrimination Against Women, *adopted* Dec. 18, 1979, *entered into force* Sept. 3, 1981, at art. 2(e), G.A. Res. 34/180, 34 U.N. GAOR, Supp. (No. 46), U.N. Doc. A/34/46 at 193, *reprinted in* 19 I.L.M. 33 (1980) [hereinafter Women's Convention]. Egypt, Iraq, and Turkey are parties, as well as Jordan, Libya, Morocco, and Tunisia.

"Discrimination" is defined to include violence against women;[121] thus states have an obligation to eliminate "traditional" attitudes which view women in a position subordinate to men, as such stereotypes "perpetuate widespread practices involving violence or coercion."[122] Neither custom, tradition, nor religious consideration may be invoked to justify violence against women.[123]

Personal Status Laws

Islamic marriage is based in contract and the contract is based in the different fundamental duties of the spouses, as well as the double function of the wife as a contracting party receiving the dowry and as the object of exchange.[124] It is integral to the contract that the woman promises to obey and the man agrees to support her material needs. These rights and duties are not equal, but are called equivalent or complementary. The nature of this equivalency is exemplified by the representative of Egypt's discussion of nondiscrimination in society to the Committee on the Elimination of Discrimination Against Women [hereinafter the Committee or CEDAW]. While asserting that the state believed that equality was important to the full development potential of women, she added that Islam guaranteed their rights and responsibilities as daughters, sisters, mothers, and wives.[125] Thus, the obligations of a woman toward her husband and family are more than part of a mutual exchange; they take over the role of a woman to the extent that she can only be defined through her relationship to men.

Egypt has made a general reservation to art. 2 (concerning active pursuance of eliminating discrimination against women) that it will comply with the content as long as it is not counter to the *Shari'ah,* while Iraq has stated that it does not consider itself bound the sections of art. 2 requiring all appropriate measures to modify or abolish laws and customs which discriminate against women and repeal of all discriminatory penal legislation. Egypt and Iraq have also made reservations with respect to art. 9 concerning equal nationality rights, art. 29 concerning submission of disputes between states concerning interpretation to arbitration, and art. 16 concerning the equality of men and women in all matters relating to marriage and family relations during marriage and at its dissolution. Both countries qualify their reservations to art. 16 by saying "without prejudice to the Islamic *Shari'ah*" under which women have equivalent rights to men. Turkey has reserved with respect to arts. 16 and 29 as well as art. 15 concerning equality of legal capacity in civil matters, freedom of movement, and choice of residence and domicile. It has made a declaration with respect to art. 9 that the intent of the nationality provisions are to prevent statelessness.

121. General recommendation 19, *supra* note 119, at para. 6.

122. *Id.* at para. 11.

123. Declaration on the Elimination of Violence against Women, G.A. Res. 48/104, U.N. GAOR Supp. No. 49 at 217, art. 4, U.N. Doc. A/48/49 (1993) ("States should condemn violence against women and should not invoke any custom, tradition or religious consideration to avoid their obligations with respect to its elimination."). The Declaration has been called "a comprehensive statement of international standards with regard to the protection of women from violence." Coomaraswamy, *supra* note 119, at 22.

124. *See* Shahla Haeri, *Divorce in Contemporary Iran: A Male Prerogative in Self-Will, in* ISLAMIC FAMILY LAW 55, 57–58 (Chibli Mallat & Jane Connors eds., 1990).

125. U.N. Doc. CEDAW/C/SR.34, 39 (Egypt) (1984).

When justifying the unequal obligations between a married man and woman, states often argue that the burden of a husband's financial responsibility to his wife is in contrast with the wife's right to spend her money as she wishes. For example, in Egypt's reservation to the Women's Convention with regard to the equality of men and women in marriage, limitations on a woman's right to divorce are explained by the fact that "the husband shall pay bridal money to the wife and maintain her fully and shall also make a payment to her upon divorce, whereas the wife retains full rights over her property and is not obliged to spend anything on her upkeep."[126] Since women are legally entitled to choose their domestic arrangements, they should not be coerced into trading physical autonomy for financial independence. In practice most women are required to contribute to their family's survival, yet they often do not retain control of the proceeds from their labor.

The rights of women to divorce are also severely limited compared to those of men. While a man can divorce his wife at any time, a woman must prove a limited set of circumstances to a judge and may also have to obtain the permission of her husband. Although her right to include divorce provisions in the marriage contract provides the appearance of equal contracting rights, in practice, most women do not utilize this prerogative.[127] Mohsen has found that pressures including the potential loss of child custody, difficulty in collecting child support, economic obstacles, and the customs disfavoring women living alone make it difficult for middle-class women in Egypt to seek divorce.[128] Hegland's research in Iran shows that despite the psychological independence and confidence some women acquire from close social and religious networks with other women, most lack the economic independence to assert themselves in their families. For instance, she found that most "traditional" Iranian women obey and placate their husbands by conforming to socially accepted (and expected) behavior in order to maintain their financial security.[129] Widowed and divorced women who cannot obtain support from male relatives often end up losing their social status, as well as their only means for economic support. Hegland says that, because of this, "most often they chose to put up with abuse rather than leaving their husbands or disregarding the wishes of other men on whom they may be economically dependent."[130]

These states' child custody laws also act to coerce women to remain within marriage. For example, in Egypt, women are given custody of their sons up to age ten and daughters up to age twelve. Custody can be prolonged up to the age of fifteen for boys and until marriage for women and girls with a judge's approval. In Iraq, women lose custody of their daughters at age nine and their sons at age seven, and in Iran, woman are only allowed custody of their daughters until they are nine and their

---

126. The Women's Convention, *supra* note 120, reservation to art. 16.

127. U.N. Doc. CEDAW/C/SR.164, 165 (1990) (reply of the representative of Egypt).

128. Safia K. Mohsen, *New Images, Old Reflections: Working Middle-Class Women in Egypt, in* WOMEN AND THE FAMILY IN THE MIDDLE EAST: NEW VOICES OF CHANGE, *supra* note 103, at 56, 67.

129. Hegland, *supra* note 106, at 488.

130. *Id.* at 489.

sons until they are two. Of course, these are guidelines. Many women lose custody when they divorce no matter what the age of their children. The distinction these governments have made between women's and men's importance in their children's lives and their capacity as role models reveals the assumptions behind all personal status law—that a woman's abilities are constrained by her domestic functions.

Employment

Employment patterns vary between countries in the Middle East based on their economic base and system. A general distinction can be made between states that import labor and states that export labor. Some, such as Egypt, do both. In Saudi Arabia, as with most of the Gulf states, imported labor accounts for more than half of the population. In all countries, women are still tied to traditional attitudes toward women's employment, especially in regard to the types of work they can perform. Despite these biases, most women work, though only a minority participate in formal wage work. Most non-household labor is in unpaid family agriculture where, despite their significant contribution to production, the worker's labor is not socially recognized and they remain financially dependent on their male relatives.

The treatment of imported labor is receiving greater attention as a result of the Gulf War, especially the situation of Filipino maids in Kuwait.[131] Female migrant workers to the Gulf region are often excluded as a group from the protections of labor laws. Where this is not the case, they are concentrated in types of work that are unprotected, so the result is the same. Migrant women are also often unfamiliar with the language and laws of their host country and are therefore unable to assert any rights that they may have. For example, it is not uncommon for migrant domestic servants to work with no days off and to be forbidden to leave the house. In Kuwait, women who face abuse at the hands of their employers and have tried to leave have been returned by local authorities to their employer, even after attempted suicide.[132] Many are unable to leave the country because of the widespread practice whereby employers confiscate their passports upon arrival.[133] Such women are often the objects of sexual assault or other violence.

Middle Eastern women commonly work in agriculture; the textile and clothing industries; food and health care services; and secretarial, clerical, and assembly work.[134] Within occupations acceptable for women, they earn less and occupy lower-skilled jobs than their male counterparts. Lack of educational opportunities as well as traditional attitudes about women's abilities and/or willingness to accept low-status positions may provide some explanation for this situation. Legal protections for workers often exclude most women because of exemptions for agriculture and the informal

---

131. While most of the reports have come from the Gulf countries, domestic servants in Egypt have also alleged physical and sexual abuse. *See, e.g.,* Kimberly Dozier, *New Focus of Outrage at Abuse of Emigres,* S.F. CHRONICLE, Sept. 29, 1995, at D1.

132. THE HUMAN RIGHTS WATCH, GLOBAL REPORT ON WOMEN'S HUMAN RIGHTS 295 (1995).

133. *Id.* at 292.

134. ZISKIND, *supra* note 63, at 109.

sector (including domestic work) as well as for the small industries in which women are concentrated.

Maternity leave is usually provided for wage workers, both before and after giving birth. Some, but not all, also guarantee women the right to return to their jobs. Extra breaks are usually mandated in such laws, and a few provide for nursery services. In many situations however, employers circumvent these laws.[135] Even when the employer adhered to the laws, in practice these special provisions only benefit the elite groups since most women work in exempted fields. Only Iraq includes all employees who work in businesses hiring one or more persons. Free medical services are also available in most countries but, once again, exclusions apply to agricultural, informal, or temporary workers. Unemployment benefits are uniformly absent in the region except in Israel and Iraq.

Besides protections for pregnant women, there are prohibitions on arduous or hazardous work and night work in Iraq, Iran, and Saudi Arabia, among others. Egypt, Saudi Arabia, and Turkey are members of the ILO Convention No. 45 Concerning Women and Work in Underground Mines; and Egypt, Iraq, and Saudi Arabia are parties to the ILO Convention No. 89 Concerning Night Work of Women Employed in Industry. In practice, such protections limit women's access to higher-paid employment. Thus, the necessity for such conventions and their legality under international law should be reexamined in the light of contemporary standards. For the present, however, they remain in force and the signatories do not appear to be in violation. Further, some observers claim that many Middle Eastern women do not find such measures paternalistic or undesirable.[136]

Agriculture has traditionally provided most work for women but, as discussed above, workers in this field are exempted in most countries from labor protection of any kind. Iraq is alone in being a party to ILO Conventions providing agricultural workers with minimum wage and worker's compensation, but Turkey also provides them a minimum wage. A majority of female agricultural workers labor informally for their families and receive no compensation, so their work is not regulated or included in official statistics. Rural women have been disproportionately impacted by the growing integration of the region into the international economy. As men from countries with a labor surplus have migrated to labor-poor countries, women have needed to take charge of family holdings in rural areas and perform typically male responsibilities. Although this has enlarged women's production burden, it has not necessarily augmented their control over resources. Economic integration has also changed the agricultural market as small holdings have given way to larger farms producing for export. One effect of this is that "as incentives arise in the context of structural adjustment for the production of cash crops and as Governments stop subsidizing agricultural inputs, women lose in terms of access to land and credit and consequently

---

135. *See, e.g.,* Turkey, *supra* at text following note 35 (discussing the enforcement of Regulation on Conditions of Work for Pregnant or Nursing Workers, Nursing Rooms and Day Nurseries).

136. ZISKIND, *supra* note 63, at 110.

in terms of the income accruing to them and their families."[137] Another consequence has been escalating migration to urban areas, resulting in increased cultural alienation and tightened restrictions over women's behavior.[138]

The public sector has provided most wage employment and labor rights for women. For example, in the late 1970s, women in Iraq were encouraged to work for the state. Similarly, in Egypt, the Nasser State guaranteed a job to all graduates, enabling women from the lower classes to benefit from obtaining an education. Egypt's Labor Law of 1954 guaranteed equal rights and wages for women with special provisions regarding women with children, but these laws were primarily applicable to the public sector. In Iran, most women working for a wage are employed by the government, where they are provided benefits including pensions and maternity leave. In Saudi Arabia, women's separate education and employment has been facilitated by seemingly unlimited government finances, but the government's ability to provide parallel facilities even somewhat comparable in quality is dependent on the continued exploitation of oil resources. How long this can last is uncertain but, even now, there are difficulties because of the current budget deficit and reduction in the real price of oil. On top of this, structural adjustment in the region has resulted in policies reducing the public sector and increasing private employment. Women's ability to compete in the market is shrinking because there are now fewer jobs, and men are favored by private employers.

The impact of structural adjustment programs on women is recognized to be significantly greater than it is on men. As rural families find it harder to compete in a deregulated market and urban families find it harder to pay their bills or find jobs, women compensate by working harder and working longer hours. Türk writes, "In many instances, women play a major role in cushioning the adverse social impact of adjustment programs by taking over many of the functions which are increasingly abandoned by the State."[139] Women are becoming poorer, their health is suffering and they have less time or energy for activities outside the family. Compounding these effects, with fewer jobs and more women needing to find paid employment, discrimination against women and pressure for women to stay away from "men's work" increases. As mentioned above, in Egypt, despite legal prohibitions against gender discrimination, job advertisements increasingly request that only men apply. In this way, policies imposed by Western countries as a precondition to integration into international markets have acted to reinforce traditional prejudices relegating women to unpaid or underpaid labor.

Overall, increased participation in production has not necessarily resulted in expanded status and decisionmaking for women. Women who earn wages are valued more than those who work for the family through informal labor. However, their work

---

137. Report of the Secretary-General, *supra* note 17, at para. 108.

138. *See infra* notes 158–63, and accompanying text (discussing restrictions on movement and veiling.)

139. Danilo Türk, The Realization of Economic, Social and Cultural Rights, U.N. Doc. E/CN.4/Sub.2/1991/17 at 49.

outside the home is usually undervalued if not resented and they often do not retain control over their earnings. Lack of financial control limits their ability to make decisions within the family. Lynch and Fahmy write of craftswomen in an Egyptian village:

> We notice that most of the women in the study are financially dependent upon their husbands, despite their productive life, and are unpaid if they work for their husbands. Husbands in most cases are decision-makers in family planning and other matters, and therefore, even where wives feel exhausted from many pregnancies or desire to limit births, they may feel obliged to comply with their husband's wishes and are often reluctant to express opposing opinions. This is most evident in those cases where women are totally dependent, and is unrelated to the degree of their participation in production. . . .[140]

Women's access to employment is not sufficient in itself to increase their influence in the family and society. Cultural perceptions of women's work as supplementary limit women's ability to retain the proceeds of their labor, or to increase their authority within the family based on their productive contributions. Societal attitudes greatly impact how women view their own labor compared to that of men. This devaluation of women's work reduces their ability to take charge of all major decisions in life, and is perpetuated through gender-biased definitions of work and women's role in the family in national laws. The policies mandated by international financial institutions reinforce women's lack of power by undermining the very means by which women have been integrating themselves in public life. The Special Rapporteur on Violence Against Women has identified economic and social forces that exploit women's labor and bodies, especially the denial of economic independence, as one of the historical power relations underlying violence against women.[141]

Violence Against Women

Violence against women has been defined to include cultural prejudice and religious extremism.[142] Yet, it is in this area that there has been the most debate about the universality of human rights law; some claim that international standards impose Western concepts, while others find that a reduction of women's experiences to gender oppression hides other types of subjugation. However, as stated by the Special Rapporteur on Violence Against Women, "[I]t must be accepted that there are patterns of patriarchal domination which are universal, though this domination takes a number of different forms as a result of particular and different historical experiences."[143]

---

140. Patricia D. Lynch & Hoda Fahmy, *Craftswomen in Kerdassa, Egypt, in* Women, Work and Development #7, 44 (I.L.O. 1984).

141. Coomaraswamy, *supra* note 119, at para. 53.

142. Coomaraswamy, *supra* note 119, at para. 7; Report of the World Conference on Human Rights, Vienna, June 14–25, 1993, U.N. Doc. A/CONF.157/24 (Part I) para. 18; General recommendation 19, *supra* note 119, at para 11.

143. Coomaraswamy, *supra* note 119, at para. 50.

Gender segregation, including restrictions on movement and dress, is usually an attempt by men to maintain control over women's bodies. Violence against women based on crimes of honor—that is, purportedly in reprisal for actions which are perceived transgressions against the family—are an attempt to reassert or maintain this control and reestablish patriarchal power relations. With the rapid changes in Middle Eastern society, including the economic necessity of women leaving the home to work, the boundaries between acceptable and forbidden behavior have become less clear. Not only are men losing their ability to monitor women's behavior, but they are increasingly unable to fulfill their own side of the traditional gender contract—supporting their families. The resultant frustration often manifests itself in violence against women, partially because women are one of the most visible symbols of a general loss of economic and social security.

At the public level, this same attitude manifests itself in the lack of criminalization of domestic violence, discriminatory laws and, in some cases, condoning or encouraging violence. As an illustration, while Iraq has enacted many reforms for the advancement of women and is a party to the Women's Convention, in 1990 the Revolutionary Command Council announced that the killing of a female family member accused of *zina* (fornication and adultery) would no longer be treated as a crime.[144] An example of discriminatory legislation is Turkish criminal law, which defines many sexual crimes against women in terms of the "honor" of the victim and her family and whether or not she was a virgin.[145] Such crimes are called "Felonies Against Pubic Decency and Family Order," rather than crimes against the women themselves. Medical exams to determine whether women are virgins are automatically performed on Turkish women who report a sexual assault and on female prisoners.[146] In both Saudi Arabia and Iran, groups who have been condoned (if not encouraged) by their governments physically attack women and their companions when they are perceived to be violating the dress code or other "moral" prescriptions.[147] All such acts constitute violence against women by the state and not only contravene international human rights standards but also demoralize all women and the society as a whole.

The state can also breach its obligations to eradicate violence against women by failing to provide adequate remedies.[148] This is the case where women have legal remedies for gender-based violence, but only if they surmount an onerous burden. For

---

144. Marie-Aimée Hélie-Lucas, *The Preferential Symbol for Islamic Identity: Women in the Muslim Personal Laws, in* IDENTITY POLITICS & WOMEN: CULTURAL REASSERTIONS AND FEMINISMS IN INTERNATIONAL PERSPECTIVE 391, 405 n.15 (Valentine M. Moghadam ed., 1994).

145. THE HUMAN RIGHTS WATCH, *supra* note 132, at 422.

146. *See generally id.*

147. *See e.g.,* Aba-Namay, *supra* note 94, at 326; Megalli, *supra* note 96; Doublas Jehl, *Iranian Militants Enforce Religious Standards,* N.Y. TIMES, May 9, 1996.

148. *See generally Chorzow Factory,* 1928 P.C.I.J. (ser. A.) No. 17; Karen Parker & Jennifer F. Chew, *Compensation for Japan's World War II War-Rape Victims*, 17 HASTINGS INT'L & COMP. L. REV. 479, 523–28 n.3 (1994); Coomaraswamy, *supra* note 119, at para. 100 ("It is a recognized part of general international human rights law that States are responsible for . . . provision of effective remedies for the victims of human rights violations.").

example, in Iraq, one of the most legally progressive states in the region, in cases of marital violence a woman must request a separation from the court and institute legal proceedings or ask for compensation for her harm. The court's condemnation of the husband, including possible imprisonment or monetary fine, is then used as a ground for a divorce.[149] Another option for women who are living with domestic violence is to go to a family counseling center where an attempt is made to resolve the dispute or, once again, it is referred to the court.[150] These remedies do not give women the ability to flee a dangerous situation, but instead require her to obtain permission from authorities, depriving her of autonomous decisionmaking and prolonging her subjection to violence.

Cultural Practices

Practices stemming from culture, religion, customs, and traditions "which jeopardize the health, well-being, and dignity of women" violate human rights law and should be abolished.[151]

Despite legal restrictions on the age of marriage, child marriage continues to be accepted practice among many people in all countries of the region.[152] It allows poor families to reduce their economic burden and to guarantee their daughter's virginity to potential mates. However, child marriage significantly reduces the likelihood of girls continuing their education and is connected with early pregnancy and its attendant health concerns. Cultural practices which prize girls' virginity and devalue girls' education are endorsed by national legislation that differentiates legal age for marriage by gender.[153]

Temporary marriage is unique to Shi'a Islam and is only legally sanctioned in Iran, although it is also practiced in other Shi'a areas such as Iraq. Its actual practice, however, is not widespread and is often centered around pilgrimages.[154] The contract, which is between any man and any unmarried woman, has been compared to a lease.[155] Men can have an unlimited number of temporary marriages at one time, but a woman

---

149. U.N. Doc. CEDAW/C/SR.212, 213, 216 (1993).

150. *Id.*

151. Halima Embarek Warzazi, *Traditional Practices Affecting the Health of Women and Children,* U.N. Doc. E/CN.4/Sub.2/1995/6 at para. 19.

152. *See* JOHN L. ESPOSITO, WOMEN IN MUSLIM FAMILY LAW 52 (1982).

153. The legal age for marriage in Turkey is eighteen for men and sixteen for girls. With justifiable reasons and approval of parents or guardians, a court may approve marriage at the age of fifteen for boys and fourteen for girls. In Egypt, girls may marry at sixteen and boys at eighteen while in Iran the minimum age for marriage is thirteen. Iraq's law allows marriage for both genders only when they are eighteen, or at fifteen with parental approval.

154. *See generally* Hanna Papanek, *Ideal Woman and Ideal Society: Control and Autonomy in the Construction of Identity, in* IDENTITY POLITICS & WOMEN: CULTURAL REASSERTIONS AND FEMINISMS IN INTERNATIONAL PERSPECTIVE *supra* note 144 at 42, 64–68 (discussing the contemporary practice of *mut'a* in Iran).

155. *Id.* at 65; Haeri, *supra* note 124, at 60.

can only have one. The woman receives a fixed sum for being available for sex. The union lasts a specified period of time and then ends automatically, and can be for as short or as long a time as agreed by the parties. If any children are born they are legally recognized, but socially stigmatized, and the father is not financially obligated.

Legally sanctioned gender segregation can take many forms, including limitations on the activities women may perform, restrictions on mobility, and physical separation from men in the household, in public and through veiling. Before 1990, women in Turkey needed permission from their husbands to work outside the home. Women's physical mobility is restricted in many countries of the region. Under Egyptian law, women need permission from their male guardian to travel, even for business.[156] Since 1990, women in Iraq have been restricted from traveling abroad without an accompanying male. The Iraqi government claims this restriction is a necessary measure to reduce unnecessary expenditure in the face of economic sanctions.[157] In Saudi Arabia, no women are allowed to go abroad without the written permission of their legal guardian. Within the country, Saudi women are not supposed to leave the home without their husband's permission, even to visit relatives. However, younger women are challenging this prohibition and laying the groundwork for a right to leave the home without making a specific request each time.

Seclusion in the household has been practiced throughout the region to varying degrees, but primarily by the privileged in the Gulf countries. On the other hand, women from the upper classes have also had the opportunity to attend school and find wage employment. Among the elite of Saudi Arabia, Altorki has identified a trend toward neolocal residence and, within these new arrangements, a move toward less gender-based separation within the home itself.[158] Smaller households have made spacial segregation prohibitively expensive for many, and younger couples who are influenced by their travels are increasingly socializing as a couple. However, economic affluence does not necessarily result in increased autonomy for women however. Hegland notes that financial prosperity for rural and village migrant families in Iran has actually resulted in less independence for women; because social prestige is based on traditional values including seclusion of women, women were pressed into greater isolation as the need for their labor decreased.[159]

Different forms of veiling have been present in the Middle East since before Islamic times. Regional and class variations can include anything from a headscarf to a combination of face veil and long robe. The modern veil (*hijab*) usually includes a headscarf and covering clothing. It is not the traditional garment of any region, but a recent manifestation which some trace to the defeat to Israel in 1973. Although it

---

156. Moghadam, *supra* note 51, at 114.

157. Committee on Economic, Social and Cultural Rights, U.N. Doc. E/C.12/1994/SR.14 (1994)(reply of Mr. Hamash, Iraq).

158. ALTORKI, *supra* note 89, at 34. Segregation in the home consists of dual quarters for female and male family members with restrictions on women's participation in male socialization as well as on male family members' access to the women's apartment.

159. *See, e.g,* Hegland, *supra* note 106, at 495–96.

is most often associated with Islamist movements, many women who veil are not associated with these groups, nor are they necessarily highly religious. It is not a return to the segregation of the past, a practice which only the elite could afford, but is used by students and working women, among others, to practice seclusion yet continue their activities in public life. Among the urban middle class, the veil had virtually disappeared in Egypt, Turkey, Iran, and Iraq until the 1970s and been replaced with Western attire. By contrast, rural and lower class women have remained relatively unaffected by both the unveiling and reveiling trends, continuing to dress in more traditional modest attire. Women in Saudi Arabia have never unveiled, but some are unveiling in and around an expanding number of places and people. Currently, women in both Iran and Saudi Arabia are legally required to veil.

Women from many different socioeconomic classes have, to varying degrees of voluntariness, adopted the *hijab*. The primary group is comprised of women under thirty, many of them students. Zuhur found that most of the younger veiled women she spoke to in Egypt considered the *hijab* to be a symbol of change.[160] Some authors tie the practice to the alienation of increasing urbanization. Hegland found that in Iran, women from "traditional" groups living in urban areas were "far more secluded and were forced to obey stricter rules of modesty than women in rural areas."[161] This may be because crowded conditions in the cities and the loss of extended family living narrows the space in which these women have customarily acted.[162] Status may also play a part. Some women may welcome the loss of independence because it can mean less responsibility for work, social recognition, and fulfillment of culturally accepted roles. Morsy writes, "This type of dress is no more modest than the traditional peasant style, but it does stand out as a status-marker, symbolizing not simply its wearer's piety but her 'de-peasantization.'"[163]

Economic factors are also significant. In Egypt, as in the rest of the region, the drop in oil prices, a rise in inflation, and growing unemployment has led to the necessity of two-income families. While it is accepted in urban areas that unmarried women will work to meet potential husbands and to acquire a trousseau, there still is the expectation that married women have no need to work. Societal biases view working married women as earning money solely to buy extras and not to support the family. There is also a perception that men lose honor when their wives work, because it means they are not fulfilling their obligation of maintenance. In analyzing the new veiling in Egypt among the lower-middle class, Macleod finds women are, for the most part, doing it by "choice"—using the symbolism both as a means of resistance and of acquiescence.[164] She finds that women feel the need to work outside the home

---

160. SHERIFA ZUHUR, REVEALING REVEILING: ISLAMIST GENDER IDEOLOGY IN CONTEMPORARY EGYPT 76 (1992).

161. Hegland, *supra* note 106, at 494.

162. *See, e.g.,* AYUBI, *supra* note 22, at 38–39.

163. MORSY, *supra* note 105, at 138.

164. ARLENE ELOWE MACLEOD, ACCOMMODATING PROTEST: WORKING WOMEN, THE NEW VEILING, AND CHANGE IN CAIRO 127 (1991).

has devalued their traditional role in society (that of wife and mother) without providing an alternative identity that commands respect.[165]

Some women also feel guilt that they don't spend more time with their children or taking care of the household, despite the needed income their wage labor provides. Working women are still expected to perform all the household tasks and to have meals prepared by the time their husband comes home. Their inability to perform these tasks up to society's—and their husbands'—expectations creates an internal conflict that some are able to resolve with the veil. Because the *hijab* commands respect, it provides a way of showing that despite their need to work, they are good Islamic women and place primary value on their role in the family. Thus, some say that through their clothing choices, women are taking control and defining themselves in a period of transition. Macleod also asserts, however, that this act betrays the limits on women's power.[166]

Another side of the economic crisis is that the importation of Western values and consumption patterns has raised financial expectations among the middle classes, yet not provided the means of fulfillment. The *hijab* can act as a uniform that hides economic disparities and eliminates the need for middle class women to purchase expensive Western fashions.[167] Macleod found that Egyptian women from the lower classes are not working outside the home, while most lower-middle-class women are doing so. She attributes this to the economic ideology of the group—a desire to achieve middle-class status and acquire the consumer goods associated with it.[168] Similarly, Hatem writes, "Islamicism became a powerful political tool used by the young (male and female) urban professionals to compensate for their alienation, and the limited channels of mobility and participation in the current secular, capitalist society."[169]

A further factor in the reveiling trend may be that in a time of cultural conservatism and growing Islamist movements, women who want to continue their public role find it facilitated by visually reaffirming their Islamic identity. Some argue that for women who are increasingly exposed to the public gaze at school or work, it provides a symbol of morality that places the women off-limits. Many writers discuss how the *hijab* facilitates women's autonomy by acting as a visible barrier to male harassment in a society where men have not yet internalized such limitations.[170]

In Saudi Arabia, girls' veiling becomes mandatory with the onset of puberty and menstruation. The veil has two parts: a black cloak reaching to the ground worn over

---

165. *Id.* at 132–33.

166. *Id.* at 101–102, 137–40; *See also* Hegland, *supra* note 106, at 501 (discussing traditional Iranian woman maneuvering within limits imposed by men because of economic dependency).

167. *See, e.g.,* ZUHUR, *supra* note 160, at 13–14.

168. MACLEOD, *supra* note 164, at 85–86.

169. Mervat Hatem, *Egypt's Middle Class in Crisis: The Sexual Division of Labor,* 42 MIDDLE EAST J. 407, 410 n.3 (1988).

170. *See, e.g.,* AYUBI, *supra* note 22, at 46–47; MACLEOD, *supra* note 164, at 113–14; ZUHUR, *supra* note 160, at 78.

other clothing, and a shawl wrapped around the head several times covering the face. Veiling is viewed as a religious requirement; not veiling is considered to be a sin. The veil's primary social use is supposedly to hide eligible girls from potential husbands. A lapse in veiling etiquette is a lapse on the part of the woman, but is also considered to be one on the part of the head male of the household. Thus men use the injunctions to monitor women's behavior, especially outside of the home. Veiling practices, however, are becoming incrementally liberalized among younger married women. Primarily when traveling abroad, women have modified their veil, and today, some do not use it at all while outside of the country. Most recently, some women outside the country are not veiling even in front of Saudi men outside their family. Within the country, younger women are modifying veiling practices within the home, increasing the number of men in front of whom it is acceptable to appear unveiled.

The *hijab* was used by Iranian women during the revolution, both as a symbol of their disenchantment with the Shah's ties to the United States and its consumerist values as well as a means to evade the eyes of SAVAK. It was used as an assertion of cultural identity and as a rejection of economic dependence. However, many women were surprised when shortly after the success of the revolution, Khomeini announced that veiling would be mandatory. Since that time, there have been criminal penalties, including lashing, for not veiling or mal-veiling.[171] Additionally, government employees who are accused of violating the dress code may be suspended from work for up to two years; a husband who works for the government may also be penalized for his wife's transgressions.[172]

Islamist movements in the region sometimes coerce women to wear the veil, violently or otherwise, and they encourage segregation between men and women, but they do not uniformly discourage women from continuing their public role. Even in Iran, although many women were originally dismissed from their government jobs and have been forbidden from working in some positions (such as judges), due to circumstances such as the mobilization of men for the Iran-Iraq War, women have increasingly been allowed to return to work, and they are being encouraged to continue their education. In other countries, Islamist groups have provided networks of support, including financial backing, for women who are pursuing university education and plan to work after school. Moghissi argues that women's involvement in the Iranian revolution is not fully explained as a desire to preserve traditional ways of life. "On the contrary," she writes, "it was because the material rewards of modernization affected only few women and then only in superficial ways."[173] Thus, Islamist groups are not simply pursuing an idealized past where women were totally excluded from public life; their utilization of veiling as a potent symbol of their values encompasses other goals. In this way, they are consistent with previous political movements

---

171. The dress code requires all women to wear the *chador*, a long loose smock and trousers in dark colors and a headscarf.

172. NATIONAL COUNCIL OF RESISTANCE OF IRAN, *supra* note 65, at 21.

173. MOGHISSI, *supra* note 52, at 43.

employing the image of women, including "modernizers," and this tactic may ultimately prove limiting for women for the same reasons.

Toprak sees the Islamist movement in Turkey not only as a rejection of alien culture, but as a response to structural changes in the economy.[174] For her, the question is the same one that confronted the Ottoman Empire: how to respond to Western technological and industrial advances. She says that the debate between secular and Islamist groups in Turkey is about "the meaning and consequences of integration with the modern technostructures."[175] As she and others have emphasized, Islamist groups have utilized technology to disseminate information and also have sophisticated networks to support themselves. Ayubi says of Egypt, "The Islamist discourse of [militant political Islamists] is better seen as the moralist/culturalist expression of a development crisis, that has resulted in the frustration of the rising expectations of the lower-middle class in general and of the intelligentsia and the students in particular."[176] She sees the contemporary radical Islamist movements as a result of the failure of the post-independence development process.[177] Thus, for many observers, the new debate surrounding veiling is rooted in the old question of what development means for peoples integrating into an international economic and cultural order that is dominated and defined by external powers.

Armed Conflict

All the countries of the Middle East have been profoundly affected by the "Palestinian question," the denial of the right of the Palestinian people to their legally recognized right to self-determination.[178] The nonfulfillment of the General Assembly's partition plan for the creation of a Palestinian State, three regional wars, the consequent flight of Arabs and creation of a stateless refugee population, and the refusal of Israel to return the occupied territories has influenced the agenda and rhetoric of every state. The link between this and women's human rights is exemplified by Iraq's habitual disclaimer when acceding to multilateral treaties, including the Women's Convention and the Human Rights Covenants: "The approval in no way implies recognition of or entry into any relation with Israel." Likewise, regional preparatory documents and statements at Beijing refer to the occupation. The Arab Plan of Action asserts that "comprehensive and just peace and stability in the region are prerequisites to development and equality" of women in the region.[179]

---

174. Binnaz Toprak, *Women and Fundamentalism: The Case of Turkey, in* IDENTITY POLITICS & WOMEN: CULTURAL REASSERTIONS AND FEMINISMS IN INTERNATIONAL PERSPECTIVE, *supra* note 144, at 293, 295.

175. *Id.*

176. AYUBI, *supra* note 22, at 158.

177. *Id.* at 176–177.

178. *See* G.A. Res. 3236 (XXIX) (1974) ("[T]he Palestinian people are entitled to self-determination in accordance with the Charter of the United Nations."). *See generally* Adrien Katherine Wing, *Palestinian Women and Human Rights, supra* Section IV, this volume.

179. Arab Plan of Action, *supra* note 3, at para 14.

Every recent struggle for independence from foreign influence in the region has been combined with promises of liberation for Palestine and images of Israel's existence as a growth of imperialistic designs. This has perpetuated a colonized mentality whereby independence is the priority concern and all "peripheral" issues of development are postponed. Women's capacity for advancement has been retarded as high expenditures for weaponry have resulted in reduced funding of development programs; many women have been living as perpetual refugees, and others have devoted their efforts to participating in armed conflict.[180] Many of the region viewed the virility of the U.N.-sanctioned, United States-led attack on Iraq through the experience of almost fifty years of inaction against the illegal occupation of Palestinian lands by Israel. Resentment toward this disparity of response led many to defend Saddam Hussein's actions despite the catastrophe it meant for the region, Iraq, and its people, coming as it did on the heels of the devastating Iran-Iraq War. Approval grew when Hussein linked Iraq's withdrawal from Kuwait with Israel's return of the occupied territories.

All economic, social, and political development has been skewed toward the industry of war. Financially, the region has been hurt through its refusal to trade with Israel or to do business there, wars have destroyed human and environmental resources as well as development potential, and the expenditure of a large percentage of the region's wealth on high-tech weaponry from the Western states has contributed to rapidly increasing debt burdens. Socially, there has been immeasurable damage to communities' efforts to improve their quality of life. For women, the unending state of war has had an additional effect—a culture of violence that permeates all aspects of society, reinforcing patriarchal power relations and encouraging a loss of respect for human rights.

The Gulf War in 1991 was the most recent conflict to devastate the region. The civilian populations of Kuwait and Iraq have suffered the most, especially women, children, the elderly, and the poor. In Iraq, the war's effects continue year by year to reduce women's equality within society through the imposition of economic sanctions in disregard of international law humanitarian protections. These effects include: a fifth of the population (four million people) at severe nutritional risk; severe malnourishment and stunting of 29 percent of children under five (nearly 900,000 children); epidemics of malaria, cholera, typhoid, and other infectious diseases caused by polluted water resulting from the destruction of water and electrical plants; a lack of even basic medical supplies including anesthetics and antibiotics; a 600 percent increase in mortality of children; and a critical increase in maternal mortality.[181] It

---

180. *See generally* Karen Parker, *Human Rights of Women During Armed Conflict, supra* Section II, this volume.

181. *See generally* Julia Devin, Hearings on the Humanitarian Crisis in Iraq before the International Task Force of the House Select Committee on Hunger, 102d Cong., 1st Sess. 102–18 (1991); Adeeb Abed & Gavrielle Gemma, *Impact of the War on Iraqi Society* and Nawal El Saadawi, *The Impact of the Gulf War on Women and Children, in* RAMSEY CLARK AND OTHERS, WAR CRIMES: A REPORT ON UNITED STATES WAR CRIMES AGAINST IRAQ 180 (1992); Thalif Deen, *United Nations: U.N. Seeks Humane Approach to Sanction,* INTER PRESS SERVICE, Feb. 1, 1996; Johanna

has been estimated that at least 250,000 people (mostly civilians) died during the Gulf War and that 570,000 have died since the war due to starvation and other diseases.[182] An estimated 4,500 children under the age of five continue to die every month as a result of the shortage of food and medicine.[183] The Iraqi economy has collapsed, leaving many people unemployed, while others make only 7 percent of their former earnings because of the devaluation of the dinar.

The destruction of Iraqi society and its infrastructure has been devastating to women. Whereas previously the cost of medical care of all kinds was either free or minimal and the country supported renowned medical clinics, there is now little, if any, pre- and post-natal care, or even medical supplies for the injured or ill. Obtaining subsistence amounts of food and water is now a daily preoccupation for most women. With high unemployment, women (who had been making great advances in entering the workforce) have been first to lose their jobs and the last to find work. Girls are dropping out of school to help their families, and crime and prostitution have become serious social problems for the first time. Many women lost their husbands, and thus their financial support, because of the war. As a result of this, after both the Iran-Iraq War and the Gulf War, Iraq (and Iran in the first case) began advocating polygamy as a solution. In 1991, Iraq offered 7,000 dinars to any man who married a war widow. As mentioned previously, Iraq also decriminalized "crimes of honor" against women and forbade women from traveling abroad unaccompanied. Women in Saudi Arabia are also still suffering from the Gulf War as the government uses increased restrictions on their behavior to fend off criticism from Islamist groups radicalized by the presence of American troops.

Protocol I to the Geneva Conventions prohibits attacks on civilian populations which employ a method that cannot be limited in scope and "are of a nature to strike military objectives and civilians or civilian objects without distinction."[184] Further, it is prohibited to destroy "objects indispensable to the survival of the civilian population," including drinking water installations.[185] Likewise, economic sanctions imposed

Kristjonsdottir, *A Struggle Unveiled: Iraqi Women Speak Up*, JERUSALEM POST, Aug. 31, 1995; Margarita Papandreou, *Perspective on Iraq: Barbs Aimed at Saddam Misfire; The U.N. Embargo Has Shattered Once-Substantial Social and Political Rights Held by Women*, L.A. TIMES, May 29, 1994, at M5.

182. DR. BEATRICE BOCTOR, REPORT BY THE INTERNATIONAL COMMISSION OF INQUIRY ON ECONOMIC SANCTIONS 3 (1996) (distributed to the United Nations Commission on Human Rights.)

183. *See* Scott Peterson, *The Hungry Iraqis: What's Behind the Blame Game*, CHRISTIAN SCIENCE MONITOR, May 7, 1997, at 6.

184. Protocol Additional I to the Geneva Conventions of 1949, at art. 51 §4, *in force* Dec. 7, 1978, 1125 U.N.T.S. 3, *reprinted in* 16 I.L.M. 1391 (1977) [hereinafter Protocol I]. The Geneva Conventions apply during armed conflicts and during partial or total occupation of a party's territory until the termination of that occupation (art. 3). The Iraqi government has been excluded from a significant portion of Northern Iraq by the military presence of the United States since 1991 and has been bombed by the United States for entering this territory as recently as 1996.

185. *Id.* art. 54 § 2. Section 2 reads in full:

"It is prohibited to attack, destroy, remove or render useless objects indispensable to the survival of the civilian population, such as foodstuffs, agricultural areas for the

during an armed conflict must comply with the humanitarian exceptions to the Geneva Conventions.[186] Governments are required not only to obey the Geneva Conventions when they are parties to a conflict, they are obligated to ensure respect for the Conventions "in all circumstances."[187] The General Assembly has recently reaffirmed that economic sanctions in violation of international law obligations and the U.N. Charter for political or economic coercion are forbidden.[188]

Conventions and Declarations Regarding Women

Of the five countries discussed, only Egypt, Iraq, and Turkey are parties to the Convention on the Elimination of All Forms of Discrimination against Women.[189] However, as explained above and as expressed by the Secretary-General, the Women's Convention codified many customary or conventional rights already existing in international law, including that: "All are equal before the law and are entitled without any

---

production of foodstuffs, crops, livestock, drinking water installations and supplies and irrigation works, for the specific purpose of denying them for their sustenance value to the civilian population or to the adverse Party, whatever the motive, whether in order to starve out civilians, to cause them to move away, *or for any other motive.*" (Emphasis added.)

186. *See* Geneva Convention Relative to the Protection of Civilian Persons in Times of War, *opened for signature* Aug. 12, 1948, *entered into force* Oct. 21, 1950, at art. 23, 55, 59, 75 U.N.T.S. 287 [hereinafter Fourth Geneva Convention].

While foodstuffs and medical supplies were formally excepted from the Security Council sanctions because Iraq was primarily dependent on oil for importing the majority of its humanitarian needs, it was foreseeable that the civilian population would suffer these appalling consequences due to the extraordinary length of their imposition. *See* The Health Conditions of the Population in Iraq Since the Gulf Crisis, WHO/EHA/96.1 (1996). The World Health Organization's report documents that more than 70 percent of Iraq's food requirements were imported prior to 1991 and concludes that "*[f]inancial constraints* as a result of the sanctions have prevented the necessary import of food and medicine." (Italics in original.) The report adds further that, "Assessment reports rightly remarked that the quality of health care in Iraq, due to the six-week 1991 war and the subsequent sanctions imposed on the country, has been literally put back by at least 50 years." *Id.*

187. Fourth Geneva Convention, *supra* note 186, at common art. 1. The International Court of Justice has implicitly recognized the *jus cogens* nature of art. 1 and 3 of the Geneva Conventions. (Nicar. v. U.S.) 1986 I.C.J. 14 at 100–01, 113–15 (opinion of the Court), 151–53 (Singh, J., separate opinion), 199–200 (Sette-Camara, J., separate opinion). *See generally* Parker & Neylon, *supra* note 8, at 432–35 (discussing the *jus cogens* nature of humanitarian law). Thus all states were arguably under a legal and moral obligation to end the oil embargo as soon as the consequences to the civilian people of Iraq first became apparent. Ignoring the effect of international sanctions on the most vulnerable social groups in the pursuit of political aims caused or exacerbated many women's human rights violations.

188. Economic measures as a means of political and economic coercion against developing countries, G.A. Res. 44/215 (Dec. 22, 1989) ("[r]eaffirms that developed countries should refrain from threatening or applying . . . economic sanctions, incompatible with the provision of the Charter of the United Nations and in violation of undertakings contracted multilaterally and bilaterally, against developing countries as a form of political and economic coercion that affects their political, economic and social development.").

189. Women's Convention, *supra* note 120.

discrimination to equal protection of the law."[190] All three countries have made reservations that have been criticized as incompatible with the Convention's object and purpose.[191] They include the articles regarding equality of nationality rights, equality within the family, and the need to take all appropriate measures for the Convention's implementation.

Iraq and Egypt have made reservations to Article 9 on equality of nationality rights, while Turkey has made a declaration that the article is not in conflict with its Civil Code since its national provisions have the intent of preventing statelessness. Under Iraq's Nationality Act of 1961, when an Iraqi woman marries a foreigner, the man cannot acquire Iraqi nationality and their children are not entitled to Iraqi nationality. In Turkey, although both foreign men and women married to nationals may acquire citizenship, a foreign woman merely needs to express her willingness to the marriage officer at the time of her marriage. However, a foreign man needs to apply to the Ministry of Interior, obtain a proposal of the Ministry, and obtain a decision of the Council of Ministers. A Turkish woman can lose her nationality if her husband's state attributes nationality to her and she declares willingness to acquire it. This, however, does not apply to Turkish men. In Egypt, when a woman marries a foreign man, the child takes the father's nationality, unless the child obtains permission from the Minister of the Interior to acquire the mother's nationality. This *de jure* discrimination violates these countries' international law obligations.

All three states have reservations to Article 16 regarding the elimination of discrimination against women in all matters relating to marriage and family relations. The underlying issue is the previously discussed distinction between equal rights and equivalent rights. In the view of the Committee (CEDAW), they are not synonymous, but actually opposing concepts used in male-dominated societies to sidestep the need to achieve equality.[192] Egypt and Iraq have also made reservations to the requirement in Article 2 to take "all appropriate measures" in eliminating discrimination against women. Although Turkey has not reserved to this section, it has not yet revised its legislation to fulfill its obligation under this article.

In introducing their reports to the Committee, Turkey, Egypt, and Iraq have claimed to be in compliance with the Convention and often attribute societal inequalities to the preferences of women or cultural attitudes. Further, in situations where no explicit legal barriers exist, these states assert they have fulfilled their obligations. For example, a representative of Turkey has said that while there is no discrimination between men and women in employment, the low number of women in management positions is a result of lower levels of education and vocational training received by

---

190. Report of the Secretary-General, Second Review and Appraisal of the Implementation of the Nairobi Forward-Looking Strategies for the Advancement of Women, U.N. Doc. E/CN.6/1995/3/Add.7, at para 3 (*quoting* Universal Declaration, *supra* note 7, at art. 7).

191. As of 1993, Turkey's reservations to the Women's Convention had yet to be published in the Official Gazette, a prerequisite to their becoming effective under Turkish law.

192. U.N. Doc. CEDAW/C/SR.35 (1984) (statement of Mr. Nordenfelt).

women.[193] In explaining women's low participation in political organizations, the judiciary, and at high levels of the executive branch, the representative said that problems included illiteracy, women's unawareness of their political rights, and their preference to family obligations.[194] However, states have an obligation to eliminate inequality based in cultural biases, as discussed above. Egypt has said that "aside from matters relating to equality between men and women in connection with marriage and with family relations during marriage and after divorce, it could be seen that Islamic law had guaranteed to women all the rights and all the kinds of equality provided for by the Convention."[195] Since women's inequality begins in the family, law that fails to confront it only serves to perpetuate gender discrimination in all areas.

Egypt, Iran, and Iraq also have obligations under the Human Rights Covenants to "undertake to ensure the equal right of men and women" to the enjoyment of all economic, social, cultural, civil, and political rights in the Covenants.[196] Regarding Iran, the Human Rights Committee has found "the persistence and extent of discrimination against women" to be incompatible with this duty. They singled out the treatment of women who do not conform to the dress code, the need for permission to leave the home, and exclusion from the magistracy, among others, as incompatible with the International Covenant on Civil and Political Rights.[197] The Committee on Economic, Social, and Cultural Rights has found that restrictions referring to Islamic standards "negatively affect the application of the Covenant," including the provisions on non-discrimination; equality between men and women; and the right to work, health, education, and to take part in cultural life.[198] It found that Iran was using religion as a pretext to abuse these rights.[199] The use of such provisions by any country should therefore be seen to be in violation of the Human Rights Covenants.

All five states are parties to International Labor Organization (ILO) Convention No. 100 Concerning Equal Renumeration for Men and Women Workers for Work of Equal Value and No. 111 Concerning Discrimination in Respect of Employment and

---

193. U.N. Doc. CEDAW/C/SR.161, 165 (Turkey) (1990).

194. *Id.*

195. U.N. Doc. CEDAW/C/SR.39 (Egypt) (1984).

196. Among others, additional human rights treaty commitments of these countries include: Convention on the Political Rights of Women, *adopted* Dec. 20, 1952, *entered into force* July 7, 1954, 193 U.N.T.S. 135 (Egypt, Turkey); Convention on the Rights of the Child, *adopted* Nov. 20, 1989 *entered into force* Sept. 2, 1990 (Egypt, Iran, Iraq); Convention against Torture and other Cruel, Inhuman or Degrading Treatment or Punishment, *adopted* Dec. 10, 1984, *entered into force* June 28, 1987, G.A. Res. 39/46, 39 U.N. GAOR, Supp. (No. 51), U.N. Doc. A/39/51, at 197 (1984) (Egypt, Turkey); and UNESCO Convention against Discrimination in Education, *adopted* Dec. 14, 1960, *entered into force* May 22, 1962, 429 U.N.T.S. 93 (Egypt, Iran, Iraq, Saudi Arabia).

197. Human Rights Committee, Comments on Iran (Islamic Republic of), U.N. Doc. CCPR/C/79/Add.25 (1993).

198. Committee on Economic, Social and Cultural Rights, Concluding Observations on Iran, U.N. Doc. E/C.12/1993/7.

199. *Id.*

Occupation.[200] These Conventions require parties to promote equality in employment through national policies with the aim of eliminating any discrimination of opportunity or treatment.[201] The right to equal renumeration for work of equal value requires not only that women are paid the same as men for equivalent work, but it also "challenges both a purely market-based definition of value and deeply rooted cultural assumptions about the value of women's labor within and outside the home."[202] Thus, these states' non-regulation of the work that women customarily perform, and the lower (or lack of) renumeration received by women in their traditional occupations contravene their obligations under these Conventions.

Presently, and despite its unanimous adoption by Arab labor ministers in 1976, only Iraq and Palestine have signed the League of Arab States (ALO) Convention 5 on Women at Work, which would provide for equality of men and women in placement, renumeration, and working conditions. Under the rules of the League, three ratifications are needed for it to come into force.

Self-Determination and the Right to Development

The preamble to the Women's Convention affirms the fundamental relationship between the realization of self-determination and the achievement of gender equality.[203] Cultural attitudes that perpetuate women's subordination cannot be seen in a vacuum; the history of these Middle Eastern countries shows that women's legal status has been tied for better or worse to defensive strategies against perceived subjugation by Western powers. The representative of Iraq has said that the main obstacles to implementation of the Women's Convention were the result of prevailing traditions and customs and society's vision of women; the economic, social, and cultural backwardness of developing countries; and the unjust world economic order. She identified the economic blockade as the most serious circumstance hampering implementation.[204] The representative of Egypt has likewise associated both social and economic problems with the inability of women to exercise their full rights.[205]

---

200. I.L.O. No. 100, *adopted* June 29, 1951, *entered into force* May 23, 1953, 165 U.N.T.S. 303; I.L.O. No. 111, *adopted* June 25, 1958, *entered into force* June 15, 1960, 362 U.N.T.S. 31.

201. I.L.O. No. 111, *supra* note 201.

202. Report of the Secretary-General, Equality: Equal Pay for Work of Equal Value, at para. 13, U.N. Doc. E/CN.6/1994/2.

203. The Women's Convention, *supra* note 120 ("*Emphasizing* that the eradication of apartheid, all forms of racism, racial discrimination, colonialism, neo-colonialism, aggression, foreign occupation and domination and interference in the affairs of states is essential to the full enjoyment of the rights of men and women . . . ;" "*Affirming* that the . . . realization of the right of peoples under alien and colonial domination and foreign occupation to self-determination and independence, as well as respect for national sovereignty and territorial integrity, will promote social progress and development and as a consequence will contribute to the attainment of full equality between men and women.") [Emphasis in original].

204. U.N. Doc. CEDAW/C/SR.212, 213, 216 (Iraq) (1993).

205. U.N. Doc. CEDAW/C/SR.164, 165 (1990).

The Middle East has been under political, economic, and cultural domination from the West for over a century. Independence and equal rights for women are often being treated as mutually exclusive. Women took an active role during national liberation struggles with the understanding that their liberation would have to wait for their people's. After independence, there were increased education and work opportunities for women, but traditional prejudices continued to flourish. With neverending confrontations over Palestine, battles over disposition of natural resources, and states' inability to chart an economic course independent of Western interference, women's rights became seen as an issue of cultural imperialism and was viewed in opposition to authentic national development. All discussions of human rights emanating from the region, whether from states or women themselves, refer to one or more self-determination issues. This linkage is mirrored in international standards that recognize self-determination to be an indispensable foundation for the endurance of all human rights.

Self-determination is intimately connected with the prevention of violence. The Charter of the United Nations provides the right to self-determination, stating that one of the purposes of the United Nations is "[t]o develop friendly relations among nations based on respect for the principle of equal rights and self-determination of peoples, and to take other appropriate measures to strengthen universal peace."[206] Article 55 of the Charter connects peace between nations with self-determination and the observance of human rights.[207] Subsequent General Assembly resolutions have affirmed that the purpose of guaranteeing this right to peoples is to prevent war and other types of violence that hinder fulfillment of fundamental human rights.[208] At the same time, peace cannot last without social justice for both men and women.

The association between self-determination, peace between nations, and women's human rights is clearly shown in the case of the Middle East. The persistent denial of statehood to Palestine despite U.N. recognition of its right has resulted in continuous conflict in the region, including international armed conflict, civil war, massive budgets for defense, and a siege mentality. The impact on human rights (especially those of women) is direct. Besides loss of family members (including those who provide

---

206. U.N. Charter, June 26, 1945, 59 Stat. 1031, T.S. No. 933, 3 Bevans 1153, *entered into force* Oct. 24, 1945, at art. 1, para. 2.

207. *Id.* Art. 5 states:

   With a view to the creation of conditions of stability and well being which are necessary for peaceful and friendly relations among nations based on respect for the principle of equal rights and self-determination of peoples, the United Nations shall promote . . . universal respect for, and observance of, human rights and fundamental freedoms for all without distinction as to race, sex, language or religion.

208. *See* Inclusion in the International Covenant or Covenants on Human Rights of an article relating to the right of peoples to self-determination, G.A. Res. 545 (VI) (1952), where the General Assembly decided to include the right in the International Covenants on Human Rights, "[t]o save the present and succeeding generations from the scourge of war. . . ."; *See, e.g.,* Declaration on Principles of International Law concerning Friendly Relations and Cooperation among States in Accordance with the Charter of the United Nations, G.A. Res. 2625 (1970).

financial and social support) and increased production burdens, women suffer as the objects of increasing violence and conservatism. As mentioned above, in Iraq, Iran, and Saudi Arabia, recent armed conflicts have resulted in expanded constraints on women's participation in society as well as increased sexual violence. There is a long history in the region of militants fighting against colonialism and neocolonialism through advocating a return to "authentic culture." Both groups and governments who have felt the need to respond and to justify their legitimacy have utilized restrictions on women to demonstrate their commitment to independence from foreign pressures.

Self-determination also promotes economic, social, and cultural development. The primary responsibility to advance development lies with the state, but as a corollary, states have the right to choose the method of development and to control the disposition of their natural wealth and resources.[209] Coercion or interference with these prerogatives by other states is forbidden.[210] Unequal trade relations, debt servicing, and the activities of transnational corporations are recognized as having a negative impact on the fulfillment of states' developmental responsibilities.[211] The activities of transnational corporations are viewed as "neo-colonial," in that they play a similar role to colonial powers of the past.[212] Because their investment policies often reflect these past colonial relationships (including location and concentration), they "tend to consolidate inequality between countries and to perpetuate structures of trade dependence."[213] Additionally, their products often do not correspond to the needs of the host country and therefore contribute to the transfer of patterns of consumption that do not reflect local conditions.[214] Similarly, the Special Rapporteur on Economic, Social, and Cultural rights has found that structural adjustment programs are incompatible with the realization of development rights.[215] Such programs interfere with states' sovereignty by reducing national control of economic, social, and cultural decisions.

---

209. Charter of Economic Rights and Duties of States, G.A. Res. 3281 (XXIX) (1974), art.7. ("[E]ach State has the right and the responsibility to choose its means and goals of development, to fully mobilize and use its resources, to implement progressive economic and social reforms and to ensure the full participation of its people in the process and benefits of development".); *See also* Declaration on Social Progress and Development, *supra* note 11, at art. 3.

210. Charter of Economic Rights and Duties of States, *supra* note 210, at art. 32 ("No State may use or encourage the use of economic, political or any other type of measures to coerce another State in order to obtain from it the subordination of the exercise of its sovereign rights"); Permanent Sovereignty over Natural Resources, G.A. Res. 1803 (XVII) (1962), preambular para. 8 ("[T]he provision of economic and technical assistance, loans and increased foreign investment must not be subject to conditions which conflict with the interests of the recipient State.").

211. *Report of the Secretary General, The Relationship Between the Enjoyment of Human Rights, in Particular, International Labor and Trade Union Rights, and the Working Methods and Activities of Transnational Corporations*, U.N. Doc. E/CN.4/Sub.2/1995/11 at para. 89.

212. *Id.* at para. 91; GROS ESPIELL, *supra* note 15, at 4.

213. *Report of the Secretary General*, *supra* note 211, at para. 91.

214. *Id.* at para. 93.

215. Danilo Türk, *Final Report on the Realization of Economic, Social and Cultural Rights*, U.N. Doc. E/CN.4/Sub.2/1992/16 at para. 50.

International financial bodies such as the IMF not only influence domestic development goals directly through their policies, but also indirectly through loans and their
impact on investment choices of foreign private actors.[216]

Cristescu states that "[e]conomic development is only a means of achieving certain social objectives, and economic growth and social development are interdependent. The benefits of economic advancement should serve not merely an already
privileged few but the many who are in dire want."[217] Austerity measures do not take
into account the specific social conditions of the country, but are applied with economic principles in mind. The uniform result has been reduced public spending on
social services affecting economic, social, and cultural rights such as health care and
education and causing a "growing income disparity within and between states."[218]
Egypt provides a perfect example of this. Sadat's "open door" policy, intended to
increase foreign investment and encourage economic development along IMF lines,
resulted in "an inflationary spiral of rising prices not matched by rising wages, an
influx of foreign luxury goods accompanied by aggressive advertising to promote
conspicuous consumption, and an increasing disparity between social classes due to
the growth of a relatively wealthy upper-middle class working in the private sector."[219]
Across the region, the large agricultural holdings facilitated by IMF policies and integration into the world economy are undermining traditional farming and resulting in
mass migration to urban centers. This is in turn undermining traditional socio-
economic systems without contributing to the growth of new ones. Women now work
more for less money and recognition, have fewer employment opportunities, and participate less in social decision making.[220]

The right of self-determination guarantees people the right to define their cultural development.[221] For a developing nation, the right to culture "is closely linked
with the political right of self-determination, with the quest for an indigenous culture
as a means of liberation and rebirth, a new meaning for national dignity."[222] The rapid

---

216. Danilo Türk, *Preliminary Report on the Realization of Economic, Social and Cultural Rights*, U.N. Doc. E/CN.4/Sub.2/1989/19 at para. 80.

217. Cristescu, *supra* note 11, at 94; *See generally* Declaration on the Right to Development, *supra* note 13.

218. Türk, Final Report, *supra* note 215, at para. 76–84.

219. MACLEOD, *supra* note 164, at 87.

220. Hegland's research on traditional Iranian women has shown that economic prosperity led men to seek prestige through utilization of traditional status-conferring norms such as seclusion of women. She says that, "Economic 'development' thus did not necessarily improve the position of women. Quite to the contrary, increased economic prosperity enabled men to utilize more effec-tively the symbolic function of women for their own personal advantage." Hegland, *supra* note 106, at 495–96.

221. Declaration of the Principles of International Cultural Co-operation, UNESCO (1966); CRISTESCU, *supra* note 11, at 71 ("Cultural interaction precludes the imposition of a culture on another people, and also does not permit the absorption, the submission or the holding back of the cultural development of another nation.").

222. *Id.* at 113.

and jarring transformations in the region are causing people to reevaluate the essence of their society and to strive to retain that which is culturally legitimate and specific to them. Activities which prevent self-determination may increase cultural conservatism and entrench women's subordinate status, thereby preventing cultural evolution. For individuals, a right to culture means a right of access to knowledge, to develop his or her personality, and "to an active participation in creating material and spiritual values and using them for the further progress of modern civilization."[223] Thus, the realization of self-determination assures women's right to have a voice in the creation of a Middle Eastern culture that can accommodate both equality and an unique regional identity.

CONCLUSIONS

Islam is not inherently hostile to women; for a time, it fostered some of the most advanced legal protections for women in the world. The most vital force working against women's development within society is the continuance of patriarchal relations in the family and at the state level, exacerbated by unrealized self-determination. The Middle Eastern states integrated into the Western-dominated international economy with their traditional power relations preserved and consolidated. As women have not controlled or been allowed equal access to culturally recognized sources of power, they have not had any structural basis from which they could direct and define their role in society. Decisions regarding economic and political priorities must begin with existing social conditions. However, states, as well as international financial institutions, continue to follow agendas that reinforce a devaluation of women's productive role in national and international development. Thus, while Egypt's current Third Five Year Plan emphasizes motherhood in a special section, it does not recognize women's contribution to economic development.[224] Likewise, World Bank and IMF policies reflect general economic priorities and do not take account of their impact on human rights concerns. Economic and social development should be united. National policies, U.N. bodies, and the practices of international financial institutions must be held fully accountable to international human rights standards. For development to be sustained, women must be given the opportunity to characterize their needs and to create a power base that will allow them to participate equally in societal decision-making.

Patriarchal relations prosper where there is a continuing threat of conflict. To prevent violence, all states must be held accountable to humanitarian law rules. If the law is selectively applied so that countries with the means to control international forums remain unaccountable for their violations of the Geneva Conventions, the rule of law is itself denigrated and turned into a means to legitimize and perpetuate the subordinate status of developing nations and of vulnerable social groups. Accordingly, the failure to recognize the devastating consequences of economic sanctions on women and children aids the reinforcement of cultural prejudices and cripples women's advances.

---

223. Cristescu, *supra* note 11, at 113.
224. Moghadam, *supra* note 51, at 115.

States have the responsibility to comply with human rights standards through legislating *de jure* equality and through promoting the elimination of traditional attitudes that discriminate against women, but domestic policies are not enough. States must be able to make and implement decisions with their people's interests in mind and without the constraints imposed by neo-colonial practices. Self-determination and women's full and equal participation in society are mutually reinforcing and inter-dependent, and neither can be achieved without the other.

PALESTINIAN WOMEN AND HUMAN RIGHTS

Adrien Katherine Wing

INTRODUCTION

After thirty years under Israeli occupation, the newly emerging Palestinian entity[1] must address many different human rights issues. One area that must not be overlooked in the development of human rights policy is women's status. This chapter analyzes the issues that define and affect women's lives and offers suggestions to enhance women's role within Palestinian society.[2] Namely, efforts should be made to provide legal rights for women commensurate with international human rights norms.

The traditional status of women in Palestinian society creates a tension for adopting international human rights that improve women's rights within the domestic legal system. This tension is evidenced by the fact that both customary and Islamic[3] traditions sanction differential treatment on the basis of gender.[4] The 1988 Palestine National Council (PNC) Declaration of Independence, however, expresses the desire to improve the legal status of women.[5] Later, a women's technical committee headed

---

1.   Palestine refers to the West Bank, Gaza Strip, and East Jerusalem, which was formerly known as the Occupied Territories. This area is still occupied despite the partial Israeli withdrawal from most of the Gaza Strip and 3 percent of the West Bank.

2.   This chapter draws upon Adrien Katherine Wing, *Custom, Religion and Rights: The Future Legal Status of Palestinian Women*, 35 HARV. INT'L L.J. 149 (1994).

3.   Outside of Tunisia, which has a uniform personal status law for all citizens, the trend in the Islamic world has been to continue a system of legal pluralism in which a person's religion determines the applicable law. Ann Elizabeth Mayer, *Islam and the State*, 12 CARD. L. REV. 1015, 1027–28 (1991). Islam is the religion discussed here because 92 percent of Palestinians are Sunni Muslim, with a Christian minority composed of several denominations centered in Jerusalem, Ramallah, and Bethlehem. GEORGE BISHARAT, PALESTINIAN LAWYERS AND ISRAELI RULE: LAW AND DISORDER IN THE WEST BANK 11 (1989).

4.   A number of articles discuss whether religion is the source of women's oppression. Many feminists view patriarchy as the source of oppression, whether manifested in religion, custom or elsewhere.

5.   Declaration of Independence, U.N. Doc. A/43/827, S/20278, Annex III at 15, *reported in* 27 I.L.M. 1668, 1670 (1988) [hereinafter Declaration of Independence]. On Nov. 15, 1988, nearly eleven months into the *intifada* movement, the PNC issued the Declaration of Independence, which unilaterally proclaimed Palestine an independent state. Among its several features, the Declaration enumerated democratic principles that would form the basis for future Palestinian governing institutions such as a commitment to non-discrimination regardless of race, color, religious beliefs, or gender. *See* Michael Ross, *PLO Proclaims Palestinian State*, L.A. TIMES, Nov. 15, 1988, at 1.

by leading activist Zahira Kamal designed a draft women's bill of rights, which was "seen as a mobilizing tool to show the interests and strength of women prior to the introduction of key pieces of legislation, like a constitution."[6] The most recently proposed draft Basic Law also seems committed to the rights of women, as it contains an article declaring that men and women are equal under the law and that there shall be no discrimination on the basis of sex.[7]

Improving women's status is profoundly important, because gender equality ultimately impacts social progress. Ensuring that not only men, but also women, are equally protected under the law challenges deeply rooted Palestinian customary and religious attitudes. These behavior and thought patterns can be difficult to eradicate through the passage of new laws, even if enacted by a popularly elected legislative body. When religious, social, and cultural norms conflict with legal rights, efforts to elevate women's status often fail for lack of community support. Sometimes women enjoy greater equality under custom than religious law; secular law, however, offers women more formal equality than either customary or religious law.[8] While some sectors of Palestinian society will favor equal rights for women, other sectors will likely oppose such action as antithetical to religious values. Palestine has sizable communities of Islamic fundamentalists and other traditionalists who oppose such reform. It must be recognized, however, that Palestine's social and economic development will depend on women's full participation and contribution in all aspects of life.

Women's current status within Palestinian society is intricately intertwined with the development of customary and religious heritages.[9] Many Islamic doctrines and principles were drawn from pre-existing seventh century customary law, while at the same time customary law has been influenced by Islamic precepts.[10] The fusion of religious and customary law has been central to the general process of legal development in Islam.[11] Islamic and customary law have also been influenced by Ottoman and British colonial law.[12] The second section of this chapter attempts to analyze the historical roles that custom and religion have played in shaping women's rights. The

---

6. Rita Giacaman & Penny Johnson, *The Palestinian Women's Movement in the New Era*, MIDDLE E. REP. 24–25 (1994).

7. The Palestinian Authority Basic Law, 9th draft, art. 9 [hereinafter Draft Basic Law] (on file with the author). During the summer of 1996, the author was hired as an independent contractor by the United States Agency for International Development to advise the newly elected Palestinian Legislative Council on the drafting of the Basic Law.

8. AHARON LAYISH, WOMEN AND ISLAMIC LAW IN A NON-MUSLIM STATE: A STUDY BASED ON DECISIONS OF THE SHARIA COURTS IN ISRAEL 328 (1975).

9. Julie M. Peteet, *Socio-Political Integration and Conflict Resolution in the Palestinian Camps in Lebanon*, J. PALESTINE STUD. 29, 40 (1987) (noting that custom and religion are often confused in the Arab world).

10. MOHAMMED HASHIM KAMALI, PRINCIPLES OF ISLAMIC JURISPRUDENCE 285 (1991).

11. Daisy Hilse Dwyer, *Law and Islam in the Middle East: An Introduction, in* LAW AND ISLAM IN THE MIDDLE EAST 1, 3 (Daisy Hilse Dwyer ed., 1990); NOEL J. COULSON, SUCCESSION IN THE MUSLIM FAMILY 2 (1971).

12. *See* BISHARAT, *supra* note 3, at 191 n.35.

third section considers the socio-legal status of women during the Palestinian *intifada*[13] from 1987 to 1993. Then the fourth section examines the ninth draft of the Basic Law in terms of its guarantees for women's rights. The fifth section discusses the Women's Charter of 1994, which delineates a more comprehensive framework for extending fundamental rights and freedoms to women. While there are many possibilities for improving the status of women, the sixth section analyzes three interrelated options: it first discusses current Islamic and feminist theories for improving women's status through Islamic reinterpretation, then highlights options for codifying constitutional rights through the adoption of international human rights norms, and finally proposes that women's status must also be built upon the changes wrought by the *intifada* and asserts legal reform will be successful only to the degree that it reflects other societal change.[14]

THE INFLUENCE OF CUSTOMARY AND ISLAMIC LAW ON WOMEN'S RIGHTS

Customary Law

Customary law includes a whole range of offenses concerning women, who are considered repositories of family and clan honor.[15] If female chastity and purity are not maintained, the family and clan are greatly disgraced.[16] To understand the importance of these norms within the Palestinian social context, the intermingling of custom and religion must be recognized.[17]

Historically, women—particularly upper- and middle-class women—were "ideally" secluded in their homes, behind veils or, more recently, *hijab* (head scarves).[18] By requiring that women be confined to their homes and wear modest clothing, customary law protected both men and women from female sexuality.[19] This physical separation represented "the polarization of what cannot be controlled," and women's sexuality was regarded as "a lurking danger with a threatening potential."[20]

---

13. The term *intifada* derives from the Arabic verb "to shake" and connotes an attempt to shake off twenty-five years of Israeli occupation.

14. Nawal el Saadawi, The Hidden Face of Eve: Women in the Arab World xiv (1980).

15. *Id.* For a discussion of these offenses among Palestinian bedouins during the British mandate period, *see* Aref el-Aref, Bedouin Love Law and Legend 79 (1944). For a comparison, *see* Paul Dresch, Tribes, Government, and History in Yemen 56 (1989).

16. Philippa Strum, The Women are Marching: The Second Sex and the Palestinian Revolution 27 (1992).

17. For a discussion of the religious aspects of this heritage, *see infra* notes 41–91 and accompanying text.

18. Abdullahi A. An-Na'im, *Human Rights in the Muslim World: Socio-Political Conditions and Scriptural Imperatives*, 3 Harv. Hum. Rts. J. 13, 38 (1990).

19. Strum, *supra* note 16, at 25.

20. Fatima Mernissi, Beyond the Veil: Male-Female Dynamic in Modern Muslim Society (1987).

The birth of a girl was not considered a joyous occasion by the family and clan, because it is through the birth of sons that the father's line is continued. Girls received a limited education, which, when available, was administered separately from the boys'.[21] Upon reaching puberty, young girls were required to wear clothing that covered most of the body, which included *hijab* and long skirts. Girls customarily entered into arranged marriages soon after puberty—often to someone in the same clan, because marriage was the uniting of families as well as individuals.[22] This type of kinship marriage reinforced familial ties by keeping land in the family and by paying a lower *mahr*, or bride price, to the woman.[23] There was no equivalent to the Western concept of adolescent dating and social fraternization with the opposite sex, and if a bride failed to prove her virginity on the wedding night, the family suffered severe social embarrassment.[24] The status of a wife in the new family and the community rose significantly by the birth of a son, especially if the birth occurred within a year after the wedding. The new mother then became known as "*Um* (mother of) [oldest son's name]," for example, "Um Khalil."[25] The subsequent production of more sons further enhanced her status. An adult woman could not live on her own, but had to live either with her father's family or her husband's family. If divorced, she had to return to her father's home in disgrace, since custom required a woman to live under the authority of a male relative at all times.[26] In certain families and communities, many of these customs apply today.

When a woman is sexually assaulted, it is often considered a case of honor (*qadiyat arad*),[27] and the way these cases are dealt with present a poignant example of the continuing relevance of customary law for Palestinian women. These cases are heard by special customary adjudicators known as *manshad* (one who is implored). Only three *manshads* reside in the West Bank, and the position tends to be held by certain families.[28] The judgements can amount to thousands of Jordanian dinars,[29]

---

21.   A 1982 study reported that the female education rate was half that of males. STRUM, *supra* note 16, at 36.

22.   For a dispute that arose in 1958 when a girl did not want to marry someone within the *hamula* (clan), *see* ABNER COHEN, ARAB BORDER-VILLAGES IN ISRAEL: A STUDY OF CONTINUITY AND CHANGE IN SOCIAL ORGANIZATION 71 (1965).

23.   Payment by a relative for the bride was customarily less than payment by a non-relative. STRUM, *supra* note 16, at 28. *Mahr* is an amount of money given by the bridegroom to his wife, which she keeps for her own use. It is not the sale of the bride to the husband. He does not get to keep or control the money. ABDUL RAHMAN I. DOI, WOMEN IN SHARI'AH 154 (1989). For more on the bride price, *see* ANNALIES MOORS, WOMEN, PROPERTY AND ISLAM: PALESTINIAN EXPERIENCES 1920–1990 (1990) (two-year study in Jabal Nablus, West Bank).

24.   Proof of virginity was usually evidenced by a bloody sheet indicating rupture of the hymen. SAADAWI, *supra* note 14, at 25.

25.   ANGELA BENDT & JAMES DOWNING, WE SHALL RETURN: WOMEN OF PALESTINE 89, 25 (1980).

26.   STRUM, *supra* note 16, at 28.

27.   BISHARAT, *supra* note 3, at 37.

28.   *Id.* at 40, 191 n.33.

29.   *Id.* at 40.

depending on whether the violation was physical or verbal, whether she was fondled through her clothing or her dress was actually lifted, and the distance the violation occurred from the victim's home.[30] If it is decided that the violation was the woman's fault, the men in her "dishonored" family often feel justified in severely punishing or even killing her.[31] While the jurisprudence is customary law, it is represented as consistent with, if not identical to, Islamic law,[32] thereby demonstrating the intertwined nature of the two traditions. In actuality, none of these *arad* determinations are covered by Islamic law.[33]

Feminist scholars argue that the differential treatment of women under customary law is a result of the ongoing existence of patriarchy within Palestinian society.[34] This patriarchy stems from historical realities that existed when the physically stronger members of the clan were responsible for the protection of the family. Thus, gender roles developed according to societal needs: men were the protectors and providers and women were the child rearers and nurturers.

This customary bifurcation of gender roles was emphasized further during the territorial occupations by the Ottomen, British, Jordanians, Egyptians, and Israelis. Custom and religion[35] became psychological and social refuges against unwanted foreign penetration[36] and provided a basis on which to confront, or at least survive, the incursions. During occupations, one of the few areas still controlled by the subordinated men was oversight of their women. For example, if men were asked why they would not let women have more freedom some would respond, "What is left for us? We don't have land, homes, or identity—at least let's have our honor."[37] Moreover, the protection of *arad* (honor) was intertwined with the protection of *ard* (land).[38] According to Egyptian feminist Dr. Nawal el Saadawi, some Palestinians left the West Bank during the 1967 war because of the perceived need to protect the honor of their women.[39] Therefore, loss of control over the important public aspects of male lives, including land, was counterbalanced by the maintenance and strengthening of male

---

30. The notion was that the closer to the home an offense occurred, the greater the dishonor to the family. *Id.* at 191 n.32.

31. BENDT & DOWNING, *supra* note 25, at 89. For more on honor killings, *see* Lama Abu-Odeh, *Crimes of Honor and the Construction of Gender, in* ARAB SOCIETIES, IN FEMINISM AND ISLAM: LEGAL AND LITERARY PERSPECTIVES 141 (Mai Yamani ed., 1996).

32. BISHARAT, *supra* note 3, at 40.

33. *Id.* at 191 n.32.

34. *See, e.g.,* SAADAWI, *supra* note 14, at 4.

35. Custom and religion were traditions with which the occupiers tampered the least. The occupiers' concern was primarily with areas affecting their ability to physically or militarily control the population.

36. SAADAWI, *supra* note 14, at ix.

37. PAUL COSSALI & CLIVE ROBSON, STATELESS IN GAZA 38 (1986).

38. SAADAWI, *supra* note 14, at 2.

39. *Id.*

control over private aspects, including female lives. The centrality of honor and male domination thus remained intact in the private sphere.

Women have rarely been able to challenge the notion of their own subordination, especially in the context of foreign occupation that threatens the entire social fabric. While a few may see women's liberation from patriarchy as inextricably linked with the national liberation struggle, many more women—including the politically active—are concerned with day-to-day physical and mental survival. Like many men, these women view custom as both necessary and desirable, one area in which their own culture is reaffirmed. As one female political activist stated, "If a family cannot educate all the children, the man must be chosen, because he will be the breadwinner and the head of the household."[40] Yet the current social reality and historical lack of educational opportunity demonstrates the need for girls to receive special attention.

In conclusion, custom and customary law within the Palestinian community has been influenced not only by patriarchy, but also by foreign domination and occupation. This combination has resulted in Palestinian women's continued social and legal subordination. Men still govern the public and private lives of women, often limiting them to their historical roles as nurturers and repositories of family honor. As will be discussed *infra*, the *intifada* affected the traditional gender roles to a certain degree.

Islamic Religious Law

With respect to the rights of women, the *sharia*, or Islamic law, offered women a vast improvement over seventh century customary law.[41] Instead of being regarded as mere chattels of their husbands, women were given an independent legal personality, which gave them the right to own and inherit property. The *sharia* also restricted polygamy to four wives, permitted women to obtain divorces on limited grounds, and provided for maintenance. While these rights may appear insignificant to those in the Western world, they must be viewed in the international historical context, in which they compared quite favorably until relatively recently.[42]

On the negative side, however, the *sharia* sanctions differential treatment that is disadvantageous to women. Women receive only half the inheritance share of a

---

40. Cossali & Robson, *supra* note 37, at 35.

41. For a discussion of the rights of women during *jahiliya* (the period of ignorance, or pre-Islamic period), *see* Asghar Ali Engineer, The Rights of Women in Islam 20 (1992).

42. Abdullahi An-Na'im, *The Rights of Women and International Law in the Muslim Context*, 9 Whittier L. Rev. 491, 495 (1987). For more on the rights of women, *see* Engineer, *supra* note 41; Jamal J. Nasir, The Status of Women Under Islamic Law (1990); Doi, *supra* note 23, at 154; Judith Romney Wegner, *The Status of Women in Jewish and Islamic Marriage and Divorce Law*, 5 Harv. Wom. L.J. 1 (1982); Mernissi, *supra* note 20; Fatima Mernissi, Woman and Islam (1991) [hereinafter Mernissi, Woman]; Fatima Mernissi, The Veil and the Male Elite (1991) [hereinafter Mernissi, Male Elite]; Naila Minai, Women in Islam: Tradition and Transition in the Middle East (1981); Afzular Rahman, Role of Muslim Woman in Society (1986); Women in the Muslim World (Lois Beck & Nikki Keddie eds., 1978); Women in Islamic Societies: Social Attitudes and Historical Perspectives (Bo Utas ed., 1983).

man, even if they have the same degree of relationship to the deceased.[43] A man can have up to four wives, while a woman is allowed only one husband. Islamic law allows a husband to divorce his wife at will, while a wife must prove she has grounds.[44] As long as the threat of polygamy exists, a wife will have difficulty in challenging her husband's and his family's authority. A "challenging" woman may find herself displaced by a new wife coming into the home, thereby having to share the family's resources and the husband's affections. Under custom, a wife who is unable to produce sons quickly is also under the threat of being replaced by a wife who can offer sons.[45]

Men have the right to beat their wives for not submitting to their authority, and wives must accept and endure these punishments.[46] Muslim women must marry Muslim men, but Muslim men can marry Muslim, Christian, or Jewish women.[47] Custody is awarded to women only if the children are very young.[48] The notion of *qawama*, or guardianship, also has affected the status of women.[49] In the private realm, women have not been able to control their own lives; in the public realm, women often have not been allowed to hold public offices, as this would entail supervising men.[50]

In the Middle East, *sharia* courts do not interpret personal status matters based directly on Koranic sources. Most countries have adopted the European Civil Code model and have personal status codes that incorporate pre-existing Islamic jurisprudential schools of thought. Because Jordanian law still generally applies in the West Bank,[51] the *sharia* courts utilize the 1976 Jordanian Law of Personal Status.[52] The

---

43. For more on inheritance, *see* MOORS, *supra* note 23.

44. An-Na'im, *supra* note 42, at 496. Polygamy is based on Koranic verse 4:3. The idea that only the male can unilaterally divorce comes from verse 2:237, which says that the marriage tie is in the hands of the man (*bi yadithi 'uqdatun nikah*). Inheritance is covered by verses 4:11 and 4:176.

45. Elizabeth H. White, *Legal Reform as an Indicator of Women's Status in Muslim Nations, in* WOMEN IN THE MUSLIM WORLD 52, 58 (Lois Beck & Nikki Keddie eds., 1978).

46. An-Na'im, *supra* note 18, at 39. Verse 4:34 covers the husband's right to chastise his wife to the extent of beating. For more on domestic violence, *see* Adrien Katherine Wing, *A Critical Race Feminist Conceptualization of Violence: South African and Palestinian Women*, 60 ALB. L. REV. 943 (1997).

47. Ann Elizabeth Mayer, *Law and Religion in the Muslim Middle East*, 25 AM. J. COMP. L. 127, 144 (1987).

48. *Id.*

49. Verse 4:34 of the Koran states: "Men have *qawama* over women because of the advantage the (men) have over them (women) and because they (men) spend their property in supporting them (women)." HOLY QUR'AN (A. Ali trans. & commentary).

50. An-Na'im, *supra* note 18, at 39.

51. For an analysis of how these laws have been altered by the Israeli occupation, *see* RAJA SHE-HADEH, OCCUPIERS LAW: ISRAEL AND THE WEST BANK (1988).

52. Jordanian Law of Personal Status, Temporary Law No. 61/1976, Official Gazette No. 2668 of Dec. 1, 1976, which replaced the 1951 Code. One of the exceptions to the 1988 renunciation of all legal claims to the West Bank by Jordan's King Hussein was the *sharia* courts, so the judges

Jordanian Code stipulates that the legal age for marriage is fifteen for women and sixteen for men.[53] Following the *qawama* concept of guardianship, a woman must obtain the consent of her closest male relative on her father's side, regardless of her age, when marrying for the first time.[54] A male guardian, or *wali*, must contract a woman's marriage, whereas a man may contract his own marriage. If a woman has no male relative, the *sharia* judge has the power to act as guardian.[55] For a marriage contract to be valid, at least one man must act as a witness. It takes two female witnesses in lieu of one male to constitute a valid contract.[56] The *mahr*, which exists under both custom and religion, must be paid to the woman,[57] and she is not required to use the money on furnishing her new home.[58] One problem, however, is that the father or grandfather is authorized to receive the amount on behalf of the bride. This clearly invites abuse, and women often do not receive their *mahr*.[59]

The Jordanian Code also provides that a husband is obligated to support his wife, while a wife has the corresponding duty to obey her husband (*taa*). The husband is not duty bound, however, to provide housing, food, clothing, and medication.[60] The Code permits polygamy[61] and does not require the husband to inform his wife or wives of his intent to wed.[62] He cannot, however, house his wives together without their specific consent.[63] If a wife refuses to move wherever a husband requests, she risks los-

---

retain their Jordanian appointments, salaries, and supervision. Lynn Welchman, *Family Law under Occupation: Islamic Law and the Shariah Courts in the West Bank, in* ISLAMIC FAMILY LAW 93 (Chibli Mallat & Jane Connors ed., 1990) [hereinafter Welchman, *Occupation*]. For a discussion of the contents of the 1976 law, *see* Lynn Welchman, *The Development of Islamic Family Law in the Legal System of Jordan*, 37 INT'L & COMP. L.Q. 868 (1988) [hereinafter Welchman, *Islamic Family Law*]. Since access to Jordan has been cut off, these courts no longer refer those in violation of the family code to the West Bank criminal courts because these were under Israeli control. Welchman, *Occupation*, at 99. During the British Mandate period from the end of World War I, the 1917 Ottoman Law of Family Rights was in effect for all Muslims. ROBERT EISENMAN, ISLAMIC LAW IN PALESTINE AND ISRAEL: A HISTORY OF THE SURVIVAL OF TANZIMAT AND SHARIA IN THE BRITISH MANDATE AND THE JEWISH STATE 34 (1978). A new draft is under consideration in Jordan, and its provisions are described by Welchman, *Islamic Family Law*, at 872.

53.   Jordanian Personal Status Law, *supra* note 52, art. 5.

54.   *Id*. art. 13.

55.   *Id*. arts. 9–13.

56.   *Id*. art 16.

57.   *Id*. art 44. *Mahr* is mentioned in the Koranic verse 4:4.

58.   Jordanian Personal Status Law, *supra* note 52, art. 61.

59.   *Id*. art. 63. For a description of how the father of the bride kept the *mahr, see* KITTY WARNOCK, LAND BEFORE HONOUR: PALESTINIAN WOMEN IN THE OCCUPIED TERRITORIES 30 (1990).

60.   Jordanian Personal Status Law, *supra* note 52, arts. 36, 66, 67.

61.   It has been estimated that the rate of polygamy is 5–10 percent in some villages. STRUM, *supra* note 16, at 234.

62.   Jordanian Personal Status Law, *supra* note 52, art. 28.

63.   *Id*. art. 39.

ing her maintenance rights.[64] A wife may also lose rights to her maintenance if she leaves the house without permission, even if she is merely going to work.[65]

With respect to divorce, the Code permits a husband the right to unilateral divorce without judicial action (*talaq*).[66] Divorce is a revocable event that later becomes permanent. A husband is able to divorce his wife without fully terminating the marriage, just by announcing three times, "I divorce you."[67] The wife must wait a three-month period (*idda*) before she can remarry.[68] If the husband changes his mind before the three-month period expires, the wife must return to him and resume the marriage.[69] The divorce becomes final only when he divorces her three times on three separate occasions.[70] Each time a husband divorces a wife, she must leave the marital home.[71] The Code requires a husband to pay alimony only to meet minimal needs.[72] If the *sharia* judge with whom the husband registered the divorce thinks the divorce was arbitrary, he can order compensation of up to one year's alimony.[73] The divorced woman is not only left in a financially precarious position, but she must also return to her father's home in disgrace.

As under general *sharia* principles, Palestinian women can divorce under Jordanian law only if one of the authorized grounds is met: impiety;[74] incurable skin or sexual disease;[75] mental disease;[76] desertion of more than one year;[77] inability to pay *mahr*;[78] inability to provide maintenance;[79] or inability of the wife to live with the husband.[80] If the divorce is requested on medical grounds, the husband is allowed

---

64.   *Id* art. 37.

65.   *Id*. arts. 68–69.

66.   *Id*. art. 85.

67.   *Id*. art. 97.

68.   *Id*. art. 135.

69.   *Id*. art. 94.

70.   *Id*. art. 98.

71.   *Id*. art. 36.

72.   *Id*. art. 36.

73.   *Id*. art. 134. The Jordanian courts have supplemented this provision by ruling that any *talaq* pronounced without the consent of the wife is arbitrary, with the burden of proof then falling on the husband to establish the existence of a *sharia* reason for the divorce to defeat his wife's claim for compensation. Welchman, *Islamic Family Law, supra* note 52, at 881.

74.   Jordanian Personal Status Law, *supra* note 52, arts. 113–15.

75.   *Id*. art. 116.

76.   *Id*. art. 120.

77.   *Id*. art. 123.

78.   *Id*. art. 126.

79.   *Id*. art. 127.

80.   *Id*. art. 132.

one year to seek medical assistance;[81] the divorce is granted only if the husband does not recover during that year. Unlike traditional religious doctrines, beating constitutes grounds for a divorce under the Code.[82] The Code also stipulates that a woman may specify in the marriage contract that she can get divorced without judicial process, that polygamy is a grounds for divorce, and that she has the right to work.[83] Such stipulations are rare,[84] however, indicating either a reluctance to defy local custom or a lack of knowledge about this option.

With respect to child custody, the Code provisions attempt to ensure that the children remain in control of the father's family. The ex-wife may care for the children until they reach puberty,[85] unless she remarries before then to someone outside her husband's family. If this occurs, she may lose custody of a son at age nine and a daughter at age eleven.[86]

Religious courts have often been ineffectual, primarily because of an Israeli military prohibition on enforcement of their orders.[87] Some of the courts' functions in the Occupied Territories were taken over by institutions of the *intifada*.[88] Women activists view the replacement of the *sharia* norms with egalitarian civil legislation as a critical step in improving the status of Palestinian women.[89] On the other hand, more traditional women have stated: "Our role as women is clear. . . . We are able to raise scores of courageous men. . . . It is the women's obligation to bring up her children in the true Islamic way—to spur them on to Jihad in the path of God to elevate the glory of their religion."[90]

---

81. *Id.* arts. 115–16.

82. *Id.* art. 69.

83. Welchman, *Islamic Family Law, supra* note 52, at 875.

84. Jordanian Personal Status Law, *supra* note 52, art. 19. Lynn Welchman researched 8,500 marriage contracts registered in the *sharia* courts of the West Bank over the past twenty years and discovered only 1.5 percent contained any stipulations. Welchman, *Islamic Family Law, supra* note 52, at 874 n.10.

85. Jordanian Personal Status Law, *supra* note 52, art. 162.

86. *Id.* art. 156.

87. JOHN HENDY, OCCUPIED PALESTINE: TRADE UNIONS AND THE LAW 30 (1989). Decisions of *sharia* courts of the Territories are not recognized in Israel, forcing claimants to start new suits in *sharia* courts in Israel if they want the judgement enforced there. BISHARAT, *supra* note 3, at 141.

88. During the *intifada*, justice committees, women's committees, the Unified National Leadership of the Uprising (UNLU), and private individuals often handle various personal status matters. *See* Adrien K. Wing, *Legal Decision-Making During the Palestinian Intifada: Embryonic Self-Rule*, 18 YALE J. INT'L L. 95, 134–139 (1993).

89. Marwan Darweish, *The Intifada: Social Change, in* RACE & CLASS 47–56 (1989). Rita Giacaman & Penny Johnson, *Palestine Women: Building Barricades and Breaking Barriers, in* INTIFADA: THE PALESTINIAN UPRISING AGAINST ISRAELI OCCUPATION 155, 168 (Zachary Lockman & Joel Beinin eds., 1989).

90. COSSALI & ROBSON, *supra* note 37, at 41.

In conclusion, the *sharia* as codified by the Jordanian Personal Status Law and intermixed with customary practice has contributed to the continued legal and social subservience of women. As is the case with custom, the status quo was altered to some degree by the *intifada*.[91]

SOCIO-LEGAL STATUS OF WOMEN DURING THE INTIFADA: 1987–1993

The Palestinian uprising, known as the *intifada*,[92] was primarily aimed at obtaining political rights for Palestinian society, not at obtaining rights for women. Yet women's participation in the *intifada* was so extensive that it altered traditional images of women to some degree. Women's participation in the *intifada* was "comprehensive, direct and active."[93] They were encouraged by the Underground Leadership of the Uprising (UNLU)[94] to become involved in executive functions of the newly formed popular committees.[95] They were especially involved in those functions relating to their traditional role as "sustainers,"[96] such as medical relief, food distribution, and fund raising.[97] Women collected donations; ran blood banks; passed out leaflets;

---

91. *See* Wing, *supra* note 88, at 134–39.

92. *See supra* note 13 for term usage. This section of the chapter will not discuss justifications for the *intifada*. *See, e.g.,* Richard Falk & Burns Weston, *The Relevance of International Law to Palestinian Rights in the West Bank and Gaza: In Legal Defense of the Intifada*, 32 Harv. Int'l L.J. 129 (1991) (arguing that Israeli occupation of the West Bank and Gaza challenges international law, violates traditional human rights policies, and thus justifies Palestinian resistance); *The Intifadah—An Act of Self-Defense*, 4 Palestine Y.B. Int'l L. 85 (1987–88) (justifying Palestinian revolt against Israeli administration of Occupied Territories).

93. Rita Giacaman, *Palestinian Women in the Uprising*, 2 J. Refugee Stud. 139, 142 (1989).

94. Darweish, *supra* note 89, at 59.

95. Ziad Abu-Amr, *The Palestinian Uprising in the West Bank and Gaza Strip*, 10 Arab Stud. Q. 384, 399. For a discussion of the liberating role of women, *see* Darweish, *supra* note 89, at 59; Aaron David Miller et al., *Two Years of Intifada: Its Impact on American, Israeli, and Palestinian Political Climates*, 31 Am. Arab Aff. 29, 36 (1989–1990) (*quoting* Professor Hanan Ashrawi); Giacaman & Johnson, *supra* note 89, at 155; Eileen Kuttab, *Community Development Under Occupation: An Alternative Strategy*, 2 J. Refugee Stud. 131, 135; Yezid Sayigh, *The Intifada Continues: Legacy, Dynamics, and Challenges*, 11 Third World Q. 20, 37 (1989); Islah Jad, *From Salons to the Popular Committees: Palestinian Women 1919–1989, in* Intifada: Palestine at the Crossroads 126 (Jamal Nassar & Roger Heacock eds., 1990).

96. Don Peretz, Intifada 96 (1991). Hiltermann also saw women's gains as an extension of their traditional teaching and rendering service. Joost R. Hiltermann, Behind the Intifada: Labor & Women's Movement in the Occupied Territories 197 (1991); Joost R. Hiltermann, *The Women's Movement During the Intifada*, J. Palestine Stud. 52–53 (1991) [hereinafter Hiltermann, *The Women's Movement*]; Jad, *supra* note 95, at 135. According to Professor Peteet, "long-term conflict makes for flux as gender roles and ideologies are blurred and subject to conscious reexamination. Households are mobilized for communal defense, and women take on tasks usually associated with men. Yet there also occurs a process of feminization of specific sectors of the national movement. Both processes involve a complex reconceptualization of gender." Julie M. Peteet, Gender in Crisis: Women & the Palestine Resistance Movement 8 (1991).

97. Darweish, *supra* note 89, at 59. For a comparison with the roles of women in Lebanon from 1969–1982, see Peteet, *supra* note 96, at 8.

watched for soldiers; and nurtured families of the dead, arrested and wounded.[98] Because of their involvement in the cause, women too were arrested, killed, and wounded.[99] Moreover, women became the core of the home economy movement to develop Palestinian self-sufficiency and boycott Israeli goods. Women also organized and operated income-generating projects outside their homes.[100] Among the efforts to mobilize women was a December 1990 conference by the Bisan Center in Jerusalem entitled "The *Intifada* and Some Women's Social Issues." Nearly 500 women attended the conference to discuss such critical issues as the *hijab* campaign in Gaza to force all women to wear headscarves, marital age reduction, and comparative family law.[101] Clearly, the *intifada* modified the traditional role and status of Palestinian women.

A concrete, albeit atypical, example of the change in the traditional status of women was the PLO's 1991 selection of Professor Hanan Mikhail Ashrawi, Birzeit University Dean of Faculty of Arts, as the principal spokesperson for the Palestinian negotiating team.[102] While her Western-educated, urbane demeanor has won admiration in many circles, there are vociferous critics at home who feel that these very characteristics as well as her minority Christian status make her an inappropriate representative of the Palestinian masses.[103] For example, the fundamentalist group *Hamas* has called her a "loose woman,"[104] which is consistent with fundamentalist philosophy that regards women's public participation as anathema to Islamic principles. Therefore, the significance of the selection of a female should not be overstated; it was aberrational at this point in time.[105] Nevertheless, one indication of her overall popularity was the fact that she was one of five women elected to the new eighty-eight-member Palestinian Legislative Council in the January 20, 1996, elections. Palestinian Authority President Yasser Arafat subsequently named her the Minister of Higher Education.

---

98.   ZE'EV SCHIFF & EHUD YA'ARI, INTIFADA: THE PALESTINIAN UPRISING—ISRAEL'S THIRD FRONT 247 (Ina Friedman ed. & trans., 1990).

99.   According to Schiff and Yaari, women constituted one-fifth of those wounded in the first three months. *Id*. at 126.

100. Jad, *supra* note 95, at 136.

101. BISAN CENTRE, THE INTIFADA AND SOME WOMEN'S SOCIAL ISSUES (1991). *Hijab* campaign is discussed in Wing, *supra* note 88, at 134–39.

102. JOHN WALLACH & JANET WALLACH, THE NEW PALESTINIANS: THE EMERGING GENERATION OF LEADERS 3 (1992).

103. *Id*. at 3.

104. *Id*. at 30.

105. The selection of female national leaders—Benazir Bhutto of Pakistan, Indira Gandhi of India, Golda Meir of Israel, and Corazon Aquino of Philippines—may not represent generalized higher female political participation in those countries, but instead derive from unique historical and political circumstances. ESCHEL M. RHOODIE, DISCRIMINATION AGAINST WOMEN: A GLOBAL SURVEY 31 (1989). There were two other women in the Palestinian negotiating team, Suad Amiry and Zahira Kamal, but they received far less media coverage than Professor Ashrawi. WALLACH & WALLACH, *supra* note 102, at 102.

According to Professor Joost Hiltermann, most women were unable to fill promi-nent leadership roles within the *intifada*.[106] This was due, in part, to a combination of factors, including customary norms and community values restricting leadership to males and the growing influence of Islamic fundamentalism in the territories. Another important factor was that women assumed major responsibilities as de facto heads of large households while several male family members were in prison, in hiding, injured, deported, or dead. Although the UNLU included women at various times and stages of the uprising, an analysis of the Communiqués and the pattern of arrests and depor-tations suggests that the leadership was generally male.[107]

Custom and religion were greatly influenced by the *intifada*.[108] For example, Palestinian legal actors have traditionally been highly respected senior men who have served as religious or customary law mediators (*qadis*) and lawyers (*muhamein*).[109] The numbers and types of legal actors expanded during the *intifada*. The UNLU, pop-ular justice committees, and private individuals mediated spousal quarrels and regu-lated *mahr* reductions. These organizations and individuals gained respect and legitimacy for the roles they played during the *intifada*, rather than through any cus-tomary or religious status. Of course, individuals such as Faisal Husseini enjoyed great respect both before and during the *intifada*.

Yet the *intifada* was not successful in eradicating customary and religious norms about women's roles in society. After the initial upsurge in women's political activ-ity, the position of women basically stagnated or reversed.[110] An important illustra-tion of this retrenchment is the *hijab* campaign launched by *Hamas* in 1989, which resulted in the imposition of headscarves on all women in Gaza. The traditionalists portrayed the wearing of the *hijab* as a sign of political commitment to the *intifada*, cultural struggle, and national heritage.[111] Women who refused to wear the scarf were subjected to graffiti attacks and verbal abuse. Some men even threw stones at these women, which was ironic given that the stone had come to symbolize the Palestinian struggle against the Israelis. Because stoning is a traditional Islamic punishment used against "loose" people who may be adulterers or fornicators, such attacks had a potential double meaning, implying that these women were "vain, frivolous, or anti-nationalist."[112]

The situation reached a crescendo when traditionalists threatened two women activists, who had donned the *hijab*, because their heads were not completely cov-ered. When one woman attempted to protect herself by claiming possession of a knife

---

106. Hiltermann, *The Women's Movement, supra* note 96, at 53.

107. *Id.*; Giacaman & Johnson, *supra* note 6, at 165.

108. Throughout the *intifada*, the Palestinian Press featured articles on the return to customary law. ROBERT HUNTER, THE PALESTINIAN UPRISING: A WAR BY OTHER MEANS 3 (1991).

109. *See generally* BISHARAT, *supra* note 3.

110. HILTERMANN, *supra* note 96, at 193. *See generally* STRUM, *supra* note 16.

111. Rema Hammami, *Women, the Hijab, and the Intifada*, MIDDLE E. REP. 25, 26 (1990).

112. *Id.* at 26.

and began to unzip her bag, the men retaliated. The group shouted that the women had a tape recorder in the bag and were "collaborators."[113] This is the ultimate insult to a Palestinian nationalist and invokes the most serious consequences for the accused; numerous alleged collaborators have been killed by their fellow Palestinians on frequently unsubstantiated grounds.[114] The crowd chased the women and grabbed the bag, but found no recorder and subsequently dispersed.[115]

An *intifada* justice committee[116] tried the three male instigators and sentenced them to pay a fine of 3000 JD ($4,500) to the women and their families.[117] The next UNLU communiqué (*bayan*) condemned "attacks by radical groups on Palestinian women in Jerusalem, Hebron and Gaza."[118] An appendix attached to the communiqué elaborated on the role of women in the *intifada:*

> Woman as we perceive her, besides being a mother, daughter, sister or wife, is an effective human being and full citizen with all rights and responsibilities. . . .
>
> We specify the following points:
>
> (1) We are against excessive vanity in personal dress and use of cosmetics during these times. This is applied to the same degree for men and women.
>
> (2) We believe that any dispute outside the purview of the occupation and its various offices should be resolved and settled in a democratic way with any suggestions offered in the course of normal constructive discussion or advice.
>
> (3) We should value highly the role women have played in our society during these times in achieving our national goals and confronting the occupation and they should not be punished without cause.
>
> (4) The phenomenon of harassing women contradicts the traditions and norms of our society as well as our accepted attitudes about women. At the same time it denigrates the patriotism and humanity of each female citizen.
>
> (5) Nobody has the right to accost women and girls in the street on the basis of their dress or the absence of a headscarf.
>
> (6) The Unified National Leadership will chase these hooligans and will stop such immature and unpatriotic actions, especially when it is found that many such hooligans consistently engage in their own suspicious activities.[119]

This appendix reveals the intertwining of custom, religion, and rights during the *intifada.* The Preamble clearly establishes that women are entitled to the full array of human rights. It does not limit itself to the public arena as did the Palestinian

---

113. *Id.*

114. For more on the treatment of collaborators, *see* Wing, *supra* note 88, at 139.

115. Hammami, *supra* note 111, at 26.

116. Such committees were formed to take the place of the Israeli administered legal regime, which has no legitimacy in the Palestinian community. *See* Wing, *supra* note 88, at 121.

117. Hammami, *supra* note 111, at 27.

118. Communiqué No. 43, *cited in id.*

119. *Id.* at 27.

Declaration of Independence.[120] While section 5 does not mandate that women wear the *hijab*, section 1 implies that modest dress, in keeping with custom and religious traditions, was required. Section 4 clearly criticizes the harrassment of women as inconsistent with Palestinian legal and social norms, but does not address the social custom of harassing, ogling, and whistling at women dressed "immodestly." Thus, one counter-interpretation of the appendix is that it implicitly authorizes harassment of women who are dressed "excessively."

Patriotic graffiti appeared soon after, proclaiming "[t]hose caught throwing stones [at women] will be treated as collaborators."[121] In a display of the UNLU's legitimacy and influence on Palestinian society, the atmosphere changed dramatically in a few days, and "women without head scarves no longer felt so threatened. Few men dared tell a woman to cover her head, and those who did were accused of considering themselves greater than the unified leadership."[122]

Nevertheless, it proved impossible to eradicate traditionalist beliefs and tendencies. Despite the warning by the UNLU to permit women flexibility in their dress, no action was taken to enforce the provisions in the appendix of Communiqué No. 43. Thus, in February 1990 fundamentalists felt free to renew the *hijab* campaign and attempted to impose the *jilbaab* (full length dress) as well.[123] *Hamas* activists continued to patrol the Gaza streets looking for inappropriately attired women to douse with vegetable dye as punishment.[124] In March 1993 informants stated that women had been attacked with acid, and many secular women confided that they dared not leave the house without wearing a head scarf. One elite woman refused to leave her family compound, because she refused to wear the *hijab*.[125] Only Christian women went about without scarves.[126] Women in parts of the West Bank feared being attacked with stones and pelted with fruit.[127] The UNLU and other nationalists were clearly unable, or perhaps unwilling, to counter the growing fundamentalist dictates.[128] Feminists tried to justify the inability of the UNLU to defeat the fundamentalist forces by stressing the need for solidarity in fighting the occupation.[129] Once again, however, it was *women's* rights that were sacrificed to accommodate nationalist aims.

---

120. *Id.*

121. *Id.*

122. *Id.*

123. Communiqué No. 43, *cited in* Hammami, *supra* note 111, at 28.

124. Sara Roy, *The Political Economy of Despair: Changing Political Attitudes among Gaza Refugees*, J. Palestine Stud. 65 (1989).

125. Personal interviews conducted by the author in Gaza in March 1993 (interview notes on file with author).

126. Based on personal observation by the author in Gaza, March 1993.

127. Strum, *supra* note 16, at 222.

128. Hiltermann, *supra* note 96, at 207.

129. Interview with woman activist in Ramallah (June 5, 1990), *in* Hiltermann, *supra* note 96, at 204.

The UNLU and justice committee's handling of the *hijab* campaign, using both customs and new norms espousing women's equality to resolve a societal problem, had both positive and negative implications for women's status. On the beneficial side, the UNLU defined attacks on women as a political and social crime. On the negative side, "the *sulha* (settlement) only [fed] into traditional conceptions of women by [involving] the women's families and treating the issue as a question of honor and the women not as political individuals but as family property."[130]

In addition to the handling of the *hijab*, UNLU communiqués also supported the continuance of patriarchy. Participants in the *intifada* were usually referred to as "our sons," "brother doctors," "brother workers," or "brother businessmen and grocers."[131] When *bayanat* mentioned women, it was usually as among the people "who are suffering,"[132] or as "mothers," rather than as women in their own right.[133] Some communiqués excluded women altogether, despite the ongoing activity of the women's committees.[134]

A few *bayanat* departed from this marginalizing pattern. For example, Communiqué No. 5 called on "mothers, sisters, and daughters to work side by side with their husbands, sons, and brothers."[135] In August 1988, the UNLU reminded women's committees that they had to "shoulder a special responsibility in organizing sit-ins and other appropriate activities" in solidarity with male and female prisoners.[136] Furthermore, the UNLU consistently recognized International Women's Day, and with each year of the uprising the emphasis on this day increased. In 1988, the UNLU merely called for demonstrations on March 8 as part of its weekly schedule.[137] The following year, the UNLU expanded its references to "salute the Palestinian woman" and to declare its "admiration for her heroism in the national struggle."[138] The UNLU also urged "strengthening the unity of the women's movement in the State of Palestine within the framework of the Unified Women's Council."[139]

---

130. Hammani, *supra* note 111, at 27.

131. UNLU Communiqués Nos. 3, 9, and 23, *reprinted in* Hiltermann, *supra* note 96, at 53–54. *See also* UNLU Communiqués Nos. 1 and 14, *reprinted in* INTIFADA: THE PALESTINIAN UPRISING, *supra* note 89, at 328, 347.

132. UNLU Communiqué No. 24, *reprinted in id.* at 377.

133. Communiqués Nos. 8, 29, and 53, *in* Hiltermann, *supra* note 96, at 54.

134. UNLU Communiqué No. 21, *in* HILTERMANN, *supra* note 96 at 20.

135. HILTERMANN, *supra* note 96, at 201.

136. UNLU Communiqué No. 23, *reprinted in* INTIFADA: THE PALESTINIAN UPRISING, *supra* note 89, at 372.

137. Hiltermann, *supra* note 96, at 54.

138. *Id.*

139. *Id.*

PLO leadership outside of the Occupied Territories also issued documents that may be interpreted as restrictive of women's rights. As previously discussed, the Palestinian Declaration of Independence states that "[g]overnance will be based on principles of social justice, equality, and nondiscrimination in public rights on grounds of race, religion, color or sex."[140] It appears that this call for equality is limited to the public sphere, as the dichotomy between private and public realms is maintained. Thus, change in personal status matters, most impacted by religion and custom, was apparently not contemplated.

The Declaration later "render[s] special tribute to the brave Palestinian woman, guardian of sustenance and life, keeper of our people's perennial flame."[141] Professor Hiltermann interprets the Declaration to mean that "the only roles assigned to women in the new state are to protect, preserve, and procreate."[142] A preferable interpretation might be that women are free to participate in public life and obtain the public, civil and political rights in addition to, but not instead of, their traditional roles.

Despite questions raised about their public participation, women continued to play an active role in the *intifada*. For instance, the decrease in the amount of *mahr* paid during marriage was achieved in some cases as a result of the active participation of women's groups.[143] Some women contended that *mahr* was an outdated custom that failed to improve women's social status and was inconsistent with the goals of the national liberation movement.

The role of women changed as Palestinian women prepared themselves to participate in the socioeconomic and political playing fields of a new Palestine. During the *intifada*, resource centers that educated women about their legal rights were established.[144] The purpose of these centers was also to initiate an informal legislative drafting process, and legislation pertaining to women's issues was discussed among the various committees.[145]

In conclusion, despite the advances made by women during the *intifada*, the fact remains that women were, and still are, subject to the oppressive practices dictated by customary and religious law. *Hamas' hijab* campaign was but one example of the perpetuation of the oppression of women.[146] Women's participation in the *intifada* did challenge and change certain traditional norms. By no means, however, did women secure an equal footing with men, or become first-class citizens.

---

140. Proclamation of the Independent Palestinian State, 19th Session of Palestine National Council, Algiers, Nov. 15, 1988, *reprinted in* INTIFADA: THE PALESTINIAN UPRISING, *supra* note 89, at 397–99.

141. *Id.*

142. HILTERMANN, *supra* note 96, at 202.

143. WARNOCK, *supra* note 59, at 63.

144. MARIA HOLT, HALF THE PEOPLE: WOMEN'S HISTORY AND THE PALESTINIAN INTIFADA 14 (1992).

145. *Id.* at 43.

146. Hammani, *supra* note 111, at 25–26.

THE PALESTINIAN AUTHORITY DRAFT BASIC LAW AND ITS IMPACT ON THE STATUS OF WOMEN

In December 1993, the PLO published an interim constitution known as the "Draft Basic Law for the National Authority in the Transitional Period."[147] Palestinian jurists, scholars, and activists later met to modify the document and published the third version in April 1994.[148] This document was superseded by a fourth draft, which was submitted to the newly elected Palestine Legislative Council (PLC) for its consideration in May 1996. The PLC turned the fourth draft over to its Legal Committee, which considered it along with a fifth draft that had been produced by the Birzeit Law Center. The Legal Committee produced a sixth draft that was published and circulated within Palestine and abroad. While the sixth draft was being prepared for circulation, the Executive Branch presented a seventh draft to the Council as well. After a period of commentary, the Legal Committee produced an eighth draft for initial consideration by the full Council.[149] The Council deliberated during August and September and produced a ninth draft, which is also known as the First Reading. The ninth draft was then sent back to the Executive Branch for consideration, where it has since remained. As of October 2000, it is unclear when or if the Basic Law draft will be returned to the PLC for its proposed second and third reading and final adoption. Furthermore, the Basic Law, if finalized, is intended only to be utilized during the autonomy period.

Chapter 2 of the Basic Law on Fundamental Rights and Freedoms addresses the topic of women's rights. It is an important portion of the document, because it explicitly guarantees all Palestinians inalienable rights for which thousands of Palestinians—male and female—have given their lives.

Article 10 states that the government will work "without delay to incorporate the international and national declarations and agreements that protect human rights."[150] Article 9 sets forth the principle that women and men should be afforded equal rights under the law.[151] Articles 12 through 32 emphasize criminal procedural rights, freedom of religion, opinion, press, residency, movement, economic activity, and the right to private property, housing, care for martyrs families, education, work, political life, litigation, etc.[152] Article 29 states that "care of motherhood and children

---

147. Nasser H. Aruri & John J. Carroll, *A New Palestine Charter*, 4 J. OF PALESTINE STUD. 5 (1994).

148. *Id.*

149. The author participated as an independent consultant with the Council in this process.

150. Draft Basic Law, *supra* note 7, art. 10. The fourth draft specifically mentioned various conventions, including the Convention on the Elimination of All Forms of Discrimination Against Women (Women's Convention). G.A. Res. 34/180, 34 U.N. GAOR Supp. (No. 710.46) at 193, U.N. Doc. A/34/46 (1979) (*entered into force* Sept. 3, 1981) (fourth draft on file with author).

151. *Id.* art. 9.

152. *See supra* note 7.

is a national obligation,"[153] language reminiscent of the UNLU communiqués.[154] These fundamental rights and freedoms are guaranteed by allowing individuals the ability to challenge violations within the judicial system.[155]

While Chapter 2 has several positive attributes with respect to women's rights, it must be read in conjunction with Chapter 1. Article 4 states that Islam is the official religion,[156] a clause added in the sixth draft and found in all Arab constitutions.[157] As discussed above, Islam, as strictly and commonly interpreted, sanctions a variety of inequalities between men and women. Thus an inherent contradiction exists between Chapters 1 and 2. Moreover, because the ninth draft has omitted the specific delineation of all the human rights conventions found in the fourth draft, it is unclear if the Women's Convention would be specifically endorsed by the new government, especially given Islamist forces and the language of Chapter 1.

Endorsement of the Women's Convention is particularly critical because it is very explicit about the rights of women in various spheres of their lives. Article 1 of the Women's Convention defines discrimination as:

> any distinction, exclusion or restriction made on the basis of sex that has the effect or purpose of impairing or nullifying the recognition, enjoyment or exercise by women, irrespective of their marital status on a basis of equality of men and women, of human rights and fundamental freedoms in the political, economic, social, cultural, civil, or any other field.[158]

The Women's Convention also contains fifteen articles detailing when states must take "appropriate measures" in the fields of education;[159] health care;[160] nationality;[161]

---

153. *Id.* art. 29.

154. *See supra* note 131 and accompanying text.

155. Draft Basic Law, *supra* note 7, art. 32. Article 32 states: "Every trespass to any of the personal freedoms or personal sanctity of life for humans or other civic rights and freedoms that are guaranteed in the basic or (other) law is a crime in which such a case, founded on civil or criminal precedents, cannot be dismissed. The Palestinian National Authority shall assure a just compensation to anyone whom incurred such harm."

156. *Id.* art. 4.

157. The author was present when this clause was added in to the sixth draft.

158. *Id.*

159. The Women's Convention, *supra* note 150, art. 10. Article 10(c) and (h) states: to "take all appropriate measures . . .to ensure . . .[t]he elimination of any stereotyped concept of the roles of men and women at all levels and in all forms of education . . . and, in particular, by the revision of textbooks and school programmes and the adaptation of teaching methods" as well as by "[a]ccess to specific educational information on family planning." It does not mandate coeducation, but merely encourages it. *Id.* art. 10(c).

160. *Id.* art. 12. Article 12(1) and (2) states: to "take all appropriate measures to eliminate discrimination . . . in health care . . . including [services] related to family planning" and to ensure access to services: in connection with pregnancy, confinement and the post-natal period, granting free services where necessary, as well as adequate nutrition during pregnancy and lactation.

161. *Id.* art. 9.

culture;[162] family and personal status;[163] legal and political activities;[164] employment;[165] recreation;[166] and mortgages and other forms of credit.[167]

Thus, although the Basic Law affirms some important human rights norms, it lacks the specificity to address several women's human rights issues. Because the early drafts (one through three) failed to discuss the full panoply of political, economic, and civil rights that many Palestinian women desire, several women's committees, the PLO's General Union of Palestinian Women, and other advocates assembled in January 1994 to draft a "Document of Principles of Women's Rights" (Women's Charter).[168] Because the ninth draft fails to rectify these inadequacies, the following section outlines the substance of the Women's Charter.

---

162. *Id.* art. 5. Article 5 states: to "take all appropriate measures . . . [t]o modify . . . social and cultural patterns of conduct . . . with a view to achieving the elimination of prejudices . . . that are based on the idea of the inferiority or superiority of either of the sexes or on stereotyped roles."

163. *Id.* art. 5. Article 5 also states: to "ensure that family education includes a proper understanding of maternity as a social function and the recognition of the common responsibility of men and women in the upbringing . . . of their children." Article 16(1)(d) and (e) states: to "take all appropriate measures to eliminate discrimination . . . in . . . marriage," including to ensure "[t]he same rights and responsibilities as parents" and "[t]he same rights to decide . . . responsibly on the number and spacing of their children."

164. *Id.* art. 2. Article 2(a) states: "to embody the principle of the equality of men and women in their national constitutions or other appropriate legislation." Article 6 states: to "take all appropriate measures . . . to suppress all forms of traffic in women and exploitation of [and] prostitution of women." Article 7(b) and (c) states: to ensure that women "participate in the formulation of government policy and the implementation thereof and to hold public office and perform all public functions at all levels of government" as well as in "non-governmental organizations and associations concerned with the public and political life of the country."

165. *Id.* art. 11. Articles 11(1)(b), (1)(d), (2)(b), and (2)(c) states: to take all appropriate measures to eliminate employment discrimination against women, including ensuring "[t]he right to the same employment opportunities, including the application of the same criteria for selection in matters of employment;" "[t]he right to equal remuneration, including benefits, and to equal treatment in respect of work of equal value;" "maternity leave with pay or with comparable social benefits without loss of former employment, seniority or social allowances;" and "the provision of the necessary supporting social services to enable parents to combine family obligations with work responsibilities . . . in particular through . . .child-care facilities." Article 11 also provides "special protection to women during pregnancy in types of work proved to be harmful to them." Art. 11(1)(f). There is a caveat that such legislation "shall be reviewed periodically in light of scientific and technological knowledge and shall be revised, repealed or extended as necessary." Art. 11(3). Clearly there is great potential for abuse where states could draft protective legislation as a means of discriminating against women. The Convention does not prohibit discrimination in hiring or job assignment of pregnant women. For a United States case involving protective conditions for women, *see International Union, UAW v. Johnson Controls, Inc.*, 111 S. Ct. 1196 (1991), where the Supreme Court held that a company sex-specific fetal protection policy is forbidden under Title VII of the Civil Rights Act as impermissible sex discrimination. Medical evidence showed that exposure to the lead used to manufacture batteries also hurt men's reproductive capabilities, but only women were banned from working, unless they could prove they were infertile.

166. Draft Basic Law, *supra* note 7, art. 13(c).

167. *Id.* art. 13(b).

168. It is interesting to note that South African women gathered together in February 1994 to dis-

DOCUMENT OF PRINCIPLES OF WOMEN'S RIGHTS

The Women's Charter, also known as a women's bill of rights, was published in August 1994.[169] This document is comprised of a Preamble and General Provisions that specify the political, civil, economic, and cultural rights of Palestinian women. The Preamble states that the state of Palestine is for all Palestinians regardless of their present residence. It adds that "human dignity will be safeguarded by means of a parliamentary democratic system of governance, itself based on freedom of expression. . . ."[170] More important, the Preamble emphasizes that minorities and women are to be afforded protection and equal treatment under the law.[171] Interestingly, the Preamble also mandates that this document be ratified and included in the new Palestinian constitution. In essence, the Preamble challenges the traditional role of women and in so doing, attempts to liberate Palestinian women for the twenty-first century.[172]

The section termed "General Provisions" reiterates the need to "abolish all forms of discrimination and inequality against women that were propagated by the different forms of colonialism . . . and that were reinforced by the conglomeration of customs and traditions prejudiced against women embodied in a number of laws and legislation."[173] Moreover, this section restates the importance of endorsing and following the 1979 Convention on the Elimination of All Forms of Discrimination Against Women.[174] This document, unlike the Basic Law, consistently echoes the need

---

cuss a Women's Charter that goes beyond the interim constitution. See Adrien K. Wing and Eunice deCarvalho, *South African Women: Towards Equal Rights*, 8 HARV. HUM. RTS J. (1995).

169. Draft Document of Principles of Women's Rights, Aug. 1994, *reprinted in* J. PALESTINE STUD. 137 (1994) [hereinafter Women's Charter].

170. *Id.* The Preamble states:

> The State of Palestine is a state for all Palestinians wherever they may be. It is the state where individuals enjoy collective national and cultural identity, and pursue complete equality of rights. In this state, their political and religious convictions and their human dignity will be safeguarded by means of a parliamentary democratic system of governance, itself based on freedom of expression and freedom to form parties. . . .

171. *Id.*

172. *Id.*

173. *Id.* The General Provisions, para. 1 states:

> We, the women of Palestine, from all social categories and the various faiths, including workers, farmers, housewives, students, professionals, and politicians promulgate our determination to proceed with our struggle to abolish all forms of discrimination and inequality against women, which were propagated by the different forms of colonialism on our land, ending with the Israeli occupation, and which were reinforced by the conglomeration of customs and traditions prejudiced against women, embodied in a number of existing laws and legislation. In order to build a democratic society that ensures equal opportunities for women in rights and obligations within the following principles. . . .

174. *Id.* para. 2 states: "The future Palestinian state and the PNA must be committed, regardless of its jurisdiction, to the Declaration of Independence and to all international declarations and conventions pertaining to human rights, particularly the 1979 Convention on the Elimination of All Forms of Discrimination Against Women."

to use legislative and administrative means to provide safeguards for all aspects of women's lives. This section further states that a woman, elected or appointed, to any governmental body "should be on equal footing with men" and that laws should be "compel[ling], functional and executable."[175]

Additionally, this document tries to incorporate the positive aspects of Palestinian and Arab culture in its vision of a new Palestinian state. The Charter examines the pertinent roles and definitive contributions made by women during the national liberation movement[176] and outlines women's commitment to the movement by focusing on how women promoted the struggle for free Palestine instead of advocating women's issues. In this respect, the drafters argue that it is "the time to affirm that the issue of women's legal rights in all aspects is a cornerstone for building a democratic Palestine society."[177]

The document also contemplates women's emancipation. To ensure that this vision becomes a reality, the drafters specify that three measures must be taken. First, that a clear and unambiguous statement regarding equality be promulgated. Second, that the state implement and enforce the laws. Third, that Palestinian society abide by the principles of law and human dignity.[178]

The most germane portions of the General Provision are ones that assert the political, civil, economic, and cultural rights of women. Under political rights, the

---

175. *Id.*

176. *Id.* The General Provisions, para. 5 states:

From the vision of the Palestinian women for a society of justice and equality, the general provisions stated above are basic guidelines from which we acquire support in order to:

- Preserve a cohesive Palestinian society . . .

- Enhance Palestinian culture and uniqueness . . . and

- Reinforce the national social struggle of Palestinian women: The Palestinian women's struggle has been depicted over the decades of the Palestinian national struggle as an immeasurable contribution in all spheres: women were martyred and thousands imprisoned. Palestinian women also played a vital role in the preservation of the unity of the Palestinian family as a social base to support individuals in the absence of the Palestinian national authority. Palestinian women were forced to delay many tasks associated with their social position and instead focused all their attention toward issues of the national and political struggle. It is now the time to affirm that the issue of women's legal rights in all aspects is a cornerstone for building a democratic Palestinian society. . . .

177. *Id.*

178. *Id.* Paragraph 5 also states:

We, the women of Palestine, see equal rights between men and women in all spheres as a basic principle for the emancipation of women and men. This requires having legislative and administrative procedures to ensure its implementation. This demands that we unite our efforts to remove those social norms that prohibit women from success in society, in order to guarantee the respect of human rights and the principle of law.

drafters asked that women obtain the right to vote; be allowed to participate in public referendums; have the ability to hold office; be treated equally in non-governmental bodies; and be allowed to participate in the diplomatic corps.[179] The drafters also requested that women be given civil rights, such as the ability to preserve or change nationality; the choice to marry a non-Palestinian; freedom to travel; the right to adequate housing; protection from violence; treatment of house chores as a social task; the right to expression and assembly; and the right to bring suit in court.[180] Under economic, social, and cultural rights, the drafters asked for the right to equal pay for equal work; equal opportunities; equality in making contracts; and equality in social welfare.[181]

The advantages of the Women's Charter over the Basic Law are many. First, in contrast to the Basic Law, the Women's Charter explicitly discusses the political, social, and other rights that must be made available to women. This explicitness is very important because it conveys the expectations of Palestinian women for a new Palestine state. Second, this document directly and unapologetically recognizes that Palestinian custom and tradition have contributed to the domination of women. This recognition is key, because it amounts to a tacit promise that such oppression will not be a part of the newly emerging Palestinian state. Third, the Women's Charter empha-

---

179. *Id*. The General Provisions, Political Rights states:

> To guarantee the right of women in voting, running for office, involvement in public referendums, and the ability to hold political and public judicial posts on all levels. This is in addition to equal opportunity with men in political parties, non-governmental organizations concerned with political and public life in Palestine, and the representation of the state in international and regional organizations as well as in diplomatic corps.

180. *Id*. The General Provisions, Section on Civil Rights states:

> To grant the woman her right to acquire, preserve or change her nationality. Legislation must also guarantee that her marriage to a non-Palestinian, or a change of her husband's nationality, while married, will not necessarily change the citizenship of the wife. This includes her freedom from imposition of her husband's citizenship. Women should also be granted the right to give citizenship to her husband and children, be guaranteed full freedom to move, travel, and choose her place of residency, have guaranteed her right to adequate housing. Motherhood should be looked upon as a social post. House chores should be regarded as a task of social and economic value. The law should stand next to the women to protect her family from violence and practices that infringe on any of her guaranteed rights, including her right to join any activity, assembly, or association by guaranteeing her right to go to court as a citizen with full rights.

181. *Id*. The General Provisions, Section on Economic, Social and Cultural Rights states:

> The Constitution and Palestinian legislation must guarantee the equality of women at work ensuring equal pay with men working in the same work, providing equal opportunities in promotion, training, compensation, rewards, health insurance and maternity rights. Equality in making contracts, administering property, obtaining banking contracts and property mortgage in all procedures practiced in courts and judicial bodies must also be guaranteed. We also affirm the importance of equality in social welfare, the benefit of health, education, and training services, and the guarantee of her full equality regarding issues pertaining to personal status.

sizes the role and contributions of women during the national liberation period, which is significant as it provides an explanation, or justification, as to why Palestinian women should be treated equally in society and under the law.

Despite its positive attributes, critics of the Women's Charter may find that it is too drastic and too bold. A society that continues to see women as repositories of family honor may not be politically, socially, and economically prepared to grant women equality. The growing political and cultural power of *Hamas* and other Islamic fundamentalists makes the Charter's adoption unlikely. And, even if the Charter were adopted, there is no guarantee that women would actually benefit. The Charter merely declares women's rights; it provides no means for enforcing them.

Reconciling the views of the traditionalists with the views of the burgeoning women's advocates is a difficult task. Although the Women's Charter goes a step further than the Basic Law and traditional norms by advocating an equity-based state, fundamentalist groups will continue to oppose the transformation of women's traditional roles within Palestinian society. Hopefully, the Palestinian decisionmakers will realize the importance of women's rights and incorporate measures ensuring women's political, social, and economic equality. Suggestions that Palestinian decisionmakers should consider for the implementation of women's rights are discussed below.

ENHANCING THE STATUS OF PALESTINIAN WOMEN

To their credit, the Palestinians have already begun the process of establishing institutions that will monitor human rights compliance. For instance, Article 31 of the ninth draft calls for the formation of "an independent body to assure human rights . . . [which] shall present periodical reports to the Legislative Council."[182] The body's effectiveness will depend on its willingness to act independently and to review critically the new government's actions. It is only natural to anticipate that numerous problems will emerge as the new decisionmakers have little or no experience in implementing international human rights norms. Non-governmental watchdog groups such as the Palestinian Centre for Human Rights in Gaza have already faced harassment from the new government.

In formulating legal rules and processes, Palestinian leaders must consider whether to adopt tinkering, following, or leading law reform in each of the areas under consideration.[183] "Tinkering law reform" implies accepting the legal status quo by making tiny adjustments at the margins. For example, this type of reform would entail hiring more judges when the backlog becomes overwhelming.[184] "Following law reform" responds to societal change, e.g., lowering the voting age to reflect the perceived increased maturity of youth. Tinkering and following law reforms are least likely to be resisted by the public because they do not greatly impact the existing legal regime and social customs. "Leading law reform," on the other hand, utilizes law to

---

182. Draft Basic Law, *supra* note 7.

183. JOHN BARTON ET AL., LAW IN RADICALLY DIFFERENT CULTURES 8 (1983).

184. *Id.* at 8.

implement societal change instead of merely responding with minor modifications. While leading law reform characterizes the bulk of modern major law reform,[185] it is often the most likely to be resisted because it restructures existing societal customs and religious norms. In some instances, Palestinian leaders may prefer tinkering or following law reforms to minimize societal upheaval in a population that has undergone massive disruption over the thirty years of occupation. In other cases, decisionmakers may decide that a particular legal principle is important enough to undertake leading reform, in spite of predictable opposition from fundamentalist and traditionalist groups.

In addition to the equality and anti-discrimination clauses already in the Basic Law, Palestinian decisionmakers should adopt additional leading law reform measures. The Basic Law should include a clause that assures affirmative action, or positive measures, to improve women's status. These proposals will probably encounter substantial resistance. The following sections discuss three possible justifications for their implementation: reinterpretation of Islam; compliance with international human rights norms; and building upon changes wrought in Palestinian society by the *intifada*.

Islamic Reinterpretation

This section discusses reinterpreting the *sharia* as a means to enhance legal arguments in favor of women's equality.[186] Many Muslims have a strong commitment to the *sharia* and may resist proposed reforms that challenge centuries of learned behavior based on patriarchy and male dominance. Women themselves are often reluctant to abandon social practices that define their religious beliefs. On the other hand, secularization, external cultural influences, and international human rights conventions have persuaded many women and men to accept less inequality between the sexes. They grapple with how to implement policies based on equality in the face of those who interpret the *sharia* more conservatively.[187]

As early as the nineteenth century, Muslim feminists, liberals, and leftists called for *sharia* reform, especially in the area of personal status. Today, a dialectical relationship between religion and government is emerging, in which Islamic doctrines and clerics espousing conservative reform are transforming governments and legal systems. Even in the face of such strong opposition, governments have been increasingly able to reform and control many aspects of Islamic law and religion.[188] With the exception of Saudi Arabia, nations have revised these laws in a piecemeal fashion; in a few countries, the modifications have been quite extensive examples of leading law reform.[189] Because of fundamentalist pressures and the increasing influence of reli-

---

185. The adoption of modern constitutions and civil codes, formation of law reform commissions, and "law making" judicial activity are all examples of leading law reform. *Id.* at 9.

186. Abdullahi An-Na'im, *Civil Rights in the Islamic Constitutional Tradition: Shared Ideals and Divergent Regimes*, 25 John Marshall L. Rev. 267, 284 (1992).

187. An-Na'im, *supra* note 42, at 514.

188. Mayer, *supra* note 47, at 184.

189. *See* Tunisian Code of Personal Status of 1956; Iranian Family Protection Act of 1967, as

gion in Muslim societies, many current reform movements demand change through a re-examination of the *sharia* principles and other sources of law.[190] This adaptation of *sharia* law can be characterized as tinkering legal reform, rather than leading reform that often inspires organized opposition. Reformers believe that Islam cannot be abandoned to the sole province of traditionalists, and thus want to show that the rights of women are consistent with Islamic law and not alien Western notions. They realize that imaginative techniques must be formulated to maintain and enhance the legitimacy of Islam while improving the status and rights of women.[191]

Some reformers are thus involved in reappraising the theological justifications for restrictions on women's rights by arguing that "patriarchal attitudes and cultural traditions [are] disguised as religious norms."[192] These reformers, however, realize that facile adoption of Western feminist notions would constitute leading law reform that would not be effective in changing Palestinian society.[193] Instead they are attempting to theorize methodologies based upon the historical and cultural realities of Muslim women.

To counter this liberalization movement, fundamentalists and other traditionalists have called for strict interpretation of Islamic principles by rejecting new reform and repealing pre-existing reforms. For several reasons, Islamic fundamentalism throughout the Islamic world is on the rise, even among Palestinians. First, Islamic nations have become disenchanted with Western and socialist ideologies that stress individualism and modernism as the method to solve problems. These "solutions" are viewed as alien intrusions, and as neo-colonialist and imperialist in nature. Second, secular Arab nationalism, as espoused by leaders such as the late Egyptian president Gamal Abdel Nasser, failed to solve economic and political problems. Third, important oil-rich nations continue to stress Islamic, as opposed to nationalistic, solutions; these nations have the resources to fund Islamic groups in various countries. Fourth, many take pride in an indigenous legal system that is often considered to represent the genius of the Islamic community. Fifth, many believe that the *sharia* is the will of God, and thus must be strictly obeyed.[194]

Fundamentalists reject twentieth century secular reforms as "heretical innovations inspired by western examples that lead to decadence, immorality and the destruction of the family."[195] Thus, reformers have often been attacked as Western lackeys

---

amended in 1975 (abrogated in 1979 by Khomeini government); Pakistan Muslim Family Laws Ordinance of 1961, *discussed in* Mayer, *supra* note 47, at 141–42.

190. Mayer, *supra* note 47, at 178. Examples of the new critics of inequality are WOMEN AND ISLAM (al-Hibri ed., 1982); MERNISSI, *supra* note 20; MERNISSI, WOMAN, *supra* note 42; MERNISSI, MALE ELITE, *supra* note 42.

191. An-Na'im, *supra* note 42, at 501.

192. ANN ELIZABETH MAYER, ISLAM AND HUMAN RIGHTS: TRADITION AND POLITICS 113 (1991). *See also* works of Fatima Mernissi, *supra* note 42.

193. An-Na'im, *supra* note 42, at 516.

194. Farhat J. Ziadeh, *Permanence and Change in Arab Legal Systems*, 9 ARAB STUD. Q. 20, 20, 33 (1987).

and agents of Western cultural imperialism.[196] Fundamentalists want women to wear veils or head scarves and long dresses and attend all-female schools. They want to exclude women from public functions, repeal any personal status reforms and restrict female education to suitable subjects such as religion, nursing, teacher training, home economics, and gynecology.[197] One problem that confronts the implementation of progressive reforms is the restrictive views of individual *qadis* who may constitute latent opposition to change. For example, it was not until 1964—eight years after the Tunisian Personal Status Law prohibited polygamy—that the courts declared a polygamous marriage invalid.[198] They refused to implement leading law reform. In many countries, the current ideological battle is still between the forces for liberal reform and the traditional view shared by fundamentalists.[199]

Palestinian decisionmakers interested in a religious justification of women's rights reforms must examine reinterpretations of the *sharia* that have been adopted by various countries.[200] For example, Tunisia found an Islamic justification for abolishing polygamy: The Koran states that men must treat each wife equally; because it is physically impossible to treat individuals in an identical fashion, polygamy cannot be rationalized.[201] Traditionalists often respond to this analysis by arguing that the Koran would not permit polygamy if it were impossible to effectuate. A potential rebuttal to this fundamentalist argument is that Prophet Muhammad was not in favor of polygamy and wanted to ensure that it would be extremely difficult to undertake.[202]

In another example of leading law reform, Tunisia abolished the *talaq*, the unilateral divorce by a husband without judicial intervention. To justify their reforms, Tunisian decisionmakers cited several Koranic verses that stress the undesirability of divorce and the need to seek arbitration whenever there is spousal discord. Because a husband's desire to pronounce *talaq* is certainly evidence of marital discord, Tunisian jurists reasoned, judicial intervention is always required.[203] Palestinian framers could adopt similar reasoning and justifications for banning *talaq*.

---

195. Mayer, *supra* note 47, at 143.

196. ABUL ALA MAWDUDI, PURDAH AND THE STATUS OF WOMEN IN ISLAM 40 (1979).

197. Mayer, *supra* note 47, at 175.

198. Noel Coulson & Doreen Hinchcliffe, *Women and Law Reform in Contemporary Islam, in* WOMEN IN THE MUSLIM WORLD 48–49 (Lois Beck & Nikki Keddi eds., 1978) .

199. Mayer mentions Algeria, Egypt, and Pakistan as places where the battle continues. Mayer, *supra* note 47, at 177.

200. *See* An-Na'im, *supra* note 42; JOHN L. ESPOSITO, WOMEN IN MUSLIM FAMILY LAW 1116 (1982); An-Na'im, *supra* note 18, at 46; ABDULLAHI A. AN-NA'IM, TOWARDS AN ISLAMIC REFORMATION: CIVIL LIBERTIES, HUMAN RIGHTS, AND INTERNATIONAL LAW 52 (1990); Elizabeth H. White, *Legal Reform as an Indicator of Women's Status in Muslim Nations, in* WOMEN IN THE MUSLIM WORLD 60 (Lois Beck & Nikki Keddi eds., 1978) (containing table listing reforms affecting women's status).

201. White, *supra* note 200, at 58. For more on Tunisia, *see* RHOODIE, *supra* note 105, at 369.

202. White, *supra* note 200, at 59.

203. *Id.*

In addition to examining the experience of various countries in reinterpreting the *sharia*, Palestinians should also peruse the writings of commentators who advocate more rights for women.[204] For example, the conservative Egyptian scholar Muhammad al-Ghazali argues that women's oppression is not based on Islam, but on misinterpretation of the *sharia*. While he does not reject the inequality of the sexes in the Koran, he does not find it problematic if women occupy political positions.[205] Because he is a conservative, al-Ghazali's views may be acceptable to both conservatives and progressives.[206] To increase support for reforming traditional norms and values, Palestinian leadership should cite conservative scholars who hold progressive views in certain areas of the law.

Professor Abdullah An-Na'im of Sudan offers a reinterpretation of *qawama*, the male guardianship provision. The Koranic verse presents *qawama* as based on two conditions: male physical superiority and financial support of women. Physical strength, however, is not relevant in the modern era when the rule of law governs brute force. In addition, today more women are able to work outside the home and become economically independent of men. Because neither of the two historical conditions is currently applicable, the concept of *qawama* should be revised.[207] Professor An-Na'im also believes that reform efforts can be justified today given that other modifications of the *sharia* have been generally accepted. For example, Muslim scholars quoted from the Koran throughout the Middle Ages to justify slavery; no one would justify it today.[208] Therefore, Palestinian framers could use Professor An-Na'im's reasoning to modify *qawama* and other concepts.

Another possibility for Palestinian decisionmakers is to engage in their own reinterpretive justifications. In March 1993, this author traveled to Egypt, Israel, and the Occupied Territories and held discussions with various Palestinian lawyers, academics, and activists—both male and female. They indicated that Palestinian Islamic scholars have either not addressed reinterpretive issues regarding women's rights, or that they have not done so in public fora or journals. Informants attribute the failure to address these issues to the conservative and powerful influence of traditionalists like *Hamas*—who dominate the public fora and call for restriction of women's rights—and the crushing nature of the ongoing occupation, which does not afford these scholars the luxury of theorizing about their future.[209]

---

204. For exceptions, *see* MAHMOUD MOHAMED TAHA, THE SECOND MESSAGE OF ISLAM (A. An-Na'im trans., 1987); An-Na'im, *supra* note 42, at 497.

205. *See* Muhammad al-Ghazali, *Qadaya al-mar'ah: Bayna al-taqalid al-rakida wa al-wafida* (Women's Issues: Between Stagnant and Incoming Traditions) (1990), *described in* As'ad AbuKhalil, *A New Arab Ideology? The Rejuvenation of Arab Nationalism*, 46 MIDDLE E. J. 22, 32–33 (1992).

206. *Id.* at 33.

207. An-Na'im, *supra* note 18, at 47.

208. AN-NA'IM, ISLAMIC REFORMATION, *supra* note 200, at 91; ENGINEER, *supra* note 41, at 2.

209. Interviews in Egypt, Israel & the Occupied Territories, Mar. 16–28, 1993. The author was accompanied on this trip by two research assistants, Douglas K. Burrell and Shobhana Kasturi.

The existence of other sources of Islamic law, in addition to the Koran, could aid Palestinians in their reform efforts. For example, the *sunna* are the words and deeds of Prophet Muhammad, his closest companions, and the first generation of believers. The *sunna* are collected in reports (*ahadith*) written during the ninth century.[210] The process of interpretation by the four jurisprudential schools of the Koran and *ahadith* is known as *ijtihad*. The third source of law is the *ijma*, which represents the consensus of the ninth century Islamic scholars from each school.[211] *Qiyas*, the fourth source of law, is an interpretive method based on reasoning by analogy. Palestinian reformers could thus claim a modern right to *ijtihad* and *qiyas* to establish an enlightened *ijma*. Revisions to personal status and inheritance rules could then be justified in the same manner as the polygamy and *qawama* reforms discussed previously. Other potential revisions could include using *ijtihad* to justify raising the age of consent for marriage, which is not specifically enumerated in the Koran. If the Palestinians raised the female's age of consent from fifteen to eighteen,[212] more girls would finish high school, be more employable, and have children later in life. All these attempts could be formulated as mere tinkering reform, and thus permissible under Islamic law.

One of the theoretical problems with this approach is that *ijtihad* cannot be used if the Koran or *sunna* plainly speak on the issue.[213] Traditionalists could claim, for example, that the Koran clearly permits a man to have four wives, and that therefore *ijtihad* cannot be used to limit this right. A possible response to the traditionalist argument would necessitate adopting Tunisia's approach in interpreting the polygamy provision.[214]

The fact that custom was incorporated into Islamic law can also help Palestinian reform efforts, because "the inclusion of modern social standards or customs can be viewed as consistent with the manner in which law had been formulated to meet particular social needs in the past."[215] To use the *qawama* example again, an argument could be made that modern custom does not necessitate that all women must be under the control of the physically stronger sex. Thus, it would be consistent with the intertwining of custom and religion to conclude that Islamic practice no longer requires the implementation of customs, such as *qawama*, that have outlived their relevance within the Palestinian community.

---

210. Justin Leites, *Modernist Jurisprudence as a Vehicle for Gender Reform in the Islamic World*, 22 Colum. Hum. Rts. L. Rev. 251, 254 (1991).

211. *Id.* at 265.

212. Before the British came, Palestinian law had raised the age of marriage for girls to seventeen. Thus, it was the Western Christian British regime that lowered it. Raising it again would be restoring the Palestinian pre-existing rule. Layish, *supra* note 8, at 14–15. Women's rights activists are demanding as much. *See* Deborah Horan, *Women in Palestine: Elections Are Over, On with the Struggle!*, Inter Press Serv., Jan. 31, 1996.

213. An-Na'im, *supra* note 200, at 58.

214. An-Na'im, *supra* note 18, at 47.

215. Esposito, *supra* note 200, at 129.

In conclusion, reinterpretation of Islam holds some promise for Palestinian decisionmakers interested in constitutionally justifying the equality of women. Muslim nations and scholars both provide some examples for consideration. Any push for change, however, will be countered by fundamentalists and traditionalists, who will resist progressive interpretations as examples of inappropriate leading law reform that do not reflect the social consensus of the community. In spite of such opposition, proposed reforms could either be justified solely through non-codified interpretations as suggested above, or they could be justified based upon implementation of human rights norms as discussed in the following section.

Adoption of International Human Rights Norms

This section discusses the possibilities for justifying gender equality based upon the adoption of international human rights norms. The Palestinians could engage in leading law reform by adopting wholesale revision of various laws based on norms proffered by international human rights conventions. Palestine could achieve this by signing and ratifying into law the various international treaties and agreements. Even if Palestine does not achieve independent statehood and thus is incapable of becoming a signatory to international treaties, the Palestinian Authority could incorporate the substance of these norms into the Basic Law.

Professor Louis Henkin notes, however, that the strongest challenge to the universal application of human rights has been culturally based resistance.[216] In the Middle East this resistance comes from the traditionalists and the fundamentalists. While there are those who support the full endorsement of international human rights standards, many find these principles antithetical to Islam.[217] Regimes like Iran have wholeheartedly embraced Islamization; on the other hand, regimes like those led by Saddam Hussein in Iraq and Hafez al-Assad in Syria have successfully crushed opposition groups calling for Islamization.[218] Some scholars have postulated that adopting some form of Islamization is a "strategy adopted by beleaguered elites in an attempt to trump growing Muslim demands for democratization and human rights."[219]

Cultural relativists argue that international human rights are Western in nature, and thus not suitable for those in the developing world.[220] The cultural imperialism argument can be countered by noting that cannibalism and slavery were once hallowed traditions in certain cultures, and no one attempts to justify them today.[221]

---

216. Louis Henkin, *The Universality of the Concept of Human Rights*, 506 ANNALS 12, 14–15 (1989).

217. MAYER, *supra* note 193, at 29.

218. *Id.* at 30–31.

219. *Id.* at 31.

220. These arguments are discussed in the context of female circumcision by Alison T. Slack, *Female Circumcision: A Critical Appraisal*, 10 HUM. RTS. Q. 437 (1988). *See also* Jack Donnelly, *Cultural Relativism and Universal Human Rights*, 6 HUM. RTS. Q. 400 (1984).

221. Riane Eisler, *Toward an Integrated Theory of Action*, 9 HUM. RTS. Q. 296 (1987).

Despite opposition from cultural relativists, Professor Abdullah An-Na'im of Sudan states that the Muslim world must struggle to reconcile Islam with human rights standards.[222]

This section examines selected aspects of the more than twenty-two international documents related to the status of women[223] to highlight potentially suitable provisions for implementation in Palestine. The Islamic nations have devised some mechanisms. In September 1968, the Arab League established the Permanent Arab Regional Commission on Human Rights to advise the League on ways to protect human rights.[224] This Commission has not yet generated an Arab Convention on Human Rights, but has focused its attention on the promotion rather than the protection of human rights.[225] A draft Charter on Human and Peoples Rights in the Arab World,[226] however, has been drafted by the Islamic Conference, of which all Muslim countries are members. The Charter endorses human rights as compatible with Islamic norms and doctrines.[227]

The major protections of rights, however, are found in the United Nations Charter; the Universal Declaration of Human Rights (Universal Declaration);[228] the Women's Convention;[229] the International Covenant on Civil and Political Rights (ICCPR);[230] and the International Covenant on Economic, Social and Cultural Rights (ICESCR).[231] The Preamble of the United Nations Charter reaffirms "the equal rights of men and women."[232] Among the purposes of the United Nations is "promoting and encouraging respect for human rights and fundamental freedoms for all without dis-

---

222. An-Na'im, *supra* note 18, at 51.

223. *See* Natalie K. Hevener, *An Analysis of Gender Based Treaty Law: Contemporary Developments in Historical Perspective*, 8 Hum. Rts. Q. 70 (1986).

224. *See* Council of the Arab League, Res. 2443/48, Sept. 3, 1968; Istvan Pogany, *Arab Attitudes Toward International Human Rights Law*, 2 Conn. J. Int'l L. 367, 373 (1987).

225. Burns H. Weston et al., *Regional Human Rights Regimes: A Comparison and Appraisal*, 20 Vand. J. Transnat'l L. 585 (1987).

226. Karen Engle, *International Human Rights and Feminism: When Discourses Meet*, 13 Mich. J. Int'l L. 517, 537 n.67 (1992).

227. "Reaffirming their commitment to the UN Charter and fundamental Human Rights, the purposes and principles of which provide the basis for fruitful co-operation amongst all people," *quoted in* Mayer, *supra* note 193, at 14.

228. U.N. Doc. A/810, G.A. Res. 217 (III) at 71 (1948) [hereinafter Universal Declaration].

229. *Supra* note 150.

230. G.A. Res. 2200 (XXI), 21 U.N. GAOR Supp. (No. 16) at 53–56, U.N. Doc. A/6316 (1967) (*entered into force* Mar. 23, 1976). *See also* the Convention on the Political Rights of Women, which was adopted by the General Assembly in 1952, and entered into force on July 7, 1954. 27 U.S.T. 1909; T.I.A.S. No. 8289; 193 U.N.T.S. 135, 7 U.N. GAOR Supp. (No. 20) at 28, U.N. Doc. A./2334 (1952).

231. G.A. Res. 2200 (XXI), 21 U.N. GAOR Supp. (No. 16)) at 49–50, U.N. Doc. A/6316 (1967) (entered into force Jan. 3, 1976).

232. Preamble, U. N. Charter, 59 Stat. 1031, T.S. No. 993, 3 Bevans 1153, 1976 Y.B.U.N. 1043.

tinction as to race, sex, language, and religion."[233] Article 13 of the U.N. Charter directs the General Assembly to "initiate studies and make recommendations for the purpose of . . . assisting in the realization of human rights and fundamental freedoms for all without distinction as to . . . sex."[234]

The Universal Declaration elaborates those provisions outlined in the Charter. It is not a treaty, nor does it seek to enforce legal obligations, but rather it delineates "a common standard of achievement for all peoples and all nations."[235] The Preamble to the Universal Declaration recognizes "the equal and inalienable rights of all members of the human family" and reaffirms "faith . . . in the equal rights of men and women."[236] Despite its original non-binding status, the Declaration has acquired greater force because domestic courts have used it as a way to determine compliance with the United Nations Charter.[237]

The ICESCR asserts a right to sexual equality. The parties to the Covenant "undertake to ensure the equal right of men and women to the enjoyment of all economic, social and cultural rights."[238] Women are "guaranteed conditions of work not inferior to those enjoyed by men, with equal pay for equal work."[239] It includes a provision that marriage must be entered into with the free consent of the intending spouses.[240] The ICCPR also forbids discrimination on the basis of sex[241] and ensures the "equal right of men and women to the enjoyment of all civil and political rights."[242] It also guarantees to all citizens, without distinction on the basis of sex, the right to take part in public affairs,[243] to vote and be elected,[244] and to have access to public services.[245] Another section requires parties to "insure equality of rights and responsibilities of spouses as to marriage, during marriage and at dissolution."[246] Among the Middle East countries ratifying ICCPR and ICESCR are Afghanistan, Egypt, pre-

---

233. *Id.* art. 1(3).

234. *Id.* art. 13.

235. Burns Weston, *Human Rights, in* Human Rights in the World Community: Issues and Action 22–23 (Richard Pierre Claude & Burns H. Weston eds., 1989).

236. Preamble, *supra* note 228.

237. Weston, *supra* note 235, at 23. An-Na'im finds that it has both political and moral force. An-Naim, *supra* note 18, at 491.

238. *Supra* note 231.

239. *Id.* art. 7(a)(i).

240. *Id.* art. 10(1).

241. *Supra* note 230.

242. *Id.* art. 3.

243. *Id.* art. 25.

244. *Id.*

245. *Id.*

246. *Id.* art. 23.

1979 Iran, Jordan, Libya, Morocco, Syria, and Tunisia (Algeria intends to ratify).[247] Some commentators argue that these norms are now part of customary international law, and therefore bind states regardless of whether they are signatories.[248]

The Women's Convention, however, contains the most extensive provisions.[249] Yemen, Egypt, Iraq, Libya, and Tunisia are among the over one hundred countries that have ratified it.[250] This document is critically important, because it covers a large amount of discrimination that takes place within the private sphere, an "area[] in which the majority of the world's women live out their days."[251] Palestinian decisionmakers should consider adoption of some of its provisions, including those affecting women within the private sphere.

Although a majority of nations have ratified the various covenants protecting the rights of women, the problem of inequality nevertheless persists.[252] With respect to the Women's Convention in particular, a major impediment to equality is that many signatories have ratified the treaty with reservations; at least twenty-three of the one hundred states that ratified the Convention made eighty-eight substantive reservations.[253] The conflicts between the status of women under religion and custom and their status under the Convention seem to be the major reason for so many reservations.[254] Some of these reservations literally strip the Convention of its merit. For example, Egypt ratified the Convention, but made a substantive reservation "concerning the equality of men and women in all matters relating to marriage and the family," thus purporting to ratify "without prejudice to the Islamic Sharia's provisions."[255]

Palestinians must examine the world's experience in implementing the Women's Convention. Following the Egyptian model reveals an exercise in mere tinkering, because the major area of private discrimination is left totally untouched. On the other hand, the acceptance of a reservation based on religious grounds may increase support from the traditionalist sectors of Palestinian society.

---

247. Mayer, *supra* note 193, at 24.

248. *Id.*

249. *See supra* note 150 and accompanying text.

250. Sarah C. Zearfoss, *Note, The Convention for the Elimination of All Forms of Discrimination Against Women: Radical, Reasonable, or Reactionary?*, 12 Mich. J. Int'l L. 903, 903 n. 2 (1991).

251. Noreen Burrows, *International Law and Human Rights: The Case of Women's Rights, in* Human Rights From Rhetoric to Reality 82 (Tom Campbell et al. eds., 1986).

252. Albert P. Blaustein, *Foreword, in* Rhoodie, *supra* note 105, at xi.

253. Zearfoss, *supra* note 250, at 925. This can be contrasted to the Race Discrimination Convention where only two parties out of 127 made substantive reservations (Afghanistan and the German Democratic Republic).

254. *See* A Report on the Ninth Session of the Committee on the Elimination of Discrimination Against Women 10 (International Women's Rights Action Watch CEDAW #9, May 1990), *cited in* Zearfoss, *supra* note 250, at 925 n.112.

255. Multilateral Treaties Deposited with the Secretary General: Status as of Dec. 31, 1986, at 162, U.N. Doc. ST/LEG/SER.E/3 (1985).

Professor Theodor Meron has observed serious problems with the Women's Convention's concern with the private sphere, particularly in the area of religion.[256] Although he recognizes that much of women's oppression is located in the private sphere, he is opposed to regulation as a solution because it "might require invasive state action to determine compliance, including inquiry into political and religious beliefs."[257] He recommends the modification of cultural and social patterns through education and government incentives rather than state encroachment into the private sphere.[258] Because Meron is unable to reconcile the Women's Convention with the Declaration on Religion,[259] he believes that both women's rights and religious freedom will suffer: "The attainment of the goal of equality of women may therefore require encroachment upon religious freedom."[260]

Palestinians should balance the interference with religious norms against the realization of equality. In so doing, Palestinian decisionmakers should realize the importance of equality, a self-professed goal of the national movement. They could adopt Professor Meron's recommendations for changing social and cultural patterns through education and government incentives and couple that with tinkering, following, and leading law reform envisioned by international human rights agreements.

Professor An-Na'im, however, cautions that legal reform must not move too rapidly: "It is irresponsible and inhumane to encourage these women to move too fast, too soon and to repudiate many of the established norms of their culture or religious law, without due regard to the full implications of such action."[261] While it can be argued that the moral force of international agreements signed by a majority of the world is powerful, the reality is that "without a translation of the rhetoric of human rights into enforceable legal rules the individual is in a very weak position in respect of a very powerful state."[262] At one extreme, women may find themselves confronted by a backlash from traditionalist forces that places them in personal danger; this actually happened in the Palestinian *hijab* campaign described above.[263] Alternatively, women may find that progressive rights are not enforced by governmental officials and agencies, thereby negating whatever substantive value the enactment of rights was to achieve.

---

256. THEODOR MERON, HUMAN RIGHTS LAWMAKING IN THE UNITED NATIONS: A CRITIQUE OF INSTRUMENTS AND PROCESS 62 (1986).

257. *Id.*

258. *Id.* at 62–63.

259. There is a specific declaration, but no Convention yet on religious discrimination. Declaration on the Elimination of All Forms of Intolerance and of Discrimination Based on Religion or Belief, G.A. Res. 55, 36 U.N. GAOR Supp. (No. 51) at 171, U.N. Doc. A/RES/36/55 (1982).

260. MERON, *supra* note 256, at 155.

261. An-Na'im, *supra* note 42, at 516.

262. Burrows, *supra* note 251, at 91.

263. *See* Wing, *supra* note 88, at 134–39.

In selecting which internationally recognized rights to adopt, Palestinians must carefully evaluate the various proposed rights schemes. Because of the increasing international acceptance of human rights norms, opponents of such norms use sophisticated rationales often cloaked in the language of human rights.[264] The patterns of diluted rights in Islamic human rights schemes should not be ascribed to peculiar features of Islam or Islamic culture but should be seen as part of a broader phenomenon of attempts by beneficiaries of undemocratic and hierarchical systems to legitimize their opposition to human rights by appeals to supposedly distinctive cultural traditions.[265]

As an example of a nuanced attempt by opponents to implement international norms, consider the following. The Universal Declaration of Human Rights states, "Men and women of full age, without any limitation due to race, nationality, or religion, have the right to marry and found a family."[266] The 1981 Universal Islamic Declaration of Human Rights, which was prepared under the auspices of the Muslim World League and which represents the interests of conservative Muslims,[267] contains a similar provision: "Every person is entitled to marry, to found a family, and to bring up children in conformity with his religion, tradition and culture."[268] The language concerning conformity with religion actually means that *sharia* still governs a Muslim's personal status. *Sharia* restricts Muslim women from marrying non-Muslim men. Therefore, the Universal Declaration's provision was subtly limited by using language that appeared innocuous to the unknowledgable, thereby maintaining the discriminatory strictures of Islamic law.

Professor Mayer also notes that the English and Arabic versions of this document vary considerably because the English version attempts to approximate Western notions of human rights that are not delineated in the Arabic version.[269] Thus, Palestinians and scholars must carefully consult bilingual versions of the proposed reforms to ensure that English versions written for Western audiences are not providing greater rights than Arabic versions prepared for domestic constituencies. If documents are printed in both languages, a clause asserting the validity of both versions must be included.

It is also important to note that some alleged proponents of reform who write extensively on the topic of equality for all Muslims may actually oppose change. A careful reading of their proposals indicates that they do not advocate equality between the sexes. Professor Mayer analogizes this to the Western notion that equality does not include rights for children. For example, young people do not have the right to vote or marry. She further provides the example of the American founding fathers of

---

264. MAYER, *supra* note 193, at 214.

265. *Id*. at 215.

266. Universal Declaration, *supra* note 228, art. 16(1).

267. For a thorough discussion of this document, *see* MAYER, *supra* note 193.

268. Art. 19a, discussed *id*. at 120.

269. *Id*.

the Constitution whose notion of political and social equality did not include women, blacks, or Native Americans.[270] The broad, sweeping leading law reform that the U.S. Constitution represented was seen, at the time, as having no relevance to the status of these particular groups. Thus, it is critical for Palestinian leaders to differentiate between proposals for true equality, and those for equal treatment of all men among themselves and equal treatment of all women among themselves. Palestinian decisionmakers should not enact leading law reforms that appear facially valid for everyone, but in actuality do not apply to half of the population.

Another problem facing the Palestinians in adopting international human rights norms is that of enforcement. Institutions that enforce the international conventions include the Commission on Human Rights, the Human Rights Committee, the Commission on the Status of Women, and the Committee on the Elimination of Discrimination Against Women (CEDAW).[271] The Commission on the Status of Women, established in 1946 by the U.N. Economic and Social Council, has a mandate to prepare reports on the promotion of women's rights.[272] The Optional Protocol to the ICCPR empowers the Human Rights Committee to act on individual complaints.[273] None of these institutions, however, has properly enforced women's rights.[274]

Human rights agreements are notorious for weak enforcement provisions, but the Women's Convention's enforcement mechanisms are unusually insubstantial.[275] A twenty-three person committee meets for approximately two weeks on an annual basis[276] to review reports submitted by parties to the Convention. These parties must submit their first report within one year after the Convention enters into force and then every four years thereafter.[277] This procedure fails for several major reasons. First, two weeks is an insufficient amount of time to analyze the reports, as evidenced by the backlog of unread reports. The committee is so backlogged that a member has estimated that it would take until the year 2000 just to read the reports submitted as of 1986.[278] No other human rights treaty organ is subjected to such a

---

270. *Id.* at 136. *See* DERRICK BELL, RACE, RACISM, AND AMERICAN LAW 2 (1992).

271. The Commission on Human Rights and Commission on the Status of Women are under the ECOSOC Council. The Human Rights Committee is set up to enforce the Political Covenant, and CEDAW to enforce the Women's Convention.

272. U.N. Doc. E/CN.6/124, at 7 (1949). For more on the Commission, *see* Malvina H. Guggenheim, *The Implementation of Human Rights by the U.N. Commission on the Status of Women: A Brief Comment*, 12 TEXAS J. INT'L L. 239 (1977).

273. ICCPR, *supra* note 230, at 254.

274. Laura Reanda, *Human Rights and Women's Rights: The United Nations Approach*, HUM. RTS. Q. 11–12 (Spring 1981).

275. Zearfoss, *supra* note 250, at 922; Detlev Vagts & W. Bronson Howell, *Book Review of HUMAN RIGHTS: FROM RHETORIC TO REALITY* (Tom Campell, David Goldberg, Sheila McLean, & Tom Mullen eds., 1986), 81 AM. J. INT'L L. 474, 477 (1987). ("As with international law in general, enforceability is a serious problem for international human rights provisions regarding women.").

276. Women's Convention, *supra* note 150, arts. 20, 21.

277. *Id.* arts. 17, 18.

278. MERON, *supra* note 256, at 80–82.

constraint.[279] Second, the committee has no authority to do anything other than examine reports; it cannot consider individual complaints.[280] The committee cannot find that a party is in violation of the Convention, but instead must rely on the public reporting system and on the ability of parties to negotiate their disputes.[281] Finally, the committee is isolated geographically; the Commission on Human Rights meets in Geneva and the committee meets in Vienna.[282]

Thus, Palestinian decisionmakers cannot rely on the international enforcement mechanisms if they adopt the various human rights agreements. They must implement domestic enforcement mechanisms that will be accountable to the new government's policies. A court that holds the new rights invalid, as was the case in Egypt, is ineffective. Reliance on Islamic *qadis* or *sharia* courts that view the reforms as anti-Islamic will not work either. Instead, politically appointed executive branch officials could create new administrative institutions to enforce the implementation of rights. This could be backed by stiff penalties, including prison time, to indicate the serious nature of the offenses. An Ombud office could be established to investigate government failures to enforce rights and to hear individual human rights complaints.[283] Appointment of additional secular or religious judges could help ensure that the pre-existing institutions are more amenable to implementing new governmental policies. This should be coupled with national educational campaigns in the schools, workplaces, and other parts of civil society to gain support for societal change. The ultimate aim is for today's leading law reforms to one day be regarded as following reforms that only needed tinkering.

If constitutionally enshrining women's equality is considered too progressive at this time, decisionmakers instead could amend the Jordanian Personal Status Code. This would entail tinkering or following law reform as the fundamental patriarchal structure of religious and customary law is retained. In other Muslim countries, codes have brought changes in several areas. Some nations, for example, have introduced legislation establishing minimum ages for the capacity to marry.[284] States have restricted or banned a husband's right to be polygamous.[285] Restrictions have also been placed on a husband's right to unilaterally terminate the marriage.[286] Mothers

---

279. *Id.* at 84–85.

280. *Id.* at 56.

281. Zearfoss, *supra* note 250, at 923.

282. MERON, *supra* note 256, at 215.

283. For a discussion of the Ombud office in the new nation of Namibia and as proposed for South Africa, *see* Adrien Katherine Wing, *Communitarianism v. Individualism: Constitutionalism in Namibia and South Africa*, 11 WISC. J. INT'L L. 296 (1993).

284. Coulson & Hinchcliffe, *supra* note 198, at 37, 39.

285. *Id.* at 40. Tunisia, Israel, Turkey, and the former Soviet Union prohibited polygamy altogether. *Id.*

286. *Id.* at 43. Most countries have restricted the husband's right to unilaterally terminate the marriage. *Id.*

have been granted longer custody of children,[287] and inheritance codes have been amended as well.[288]

Egypt provides an interesting case study of the dynamics of tinkering law reform in the area of women's rights. The Egyptian Family Law Amendments of 1979 were passed by Anwar Sadat in a presidential decree. These laws gave women some additional rights, such as requiring a husband to register his divorce and notify his wife; increasing alimony; increasing a mother's custody period of minor children; requiring a husband to provide housing for an ex-wife and children; permitting a wife to obtain a divorce if court mediation efforts at reconciliation fail; permitting automatic divorce if a husband takes a second wife; and permitting women to work without spousal permission.[289] Fundamentalists attacked these amendments and derisively called them Jihan's (Mrs. Sadat's) laws. Islamic groups believed that the First Lady of Egypt stepped beyond her proper customary role by influencing her husband and the Parliament to make unsuitable revisions to the law. Under great pressure from traditionalists, the Constitutional Court in 1985 overturned these amendments on procedural grounds.[290] In response to the Court's decision, the Parliament passed a nearly identical law, with one major exception. A wife no longer received an automatic divorce after a spouse's second marriage, but was required to obtain a judicial decree. Given its conservative nature, it would not be uncommon for the judiciary to rule against a woman seeking such a divorce.[291] Therefore, the law retained its fundamentally polygamous nature under religious and customary law.

The example of Algeria is instructive as well, although the outcome is yet to be resolved. The 1984 Personal Status Law embodied *sharia* principles that relegated women to an inferior status.[292] The law conflicts with the current 1989 Constitution, which includes provisions for equality under the law,[293] a commitment to ensure equality in rights and duties among all citizens,[294] and a guarantee of fundamental liberties and human rights.[295] It remains to be determined if the new Constitution will

---

287. *Id.* at 45.

288. Reforms in this area have been less far reaching. Tunisia, Somalia, Sudan, Egypt, and Iraq have made some changes. *Id.* at 47. A table of Islamic reforms in the various countries can be found *id.* at 49–50.

289. KEVIN DWYER, ARAB VOICES: THE HUMAN RIGHTS DEBATE IN THE MIDDLE EAST 237 n.2 (1991). For more on Egypt, *see* RHOODIE, *supra* note 105, at 363.

290. DWYER, *supra* note 289, at 237 n.2.

291. *Id.*

292. These included permitting men to have four wives, while women can only have one spouse, ALGERIAN CONST. art. 8. Women must obtain consent to get married, *id.* art. 9. The wife must obey the husband, *id.* art. 39. The husband can divorce his wife at his discretion, *id.* art. 48, whereas women must establish certain grounds, *id.* art. 53. Muslim women are barred from marrying non-Muslims, *id.* art. 62.

293. ALGERIAN CONST. art. 28.

294. *Id.* art. 30.

295. *Id.* art. 31.

empower women to challenge the 1984 law on constitutional grounds, or whether the 1984 law will be treated as inviolable.[296]

The Palestinians could similarly reform the Jordanian Personal Status law. For example, the minimum age for marriage could be raised to eighteen.[297] A husband's unrestricted *talaq* power to unilaterally terminate a marriage could be limited by requiring court mediation, registration, or other intervention. *Qawama* and *mahr* also could be modified. Alimony could be increased, and women could be given the right to work outside the home without spousal permission. (Because many Palestinian women must work outside the home for economic reasons, amending this particular provision may be seen as following law reform.) A wife's custody of children could also be extended past puberty.

The right to automatic divorce if a husband takes a second wife, may encounter the same resistance in Palestine as it did in Egypt. An alternative approach would be to inform women of their right to stipulate this option in the marriage contract. On the other hand, it is difficult to generalize about societal reaction based upon the experience of other countries. The Palestinian rate of polygamy may be lower than Egypt's, and therefore this issue might evoke less societal reaction. However, Palestinian society may view polygamy as a fundamental custom and religious right and attempts to further restrict it could meet resistance.

Gains Made by Women During the *Intifada*

This section discusses a third major way to justify constitutional reform in the area of women's equality: Palestinians could build upon societal changes introduced by the *intifada* to implement needed reforms. Changes wrought by the *intifada* must first be analyzed in the context of women's historical fight for fundamental rights and freedoms.

The political involvement of Palestinian women emerged after World War I during the British Mandate that proposed the creation of a Jewish homeland in Palestine. The Palestinian national movement developed in protest.[298] The focus of upper-class Palestinian women's efforts, like those of the nationalist movement, was to end British occupation.[299] In addition to charitable projects, women's groups also occasionally marched in demonstrations. After the first women's conference in 1929, a delegation of women protested in front of the British governor's house, crying, "To serve our

---

296. Mayer, *supra* note 47, at 1034–35.

297. *See supra* text accompanying notes 41–91.

298. Jad, *supra* note 95, at 126. For more on women's movements, *see* HILTERMANN, *supra* note 96, at 92; Hamida Kazi, *Palestinian Women and the National Liberation Movement; A Social Perspective, in* WOMEN IN THE MIDDLE EAST 26 (1987); Rita Giacaman & Muna Odeh, *Palestinian Women's Movement in the Israeli-Occupied West Bank and Gaza Strip, in* WOMEN OF THE ARAB WORLD: THE COMING CHALLENGE 57 (Nahid Toubia ed., 1988).

299. Jad, *supra* note 95, at 126.

homeland we shall take off our veil!"[300] This demonstration signified a break with religious and customary norms to support nationalist demands. The Arab Women's Committee, which primarily consisted of upper-class women and students, was soon formed.[301] Women also participated as messengers and fighters during the 1936 revolt against the British.[302] After the founding of the state of Israel in 1948, thousands of Palestinians were dislocated and considered refugees. In response, women expanded their involvement in charitable organizations to aid the displaced Palestinians.[303] After the formation of the Palestine Liberation Organization in 1964, the General Union of Palestinian women was established.[304] Since the beginning of the Occupation in 1967:

> the national question [has been] a major factor which both supports the movement for women's liberation and simultaneously limits its further development. It supports liberation by calling on women to move beyond the household realm and to face the occupation (side by side) with men. But it deters further development by emptying it of its feminist and class content and limiting it to the confines of the national liberation struggle.[305]

The various Palestinian political factions formed women's political groups, offering the same programs as did the charitable organizations. The women's groups established day care, training programs, and literacy projects.[306] The groups avoided many gender issues either because they truly believed such issues were not a priority, or because they were afraid to sow seeds of disunity in the movement.[307] In 1978, college-educated women activists established the Women's Work Committee in Ramallah,[308] which, for the first time, recruited professional, clerical, and factory workers.[309] This committee splintered into different factions allied with the four political parties affiliated with the PLO: *Fatah*, DFLP, PFLP, and the Communist Party.[310]

In December 1989, the women's organizations affiliated with *Fatah* (the Women's Committee for Social Work), the DFLP (the Palestine Federation of Women's Action Committees), the PFLP (the Palestine Federation of Women's Committees), and the Communist Party (the Association of the Palestine Working Women's Committees) formed the Higher Women's Council.[311] These groups "perceive themselves to be fully

---

300. *Id.* at 127. For more on this period, *see* Matiel Mogannam, The Arab Woman and the Palestine Problem (1937); Elise G. Young, Keepers of the History 144 (1992).

301. Jad, *supra* note 95, at 127.

302. Bendt & Downing, *supra* note 25, at 46.

303. Jad, *supra* note 95, at 127.

304. *Id.* at 128.

305. Giacaman & Odeh, *supra* note 298, at 62.

306. Jad, *supra* note 95, at 132.

307. *Id.*

308. Strum, *supra* note 16, at 59.

309. Hiltermann, *supra* note 96, at 133.

310. *Id.* at 134.

311. *Id.* at 135.

equal participants in the national movement, not mere adjuncts to the male leaders and combatants."[312] The aim of the Council is to strike a balance between the national liberation struggle and women's social struggle.[313] An incredible tension remains between the need to assert a feminist agenda and the need to support a nationalist agenda for independence. While some approach the subordination of women from a feminist perspective, others link women's oppression to the "collective weaknesses that impede liberation."[314] Some women—like Palestinian negotiating team member Zahira Kamal, a prominent activist aligned with the DFLP—do not adopt the word feminism, but state: "When we are talking about feminism, it is the right of women to work and to get an education."[315] Feminist discourse may alienate many male and female traditionalists who view it as a form of Western cultural imperialism. These same traditionalists, however, realize the need for men and women to obtain education in order to find gainful employment. Many women want to be spared the fate of Algerian women who were once again restricted to the private sphere after the national liberation movement achieved independence in the 1950s.[316] After the grueling liberation struggle, custom and religious norms were reasserted to affirm Algerian culture and patriarchy.

In addition to the formation of factional groups and charitable societies, a number of women's resource centers developed in Ramallah, Nablus, and Gaza. Their purpose was to disseminate materials and educate women from different backgrounds about their legal rights in preparation for a future Palestinian state.[317] Suha Hindiyeh, director of the Women's Resource Centre, stated:

> We have to start thinking of laying the basis for a strong women's movement. That's why we're planning to . . . attempt to put forth women's legislation in every aspect—family law, women workers, and many other issues related to women—drafting these legislations and discussing them with the other Women's Committees, with the Palestinian women's movement as a whole, so as to present it to our government when it comes.[318]

Women activists continue to express concern about the need to solidify and expand the few gains in women's status achieved during the *intifada*, so as to prevent the replication of Algerian experience in the newly emerging Palestinian state.[319] Many women want to be actively involved in the development of legislation and a consti-

---

312. PERETZ, *supra* note 96, at 97.

313. HILTERMANN, *supra* note 96, at 53.

314. Rosemary Sayigh, *Encounters with Palestinian Women under Occupation, in* OCCUPATION: ISRAEL OVER PALESTINE 269, 282 (Naseer Aruri ed., 1984).

315. *Quoted in* WALLACH & WALLACH, *supra* note 102, at 106.

316. *Id.* at 118.

317. MARIA HOLT, HALF THE PEOPLE: WOMEN'S HISTORY AND THE PALESTINIAN INTIFADA 14 (1992).

318. *Id.* at 43.

319. *See id.* at 198; The newsletter of the Union of Palestine Working Women's Committees (Communist Party) also raised this concern. *The Intifada and the Role of Palestine Women*, VOICE OF WOMEN, Sept. 1989, at 1, *cited in* Hiltermann, *The Women's Movement, supra* note 96, at 55.

tution that promote gender equality.[320] Additionally, Hanan Ashrawi stated that "there is an urgent and concentrated need to crystallize a feminist perspective and ideology."[321] Yet female Palestinian academics have expressed great frustration in obtaining scholarly, financial, and emotional support from their male colleagues when attempting to write on feminist issues.[322] Thus, the political outlook for women's issues remains unclear. Moreover, future economic and political problems make it less likely that women's rights supporters will be able to vigorously pursue a separate feminist agenda.

The stagnation and decline of women's participation during the *intifada* is further evidence of fundamentalism's increasing influence. Reinforcement of the family unit and the role of maternity has occurred to the detriment of female political organization. It appears that there are increased pressures on women to assume a more traditional lifestyle. The number of early marriages is increasing, and the average age of marriage has dropped from twenty-one to seventeen.[323] Fundamentalist groups have also attacked coeducation by calling for gender segregation.[324]

The women's movement is unable "to bring a balance between the national conflict needs on the one hand, and needs of women stemming from their class oppression and their oppression as women by a patriarchal system of social organization on the other."[325] With respect to the future role of Palestinian women, President Yasser Arafat has stated they will not suffer the fate of the Algerian women, because Palestinian women have a higher rate of education, which enables them to obtain professional positions.[326] He noted that there were thirty-seven female members in the 301-member Palestine National Council, a percentage that compares favorably to developed nations,[327] and stated:"I would say that in the new state female representation in parliament and official jobs will [be comparable] to the most advanced nations in the world."[328] Five women were elected in the eighty-eight-member Legislative Council elections of January 1996, a percentage that compares favorably to the number of women in the U.S. Congress. While admirable in the Middle Eastern context, President Arafat's statement does not address the private and public dichotomy in the

---

320. March 1989 editorial of Federation of Palestinian Women's Action Committees (DFLP), *cited in* Hiltermann, *The Women's Movement, supra* note 96, at 55. This is the position of three progressive women's groups, not *Fatah.*

321. WARNOCK, *supra* note 59, at 188. For a feminist perspective from an American Jewish author, *see* YOUNG, *supra* note 300.

322. Interviews by author in the West Bank and Egypt, Mar. 1993 (interview notes on file with author).

323. Lashar Khalife, *Women and the Intifada*, INT'L VIEWPOINT, Oct. 28, 1991, at 21.

324. Salim Tamari, *Left in Limbo: Leninist Heritage and Islamist Challenge*, MIDDLE E. REP. 16, 17 (1992).

325. Giacaman, *supra* note 93, at 141.

326. YOUNG, *supra* note 300, at 49.

327. *Id.*

328. *Id.*

Palestinian Declaration of Independence. While some Palestinian women will want to participate in the public spheres, some will certainly also be concerned with the private sphere where they spend the majority of their lives.

It appears that while social change has taken place in the nature of customary and religious norms regarding women's rights during the *intifada*, retrenchment has also occurred because of fundamentalist pressures. The full scope of legal extension[329] and legal penetration[330] of the changes must be determined to implement any future modifications to the Palestinian legal system. This is necessary to avoid problems of enforcement, because often what the legal system proposes to effect and what it actually does may be entirely different.[331]

An evaluation of women's status during the *intifada* is especially complicated, because much of the legal decision-making was based on customary and religious law that involved informal negotiation and settlement. Other societies may even consider these elements to be outside the legal system altogether. The potential extension of the legal decision-making was limited by the existence of the military occupation, which criminalized participation in any aspect of the *intifada* and imposed legal traditions and court systems upon Palestinian society. Because of the denial of freedom of the press by the Israelis, the need for secrecy, and difficulty in conducting research, it is impossible to know how far the new process actually penetrated into society. The very fact that compliance was high in the pre-Gulf war period may provide some indication of penetration at that time. On the other hand, it is possible that the compliance with the new rules was very sporadic, given its embryonic nature and inability to publicly evolve and flourish.

CONCLUSION

This chapter has set forth a number of important features of Palestinian society that will act as assets and impediments in establishing equality for women under the law. It has confronted the question of how Palestinian custom and Islamic religious practices, working separately and in conjunction, can be modified to advance the constitutional legal status of women, a professed goal of the Palestinian national movement.

Deeply held customary and religious beliefs endorse the differential treatment of women in Palestinian society. In the current climate of establishing Palestinian

---

329. Legal extension is the social reach of the law, how society defines and differentiates what is legal from what is non-legal, i.e., that which is left to custom, tradition, religion, informal negotiation, social convention, and peer and familial influence. BARTON ET AL., *supra* note 183, at 2. For example, the U.S. does not legally prohibit premarital sex (except with minors). It permits religion, the family, and social convention to regulate such behavior.

330. Legal penetration is the social grasp of the law, the degree to which the system actually penetrates and controls social life. *Id.*

331. For example, the United States legally prohibits prostitution; drug use; smoking and drinking by minors; and not wearing seatbelts. Yet all these activities exist and flourish to varying degrees depending on the law's penetrative ability.

autonomy, it is hoped that the Palestinian governing authorities will improve the status of women by ultimately guaranteeing and enforcing gender equality. The improved status of women in Palestinian society requires legal reform.

Although there are many methods to justify progressive reforms, this chapter analyzed three interrelated options. The first option, reinterpretation of Islamic doctrine, has been utilized throughout the Islamic world. This approach involves tinkering or following law reform and leaves intact the basic patriarchal structures of the legal system. When both religious and customary traditions support a given social norm, it is extremely difficult to successfully change entrenched patterns of discrimination.[332] Thus, although leading law reform can be instituted *de jure*, societal perceptions must change before *de facto* equality for women can be realized.[333]

A second approach to improving the status of women is through the implementation of codes that may be based partially on customary and religious norms and partially, or totally, on international human rights conventions. The critical problem with such leading law reform is that it is difficult to ensure *de facto* obedience from existing legal actors who may oppose reform. The constitutions of most Islamic states have clauses forbidding discrimination on the basis of gender; many states have already signed international human rights treaties guaranteeing gender equality.[334] Thus, it is the compliance, rather than the adoption, of these norms that presents the true dilemma. The state must play a major role in enforcing equality.[335] The Palestinians could publish a new family code that, at a minimum, codifies the reinterpretation of Islamic jurisprudence as found in the Jordanian Personal Status Code. This would follow the model of other secular Muslim states. Ideally, the Palestinians could adopt codes based on the international human rights principles found in various documents described previously. Palestinian decisionmakers, in finalizing the Basic Law and the subsequent constitution, may also take some guidance from the Document of Principles of Women's Rights, which was drafted by Palestinian women for Palestinian women. This document has incorporated those international human rights norms necessary to the improvement of women's status and role in the newly emerging Palestinian state.

The third approach to improving women's legal status is a Palestinian-centric emphasis on following the social reforms developed during the *intifada*. Ultimately, legal change will only be successful if societal change also occurs. Because Palestinian society indeed changed during the *intifada* to a certain degree, there is some cause for optimism about the success of proposed reforms. This optimism, however, must

---

332. Mayer, *supra* note 3, at 1035.

333. MERON, *supra* note 256, at 55.

334. An-Na'im, *supra* note 186, at 289. For a chart noting the Muslim state signatories to the human rights covenants, *see* Amyn B. Sajoo, *Islam and Human Rights: Congruence or Dichotomy*, 4 TEMP. INT'L & COMP. L.J. 23, 34 (1990).

335. Dima Abdulrahim, *Islamic Law, Gender and the Politics of Exile: The Palestinians in West Berlin: A Case Study in Islamic Family Law, in* Welchman, *Islamic Family Law, supra* note 52, at 181.

be tempered by the fact that traditional forces will likely oppose most of the changes as inconsistent with Islamic customs and doctrines.

While leading legal reform is conceivably the quickest approach by which to effect improvement in the status of Palestinian women, it is also potentially the least effective. As discussed, sweeping reforms that do not comport with the existing culture and religion may lack legitimacy among the population and will most likely be difficult, if not impossible, to enforce. A more effective approach to legal reform may be a combination of the following and tinkering reforms that would take into account Palestinian cultural and religious traditions. Although reforms achieved in this manner would take place at a slower rate, the resultant reforms would be perceived by the populace as legitimate. This perception of legitimacy, in turn, would foster voluntary compliance.

The current moment is not ripe for rapid change. The Oslo Accord and other recent agreements between Israel and the PLO have met with strong resistance or skepticism from many Palestinians.[336] Many feel that the PLO has betrayed their interests. Since the May 1996 election of Israeli Prime Minister Benyamin Netanyahu and the further breakdown of the peace process, frustrations have grown with the Palestinian Authority. Thus, it may be wiser for Palestinians to opt for gradual change instead of radical revisions of long-accepted cultural and religious precepts. Only time will tell if Palestine will be at the forefront of the Muslim world in adopting and enforcing equal rights norms that have so long been denied to both Palestinian men and women.

---

336. Chris Heges, *Palestinian's Reactions: Anger, Doubt, and Hope*, N.Y. Times, Sept. 10, 1993, at A9.

HUMAN RIGHTS OF WOMEN IN CENTRAL AND EASTERN EUROPE

Julie Mertus

INTRODUCTION*

Recent changes in Central and Eastern Europe (CEE)[1] have jeopardized, rather than enhanced, women's human rights. Most studies of women's human rights in Central and Eastern Europe have treated the region as a generic entity, as if the history and culture of the enormous region could be blended into a single phenomenon —the so-called countries in transition. Yet the nature and degree of the problems faced by women vary significantly from country to country and, within each country, from social group to social group. The elderly and disabled, single mothers and girls, refugee and migrant women, and women from minority ethnic, religious, national, or linguistic groups face the greatest obstacles to full participation in society and realization of human rights. Women living in countries recovering from or in the throes of armed conflict, as well as women in countries facing acute economic crises, have their own sets of issues and, it follows, their own strategies for promoting women's status.

International and regional governmental and non-governmental organizations have interjected their own varied agendas into the region; women advocates for human rights in CEE have shaped their particular responses to foreign interventions in line with their own historical survival tactics and existing opportunities for progress. A unified chapter on women's human rights in Central and Eastern Europe threatens to discount this multi-threaded diversity.

* This chapter was completed with the help of many individual women and women's organizations, with special thanks to those who coordinated responses to the survey: Sevdie Ahmeti and Vjosa Dobruna, Center for the Protection of Women and Children (Pristina, Kosovo); Aida Bagic (Zagreb, Croatia); Lilja Farkas (Nane!), Viola Zentai (MONA, Foundation of Women of Hungary) and Antonia Burrows (Budapest, Hungary); Vera Dakova (Sofia, Bulgaria); Delina Fico, Women's Center (Tirana, Albania); Louise Grogan, (Amsterdam); Laura Grunberg, ANA Society for Feminist Analysis (Bucharest, Romania); Jana Juranova (Bratislava, Slovakia); B.a.B.e. Women's Human Rights Groups (Zagreb, Croatia); Elena Kotchkina, Moscow Center for Gender Studies (Moscow, Russia); Kathleen Imholz (Tirana, Albania); Monika Macovei (Bucharest, Romania); Zorica Mrsevic, Women's Studies (Belgrade, Serbia); Urszula Nowakowska, Women's Rights Center (Warsaw, Poland); Kate Shaw, ProFem (Prague, Czech Republic); Suzette Schultz (Berlin, Germany); Olena Suslova (Kiev, Ukraine); Genoveva Tisheva (Sofia, Bulgaria); Tefta Zaka, Women's Bar Association (Tirana, Albania). Special appreciation is due to Jelica Todosijevic, Robin Phillips and Ann Snitow.

1. Central and Eastern Europe (CEE) refers to all of Europe other than the area identified as "west"; thus, many parts of the Newly Independent States fall into CEE.

To underscore both continuity and difference, this chapter offers a country-by-country survey of the region, drawing extensively from reports of lawyers, scholars, and activists (not mutually exclusive groups) in the region. Core information, including the selection of topics, has been drawn from the results of a ten-country[2] survey administered by the author in August 1996. The chapter begins with a survey of the status of women under prior regimes and an analysis of the impact of recent economic, political, and social changes in CEE on the human rights of women. It then turns to a country-by-country analysis, presenting factual information about the law and reality in the three areas identified by women in the region as most pressing: economic conditions and discrimination in employment; domestic violence, rape, and other forms of violence against women (including trafficking in women and forced prostitution); and women's low participation in political life. In addition, the chapter details other issues identified as areas of concern: abortion and women's health; sexual harassment; maternity leave and childcare; family law (with particular reference to divorce); and discrimination against both lesbians and single women.[3] By providing detailed information, this chapter seeks to serve as a resource for women, both in the region and elsewhere, who seek to understand the complex nature of change in CEE and its impact on women.

THE LEGACY OF FORMAL EQUALITY

Under the socialist systems of Central and Eastern Europe, women gained equality on formal grounds, including integration into the labor market, access to education, and formal inclusion into governmental structures. If discrimination is defined narrowly as "different treatment" (in other words, treating women and men differently), ideologically speaking women did not experience discrimination. Employment was equated with women's emancipation: Both men and women were workers equally obligated to contribute to their party/state. The gap between ideology and reality in

---

2.   The countries were chosen according to availability of information and in line with a desire to present regional diversity. In each country, at least three people with knowledge of both law and practice were asked about the state of the formal law and the status of women with regard to each of the topics examined below. In addition, they were encouraged to provide information as to actions taken by women's groups. Where the information provided was incomplete, the country was not included in the final report for that question. The information was supported by published sources. For the subjective parts of the survey, a cross section of at least 100 women was surveyed in the region. Although this sample is not scientific, the results were checked against and supported by other published and unpublished sources. Due to space constraints, the entries for Germany were abbreviated. Countries included in whole or in part are: Albania; Bulgaria; the Czech Republic; Croatia; Germany (primarily with respect to the former East Germany); Poland; Romania; Serbia (Yugoslavia); Slovakia; and Ukraine. In addition, the geographic region of Kosovo is considered separately from Serbia as the issues of women's human rights in Kosovo differ significantly from Serbia and as the status of Kosovo has not been resolved.

3.   Additional issues identified as sources of concern for women included: discrimination against older women; discrimination against women from particular ethno-national/racial groups; use of culture or religion to oppress women; lack of opportunities for village and rural women; drug and alcohol abuse; lack of opportunities for girls; degradation of the environment; and negative stereotypes of women in the media.

CEE, however, is renowned. As Barbara Einhorn has observed, "State socialism 'emancipated' women not as equal citizens but as worker-mothers."[4]

In order to balance the ideological attachment of full employment with the notion that women should maintain their "natural" role as mothers, the socialist system did in fact treat women differently from men. Protectionist legislation prohibited pregnant women, women with small children, and, in some cases, all women from holding dangerous or taxing jobs; and compensatory legislation granted benefits and allowed exceptions for women's motherhood role, such as maternity benefits, child care, and leave for caring for sick family members.[5] By further entrenching the patriarchal division of labor and reaffirming that women's primary role was one of reproduction and caretaking, the social benefits system "isolated women and men felt largely relieved from their responsibilities as fathers and husbands."[6] Ultimately, then, the benefits worked against women's equality.

To supplement the protectionist measures and further promote ideological equality, states enacted a number of so-called "positive" discriminatory measures, all of which had a dark underside for women. Quotas were set to ensure women's participation in the political sphere, but few women had access to positions of leadership or impact over decision-making; the doors of higher education swung open to women, but women's returns on their education were far less than those of men;[7] and the door to the labor market opened wider,[8] but women were segregated into lower paid industries and occupations.

Thus, if discrimination is defined more broadly as unequal access to power and resources, discrimination was indeed rampant, despite the formal guarantees.[9] Men

---

4.   BARBARA EINHORN, CINDERELLA GOES TO MARKET: CITIZENSHIP, GENDER AND WOMEN'S MOVEMENTS IN EAST CENTRAL EUROPE 40 (1993).

5.   Although in some countries men as well as women could take child care leave, very few men did so.

6.   United Nations Economic and Social Council, High-Level Regional Preparatory Meeting for the Fourth World Conference on Women, *The Role of Women in the Transitional Processes: Facing a Major Challenge*, at para 12, U.N. Doc. E/ECE/RW/HLM 5 (1994) [hereinafter ECOSOC, The Role of Women in the Transitional Processes].

7.   Ireneusz Bialecki & Barbara Heyns, *Educational Attainment, the Status of Women, and the Private School Movement in Poland, in* DEMOCRATIC REFORM AND THE POSITION OF WOMEN IN TRANSITIONAL ECONOMIES (Valentina M. Moghadam ed., 1993).

8.   Women's participation rate in the labor market was extremely high, between 80 and 90 percent.

9.   *See* Belinda Cooper, *The Truth About Superwoman: Women in East Germany*, 5 MICH. FEMINIST STUD. 59 (1990) *See also* BARBARA JANCAR, WOMEN UNDER COMMUNISM (1978); ALENA HEITLINGER, WOMEN AND STATE SOCIALISM: SEX INEQUALITY IN THE SOVIET UNION AND CZECHOSLOVAKIA (1979); GAIL W. LAPIDUS, WOMEN IN SOVIET SOCIETY: EQUALITY, DEVELOPMENT, AND SOCIAL CHANGE (1978); HILDA SCOTT, DOES SOCIALISM LIBERATE WOMEN? (1974); Renate Siemienska, *Women, Work and Gender Equality in Poland: Reality and Its Social Perceptions, in* WOMEN, STATE AND PARTY IN EASTERN EUROPE (Sharon Wolchik & Alfred Meyer eds., 1985) [hereinafter Siemienska, *Women, Work and Gender Equality*]; Sharon Wolchik, *Eastern Europe, in* THE POLITICS OF THE SECOND ELECTORATE: WOMEN AND POLITICAL PARTICIPATION 252–77 (Joni Lovenduski & Jill Hills eds., 1981).

earned considerably more than women,[10] both because they held higher positions and received favorable treatment within the same industries and positions, and because women were concentrated in less prestigious, lower paid industries and occupations (in particular, education and health care). As a general rule, wherever women worked, the profession was of low status and more likely to be of a clerical nature. Indeed, although a large number of women were lawyers, judges, physicians, accountants, economists, and teachers,[11] women in these professions were generally low paid and poorly regarded.[12]

The gender-segregated labor market can be at least partially explained by traditional attitudes about men as decisionmakers and women as family caretakers—attitudes that persisted both *despite* and *because of* the system. Despite the rhetoric of equality, men had careers while most women just "went to work."[13] Men were more likely to find an environment for meaning and self-realization in the workplace. Women were still expected to find fulfillment within their family; their jobs were intended to be complementary to, but never competitive with or in lieu of, their family obligations.[14] Shortage economies required someone to queue for food, to scavenge for goods. That someone was women. By holding lower-status jobs, women could more easily slip away from the workplace to attend to family "emergencies," from finding milk to taking a sick child to the clinic.

These practices, deeply ingrained into the social culture,[15] have had long-term consequences on women's image as workers, decreasing their chances of being hired

---

10. In the 1980s in Bulgaria, Poland, Hungary and the former Czechoslovakia, between professionals within the same occupational category, women earned between 73 and 78 percent of men's salaries. Larger differences between male and female workers prevailed in other categories. ECOSOC, *The Role of Women in the Transitional Processes, supra* note 6, at para. 13 (citing Sabine Hubner et al., *Women's Employment in Central and Eastern Europe: Status and Prospects, in* STRUCTURAL CHANGES IN CENTRAL AND EASTERN EUROPE: LABOUR MARKET AND SOCIAL POLICY IMPLICATIONS (Gerog Fisher & Guy Standing eds., 1993).

11. For example, in the former Soviet Union, women accounted for 89 percent of all bookkeepers; 87 percent of economists; 70 percent of teachers and 67 percent of physicians. Natalia Rimashevskaia, *Perestroika and the Status of Women in the Soviet Union, in* WOMEN IN THE FACE OF CHANGE: THE SOVIET UNION, EASTERN EUROPE AND CHINA (Rai Shirin, Hilary Pilkington & Annie Phizacklea eds., 1992).

12. Men held the more prestigious posts within each of these professions (e.g., the lawyer permitted to work on foreign business contracts; the chief of the hospital or school; the government economist in charge of economic policy, etc).

13. Jirina Siklova, *Report on Women in the Post-Communist Central Europe (Personal View From Prague)* (cir. 1996, manuscript on file with author (unpaginated)).

14. *See* SUPERWOMEN AND THE DOUBLE BURDEN: WOMEN'S EXPERIENCE OF CHANGE IN CENTRAL AND EASTERN EUROPE AND THE FORMER SOVIET UNION 78 (Chris Corrin ed., 1992).

15. The International Labour Organization (ILO) has found that such practices have survived to a certain extent in state enterprises. An ILO survey conducted in the Czech and Slovak republics in 1991–92 found that 70 percent of women could leave their workplace to "attend to urgent personal matters" without much difficulty. Thirteen percent said they could leave "any time," 24 percent "sometimes" and 33 percent "exceptionally." PORI, 1991/92, Zamestnanost Zen: Zavercna sprava z vyzkumu, Public Opinion Research, Prague (*cited in* ECOSOC, *The Role of Women in the Transitional Processes, supra* note 6, at para. 11).

for more prestigious posts and depressing chances of promotion. Actual and imagined "female" attitudes toward work emerged, such as "poor assertion skills, evading success, fear of responsibility, and determination of job satisfaction by social conditions (company atmosphere, opportunity for personal communication) rather than by objective criteria (income, promotion prospects, leverage in collective bargaining)."[16] Managers came to view women as less "reliable" and more "expensive" workers.

Thus, the notion of formal equality was used by the state for its own purposes. After all, the social system demanded such an instrumental use of women. Women became a reserve labor pool, to be pushed into jobs where needs arose and dismissed during times of surplus. Women's "natural role as mothers" and the need to "populate the nation" could always be tapped to justify segregating women into lower paid jobs, forcing women into earlier retirement, or deciding when certain activities were dangerous to women's childbearing capacities.

The rhetoric of equality was similarly used by men in an attempt to keep women from demanding actual equality: "Any claims or complaints by women about the excessive burden [of daily household chores and labor in State enterprises—the double or triple burden—] provoked aggression: 'You wanted equality. Now you've got it. You have only yourself to blame.'"[17] The state-sanctioned women's organizations offered little retreat as they only championed women's glorious role as mother-worker. Restrictions on civil and political rights curtailed further possibilities for public associations that would work for change.

The lack of equality in the economic sphere affected various groups of women differently. Single mothers, elderly women, rural women, disabled women, and members of minority ethnic groups[18] had the worst chance of earning a decent living.[19] Women fared the best if they could earn a second income, through bribes, black market barter, and, in some cases, through private, legal markets for food and goods and

---

16. ECOSOC, *The Role of Women in the Transitional Processes, id.* at para. 12 (citing Hildegard Maria Nickel, *Women in the German Democratic Republic and in the New Federal States: Looking Backward and Looking Forward (Five Theses), in* GENDER POLITICS AND POST-COMMUNISM (Nanette Funk & Magda Muller eds., 1993).

17. Irina Jurna, *Women in Russia: Building a Movement, in* FROM BASIC NEEDS TO BASIC RIGHTS: WOMEN'S CLAIMS TO HUMAN RIGHTS 477, 482 (Margaret A. Schuler ed., 1995).

18. Women of minority ethnic, national, or religious groups face discrimination everywhere: Rom (gypsies; 3 million scattered throughout Central and Eastern Europe, but particularly in Romania, Slovakia and Hungary); Hungarians in Slovakia (some 600,000) and in Romania (1.6 million according to Romanians; 2 million according to Hungarians), Serbia (300,000), and Ukraine (some 200,000); Albanians in Kosovo (2 million), Serbia proper, and Macedonia (at least 430,000); Slovaks in Hungary (20,000); Jews throughout Eastern Europe (especially in Hungary, where the Jewish population totals roughly 85,000 and in Poland where anti-Semitism is particularly strong); Germans in Poland, the Czech Republic, and Hungary; and Russians in Ukraine, Estonia, Latvia and elsewhere. *That Other Europe,* THE ECONOMIST, Dec. 25, 1993, at 17.

19. *See, e.g.,* Frances Pine, *Uneven Burden: Women in Rural Poland, in* WOMEN IN THE FACE OF CHANGE: THE SOVIET UNION, EASTERN EUROPE AND CHINA (Shirin Rai, Hilary Pilkington & Annie Phiacklear eds., 1992).

private-sector services. The possibilities for the "second economy" varied greatly from country to country and, within countries, between rural and urban areas.[20]

Women, like men, retreated into the private sphere. Societies were more of the communal type, based on family solidarity and connection, rather than modern societies based on performance, contract, and impersonal connection. Thus, "[i]t was only important to conform, to hunt for goods, arrange for kids to be accepted into schools, hold values of basic survival, [and] maintain hearth and home."[21] Women and men faced one common enemy, the regime: "Women blamed communism, or more accurately the rhetoric of communism as well as themselves for their misfortune."[22] For many women, opposing the formal equality and the double burden that went along with it was "part of opposing Communism."[23]

HUMAN RIGHTS OF WOMEN IN TRANSITION ECONOMIES

The collapse of socialist regimes raised women's expectations for realizing their human rights.[24] Indeed, almost overnight, women (and men) gained several social and political rights, such as the right to association, to travel, to speech and the press, and the freedom to organize political parties and participate freely in the political process. Yet few of these rights have led to significant improvements in the ability of women to participate in political and social life; instead, women have been losing many of the benefits acquired in the past.[25]

The changes most affecting women's human rights in CEE are part of larger shifts in the global economy. The entities that now virtually dictate global economic policies—the World Bank, the International Monetary Fund (IMF), and the U.S.— are promoting policies of "structural adjustment," rewarding states' attempts to promote the market orientation of economies (instead of valuing states' equitable distribution of social benefits). In exchange for cash grants or commodity transfers,

---

20. Women in large urban areas in Hungary, for example, had the possibility of renting out parts of their flat to tourists, while such practice was largely unheard of in rural areas within Hungary, and strictly forbidden in other countries, such as Ukraine and Romania. In some countries, such as Yugoslavia and Hungary, women with higher education, and in particular doctors and lawyers, could combine state jobs with private practice. In general, however, such private practices tended to be dominated by men.

21. Zora Butorova (FOCUS Agency for use of the Alliance of Slovak Women), *Men and Women at the Crossroads of Social Expectations* (cir. 1996, unpaginated) (monograph, draft on file with author) (citing M. Frisova) [hereinafter Slovakia Report on Women].

22. Krisztina Morvai, *Continuity and Discontinuity in the Legal System: What it Means for Women: A Female Lawyer's Perspective on Women and the Law in Hungary*, 5 UCLA WOMEN'S L.J. 63, 66 (1994).

23. *Id.*

24. *See* Elzbieta Matynia, *Women After Communism: A Bitter Freedom*, 61 SOCIAL RESEARCH 2, 356 (1994).

25. Sharon Wolchik, *International Trends in Central and Eastern Europe: Women in Transition in the Czech and Slovak Republic—The First Three Years*, 5(3) J. WOMEN'S HISTORY 100–107 (1994).

countries agree to measures "aimed toward increasing exports, promoting private and direct foreign investment, privatizing public-sector enterprises and cutting back on state provided social welfare services."[26] To various degrees across CEE, governments have withdrawn from economic management of economic activities, turning the reins over to private companies.[27] In return, private and governmental investments in CEE have soared; social conditions for the majority of the population have plummeted.[28]

Five attributes of the transition to a market economy have had a particular impact on women's human rights:[29]

(1) the dismantling of the welfare state;

(2) increased unemployment and non-employment;

(3) declining levels of income and increased poverty;

(4) overt job discrimination and continued occupational segregation; and

(5) a surge of traditional attitudes towards gender roles.

Each of these issues will be discussed separately below.

The Dismantling of the Welfare State

In the new market economies of the CEE, the very conceptualization of social and economic rights has been transformed. Under the old command (or quasi-command) economies, social and economic rights had been "defined in terms of goods and services" and social outcomes, and "employment-related rights [had] been the means through which these goods and services had been disbursed."[30] In other words, the state enterprise distributed the things that made economic and social rights real, such as child care, pensions, and health care. In contrast, under the free market economies of the industrialized west, "social and economic rights are defined within the context of the market" and thus "employment-related rights are largely limited to granting women equal access to the market."[31] This reconceptualization has resulted in a net loss for women. Women in CEE have always had access to the labor mar-

---

26.   Rebecca A. Sewall, *Reconstructing Social and Economic Rights in Transitional Economies, in* FROM BASIC NEEDS TO BASIC RIGHTS: WOMEN'S CLAIMS TO HUMAN RIGHTS 155, 159 (Margaret A. Schuler ed., 1995) [hereinafter Sewall].

27.   *See* ECE, ECONOMIC SURVEY FOR EUROPE 1992–1993 (Geneva, Sales No.E.93.II.E.1), Chapter 3 (discussing process of privatization); *see also* PRIVITIZATION IN THE TRANSITION PROCESS: RECENT EXPERIENCES IN EASTERN EUROPE (Yilmaz Akyüz et al. eds., U.N. Publications, Sales No. E.94.II.D.2S).

28.   *See* UNICEF, *Public Policy and Social Conditions, Regional Monitoring Report (Eastern Europe)*, No. 1, Nov. 1993.

29.   Similar attributes are identified in ECOSOC, *The Role of Women in the Transitional Processes, supra* note 6.

30.   Sewall, *supra* note 26, at 166.

31.   *Id.*

ket. They gain something they already had, while effectively losing social and economic rights.

Under the centrally planned economies, the social safety system had provided guaranteed employment, housing, health care, child care, vacation, education, livable pensions, and emergency support.[32] With increasing independence from the state, enterprises have discontinued most benefits, forcing the government and specialized private agencies to take up the slack.[33] Yet growing unemployment rates in CEE have strained already taxed public and private resources.[34] The message to unfortunate workers is that unless they can afford to pay, they will just have to do without.

Women bear a large share of the burden of the dismantling of the welfare state. As in other countries undergoing "structural adjustment,"[35] the protective labor laws that once favored the rights of women are now being viewed as impediments to economic growth. Child support systems, including family/child allowances, nurseries, and kindergartens, are now closed entirely or partially, or privatized and thus open only to those who can afford to pay.[36] Declines in family benefits have increased women's "caring" functions; when the state will not pay for care of the elderly, women are expected to take on this role. Many women find themselves spending more time on caretaking of family members than ever before. Thus, deteriorating economic conditions have increased pressure on women to earn more while simultaneously limiting their ability to do so.

The threat to women's economic and social rights places all women's rights in jeopardy. As long as women are impoverished and overburdened, they cannot begin to participate fully in society. Accordingly, "the shift from one economic system to another signals the need for a redefinition for women's social and economic rights, and new employment-related mechanisms to uphold these rights."[37] Women in the

---

32. Violeta Roxin & Janos Hoos, *Social Services in Eleven Central and East European Countries—Comparative Aspects, in* REFORMING SOCIAL SERVICES IN EASTERN EUROPE—AN ELEVEN NATION OVERVIEW 281–318 (Victor A. Pestoff ed., 1995).

33. *See* George Kopits, *Social Security, in* FISCAL POLICIES IN ECONOMIES IN TRANSITION (Vito Tanzi ed., 1992); REFORMING SOCIAL SERVICES IN EASTERN EUROPE—AN ELEVEN NATION OVERVIEW (Victor A. Pestoff ed., 1995).

34. *See* Lucjan T. Orlowski, *Social Safety Nets in Central Europe: Preparation for Accession to the European Union?*, 37(2) COMPARATIVE ECONOMIC STUDIES 29 (1995).

35. *See* G. Standing, *Feminism Through Flexible Labor*, 17 WORLD DEVELOPMENT 1077–1095 (1989).

36. The closures were extremely fast. Out of 773 kindergartens run by Slovak enterprises in 1989, only 196 remained in 1992; in Hungary only 1 percent of children of the relevant age group attend enterprise-run kindergartens. ECOSOC, *The Role of Women in the Transitional Processes, supra* note 6, at para. 49. Although the old system of child care was infamous in some places for its low standard of care, and in particular a high child/career ratio, many women still for long what was. *See* Ewa Ruminska-Zimny, *The Family and Society: Facing Socio-Economic and Political Crisis*, United Nations Interregional Seminar on Women in Development, Warsaw, May 29–31, 1989.

37. Sewall, *supra* note 26, at 156.

region have identified the right to return to work after pregnancy, a right once enjoyed under the old regimes, as one that must be protected in the new market systems. Some activists have also targeted maternity leave in general, arguing that the legal approach should be changed to parental leave in order to challenge the stereotype of "women's duties" and to foster the father's involvement in raising children. As the country-by-country survey, included *infra*, indicates, some of these measures have been adopted in certain countries, while others are still wanting.

Increased Unemployment and Non-Employment

Women have been the main losers in the restructuring of CEE economies with regard to access to the labor market. The decline in manufacturing employment was faster for women than for men; female administrative and clerical jobs were drastically reduced in the processing structure while male jobs on the production line experienced less drastic decreases.[38] In countries with a large agricultural sector, structural changes have had adverse effects on women's employment as women have traditionally been employed in large numbers on state farms, in particular in administration.[39] Unemployment rates for women have increased in all countries except for the Czech Republic and, apart from Hungary and Slovenia, the gap between female and male unemployment has widened.[40] In the Russian Federation and in other CIS countries, the share of women among the unemployed has reached a particular high, estimated at 70 to 80 percent.[41]

This figure tells only part of the story. A little hocus pocus with the labor statistics keeps unemployment rates far lower than the actual employment picture. One way states hide underutilization of labor is by encouraging workers to leave the work force. Early retirement schemes have been very popular throughout the CEE, particularly in the Czech Republic, Hungary, Romania, and Slovakia.[42] The "non-employment rate"—that is, the rate of the population that is not seeking work and thus cannot be counted as unemployed—has increased in CEE at a much more rapid rate than the unemployment rate. In Hungary, for instance, the non-employment rate rose from 16

---

38.   ECOSOC, *The Role of Women in the Transitional Processes*, *supra* note 6, at para. 39.

39.   *Id.* at para. 40.

40.   United Nations Economic and Social Council, High-Level Regional Preparatory Meetings for the Fourth World Conference on Women, Vienna, Oct. 17–21, 1994, *"Women's Access to Employment and Entrepreneurship,"* U.N.Doc. E/ECE/RW/HLM/4, 1994 [hereinafter ECOSOC, *Women's Access to Employment*].

41.   Guy Standing, *Structural Changes and the Labor Market Crisis in Eastern and Central Europe, in* STRUCTURAL CHANGE, EMPLOYMENT AND UNEMPLOYMENT IN THE MARKET AND TRANSITION ECONOMIES (1994); *see also* E. Gruzdeva, L. Rzhanitsyna, & S. Khotkina, *Women in the Labour Market*, 35 (10) PROBLEMS IN TRANSITION (1993).

42.   *See* Lucjan T. Orlowski, *Social Safety Nets in Central Europe: Preparation for Accession to the European Union?*, 37 COMP. ECON. STUD. 29 (1995), available on LEXIS (pg. nos. not available) (stating that rising structural unemployment has increased the number of those seeking early retirement and pension benefits.)

to 32 percent between 1990 and 1993.[43] Frequently, women have little incentive to register as unemployed, either because unemployment benefits are extremely low or other social benefits induce women to exit the workforce altogether.[44] Thus unemployment figures alone do not accurately reflect their social situation.

A survey carried out by a Bulgarian national public opinion research institute in 1992 found that 77.7 percent of all respondents saw unemployment as the most acute problem facing Bulgarian women.[45] That percentage is likely to be even greater today as economic conditions in Bulgaria have only deteriorated. Economic conditions vary greatly from country to country within the region and, as the Bulgarian example shows, conditions are subject to cyclical variations.[46] Out of over 100 women surveyed from the region nearly all, with the exception of women from the Czech Republic, listed "economic conditions," "unemployment," or "poverty" as the top concern facing women in their country.[47] When asked why, they again stressed the interrelationship between these rights and other rights.

Declining Income and Increasing Poverty

In all countries in CEE, real wages have decreased over the past five years,[48] and poverty has increased in turn. The impact on women and children has been particularly severe, since women were already at the bottom of the pay scale and were less likely to participate in black market or private sector activities that could help them make up for the decline in official wages. To make ends meet, many women in CEE now work several part-time jobs in addition to doing their household tasks. As exhaustion has set in, the overall health condition of women has fallen dramatically. For example, according to data from medical checkups in Bulgaria in 1993, only 30 percent of all women were healthy or practically healthy; in 1983, 68 percent of women

---

43. Martin Godfrey, *The Struggle Against Unemployment: Medium-Term Policy Options for Transitional Economies*, 134 (1) INT'L LABOUR REV. 3 (1995).

44. For example, under Hungarian law, mothers can receive, in addition to a five-month maternity leave, 75 percent of their previous salary until the child is two years old. The child allowance is greater than unemployment benefits and the entitlement period lasts longer. Klara Foti, *Rising Unemployment in Hungary: Causes and Remedies* (Hungarian Academy of Science, Working Paper No. 24, Aug. 1993).

45. Nacionalen Centr za Izuchavane na Obschestvenoto Mnenie (National center of Public Opinion research), Socialniat Status na Svremennata Blgarska Zhena, Oct. 1992, Sofia (*cited in* ECOSOC, The Role of Women in the Transitional Processes, *supra* note 6, at para. 42).

46. Cycles tend to be related to political crises and elections.

47. The survey of subjective preferences of women in the region was supplemented with other sources from the region. Thus, although the sample is not scientific, the finding that women tend to be most concerned with economic issues is supported by a variety of sources.

48. The cumulative fall in real wages over 1990–1993 varied from 12 to 15 percent for Hungary and the Czech Republic to around 30 percent for Poland. The fall was even worse in countries in conflict, such as the former Yugoslavia, and where the economic transition was accompanied by an abrupt disintegration of the former federal structures, such as Ukraine or Moldova. ECOSOC, The Role of Women in the Transitional Processes, *supra* note 6, at para. 44.

were said to be healthy or practically healthy.[49] Severe environmental degradation has only exacerbated health problems.

Single mothers and large families are among those most likely to be impoverished. By 1993 in Poland, "three-quarters of single mother families and over a half of families with at least four children were living below the poverty line."[50] Other particularly vulnerable social groups include elderly women, the disabled, migrants, refugees (mainly women and children),[51] and members of minority ethnic, national, or racial groups. While these groups are vulnerable everywhere, including in Western Europe and the U.S.,[52] they face particular hardships in CEE where severe poverty and lack of economic opportunities are rarely addressed by social institutions, either because such institutions do not exist or because they are inoperable.[53] In many countries, pensions for the elderly and the disabled decreased in value at an accelerated pace while the cost of public utilities and food has soared. In Bulgaria, for example, the pension for a disabled person in the spring of 1996, before the tremendous inflation, was barely enough to pay for a household's electricity and heating. After the onset of inflation, the pension was almost worthless.[54]

Sociologists within the region blame poverty and unemployment for escalating crime rates, including an overall increase in the number of crimes committed by women. In Russia, for example, women committed about 238,000 crimes in 1995, up from 142,000 in 1993. Also in 1995, over 5,600 women were convicted of premeditated murder and about 3,350 of grievous bodily harm.[55]

Poverty has also led to rapidly declining birth rates.[56] Gail Kligman has underscored that "[i]t is a significant anomaly that while the economic needs of eastern Europe may be compared with those of developing countries, demographic trends (especially declining birthrates) mirror those of Western Europe."[57] Fertility rates

---

49. *Bulgaria—Situation of Women, United Nations National and Global Development, NGO Report for Beijing,* U.N. Development Programme (1995), at 4.

50. B. Aciak, *Family Benefits and Social Policy in Poland, in* FAMILIES, POLITICS AND THE LAW: PERSPECTIVES FOR EAST AND WEST EUROPE 284 (Mavis Maclean & Jacek Kurczewski eds., 1994).

51. Xenophobia has grown in Europe in recent years. *See* Mort Rosenblum, *Europeans Target Immigrants With New Hatred,* CHI. TRIB., Nov. 16, 1995, at 8; Jennifer Monahan, *Fortress Europe: Backlash Against Refugees,* 8 (354) NEW STATESMAN & SOCIETY, June 26, 1995, at S10.

52. *See* Pauline Conroy & Niamh Flanagan, *Women and Poverty in the European Community: Issues in the Current Debate* (Commission of European Communities, V/4294–EN, 1953).

53. ECOSOC, Women's Role in the Economy, *supra* note 42, at para. 23.

54. Example drawn from actual case in Bulgaria known to author.

55. OMRI DAILY DIGEST, Feb. 1, 1996 (available at www.omri.cz). The total number of recorded crimes in 1995 was about 2.75 million. *Id.*

56. Nicholas Eberstadt, *Demographic Shocks in Eastern Germany, 1989–93,* 46 EUROPE-ASIA STUDIES 519, 520 (1994).

57. Gail Kligman, *Gendering the Postsocialist Tradition: Women in Eastern Europe,* AAASS NEWSNET, Mar. 1994, at 3.

dropped in all countries in CEE in the early 1900s.[58] In East Germany, for example, births in 1992 amounted to 44 percent of the 1989 total. Many women in CEE see eradication of poverty as an essential component to improving women's reproductive freedom. While also supporting safe and legal abortion for women and advocating for improvements in women's health care, many women find that the freedom to have children does not exist in the wake of poverty.

Overt Gender Discrimination and Continued Job Segregation

Although formal equality still exists in theory, gender discrimination has intensified in the workplace. Women have a hard time breaking into the new jobs that have been created in the transition—including high paid positions with foreign firms, the private service sector, and entrepreneurial activities. Businesses overtly give preference to male workers in recruitment, job training, and promotion.[59] The preference is particularly marked in the case of professional and technical work and skilled manual labor, except for the textile industry where women still tend to predominate.[60] Newspapers are full of gender-segregated advertisements: men with good education and training are wanted for managerial, sales, and decision-making positions; pretty, young, slim women can apply for positions as secretaries. Ads for females sometimes "feature code words like 'available' or 'open-minded' to signal that successful applicants must be sexually available to their superiors."[61] Foreign firms that could never place gender specific advertisements in their own countries take advantage of gaps in discrimination legislation in CEE.[62]

Young women face extreme obstacles in hiring. While older women may be hired for their skills and potential contribution to the workplace, younger women are hired to "improve the social climate." Romania has one of the worst records in this regard. According to government statistics, women aged fifteen to twenty-four are over twice as likely to be unemployed as men of the same age.[63]

Although in most countries in CEE women tend to be more educated than men,[64] their return on their education continues to be low. In all countries in CEE women

---

58. For statistics, *see International Child Development Centre, Central and eastern Europe in Transition: Public Policy and Social Conditions*, 1 Regional Monitoring Report 73 (1993).

59. For an ILO survey on gender discrimination in the labor market, *see* Liba Paukert, *Women's Employment in east-Central European Countries During the Period of Transition to a Market Economy* (Working Paper, ILO, Geneva, 1993).

60. *Id.*

61. Kim Lane Schepple, *Women's Rights in Eastern Europe*, East Eur. Constit. Rev. 66, 66 (Winter 1995) [hereinafter Schepple, *Women's Rights*].

62. Not only does the law not forbid gender specific advertisements, but also public opinion appears to accept such practices. In surveys conducted by the author with youth groups in Romania, for example, less than 5 percent of the young people surveyed saw any problem with gender specific advertisements. The practice, in the words of one young woman, was "natural."

63. ILO Yearbook of Labour Statistics 1993, 1994; ILO World Labour Report 1994. The official statistics are thought to be low since women are more frequently counted as "inactive" and "nonemployed" and thus not included in the labor statistics.

64. According to the United Nations Educational, Scientific and Cultural Organization

continue to earn less than men[65] due to inequalities in the distribution of men and women across occupations and industrial sectors, the low valuation attached to jobs where women predominate, and from inequality in pay across these divisions. An inverse correlation exists between the employment share of women in an industry and the relative level of pay in that industry.[66] Women continue to be segregated in lower paying jobs and occupations. In Slovakia, for example, in 1995 women comprised over half the work force in the following branches of the economy: clothing industry (90 percent); health care and social care (80 percent); textile industry (79 percent); education (78 percent); banking and insurance (70 percent); and hotels and restaurants (66 percent).[67]

Even if women have a job, they are unlikely to keep it. Job security has decreased dramatically for women in CEE.[68] New market conditions can explain only part of the decrease; discrimination explains a large share of the rest. Even in the same industries and occupations, women are likely to be the first to be fired or terminated in the name of economic efficiency.[69] Employers still view women as more expensive, more expendable workers, and fail to offer them the kind of flexible work schedules that would allow them to meet all of their multiple demands. Some women have gone through drastic measures to keep their jobs, complying with their employers' direct or indirect challenges to fundamental freedoms relating to bodily integrity, life, and health. According to Editha Beier, Secretary for Women in Saxony-Anhalt (Germany), some women are even "having themselves sterilized either because their employers tell them they must, or because they believe it to be their only chance."[70] Other women are turning a blind eye to sexual harassment—an epidemic in CEE workplaces.[71]

(UNESCO) the only countries in what could be considered Central and Eastern Europe that have more males than females in third-level education (university) are the Czech Republic, Romania and the Federal Republic of Germany (up to 1990). The highest ratio of female students to male students in the entire ECE region are in Iceland (144); Poland (127), Portugal (127); Sweden (117) and Ukraine (117); the lowest are in Turkey (52) and Switzerland (54). UNITED NATIONS EDUCATIONAL, SCIENTIFIC AND CULTURAL ORGANIZATION, STATISTICAL YEARBOOK (Paris 1993).

65.   For example, in 1990 unskilled Hungarian male workers earned on average 15 percent more than women in the same occupation. Gyorgy Sziraczki & Jim Windell, *The Impact of Employment Restructuring on Disadvantaged Groups in Bulgaria and Hungary* (Working Paper No. 62, WEP 2–43/WP.62, ILO, January 1993).

66.   United Nations Economic and Social Council, High-Level Regional Preparatory Meetings for the Fourth World Conference on Women, Vienna, Oct. 17–21, 1994, "*Women's Access to Employment and Entrepreneurship*," at para 73, U.N. Doc. E/ECE/RW/HLM/4 (1994) [hereinafter ECOSOC, *Women's Access to Employment*].

67.   Slovakia Report on Women, *supra* note 21.

68.   For an overview of the problem of women and employment in CEE, *see* FAMILY, WOMEN AND EMPLOYMENT IN CENTRAL-EASTERN EUROPE (Barbara Lobodzinska ed., 1995).

69.   ECOSOC, *The Role of Women in the Transitional Processes, supra* note 6, at para. 42.

70.   *Berlin Wall Down, Gloom and Sterilization Up*, INT'L HERALD TRIB., May 25, 1992.

71.   Women have longed faced sexual harassment in CEE workplaces: "While the display of naked female bodies is a new social phenomenon accompanying political thaw and the advent of mass culture and advertising, the communication of dirty jokes and innuendoes in the workplace is not new." The only new component is that some women are now beginning to label the behavior as impermissible and intolerable. Slovakia Report on Women, *supra* note 21.

Migrant women in and from CEE[72] are particularly susceptible to human rights abuses, as they often work in isolation and without social or legal protections as domestic workers. Similarly, employers often take advantage of women from minority ethnic, religious, or linguistic groups. Women's groups in CEE have begun to address the needs of these populations. For example, Rom (gypsy) women's groups in Hungary have organized to address human rights and labor abuses in both the public and private spheres; in Croatia, Slovenia, Bosnia-Herzegovina, and Serbia, a number of women's groups (including those organized by women refugees for women refugees) promote the social, economic, and political rights of refugees; in Russia, women from the Caucases and other areas in conflict have spearheaded anti-war and human rights campaigns.

Surge of Traditional Attitudes Toward Gender Roles

Traditional attitudes toward gender roles have (re)surfaced and gained prominence in CEE since the transition. The resurgence comes in many flavors; the ability of the ideology to influence social behavior depends on the particular history and culture of a country, its present economic and political status, and the fortification efforts already undertaken by women to resist either the traditional attitudes or alternative values of feminisms (indeed feminism has been rejected by many CEE states as another oppressive -ism or an irrelevant foreign implant).

In some areas, society trumpets the "right not to work,"[73] as a new "choice" delivered by democracy. Yet few have the option to not work. Not only does economic necessity force women into the labor force, but also many women seek fulfilling and interesting careers. After all, the female labor force in CEE is one of the most highly educated in the world. The "Cinderella complex" has limited appeal to the many women who, like men, wish to make the most of the transition, through increased professional (and personal) travel, international collegial exchanges, better working conditions, improved chances for advancement, and new avenues for personal growth and enrichment.

In other areas, traditionalism entwines itself with the platform of nationalists. Andjelka Milic has noted that "nationalism needs women, but only women constructed in a nationalist image."[74] Women's bodies become the vessel for new foot soldiers for the national cause; women's homes become the training ground in which dutiful members of the nation[75] are nurtured and indoctrinated. It is deemed that in order to do

---

72. Migration from East to West has increased due to wage differential and growing unemployment in the East and to an influx of refugees from war-affected zones. *See* RICHARD LAYARD ET. AL., EAST-WEST MIGRATION: THE ALTERNATIVES (1992).

73. *See* Laryssa Lissyutkina, *Soviet Women at the Crossroads of Perestroika, in* GENDER POLITICS AND POST-COMMUNISM (Nanette Funk & Magda Muller eds., 1993).

74. Andjelka Milic, *Nationalism and Sexism: Eastern Europe in Transition, in* EUROPE'S NEW NATIONALISM 169–83 (Richard Caplan & John Feffer eds., 1996) [hereinafter Milic].

75. The use of the word "nation" here is in line with the CEE usage. Here, "nation" (narod) signifies a people, not a state (the U.S. equation of nation). Although the people may be an "ethnic"

their part for their nation, women must fulfill their sacred role as mothers.[76] In Croatia, for example, anti-abortion forces, working closely with Croatian nationalists, have exerted pressure on Parliament to adopt measures that would foster "democratic renewal of the nation."[77] Linking their call to increase the birth rate among Croat women with the demand that immigration of non-Croats be curtailed and non-Croat refugees be "returned," anti-abortion organizations succeeded in pressuring Parliament to pass a National Program for Demographic Development. Adopted in January 1996, this program calls for a "positive spiritual atmosphere" to be created through "protection of the family as a basic social unit" and recognition that the family is the "headquarters of the renewal of the nation and state."[78] The Program simultaneously warns against massive immigration of "demographically stronger peoples" (i.e., refugees from Bosnia) and foresees privileges for (Croatian) families with three or more children.[79]

One particular variant of the resurgence in traditionalism is found in countries that are also experiencing the (re)emergence of a powerful, state-aligned religion. Poland is often held out as an example of a state closely tied to the Roman Catholic Church. There, the Church plays a crucial role in political attempts to roll back women's rights and to reinforce women's "natural" role as mother and caretaker. But the Roman Catholic Church plays a similar role, albeit with perhaps less state-sanctioned power, in Croatia and Slovakia; the Orthodox Church in Serbia and Romania has entered the ideological debate over the role of women. In these countries and elsewhere, so-called religious values are used strategically to promote the country's own particular brand of nationalism. In the power struggles that have emerged in these contested states, politicians who never professed a religious faith in the past are suddenly arguing that, in the name of church and state, women should return to the family.

---

group, ethnicity may not be the market for the nation; people from the same ethnic groups can be said to be of different nations (for example, Slavic people can be Russian, Serb, Croat, Slovak, etc.). The literature on nationalism presents conflicting definitions of the term. *See, e.g.*, ERNEST GELLNER, NATIONS AND NATIONALISM (1983); BENEDICT ANDERSON, IMAGINED COMMUNITIES (1993); JOHN BREUILLY, NATIONALISM AND THE STATE (1994); WILL KYMLICKA, MULTICULTURAL CITIZENSHIP (1995); DAVID MILLER, ON NATIONALITY (1995); SUKUMAR PERIWAL, NOTIONS OF NATIONALISM (1995); MONTSERRAT GUIBERNAU, NATIONALISM: THE NATION-STATE AND NATIONALISM IN THE TWENTIETH CENTURY (1996). For an excellent overview of the debate over "ethnicity," *see* JOHN HUTCHINSON & ANTHONY D. SMITH, ETHNICITY (1996).

76.   Julie Mertus, *Gender in the Service of Nation: Female Citizenship in Kosovar Society*, 3 (2/3) SOCIAL POLITICS: INT'L STUDIES IN GENDER, STATE AND SOCIETY (1996) [hereinafter Mertus, SOCIAL POLITICS]. For an overview of the rise of the far right in Europe, *see* LUCIANO CHELES, RONNIE FERGUSON & MICHALINA CAUGHAN, THE FAR RIGHT IN WESTERN AND EASTERN EUROPE (2d ed. 1995).

77.   *Croatian Pro-Lifers Attacking Women's Rights*, B.A.B.E BULLETIN, Jan. 31, 1996 (available at BABE_ZG@ZAMIR-ZG.ZTN.APC.ORG). The use of the term nation here refers to the people, not the state—that is, to the Croat nation.

78.   *Id.*

79.   *Id.* For a discussion of similar pronatalist policies in Serbia, *see* Mertus, SOCIAL POLITICS, *supra* note 76; and RENATA SALECL, THE SPOILS OF FREEDOM: PSYCHOANALYSIS AND FREEDOM AFTER THE FALL OF SOCIALISM (1994).

Equal enjoyment of human rights entails much more than legislation affirming equal rights for women or, in the words of many constitutions, mandating equality "between men and women." It also involves the breakdown of gender stereotyping, which alters the balance in power between men and women and prevents women from realizing their rights.[80] To date, the new free press in CEE has tended to feed into the hands of nationalists/traditionalists by promoting gender stereotyping. Several women's groups in CEE, and in particular in Russia, have launched alternative media campaigns to challenge gender stereotypes. And, despite the immediate, short-term political costs, women's groups in many countries have challenged the rhetoric of nationalists and neo-traditionalists.

EXAMINING THE STATUS OF WOMEN TODAY

At first glance, women's status under the laws of Central and Eastern Europe appears to be quite similar. The Constitutions of all countries in CEE boast a provision formally mandating gender equality. Although most provisions of the laws are gender-neutral, the Labour and Family Codes of all countries, and in some cases the Constitutions, still provide a remnant of the protectionist legislation of the prior regime, although the extent of cash and in-kind benefits varies greatly from country to country. Most of the Labor Codes prohibit sex-based discrimination as well, although none of the countries provide an effective means for explicit redress for women subjected to discrimination. None of the countries sufficiently safeguard women's right to freedom from violence, neglecting in particular marital rape, domestic violence, and sexual harassment.

Many significant differences exist between countries, some of which may be surprising to an outside reader. Albania has one of the most explicit laws on sexual harassment in Europe (although the definition of sexual harassment is rather narrow) and one of the only women-run psychological counseling centers for women and children victims of violence. The wage gap in Hungary is among the worst in all of Europe; nevertheless, Hungary, along with Slovenia, remains one of only two countries in CEE where women's official rate of unemployment is lower than men's rate. While the abortion rate has declined in nearly all countries as contraceptives have become more accessible,[81] the rate has soared in Bulgaria. Women entrepreneurs tend to progress more easily in the Czech Republic than in any other country, but women in Ukraine have been among the most active in promoting women in small business. Women's human rights education campaigns have been particularly strong in Ukraine, Russia, Kosovo, and Croatia.

---

80. General Comment N-18, in General Comments Adopted by the Human Rights Committee Under Article 40, Paragraph 4 of the International Covenant on Civil and Political Rights: Addendum, Human Rights Committee, U.N. Doc. CCR/C/21/Rev.1/Add.1, P5 (1989).

81. The only exceptions are Bulgaria and Romania. Still, abortion remains widespread, ranging from 2.5 to 4 abortions per woman (over the course of her lifetime) in the former USSR, to 1.5 in the rest of CEE. By contrast, in Western Europe and the U.S., the figure is no higher than .63 per woman. 47 (3) WORLD HEALTH 18 (Bulletin of the World Health Organization, May 1994).

Some of the differences may be anticipated: Romania is the only country in which lesbians may still be sent to prison if their mere existence causes a "public scandal" and thus Romanian lesbians are among the most invisible in all of CEE. Polish women have faced the toughest challenges to women's reproductive freedom, but Polish women's reproductive rights advocates have also been among the most highly organized and effective human rights groups in CEE; in 1996 they succeeded in pressuring the Polish legislature to liberalize the abortion law. Forced prostitution and sex trafficking is a problem for women in every country, but it has been identified as a primary concern only by women's groups in the Czech Republic (where gender studies programs are strong and individual women academics and activists have taken a primary interest in the issue) and in Ukraine and Russia (two of the main countries from which sex traffickers "recruit").

Respondents to the survey were asked, "What are the top issues facing women in your country?" Women in every country except for the Czech Republic listed "poor economic conditions" or "unemployment among women" as a primary concern. In justifying their choice, they pointed to the interconnectedness of social and economic rights and civil and political rights. Without resources, they noted, women cannot begin to form women's organizations, run for political office, or exercise their rights to free association and speech. Female workers desperate for a job are in a poor position to demand decent and fair working conditions and equitable employment opportunities. Women still burdened with the double or triple burden have little time to press for their right to be free from violence. The collapse of the welfare state and burden of privatization has taken its toll on women's ability to effectuate any of their human rights.

Another issue identified by women in nearly all countries as a primary concern is violence against women, including domestic violence, rape, and other forms of assault. Social and economic changes accompanying structural transformation have led to an increase in violence. Every country has women's groups that work specifically on the issue of violence against women; nearly all have shelters. However, these efforts are limited mainly to large urban areas and, for the most part, violence against women remains a hidden social problem.

The degree of attention to violence now paid by women's groups, some CEE women activists maintained, may be influenced greatly by the agendas of foreign women's groups (and in particular women from the United States and Western Europe) who list violence as a primary concern of their own.[82] Like women in Western Europe and the United States, women in CEE are unlikely to report instances of violence to police or to seek legal redress. Women in CEE, like many women worldwide, fear the social stigma that reporting such crimes will entail. However, CEE women are motivated by other considerations, which are perhaps only common to those faced by

---

82. Regarding outside influence, "[i]t is impossible to separate out some 'natural' urge we have to work on these issues from the influence of the West," Z., a Croatian women activist remarked, for, "Who knows what we would have done if we were somehow in a bubble?" Interview with author, Boston, Nov. 1996.

minority women in Western Europe and the United States: there is no tradition of turning to the police or the legal system for *anything*. For these women, the legal system has traditionally existed to oppress, to deny rights.[83] Addressing the problems of domestic violence and sexual assault thus entails tackling the fears of generations toward the state institutions and their agents—the police, prosecutors, and judges.

Another phenomena which Central and Eastern European women experience differently is forced prostitution and trafficking in women. Quite simply, women in CEE are likely to be the target of "the trade." In the sex trade in "the west," CEE women are increasingly being marketed since they are more likely to be AIDS-free.[84] Answering advertisements for waitresses, dancers, models, and wives, few women have any idea what they are to expect from their new position. They hope only to escape the desperate economic situation back home. Their "handlers" often take their passport as collateral, thus denying them possible escape routes. Most European organizations have done little to address the problem. For example, the European organization for police cooperation, Europol, concentrates on tracking down stolen cars in Europe; stolen women are not an issue, much less a priority.[85]

The final issue identified as a primary concern is women's low participation in political life.[86] Since women were not compromised to the same degree as men by their collaboration with the former regimes, one would expect them to be more politically active today.[87] Instead, women are grossly underrepresented in formal political life. The phenomenon is particularly acute in nationalist dominated areas, as nationalists' implicit "tactic is to retard any open politicization of women: what is called for from them instead is patience, solidarity, participation and tolerance of initial hardships."[88] When women enter the political stage set by nationalists, they often adopt "a role circumscribed for them by the very nationalist discourse they opposed—the role of mothers."[89] Hence, there has been a long chain of mothers marching for peace in Croatia, Serbia, and the Caucases.

To the extent that women are active in CEE social and political issues, their activities tend to be concentrated predominately on the local level, outside of formal pol-

---

83.   In addition, prosecutors and state attorneys are mistrusted—in the past they had cooperated closely with the state.

84.   *European Parliament Debates Growing Trade in Women and Children*, THE REUTER EUROPEAN COMMUNITY REPORT, Jan. 19, 1996 (unpaginated).

85.   The Chairperson of the European Parliament's Committee on Women's Rights is attempting to make trafficking in women a priority. *Euro Drive for Women's Rights Pledged*, THE IRISH TIMES, May 16, 1996, at 7.

86.   Only Serbian women activists gave the matter little attention; nearly all independent women's groups in Serbia have stressed refusal to cooperate with the official regime in any respect. Observation drawn from author's work in the field.

87.   *See* Siklova, *supra* note 13.

88.   Ewa Hauser, Barbara Heyns, & Jane Mansbridge, *Feminism in the Intersection of Politics and Culture, in* GENDER POLITICS AND POST-COMMUNISM 259 (Nanette Funk & Magda Mueller eds., 1993).

89.   Milic, *supra* note 74, at 181.

itics, addressing such issues as education, the social safety net, and a clean environment. Joanna Regulska has suggested two explanations for the high concentration of women in non-governmental organizations (NGOs).[90] First, the move may be calculated. The newly gained rights to association and speech provide women with an opportunity to test the benefits of transition. Women believe NGOs provide an arena through which they can make a difference—a place where the political becomes translated into practice. Second, the move to NGO work may represent a default position. NGOs may be the *only* place where women can engage in politics. Often perceived as weak by men, NGOs are one area of public activity wide open to women, although this phenomenon changes after the NGO attracts foreign funds and/or achieves power locally.[91]

Even within the new NGO structure, most women are hesitant to push for their human rights, instead concentrating efforts on humanitarian concerns more akin to "charity" than empowerment. Women try their best to not rock the boat. As Ralitsa Muharska explains in the case of Bulgaria, "In addition to coming out of a society which they denounce and accuse of having caused the ills inflicted upon them, Bulgarian women tend to have a conformist attitude toward their new society, unless they want to be associated with the left—which is really right in terms of economic power, resting on bleached communist money (it presumably having been red before)."[92] Activities of women's NGOs are also adversely affected by the existence of the former official women's organizations, which had promoted the party state and not women's rights.[93] The continuing operation of the stepdaughters of these organizations serve to give women's groups everywhere a bad name.

Many women, whose past experience with politics consisted of symbolic, mandatory activities organized by the Communist Party, are eager to withdraw from politics altogether. "Such attitudes," Sharon Wolchik has noted, "were part of a more general reaction to the fact that equality was, to a large extent, a goal imposed from

---

90.   Regulska's wording and analysis is slightly different. Joanna Regulska, Political Rights and Their Meaning for Women: Transitional Politics in Poland, at 43 (unpublished paper on file with author). *See also* Joanna Regulska, *Transition to Local Democracy in Poland: Do Polish Women Have a Chance?, in* WOMEN IN THE POLITICS OF POSTCOMMUNIST EASTERN EUROPE 35–62 (Marilyn Rueschemeyer ed., 1993).

91.   Romania provides an excellent example of this phenomenon. Few men were interested in NGO work in Romania until it became clear that through NGOs they could control foreign funding and exert power. Although most of the workers in Romanian NGOs are women, leadership positions of the most powerful and wealthiest NGOs tend to be given to men. Author's research with Romanian NGOs, Spring 1996; *Guide to Romanian NGOs* (cir. 1994, 1995, and 1996, on file with author).

92.   Ralitsa Muharska, *What Kind of Feminism for Bulgaria?, in* GAINS AND LOSES: WOMEN AND TRANSITION IN EASTERN AND CENTRAL EUROPE 74, 80 (Laura Grunberg ed., 1994).

93.   In 1988 in Prague, for example, the official women's organization announced that the issue of main concern for women in Czechoslovakia was "beautification of the cities"; "We really have to get women to stop hanging their dirty laundry out of the window," the leader of one group said. Julie A. Mertus, Behind the Veil of Equality: Voices from Czechoslovakia (unpublished manuscript, 1997–98).

above, as well as disappointment with the uneven gender role changes that resulted in the communist period."[94]

Despite the many obstacles, women in CEE are increasingly using the political sphere to advance the human rights of women. From Albanian women holding voter education workshops for women in over fourteen towns and villages, to Croatian women collecting tens of thousands of signatures on pro-choice petitions and lobbying Parliament, to Russian women monitoring their country's compliance with the Women's Convention (Convention on the Elimination of All Forms of Discrimination Against Women) and presenting their own alternative country report, to women using their country's hearings on the Women's Convention implementation to hold Parliament to new promises to promote the status of women, women in CEE are defining the issues for themselves and finding the best means to realize their goals.

The path taken by women in CEE is likely to be different than that of women in the "west," as the nature of the problem and the socio-political-historical context differs. For example, with respect to reproductive freedom, the language of human rights focuses on empowerment of women to make their own reproductive choices. In the west, the problem often is that women are not given the authority to make decisions about their lives. With few exceptions, in the east, women have the authority; they lack information and the economic means to make their choice.[95] For now, the strategies of women's groups in CEE are likely to include advancement of women's economic status and control over information.

The following survey addresses some of the many issues defined by women in CEE as central to advancing the status of women.

SURVEY ON WOMEN'S HUMAN RIGHTS IN CENTRAL AND EASTERN EUROPE

This survey is divided into three main sections: Constitutional provisions prohibiting discrimination against women; main areas of concern[96] (workplace discrimination, violence against women, and political participation); and other areas of concern (abortion and women's health, sexual harassment, maternity leave and childcare, family law, and discrimination against lesbians and single women).

---

94. Sharon L. Wolchik, *Women's Issues in Czechoslovakia and in the Communist and Postcommunist Periods, in* WOMEN AND POLITICS WORLDWIDE 210–25, 214 (Barbara J. Nelson & Najma Chowdhury eds. 1995) [hereinafter Wolchik, *Women's Issues*].

95. *See* Katarina Tomaševski, *Reproductive Rights, and Reality: How Facts and Law Can Work for Women: European Approaches to Enhancing Reproductive Freedom*, 44 AM. U. L. REV. 1037, 1039 (1995).

96. Note that these are the areas identified as "primary concerns for women" by women activists, lawyers, and scholars in Central and Eastern Europe. However, many women stressed the interconnectedness of issues, especially the relationship between economic issues and all other concerns. Thus, apart from economic considerations, which are clearly a primary concern in CEE, the order of issues in this section does not represent a ranking.

Constitutional Provisions Prohibiting Discrimination

Albania

Albania's transitional Constitution[97] contains the following equal rights clause:

> All are equal in law and before the law. No one may be discriminated against because of sex, race, ethnicity, language, religion, economic, financial, educational and social condition, political belief, parentage or any other personal circumstance. (Article 25.)

Albania is under pressure for various reasons to enact a new Constitution, but it will probably contain a similar clause (perhaps modified by the omission of the words "or any other personal circumstance").

Bulgaria

According to the Constitution of Bulgaria, citizens are equal before the law regardless of sex:

> There should be no abridgment of rights and no privileges on grounds of race, nationality, ethnic identity, sex, origin, education, personal, social or property status. (Article 6(2).)

Croatia

The Croatian Constitution contains a general equality provision:

> Citizens of the republic of Croatia shall enjoy all rights and freedoms regardless of race, color, sex, language, religion, political or other opinion, national or social origin, property, birth, education, social status or other properties. All shall be equal before the law. (Article 14.)

Czech Republic

The Charter of Fundamental Rights and Freedoms in the Constitution of the Czech Republic states:

> Fundamental rights and freedoms are guaranteed to all, regardless of difference of sex, race, skin color, language, faith or religion, political or other opinions, national or social origin, membership in a national or ethnic minority, property, gender, or other status. (Article 3(1).)

Hungary

The Constitution of Hungary ensures equal rights:

> [T]he Republic of Hungary shall ensure the equality of men and women with regard to the exercising of all civil, political, economic, social and cultural rights. (Article 66(1).)

---

97.   Albania does have a Constitution, although it is called a "transitional" Constitution as it was enacted in April 1991, when Albania completely repealed its last Communist Constitution. This document was intended to be replaced by a new Constitution, but instead it has been supplemented several times, most recently on Mar. 31, 1993, when a human rights chapter was added.

Poland

The Constitution of Poland provides that "[a]ll citizens have equal rights regardless of sex. . ." (Article 67(2).) A further article develops the general equality principle, declaring: "Women are granted equal rights to men in every field of the state, political, economic, social and cultural life." (Article 78.)

Romania

In addition to a general equality provision, the Romanian Constitution specifically provides that "[w]omen will receive the same pay as men for equal work." (Article 38.4.)

Russia

The Russian Constitution contains both a general and specific provision mandating women's equality:

> The state guarantees equality of rights and freedoms of a person and a citizen, independent of sex, race, nationality, language, ethnic background, property and job status, place of residence, religious beliefs, convictions, belonging to social organizations, and other social conditions. All forms of limiting citizens' rights on the basis of belonging to social, race, national, language, or religious groups is forbidden.

> Men and women shall have equal rights and equal freedoms and equal opportunities to use them. (Article 19(2) and (3).)

Serbia

The Constitution of the Republic of Serbia states:

> Citizens are equal in their rights and duties and have equal protection in front of state and other agencies, regardless their race, sex, birth, language, national belonging, religion, political and other believing, education, social background, marital status and any other personal characteristics. (Article 13.)

The Constitution of Federal Republic of Yugoslavia includes a similar provision, with the addition that "all are equal under law" and "all are obliged to respect freedom and rights of the others and are responsible for doing so." (Article 20).

Slovakia

The Constitution of the Slovak Republic ensures equality for all citizens, stating:

> Basic rights and liberties . . . are guaranteed to everyone regardless of sex, race, color of skin, language, creed and religion, political or other beliefs, national or social origin, affiliation to a nation or ethnic group, property, descent, or another status. No one must be harmed, preferred, or discriminated against on these grounds. (Article 12(2).)

Ukraine

The Ukrainian Constitution provides:

All citizens have equal constitutional rights and freedoms. They are equal before law. No one shall have privileges or limitations on the basis of race, colour, political or other opinion, sex, national or social origin, property, birth, language, religion or other status. (Article 24.)

Main Areas of Concern

Discrimination in Employment and Unemployment

Albania

The Labour Code prohibits discrimination against women in employment. The Labour Code reads as follows:

Equality in Pay Between the Sexes

(1) The employer shall give the same pay to women and men who perform work of an equal value.

(2) Differences in pay based on objective criteria independent of sex, such as the quality and amount of work, professional qualification and seniority, are not considered discriminatory. (Article 115.)

Despite these strong provisions, in practice men predominate in higher paid jobs. Although women's level of educational achievement in Albania is generally higher than men's, their rate of unemployment is higher at each level of education. In 1993, the official unemployment rate for women was 17.9 percent, compared with 14 percent for men.[98]

An estimated 70 percent of women work for private businesses without a contract, making them susceptible to exploitation.[99] Only a small percent of private businesses are owned by a woman. The World Bank has given small credits (up to 3,000) to families for small enterprises and other initiatives. Only 2 percent of the notes have been signed by women; few have been used to open businesses primarily employing women.[100]

The Albanian labor market has one very unique aspect (similar in degree only to Kosovo)—enormous emigration. Hundreds of thousands of Albanians, especially men, live abroad as legal or illegal "guest workers," sending most of their paychecks home to support their families. However, young women and girls also participate in the out-migration, as they are lured and tricked into prostitution in neighboring Italy or Greece, or elsewhere in Europe.

Bulgaria

The provision in the Labour Code guaranteeing the principle of equal pay for work of equal value was removed in 1992.[101] Today, women's right to freedom from

---

98. *Id.*

99. *Id.* at 19.

100. *Id.* at 20.

101. *See Bulgaria 1995: Situation of Women*, U.N. Development Programme (1995), at 3 [here-

discrimination in employment stems from general constitutional provisions. Despite constitutionally mandated equality, discrimination against women takes many forms. For example:

> [T]he private companies set an age limit to women applicants. Women are usually those offered manual, repetitive or unattractive work. Apart from that they are appointed to positions at a lower level in the hierarchy . . . [where they have] limited opportunities for career and promotion.[102]

Many women report discrimination in connection with maternity. Although the Labour Code obligates employers to transfer pregnant women and mothers of young children to less hazardous positions, employers, especially in the private sector, often terminate a woman's employment as soon as she becomes pregnant.

On average, women earn 72 to 74 percent of men's salary.[103] They are also more likely to be unemployed, especially if they are under the age of thirty. And, if employed, they are segregated into public sector employment—industry, agriculture, trade, education, and health care.

The elderly, disabled, and single parent families (i.e., women and children) have been hardest hit by economic crises in Bulgaria. In 1995, four-fifths of the population lived under the social minimum.[104] With the recent increase in inflation, that percentage is now likely to be higher.

Croatia

Article 2 of the new Labour Law prohibits, in very general terms, unequal treatment in employment. Other provisions of the Labour Law are protectionist in nature. Article 52 prohibits night work for women, and Chapter IV—"Protection of Maternity"—provides benefits for mothers, although such benefits can easily be used against women. For example, the chapter provides for mandatory maternity leave during the first six months of the child's life for the mother only, and not the father. Employers have used this provision as an excuse to avoid hiring "expensive" female workers.

Legaline, a women's human rights hotline in Zagreb, has reported a sharp rise in the number of calls connected with employment since the new Labour Act became effective in January 1996:

> There were a number of calls received from women employed by private employers, complaining that some of their basic rights were being denied to them, such as the right to weekly rest days and annual leave for the prescribed length. But they do not dare to do anything for fear that they will be fired. In some cases women who are

---

inafter UNDP Bulgaria Report] (discussing the need to restore equal pay provisions of the Labour Code.)

102. *Id.* at 2.

103. *Id.*

104. *Id.* at 19.

employed by private employers are being paid less than was mutually agreed when they took the job in question.[105]

Many women complained that employers disregard their rights pertaining to maternity leave, particularly in connection with remuneration of salary during this period.[106] Under the new Labour Act, a woman with four of more children has status as "Mother Nurturer" and is entitled to certain benefits such as a salary, health and disability protection, and recognition of working years in lieu of employment.[107] However, the legislature failed to pass a corresponding budgetary provision that would create the funds to pay the Mother Nurturers.

The new Labour Act also increases employers' ability to dismiss workers. This has intimidated working women, limiting their ability to object to their employer's labor practices. The new law makes no provision for protection of women from sexual harassment, coercion, and molestation in the work place. There are also no mechanisms built into the Act by which women are ensured equal opportunities in employment and professional promotion, advancement, or training.

Czech Republic

The Labour Code of the Czech Republic contains two primary provisions mandating equality in the workplace. First, Article 3 states:

> All citizens shall have the right to work, and to a free choice of employment, along with decent working conditions, and protection against unemployment. These rights belong to all citizens regardless of race, skin color, language, gender, social origin. . . .

Second, Article 7 provides specific gender equality language:

> Women shall have the right to the same status at work as men. Working conditions for women must not only conform to their physiological constitution, but also take into account their social role as mothers and their obligations in caring for children.

While the provisions prohibiting women from performing night work were recently revoked in response to the International Labour Organization, there remain provisions barring all women from performing various types of work, such as mineral extraction, mining,[108] and other types of work deemed "inappropriate for them physically or which are harmful to their bodies, and especially those which endanger their maternal calling."[109]

---

105. Report on the Activities of Legaline, Legal Status of Women in Croatia, Dec. 1996 (available at BABE_ZG@ZAMIR-ZG.ztn.apc.org) [hereinafter Legaline, Croatia]. Legaline reports that in order to avoid high payroll taxes, employers often register women at minimum wage, although the agreed upon wage is significantly higher. As a result women will be entitled to only minimum pensions. There is a growing trend for private employers to not register at all, and consequently their workers are left with no rights whatsoever.

106. *Id.*

107. *Id.*

108. Czech. Rep. Labour Code, art. 150(1).

109. Czech. Rep. Labour Code, art. 150(2).

Women are underrepresented in professional management positions, comprising 13 percent of top and middle-level managers. They comprise 5 percent of the top executive positions in banks, insurance companies, and financial consulting firms.[110]

Women's hourly incomes comprise approximately 74 percent of men's incomes in the blue-collar sector; the disparity is greater in the white collar sector.[111] While unemployment is remarkably low in the Czech Republic, women nevertheless constitute a majority of the unemployed, and this number is steadily increasing (57.4 percent in 1991, 58 percent in 1994, 62 percent in 1995).[112] Women remain unemployed longer than men; Roma women (gypsy) face the greatest difficulty finding a job legally. Sex-specific hiring practices are common; there is no legal precedent for combating such practices.

Surveys demonstrate that, while women tend to be dissatisfied with their employment prospects and their supervisors, they consider discriminatory practices a fact of life. According to the women's rights group Profem, "[t]he predominating attitude in the Czech Republic is that sex discrimination per se does not exist, and that these trends, which would generally be attributed to discrimination elsewhere, simply reflect women's decisions to remain dominant in the family."[113]

Hungary

Although Hungarian law formally mandates equality between men and women, discrimination is widespread in the workforce. In the private sector, employers frequently fire women for taking maternity leave;[114] and women are discriminated against in finding employment and in advertisements.[115] Women with small children, elderly women, and young women face the greatest discrimination. Although slightly more women in the workforce are university graduates than are men, educational achievements do not translate into economic security; more than 75 percent of men have some kind of skill qualifications, compared with only 44 percent of women.[116]

The wage gap in Hungary is among the worst in all of Europe (along with the United Kingdom and Luxembourg). Female manual laborers earn approximately 67 percent of male wages; non-manual workers earn between 54 and 63 percent of their

---

110. Response to author's survey, Aug. 1996 (Kate Shaw, Profem, Prague) [hereinafter Shaw Survey].

111. Figures for 1993; more recent figures are estimated to be worse for women. *See* ECOSOC, *Women's Access to Employment, supra* note 40, at Table X.

112. Shaw Survey, *supra* note 110.

113. *Id.*

114. Sharon Ladin, International Women's Rights Action Watch, *1996 IWRAW to CEDAW Country Reports*, Oct. 1995, at 52 [hereinafter IWRAW Country Reports].

115. Advertisements from Hungary on file with author.

116. Katalin Koncz, *Hungarian Women's Political Participation in the Transition to Democracy, in* WOMEN AND POLITICS WORLDWIDE 348–60, 354 (Barbara J. Nelson & Najma Chowdhury eds., 1995) [hereinafter Koncz].

male counterparts wages.[117] This gap has been steadily increasing since 1989.[118] Women workers tend to be concentrated in low-paying traditionally female jobs— such as the textile and leather industries, economics, postal services, and some medical fields.[119]

Nevertheless, Hungary remains one of only two countries in CEE (along with Slovenia) where women's official rate of unemployment is lower than men's rate.[120] It is perhaps the only country in CEE where official statistics show a higher rate of unemployment for male youth than female youth. In 1992, according to official labor statistics, 23 percent of male youth aged fifteen to twenty-four were unemployed, compared with 14 percent of female youth of the same age.[121] However, a far higher percentage of male youths are "unofficially" employed than are female youths, and females of this age bracket are far more likely than males to drop out of the labor market altogether for education or child-rearing (and thus are not counted by unemployment statistics).

After 1989, harassment and prejudice towards the Roma have intensified along with a sharp drop in their economic status. Rom women are among the lowest paid and least likely to be employed segment of the Hungarian population. Two Rom organizations deal especially with issues facing Rom women: The Association of Rom Women in Public Life and The Union of Rom Mothers; in addition, the Open Society Institute has funded education programs on diversity which include discussion of gender and ethno-national identity.

Kosovo/a[122]

Kosovo has two de facto governments: the Serbian government, which rules through the force of law, and the Albanian government that, although elected illegally,

---

117. Figures for 1993; more recent figures are estimated to be worse for women. ECOSOC, *Women's Access to Employment, supra* note 66, at Table X.

118. In 1989 manual workers earned 76 percent of men's salaries and non-manual workers earned 61 percent. *See* Koncz, *supra* note 116, at 354.

119. Koncz, *id.*

120. In 1990, the unemployment rate for women was 1.4 and for men, 1.8; in 1991, the rate was 7.6 for women, 9.2 for men; in 1992, 10.5 for women and 14.0 for men. ECOSOC, *The Role of Women in the Transitional Processes, supra* note 6, at Table 2.

121. ECOSOC, *Women's Access to Employment, supra* note 66, at Table IV.

122. Kosova is the Albanian, Kosovo the Serbian, spelling for the part of the former Yugoslavia that is almost 90 percent ethnic Albanian ("Kosovar Albanian") and 10 percent ethnic Serb. As most world atlases use the Serbian spelling, that is what will be used here. Under the 1974 Constitution of Yugoslavia, Kosovo was an autonomous province of Serbia, which in turn was a Republic of Yugoslavia. In 1989, the regime controlled by Serbian President Slobodan Milosevic revoked Kosovo's autonomous status. Kosovar Albanians contest the legitimacy of that move and argue that since Yugoslavia has disintegrated the status of Kosovo is unclear. The Milosevic government argues that Kosovo is part of Serbia and Yugoslavia (Serbia and Montenegro). Because the conditions in Kosovo differ from Serbia proper (or, alternatively, the rest of Serbia), especially with respect to women's human rights, Kosovo is included separately in this chapter. However, this separate listing does not denote recognition (or failure to recognize) Kosovo as a separate entity.

rules through the force of moral authority. The legal provisions pertaining to women's human rights thus are the same for Kosovo as for Serbia (see below). The moral force of leadership and tradition, however, differs.

Before 1990, 20.9 percent of the work force in Kosovo was women. The rate for urban areas was much higher, approximating that of women in the rest of Yugoslavia; in rural areas, most women were not counted in the workforce, although they labored on family lands and in family businesses.

When the Belgrade regime tightened control over Kosovo in the early 1990s, Albanians employed in state enterprises, including many female doctors and teachers, either were fired or quit in protest. Today, according to the Center for the Protection of Women and Children, less than 3 percent of women work for pay in the official workforce.[123] Many women, however, are employed in "volunteer" and "solidarity" labor, working as teachers, doctors, and administrators in alternative, Kosovar Albanian institutions.

Kosovo is one of the poorest areas in Europe. Women's groups in Kosovo[124] have organized projects to boost women's skills and employment, from sewing classes in villages to educating young women in journalism.[125]

Poland

The Constitution of Poland requires that men and women be given equal pay for equal work. In addition, the Labour Code, newly amended in 1996, prohibits discrimination based on gender. However, the Code does not cover hiring, the point at which discrimination is widespread. As of this writing, the law has yet to be tested through any Court action.

In the name of protecting women's health and preserving their procreative capacity, the Labour Code prohibits the employment of women in certain hazardous positions.[126] Women thus find themselves effectively banned from over ninety occupations in twenty fields of employment. These occupations and jobs are usually better paid than those available to women. Employers are obligated to transfer pregnant women to another position if performing work forbidden for pregnant women.[127] Moreover, the law bans night work, overtime work, and business trips for pregnant women and women bringing up children of less than one year of age.[128]

---

123. Response to author's survey, August 1996 (Sevdie Ahmeti, Center for the Protection of Women and Children). *Editor's Note:* This chapter was finalized prior to the 1999 conflict in Kosovo.

124. Groups include the "Centre for Protection of Women and Children," "League of Albanian Women," "Sisters Qiriazi," ALDK Women's Forum," "Women in Black of Kosova," "Aureola," "Group of Women Veterans of Teaching, Writers and Artists," and "Media Project."

125. The Media Project can be reached at CCK_PR@Zana-Pr.ztn.apc.org.

126. Labour Code, art. 176.

127. Labour Code, art. 179(1).

128. Labour Code, art. 178. *See also* Polish Committee of NGOs, *The Situation of Women in*

Women's earnings have, on average, been 30 percent lower than those of men.[129] Women also face a far greater risk of being unemployed. In 1993 the official unemployment rate was 14.9 percent for women and 11.8 percent for men; in 1991, 11.4 percent for women and 7.9 percent for men; in 1990, 3.8 percent for women and 3.2 percent for men.[130] In addition, men have an easier time finding a job, and women must change jobs more frequently than men.[131] At any given time, the available jobs are more likely to be incompatible with the skills possessed by women. Women hold far fewer management positions than men, especially in the private sector.

The group most at risk of layoffs is women over the age of forty who are employed in state sector office jobs. They have the most difficulty finding other jobs, and, due in part to age related psychological barriers, have difficulty retraining and qualifying for another field of work.

The Center of Women's Activation and Employment (Warsaw), the Association for Women and Their Families (Warsaw), and the Center for the Advancement of Women Foundation (Warsaw) organize training for women job seekers, provide legal assistance, and try to encourage the media to get involved. The Women's Rights Center in Warsaw provides legal assistance to women who allege employment discrimination.

Russia

Although Russian law formally provides for equality between women and men, women's position in the economy has continued to decline since the onset of privatization. During the process of transferring ownership and control of property to private interests, many former factory directors have obtained controlling interests in their factories. Former managers have had privileged access to information about ongoing privatization efforts, and have claimed controlling rights over inventories or essential machinery. Although women were employed to perform both the highest and least-skilled tasks in factories, they were seldom present on the boards of directors of the enterprises. As such, they have been largely excluded from decision making and profit-sharing in formerly state-owned enterprises.[132]

The problem of non-payment and late payment of the workforce leads to a further concentration of interests among the former directors of enterprises. Workers are being offered shares in the enterprise in lieu of paychecks. These shares are com-

---

Poland (Report of the Fourth World Conference on Women in Beijing, China, Aug. 1995 (Poland)), at 8 [hereinafter Poland NGO Report].

129. Poland NGO Report, *id.* at 7.

130. ECOSOC, *The Role of Women in the Transitional Processes*, *supra* note 6, at Table 2.

131. Renata Siemienska, *Polish Women as the Object and Subject of Politics During and After the Communist Period, in* WOMEN AND POLITICS WORLDWIDE 610–24, 616 (Barbara J. Nelson & Najma Chowdhury eds., 1995) [hereinafter Siemienska, *Polish Women*].

132. Survey response of Louise Grogan, Economist, in Moscow, Russia (Aug. 1995) [hereinafter Grogan Survey] (describing interview with Elena Kotchkina, Sociologist, Moscow Center for Gender Studies and Expert of the Russian State Duma).

monly bought back privately by key shareholders in the enterprise, who offer a price reflecting the desperate situation of the unpaid worker.

Mass layoffs have been common in state-owned enterprises which must now compete with an unchecked influx of products from Western Europe and Asia. Those with controlling interests in factories have adopted strategies to scale down their workforces with a minimum of organized resistance. As a group, women are poorly represented on the governing boards of enterprises and thus can only protest their lay-offs after the fact.

Popular and emerging Russian corporate culture promotes the return of women to their biologically determined roles as mothers and homemakers. The Government of the Russian Federation is actively seeking a rise in the birth rate and has begun to restrict the types of occupations and times of day in which women may work.

Women in Russia continue to earn far less than men. A 1996 poll by the Public Opinion Fund found that women make up 87 percent of employed Russian urban residents with a personal income of less than 100,000 rubles ($21) a month, far below a living wage. The higher the income bracket, the lower the proportion of women. Women constitute 71 percent of those with earnings between 200,000 and 400,000 rubles, 57 percent of those earning 400,000 to 600,000 rubles, 45 percent of those with incomes between 600,000 and 1 million, 38 percent of those earning from 1 to 1.5 million, and only 32 percent of those earning more than 1.5 million.[133]

Women also constitute 62 percent of the officially registered unemployed.[134] Older women have been disproportionately represented amongst those laid-off during the transition. Savings they accumulated during their working lives disappeared overnight during price reforms. These women were trained and educated for a different society from that in which they now live. If they are divorced or widowed, they will be expected to survive on a forty dollar monthly pension, less than a third of that which is necessary to live. Older men, unlike women, may have additional sources of income, such as pensions for participation in the armed forces.[135]

Although estimates vary, most commentators agree that at least 60 percent of Russians are living below the poverty line. Women and children are most likely to live in poverty, particularly the elderly and the disabled, and single mothers (about 15 percent of all Russian mothers are unmarried).[136]

---

133. OMRI DAILY DIGEST, Mar. 8, 1996 (available at www.omri.cz).

134. OMRI DAILY DIGEST, Mar. 5, 1996 (available at www.omri.cz). According to Economics Ministry data, at the beginning of Dec. 1994, the number of unemployed and partly unemployed totaled 10 million, or more than 13 percent of the working population. OMRI DAILY DIGEST, Jan. 12, 1995 (available at www.omri.cz).

135. Anastasia Poskadskaya, Director of the Moscow Center for Gender Studies until 1995, recently finished an oral history project on the lives of older women in Russia. Tatiana Gerasiomova, a lawyer from Saint-Petersburg, has begun research on the legal status of older generations of Russian women.

136. Nadezhda Ashgikhina, *A Movement Is Born: Russian Women Are Coming Together to Create a New Fabric of Life*, 51(4) BULLETIN OF ATOMIC SCIENTISTS 47 (1995). Workers wishing to

The political faction "Women of Russia," which lobbies in the State Duma, has initiated a special decree that would protect jobs in the textile industry, where a large portion of employees are women. Women of Russia also supported proposed minimum wage legislation that would benefit all workers, but particularly women as they are most likely to be low paid.

Serbia

Serbia and Yugoslavia do not have specific legal provisions pertaining to equal employment in the workplace, only the general constitutional provisions cited above. The "rule of law" has not operated independently in Serbia for several years; women's groups do not consider legal recourse the most effective way to advance the status of women at this time.

Women's position in the workplace worsened during the war. Women were among the first to be fired or frozen out of their jobs. Employers enjoyed considerable leverage in hiring women according to their own "conditions" including willingness to submit to harassment, sporadic pay, and irregular hours. Men were more likely to be employed in the most profitable "sectors" of the time: by foreign organizations and in the black market. Managerial positions and directorships are almost exclusively male. Accurate figures on employment and unemployment do not currently exist.

Slovakia

Women formally enjoy equality under Slovakia's Constitution. However, women are pressed into the lowest paying jobs and, even in the same jobs, women earn less than men. In 1993, the average monthly wage was 5,310 Sk. As many as 73 percent of women earned less than 5,000 Sk, while only 46 percent of men were in this wage bracket. Only about 11 percent of women earned more than 6,000 Sk, while 31 percent of men did so.[137]

Even though the percentage of women working in the private sector is increasing, for the most part women work as employees and not as self-employed entrepreneurs. In 1994, female entrepreneurs represented 21.6 percent of the total number of entrepreneurs with no employees and 19.7 percent of the total number of entrepreneurs with employees. In the second quarter of 1995, the numbers were slightly better: women comprised 25.7 percent of entrepreneurs with no employees and 25.5 percent of the entrepreneurs with employees.[138] To improve the balance in the future,

---

keep their jobs will generally continue to work for an employer who falls behind in paying salaries. After several months of working without pay, employees realize that they will never be paid the months of salary owed them if they leave the firm. In this way, workers become increasingly bound to the firm. The legal system is unwilling to take on such cases, as they account for at least 30 percent of the workforce in Russia. Grogan Survay, *supra* note 132.

137. Slovakia Report on Women, *supra* note 21.

138. *Id.*

women's groups in the Czech Republic have initiated training and support programs for women in small businesses.

Ukraine

Apart from the general provision of equality in the Constitution, no specific laws prohibit employment discrimination against women in Ukraine. By law, women may be excluded from certain hazardous jobs, night work, and overtime. In the 1980s, women in Donetsk, the eastern mining region, unsuccessfully fought the prohibition on women working in underground mines, one of the highest paid occupations in Ukraine. The court at that time reasoned that the prohibition was necessary for the children's welfare, as it assured that at least one parent would survive.[139]

According to U.N. figures, living standards in Ukraine declined 80 percent in a twenty-eight month period after independence.[140] Rural families in Ukraine face the greatest poverty; very few income-producing activities exist for rural women. About 70 percent of the unemployed are women. Among specialists with higher and specialized secondary education, women comprise 61 percent of the jobless.[141]

Very few women have opened private enterprises. To aid women entrepreneurs, the League of Ukrainian Women of Transcarpatian has built a credit union for women; Women in Agrobusiness has provided start-up support for women in business; the Women's Legal Center provides legal assistance to unemployed women; and a variety of women's groups have provided seminars and training sessions on self-employment (for example, in Soyuz Ukrainok and Lviv). In addition, after the July 1995 review of Ukraine's implementation of the Women's Convention, the Ukrainian Parliament agreed to initiate proposals that would enhance women's access to self-employment and job training. However, these proposals have yet to be implemented.

Violence Against Women

Family Violence

Albania

Albania's new Criminal Code, enacted in June 1995, does not contain specific provisions on domestic violence.[142] Instead, domestic violence may be prosecuted under general penal provisions, including the crimes of: "threat" (Article 84), "torture resulting in serious consequences" (Article 87); "serious intentional injury"

---

139. Based on author's interviews with women teachers and lawyers in Donetsk, Ukraine, Mar. 1995 (court case unavailable).

140. IWRAW Country Reports, *supra* note 114, at 59.

141. Response to author's survey, Aug. 1996 (Olena Suslova, Kiev); Swanee Hunt, *Women's Vital Voices: The Costs of Exclusion in Eastern Europe*, FOREIGN AFF., July 1, 1997.

142. The new Penal Code also provides harsher sentences for violent sexual relations, as well as for the trafficking in human beings.

(Article 86); "non-serious intentional injury" (Article 89); and "other intentional harm" (Article 90).[143]

Under the Code of Penal Procedure, domestic violence cases can only be brought if the victim files a complaint. In other words, the victim must prepare and present the entire case herself, without state assistance. Exceptions are made only if the woman has been killed or permanently injured (physically). A 1995 study by the Minnesota Advocates for Human Rights concluded that:

> Police, prosecutors and judges treat domestic violence as a situation for which each party bears equal responsibility. They invariably try to persuade women to pardon their abusers at each stage of the legal process. The result of this focus . . . is that the vast majority of women drop charges of assault before a trial is commenced. . . . In addition, the government does not provide any social services to victims of domestic assault nor does it attempt in any way to prevent these crimes from occurring.[144]

In 1995, the women's advocacy group Refleksione ("Reflections") conducted an extensive country-wide survey with 1,400 respondents.[145] It found that women of all religious faiths and social backgrounds experience violence in the family in Albania: one in five women is physically abused by her partner, one in seven by family members, one in thirteen by perpetrators qualified as known, and one in fourteen by abusers outside their home.[146] The study concluded that the political and economic transition has had a particularly detrimental effect on the incidence and severity of violence, explaining that:

> women fired from their jobs, and who have become housewives against their will, feel not respected in the individual and social sphere, they are psychologically frustrated because their professional abilities do not respond to their existing situation. [In addition], the hard economic situation and inappropriate living conditions make them more [susceptible] to aggravated physical and psychological violence.[147]

Bulgaria

Domestic violence cases are almost impossible to bring successfully under the criminal law in Bulgaria. The Penal Code in Bulgaria establishes three levels of criminal assault based on the severity of injury: grave, medium, or light injury. In order to meet the threshold requirement for a grave injury, the victim must experience permanent impairment of health;[148] for a medium injury there must be at least "short,

---

143. Minnesota Advocates for Human Rights, *Domestic Violence in Albania*, Apr. 1996 (monograph), at 15 (available at mnadvocates@igc.apc.org) [hereinafter Minnesota Advocates, Albania Report].

144. *Id.* at 3.

145. Silvana Miria, *Violence Against Women and the Psychological Taboos Favoring Violence*, (mimeograph of the Women Association "Refleksione" cir. 1996) [hereinafter Miria].

146. *Id.* at 13.

147. *Id.* at 19.

148. Bulg. Penal Code, § 128, defines grave injury as:

continuous distortion of consciousness; permanent blindness of one or both eyes; permanent deafness; loss of speech; reproductive inability; disfigurement which forever

lasting danger to health."[149] The examining physician makes the legal determination as to the severity of the injury.

In the case of light injuries, the state does not participate in the prosecution. In the case of a medium injury, the state will participate in the prosecution only where the victim and perpetrator are not related. This effectively means that women will not receive state assistance in bringing a domestic violence case unless they can show severe and permanent impairment to health. Consequently, the "victim of domestic violence who attempts to prosecute her batterer alone faces a daunting task."[150] Not surprisingly then, very few cases of domestic violence are ever brought in Bulgaria.

Minnesota Advocates for Human Rights has summarized the primary shortcomings of Bulgaria's legal system with respect to domestic violence:

> The law exempts from prosecution certain types of assault if committed by a family member, although the state prosecutes the same act if committed by a stranger. . . . Even when the woman is permanently injured, the state does not always prosecute. The courts do not take seriously their obligation to punish perpetrators of violence against women in the home. In addition, the government does not provide any social services to victims of domestic assault nor does it attempt in any way to prevent those crimes from occurring.[151]

Domestic violence appears to have increased in Bulgaria since 1989.[152] As noted in the report prepared by the United Nations Development Program for the Fourth World Conference on Women:

> Under the conditions of crisis and increasing tension in society, the family becomes a convenient place for transferring negative emotions. Most often women and children are the objects of aggression and physical violence. . . . Bulgarian men have no skills acquired to express or transform their negative moods and aggression into actions that are not directed to those close to them.[153]

> causes a disturbance of speech, or of a sense organ; loss of a kidney, the bile or a lung lobe; loss of maiming of a leg or arm; permanent general health impairment, dangerous to life.

149. Bulg. Penal Code, § 129, defines medium injury as:

> permanent weakening of eyesight or hearing; permanent embarrassment of speech, of the movement of the extremities, the body or neck, of the functions of the sexual organs without causing reproductive incapacity; breaking of a jaw or knocking out of teeth, without which chewing or speech are obstructed; disfigurement of the face or other parts of the body; permanent impairment of health not dangerous for life or impairment of health temporarily dangerous to life; injuries which penetrate into the cranial, thoracic and abdominal cavities. Anything that causes short, lasting danger to health.

150. Minnesota Advocates for Human Rights, *Domestic Violence in Bulgaria*, Mar. 1996 (monograph), at 11 (available through mnadvocates@igc.apc.org) [hereinafter Minnesota Advocates, Bulgaria Report].

151. *Id.* at 3.

152. *Id.* at 19.

153. UNDP Bulgaria Report, *supra* note 101, at 15.

Croatia

The only crimes recognized by the Criminal Code that can be applied to domestic violence cases are insult and assault and battery.[154] The Criminal Code has not recognized many forms of violence against women. For example, stalking, telephone harassment, sexual harassment on the street or in the workplace, insulting forms of address and other forms of disdainful behavior towards women are not even contemplated as criminal. No law exists to challenge abusers' attempts to forbid women from leaving their homes or communicating with friends or relatives, to prohibit women from accepting employment, or to threaten women with economic or social retribution.

Lawmakers and judges tend to view civil suits as the most appropriate remedy in cases concerning family violence. Advocates for women in Croatia find "it is almost impossible to imagine how a civil suit could provide any fair or just resolution in the case of domestic violence."[155] Plaintiffs must bear the cost of civil suits, and proceedings usually run exceptionally long. Even in those rare cases where a woman may instigate criminal proceedings against the perpetrator, the statute of limitations often expires before the case is filed.[156] Courts in Croatia tend to be overworked; no court at any level has experience or special expertise in handling domestic violence complaints. The net result is a systemic failure of the judicial system to effectively address the issue of violence against women.

Under existing law, a physician treating an injured person must submit a criminal report naming the perpetuator of violence. Wishing to avoid disclosure, some women refuse medical treatment; others fabricate the source of their injuries. However, even when women want their physician to take action, many women indicate that their physician failed to report the crime.[157] In general, physicians demonstrate little sensitivity to women who suffer from domestic violence.

There are no specialized police to deal with domestic violence. Furthermore, judges and police personnel are not educated about domestic violence. The standard operating procedure for police in domestic violence situations is to do nothing until something "serious" happens, that is until someone is killed or seriously injured. Women rarely report domestic violence.

The first hotline in CEE for women victims of violence was established in Zagreb in 1987. Since then, hotlines have spread to every major city. The first shelter in CEE for abused women and their children, the Autonomous Women's House,[158] also was

---

154. Legaline, Croatia, *supra* note 105. *See also* Response to author's survey, Aug. 1996 (B.a.B.e, Zagreb).

155. *See* Legaline, Croatia, *supra* note 154.

156. *Id.*

157. *Id.*

158. Many "trainers" from the U.S. and Western Europe have offered training to the Autonomous Women's House and other such groups. After the staff had been working on the issue for some time, however, they began to reject most would-be trainers, and instead to offer their own wisdom

begun in Zagreb, in December 1990. The Autonomous Women's Center has also provided training for sister projects in Croatia and abroad.[159] Moreover, B.a.B.e., a women's human rights group, provides free legal assistance.

Czech Republic

While family law grants men and women equal rights and assigns them equal responsibilities, both the family law and the criminal law fails to address domestic violence. A draft for a new law on the family has recently been developed, but as of this writing it has not yet been adopted.

The present criminal law and practice presents many obstacles to domestic violence claims. The Penal Code states that victims of certain criminal acts must consent to criminal proceedings if the offender is somehow related to the victim at the time when the crime is committed.[160] If the victim does not agree to press charges, criminal proceedings are not commenced, and the accused's activities go unmonitored. Once a victim decides not to prosecute, the decision cannot be reversed. If these same acts had been committed against a stranger, they would have been punishable by imprisonment, with or without the victim's consent.

A number of women's non-profit organizations offer aid to women and children who are victims of violence. Activists working with battered women report that police require that a victim of domestic violence procure a doctor's note verifying that the injuries she has sustained will prevent her from working for a period of seven days. Only then will police consider referring the case to court and the victim to a social worker.[161]

Hungary

Violence against women is perceived as a problem by the Hungarian public, but domestic violence is largely unacknowledged. Studies conducted by women's advocacy groups in Hungary have found that violence against women occurs in all strata of society throughout the country. In the context of recession, high unemployment,

---

and experience for women's groups elsewhere. Authors' conversations with Autonomous Women's House Staff, Aug. 1995.

159. *Autonomous Women's House Zagreb* (Automomous Women's Center, project description, cir. 1995). Sister projects in Croatia include The Center for Women War Victims, Rosa House, and Women's Studies; sister projects abroad include Medica—Bosnia and Herzegovina, SOS Hotline for Abused Women—Slovenia, and NaNe/SOS Telephone—Hungary.

160. Article 163 (a) of the Penal Code. *See also* Kamila Michalkova, *Coalition Protects Victims of Domestic Violence*, PRAGUE POST, May 14, 1997, at 1 (noting that law enforcement officials dismiss domestic violence as "a couple of slaps between partners," and listing the organizations making up the Coordinating Circle for the Prevention of Violence Against Women as Profem, Nadace Rosa, Gender Studies Center, and Elektra); Emma McClune, *Shelter Is Planned for Women Whose Suffering Even Language Denies*, PRAGUE POST, Mar. 22, 1995, at News Section (noting that if a woman wants to press charges against her aggressor, her doctor must certify that "she has sustained injuries sufficient to justify seven days of sick leave.")

161. Shaw Survey, *supra* note 110.

and general uncertainty about the future, frustration and tensions have escalated, and incidents of domestic violence have increased. Still, only a small number of battered women report the incidents due to fear of the police, emotional trauma, and fear of revenge and further violence. The general provisions of the Criminal Code in Hungary provide insufficient recourse to victims of domestic violence.

Hungary's first hotline for battered women and children was launched by NaNe (Women for Women Against Violence) in February 1994. Another civil organization, the Ombudswomen project in Budapest, operates, among other things, a Women's Information and Resource Center which provides the services of lawyers, social workers, and lay activists to assist women in crisis. Both governmental and non-governmental organizations have established battered women's shelters.

Kosovo

Kosovo, being subject to the laws of Serbia and Yugoslavia, does not have a specific law on domestic violence (see Serbia, *infra*). Kosovo Albanian women's groups have put "creating a law on domestic violence" on their wish list for changes should a democratically elected government take power in Kosovo. Independent Kosovar Albanian women's groups report that the incidence of domestic violence has increased since 1991, due in part to worsening economic and political conditions.

Poland

The Penal Code in Poland, unlike the law of most countries, explicitly recognizes domestic violence as a criminal act. Article 184 of the Code states that anyone who commits physical and psychological abuse over a member of his or her family (or another person in a permanent or temporary relationship of dependency to the perpetrator) could be punished with up to five years of imprisonment.[162] If the abuse results in a suicide attempt by the abused, the penalty may increase to ten years.

Other provisions of the Penal Code that could be used in cases of domestic violence include prohibitions against "violating personal untouchability" or use of vulgar words to degrade or incite violence;[163] battery at any location;[164] use of force or threats to make another person behave in a certain manner;[165] or verbal threats or threats through express body language which may lead the victim to have reason to fear that the threat is real.[166]

---

162. Pol. Penal Code, art. 184.

163. Pol. Penal Code, art. 182.

164. Pol. Penal Code, art. 156.

165. Pol. Penal Code, art. 167.

166. Pol. Penal Code, art. 166. *See* Isabel Marcus, Dark Numbers: Domestic Violence in Poland, (unpublished draft cir. 1996), at 17 (reporting on results of survey on domestic violence in Poland).

However, in Poland as elsewhere, "[t]he codified law and its application are usually two different realities."[167] Police rarely react when violence occurs in a home or between family members; most cases are dismissed or punishment is suspended. In order to make a case under Article 184 of the Penal Code, prosecutors must show "serious injury." Bruises are deemed insufficient injury. In order to meet the evidentiary standard, doctors must certify that the target of violence is unable to function for more than seven days.[168]

A 1993 survey of 1,087 women conducted by the Public Opinion Research Center found that 8 percent had been repeatedly beaten by their husbands and a further 8 percent had been beaten sporadically.[169] The actual figures are likely to be much higher. In the same survey divorced women, who apparently felt more free to speak about abuse, reported far higher incidents of violence: 41 percent said they had been beaten repeatedly; 21 percent said that it happened sporadically. When these same women were asked whether they knew about any women who were beaten by their husbands, 41 percent of the married and 61 percent of the divorced women answered in the affirmative.

Women's NGOs provide various kinds of assistance and support to victims of violence. For instance, the Women's Rights Center provides legal assistance to battered women and has launched a campaign to raise public awareness. The campaign has caught the interest of newspapers and television, and pressure has mounted for better implementation of the criminal law. Other groups concerned with violence against women include the Society for Intervention in Crisis Situation; Women Against Violence, Women's Foundation eFKa from Krakow, and Associations of Battered Wives from Bydgoszcz.

Romania

Domestic violence can be prosecuted under the general provisions applicable to assault or battery. The Romanian Penal Law defines five levels of assault: battery, bodily injury, unintentional bodily injury, aggravated bodily injury, and battery causing death.[170] The aggrieved is primarily responsible for preparing the case, unless the crime can be defined as aggravated bodily injury or battery causing death. This means that in nearly all cases the aggrieved is responsible for bringing the case.

If the parties reconcile, the case is dismissed. Sentences vary according to the level of injury, as determined by the number of days for which medical treatment is required. Women report being humiliated and further mistreated both during the mandatory examination by the physician and in the police station. Some women fear bringing cases against their batterers because the Romanian police have an infamously

---

167. Poland NGO Report, *supra* note 128, at 14.

168. *Id.* at 19.

169. Poland NGO Report, *supra* note 128, at 50.

170. Penal Code, arts. 180–84.

low respect for human rights.[171] One man who was arrested for beating his wife reportedly died from the beating he received in police custody.[172]

Police are charged only with investigating homicides and serious assault cases. A study of the Minnesota Advocates for Human Rights found:

> [I]f the police are called [in] a domestic assault case, the common practice is to counsel or advise the couple at the scene of the assault. The police may occasionally fine the abuser or require him to return the victim's property. Police do not, however, generally make arrests in these situations.[173]

Romania currently has no infrastructure to support women who have been battered. Given the severe housing shortage in Romania, few women can hope to ever leave their husbands. Moreover, few in Romania can imagine that the police or courts could ever be a source of justice.[174]

Russia

Domestic violence has been increasing in Russia in recent years. Issues of violence within the family are grossly underreported, with many cases not receiving attention until the woman is killed. The number of spousal murders in Russia has tripled in the last ten years. In 1993, out of a total of 29,213 homicides and attempted homicides, more than 6,000 perpetrators were husbands or male partners who killed or attempted to kill their wife or female partner; 9,700 were murders by other family members or relatives.[175] It is estimated that annually 7,000 children are victims of sexual violence.[176]

In 1994, Galina Sillaste began working on a new legislative bill "About Prevention of Domestic Violence." In July 1995, the Committee on Women, Family, and Youth of the State Duma of the Russian Federation included this bill in the parliamentary schedule for October 1995. Russian NGOs were not included in the development of this legislation, despite their experience with the issue. The draft provided strict regulations for crisis centers concerned with violence against women, raising objections from existing women's crisis centers.

---

171. Minnesota Advocates for Human Rights, *Lifting the Last Curtain: A Report on Domestic Violence in Romania*, Feb. 1995, at 12 [hereinafter Minnesota Advocates, Romania Report].

172. Whether or not the man actually died from police beatings is unconfirmed.

173. Minnesota Advocates, Romania Report, *supra* note 171.

174. Author's interviews with students and activists in Romania, Feb.–June 1996.

175. The Moscow Center for Gender Studies and Network of East-West Women Project of "Committee of the Rights of Women," Report on the Legal Status of Women in Russia: Contemporary Debates (Moscow, 1996) (draft on file with author) (unpaginated computer disk version) [hereinafter Moscow Gender Studies Report]. *See also* Mairead Carey, *Home News*, IRISH TIMES, Mar. 15, 1997, at 8 (reporting that, according to official reports, 14,500 women died in incidents of domestic violence in 1993; in 1994, 15,500 women died and more that 56,000 women were seriously injured).

176. *Id.*

An analysis of one of the early versions of the bill (June-July, 1995) showed that the definition of the family offered in the document was vague and unclear.[177] Among its many problems, it did not provide for inclusion of the legal status of partners or cohabitants whose marriage was not officially registered (which, according to the Moscow Gender Studies Center, account for 46 percent of all relationships). Although the bill has been modified to correct for some of the problems, as of this writing no version has been passed into law.

Serbia

The criminal law does not have a domestic violence provision per se, but the general provisions of the law cover such potentially applicable crimes as murder, serious physical injury, less-serious physical injury, unlawful deprivation of someone's freedom, menacing of someone's security, threatening the "inviolability of the apartment," incest, abusing a juvenile person, insult, slander, and coercion.

According to the Autonomous Women's Center in Belgrade, the rate of domestic violence, rape, and other forms of violence against women has increased since the 1990s war in the former Yugoslavia. Activists attribute the increase to violent men returning from battle, an increasingly misogynist and violent culture, poverty and frustration among the general population, and increased numbers of "vulnerable" women, including refugees and displaced people, young girls on the street, and drug addicts.

Women's groups in at least five cities offer SOS Hotlines, support to battered women, legal aid, shelters, and counseling. The Center for Girls in Belgrade works specifically with young women and girls, offering youth chat groups, counseling, and exercises to raise self-esteem. Women in Serbia have found especially creative ways to support their projects. One women's shelter near Belgrade supports itself from a chicken farm run out of the basement. Another group runs a second hand shop that employs women from the shelters during a transitional stage.

Rape and Trafficking in Women[178]

Albania

The Albanian Penal Code does not recognize marital rape as a crime.[179] A survey by the Albanian women's group Refleksione ("Reflections") found that 26 percent of all women had been forced by their husbands to have sexual relations against their will.[180] Another study conducted by Albanian women activists found that only

---

177. *Id.*

178. The responses to the author's questions about the trafficking in women were often incomplete. Absence of information about this issue for a particular country does not necessarily mean that it is not prevalent.

179. Response to author's survey, Aug. 1996 (Tefta Zaka and Kathleen Imhotz, Tirana).

180. Miria, *supra* note 145.

10 percent of women interviewed even had a clear understanding of what marital rape was.[181]

In June 1996, women in Tirana opened the first counseling center for women, children, and victims of sexual violence. Despite this effort and the work of other women's and health groups to publicize the issue, there are no hotlines or shelters for raped or battered women in Albania. In addition, although Albanian women are prey to the growing sex trade in Europe, women's groups are only beginning to address the issue of forced prostitution and trafficking in women.

Croatia

Under the Penal Code of Croatia, rape occurs if someone, through use of physical power, or threat to life, body, or property, or life, body, or property of someone close to her, forces a woman into a sexual act. The law does not include marital rape.[182]

Local women's groups in Croatia, often in conjunction with foreign groups, provide counseling and assistance to women who have survived wartime rape and other wartime sexual abuse. The Center for Women War Victims in Zagreb offers ongoing counseling sessions, which are frequently led by women refugees who have survived traumas themselves. Additional projects by and for women refugees exist in Osijek, Dubrovnik, Split, Rijeka, and several other cities and towns.

Czech Republic

The Penal Code of the Czech Republic defines rape in the following provision:

> Whoever, by means of violence or threat of imminent violence, coerces a woman into copulation, or takes advantage of her defenselessness for such purpose, will be punished with imprisonment for two to eight years.

> An offender will be imprisoned for five to twenty years if (a) the offender commits the crime described in paragraph 1 when the act has a serious, detrimental affect on the victim's health, or (b) commits such crime against a woman younger than 15 years.

> An offender will be imprisoned for ten to fifteen years if the crime stipulated in paragraph 1 results in the victim's death. (Article 241.)

There are no provisions which refer to marital rape.

Research conducted on sexual behavior in 1993 indicated that one-eighth of Czech Republic women had been raped; half of these women were raped by their husbands, 38 percent by acquaintances, and 11 percent by strangers. Three out of a hundred women raped reported the incident to the police.[183]

Prostitution and trafficking in women have both experienced fantastic growth in the Czech Republic since 1989. Between 1993 and 1994, criminal activities con-

---

181. Saimira Gjipali & Mimoza Xhafa, *Domestic Violence Against Women: A Violation of Human Rights*, May 1995 (monograph).

182. Response to author's survey, Aug. 1996 (B.a.B.e, Zagreb).

183. Shaw Survey, *supra* note 110.

nected with trafficking increased by 67 percent in Prague, by 264 percent in Western Bohemia, by 500 percent in Southern Moravia, and by 97 percent in the Czech Republic as a whole.[184] The women's group "Profem" has been especially active in studying and bringing attention to these issues.

Germany

Marital rape is not a crime under German law.

Hungary

The Hungarian penal legislation does not recognize marital rape, although the Constitutional Court is reviewing the matter and the law may soon change. Another peculiar provision of the criminal law, advocates are trying to change, states that if a rapist marries his victim, he is entitled to a reduction in his prison sentence.[185]

Since 1989, there has been a steady increase in forced prostitution and the trafficking in women in Hungary. Hungary is also reportedly the largest producer of pornography in the region. One main area of debate among women's groups in Hungary is whether to legalize prostitution.

Kosovo

Marital rape is not recognized as a crime under Serbian law (the law that governs Kosovo). "In the rural, traditional areas of Kosovo, women are treated as the property of their husband and mother-in-law," one Kosovar activist explained: "Most women in these areas believe that their husband can do with them as they please."[186]

Historically, nationalist leaders have used the issue of rape to ignite tensions between ethnic Serbs and Albanians. In the late 1980s, the Serbian and Yugoslav media ran numerous stories about Albanian men raping Serbian women. Nearly all of these accounts evaporated after 1991. Federal crime statistics for the late 1980s period show fewer rapes per capita in Kosovo than in any part of then-Yugoslavia, with only a small percentage of the cases involving an Albanian perpetrator and a Serbian victim.[187] But statistics matter little. The stories of rape served to spread fear and to create division. To this day, some Kosovar Albanian women fear bringing charges in rape cases where the perpretrator is of the same ethnic group (the vast

---

184. *Id.*

185. Response to author's survey, Aug. 1996.

186. Identity withheld upon request, author's interview, May 1995. *See also Editor's Note, supra* note 123.

187. Author's analysis of federal crime statistics and interviews with Serbian criminologists, Belgrade 1993–1994. *See also* Conference in Ljubljana, "Kosovo-Serbien-Jugoslawien," Ljubljana, 1989 (report on file with author); Srdja Popović et al., Kosovskič vor: Drešiti ili seći?, (Belgrad: Kronos, 1990), at 47 (giving extensive statistics); Mark Thompson., A Paper House: The Ending of Yugoslavia 130 (1992); Cornelia Sorabji, *Crimes Against Gender or Nation?*, War-report 18 (Feb.–Mar., 1993), at 16.

majority of cases)[188] as the case could be used to justify past and present discrimination against Albanian men.

Local women's groups have begun to break the silence about forced prostitution and trafficking in women. In 1994, Xerhi Bucinca, a woman journalist, published the first article about the subject to appear in an Albanian-language journal.[189] Although she was criticized heavily for the piece, it has opened discussion on the problem.

Poland

The Penal Code defines rape as an offense against personal freedom, stating that "[w]ho by means of unlawful threat, or deceit, forces a lewd act on another person is liable to penalty of one to 10 years."[190] Where the judge finds that the rapist acted with "cruelty," the penalty may increase to up to twenty-five years. Polish law permits the prosecution of marital rape, but there are few such cases.

According to data from the Ministry of Justice, 51 percent of defendants are sentenced for one to two years of imprisonment, 30 percent for two to five years, and 21 percent for more than five years. Moreover, approximately 30 percent of the judgements passed are changed to suspended sentences.[191] According to Urszula Nowakowska, of the Women's Rights Center, "in practice cases of rape are often treated as incidents resulting from the provocative behavior of women."[192]

Romania

Marital rape is not included as a crime under Romanian law. Women are deeply suspicious and fearful of the criminal justice system and thus extremely reluctant to report cases of rape. Consequently, most of the reported cases involve situations in which the woman is severely injured and left with no way to hide the crime.

A large number of Romanian girls and young women have been tricked into work in prostitution rings abroad. The issue of trafficking in women, however, has received inadequate attention in Romania and the exact extent of the problem is unknown.

Russia

Russian law identifies only females as possible victims of rape.[193] The Penal Code specifies different penalties for rape according to the nature of the crime:

---

188. *Id. See also* Mertus, Social Politics, *supra* note 76, at 264–65.

189. Xheraldina Bucinca, *Kosovaria*, Dec. 25, 1994, "*Mos me pyatni pse shes trupin tim*" (Don't ask me why I am selling my body).

190. Pol. Penal Code, art. 168.

191. Response to author's survey, Aug. 1996 (Urszula Nowakowska, Women's Rights Center, Warsaw).

192. *Id.*

193. Russian Criminal Code, art. 117.

(1) Rape, sexual intercourse with the use of physical violence or threat to victim or to an other person or with using an uninvolved bystander. Rape is punished by the deprivation of freedom for a period from three to six years.

(2) Rape,

a) when committed several times or by the person who had previously committed offenses of a sexual nature;

b) when committed by a group of persons, group of persons by a prior agreement, or by an organized group;

c) when connected with threat of murder or with threat of causing the severe injury to health, and also committed with intentional cruelty for the victim or for other people;

d) when committed against a girl under the age of 18,

is punished by deprivation of freedom from four to ten years.

(3) Rape,

a) resulting in the death of victim;

b) resulting in serious injury to the health of the victim, contamination by AIDS, or other serious consequences;

c) against victims obviously under the age of 14 years,

is punished by deprivation of freedom for the period from eight to fifteen years. (Article 132.)

There is no specific law on marital rape.

In 1993, the Moscow Crisis Center for Women was established; it now operates in several major Russian cities. Telephone hotlines were set up in Moscow by the Sexual Assault Recovery Center. In 1995, Moscow's first women's shelter was established.

Serbia

The minimum penalties for rape in Serbia are shockingly low; indeed they are amongst the lowest in Europe. The law provides:

(1) Whoever compels a female person with whom he is not living in marital community into a sexual relationship, by using force, or threatening to directly attack the life and the body of the female person or of someone close to her, will be punished by a prison term from one to ten years.

(2) If as a consequence of the deed from (section 1) of this article serious physical injury of the female person resulted or if the deed was done by a few persons, or in a specially cruel or humiliating way, the perpetrator will be punished by a prison term of at least one year (the maximum is 20).

(3) If the deed from (1) of this article was committed against a juvenile person, or if as a consequence the death of the female person occurred, the perpetrator will be punished with a prison term of at least three years. (Article 103.)

Marital rape is specifically excluded from the law. In practice, "it is the raped woman who is treated as the guilty one."[194]

---

194. Response to author's survey, Aug. 1996 (Zorica Mrsevic, Belgrade Women's Law Group).

Ukraine

In Ukraine, the definition of rape neither includes nor excludes marital rape. An extremely small number of women in Ukraine report cases of sexual violence, "because they are afraid of the police or to appear in court, and they may have nowhere to go."[195]

The trade in women and young girls—within Ukraine and abroad—is a serious problem. Newspapers commonly run advertisements for dancers, nannies, waiters, entertainers, or other positions abroad.[196] Many of these ads are thinly veiled attempts to recruit young women and girls into prostitution. Lawyers in Ukraine complain that it is virtually impossible to stop these practices under current law. In addition, the Ukrainian Criminal Code does not treat prostitution as a crime unless a third person is involved in the selling of sexual services.[197] Most advocates for women in Ukraine would probably support stricter laws on forced prostitution and the trafficking in women.[198]

Women's Political Participation

Albania

Under the old regime, women held 30 percent of the seats in Parliament. After the first free elections in March 1991, that figure dropped to 3.6 percent (nine women out of a 250 member body).[199] Thereafter, a mixed system was applied in elections, combining the majority system with proportional representation. This process appeared to facilitate women's involvement in politics. In 1995, women held 5.7 percent of the seats (eight out of 140).[200]

In 1994, women parliamentarians formed a caucus—the Group of Parliamentary Women—to work together on women's rights. The same year, the government created a department of "Woman and Family" to be a focal point for women's issues within the Ministry of Labour.

Women are extremely active in Albania in the leadership of NGOs; there are at least eighteen NGOs dedicated to women's issues.[201] Before the May 1996 elections, these NGOs developed projects to identify, train, and help women candidates. A coalition for women's groups held voter education campaigns throughout the country to increase women's turnout and political involvement.

---

195. Response to author's survey, Aug. 1996 (Olena Suslova, Kiev).

196. Advertisements from Ukraine on file with author.

197. IWRAW Country Report, *supra* note 114, at 63.

198. Summary finding based on author's field research in four cities in Ukraine, Mar. 1995 and Feb. 1996.

199. Tatjana Daci, Albania National Report, *Action for Development, Equality and Peace*, prepared for the Fourth World Conference on Women, at 7 (Sept. 1995) [hereinafter Albania NGO Report].

200. *Id.*

Despite these efforts, women's overall participation in government in Albania remains among the lowest in Europe. In the four governments formed after the first pluralist elections (1991–1995), women did not hold a single ministerial function. In 1995, out of twenty ministers, there was only one woman; only 7 percent of all deputy ministers are women.[202] While in 1991 over 40 percent of leaders in local administration were women, by 1994 no women were local leaders. Before 1991, women were prohibited from working as professional diplomats. In 1994, there were twenty-four women diplomats among 231 (10.4 percent of the total). But there has never been a woman ambassador.[203]

Bulgaria

Women's participation in government, although lower than under the prior system, is higher in Bulgaria than in some CEE countries. In 1995, women held 13 percent of the seats in Parliament; 20 percent of the elected offices in municipal councils and commissions; 13 percent of superior administrative positions; 8 percent of mayor posts in large municipalities; and 28 percent of mayor posts in small municipalities.[204]

In 1994, when a caretaker government was appointed by the President, for the first time in the country's history, a woman was appointed Prime Minister. In 1995, there was one woman serving as a minister in the federal cabinet and six women deputy ministers.[205] Bulgaria does have a women's political party, but it does not have wide political support.

Croatia

On the one hand, war has led to the creation and expansion of many women's initiatives in Croatia, particularly humanitarian efforts connected with refugees. On the other hand, war has had a particularly negative impact on women's formal political participation in Croatia, as "resurgent traditional catholic values within the context of nationalism and war also limits women's ability to speak out and take action as they would be branded as traitors if they were to criticize an act of the government that is unfavorable to women, or if they were to rebel against the propaganda encouraging women to do their job and [replenish] the nation [through reproduction]."[206]

The impact of the extremely low number of female politicians is compounded by their lack of influence over legislative decisions and exclusion from informal gatherings where a majority of decisions are made. This absence of influence and disregard of women's points of view causes general political apathy among female citizens, which in turn favors a low rate of female participation in the political process.

---

201. Brochures of Albanian women's groups on file with author.

202. Albania NGO Report, *supra* note 199, at 8.

203. *Id.*

204. UNDP NGO Report, *supra* note 49, at 26.

205. *Id.*

206. Response to author's survey, Aug. 1996 (B.a.B.e, Zagreb).

In 1996, women constituted 8 percent of all representatives in Parliament. At the local level, women hold a higher percentage of leadership positions; in Zagreb in 1996, women held 12 percent of the seats in local political bodies.[207] There is no woman's party as such, but some of the political parties have women's initiatives.

Women's NGOs in Croatia have worked together to lobby political bodies. Before the October 1995 parliamentary elections, fourteen women's groups[208] established a Women's Election Platform addressing women's concerns. The election platform demanded the establishment of a Ministry for Gender Equality, quotas for women representatives in Parliament, prevention of all forms of violence against women, governmental programs and measures for improving the economic independence and status of women, elimination of the Department on Demographic Development, and freedom of choice on reproductive rights. In elections since 1995, women's groups have promoted the candidates who address women's human rights.[209]

Czech Republic

As in other CEE countries, during the old regime women were better represented among governmental elites, although their access to power remained limited. Women were always less likely to be members of the Communist Party, despite the employment and economic advantages granted to members.[210] Unlike women in Poland, Czech women did rise to leadership positions in important dissident movements. Above all, they took an active role in Charter 77, the intellectual dissident organization which played a major role in activities leading to the fall of the Communist Party.[211] In addition, young women became more vocal in the last years of communist rule, and many emerged as leaders in independent student organizations and demonstrations of 1989.

Despite the unusually strong presence of women in dissident organizations, few women emerged as leaders in the new government. After the June 1990 federal elections, women made up a mere 10.7 percent of the deputies elected to the federal assembly.[212] This figure has risen only slightly in the intervening years. After the 1996 elections, women constituted 15 percent of the Parliament.[213] While there were no

---

207. *Id.*

208. The organizations in the coalition included the Autonomous Women's House; Ariadna-Rijeka; B.a.B.e.; Center for Women War Victims; Center for Women's Human Rights-DOS; Center for Peace, Non-Violence and Human Rights-Osijek; Rosa House; Women's Infoteka-Zagreb; Women's Group-Losinj; Women's Group-Split; Women's Peace Workshop-Rijeka; Workshop Open Doors-Split; SOS Hotline-Zagreb; Women from the Anti-War Campaign of Croatia.

209. Lobbying material from Zagreb women's groups on file with author.

210. Wolchik, *Women's Issues, supra* note 94, at 213 (citing SHARON L. WOLCHIK, CZECHOSLOVAKIA IN TRANSITION 71 (1991)).

211. *See* Barbara Jancar, *Women in the Opposition in Poland and Czechoslovakia in the 1970s, in* WOMEN, STATE, AND PARTY 169–72 (Wolchik & Meyer eds., 1985).

212. Wolchik, *Women's Issues, supra* note 94, at 214.

213. Shaw Survey, *supra* note 110.

women in the new minority cabinet, there was one woman[214] among the five chairpersons of the House of Deputies, and there was one woman chairperson[215] among the twelve expert parliamentary committees.

The Czech Republic has neither a women's party nor serious efforts to organize one. Women's NGOs have undertaken voting education efforts in an attempt to increase women's role in politics. For example, in 1996 the Gender Studies Center in Prague hosted a day-long seminar on women and politics that brought together women politicians, professionals, and academics.

Hungary

Women did not fare well in the first free elections in Hungary, held on March 25, 1990. Twenty-six women were elected to Parliament, representing 6.7 percent of all parliamentarians.[216] In contrast, in the early 1980s almost one-third of the parliamentarians had been women.

These numbers tell only part of the story. Even when women are elected, they do not hold positions of leadership and power. In 1990, there were no female ministers and only three women among the thirty-three under-secretaries.[217] Although women's representation has improved slightly, women still are dramatically underrepresented, particularly in positions of power.

This phenomenon demonstrates continuity with, and not a break from, the past. As Katalin Koncz has observed: "Under the old regime, many women were elected only to improve statistics; they did not demonstrate their abilities or their commitment to the elections."[218] Although members of the Parliament were technically elected by the public, the party organization played a heavy hand in the selection of candidates. Thus, "loyalty to the party was stronger than loyalty to group interests."[219] Under such conditions, women in Parliament rarely spoke out in favor of women's interests.

The Hungarian experience with democracy has shown that fewer women are elected where voters directly elect their representatives than where voters cast their ballots for party lists (who in turn are responsible for choosing the individuals). In the first democratic government, more than 80 percent of the women representatives in Parliament had won their seats by local and national party lists; only 18.5 percent won by direct election.[220] Still, the proportion of women in the new political parties remains low, again especially in positions of leadership. Indeed, "[i]n Hungary, pop-

---

214. *Id.*

215. Anna Roschova, Committee on Mandates and Immunities (Christian Democratic Alliance/CDA).

216. Koncz, *supra* note 116, at 350.

217. *Id.*

218. *Id.*

219. *Id.*

220. *Id.* at 351.

ular opinion supports the practices of parties promoting men in leadership positions. Electors believe that because of practical experience men can perform better as representatives than women, who are too burdened with family affairs and household chores and who do not have enough time left for the tasks expected of an MP."[221]

Kosovo

Women play a limited role in the "parallel" Kosovar Albanian government. The fourteen member Presidency of the Democratic League of Kosovo (LDK, the ruling, although illegal, Kosovar Albanian government), includes only one woman. She travels widely as a spokesperson for Kosovo, but her role is restricted by her high position to "greater" political issues—the ultimate freedom for Albanians. Women's additional involvement in LDK politics is channeled through special women's branches, more akin to a "ladies auxiliary" of the important men's work than an independent women's voice.[222]

Most Kosovar Albanian political leaders treat women's issues as a luxury that cannot be addressed until the larger political issues for Albanians are decided. Yet some Albanian women (including women affiliated in some way with the LDK), particularly intellectuals from urban areas, reject this reasoning. Since 1993, women's groups in Kosovo have become more numerous and powerful, thus increasing their indirect influence on the organization and conduct of Kosovar Albanian society.[223]

Poland

As in other CEE countries, women's formal participation in politics had been relatively high under the prior regime, yet women held few positions of leadership. In the period 1944–1979 only thirteen women held top state positions; eight of these women had been on the Central Committee of the ruling Communist Party (the Polish United Workers' Party).[224] Women were denied positions in the state administration due to "such things as officials' unwillingness to appoint women, women's fear of responsibility, and women's heavy family commitments."[225]

As Renata Siemienska has shown, "during periods of political destabilization (such as the crises of 1956 and the 1980s), when there was a struggle for power and political influence, women were the first to be deleted from candidate lists" and eliminated from positions in power.[226] The heyday of the Solidarity independent trade union movement proved to be no exception. Although women constituted about half

---

221. *Id.*

222. Mertus, Social Politics, *supra* note 76, at 271. *See Editor's Note, supra* note 123.

223. *Id.*

224. Siemienska, *Polish Women, supra* note 131, at 613.

225. *Id.*

226. *Id. See also* Siemienska, *Women and Social Movements in Poland, in* Women and Politics 6, 23–26 (1981).

of Solidarity's members, they rarely held positions of power.[227] At the onset of Solidarity's confrontation with authorities in the 1980s, "the trade union's only demands specifically concerning women included three-year paid maternity leave and a guarantee of sufficient places for children in kindergartens and nurseries[,] . . . demands . . . [which would create] conditions that would improve women's ability to fulfill their traditional roles."[228]

After the local government elections in 1994, women constituted about 13 percent of local politicians and filled 6 percent of local political leadership positions.[229] The percentage of women in the Sejm (lower house of Parliament) as well as in the Senate (upper house) was about 13 percent, a slight increase from 1991–1993.[230]

In 1991, women parliamentarians across party lines formed a Women's Parliamentary Caucus (or "The Parliamentary Group of Women") to increase women's political influence in the Parliament. Its current members cross party boundaries and number over two-thirds of women members of both houses.[231] The Caucus, along with women's human rights activists and academics, pressured the Prime Minister to fill the long-vacant position of Government Executive Officer for Women's and Family Affairs, a remnant from the old government but a post that could potentially increase attention paid to women's issues. Although the post was eventually filled in 1994, it has remained largely perfunctory and ineffective.[232]

As to women's participation in other forms of public life, in 1996 women constituted 60 percent of the active staff in education, 52 percent in health care, 49 percent in cultural institutions, 45 percent in tourism, and 35 percent in trade unions.[233]

The informal group "Women Also" was active in the local elections in 1994. "Women Also" actively campaigned to encourage women to stand for local council elections, supporting women deciding to stand for election, and canvassing the public to vote for women candidates.[234] Moreover, women's NGOs such as The Center for the Advancement of Women ran training courses for women in media relations and in conducting public meetings. The women's party in Poland has not been active in recent years. According to the Women's Legal Center in Kiev, the only party pro-

---

227. Renate Siemienska, *Women and Solidarity in Poland in the Early 1980s, in* WOMEN AND COUNTER POWER 33–45 (Yolande Cohen ed., 1989).

228. *Id.*

229. Response of Women's Law Center to author's survey, August 1996. *See also* Poland NGO Report, *supra* note 128, at 21–29.

230. In 1991, women constituted 9.1 percent of the Lower House and 6 percent of the Upper House. *Poland, in* WOMEN AND POLITICS WORLDWIDE 608–609, 609 (Barbara J. Nelson & Najma Chowdhury eds., 1995).

231. Polish NGO Report, *supra* note 128, at 22.

232. *Id.* at 23.

233. Response to author's survey, Aug. 1996 (Urszula Nowakowska, Women's Rights Center, Warsaw).

234. *Id.*

moting women is the Labour Union, which reserves 33 percent seats at the party's electoral list for women.[235]

Russia

The participation of women in Russian politics has plummeted since the onset of democratization. In 1995, of 450 Duma members, only fifty-seven were women, and there were only nine women among the 176 Federation Council members.[236]

Women's groups have criticized the lack of representation in Parliament and have organized, albeit often unsuccessfully, to elect women candidates. In July 1995, the National Council for the Fourth World Conference on Women sent a letter to President Yeltsin, the leaders of both chambers of Parliament, and Russia's political parties expressing concern about the low number of women in the Parliament.[237] Among the many other political actions undertaken by women in Russia, on March 4, 1996, representatives of fifty-three women's associations appealed to the Duma [legislature] to improve the legal status of women in the workforce. They proposed that the Duma create a body to assess all draft legislation from the point of view of equal opportunities for men and women.[238]

On the local level, women have been extremely influential in the non-governmental provision of social services.[239] Women's NGOs have established links with local governments, procured subsidies for the poor, the elderly, and handicapped, pressed for environmental and educational reforms, and advocated against abuses in and of the military.

Serbia

The situation regarding women's participation in Serbia is much different than other parts of CEE, due to the war in the former Yugoslavia and independent women's almost absolute refusal to take part in the Milosevic regime. Given the extreme policies of the present government, the high degree of corruption in both the legal and political system, the lack of an independent judiciary and the absence of the rule of law, autonomous women's groups prefer to work outside official channels.

Complicating Serbian women's decision to become involved in politics is the presence of Mirjana Markovic, President Slobodan Milosevic's wife. Markovic has at times organized "women's groups" for the purpose of holding and attending international conferences. These groups disappear after the conferences; the independent groups in Serbia that are working on women's human rights issues are not invited to

---

235. *Id.*

236. OMRI DAILY DIGEST, Aug. 1, 1995 (available at www.omri.cz).

237. *Id.*

238. OMRI DAILY DIGEST, Mar. 5, 1996 (available at www.omri.cz).

239. Nadezhda Ashgikhina, *A Movement Is Born: Russian Women Are Coming Together to Create a New Fabric of Life*, 51 (4) BULLETIN ATOMIC SCIENTISTS 47 (1995).

their gatherings or given governmental support for attending them (with few exceptions, independent women's groups in Serbia do not accept government funding for any activities). Nevertheless, the existence of Markovic's "women's efforts" causes great confusion among the general public. Widespread television coverage of Markovic's "women's meetings" leads people to equate any group working on women's issues with Markovic's agenda.[240] As a result, "[a]s long as women's political work prompts the vision of Mirjana Markovic, women will run away as fast as they can."[241]

Women are a rarity in the federal level of Serbian politics, comprising less than 5 percent of elected posts. At the local level, women make up less than 10 percent of the elected politicians.[242] Women's rights groups have not yet attempted to create a women's party.

Ukraine

In 1996, women held approximately 4 percent of the high ranking political positions. Not a single minister in the federal Parliament was female.[243] Ukraine has a woman's party—the Ukrainian Women Christian Party—but its influence on public life is "negligible."[244]

Several administrative entities in both Parliament and the Cabinet of Ministers are ostensibly concerned with women's issues. For example, Parliament has a Commission on Health Care, Mother and Child Protection; the Commission on Human Rights has a sub-commission on Enforcement of Rights of Women, Family and Children; and the Office of the President of Ukraine has a Committee for Women's Affairs, Motherhood and Childhood. However none of these entities have much say over budgetary matters and, to date, they have been largely symbolic.

Under the former regime, women received 36 percent of the seats on the Supreme Council.[245] In the first democratic elections in 1990, women won only 3 percent of the seats. In 1994, this figure increased by only one percentage point.[246] There is not a single woman minister. Political parties do not have quotas for women on their electoral lists, and do not include women in places of leadership in their activities.

Women in Ukraine have targeted "women in politics" as one of their primary goals. Groups such as Women's Fate, the Ukrainian Center of Independent Research, and the Humanitarian Initiative have held workshops and training to promote women's participation in politics. In addition, women have created coalitions to push women's

---

240. Author's observation of media coverage in Serbia, 1993–1995.

241. Author's interview with "K.", June 1996.

242. Response to author's survey, Aug. 1996 (Zorica Mrsevic, Belgrade Women's Law Group).

243. Response to author's survey, Aug. 1996 (Olena Suslova, Kiev).

244. *Id.*

245. IWRAW Country Reports, *supra* note 114, at 63.

246. Response to author's survey, Aug. 1996 (Olena Suslova, Kiev).

agendas during electoral campaigns.[247] After the July 1995 hearing on the implementation of the Women's Convention in Ukraine, the Ukrainian Parliament agreed to take steps to increase the participation of women in executive offices on parity with men.

Other Areas of Concern

Abortion and Women's Health[248]

Albania

In January 1992, the abortion law in Albania was revised to make abortion legal. Previously, abortions were only permitted when the pregnancy endangered the health of the mother. During the time in which abortions were illegal, many women turned to unsanitary, illegal procedures; an estimated 50 percent of women who had illegal abortions suffered grave health consequences.[249] The 1992 law permitted abortions before the twelfth week of pregnancy for anyone over the age of sixteen. Women seeking abortions after the twelfth week of pregnancy and younger women seeking abortions were forced to see a special commission that would decide whether the abortion was necessary.[250]

In December 1995, the Albanian Parliament passed legislation further liberalizing abortion, allowing abortion as a "family planning method," thus opening abortion to women upon demand.[251] An estimated 30,000 abortions take place every year in Albania,[252] although the number could be higher due to a large number of illegal procedures that still are performed, especially in rural areas. The number of abortions now exceeds the number of reported births. Contraceptives are scarce in Albania and accurate family planning information is hard to find.[253]

Bulgaria

Under the old regime, married women with one or no children were forbidden to have an abortion unless a medical problem existed.[254] Other women could freely

---

247. *Id.*

248. Very few respondents to the survey provided information about HIV/AIDS. Absence of data, however, does not necessarily mean that the problem does not exist. The rate of HIV infection in CEE has been rising steadily and, despite scattered education campaigns, prejudice toward the HIV positive and ignorance about the virus is high.

249. Diana Culi, Liri Shimani & Lenovefa Wdremice, *Albania, in* HELSINKI CITIZENS' ASSEMBLY, REPRODUCTIVE RIGHTS IN EAST AND CENTRAL EUROPE 13 (Helsinki Citizen's Assembly Publication Series 3, 1992).

250. *Id.*

251. OMRI DAILY DIGEST, Dec. 8, 1995 (available at www.omri.cz).

252. *Id.*

253. Response to author's survey, Aug. 1996 (Tefta Zaka and Kathleen Imhotz, Tirana).

254. Dimitrina Petrova, *Bulgaria, in* HELSINKI CITIZENS' ASSEMBLY, REPRODUCTIVE RIGHTS IN EAST AND CENTRAL EUROPE 15 (Helsinki Citizen's Assembly Publication Series 3, 1992).

obtain an abortion. The restrictions on married women were lifted in 1990 and today abortion is legal for all women under the same criteria. Abortions can be performed for any reason up to the tenth week of pregnancy (and up to the twelfth week in some cases); an abortion for medical reasons is allowed up to the twenty-second week of pregnancy.[255]

Abortion is free of charge if it is being performed for "health reasons," but otherwise a fee is required.[256] The cost of abortion procedures has risen significantly over the past three years. Due to lack of funding and information, many women continue to have higher-risk illegal procedures. A record high 120,000 women in Bulgaria had an abortion in the first five months of 1996, 100,000 of which were legal and the rest illegal. According to official data, 150,000 pregnancies were terminated in 1995, while only 72,000 babies were born.[257]

Many contraceptives, including the pill and the IUD, are available in Bulgaria without prescription. Condoms are available but are not commonly used due to social taboos. The most widely used form of birth control is the least effective—the "withdrawal method." For the most part, very little sex education exists in the school system, but family planning clinics provide contraceptive information and counseling. The rate of teenage pregnancy in Bulgaria is extremely high.[258]

The general standard of health in Bulgaria is growing worse by the year. According to data from medical checkups in 1993, only 30 percent of all women are healthy or practically healthy; in 1983, 68 percent of women were said to be healthy or practically healthy.[259] The maternal mortality index (number of deaths per 100,0000 live births) is among the highest in Europe.[260]

Croatia

The old law on abortion from the former Yugoslavia still governs access to abortion in Croatia.[261] The 1978 Act of Health Measures for Free Decisions on Child-Bearing "determines the rights and duties of people to freely make decisions in matters relating to procreation . . . [including] birth control, abortion, . . . [and] medical help for those who desire, but cannot have children."

---

255. *Id.*

256. *Id.*

257. OMRI DAILY DIGEST, June 26, 1996 (available at www.omri.cz).

258. Sociological survey of Dimitrina Panajotova, Bulgarian Free Feminist Group, Sofia, 1992; updated by author's conversations with the Bulgarian Free Feminist Group, May 1996.

259. UNDP NGO Report, *supra* note 49, at 8.

260. In 1993, the index was 20 in Bulgaria, compared with 12.8 in Poland, 8.1 in Great Britain and 1.6 in Denmark. UNDP NGO Report, *id.* at 8.

261. This section is drawn from research the author conducted in Croatia in January and February 1993. *See* The Center for Reproductive Law and Policy, *Meeting the Health Care Needs of Women Survivors of the Balkan Conflict* 17–20 (1993) (monograph).

The 1978 Act establishes a general right to procreative liberty, declaring that "[t]he right of a person to make autonomous decisions on issues relating to procreation can only be restricted because of health reasons and under circumstances prescribed by this act." (Article 2.) The 1978 Act establishes a specific "right to be informed of the advantages and methods of family planning. . ." (Article 6), a "right to use birth control devices . . ." (Article 6), a limited right to abortion (Articles 15–27), and a "right to medical help" for "women and men who cannot fulfill their desire to have descendants on their own" (a limited right to artificial insemination) (Articles 29–34.)

Abortions are permitted under the 1978 Act for any reason up to ten weeks after conception. After ten weeks, a woman must obtain permission from a special Commission, composed of two physicians and one social worker or registered nurse. Young women under the age of sixteen seeking abortions must also receive the consent of one parent or guardian.

The Commissions are legally able to grant exceptions when "it is medically established that it would be impossible to save [the women's] life or prevent damage to her health during pregnancy, delivery or postpartum condition," "when there is a medically established probability that the child would be born with serious congenital, physical or psychological handicaps," or "when the conception is the consequence of a criminal act of rape, a criminal act of sexual intercourse with an incompetent person, a criminal act of sexual intercourse that is a consequence of an abuse of authority, a criminal act of sexual intercourse with a child, or a criminal act of incest." (Article 22.)

In addition, abortions can be performed at any time "where there is immediate danger to the life or health of the pregnant woman; [or] where the abortion has already been initiated." (Article 25.) If the Commission denies a woman's request, she has the right to appeal to a second Commission.

While the 1978 Act sets no time limit for abortions, most hospitals will not perform an abortion after twenty-two weeks gestation; others set the time limit at twenty or even fourteen weeks.[262] Advocates for women in Croatia report that accessibility to second trimester abortions varies widely from hospital to hospital and from physician to physician. Women who can show that their pregnancy causes only psychiatric distress are unlikely to be able to obtain a legal abortion.[263] According to the women's advocacy group B.a.B.e., "doctors and hospital workers fear the reactions of the government supported[264] pro-life movement and the [Roman

---

262. *Id.* at 19.

263. *Id.* at 18.

264. In Spring 1992, the Croatian government established the Ministry for Renewal with a special Department for Demographic Renewal, headed at that time by Don Ante Bakovic, a former priest and staunch nationalist anti-abortionist. The Department proposed motherhood as the highest vocation for women and presented a strategy for the development of an "ethnically clean" birth rate. Local and international pressure led to the removal of Bakovic from this post and the formal dismantling of the Department. Bakovic, with support of leading politicians including President

Catholic] Church."[265] The cost for abortion varies, but the average cost in August 1996 was 1.500 kuna, approximately an average monthly salary.

An abortion law proposed in 1995 would require obligatory counseling for women (with a doctor, social worker, and a priest) and shorten the legal time for abortions to ten weeks. Some anti-abortionists in Croatia, who are often tied closely to the Roman Catholic Church and/or nationalist groups, advocate that a ban on abortion be accompanied by pro-natalist and anti-immigrant policies to support an increase in the Croat birth rate.[266]

Contraception is still legal but inaccessible for many women as the services are not covered by social insurance. Under increasing pressure from the Church, sex education has disappeared from most schools.

Czech Republic

In the former Czecheslovakia, the first abortion law passed in 1958 permitted abortions based on the decision of a special commission.[267] After 1986, the law was liberalized. Early procedures (up to the forty-second day of pregnancy) were not even counted as abortions, but instead called "menstrual regulation."[268] Women could receive two abortions free each year, as long as they were performed within the first eight weeks of pregnancy, otherwise they would pay a fee.[269]

Despite the efforts of a small but vocal Catholic anti-abortion movement, abortion remains legal and widely available in the Czech Republic. However, women now must pay for the procedure. The Ministry of Health establishes the cost of abortions: procedures performed in the first eight weeks of pregnancy cost CZK 2, 876 (41 percent average monthly wage); procedures performed between the eighth and the end of the twelfth week of pregnancy cost CZK 3,634 (52 percent average monthly wage).[270] Physicians are prohibited from performing abortions on women who are neither citizens nor long-term residents.

Tudjman, subsequently established a quasi-NGO, the Croatian Population Movement, to carry out his agenda. Meanwhile, the Department, renamed the National Program for Demographic Development, was recognized by Parliament in January 1996. The proposed work of the new Program includes much of Bakovic's original agenda, including elimination of non-Croat immigration and return of refugees, accompanied by incentives to increase the Croat birth rate. *Croatian Pro-Lifers Attacking Women's Rights, supra* note 77; author's interview with B.a.B.e, Feb. 1996.

265. Response to author's survey, Aug. 1996.

266. *See Croatian Pro-Lifers Attacking Women's Rights, supra* note 77.

267. *See* G. Niksova, *The Legal Provisions Governing Abortions in Czechoslovakia,* 20 BULLETIN OF CZECH LAW 172, 176 (1981) (discussing § 227 of the Penal Code).

268. *See* HELSINKI CITIZENS ASSEMBLY WOMEN'S COMMISSION, REPRODUCTIVE RIGHTS IN CENTRAL AND EASTERN EUROPE 18 (1992) [hereinafter REPRODUCTIVE RIGHTS IN CEE].

269. *Id.* at 19.

270. Rate for 1996. At that time, the average monthly salary was approximately CZK 7,000. Shaw Survey, *supra* note 110.

After an initial increase in abortions in the late 1980s, the incidence of abortion has been declining steadily. The number of abortions fell from 49.7 abortions per 1,000 women in 1988 to 23.3 in 1994. In 1993 alone, the abortion rate dropped 23 percent.[271] While this marks a significant decrease, the incidence of abortion in the Czech Republic is still much higher than it is in Western Europe. The decrease has been attributed in part to the greater availability of contraceptives. However, the price of contraceptives has risen; until recently contraceptives were state-subsidized. While family planning services are available and sex education ("family life education") can be found in some form in schools, family planning specialists in the country decry the education as grossly inadequate.

Germany

The abortion law of the former East Germany, from 1972 onward, made abortions legal for any reason up to the twelfth week of pregnancy. After the twelfth week, abortions were available only in cases of serious medical reasons, as determined by a special medical committee. Generally women were not allowed to have abortions more than once within a six-month period. Women under the age of eighteen needed parental consent.[272]

In contrast, the law on abortion in the former West Germany, from 1976 onward, prohibited nearly all abortions. Abortions could only be performed when one of four indications were present:

(1) a medical indication of danger to the life or health of the pregnant woman;

(2) a eugenic indication of a child's physical or mental handicap;

(3) an ethical indication in the case of rape; or

(4) a social indication of an emergency situation in the life of the pregnant woman.[273]

The law further required a woman to undergo counseling with a doctor other than the one who would perform the procedure.

After unification, as an interim solution, East Germany's abortion law was allowed to remain in effect until the end of 1992.[274] In 1993, the Federal Constitutional

---

271. Schepple, *Women's Rights, supra* note 61, at 68.

272. Kerstin Koanbek & Christiana Schubert, *Germany, in* Helsinki Citizens' Assembly, Reproductive Rights in East and Central Europe 21 (Helsinki Citizen's Assembly Publication Series 3, 1992).

273. *Id.* at 22. Art. 218 of the German Penal Code.

274. Section 153 of the East German Criminal Code of Jan. 12, 1968, in its new version of Dec. 14, 1988 (Gesetzbl. DDR I, 1989, 33), amended in the 6th Criminal Law Amendment Act of June 29, 1990 (Gesetzbl. DDR I, 526), remained in force on eastern German territory. This was also true of the provisions of the Law on Interruption of Pregnancy of Mar. 9, 1972 (Gesetzbl. DDR I, 89) and its implementing regulations (Gesetzbl. DDR II, 149).

Court held that Basic Law protects the right to life of the unborn and thus, abortion was to be generally regarded as unlawful. The compromise law, the Court ruled, did not adequately protect the life of the unborn. In particular, the Court found that the neutral counseling required by the compromise law was insufficient and that a more explicitly normative form of counseling was warranted. In a lengthy and complex decision, the Court essentially made "detailed and substantive policy more so than in virtually any other Constitutional Court decision, thereby limiting legislative prerogative."[275] Legislatures were still free, however, to permit abortions in exceptional circumstances.

The Penal Code of the united Germany thereafter permitted abortions on two limited grounds: if a physician determined that the continued pregnancy would endanger the life of the woman or pose injury to her physical or mental health, or if the physician determined that the fetus suffered from irremediable damage. In the latter case, the abortion had to be performed within the first twenty-two weeks of pregnancy[276] and the pregnant woman had to receive counseling at least three days before the performance of the abortion and obtain permission from her doctor or a public health official.[277]

Germany's new abortion law, which took effect in January 1996, expands the circumstances under which women may have early abortions. As long as an abortion is performed within the first twelve weeks of pregnancy, a woman may receive an abortion provided that she receives counseling from her doctor and from an outside counseling center. In addition, abortions may be performed in cases of rape or when the pregnancy poses a threat to the health or life of the pregnant woman.[278] Under the new law, physicians can be fined 10,000 DM for failing to provide the mandatory counseling prior to performing abortions, and family members who pressure women to terminate their pregnancy could face up to five years in prison.[279]

The Social Security Code reimburses the cost of legal abortions performed for insured persons in hospitals or other designated institutions. The statutory health insurance schemes also cover the cost of abortion services for low-income women and generally reimburse patients for medical treatment, counseling, examinations, and the provision of medications.[280] Furthermore, insured persons have the right to state-subsidized birth control and family planning.[281] The 1990 Unification Agreement

---

275. Decision of the Second Senate, German Constitutional Court of May 28, 1993 (2BvF 2/90 (BGBI.I S 820).

276. Ger. Penal Code, art. 218a(3).

277. Ger. Penal Code, art. 218(1).

278. International Program, The Center for Reproductive Law and Policy, *Women of the World: Formal Laws and Policies Affecting their Reproductive Lives* (monograph) 1995, at 18 (citing *Germany: Abortion Compromise Clears Final Hurdle*, International Briefing, The Abortion Report, American Political Network, July 19, 1995).

279. Ger. Penal Code, art. 218c.

280. Ger. Social Code, art. 24b(1).

281. Ger. Social Code, art. 24a(1).

between East and West Germany[282] specifically advocated providing sufficient and equal health care services for all persons residing within Germany. To this end, the German Social Code extends the former West Germany's extensive system of health insurance policies[283] and medical care to the former East Germany.

The Family Support Act of 1992 recognizes a right to family planning counseling. According to women's rights activists in Germany[284] and international health specialists,[285] this provision has been read as a mandate for information encouraging a woman to continue her pregnancy. Sex education is provided in schools, but some activists warn that it is frequently heavily weighted against abortion.

Germany's restrictions on new reproductive technologies are among the strictest in the world.[286] Surrogate motherhood arrangements, transferring an embryo from one woman to another, and many methods of artificial insemination are strictly prohibited.[287] Activists for women's human rights in Germany (and especially West Germany) have identified revision of the laws on reproductive technologies as one of the main issues on their agenda.[288]

Hungary

The 1973 abortion law in Hungary permitted abortions for any reason, for single and divorced women, widowed women, married women over the age of thirty-five, and women who have undergone two or more births. Other women had to plead their case before a special commission. Minors could obtain an abortion up to the eighteenth week of pregnancy; in the case of rape or incest, abortions were permitted up to twenty weeks of pregnancy.

The new abortion law, passed by Parliament in 1992, allows for abortions under a set of enumerated medical and social circumstances, including certification by the woman that she is in crisis. Although the reasons allowed for having an abortion appear to be relatively liberal, the law contains several new, restrictive provisions. Women

---

282. Art. 31 (IV) of the *Vertrag zwischen der Bundesrepublik Deutschland und deer Deutschen Demokratischen Republik hber die Herstellung der Einheit Deutschlands (Einigungsvertrag)* [Unification Treaty] of Aug. 31, 1990, BGBl II at p. 889. *See also* KLAUS STERN & BRUNO SCHMIDT-BLEIBTREU, EINIGUNGSVERTRAG UND WAHLVERTRAG (1990).

283. *See* Karsten Schroeder, *The Statutory Health Insurance Scheme: Fundamentals of the German Health Service*, IN PRESS SOCIAL REPORT, Sept. 1994.

284. Responses to authors' survey, Aug. 1996 (Suzette Schultz, Berlin).

285. *See* Joachim von Bross, *The 'Yo-Yo' Effect of Public Family Planning Funding in Germany*, 23 PLANNED PARENTHOOD IN EUROPE 6 (Mar. 1994); International Program, The Center for Reproductive Law and Policy, *Women of the World: Formal Laws and Policies Affecting their Reproductive Lives* (monograph) 1995, at 19.

286. *Political and Religious Leaders Take Up Debate on In Vitro Fertilization of Older Women*, THE WEEK IN GERMANY, Jan. 21, 1994, at 6.

287. *See* the Embryo Protection Law of Dec. 19, 1990, Bundesgesetzblatt, Pt. I, 19 Dec. 1990, 2746–48.

288. Response to author's survey, Aug. 1996 (Suzette Schultz, Berlin).

must wait at least three days before having the procedure. In addition, they must undergo counseling that provides information about contraceptives and the risks of abortion.[289] These provisions are particularly burdensome to rural women who must travel great distances for gynecological health care and for young and low-income women. After the law went into effect, the number of abortions declined by 22 percent.[290]

Parliament had been forced to create a new abortion law after the Constitutional Court in 1991 struck down the old abortion provisions, comprised of administrative regulations, not statutes. The Court ruled that the issue of abortion, like other questions implicating fundamental rights, had to be governed by statute. The legislature, the Court found, had the discretion to fashion a law by balancing the interests at stake. The legislature could neither find the fetus a legal person with rights equal to the pregnant woman, nor could the legislature find that the fetus was entitled to no rights whatsoever.[291] By including waiting periods and mandatory counseling, Parliament apparently attempted to make this balance.

Not satisfied with the outcome, a vocal group of anti-abortionists continues to pressure the government to enact a more restrictive law. Some of the anti-abortionists are tied closely with Hungarian nationalists who see returning women to their role as mothers and banning abortion as necessary to return to "Christian values" and restore the "Hungarian nation."[292]

Sex education is very limited in Hungary. The Catholic Church, which has been given back control of many schools by the government, has campaigned against sex education as a dangerous influence on young minds. The rate of teenage pregnancy is high in Hungary.

Kosovo

The law on abortion in Kosovo is still governed by the law of former Yugoslavia, that is, the "1978 Act on Health Measures for Free Decisions on Child Bearing."[293]

Some human rights activists have long reported that Kosovar Albanian women are encouraged to have abortions, while Serbian women are encouraged to carry until term. Indeed, in 1990, the Serbian legislature attempted to pass a measure that would have encouraged Serbian women to have children while discouraging Kosovo women from having children;[294] because rural Kosovar Albanian women tend to have larger

---

289. Schepple, *Women's Rights, supra* note 61, at 68. According to IWRAW, "[t]he counseling is designed to prevent future abortions, and to ensure that the woman is not being coerced by someone else into having an abortion." IWRAW Country Report, *supra* note 114, at 57.

290. *Id.*

291. Case 64/1991 (XII.17) (*cited in* Schepple, *Women's Rights, supra* note 61, at 68).

292. Antonia Burrows, *Hungary, in* HELSINKI CITIZENS' ASSEMBLY, REPRODUCTIVE RIGHTS IN EAST AND CENTRAL EUROPE 25 (Helsinki Citizen's Assembly Publication Series 3, 1992).

293. *See* Croatia, *supra.*

294. *See infra* note 331, and accompanying text.

families than Serbian families, the proposal, which failed to pass, would have had a disproportionately negative impact on Kosovar Albanian women.[295] The abortion rate has always been low among Kosovar Albanian women; even fewer abortions have been performed since the crisis began in Kosovo in 1989.

The health system has suffered under the current political crisis. Beginning in 1989, many Albanian health care workers were fired from or resigned from their positions. To the greatest extent possible, the Albanian population boycotted the Serbian-run hospitals and clinics, turning instead to private, Albanian-run health care. Still, many Albanians had no choice but to turn to state hospitals for maternity care. Due to substandard conditions and inadequate training of physicians in state hospitals, the maternal morbidity and mortality rate in Kosovo hospitals has been among the highest in Europe.[296]

In June 1995, Kosovar women activists opened the first women's and children's health care clinic in Kosovo, the Centre for Protection of Women and Children.[297] The Pristina-based clinic is the only facility offering pap smears and other preventative gynecological health care to a population of approximately two million.

Poland

On May 28, 1997, the Constitutional Tribunal of Poland struck down the country's liberalized abortion law, which permitted abortions, for compelling social and financial reasons, until the twelfth week of pregnancy, and in certain cases of rape, incest, and gross fetal defects. The court found that the provision permitting abortions for social reasons did not uphold the constitutional guarantees to the right to life and was thus violative of the country's democratic order. "The first article of our constitution names Poland as a democratic state based on the rule of law," said Tribunal President Andrej Zoll. "The highest value in a democracy is human life, which must be protected from its beginning to the end." The provisions relating to incest, rape, and fetal defects were not affected by the ruling.[298]

The law that was struck down had taken effect in January 1997. The Sejm, one branch of the bicameral Polish Parliament, had voted in favor of the controversial law in October 1996, with a count of 228 to 195 (with sixteen abstentions). That vote

---

295. Mertus, SOCIAL POLITICS, *supra* note 76, at 267. *See Editor's Note, supra* note 123.

296. *See* JULIE MERTUS & VLATKA MIHELIC, OPEN WOUNDS: HUMAN RIGHTS ABUSES IN KOSOVO 132 (1994).

297. Brochures and publications of Centre on file with author.

298. *See Polish Court Rejects Bulk of Abortion Law*, THE BALT. SUN, May 29, 1997 (1997 WL 5513578); Dean F. Murphy, *Polish Court Restricts Abortion Rights in Europe: Judges Rule Recent Statute Violates Country's Nacent Democratic Order*, L.A. TIMES, May 19, 1997 (1997 WL 2215001). Note that within six months of such a constitutional decision, a two-thirds majority of the Sejm (the lower house of Parliament) could void the decision. In the case of the abortion law, a two-thirds majority would likely be hard to find. *See* Michel Viatteau, *Referendum Urged for Poland After Abortion Ruled Unconstitutional*, AGENCE FRANCE-PRESSE, May 19, 1997 (1997 WL 2123408). As of this writing, the Sejm did not take such action.

overturned a Senate veto of the draft law earlier in the month. A poll conducted by the Public Opinion Research Center at the time of the signing showed that 56 percent of respondents supported the amendments to the abortion law while 33 percent were against.[299]

Previously, a 1993 law, the Family Planning, Fetus Protection and Conditions of Admissibility of Abortion Act, permitted abortions only if a pregnancy threatened a woman's life or health, resulted from incest or rape, or if a fetus was irreparably damaged. In practice, the 1993 law prohibited nearly all abortions, with a penalty of two years imprisonment imposed on those caught performing it.[300] At least three women died from illegal abortions while the 1993 law was in effect.[301]

Doctors' fear of authorizing abortions, due to a lack of precise definitions of proper medical grounds in the law, compelled many women to go to very expensive and illegal private practices. Women's options outside the law included finding a private doctor who would induce an illegal abortion for a high fee; inducing miscarriages by using primitive and risky methods; or finding agencies specializing in organizing trips abroad (abortions in Russia are relatively-inexpensive while abortions in West European countries are much more expensive).

Under both old and new laws, abortions in public hospitals are covered by social insurance, but a great many women do not receive the financial support they are entitled to by law because of a lack of government resources.[302] Women's groups in Poland, such as the Federation for Women and Family Planning, the Women's Rights Center (Warsaw), and Pro-Femina have been active forces behind the campaign to make reproductive health care safe and available.

In Poland, the authorities are duty-bound to provide easy access to information about reproduction to all citizens. In reality, however, there is no guarantee of wide availability of contraceptives. Devices on sale in pharmacies are often too expensive for the average citizen, because contraceptives are not eligible for the 30 percent discount that applies to most medications. Neither knowledge about, nor access to, contraceptives devices is sufficient in Poland. Sex education in schools is non-existent or incomplete, and family planning information does not reach most rural women. Nevertheless, the Federation for Family Planning and other local and international

---

299. *See Abortion Law Liberalized in Poland*, OMRI Daily Dig., Oct. 24, 1996; Ann Snitow, *Poland's Anti-Abortion Law: The Church Wins, Women Lose*, The Nation, Apr. 26, 1993, at 16 (noting that abortions had been legal and widely available in Poland from 1956 until 1993); *Reactions to Abortion Liberalization in Poland*, OMRI Daily Digest, Nov. 27, 1996.

300. *Reactions to Abortion Liberalization in Poland, id.*; Viatteau, *supra* note 298; Snitow, *supra* note 299 (explaining the 1993 abortion law, which stated that one who causes the death of a conceived child (someone other than the mother) is subject to two years imprisonment, unless certain circumstances regarding the woman's health exist).

301. Schepple, *Women's Rights, supra* note 61, at 67.

302. Eleanora Zielinska, *Recent Trends in Abortion Legislation in Eastern Europe with Particular Reference to Poland*, 4 Crim. L.F. 47, 29 (1993).

health and women's groups have made significant inroads over the past three years in increasing access to contraceptives.[303]

Preventative gynecological care in Poland is the exception, not the rule. Eight thousand women in Poland suffer from breast cancer; half of them die because the diagnosis was made too late.[304] Environmental problems compound generally poor health conditions. An estimated 30 percent of the Polish population lives in areas of ecological disaster.[305]

HIV-AIDS Education in Poland is minimal. Women and children are increasingly infected. In 1988, the ratio of HIV positive women to HIV positive men was 1:20; in 1994, the ratio was 1:4.[306]

Romania

The abortion restrictions and pronatalist policies of the Ceausescu regime were among the most severe in the modern world.[307] From 1967 until 1985, only women with four or more children could obtain a legal abortion. In 1985, the law was tightened further to permit abortions only to women with five children under the age of eighteen. A series of additional measures was enacted to encourage reproduction and prevent abortion. Women workers at state enterprises were subject to spot "health" checks at the workplace to ensure that they were not secretly having abortions. Women who bore many children were awarded decorations and minor privileges.[308] Contraceptives were unavailable through legal channels. During this time, 86 percent of female mortality was connected to illegal abortions.[309]

One of the first acts of the post-Ceausescu government was to liberalize abortion laws and to make it widely available for a low price. In the first three months following legalization, female mortality fell by 317 percent.[310] In the first year, over one million women had abortions.[311]

Although contraceptives are available today in Romania, few people use them because of the lack of accurate information. Although the state does not sponsor sex

---

303. Survey response of Urszula Nowakowska, Women's Rights Center, Warsaw (Aug. 1996).

304. Poland NGO Report, *supra* note 128, at 35.

305. *Id.*

306. *Id.* at 37.

307. *See* Mary Ellen Fischer, *Women in Romanian Politics: Elena Ceausescu, Pronatalism, and the Promotion of Women, in* WOMEN, STATE, AND PARTY 153–62 (Wolchik & Meyer eds., 1985).

308. *See* Gail Kligman, *Women and Reproductive Legislation in Romania: Implications for Transition, in* DILEMMAS IN TRANSITION IN THE SOVIET UNION AND EASTERN EUROPE 141, 148 (George W. Breslauer ed., 1991).

309. Borica Koo & Carmen Jaorjascu, *"Romania," in* HELSINKI CITIZENS' ASSEMBLY, REPRODUCTIVE RIGHTS IN EAST AND CENTRAL EUROPE (Helsinki Citizen's Assembly Publication Series 3, 1992.)

310. *Id.*

311. *Id.*

education programs, private NGOs have established family planning clinics. One of the most active, the Society for Sex Education and Contraceptive Services (SECS), has established family planning clinics in at least six locations, published educational material for wide distribution, and undertaken media campaigns to increase public awareness.[312]

The overall standard of health care in Romania is very low. Many women do not have preventative care such as pap tests. In Romania very few women ever have pap tests—and the mortality rate from cervical cancer is the highest in Europe (10.68 per 100,000 versus the European average of 3.55 per 100,000).[313]

Russia

Russian law provides that each person has the right to the protection of their health, and to medical aid.[314] The provison in the law pertaining to expenditures of social funds—on the basis of resources corresponding to the budget—has been applied in such a way as to eliminate and privatize many aspects of health. According to Russian women human rights advocates, "local governments do not prioritize health in their limited budgets and, as a result, women must take care of sick children and ailing parents in the home, without necessary medicines."[315]

Abortion, however, is legal and widely available. The number of abortions for every 100 births is 217; almost two out of every three pregnancies end in abortion. However, the number of abortions in Russia has been steadily declining, largely because of increased access to contraceptives (although access to contraceptives is far from satisfactory). Less than 2.9 million abortions were performed in 1993, as compared with 4.4 million in 1988.[316] An abortion in Russia costs roughly one hundred dollars, more than an entire month's wage for many women (and four to five times the monthly wage for some); contraception is also expensive and more difficult to find than abortion services.[317]

A revision of the family law, proposed in 1993, would have added that the state recognizes a "child's right to life" and that men and women have "equal rights in deciding all issues of family life, including family planning."[318] Women advocates argued that the proposal could have been used to prohibit abortions. The Bill has not been discussed seriously since 1993.

---

312. Public Education Material of Society for Sex Education and Contraceptive Services (SECS) on file with author.

313. Koo & Jaorjascu, *supra* note 309.

314. Response to author's survey, Aug. 1995.

315. Grogan Survey, *supra* note 132.

316. Schepple, *Women's Rights, supra* note 61, at 68.

317. Grogan Survey, *supra* note 132.

318. *Women's Rights, supra* note 61, at 67.

Although the pro-life movement has not made much headway in Russia, it is considered to be connected with the introduction of a new provision of the Criminal Code prohibiting the "murder of a newly born infant by the mother." Article 106 of the Criminal Code provides that "murder of the infant at the time or right after birth in a psychologically traumatic situation or in a state of psychic disorder, which does not exclude mental sanity is punishable by imprisonment for up to 5 years."[319] The Moscow Gender Studies Center states that "concerning the fact that there is no rise in statistics for this crime, the appearance of this particular Criminal Code provision is connected with the newly developing "pro-life" movement in Russia."[320]

Health care has deteriorated in recent years. Consider the following statistics: According to the Labour Ministry, the number of Russian women who die during childbirth has risen sharply in the past few years. Since 1992, the childbirth mortality rate has increased from forty-seven per 100,000 to fifty-two per 100,000. This rate is ten times higher than in industrialized European countries.[321] There has been a reduction in the number of hospital beds (medical and obstetrical) for pregnant women and women giving birth. In 1994 the total was 29.1 per 10,000 women aged fifteen to forty-nine, whereas, in 1985, this total was 32.4 per 10,000 women of childbearing age.[322] According to information gathered from the Moscow Gender Studies Report:[323]

- There are five gynecologists per 10,000 women in the state health care system.

- The breast cancer rate has increased from 27.9 thousand cases (36.4 per 10,000 women) in 1985 to 37.0 thousand cases (47.1 per 10,000 women) in 1994. For cancers of the cervix, uterus, and placenta, the rate has gone from 15.0 thousand cases in 1985 to 24.8 thousand cases in 1994. For sexually transmitted diseases such as syphilis, the rate has gone from 6.7 thousand cases (8.7 per 10,000 women) in 1985 to 62.6 thousand cases (79.6 per 10,000 women) in 1994.

- In 1994, the rate of anemia among pregnant women was more than three times the number in 1985 and the rate of illnesses of the urinary-genital system was twice as high by 1994.

- The number of birth complications has increased by 61.3 percent. More than 50 percent of the children who are born have health problems.

- The registered level of infant and child deaths and the number of abortions in Russia has reached proportions unprecedented in the second half of the twen-

---

319. Russian Criminal Code, art. 107 (1996).

320. *See* Moscow Gender Studies Report, *supra* note 175. Russian Criminal Code, art. 134 (1996).

321. OMRI Daily Digest, June 26, 1995 (available at www.omri.cz).

322. Moscow Gender Studies Report, *supra* note 175.

323. The following statistics were compiled from the Moscow Gender Studies Report, *id.*

tieth century. In 1994, infant deaths totaled 18.6 per 1000 births. The number of abortions stands at 83.4 per 1,000 women (aged fifteen to forty-nine).

Serbia

Like Croatia, abortion in Serbia is still governed by the law of former Yugoslavia, the 1978 Act on Measures for Free Decisions Regarding Child-Bearing (see section on Croatia, *supra*). According to some advocates for women in Serbia, however, women are in fact required to obtain permission from a special Commission for an abortion after the eighth week of pregnancy (although the law specifies ten weeks). In addition, in Serbia the Commission rarely grants permission to married women with one or no children.[324]

Since 1991, an increasing number of women have died from illegal and unsafe abortions as anti-abortion forces have grown and legal procedures have become harder to obtain, especially for ethnic Serbs.[325] The most common tactic of anti-abortionists in wartime Serbia is to brand women who forego childbearing and child-raising roles as "unpatriotic" and "selfish" to their nation, which "needs them."[326] The Serbian Orthodox Church established the tenor for the campaign in March 1994, when Vasilije Kacavenda, one of the highest ranking people in the Church, proclaimed that "abortion is the unspeakable slaughter of little Serbs" and that "Serbian people are dying and bleeding at the same time, both on the battle field and on the medical table."[327]

Belgrade women's groups have noticed that since the war began, the so-called abortion commission has started denying abortions to more Serbian women when the grounds were "social reasons" but has continued to permit abortions for the same reasons for Rom (Gypsy) and Albanian women.[328] Nevertheless, most abortions performed in Serbia are on Serbian women during the first twelve weeks of pregnancy (when the Commission plays no role).[329] Knowing that selective use of the Commission is not enough to limit significantly Serbian women's abortions, the

---

324. Response to author's survey, Aug. 1996 (Zorica Mrsevic, Belgrade Women's Law Group).

325. Author's interview with Autonomous Women's Center, May 1995.

326. *See* Dasa Duhacek, *Women's Time in the Former Yugoslavia, in* GENDER POLITICS AND POST-COMMUNISM: REFLECTIONS FROM EASTERN EUROPE AND THE FORMER SOVIET UNION 131 (Nanette Funk & Magda Mueller eds., 1993); "Zenski dokumenti 1990–1993" at 1, 5 ("Women's Documents 1990–1993"), Feministicke sveske (Feminist Notebooks) (Winter 1995) (chronology of documents on abortion in Serbia).

327. Gordana Radisavljevic, *Neprikosnoveno pravo* (Inviolable Right), POLITIKA (daily), Dec. 1994. In his 1994 Christmas address to the nation, Patriarch Pavle's proclaimed that "not allowing your children to see the bright of the day is a greater sin than murder." I. Kisic & N. Kovacevic, *Zenski gnev i popovska zloba* (Women's Rage and the Evils of Priests), NASA BORBA (independent daily), Jan. 16, 1995.

328. Author's interviews with Autonomous Women's Center, SOS Hotline, and Women's Shelter, Belgrade, Apr. 1995.

329. Author's interviews with doctors Stanislava Otasevic and Vera Litricin, Autonomous Women's Center and SOS for Girls, Belgrade, Apr. 1995.

Serbian Parliament passed a restrictive abortion law in May 1994, but President Milosevic refused to sign the measure.

In 1994, another proposed restrictive abortion law, more onerous than the earlier proposal, surfaced in Parliament, banning all abortions after ten weeks except for very limited medical reasons (when pregnancy or childbirth endangers the woman's life or when there is evidence of grave fetal defects).[330] Various versions of this proposal were contemplated again in 1995 and 1996, but as of this writing none have been adopted. The most recent proposal forbids all procedures after the tenth week of pregnancy unless the pregnancy is the result of rape or another crime, is threatening to the woman's life, or if the child would be born with grave defects.

Women in Serbia have long had access to contraceptives. During the war, Serbia faced a shortage of "the pill" as contraceptives had been manufactured elsewhere in the former Yugoslavia or abroad. For the most part, today nearly anything can be found in private pharmacies as long as the woman has sufficient finances. Still, due to a lack of information and finances, many women do not use contraceptives. Sex education does not exist in schools.

In 1990, the Serbian Parliament considered a law that was designed to raise the birth rate among Serb women while also indirectly discouraging Albanian women from having children. The proposal would have permitted families with two children to pay less than families with only one child; families with three or more children would have been free from paying taxes regardless of income.[331] The law would have applied only in regions with a low birth rate—in other words, it would have applied to areas dominated by ethnic Serbs and not to Kosovo, where the birth rate is high and the population is approximately 90 percent ethnic Albanian. This proposal received great attention in the media, leading to the creation of many new women's groups.

Although the 1990 proposal was defeated, nationalist-leaning political parties continue to discuss the need to raise the Serbian birth rate, and to decrease the non-Serb (that is, the Albanian) rate. Periodically, demographers predict that by the end of the next century Albanians will out-populate Serbs; physicians speak on national television about the "time bomb" in the womb of Albanian women.[332] In fact, although

---

330. Nadezda Cetkovic, *Nedvoljna argumentacija* (Insufficient Argumentation), Politika, Jan. 13, 1995 (Rajko Sudzum, Assistant Minister of Health of Serbia, claims that abortions in cases in which pregnancy results from rape and incest are allowed, but Cetovic argues otherwise.)

331. Ivana Balen & Natasha Acimovic, *Helsinki Citizens' Assembly, Reproductive Rights in East and Central Europe* 35 (Helsinki Citizen's Assembly Publication Series 3, 1992).

332. Author's observation of Belgrade television newscasts, 1993–1995. For example, in 1994 the daily Borba reported:

According to the research of Mrs. Gordana Matkovi from the Economic Institute, in the year 2050 in central Serbia, the number of children will decrease from 67,000 to only 27,000; in Vojvodina, from 20,000 to 9,000, and in Montenegro from 9,600 to 3,600 children. During that time in Kosovo and Metohija, the decrease will be negligible from today's 52,000 to 48,000 children. In other words, in one year there will be more newborn children in Kosovo than in all other areas together.

the overall Albanian birth rate is higher than the Serbian rate, the figures are almost identical for educated, urban women, regardless of ethnicity.[333]

Slovakia

Although abortion is now available freely, pressure is growing for restrictions. Anti-abortion forces, often working closely with religious groups and at times with foreign groups, have proposed a nearly absolute ban on abortions. As of this writing, a draft law has yet to materialize.

In 1994, the abortion rate was 61.9 abortions per 100 children born.[334] After the liberalization of abortion laws in the mid-1980s, the abortion rate sharply increased but, beginning in 1988 as contraceptives became more available, the abortion rate displayed a downward trend. In over 75 percent of the cases, abortions are performed on married women with one or more children.[335]

Ukraine

Abortion and contraception are theoretically available to all women. However, rural women must often travel prohibitively long distances to have the procedure, and younger women may not be able to afford the "incidental" costs of the procedure. Although most health services are still covered by social insurance, in reality women must pay from $15 to $100 for abortions (from 15 percent to an entire average monthly salary).[336] Physicians can prohibit abortions in individual cases after finding a danger to the women's health.

The main health problems facing women in Ukraine stem from industrial pollution and the continuing effects of the Chernobyl disaster:

> According to the Ukrainian Institute of Gynecology and Obstetrics, seventy percent of children are now born with some developmental defect. Of the thirty percent who are born healthy, only twenty percent are still healthy by the time they graduate from

---

The article also detailed the results of a survey of four hundred Belgrade women who decided to have an abortion:

> Those women accept lack of renewal of the population as a problem demanding attention. . . . [They exhibit the] feeling of the nation being in danger because of the demographic explosion in Kosovo but also they point out the long-term consequences of the present reproductive model such as growing old and high depopulation.

M. Jankovi, *Da li dr`ava `eli decu?* (Does the state want children?), BORBA (Belgrade daily), June 2, 1994.

333. In fact, Srdjan Bogosavljevi, a Serbian academic, has found that the average number of live births among the educated inhabitants of Kosovo is less than in Central Serbia. Srdjan Bogosavljevi, *A Statistical Picture of Serbo-Albanian Relations*, REPUBLIKA 19 (vol. VI, Special Issue 9, Feb. 1994) (*published also in* DUSAN JANJIC & SHKELZEN MALIQI, CONFLICT OR DIALOGUE: SERBIAN-ALBANIAN RELATIONS AND THE INTEGRATION OF THE BALKANS 17–29 (1994)).

334. Slovakia Report on Women, *supra* note 21 (unpaginated).

335. *Id.*

336. Response to author's survey, Aug. 1996 (Olena Suslova, Kiev).

school. Forty percent of Ukrainian women are not able to carry out a normal pregnancy, and one out of every six is infertile. The male population, suffering from a near-epidemic of heart attacks, strokes and other alcohol or stress related diseases, has been dying steadily younger since the transition began.[337]

In their tradition role as caretakers of the family, women bear the greatest burden for the many illnesses related to environmental disasters. The crumbling social service system in Ukraine has "utterly failed"[338] to meet their needs.

Sexual Harassment

Albania

Albania has one of the most explicit laws on sexual harassment in Europe, although the definition of sexual harassment appears to be narrow. The new Labour Code, enacted in August 1995, states:

Protection of the Personality: [in the sense of personhood, or reputation].

(1) The employer shall respect the personality of the employee and protect it in Labour relations.

(2) He must avoid any position that infringes on the dignity of the employee.

(3) The employer is forbidden to perform any act that constitutes sexual harassment [the word is actually "shqetesim," which means something that is disturbing or uncomfortable] against the employee and shall not permit the performance of such acts by other employees.

By "sexual harassment" is understood as any harassment [shqetesim] that clearly damages the psychological condition of the employee because of sex. [Me shqetesim seksual kuptohet cdo shqetesim qe demton ne menyre te dukshme gjendjen psikologjike te punemarresit per shkak te seksit]. (Article 32.)[339]

This clause, developed by the Women's Legal Group, an Albanian NGO, represented a compromise between advocates for women who wanted a broader definition of sexual harassment and legislators who resisted making any changes. Women's groups in Tirana have applauded the new law as a significant advance in a society in which sexual harassment is a taboo subject.[340]

Croatia

There is no specific law on sexual harassment. Cases of sexual harassment may be brought only under the general Criminal Code. Advocates for women's rights in Croatia say that courts are unlikely to apply criminal law to a case of sexual harassment unless it results in rape or some other kind of physical assault: "Using power in the working place to force women to [perform] sexual acts . . . , acts such as harassment, stalking or sleazy phone-calls are not recognized as sexual crimes."[341]

---

337. IWRAW Country Reports, *supra* note 114, at 59.

338. Response to author's survey, Aug. 1996 (Olena Suslova, Kiev).

339. Translation by Kathleen Imholz.

340. Response to author's survey, Aug. 1996 (Tefta Zaka and Kathleen Imholz, Tirana, Albania).

341. Response to author's survey, Aug. 1996 (B.a.B.e, Zagreb).

Sexual harassment "is not recognized as an act that men should not commit," according to a representative of B.a.B.e., explaining that "[s]exual harassment is widespread, but considered a 'non-topic,' in other words you just shouldn't talk about it."[342] Refugee women in Croatia are particularly subject to harassment, as they are often hired illegally.

Czech Republic

The Czech Republic has no laws that specifically address sexual harassment. A woman can file a claim based on violation of personal dignity, or extortion, if an employer fires her for failure to comply. Neither of these options, however, is particularly viable.

Refugee, migrant, and Rom (gypsy) women are frequently hired in short-term, unregulated jobs where the potential for exploitation and harassment is extremely high. However, no data is available about sexual harassment among these populations.

Hungary

Sexual harassment is virtually an epidemic.[343] In 1994, when liberal MPs tried to add an amendment concerning sexual harassment to the Labour Bill, the Labour committee ridiculed the suggestion and failed to vote the amendment out of committee, even though such a procedure requires only one third of the committee to vote positively.[344]

Workplace harassment does not appear as a concrete charge under the current Penal Code, yet it could be judged equivalent to the crime of defamation through aggression. Alternatively, the perpetrator may be held responsible for duress, restriction of personal freedom, or public acts of indecency.

Kosovo

The topic of sexual harassment is strictly socially taboo. No study has ever been conducted on sexual harassment in employment in Kosovo.

Poland

The Penal Code states that anyone who uses his or her superior position to force another person to provide sexual favors may be sentenced to up to five years in prison. According to advocates for women in Poland, in the few cases in which the provision has been invoked, it has been applied only to the case of rape or attempted rape. This has fostered the general belief that any harassment that does not include rape is permissible.

---

342. *Id.*

343. IWRAW NGO Report, *supra* note 197, at 53.

344. Response to author's survey, Aug. 1996.

A provision in the Labour Code, effective in July 1996, imposes a duty on employers to protect workers' dignity. The new provision does not cover employee to employee behavior, nor does it oblige employers to create a friendly work environment.[345]

Romania

Romanian labor law does not include sexual harassment. Cases could potentially be brought under the Criminal Code, but Courts are unlikely to apply the Criminal Code to situations not involving rape or attempted rape. In Romania, there is little or no awareness about sexual harassment. According to Laura Grunberg, of the Society for Feminist Analysis: "Women are exposed to sexual harassment when going to interviews, when being secretaries, as students. . . . But the issue has never been studied." She explains that "it is considered as an extravagance to speak about it in the context of the other problems of transition."[346]

Slovakia

Slovak labor law does not specifically define and prohibit sexual harassment even though it is quite prevalent in the workplace. In a recent survey of over 1,000 people throughout Slovakia, almost half of the respondents regularly encountered sexual jokes, stories, and innuendoes.[347] Women in Slovakia tend to accept hostile work environments as "natural" or inevitable.

Russia

The definition of sexual harassment in the old Criminal Code prohibited sexual harassment only when it involved sexual intercourse. Under this law, Clause 118 defined sexual harassment as: "Forcing a woman to have intercourse or to satisfy sexual needs in other form by a person on whom the woman is dependent in material by professional status."[348] On June 19, 1995, the Duma voted for a new Criminal Code. The new Code eliminated the requirement of sexual intercourse, defining sexual harassment instead in Clause 134 as "[t]he forcing of a person to actions of a sexual character," including "forcing a person to commit sexual intercourse, sodomy, lesbianity, or other actions of sexual character by blackmail, threats, destruction, damage or removal of property, or by using the dependent position of the victim."[349] The Labour Code does not mention sexual harassment.

---

345. Response to author's survey, Aug. 1996 (Urszula Nowakowska, Women's Rights Center, Warsaw).

346. Response to author's survey, Aug. 1996 (Laura Grunberg, ANA, the Society for Feminist Analysis, Bucharest).

347. Slovakia Report on Women, *supra* note 21.

348. Art. 118, Russian Criminal Code (pre-1996).

349. Art. 134, Russian Criminal Code (1996).

The addition of the clause prohibiting coercion into homosexual relations is particularly curious. "The new law confuses the issue and weakens possibilities for enforcement by law combining sexual harassment with the forcing men and women to enter into homosexual relationships." Elena Kotchkina, Expert of the Russian State Duma warns, "A claim of sexual harassment now also invokes the popular stereotypes regarding homosexuality."[350] Few women even contemplate bringing a sexual harassment case: "For most women, the fact of having a job is more important that the degradation [they experience from their] employer's indiscretions."[351]

Serbia

Although Serbia's labor law does not include sexual harassment, the criminal law prohibits men from using their position to force sexual relations on a woman:

(1) Who abuses his position to lead into sexual relationship or unnatural chastity (buggery) a female person who is in a subordinate position or dependence to him, will be punished with a prison term from three months to three years.

(2) Teachers, educators, guardians, curators, foster fathers, or step fathers or any other person who abuses his position and commits a sexual relationship or unnatural chastity (buggery) with a juvenile person older than 14, who was dedicated to the perpetrator for learning, studying, education, care, or curing, will be punished by prison term from 6 months to 5 years.

(3) If the deed from section (2) of this article was committed against the person who was younger than 14, the perpetrator will be punished with a prison term from one to eight years. (Article 107.)[352]

This provision has rarely been applied. Courts would likely read it to cover only rape, sodomy, and other physical sexual acts.

Ukraine

Ukrainian labor law does not include sexual harassment, however the general provisions of the labor law could be read as applicable. In 1996, in the western town of Lviv, a woman won a criminal case concerning sexual harassment. Ukrainian activists believe that this is the first successful sexual harassment case in the country.[353]

Maternity Leave and Child Care

Albania

The new Labour Code permits both men and women to take child care leave.

---

350. Grogan Survey, *supra* note 132.

351. *Id.*

352. Serbia Penal Code, art. 107, translation by Zorica Mrsevic.

353. Response to author's survey, Aug. 1996 (Olena Suslova, Kiev) (case citation unavailable).

Bulgaria

Mothers receive special protections under the Bulgarian Constitution:

> Mothers shall enjoy special protection from the state which shall guarantee them paid leave before and after confinement, free obstetrical care, relaxed conditions of work and other types of social assistance. (Article 47(2).)

According to the Labour Code, either parent may receive child care leave. Maternity leave is to last for a period of two years, after which the mother may receive one additional year of unpaid leave. The duration of leaves counts toward the length of work service for purposes of determining pensions.

Practice differs greatly from the written law, however. According to the Bulgaria office of the UNDP, "[t]hese regulations do not reflect the real capacity of the state to provide the mentioned guarantees to women—neither through resources nor through mechanisms of control."[354]

Croatia

Croatian law contains several provisions designed to encourage women to have children and to "protect" mothers in their reproductive and caretaking roles. The Constitution provides guiding language:

> The Republic shall protect maternity, children, and young people and shall create social, cultural, educational, material, and other conditions conducive to the realization of the rights to a decent life. (Article 62.)

The labor law specifies that when a woman has multiple births, a third child, or any child after the third, she may take full maternity leave up to the time the youngest child turns three. Fathers have the right to childcare leave after the child reaches the age of six months.[355]

Article 63 of the Labour Law introduces special rights for "Mother educators."[356] A mother with four or more children has the right to status as a Mother Child-Nurturer, according to special regulations. These regulations provide for female parents, but not for male parents, financial remuneration (according to professional status and salary), as well as pensions and health insurance. Women's human rights advocates in Croatia fear "the law only seemingly protects women, but according to cultural practices it will end up pushing women out of the workforce."[357] Due to the potentially high cost of maternity benefits, employers have become increasing reluctant to hire women.

---

354. UNDP Bulgaria Report, *supra* note 101, at 2.

355. Labour Law, art. 38. Response to author's survey, Aug. 1996 (B.a.B.e, Zagreb).

356. Response to author's survey, Aug. 1996 (B.a.B.e, Zagreb).

357. *Id.*

Czech Republic

Under current law, married women are granted paid maternity leave of twenty-eight weeks, and single women are granted maternity leave of thirty-seven weeks.[358] A mother may request an additional three years of maternity leave. Women are "guaranteed" their previous (or equivalent) position when they return to the workplace.

After maternity leave is completed, a parental allowance is granted if a parent (male or female) must stay at home full time to take care of a child younger than four years old, or younger than seven years if the child suffers from a long-term illness. "Parent" is understood in this case to be a person who has assumed long-term care of the child.[359]

While the more extensive portion of the leave (parental leave) is not gender-specific, young women are reputed to be less reliable employees, as they are more likely than men to take parental leave. Thus, the benefits have effectively placed obstacles in the path of young women seeking employment.

Germany

Women receive fourteen weeks of paid maternity leave: six weeks before the birth and eight weeks thereafter. In addition, a parent may take up to eighteen months of postnatal leave, during which time they receive a small allowance and protection from dismissal from employment.[360] In addition, under the German Federal Law on Financial Support for Rearing Children, the parent raising the child receives an allowance until the child's second birthday.

Although many nurseries and kindergartens are state subsidized, conditions may be substandard. Closure of state enterprise-supported nurseries and kindergartens in the former East Germany have led to a serious shortage in facilities. In 1991, educators and workers in kindergartens went on strike for three weeks to protest the large size of classes and low pay.[361] Higher income parents tend to opt for autonomous, private "kinder-shops."

Hungary

Hungary's benefits for women with small children have long been among the most generous in Europe. Mothers are entitled to twenty-four weeks of maternity leave with full salary. After this period and up to the child's second birthday, mothers who remain at home can receive a childcare allowance, which is adjusted to their

---

358. The old law, Labour Code § 157(a), Act No. 42, May 6, 1970 *as reprinted in* 13 BULLETIN OF CZECH LAW 128–129 (1973) provided that "a woman shall be entitled to maternity leave for a period of 26 weeks."

359. Shaw survey, *supra* note 110.

360. Martina I. Kischke & Karsten Schroeder, *Equal Rights—But Also Equal Opportunities? The Situation in the Federal Republic of Germany*, IN PRESS, SOCIAL REPORT, Mar. 1990, at 6.

361. Response to author's survey, Aug. 1996 (Suzette Wahren, Berlin).

prior wage (usually 65 to 75 percent of salary).[362] After the child's second year, women can receive a significantly lower, flat-rate allowance based on the number of children in the family. Either parent can draw either type of allowance after the child's first year.[363]

In April 1995, the legislature voted to reduce maternity leave to three months; pregnancy and infant benefits were to be cut as well.[364] Nevertheless, the Constitutional Court struck down the parts of the budget legislation pertaining to family support programs. The court ruled the right to social security and family protection are explicit in the Constitution and, thus, the legislature could not abruptly cut off all benefits (although it could implement a means test). The court further ruled that pregnancy and maternity benefits were protected from government cuts, because the Constitution explicitly protects mothers and children and because the country's abortion jurisprudence requires the government to respect women's decision to have children by establishing the conditions for making such a choice freely. To date then, maternity benefits have continued in Hungary.

More than half of all children below the age of four go to nurseries or kindergartens. With the onset of privitization, many childcare facilities have closed in recent years or gone out of business. Existing facilities are most often overcrowded and understaffed. Kindergartens and nurseries are no longer free of charge, and the amount of the admission depends on whether the organization is state-owned or private. Recently, mothers have been more likely to leave older children home unattended.

The Constitutional Court in Hungary has read the Constitutional provisions mandating equality between men and women to strike down regulations that benefited women and not men. A poor, widowed father had challenged a social security regulation that allowed only women to collect permanent widow's pensions when their spouse died. The court ruled that equality between men and women (Article 66 of the Constitution) required men to receive the same benefits from the government as women and, thus, the law was discriminatory.[365] Whether this decision will have an impact on other work-related benefits is unclear.

Poland

Women have the right to paid maternity leave for the duration of sixteen weeks for the first child; eighteen weeks for each additional birth; and twenty-six weeks in the case of multiple births.[366] Childcare leave is now available to both mother and the father on a equal basis, as long as the parent has been employed for at least six months. In principle, the duration of such leave is three years, that is, up to the fourth year of

---

362. Koncz, *supra* note 116, at 355.

363. *Id.*

364. IWRAW Country Reports, *supra* note 114, at 51.

365. Case No. 10/1990 (*cited in* Kim Lane Schepple, *Women's Rights in Eastern Europe*, EAST EUR. CONSTIT. REV. 69 (1995).

366. Poland NGO Report, *supra* note 128, at 8.

a child's life. It is, however, possible to extend it for a further three years in the case of a child's chronic disease, disability, or mental deficiency.[367]

Unlike in earlier times,[368] childcare leave is unpaid. If women do not have sufficient means of subsistence, they can apply for childcare benefits, a social security benefit. The parent taking childcare leave has the right to come back to the same position at work and his/her contract can be terminated only if the employer declares bankruptcy. In practice, employers circumvent this requirement by dismissing women a few days after they return to work.

In the last few years, the number of kindergartens and nurseries has diminished and fees have increased. Many women report a high degree of dissatisfaction with the standard of care; some believe nurseries to be harmful to the development of children.[369]

Russia

During the Soviet era, employees received salaries and social subsidies in exchange for their labor. These benefits included medical care, clothing, education for children, and inexpensive childcare. The costs of these social subsidies were borne by the federal government, which in turn compensated the spheres of industry and enterprises for providing the services.

Since the transition began, there has been a four-fold decrease in the portion of the federal budget ascribed to social provisions.[370] Responsibility for compensating enterprises has been reassigned to local governments. Given the high bankruptcy rate of state-owned enterprises, and the lack of cash flow to regional governments, very little money is actually now spent on secondary benefits to employees. As a result, kindergartens have been closed and privatized on a massive scale. Many women cannot afford to work because the cost of childcare has become prohibitive. The number of children of pre-school age far exceeds the number of places available in community kindergartens. In the southern city of Novochekarsk, for example, there are 240,000 inhabitants. Over a six-month period in 1993, there were fifty places available for children in the city's two kindergartens.[371] According to government statistics, the number of kindergarten spaces decreased from nine to six million from 1990 to 1994.[372] The Moscow Center for Gender Studies believes that this figure far underestimates the extent of the closings.

---

367. *Id.*

368. *See* Siemienska, *Polish Women, supra* note 131, at 616.

369. Poland NGO Report, *supra* note 128, at 33.

370. Grogan Survey, *supra* note 132. *See also Russia's Chernomyrdin Pledges Social Benefits,* Dow Jones Int'l News, Dec. 10, 1996 (available in Westlaw, Euronews Lib, Down Jones File).

371. Grogan Survey, *id.*

372. *Id.*

Although the Constitution guarantees free preschool education as a right,[373] it is not a priority of the administration and thus it remains severely underfunded. The federal government has operated a poorly funded program entitled "Children of Russia" since 1994. At a regional level, women's groups have brought the issue of childcare to the forefront of political debates. They have actively campaigned against the privatization of kindergartens, and pushed childcare to the top of local budget discussions. Nevertheless, affordable childcare does not exist in Russia.

Ukraine

Unlike some other CEE countries, the system of maternity and childcare benefits in Ukraine does not encourage women to stay at home and have children because the level of assistance is extremely low. "Only if the family has appropriate support from some other place," says Olena Suslova, "can couples even think of having children."[374]

Men as well as women can take childcare leave in Ukraine. However, in practice, men invoke the benefit only when the mother has died or become seriously ill. Parents who take childcare leave are guaranteed their jobs upon their return. Nevertheless, due to the harsh economic circumstances, most parents, women and men, take as short a leave from their paid work as possible.

Family Law (with Particular Reference to Divorce)

Albania

The divorce rate in Albania traditionally was extremely low. After the Albanian Parliament enacted a no-fault divorce law, the rate rose significantly as the procedure became more easy to obtain.[375] Some advocates for women's rights in Albania are working further to modernize divorce and child support procedures.[376] Presently, severe housing shortages present a significant obstacle to divorce. According to a recent survey by the Albanian women's group "Reflections," most marriages in the country are still arranged (58 percent).[377] Women report a far greater incidence of violence in these marriages than in "love marriages."[378] At the same time, women who are divorced or single also face great risk of violence and harassment.

---

373. Russian Constitution, art. 43(2).

374. Response to author's survey, Aug. 1996 (Olena Suslova, Kiev).

375. Minnesota Advocates, Albania Report, *supra* note 143, at 19.

376. Response to author's survey, Aug. 1996 (Tefta Zaka and Kathleen Imhotz, Tirana).

377. Miria, *supra* note 145, at 7.

378. *Id.*

Bulgaria

The Bulgarian Family Code permits divorce by mutual consent.[379] When both parties agree to the divorce, the court does not inquire into the reasons for the dissolution. However, if only one party wants the divorce, the court must establish fault.[380] Poor economic conditions and a shortage of housing often prevent women from seeking divorce.

Croatia[381]

The process of divorce in Croatia commences with a mandatory visit to a Social Service Centre, where the couple will be counseled to reconcile. The reconciliation attempt is mandatory in all cases except when the parties do not have minor children and the parties have agreed to a divorce. If the reconciliation attempt is unsuccessful, the party seeking divorce can file an action in the court of first instance.

The divorce resolves all questions concerning the dissolution of the marriage, custody (including care and upbringing) of the children, access to the children, and support payments for the spouse. Women have expressed fear that, when they initiate a divorce, their spouse may react with violence against them or their children or simply take the children away from them. A further difficulty lies in the high cost of the process, which the woman must pay with little probability she will ever recover her costs. The average divorce process lasts for one to two years.

There is no legal mechanism to grant the woman exclusive possession of the matrimonial home pending the divorce proceedings. Women often encounter great resistance from their spouse, which may include threats to the children's safety, threats to take the children away from her, and allegations in court that she is an unfit mother. Women complain that their husbands frequently violate child visiting agreements and that the legal system provides inadequate recourse in these situations. Women report that even in custody disputes they ultimately win, they are reduced to a state of despair, panic, and helplessness by the process. Added to the trauma of the divorce proceedings, a spouse can create unnecessarily long delays by simply not appearing for the court proceedings. In most cases, a divorce cannot be issued without both parties being heard in court.

When children are involved, the courts issue a decision on alimony, based on the child's needs and the ability of both parents to offer financial support. Other support obligations and additional earning opportunities are also taken into consideration. The parent who has not been given custody is obligated to pay a fixed percentage of his or her monthly salary as alimony. If the person concerned does not have a fixed monthly income, the alimony is set at a fixed percentage of the minimum wage in the Republic of Croatia. Usually, between 20 and 30 percent of the salary is payable for

---

379. Family Code, art. 100.

380. Family Code, art. 99.

381. The source for this entire section is Legaline, Croatia, *supra* note 105.

each child, or 70 to 100 percent of the minimum wage in the Republic of Croatia. At times, in cases in which a percentage of actual salary is awarded, the parent takes a private job and reports lower earnings than actually received, or the parent simply stops working.

The court can also require alimony for the support of one of the marriage partners. This occurs where the partner seeking such support cannot find employment, is not capable of working and has no income, or has no property which could be a source of income. Women have often stayed at home to care for children and the household during the course of the marriage. When the marriage breaks down these women often find themselves working outside the home for the first time in their lives. The employment that is available to them is usually low paid. The system does not recognize and compensate women for the work they performed in the home by raising the children and maintaining the household.

Along with the divorce, or after it has been finalized, the couple's joint property is divided. In cases where the parties cannot reach a decision, either party can file a claim for the division of the property of the marriage with the court. Women are often not informed of their rights regarding joint property. Often the husband assures that he is sole owner since the property is in his name and he paid for it with his income. However, the law considers all property acquired in marriage to be joint property; women are deemed to have contributed to the joint property of the marriage by caring for children and maintaining the household. A new proposal in the Act on Marriage and Family Relations envisions that the joint property of married couples shall be divided equally. Enforcement of court decrees related to the dissolution of marriage requires an expensive and time consuming process.

Czech Republic

Courts have great discretion to determine custody of children under the law of the Czech Republic, as the Family Code states:

> (1) If the parents of a dependent child decide to revoke their marriage, a court will administer their rights and obligations to the child for the period following the divorce, and will determine, in particular, to whom the child will be entrusted, and how each of the parents will contribute to his sustenance.
>
> (2) This decision regarding the administration of rights and obligations of the parents to the child may be substituted by their agreement, which requires approval of a court to be considered valid. (Article 26.)

In practice, most children, especially young children, are given to their mother's custody.

In the case of divorce a spouse is entitled to alimony if he or she is unable to support herself or himself.[382] If the parties cannot reach an agreement on alimony, a court of law will decide.

---

382. Family Code, art. 92.

The law contemplates only a very limited amount of child support, which is to be given to the mother. The Family Code is clear:

> The father of a child whose mother is not married is obligated to provide the mother with a contribution to pay for sustenance for the period of one year, as well as for costs related to pregnancy and childbirth. (Article 95.)

Both spouses have an equal right to all property acquired during the duration of the marriage, with the exception of things received through inheritance and gift-giving, or which are considered vital to the spouse's occupation.[383] According to advocates for women's rights in the Czech Republic, despite these regulations, women are very negatively impacted by divorce.[384]

Hungary

One in every three marriages in Hungary ends in divorce.[385] In line with other European laws, Hungarian family legislation provides an opportunity to dissolve a marriage if it has finally and irreversibly broken down. Such dissolution is not associated in the legislation with any specific list of conditions and neither is it conditioned upon either party's culpability. The parties may seek dissolution jointly as well as separately. Family related legislation requires a mandatory reconciliation procedure, without which the diverse process may not begin.

In the case of divorce, either the mother or the father can obtain custody of the child. The divorced wife does not receive alimony unless the parties mutually agree to an arrangement. The division of property depends upon whether the couple has a marriage contract; where no contract exists, joint property will be divided according to the spouses' contribution. The present judicial system has no effective mechanisms to enforce ex-husbands' financial obligations following a divorce.[386]

Poland

The law on divorce in Poland is like no other in CEE. Spouses cannot obtain a divorce by mutual consent in Poland. Rather, they must obtain a court determination that there has been a "complete and irretrievable disintegration of matrimonial life (physical, spiritual, and economic)."[387] The court procedure, usually undertaken at great financial and emotional expense, may last for several years. Despite the consent of the parties, the court may not grant a divorce if it determines that the dissolution is in conflict with the interest of juvenile children, with the principle of

---

383. The former Czechoslovakia had also similarly subscribed to the law of community property. *See* Civil Code, 143–151, Act No. 40 of Feb. 26, 1964, Collection of Laws. *See generally*, G.E. GLOS, THE LAW OF MARITAL PROPERTY IN CZECHOSLOVAKIA AND THE SOVIET UNION 24–33 (1981).

384. Shaw Survey, *supra* note 110.

385. IWRAW Country Reports, *supra* note 114, at 52.

386. IWRAW Country Report, *supra* note 114, at 57.

387. Family and Guardianship Code, art. 56.

community life, or if the divorce is sought by the spouse who is exclusively guilty of the breakdown of the marriage.

The court may grant custody to one or both parents, but in practice the mother most often retains custody and the father is granted visitation rights. Parents are rarely deprived of their parental rights; even in the case of family violence, the court may grant custody to both parents.[388] Child support depends on the needs of the child and the potential of the parent to provide support. Theoretically, a spouse who fails to pay support may be imprisoned. The principle of the "best interests of the child" is supposed to guide judges in family matters, although in abduction cases the court often gives custody to the parent who abducted the child. In these cases, the judicial process is so slow that, by the time a solution has been reached, the child has lost contact with the other parent, and "in the child's best interest," custody is given to the parent with whom the child is most familiar.

In Poland, division of property upon dissolution of a marriage is governed either by a premarital contract or, in absence of such an agreement, through a default option. Under this latter course, only property acquired during the term of marriage will be divided. Each party will receive exactly half of the joint property unless one party contributed significantly more to the existence of the joint property (a proviso that is rarely invoked).

Alimony may be granted under limited circumstances. If the divorce is on any grounds other than fault, and one of the parties does not have means to support him/herself, the other party is bound to provide alimony for a maximum of five years after the divorce. If the judge finds that one party is at fault for the dissolution of the marriage, that party cannot claim alimony at all, while the "innocent" party can demand alimony for an unlimited time. In practice, in Poland it is the woman who most often seeks divorce; she rarely receives alimony.

The most common reason for women seeking a divorce is domestic violence. Instead of providing relief, the cumbersome divorce procedure often exacerbates and prolongs domestic violence.[389] In 1990, divorce cases were transferred from Family Court to Provincial Courts, courts of general jurisdiction with no prior history of involvement with divorce. This move made divorce less available, increased the cost of the divorce, and protracted the proceedings. As a consequence, "unhappy couples in situations where violence has occurred may have to stay together and their misery may be compounded by economic conditions, dire necessity and the unavailability of other housing."[390]

Beyond the protracted divorce provisions, the Family Code in Poland overtly discriminates with respect to the age of marriage and the use of surnames. The min-

---

388. Response to author's survey, Aug. 1996 (Urszula Nowakowska, Women's Rights Center, Warsaw). This section is drawn almost exclusively from the response to author's survey.

389. Many women attribute ongoing domestic violence in their families to the difficulty of a divorce. *See* Marcus, *supra* note 166, at 14.

390. *Id.*

imum age of marriage is set at twenty-one for men and at eighteen for women.[391] In addition, a woman, while contracting a marriage, must make a declaration if she wishes to keep her surname. If she does not make such a declaration, she automatically assumes her husband's surname.[392] Both of these provisions work to deny women's competency to make decisions and perpetuate a male role as decision-maker and head of household.

Romania

Romania has a no-fault divorce law. After enactment of this law, the number of divorces increased significantly. Family violence motivates many women to seek divorce. Still, roadblocks to dissolution of marriage remain, such as a shortage in housing that forces couples to continue living together, a lack of information about divorce, and the high cost of the procedure.[393]

Russia

The Russian Family Code permits termination of marriage "by means of annulment by application of one or both of the spouses, or by the guardian of a spouse who has been found by the court to be incompetent."[394]

Spouses may establish a Marital Contract prior to marriage, which stipulates control of assets possessed by each before marriage, and the status of property accumulated during marriage.[395] In the event of disagreement or where the parties have not made a marriage contract, the matter is taken to court. Courts generally divide property acquired during the marriage evenly between the parties. If one of the spouses is deemed to be incompetent, due, for instance, to alcoholism or because of criminal behavior or family violence, the legal principle of equal sharing of accumulated common property may be abandoned. In this case, the court is instructed to act in the interests of underage children and of spouses who have been performing unremunerated labor for the household.[396] Although the Family Code also provides for alimony[397] in the case of dire economic circumstances, women seldom receive alimony, but if they do, rarely is the award sufficient or enforceable.

Serbia

The Serbian law and practice on divorce and other family issues is almost identical to that of Croatia, discussed *supra*. As in Croatia, a couple that has children must

---

391. Art. 10(1) of the Family Code.

392. Art. 25(1) of the Family Code. *See* Poland NGO Report, *supra* note 128, at 8.

393. Response to author's survey, Aug. 1996 (Laura Grunberg, ANA, the Society for Feminist Analysis, Bucharest).

394. Family Code, art. 16.

395. Family Code, art. 34(1).

396. Family Code, art. 38(3).

397. Family Code, art. 13.

first appear at a Center for Social Work to try to solve their problems without divorce. In practice, "that means trying to convince women to continue to suffer violence. . . . [T]hey will say, 'if anybody will divorce just because of one slap, marriages will disappear. . . .' [T]hey are not on women's side at all, but [rather] their role is to save marriages under all conditions."[398]

Should the attempt at reconciliation not succeed in keeping the couple together, either party may file for divorce. During the extremely protracted divorce process, most women have no choice but to remain with their husband in the family home. Women's rights advocates in Belgrade report that many cases of severe domestic violence occur after women have already initiated divorce proceedings against their husbands.[399]

Under the Family Code in Serbia, everything gained during marriage should be split evenly between the partners. If a woman was not employed, she still may ask for one half of everything because of her unremunerated contribution to the family. Although either parent may obtain custody according to the interests of the child, juvenile children are almost always given to the mother.

Ukraine

Either spouse may apply for divorce in Ukraine, although somewhat unique restrictions on the husband's ability to seek divorce exist. The Family Code provides:

> The husband does not have the right, without the wife's consent, to bring a suit to terminate the marriage, while the wife is pregnant, or within one year after the birth of a child. The termination of marriage takes place in a legal process, although, if there is mutual agreement by the spouses about terminating the marriage, they can do so at the organs where acts of civil marriage are registered, if they do not have any children who are minors of 16 years. (Article 38.)

These provisions purportedly are designed to protect pregnant women, women with young children, and young children in marriage.

Martial property is divided evenly according to Ukrainian law: "Spouses have equal rights to property even in the case where one of them was occupied with housework, childcare, and/or for other legitimate reasons did not have an independent source of income."[400] Parents have equal rights, and carry equal responsibilities regarding their children, even in cases where the marriage is terminated. However, child support awards are neither adequate nor enforceable.

---

398. Response to author's survey, Aug. 1996 (Zorica Mrsevic, Belgrade Women's Law Group).

399. Author's interview with Lepa Mladjenovic, Women's Center, Belgrade, Mar. 1996.

400. Family Law, art. 22.

Lesbians and Single Women[401]

Albania

There is no mention of lesbian relationships in the Criminal Code. The previous Criminal Code had criminalized male homosexual relationships. Therefore, at this time, neither male nor female same-sex relationships are criminal offenses in Albania.[402] The issue of lesbianism is taboo in Albania; single women are treated as "abnormal" or "unfortunate."

Croatia

None of the laws mention lesbian relationships. Both single women and lesbians are in practice treated as "out groups." The word "lesbian" is used as a derogatory and insulting word to any woman. Single women, if young, are regarded as being "hunting" for a husband. If older, they are regarded as having "failed" in their life.

Czech Republic

The Czech Republic has no laws which specifically address lesbians. Although a growing lesbian culture exists in major cities, the topic is still mainly taboo.[403] Women marry at a very young age in the Czech Republic; never-married single women are a rare but growing population. The number of single mothers has increased dramatically in the 1990s. The Labour Code specifically recognizes single mothers, granting them extended leave for pregnancy and childcare. The law further stipulates that a single woman worker who is taking care of a child younger than three years old may not be fired (unless the organization ceases to exist, is relocated, or is transferred to another ownership).[404]

Germany

Since 1957, female homosexuality has not been a crime. In some of the new federal states (in the former GDR), such as Brandenburg, the State Constitution prohibits discrimination against homosexuals.[405]

---

401. The category "lesbians and single women" has been used because of the similarities in discriminatory treatment that lesbians and single women face. Many unmarried women in CEE state that they are given the worst jobs and denied apartments and other social benefits because they are not with men. Whether they are lesbians or not is rarely the motivating factor. Single women, and in particular single mothers, have long faced discrimination. *See* Katarina Tomaševski, *Reproductive Rights, and Reality: How Facts and Law Can Work for Women: European Approaches to Enhancing Reproductive Freedom*, 44 Am. U.L. Rev. 1037, 1039–1040 (1995).

402. Response to author's survey, Aug. 1996 (Tefka Zaka and Kathleen Imholz, Tirana).

403. Response to author's survey, Aug. 1996 (Kate Shaw, Profem, Prague).

404. Labour Code, art. (1) (a).

405. Response to author's survey, Aug. 1996 (Suzette Schultz, Berlin).

Hungary

Hungarian law does not criminalize homosexuality. Single women are not discriminated against in cities; in urban areas, being single is considered a shame.

Kosovo

Although the law does not mention lesbians, the medical establishment continues to treat lesbians as sick women and social taboos are quite strong. Some Kosovar Albanian women's groups are beginning to use workshops and publications to change social attitudes toward lesbians.[406] Although single women are in a better position than lesbians, single women face social pressure in Kosovar society as well.

Poland

Lesbian relationships are not mentioned in the law of Poland.[407] Treatment of lesbians varies greatly from indifference in some large cities to hostility in more rural areas. The lustration act, "on the initial conditions to take high positions in the Republic of Poland" provides that candidates for office can be disqualified for moral reasons. According to some interpretations, a questionnaire for candidates should include questions about sexual preference.[408] This approach, although feared by human rights activists, has not been implemented.

Single women are mentioned in the law of Poland only in the context of single mothers. Single women may be stigmatized as they are not deemed to be "complete" women unless they have a husband and children.[409] The rate of marriages, especially in cities, is decreasing and the number of single mothers is increasing.

Romania

On September 26, 1996, the Romanian Parliament voted to retain the infamous Article 200 of the Romanian Penal Code. While the newly adopted version of Article 200 no longer criminalizes all homosexual acts, it retains legal penalties for consensual homosexual acts between adult Romanian citizens. The law criminalizes sexual relations between persons of the same sex taking place in public or which cause a "public scandal" with a penalty of between one to five years imprisonment. A 1938 Romanian law defines "public scandal" as "an act which becomes known to more than two persons who disapprove of it." This vague language has allowed continued persecution, blackmail, and police harassment of gay men and lesbians in Romania.

---

406. Response to author's survey, Aug. 1996 (Sevdie Ahmeti, Center for the Protection of Women and Children).

407. However, in Poland on Apr. 11, 1995, the Polish Constitutional Committee did propose a clause prohibiting discrimination based on sexual orientation. *See* Piotr Dukaczewsk, *Homosexual Rights Provision*, WARSAW VOICE, Apr. 24, 1995.

408. Poland NGO Report, *supra* note 128, at 64.

409. Response to author's survey, Aug. 1996 (Urszula Nowakowska, Women's Rights Center, Warsaw).

The only comparable provision regarding heterosexual acts is Article 321, which punishes "acts, gestures, words, or expressions which offend against good manners or cause public scandal," and imposes a penalty of three months to two years imprisonment. Paragraph 5 prohibits, with a similar penalty, "propositioning or enticing a person to take part in sexual relations with a person of the same sex, as well as propaganda or association or any other acts of proselytism with the same purpose." This provision could be applied in such a manner as to infringe upon fundamental rights to freedom of speech, assembly, and association, and as to be used to persecute Romanian citizens who even present homosexuality in a positive light.

The number of single women in Romania is rising, although early marriage tends to be the norm. While single women are usually accepted in cities, in rural areas never-married single women are treated as abnormal.

Russia

Russian criminal law no longer penalizes homosexual relationships. However, the Penal Code penalizes coercion to enter into a homosexual relationship, as discussed under Sexual Harassment, *supra*.

Popular perceptions about homosexuality are "overwhelmingly negative."[410] As such, lesbians have reasons to fear for their professional and physical security. For women living in communal flats,[411] for example, it is impossible to justify the long-term presence of a friend by explaining that this woman is a same-sex partner. Russia has a long history of institutionalizing and forcibly "treating" lesbians as mentally ill.[412] Although this practice has abated somewhat, some Russian lesbians still report being forced to undergo "medical treatment" and family violence designed to "cure them."[413] Under such circumstances, many lesbians marry men in order to protect their economic, physical, and social well-being.

Serbia

Unlike in Russia and Romania, Serbian law never explicitly prohibited lesbian relationships or specified forced institutionalization of lesbians. Until July 1994, male homosexuality was banned by the Serbian Criminal Law (Article 101, Section on Indecent Acts Against Nature) but it did not affect the position of lesbians before the law and in the society. The general attitude towards lesbians in Serbia is negative and the relationship between two women is not taken seriously by other members of the community. The role of the woman is strictly determined by the tradition and there is little tolerance and understanding for those who do not fit the preconceived image of a "decent woman."

---

410. Grogan survey, *supra* note 132.

411. Communal flats, apartments shared by many families, were a common arrangement in the Soviet Union, and they remain common in post-Soviet Russia.

412. MASHA GESSEN, THE RIGHTS OF LESBIANS AND GAY MEN IN THE RUSSIAN FEDERATION (1994).

413. Author's interviews with "L." and "M.", Moscow, Feb. 1995.

Slovakia

There are no legal prohibitions against lesbians, but social taboos are strong. The number of single mothers is rising, as are the number of single women generally. A recent survey found that 80 percent of women and 72 percent of men support the statement: "If a woman wants to have a child and bring it up without a man, it is her undeniable right."[414]

Ukraine

The law does not mention lesbian relationships and there are no provisions pertaining to single women. In practice, lesbians are invisible in the life of society. However, international congresses of gays and lesbians have been held in Kiev. Single women are becoming more and more common in Ukraine and, according to women's rights activist Olena Suslova, they face no discrimination.[415]

---

414. Slovak Women's Report, *supra* note 21 (unpaginated).

415. Response to author's survey, Aug. 1995 (Olena Suslova, Kiev).

WOMEN'S RIGHTS IN UKRAINE

Myroslava Antonovych

INTRODUCTION

The independence of Ukraine from the Soviet Union in 1991 meant not only political liberation but the assumption of new obligations concerning human rights. Questions arose in Ukraine regarding Ukraine's existing treaty commitments and the possible ratification of new human rights treaties. By 1995, Ukraine's human rights record received a better-than-passing grade in the U.S. Department of State's Country Report on Human Rights Practices.[1] Yet, much remains to be done in the sphere of human rights in Ukraine, particularly concerning the human rights of women.

A review of the literature on women's issues in Ukraine showed that the legal rights of Ukrainian women have not been the subject of separate research. However, there are several publications which focus on the role of women in Ukrainian public life.[2] Further, several books and papers are devoted to famous Ukrainian women who played important roles in Ukrainian and world political affairs.[3] Numerous monographs reveal the status of women in the Soviet Union.[4] Furthermore, articles regard-

---

1.   1 U.S. DEP'T OF STATE, COUNTRY REPORTS ON HUMAN RIGHTS PRACTICES FOR 1995 (Mar. 1996). In March 1996, this report was submitted to the Committee on Foreign Relations of the U.S. Senate, and to the Committee on Foreign Affairs of the U.S. House of Representatives. *See* Yaro Bihun, *State Department Says Ukraine Makes Progress on Human Rights*, UKRAINIAN WEEKLY, Mar. 24, 1996, at 1.

2.   MARTHA BOHACHEVSKY-CHOMIAK, FEMINISTS DESPITE THEMSELVES: WOMEN IN UKRAINIAN COMMUNITY LIFE 1884–1939 (1988); MARTHA BOHACHEVSKY-CHOMIAK, DUMA UKRAINY: ZHINOCHOHO RODU (1993) (Duma of Ukraine of the Feminine Gender), which includes a section entitled, *Women, History, and Human Rights*. The role of women in Ukrainian history is further analyzed in other books, including *A Woman and a State:* IVAN KUZYCH-BEREZOVSKYI, ZHINKA I DERZHAVA (2d ed.1994); *Women in the History of Ukraine:* OLES' KOZULYA, ZHINKY V ISTORIYI UKRAINY (1993); *Outstanding Women of Ukraine:* OL LUHOVYI, VYZNACHNE ZHINOTSTVO UKRAYINI (2d ed. 1994); FRANSES SVYRIPA, WEDDED TO THE CAUSE: UKRAINIAN-CANADIAN WOMEN AND ETHNIC IDENTITY 1891–1991 (1992); and WOMAN OF UKRAINE: HER PART ON THE SCENE OF HISTORY, IN LITERATURE, ARTS, AND STRUGGLE FOR FREEDOM (1955) [hereinafter WOMAN OF UKRAINE], published by the Ukrainian National Women's League of America, and 500 UKRAINIAN MARTYRED WOMEN (Stephanie Halychyn ed., 1956).

3.   *See, e.g.,* Y. ROLLE, ZHINKY PRY CHYHYRUNSKOMU DVORI (1996); DE KE DE SENT-EMUR, ANNA RUSSE, REINE DE FRANCE; I. FYLYPCHAK, ANNA YAROSLAVNA-KOROLEVA FRANTSIYI (1995); A. LOBANOV-ROSTOVSKY, UNE PRINCESSES RUSSE, REINE DE FRANCE AU XI SIECLE (1829).

4.   *See, e.g.,* THE ROLE AND STATUS OF WOMEN IN THE SOVIET UNION (Donald Brown ed., 1968); NORTON DODGE, WOMEN IN THE SOVIET ECONOMY; THEIR ROLE IN ECONOMIC, SCIENTIFIC, AND TECHNI-

ing Ukrainian women have regularly appeared in *Our Life,* a journal published in New York by the Ukrainian National Women's League of America. And a number of articles on Ukrainian feminism by Professor Bohachevsky-Chomiak and Maxim Tarnawshy have been published in several American journals.[5] Nevertheless, the topic of women's rights in Ukraine still needs a thorough and detailed interpretation and expansion.

In an attempt to conform to international standards, Ukraine is a signatory to many international human rights instruments. Ukraine was among the first of the former Soviet Republics to ratify the Convention on the Elimination of All Forms of Discrimination against Women.[6] Subsequently, Ukraine ratified the Convention on the Political Rights of Women,[7] the Convention on the Nationality of Married Women,[8] and the Convention for the Suppression of Traffic in Persons and of the Exploitation of the Prostitution of Others.[9] Among the conventions of the ILO concerning women's rights, Ukraine has ratified the Convention on the Use of Women Workers in Underground Jobs,[10] the Convention on Equal Pay to Men and Women Work Force for Equal Jobs,[11] and the Convention on the Protection of Maternity.[12] The process of

---

CAL DEVELOPMENT (1966); ALENA HEITLINGER, WOMEN AND STATE SOCIALISM: SEX INEQUALITY IN THE SOVIET UNION AND CZECHOSLOVAKIA (1979); BARBARA WOLFE JANKA, WOMAN UNDER COMMUNISM (1978); GAIL WARSHOFSKY LAPIDUS, WOMEN IN SOVIET SOCIETY: EQUALITY, DEVELOPMENT, AND SOCIAL CHANGE (1978); WILLIAM M. MANDEL, SOVIET WOMEN (1975); SOVIET LEGISLATION ON WOMEN'S RIGHTS: COLLECTION OF NORMATIVE ACTS (1978).

5. *See, e.g.,* Martha Bohachevsky-Chomiak, *Socialism and Feminism: The First Stage of Women's Organizations in the Eastern Part of the Austrian Empire, in* WOMEN IN EASTERN EUROPE AND THE SOVIET UNION 44 (Tova Yedlin ed., 1980); Martha Bohachevsky-Chomiak, *Feminism in Ukrainian History,* 12 J. UKRAINIAN STUD. 16 (1982); Martha Bohachevsky-Chomiak, *Feminism in Action: The Ukrainian Women's Union Between the World Wars,* 2 WOMEN'S STUD. INT'L 20 (1982); Maxim Tarnawsky, *Feminism, Modernism, and Ukrainian Women,* 19 J. UKRAINIAN STUD. 31 (1994). After Ukraine gained independence in 1991 from the Soviet Union, several articles and papers were presented at women's conferences held in Ukraine. For example, in July 1993, Professor Zoreslava Romovska of Lviv University presented a paper that analyzed legal problems dealing with women and power at The Ukrainian Woman and Democracy Conference sponsored by the Union of Ukrainian Women and the World Federation of Ukrainian Women organizations. *See* ZORESLAVA ROMOVSKA, ZHINKA I VLADA: PERSHA MIZHNARODNA ZHINOCHA CONFERENTSIYA— UKRAYINKA I DEMOCRATIYA 151 (1993).

6. Convention on the Elimination of All Forms of Discrimination against Women, G.A. Res. 34/180, UN GAOR, Supp. No. 46, at 193, U.N. Doc. A/34/46 (1979) [Women's Convention].

7. Convention on the Political Rights of Women, 193 U.N.T.S. 135 (1953)

8. Convention on the Nationality of Married Women, 309 U.N.T.S. 65 (1957).

9. Convention for the Suppression of the Traffic in Persons and of the Exploitation of the Prostitution of Others, 96 U.N. T.S. 271 (1949).

10. Convention Concerning the Employment of Women in Underground Work in Mines of All Kinds, No. 45, 40 U.N.T.S. 63 (1935).

11. Convention Concerning Equal Remuneration for Men and Women Workers for Equal Value, No. 100, 165 U.N.T.S. 303 (1951).

12. Convention Concerning the Employment of Women Before and After Childbirth, No. 3, 38 U.N.T.S. 53 (1919) [Maternity Protection Convention].

implementing other international human rights instruments and standards affecting women is a continuing one.

HISTORY OF WOMEN IN UKRAINE

There was a time when Ukraine demonstrated high esteem for and favorable treatment of women. In 900 A.D., in the Ukrainian state of Kyivan Rus with its famous princess Olha, women were highly educated and occupied powerful positions in society. In the Kyivan Rus family, a woman played a significant role. Comparatively, a woman's position in the Kyivan Rus family was much higher than under the Roman or Old-Germanic law. Unlike a woman in Roman or Old-Germanic systems, a woman in Kyivan Rus was considered legally competent and needed no trustee.[13] Indeed, in Kyivan Rus, a woman retained title of her pre-marital property during the marriage, and it was never subject to a common legacy after the husband's death.[14] Furthermore, a woman, in her own right, could be considered the head of the family.[15] Under a 912 treaty between Kyivan Prince Oleh and the Byzantine Church, a wife maintained separate ownership of property, which was not confiscated by the state even when her husband was incarcerated or escaped from prison.[16] Additionally, women could sue or be sued and could appear in courts as advocates and witnesses.

There are several examples of the active role women played in state affairs and diplomatic relations in the periods of Kyivan Rus and the Halych-Volyn Princedom. Princess Olha wisely ruled the Kyivan Rus state for almost twenty years. She was an authoritative woman who maintained tradition, raised her children, and promoted order in the state. She never remarried—even forgoing a proposal from a Greek king. Under the Rus Chronicle, Olha led a diplomatic mission to Constantinople in 957.[17] According to his writings, Byzantine Emperor Constantine VII, Porphyrogenitus, sought to marry Olha. Cleverly, Olha asked the king to be her godfather, and the king obliged. Since the king was her godfather, a marriage between godfather and goddaughter would be impermissible. Shortly thereafter, in 959, Olha sent her ambassadors on a political mission to the German king, Otto I the Great, who governed as the Holy Roman Emperor.[18] It is likely that she asked the German king to send Western missionaries to Kyivan Rus.

There were also several royal marriages that elevated the image of Kyivan Rus in the world. Anna, daughter of the Kyivan Prince Yaroslav the Wise, married the king of France, Henri I (son of Robert II).[19] After Henri's death in 1060, Anna became the

---

13. MYKHAILO HRUSHEVSKYI, 3 ISTORIYA UKRAYINY-RUSY 376–77 (1993).

14. 2 PRAVDA RUSKA 99 (B. Grekov ed., 1947).

15. NATALIYA POLONSKA-VASYLENKO, 1 ISTORIYA UKRAYINY 254 (2d ed. 1976).

16. LITOPYS RUS'KYI 20 (1989).

17. *See id.* at 35–36.

18. *See, e.g.,* HRUSHEVSKYI, *supra* note 13, at 451.

19. *See* MYKHAILO HRUSHEVSKYI, 2 ISTORIYA UKRAYINY-RUSY 33 (1993).

regent of the French throne. Another of Yaroslav's daughters, Yelyzaveta, married the king of Norway, Harald III.[20] Furthermore, one of Yaroslav's granddaughters, Yevprasksiya, married Henry IV, and became the courageous German Empress Adelgeida.[21] Ultimately, these marriages served to further the interests of Kyivan Rus in the international community.

Women also assumed great responsibility in the affairs of the Kyivan Rus state. In 1097, Prince Vsevolod's widow was selected to conduct negotiations with Volodymyr Monomach. Likewise, Prince Volodymyr Vasylkovych entrusted his wife with carrying on negotiations with Konrad Mazovetskyi. And Anna, Prince Roman Halytskyi's widow, pursued a complicated policy of preserving Halych-Volyn Princedom for her sons for more than fifteen years.[22]

During the period of the Lithuanian-Ruthenian state, women's legal status was defined by the "Lithuanian Statute," which incorporated the principle of gender equality into its criminal and civil articles. Like men, women were subject to laws and regulations, and they were granted legal rights without restriction due to their sex. The criminal system provided protection for women, and even greater protection under certain circumstances—during pregnancy, for example. There were also certain spousal protective devices to safeguard a wife's financial interests. In particular, a husband was required to give his wife a writ conveying one-third of his real property. However, daughters were not eligible to inherit real property, purportedly because land ownership was derived from military service.[23]

During the perpetual wars of the Cossack period, women not only ran the household but physically defended the home and family. Therefore, many women were captured by the Tartars and sold as slaves for Turkish harems. Among the slaves was a Ukrainian girl, Roksoliana, who became the wife of Sultan Suleiman I Canuni and managed to prevent Tartar invasions of Ukraine from 1520 until 1550.[24] The 1710 Constitution, written by Cossack Hetman (commander-in-chief) Pylyp Orlyk, included a widow's right to own land if she was without issue and the right of a woman whose husband was in military service to be free of taxes and common obligations.[25] Furthermore, in 1743, the Code of Laws adopted harsher penalties for the killing or insulting of a woman than for the same crime against a man.[26] Nonetheless, the Code of Laws merely fined—holovshchyna obligation—the murderer of an unmarried woman, serf, slave, or prisoner of war.[27] Finally, the Constitution of the Ukrainian

---

20. *See id.* at 31–32.

21. *See id.* at 79.

22. *See* POLONSKA-VASYLENKO, *supra* note 15, at 254.

23. ENCYCLOPEDIA OF UKRAINE 705 (Danylo Husar Struk ed., 1993).

24. *See id.*

25. *Pacty ta Constytusii Zakoniv ta Volnostey Viyska Zaporozhskoho, reprinted in* HISTORY OF UKRAINIAN CONSTITUTIONALISM (in documents) 10 (1996) [hereinafter *Constytusii*].

26. ENCYCLOPEDIA OF UKRAINE, *supra* note 23.

27. *See id.*

National Republic in 1918 proclaimed the equality of men and women regarding legal rights and duties.[28]

Interestingly, whenever Ukraine lost independence and became part of another state, the position of Ukrainian women became very difficult. For example, when Ukraine was part of the Austrian Empire, under Austrian civil law women were on the same legal footing as the mentally incompetent, the blind, and the deaf—unable to attest to the making of wills.[29]

The Ukrainian women's movement became very active in the late nineteenth and early twentieth centuries. In 1884, Natalia Kobrynska organized Ukrainian women in Stanislaviv (now Ivano-Frankivsk) primarily for educational purposes. That same year, Olena Dobrohrayeva founded Higher Courses for Women in Kyiv.[30] In 1909, Ukrainian women's groups in Lviv formed an organization, which in 1917 became known as the Ukrainian Women's Association. After the October Revolution in Russia, the Ukrainian parliament, the Ukrainian Central Rada, granted women equal rights with men to vote and to be elected to political office. There were eleven women members of the Rada, and two women, Lyudmyla Starytsha-Chernyakhivska and Zinaida Myrna, were elevated to the executive committee of the Rada, the Mala Rada.[31] Later, in 1920, the Ukrainian National Council of Women was formed in Kamyanets Podilsky as the superstructure for all Ukrainian women's organizations. The Council, which was headed by Sophia Russova, was accepted as a member of the International Council of Women. A section of the International Women's League for Peace and Freedom was formed in Lviv under the leadership of Blanca Baranova, and in 1921 the section was admitted to the League in Vienna.[32]

After World War I, western Ukraine was divided among Poland, Romania, and Czechoslovakia. Halychyna, the largest portion of Ukraine, suffered under Polish rule. Olha Bassarab, a prominent member of several Ukrainian women's organizations and International Red Cross award recipient, was imprisoned and tortured to death by Polish police.[33] In 1928, Ukrainian women took the first steps toward participation in the parliamentary elections in Poland. Two women on the Ukrainian National Democratic Party ticket, Olena Kiselevska and Milena Rudnytska, were elected. The World Union of Ukrainian Women was founded in 1937 and served to unite the majority of the Ukrainian women's organizations.[34] The first post-World War II Congress of Ukrainian Women, held in Philadelphia in 1948, founded the World Federation of Ukrainian Women's Organizations.[35]

---

28. *See Constytusii, supra* note 25, § 2.11.

29. Dora Klushynska, Chomuzhinky Zhadaiut Politychnykh Prav 17 (1918).

30. *See* Woman of Ukraine, *supra* note 2, at 12.

31. *See id.* at 13.

32. *See id.* at 14.

33. *See id.* at 16.

34. *See id.* at 17.

35. *See id.* at 19.

THE EMERGING FEMINISM OF WOMEN IN UKRAINE

Unlike many American and European women struggling for emancipation and equal rights, Ukrainian women sought personal liberation and inclusion in the developing economic structure. They did not struggle for equality but rather took responsibility by accepting meaningful public work. Professor Bohachevsky-Chomiak terms this phenomenon "pragmatic feminism."[36]

Ukrainian women worked for the public good, not only for women. Thus, Ukrainian feminism became the result of the *activity* of women and not a factor of its appearance. According to Maxym Tarnawsky, Martha Bohachevsky-Chomiak's groundbreaking study of the western Ukrainian women's movement, *Feminists Despite Themselves*, emphasizes the provisional, contingent nature of Ukrainian feminism. Tarnawsky offers an illustration of how this worked in literature (rather than social organizations) and points to some of the complex ideological problems that have hindered, and continue to hinder, the Ukrainian women's movement.[37]

Ukrainian feminist writers at the turn of the twentieth century revealed the conditions that women endured in Ukrainian society, reasoning that it would be necessary to show first a need for change before advocacy for change would be seriously considered. Two of the most important leaders and spokespersons for the Ukrainian women's movement in the early 1900s, Lesia Ukrainka and Olha Kobylianska, identified various social, domestic, and personal difficulties facing Ukrainian women and offered thoughtful and concrete solutions.[38] Although these leaders promoted feminism, both Ukrainka and Kobylianska were heavily influenced by Friedrich Nietzsche, a notorious misogynist. It is perhaps thus fair to conclude that these heroines struggled for personal freedom rather than for women's rights *per se*.[39]

The Ukrainian Soviet Republic promulgated legislation to protect women during maternity and childrearing, to secure women's rights in the family and in the workplace, and to create social insurance and welfare. These laws should have galvanized women into a potent force, but they did not improve women's position in practice, principally because survival conditions were horrific. Between 1932 and 1933, some seven million Ukrainians died from famine despite living on what may be the richest soil in the world. The famine was the result of a well planned Soviet policy of extermination of Ukrainians. This crime of genocide, which was committed against the Ukrainian people, impacted especially upon women and children.

Women also carried difficult burdens in everyday life. These day-to-day survival obligations proved disadvantageous and deterred any professional advancement. Yet, together with men, women struggled for their rights during these times. Thousands of women were imprisoned in Stalin's prisons and labor camps. Two out of ten

---

36.   *See* BOHACHEVSKY-CHOMIAK, FEMINISTS DESPITE THEMSELVES, *supra* note 2.

37.   *See* Tarnawsky, *supra* note 5, at 41.

38.   *See id*. at 31–32.

39.   *See id*. at 32, 37, 40.

founders of the Ukrainian Helsinki Group were women, and they signed the Declaration of the Ukrainian Public Group to Promote the Implementation of the Helsinki Accords.[40] One signatory was Oksana Meshko, a prisoner of Beria's concentration camp. She was part of a family of dissidents; her son was imprisoned for his political beliefs. The other signatory, Nina Strokata, a microbiologist, was sentenced to four years in prison for defending her husband, a well-known Ukrainian political prisoner, Svyatoslav Karavansky. Once she was released from prison and relocated to the Kaluga Region of Russia, Strokata was still kept under police surveillance.[41]

UKRAINIAN WOMEN IN MODERN SOCIETY

The contemporary status of women in Ukraine reflects the process of a country straining to change its political system from a totalitarian superstate to a democracy. Armed conflicts in nearby territories have also impacted Ukraine. Women constitute 54 percent of the Ukrainian population. According to the Constitution, the equality of men and women is guaranteed in regards to political and cultural activities, in employment and wages, and in education and vocational training.[42] This equality is further guaranteed by special measures for women, including retirement benefits, maternity accommodations in the workplace, and maternity leave with pay for pregnant women and mothers.[43]

Yet, as elsewhere, rights on paper do not translate into rights in reality. For women's rights to be realized, a mechanism for enforcement is necessary. The statistics tell an unfortunate story. Sixty-one percent of Ukrainian women have received higher education, but only 5 percent of women are chairpersons.[44] At the same time, women constitute 42 percent of all agricultural workers, 48 percent of all industrial workers, and 80 percent of those holding trade and service jobs. Generally, the higher the income bracket, the lower the proportion of women. All these figures lead to a conclusion that economic discrimination against women is firmly established in Ukraine. An example of blatant discrimination against women is found in the joint Ukrainian-German venture, TDC. The joint venture company announced twenty-four job openings, but twelve were exclusively for men: these positions were for service managers, marketing representatives, and reviewers. Quite clearly, the nature of these jobs does not require that they be filled by men.[45]

---

40. THE HUMAN RIGHTS MOVEMENT IN UKRAINE: DOCUMENTS OF THE UKRAINIAN HELSINKI GROUP 1976–1980 32–33 (Lesya Verba & Bohdan Yasen eds., 1980).

41. *See id.*

42. UKRAINIAN CONST., *reprinted in* 611 UKRAINIAN Q. 230 (1996).

43. *See id.*

44. Natalia Lakiza-Sachuk, *"Zhinoche Pytannya" v Konteksti Demokratyzatsiyi*, 11 POLITYKA I CHAS 36 (1994).

45. OLENA SUSLOVA, PERSHA MIZHNARODNA ZHINOCHA CONFERENTSIYA "UKRAYINKA I DEMOCRATIYA" 157–58 (1993).

Furthermore, there have been cases of women being dismissed from their jobs due to discriminatory motives. During periods of market reform in Ukraine, these types of dismissals have increased. For instance, 70 percent of the unemployed are women, but among unemployed youth, only 45 percent are women.[46] Women reentering the workforce after raising children suffer the greatest discrimination, as 83 percent of workers dismissed before retirement are women. Women of childbearing age are also subject to employment discrimination. Hence, it is unremarkable that 83 percent of the unemployed at state training centers are women. Meanwhile, 86 percent of those who lost their jobs and sought further qualifications are women. Unfortunately, the process of retraining women who have reentered the job force after years working in the home, has had very little success.[47]

The proportion of women employed in heavy industrial work is twice that of men. In response to this, the Ukrainian Cabinet of Ministers implemented a program in April 1996 that requires the removal of women from jobs involving heavy manual labor and harmful work conditions. The program also places limitations on women working nightshifts and forecasts the removal of women from positions in iron-processing, foundries, galvanic and etching works, nickel- and chromium-plating, ferrous metallurgy, some types of furniture manufacturing, and driving trucks with a carrying capacity over one ton.[48] Subsequently, the training of women for these positions has ceased. This demonstrates that the state intends to afford protection to women in regards to their "role" as mothers or future mothers. Many feminists consider these limitations to be impermissibly discriminatory, because women should have the right to pursue the same employment opportunities as men if they so choose.[49]

Some positive changes have taken place in respect to Ukrainian hiring practices. In recent years, women have occupied posts previously considered exclusively for men, for example, women are now in positions of authority in police departments (militia) and in the armed forces.[50] For example, General Larysa Melnyk is the highest ranking woman in the Ukrainian Armed Forces, holding the post of Deputy Chief of the Main Command of Educative Work on Social and Legal Problems.[51] Some 23,000 women serve in the Ukrainian army, including 336 commissioned officers, 2,316 warrant officers and more than 20,000 enlisted personnel.[52] Such advancements

---

46. *See id.* at 156.

47. *See id.*

48. INTEL NEWS, Apr. 9, 1996.

49. *See* Anne Trebilcock, *ILO Conventions and Women Workers*, and Natalie H. Kaufman, *Assorted Instruments Affecting Women's International Human Rights*, in Vol. 2 of this treatise.

50. Vira Valerko, *Persha Zhinka-Nachalnyk Raividdilu*, URYADOVYI KURYER, July 23, 1996, at 6.

51. Volodymyr Chykalin, *Zakhysnyky Ukrayiny Potrebuyut Zakhystu*, URYADOVYI KURYER, July 20, 1996, at 8.

52. INTEL NEWS, Mar. 8–9, 1996.

in the armed forces and police departments mark the process of feminization of organizations traditionally reserved for men.

Additionally, women are gaining a stronghold in Ukrainian business communities. Members of the Organization of Business Women of Western Ukraine are heads of agricultural firms, directors of plants, and serve to involve women in the management of state affairs. As a result, women now aspire to political and economic positions of power and authority. While it is true that women have made gains in Ukrainian society, it is also true that the Ukrainian government should implement additional policies that ensure a woman's ability to combine family and career.

In an effort to promote the ability of women to participate in government, Articles 7 and 8 of the Convention on the Elimination of all Forms of Discrimination Against Women requires the state to take affirmative measures to eliminate discrimination against women in the political and public sectors of society.[53] Consequently, women are guaranteed the right to participate in the formulation of governmental policy, the right to hold public office, and the right to represent their country at the international level. However, Ukraine cannot boast of implementing these rights. In fact, in the late 1990s, there were only eighteen women (out of 400 people's deputies) in the Verkhovna Rada (Ukrainian Parliament). This provides inadequate representation of the female population. Some politicians and scholars propose to establish a quota of people's deputy positions for women, thus following the example of many European states. In Sweden, for example, in the mid-1990s, half of the governmental officers and 43 percent of its Parliament were women.[54] Another example is Iceland, which had a female President, Vigdis Finnbogadottyr, for sixteen years.[55]

In Ukraine, women's resource organs include the Parliamentary Health, Maternity and Childhood Protection Committee, and the Ministry on Family and Youth, which was created on July 26, 1996 by President Leonid Kuchma.[56] These agencies replaced the Ministry on Youth and Sport, the Committee on Minors by the Cabinet of Ministers, and the President's Committee on Women, Maternity and Childhood. The Parliamentary Committee on Health, Maternity and Childhood Protection represents women's interests on a national level and takes part in solving important problems facing women today. Notably, the Committee initiated a plan to eliminate the advertising of tobacco and alcohol in an effort to head off a growing substance abuse problem in the Ukraine.[57] Yet this Committee has few women deputies and cannot adequately protect women's rights on the national level.

---

53. *See* Women's Convention, *supra* note 6.

54. Serhiy Pravdenko, *Stokholm: Solo Ukrayiny v Orkestri Yevropy i Planety*, HOLOS UKRAYINY, July 12, 1996, at 3.

55. *Ivid Narodnoyi Lyubovi Vtomlyuyutsya*, HOLOS UKRAYINY, July 2, 1996, at 6.

56. *Ukaz Prezydenta Ukrayiny "Prozminy v Sytemi Tsentralnukh Orhaniv Vykonavchoyi Vlady Ukrayiny" July 26, 1996*, HOLOS UKRAYINY, July 31, 1996, at 2.

57. INTEL NEWS, Mar. 8–9, 1996.

In accordance with the Act "On Citizenship of Ukraine," promulgated in October 1991, women are granted equal rights with men in acquiring, changing, or retaining Ukrainian citizenship.[58] In an effort to correspond with international legal principles, Ukraine has simplified the process of granting Ukrainian citizenship to foreign women who are married to Ukrainian citizens.[59] This new process complies with the Convention on the Nationality of Married Women, of which Article 3.1 provides:

> Each Contracting State agrees that the alien wife of one of its nationals may, at her request, acquire the nationality of her husband through specially privileged natural-ization procedures, the grant of such nationality may be subject to such limitations as may be imposed in the interests of national security or public policy.[60]

Ukrainian legislation, such as The Code of Laws on Work[61] and "On State Help to Families with Children,"[62] guarantee the right of women to work and to receive social security, respectively. Another Act, The Decree of the Cabinet of Ministers No. 832, "On Rise of State Help to Some Categories of Citizens," determines the amount of the entitlement to the unemployed, to single-mothers, to families with four or more children under the age of sixteen, to persons who care for a child under the age of three, and to other special classes.[63] In fact, families with children are offered eight different types of state benefits. This legislation further prohibits the dismissal of women due to pregnancy or maternity leave. Women are provided maternity leave for three years with pay (full pay for four months during pre-natal and post-natal peri-ods) and without loss of employment. And women who attend universities or who are unemployed also benefit by this legislation.[64] These are but a few of the social secu-rity benefits granted to women under Ukrainian legislation.

Although such benefits may sound generous, they provide the bare minimum to ensure the health and nutrition of mothers and their children. Indeed, many women do not use their maternity leave but instead enroll their newborns in childcare facil-ities and return to work as soon as possible. Other women are forced to take mater-nity leave because of the dire economic conditions, which make jobs difficult to obtain. This phenomenon has contributed to disturbing statistics. The Ukrainian death rate has recently outpaced an ever-declining birth rate. According to Health Minister Yevhen Korolenko, this disparity is Ukraine's most crucial health issue. Specifically, in the mid-1990s, Ukraine's population growth had decreased to 9.6 births per 1,000 people, while the death rate increased from 5.15 to 12.1. Minister Korolenko reported that 45 percent of the nation's births were premature and 380 out of every 1,000 new-

58. *Pro Hromadyanstvo Ukrainy*, HOLOS UKRAYINY, Nov. 13, 1991, at 12–13.

59. *See id.*

60. Convention on the Nationality of Married Women, adopted Jan. 29, 1957, 309 U.N.T.S. 65 G.A. Res 1040 (1958).

61. KODEKS ZAKONIV PRO PRATSYU, NOVE ZAONODAVSTVO UKRAINY PRO PRATSYU 63–67 (1991).

62. *Pro Derzhavnu Dopomohu Simyam z Ditmy Nov. 21, 1992, reprinted in* PRAVO UKRAINY 43–63 (1993).

63. *Dopomoha na Ditey*, URYADOVYI KURYER, Aug. 10, 1996, at 8.

64. *See id.*

borns suffered birth defects.[65] This tragedy can be attributed primarily to the Chernobyl disaster, to other environmental degradation, and to the economic crisis in Ukraine.

Women in Ukraine enjoy the right of reproductive freedom. Nevertheless, women still need information on reproductive health and family planning and corresponding health services. The lack of reproductive education and contraceptives has resulted in a large number of abortions. Each year Ukrainian physicians perform about one million abortions.[66] In 1991, there were 152 abortions for every 100 births.[67] However, this high abortion rate will likely decrease in the future, perhaps partially because people will turn to the religions once prohibited under the Soviet system. Ukraine is historically a Christian state with Christian traditions since Kyivan Rus, and the two leading Christian confessions in Ukraine, Orthodox and Greek-Catholic, forbid abortions.

WOMEN'S POLITICAL ORGANIZATIONS

One of the predominant characteristics of the Ukrainian women's movement is its ever-increasing public activity. There are some 100 registered non-governmental organizations dealing with issues affecting women, maternity, and children. They all claim to represent women in some way. However, the proliferation of these organizations (which are meant to promote political, educational, national, and cultural agendas too) should not be construed to indicate a powerful women's movement in Ukraine. According to Natalya Lavrynenko of the Democratic Initiatives, the women's movement in Ukraine has very little influence and only one-half of 1 percent of Ukrainian women are actively involved.[68]

Until relatively recently, there was one primary political party dedicated to women's issues in Ukraine—The Ukrainian Christian Party of Women. The main goals of the party are to promote the physical and spiritual revival of those people suffering from ecological disaster and biological degeneration and to struggle for a sovereign Ukraine founded on real equality for women and their participation in government.[69] Hence, the main directions of party activity include: state, structure, society, ecology, economic structure, culture of language, education, social protections, and justice.[70] In January 1997, the Political Party of Women of Ukraine was created. Of the other forty political parties in Ukraine, only one has a female chairperson. Slava Stetko leads the Congress of Ukrainian Nationalists.[71]

---

65.   *EcoRev*, INTEL NEWS, Feb. 26, 1996.

66.   *See* ROMOVSKA, *supra* note 5, at 155.

67.   *See id.*

68.   *The Women's Movement in Ukraine: Many Organizations Achieving Little*, INTEL NEWS, Mar. 8–9, 1996 [hereinafter *Women's Movement in Ukraine*].

69.   Prohrama i Statut Ukrayinskoyi Khrystyianskoyi Partiyi Zhinok.

70.   *See id.*

71.   Among the major non-governmental women's organizations in Ukraine are: the Women's

The Union of Ukrainian Women (UUW) boasts more than 10,000 female members. According to the head of the UUW, the Union promotes advancements in education, charity, and commerce.[72] Although Ukrainian women are conscious of purely feminist and social problems worldwide, a number of domestic problems demand their immediate attention. Since the inception of the UUW in the early 1990s, its foremost effort has been to overcome the difficult obstacles surrounding the communist nomenclature. Under the Soviet system, branches of the UUW were considered underground organizations. Presently, the UUW is primarily concerned with providing assistance to the needy, organizing summer health clinics for Chernobyl and Prednister children, and caring for the pecuniary and psychological needs of orphans, the elderly, the disabled, and battered women.[73]

Another active women's organization in Ukraine is The Women's Union of Ukraine (WUU). The WUU is the successor organization to the former Ukrainian branch of the Soviet Women's Committee and has affected change by using the network of regional women's councils established in the Soviet era. According to the WUU head, Maria Orlyk, the organization maintains about 40,000 members and assists women in finding employment during this period of economic reform.[74] At a 1993 nationwide conference, the WUU defined its main task as protecting the rights of women engaged in business activities.

The Women's Community was organized in 1994 under the auspices of the Women's Council of the Rukh (one of the largest political parties in Ukraine). According to its leader, Maria Drach, one of its slogans is: "From the well-being of every family to the well-being of the Ukrainian state."[75]

The Organization of Soldiers' Mothers defines its struggle as opposition to illegality and violence in the military, and many "women managed to obtain their official representation in the headquarters of armed forces of Ukraine."[76] The Jewish women's organization, Rakhamim, was created in 1993 to assist elderly Jews who do not receive any support from their children or who suffer some type of disability.[77] Rakhamim also helps poor families pay for funerals.

Union of Ukraine, the Women-Workers Union For the Future of Children of Ukraine, the Union of Ukrainian Women, Women's Community, Organization of Soldiers' Mothers, All-Ukrainian Federation of Mothers with Many Children, the League of Ukrainian Women, and professional groups such as the Federation of Ukrainian Women of Business and the Organization of Women Farmers.

72.   Atena Pashko, *Vidnoolenyi z Popelu*, 10 Our Life 8, 8–11 (1993). The UUW has played an active role in the international women's movement by participating in the International Conference in Prague organized by UNESCO in December 1991, by attending the Helsinki Public Assembly in Bratislava in March 1992, and the Women's Conference in Freinurg in May 1992. The UUW was admitted to the International Alliance of Women Organizations in October 1992, at the meeting of the XXIX Congress in Athens, Greece. *Id.*

73.   *See id.*

74.   *Women's Movement in Ukraine, supra* note 68, at 8–9.

75.   *See id.*

76.   *See id.*

77.   *See id.*

There are many more non-governmental organizations, but, despite their great number, they have achieved relatively little. The women's movement in Ukraine has failed to become a social phenomenon. Many organizations have learned that greater results can be achieved by combining forces, so many women's organizations have started to consider consolidations or coalitions. This does not mean unification; they may be too different to unite. Yet, the Consultative Council of Women's Organizations Leaders has been created as a coordinative organ for common activities. For example, the Consultative Council allied a block of eighteen women's organizations in support of the Constitution of Ukraine.

The problems facing Ukrainian women have been discussed at several conferences.[78] Further, a delegation of Ukrainian women took part in the Fourth World Conference on Women in Beijing in September 1995. The major strategies accentuated at the Beijing conference were accepted as the foundation of the *Program of Action* adopted by the All-Ukrainian Women Conference in Kyiv in June 1996. The *Draft Program* was prepared by the Political Council of the international committee of the Women Community under the legal guidance of Professor Tamara Melnyk of the Ukrainian Transport University. In accordance with the Beijing directives, Ukrainian women must seek to remove the obstacles that block women from meaningful and equal participation in the economic, political, spiritual, and cultural decisions facing Ukraine. They must also strengthen principles of equality of men and women in respect to family, to employment, and other basic human rights. Ultimately, women must reach out in a thoughtful effort to achieve gender equality in Ukraine and in the world.

The United States Agency for International Development (USAID) has provided significant support and development assistance to Ukrainian women's organizations. USAID/Kyiv considers the participation of women in the political process to be central to the success of democratic and economic reform.[79] The US-NIS Women's Consortium, funded by an ENI Bureau grant to the Winrock Foundation, focuses on participatory decision making, women's rights, and leadership training. It has also made smaller grants to launch grassroots women's organizations such as the Kyiv Women's Legal Center and the Kyiv Women's Crisis Center. The Consortium teaches hands-on democracy techniques. As a result of this training, a member of the Consortium, the US League of Women Voters, brought ten Ukrainian women to the United States, where the Ukrainians could learn NGO management and lobbying first-hand.[80]

---

78.   These include: *Strategies of the IV World Conference of Women and the Program of Actions in Ukraine*, hosted by the Women's Community organization (Kyiv, June 1996); *Women of Ukraine: History, the Present and a Look into the Future*, organized by the UUW (Dnipropetrovsk, November 1995); the international conference on *The Ukrainian Woman and Democracy*, organized in conjunction with the World Federation of Ukrainian Women Organizations (Kyiv, 1993); and *A Woman in Struggle for Freedom of Ukraine*, organized by the UUW (Lviv, 1990), among many others.

79.   Activities of the United States Agency for International Development (USAID) (relating to Women's Issues).

80.   *See id.* Similarly, six grassroots Ukrainian women's organizations (Kharkiv Gender Center,

CONCLUSION

Because of decreasing living standards, rising unemployment, threats of corruption, trafficking problems, and organized crime, women do not have the ability to exercise their rights fully. More importantly, women's rights can only be guaranteed in a politically and economically stable country. To preserve Ukraine from internal instability continues to be the primary goal of the Ukrainian women's movement. However, special attention should be paid to women's interests concerning economic advancement, health, welfare, safety, housing, public services, and the enforcement and promulgation of laws that address women's concerns.

Kharkiv Women's Fund, Lyubystok Women's Club, Women's Information-Consultation Center of Kyiv, Kyiv Women's Legal Center, and the Women's Crisis Center of Kyiv) have received grants from the Eurasia and International Renaissance Foundation (Soros).

ISSUES AFFECTING WOMEN IN THE SOUTH PACIFIC ISLANDS

Cynthia L. Ambrose

INTRODUCTION

The South Pacific is a vast area of blue ocean with splatters of volcanic land masses known as the South Pacific Islands. These islands share the separation and remoteness that such waters inevitably dictate. This chapter on women in the South Pacific Islands will focus primarily on the Federated States of Micronesia, Papua New Guinea, the Cook Islands, and the Republic of the Marshall Islands. While these island nations were chosen as a focus because of the availability of resources, the issues faced by the women of these specific islands are representative of the issues faced by women throughout the South Pacific region.[1]

The islands in the South Pacific differ in the details of their histories, cultures, and traditions, but gender-based norms and practices throughout this region are somewhat similar from island to island.[2] All of the islands have shared in a struggle for independence and are now continuing to work towards developing and maintaining their countries' independence. As these islands continue to develop, true positive progress will only be achieved by recognizing that discrimination and harmful gender practices are a hindrance to the countries' development and must be eliminated. The historical cultures and traditions, combined with the introduction of new systems and governments, have fostered and developed discriminatory treatment in the islands. Indeed, "[a]lthough the region is marked by tremendous diversities in levels of social and economic development, and the extent of gender differences along differential dimensions varies from one country to another, the pattern is broadly similar everywhere."[3] The pattern of subordination, a pattern of limiting and restricting women's access to and participation in all aspects of public and private society, must be confronted and remedied.

As the Pacific Islands struggle for their independence, the women of these island countries also struggle for their own independence—for equal rights and equitable

---

1. *Federated States of Micronesia*, 1993 NATIONAL REVIEWS OF THE NAIROBI FORWARD-LOOKING STRATEGIES FOR THE ADVANCEMENT OF WOMEN 5 [hereinafter *FSM*].

2. *Ministerial Conference on Women and Sustainable Development*, 9 WOMEN'S NEWS QUARTERLY NEWSLETTER OF THE PACIFIC WOMEN'S RESOURCE BUREAU 7 (South Pacific Commission, New Caledonia, June 1994).

3. *Id.*

treatment. During this time when the countries are working towards independence and stability, the positive efforts of all of the countries' people, men and women alike, are necessary to survival and development. The development and future of the Pacific Island people will continue to be deficient until women are afforded full participation, indeed "[i]ssues relating to women affect nearly all human development goal[s]."[4] The importance of women and equality to the future development and independence of these island countries must be recognized because "[t]he roles of women are the key for family, community and a nation's success."[5] Women can and should be contributing their knowledge and abilities to the future of the developing island nations.

In the South Pacific, women are subjected to violence, are less educated than males, hold a smaller share of the job markets, are paid less, have minimal control over health issues that affect them, and are underrepresented in government and politics.[6] Although programs providing opportunities for women in education and politics would be advantageous to all of the Pacific Islands, such programs are very limited.[7] Clearly, women need improved health care, educational access, employment opportunities, and broader participation in government in order to make a maximum contribution to society.[8]

Women are important to a nation's overall development and independence. Because "[i]ssues relating to women affect nearly all human development goals"[9] in the South Pacific, as elsewhere, "[w]omen must become an integral part of the nation's development on all fronts."[10] The focus needs to be at all levels of public and private life, and even "between the entire Pacific region, to promote sustainable development and increase the role of women in the development of the nations."[11]

This chapter will concentrate on the major issues affecting women in the South Pacific as they struggle for equality and independence as do their countries. The issues that the women of the South Pacific face are in many ways linked to the introduction of colonization and Western values and systems into the traditional societies and cultures of these islands. It is not that the historical traditional societies were ones of equality, but the colonization in many ways seemed to enhance and extend the traditional inequalities. Therefore, "[t]he challenge facing the Pacific people is to carry

---

4.   PACIFIC HUMAN DEVELOPMENT REPORT, UNITED NATIONS DEVELOPMENT PROGRAM 68 (1994) [hereinafter PACIFIC].

5.   THIRD MICRONESIAN SUBREGION WOMEN'S CAUCUS REPORT 1994, 1 (South Pacific Commission, New Caledonia).

6.   *FSM, supra* note 1, at 6.

7.   Ministry of Social Services, National Women's Policy-Republic of the Marshall Islands 1996–2001 2 (July 1995) (unpublished statement) (on file with the Marshall Islands Ministry of Social Services) [hereinafter Ministry].

8.   *Id.* at 4.

9.   PACIFIC, *supra* note 4, at 68.

10.   Ministry, *supra* note 7, at 24.

11.   *Id.* at 3.

forward the strengths of their cultures, at the same time adopting and adapting as they interact with other cultures and as they inevitably integrate more fully into the world political economy."[12] Although past cultures and traditions were not ones of true equality or equity, there were some positive aspects in that women served important roles that had acknowledged value. However, many injustices of the past were never openly recognized and thus never addressed. When the new ideas and influences of the patriarchal Western world invaded the islands, discrimination increased and even erased any positive gender roles and values from the cultural past. Currently, the women of the islands are in a changed, more Western, society, and face both old and new issues.

TRADITION AND CULTURE

The islands of the South Pacific were traditionally matrilineal.[13] That is, descent was based on the mother's line. Women were the history and foundation of the families, "the giver and sustainer of life."[14] Women—mothers, sisters and daughters— had special value through the family heritage and the land that they owned.[15] They were the protectors and caretakers of the land, and the land was everything to these people.[16] Land defined who you were; you were nothing without land.[17] However, matriarchy did not confer equality, or even a good life, upon women. One author, in discussing a girl's entry into womanhood in the Marshall Islands, provides a detailed description of the difficulty women face in growing from girlhood to womanhood. A beautiful ceremony is held for the girl-child, although it is actually a sad occasion for her because she must now begin the hard life of a woman: "They do not herald her entry into womanhood, but give her a last fling to console her before she passes irrevocably from the desirable condition of girlhood to a woman's life of drudgery."[18]

The culture, although matrilineal, was male dominated.[19] The term "role separation" is often used to describe the traditional relationship between men and women

---

12.   PACIFIC, *supra* note 4, at 63.

13.   P. Thomas, *The Impact of Aid, Development and Technological Change on the Status of Women in Developing Countries*, 29 WOMEN AND DEVELOPMENT COURIER 1, 3 (Dec. 1983) (on file with the Micronesian Seminar Library, Box 220, Pohnpei, FM 96941) [hereinafter Thomas].

14.   Ministry, *supra* note 7, at 6.

15.   Thomas, *supra* note 13, at 3; Ministry, *supra* note 7, at 6.

16.   Beatriz Moral, Chuukese Women's Status—Traditional and Modern Elements (unpublished paper) (on file with the Micronesian Seminar Library, Box 220, Pohnpei, FM 96941) [hereinafter Moral]; Videotape: Changing Roles of Women (Micronesian Seminar 1995) (on file with the Micronesian Seminar Library, Box 220, Pohnpei, FM 96941) [hereinafter Changing Roles]; FSM Women's Interest Program, The Enhancement of the Status of Women in the FSM by Encouraging their Full and Active Participation in the Development Process, (Nov. 20–24, 1995) (on file with the FSM Women's Affairs Office, Pohnpei, FM 96941) [hereinafter FSM Interest Program]; *Marshall Islands*, 1993 NATIONAL REVIEWS OF THE NAIROBI FORWARD-LOOKING STRATEGIES FOR THE ADVANCEMENT OF WOMEN [hereinafter *Marshall Islands*].

17.   Moral, *supra* note 16.

18.   Wedgewood, *Notes on the Marshall Islands*, XIII OCEANIA JOURNAL 1,10 (Sept. 1942).

19.   Moral, *supra* note 16.

in the South Pacific Islands;[20] a relationship that resembles socialism in that they work together for the common good, with complementary, but different roles.[21] In Papua New Guinea, for example, the women raised the pigs, and the pigs were the basis for men's status, thus women participated in the men's economic position.[22] Both men and women were seen as necessary to the community.[23] The women did have some power and control, but it was indirect, "behind the scenes" power and control.[24] Tina Takashy's report on women in the Federated States of Micronesia (FSM) discusses the complementary roles men and women traditionally held, and the loss of this complementary role system with the introduction of Western systems.[25] However, Takashy's report, like some others, indicates that the traditional relationship of complementary roles between men and women was satisfactory and desired.[26] Similarly, the National Women's Report for the Republic of the Marshall Islands advocates returning to a past where women had clearly defined roles.[27] There are others who have written on South Pacific women's rights, roles, and status who have likewise described the past and the historical standards as acceptable.[28] In some areas women are no longer allowed to fish and build canoes as they had in the past. This difference between roles in the past and present has caused some to remember the past as purely positive, and to urge a return.[29]

Even with role separation and "indirect power," severe restrictions on women's access to economic activities outside of the home still prevailed.[30] Traditionally, women had defined, valued roles, but to a large extent the roles were limited to domestic responsibilities because they were taught to "complement men instead of compete."[31] Women had the domestic roles, and men had the public ones. Men were, therefore, "culturally designated communicators of decision making processes as well as providers of leadership."[32] The men dominated and controlled, while women were restricted to the home and silenced.

20.　Changing Roles, *supra* note 16; *FSM, supra* note 1, at 3.

21.　*Id.*

22.　Thomas, *supra* note 13.

23.　Changing Roles, *supra* note 16.

24.　*Id.*

25.　*FSM, supra* note 1, at 6.

26.　*Id.*

27.　Ministry, *supra* note 7, at 4.

28.　Statement from Sizue G. Yoma, on women's issues to the Second Asian and Pacific Ministerial Conference on Women in Development (June 7–14, 1994) (on file with the Micronesian Seminar Library, Box 220, Pohnpei, FM 96941); Thomas, *supra* note 13, at 3, 8.

29.　Ministry, *supra* note 7, at 2.

30.　*Id.*

31.　Ministry, *supra* note 7, at 2; Changing Roles, *supra* note 16.

32.　*FSM, supra* note 1, at 7.

Beatriz Moral, an anthropologist in the South Pacific, discusses the "incest taboos" as the root of cultural male superiority and domination.[33] Because all men in a family clan were viewed as the female clan members' brothers, she had to avoid all contact with them.[34] A woman was taught to never draw attention to herself and to try to be "non-existent."[35] Women thus learned to remain quiet, to never speak or interact in public; women worked very hard to disappear.[36] Men became the public speakers and players, the spokespersons for all, and from this grew the belief that men were superior and better able to lead and control.[37] Men dominated, and women, willingly or not, submitted to the domination.

Women's learned passiveness was reinforced by the introduction of outside influences. After "incest taboo" came the introduction of Christianity, followed by Western patriarchal culture and values, both of which strengthened male superiority.[38] The shape of the family and culture changed with these religious, social, economic, and political influences. It should naturally follow that women's roles would evolve to meet the influences and cultural changes; unfortunately this did not occur.[39] The introduction of missionaries, colonization, imported Western value systems, technology, and the more recent aid and development programs have caused women to lose their status, value, and "indirect power" of the past. These outside influences have contributed to the erosion of the traditional "complementary hierarchical power-sharing status" between men and women.[40] Pacific cultures, which served as a basis for social cohesion and provided social safety nets, were strained as expectations were altered by modern development.[41]

Christianity reinforced male superiority by bringing only men into leadership and domination roles as priests, ministers, missionaries and teachers.[42] The missionaries also brought the Bible, quoting: "Wives, submit yourselves unto your husband, as unto the Lord, for the husband is the head of the wife, even as Christ is the head of the Church."[43] Women were told to obey their husbands and to take care of the household.

---

33. Beatriz Moral, *supra* note 16.

34. *Id.*

35. *Id.*

36. *Id.*

37. *Id.*

38. *Id.*

39. Ministry, *supra* note 7, at 6.

40. Statement from Sizue G. Yoma, on women's issues to the Second Asian and Pacific Ministerial Conference on Women in Development (June 7–14, 1994) (on file with the Micronesian Seminar Library, Box 220, Pohnpei, FM 96941); Thomas, *supra* note 13, at 3, 8.

41. Pacific, *supra* note 4, at 63.

42. *Id.*

43. Ephesians 5:22–23 *reprinted in* Thomas, *supra* note 13, at 5.

Similarly, in the aftermath of World War II, the United States brought a limited democracy to the islands: a government of men.[44] The leaders and representatives "administering" the South Pacific under the Trust Territory were men. Even today, the representatives from the United States visiting and overseeing the South Pacific are primarily men. Male superiority and domination was now legitimized. Colonization and modernization brought increased male domination to the islands.[45] The South Pacific followed in the steps of the "parent"—the United States of America. Men became the leaders and decision makers of the new democratic society.

As the new, more modern, imported value systems were introduced to the islands, a male oriented society continued to develop, "causing the [complete] disempowerment of women."[46] These foreign influences and value systems took the South Pacific Islands from subsistence economies to cash economies, from extended families to nuclear families, from traditional societies to modern societies. These transitions compounded and diminished any roles and value the women had, reinforcing inequality between men and women.[47]

While women were not equal to men traditionally, they did have roles and value. But, with the new influences, these traditional women's roles were no longer available and women lost all perceived value.[48] Further, women were not allowed to enter into new roles.[49] The life of the South Pacific Island women deteriorated, and role separation, which was unequal and unfair in the past, was gone, and they were left with even less.

The women of the South Pacific Islands today have little or no voice about the inadequate health services available. They are less educated than men, have fewer employment opportunities and receive less money in the employment sector than men; they have little or no voice in the decision-making political bodies, and they suffer from domestic violence.[50] Each of these areas will be examined separately in the following sections.

HEALTH

"Health" reaches beyond physical ailments; it refers to general well being and quality of life.[51] Women's health issues affect the entire population because "health problems faced by women have a negative impact on the development of family, cul-

---

44. Moral, *supra* note 16.

45. Thomas, *supra* note 13, at 5.

46. FSM Interest Program, *supra* note 16.

47. *Third Micronesian Subregion Women's Caucus Report 1994* (South Pacific Commission, New Caledonia), at 8 [hereinafter *Caucus*]; Changing Roles, *supra* note 16.

48. *Caucus, supra* note 47; Changing Roles, *supra* note 16.

49. *Id.*

50. FSM Interest Program, *supra* note 16.

51. *FSM, supra* note 1, at 7 (footnote omitted).

ture, and nation."[52] Health status affects all aspects of one's life and extends beyond the individual to the family, community, and society as a whole.

Health in general in the South Pacific Islands is poor.[53] The health situation for women in the South Pacific Islands is both different, and in some ways more severe, than the situation for men. The major health problems faced by women in the South Pacific largely concern issues relating to reproduction. The health problems throughout the South Pacific Islands are similar, and a "rapid cultural change can lead to a serious rise in fertility and a rapid deterioration in the health status of women and children."[54] Prior to 1958, population growth in the Marshall Islands was less than 1 percent per annum.[55] However, the introduction of a cash economy and foreign funded development programs brought a decrease in cultural traditions regarding marriage and reproduction, and an increase in health problems.[56] For example, women began to marry younger, rather than waiting until the age of twenty. Women also began to bear one child immediately following another, rather than waiting at least a full breast-feeding cycle as they had in the past.[57] In the Marshall Islands:

> Undoubtedly, health status is the major issue of concern for women. High rates of fertility combined with short birth spacing, inadequate nutrition and sanitation, obesity, teenage pregnancies, high rates of sexually transmitted diseases (STDs), and inadequate access to health care . . . are [some of] the major health problems confronting women.[58]

The greatest health problem in the Marshall Islands is poor nutrition combined with reproduction, which may lead to diabetes, STDs, gynecological problems, obesity, and anemia.[59] In fact, throughout the South Pacific region, women's major health risks are largely centered around the combination of reproduction and malnutrition.[60]

---

52. Ministry, *supra* note 7, at 9.

53. Ministry, *supra* note 7, at 9; Chris Peteru, *Food for Thought*, Pacific Islands Monthly, July 1996, at 41 (With the new modern Western influences, imports have increased drastically. Traditionally, the South Pacific people relied on the "highly nutritious locally produced food." Along with the Western influences came Western foods: "While gathering fresh food has never been a problem for people on the tiny islands scattered around the Pacific, a growing mountain of imported foods is making some far-reaching impact on the way they live." The imported foods are seen as "luxury goods." The increase and growth in imports has caused a "nutritional nightmare." People have replaced the fresh local fruits and vegetables with imports such as sugar, white rice, and white flour. The South Pacific people's digestive systems have not been able to safely handle the new diet, and thus health problems continue to grow. One result has been a surge in deaths caused by heart disease, obesity, and diabetes. The South Pacific Islands need to decrease imports, and go back to local fruits and vegetables to regain control over their health and eliminate the health risks associate with diets of imported foods.).

54. Pacific, *supra* note 4, at 30.

55. *Id.* at 31.

56. *Id.*

57. *Id.*

58. Pacific, *supra* note 4, at 31 (*quoting* ADB Report 1991).

59. Ministry, *supra* note 7, at 9.

60. U.N., The Women's World 1995 Trends and Statistics 71–75, U.N. Doc. ST/ESCAP/1489 (1995) [hereinafter Women's World].

As mentioned briefly above, outside influences have weakened tradition's influence on sexual activity and reproduction. Thus, women have neither control nor power over their reproductive rights. While Family Planning Programs were introduced to the Federated States of Micronesia (FSM) as early as the mid-1960s, the FSM national and state governments neither promote nor encourage the programs.[61] The programs are administered quietly and slowly because of a conflict with the religious and cultural sectors of society.[62] After over thirty years of Family Planning Programs in the FSM, the rate of fertility continues to increase.[63]

For women, the health picture has continued to worsen.[64] Approximately 350 million women in the developing world suffer from malnutrition.[65] Management, research, and development of health care is generally conducted by men.[66] Thus, the issues and concerns of women are seldom addressed.[67]

Health concerns of women and men may differ because of biological and socioeconomic factors.[68] There exists a wide gap in available preventative and curative care.[69] The availability and quality of care provided, and the success and failure of disease control programs, is affected by gender.[70] Women's health concerns must be known and understood by the medical professionals, and women need to be involved in the health care field. In addition, information about South Pacific women's health issues must be readily available in an understandable manner so that women can take control of and make appropriate decisions regarding their bodies.

EDUCATION

The education of women in the South Pacific Islands is rarely promoted or supported. There is a high illiteracy rate among women.[71] Major impediments to the independence and education of women are found in the customs, traditions, and influences which dictate that women belong in the home, effectively eliminating women's opportunity for education, equality, and self-determination.[72]

---

61. *FSM, supra* note 1, at 9.

62. *Id.*

63. *Id.*

64. *FSM, supra* note 1, at 7–8.

65. *Empowering Women*, UNICEF EAST ASIA AND PACIFIC REGIONAL OFFICE, at 18 (on file with author)[hereinafter *Empowering Women*].

66. *FSM, supra* note 1, at 9.

67. *Id.* at 7–10.

68. WOMEN'S WORLD, *supra* note 60, at 71.

69. *Id.*

70. *Id.* (*citing* WORLD HEALTH ORGANIZATION, WOMEN AND TROPICAL DISEASES (Pandu Wijeyarantne, Eva M. Rathgenbar & Evelyn St. Onge eds., Ottawa, International Development Research Center, and Geneva, World Health Organization, 1992)).

71. 1995 TRENDS AND STATISTICS at 89, U.N. Doc. ST/ESCAP/1489 (1995).

72. *FSM, supra* note 1, at 11.

In 1992, in the FSM, only 32 percent of women completed high school, compared to 52 percent of men.[73] In the Marshall Islands, the rate of women dropping out of high school has been high because of pregnancy, cultural restraints, and lack of family encouragement or support.[74] In 1990, in Papua New Guinea, there was an estimated sixty-one females for every 100 males enrolled in school.[75]

Historically, when colonization came to the South Pacific Islands, only the education of men was promoted.[76] The value of educating women was, and still is, regularly questioned. There exists the notion that "formal education is not an attractive option for women as it does not prepare them for productive married life and its obligations."[77]

Education provides opportunities and alternatives; it provides a future. Education affects most of the issues facing women in the South Pacific. Education provides opportunities outside of the home, unconnected to and independent of men, where women can participate in society as productive contributors to the nation's future. With greater options and opportunities, pregnancies may decrease, because educated women usually marry later and have fewer children.[78] As fertility decreases, development of the South Pacific Island countries increases.[79] With education and opportunities, women can begin to address reproduction and pregnancy health risks. As women are educated they will have greater access to the political arena and decision-making bodies. Education also increases confidence and respect—women will gain self-confidence and be better able to confront and battle other obstacles. Education is a major key to the South Pacific women's struggle for equality.

Education of women will benefit the entire region's growth and development.[80] It is one of the most proven means of ensuring women's active participation in their nation's development and future.[81] Education is an investment in the people of the nation, and it is perhaps the most worthwhile investment for developing countries.[82]

Obstacles must be removed, and access to education for women must be improved.[83] In the Marshall Islands, a new policy awards education grants to appropriate numbers of female and male recipients.[84] There need to be more policies pro-

---

73. *Id.*
74. Ministry, *supra* note 7, at 17.
75. WOMEN'S WORLD, *supra* note 60, at 89.
76. Thomas, *supra* note 13, at 6.
77. *FSM, supra* note 1, at 11–12.
78. WOMEN'S WORLD, *supra* note 60, at 92.
79. *Empowering Women, supra* note 65, at 20; WOMEN'S WORLD, *supra* note 60, at 89, 92.
80. PACIFIC, *supra* note 4, at 29.
81. WOMEN'S WORLD, *supra* note 60, at 89.
82. *FSM, supra* note 1, at 11–12.
83. WOMEN'S WORLD, *supra* note 60, at 89.
84. Ministry, *supra* note 7, at 17.

moting the education of women and girls; these policies require active support and implementation. Educating women and girls ensures the education of the nation. There are no disadvantages.

EMPLOYMENT OPPORTUNITIES

To understand the prevailing sexist attitudes and the lack of employment opportunities for women in the Pacific, consider the words of Sitaleki Finau to the South Pacific Commission on Woman's World Community Training.[85] Finau stated that allowing women access to the private sphere is "like letting the cows go while we try to get milk out of the bulls."[86] The speech discusses the inherent division of labor recognized and accepted in Tonga and most South Pacific Island societies.[87] Women are responsible for the children, the home, and the health of the family; men are responsible for the "out of home" needs.[88] Finau's speech is full of patriarchal insights on why women should stay home and not enter the arena of public life, a belief shared by many government leaders in addition to the speaker.

The facts establish that Finau's ideas, as alarming as they are, are not far from the real situation. In 1992, less than 10 percent of women in the FSM held administration level positions.[89] According to the 1988 census, in the Marshall Islands, 70 percent of the labor force was male.[90] Even in some of the more developed and progressive Pacific Islands, like the Cook Islands, the employment positions available for women are usually low level and low paying: "Like a pyramid, the lower one goes through the rank, the more women one finds. And like any other country, the Cook Islands is another example of the gender inequalities that exist in the workplace."[91] Women's attempts to break from traditional roles and responsibilities are often viewed as neglect of the family and home.[92]

Historically, the culture and traditions have taught the people of the South Pacific, men and women alike, that a woman's place is in the home. Women have value only as homemakers, child bearers, and child rearers.

The employment pattern in the developing Pacific region is made up of three sectors: (1) the formal sector of government and family businesses; (2) the informal sector of street vendor type businesses; and (3) agriculture and fishing.[93] In the

---

85. Sitaleki A. Finau, speech to women trainees at the South Pacific Commission Training Workshop (July 4, 1987) (on file with the Micronesian Seminar Library, Box 220, Pohnpei, FM 96941) [hereinafter Finau].

86. *Id.*

87. *Id.*

88. *Id.*

89. *FSM, supra* note 1, at 11.

90. *Marshall Islands, supra* note 16, at 91.

91. Williams, *Cook Islands Women Still Await Their Moment,* PACIFIC ISLANDS MONTHLY, July 1996, at 50.

92. Finau, *supra* note 85.

Marshall Islands, while women do hold positions in each sector, they receive the lower-level jobs and lower pay.[94] In the FSM, as of 1990, 12 percent of the males held professional positions, compared to 4 percent of females.[95] Thus, it is clear that women "work in different jobs and occupations than men, almost always with lower status and pay."[96] In addition, women are also responsible (usually solely) for the family and the home, which are universally unpaid, unrecognized, and unvalued positions: "For most women, family and work are constantly tied together. . . . For most men, work means an income-producing job with a fixed schedule outside the house."[97]

Access to employment opportunities brings unlimited benefits to a woman herself, to those who rely on her, and to society.[98] Women in the work force are necessary for the future development of a country. It is a great disadvantage to a country to deny women employment opportunities.

GOVERNMENT AND POLITICS

The independent island nations of the South Pacific have constitutions that grant equality to all citizens, regardless of gender.[99] However, as in the United States and throughout the world, this constitutional right to equality is far from the reality women face.[100] Although women have the right to vote they are nonetheless "excluded from participating in the decision-making processes."[101] Thus, words of equality written into the constitutions are merely words, and to most, empty words.[102] Cultural traditions and present-day society make equality provisions essentially moot in the South Pacific.[103]

All over the world, men dominate politics and fill decision-making positions.[104] In the South Pacific, women hold few positions in government and have little, if any, influence on governmental decisions.[105] Even those studying women's issues in the South Pacific do not always realize the severity of the situation, for a variety of rea-

---

93. Ministry, *supra* note 7, at 28.

94. *Id.* at 8.

95. *FSM, supra* note 1, at 11.

96. WOMEN'S WORLD, *supra* note 60, at 105.

97. *Id.*

98. *Id.*

99. F.S.M. CONST. art. IV, § 4; CONST. OF THE MARSHALL ISLANDS ART. II, §12; CONST. OF THE INDE-PENDENT STATE OF PAPUA NEW GUINEA, preamble, # 2 and Part III, #55; CONST. OF THE SOVEREIGN DEMOCRATIC REPUBLIC OF FIJI ch. II, # 16 (these constitutions are similar to the Constitution of the United States).

100. ACHIEVEMENTS AND DIRECTIVES 246 (Ron Crocombe et al. eds., 1992).

101. *Empowering Women, supra* note 65, at 18.

102. *FSM, supra* note 1, at 16.

103. *Id.*

104. THE FUTURE OF DEMOCRACY IN THE PACIFIC 17 (Ron Crocombe et al. eds., 1992).

105. Ministry, *supra* note 7, at 24.

sons, from economic or technological restrictions to inadequate training or personal obstacles. While the FSM has only "a handful" of women in government positions, the Assistant Secretary of External Affairs for Asian, Pacific, African and Multilateral Affairs relies on increased awareness to change this present situation.[106]

Even in South Pacific Island countries where women still retain some traditional power, they are not represented in the formal government.[107] In the Cook Islands, where women own land and occupy most of the traditional leadership positions, only one woman has held a position in the formal ruling government: Cabinet Minister Fanaura Kingstone.[108] Kingstone recalls her time in the government as "bittersweet; definitely a boys club" where Kingstone was rarely asked for her opinion and frequently "had to deal with condescending attitudes to women."[109]

The lack of women in politics and decision making is the result of a tradition and culture that created and reinforced passive women with little self confidence. A constantly developing patriarchal system encourages such traits.[110] Tradition and culture have taught women to be submissive and to not question men's decisions.[111] Women are taught, and have learned, to yield to men and to depend on men, with a cost to self.[112] This is compounded by little or no access to education and employment.[113]

Even after the introduction of democracy, change did not and has not been forthcoming. For instance, in Papua New Guinea, "women's integration into the political domain as part of post-independence 'development' has not occurred."[114] Women in the South Pacific have always had limited opportunities. Their history did not provide them with marketable skills, nor did it give them the confidence for involvement in the public arena.[115] Women face a public domain of men—created by men, for men:

> This political isolation of women, along with that of other less-advantaged people in our society, is a weakness in our liberal democratic system of government. The absence of (meaningful) mass participation in the political process raises questions about the accountability and legitimacy of government.[116]

---

106. *FSM, supra* note 1, at 3.

107. Williams, *supra* note 91, at 50.

108. *Id.*

109. *Id.* at 51.

110. THIRD MICRONESIAN SUBREGION WOMEN'S CAUCUS REPORT 1994, SOUTH PACIFIC COMMISSION, NEW CALEDONIA 9 (1995) [hereinafter CAUCUS REPORT].

111. Ministry, *supra* note 7, at 24.

112. CAUCUS REPORT, *supra* note 110, at 9.

113. *Id.*

114. SUSTAINABLE DEVELOPMENT OR MALIGNANT GROWTH? PERSPECTIVES OF PACIFIC ISLAND WOMEN 251 (Atu Emberson-Bain ed., 1994) [hereinafter PERSPECTIVES].

115. *Id.*

116. PERSPECTIVES, *supra* note 114, at 260.

The development of women's organizations that encourage and promote training and support will help make changes.[117] But more is needed. Education and support are necessary. Women must be armed with the skills, knowledge, and confidence to assume the highest level of governmental positions, and access to these positions must be provided. The women's groups in the South Pacific are providing a foundation, and women themselves are beginning to take action to challenge the male dominated political arena: "Times have changed now, we have to stand up and speak our minds."[118]

DOMESTIC VIOLENCE

It is now a well-documented fact that "[g]ender based violence against women crosses all cultural, religious and regional boundaries and is a major problem in every country in which it has been studied."[119] Gender abuse is a universal problem in all cultures, threatening all families and all societies.[120] The current statistics on domestic violence in the South Pacific region indicate a serious problem; the rates are astounding.[121] Reports assert that: "Women from all age groups and economic strata and in both urban and rural areas can tell stories of injuries suffered at the hands of their husbands and boyfriends."[122] A survey in Western Samoa concluded that 30 percent of the women surveyed had suffered "bashing or sexual abuse."[123] The women often knew the offenders, who were mostly husbands, partners, or other male friends.[124] Just as violence against women is common all over the world, it is also prevalent in the South Pacific region.[125]

One explanation for the increase in domestic violence in the South Pacific is the elimination of the extended clan family system and matrilineal rule.[126] The replacement of extended families with nuclear families has contributed to the violence, as has a decline in the appreciation and protection of the mothers, sisters, and wives.[127] Traditionally, the clan men protected the clan women, but this protection no longer exists.[128] Other explanations for the rise in domestic violence

---

117. *Empowering Women, supra* note 65, at 21.

118. Williams, *supra* note 91, at 50.

119. WOMEN'S WORLD, *supra* note 60, at 158.

120. Chris Peteru, *Breaking the Silence*, PACIFIC ISLANDS MONTHLY, June 1996, at 26.

121. Videotape: Beneath Paradise (Micronesian Seminar 1995) (on file with Micronesian Seminar Library, Box 220, Pohnpei, FM 96941) [hereinafter Beneath Paradise]; *Empowering Women, supra* note 65, at 18.

122. Ministry, *supra* note 7, at 21.

123. *Id.*

124. *Id.*

125. Beneath Paradise, *supra* note 121.

126. *Marshall Islands, supra* note 16, at 13; Ministry, *supra* note 7, at 13.

127. *Marshall Islands, supra* note 16, at 13; Ministry, *supra* note 7, at 22.

128. *Marshall Islands, supra* note 16, at 13; Ministry, *supra* note 7, at 22.

include alcohol abuse and increased stresses associated with modern society.[129]

Annette Zimmerman, director of mental health services in the FSM, gives four reasons for violence against women in this region: (1) the need to control/power; (2) stress from work and family; (3) learned behavior; and (4) isolation and loss of family support systems.[130] A survey conducted in Western Samoa found that 53 percent of the incidents of domestic violence were attributed to anger, followed by 28 percent that were alcohol related.[131] In this study, "a mere 3 percent of the women who had been violated reported the incident to the police."[132]

The establishment of women's groups, and the concurrent education on all levels of society about gender violence, is a prerequisite toward eradicating domestic violence.[133] In efforts to combat gender-based violence, it is crucial to "dispel myths and biases that [suggest] violent behavior against a woman [is] all right."[134] Thus, at a minimum, there must be incentives and support for reporting the crime. There must also be counseling and support services available for survivors, education and training for police and judges; and adequate and appropriate punishment for perpetrators.[135]

RECOMMENDATIONS

The numerous and complicated impediments to women's rights must be examined and addressed at all levels of public and private spheres. Most of the Pacific Island nations are not bound by international human rights treaties because they are not parties to those treaties.[136] Thus, unless the violations have become a part of customary international law or constitute *jus cogens* norms, little redress in international bodies is available. Governmental and non-governmental organizations must work together to bring about change. As Suzie Yoma states: "A greater task remains and that is to bring wider and better understanding and awareness to the people . . . about the global efforts and activities in promoting . . . equality."[137] Although remedial mea-

---

129. Ministry, *supra* note 7, at 22; Beneath Paradise, *supra* note 121.

130. Beneath Paradise, *supra* note 121.

131. Peteru, *supra* note 120, at 26.

132. *Id.*

133. Beneath Paradise, *supra* note 121; *Empowering Women, supra* note 65, at 18.

134. Peteru, *supra* note 120, at 27.

135. Beneath Paradise, *supra* note 121.

136. None of the nations discussed in this chapter are a party to the Convenant on Civil and Political Rights, 999 U.N.T.S. 171 (Dec. 16, 1966). The Solomon Islands is a party to the Covenant on Economic, Social and Cultural Rights, 993 U.N.T.S. 3 (Dec. 16, 1966). On Jan. 12, 1995, Papua New Guinea acceded to the Convention on the Elimination of all Forms of Discrimination Against Women, 19 I.L.M. 33 (1980) (Dec. 18, 1979). *See* BARRY E. CARTER & PHILLIP R. TRIMBLE, INTERNATIONAL LAW, SELECTED DOCUMENTS AND NEW DEVELOPMENTS (1994).

137. Statement from Sizue G. Yoma on women's issues to the Second Asian and Pacific Ministerial Conference on Women in Development (June 7–14, 1994) (on file with the Micronesian Seminar Library, Box 220, Pohnpei, FM 96941).

sures are often complex and controversial, action must clearly be initiated in order to promote and protect women's human rights in the South Pacific region. Thus far, there has been little or no action by the Pacific Island governments and people to address and remedy the unequal status and harmful treatment of women.[138] There are no easy solutions to deeply entrenched gender biases, for "[s]ocietal differences are difficult to overcome and the struggle for equality must therefore be recognized as a long-term continuous one."[139]

In recent years, many women's groups and advocacy organizations have been formed in the South Pacific region.[140] Although these groups face numerous financial, procedural, and practical restraints, it is crucial that these groups endeavor to promote and protect the basic human rights of all members of society—men, women, and children. Women must continue their struggle to move into the public sector, including high-ranking positions in the fields of education, employment, and governmental leadership. Donors giving aid and assistance to the South Pacific Islands must require that women's voices and abilities be utilized in their projects, and demand an "equitable spread of benefits and opportunities."[141]

The undervalued and underutilized qualities and assets of women's resources must be fully integrated into the development of the nation, because "[w]omen are by nature the true and natural leaders of our society—they are our mothers, they gave us our first breath of fresh air and rear us to today so surely they are the ones to show us tomorrow as well."[142] Thus, for the islands of the South Pacific to succeed in their independence and positive development, they must recognize that maximum progress can only be achieved by respecting the basic human rights and dignity of all people, including women.[143]

---

138. *Id.*

139. Ministry, *supra* note 7, at 4; PERSPECTIVES, *supra* note 114, at 259.

140. UNITED NATIONS, DIRECTORY OF NATIONAL AND FOCAL POINTS FOR THE ADVANCEMENT OF WOMEN IN ASIA AND THE PACIFIC, U.N. Doc. ST/ESCAP/1489 (1995).

141. Thomas, *supra* note 13, at 8. For example, the United Nations, in a new pilot project called Incorporation of Women in Mainstream Development Planning, promotes full participation of women and men in all stages of the development process. Ministry, *supra* note 7, at 24.

142. *FSM, supra* note 1, at 3.

143. *Id.*

ABORIGINAL WOMEN IN AUSTRALIA AND HUMAN RIGHTS

Penelope Andrews

This chapter provides an overview of the contemporary condition of Aboriginal women in Australia. It suggests certain ways in which the application of international human rights law may have an impact in removing some of the structural obstacles that trap Aboriginal women in a spiral of dislocation, desperation, and poverty. It recognizes the multi-faceted nature of the situation of Aboriginal women across the Australian continent, and the divergence in lifestyles, income, educational levels, political opinions, and aspirations. However, because the chapter focuses on the *overall* situation of Aboriginal women, of necessity, certain generalities are conscripted.

INTRODUCTION

Australia's international reputation as a responsible global partner is reasonably intact. Australia has been a committed signatory to a host of United Nations treaties and conventions aimed at stamping out torture globally,[1] ensuring that refugees are accorded certain rights as they flee persecution,[2] and according fundamental rights to the world's most precious resource—its children.[3] These actions indicate some willingness on the part of successive Australian governments to allow international access and scrutiny of relevant laws and policies, and also to provide Australian citizens some external recourse when human rights violations occur locally.[4]

---

1.   *See* Convention Against Torture and other Cruel, Inhuman or Degrading Punishment or Treatment, *adopted* Dec. 10, 1984, *entered into force* June 26, 1987, G.A. Res. 39/46, 39 U.N. GAOR, Supp. No. 51, U.N. Doc. A/39/51, at 197 (1984), *reprinted in* 23 I.L.M. 1027 (1984), minor changes *reprinted in* 24 I.L.M. 535 (1985).

2.   Convention Relating to the Status of Refugees, July 28, 1951, 189 U.N.T.S. 150 (*entered into force* Apr. 22, 1954).

3.   Convention on the Rights of the Child, *adopted* Nov. 20, 1989, G.A. Res. 44/25, 44 U.N. GAOR, Supp. No. 49, U.N. Doc. A/44/49, at 166 (1989), *reprinted in* 28 I.L.M. 1448 (1989) (*entered into force* Sept. 20, 1990). For an interesting discussion on the increasing relevance of international human rights norms to Australian law, *see* M. Kirby, *The Australian Use of International Human Rights Norms: From Bangalore to Balliol—A View from the Antipodes*, 16 U. New S. Wales L.J. 363 (1993).

4.   For a comprehensive list of major human rights instruments relevant to Australia, *see* Nick O'Neill & Robin Handley, Retreat into Injustice: Human Rights in Australian Law 141–43 (1994).

Significantly, Australia has ratified the International Covenant on Civil and Political Rights,[5] the International Covenant on Economic, Social and Cultural Rights,[6] the International Convention on the Elimination of All Forms of Racial Discrimination (Race Convention)[7] and the Convention on the Elimination of Discrimination Against Women (Women's Convention).[8] But despite Australia's international image and standing, the situation of Australia's indigenous population remains desperate.[9] In 1985, a leading newspaper in Melbourne observed:

> After 197 years of white settlement, this is the statistical profile of the descendants of the people who have lived in this country for at least 40,000 years: an infant mortality rate three or four times greater than that of all Australians; life expectancy about 20 years less than that of all Australians; a median family income slightly more than half of that of other Australians; an unemployment rate that has tripled since 1971 to be four times that of other Australians; a disproportionate number uneducated, under-educated and imprisoned.[10]

All social and economic indicators suggest that Aborigines are the most disadvantaged Australians.[11] Within Aboriginal communities, women fare the worst.[12] This

---

5. International Covenant on Civil and Political Rights, *adopted* Dec. 19, 1966, 999 U.N.T.S. 171.

6. International Covenant on Economic, Social and Cultural Rights, *adopted* Dec. 16, 1966, 993 U.N.T.S. 3 (*entered into force* Jan. 3, 1976).

7. International Convention on the Elimination of all Forms of Racial Discrimination, *opened for signature* Mar. 7, 1966, 660 U.N.T.S. 195.

8. Convention on the Elimination of all Forms of Discrimination Against Women, *opened for signature* Mar. 1, 1979, 1429 U.N.T.S. 13 (*entered into force* Sept. 3, 1981). All of these documents bear directly on the issues to be discussed in this chapter. It is worth noting that Australia passed the Racial Discrimination Act in 1975 and the Sex Discrimination Act in 1984 in pursuance of its ratification of the Race Convention and the Women's Convention. In addition, there have been various legislative attempts (referred to below) to address the plight of Australia's indigenous population.

9. Although Aborigines or Aboriginal peoples are referred to throughout this chapter, the reference includes both Aborigines and Torres Strait Islanders. The latter occupy the islands off the Australian coast, where European colonization was less invasive. The terms "Aborigines," "Aboriginal peoples," and "indigenous peoples" are used here interchangeably. In *Commonwealth v. Tasmania*, 46 A.L.R. 625 (1983), the High Court of Australia provided a definition of "Aborigine" for constitutional and administrative purposes and stated that "[b]y 'Australian Aboriginal' I mean, in accordance with what I understand to be the conventional meaning of that term, a person of Aboriginal descent, albeit mixed, who identifies himself [or herself] as such and who is recognized by the Aboriginal community as an Aboriginal." *Id.* at 817.

10. PHYLLIS DAYLIGHT & MARY JOHNSTONE, WOMEN'S BUSINESS: REPORT OF THE ABORIGINAL WOMEN'S TASK FORCE 22 (1986) [hereinafter ABORIGINAL WOMEN'S TASK FORCE] (*quoting Editorial*, THE AGE, Sept. 13, 1985).

11. The 1988–1989 Report of the Department of Aboriginal Affairs states the number of Aborigines and Torres Strait Islanders as 227,638, or 1.46 percent of the total Australian population. The life expectancy of Aborigines is approximately twenty years less than that for all Australians. The imprisonment rate of Aborigines is estimated to be sixteen to twenty times that for the non-Aboriginal population. *See* H. McRAE, G. NETTHEIM & L. BEACROFT, ABORIGINAL LEGAL ISSUES 33–35 (1991). In *Mabo v. Queensland*, 107 A.L.R. 1 (1992), Justices Deane and Gaudron spoke of a "national legacy of unutterable shame." *Id.* at 79.

12. For example, the rate of labor force participation for Aboriginal women is substantially

is despite the fact that the role of Aboriginal women was significant in both the public and private spheres of Aboriginal society. Indeed:

> Traditionally, women in Aboriginal culture have a status comparable with and equal to men. They have their own ceremonies and sacred knowledge, as well as being custodians of family laws and secrets. They supplied most of the reliable food and had substantial control over its distribution. They were the providers of child and health care and under the kinship system, the woman's or mother's line was essential in determining marriage partners and the moiety (or tribal division) of the children.[13]

Aboriginal women in Australia have to contend with the legacy of cultural deprivation and denigration, as well as the double bind of racism and sexism.[14] The lives of Aboriginal women in Australia today are varied significantly by geography, economic status, lifestyle, and age, which makes the task of the observer fairly daunting. This reality is further complicated by the fact that it is unclear how many Aboriginal women continue to have large parts of their personal lives governed by aspects of traditional law, or live a customary lifestyle, that is, Aboriginal women who continue to have close ties to the land.

The relevance of this point might not be obvious, but any focus on the status of Aboriginal women needs to address the issue of Aboriginal spirituality—"The Dreamtime"—and how land is central to this spirituality,[15] or Aboriginal identity:

---

lower than the total Australian female population. The 1981 census showed that 22.1 percent of Aboriginal females were unemployed, as compared to 6.8 percent of the total female population. Only 1.8 percent of Aboriginal women, as compared to 7.5 percent of all Australian women, earned more than $15,000 per annum. ABORIGINAL WOMEN'S TASK FORCE, *supra* note 10, at 135, 137. *See also* ABORIGINAL AND TORRES STRAIT ISLAND COMM'N, EVALUATION: (1) THE OFFICE OF INDIGENOUS WOMEN; (2) ONGOING WOMEN'S INITIATIVES; (3) WOMEN'S NEW INITIATIVES (1990).

13.   Sharon Payne, *Aboriginal Women and the Law, in* ABORIGINAL PERSPECTIVES ON CRIMINAL JUSTICE 31 (Chris Cunneen ed.,1992).

14.   The literature about Aboriginal people is voluminous. Indeed Aboriginal people have continually complained of being the most widely researched community in Australia, without the concomitant benefits of such endless inquiry. *See* ABORIGINAL WOMEN'S TASK FORCE, *supra* note 10, at 1. However, most of the research has focused on Aboriginal society from the perspectives of males within the communities, and very often at the pens of male anthropologists. *See* J. Scutt, *Invisible Women?: Projecting White Cultural Invisibility on Black Australian Women*, 46 ABORIGINAL L. BULL. 4 (1990).

A major breakthrough for Aboriginal women, in terms of their voices being heard, was provided by the Report of the Aboriginal Women's Task Force under the auspices of the Prime Minister and Cabinet, Office of the Status of Women. The Task Force conducted lengthy interviews with, and surveys of, Aboriginal women throughout Australia and produced a comprehensive set of recommendations in relation to Aboriginal women in 1986. The recommendations covered a host of issues including children, employment, legal aid, land rights, culture, and community services. *See generally* ABORIGINAL WOMEN'S TASK FORCE, *supra* note 10.

15.   *See generally* DIANE BELL, DAUGHTERS OF THE DREAMING (1983). Besides other ceremonies, Bell also explores the ceremonies of Aboriginal women in Central Australia. A particularly poignant illustration of Aboriginal spiritual ties to the land is found in BRUCE CHATWIN, THE SONGLINES (1987). The issue of Aboriginality and spirituality is also explored in EUGENE STOCKTON, THE ABORIGINAL GIFT: SPIRITUALITY FOR A NATION (1995). It has been noted that "to discuss culture and the history of the country without proper consideration of the 'ceremony' perpetuates an alien-

> To understand our law, our culture and our relationship to the physical and spiritual world, you must begin with the land. . . . For indigenous peoples from every part of the earth, land has always been the foundation and map for our spiritual and physical survival, memory and development. It is near impossible to use a non-indigenous language to describe the nature of the connection indigenous peoples have to our traditional lands.[16]

Exploring the possibility of the applicability of international human rights norms places this spirituality in stark contrast to the highly formalized, process-driven, and modern system of enforcement that international human rights law mandates.[17]

It is not within the scope of this chapter to analyze the details or features of Aboriginal spirituality.[18] The intention is merely to signify an aspect of Aboriginal life that might provide some understanding of the complexity of the contemporary conditions of Aboriginal women and how the pursuit of human rights has to recognize and embrace the spiritual realm.

Aboriginal spirituality coexists alongside the harsh economic and social realities of Aboriginal women's lives, and arguably is distorted by these material factors. The imperative to recognize the spiritual dimensions of Aboriginal existence provides a formidable challenge for Aboriginal women activists and their allies in the international human rights arena, and undergirds attempts to alter the situation of many Aboriginal women.

Moreover, attempts by Aboriginal women to improve their lives are hampered to some extent by Australia's federal system of government.[19] Although legal responsibility for the welfare of Aboriginal people vests with the federal government, the different states in the Commonwealth, with dissimilar ideologies, have administered programs and projects for Aboriginal peoples. This has a direct impact on the suc-

---

ation from the mother earth; the spiritual centre of ourselves as Aboriginal peoples." Irene Watson, *Law and Indigenous Peoples: The Impact of Colonialism on Indigenous Cultures, in* CROSS CURRENTS: INTERNATIONALISM, NATIONAL IDENTITY AND LAW 107 (Christopher Arup and Lee Ann Marks eds., 1996).

16. Speech by Mick Dodson, Aboriginal Social Justice Commissioner, to Conference on Twentieth Anniversary of the Aboriginal Land Rights Act (N. Terr.) at the Old Parliament House, Canberra (August 1996) (on file with the author).

17. Andrew Byrnes, *Enforcement Through International Law and Procedures, in* HUMAN RIGHTS OF WOMEN: NATIONAL AND INTERNATIONAL PERSPECTIVES 189 (Rebecca Cook ed.,1994).

18. The legacy for Aboriginal Australians of European colonialism in Australia is not confined to issues of economic exploitation or legal dispossession. The legacy entails a history of cultural deprivation that involved, for example, the theft of Aboriginal religious and cultural artifacts; attempts by various colonial administrations to "Christianize" and "civilize" Aborigines; and a total disregard for Aboriginal ceremonies that demanded a certain level of secrecy. For a thoughtful exploration of these issues, *see generally* GRETA BIRD, THE PROCESS OF LAW IN AUSTRALIA (1988); *see also* C. Golvan, *Aboriginal Art and the Protection of Indigenous Cultural Rights*, 56 ABORIGINAL L. BULL. 5 (1992).

19. *See generally* ZELMAN COWAN & LESLIE ZINES, FEDERAL JURISDICTION IN AUSTRALIA (2d ed. 1978).

cess or failure of various measures taken to improve the lives of Aborigines. It also results in uneven outcomes for different Aboriginal communities.[20]

Another significant impediment for Aboriginal women in their quest for equality is the privileging of the male Aboriginal voice in all matters of concern to their communities. Until the mid-1980s,[21] it was uncommon for women to be consulted by outsiders about their needs, preferences, and life choices. The many fact-finding missions that regularly visited Aboriginal communities simply ignored women's voices—their opinions appeared not to matter. And yet numerous programs and policies on health, housing, education, and other important community concerns were predicated on the findings of these missions. In all of these, women's voices were simply absent.[22] As two researchers explain:

> Research, which forms the basis of policy and general understanding of Aboriginal society, has focussed on men for reasons other than the practical issue of discrete male and female domains. Deeply entrenched preconceptions of the role of women as insignificant in Aboriginal society constrains research and policy as surely as does the predominance of men in the field. . . . In the course of our research we scanned the ethnographic literature for references to women, but found little of relevance, many inaccuracies and much sexism later in the reporting. . . .[23]

This chapter highlights the major issues concerning Aboriginal women in Australia today. The first section assesses the history of racism in Australia and the failure of the British system of justice to protect Australia's indigenous population. It refers to the various laws and policies that operated under the guise of "Native Protection," and that separated families, culminating in cultural destruction that has left a lasting blight on Aboriginal people. The section also highlights the struggle for land rights and sovereignty in Australia, with reference to the landmark 1992 *Mabo* decision, the subsequent passage of the Native Title Act in 1993, and the 1996 *Wik* decision.

The second section focuses on two issues related to the status of Aboriginal women in Australian society. First, it examines women and customary or traditional law, with reference to the Australian Law Reform Commission's Report on the recognition of Aboriginal customary law, and considers the access that Aboriginal women have to the wider Australian legal system. The second issue covered in this section is violence to which Aboriginal women are subjected.

The third section highlights the application of international human rights law to promote and protect women's rights, and suggests strategies that might assist in ameliorating some of the conditions that Aboriginal women face. These strategies flow from recommendations listed by Aboriginal women in various reports.

---

20.   Peter Hanks, *Aborigines and Government: The Developing Framework, in* Aborigines and the Law 19 (Peter Hanks and Bryan Keon-Cohen eds., 1984).

21.   *See generally* Aboriginal Women's Task Force, *supra* note 10.

22.   Diane Bell & Pamela Ditton, Law: The Old and the New: Aboriginal Women in Central Australia Speak Out 5 (1980).

23.   *Id.* at 7.

THE HISTORY OF RACISM

Land Grabs and Dispossession

Aboriginal occupation of Australia dates back approximately 40,000 years, during which Aborigines settled and traversed the continent continuously.[24] The invasion of Australia and the brutal decimation of the Aboriginal population commenced just over 200 years ago.[25] The history of colonization and the subsequent dispossession of the indigenous population has been well documented.[26] Most of these texts attest to, and suggest reasons for, the dire circumstances in which Aborigines find themselves.

The last 200 years of European colonization has been characterized and tabulated according to the following phases:

(1) first contacts and conciliation;

(2) displacement, conflict and extermination;

(3) protection and segregation;

(4) assimilation; and

(5) integration.[27]

In the historical literature these phases have been outlined in a rather broad manner, and do not necessarily indicate that each phase represented policy progression in a chronological manner, or consistently across regions. So, for example, in one state the protection policy might still be in place, at the same time that another state was moving towards a more integrationist model.[28] Any semblance of coherence or consistency in relation to the administration of the welfare of Aboriginal peoples only became a constitutional possibility after a referendum in 1967 that handed the Commonwealth Parliament legislative power over Aboriginal peoples.[29] The first two phases have resulted in the near annihilation of Aboriginal communities, and it has been argued that the idea of Aboriginal people dying out as a race underpinned the activities of the settlers (both official and unofficial).[30]

---

24. *See generally* G. BLAINEY, THE TRIUMPH OF THE NOMADS (1975); D.J. MULVANEY, THE PREHISTORY OF AUSTRALIA (1975).

25. *See generally* C. ROWLEY, THE DESTRUCTION OF ABORIGINAL SOCIETY (1970); R. EVANS, K. SAUNDERS & K. CRONIN, EXCLUSION, EXPLOITATION AND EXTERMINATION (1975).

26. For an abbreviated list, *see* RICHARD BROOME, ABORIGINAL AUSTRALIANS (1982); HENRY REYNOLDS, THE OTHER SIDE OF THE FRONTIER (1982); and CHARLES ROWLEY, THE DESTRUCTION OF ABORIGINAL SOCIETY (1970).

27. There have been indications that a new phase, self-determination, has been underway in the last few years. *See* McRAE, NETTHEIM & BEACROFT, *supra* note 11, at 9. *See generally* CHRIS CUNEEN & TERRY LIBESMAN, INDIGENOUS PEOPLE AND THE LAW IN AUSTRALIA (1995).

28. *See* McRAE, NETTHEIM & BEACROFT, *supra* note 11, at 9.

29. *Id.* at 10.

30. ROWLEY, *supra* note 25. *See also* Iris Clayton, *Anybody Could Afford Us, in* BEING ABORIGINAL 74 (Ross Bowden & Bill Bunbury eds., 1990).

There is some controversy in the literature about the extent of official authorization (as opposed to condonation or ignorance) of displacement of Aboriginal communities and/or massacres. For example, some evidence suggests that the first occupiers carried strict instructions from the British Crown about their first contact with the local people:

> You are likewise to observe the genius, temper, disposition and number of the natives, if there be any, and endeavour by all proper means to cultivate a friendship and alliance with them . . . showing them every kind of civility and regard. . . . You are always with the *consent* of the natives to take possession of convenient situations in the country in the name of the King of Great Britain. . . .[31]

However, there is every indication that consent was neither sought nor obtained from the Aborigines before their land was seized.[32]

The literature on the history of colonization points to substantial resistance on the part of Aboriginal people.[33] However, this did not prevent drastic reductions of their numbers from disease. The denial of access to their land deprived them of food and resources, and interfered with the ceremonial religious practices that were part of their culture and identity. White intrusion on the land made it extremely difficult for Aboriginal people to protect their sacred sites.[34] The basis of Aboriginal society—the traditional systems of law, spirituality, and kinship—was completely disrupted. The implementation of the British system of laws rendered Aboriginal people aliens in their own land. More significantly, Aborigines were once self-sufficient, nomadic, and hunting peoples, who lived in spiritual, as well as economic, harmony with the land, but this British feat left them without the mobility which was their life-blood.[35] This forced immobility resulted in a dependency on European food and welfare rations for survival. With their cultural integrity completely undermined, Aborigines became increasingly vulnerable to European influences, particularly alcohol.[36]

The choices of survival for Aboriginal people were slim. The settlers wanted control of their land, not their labor, which was provided by convicts.[37] Aborigines were therefore of absolutely no economic value to the settlers.[38] The ideology of racism

---

31. J.M. Bennet & A.C. Castles, A Source Book of Australian Legal History 253–254 (1979) (emphasis added).

32. *See generally* Henry Reynolds, Frontier (1987). *See also* W.E.H. Stanner, *The History of Indifference Thus Begins, in* White Man Got No Dreaming 165 (1979).

33. *See generally* Neville Green, The Forest River Massacres (1995).

34. *See generally* G. Blainey, A Land Half Won (1980).

35. *Id.*

36. *See generally* Reynolds, The Other Side of the Frontier, *supra* note 26.

37. Among the first settlers in Australia after 1788 were large numbers of convicts who had been transported there as part of Britain's penal policy. For the first decades of settlement, they provided a source of cheap labor for the free settlers. *See generally* Henry Reynolds, Aborigines and Settlers: The Australian Experience 1788–1939 (1972).

38. Colin Bourke, *Economics, Independence or Welfare, in* Aboriginal Australia 179 (Colin Bourke et al. eds., 1994).

and the particularly obnoxious stereotype of Aborigines were prevalent among the settlers; Aboriginal people were, at best, a source of irritation, and at worst, a scourge to be eliminated.[39]

Colonization, coupled with the ravages on their communities, deprived women of their status and role within their communities. In addition, being female made them more vulnerable to sexual exploitation from the settlers:

> Aboriginal women carried a double burden. As women they were seen as sexual objects and fair game for white men; as members of a subject people they were also victims of the whole range of indignities bestowed by a brutal invading colonialism which considered itself to be the master race.[40]

Most important, the imposition of a highly patriarchal European legal and value system ensured that Aboriginal women would be relegated to a second class status within their communities.[41] The British colonial administration, with its patriarchal attitudes, largely rendered Aboriginal women invisible. If traditional Aboriginal society harbored gender inequality,[42] the imposition of colonial policies cemented this inequality by ensuring that the male Aboriginal view was the dominant reflection and interpretation of Aboriginal society.[43] This situation has continued to the present, and in most of the areas of concern to Aboriginal communities, it is the Aboriginal male perspective that is sought and considered.[44] This is most apparent in the area of land rights, and has resulted in profound injustice to Aboriginal women.[45]

Protection and Assimilation: Mothers and Children and Forced Separation

The cumulative impact of the first contact with Europeans had a devastating impact on Aboriginal society. Within a few decades, their numbers were dramatically reduced.[46] This was a concern to some in Britain, so in 1837, the House of Commons Select Committee on Aborigines recommended laws and policies for the establishment of mission stations and protectors.[47] These missionaries and protectors were ostensibly to shield Aborigines from the most egregious aspects and abuses of

---

39. *See generally* TONY AUSTIN, SIMPLY THE SURVIVAL OF THE FITTEST (1992).

40. ANNE SUMMERS, DAMNED WHORES AND GOD'S POLICE: THE COLONIZATION OF WOMEN IN AUSTRALIA 276 (1975).

41. *See generally* BELL & DITTON, *supra* note 22. "If one complaint about the interaction of the two laws [Aboriginal and European] was consistent, it was that in the past women had a voice, which was heeded and that today they were habitually denied that voice." *Id.* at 4.

42. *See generally* BELL & DITTON, *supra* note 22.

43. Fay Gale, *Seeing Women in the Landscape: Alternative Views of the World Around Us, in* WOMEN, SOCIAL SCIENCE & PUBLIC POLICY 65 (Jacqueline Goodnow and Carole Pateman eds., 1985).

44. *Id.*

45. *Id.* at pt. 1, sec.(c).

46. *See generally* REYNOLDS, *supra* note 37.

47. *See generally* ROWLEY, *supra* note 25.

European contact. Whatever good intentions might have prompted these developments, in time, the Office of Protector and, to a lesser extent, the missionaries, came to represent some of the most pernicious official institutions of the colonial period.[48]

During the first half of the twentieth century, an assortment of laws and policies within the various states, in relation to Aborigines and under the guise of "protection," cemented the separate and inferior status of Aboriginal people. The constitutional paradigm, which mandated federal government authority over Aborigines in the Northern Territory (after 1911) and the Australian Capital Territories, also limited federal influence over the various states.[49] Moreover, an elaborate system of racial classification predicated on Aboriginal "blood" content, the contradictory demands for Aboriginal labor and differing minimum wage rates, and inconsistencies in liquor restrictions imposed on Aboriginal communities, exacerbated this intrastate legislative labyrinth.[50]

Discussion about the legal status of Aboriginal people was complicated by state administration of legislation and policies. It was only after a referendum in 1967 that an amendment to the Australian Constitution empowered the Commonwealth government to make laws relating to Aboriginal people for Australia as a whole. Only then did Aborigines win citizenship and the right to vote in elections.[51]

But arguably the most horrific aspect of the official assimilation policy was the forced removal of Aboriginal children from their families to propagate European civilization and Christian values.[52] These events have been described as genocidal because of the devastating impact on individual and group identity. As one report states, "[i]n its crudest form the policy of assimilation fell within the modern definition of genocide, and in particular the attempt to 'solve the Aboriginal problem' by the taking away of children and merging them into white society. . . ."[53] The "stolen generations" case,[54] before the High Court of Australia, represents a cause of action by Aboriginal plaintiffs who seek redress for children removed from families and institutionalized or placed in foster care.

The assimilation policy has been interpreted as one of the "most disempowering acts of all" for Aboriginal women,[55] and a significant cause of the profound despair

---

48.   *See generally* PAT JACOBS, MISTER NEVILLE (1990).

49.   KEITH McCONNOCHIE, DAVID HOLLINSWORTH & JAN PETTMAN, RACE AND RACISM IN AUSTRALIA 111 (1988).

50.   *Id. See also generally* ANNA HAEBICH, FOR THEIR OWN GOOD (1988); ELLA SIMON, THROUGH MY EYES (1987).

51.   I. Mitchell, *Epilogue to a Referendum,* 3 AUSTL. J. SOC. ISSUES 4, 12 (1968).

52.   *See generally* MARGARET TUCKER, IF EVERYONE CARED (1977).

53.   ROYAL COMM'N INTO BLACK DEATHS IN CUSTODY, REPORT OF COMM'R J. H. WOOTEN, Q.C., at 75–77 (1988).

54.   Kruger & Ors v. The Commonwealth of Australia (Proceeding No. M 21 of 1995, pending judgement).

55.   Payne, *supra* note 13, at 32.

that continues to tear at the Aboriginal psyche.[56] In later decades, official policy moved toward a model of integration, in which access to health, housing, and education were seen as rights to which Aboriginal people were entitled, as were all Australians.[57] The last two decades have witnessed increasing political organization and activism on the part of Aboriginal Australians, and successive governments have been more receptive to the demands of the indigenous population. The late 1980s and early 1990s brought significant gains for Aboriginal people in their quest for self-determination.[58] Nowhere have these gains been more pronounced than in the area of land rights.

Land Rights

The Aboriginal peoples' campaign to regain their traditional land, and to own legal title to such land, gained momentum in the late 1960s. This period coincided with widespread political activism on the part of Aboriginal Australians for greater political rights, and for equal access to the economic benefits of Australian citizenship.[59] After an unsuccessful lawsuit[60] in which the Northern Territory Supreme Court failed to recognize the land rights demands made by a group of Aborigines in that Territory, the Commonwealth Government passed the Aboriginal Land Rights Act (N. Terr.).[61] This Act gave the traditional owners freehold title (the most secure title under Australian law) to all Crown land in the Northern Territory which was then designated as "Aboriginal Reserve Land."[62]

The Act provided for the appointment of an Aboriginal Land Commissioner, and permitted Aboriginal people to gain freehold title to other land by demonstrating to the Commissioner that they were the owners of that land according to spiritual tradition. However, the only land covered by the Act was land over which no one else held a lease or freehold title; privately owned property was not included.[63]

Land claims under the Act proved to be a daunting and costly legal process. Despite this fact, there were notable successful claims,[64] and some 34 percent of all Northern Territory land has reverted to Aboriginal lands.[65]

---

56. *See generally* STUART RINTOUL, THE WAILING: A NATIONAL BLACK ORAL HISTORY (1993).

57. *See generally* REYNOLDS, *supra* note 37.

58. Frank Brennan, *Aboriginal Self-Determination: The New Partnership of the 1990's*, 17 ALTERNATIVE L.J. 53 (1992).

59. *Id.*

60. Millirpum v. Nabalco, 17 F.L.R. 141(1971).

61. Act No. 191 of 1976 (Cth).

62. *Id. See* sched. 1.

63. *Id.*

64. The Uluru, formerly Ayers Rock, a huge rock of immense archaeological and cultural significance, situated in the center of the country, was handed back to the Aboriginal traditional owners under the legislation. *See generally* PHILLIP TOYNE & DANIEL VACHON, GROWING UP THE COUNTRY: THE PITJANTJATJARA STRUGGLE FOR THEIR LAND (1984).

65. It has been pointed out that most of the land reverting to the traditional Aboriginal owners has been primarily the less fertile land. *See* BRENNAN, SHARING THE COUNTRY 22, 38 (1991).

The benefits to Aboriginal communities of successful land claims are enormous: freehold title carries with it the right to control mining and development on the land, and to receive royalties from all past and present mines. The money obtained through this process is distributed to the benefit of traditional owners and other Aboriginal people in the Territory.[66] Such revenue also provides the major funding source for the Aboriginal Land Councils in the Northern Territory, which have the statutory power to make land claims on behalf of the traditional owners and to generally protect their interests.[67]

After the passage of the Aboriginal Land Rights Act, various states across Australia passed land rights legislation in response to demands by local Aboriginal groups. The situation was however, uneven, and huge disparities existed across the states.[68]

At the federal level, the Labour government, which was elected to office in 1983 and initially voiced a strong commitment to the passage of national land rights legislation, essentially abandoned the pledge made at the end of the decade.[69] The Aboriginal community and its allies in non-Aboriginal Australia, in response to the inadequacies of the various states' attempts at land rights legislation, eventually turned to the Australian judiciary to advance their land rights cause.

Mabo v. Queensland[70] proved a turning point in the 200-year-old legal approach to the colonization of Australia and, specifically, a turning point for property rights of the original inhabitants of the Australian continent. In a landmark decision, the judges of the Australian High Court overturned the settled legal doctrine of *terra nullius*,[71] recognizing the reality that Australia was "owned" by Aborigines at the time of British settlement.[72] It appeared that Australia's High Court was willing to embrace the growing international judicial trend of recognizing the prior rights of indigenous peoples.

---

66. Within the wider Australian society, there is a growing hostility to land rights. *See* Rosemary Neill, *Dialogue of the Deaf*, THE WEEKEND AUSTRALIAN, June 29–30, 1996, at 28. Tension also exists between Aboriginal activists who demand sovereignty as part and parcel of land rights claims, and those who recognize the incremental nature of land rights and other gains. *See* M. Mansell, *The Court Gives an Inch but Takes Another Mile*, 2 ABORIGINAL L. BULL. No. 57, 4 (Aug. 1992); *see also* Noel Pearson, *Reconciliation: To Be or Not to Be*, 3 ABORIGINAL L. BULL. No. 61, 14 (Apr. 1993).

67. Robert Blowes, *From Terra Nullius to Every Person's Land*, 52 ABORIGINAL L. BULL. No. 2, 4 (Oct.1991).

68. *See generally* BRENNAN, *supra* note 65.

69. Galarrwuy Yunupingu, From Bark Petition to Native Title: 20 Years of Land Rights, (paper presented at Conference to Celebrate 20th Anniversary of Land Rights Act (N. Terr.), Canberra (August 1996) (on file with the author)).

70. 107 A.L.R. 1 (1992).

71. The legal fiction of *terra nullius*—that Australia was uninhabited and belonged to no one— was sustained throughout the whole period of Australian colonization. *See generally* HENRY REYNOLDS, THE LAW OF THE LAND (1987).

72. 107 A.L.R. at 27–29. "The lands of the continent were not *terra nullius* or 'practically unoc-

The legal victory of the indigenous community of Murray Island (who had successfully launched the challenge) gave a momentous psychological impetus to land rights activists, and spurred the passage of the Native Title Act by the Commonwealth Government.[73] The purpose of the Act was not only to clarify uncertainty around the *Mabo* decision, but also to create the opportunity for Aboriginal people to pursue native title rights in a non-litigious setting.[74] A significant provision of the Act was the establishment of a land acquisition fund for Aborigines to compensate them for the loss of their native title rights.[75]

The *Mabo* decision and the Native Title Act left unanswered some crucial questions about native title.[76] The most recent decision of the Australian High Court (1996) was an attempt to deal with one of those questions, namely, the existence of native title on pastoral leases.[77] A deeply divided court held that pastoral leases and native title could coexist, but that in a conflict of interests, the pastoral lease would prevail.[78]

Obtaining rights to land is crucial for Aboriginal women. In a 1986 national task force study on Aboriginal women's rights, Aboriginal women considered land rights a "major way to achieve self-determination and maintain the integrity of Aboriginal culture."[79] The study outlined the importance of land rights gains, and the benefits for women who are custodians of the land and who share responsibility for land maintenance and religious ceremonies alongside men.[80] However, in the same study, women pointed out that various government agencies do not recognize this role as evidenced by their failure to appoint women in significant numbers to land councils around the country, and by their failure to disseminate information about land rights in simple and accessible language.[81]

---

cupied' in 1788. The Crown's property . . . was, under the Common law which became applicable upon the establishment of the colony in 1789, reduced or qualified by the burden of the Common law native title of the Aboriginal tribes and clans to the particular areas of land on which they lived or which they used for traditional purposes." *Id.* at 4.

73. Native Title Act No.110 of 1993 (Cth). The preamble to the Act provides that state governments should, where appropriate, facilitate negotiations at the regional level for land claims. *Id.*

74. To this end the Act established the National Native Title Tribunal to navigate these claims around native title. *See* Act No.110 of 1993, pt. 6, sec. 107. *Id.*

75. *Id.* at pt.10, sec. 201.

76. Even though the court in *Mabo* recognized Aboriginal native title under the common law, it stated that those rights had been largely extinguished by subsequent legislation, particularly in the granting of freehold title. The court left open the question of the status of native title on pastoral leases. *See* H.A. Amankwah, *Post-Mabo: The Prospect of the Recognition of a Regime of Customary (Indigenous) Law in Australia*, 18 U. QUEENSL. L.J. 15 (1994).

77. Wik Peoples v. Queensland, 71 A.L.R. 173 (1996); Thayorre People v. Queensland, 141 A.L.R. 129 (1996).

78. *Id.* at 132.

79. ABORIGINAL WOMEN'S TASK FORCE, *supra* note 10, at 9.

80. *Id.* at 9–10.

81. *Id.*

ABORIGINAL WOMEN IN AUSTRALIAN SOCIETY

Women and Customary Law

As previously noted, the literature on Aboriginal women is sparse. Lawyers and policy makers have historically had to depend on the research and findings of anthropologists, particularly female anthropologists, to determine the role and status of women in Australian Aboriginal society.[82] About this there is divergent opinion. One view holds that women are universally subordinated and perceived as the "pawns, chattels and slaves of their menfolk, maltreated and neglected,"[83] while another discerns the position of Aboriginal women as superior to Western women in terms of their independent economic status and the high social value placed on their roles and rituals.[84] Yet another view has advocated a certain interdependence and mutuality between Aboriginal women and men,[85] an approach coinciding increasingly with research findings that highlight the communitarian bases of many non-Western societies where such interdependence is mandated for community survival.[86]

After an impressive and thorough study on the impact of the imposed (European) law in combination with traditional (Aboriginal) law on women, and their disempowerment as a consequence of this legal fusion, the independence and autonomy of women in traditional Aboriginal society has been asserted as follows:

> Men and women played fundamentally different roles but each jointly subscribed to a code which they maintained in a co-operative manner. Their roles were essentially interdependent and complementary. Law was conceived of as an unchanging, all powerful force in their lives. Both men and women played important roles in teaching and sustaining this law. The basis of women's authority, like that of the men, rested upon ritual knowledge and expertise, rights in land and seniority.[87]

The determination of the role and status of Aboriginal women vis à vis Aboriginal males defies simple analysis. It is permeated by unstated assumptions which the inquirer brings to bear on the inquiry and that often cause an obfuscation of highly complex interactions within the relevant community. The responses of Aboriginal women also become enmeshed in conflicting expectations and mechanical responses that further erode the issues.[88]

---

82.   *See generally* AUSTRALIAN INSTITUTE OF ABORIGINAL STUDIES, CANBERRA, WOMEN'S ROLE IN ABORIGINAL SOCIETY (Fay Gale ed., 1974).

83.   Annette Hamilton, *A Complex Strategical Situation: Gender and Power in Aboriginal Australia, in* AUSTRALIAN WOMEN: FEMINIST PERSPECTIVES 69, 72 (N. Grieve and P. Grimshaw eds., 1981) [hereinafter *A Complex Strategical Situation*].

84.   *Id.*

85.   *See generally* BELL & DITTON, *supra* note 22.

86.   Isabelle R. Gunning, *Arrogant Perception, World Travelling and Multicultural Feminism: The Case of Female Genital Surgeries*, 23 COLUM. HUM. RTS. L. REV. 189 (1991–92).

87.   BELL & DITTON, *supra* note 22, at 114.

88.   It has been argued that:

> [T]he apparent position of Aboriginal women depends very much on the ethnographer describing the situation. Male anthropologists report that men have power and

Aboriginal women activists have continually asserted an equality with men in traditional Aboriginal society.[89] Such assertions are understandable in the face of persistent denigration of Aboriginal society, and in response to attempts by white women to find a symmetry of oppression between Aboriginal and non-Aboriginal women and to project the idea of a "sisterhood" that transcends racial hierarchies.[90] For many Aboriginal women, their struggle for equality appears to be inextricably bound to the struggle of all Aboriginal peoples.[91] In the global struggle of racial minorities and colonized peoples, race is regularly privileged over gender.[92]

But any avowal of equality for the legitimate political purpose of racial solidarity still requires a credible empirical basis.[93] A useful way to analyze the question of women's status or role under traditional law, or the access that women have to the power structures within their communities, is to shift the paradigm to one that focuses on the power dynamics within any given community. It has been suggested that the status of women:

> cannot be conceptualized as a see-saw balanced on a central fulcrum, with women sitting on one end and men on the other. Debates about "oppression," "subordination," "asymmetry" and so on are basically concerned with questions of power: the implicit question is, which sex is the more powerful, in which contexts, and how is the pattern of those power relations maintained, reproduced and sometimes transcended?[94]

---

control over women such that female subordination appears to be unquestionable. Most female ethnographers . . . report more favourably on women's status. . . . [T]he male scholars who are androcentric are also misanthropic, for they misrepresent the Australian men as brutal, domineering, and oblivious to the humanity of the women. . . . The women ethnographers . . . show us men and women living together in equal partnership, the rights, self-respect, and dignity of the members of both sexes being guaranteed.

Rohrlich-Leavit et al., *Aboriginal Women: Male and Female Perspectives, in* TOWARDS AN ANTHROPOLOGY OF WOMEN (R. Reiter ed., 1975), *in* Hamilton, *supra* note 83, at 74.

89.   *See generally* Payne, *supra* note 13.

90.   *See* Patricia Grimshaw, *Aboriginal Women: A Study of Culture Contact, in* AUSTRALIAN WOMEN: FEMINIST PERSPECTIVES, supra note 83, at 86; Melissa Lucashenko, *No Other Truth: Aboriginal Women and Australian Feminism,* 2 SOC. ALTERNATIVES No. 4, 21 (Jan. 1994).

91.   An obvious consideration for Aboriginal women is the potential for divisiveness of feminism within the Aboriginal community. These sentiments were echoed repeatedly by Aboriginal women in a series of interviews published in 1977. Typical were comments like: "I can't get interested in women's liberation. To me, as an Aboriginal, its not relevant, for the simple reason that our whole people have to be liberated. I don't consider that we split forces, between women and men. I can only identify with the idea of lib. (sic) for the whole people." LIVING BLACKS: BLACKS TALK TO KEVIN GILBERT 21 (Kevin Gilbert ed., 1977).

92.   *See generally* ANGELA DAVIS, WOMEN, RACE AND CLASS (1982).

93.   This is not to suggest that Aboriginal women have no credible research support for their position. However, there should be a recognition of the dialectic posed by alternative visions of Aboriginal society among anthropologists. *See supra* note 88.

94.   *See* Hamilton, *A Complex Strategical Situation, supra* note 83, at 74.

This paradigm creates the theoretical space for articulating a narrative that recognizes the intricacies of contemporary Aboriginal existence in Australia; reasons that point to different geographical locations, lifestyles (urban or rural, traditional or semi-traditional), class, and associated variables. A discussion of Aboriginal customary law has to be predicated on a recognition of the diverse conditions within which Aboriginal women find themselves, and how different aspects of customary law affect their lives.

Since the origins of the colonial state, the recognition of indigenous law has been touted in several contexts in Australian courts.[95] It has been most pronounced in the criminal law area, where the specter of an Aboriginal defendant being punished twice (by the common law and traditional law) has been raised.[96] The recognition of traditional law raises specific issues in relation to Aboriginal women, because recognition of certain traditional practices might contradict international treaties, such as the Women's Convention, to which Australia is a signatory. In 1986, after extensive consultation, the Australian Law Reform Commission published a comprehensive report on the recognition of Aboriginal customary laws.[97] Although the submissions to the Commission raised multiple arguments in relation to questions of procedural and substantive rights, and the benefits and disadvantages of recognition, very few submissions dealt with the question of recognition of and the consequences for Aboriginal women.[98] For the most part, those who articulated the special interests of women pointed to a possible deleterious effect of the recognition of certain practices that discriminate against women.[99]

The Commission's report suggested a host of ways that traditional law might coexist with the Australian common law. Specifically in relation to women, the Commission's report recommended the limited recognition of tribal marriages[100] and expanded rights around child custody.[101] Bell and Ditton have expressed concern at certain of the Commission's recommendations:

> The mode of recognition of customary law finally recommended by the Law Reform Commission is however of concern to us in that we believe it must recognize women as having a role in the maintenance of customary law, in the socialization of children

---

95. R v. Jack Congo Murrell, 1 Legge Rep. 72 (1836) (N.S.W.S. Ct.). In this murder trial, the defendant unsuccessfully argued that the court had no jurisdiction over crimes committed by one Aborigine against another, because Aboriginal people had their own laws and customs. In *R v. Wedge*, 1 N.S.W.L.R. 581 (1976), on similar facts, the court again rejected the defendant's assertions of Aboriginal sovereignty.

96. The question has also surfaced where an Aboriginal defendant has acted in accordance with traditional law, but in so doing has contravened the common law. Kenneth Maddock, *Aboriginal Customary Law, in* ABORIGINES AND THE LAW, *supra* note 20, at 212.

97. AUSTRALIAN LAW REFORM COMM'N, REPORT NO. 31, THE RECOGNITION OF ABORIGINAL CUSTOMARY LAWS (1986).

98. *Id.*

99. *Id.* paras. 11, 17 and 18.

100. *Id.* para 80.

101. *Id.* paras. 365–71.

into the value system, in dispute settlement procedures and in the performance of religious rituals, which maintain harmony and resolve conflict.[102]

Some of these recommendations have been adopted in certain states, but most of the Commission's overall recommendations have been shelved.[103] The conundrum for Australian legislators centers on the uneasy fact that ultimately any recognition of Aboriginal customary law carries with it the imperative to recognize the *values* that underlie the law.

Tensions around recognition are most profound in relation to the question of violence against Aboriginal women, where crucial questions of identity and justice arise. The process of colonialism mentioned earlier in this chapter has resulted in a wholesale legal disenfranchisement of Aboriginal people, and has, not surprisingly, led to a widespread Aboriginal skepticism of the Australian legal system.[104] These consequences impact enormously on all Aboriginal people, but it is Aboriginal women who are the "least well served by the legal system."[105]

For Aboriginal women, the question goes beyond access to legal representation and information about rights, although that contributes to the problem. The issue acquires a certain sad irony when Aboriginal men utilize cultural defenses as a shield when charged with crimes of violence against Aboriginal women.[106]

Many Aboriginal women have attempted to educate the wider Australian society about this dilemma, and have organized to distinguish cultural practices that bolster traditional (communitarian) values from those that serve as smokescreens for male dominance and violence.[107] They are therefore able to agitate for demands around self-determination, including recognition of aspects of traditional law that will not render them subordinate.

Violence Against Aboriginal Women

The relatively suburban term "domestic violence" does not come close to adequately describing the levels of violence perpetrated against Aboriginal women—typically by male perpetrators (not only the spouse), over a longer period, more commonly with weapons and more frequently resulting in severe injury.[108]

---

102. BELL & DITTON, *supra* note 22, at 11.

103. James Crawford, *Legal Pluralism and the Indigenous People of Australia, in* THE RIGHTS OF SUBORDINATED PEOPLES 178 (Oliver Mendelsohn and Upendra Baxi eds., 1994).

104. *See generally* AUSTRALIAN ROYAL COMM'N, REPORT OF THE ROYAL COMM'N INTO ABORIGINAL DEATHS IN CUSTODY (1991).

105. *See generally* AUSTRALIAN LAW REFORM COMM'N, REPORT NO. 69, EQUALITY BEFORE THE LAW: WOMEN'S EQUALITY (1994) [hereinafter A.L.R.C. REPORT NO. 69].

106. DIANE BELL, *Representing Aboriginal Women: Who Speaks for Whom?, in* THE RIGHTS OF SUBORDINATED PEOPLES, *supra* note 103, at 221.

107. *Id.*

108. A.L.R.C. REPORT NO. 69, *supra* note 105, at 119.

The incidence and severity of violence against Aboriginal women, both from within the Aboriginal community and outside it, has reached such crisis proportions that it has been interpreted as a continuing violation of their human rights.[109] The lingering effects of colonialism, the pervasive racism, their minority status, and the desperate socio-economic conditions of many Aboriginal communities all contribute to this situation.[110]

Our knowledge of violence against Aboriginal women is still insipient. Its historical neglect explains the lack of accounting for outsider violence against Aboriginal women.[111] However, the vulnerability of Aboriginal women within the criminal justice system has been noted. In 1991, the National Inquiry into Racist Violence referred to widespread sexual abuse of Aboriginal women by police officers.[112] The Inquiry received evidence pointing to the rape of young Aboriginal girls at police stations, who were then too traumatized or fearful to lodge complaints.[113] This abuse was not confined to women in police custody.[114] A white individual testified to the Inquiry about the police practice in one town of detaining young Aboriginal women patrons at a bar, and then offering them to white male patrons for sex.[115]

In 1991, the Royal Commission Inquiry Into Black Deaths in Custody included the deaths of twelve Aboriginal women. Its recommendations, however, failed to address adequately the specific issue of violence against Aboriginal women.[116] The Commission has been accused of representing "attitudes and actions contained within a hierarchical patriarchy that dominates much of Australia. Unless it is able to consider how this patriarchy has subjugated women, any 'solution' it offers only can create venues for further oppression, of both Aboriginal men, and women."[117]

Even within their own communities, Aboriginal women have been victims of disturbing levels of violence. However, widespread discussion of this situation outside Aboriginal communities has always been taboo for fairly obvious reasons. First, the struggle that Aboriginal people have been involved in since colonization has demanded a focus on the elimination of colonialism and racism. The issue of the con-

---

109. *See* BELL, *supra* note 106.

110. *See supra* notes 11 and 12.

111. Marie Brooks, Aboriginal and Torres Strait Islander Women in Custody, Paper at Conference *Aboriginal Justice Issues II,* Australian Institute of Criminology (June 14–17, 1994) (on file with the author).

112. *See generally* REPORT OF THE NATIONAL INQUIRY INTO RACIST VIOLENCE IN AUSTRALIA, RACIST VIOLENCE (1991) [hereinafter RACIST VIOLENCE REPORT].

113. *Id.* at 89.

114. The 1992 National Census stated that 14.1 percent of male prisoners and 18 percent of female prisoners are Aboriginal. *See* A.L.R.C. REPORT No. 69, *supra* note 105, at 119.

115. *See* RACIST VIOLENCE REPORT, *supra* note 112, at 88.

116. *See generally* Payne, *supra* note 13.

117. Judy Atkinson, *Violence Against Aboriginal Women: Reconstitution of Community Law— The Way Forward,* 2 ABORIGINAL L. BULL. No. 46, 6 (1990).

tinued subordination of women within the Aboriginal community was subsumed under the rubric of this struggle. Second, their situation in a racially bifurcated society resulted in Aboriginal women being precluded from engaging in productive coalitions with their white feminist counterparts. The latter were also reluctant to engage the issue of violence against Aboriginal women for fear of accusations of prioritizing sexism over racism.[118] However, the statistics of intra-community violence against Aboriginal women have been compelling, and Aboriginal women are increasingly organizing around this problem.[119]

The research on the causes of violence against Aboriginal women suggest an interplay of a complex set of factors. They include a culturally accepted system of sexual subordination that is buttressed by the wider patriarchal Australian society.[120] Although there is some divergence between Aboriginal activists and scholars and their non-Aboriginal counterparts about the extent of sexual subordination in Aboriginal society,[121] there appears to be a general consensus that a combination of values in both societies has resulted in the diminished status and vulnerable conditions of Aboriginal women.[122] Marcia Langton, Aboriginal anthropologist and activist, refers to "the ability of men to use force in the final analysis, to preserve male dominance in ideology, in structures and relationships. This was so in traditional times and remains so, but in vastly changed circumstances."[123] Other factors suggested are the appalling socio-economic conditions within which many indigenous people find themselves, the cultural dislocation, and the resultant breakdown of social control.[124]

By far, the most devastating factor appears to be the abuse of alcohol in many communities.[125] Although the research is inconclusive on the role of alcohol relative to the increased incidence of violence, there appears to be a general recognition of the significant correlation between excessive alcohol consumption and violence.[126] A number of Aboriginal women's groups have been active in local campaigns to designate their communities alcohol-free, based on their perceptions that alcohol consumption contributes to the violence.[127]

---

118. *See* Bell, *supra* note 106, at 225.

119. *See generally* EDIE CARTER, ADELAIDE RAPE CRISIS, INC., ABORIGINAL WOMEN SPEAK OUT (1987).

120. *See generally* Bell, *supra* note 106.

121. *See generally* AUDREY BOLGER, ABORIGINAL WOMEN AND VIOLENCE (1991).

122. This is not to suggest that Aboriginal women are hapless victims of violence. In VICTORIA KATHERINE BURBANK, FIGHTING WOMEN (1994), Burbank vividly describes the resistance of Aboriginal women to violence, and their refusal to submit to victimhood.

123. Marcia Langton, *Feminism: What Do Aboriginal Women Gain?*, BROADSIDE NATIONAL FOUNDATION FOR AUSTRALIAN WOMEN NEWS (1989), *cited in* BOLGER, *supra* note 121, at 53.

124. *See* BOLGER, *supra* note 121, at 53.

125. *Id.*

126. Judy Atkinson, *Stinkin Thinkin—Alcohol, Violence and Government Responses*, 51 ABORIGINAL L. BULL. No. 2, 4 (Aug. 1991). *See also* Patrick Dodson, *Reconciliation and the High Court's Decision on Native Title*, 61 ABORIGINAL L. BULL. No.3, 6 (Apr. 1993).

127. BOLGER, *supra* note 121, at 47.

ABORIGINAL WOMEN AND INTERNATIONAL HUMAN RIGHTS

As noted in the introduction to this chapter, Australia's attempts at satisfying her obligations under international human rights law, and her human rights record, have been generally satisfactory.[128] However, the situation of Aboriginal Australians is still a cause for concern, and Australia's inadequacies in this regard have been well documented.[129] The different processes of reconciliation attempted over the past few decades, ranging from the attempts at land rights restoration (albeit limited), to negotiations for a treaty, to various mechanisms of self-determination or management on the part of Aboriginal peoples, all reflect some concordant endeavors by the Australian government and indigenous peoples to pursue a vision for a more equitable Australia.[130] These processes are ongoing, and no doubt they will tap the resources and imagination of Aboriginal activists and their allies for some time to come.

The issue of Aboriginal women and international human rights raises parallel concerns. There is no question that international human rights law has some useful application to Aboriginal women; the utilization of pertinent treaties and conventions might in some respects improve certain aspects of Aboriginal women's lives. But those who agitate for a global vision steeped in human rights discourse, and who sometimes adopt a crusading, almost evangelical, approach to the pursuit of these rights, might benefit from some tempering of this vision.[131]

In this regard two significant factors are worth highlighting. First, human rights practice and discourse operates within constraining paradigms that have been the targets of detailed critique.[132] Second, the global terrain of struggle on behalf of women, and the identification and pursuit of universal strategies have been subjected to a fundamental reorientation.[133] Any strategy invoking human rights law needs to take cognizance of these dialectic strands within the international human rights framework and tread with contextualized boldness.[134]

---

128. For example, Australia is not regularly cited in Amnesty International and other human rights monitoring reports on political detentions and other security force violations. The World Human Rights Guide gives Australia a 91 percent rating on human rights. WORLD HUMAN RIGHTS GUIDE 26 (Charles Humana ed., 1992).

129. E.I.A. DAES, Chairwoman-Rapporteur of the United Nations Working Group on Indigenous Populations, Australia 7–22 (Dec. 12–Jan. 2, 1988), *cited in* Crawford, *Legal Pluralism and Indigenous Peoples, supra* note 103, at 188.

130. *See generally* JUDITH WRIGHT, WE CALL FOR A TREATY (1985); REPORT BY THE SENATE COMMITTEE ON CONSTITUTIONAL AND LEGAL AFFAIRS, TWO HUNDRED YEARS LATERV (1983); Patrick Dodson, *Reconciliation and the High Court's Decision, supra* note 126.

131. For a thoughtful analysis of these issues, *see* J. Oloka-Onyango, *The Plight of the Larger Half: Human Rights, Gender Violence and the Legal Status of Refugee and Internally Displaced Women in Africa*, 24 DENV. J. INT'L L. & POL'Y No. 2/3, 349 (Spring 1996).

132. Peter Vale, *Engaging the World's Marginalized and Promoting Global Change: Challenges for the United Nations at Fifty*, 36 HARV. INT'L L.J. 283 (Spring 1995).

133. Chandra Talpade Mohanty, *Cartographies of Struggle: Third World Women and the Politics of Feminism, in* THIRD WORLD WOMEN AND THE POLITICS OF FEMINISM 1 (Chandra Talpade Mohanty, Ann Russo, Lourdes Torres eds., 1991).

134. This is a suggestion that goes beyond the hackneyed universal versus relativist debate.

Aboriginal women live within communities with strong communitarian ties, and where interdependence typifies intracommunity relations. Although this situation is best exemplified in traditional and rural communities, urban Aboriginal societies also exhibit these same traits.[135] Any approach focusing on the possibility of improving the lives of Aboriginal women through the application of international human rights norms needs to recognize that this quest has to address the improvement of the lives of *all* Aboriginal people. The varying demands for self-determination or self-management, or other mechanisms for attaining equality in Australia, whether they be land rights or the recognition of Aboriginal customary law or sovereignty, reflect the communities' aspirations.[136]

Since the 1970s, Australia's Aboriginal population has utilized international legal mechanisms in their quest for land rights and other methods of self-determination.[137] In tandem with indigenous activists from around the globe, they have combined political strategies with justiciable legal claims.[138]

Aboriginal women have been involved in these various campaigns, but have directed their efforts at issues that affect the Aboriginal community as a whole.[139] There has been no concerted effort, in the international arena, by Aboriginal women focusing on the issues of women qua women. There is, however, increasing recognition by Aboriginal women of the need to create an organizational space around their issues in the wider Aboriginal struggle in the global arena.[140]

Aboriginal women have made demands in a variety of local contexts to pursue their collective rights as women. A few major projects pursued at the national level among Aboriginal women in the last decade have been highlighted and might provide some useful insights.[141] These projects were selected because their research and

---

Rather, it suggests an approach that engages competing visions and strategies and incorporates these in the feminist transformative project.

135. Larissa Behrendt, *Aboriginal Urban Identity: Preserving the Spirit, Protecting the Traditional in Non-Traditional Settings*, 4 THE AUSTL. FEMINIST L.J. 55 (1995).

136. *See generally* Grimshaw, *supra* note 90. "Black women have yet to see even their menfolk attain positions of power and influence in the mainstream culture. It is understandable then, that in terms of priorities, black women seek to raise the life chances of the whole group. They view disadvantages of race and class before disadvantages of sex." *Id.* at 94.

137. Even where legal avenues were not possible, the Aboriginal population has increasingly seen international forums, such as the United Nations Working Group on Indigenous Populations, as an appropriate venue to interact with representatives of indigenous populations from around the globe. *See generally*, B. HOCKING, INTERNATIONAL LAW AND ABORIGINAL HUMAN RIGHTS (1988).

138. Tony Simpson, *On the Track to Geneva, in* VOICES OF ABORIGINAL AUSTRALIA 170 (Irene Moores ed., 1995).

139. Helen Corbett, *International Efforts, in* VOICES FROM THE LAND 76 (Mandawuy Yunupingu et al. eds., 1994).

140. *See generally* Behrendt, *Aboriginal Urban Identity, supra* note 135.

141. They are: ABORIGINAL WOMEN'S TASK FORCE, *supra* note 10; ABORIGINAL AND TORRES STRAIT ISLAND COMM'N, OFFICE OF EVALUATION AND AUDIT; (1) The Office of Indigenous Women, (2) Ongoing Women's Initiatives, (3) Women's New Initiatives (1990); THE CONSULTATION PROJECT WITH

reports are the most comprehensive, and their methodology indicates reasonably successful attempts at soliciting the opinions of as wide a range as possible of Aboriginal women.[142]

These research endeavors and reports are predicated on certain assumptions and factual assertions. They include the fact that Aboriginal women are the most socially and economically disadvantaged group in Australia, and that it is imperative that federal, state, and local governments embark on culturally sensitive programs, controlled by Aboriginal women, which will enhance their status and lead to full equality in Australian society.[143] Implicit in the projects is the recognition that Aboriginal women have valuable skills and rich talents to offer the wider Australian community.

ABORIGINAL AND ISLANDER WOMEN UNDER THE AUSPICES OF THE SEX DISCRIMINATION COMM'R (1994); ALRC REPORT NO. 69, *supra* note 105.

142. Other Aboriginal women's projects at the state and local level are worth noting. For example, ABORIGINAL WOMEN SPEAK OUT, *supra* note 119; REPORT OF THE CHIEF JUSTICE'S TASK FORCE ON GENDER BIAS (W. Austl., June 1994); BEYOND VIOLENCE: FINDING THE DREAM (Judy Atkinson ed.,1990).

143. *See* Aboriginal and Torres Strait Islander Commission, Office of Evaluation and Audit: Evaluation of (1) The Office of Indigenous Women; (2) Ongoing Women's Initiatives; (3) Women's New Initiatives (Dec. 1990). According to this evaluation, the following miscellaneous statistics have been noted:

1. In the Northern Territory:

   (a) the Aboriginal death rate from family violence was ten times higher than that of the white population;

   (b) 53% of Aboriginal men who died in prison cells over the last ten years were jailed for acts of violence: 9% for homicide, 12% for assault and 32% for crimes of sexual assault;

   (c) Aboriginal women represent 50% of all women in custody in Australia; and

   (d) 70–80% of all young women going through the court system have been sexually assaulted.

2. In the ACT (Australian Capital Territory) only 17 percent of Aboriginal women earn an income greater than $12,000.

3. In Western Australia and New South Wales only 1.7 percent and 2.0 percent respectively of Aboriginal women earn an income in excess of $12,000.

4. One in five Aboriginal female marriages end in divorce compared to one in ten for the total Australian female population.

5. 20.6 percent of female children aged five to fifteen years were not attending educational institutions.

6. Aboriginal women were victims of 79 percent of total deaths involving chargeable homicides in the Northern Territory in 1987.

7. In a report entitled "Aboriginal Women Speak Out" which was based on a survey in South Australia in September 1987, it was established that:

   (a) 90 percent of rape victims were women and girls; and

   (b) 20 percent were pack raped.

The recommendations that they highlight represent the best possible means, from the perspective of Aboriginal women, to overcome the attitudinal and structural disadvantage to which they are exposed. The recommendations listed incorporate a panoply of civil, political, social, economic, and cultural rights.[144] All the reports echo a need for regular and ongoing consultation with Aboriginal women about the impact of various government programs on their lives. They also reflect a widespread desire that the development and design of these programs involve Aboriginal women and that the relevant information be disseminated in a linguistically and culturally appropriate manner to Aboriginal communities.

In the area of social and economic rights, the recommendations reflect the basic conditions in which many Aboriginal communities still find themselves.[145] They evince attempts to provide for Aboriginal Australians what most other Australians take for granted: access to proper shelter, education, employment, and health services. In the area of civil and political rights, the recommendations point to the discrepancy in the provision of legal and other official services between Aboriginal and non-Aboriginal Australians, and between Aboriginal men and women.[146] The reports also reflect a widespread ignorance of rights among Aboriginal women, and the accompanying lack of expectation that certain rights will be protected.[147]

The issue of cultural rights remains the most troubling. Most of the recommendations manifest a desperate need for culturally appropriate approaches and structures to administer Aboriginal affairs. These cultural concerns traverse the range of socio-economic and civil and political rights, and reflect a major preoccupation among Aboriginal women. They reflect the ongoing struggle of Aboriginal women to ensure that their cultural identities are not only respected, but will not be further eroded even as their material conditions improve.[148]

---

144. In the various reports they are categorized as follows: (1) Policy; (2) Access to the Legal System; (3) Housing; (4) Education; (5) Health; (6) Community, Family, and Personal Matters; (7) Employment; (8) Land Rights; (9) Violence; and (10) Culture. Some of these categories are identical to those outlined in the various reports; others represent the author's categorization.

145. Note for example the recommendations in the areas of housing, education, health, and employment: the need for coordination of various government services; for courses in household management; for steps to improve the retention rates of Aboriginal school children; for the provision of essential services to improve the health of all Aborigines; for greater Aboriginal control in all these areas; and for specific women's policies in these areas. *See* ABORIGINAL WOMEN'S TASK FORCE, *supra* note 10, at 11–19.

146. Both the ABORIGINAL WOMEN'S TASK FORCE, *supra* note 10, and the A.L.R.C. REPORT No. 69, *supra* note 105, reflect major shortcomings (from the perspective of women) of the services offered by Aboriginal Legal Services: they provide legal representation for criminal defendants, and do not engage in civil litigation. Moreover, many of the clients of the Aboriginal Legal Services are Aboriginal males who have perpetrated violence on females within their communities. Women therefore do not have access to the kinds of legal services that would best address their concerns.

147. ABORIGINAL WOMEN'S TASK FORCE, *supra* note 10, at 15.

148. *Id.*

Human Rights Strategies

Discrete legislative packages enacted by the Australian legislature, for example, the Race Discrimination Act,[149] the Sex Discrimination Act,[150] the Northern Territory Land Rights Act,[151] and the National Native Title Act,[152] reflect some formal national consensus around the elimination of racial and sex-based discrimination. These statutes reflect the Australian government's commitment to its international obligations under the Race Convention and the Women's Convention. The pivotal issue in relation to these legislative incursions is the translation of these formal legal rights into substantive socio-economic rights.[153]

The struggle to overcome the fundamental obstacles which have resulted in the dire conditions within which a large number of Aboriginal women find themselves, necessitates a focus on the intersectionality of a diverse array of factors that contribute to their subordinate status in Australian society.[154] The international human rights norms embodied in the Women's Convention and the Race Convention should be "indigenized" to accommodate the peculiar situation of Aboriginal women.[155] The effectiveness of local versions of these instruments will rest on such an accommodation.

It is this author's contention that the following strategies might be worth pursuing in an endeavor to implement internationally recognized rights for women and to improve the socio-economic conditions of Aboriginal women.[156] These strategies are not exhaustive, nor are they without certain weaknesses; they merely point out ways of effectuating human rights gains.

Federal and State Human Rights Tribunals

Within the Australian context there is some organizational base from which to pursue rights for Aboriginal women that mirror those found in international instruments to which Australia is a signatory. The federal and state structures designed to

---

149. Act No. 52 of 1975 (Cth).

150. Act No. 4 of 1984 (Cth).

151. *See supra* note 61.

152. *See supra* note 73.

153. *See generally* STUART SCHEINGOLD, THE POLITICS OF RIGHTS (1974).

154. Larissa Behrendt, *Aboriginal Women and the White Lies of the Feminist Movement: Implications for Aboriginal Women in Rights Discourse*, 1 AUSTL. FEMINIST L.J. 27 (1993) [hereinafter *The White Lies of the Feminist Movement*].

155. For Aboriginal women, the issues are not just about better socio-economic conditions, or equality with men; they revolve around crucial *identity* questions that impact on all indigenous peoples.

156. These recommendations are made not for their novel value, but because they represent an alchemy of cumulative struggles, which have been pursued in Australia and in other contexts, with differential success. *See generally* HESTER EISENSTEIN, INSIDE AGITATORS: AUSTRALIAN FEMOCRATS AND THE STATE (1995). *See also* PUTTING WOMEN ON THE AGENDA (Susan Bazilli ed., 1994).

administer the various statutes promulgated in pursuance of Australia's ratification of various covenants are well placed to vigorously enforce their mandates.[157] Many of these governmental human rights agencies are empowered with a plethora of strategies at their disposal, including conciliation, adjudication, education, and lobbying.[158] However, perennial problems for these tribunals include the lack of a prominent profile among Aboriginal women, and the limited resources allocated to pursue the tasks.[159] The success of the tribunals depends on their commitment to constructively engage with Aboriginal women and to devise strategies that will achieve the desired purposes.

The various commissions and projects focusing on the needs and aspirations of Aboriginal women provide some blueprints from which comprehensive policies and programs can be articulated and developed:

> [T]he initiatives which have improved access to justice for Aboriginal and Torres Strait Islander women demonstrate that solutions reside in the women and in the communities. . . . It is essential that measures to increase indigenous women's access to justice begin by giving status to women. This requires that women determine the nature of the service and control the delivery of the service.[160]

Public Interest Litigation and NGO Campaigning

Australia has ratified a number of international human rights instruments that Aboriginal women might use to address local grievances.[161] Specifically, the Australian government reports regularly to the following international human rights bodies:

- The Committee for the Elimination of Discrimination Against Women [in relation to the Women's Convention];

- The Committee for the Elimination of Racial Discrimination [in relation to the Race Convention];

- The Human Rights Committee [in relation to the International Covenant on Civil and Political Rights];

- The Committee on Economic, Social and Cultural Rights [in relation to the International Covenant on Economic, Social and Cultural Rights].[162]

---

157. The project of the Sex Discrimination Commissioner is an indication of these possibilities. *See supra* note 141.

158. At the federal level, the Race Discrimination Commissioner administers the Racial Discrimination Act (1975) and the Sex Discrimination Commissioner administers the Sex Discrimination Act (1984). The Social Justice Commissioner addresses the needs of indigenous people, and the Human Rights Commissioner administers the Human Rights and Equal Opportunity Commission Act (1986), as well as the International Covenant on Civil and Political Rights, and the International Covenant on Economic, Social and Cultural Rights. *See generally*, HUMAN RIGHTS: THE AUSTRALIAN DEBATE (Lynne Spender ed., 1987).

159. *See generally* REPORT OF SEX DISCRIMINATION COMMISSIONER, *supra* note 141. *See also* A.L.R.C. REPORT NO. 69, *supra* note 105.

160. A.L.R.C. REPORT NO. 69, *supra* note 105.

161. *See supra* note 4.

162. *Id.*

The use of public interest litigation to pursue rights has increasingly become part of the Australian legal landscape.[163] Additionally, an extensive and vigorous NGO network has developed in the last few decades to provide support and assistance.[164] These organizations are well placed to pursue strategies holding the Australian government to their official international commitments. For Aboriginal people, the use of litigation to pursue land rights and other claims is now commonplace, and has produced remarkable results.[165] While the use of litigation to pursue rights has been most pronounced in the land rights situation, in other areas there has been limited success as well.[166]

In many ways, Aboriginal women are now better placed to utilize legal tactics combined with political campaigning and organizing to pursue their own goals. Reports of successful local community interventions by Aboriginal women indicate a trend in that direction, and suggest that a strategic legal and political campaign, combined with effective coalition building, offer a window through which Aboriginal women could press their human rights claims.[167]

Aboriginal Women's Groups and Coalition Building

Aboriginal women's organizations have and continue to play a significant role in the lives of large numbers of Aboriginal women.[168] The Australian Law Reform Commission Report on Gender Equality and the Law[169] detailed reasonably successful programs initiated and maintained by groups of Aboriginal women throughout Australia.[170] Increasingly women are establishing local projects to deal with "family fighting"[171] and

---

163. *See generally* JON FAINE, LAWYERS IN THE ALICE: ABORIGINALS AND WHITEFELLAS LAW (1993).

164. Some NGOs include the Public Interest Advocacy Centre; the Aboriginal Women's Legal Resource Centre; and many women's, consumer, environmental and refugee support groups. Alongside these organizations exist a host of state-sponsored legal aid and other support groups.

165. Until recently, lawsuits were seldom successful, particularly when the question of the issue of recognition of traditional law arose, or where the plaintiffs challenged Australian sovereignty over Aborigines. *See, e.g.*, Coe v. Commonwealth, 24 A.L.R. 118 (1979).

166. *See generally* FAINE, *supra* note 163. The network of Aboriginal Legal Services has been the major provider of legal representation to Aboriginal defendants in criminal matters. These services are officially funded by the Aboriginal and Torres Strait Islander Commission. *See* A.L.R.C. REPORT NO. 69, *supra* note 105, at 123.

167. A.L.R.C. REPORT NO. 69, *supra* note 105, at 124.

168. *See generally* BELL, *supra* note 15.

169. *See generally* A.L.R.C. REPORT NO. 69, *supra* note 105.

170. These programs include a system of night patrols run by women in certain Aboriginal communities in Central Australia; women's councils which initiate a diverse range of programs in their communities including family violence prevention programs; a "Women's Business Project" in New South Wales which aims, among other things, to increase women's access to legal and other services. *See* A.L.R.C. REPORT NO. 69, *supra* note 105, at 124–25.

171. Audrey Bolger, in her comprehensive study on violence against Aboriginal women, found that Aboriginal people prefer the term "family fighting" to "domestic violence." *See* BOLGER, *supra* note 121, at 6.

related concerns.[172] The significance and success of many of these endeavors arose from their grounding in traditional structures and their cultural symmetry.[173] However, these endeavors by Aboriginal women are still rare, and do not indicate their systematic adoption across Australia.

In the reports mentioned earlier in this chapter, reference is made to specific issues raised and demands made by Aboriginal women.[174] From these reports it is possible to deconstruct the major problems that bedevil programs designed specifically in the interests of Aboriginal women. First, many programs are under-resourced because of the lack of availability of skilled Aboriginal women. This is linked to the fact that often insufficient attention is paid to the kind of resources needed to implement specific strategies. Generally the question of dollar amounts does not raise problems, but their effective use does; often funding appears ad hoc, not sufficiently programmatic, and arbitrarily allocated. Second, programs frequently do not distinguish between those issues that only affect women, and larger community issues that also require particular input from women. Third, often the mechanisms for evaluating and assessing programs and their impact on women are either unavailable or inadequate. This is linked to the overall problem with streamlining available data in relation to women.[175] Fourth, very often programs are initiated with enthusiasm, but there is a lack of commitment to follow them through. Fifth, there is a regular failure to integrate or incorporate women's programs with overall community development programs or goals.[176] And sixth, the goals, objectives, and strategies for the programs are frequently unclear and undefined.

The articulation and listing of these programmatic shortcomings creates the space for Aboriginal women to structure and implement programs that can most effectively advance their human rights claims. Their relatively small numbers within the wider Australian population requires that Aboriginal women engage in coalition building with their white counterparts.[177] This engagement with the largely white feminist movement has been subjected to some critique in the last few years as Aboriginal women have attempted to balance their bifurcated political demands: the pursuit of

---

172. Ester Alvares, A Women's Refuge for Bourke—A Community Initiative, Paper delivered at conference *Aboriginal Justice Issues* Australian Institute of Criminology, Cairns (June 23–25, 1992).

173. *See generally* A.L.R.C. Report No. 69, *supra* note 105.

174. *See supra* note 141.

175. Although there are a host of government departments and NGOs focusing on Aboriginal women, there appears to be a general lack of synthesis and gathering of data to make effective program implementation possible.

176. For example, an analysis of the poor education statistics of Aboriginal women demands a focus on the living conditions in the home, the unemployment rates of Aborigines, health and other socio-economic issues. Programs therefore have to be more integrative and systematic in their conception and conduct.

177. Verity Burgmann, Power and Protest: Movements for Change in Australian Society 24 (1993). *See also* Lorna Lippmann, Generations of Resistance: The Aboriginal Struggle for Justice 46 (1981).

a negotiated self-determination or autonomy for all Aborigines, and a place in the wider Aboriginal community where their female role and status will not be undermined, and where violence against them will not be tolerated.[178] But the habits of political struggle, harnessed by years of engagement in broader Aboriginal political struggle, ensure that Aboriginal women will determine for themselves the shape or structure such coalitions will take.[179]

CONCLUSION

Aboriginal women are increasingly carving out a niche for themselves on the Australian political and legal stage, as evidenced by their demands for greater rights and protection inside and outside the home,[180] for compensation for being forcibly separated from their children and loved ones,[181] for a place at the negotiating table regarding local struggles, land rights, and sovereignty,[182] and for recognition for participation in all the struggles that Aboriginal people are engaged in for full citizenship.[183] In short, Aboriginal women's issues are increasingly moving from the margins of discussion to a more central place on the Aboriginal political and legal agenda.

The foregoing discussion regarding the increasing use of international human rights norms comes in the wake of the continuing debate between "Western" and "Third World" or non-Western feminists about the "universality" of women's rights and the shape such rights should take in the local context, and the privileging of certain voices over others. The debate involves a critique of the "corporatist" structure of international law and the constraints posed. These are perennial issues incapable of swift, simple resolution, but nevertheless important in infusing into the feminist transformative agenda the necessity to engage with marginalized minority peoples such as Aboriginal Australians. These divergent interpretations of international human

---

178. *See generally* Behrendt, *The White Lies of the Feminist Movement, supra* note 154. *See also* Rosemary Hunter, *Deconstructing the Subjects of Feminism: The Essentialism Debate in Feminist Theory and Practice,* 6 THE AUSTL. FEMINIST L.J. 135 (1996).

179. For a thoughtful discussion on difference, diversity, and coalition building, *see* CHARLOTTE BUNCH, PASSIONATE POLITICS: FEMINIST THEORY IN ACTION 140 (1987). *See also* AUDRE LORD, SISTER OUTSIDER 114 (1984).

180. *See* A.L.R.C. REPORT No. 69, *supra* note 105.

181. *See supra* text accompanying note 54.

182. For example, in their research, Bell and Ditton found Aboriginal women have huge misgivings about village councils as consisting of "self serving drunkards," and councils on Aboriginal settlements as not reflecting indigenous local authority structures. They also found that women resented the male bias in council composition and decision making, a throwback from earlier white perceptions of authority in Aboriginal society. *See* BELL & DITTON, *supra* note 22, at 12. Many Aboriginal women also felt that the "democratic bodies" set up to represent Aboriginal communities were formalized because their membership was largely male, whereas female representative organizations were often relegated to a non-formal, therefore uninfluential, status. *Id.* at 115–16.

183. These developments are apparent in the increasingly vocal presence of Aboriginal women in areas previously monopolized by outside "expert" opinions. *See generally* Behrendt, *The White Lies of the Feminist Movement, supra* note 154.

rights norms create the space for positive action in a world where the intersectionality of economic status, and racial or ethnic identity is increasingly hostage to political opportunism.[184]

Aboriginal women have survived widespread tyranny against their communities since the earliest European contact. They have also overcome tremendous levels of personal violence while continuing to organize and agitate for full participation in the wider Australian society. They demand no less than non-Aboriginal women: a place where their humanity and cultural integrity will not be compromised. In this endeavor, the international human rights framework provides the symbolic and substantive backdrop.

---

184. *See generally* Sharon Hom, *Commentary: Re-positioning Human Rights Discourse on "Asian" Perspectives*, Buff. J. Int'l L. (Spring 1997).

Section V

Other Issues

THE "EQUALITY OF PUPPIES": WOMEN AND THE INTERNATIONAL MONETARY FUND

Jane Lee Saber

INTRODUCTION

Women in developing countries are "the poorest of the poor."[1] Indeed, of the estimated 1.2 billion people living in extreme poverty in undeveloped countries, 59 percent are female.[2] Of the 12,000 people who die each year due to malnutrition, many are women and female children. Two-thirds of developing country women suffer from anemia and malnutrition, and over one billion people, the majority of these being females, have deficient daily diets.[3]

One of the reasons that developing country women's disparate poverty is escalating is that contemporary notions of development are inappropriate to promote the goals of financial and human growth while also preventing discriminatory impact.[4] In particular, notions of development, as defined by the white, Western patriarchy, are in tension with improving the lives of those in developing countries. Contemporary standards of development focus on the measurement of economic development, using indicators such as Gross National Product (GNP), Gross Domestic Product (GDP), balance-of-payments, and others. This system of measurement is commonly known as the "neo-classical monetarist model." This model assumes that development can be numerically measured by the consideration of a country's balance sheets; it does not consider distributional effects on developing country populations, and thus, generally does not concern itself with the fulfilment of the basic needs of the poor.

The International Monetary Fund (IMF) is an example of an institution applying this neo-classical monetarist development model in its transactions with developing countries. In applying these notions, the IMF seeks to increase the monetary prosperity of its developing country members. Unfortunately, the application of these principles does not generally lead to economic improvement for developing countries. In addition, other significant negative economic consequences, many of which disproportionately affect women, arise as a result of the IMF programs. While IMF

---

1. VANDANA SHIVA & MARIA MIES, ECOFEMINISM (1993); MAYRA BUVINIC & SALLY YUDELMAN, WOMEN, POVERTY AND PROGRESS IN THE THIRD WORLD 15 (1989).

2. Katherine McAfee, *What is Development*, 4 OXFAM AM. NEWS 6, 7–8 (1991–1992).

3. *Id.* at 19.

4. The discussion will be limited to this point, although clearly there are other reasons for developing country poverty. *See generally* PETER KORNER ET AL., THE IMF AND THE DEBT CRISIS, A GUIDE TO THE THIRD WORLD'S DILEMMA 20–42 (1986).

involvement in developing countries is not the primary reason that poverty exists in them, and IMF policies and programs are not deliberately biased against developing country women,[5] these programs nevertheless systematically and disparately disenfranchise poor women in developing countries.

This chapter is organized into several parts. First, a brief description of the model of development used by the IMF will be presented. Second, the specific details of the IMF's structure, operations, and policies, including the types of transactions that occur between developing countries and the IMF will be characterized. Third, a description of the economic and social effects that occur as a result of the IMF's application of conditionality will be presented. Fourth, it will be shown how IMF policies and procedures disparately affect women in developing countries. Finally, short-, medium-, and long-term recommendations that may be used to alleviate the negative impact of IMF programs on poor women in developing countries will be discussed. Changes must be made to development principles, institutions, and the international society to prevent the continued poverty of developing country women. Otherwise, no equality for women will ever exist, and the convictions espoused by Clinton P. Anderson, U.S. Secretary of Agriculture in 1946 will simply continue:

> There is no pleasant solution. The fact that in certain countries people die of hunger is not sufficient reason to provide [assistance]. . . . We are in the position of a family who has a litter of puppies; we have to decide which ones will be drowned.[6]

By default, because of their gender, poor women in developing countries routinely are the selected "puppies" that are "drowned."

DEVELOPMENT PRINCIPLES USED BY THE IMF

IMF's application of contemporary development principles disenfranchises poor women of developing countries. IMF notions of development are based on numerical indices, such as GNP, GDP, and balance of payments, and seem to be simply defined as the relative wealth and industrialization of countries, as measured by numerical, economic indices. Positive relative measurement of these indices is defined as development, while negative relative measurement is defined as underdevelopment or maldevelopment.[7] Many authors have concluded that this numerical definition of development is the dominant viewpoint of the IMF.[8] The IMF model appears to par-

---

5.   IMF policies could be described as "gender-blind." However, because the effects of these policies have a disparate impact on women, the policies are biased in their results.

6.   As reported in BUVINIC & YUDELMAN, *supra* note 1, at 18–19. *See generally* S. GEORGE, How THE OTHER HALF DIES, THE REAL REASONS FOR WORLD HUNGER (1976).

7.   Lombardi similarly agrees that economic indicators and numerical measurement typically define development. *See generally* RICHARD LOMBARDI, THE DEBT TRAP, RETHINKING THE LOGIC OF DEVELOPMENT 36 (1985).

8.   *See e.g.*, VANDANA SHIVA, ECOLOGY AND THE POLITICS OF SURVIVAL, CONFLICTS OVER NATURAL RESOURCES IN INDIA 20–35 (1991); R. DORNBUSCH, STABILIZATION, DEBT AND REFORM, POLICY ANALYSIS FOR DEVELOPING COUNTRIES (1994). The phrase "dominant viewpoint of contemporary society" is used to describe the viewpoint held by those countries, institutions, and individuals that have social, political, and economic power generally. This does not mean to imply that there are not

allel the model described by Bartelmus as the "neo-classical growth model," which is based on "individual planning, market mechanisms, and increased saving and capital injection by foreign aid for investment."[9] With respect to this model, Shiva notes that current development theories:

> focused exclusively on a model of progress derived from Western industrialized economies, on the assumption that Western style progress was possible for all. Development, as the improved well-being of all, was thus equated with the Westernization of categories—human needs, productivity and growth. . . . "[D]evelopment" as capital accumulation and the commercialization of the economy for the generation of "surplus and profits" thus involved the reproduction of not only a particular form of wealth creation, but also of the associated creation of poverty and dispossession. . . . [I]t became an extension of the project of wealth creation in modern Western patriarchy's economic vision.[10]

The IMF applies these notions of development in its involvement with developing countries. As such, the IMF "values"[11] countries based on their economic prosperity rather than the level of basic needs fulfilment of the developing country population.[12]

THE INTERNATIONAL MONETARY FUND

The IMF is a specialized agency of the United Nations (U.N.)[13] that is owned and controlled by member national governments in conjunction with national central banks. The IMF possesses full juridical personality[14] and has certain privileges and immunities, as set out in its articles.[15] It consists of three separate bodies: the Board of Governors, the Executive Board, and the Managing Director. The highest authority of the IMF is the Board of Governors, and all power vests specifically in the Board, unless stipulated otherwise by the articles. Each member country appoints one governor and an alternate for Board membership.

The Executive Board is the most substantial decision-making body of the IMF. It has a limited membership of twenty-two;[16] five members are appointed and the balance are elected. Representation on the Executive Board ensures that a member coun-

---

other viewpoints. The term is used simply to connote the views of the majority of the affluent and influential.

9.   PETER BARTELMUS, ENVIRONMENT AND DEVELOPMENT 4–6 (1986).

10.   SHIVA, *supra* note 8, at 71.

11.   Such as poverty, starvation, fulfilment of basic needs, and quality of life measurements.

12.   NAILA KABEER, REVERSED REALITIES: GENDER HIERARCHIES IN DEVELOPMENT THOUGHT 224 (1994).

13.   The IMF reports to the Economic and Social Council of the United Nations.

14.   Reparation for Injuries Suffered in the Service of the U.N., 1949 I.C.J. 174 (Advisory Opinion).

15.   Articles of Agreement of the International Monetary Fund, July 22, 1944, 69 Stat. 1401, 1402, T.I.A.S. No. 1501, 1, 2, UNTS 39, 40 [hereinafter Articles].

16.   H.K. JACOBSON, NETWORKS OF INTERDEPENDENCE: INTERNATIONAL ORGANIZATIONS AND THE GLOBAL POLITICAL SYSTEM 96 (1979).

try will have a measure of influence with the IMF. The other body, the Managing Director and staff, runs the day to day operations of the IMF, including membership and other departments.[17]

The IMF funds its basic resources through the contributions of members, called "quotas."[18] Initially, each country disburses funds to the IMF.[19] These contributed disbursements or quotas are significant to the influence that a member has in IMF decisions,[20] because most IMF decisions are made on a weighted voting system. Under the articles, each IMF member receives two hundred and fifty basic votes, plus one additional vote for each part of its contributed quota equivalent to one hundred thousand U.S. dollars.[21] This weighted voting system was designed to be technically biased in favor of "less economically potent" members, although this concept has been open to significant criticism.[22] Voting quotas are currently valued, based on the IMF-member "currency" called Standard Drawing Rights (SDRs). The quota determines a member's borrowing rights and primary lending commitments, therefore, the quantum of the quota is the most important figure for an IMF member, should the member wish to participate in IMF transactions.

Transactions through the IMF are comprised of exchanges of currencies through purchase and repurchase. In these transactions, the IMF exchanges "hard currency for a member country's soft currency, thereby reducing its fungible assets."[23] This procedure is called a "draw." The drawn currencies come from the SDR quota contributions or from contributions from other members under the "General Arrangements to Borrow."[24] Members draw other member's currencies from the IMF by purchasing

---

17. *See generally* KENNETH W. DAM, THE RULES OF THE GAME, REFORM AND EVOLUTION IN THE INTERNATIONAL MONETARY SYSTEM 78–82 (1982).

18. Quotas are related to "(1) members' subscription to the IMF [i.e., their contributions to IMF resources]; (2) member's drawing rights under regular and special facilities; (3) member's voting power; and (4) member's share of any allocation of SDRs." *See generally* W.L. DAVID, THE IMF POLICY PARADIGM, THE MACROECONOMICS OF STABILIZATION, STRUCTURAL ADJUSTMENT AND ECONOMIC DEVELOPMENT 15 (1985).

19. *See* J.J. POLACK, SOME REFLECTIONS ON THE NATURE OF SPECIAL DRAWING RIGHTS 12 (1969) (Washington, D.C.: International Monetary Fund Pamphlet Series).

20. J. GOLD, THE INTERNATIONAL MONETARY FUND AND INTERNATIONAL LAW, AN INTRODUCTION 10 (Washington, D.C.: International Monetary Fund, 1965).

21. Today, the same basic formula applies, except that Standard Drawing Rights (SDRs) are now substituted for U.S. dollars as a basis for voting valuation.

22. Although the voting weights technically could have meant more influence for economically smaller members, in actual fact, the votes have been significantly diluted by increased quotas for larger members. Ferguson shows the actual percentage of total voting power that basic votes give to each member: 1946: 11.3 percent of total, 1960: 10.3 percent of total, 1970: 10.3 percent of total, 1975: 9.9 percent of total, 1980: 5.1 percent of total, 1982: 5.6 percent of total. *See* T. FERGUSON, THE THIRD WORLD AND DECISION MAKING IN THE INTERNATIONAL MONETARY FUND, THE QUEST FOR FULL AND EFFECTIVE PARTICIPATION 63 (1988).

23. *See* K. STILES, NEGOTIATING DEBT, THE IMF LENDING PROCESS 22 (1991).

24. General Arrangements to Borrow will not be further discussed. For additional information, *see* DAM, *supra* note 17, at 149–50.

the foreign currencies in exchange for a further payment of their own currencies into the IMF. These drawings are permitted virtually automatically, up to the initial 25 percent member's gold contribution. Of course, all such drawings have to be repaid to the IMF.

If a member needs further foreign currencies, the IMF will continue to advance this currency, as long as the IMF is satisfied that the requesting member is taking steps to rectify its balance of payment problems. Drawings from the next credit level, known as the "first credit tranche," may go as high as 125 percent of the member's quota.[25] Any drawings beyond this level need extensive justification from the requesting member country. The normal drawing limit is 200 percent of the member's quota.[26] The articles specify that there are no time limits for drawings, although the IMF requires a portion of any increases in monetary reserves to be used for repurchases, unless reserves are abnormally low.[27] All repayments must be completed within three to five years, and any drawings made by standby agreements or conditionality, as discussed below, must be repaid within three years.

The IMF conditions access to its extended resources on the adoption of a "stabilization programme," also known as "conditionality" or "structural adjustment," by the drawing member.[28] The stabilization programme, which consists of IMF-approved "performance criteria" to be completed over a specified time frame, requires members to use devaluation and modified monetary and fiscal policies to decrease the demand for imports, which will hypothetically release resources for the balance of payments improvements. The IMF enforces this programme by requiring members to enter into "standby agreements" or arrangements, whereby members receive funds in installments and only receive the funds if the IMF is satisfied that its performance requirements are being satisfied by the drawing member.[29]

Theoretically, these policies and declarations "should help a member to overcome its balance of payments problems, avoid the temptation to resort to measures detrimental to itself or to the general welfare, and help it to achieve and maintain a sustainable balance of payments position over a reasonable period ahead."[30] However, for seventy-nine standby arrangements negotiated from 1963 to 1972, less than one-quarter improved the member's balance of payments in a statistically significant manner.[31] Sachs summarizes the economic results of IMF programs:

---

25. *See* GOLD, *supra* note 20, at 15 for a discussion on the types and levels of credit available.

26. *See* DAVID, *supra* note 18, at 23.

27. As designated by the IMF. *Id.* at 25.

28. Failure to meet performance criteria does not interrupt drawings in the first tranche. *See* J. GOLD, LEGAL AND INSTITUTIONAL ASPECTS OF THE INTERNATIONAL MONETARY SYSTEM 36 (International Monetary Fund, 1979).

29. Borrowers of IMF funds are known as "drawing members." *See* J. GOLD, STANDBY ARRANGEMENTS 147 (International Monetary Fund 1970).

30. J. Gold, *Use of the International Monetary Fund's Resources: Conditionality and Unconditionality as Legal Categories*, 6(1) J. INT. L. & ECON. 18, 21 (1971).

31. There are many empirical studies that confirm the lack of success of various aspects of the

The IMF's recent record in the debtor countries is one of failure. The failure was predictable, and the IMF could have done much better. The IMF is committed to restoring balance-of payments viability in the medium term to countries with an external financing crisis. Viability here refers to the capacity of a country to meet its international financial obligations without undermining national prosperity and on a *routine* basis (i.e., without further rescheduling, new concerted loans or further negotiated reductions in the debt). Viability by this standard has been restored for few if any of the thirty-nine or so countries that have been engaged in the past decade in the restructuring of their commercial bank debt. . . . [M]ost of the problem debtor countries are further away than ever from renewed creditworthiness.[32]

These results are even more undesirable when they are considered in the context of recent global trends, such as increased poverty and developing country populations, increased numbers of multinational corporations and the lessening of economic barriers to trade, increased availability of electronic financial communications and transfers, increases in automation and biotechnological agricultural products, and the degradation of the environment.[33] Although a discussion of these trends will not be undertaken here, all of these factors will tend to make the lives of the poor in developing countries worse in terms of the ability of the poor to meet their basic survival needs.[34] Thus, it is even more crucial to find an acceptable means of application of population and basic needs oriented development principles by institutions such as the IMF. Currently, however, the survival of poor populations does not appear to be a main consideration in IMF policy and procedure.

SOCIAL COSTS OF IMF ASSISTANCE

Coupled with the lack of empirical success of IMF programs are the other costs arising as a result of the IMF's involvement with developing countries. Public issues, such as loss of sovereignty and political stability, have been noted once IMF assistance is extended.[35] In addition to these "public-domain" problems, other private factors arise once IMF programs are instituted.[36] Specifically, there are a number of social costs that occur which tend to deepen the impoverishment of disenfranchised people in developing countries.[37]

IMF programs. *See, e.g.*, Sebastian Edwards & Julio Santaella, *Devaluation Controversies in the Developing Countries: Lessons from the Bretton Woods Era, in* A RETROSPECTIVE ON THE BRETTON WOODS SYSTEM, LESSONS FOR INTERNATIONAL MONETARY REFORM 420 (Michael D. Bordo & Barry Eichengreen eds., 1993).

32.　*See* Jeffrey Sachs, *Social Conflict and Populist Policies in Latin America, in* NATIONAL BUREAU OF ECONOMIC RESEARCH WORKING PAPER No. 2897 103 (Cambridge, Mass., March 1989).

33.　*See, e.g.*, PAUL KENNEDY, PREPARING FOR THE TWENTY-FIRST CENTURY 290–328 (1993).

34.　For a full description of these trends and their effects on the poor, see Jane Saber, The Equality of Puppies: The Disparate Effects of IMF Development Application on Developing Country Women, at 89–91 (unpublished LLM. Thesis, University of Alberta, 1996 on file with author).

35.　*See generally* DAVIDSON BUDHOO, ENOUGH IS ENOUGH, DEAR MR. CAMDESSUS . . . OPEN LETTER OF RESIGNATION TO THE MANAGING DIRECTOR OF THE INTERNATIONAL MONETARY FUND (Apex 1990).

36.　*See* BUVINIC & YUDELMAN, *supra* note 1; and KORNER ET AL., *supra* note 4.

37.　*See, e.g.*, ADJUSTMENT WITH A HUMAN FACE, PROTECTING THE VULNERABLE AND PROMOTING GROWTH (G.Cornia, R. Jolly & F. Stewart, eds., 1987) [hereinafter ADJUSTMENT WITH A HUMAN FACE].

In her article on conditionality, Stewart describes these costs: contraction in per capita incomes,[38] rising unemployment, rising urban poverty, reduced government per capita expenditure (including expenditure on the social services and food subsidies), rising malnutrition, stagnant or falling levels of real investment, and no improvement (and in some cases deterioration) in the current account of the balance of payments in many countries with IMF programs.[39] Although recognizing that the IMF was not a causal factor in the initial economic difficulties of drawing countries, she concludes:

> Developments associated with conditionality in the 1980s were highly unsatisfactory, [and] for the most part—despite heavy social costs—conditionality in the 1980s did not succeed in eliminating imbalances and restoring countries to a position of sustainable growth.... [T]he programmes may have contributed to the worsening terms of trade suffered by primary producers, which were, in turn, partly responsible for the limited improvements in the current account balance of many Third World Countries.[40]

In addition, Dell identifies other difficulties arising from declining real wages in some developing countries as a result of IMF conditionality.[41] He notes that in some instances, real wages decreased on the order of 20 to 40 percent within several months of IMF conditionality being instituted in drawing countries.[42] He finds that this drastic decrease led to 20 to 40 percent less purchasing power for the population. This, in turn, caused a decrease in the quality of life and the fulfilment of basic needs of the people.[43] Shiva,[44] David,[45] Budhoo,[46] and others, as described below, suggest that the IMF is at least partly responsible for the worsening conditions of the poor in IMF-assisted countries.

Cornia *et al.* prepared several studies regarding this deterioration, including fulfilment of basic human needs, and the distributional and poverty implications for developing country populations as a result of IMF involvement in these countries.[47]

---

38. Per capita income fell in over 70 percent of IMF assisted countries in Africa and Latin America, *id.* at 32.

39. Frances Stewart, *Should Conditionality Change?, in* THE IMF AND THE WORLD BANK IN AFRICA, CONDITIONALITY, IMPACT AND ALTERNATIVES, SEMINAR PROCEEDINGS NO. 18, 29–45 (Havnevik ed., Scandinavian Institute of African Studies, 1987). Stewart states: "Real government consumption per head fell in 55% of African countries (1980–84) and 70% of Latin American countries.... [R]eal expenditure on food subsidies per head fell in nine out of ten countries for which information has been collected, eight of which had fund programmes." *Id.* at 33.

40. Stewart, *id.* at 33–34.

41. *See generally* Sidney Dell, *The Future of the International Monetary System, in* THE FUTURE OF THE INTERNATIONAL MONETARY SYSTEM, CHANGE CO-ORDINATION OR INSTABILITY? 201 (Omar Hmouda et al. eds., 1989).

42. *Id.* at 214.

43. *Id.* at 210–16.

44. VANDANA SHIVA, STAYING ALIVE, WOMEN ECOLOGY AND DEVELOPMENT 25 (1988).

45. DAVID, *supra* note 18, at 121.

46. BUDHOO, *supra* note 35, at 65–70.

47. Giovanni Andrea Cornia, *Economic Decline and Human Welfare in the First Half of the 1980s, in* ADJUSTMENT WITH A HUMAN FACE, *supra* note 37, at 47 [hereinafter *Economic Decline*].

One study addresses the deterioration of living standards that has occurred in developing countries after IMF applications of conditionality in the first half of the 1980s. Although this analysis is primarily concerned with the deterioration of the welfare of children, Cornia identifies statistics that are pertinent to general deterioration of living conditions in developing countries.[48] Cornia first examines the availability of resources for basic need fulfilment. With the exception of Sri Lanka, all sample countries experienced some type of recession in their economies once IMF assistance was instituted.[49] Unemployment rates increased in all but one of the countries examined. Real salaries similarly showed a general decline in all countries except South Korea. Because of the reduction in employment levels, and the reduction of real wages, women have had to increase their participation in the labor force "in order to offset the drop in earnings of (male) breadwinners."[50] Inflation (measured using the Consumer Price Index) also accelerated substantially, and this similarly increased the need for female labor force participation.[51] The need to offset reduced household buying power typically fell to women, who are, by and large, responsible for family sustenance.[52] As a result, it is the women's time and energy that is most affected by these decreases, as discussed *infra*.

Even with the increased female participation in family sustenance, the net effects of these factors indicate a disparate drop in the household resources, particularly for the impoverished.[53] In Ghana, the Philippines, Chile, Jamaica, Peru, and Brazil, the number of people living below the poverty line increased.[54]

In addition, in most IMF adjustment programs, social sector spending is reduced.[55] The results of one study describe the impact of adjustment programs on government expenditures:

---

48.   The statistics were gleaned from a sample of ten developing countries: Botswana, Ghana, Zimbabwe, the Philippines, South Korea, Sri Lanka, the state of Sao Paulo (Brazil), Chile, Jamaica, and Peru. *Id*. at 21–22.

49.   In the Philippines, Ghana, Jamaica, and Peru, the cumulative decline in GDP per capita was 15 percent or more. Chile and Brazil had declines of -6.8 and -9 percent, whereas south Korea, Zimbabwe, and Botswana recorded overall increases in GDP, even though recession was, in fact, experienced during some time in the sample period. *Id*. at 22–23.

50.   Specifically stating: "With the exception of South Korea, real salaries (i.e. money salaries deflated by the Consumer Price Index (CPI) or by the GDP deflator), have generally declined faster than the observed drop in GDP per capita. This was also the case in Sri Lanka and Zimbabwe, and possibly Botswana, where real salaries declined despite the increase in GDP per capita." *Id*. at 22.

51.   "Reaching two or more digits in the early 1980s for all countries included in the sample," *id*. at 27.

52.   Including food collection, food preparation, fuel and water collection, child care, health, education, and so on.

53.   Due to real wages declining faster than GDP per capita, and rates of inflation for wage goods being higher than the consumer price index, which is the price paid for consumers of a standard assortment of goods, at a given point in time. *See* Cornia, *Economic Decline, supra* note 47, at 25–27. These effects have been greatly underestimated.

54.   Until 1984. *Id*. at 27.

55.   CHERYL PAYER, THE DEBT TRAP, THE IMF AND THE THIRD WORLD 81 (1974).

> In Ghana, where prolonged crisis resulted in a cut of health expenditure per capita in 1982/83 to 80 per cent of the 1974 level, a project to immunize against yellow fever met only 50 per cent of its target. . . . [I]n Mozambique, the drugs and equipment needed to maintain the primary health care infrastructure cannot be maintained. . . . In Zaire, 7,000 teachers were taken off the government payroll. . . . In Ethiopia, even in the primary schools . . . a textbook is shared by at least four students. . . . [T]he visibly deteriorating conditions of basic services in many countries are due to the compounded effects of the general financial crisis together with specific cuts in health and education expenditures.[56]

This is not to say that health and education were the most reduced sectors of government expenditures. In fact, cuts in government expenditures tended to fall most on economic services and least on defense, with education and health in a median position.[57] Capital expenditure was reduced most, followed by subsidies. Wages were most protected, followed by purchase of goods.[58] Governments in question made choices of which sectors to cut, and by what amounts, and noted that there was "no inevitability about the connection between declining GDP per capita and declining (lifestyles)."[59] The governments of developing countries had some power to change their own development policy decisions to account for basic needs fulfilment of the poor, but they did not do so. Developing country governments made the "reasoned" choice not to consider the deteriorating lives of the poor.

Decreases in food subsidies were also common once IMF conditionality was initiated. Specifically, "capping or reducing food subsidies was part of about one-third of adjustment programs supported by the IMF in recent years."[60] Statistics indicated that government food subsidy expenditures "have increased less than the domestic inflation and also less than the combined effect of inflation and devaluation against the dollar," and that the increases in government expenditures on food subsidies have increased less than other government expenditures.[61] Thus, "it appears that there has been a general decrease in government expenditures on food subsidies during the period 1980–1985 both in real terms and as a share of total government budgets and GDP."[62] For those who are already poor, these reductions are life-threatening.[63]

This study also found a significant contraction in "key social service" availability, rapidly escalating user costs, and a general deterioration in the quality of the

---

56. Per Pinstrup-Andersen, Maurice Jaramillo & Francis Stewart, *The Impact on Government Expenditures, in* ADJUSTMENT WITH A HUMAN FACE, *supra* note 37, at 73–74 [hereinafter *Impact on Government Expenditures*].

57. *Id.* at 73.

58. *Id.* at 77–79.

59. *Id.* at 81.

60. *Id.* at 83.

61. *Id.* at 85.

62. *Id.* at 87.

63. *See generally* BUDHOO, *supra* note 35.

services delivered in most of the countries.[64] Declines in food intake or availability for the bottom 20 to 40 percent of the population were found,[65] as well as declines in educational services available, increased infant mortality and child deaths, increased malnutrition, and reduced educational attainment.[66] Although the IMF adjustment programs were not the sole cause of these upheavals, it appeared that when these programs are combined with already existing financial crises, the results were augmented.

These observed decreases in the real value of government expenditures on food subsidies were not only due to explicit policy action aimed at subsidy programs. Devaluations of national currencies and rising import prices of subsidized goods contributed to falling subsidy costs in dollars in many countries with little or no explicit policy action toward food subsidies.[67] The net effect of the reduction of subsidies was higher prices.

Thus, because IMF development principles do not consider the social costs resulting from conditionality, developing countries must struggle to achieve quantitative improvement at the expense of the survival of the poor. These results are unacceptable. No individual, regardless of gender, should be subjected to increasing disenfranchisement and poverty because of inappropriate development principles such as those employed by the IMF. Unfortunately, as examined below, poor women, more than men, suffer the consequences of this style of development.

EFFECTS OF IMF ON WOMEN

Women in developing countries disproportionately bear the costs associated with development, as applied by the IMF. This is because there are inherent, interrelated flaws in contemporary development principles and in IMF conditionality. Prior to the analysis of this issue, two factors must be addressed. First, the colonization of developing countries and the influence of the white, Western patriarchy are not the exclusive causes of gender-biased effects in developing countries. In some societies, gender bias, in the form of cultural-specific male dominance over women existed throughout recorded history. However, because this history was chronicled by the students of patriarchy, namely Western academics and historians, the true nature of these relations and their relative effects on the lives of women are not clearly ascertainable. Nevertheless, although contemporary development principles and IMF conditionality contribute to the current disenfranchisement of women in developing countries, the causal bases of gender bias could have resulted from pre-existing cultural practices.

---

64. *Impact on Government Expenditures, supra* note 56, at 82–85. The authors neglect to specifically state what these key social services are.

65. In Sri Lanka, Brazil, Peru, Philippines and Ghana. *Id.* at 28.

66. *Id.* at 11, 29–33.

67. *Id.* at 87.

Second, although contemporary notions and applications of development and IMF conditionality originate with the white, Western patriarchy, these prescriptions may be affected by pre-existing ideologies existing in various regions. For example, cultures already demonstrating gender biases would apply these biases in interpreting and applying the white, Western, patriarchal epistemologies, methodologies, information, and "directives." Regardless of its origin, patriarchal notions and applications of development in general, and IMF conditionality in particular, cause detrimental effects in the lives of poor women in developing countries.

Irrespective of these two factors, it is clear that white, Western, patriarchal development principles have exacerbated the poverty of poor women in developing countries for several reasons. First, contemporary development principles only contemplate developing country women's contributions in their roles in the family. This work is not deemed "valuable," since value is defined by numerical measurements in the marketplace. According to the model, that which cannot be valued in the marketplace is valueless. This results in the general exclusion of the work of many women from the scope of developmental "consideration."

Second, development principles presuppose that women are dependant on, and "taken care of" by patriarchal structures. Even if there is no authority providing for the needs of developing country women, the patriarchal institution of welfare is assumed to deal with any anomalies.[68] Therefore, when development principles are envisaged, there seems to be little consideration of meeting the unique requirements of the "unconventional," female "aberrations" to the current developmental categorizations of women.[69] Therefore, independent, "non-welfare" women's issues are not generally or specifically addressed by current development theories and practices, as the very existence of these issues is virtually unrecognized.

This is particularly disturbing when noting that women in developing countries frequently must be the primary breadwinner for their families. Indeed, "roughly one-third of all households in the Third World are headed by women, and in some regions, such as the cities of Latin America and the rural areas of some African countries, the percentage is closer to one-half."[70] For example:

> In a squatter settlement near Nairobi, Kenya, Nelson estimated that 60 to 80 per cent of women in the settlement were independent heads of households. In the Caribbean, female urban migrants often leave their children behind with their mothers, so that the rural areas of many territories become dominated by households headed by grandmothers.[71]

---

68. *See generally* Bould, *Development and the Family, Third World Women and Inequality, in* WOMEN, DEVELOPMENT AND CHANGE, THE THIRD WORLD EXPERIENCE 50, 55 (M.F. Abraham & P.S. Abraham eds., 1988).

69. This lack of consideration is changing, but haltingly. *See* KABEER, *supra* note 12, at 245.

70. BUVINIC & YUDELMAN, *supra* note 1, at 9.

71. Janet Townsend & Janet Henshall Momsen, *Towards a Geography of Gender in Developing Economies, in* GEOGRAPHY OF GENDER IN THE THIRD WORLD 27, 53 (Janet Henshall Momsen & Janet G. Townsend eds., 1987).

Many developing country women do not have the so-called "luxury" of being part of a traditional nuclear family,[72] which includes a primary male breadwinner, a mother/wife, and children.[73]

Thus, one of the major reasons that deterioration in the lives of developing country females is occurring is the failure of development to recognize the triple role women must fulfill in developing countries.[74] The roles include reproductive work (including childbearing and rearing), productive work (as wage earners), and community management work involving assistance for the collective consumption of the community. The reproductive and management roles are specifically not recognized, as they are deemed natural and non-productive, and are therefore not valued.[75] This situation causes most of the work of women to be invisible. Women, as a result, are in a worse position than men, whose productive, wage earning activities are both rewarded and sanctioned by current development principles, even though "women (still) perform two-thirds of the world's work hours."[76] Thus, because women's work consists of both paid and unpaid activities, much of women's work is excluded from the numerical indices of development:

> In much of the Third world, this type of "development" has eroded women's status relative to men's and usurped their productive roles in agriculture and handicrafts production. Women have frequently failed to find in the modern sector adequate replacements for their traditional roles, both because they rarely have the educational qualifications and because they have internalized patriarchal definitions of appropriate female roles. Thus while modernization has improved the situation of some groups, it has threatened the material well-being of a substantial proportion of the Third World women.[77]

Returning to the example of the IMF, it can be specifically seen how women are disenfranchised by these development principles, as applied by this institution.

As described previously, the IMF typically requires devaluation and monetary and fiscal modifications in the country of conditionality application. A number of consequences occur as a result of these policy revisions, including: reduced govern-

---

72. Bould, *supra* note 68, at 51.

73. *See generally* M. Zelditch, *Role Differentiation in the Nuclear Family: A Comparative Study, in* FAMILY SOCIALIZATION AND INTERACTION PROCESS 301, 307–51 (T. Parsons & R.F. Bales eds., 1955).

74. Caroline Moser, *Women, Human Settlements and Housing: a Conceptual Framework for Analysis and Policy-making, in* WOMEN, HUMAN SETTLEMENTS AND HOUSING 12, 13 (C. Moser & L. Peake eds., 1987). Some authors, like Kabeer, hold that women have a dual role, rather than a triple role. Kabeer sees women's roles to consist of domestic duties and employment duties. KABEER, *supra* note 12, at 98. Moser's characterization, at 13–15, may be more valid. In subsistence economies, it is not uncommon for women to pool their meager resources for the collective use. SHIVA, STAYING ALIVE, *supra* note 44, at 32. This cooperation only occurs if it is organized by the women. Therefore, if these cooperative activities are taking place in the community, women do indeed have a triple role.

75. Moser, *supra* note 74, at 13.

76. *Id.*

77. ESTER BOSERUP, WOMEN'S ROLE IN ECONOMIC DEVELOPMENT (1970).

ment spending on education, social programs, welfare, food subsidies, health, and increased violence. Further, the IMF's conditionality requirements reduces the purchasing power of the poor, which specifically causes increased workloads for developing country women. In addition, access to development programs for women, which might alleviate their poverty, is limited through gender-blind institutional policies. As analyzed below, the IMF's application of conditionality in developing countries clearly has a disproportionate impact on women.

When the IMF applies conditionality, generally there are fewer jobs available, and the employment that is available will have reduced wages, because devaluations and monetary and fiscal policies tend to reduce profitability of business. When profits fall, owners of capital and production typically re-evaluate the "bottom line" of their businesses. Layoffs and reductions of wages and staff levels tend to occur when profits fall.[78] Low-level staff are often categorized as redundant and thus are "laid off."[79] If these workers are replaced, they are often replaced with less adequately trained individuals, who will work for significantly reduced wages.[80] The net effect of these changes is that the poor and middle classes become poorer, and generally, there is less disposable income in the country.[81] Recession may result from these policies.[82] This is particularly damaging to women, as most often they are at the bottom of the employment hierarchy:

> The adjustment measures mandated by . . . the IMF have had an impact on women's employment and income-earning opportunities. Women are often the last hired and the first fired. They also find themselves "bumped down" the employment ladder when jobs of men on rungs above are eliminated. During times of prosperity, women fill jobs in the modern economy, but lose them to men during recessions. Women perform low-paid, menial work outside the modern economy—work not covered by modern labour regulations. Basically they take any work they can find to supplement a reduced household budget. Furthermore, when the economy declines, people cut back on expenditures. As a result of currency devaluation in Latin America, for example, many jobs in the service sector, in which women predominate, have been eliminated. Cutbacks in social service budgets also have more of an effect on women because they are more likely to be employed by agencies that deal with health, education and welfare.[83]

Women are often at the bottom of the employment hierarchy simply because they have been discriminated against in education. Poor education of developing country populations is often exacerbated by reduced education budgets that are cut when government spending reductions are necessary. Buvinic has provided statistics which set

---

78. LOMBARDI, *supra* note 7, at 229.

79. Sachs, *supra* note 32, at 117–19.

80. BUDHOO, *supra* note 35, at 78.

81. Besides a reduction in the quality of the goods and services available, because of untrained staff.

82. *See* Dell, *supra* note 41, who has suggested that real wages in developing countries were decreased between 20 to 40 percent over a short time frame. This decrease would clearly be dangerous for individuals or family units already perilously close to starvation.

83. BUVINIC & YUDELMAN, *supra* note 1, at 16.

out the changes in education budgets of various governments.[84] She states that according to the United Nations Children's Fund (UNICEF), "the world's least-developed countries have cut these budgets by twenty-five percent."[85]

This reduction on educational spending has a greater negative effect on women than on men. As education expenditures decline and school fees increase, females are at a particular disadvantage. Parents prefer to educate sons because their job prospects are better.[86] In addition, there is the ongoing perception that males will be the primary breadwinners in the families. Therefore, when a choice must be made, parents harmfully tend to give sons preferential education over daughters:

> Schooling for girls is not considered as important because they are not perceived as potential breadwinners. This myth goes hand in hand with the belief that women's education and women's work have little value and are of less importance to family welfare. But mothers', not father's, education, is the most important factor contributing to children's health.[87]

Lower education levels for women in developing countries mean that the jobs that women are qualified to take are more limited than those available to men. Obviously, managerial, governmental, or any technical jobs requiring training are not available to those individuals without the requisite preliminary training. As a result, many women are unemployed or under-employed, and have, it seems, no legal entitlement to a decent, adequately paid job with reasonable working conditions. This effect is further amplified by the fact that in many cultures, it is perceived as socially undesirable for women to work.[88] It is a vicious circle for developing country women. They hold menial, low-paying jobs because they are not educated, but cannot become educated because they are poor women. Further, if the primary wage earner of a family unit is not able to get employment, the family unit must then rely on seasonal, low-paying work that is temporary in nature, or rely on government social programs for survival.[89] However, even these government programs are more difficult to attain when the IMF applies conditionality.

---

84. *Id.* at 16–20. Specifically, Buvinic found decreases in education expenditures as a percentage of total government expenditure. There are no statistics indicating when the IMF conditionality was instituted in these countries. Further, there are no statistics showing the actual effect of the IMF conditionality on education expenditures. However, the relationship between IMF entrance into a country and the cutbacks in education should be the subject of further study. Such a study is beyond the scope of this work. Bould states the following with respect to the status of women in India, based on the 1974 report by the Committee on the status of women in India: female illiteracy among women rose from 142 to 215 million. Bould, *supra* note 68, at 59.

85. Buvinic & Yudelman, *supra* note 1, at 14.

86. *Id.* at 14.

87. *Id.* at 22.

88. Veronica Beechey, *Women in Production a Critical Analysis of Some Sociological Theories of Women's Work, in* Feminism and Materialism 155, 186 (A. Kuhn & A. Wolfe eds., 1978).

89. When jobs are not available, men tend to migrate to the cities, while the women and children are left behind to fend for themselves. Buvinic & Yudelman, *supra* note 1, at 4.

As previously indicated, social sector spending is also often reduced as a result of IMF programs. This causes less funding to be available for other basic needs such as clean water, sanitation, health, education, government funding of self-help development programs, and deteriorating transportation systems. Although Cornia notes that most cuts are made in the economic service area, even the most minor cuts in any of these areas can be disastrous for those already impoverished.[90] Women, as the poorest of the poor, bear the greatest burden of these cuts. Women will need to forage for extra food in the common land in order to make up for their loss.[91] However, given that the common land is being reduced because of capitalist demands for production for export, even this resource is becoming increasingly scarce. Women must walk further and further, and spend increased hours looking for food, fodder, and adequate water. Even with this increased effort, food intake has declined for the bottom 20 to 40 percent of developing country populations.[92]

It must also be noted that prior to any cutbacks in social programs, women already suffer from less nourishment and fulfilment of other basic needs than their male counterparts. Buvinic, for example, notes the disparity of food availability of males and females:

> Benefits are often unequally distributed within families, with men and boys usually favoured over women and girls. In times of scarcity, women and girls lose out in terms of quality and quantity of food as well as other resources. The reasons for this discrimination are grounded on the belief that males are more critical to family survival than females. It does not mean that men do not care for their womenfolk. But poverty dictates painful choices, and the belief that males are the breadwinners guides decisions in favour of men and boys.[93]

Statistically, pregnant and lactating women are the most disadvantaged in terms of proportionate caloric requirements being fulfilled. This situation is particularly desperate, since two-thirds of the women of reproductive age (fifteen–forty-five) are pregnant, lactating, or both.[94] Further, 59 percent of girls, as compared to 56 percent of boys, suffer chronic malnutrition, while 10 percent of girls and 7 percent of boys suffer acute malnutrition.[95] By the 1980s, the average weight of boys had improved, whereas girls showed little or no improvement.[96]

---

90. Giovanni Andrea Cornia & Francis Stewart, *Country Experience with Adjustment, in* ADJUSTMENT WITH A HUMAN FACE, *supra* note 46, at 124 [hereinafter *Country Experience*].

91. SHIVA, ECOLOGY & POLITICS OF SURVIVAL, *supra* note 8, at 124–132.

92. *Id.* at 126.

93. BUVINIC & YUDELMAN, *supra* note 1, at 21–22. Kabeer also notes the disparity in food availability between women and men, in considering the situation in Bangladesh. However, she also seems to make some generalizations on food availability for women in this section. KABEER, *supra* note 12, at 142–146.

94. W. MAHMUD & S. MAHMUD, ASPECTS OF THE FOOD AND NUTRITIONAL PROBLEM IN RURAL BANGLADESH, ILO/WEP Research Working Paper 10–6/wp74 (1985), as cited in KABEER, *supra* note 12, at 147.

95. KABEER, *supra* note 12, at 143, citing UNICEF, ANALYSIS OF THE SITUATION OF CHILDREN IN BANGLADESH (Dhaka, UNICEF, 1987).

96. This study was specific to Bangladesh. M.K. CHOWDHURY, A. RAZZAQUE, S. BECKER, A.M.

Cultural practices have a significant impact on the fulfilment of nutritional requirements. Indeed, "practices that lead to inequitable gender distribution of food in the family include feeding males first, particularly adult males, and giving them the choicest and largest servings."[97] Once the conditionality programs are implemented, women's nutritional status deteriorates further because of the loss of purchasing power and resource availability. And should the calories, distribution, and diversity of the food not be satisfactory to the household males, violence can result from disputes over food, such that women may have to choose between black eyes or empty stomachs. Most choose empty stomachs.[98]

No matter what concessions they make to men, many poor women experience increased violence once IMF conditionality is imposed. Bould states that "a deterioration of the relative or absolute economic situation of families puts new and heavy stress on family relationships. One or both marital partners is likely to be blamed for failure to meet their economic obligations. . . . [T]he woman is more likely to see her household position deteriorate further than the man's under the process of dualistic development."[99] It is important to understand that one of the reasons why this abuse is occurring is the high level of anxiety developing country populations feel with respect to their own chances of survival. Conditions of scarcity cause frustration and uncertainty in all people. Developing country men are faced with the perception that they should be providing for their families. When they cannot, they may turn to take out their frustrations and uncertainties on those over whom they have power, including their wives and children.[100] As economic situations deteriorate, and all the assets of the women are sold, men become increasingly frustrated.[101] This frustration is evident in the occurrence of "IMF riots,"[102] political uprisings, and coups that occur after the IMF imposes its programs.[103] Women will likely continue to experience violence against them, usually at an increased frequency and intensity.[104]

Besides having their survival threatened by violence against them, women's health is also threatened by government cutbacks. The previously described social expenditure reduction also affect levels of health care in developing countries. Pre-existing gender biases occur in the health standard of men and women in developing

---

SARDER, & S. D'SOUZA, DEMOGRAPHIC SURVEILLANCE SYSTEM—MATLAB. VOLUME NINE. VITAL EVENTS AND MIGRATION—1979 (Dhaka: International Centre for Diarrhoeal Disease Research Bangladesh, 1982).

97. KABEER, *supra* note 12, at 143.

98. *Id.* at 144–45.

99. Bould, *supra* note 68, at 62.

100. KABEER, *supra* note 12, at 146–153.

101. Which happens regularly, according to Kabeer. *See* KABEER, *supra*, note 12, at 207.

102. *See* Saber, *supra* note 34, at 90–105.

103. Although it is difficult to prove that the riots resulted directly from IMF involvement.

104. KABEER, *supra* note 12, at 211. The hypothesized increased violence against poor women, once IMF conditionality is instituted, should be the subject of further study.

countries.[105] For example, mortality rates in developing countries are very high, and are higher among women who "have not been successful in producing a live birth or healthy children, particularly healthy sons, and who are usually under intense pressure to undergo a succession of closely spaced births."[106] Further, D'Souza and Chen show that although females have a biological advantage of survival for the first month of birth, in the first four years of life, twice as many girls are likely to die than boys.[107] High maternal deaths are also commonplace among poor, developing country women.[108] Illness is quite likely considering the lower availability of health care, and the previously mentioned reduced access to food. Thus, the IMF, by recommending developing country austerity, indirectly ensures that what little health expenditures were being made on women are transferred to men.

As noted previously, IMF conditionality usually includes devaluation. As a result, exports become more expensive, and there will be a correspondingly increased demand for local products. Further, because of increased demand for scarce local products, it is likely that the price of local products will also increase. Immediate actual cost increases for imported products and a longer-term increase in price of domestic products are typical results.[109] This leads to decreased purchasing power of consumers, causing decreased fulfilment of the basic needs of women.

Often, there are no local products that can be consumed alternatively to imports. Further, many production facilities are used to produce high demand products, rather than basic needs products.[110] If there are no local comparable products, basic goods that the household had consumed simply are more expensive or not available. This lack of basic goods compromises the health and survival of the family. As described above, loss of goods available to the population usually falls on the shoulders of women.[111]

---

105. Since women in developing countries have not had the same levels of care that men have had, once development notions are imported into these countries, women and men may be used to the fact that women are only entitled to minimal health care. See *Impact on Government Expenditures, supra* note 56, at Chapter Five for a discussion of this point. *See also* L. Chen, A. Chowdhury & S. Huffman, *Anthropometric Assessment of Energy Protein Malnutrition and Subsequent Risk of Mortality Among Pre-School Aged Children,* 5(11) Studies in Family Planning 322, 334–41 (1980); N. Sabir & G. Ebrahim, *Are Daughters More at Risk than Sons in Some Societies?,* 30 J. Trop. Paediatrics 25, 27 (1984).

106. Kabeer, *supra* note 12, at 147, uses the example of Bangladesh, where mortality is 5–7 percent per live thousand births.

107. S. D'Souza & L. Chen, *Sex Differentials in Mortality in Rural Bangladesh,* 6(2) Pop. & Dev. Rev. 257, 265 (1980).

108. Kabeer, *supra* note 12, at 148–150; Mahmud & Mahmud, *supra* note 94, at 17.

109. Lombardi, *supra* note 7, at 28–29. This increase in prices could also be noticed on a shorter term, but the length of time between the devaluation and the price change would depend strongly on the elasticities of supply and demand for the product in question. If there is a shortage of the product, production for other products may be changed to produce more of the high demand product. With deteriorating land use for women, their access to agricultural lands, for example, would be reduced because of these devaluations.

110. *Id.* at 25–26.

111. Kabeer, *supra* note 12, at 20–26.

The governments of developing countries have attempted to defend themselves from the criticism of ignoring the impoverishment of the population by stating that there are development programs in place to assist people in finding suitable self-employment or income earning opportunities.[112] Although these programs may be beneficial for some segments of the population, women's access to these programs is limited.[113] The programs that are available to women are typically staffed by men, who may not understand women's needs and issues. In order to rectify this, some gender training has been instituted by various agencies.[114] However, even though this training may have made some agencies aware of women's issues, many of the programs have not yet incorporated gender issues:

> The failure of modernization to benefit women was attributed to a variety of factors reflecting these different cultural contexts. In female farming systems, particularly in sub-Saharan Africa, women had been deprived of access to training, land rights, education and technology by colonial and post-colonial administrators whose biased perceptions led them to favour male farmers. In the market economies of the Third World, employers demonstrated a preference for men, creating a sex-stereotyped job hierarchy, while women's own prejudices and preferences inhibited them from seeking employment in the modern sector. This led to a divergence in attitudes since employment in the modern sector requires not only formal training but also a certain attitude to work which may be best described as the capacity to work regularly and attentively . . . those who work within the confines of the family are not likely to acquire this attitude.[115]

The major consequence of this is that women are not seen as appropriate recipients of these programs: "Planners, generally men—whether in donor-country agencies or in recipient countries—have been unable to deal with the fact that women must perform (many) roles in society, while men perform only one."[116] Rogers also concludes that existing programs are discriminatory.[117] She found that Western planners perceive women as illogical and irrational and see no reason to offer them incentives to participate in the development process.[118]

In addition, statistical data collection procedures concerning the status of women in developing countries by development agencies have a negative effect on the dis-

---

112. *Id.* at 20.

113. Boserup provides the example of farming, where women have essential roles but are not recognized as farmers, but still as housewives and mothers only. BOSERUP, *supra* note 77, at 25–49.

114. KABEER, *supra* note 12, at 7; Moser, *supra* note 74, at 6–7, 214.

115. KABEER, *supra* note 12, at 20.

116. BOSERUP, *supra* note 77, at 22; KABEER, *supra* note 12.

117. B. ROGERS, THE DOMESTICATION OF WOMEN: DISCRIMINATION IN DEVELOPING SOCIETIES 34–36 (1980).

118. As found in KABEER, *supra* note 12, at 23. A common response of development agency officials was as follows: The most consistent responses of male planners to the introduction of discussion about women in development is to base their arguments against change on the domestic model familiar to them: '*my* wife doesn't work,' 'I get on very well with my daughters,' 'my mother always said a woman's place is in the home,' and other variations on the theme that women should follow the model of feminine deportment which they consider correct. *See* ROGERS, *supra* note 117, at 50.

crimination in labor and development programs for women. There are very few reliable statistics.[119] Because of this lack of information regarding the true nature of developing country women's lives, coupled with the gender-blind developmental biases against females, women's economic contributions have not been met with proportionate contributions in assistance: "It is the blindness to these inequities more than the blindness of invisibility that stands in women's way. The blindness has an institutional and political base."[120]

Once IMF conditionality is imposed, even if there was the initial possibility of access to programs, the reduction of government spending in this area presumably would further exclude women from benefitting from these programs. In addition, if men lose access to these programs, it will be the women who will have to make up the shortfall, shouldering the burdens of the adjustment.[121]

RECOMMENDATIONS FOR CHANGE

Thus far, it has been shown that the notions of development applied by the IMF largely do not consider the welfare of poor women in developing countries. To lessen or prevent these effects from occurring, there are a number of changes that can be made, which include redefining the following: development principles, developing country policies, the IMF, and the status of women generally. The best answer to the disenfranchisement of developing country women would be a combination of each of these solutions, because of the varying time periods that will be required to make modifications in these areas. In any event, it is clear that change is necessary to ensure the survival of poor women in developing countries. Hopefully, an effective remedy will be found to redress the decreasing quality of life and ability to survive that poor, developing country women face.

Redefining Development

The first problem that must be addressed is the question of how to change the currently inappropriate notions of development. These notions must be replaced with a more distributively fair theory, which does not place the increasing burden of poverty on the poor. The following U.N. resolution provides a starting point for the necessary changes. This resolution states that the ideal goals for development include efforts:

> (i) to effect structural change which favours national development and to activate all sectors of the population to participate in the development process;
>
> (ii) to aim at social equity, including the achievement of an equitable distribution of income and wealth in the nation;

---

119. KABEER, *supra* note 12, at 24.

120. R.B. Dixon, *Seeing the Invisible Women Farmers in Africa; Improving Research and Data Collection Methods, in* WOMEN AS FOOD PRODUCERS IN DEVELOPING COUNTRIES 29, 32 (J. Monson & M. Kalb eds., 1985).

121. *Id.* at 48.

(iii) to give high priority to the development of the human potentials including vocational and technical training and the provision of employment opportunities and meeting the needs of the children.[122]

Growth, as described by the U.N. resolution above, would include: (1) adequate employment creation; (2) meeting the basic human needs of all segments of the population; (3) reduction in inequalities, for example, through a more equitable distribution of income and wealth; and, in general, (4) the provision of a better quality of life.[123] David suggests that development principles should be focused on human development, as compared to simple economic development.[124]

In order to achieve these goals, the "neo-classical growth model" should be replaced with a model that concentrates on the attainment of life essentials,[125] known as the "basic needs model."[126] However, because this model does not specifically address the needs of developing country women, an extension of this model, called the "subsistence model," is more appropriate.[127] The basic premise of this model is that development should be measured by the attainment of basic needs by poor women. The main characteristics of this model include a retreat from monetary value as the prime focus of development, and a revision of white, Western patriarchy to incorporate the recognition of value of those things and people which cannot be valued in the marketplace.[128] In essence, this change would require a dismantling of the bases of contemporary development ideologies.[129]

To coincide with the subsistence perspective, the value of any person or any object would not be defined solely by its value in the marketplace. Notions that people and countries are only as valuable as the numerical wealth that they generate should be discarded. All endeavors contributing to subsistence should be recognized, whether wage producing or not. Specifically, women's triple role of nurturer, community organizer, and income earner should be recognized. Other indicators, such as family time contributions, levels of basic need fulfilment through subsistence production, and other factors would also be used, in order to recognize non-market contributions.[130]

---

122. U.N. General Assembly Resolution No. 2681 (XXV) of Dec. 11, 1970.

123. DAVID, *supra* note 18, at 112.

124. *Id*. at 105.

125. Nine fundamental human needs have been identified, namely: subsistence, protection, affection, understanding, participation, leisure/idleness, identity, self-esteem, and freedom: M. MAX NEEF ET AL., HUMAN SCALE DEVELOPMENT: AN OPTION FOR THE FUTURE, DEVELOPMENT DIALOGUE. (CEPAUR Dag Hammarskjold Foundation, 1989, Eng. ed. 1992).

126. *See generally* W. LEISS, THE DOMINATION OF NATURE 125–146 (1994) for a discussion of this model.

127. SHIVA & MIES, *supra* note 1, at 297–322. *See also* KABEER, *supra* note 12, at 80–96.

128. *See* JONI SEAGER, EARTH FOLLIES 282 (1993); KABEER, *supra* note 12, at 84.

129. SHIVA & MIES, *supra* note 1, at 319–322.

130. *Id*.

In conjunction with this new valuation system, the dichotomy between work and home should be removed. Once this distinction is eliminated, and the status of non-market roles is increased, it may very well be that there will be an increase in the proportion of men involved in these roles. If men participate in the subsistence survival of developing country populations, the burden of increased workloads would fall less on women. Mies recommends that both men and women be involved in subsistence.[131] Patriarchal notions that separate women's work from men's work must be attacked and replaced with the valuation, outside the neo-classical monetarist markets, of *all* types of work. Notions of reductionist white, Western patriarchy, and in particular notions of gender roles, must be changed to achieve these goals.

Redefining Developing Country Development

Developing countries have many pre-existing problems, including indebted industrialization, agricultural maldevelopment, political unrest, and excessive government expenditures.[132] Indeed, although these areas of expenditure must be examined to ensure that the funds are being put to the best and most appropriate use, cutbacks in this area must be viewed with caution. This is because, as noted previously, when these expenditures are cut, it is usually the lives of poor women that deteriorate as a result. Therefore, although frugality may be necessary, the spending that does take place must be targeted towards programs that actually assist poor women.

Rather than cutting social programs, governments should choose to cut spending in other areas, and in particular, in the area of armaments and the military.[133] Many developing countries spend a good deal of their budgets on military expenditures.[134] Indeed:

> In India, a country with over one-third of its population living below the poverty line, the government spends 14 percent of its revenue on defence; in Saudia Arabia, military spending, as a percent of GNP jumped from 5 percent in 1960 to 22 percent by the late 1980s; in the Sudan . . . military spending increased by a factor of four.[135]

These expenditures do not directly assist the poor;[136] the segments of society that seem to benefit the most from these expenditures are the companies making profits off

---

131. *Id.* Mies suggests that one of the reasons men will not become involved in roles other than income earning is because these other roles have no status or social recognition attached to them. She hypothesizes that increased recognition would increase the number of men involved in these activities.

132. KORNER ET AL., *supra* note 4, at 36–45.

133. DAVID, *supra* note 18, at 121 ("The conditions under which governments can effectively cut subsidies are not well known and need to be further researched.").

134. Stewart, *supra* note 39, at 45 ("Expenditure on defence and internal security has increasingly become one of the most important expenditures in the recurrent government budget in developing countries. Yet stabilization programs do not pay much attention to this form of expenditure.")

135. RUTH LEGER SIVARD, WORLD MILITARY AND SOCIAL EXPENDITURES 20–45 (Washington: World Priorities Institute, 1991).

136. *See* Stewart, *supra* note 39, at 39–44 for further statistics on increasing military expenditures.

armaments sales, and perhaps public officials.[137] This spending is justified by the authorities as protecting a developing country's sovereignty. However, this justification begs the question as to who exactly is going to want to take over a country whose people are starving and whose environment is destroyed. Priorities of spending have to be moved away from expenditures like these, and instead put towards measures designed to assist the poor who are literally perishing from the lack of fulfilment of basic needs. It is difficult to imagine that any person or group of people would prefer "one more helicopter" over saving the lives of many. This, unfortunately, is today's reality.

Another hypothesized reason for the debt crisis is the increase in developing country population levels, which causes overuse of the natural resources.[138] Procreation is one method to ensure the survival of the family unit, because more family unit members means a greater labor force to provide for basic needs. If notions of development, and social programs were targeted towards the achievement of a subsistence lifestyle and women's needs in particular were addressed, it is possible that the need for high fertility may decrease.[139] This relationship between levels of procreation, education, social spending and levels of poverty warrants further consideration.[140]

Once these recommendations are instituted, it is likely that there will be less poverty among the populations of developing countries. When populations feel more secure, they will also be less inclined to have political insurgence events,[141] and if governments are more stable, they will be more able to make difficult expenditure decisions without repercussions and will more likely have a commitment to any programs that are undertaken.[142] Thus, the above recommendations will achieve the lessening of general violence and upheaval in developing countries, which will greatly contribute to the improved lifestyles of women in those countries.

Although the implementation of a subsistence perspective for development is desirable, there are many problems with its implementation.[143] Primarily, there are many individuals, businesses and governments that base their operations on white, Western patriarchal values and profit from these epistemologies. Clearly, without some significant advantage arising from this changed perspective, these entities will not be willing to readily give up the benefits that they currently enjoy. The power of

---

137. It must be noted that there is increased employment that arises as a result of military expenditures. However, these funds could be re-directed to other employment generating activities.

138. KORNER ET AL., *supra* note 4, at 125–129.

139. BUVINIC & YUDELMAN, *supra* note 1, at 36.

140. KENNEDY, *supra* note 33, at 342, provides statistics relating adult female literacy rates to total fertility rates, as well as the average number of children by mother's years of education. Generally, the more literate and more educated women are, the fewer children they have. See Tables 13 and 14, at 342, for the specific statistics.

141. Edwards & Santaella, *supra* note 31, at 445.

142. Stewart, *supra* note 39, at 37.

143. For a description of other implementation problems, *see* Dell, *supra* note 41, at 58–60.

those who have interests in keeping the *status quo* is significant. In contemporary society, those entities that have money can have their interests represented and also have the ability to make their own opinions heard. Poor women in developing countries will not have the time or the resources available to voice their own opinions to the proper authorities.[144] It will be thus challenging to gain acceptance of the subsistence model from those who currently enjoy power and wealth arising from the neo-classical model of development.

The adoption of the subsistence standard would also require analyzation of whether others should be allowed to consume excessively, as is the case in some parts of the affluent West.[145] It is questionable whether "the affluent" would be willing to give up their current, excessive lifestyles in order to ensure the survival of the global poor. But this reduction of excess must be strived for, if the lives of the poor are to be improved. The environment cannot possibly sustain the consumption of the world's populations at the levels of consumption of the affluent societies.[146] Compromises and reductions must be made, or the destruction of the ecosystem and its peoples will be virtually assured.[147]

It is apparent, then, that any changes in this perception and use of development will have to be accomplished in the long term, since current development notions are firmly entrenched internationally. From a practical point of view, these changes will not be made rapidly, but instead will be the result of many studies, many statistics, and the uprising of the poor and disenfranchised, and their advocates. Eventually, however, this subsistence notion of development must be adopted to ensure the changes required for the improvement of women's lives. Fortunately, progress on this front is being made:

> There appears to be a growing recognition in international policy circles that both economic growth and poverty alleviation are better served by governed rather than untrammelled market forces. While the arguments which have roused greatest interest predictably relate to the need for "market friendly" interventions for greater economic growth, there is also an increased interest in a "human development", which combines labour-intensive growth strategies to generate employment opportunities for the poor with public provision of key welfare resources. While this offers a more hospitable environment for a "reversed" agenda than a neo-liberal driven one, we need to continue to argue for policies that go beyond "market-friendly" interventions to

---

144. The authorities, have the power to change development to coincide with the subsistence perspective. It may also be that these authorities, themselves, have vested interests in maintaining the status quo. BUVINIC & YUDELMAN, *supra* note 1, at 42.

145. This is not to imply that the West is not fraught with the problems of poverty.

146. VANDANA SHIVA, THE VIOLENCE OF THE GREEN REVOLUTION, THIRD WORLD AGRICULTURE, ECOLOGY AND POLITICS 24 (1991). ("Ghandi suggests that if these consumption levels were to occur world-wide, the earth would be stripped bare as if by locusts.")

147. Due to the limited nature of this chapter, an analysis of affluent society's consumption patterns on the ecosystem will not be undertaken here. For more discussion on this issue, see generally LEISS, *supra* note 126, Chapter Two; BARTELMUS, *supra* note 9; and BILL DEVALL & GEORGE SESSIONS, DEEP ECOLOGY, LIVING AS IF NATURE MATTERED (Gibbs Smith, 1985).

policy approaches which are designed to equalize access to market opportunities as well as to welfare provision.[148]

The use of the subsistence development theory would not only lead to an improved lifestyle for women, but would also lead to more satisfying and less superficial lives for all peoples. Subsistence lifestyles must be achieved because the current notions of development are not equipped to handle the problems facing developing countries, their natural environments, and women:

> The growth of the market cannot solve the very crisis it creates. Further while natural resources can be converted into cash, cash cannot be converted into nature's ecological processes. . . . [I]n nature's economy, the currency is not money, it is life. . . . The business groups encouraging cash cropping can opt out when the productivity of newly opened lands declines. They have no compulsion towards the ecological rehabilitation of the ravaged land. They command the resource base by making decisions that transcend their basis in legal ownership, but do not have to bear the ecological costs of the destruction of soil and water systems.[149]

Change must be made in both the contemporary notions of development and the government practices, ideologies, and procedures that have caused development to turn from an ideology of economic growth into the development disaster that is now becoming apparent. In the shorter term, however, specific changes to the IMF will also assist in achieving the goal of a better life for developing country women.

Redefining the IMF

The next focus of change should be modifications to the design, policies and procedures of the IMF. One of the first changes that must be addressed is the sharing of the burden of adjustment by *all* members of the IMF, not just the developing countries. In identifying the recommendation to share adjustment, it must be remembered that balance-of-payments difficulties frequently are not the "fault" of the borrowing developing countries. Often, poor balance-of-payment levels occur as a result of the deterioration of commodity prices for developing country exports, as well as increased costs of imports, including imports for production.[150] The developed countries, which typically profit from these decreased commodity costs and increased payments for their exports to developing countries usually absorb the extra profits or value, and do not suggest that they, themselves, should contribute their resources to those developing countries from which they glean their profits.

Instead, the developed countries and their commercial bankers temporarily lend back the profits and expect a rate of interest to be paid on those profits. This should not be allowed to continue in such a wholesale fashion. Stewart recognizes this need for change and recommends that there be an imposed *symmetry of adjustment*, whereby the current burden of policy change and adjustment be shared among all

---

148. KABEER, *supra* note 12, at 84–85.

149. SHIVA & MIES, *supra* note 1, at 342.

150. There are also external economic considerations that add to balance-of-payments problems. *See* LOMBARDI, *supra* note 7, at 220–41.

countries, not just the developing countries. She suggests that the surplus countries should expand their domestic absorption, which would reduce deficits without such extreme policy changes for developing countries. She also recommends support for commodity prices through commodity price agreements, which would have a floor price and be supported in supply by primary producers. These features, Stewart anticipates, would stimulate the global economy, and cause the imbalances in exports and imports for developing countries to stabilize at an acceptable level.[151]

However, if these features were not effective, a distribution scheme that would force more affluent countries to contribute a fair share of their monetary surpluses to the less financially fortunate countries would be indicated. Clearly, in order to have such a distribution system function, affluent countries would have to give the needs of developing countries more importance. This can be partially achieved by increasing the influence that the developing countries have in the IMF, as discussed below.

Developing country needs could be made more apparent by changing the allocation of votes given to the developing countries in the IMF. There are two theoretical methods to modify the voting structures of the IMF. First, changes can be made in the quantum of basic votes given to each member. Developing countries could simply be given more votes. Alternatively, changes could be made in the criteria used for the allocation of quotas. Votes could be allocated for both contributions and drawings from the IMF. It is unlikely, however, that these alternatives would be acceptable to the developed, contributing countries of the IMF.

Since it is not likely that the developing countries will be in a position to *lend* the IMF resources, the voting structure itself and the ideologies of what constitutes worth in relation to quotas must be re-evaluated, so that not only the developing countries bear the burden of adjustment. The status of developing countries compared to industrialized nations can be analogized to the position of women as compared to men. Developing countries and women both have no real relative power and are governed generally by the will of others. Alternatively, they are left alone, with no assistance for their needs except for welfare or aid provisions, which are generally ineffective.[152] Therefore, an alternative to the current voting allocation could consider not only giving votes for contribution of resources, but also giving votes for the *use* of resources. This solution would require the virtual reconstitution of the IMF's Articles of Agreement, to which, doubtless, the developed countries would probably not readily agree. Instead, the developing countries must, as recommended by Ferguson, consolidate their voting power to form a common front by which to assure that their opinions are heard.[153] These changes will stop the "feminine pauperization" of both women and developing countries.

---

151. Stewart, *supra* note 39, at 37.

152. SHIVA, STAYING ALIVE, *supra* note 44, at 24–32.

153. FERGUSON, *supra* note 22, at 227.

However, this solution assumes that there is only one opinion that is shared by all developing countries. This is clearly not the case.[154] In the category of developing countries, there are many levels of poverty, as well as many different political and social philosophies which underlie the individual countries and the decisions that are made within them. The needs of women may not specifically be addressed. Therefore, finding a united front may be more difficult than it appears at first glance. However, the developing countries must be prepared to put away all but their most fundamental objections if they hope to have power within the ambit of the IMF.

Essential to any policy changes within the current IMF structure itself is the change of IMF economic models away from the current neo-classical monetarist model with its insistent focus on profits and net financial gains and indicators. Many authors recommend that the IMF change its neo-classical monetarist assumptions to premises that recognize the interconnectedness of the world economies,[155] because, as pointed out by Havnevik, neo-classical monetarism is simply unproven and incorrect.[156] Sachs suggests that because the IMF uses rudimentary methods in setting performance criterion, and errors are made, these methods must be changed.[157]

The targets that the IMF uses for adjustment must also be modified, since they are based on these neo-classical monetarist model assumptions. Instead of specific targets, ranges of acceptability, or ceilings of expenditures could be used.[158] Further,

> an additional way to provide a little more flexibility would be to distinguish between ceilings and targets. . . . [It] would be better if it were agreed that the projections would provide targets and that the sanctions associated with performance criteria would come into play only if the targets were exceeded by such a wide margin as to breach a ceiling set a specified distance from the target.[159]

The current adjustment programs and their results have been rather dismal failures. Thus, change must include targets and programs flexible enough to account for the many country variations. As suggested by Dell, stabilization programs should indicate objectives and directions for the economy but should avoid standard formulas and pinpoint targetry.[160]

Related to the modification of targets is the recommendation that the IMF tailor its packages more closely to the drawing member's needs. IMF programs may be criticized on the grounds that they appear to be standard in nature, with the same

---

154. DAVID, *supra* note 18, at 117.

155. *Id.* at 116; STILES, *supra* note 23, at 142; K. Havenik, *Classical Concepts of Monetarism, or How to Fail at Adjustment, in* THE IMF AND THE WORLD BANK IN AFRICA, CONDITIONALITY, IMPACT AND ALTERNATIVES (Seminar Proceedings No. 18, 14, at 20) (K. Havenik ed., Uppsala: Scandinavian Institute of African Studies, 1987).

156. *Id.* at 21.

157. Sachs, *supra* note 32, at 116.

158. *See* DAVID, *supra* note 18, at 118.

159. *Id.*

160. Dell, *supra* note 41, at 194.

types of requirements applied, irrespective of the actual conditions of the individual developing countries. If IMF conditionality included heightened consideration of the unique positions of each drawing member, it would lead to "less draconian, more gradual adjustment programmes for poorer developing countries."[161] One can certainly identify immense differences between individual countries in areas such as culture, environment, education, poverty levels, water availability, transportation infrastructure, and an infinite number of other variables. A common application of conditionality requirements is not the appropriate answer for all drawing members. However, according to the actual documents that have been made available from various sources, this standardized application is generally what has occurred.[162] Clearly, this type of one solution answer to diverse problems is not the most effective manner in which to ensure financial stability of developing countries.

Unfortunately, it is difficult to determine exactly what policies and requirements the IMF considers, since the IMF has immunity from disclosure for all inquiries.[163] This should be rectified. The IMF effectively holds a country's economic destiny in its hands, and yet these countries are not allowed to ascertain the exact policies, procedures, and requirements of the IMF. To alleviate this problem, all documents, except the most highly confidential, should be available to the public.

Timing is another change that must be made in the application of conditionality programs. Currently, there are no programs in the IMF that allow for adjustment over a longer time frame. Stewart and Cooper recommend a more gradual timing of adjustment.[164] If a longer time frame for adjustment was allowed, cuts in employment, social programs, food subsidies, and other poverty alleviating programs could take place in a manner that would not immediately jettison the burden of conditionality on the poor. Their lives would not be changed so rapidly and in such a significantly negative fashion.

Another solution to alleviate short-term funding concerns for developing countries is the establishment of a low conditionality, easily accessible resource fund[165] to address the needs of drawing members facing balance-of-payments difficulties.[166] The IMF does, technically, have such resources available in the Compensatory Financing Facility (CFF). Although the CFF helped shield weaker members from international market fluctuations, after September 1983, the CFF was no longer widely

---

161. *See* T. KILLICK, THE IMF AND STABILIZATION: DEVELOPING COUNTRY EXPERIENCES 284–298 (1984).

162. Again, the IMF does not typically let the outside world see its documents, and has immunity from such disclosure. *See* BUDHOO, *supra* note 35.

163. BUDHOO, *supra* note 35, at 84–87.

164. Stewart, *supra* note 39, at 41; Richard N. Cooper, as found in Sachs, *supra* note 32, at 117.

165. Easily accessible does not mean without any conditionality. If, in fact, requesting governments have shown no fiscal responsibility, more difficult access to these funds would probably be warranted. However, especially in cases where the fiscal imbalance is beyond the requesting member's control, low conditionality funds should be available.

166. This recommendation was put forward by Dell, *supra* note 41, at 255–73.

used, due to lack of financial support from the developed countries[167] and the inability of developing countries to meet the terms of acceptance into the programs.[168] The effective removal of this low conditionality financing made financing availability without intrusion on domestic polices even more difficult to achieve. The lack of availability of low conditionality resources must be remedied.[169] The reinstatement of the original form of the CFF, or a similar financing facility, is a short-term solution to the financing problems of some developing countries.[170]

Related to low conditionality financing is the recommendation that quotas, which are the amount of drawings available to a needy member, should be increased. In particular, quotas need to be large enough to enable the IMF to fulfill its traditional role as the major source of temporary balance of payments finance to those countries that have not achieved significant access to the international capital market, preferably by the extension of low-conditionality financing where balance-of-payments problems arise because of external factors.[171] If the IMF does not make resources reasonably available to lend to its drawing members, the conditions of the poor will worsen. Quotas, coupled with low conditionality facilities, such as the CFF, will protect the social programs which, if cut, will cause a significant deterioration of the quality of life of the poor. Since women are the most affected by expenditure cuts, as previously noted, these changes could provide them with a higher quality of life.

Poor women should also be protected by other measures in IMF policies and procedures. Stewart recommends that the IMF policies should concern themselves with restructuring social sector spending in a balance which will facilitate both subsistence survival and economic growth.[172] In doing so, some compensatory policies should be used to protect basic needs, including health and nutrition, particularly for women, who are typically the most disenfranchised in these areas. After implementation of such ideas, the results of these changes should be monitored to include economic growth, as well as subsistence survival rates.[173]

Cornia *et al.* suggest that the distributional inequities necessitated by the use of development principles also be modified. These authors suggest that more expansive polices with sustainable levels of output, investment, and fulfilment of human needs be used in a more gradual period of adjustment. In addition, the authors recognize that specific policies must be instituted for the poor, including modified policies of taxation, government expenditure, aid, credit, foreign exchange, and

---

167. *Id.* at 250–56 and 261.

168. Notably, if balance-of-payments difficulties are not short-term in nature, CFF funding will not be possible: DAM, *supra* note 17, at 214.

169. Dell, *supra* note 41, at 194.

170. *Id.* at 255–63.

171. *See* FERGUSON, *supra* note 22, at 225–30 and DAVID, *supra* note 18, at 114–20.

172. Stewart, *supra* note 39, at 42.

173. Killick also recommends that the IMF review its policies to take into account their distributional impact on the poor. KILLICK, *supra* note 161, at 284–98.

asset distribution.[174] These policies will achieve the "prioritizing, selectivity, redistribution, and restructuring"[175] necessary for the subsistence survival of the poor. Cornia *et al.* term this "adjustment with a human face."[176]

Further, Budhoo recommends that there be *internal* checks and balances on the IMF. He recommends that a fully independent IMF council with broad decision-making powers and more extensive geographic representation be instituted. Next, he envisions *external* checks and balances on the IMF, with the establishment of an advisory and review commission to evaluate IMF and World Bank activities. This commission would act as a final court of appeal on three subjects: IMF or World Bank disputes, charges by members of institutional bias or inconsistencies, and issues of non-compliance of members brought to it by the IMF. This committee would also review major policy decisions of the IMF and World Bank. It would be comprised of a wide range of professional disciplines, with a majority of members from developing countries.[177]

In addition, there should be regional coordinating committees to examine national economic performance from the perspective of the drawing country's own system of priorities of development, which would review any subjective value judgements underlying the incidents of conditionality and would have grievance procedures for problems. The members would be elected by IMF and World Bank Governors. A watchdog committee must be established by the developing countries to oversee the activities of the IMF. All IMF activities and policies must be monitored, particularly in terms of their effects on the poor. The implementation of these monitoring bodies would likely ensure more equity amongst IMF members.

A final recommendation for IMF change consists of measures to ensure its cooperation with the World Bank, the commercial banks, and other national and international entities. Stewart recommends that developing country governments be given alternative, combined methods of adjustment by the IMF and the World Bank together, as well as technical assistance, collective discussions among recipient governments, and the establishment of independent commissions to develop adjustment programs.[178]

If the World Bank and the IMF were to cooperate, it is likely that a more comprehensive package of subsistence development could be devised. In this new subsistence cooperation, according to Brainard and Shelto-Colby, commercial banks would agree to maintain and increase financing, the World Bank would coordinate medium term growth, and the IMF would provide input on balance-of-payments and

---

174. G. Cornia, R. Jolly, & F. Stewart, *An Overview of An Alternative Approach, in* ADJUSTMENT WITH A HUMAN FACE, *supra* note 37, at 131–35 [hereinafter *Overview*].

175. *Id.* at 134.

176. *Id.* at 134–35.

177. BUDHOO, *supra* note 35, at 84–87.

178. Stewart, *supra* note 39, at 43.

exchange policies.[179] The drawing countries themselves would have to agree to maintain open markets with increased export credits and direct bilateral aid and to provide financing and rescheduling of previous debts. Developing countries would also have to agree to structural changes for their medium term financial commitments. This recommendation would ensure economic coordination between these bodies, which would lead to better and more efficient distribution and use of resources for the purpose of subsistence development.

It has also been suggested that the establishment of a World Central Bank would in the long term solve many problems that exist in the IMF:

> One possible solution to the problems of international cooperation would be to develop *supranational institutions*. But the evolution of cooperation among banking supervisors has not yet reached the supranational plane, even in the European Community; surprisingly, even the European Central Bank has been given only limited regulatory powers by its framers. Supranational cooperation would require that supervisors hand over their responsibilities to a global agency, which makes some intuitive sense in a world of global finance. Given that states still wish to maintain some control over their domestic financial firms in order to pursue national interest, however, supranational solutions lose their attraction.[180]

The problem with implementing such an institution is the required level of political unity that would be necessary to initiate it.[181] Thus, at least in the short term, this alternative is not wholly feasible.[182] Perhaps a less intrusive alternative, such as the strengthening of IMF ties with the World Bank, the World Trade Organization, and GATT, would be a more realistic approach:

> The Fund's ties with the GATT should be strengthened as should its activities to help assure that the rising tide of protectionism does not lead to intensification of trade restrictions by industrial countries. . . . [O]therwise the world can slip back to widespread use of restrictions on international trade and inevitably to widespread bilateralism. . . . In addition, the Fund may find it increasingly necessary to play an active role in cases of pure protectionism, i.e. protection of domestic industry and employment not related to balance-of-payments reasons.[183]

The goals of subsistence development could be reached, to a certain extent, with the strengthening of these interactions. A World Central Bank, however, would be much more effective at coordinating political, social, and economic forces and would lead

---

179. Lawrence J. Brainard & Sally Shelto-Colby, *Prospects for Cooperation between Commercial Banks and Multilateral Financial Institutions: The Future of the Baker Plan, in* THE POLITICAL MORALITY OF THE INTERNATIONAL MONETARY FUND 65, 74 (R. Myers ed., 1987).

180. ETHAN B. KAPSTEIN, GOVERNING THE GLOBAL ECONOMY: INTERNATIONAL FINANCE AND THE STATE 14 (1994).

181. Dell, *supra* note 41, at 94.

182. For a description of the possibilities of a world economic and political institution, see HAL LINSEY, THE COMING NEW WORLD ORDER 35–76 (1993).

183. Irving S. Friedman, *The International Monetary Fund: A Founder's Evaluation, in* THE POLITICAL MORALITY OF THE INTERNATIONAL MONETARY FUND 27 (R. Myers ed., 1987).

to a holistic approach to development. As a future possibility, this option does have some appeal.[184]

These suggestions and recommendations can be used, in part or in whole, to allow for less deterioration in the financial position of developing countries. This, in turn, may alleviate the disenfranchisement of the poor, and in particular, poor women. However, there is a strong probability that women's disparate poverty will not be completely resolved by the modifications of merely one institution. Therefore, the problems facing women in developing countries must be specifically addressed with separate solutions.

REDEFINING WOMEN'S LIVES IN DEVELOPING COUNTRIES

Developing country women's issues may be handled in a variety of ways. In the past it had been assumed that benefits would "trickle down" to women, but this has proved largely inaccurate,[185] so there is a need to address women's issues specifically.

The underlying developmental gender biases against women that result in the overall devaluation of women and girls and their contributions must be rectified. Scholarship, educational campaigns, activism, and other measures may be used to increase the awareness of governments and institutions regarding the status of women. Governments should introduce gender training for both themselves and the development institutions with which they interact. This training would educate both the men and women about the existence of gender bias against women, identify where the bias occurs, and promote a strategy to alleviate these problems. Gender training would also have to include numerical data regarding the status of women as household heads and specifically provide reliable statistics showing the numbers of households headed by women, their average incomes, their average expenditures for basic needs, and the shortfalls in income that they have.[186] Once the problem of bias is adequately recognized, more action can be taken to lessen it.

Women and girl-children must also become empowered through education, employment, and political participation.[187] Deeply entrenched gender biases will not automatically disappear because of women's education and empowerment, but redressing the power imbalances will help give women a voice that is recognized by the institutions that hold them captive in poverty.[188] Organization and empowerment must

---

184. There are other options to assist the developing countries in their search for financial stability, including increased aid, changed development bank policies and practices, commercial bank modifications, and so on. LOMBARDI, *supra* note 7, at 183–85.

185. KABEER, *supra* note 12, at 118.

186. As recommended by KABEER, *id.* at 239, 264.

187. *See* SHIVA, ECOLOGY & POLITICS OF SURVIVAL, *supra* note 8, at 28–45.

188. Further changes in education could also be made: Increase the share of females in primary education, change the times of the school year to account for employment and obtain resources for the education of women from abroad. *See, e.g.* Richard Jolly, *Education, in* ADJUSTMENT WITH A HUMAN FACE, *supra* note 37, at 238–39.

occur at all levels, in particular at a grassroots level, and women must continue to struggle to help themselves and others.[189]

With respect to employment, improvements for women could be achieved using several methods. First, legislation mandating minimum wages and types of working conditions should be either put into place or strengthened, with high penalties payable by those who disregard these regulations. This recommendation would hopefully prevent the below-minimum-wage, dangerous working conditions jobs that many developing country women are forced to endure. Of course, the disadvantage of this recommendation is that employers could simply refuse either to open businesses in those developing countries with stringent legislation or substitute adult labor with child labor.[190] However, if this recommendation is implemented on an international scale, there would be no alternative but to comply with the legislation. Only the strongest of central legislative authorities would be able to enforce such requirements. This authority does not currently exist. However, in the context of already available institutions, unions or some alternative form of labor organization could provide the collective strength for poor women to demand better conditions of work. However, such processes are resource and time consuming, both of which are scarce commodities for the poor. In addition, the organization of workers is likely to be strenuously opposed by employers and may be accompanied by threats of automation, layoffs, or worse.[191]

Second, a child care system, whether it be government or community based would allow women more time to pursue employment and educational opportunites. Community-based child care is already available in some communities,[192] and it should be extended to other geographic regions. Again, this organization must come primarily from within communities, and women must be the ones to implement such plans. This change would clearly decrease the onerous time constraints that child rearing requires.

Third, women should be paid for their work in cash if they cannot (for instance, because of discriminatory familial, social, or legal restriction) open bank accounts or sign their own names on employers' checks.[193] Jolly cites examples of institutions that can help the poor, such as the Grameen Bank in Bangladesh.[194] This bank had simple operations, and went from community to community in order to allow the poor women to open bank accounts, thus increasing greatly women's accessibility to money. There are other groups, such as the self-employed women's association in India, or

---

189. If women wait for the so-called developed nations to improve their lives, the wait may be long indeed. *See* M. DALY, GYN/ECOLOGY: THE METAETHICS OF RADICAL FEMINISM 26 (1980).

190. This is already common practice. *See* Frances Stewart, *Supporting Productive Employment Among Vulnerable Groups, in* ADJUSTMENT WITH A HUMAN FACE, *supra* note 37, at 214.

191. *See* KENNEDY, *supra* note 33, at 47–65, 88.

192. BUVINIC & YUDELMAN, *supra* note 1, at 32.

193. Stewart, *supra* note 39, at 217.

194. *Id.* at 216–21.

the Banco Popular in Costa Rica, which also have increased access to money for women as their goal.[195] Women should especially be allowed to control the monies arising from their work outside the home, as this leads to greater survival rates for members of the family unit. Moreover, if women were to receive not only their own incomes, but also the incomes of their male counterparts, the fulfilment of all the members of the family unit's basic needs would be more likely met.[196]

An increase in women's control over income would likely lead to other improvements in the lives of women. Women would possibly become entitled to more food, since they would have increased economic status in the family.[197] Further, the health of the family would probably improve, because there would be more money available for this basic needs fulfilment.[198]

Fourth, there also should be some requirement or at least incentive for men to play a greater role in child rearing.[199] Further, as Bould suggests,[200] child support and family unit support should be required as a percentage of the male's income.

Fifth, the lives of all members of the family unit would be greatly improved by changes to the land use systems and land distribution systems of developing countries. Women's lives deteriorate significantly when they no longer have access to land, which supplements the deficiencies in basic necessities that they face.[201] Although it would be difficult to achieve a redistribution of these lands, once the notions of development are changed to consider subsistence as an acceptable alternative, it is possible that land use patterns can also be changed.[202] If agricultural emphasis is placed on subsistence, rather than production for export, women in developing countries would have fewer demands on their time. This change would give the women more time to pursue education, business, or any number of other alternatives. Alternatively, it would relieve them of the constant pressure to search for resources to fulfill their basic needs. Increased natural resource availability through land use changes would thus improve the living conditions of developing country women.

---

195. *Id.* at 214–16.

196. *See* Maria Mies, *Women Have No Fatherland, in* ECOFEMINISM 116, 117–18 (Vandana Shiva & Maria Mies eds., 1993) for a discussion of males having a greater tendency to spend their incomes on luxury items.

197. According to BUVINIC & YUDELMAN, *supra* note 1, at 124.

198. Richard Jolly, *Education, in* ADJUSTMENT WITH A HUMAN FACE, *supra* note 37, at 224.

199. Legislation has not been successful even in developed countries, as there are often males who prefer to go bankrupt, or otherwise hide their incomes, so as not to pay support. In order for this scheme to be successful, the punishment for non-compliance must be both socially and economically severe. KABEER, *supra* note 12, at 231.

200. Bould, *supra* note 68, at 67.

201. Not only must women spend more time, but also young females must help their mothers in their basic need gathering tasks. As pointed out by Buvinic, it is the girls who are forced to take more responsibilities when either the mother has to work or has to spend more time in subsistence provision. *See* BUVINIC & YUDELMAN, *supra* note 1, at 33.

202. Land use changes have been described by SHIVA, ECOLOGY & POLITICS OF SURVIVAL, *supra* note 8, at 186–95.

Sixth, Cornia also suggests improving and supporting self-help practices at the household level, especially those promoting health, food provision, and child care.[203] Nutritional programs could include food-for-work programs, subsidized employment programs, programs to expand at-home production, increasing production on small farms, food stamp programs, social and poverty relief programs, unemployment compensation, on-site feeding, take-home food schemes, and nutritional rehabilitation centers.[204] Work cooperatives, whereby women work as a collective group to produce a certain result, are another alternative.[205]

Other types of social programs currently available must also be reformed to specifically target women or, at a minimum, ensure that women are not disenfranchised by the programs. Such social programs would consist of welfare-type programs as well as self-help programs. Welfare-type programs, although somewhat helpful in the short term, for certain recipients, tend to degrade women to the status of "takers from the economy," since they are not considered to be producing in the capitalist sense. Gender bias had traditionally limited women's access to self-help programs. Women must play a larger role in establishing community self-help programs, which enable them to pool their resources and energies for the achievement of basic needs fulfilment.[206] In addition, through scholarship and legislative articulations of women's human rights, development agencies may eventually deconstruct and redress their own biases against women.

One of the most crucial elements in changing the lives of developing country women is the removal of the gender biases that underlie the disparate pauperization of women. These biases characterize women as "dependant" and undervalue the non-market work that they produce. Once recognition of the inappropriateness of these characterizations is achieved, the attainment of the other suggested changes will be facilitated. Nonetheless, a number of external factors will hinder the realization of these recommendations.[207] Those in a more fortunate educational and economic position must voice the opinions of disenfranchised developing country women. If the message is repetitive and persistent, it is possible that these institutions and governments could change their policies to allow for the "positive" discrimination that is required for the promotion of the needs of developing country women. It is the duty

---

203. G. Cornia, *Social Policymaking: Restructuring, Targeting Efficiency, in* ADJUSTMENT WITH A HUMAN FACE, *supra* note 37, at 174–80.

204. Jolly, *supra* note 198, at 244–45.

205. Cornia & Stewart, *Country Experience, supra* note 90, at 174–89.

206. The Grameen Bank in India, for example, teaches women how to sign their names, open bank accounts, and be responsible for their own finances. Another example of the ability of women to organize themselves for the benefit of all can be found in Housing book. In this example, women pooled their resources to purchase a van, in order to buy supplies in bulk, which, of course, was less expensive than individual purchases. This sort of initiative is exactly the type of self-help programs that women must develop for themselves, in order to rid themselves of the yoke that patriarchal capitalism has imposed upon them. *See* KABEER, *supra* note 12, at 298–303.

207. Such as lack of resources, lack of receptiveness of governments, difficulties in organizing, and presenting a consensus decision.

of female scholars and women of influence to pursue this goal of bettering the lives of women in developing countries.

CONCLUSION

Women continue to occupy a marginalized place in development thought and policy. As noted by the United Nations' World Survey on the Role of Women in Development:

> Ironically, poverty among women has increased, even within the richest countries, resulting in a "feminization of poverty". Poverty particularly afflicted families in which women are the sole income earners, a growing phenomenon. . . . [I]increases in maternal and infant mortality in some developing countries have been observed for the first time in decades as social services have been cut as part of adjustment packages. . . . Women have been at the epicentre of the crisis and have borne the brunt of the adjustment efforts. They have been the most affected by the deteriorating balance between incomes and prices, by the cuts in social services, and by the rising morbidity and child deaths. It is women who have had to find the means for families to survive. To achieve this they have had to work longer and harder.[208]

In this chapter, the IMF was used as an example of a contemporary institution applying contemporary development principles in its interactions with developing countries. Not only does the empirical evidence show that improvements in the numerical indices of development were not likely to occur as a result of this application, but also, it was shown that economic and social disturbances were likely to result. It was also demonstrated that these applications disproportionately affect women in developing countries; their lives deteriorate as a direct and indirect result of IMF programs.

Short- to medium-term changes were recommended, and involved restructuring and changing the IMF specifically. These modifications would alleviate some of the IMF-specific poverty that developing country women disproportionately face. Further, as a medium- to long-term goal, it was recommended that the general contemporary status of women be improved by the modification of contemporary notions of development. It is hypothesized that the underlying biases against women can be removed through gender training of both society, and women, themselves. This would lead to the re-evaluation of women's work in society, and would directly reduce the negative effects of development on women.

Although neither women nor men should be subjected to the inappropriate development paradigms currently in place, it is the developing country women who are disparately affected by these epistemologies. At a minimum, these women should be guaranteed equality to men. Further, because women have, in the past, been disparately pauperized by these notions, strong positive action to assist them should be taken. If such action is not pursued, developing country women, by default, will continue to be the "puppies" of the "litter" that are selected to be "drowned."[209] Change is imperative.

---

208. UNITED NATIONS, WORLD SURVEY ON THE ROLE OF WOMEN IN DEVELOPMENT 5 (United Nations, 1989b).

209. BUVINIC & YUDELMAN, *supra* note 1, at 15.

HISTORICAL PRECURSORS TO MODERN CAMPAIGNS FOR WOMEN'S HUMAN RIGHTS: CAMPAIGNS AGAINST FOOTBINDING AND FEMALE CIRCUMCISION

Kathryn Sikkink*

INTRODUCTION

Historical campaigns around women's rights enhance our understanding of modern networks by providing an historical backdrop to modern campaigns for women's rights and to violence against women. These cases provide an historical perspective to help us think about questions often asked about campaigns for women's human rights. In particular, modern campaigns for women's rights have often raised questions about cultural imperialism, including whether those efforts are inappropriate attempts to impose Western values and culture upon societies that neither desire nor will benefit from them. Furthermore, cultural defenses of traditional practices are particularly common around issues involving women's role in the family and society. In this context, it may be useful to explore historical campaigns that attempted to change strongly embedded cultural practices that today would be called violence against women, and ask under what conditions such campaigns succeeded in bringing about changes in policy and practices.

This chapter focuses on the 1874–1911 campaign by Western missionaries and Chinese reformers to eradicate footbinding in China, and the efforts by Western missionaries and British colonial authorities to end the practice of female circumcision among the Kikuyu of Kenya in 1920–1931. For each campaign, there are comparable "non-campaigns," or related issues around which activists did not organize. In the case of footbinding, related "non-campaigns" included the issues of female infanticide and concubinage in China. In Kenya, the absence of a campaign among other cultural groups that also practiced female circumcision (e.g., the Maasai) was a puzzle even to reformers at the time.

This study differs from other work on historical social movements in that it focuses explicitly and primarily on the transnational dimension of movement activity, exploring campaigns in which foreign linkages or actors were central to the organizing effort.[1] Modern research on networks suggests the importance of domestic

---

*   Adapted from chapter II of ACTIVISTS BEYOND BORDERS: ADVOCACY NETWORKS IN INTERNATIONAL POLITICS by Margaret Keck and Kathryn Sikkink, New York: Cornell University Press, 1998.

1.   *See, e.g.,* SIDNEY TARROW, POWER IN MOVEMENT: SOCIAL MOVEMENTS, COLLECTIVE ACTION, AND

political structures for explaining the success of transnational networks in influencing state policy.[2] These two historical precursors provide extreme variation of domestic structures of the target state: the footbinding campaign was carried on in the final years of Imperial China, and the female circumcision debate took place in a British colony. A domestic structures argument might lead us to expect that transnational campaigns initiated primarily by British citizens would be most effective in a British colony, and much less effective in a foreign and culturally distant empire. The measure of effectiveness in the two cases is exactly the reverse: in terms of outcomes, the footbinding campaign led to the most rapid change, while the campaign against female circumcision did not succeed in changing important attitudes or practices.

Many historical campaigns begin with an idea that is almost unimaginable, even to early proponents. When first proposed, for example, the ideas that slavery could be abolished, that women would vote, that footbinding would be a relic of the past, were dim and radical prospects. How the unimaginable became a possibility, and how that possibility was, in some cases, later seen as inevitable, is one of the main questions of this chapter. At the same time, the case of female circumcision reminds us that such changes are neither inevitable, obvious, nor linear, but the contingent result of contestations of meaning and resources waged by specific actors in an historical context that colors the interpretations and policies that emerge.

CAMPAIGNS AGAINST FOOTBINDING AND FEMALE CIRCUMCISION

Both female circumcision and footbinding represent early examples of practices we would now call violence against women, practices that resulted in bodily mutilation with long-lasting impact on the health and activity level of women. Both practices were ancient and deeply embedded culturally, involving highly ritualized rites of passage from girlhood to womanhood; indeed, these characteristics defined womanhood. Both were prerequisites for marriage.

Although the origins of female circumcision are not fully understood, there is evidence that it was practiced by the ancient Egyptians. Whatever the exact origins, female circumcision was not a custom connected to any particular religion, but was practiced by many cultural groups in Africa and parts of the Middle East, including

---

POLITICS (1994). Tarrow, in his historical survey of social movements, focuses mainly on national social movements, although he discusses the transnational diffusion of repertoires of collective action, and concludes with a section on the increasing transnationalization of modern social movements. *Id.* at 193–98. In a recent paper, Tarrow expresses some skepticism that the world is now entering an "unheralded age of global movements," and encourages "comparatively bold historical studies" of transnational movements. Sidney Tarrow, Fishnets, Internets, and Catnets: Globalization and Social Movements 22 (June 1995) (paper prepared for the Conference on Structure, Identity, and Power: The Past and Future of Collective Action, Amsterdam, June 2–4, 1995).

2.   Here, "domestic political structures" refers to political institutions, state-society relations, and the values and norms embedded in its political culture. Thomas Risse-Kappen, *Ideas Do Not Float Freely: Transnational Coalitions, Domestic Structures, and the End of the Cold War*, 48 INT'L ORG. 187 (1994).

Animists, Moslems, and Christians. Catholic missionaries who went to Abyssinia in the sixteenth century first tried to prohibit it among their converts. When they discovered that men rejected the Catholic converts when it came time to choose a wife, missionaries later condoned the practice so as not to undermine their efforts at conversion.[3]

Footbinding also has ancient roots. Although the Chinese had admired small feet since antiquity, there is little verifiable proof that women bound their feet before the tenth century.[4] The practice became more widespread during the Sung dynasty, and was widely practiced by all classes during the Ming (1368–1644) and Ch'ing (1644–1911) dynasties.[5] The origins of the practice are rooted in traditional folklore and aesthetic appeal. It has also been explained as a symbol of conspicuous leisure, and as a means to control women's movement, keep women at home, and protect chastity.[6] It was widely believed that women without bound feet would not find husbands.

The two distinct practices have some interesting similarities. Both were seen as protecting women's chastity, and necessary for marriageability. Both practices were socially mandated but never legally enforced or required, and the rituals were carried out by mothers and females on girl children. Both were widespread social practices affecting girls of diverse classes and backgrounds.[7] After concerted campaigns against both practices, footbinding was totally eradicated in China in the early twentieth century, while female circumcision continues to be practiced extensively throughout the world, particularly in parts of Africa, today.

The Campaign Against Footbinding in China

Although footbinding is analogous to the Western practice of corseting (binding the torso), to which it has been compared, the physical pain and toll it involved was much more extensive. Young girls, between four and eight years old, had their feet tightly wrapped to prevent growth. After years of intense pain, the toes were broken and flesh had fallen off to produce a narrow foot of three- to five-inches long.[8]

---

3.   Fran P. Hosken, The Hosken Report: Genital and Sexual Mutilation of Females 74, 76, 78 (4th ed. 1993).

4.   Howard Levy, The Lotus Lovers: The Complete History of the Curious Erotic Custom of Footbinding in China 38 (1992).

5.   Alison R. Drucker, *The Influence of Western Women on the Anti-Footbinding Movement 1840–1911,* 8:3 Historical Reflections 179 (1981).

6.   Levy, *supra* note 4, at 41, 44; Drucker, *supra* note 5, at 179.

7.   There is some debate about how widespread footbinding was among lower classes, and this differed from region to region, but observers of the time report footbinding as an almost universal practice in some regions, even among poor peasants. Isabela Bird, The Yangtze Valley and Beyond 346 (1900). One survey found that 99 percent of women born before 1890 in one region had bound feet. Sidney Gamble, *The Disappearance of Footbinding in Tinghsien,* Am. J. Soc. 181–83 (Sept. 1943).

8.   For a detailed description of the process, including illustrations and first-person testimony, see Levy, *supra* note 4, at 23–35.

In modern parlance, this would be called a human rights abuse—even most forms of modern torture do not leave physical effects as deforming and permanent as those of footbinding. Yet, narratives of women who experienced footbinding testify to the physical pain of the practice, the pride women felt in their small feet, and the central role of the ritual of footbinding in female life. Some historians dispute the standard verdict that footbinding was "a men's conspiracy to keep women crippled and submissive;" indeed, "[f]or all its erotic appeal to men, without the cooperation of women footbinding could not have been perpetuated."[9] Instead, they stress the functions that footbinding served in socialization, appropriation of female labor, defining nationhood and gender roles, and as a central event in domestic women's culture: "Footbinding prepared a girl physically and psychologically for her future role as wife and a dependent family member. . . . Through footbinding, the doctrine of separate spheres was engraved onto the bodies of female children."[10]

For all the functions that footbinding may have served, it was ended after a focused campaign against it, initially spearheaded by Western missionary women. For hundreds of years some Chinese intellectuals and dynastic leaders had spoken out against footbinding, but their positions had no impact on changing practice. Although footbinding was widespread in China, it varied by class, ethnic group, and region. Certain ethnic groups, such as the Manchu, Mongols, Tibetans, and the Hakka, did not practice footbinding; upper-class women were more likely than lower-class women to have their feet bound; and footbinding was less common in rural areas and in the rice-growing regions of China than it was elsewhere. Yet, in 1835, one writer noted that it prevailed throughout the empire, and estimated that five to eight out of every ten women had bound feet, depending on the locality.[11] Although footbinding was often seen as an urban and upper-class phenomenon, one of the few systematic surveys from a rural area about 125 miles south of Beijing showed that 99.2 percent of women in this region born before 1890 had bound their feet.[12]

The Manchu women had never bound their feet and, in the mid-1600s, the Manchu imperial court issued edicts to prohibit footbinding, but people evaded the edicts and the court was obliged to give tacit consent to the practice.[13] Resistance to the decrees may have been a way for the majority Han ethnic group to assert its identity in the face of Manchu conquest. It is interesting that the Manchu were able to force every man to change his hairstyle and wear the queue, and yet they were not able to affect the practice of footbinding.[14]

---

9.   DOROTHY KO, TEACHERS OF THE INNER CHAMBERS: WOMEN AND CULTURE IN SEVENTEENTH-CENTURY CHINA 148, 150 (1994). *See also* C. Fred Blake, *Foot-binding in Neo-Confucian China and the Appropriation of Female Labor*, 19 SIGNS: J. WOMEN & SOC'Y 78 (1994).

10.   KO, *supra* note 9, at 149.

11.   LEVY, *supra* note 4, at 52, 53.

12.   Gamble, *supra* note 7, at 181–83.

13.   Virginia Chui-tin Chau, The Anti-Footbinding Movement in China (1850–1912) 10 (1966) (unpublished M.A. thesis, Columbia University) (on file with author).

14.   The author is indebted to Ann Waltner for this observation.

A vigorous movement to abolish footbinding originated in the late 1800s among foreigners in China's treaty ports, later spreading among those Chinese who had been most exposed to Western ideas.[15] Later, and before it became truly widespread and effective, the campaign was embraced and taken over by Chinese intellectuals and politicians, until it culminated in the decree banning footbinding after the 1911 revolution.

The campaign against footbinding had its most active phase and greatest impact at the turn of the century, well before the May Fourth Movement of 1919–1920, often seen as a peak period of political, cultural, and social innovation, and before the formation of the Chinese Communist Party in 1921. After the turn of the century, progressive literature by and about women moved on to other issues.[16] In other words, changes in footbinding preceded rather than followed the main wave of reform. It appears that anti-footbinding organizations provided fora where "larger issues of female emancipation from psychological and intellectual confinement could be raised."[17]

The defeat of China in the Opium War in 1842 led to the opening of treaty ports to foreign nationals and to the influx of missionaries and Western ideas. Chinese intellectuals began to argue that China needed reforms to avoid further humiliating defeat. At first, intellectuals argued for technological innovations and modern weapons, which were introduced between 1860 and 1894. Following China's defeat by the Japanese in 1895, intellectuals began to focus on the need to make social, cultural, and political reforms as well.[18] A national reform movement emerged in the late 1890s and included the abolition of footbinding and the improvement of the status of women among its goals. The reform movement spread its message mainly through periodicals and study societies.[19] Male reformers argued that improvements in women's status were a necessary part of their program for national self-strengthening.[20]

The repression of 1898 left key reformers dead or in prison. But despite the increased anti-foreign sentiment during the Boxer Rebellion, the anti-footbinding movement continued to grow.[21] After the Boxer Rebellion, the Imperial Court saw the need to implement gradual reforms. One of the earliest reforms came when the Court issued an anti-footbinding edict in 1902.[22] Earlier Imperial decrees had had no effect,

---

15.   JANE HUNTER, THE GOSPEL OF GENTILITY: AMERICAN WOMEN MISSIONARIES IN TURN OF THE CENTURY CHINA 23–24 (1984).

16.   Roxane Witke, Transformation of Attitudes Towards Women During the May Fourth Era of Modern China 6, 42 (1970) (unpublished Ph.D. dissertation, University of California, Berkeley) (on file with author).

17.   *Id.* at 27.

18.   Chau, *supra* note 13, at 27.

19.   *Id.* at 28.

20.   HUNTER, *supra* note 15, at 23–24.

21.   Chau, *supra* note 13, at 126–28.

22.   HUNTER, *supra* note 15, at 24.

but the 1902 decree was the beginning of the end of footbinding in China. When the new republican and nationalist government came into power in 1911, it banned footbinding altogether.

Three groups were involved in the initial campaigns against footbinding in China: 1) the Western missionary effort aimed at Chinese Christians; 2) a Western-led campaign focused on non-Christian Chinese elites; and 3) a Chinese-led campaign focused on non-Christian Chinese elites. The missionaries were the first to launch an organized campaign against footbinding when Reverend John Macgowan of the London Missionary Society founded the first anti-footbinding society in 1874. In 1895, ten women of different nationalities, led by Mrs. Archibald Little, the wife of a British merchant, founded the *T'ien tsu hui* (Natural Foot Society), a non-denominational umbrella organization. The first Chinese-initiated Anti-Footbinding Societies were set up in 1883 and again 1895, but local opposition led to their collapse. In 1897, K'ang Kuang-jen and Liang Ch'i-ch'ao founded the *Pu'ch'an-tsu hui* (Anti-footbinding Society), China's largest non-Christian anti-footbinding organization, which later established branches in other cities and had a membership of 300,000.[23]

Each of the three actors took a characteristic approach to the issue. The missionary approach was more aggressive and moralistic.[24] Missionary schools promoted "natural feet" by first only offering scholarships only to girls with unbound feet, and later by refusing entry to girls with bound feet, and not employing any teachers with bound feet. The missionary schools focused their attention on Christian converts, usually not members of the Chinese elite. But perhaps the most innovative technique of the anti-footbinding society was to take on directly one social issue at the core of footbinding. Chinese families feared that daughters with unbound feet were unmarriageable. So the members of anti-footbinding societies pledged both not to bind the feet of their daughters, and to marry their sons only to women with unbound feet. Teachers in missionary schools also took responsibility for arranging marriages for their students with unbound feet. One American missionary wrote that "anti-footbinding seems to be very much entangled with match-making on my part."[25]

One author argues that missionary efforts to convert Chinese women to Christianity were frustrated because Chinese women led such secluded lives. Thus, missionary women fought against footbinding and for education of women in order to be able to convert them more successfully.[26] Other missionaries, however, were afraid that attacking footbinding could hinder their work in converting people to Christianity. Essentially missionaries disagreed about how to deal with footbinding and the effect it would have on their work. It is not clear at all that missionaries tried to abolish footbinding because they needed to do it to carry out their conversions.

---

23. Drucker, *supra* note 5, at 194.

24. Witke, *supra* note 16, at 20.

25. ALICIA HELEN LITTLE, INTIMATE CHINA 147 (1899).

26. HUNTER, *supra* note 15, at 175.

Rather it seems that some missionaries, especially missionary women, worked against footbinding because they thought it was wrong.[27]

Mrs. Little's Natural Foot Society focused on influencing powerful officials and non-Christian Chinese women "of wealth and fashion," thus partially divorcing the issue from the Christian context. Perhaps exactly because Little was not a missionary, she was able to take a less rigid and more strategic position on the issue, recognizing the social and cultural implications of the campaign. Mrs. Little was quite explicit about her strategy, saying:

> It would be much better to work in this way, with the upper classes and as a simple matter of footbinding alone, rather than to begin at the lower classes and mix it up with religion. To work mainly among converts was not so good, first because Christian Chinese were chiefly of the humbler classes and so would exercise no influence to spread the movement, and in the second place the unbinding made the women a mark for violence in the event of anti-Christian outbreaks.[28]

In a country where Christians were a small and marginal minority, less than one percent of the population, this strategy was probably essential to the success of the message.

One of the first activities of the Natural Foot Society was to send a petition to the Dowager-Empress, inscribed in gold letters on white satin, enclosed in a silver casket, and signed by "pretty well every foreign lady in the Far East at that time."[29] Although none of the original founders of the Natural Foot Society could read Chinese, they immediately began an outreach campaign, holding meetings and translating materials into Chinese. They even had long debates about which dialect of Chinese would be most appropriate. "We knew, of course . . . that feet are the most risque subject of conversation in China. . . . In the end we took refuge in the dignified Wenli of the Chinese classics, confident that thus anti-footbinding would be brought with as great decorum as possible before the Chinese public."[30] The Natural Foot Society also had a policy of getting their Chinese advisors to approve all their literature prior to publication to avoid any cultural or linguistic mistakes.[31]

The Natural Foot Society meetings were social as well as political events. Mrs. Little described a drawing room meeting in Szechuan as:

> [a] most brilliant affair. . . . [A]ll the Chinese ladies laughed so gaily and were so brilliant in their attire that the few missionary ladies among them looked like sober moths caught in a flight of broidered butterflies. . . . [After speeches and cakes] the meeting was then thrown open and at once the very smartest of the Chinese ladies present came forward to make a speech in her turn. All present were agreed that footbinding

27. Chau, *supra* note 13, at 35, 39; *see also* Drucker, *supra* note 5, at 183.

28. *Anti-Footbinding Society Conference*, NORTH CHINA HERALD, Jan. 23, 1901, at 159–60, (microform collection at Wilson Library at the Univ. of Minn.).

29. *Summary of Work Done by the Tien Tsu Hui*, 38 CHINESE RECORDER 32 (Jan. 1907) (microform collection at Wilson Library at the Univ. of Minn.).

30. LITTLE, *supra* note 25, at 147, 150.

31. Chau, *supra* note 13, 80.

was of no use but it could only be given up by degrees. . . . But what did the men say? . . . [T]he husband of one of the ladies said next day rather crossly, "Oh, of course the women liked it! They don't want to bind their feet!"[32]

The members of the Natural Foot Society did engage in some international networking, although this was not the central part of their work. At one meeting in China, the members decided to contact a U.S. envoy in China, a Mr. Conger, and discussed whether there was sufficient interest in footbinding in the U.S. to pressure the U.S. government to send instructions to Mr. Conger on the issue.[33] This would have been a classic "boomerang" maneuver predating current network tactics by ninety years, but there is no evidence that there was sufficient interest in the United States, or that the U.S. or other foreign governments ever got involved in the issue of footbinding. Although most of the initial financial support, as well as labor power, came from foreigners, by 1908, the Natural Foot Society set up by Mrs. Little and her associates was operating entirely under the leadership of Chinese women, who continued the vigorous campaign.[34] The foreign leaders of the Society argued in 1907 that is was "high time to trust the movement more to Chinese direction."[35] This transfer from foreign to domestic leadership serves as a mark of the success of the campaign.

The Natural Foot Society attempted to turn the tide against footbinding among influential Chinese through lobbying, publications, speaking engagements, petitions, essay competitions, and submitting materials to local newspapers. A 1907 letter summarizing the work of the Natural Foot Society discusses 162 recorded meetings in thirty-three different cities, some with as many as 2,000 people present; over a million tracts, leaflets, and placards printed and circulated from the Shanghai office alone; as well as letters to the editor, and prize competitions for the best essays against binding.[36] The Chinese anti-footbinding societies focused in particular on shifting ideas and on encouraging families opposed to footbinding to marry their sons to natural-footed girls. When registering in the societies, for example, families listed the ages of their children for more convenient matchmaking.[37]

Only sixteen years passed between the formation of the first umbrella organization to the 1911 ban against footbinding; this is very rapid progress in the history of transnational campaigns. A corresponding behavioral change evolved slowly but surely. A source indicates that, in 1905, 70 percent of female children still had their feet bound.[38] But by 1912, one of the missionaries described footbinding as "doomed" and "a social practice now on the wane and destined in course of time to disappear."[39]

---

32. Little, *supra* note 25, at 151.

33. *Anti-Footbinding Society Conference, supra* note 28, at 160.

34. Drucker, *supra* note 5, at 187–89.

35. *Summary of the Work Done by the Tien Tsu Hui, supra* note 29, at 34.

36. *Id.* at 32–33.

37. Chau, *supra* note 13, at 107–08.

38. *Id.* at 135.

39. *Id.* at 149.

The only systematic study of the practice, a 1929 study of a region to the south of Peking, shows very dramatic change over a short period of time: "99.2 % of those born prior to 1890 had bound feet, only 59.7% of those born between 1905 and 1909, and 19.5% of those born from 1910 to 1914, had bound feet; no new cases at all were found among those born after 1919."[40]

Such rapid eradication of a very culturally embedded practice is surprising. Historians of China differ about the relative weight of international and domestic actors in the campaign to abolish footbinding in China. Some have stressed the role of foreign missionary groups,[41] while others place more importance on Chinese intellectuals.[42] One Chinese scholar wrote in the 1930s:

> In my opinion, for all the wrongs that Western culture might have done in China, one thing alone would have redeemed them, and that is, the conviction that their early missionaries aroused in the Chinese mind that the practice of footbinding was absurd and wrong. Prior to this, scholars did sometimes criticize this absurd custom, but the criticism was always casual, and no serious thought was ever given nor effort made, for the abolishment of this custom until the end of the last century. . . . [T]he first rolling of the stone, so to speak, was started by our sisters from the west.[43]

The most in-depth treatment of the anti-footbinding movement concludes that it should be seen as part of a reform movement carried on "as a result of contact with the west."[44] The campaign appeared to form a pattern characteristic of modern networks, where both foreign and domestic actors were crucial to the success of the campaign, with foreign actors instrumental in "first rolling the stone" and domestic actors leading the way for framing the issue in ways that resonated with the domestic audiences, and generating broad-based support necessary for the success of the movement.

Some would argue that something inherent in the practice itself might have contributed to its demise. Footbinding incapacitated women, making it difficult for them to perform heavy physical labor or work out of the home. It is this very attribute that apparently made the practice attractive in the first place; it involved a display of wealth, since the household explicitly signaled that it could afford the luxury of a wife who didn't work. Footbinding in China lasted for almost 1,000 years. No key economic change occurred around the turn of the century that suddenly rendered the practice additionally dysfunctional from a material point of view. Industrial change in China had not yet reached the point where large numbers of women were needed to work outside the home at the time that footbinding began to end.

---

40. Gamble, *supra* note 7, at 181–83.

41. *See* Drucker, *supra* note 5. *See also* Chau, *supra* note 13.

42. For example, Witke argues, that "[d]espite missionary claims to the contrary, opposition to footbinding did not originate with them." Witke, *supra* note 16, at 22.

43. Ch'en Heng-che, *Influences of Foreign Cultures on the Chinese Woman* (1934) *reprinted in* CHINESE WOMEN THROUGH CHINESE EYES 64 (Li Yu-ning ed., 1992).

44. Chau, *supra* note 13, at 26.

Although the anti-footbinding movement was initiated by foreign women, it was embraced by nationalist intellectuals and reformers. In China, footbinding became associated with nationalist reform sentiment that was both anti-feudal and anti-foreign. In the context of the military defeat by foreigners, improving the status of women and ending footbinding were seen as tools to modernize and strengthen China so it could resist foreign intervention. "Although missionaries and reformers differed in their ultimate goals—national salvation and religious conversion, they shared a common strategy—social reform, of which women's emancipation was an important part."[45] Furthermore, "[n]ot until such efforts were perceived as Chinese phenomena in a nationalistic context did a majority of Chinese . . . espouse them. . . . [T]he foreign and Christian roots of the anti-footbinding campaign had to be renounced in order for victory to be achieved. Yet Western women laid many of the foundations for the eradication of footbinding."[46]

Chinese nationalists argued that one needed to adopt some of the practices of the West in order to resist more effectively Western domination. In an anti-footbinding tract, a Chinese literati argued: "To learn what the foreigners excel at in order to fight against them doesn't mean to respect or admire them. . . . In fact women with bound feet, who are completely useless, include one half of the population. . . . Useless women are an obstacle to progress."[47]

Every campaign to change practices of this sort is a struggle about redefining the meaning of the practice. This is why foreign or international actors alone rarely succeed in changing embedded practices, because they do not understand how to frame debates in convincing and accessible ways for the domestic audience. The Chinese reformers who were at the forefront of the anti-footbinding campaign used very different arguments than the ones used by the foreign missionaries, and yet their messages resonated better with the prevailing discourse of the time in China. The message was an unusual blend of appeals to modernity and tradition. For example, Chinese intellectuals stressed that footbinding was contrary to the ancient way of doing things, and that the Chinese classics offered no mention or words of praise for footbinding.[48] Thus, to eradicate a traditional practice, intellectuals appealed to even more ancient tradition. They referred to issues of filial piety, stressing that footbinding damaged the body, a gift from one's parents, and that "natural footed woman could buy medicine for a sick parent in less time than it took a bound foot woman."[49] Yet at the same time, reformers referred to international public opinion when they pointed out that the custom "became the laughing stock of foreigners."[50]

---

45. Judy Yung, Unbinding the Feet, Unbinding their Lives: Social Change for Chinese Women in San Francisco 1902–1945 21–22 (1990) (unpublished Ph.D. thesis, University of California) (on file with the author).

46. Drucker, *supra* note 5, at 199.

47. Chau, *supra* note 13, at 60–61.

48. Chau, *supra* note 13, at 21, 26.

49. Drucker, *supra* note 5, at 182. *See also* Witke, *supra* note 16, at 27.

50. Chau, *supra* note 13, at 98, 104 (*quoting* Liang Ch'i-Ch'ao's and K'ang Yu-Wei).

In the context of military defeat, the connection that Chinese reformers made between footbinding and weakness, and between individual weakness and the collective weakness of the country, appears to have been a powerful rhetorical device in opposition to binding. Ironically, one of the more successful arguments against footbinding was a then popular, but scientifically erroneous one, based on the idea of the inheritance of acquired traits, leading to the claim that not only would women with bound feet be unable to resist foreign invaders, but that they would pass on weakness to their sons.[51] The argument is factually incorrect, but it illustrates the broader point of the importance of the meaning that ideas take on within a particular political, cultural, and historical context.

Once the anti-footbinding campaign was launched and embraced by Chinese intellectuals, no strong organized opposition emerged. In one report on the work of the Natural Foot Society, Mrs. Little argued that is was a difficulty for the movement to have found "no devil's advocate," because "nothing advanced a cause so much as controversy."[52] That may be true, but the absence of strong opposition to the movement from Chinese intellectuals and nationalists, or from the Imperial Court, surely helps explain the speed with which the anti-footbinding movement achieved its goals.

The Campaign Against Female Circumcision in Kenya

The changing names given to this practice reveal the intense debate over meaning, and the ways in which words and names convey meaning. The practice can be referred to by more technical, "neutral" terms such as "female circumcision," "clitoridectomy," or "infibulation." These operations involve damage to the female sexual and /or reproductive organs, almost always including the removal of part or all of the clitoris (clitoridectomy/excision), and sometimes also involving the removal of the labia minora, the inner walls of the labia majora, and the sewing together of the vulva (infibulation).[53] The term "female circumcision" likens the operation to male circumcision with which it bears only superficial similarities. Male circumcision does not lead to any lasting pain or significant health problems, nor does it lessen male sexual pleasure. Female circumcision, on the other hand, has a number of short-term dangers, including hemorrhage, infection, and death from the operation itself. It can lead to such long-term medical problems as chronic infection, painful urination and menstrual difficulty, malformations and scarring, and vaginal abscesses, as well as reduced sexual response and pleasure. Although infibulation is the more severe form of female circumcision, health risks are associated with both clitoridectomy/excision and infibulation.[54]

---

51. *Id.* at 101.

52. *Id.* at 83.

53. Leonard J. Kouba & Judith Muasher, *Female Circumcision in Africa: An Overview*, 28 AFR. STUD. REV. 96 (Mar. 1985).

54. Alison T. Slack, *Female Circumcision: A Critical Appraisal*, 10 HUM. RTS. Q. 445, 450–55 (1988).

Yet in the Kikuyu language and culture, the practice of and the ceremonies surrounding female circumcision were exact parallels of those surrounding male circumcision. Both female and male circumcision were essential parts of initiation ceremonies that took place during early puberty, and marked the transition of the girl/boy from childhood to adulthood. The names for both practices were the same for men and women, and the ceremonies often took place at the same time in villages, although the males and females were separated for the actual physical operation.[55]

Modern campaigns in the 1970s and 1980s around the practice of female circumcision later drew attention to the issue by "re-framing" and renaming the problem as "female genital mutilation." By renaming the practice, the network severed the link to male circumcision and implied a link with a more feared procedure—castration—and re-framed the issue as one of violence against women. Because "female circumcision" was the main term used by both those who supported and those who opposed the practice in the period under study (1920s and 1930s), this chapter uses that term.

The clitoridectomy or excision form of female circumcision was widely practiced in Kenya among the Kikuyu and many other related cultural groups. In Kikuyu culture, "only a circumcised girl could be considered a woman. It was widely believed that uncircumcised girls would not physically be able to bear children. . . . In Kikuyu eyes an uncircumcised girl of marriageable age was an object of derision, indeed almost of disgust."[56]

Concerted efforts against female circumcision in Kenya began in the 1920s when Protestant missionaries led by the Church of Scotland Missionary Society (CSM) prohibited the operation for their converts and campaigned against the practice. The leader of the campaign was a Church of Scotland medical missionary, Dr. John Arthur, who had witnessed the impact of the operation on women in mission hospitals. Dr. Arthur threw all of his considerable energy into the church's efforts to stamp out the practice, but his manner alienated many among the Kikuyu and his fellow missionaries. The four major Protestant church missions in Kenya each took a position against female circumcision, but the Church of Scotland, the most puritan in belief, campaigned most actively for the eradication of the practice.

Perhaps the most curious question is why the missionaries focused so much energy on eradicating the practice among the Kikuyu, when related practices of female circumcision existed widely in other parts of Africa as well. Female circumcision was common in Ethiopia and in Sudan; in Somalia the more severe form of genital mutilation—infibulation—was practiced. Even in Kenya and Tanzania itself, other groups that practiced circumcision, like the Maasai, were not the object of the kinds of mis-

---

55.   Jocelyn Margaret Murray, The Kikuyu Female Circumcision Controversy, with Special Reference to the Church Missionary Society's Sphere of Influence 19–20 (1974) (unpublished Ph.D. dissertation, University of California (Los Angeles) (on file with author).

56.   CARL G. ROSBERG, JR. & JOHN NOTTINGHAM, THE MYTH OF "MAU MAU": NATIONALISM IN KENYA 112 (1966) [hereinafter ROSBERG & NOTTINGHAM].

sionary pressures placed on the Kikuyu.[57] So this single case embodies multiple cases of non-campaigns—in Ethiopia, Sudan, and Somalia, and a non-campaign against the practice among the Kenyan Maasai. European influence was weaker in Ethiopia (Abyssinia), but Sudan was settled by the British, after the dispute was resolved with the French at Fashoda in 1898, and Somalialand was divided among the French, the British, and the Italians.[58] The concentration of British missionaries in Kenya may explain why the campaign focused there. More British missionaries and settlers lived and worked in Kenya than elsewhere; there were also more girls schools and medical missions, so missionaries were frequently exposed to the medical problems confronted by circumcised girls and the social pressure for circumcision.

Still, what about the Maasai and other cultural groups in Kenya? Jocelyn Murray, who has conducted the most complete research on the controversy, argues that the campaign was focused on the Kikuyu because eradication was seen as possible among them and as impossible among the Maasai or Somali's. The Kikuyu had responded in greater numbers and with more enthusiasm to the education, religion, and technologies offered by the missionaries: "Neither missionaries nor administrators had any 'leverage' to implement change among the Masai. With the Kikuyu the position was very different. Both missionaries and administrators had a great deal of leverage."[59] The campaign among the Kikuyu was possible in the first place because a small but consistent group of Kikuyu supported the missionaries. The missionaries overestimated this support, but without it, "not even the most determined of Scottish missionary crusaders would have been able to carry the campaign through."[60] This suggests that transnational campaigns are possible even when domestic populations themselves are divided over a practice.

In Kenya, British colonial administrators and missionaries used some tactics similar to those used during the anti-footbinding campaign in China to try to discourage female circumcision. Missionary schools refused to admit girls who were circumcised, and church members could be suspended for requiring their girls to be circumcised. This position was advocated for medical, religious, and cultural reasons. The European missionaries argued that the operation was medically unnecessary and dangerous, and that it was un-Christian because the associated rituals were pagan and overtly sexual.[61] Four missionaries who were also physicians, led by Dr. John Arthur,

---

57.   Murray, *supra* note 55, at 3.

58.   In Sudan in 1946, the British administration did add an amendment to the Sudanese penal code prohibiting more severe forms of female circumcision, and specifying a punishment of five years in prison and/or a fine. Just as in Kenya, the law provoked a nationalist reaction, and a leader in the independence movement was jailed for opposing the law. Asthma Mohammed A'Haleem, *Claiming Our Bodies and Our Rights: Exploring Female Circumcision as an Act of Violence in Africa, in* FREEDOM FROM VIOLENCE: WOMEN'S STRATEGIES FROM AROUND THE WORLD 152 (Margaret Schuler ed., 1992).

59.   Murray, *supra* note 55, at 4.

60.   *Id.* at 7.

61.   MARSHALL S. CLOUGH, FIGHTING TWO SIDES: KENYAN CHIEFS AND POLITICIANS, 1918–1940 138–39 (1990).

prepared a Church of Scotland Memorandum against female circumcision. They argued then that the operation itself was painful, that it led to infections of the bladder, sterility, and, in particular, to a lack of elasticity in the birth canal that delayed births and led in some cases to the death of the child.[62]

Many African members of the CSM chose to leave the church to protest its position on this issue. Some accused the church leaders of adding "an eleventh commandment" that was not in the Bible. One leader said, "I was a Christian, but if the choice lay between God and circumcision, we choose circumcision. But it is a false European choice."[63] As the issue became more heated, the CSM and other missionary societies lost substantial numbers of their members.

This campaign took place in the context of increasing African opposition to British colonial practices, such as land alienation for European settlers, heavy hut and poll taxes, and an oppressive labor recruiting system.[64] Nascent Kikuyu nationalism was represented by the Kikuyu Central Association (KCA), set up by young, mainly mission-educated Kikuyu men. The female circumcision controversy exacerbated a growing split within internal Kikuyu politics between the younger and more militant KCA and the older Kikuyu leadership represented by chiefs associated with the Christian missions.[65] The KCA embraced some Western values but also attempted to preserve some traditional cultural practices, especially female circumcision, and it was over this issue that a major conflict developed between the KCA and the missionaries.[66]

Because the male and female circumcisions were exact parallels in the eyes of the Kikuyu, they did not understand why the missionaries worked so hard to end female, but not male, circumcision. Rumors and songs even circulated that suggested that the British administrators wanted uncircumcised Kikuyu girls for themselves, which in turn would let them increase their control of Kikuyu land.[67] Thus "the defense of Kikuyu culture and Kikuyu land became intertwined" with the KCA poised "as the principal defender of both."[68]

The campaign against female circumcision became a symbol for colonial attempts to impose Western values and rules upon the population. The Kikuyu nationalist elite defended the practice as necessary to the preservation of traditional culture, and attacked foreign intervention in trying to eradicate it. "Adherence to the custom

---

62. *Memorandum Prepared by the Mission Council of the Church of Scotland, Female Circumcision*, app. I, at ii, *in* HOSKEN, *supra* note 3, at 159.

63. ROSBERG & NOTTINGHAM, *supra* note 56, at 119.

64. Bethwell A. Ogot, *Kenya Under the British: 1895–1963, in* ZAMANI: A SURVEY OF EAST AFRICAN HISTORY 266–68, 278 (1974); *see also* CLOUGH, *supra* note 61, at 66–72.

65. CLOUGH, *supra* note 61, at 142–46.

66. ROSBERG & NOTTINGHAM, *supra* note 56, at 86–87.

67. Murray, *supra* note 55, at 144–45, 162.

68. CLOUGH, *supra* note 61, at 144.

became a symbol of Kikuyu self-assertion."[69] Because the KCA was the leading voice of Kikuyu nationalism, and because they had taken up the crusade in favor of circumcision, female circumcision became associated with Kikuyu nationalism. Many Protestant leaders were opposed to and suspicious of the KCA, and their opposition to circumcision was viewed as a tool to oppose the Association. Dr. John Arthur drew up a petition opposing circumcision which not only asked teachers and other mission employees to renounce circumcision, but also to repudiate the KCA.[70]

Jomo Kenyatta, the General Secretary of the KCA and later the main leader of the anti-colonial struggle, wrote a stirring defense of female circumcision in his study of Kikuyu culture, *Facing Mount Kenya*, composed in 1935 when Kenyatta was an anthropology student at the London School of Economics. He stated: "For the present it is impossible for a member of the tribe to imagine an initiation without clitoridectomy. Therefore the abolition of the surgical element in this custom means to the Gikuyu the abolition of the whole institution. . . . [C]litoridectomy, like Jewish circumcision, is a mere bodily mutilation which, however, is regarded as the condition sine qua non of the whole teaching of tribal law, religion, and morality."[71] One of Kenyatta's concerns was the decline of sexual morality among young Kikuyu, which he saw as a result of the interference of the missionaries and their disbelief in traditional morality.[72]

In 1929–30, Jomo Kenyatta traveled to Britain to meet with British officials and church members. The debate over female circumcision was one of the major themes of his talks. Because the relations between the KCA and the European settlers in Kenya were strained, Kenyatta sought out contacts in London to whom he could present the KCA position directly. He met with Committees of the House of Commons, a member of the House of Lords, the Under-Secretary of State for the Colonies in London, and with church officials to present the concerns of his organization, which were embodied in a formal Petition.[73] While in England, Kenyatta also established contacts with members of the League against Imperialism, and with former colleagues he had met in Kenya.

During his meeting with officials of the Scottish Church, Kenyatta acted to defuse the tension with the Church, stressing that the major difference was one of strategy, that the KCA believed that "the way of gradual conviction is to be preferred to that of direct attack by means of spear and shield."[74] In a convincing letter to the

---

69. ANN BECK, A HISTORY OF THE BRITISH MEDICAL ASSOCIATION OF EAST AFRICA 103 (1970).

70. CLOUGH, *supra* note 61, at 143.

71. ROSBERG & NOTTINGHAM, *supra* note 56, at 133.

72. Kenyatta's experience with anthropology allowed him to engage in "redemptive criticism—the present employment of the past in the hopes of reshaping the future." Bruce Berman & John Lonsdale, *Louis Leakey's Mau Mau: A Study in the Politics of Knowledge*, 5 HIST. & ANTHROPOLOGY 172, 193 (1991).

73. Ann Beck, *Some Observations on Jomo Kenyatta in Britain 1929–1930*, 6 CAHIERS D'ETUDES AFRICAINES 308, 313 (1966).

74. *Id.* at 322.

Times, Kenyatta presented the Association's positions on five other key issues, appealing to the fair-mindedness of Britons by arguing that the repression of native views was a "short-sighted tightening of the safety valve of free speech which must inevitably result in dangerous explosion—the one thing all men wish to avoid."[75]

What is most striking about this trip is that it represents a very effective attempt to counter pressures within Kenya by circumventing the inattentive or hostile colonial and church authorities in Kenya and going over their heads to their superiors in Britain. Kenyatta impressed the people with whom he had contact with his seriousness, persistence, and moderation, and presented to them a different version of the events than they received from the British missionaries in Kenya.

By late 1929, the controversy in Kenya became more heated. The pro-circumcision forces circulated a satirical song, the "Muthirigu," that ridiculed missionaries, chiefs, and officials, and praised Kenyatta. The government and missionaries, fearing a threat to public order, repressed the singers by flogging them, sentencing people to detention camps, and prohibiting public meetings.[76] In this context, colonial authorities backed away from the missionaries' campaign against female circumcision. Kenyatta and his organization had helped re-frame the debate from one about health and Christianity to a discussion of nationalism, land, and the integrity of traditional culture. The public singing of the "Muthirigu" convinced colonial authorities that the issue was exacerbating relations between Kikuyu and Europeans. Colonial authorities asked the main opponent of female circumcision, Dr. John Arthur, to resign from the Executive Council. Some officials advocated more gradual policies that stressed education rather than prohibition. One official recommended "masterly inactivity," another counseled "the less talked about the operation of circumcision the better."[77] One of the political results of the controversy was to delegitimize Kikuyu leaders associated with the missions, and to increase the influence and membership of the KCA. It was one of a series of controversies among Kikuyu and between the Kikuyu and the British that contributed to the tensions that twenty years later found expression in the mass movement that Europeans called "Mau Mau."

Although there is very little data indicating how much change took place in the practice during the period of the controversy, research conducted in 1973 shows how slow changes in female circumcision have been in Kenya. At the time of the controversy, it appears that 100 percent of Kikuyu girls were circumcised. Even among the missionaries' strongest supporters, the number who decided not to circumcise their daughters was very small.[78] Orphan girls themselves often ran away from the missionary schools to get circumcised. Nevertheless, those religious groups that adopted the most intransigent position against female circumcision in the 1920s and 1930s did later see far fewer circumcised girls among their members. In a survey of high school girls in Kenya conducted in 1973, Murray found that 59 percent were not cir-

---

75. *Id.* at 325.

76. CLOUGH, *supra* note 61, at 145.

77. BECK, *supra* note 69, at 101–02.

78. Murray, *supra* note 55, at 244.

cumcised, and that this number was much higher (93 percent) among the members of the old Scottish Presbyterian Church which had led the campaign in the 1920s.[79] Yet, Murray argues that high school girls don't represent an accurate sample of the young female population as a whole, as they are more likely to come from Protestant religious backgrounds; she estimates that as much as 75 percent of adolescent Kikuyu girls were still circumcised in the mid-1970s.[80] By the 1990s, a study of female genital mutilation in Africa estimates that 50 percent of Kenyan girls and women have been circumcised, as compared to 80 percent in the Sudan, 90 percent in Ethiopia, and 98 percent in Somalia, where more severe forms of the operation are common.[81] These figures suggest that the missionary campaign did have some effect, but that the effect was far more limited than the missionaries hoped for or than that of other similar campaigns.

Notably, women were mainly absent in the anti-circumcision campaign. Women missionaries in Kenya were in a subordinate position within the mission. They were not represented in the decision-making bodies of the mission, and men often disregarded the recommendations of the Women's Conferences.[82] The rather extensive literature on the controversy does not mention any key role played by Kikuyu women in internal Kikuyu debates. Also, no associations separate from the missionary churches were ever set up to promote anti-circumcision. Even the involvement of Kikuyu themselves in the campaign came only through their involvement with missions, where they were often employed.

CONCLUSIONS

What are some implications of the historical case studies for our theorizing about the emergence and impact of transnational networks and campaigns? Despite many differences, some of the patterns revealed in these early campaigns are relevant to discussions of the conditions under which campaigns succeed or fail. In these historical cases, internationally instigated campaigns are successful when they are embraced by influential domestic groups, and when the message or "frame" of the movement resonates with powerful domestic symbols and stories. Like modern campaigns, the central conflicts in these campaigns were the interpretive struggles over the meaning of certain practices within the domestic context.

The cases provide support for the argument that transnational actors must align with domestic actors in the target state in order to have an impact.[83] The ability of the

---

79. *Id.* at 354.

80. *Id.* at 352. It is interesting, however, that the initiation ceremonies that surrounded circumcision were virtually abandoned over time, while the physical operation was maintained. *Id.* at 25.

81. HOSKEN, *supra* note 3, at 43–44.

82. ROBERT STRAYER, THE MAKING OF MISSION COMMUNITIES IN EAST AFRICA: ANGLICANS AND AFRICANS IN COLONIAL KENYA, 1875–1935 6 (1978).

83. Risse-Kappen, *supra* note 2, at 187. Kathryn Sikkink, *Human Rights, Principled Issue—Networks, and Sovereignty in Latin America*, 47 INT'L ORG. 435 (1993). These arguments connect to one aspect of political opportunity structure signaled by Tarrow—the availability of influential allies. TARROW, *supra* note 1, at 18.

anti-footbinding movement to secure alliances with the most influential members of the Chinese reformist and intellectual elite was without doubt a fundamental part of its ability to influence politics. The inability of the Scottish missionaries in Kenya to secure alliances with anyone but the most loyal of their mission converts and employees hampered their chances at success. The cases differ not so much in the availability of influential allies, as in the ability of the movements to attract and maintain allies. And paradoxically, the transnational efforts were most influential at the point before the domestic movement secured its most influential allies.

But the strength or density of the network does not operate in a political vacuum. The strength and alliances of the network must be considered in relation to the strength of the opposition. In the language of social movement theory, networks must be considered within "multi-organizational fields," which consist of actors both supportive of and antagonistic to the movements.[84] In the case of Kenya, a group of missionaries with tepid support from colonial authorities confronted a politically weak, but ideologically strong, opposition that had made the symbolic connection between the powerful issue of nationalism and the support of female circumcision. In China, a well-organized set of anti-footbinding societies faced strongly entrenched cultural beliefs, but no effectively organized political opposition. When the societies gained the support of both the Imperial Court and the nationalist reformer politicians, the eventual success of their campaign was assured.

The case studies appear to call into question, however, the argument that domestic structures are the key explanation for the differing impact of networks. If domestic structures such as political institutions, state society relations, and political culture are so central, surely a colonial administration would offer the most access to the British missionaries and the fewest opportunities to the Kikuyu nationalists. Not only did the British exercise political control, but the Christian churches in Africa had been much more successful in their conversion efforts there than in India and China.[85] Yet the Kikuyu most successfully resisted pressures and re-framed the debate to neutralize the missionaries. In contrast, Imperial China would appear to be an example of one of the least permeable domestic structures for foreign women without substantial support from their governments. Both the Kenyan and the Chinese campaigns took place at a period when domestic structures were entering a transitional period, signaling future shifts in political institutions, but the campaigns preceded the shifts rather than paralleled them.

Why did reformers choose to focus campaigns on these issues in the first place? There is no obvious connection between either footbinding or female circumcision and conversion, as evidenced by the missionary debate as to whether these campaigns helped or hindered conversion. In Kenya, for example, the campaign led to a profound drop in church membership. The Catholic Church in both places avoided par-

---

84.   Bert Klandermans, *The Social Construction of Protest and Multi-Organizational Fields, in* FRONTIERS IN SOCIAL MOVEMENT THEORY (Carol McClurg Mueller & Aldon D. Morris eds., 1992).

85.   STRAYER, *supra* note 82, at 2.

ticipating in the campaigns because it feared the effect they would have on their efforts at conversion.

The morality of evangelical groups was involved in each of these cases. The missionaries in Kenya were "puritan 'Victorians' in the fullest sense of the word: drinking, smoking, dancing, and the other worldly amusements were regarded as sinful, and in sexual matters premarital virginity, chastity within marriage and no divorce were absolute requirements."[86] Yet many other practices that were morally condemned—in Kenya, polygamy, witchcraft, and traditional medicine; in China, female infanticide, concubinage, and opium smoking—did not lead to parallel campaigns.

Some political theorists have argued for essentialist understandings of a set of basic capacities that permit "human flourishing."[87] The set of issues around which campaigns have been organized historically, however, is much more basic and focused than even the essentialist understanding. Given the various Chinese practices that the missionaries thought were wrong—female infanticide, opium smoking, concubinage—why did only footbinding generate a concerted organized campaign? Probably missionaries did not organize actively on female infanticide in China because it was a much less public and well-documented practice than was footbinding. Although female infanticide was a topic of discussion among foreigners and missionaries during this period, they mainly relied on hearsay, and could not determine or agree on the true extent of the custom.[88] Likewise, missionaries did not campaign against opium smoking or concubinage, although they certainly preached against them to their converts.

These transnational activists worked on the issues that they perceived to be the most severe for vulnerable individuals, and thus bodily mutilation of children and the accompanying physical pain generated more concern than the morally charged issues of concubinage in China or polygamy in Kenya. In this sense, the "rights" focus on the protection of individuals from bodily harm was already a "master frame" of early campaigns, although the language of human rights was usually not used.

This individualistic focus may be the result of a common evangelical Protestant background shared by many of the activists in the campaigns considered here, as well as the prevailing Enlightenment and post-Enlightenment discourses. Many of the missionaries were influenced by the Protestant revivals of the so-called Great Awakening; missionaries in Kenya came from a Protestant context, influenced by evangelical revivals such as the Keswick movement, and the Moody and Sankey Revival. John Arthur, the leading activist against female circumcision, "grew up in that evangelical atmosphere and his whole life was molded by it."[89]

---

86. Murray, *supra* note 55, 48.

87. Martha C. Nussbaum, *Human Functioning and Social Justice: In Defense of Aristotelian Essentialism*, 20 POLITICAL THEORY 202 (1992).

88. Bernice J. Lee, *Female Infanticide in China*, 8 HIS. REFLECTIONS 168–70 (1981). Missionaries did set up orphanages in China at the time, in part as a response to female infanticide.

89. Murray, *supra* note 55, at 46–47.

One of the crucial differences in these cases appears to have been the ability of the activists to shape understandings and re-frame an issue and message in a way that resonated with domestic concerns, culture, and ideology. In the context of these campaigns against footbinding, for example, the meaning of the practice changed so that what was once a source of pride for women and a "central motif in her interaction with other women"[90] became a symbol of the past, and an object of shame or derision. In Kenya, this same symbolic transference did not occur, and the uncircumcised girl continued to be an object of shame, not quite a woman.

In Kenya and China, the way that the campaigns interacted with nationalist movements at the time was crucial for the reception of the message. Despite strong anti-foreign sentiment in China around the turn of the century, the footbinding issue was not associated with anti-nationalism. Although originally associated with Christian missionaries, anti-footbinding sentiment eventually was adopted as part of the rhetoric of the nationalist and modernizing elite in China. The Chinese elite (mainly men) took leadership roles in the campaign against footbinding, which was a key part of the political, social, and cultural change necessary as part of the modernization project they advocated. By 1900, footbinding became identified as one of the most extreme practices that prevented China's advancement, and once that meaning emerged, the change in practice followed relatively quickly. In this sense, the nationalist movement in China in the late nineteenth century differed from that of nationalists in India in the same period who argued that it was necessary to learn about the material techniques of the West, but that the inner core of national culture had to be protected against the colonizer. This "inner core" or spiritual side of national culture was identified with the home, and with women.[91] One possible reason for the difference was that China, despite massive foreign intervention, continued to be an autonomous country, while both Kenya and India were colonies administered by the British. As such, anti-British and anti-foreign sentiment was stronger in the independence movement in Kenya than it was in China.

By the mid-twentieth century, African intellectuals like Kenyatta and Nyerere were holding up an idealized version of the traditional past as an alternative to the Western lifestyles and "progress" that they feared were inappropriate for their countries. The debate over female circumcision became embroiled in this controversy, so that the campaign against female circumcision became associated with colonialism and interference, and the practice of female circumcision with independence, nationalism, and tradition. In this sense, nationalism in Kenya articulated a similar material/spiritual distinction to the one made by Indian nationalists in the nineteenth century, where the material corresponded to the outside world, and the spiritual realm to the home.[92] Nationalist ideology in both India and Kenya assigned to the home sphere a key role as the main site for retaining national culture. As such, the struggle over

---

90. Ko, *supra* note 9, at 150.

91. Partha Chatterjee, *Colonialism, Nationalism, and Colonialized Women: The Contest in India*, 16 AM. ETHNOLOGIST 624–25 (1989).

92. *Id.* at 625–26.

nationalism became firmly connected to the struggle over women's role at home and in society.

In Chinese nationalist discourse, the whole realm of the home was not preserved from nationalist reforms. In China, especially through the activities of Mrs. Little's Natural Foot Society, the practice of footbinding was singled out and separated from the religious message, and from a range of other cultural issues. Although the anti-footbinding movement was part of a broader reform movement, natural foot advocates didn't demand a comprehensive package of cultural change. In Kenya, on the other hand, where the campaign against female circumcision was carried out only by missionaries in the context of the colonial state, the missionary church demanded "total cultural transformation," excluding the possibility of "selective change, by which the Kikuyu might absorb some elements of Western culture while rejecting others as unacceptable to their values or social institutions."[93] The Natural Foot Societies, however, offered, indeed advocated, this selective change, explicitly divorcing it from the totalizing context of Christian conversion. This made the message more acceptable to non-Christian nationalist Chinese reformers, who embraced it as their own.

One author argues that, in Kenya, the missionaries were tampering with one of the "deepest-felt customs" embedded in "complex emotions and attitudes," but such a description could equally apply to footbinding. The eradication of footbinding illustrates that even profoundly culturally embedded practice can be overcome rather quickly with a concerted campaign against it and widespread support from nationalist elites.

Do these cases support the argument that moral campaigns are thinly disguised attempts to further more fundamental interests? In the case of the female circumcision controversy in Kenya, the struggle over female circumcision was directly related to struggles over colonial authority and Kikuyu self-determination. Some missionaries and colonial authorities used their opposition to female circumcision as a means of furthering their campaign against the KCA. It is probably not accidental that the less successful moral campaign was the one in which moral causes and colonial interests were more intertwined. The Kenyan case provides perhaps a cautionary tale for modern transnational reformers of the dangers of reform campaigns too closely associated with state power in the context of coercive interstate practices.

Some statements of missionaries or reformers in the campaigns against footbinding and female circumcision contain examples of repugnant beliefs in moral and cultural superiority, racism, and paternalism. Nothing in the background or education or these reformers, nor the prevailing European attitudes towards foreigners, provided them with "broad vision, imagination, or sympathy" toward other non-Western cultures.[94] These campaigns proceeded by holding up a Westernized ideal of progress, and by constructing the "target" as the "other" engaged in outmoded or inhuman prac-

---

93.   Rosberg & Nottingham, *supra* note 56, at 105.

94.   Strayer, *supra* note 82, at 7.

tices and standing in the way of progress and modernity. Activists saw the victim as an unproblematic "other" who needed their assistance, but the victims rarely participated in the campaign and the reformers were rarely self-reflective about their own paternalism. In Kenya, it is curious that so few women's voices—African or European—were heard in the early debate over female circumcision. Although it took place thirty years earlier, women were more present in the anti-footbinding campaign in China than in the anti-circumcision campaign, despite the severe limitations on the participation of women in public life in China at the time.

It appears that the intransigence and paternalism that some activists brought to their campaigns compromised the success of the campaign itself because it hampered their ability to build enduring alliances across cultural and political divides. Modern networks differ in that they cannot simply impose the dichotomy of the "We vs. the Other," because more diverse individuals are present in the construction of meanings and of the campaigns themselves. While individuals continue to bring their culturally bound beliefs to debates, building modern transnational networks requires a multiplicity of voices. Surprisingly, this new multiplicity of voices may strengthen rather than weaken "rights" as the master frame of modern networks. Despite the differences among activists, the common denominator is often a concern with protecting individual human dignity against the gravest forms of physical assault. One dilemma at the core of many campaigns for human rights is that these groups are profoundly motivated by principles and morals, but are nonetheless acting politically, which involves building alliances and coalitions and inevitably entails strategizing and compromising. The way modern movements resolve this dilemma will determine whether modern networks are more successful in avoiding the arrogance of cultural imperialism evident in some historical campaigns.

WOMEN AND CIVIL SOCIETY:
NGOS AND INTERNATIONAL CRIMINAL LAW

Helen Durham

INTRODUCTION

This chapter examines the role women's non-governmental organizations (NGOs) play in international criminal law. Using case studies of the development of the Statute for an International Criminal Court and the proceedings at the *ad hoc* international criminal tribunals both in the former Yugoslavia and Rwanda, the chapter argues that women's groups have had a significant impact on the creation and enforcement of this area of law. While it must be acknowledged that NGOs are outside the formal parameters of international legal decision-making, the impact of women's NGOs on the advancement and enforcement of norms dealing with gender justice should not be underestimated.

The past few years have seen a shift in the focus of international global governance away from an exclusively state dominated approach to the development of international law toward a recognition of the important role of international civil society. Therefore, examining the role that NGOs play in forming and implementing international law, in particular international criminal law, is a timely endeavor. The active emergence of the non-state actor has allowed women to play a greater role in international governance, an area from which they traditionally have been excluded. NGOs offer women the chance to participate in global governance, both formally and informally and allow them the opportunity to advance their particular views on the international stage. NGOs are currently the most basic form of popular participation and representation in the modern world, allowing women some say in the form of global governance.

The impact of NGOs in international law is demonstrated by their recent increased involvement in international criminal law, both with the creation of the Rome Statute of the International Criminal Court (ICC)[1] and the prosecutions at the international criminal tribunals for Yugoslavia[2] and Rwanda.[3] Traditionally, only states

---

1.   Rome Statute of the International Criminal Court, adopted by the United Nations Diplomatic Conference of Plenipotentiaries on the Establishment of an International Criminal Court, July 17, 1998, U.N. Doc.A/CONF.183/9 (1998), 37 I.L.M. 999 (1998), *www.un.org/icc.* [hereinafter ICC Statute].

2.   The International Tribunal for the Prosecution of Persons Responsible for Serious Violations of International Humanitarian Law Committed in the Territory of the Former Yugoslavia since 1991, U.N. Doc. S/25704, annex (1993), *reprinted in* 32 I.L.M. 1192 (1993) [hereinafter ICTY Statute].

3.   The International Tribunal for the Prosecution of Persons Responsible for Genocide and

are the subjects of international regulation and prosecution. However, international criminal law is unique, representing a departure from the traditional approach in its imposition of criminal responsibility upon individuals rather than states. It takes the political and makes it personal. It puts names and faces to horrible and complex historical events. It dissects activities often sanctioned by states and lays blame upon individuals, be they citizens, members of the military, or high government officials. Focusing upon individuals rather than states highlights the point that:

> crimes against international law are committed by men, not by abstract entities, and only by punishing individuals who commit such crimes can the provisions of international law be enforced.[4]

Non-state actors, in particular women's NGOs, also create synergies between the political and personal. They connect the global with the local. Over the last few decades, women's groups all over the world have minimized the separation between the private and public, making domestic violence, prostitution, and "disappeared" children public issues. As human rights activist Eleanor Roosevelt, former U.S. First Lady, wrote:

> Where, after all, do universal human rights begin? In small places, close to home—so small that they cannot be seen on any maps of the world. . . . Unless these rights have meaning there, they have little meaning anywhere. Without concerted citizen action to uphold them close to home, we shall look in vain for progress in the larger world.[5]

This chapter will commence with an examination of the entities known as NGOs and consider their relationship with the formal United Nations system. The role of women's NGOs will be emphasized and examined. Following this, consideration will be given to the role of NGOs, particularly women's groups, in the development of modern international criminal law and the creation of the International Criminal Court. This chapter will focus on the impact of the Women's Caucus for Gender Justice in the Preparatory Committees (pre-ICC) and the Diplomatic Conference for the establishment of the ICC, particularly on issues as diverse as witness protection and the definition of "forced pregnancy" and "gender." It will also briefly look at the Women's Caucus contributions to the Preparatory Commissions (post-ICC).

The chapter will then provide a number of detailed case studies on the impact of individual women's NGOs in influencing the work of the two *ad hoc* international criminal tribunals. A case study will be presented on the operations of the Australian Committee of Investigation into War Crimes and comment will be made on the

---

Other Serious Violations of International Humanitarian Law Committed in the Territory of Rwanda and Rwandan Citizens responsible for genocide and other such violations committed in the territory of neighboring states, between Jan. 1, 1994, and Dec. 31, 1994, S.C. Res. 955, annex, U.N. SCOR, 49th Sess., Res. & Dec., at 15, U.N. Doc. S/INF/50 (1994), *reprinted in* 33 I.L.M. 1602 (1994) [hereinafter ICTR Statute].

4. TRIAL OF THE MAJOR WAR CRIMINALS BEFORE THE INTERNATIONAL MILITARY TRIBUNAL, NUREMBERG (1945–1946), *Judgement*, at 41; *reprinted in Judicial Decisions*, 41 AM. J. INT'L L. 17, 221 (1947).

5. E. Roosevelt, *In Your Hands: A Guide for Community Action for the Tenth Anniversary of the Universal Declaration of Human Rights*, Mar. 1958.

American Serbian Women's Caucus as examples of the impact of women's NGOs in affecting the focus of international criminal law. Finally, discussion will turn to the use of *amicus curiae* briefs, whereby NGOs and individuals can bring to the attention of the judiciary specific issues often overlooked in international trials. A case study at the International Criminal Tribunal for Rwanda will highlight the use of *amicus* briefs in ensuring that sexual violence is placed on the agenda of war crimes investigations.

NON-GOVERNMENTAL ORGANIZATIONS (NGOS)

Defining NGOs

Defining NGOs is not an easy task. Domestically, such groups can be called "interest groups," "pressure groups," "community based groups," or even "private voluntary organizations." NGOs are diverse in size, subject matter, structure, and membership and can be informal or formal associations. To generalize about them is to obscure their most salient feature—diversity. As Steiner notes, the "NGO movement has no single inspiration or aspiration, neither a spiritual nor secular authority to define one belief for all within it, no pope and no central committee."[6]

NGOs can also be found along every part of the political spectrum—from radical to extremely conservative. One commentator has sought to define NGOs after reviewing a large range of such actors by stating that:

> An NGO is any non-profit-making, non-violent, organized group of people who are not seeking government office. An international NGO is a non-violent, organized group of individuals who are not seeking government. The members of an international NGO will usually be NGOs from different countries, but they can also have any mixture of individuals, companies, political parties, NGOs or other international NGOs as members.[7]

This is a very broad interpretation and is not ideal. However, it does highlight the magnitude of organizations that could fit the definition of an NGO.

NGOs and the *U.N.*

The United Nations (U.N.) first used the word "non-Governmental organization" in its Charter, allowing for specific NGOs to have consultative status within the U.N. Economic and Social Council (ECOSOC).[8] The fact that NGOs are limited to a consultative status rather than participating indicates states' defensive attitude

---

6.   H. STEINER, DIVERSE PARTNERS: NON-GOVERNMENTAL ORGANIZATIONS IN THE HUMAN RIGHTS MOVEMENT: THE REPORT OF A RETREAT OF HUMAN RIGHTS ACTIVISTS 8 (1991).

7.   Peter Willetts, *Introduction, in* THE CONSCIENCE OF THE WORLD: THE INFLUENCE OF NON-GOVERNMENTAL ORGANIZATIONS IN THE UN SYSTEM 5 (Peter Willetts ed., 1996).

8.   Art. 71 of the U.N. Charter states that "The Economic and Social Council may make suitable arrangements for consultation with non-governmental organizations which are concerned with matters within its competence." Certain criteria as set out by ECOSOC must be satisfied to fit within one of three categories for consultation with ECOSOC. *See* E.S.C. Res. 31, U.N. ESCOR, 49th plen. mtg, U.N. Doc. E/1996/31 (1996).

towards such organizations.[9] The exclusion of formal power means that much of the work of NGOs is undertaken in informal environments, building upon webs of relationships, networks, lobbying, and the mobilization of shame. This position has not altered significantly in the last fifty years. While NGO involvement in the U.N. has dramatically transcended the original drafters' intentions, the regulations articulating NGOs formal standing remain restrictive. This may account for the plethora of "informal" work and relationships many NGOs have adopted within the U.N. system.

Since the 1945 San Francisco conference creating the U.N., NGOs have been a driving force behind the U.N.'s policies on human rights. Recently, a number of factors relating to the emerging global community have heightened NGO activities and standing.[10] The dramatic increase in the number of NGOs working directly with the U.N., [11] the ample NGO representation at U.N. conferences and the credibility given to NGO "counter-conferences"[12] all demonstrate the important positions these organizations now occupy. The increased ease of international communication, which states are often powerless to control, has resulted in a new paradigm in which NGOs are becoming a significant force in global politics. Technological developments, particularly in the area of communications, such as e-mail, the internet, and facsimile are independent of territory and relatively easily accessible. Some observers perceive such changes as increasing signs of pluralism and global democratization.[13] Classical power structures are no longer able to claim complete centralization. In such a changing environment, international and national NGOs have become an increasingly powerful "voicepiece for multi-layered transnational identities that are barely audible in the current State-dominated systems."[14]

Some commentators have labelled NGOs as "shadow states," bodies without power whose role is to provide alternative policies and criticism.[15] Concerns have

---

9. In contrast, art. 69 allows any Member of the U.N. to participate in ECOSOC deliberations and art. 70 accords the same rights to specialized agencies.

10. *See* Anne Marie Clark, *Non-Government Organziations and their Influence on International Society*, 48 J. INT'L AFFAIRS 513 (1995).

11. By mid-1999, there were 1,515 NGOs in consultative status with the Economic and Social Council (ECOSOC) and 400 NGOs accredited to the Commission on Sustainable Development, a subsidiary body of ECOSOC. See *Consultative Relationships between the ECOSOC and NGOs*, <http://www.un.org/eas/coordination/ngo/>, July 25, 1999.

12. *See, e.g.*, R. Dawson, *When Women Gather: The NGO Forum of the Fourth World Conference on Women, Beijing 1995*, 10 INT'L J. POLITICS, CULTURE & SOCIETY 7 (1996).

13. *See, e.g.*, Paul Ghils, *International Civil Society: International non-Governmental Organizations in the International System*, 44 INT'L SOC. SCI. J. 417 (1992); Lester Salamon, *The Rise of the Nonprofit Sector,* 73 FOREIGN AFFAIRS 109 (1994); William Fisher, *Doing Good? The Politcs and Antipolitics of NGO Practices*, 26 ANN. REV. ANTHROPOLOGY 439 (1997); John Boli & George Thomas, *World Culture in the World Polity: A Century of International Non-Governmental Organizations*, 62 AM. SOC. REV. 171 (1997); James Paul, *NGOs, Civil Society and Global Policy-Making*, GLOBAL POL'Y FORUM (1996), <http://www.globalpolicy@globalpolicy.org>.

14. Di Otto, *Non-Governmental Organisations in the United Nations System: The emerging role of international civil society*, 18 HUM. RTS. Q. 107 (1996).

15. Ghils, *supra* note 13, at 420.

been raised that much of the coordination between NGOs and the U.N., especially in forums such as drafting committees, is *ad hoc*, informal, and not procedurally based. As one commentator writes: "NGO influence should not hinge on which groups happen to best ingratiate themselves with nation-State representatives."[16] NGOs must continue to struggle to maintain their unique identity as the main social countervailing power to the state, without being co-opted or rendered irrelevant. This dichotomy between principle and pragmatism plays itself out within NGOs in the trade-offs between voluntarism and professionalism, informality and the institutionalization necessary to implement long-term changes.

Yet, the terminology used to describe NGOs—as *non* governmental—indicates that their relevance, input, and usefulness comes from being "outside" the formal parameters of governance. Many of the activities undertaken by NGOs at the U.N. do not have to be limited to the practicalities of pragmatism that restricts states. NGOs are generally not burdened with large bureaucracies, and are relatively flexible, open to innovations, and able to identify and respond quickly to grassroot needs.[17] The avoidance of formal power and accountability to a broad audience can allow certain freedoms of thought and the ability to focus upon specific non-national issues such as gender, universal human rights, environment, and indigenous rights.

THE ROLE OF WOMEN'S NGOS

Women's NGOs have played a part in the formation of international law from the League of Nations to the formation of the United Nations Charter, and in particular in numerous recent instances have been a driving force behind treaties, particularly those dealing broadly with gender issues. The United Nations Charter was influenced by a number of women's activists and organizations working as the Inter-American Commission on the Status of Women, which was successful in ensuring that equal treatment of men and women was included as a principle in the Charter.[18] Yet, in the early years of the United Nations, very few women's NGOs were accredited with ECOSOC—the main women's NGOs consisted of European or North American groups such as the World Association of Girl Guides and Girl Scouts and the World Young Women's Christian Association.[19] However, despite the limited numbers of early women's NGOs, these women's groups were able to lobby successfully for the important establishment by ECOSOC of a Commission on the Status of Women.[20]

---

16. Peter Spiro, *New Global Communities: Non-Governmental Organizations in International Decision-Making Institutions*, 18 THE WASH. QUARTERLY 50, 64 (1995).

17. William Fisher, *Doing Good? The Politics and Antipolitics of NGO Practices*, 26 ANN. REV. ANTHROPOLOGY 444 (1997).

18. *See* U.N. CHARTER, arts. 1, 8, 13, 55, and 76; Jane Connors, *NGOs and the Human Rights of Women at the United Nations, in* THE CONSCIENCE OF THE WORLD: THE INFLUENCE OF NON-GOVERNMENTAL ORGANISATIONS IN THE U.N. SYSTEM 147, 150–51 (Peter Willetts ed., 1996).

19. Martha Alter Chen, *Engendering World Conferences: The International Women's Movement and the UN, in* NGOs, THE UN, AND GLOBAL GOVERNANCE 139, 140 (Thomas G. Weiss & Leon Gordenker eds., 1996).

20. ECOSOC Res. 1/5 of Feb. 16 and 18, 1946, and Res. 2/11 of June 21, 1946.

Women's NGOs played a notable role in the drafting of the Universal Declaration of Human Rights. Women's NGOs have used their accumulated experience and expertise to influence the global policy agenda, and have worked to do so both within and outside the formal U.N. structure. Thus, women's NGOs have organized World Conferences on Women, attended by thousands of women NGO groups, participated by the hundreds at other U.N. Conferences and assisted in the development of U.N. declarations, treaties and Conventions, in particular the Convention on the Elimination of Discrimination Against Women (Women's Convention).[21] It is well known that the high profile of women's NGOs at the 1993 World Conference on Human Rights in Vienna resulted in the first U.N. affirmation of women's rights as human rights and the condemnation of all forms of violence against women. The recommendations from this Conference also lead to the U.N. appointment of a Special Rapporteur on Violence against Women.[22]

Women's groups were extremely active in the recent development of an Optional Protocol to CEDAW and in the creation of treaties on topics as diverse as the Convention on the Rights of the Child and the Ottawa Treaty banning anti-personnel landmines. Today the international women's movement has grown and diversified. As Martha Alter Chen notes:

> They have learned how to operate on the global stage and how to make themselves seen and heard. Moreover, they have provided effective leadership to the development, environment, human rights and population fields.[23]

As well as playing a strong role in the push for the development of new international legal norms, women's NGOs also play a crucial role in the process of enforcing international law. Studies in this area have indicated that at a grassroots level, women's NGOs have the potential to increase government accountability and implementation of international law.[24] Using a range of methods, including education, lobbying, accessing the media, and writing papers, women's groups can exert pressure and increase national government's accountability and implementation. In particular, within the U.N. system, women's NGOs have participated in the reporting and evaluation process and have written "counter" reports to those submitted by states.[25]

In the past, women's NGOs have tended to focus on issues relating to the health and development of women, as initially there was a clear demarcation between women's groups and the traditional human rights movements. The human rights movement took time to appreciate the rights of women as an intrinsic part of the

---

21.   34 GAOR Supp. (No. 46) 193, U.N. Doc A/RES/34/180 (1980), *adopted* Dec. 18, 1979, *entered into force* Sept. 3, 1981.

22.   Christine Chinkin, *Global Summits: Democratising International Law-making?*, 7 Pub. L. Rev. 208 (1996).

23.   Chen, *supra* note 19.

24.   *See* Afra Afsharipour, *Empowering Ourselves: The Role of Women's NGOs in the Enforcement of the Women's Convention*, 99 Colum. L. Rev. 129 (1999).

25.   *See* Susan Brennan, *Having our say: Australian women's organizations and the treaty making process*, 5(2) Austr. J. Hum. Rts. 94 (1999).

human rights question, as its concerns regarding human rights came from the male dominated international legal framework.[26] This framework places greater emphasis on the public curtailment by the state of the rights of an individual, as outlined in the International Covenant on Civil and Political Rights. Yet, economic and developmental rights and violations of rights in the private sphere by non-state actors are generally seen as "soft" rights and are not accorded the same status in the human rights discourse. Thus, the mandate of many human rights NGOs focuses on violations of human rights in the public sphere by the state and its agents. However, issues often of most relevance to the majority of the world's women are not civil and political rights, but economic, social, and cultural rights. Until recently, domestic violence, sexual discrimination, harassment and the like, although often a result of state sanctioned cultural or social practices, did not rank as human rights abuses for many NGOs. Today, as a result of the work of women's NGOs, violence against women and sexual exploitation and trafficking have been recognized formally as human rights violations.[27]

There are, however, important questions to raise in relation to the representative nature of women's NGOs. With billions of women in the world, it is inevitable that each women's NGO cannot claim to represent all women and their differing ideological viewpoints. There is no doubt that since 1975, leadership of the women's NGO movement has somewhat shifted from women in the North to women in the South, making it more representative. However, the fact that the ideology and origin of NGOs within the U.N. system is predominantly Western-oriented must not be forgotten.[28] Within the human rights dialogue, this results in stress between the Western focus upon civil and political rights and developing nations economic, social, and cultural agendas.[29] It must also be stressed that NGOs in general are only able to flourish domestically in "sympathetic public spaces provided by Governments."[30] Not all governments are sympathetic or provide such public spaces. While NGOs can be very effective in pushing responsive states to adhere to international human rights norms, stress must be placed upon the word "responsive." To a vast number of the world's population, particularly women, concepts such as participation and empowerment are not relevant to their daily lives and thus there is great difficulty in establishing a dialogue on the topic.[31] Even within countries with a robust civil society, inevitable ten-

---

26. As Friedman states: "To counter this neglect, some women employed an old strategy in a new way: they began to use the human rights framework to advance women's rights. Instead of claiming rights as *women*, they claimed the human rights of *half of humanity*." Elisabeth Friedman, *Women's Human Rights: The Emergence of a Movement' in* WOMEN'S RIGHTS, HUMAN RIGHTS: INTERNATIONAL FEMINIST PERSPECTIVES 22 (Julie Peters & Andrea Wolper eds., 1995).

27. *See* Connors, *supra* note 18, at 170.

28. CHIANG PEI-HENG, NON-GOVERNMENTAL ORGANIZATIONS AT THE UNITED NATIONS: IDENTITY, ROLE AND FUNCTION 257 (1981).

29. *See, e.g.*, Dianne Otto, *Rethinking Universals: Opening Transformative Possibilities in International Human Rights Law*, 18 AUSTR. Y.B. INT'L L. 1 (1997).

30. Fischer, *supra* note 17, at 451.

31. For example, there is no word in the Arabic language for "gender."

sions arise when NGOs criticize the state. The relationship between NGOs aiming to influence governments and the state will never be easy.

A critical question often posed is what gives certain stakeholders the representative authority to speak for the broader community? Do articulate, well educated, Western feminist activists speak for "all women" or only those of a certain eco-social and cultural background? As many feminists have recognized, "feminist analyses have often presumed that a white, middle-class, heterosexual, Christian, and able-bodied person is the norm behind women's experience."[32]

Similarly, it is important to question whether NGOs that purport to represent "women's interests" are actually representative of all cultural, economic, social, political, racial and religious groups. The details and validity of the concept of "popular sovereignty" is, as yet, widely unexplored. Furthermore, in relation to the role of women's NGOs in the process of international lawmaking, it is dangerous to overestimate NGOs capacity to contribute to the formal development of law. As previously stated, NGOs are not part of the formal process of treaty making as are states. Being outside the paradigm of power means that NGOs can be ignored, and NGOs papers and voices are not always incorporated into the debates. In the area of customary law, only states can establish practice and *opinio juris*. Yet, as Christine Chinkin argues:

> [T]he international law-making process is more complex and deeply layered than this reasoning might suggest. It defies simple categorisation into "treaty or non-treaty," "hard or soft," "binding or non-binding," and requires instead an analysis of expectations of conformity, institutional support and subsequent actions.[33]

Thus despite these uncertainties and issues of concern, the powerful and multifaceted nature of NGOs in international law cannot be underestimated and their importance to issues of gender quality is essential.

THE ROLE OF NGOS IN CREATING AND CRAFTING THE ICC STATUTE

On July 17, 1998, the international community agreed to adopt a Statute for an International Criminal Court (ICC), which is designed to organize a court able to try individuals accused of some of the most serious international offenses.[34] This decision was a result of over fifty years of discussion, five years of debate at the United Nations, and an intense five-week Diplomatic Conference. In the years of debate at the United Nations and at the Conference, NGOs played an important role in creating and moulding the Statute for the ICC.

The first Preparatory Committee on the Establishment of an International Criminal Court (hereafter PrepCom) was established in December 1995 by the United

---

32. Martha Minow, *Feminist Reason: Getting It and Losing It, in* FEMINIST LEGAL THEORY: FOUNDATIONS 339, 339 (D. Kelly Weisberg ed., 1993).

33. Chinkin, *supra* note 22.

34. *See* ICC Statute, *supra* note 1.

Nations General Assembly.[35] This Committee was directed to review the major substantive and administrative issues arising from the Draft Statute and to draft texts with a view toward preparing a widely accepted consolidated text. The PrepComs were attended not only by a large number of state delegations but also a wide range of NGOs. The largest NGO group working towards the creation of an ICC was the Coalition for an International Criminal Court (the Coalition). This Coalition brought together a broad-based network of NGOs and international law experts to develop strategies on substantive legal and political issues relating to the proposed Statute. Its key goal was to foster awareness and support among a wide range of civil society organizations: human rights, international law, judicial, humanitarian, religious, peace, women's groups, children's groups, victim's groups, and others.

The Women's Caucus for Gender Justice in the International Criminal Court (Women's Caucus) is an example of a specific focus member of the Coalition. Created in February 1997 with the assistance of the Coalition, the Women's Caucus aimed to advocate for the incorporation of a gender perspective in the proposed International Criminal Court. The primary goals of the Women's Caucus included:

- ensuring the participation of women's human rights advocates from all regions in developing positions that should be incorporated into the ICC treaty;

- building a political force that will influence governments negotiating the ICC through advocacy with foreign ministries at home;

- building a delegation of women to participate in developing and lobbying the positions of the Caucus at the U.N. meetings;

- using the occasion of the negotiation for popular education in women's human rights and strategies, including the ICC, for holding perpetrators accountable.[36]

Among their various activities, the Women's Caucus was responsible for a number of influential written recommendations and commentaries. In particular, the Women's Caucus played a major role in pushing for the inclusion within the ICC's jurisdiction of a broad range of sexually violent acts as both crimes against humanity and as war crimes during international and internal armed conflict. The Caucus also successfully lobbied for the inclusion of gender representation on the bench in the ICC Statute (Article 37) and other matters of equity.[37] With careful coordination, it created a Legal Text Drafting and Vetting Group, identifying relevant areas of the Statute and allocating work to various legal experts on gender issues around the world.

---

35. GA Res. 50/46, 50 U.N. GAOR 87th plen. mtg., U.N. Doc A/Res/46 (1995).

36. Letter from the Women's Caucus for Gender Justice in the International Criminal Court (1997) (on file with author).

37. *See Achievements Resulting out of Interventions Made by the Women's Caucus in the Four Preparatory Committee (Prepcom) Meetings prior to the Diplomatic Treaty Conference in Rome*, 1999, at <www.iccwomen.org.icc/internventions.htm>.

Utilizing a strong international women's legal network and information technology, the Women's Caucus was able to develop comprehensive and articulate papers to impress upon delegates that a gender perspective was essential to the ICC.

During the PrepCom of August 1997, one of the many areas of concern to the Women's Caucus and other NGOs was the provision of appropriate and effective witness protection procedures. The International Law Commission's (ILC) Draft Statute of the ICC had made limited reference to this issue. Concern was expressed by the Women's Caucus as to the numerous instances in the Draft Statute where the accused was included in the same category as victims and witnesses. In a document making recommendations in this area the Women's Caucus wrote:

> It is essential to distinguish between the degree and type of protection required by the accused and that which should be accorded to victim and "witnesses." In this context witnesses refers to individuals giving evidence for both the prosecution and the defence. In some circumstances the accused may lose certain rights (such as privacy) which are particularly important to witnesses and victims. A lack of distinction between these two groups, the accused on one side and victims/witnesses on the other, may be legally confusing or incorrect.[38]

The document then continued:

> It must also be recognized that certain rights given to witnesses and victims encourage individuals to give evidence and report offences. Unlike the situation of the accused, the appearance of the witnesses before the court and the reporting of offences by victims is likely to be discretionary and depends on their willingness to participate. Ensuring that witnesses are available to testify at trials is essential to the integrity of an international criminal proceeding. Providing suitable environments and conditions for victims and witnesses to provide investigatory bodies with evidence will provide momentum for prosecution. This is of particular importance in cases of sexual and gender violence where the protection of identity and privacy, and the avoidance of intimidation, retraumatisation, and retaliation against witnesses and family members must be an inextricable part of the Court's assessment of the rights of the accused and the guarantee of a fair and impartial trial.[39]

A number of specific suggestions made by the Women's Caucus in relation to the wording of the provision dealing with protective measures were not adopted.[40] However, the final text of the Statute differs greatly from that recommended by the ILC and incorporates many of the concerns expressed by the Women's Caucus and other NGOs writing on this topic.[41] This evolution and "fleshing out" of articles deal-

---

38. *Recommended Amendment to Article 27* (Paper produced by Women's Caucus for Gender Justice in the International Criminal Court, Aug. 1997).

39. *Id.*

40. *See, e.g., Recommendations and Commentary for August 1997 PrepCom on the Establishing of an International Criminal Court—Part II: Procedural Matters* (Paper produced by Women's Caucus for Gender Justice in the International Criminal Court, Aug. 1997), at 3.

41. *See* art. 68 of the ICC Statute, *supra* note 1, which provides:

> (1) The Court shall take appropriate measures to protect the safety, physical and psychological well-being, dignity and privacy of victims and witnesses. In so doing, the Court shall have regard to all relevant factors, including age, gender as defined in article 2, paragraph 3, health, and the nature of the crime, in particular, but not limited

ing with the protection and right of victims and witnesses was the result of the efforts of numerous Coalition members[42] and many delegates committed to this issue. The writings of the Women's Caucus on this and other topics, particularly the area of sexual violence, contributed greatly to the discussions and variety of options states had to eventually consider. With the active work undertaken by the Women's Caucus, the issue of gender within the ICC could not be ignored by delegates attending the PrepComs.

THE ROME CONFERENCE ON THE ESTABLISHMENT OF THE ICC

For five weeks during June and July 1998, the United Nations Diplomatic Conference of Plenipotentiaries on the Establishment of an International Criminal Court (the Conference) was held in Rome, Italy. Participants included state delegates; as a result of General Assembly Resolution 160 of December 15, 1997, over 250 worldwide NGOs accredited by the Preparatory Committee were also invited to participate.[43] All activities had to be performed in accordance with the Rules of Procedure adopted by the Conference.[44] It is interesting to note that this was the first formal resolution dealing directly with NGOs. Previous NGO participation in the ICC debates was an example of the informal relationship between such organizations and the U.N.

A number of powerful NGO organizations and affiliations were present at the Conference, and made their presence known. The Women's Caucus was one such example, having powerful affiliations with over 300 other international organizations. Its strength lay in its numbers so that when, in the final week of the Conference, the Caucus became concerned at the direction negotiations were taking on certain key issues, the Women's Caucus cautioned that "if these minimal criteria are not present in the final Statute, the Women's Caucus will not support the resulting weak court and will consider actively lobbying their governments against ratification."[45]

The issue of paramount concern to the Women's Caucus was that of gender justice and the ICC, an issue that also generated controversy and tension between states and NGOs and between the various NGO groups. All issues dealing with gender became extremely controversial, in particular whether or not forced pregnancy should

---

to, where the crime involves sexual or gender violence or violence against children. The Prosecutor shall take such measures particularly during the investigation and prosecution of such crimes. These measures shall not be prejudicial to or inconsistent with the rights of the accused and a fair and impartial trial.

42. *See Role of Victims in the Proceedings* (Working paper, The European Law Students Association, 1997); *Promoting the Right to Reparation for Survivors of Torture: What Role for a Permanent International Criminal Court,* (Paper produced by REDRESS, London, 1997). Much work on this topic was also done by the Caucus on Children's Rights in the ICC and Yael Danieli.

43. Due regard was given as to the provisions of part VII of the Economic and Social Council Res. 31 of July 25, 1996, and in particular to the relevance of their activities to the work of the Conference.

44. *Rules of Procedure for the United Nations Diplomatic Conference of Plenipotentiaries on the Establishment of an International Criminal Court,* U.N. Doc A/CONF.183/6, June 23, 1998.

45. *No More Compromises: Bring The Issues of Justice to a Vote* (Women's Caucus for Gender Justice in the International Criminal Court, Rome, 1998).

be included within the jurisdiction of the Court. A number of states, as well as the Vatican and an NGO calling itself the REAL Women of Canada[46] (REAL Women), expressed concern that including the crime of forced pregnancy may impact upon domestic laws relating to abortion. This view was vehemently opposed by other states and Coalition members such as the Women's Caucus. Also extremely contentious, and impacting upon the inclusion of forced pregnancy, was the definition of "gender." On this topic, REAL Women wrote papers directly expressing their concern with policies advocated by the Women's Caucus:

> Groups advocating "gender justice" have argued recently that "a small minority of delegations" are "systematically attacking . . . the essential components of justice for women". Before one can assess the validity of that accusation, however, one must know exactly what is meant by "gender justice" and "the essential components of justice for women."[47]

The paper reviewed the various definitions of "gender justice," from equal treatment before the law to a more expanded definition. It advocated that the Beijing Platform was not a "consensus" document, in particular, in relation to abortion. The paper warned against expanding the definition of "gender" from the male and female sexes to a broader interpretation, stating that the dangers inherent in this move included allowing the ICC to have a potential impact upon the law pertaining to sexual orientation and abortion. The paper reminded readers that French and Arabic texts do not use the word gender and rather refer to "the two sexes." The paper concluded:

> One might ask what fuels the continual quest for "gender justice". No one opposes equal treatment of women and men before the law. If "gender justice" means more than this, the concept dramatically expands the role of the International Criminal Court, changing the Court from a Court aimed at the "most serious crimes" of "international concern", into a potent judicial engine for social engineering.[48]

The Women's Caucus had written a position paper highlighting the use of the term "gender" and "gender-based violence" within the Vienna Declaration and Programme of Action; the Declaration on the Elimination of Violence against Women adopted February 23, 1994; the Beijing Platform for Action adopted September 15, 1995; and a number of U.N. General Assembly Resolutions. The paper concluded with a quote from the Report of the Secretary General on Integrating the Human Rights of Women Throughout the United Nations System:[49]

> As sex refers to biologically determined differences between men and women that are universal, so gender refers to the social difference between men and women that are learned, changeable over time and have wide variations both within and between cultures. Gender is a socio-economic variable in the analysis of roles, responsibilities, constraints, opportunities and needs of men and women in any context. The use of the

---

46.   This NGO was not a member of the Coalition.

47.   David M. Kennedy Center for International Studies, *What's the Argument for Gender Justice* (Position Paper, REAL Women of Canada, 1998) (on file with author).

48.   *Id.*

49.   *Report of the Secretary General on Integrating the Human Rights of Women Throughout the United Nations System*, U.N. Doc. E/CN.4/1997/40, Dec. 20, 1996, at 10.

term "gender" as an analytical tool focuses not on women as an isolated group, but on the roles and needs of men and women. Given that women are usually in a disadvantaged position as compared to men of the same socio-economic level, promotion of gender equality usually means giving explicit attention to women's needs, interests and perspectives.[50]

The final Statute of the ICC has a limited definition of "gender." Article 7 of the Statute of the ICC addressing crimes against humanity deals with this term, stating:

> For the purpose of this statute it is understood that the term "gender" refers to the two sexes, male and female, within the context of society. The term "gender" does not indicate any meaning different from the above.[51]

Forced pregnancy was finally included in the Statute, both as a crime against humanity in Article 7(1)(g) and as a war crime in Article 8(B)(xxii) (dealing with international armed conflict) and Article 8(C)(vi) (in non-international armed conflict). However, the compromise required to win the inclusion of this crime involved articulation of a high threshold for intent in the section dealing with the elements of "forced pregnancy." The Statute provides that:

> Forced pregnancy means the unlawful confinement of a woman forcibly made pregnant, with the intent of affecting the ethnic composition of any population or carrying out other grave violations of international law. This definition shall not in any way be interpreted as affecting national law relating to pregnancy.[52]

An analysis of the debates between NGOs at the Conference on issues relating to gender highlights some interesting considerations relating to the role of civil society at international negotiations. The tension between informality or a structured approach to the position and internal workings of NGOs is sharply emphasized when philosophical differences arise within such groups. Without a centralized body regulating policy in a democratic sense, who has the right to speak on behalf of whom? In some cases, it is those with the most resources, despite their narrow focus and representation of a minority, who are able to make the most impact. On the other hand, questions could be asked as to what constitutes a "minority" in such a context. Most NGOs tend to be progressive, and thus conservative NGOs appear as a "minority" in circumstances such as the ICC Conference. The underlying issue needing consideration is this: if NGOs are tasked with being the "other" voice, does internal fragmentation of views strengthen this position or weaken civil society's credibility? As raised on numerous occasions in this chapter, the most precious resource NGOs supply to discussions at an international level is the variance of views. The freedom

---

50. *The International Community has Repeatedly Reaffirmed the Need to Eliminate Gender Violence* (Position Paper, Women's Caucus for Gender Justice in the International Criminal Court, 1998).

51. ICC Statute, *supra* note 1, at art. 7(3). *See also* Kelly D. Askin, *Women's Issues in International Criminal Law: Recent Developments and the Potential Contribution of the ICC, in* INTERNATIONAL CRIMES, PEACE AND HUMAN RIGHTS: THE ROLE OF THE INTERNATIONAL CRIMINAL COURT (Dinah Shelton ed., 2000).

52. ICC Statute, *supra* note 1, at art. 7(2)(f). *See also* H. Durham, *The International Criminal Court and Gender Issues*, 4 AUSTR. RED CROSS: ICC UP-DATE 19 (1998).

accompanying informality may provide benefits far greater than that correlating structure. The price of true democratic involvement of NGOs at the Conference may have been the lack of a united front on issues, different styles of lobbying, and energies spent on internal, and at times bitter, debates.

It is impossible to quantify the level of achievement of women's and other NGOs at the Conference. Measuring the success of civil society in the creation of international legal norms is not easy. Extracting the exact value of input from one group is complex due to the range of contributions from various forces and actors. As one commentator suggests:

> This makes measuring "strategic" accountability in its most fundamental sense almost impossible—no organisation can be held accountable for the impact of forces which are beyond its control.[53]

However, despite the difficulties of quantifying precise contributions, some conclusions must be drawn from the experience. In an analysis of topics discussed in detail at the Conference and those not deeply considered, some correlation can be made to the presence of NGOs. The provision dealing with illegal weapons in the ICC Statute, for example, is extremely weak, with a limited list of prohibited weapons and no such provision for non-international armed conflict. There is no guarantee that a strong presence of anti-weapon campaigners would have changed the Statute, but it would have ensured that states could not ignore the subject as they did. On the other hand, the ample voices from women's NGOs relating to matters such as gender issues forced delegates to debate this topic at length and the final Statute has a number of advancements in the area of sexual violence and international criminal law.[54]

Attending PrepComs and the Conference, using information technology and the media to amplify their concerns, women's NGOs created a debate within and across state borders on whether the international community was serious about putting an end to impunity and creating an effective ICC to assist with international gender justice. Through quiet and loud diplomacy, emotion, extensive expertise, highly technical analysis, and influencing individuals and "shaming" governments, NGOs, including women's groups, ensured that the global dialogue on developing an effective ICC was not the exclusive domain of states.

Indeed, after the ICC Statute was adopted, the Final Act attached to the Statute created post-Rome Preparatory Commissions (PrepComs) to negotiate such things as elements of crimes and Rules of Procedure and Evidence to be used by the Court. The Women's Caucus has continued to be a major influence in attempting

---

53. Michael Edwards & David Hulme, *NGO Performance and Accountability: Introduction and Overview, in* NGOS—PERFORMANCE AND ACCOUNTABILITY—BEYOND THE MAGIC BULLET 6 (M Edwards & D. Hulme eds., 1995).

54. For further details on the ICC Statute, *see* N. Erb, *Gender-based crimes under the Draft Statute for the Permanent International Criminal Court,* 29 COLUM. HUM. RTS. REV. 401 (1998). *See also* Dorean M. Koenig & Kelly D. Askin, *International Criminal Law and the International Criminal Court Status: Crimes Against Women, in* Volume 2 of this treatise; Kelly D. Askin, *Crimes Within the Jurisdiction of the ICC,* 10 CRIM. L.F. 33 (1999).

to ensure, *inter alia*, that women's issues and gender-based crimes are not neglected, that the definitions and rules are drafted in a way to enable appropriate prosecution of sex-based crimes, and that gender inclusion and awareness is incorporated in the process.

NGOS AND THE *AD HOC* TRIBUNALS

The creation of the ICC can be seen as deriving much of its impetus from the establishment five years earlier of the International Criminal Tribunal for the former Yugoslavia (ICTY)[55] and later the International Criminal Tribunal for Rwanda (ICTR).[56] The role of NGOs in the creation of these Tribunals was significant, as NGOs brought breaches of international humanitarian law and human rights occurring within the Balkans in the early 1990s to the attention of the world's media. In particular, the reports of mass rapes of women in the former Yugoslavia "had an electrifying effect and became a significant factor in the demand for the creation of the International Tribunal."[57] In disseminating the horrors of the conflict, a large number of NGOs suggested solutions in the form of the prosecution of those responsible. NGOs also greatly assisted the Commission of Experts[58] in the gathering of initial details, particularly relating to sexual violence, for the United Nations before it decided whether to create the ICTY.[59]

NGOS GATHERING EVIDENCE

NGOs have perhaps the greatest potential to assist the future ICC, and the current Tribunals, in the area of gathering evidence due to NGOs capacity to identify potential witnesses and provide access to vital information. It is also the area fraught with the most dangers if not handled carefully by both the Tribunal and the relevant organizations.

NGOs have access to networks and grassroot information in a way that officials cannot and do not have. Very often survivors and witnesses are suspicious and fearful of formal bodies. In many instances, representatives of the state, such as the military or political parties, have caused the harm. Thus, witnesses often prefer to talk to non-state actors, either in the form of local community groups or established and well-known international NGOs.

In the area of sexual assault and gender-related crimes, women's NGOs have been the most active and efficient of all non-state actors.[60] The Sexual Assault Unit

---

55.   ICTY Statute, *supra* note 2.

56.   ICTR Statute, *supra* note 3.

57.   Rhonda Copeland, *Surfacing Gender*, 5(2) HASTINGS WOMEN'S L.J. 248 (1994).

58.   *Final Report of the Commission of Experts Pursuant to Security Council Resolution 780* (1992), SC Res. 780, 47 U.N. SCOR (3119th mtg), U.N. Doc S/Res/780 (1992); 31 I.L.M. 1476; U.N. Doc, S/674/1994 Annex (1994) (Final Report).

59.   Interview with Donato Kiniger-Passigli, External Relations Officer, ICTY (The Hague, Nov. 5, 1996) (transcript on file with author).

60.   Interview with Patricia Sellers, Legal Adviser on Gender Issues, ICTY (The Hague, Sept. 7, 1997) (transcript on file with author).

at the ICTY states that without the cooperation of such groups, it would have only limited evidence of crimes of sexual violence, such as rape.[61] Due to the personal nature of these crimes, women's groups have played a vital role in locating witnesses, encouraging them to speak out, and taking limited statements. Work is done with women who have survived sexual violence during armed conflict, and the work is at a number of levels or fora, from local "clubs" in places such as Zagreb and Tuzla to formal settings such as the Dublin Rape Crisis Centre, which assists refugees from the former Yugoslavia. It is necessary for the ICTY to develop relationships with such organizations and to identify what the NGO can do and should not do to assist the Tribunal. Not every organization dealing with survivors of sexual violence wishes to set up a partnership with the ICTY, as there is a limit to the type of work NGOs can undertake. Thus an important element of the ICTY's work is identifying potential non-state actors who may be able to assist. Such networking has been undertaken using e-mail, women's conferences, and local Legal Aid Centres, which often have details of such groups. If the relationship is to be effective, clear communication and the creation of trust is essential.[62]

CASE STUDIES

An example of the ability of women's NGOs to assist international criminal law has been demonstrated by the work of a number of NGOs in gathering evidence of sexual and other violence for use by the ICTY. Moreover, the use of *amicus curie* briefs by a number of women's NGOs in attempts to include sexual violence charges in indictments illustrates the influence of women's NGOs in international criminal law. The following case studies demonstrate the potential ability of NGOs to impact on the future ICC.

Australian Committee of Investigation into War Crimes (ACIWC)

ACIWC was established in 1994 in Melbourne, Australia in response to a specific request from a Women's Centre in Zagreb called *Tresnjevka*. An Australian woman, Jane Gronow, was sent by Austcare[63] to *Tresnjevka* to assist women survivors of the conflict in the former Yugoslavia. While Gronow was working in Zagreb, a women's group in Melbourne, Women's Interlink (WIL), wrote to her asking what could be done back in Australia to assist those in *Tresnjevka*. After discussing the matter with the women in the Zagreb Centre, Gronow responded that the women wished rape to be condemned as a war crime and for it to be prosecuted at the ICTY.

With limited resources and no access to the Tribunal, WIL decided to investigate what procedures were available within Australia to allow refugees from the region of the former Yugoslavia to give evidence to the ICTY. It was deemed that the best way to ensure the prosecution of the crime of sexual assault, and thus to create a clear

---

61.   Interviews with Nancy Patterson, Legal Officer, and Agnes Inderhaug, Investigation Team Leader, Sexual Assault Unit, ICTY (The Hague, Nov. 7, 1996) (transcript on file with author).

62.   *Id.*

63.   Austcare is an Australian NGO that deals with the problems experienced by refugees.

legal precedent, was to encourage women who were survivors to give evidence. It became apparent that there was no governmental department responsible for, or willing to assist in, the gathering of evidence in Australia. Neither was there any NGO or international legal academic group working on the issue. These conclusions led a number of members of WIL and a few other interested individuals to create ACIWC.

In 1995, ACIWC contacted the Deputy Prosecutor at the ICTY, Graham Blewitt, to enquire whether there was any role for a small and non-funded Australian NGO. Blewitt advised that it would be extremely useful if potential witnesses could be identified and screened so that the Tribunal would be able to know the quality and quantity of evidence available within the relevant refugee population in Australia.

Numerous informal meetings were arranged with community leaders, and personal relationships were established between members of ACIWC and representatives from the relevant ethnic groups. After discussing the proposed screening of witnesses with community members from the former Yugoslavia, it was decided that ACIWC's mandate should be broadened to include any individual (both sexes and all ethnic groups involved in the conflict) who wished to give evidence of any crime within the ICTY's jurisdiction.

ACIWC believed that it was important to raise the issue of the prosecution of rape as a war crime with governmental authorities and the general public. In a submission to the Joint Standing Committee on Foreign Affairs and Trade dealing with Australia's response to the conflict in the former Yugoslavia, the Committee listed its aims as:

> The identification of victims or witnesses of war crimes (especially rape and sexual assault) committed in the territory of the former Yugoslavia, from the refugee population in Australia, and passing this information to the Tribunal.[64]

Attached to the submission was an appendix outlining the need to create a strong legal precedent at the ICTY for sexual crimes. In concluding, the Committee stated:

> ACIWC believes that the identification of individuals who could assist the Tribunal is vitally important, not only for the resettlement process of refugees from the Yugoslavian region, but also for the future of international peace and security.[65]

ACIWC developed a screening kit for potential witnesses that was later amended to clearly indicate that ACIWC was solely interested in victims of war crimes, not criminals: "It is important to note that ACIWC is assisting war victims in Australia, but is neither hunting nor investigating war criminals. That task is left solely to the Prosecutor."[66]

To encourage protection, developing adequate systems of confidentiality was essential. In previous international criminal war crimes tribunals, such as Nuremberg

---

64. Australian Committee of Investigation Into War Crimes, *Papers submitted to the Joint Standing Committee in Foreign Affairs and Trade by the Australian Committee of Investigation Into War Crimes* (1996).

65. *Id.* at 3.

66. Australian Committee of Investigation into War Crimes, *Screening Kit* (1995) 1.

and Tokyo, prosecutions were held at the end of the armed conflict, and there was no fear from those giving evidence that immediate retribution would occur to loved ones still caught in the conflict. With the ICTY, this was not the case. To overcome these fears, ACIWC implemented a code system to ensure that those undertaking the screening process could not be identified.

As a result of the work of ACIWC in identifying potential witnesses, the Prosecutor of the ICTY sent a Senior Legal Adviser and an Investigator to Australia in late 1995 to undertake detailed interviews with a number of the identified witnesses. ACIWC disbanded in late 1996 due to reduced responses from the community groups, difficulty with resources, and the time consuming nature of the process. ACIWC's work did assist the ICTY in gathering important evidence. The Office of the Prosecutor expressed its approval of the work undertaken by ACIWC, stating:

> From the Tribunal's point of view NGOs play a very important part in our work, and I am sure that in the event that a Permanent International Criminal Court is established, NGOs will continue to play a critical role. In particular the work of the ACIWC in Australia has lead to the discovery of several important witnesses and I am confident that further witnesses will be identified in the future. The ACIWC is one of the most professional NGOs that the Tribunal is currently dealing with and I applaud the work that it is doing.[67]

American Serbian Women's Caucus

Another example of a women's organization assisting the ICTY is that of the American Serbian Women's Caucus (ASWC). This group was established to investigate crimes committed against Serbs during the war in the Balkans and to gather evidence to present to the ICTY. Eventually the ICTY requested the assistance of the ASWC in preparing statements of witnesses for the Tribunal, and as a direct consequence of the information supplied by the ASWC to the ICTY, the first indictments against Bosnian Muslims and Croats were issued.

The work undertaken by ASWC is another example of a women's NGO utilizing unique skills and relationships to "fill the gap" where international institutions are unable to work. The ASWC were able to not only identify and contact potential witnesses from a very cynical ethnic group, they were also able to set up complex systems to facilitate the process of gathering evidence. The personal relationships and capacity to build trust were essential. As NGOs do not rely upon governments for permission to work, they have more freedom, can be more creative in their attitudes, and are not restricted by factors such as state sovereignty and national borders. Furthermore, they can harness the goodwill of business and gain funds from community groups in a way that formal authorities cannot.

Amicus Curiae Briefs

Another way NGOs have assisted in the international criminal law process is through the submission of *amicus curiae* briefs. Non-state actors have formal capac-

---

67. Letter from Graham Blewitt, Deputy Prosecutor, ICTY (The Hague, Sept. 26, 1995) (on file with author).

ity to submit *amicus curiae* briefs to the ICTY and ICTR, which will also be available in the future ICC. The *Akayesu* case demonstrated the effectiveness of *amicus curiae* briefs.

Jean-Paul Akayesu was indicted by the ICTR in February 1996, and was charged with a range of crimes constituting Genocide, Crimes Against Humanity and Violations of Article 3 common to the Geneva Conventions.[68] The indictment charged Akayesu with acts including murder, extermination, torture, cruel treatment, other inhumane acts, and incitement to commit genocide. Rape and other forms of sexual violence were not included in the initial indictment.

In early 1997, a number of women's human rights legal scholars and non-governmental organizations[69] (Women's Coalition) submitted an *amicus* brief to the Trial Chamber of the ICTR. The brief, entitled "Respecting Amendment of the Indictment and Supplementation of the Evidence to Ensure the Prosecution of Rape and other Sexual Violence within the Competence of the Tribunal, Re: The Prosecutor of the Tribunal against Jean-Paul Akayesu,"[70] called upon the Tribunal to examine the failure of the Prosecutor to thoroughly investigate sexual violence and accordingly indict Akayesu, the first defendant brought to trial in Rwanda, with rape crimes, as their commission was prevalent in all areas of the conflict, including the territory where Akayesu held a position of authority.

The brief was conceptualized from a report published in late 1996 by Human Rights Watch entitled *Shattered Lives: Sexual Violence During the Rwandan Genocide and Its Aftermath*.[71] *Shattered Lives* stated that during the 1994 genocide, Rwandan women were subjected to sexual violence on a massive scale, and:

[a]lthough the exact number of women raped will never be known, testimonies from survivors confirm that rape was extremely widespread and that thousands of women were individually raped, gang-raped, raped with objects such as sharpened sticks or gun barrels, held in sexual slavery (either collectively or through forced "marriage") or sexually mutilated.[72]

---

68.   Prosecutor v. Jean-Paul Akayesu, Indictment, ICTR-96–4–I (Feb. 13, 1996). The indictment was amended June 17, 1997.

69.   This group consisted of: the Centre for Constitutional Rights; Centre for Women's Global Leadership; International Centre for Human Rights and Democratic Development; the International Women's Human Rights Law Clinic of the City University of New York School of Law; the Jacob Blaustein Institute for the Advancement of Human Rights; the Latin American and Caribbean Women's Health Network; the Lawyers' International Forum for Women's Human Rights, *Rassemblement Algerien Des Femmes Democratiques*; the United Methodist Office for the United Nations; Women Living Under Muslim Laws; Women Refugees Project; the Cambridge-Somerville Legal Services and the Working Group on Engendering the Rwanda Tribunal.

70.   Prosecutor v. Jean-Paul Akayesu (*Amicus* Brief Respecting Amendment of the Indictment and Supplementation of the Evidence within the Competence of the Tribunal), ICTR-96–4–T (1996) (hereinafter "*Amendment Brief*"). Original copy of the brief supplied by Professor Rhonda Copelon.

71.   AFRICA/HUMAN RIGHTS WATCH, SHATTERED LIVES : SEXUAL VIOLENCE DURING THE RWANDAN GENOCIDE AND ITS AFTERMATH (1996).

72.   *Id*. at 1.

However, more importantly for the submission of the *amicus* brief, the Human Rights Watch Report indicated that the ICTR had both the authority and the duty to prosecute crimes of sexual violence. The coalition of women's human rights NGOs reported that:

> contrary to the assertions of the ICTR's prosecutors that women would not speak of rape and that, therefore, it could not be prosecuted, there were many women who could provide evidence of rape and sexual violence in the Taba commune . . . *Shattered Lives* also documents the systemic failure of the ICTR to properly investigate sexual violence and provide meaningful witness protection.[73]

Shattered Lives not only provided pages of detailed evidence of sexual assault (in many cases provided by the survivors themselves), it also expressed strong recommendations to the ICTR. It stated that the ICTR must fully and fairly investigate and prosecute sexual violence. Furthermore it stipulated that rape, sexual slavery, and sexual mutilation should be recognized and prosecuted as crimes against humanity, genocide, and/or war crimes. In particular, it insisted that:

> The International Tribunal must step up its efforts to integrate a gender perspective into its investigations. Previous investigative methodology and procedures, which have failed to elicit rape testimonies, must be amended. In particular, the Tribunal must ensure that the issue of violence against women is treated with the same gravity as other crimes against humanity within its jurisdiction. Investigation of rape and other forms of sexual violence should be conducted by teams that include women investigators and interpreters (preferably women) skilled in interviewing women survivors of gender-based violence in the larger context of the atrocities which occurred.[74]

Upon the release of the Human Rights Report, the Women's Coalition sent an urgent letter to the Chief Prosecutor, requesting that internal reforms be carried out within the Rwandan Tribunal to ensure effective investigation into sexual violence perpetrated as part of the Rwandan genocide. In particular, the Coalition was concerned with the fact that Akayesu, the first defendant indicted, had not been charged with any crimes of sexual violence despite the fact that he was the powerful mayor of the Taba community, an area in which rapes had occurred.

The Chief Prosecutor responded positively to the letter sent by the Coalition; however, no changes were made to the indictments and the *Akayesu* trial began in late 1996 without the inclusion of charges of sexual violence.[75] During the *Akayesu* trial, information surfaced, while a judge was questioning witnesses, pertaining to Akayesu's responsibility in relation to the occurrences of sexual violence. Frustrated at the continued exclusion of sexual assault charges against Akayesu, an *amicus* brief was drafted by the Women's Coalition and submitted to the Registrar.[76]

The Women's Coalition asserted that the ICTR had the power to amend the indictment of the defendant Akayesu. It was claimed that a failure to do so, where there has

---

73. V. Oosterveld & R. Copelon, *First Rape Charges Brought at the Rwandan Tribunal*, 4 Hum. Rts. Tribune 16 (1997).

74. *Id*. at 9.

75. *Id*. at 16.

76. Discussions with Professor Rhonda Copelon at the International Women's Human Rights Law Clinic (City University of New York Law School (Sept. 27, 1997) (transcript on file with author).

been clear evidence at trial of sexual violence and further evidence available through documentation, produces unfairness and constitutes a miscarriage of justice.

The brief argued that rape is explicitly cited as a crime against humanity in Article 3(g)(f) of the Statute of the ICTR, as well as a serious violation of Article 3 of the Geneva Convention and Additional Protocol II in Article 4(e). The Women's Coalition also argued that sexual violence can be pleaded as a form of torture and cruel treatment pursuant to Article 4(a). In certain circumstances, the *amicus* submitted, rape and other forms of sexual violence, such as the killing of pregnant women, could constitute genocide referred to in Article 2(2)(a)–(d) of the Statute.[77] Thus the brief advised that the ICTR "is unquestionably mandated to prosecute persons who have raped or been responsible for rape . . . or other sexual violence."[78]

In June 1997, during the *Akayesu* trial, the Prosecutor amended the indictment to include three more counts and add three additional paragraphs dealing with acts of sexual violence. These new charges included rape (Crimes Against Humanity, Article 3(g) of the Statute of the ICTR), and outrages upon personal dignity (in particular rape), degrading and humiliating treatment, and indecent assault (Violations of Article 3 common to the Geneva Conventions and Additional Protocol II, Article 4(e) of the ICTR Statute). Akayesu pleaded not guilty to all counts in the original and subsequently amended indictment.

The Women's Coalition maintained that excerpts from the testimony from Jean-Paul Akayesu's trial as well as reports from bodies such as the U.N. Commission of Experts,[79] Africa Rights,[80] Human Rights Watch,[81] and UNHCR[82] disclosed that sexual assaults were an integral part of the widespread genocidal violence against Tutsi women. Furthermore, testimony from Akayesu's trial showed the availability of probative evidence, particularly from witnesses "H" and "J."[83] Witness "H" testified to having been raped and having witnessed the rape of other women who had taken refuge in the Bureau Communal under the control of Akayesu. Witness "J" testified that she had witnessed the rape of her six-year-old daughter by three Hutu men when they came to kill her father.[84]

---

77. For sexual violence to be pleaded as genocide it is necessary to prove that it was an integral part of a genocidal campaign, designed to result in death or destroy a women from a physical, mental, or social perspective, and to destroy her capacity to participate in the reproduction of the community. *See* KELLY DAWN ASKIN, WAR CRIMES AGAINST WOMEN: PROSECUTION IN INTERNATIONAL WAR CRIMES TRIBUNALS (1997).

78. *Amendment Brief, supra* note 70, at 7.

79. *Final Report of the Commission of Experts Established Pursuant to Security Council Resolution 935 (1994)*, 49 U.N. SCOR (3400th mtg), U.N. Doc. S/Res/935 (1994), Annex, 3 (1994) (*"Commission of Experts' Final Report"*).

80. AFRICAN RIGHTS, RWANDA: DEATH, DESPAIR AND DEFIANCE (1994).

81. SHATTERED LIVES, *supra* note 71.

82. M. Daniel, Community Services Coordinator, UNHCR, Kigali, *Report on Assignment to Rwanda* (June 12–July 24, 1995).

83. *Amendment Brief, supra* note 70, at 9.

84. *Id.* at 10.

The Women's Coalition pointed out that the Prosecutor opened his case with a statement that referred to sexual violence in the following terms:

> Our evidence will show that in 1994 in Rwanda, there was systematic and widespread murder, imprisonment, torture, persecution and *sexual assault and mutilations . . .* against the Tutsi population.[85]

The brief reviewed, in some detail, Akayesu's criminal responsibility for the rape of Tutsi women in Taba and stated:

> On the basis of the evidence of witnesses "H" and "J," on the documented cases of rape in the Taba commune and the available evidence concerning Akayesu's criminal responsibility for these acts of sexual violence, it is submitted that the Prosecutor should, as provided for by the Statute, seek leave of the Trial Chamber to add charges of rape to Akayesu's indictment.[86]

It was claimed by the Women's Coalition that the absence of charges of rape in the Akayesu indictment was not unique to the ICTR and that there were methodological and staffing problems in the Prosecutor's Office that contributed to the omission of sexual assault charges. The brief deemed that such failures deny Rwandan women who have survived sexual violence equal justice, recognition, and vindication of their suffering.

On September 2, 1998, the Trial Chamber of the ICTR found Akayesu guilty of nine counts and not guilty of six counts listed in the indictment.[87] He was found guilty of rape and other inhumane acts pleaded as a Crime Against Humanity, but not guilty of outrages upon the personal dignity, in particular rape, as pleaded as a Violation of Article 3 common to the Geneva Conventions and Additional Protocol II. Akayesu was also found guilty of Genocide, murder and torture as pleaded as a Crime Against Humanity.

The judgement makes no specific mention of the *amicus* submission of the Women's Coalition. However, there is an interesting discussion relating to the Prosecutor's decision to amend the indictment to include charges of sexual violence. The section is worth quoting in full:

> [O]n 17 June 1997, the indictment was amended to include allegations of sexual violence and additional charges against the Accused under Article 3(g), Article 3(I) and Article 4(2)(e) of the ICTR Statute. In introducing these amendments, the Prosecutor stated that the testimony of Witness H motivated them to renew their investigation of sexual violence in connection with events which took place in Taba at the bureau communal. The Prosecutor stated that evidence previously available was not sufficient to link the Accused to acts of sexual violence and acknowledged that factors to explain this lack of evidence might include the shame that accompanies acts of sexual violence as well as insensitivity in the investigation of sexual violence. The Chamber notes that the Defence in its closing statement questioned whether the Indictment was amended in response to public pressure concerning the prosecution of sexual violence. The Chamber understands that the amendment of the Indictment

---

85. *Id.* at 9.

86. *Id.* at 16.

87. *Prosecutor v. Jean-Paul Akayesu,* Judgement Sept. 2, 1998, ICTR–96–4–T.

resulted from the spontaneous testimony of sexual violence by Witness J and Witness H during the course of this trial and the subsequent investigation of the Prosecution, rather than from public pressure. Nevertheless, the Chamber takes note of the interest shown in this issue by non-Governmental organizations, which it considers as indicative of public concern over the historical exclusion of rape and other forms of sexual violence from the investigation and prosecution of war crimes. The investigation and presentation of evidence relating to sexual violence is in the interest of justice.[88]

This clearly indicates that the judges were aware of the *amicus* and examined issues such as the international judicial need to prosecute those alleged to have perpetrated sexual crimes as well as the special methodological requirements necessary to gather evidence. The *Akayesu* judgement greatly advances international legal jurisprudence in regard to sexual assault and is the first to examine, in detail, sexual violence during armed conflict.[89] It acknowledged that there is no commonly accepted definition of rape in international law, indicated the limited precedents of prosecutions for sexual violence in international humanitarian law, and determined:

The Tribunal defines rape as a physical invasion of a sexual nature, committed on a person under circumstances which are coercive. The Tribunal considers sexual violence, which includes rape, as any act of a sexual nature which is committed on a person under circumstances as coercive. Sexual violence is not limited to physical invasion of the human body and may include acts which do not involve penetration or even physical contact.[90]

Furthermore, while Akayesu's indictment did not explicitly charge him with sexual assault pursuant to the crime of genocide, the judges dealt with the issue anyway and stated that sexual assault could be included in Article 2(2)(d) of the Statute of the ICTR (imposing measures intended to prevent births within the group), and added, "[f]or instance, rape can be a measure to prevent births when the person raped refuses subsequently to procreate".[91] Thus, in certain circumstances rape could be deemed part of the genocide. This was reinforced later in the judgement, which reads, "[s]exual violence was a step in the process of destruction of the Tutsi group—destruction of the spirit, of the will to live, and of life itself."[92]

It is interesting to note that this brief included matters of fact as well as those relevant to the law, despite the regulations of the International Tribunals cautioning that *amicus* are generally limited to matters only of law.[93] However, all facts were

---

88. *Id.* at paras. 170–71.

89. *See* Kelly Dawn Askin, *The International Criminal Tribunal for Rwanda and Its Treatment of Crimes Against Women, in* INTERNATIONAL HUMANITARIAN LAW: ORIGINS, CHALLENGES & PROSPECTS (John Carey & John Pritchard eds., vol. II, 2000). Catherine Cisse, *The End of a Culture of Impunity in Rwanda? Prosecution of Genocide before Rwandan Courts and the International Criminal Tribunal for Rwanda*, 1 Y.B. INT'L HUMANITARIAN L. 171 (1998).

90. Akayesu Judgement, *supra* note 87, at para. 275.

91. *Id.* at para. 208.

92. *Id.* at para. 289.

93. *Information concerning the submission of amicus curiae briefs*, IT/122 27 (1997), U.N. Doc. IT/122 (1997).

couched in the context of the Trial Chamber's supervisory authority and the legal question of the amendment of indictments.

Questions must be raised as to what role NGOs played in the eventual inclusion of charges relating to sexual assault. There is evidence to indicate that, before the submission of the brief, the Prosecutor, despite hearing the evidence of witness "H," had not yet indicted Akayesu on sexual assault charges. After the *amicus curiae* submission was made, the indictment was amended. However, the Prosecutor's Office, as demonstrated in the judgement, would be likely to deny that it was influenced by "public pressure," it may be that it was merely a matter of time, not lack of intention, before the indictment was changed. It is important to acknowledge the potential dangers faced by the Office of the Prosecutor if it is perceived by the defense or the international community as undertaking actions due to pressure from NGOs rather than based on evidence and due process. As there was ample evidence of sexual violence in the Taba commune available, this is not an example of such "political pressure," but the matter must be carefully considered to ensure that the International Tribunals are accorded credibility.

Whether the Women's Coalition brief was a catalyst to amending the indictment will be debated by all sides involved. However, there can be little doubt that the brief advanced and strengthened arguments on the duty of the ICTR to investigate and prosecute rape and other forms of sexual violence. It also raised a number of issues, such as genocidal rape, not previously addressed formally by either the Prosecutor's Office or by the international criminal legal system and reflected in the considerations of the Judges. In the wake of the *Akayesu* decision, prosecutors amended two other indictments to include charges of rape.[94]

The lessons learned from the submission of *amicus curiae* briefs at the ICTR must be carefully studied and understood in order to continue the advancement of international gender justice when the ICC enters into force. There are also ample examples of briefs being used at the ICTY on topics such as the protection of witnesses[95] and issues relating to the quality of the testimony of rape survivors.[96] The need to educate a range of women's NGOs on the procedures involved in the submission of such briefs as well as to provide updated information on pending cases will enhance the capacity for civil society to assist in the enforcement of international criminal law.

---

94. HUMAN RIGHTS WATCH, WORLD REPORT 2000, EVENTS OF 1999 449 (1999). *See also* Kelly D. Askin, *Sexual Violence in Decisions and Indictments of the Yugoslav and Rwanda Tribunals: Current Status*, 93 AM. J. INT'L L. 97 (1999).

95. *See* Christine Chinkin, *Amicus Curiae Brief on Protective Measures for Victims and Witnesses*, 7 CRIM. L. FORUM 179, 182 (1996).

96. "Amicus Brief Respecting the Decision and Order of the Tribunal of July 16, 1998 Requesting that the Tribunal Reconsider Its Decision having regard to the rights of Witness 'A' to equity, privacy and security of the person, and to the presentation by Counsel."

CONCLUSION

To overestimate the capacity of women's NGOs in the area of international criminal law is as dangerous as underestimating their power and potential. While NGOs continue to work outside the "mainstream" in both the creation of treaties and the gathering and submission of evidence to international prosecutions, they have an increasingly important role to play. This chapter has presented practical case studies to demonstrate that women's groups have contributed significantly to the creation of the ICC Statute and the prosecution of those accused of atrocities at both the ICTY and ICTR. Considering in particular that many of the victims of these crimes are women, and the crimes committed against them are gender-based, it is essential that women continue to advocate for international criminal justice at all levels and with a range of creative strategies.

GENDER, PROPERTY, AND LAND RIGHTS: BRIDGING A CRITICAL GAP IN ECONOMIC ANALYSIS AND POLICY

*Bina Agarwal**

Please go and ask the *sarkar* [government] why when it distributes land we don't get a title. Are we not peasants? If my husband throws me out, what is my security?[1]

Economic analysis and policies concerning women have long been preoccupied with employment to the neglect of a crucial determinant of women's situation, namely, the gender gap in command over property. This is especially (but not only) true of analysis relating to South Asia. It is argued here that the gender gap in the ownership and control of property is the single most critical contributor to the gender gap existing in economic well-being, social status, and empowerment. In primarily agrarian economies the most important form of property is arable land. A struggle for gender equality in command over landed property will therefore need to occupy center stage in rural women's struggle for egalitarian gender relations.

The discussion below is divided into five sections. Section 1 examines the broad conceptual links between gender, property, and land rights. The subsequent sections focus on gender and landed property in agrarian economies, using South Asia as the illustrative context. Section 2 elaborates why it is important for rural women to have independent rights in land, especially with regard to women's empowerment. Section 3 looks at historical gender relations in those South Asian communities in which women traditionally enjoyed land rights. Section 4 identifies the obstacles women face in realizing effective land rights in most parts of South Asia today and illustrates how women's command over economic resources is crucially mediated by non-economic factors. Finally, section 5 highlights some aspects of the interventions needed for change.

Although a substantial part of the analysis below focuses on South Asia, with its particular historical and cultural specificities, the theoretical framework, conceptual linkages, and many of the arguments (especially those concerning the importance of land rights for women), also have relevance for other developing countries, in par-

---

* Reproduced with permission from Out of the Margin: Feminist Perspectives on Economics (Jolande Sap and Edith Kuiper eds., Amsterdam: Routledge, 1995).

1. Message conveyed by poor peasant women to the government of West Bengal (India) in 1979 through the elected village council, personal communication, Vina Mazumdar, Center for Women's Development Studies, New Delhi.

ticular those with substantial rural economies,[2] and for countries where new windows of opportunity for addressing women's concerns regarding property rights are now opening, as in South Africa (which is in the process of framing new land reform laws and policies) and the economies of Eastern Europe and the former Soviet Union (where private property rights are now emerging).[3]

GENDER, PROPERTY, AND LAND: SOME CONCEPTUAL LINKS

In examining the relationship between gender and property, five interrelated issues need particular focus: gender relations and a household's property status; gender relations and women's property status; the distinction between ownership and control of property; the distinctiveness of land as property; and what is meant by rights in land. The first three issues are discussed in the subsection below, and the last two in separate subsections.

Household Property and Women's Property

The links between gender subordination and property need to be sought in not only the distribution of property between households but also in its distribution between men and women, in not only who owns the property but also who controls it, and in relation not only to private property but also to communal property. Further, gender equality in legal rights to own property does not guarantee gender equality in actual ownership, nor does ownership guarantee control. The distinctions between law and practice and between ownership and control are especially critical in relation to women.

This formulation departs significantly from standard Marxist analysis, particularly from that of Engels' still-influential though much criticized exposition, where intra-family gender relations are seen as structured primarily by two overlapping economic factors: the property status of the households to which the women belong, and women's participation in wage labor. Engels argued that in capitalist societies, gender relations would be hierarchical among the property-owning families of the bourgeoisie where women did not go out to work and were economically dependent on men, and egalitarian in propertyless proletarian families where women were in the labor force. The ultimate restoration of women to their rightful status, in his view, required the total abolition of private property (i.e., a move to socialism), the socialization of housework and childcare, and the full participation of women in the labor force.[4]

---

2. For some discussions on gender, land and agriculture in the African context see AGRICULTURE, WOMEN AND LAND: THE AFRICAN EXPERIENCE (J. Davidson ed., 1988); and Carmen Diana Deere, *Rural Women and State Policy: The Latin American Agrarian Reform Experience*, 13 (9) WORLD DEVELOPMENT 1037–53 (1985).

3. *See, e.g.*, K. Verdery, *Processes: Transforming Property, Markets and States, in* WHAT WAS SOCIALISM, AND WHAT COMES NEXT? 131–203 (1996).

4. F.A. ENGELS, THE ORIGIN OF THE FAMILY, PRIVATE PROPERTY AND THE STATE (1972) [1884]. This is not meant as a summary of Engels's complex thesis, but merely of one part of it. Critiques of his analysis abound: see, K. Sacks, *Engles Revisitied: Women: The Organization of Production, and Private Property, in* TOWARD AN ANTHROPOLOGY OF WOMEN (R. R. Reiter ed., 1975); R. Delmar,

In this analysis, therefore, the presumed equality of gender relations in a working class family rested on *both* husband and wife being propertyless and in the labor force, and the inequality in the bourgeois family rested on men being propertied and women being both propertyless and outside the labor force. This underlying emphasis on the *relational* aspect of gender is clearly important. So is the emphasis on women's economic dependency as a critical constituent of the material basis of gender oppression. However, by advocating the abolition of all private property as the solution, Engels by-passed the issue of women's property rights altogether and left open the question: What would be the impact on gender relations in propertied households if women too were propertied as individuals? Entry into the labor force is not the only way to reduce economic dependence; independent rights in property would be another, and more effective, way.

Engels' emphasis on women's entry into the labor force as a necessary condition for their emancipation has been enormously influential in shaping thinking on this issue not only in socialist countries,[5] but even among left-wing political parties and non-party groups elsewhere, including left-wing women's groups in South Asia. They too give centrality to women's employment, but the necessary accompaniments emphasized by Engels, namely the abolition of private property in male hands and the socialization of housework and childcare, have largely been neglected, as has the question of women's property rights.

A critical additional point (missed in Engels' analysis and associated discussions) is that of property control. Property advantage stems not only from ownership, but also from effective control over it. In societies that underwent socialist revolutions, while private property ownership was legally abolished, control over wealth-generating property remained mainly with men; any positive effects on gender relations that could have stemmed from the change in ownership, if accompanied by gender-egalitarian mechanisms of control, thus went unrealized.[6] Indeed in most societies today it is men *as a gender* (even if not all men as individuals) who largely control wealth-generating property, whether or not it is privately owned, including as managers in large corporations. Even property that is under state, community, or clan ownership remains effectively under the managerial control of selected men through their dominance in both traditional and modern institutions: caste or clan councils,

---

Looking Again at Engels's Origin of the Family, Provate Property and the State, in THE RIGHTS AND WRONGS OF WOMEN (J. Mitchell & A. Oakely eds., 1976); M. Molyneux, *Socialist Societies Old and New: Progress Towards Women's Emancipation*, 8 FEM. REV. 1–34 (1981); and ENGELS REVISITED: NEW FEMINIST ESSAYS (J. Sayers, M. Evans & N. Redclift eds., 1987). In particular, Engels assumption that gender relations within propertyless groups, such as the industrial proletariat, and under socialism would necessarily be egalitarian has been widely criticized.

5.   In socialist countries (including those that were socialist until recently), the influence of Engels' analysis led to a significant preoccupation with women's employment as the major means of eliminating gender oppression. Molyneux, *supra* note 4.

6.   Women's representation in top political and economic decision-making bodies in such countries remained minimal. For instance, in the late 1970s, in the USSR, Czechoslovakia, Poland, and Yugoslavia under 5 percent of government posts were filled by women. *Id.*

village elected bodies, state bureaucracies at all levels,[7] and so on. Also in most countries, men as a gender exercise dominance over the instruments through which their existing advantages of property ownership and control are perpetuated, such as the institutions that enact and implement laws,[8] the mechanisms of recruitment into bodies that exercise control over (private or public) property, the institutions that play an important role in shaping gender ideology, and so on.

A second issue concerning the relationship between gender and property is: How do we define a woman's class? Marxist analysis, for instance, implicitly assumes that women belong to the class of their husbands or fathers. Hence women of propertied "bourgeois" households are part of the bourgeoisie and those of proletarian households are counted as proletarian. However, there are at least two well-recognized problems with this characterization:

- A woman's class position defined through that of a man is more open to change than that of a man: a well-placed marriage can raise it; divorce or widowhood can lower it.

- To the extent that women, even of propertied households, do not own property themselves, it is difficult to characterize their class position; some have even argued that women constitute a class in themselves.[9]

In fact, neither deriving women's class from the property status of men nor deriving it from their own propertyless status appears adequate, although both positions reflect dimensions of reality. Women of rich households do gain economically and socially from their parents' or husbands' class positions. But women also share common concerns which cut across derived class privilege (or deprivation), such as vulnerability to domestic violence; responsibility for housework and childcare (even if not all women perform such labor themselves—the more affluent women can hire helpers); gender inequalities in legal rights; and the risk of poverty if (parental or marital) family support ceases. This ambiguity in women's class position impinges with critical force on the possibilities of collective action among women. On the one hand,

---

7. In India, for instance, male dominance is apparent in the judiciary (in 1985, women constituted only 3.6 percent of the state bar council advocates and 2.8 percent of High Court and Supreme Court judges), the government administration (in 1987 only 7.4 percent of the Indian Administrative Service Officers were women), and the legislature (in 1984, only 8 percent of elected candidates in the Lok Sabha (lower house of Parliament) were women). All figures are taken from Government of India, *Women in India: A Statistical Profile–1988* (New Delhi: Ministry of Human Resource Development, 1988), at 119, 126–27, 173.

8. Scandinavian countries have a relatively better record on this: in Norway and Finland, women constituted 34 and 32 percent of all elected and appointed members of national legislative bodies in 1985–87, in sharp contrast to the 9–10 percent in India, Bangladesh and Pakistan, and 5–6 percent in the USA and UK. United Nations, *The Situation of Women: Selected Indicators 1990* (Vienna: Dept. Of International Economics and Social Affairs, Statistical Office, 1990).

9. K. MILLET, SEXUAL POLITICS (1970), S. FIRESTONE, THE DIALECTIC OF SEX: THE CASE FOR FEMINIST REVOLUTION (1970), and C. DELPHY, THE MAIN ENEMY: A MATERIALIST ANALYSIS OF WOMEN'S OPPRESSION (1977), all deny the significance of class divisions between women but from different standpoints.

class differences among women, derived through men, can be divisive. On the other hand, the noted commonalities between women's situations and the relatively vicarious character of their class privilege make class distinctions between them less sharp than those between men, and could provide the basis for collective action on several counts.[10]

A third aspect of the relationship between gender and property concerns the links between gender ideology and property. For instance:

- Gender ideologies can obstruct women from obtaining property rights. Assumptions about women's needs, roles, and capabilities impinge on the framing and implementation of public policies and property laws. Again, ideas about gender underlie practices such as female seclusion, which restrict women's ability both to exercise their existing property claims and to successfully challenge persisting gender inequalities in law, policy, and practice in relation to such claims. Hence ideological struggles are integrally linked to women's struggles over property rights.

- Those who own and/or control wealth-generating property can directly or indirectly control the principal institutions that shape ideology, such as educational and religious establishments and the media (including newspapers, TV, radio, film, theater, literature, and the arts). These can shape views in either gender-progressive or gender-retrogressive directions.

- The impact of gender ideologies can vary by a household's property status. For instance, both propertied and propertyless households may espouse the ideology of female seclusion, but the former group would be in a better economic position to enforce its practice, and in so doing reinforce its emulation by unpropertied households as a mark of social status. At the same time, gender ideologies and associated practices are not derived from property differences alone, nor can they be seen in purely economic-functional terms. Rather they would tend to shift and change *in interaction with* economic shifts.

A fourth issue that arises in relation to women and property is the possible linkage of women's property rights with control over women's sexuality, marriage practices, and kinship structures. For instance, would women with independent property rights be subject to greater or lesser familial control over their sexual freedom than those without them? It would also be important to examine whether societies which historically recognized women's inheritance rights in immovable property, in order to keep the property intact and within their purview, tended to control women's choice of marriage partners and post-marital residence.

---

10. Of course aspects of a person's identity other than class can also be divisive or adhesive, such as caste, race, ethnicity, and religion.

The Significance of Land as Property

Thus far the discussion has covered property in general, but not all forms of property are equally significant in all contexts, nor equally coveted. In agrarian economies, arable land is the most valued form of property, for its economic, political, and symbolic significance. It is a productive, wealth-creating, and livelihood-sustaining asset. Traditionally it has been the basis of political power and social status. For many, it provides a sense of identity and rootedness within the village; and often in people's minds land has a durability and permanence which no other asset possesses. Although other types of property—such as cash, jewelery, cattle, and even domestic goods (the usual content of, say, dowry in rural India and Nepal)—could in principle be converted into land, in practice rural land markets are often constrained, and land is not always readily available for sale.[11] In any case, ancestral land often has a symbolic meaning[12] or ritual importance[13] that purchased land does not. Hence in land disputes people may end up spending more to retain a disputed ancestral plot than its market value would justify. In other words, both the form that property takes and its origin are important in defining its significance and the associated possibility of conflict over it.

What Do We Mean by Rights in Land?

Rights are defined here as claims that are legally and socially recognized and enforceable by an external legitimized authority, be it a village-level institution or some higher-level judicial or executive body of the state. Rights in land can be in the form of ownership or of usufruct (rights of use), associated with differing degrees of freedom to lease out, mortgage, bequeath, or sell. Land rights can stem from inheritance, community membership, transfers by the state, tenancy arrangements, purchase, and so on. Rights in land also have a temporal and sometimes locational dimension: they may be hereditary, accrue only for a person's lifetime, or for a lesser period, and they may be conditioned on the person residing where the land is located.

As distinct from rights in land, a woman may, in theory, also have "access" to land in other ways, including through informal concessions granted by kin or friends. For instance, a man may allow his sister the use of a plot of his land out of goodwill. But she cannot claim it as a right and call for its enforcement. Having "rights" thus provides a measure of security that other forms of access typically do not.

Four additional distinctions are relevant here. First is the need to distinguish between the legal recognition of a claim and its social recognition, and between recog-

---

11.   M.R. Rosenzweig & K.I. Wolpin, *Specific Experience, Household Structure, and Intergenerational Transfers: Farm Family Land and Labour Arrangements in Developing Countries*, 100 Q. J. OF ECON. 961–87 (Supp. 1985).

12.   A.J. Selvaduri, *Land, Personhood and Sorcery in a Sinhalese Village*, in RELIGION AND SOCIAL CONFLICT IN SOUTH ASIA 82–96 (L. Smith ed., 1976).

13.   I-B. Krause, Kinship and Economics in North-West Nepal, unpublished PhD dissertation in Social Anthopology, London School of Economics, University of London, 1982.

nition and enforcement. A woman may have the legal right to inherit property, but this may remain merely a right on paper if the law is not enforced, or if the claim is not socially recognized as legitimate and family members exert pressure on her to forfeit her share in favor, say, of her brothers. Second is the earlier-noted distinction between the ownership of land and its effective *control*. (Control itself can have multiple meanings, such as the ability to decide how the land is used, how its produce is disposed of, whether it can be leased out, mortgaged, bequeathed, sold, and so on.) It is sometimes assumed incorrectly that legal ownership carries with it the right of control in all these senses. In fact legal ownership may be accompanied by legal restrictions on disposal: for instance, among the Jaffna Tamils in Sri Lanka, under the *Thesawalami* legal code, a married woman needs her husband's consent to alienate land that she legally owns. Third, it is important to distinguish between ownership and use rights vested in individuals and those vested in a group. And fourth, one might distinguish between rights conferred via inheritance and those conferred by state transfers of land.

Given the different forms (ownership and usufruct, as vested in individuals or in groups, etc.) that land rights can take, and the varying organization of production and distribution that can accompany them, it is not always possible to specify *a priori* what would be the most desirable form for women's land rights to take. But a broad specification can be attempted. When speaking here of women having rights, the rights discussed must be effective, that is, rights not just in law but in practice. The term "independent" rights is used to mean rights independent of male ownership or control (that is, excluding joint titles with men). Independent rights would be preferable to joint titles with husbands for several reasons. One, with joint titles it could prove difficult for women to gain control over their share in case of marital breakup. Two, women would also be less in a position to escape from marital violence: as some Bihari village women have said, "for retaining the land we would be tied to the man, even if he beat us."[14] Three, wives may have different land use priorities from husbands, which they would be in a better position to act upon with independent land rights. Four, women with independent rights would be better placed to control the produce. Five, with joint titles, the question of how the land would be inherited could prove a contentious one. This is not to deny that joint titles with husbands would be better than having no titles at all; but many of the advantages of possessing land would not accrue to women by joint titles alone.

Here the distinctions mentioned earlier between rights vested in individuals and those vested in groups, and between privatized land transfers via inheritance and land transfers by the state, need elaboration. In relation to privatized inheritable landed property, effective land rights would mean inheritance as individuals linked with full rights of control over land use and its produce. In state transfers of land to women, effective rights could either mean individual titles conferring ownership and control rights exactly as with private land; or they could mean rights in land held by a group of women through joint ownership or long lease, and allowing full control over land

---

14. Unpublished Conversation with author (on file with author).

use and its produce but excluding the right to sell or bequeath it. While individually owned land could be advantageous in distress circumstances in that it can be mortgaged or sold, group rights could protect the land from moneylenders or scheming relatives and enable its more productive use through group investment (as elaborated later).

Some South Asian Specificities

With the decline in communal land in South Asia, access to privatized land acquires a critical importance today which it did not have even a century ago. In India, for instance, by a rough estimate, about 87 percent of arable land is in private hands.[15] Hence, the importance of women's land rights spelled out in the next section, while couched in general terms, is especially focused on rights in privatized land, with two caveats. One, given the importance of communal land (e.g., village commons) to the rural poor, and especially to poor women (who depend on it for firewood, fodder, and other items basic for survival), there is a strong case for protecting the communal nature of any land which still exists in that form.[16] Two, it is necessary to explore the possibilities of new institutional arrangements for jointly owned/controlled land holdings by groups of women, rather than by groups of households (as is the usual focus).

In legal terms, women's property rights in South Asia are governed by "personal laws" that form a complex mosaic, varying a good deal by religion and region. Most of these legal systems give women considerable inheritance rights, and in traditionally patrilineal groups much greater rights than are enjoyed by custom, as a result of legal reform, especially after 1950.[17] But in virtually all the legal systems, some gender inequalities remain. For instance, some systems prescribe lower shares for women (Islamic law, for example, prescribes a daughter's share as half that of a son); some others restrict the conditions under which women can inherit and retain that inheritance (e.g., the *Muluki Ain* in Nepal only allows unmarried daughters over the age of thirty-five to inherit, and they forfeit their claims on subsequent marriage). Yet other legal systems restrict women's freedom to dispose of their inherited land (as noted for the Jaffna Tamils in Sri Lanka).

Inequalities also stem from gender discriminatory tenurial enactments that affect women's rights specifically in agricultural land. For instance, in India, agricultural land under tenancy is exempt from the scope of the Hindu Succession Act (HSA) of 1956 (which gave Hindu women considerable inheritance rights across India): such land is governed instead by the rules of devolution specified in state-level enact-

---

15. This was calculated from India's land use statistics for 1990–91. Government of India, *Statistical Abstract*, Central Statistical Organization, Dept of Statistics, Ministry of Planning and Programme Implementation, Delhi, 1994.

16. B. Agarwal, *The Gender and Environment Debate: Lessons from India*, 18 (1) FEM. STUD. 119–58 (1992).

17. As detailed in B. AGARWAL, A FIELD OF ONE'S OWN: GENDER AND LAND RIGHTS IN SOUTH ASIA (1994).

ments.[18] In a number of states, mostly in northwest India, these enactments specify succession rules prevailing before the HSA was passed, and which give priority to male agnatic heirs. Again in the fixation of ceilings under land reform laws, many states allow the cutivating household to retain additional land on account of adult sons but not adult daughters. Also, in most states, the holdings of both spouses are aggregated in assessing "family" land, and there is considerable arbitrariness in deciding whose portion will be declared surplus and forfeited. As a result, in several cases the wife's land (and not many women have land) has been declared surplus and taken over by the government, while the husband's land has remained intact.[19]

Even more critical than the persisting legal inequities is the gap between women's legal rights in land and actual ownership, and between ownership and effective control. Although economic surveys typically do not collect gender-disaggregated data, village studies (especially anthropological accounts) and sample surveys indicate that in most parts of South Asia women do not own land and even fewer are able to exercise effective control over it.[20] A recent sample survey of widows in rural India found that only 13 percent of the women with landowning fathers inherited land as daughters and 51 percent of women with landowning husbands inherited some as widows.[21] This gap between law and practice is especially apparent in communities that customarily practiced patrilineal inheritance.[22] Communities traditionally practicing matrilineal or bilateral inheritance were few and limited to northeast India, parts of south India, and Sri Lanka. Before examining the nature of gender relations in the latter communities, consider below why having independent rights in land is important for women's well-being and overall empowerment. (Again although the illustrative examples relate to South Asia the arguments would have relevance also for many other regions.)

---

18.   In India, the term "state" relates to administrative divisions within the country and is not to be confused with other uses of "state" throughout the chapter in the political economy sense of the word. In Pakistan and Sri Lanka, these administrative divisions are termed provinces.

19.   K. Saradamoni, *Changing Land Relations and Women: A Case Study of Palghat District, Kerala, in* WOMEN AND RURAL TRANSFORMATION 35–171 (V. Mazumdar ed., 1983).

20.   None of the countries in the region, except Sri Lanka, collects gender-disaggregated land ownership and use data in its agricultural and centennial censuses or other large-scale rural surveys. Even in Sri Lanka, such data, collected in the 1981 agricultural census, covered only agricultural operators (that is, cultivators as well as purely livestock and poultry operators) and not all rural households. Also the published data do not give a gender breakdown of land ownership even among agricultural operators. Again, most studies of village agrarian structures by economists have confined themselves to the household unit. Hence to gain an idea of where women have been given or have claimed their shares in landed property and under what circumstances, the author has drawn on anthropological, historical, and legal sources, supplemented by fieldwork observations and a recent sample survey.

21.   For details, *see* B. Agarwal, *Widows versus Daughters or Widows as Daughters: Property, Land and Economic Security in Rural India,* MODERN ASIAN STUDIES, *forthcoming.*

22.   Patrilineal inheritance: ancestral property passes through the male line. Matrilineal inheritance: ancestral property passes through the female line. Bilateral inheritance: ancestral property passes to and through both sons and daughters.

WHY WOMEN NEED INDEPENDENT RIGHTS IN LAND

The importance of rural women having independent rights in arable land rests on several interconnected arguments which can be grouped into four broad categories: welfare, efficiency, equality, and empowerment.[23]

The Welfare Argument

Especially among poor rural households, rights in land could reduce women's own and, more generally, the household's risk of poverty and destitution. This is due partly to the general positive effect of giving women access to economic resources independently of men; and partly to the specific advantages of possessing land.

Consider first the general case. In large parts of South Asia a systematic bias is noted against women and female children in intra-household access to resources for basic necessities such as health care, and, in some degree, to food. This is revealed in gender differences in one or more of the following indicators: malnourishment, morbidity, mortality, hospital admissions, health expenditures, and female-adverse sex ratios (females per 1,000 males),[24] although the evidence on food allocation *per se* is less conclusive.[25] The extent of this anti-female bias varies regionally, but it exists in some degree almost everywhere, particularly as revealed by the sex ratios which are female-adverse across all of South Asia, except Kerala in southwest India. The bias is strongest in northwest India, Pakistan, and Bangladesh, and much less stark in south India and Sri Lanka, where the sex ratios, although still female-adverse, are closer to parity.

Further, notable differences have been found in how men and women of poor rural households spend the incomes under their control: women typically spend almost all their income on the family's basic needs; men usually spend a significant part on their personal needs (tobacco, liquor, etc).[26] Research findings also suggest that children's nutritional status tends to be much more positively linked to the mother's earnings than the father's.[27]

---

23. The discussion here concerns land linked to rural livelihoods, especially arable land, but excludes homesites, even though the available data on land ownership do not always separate land under homesites from the rest.

24. B. Agarwal, *Women, Poverty and Agricultural Growth in India*, J. PEASANT STUD. 165–220 (1986), and AGRAWAL, A FIELD OF ONE'S OWN, *supra* note 17.

25. B. Harriss, *The Intrafamily Distribution of Hunger in South Asia, in* THE POLITICAL ECONOMY OF HUNGER 351–424 (J. Dreze & A.K. Sen eds., 1990).

26. *See* J. Mencher, *Women's Work and Poverty: Contribution to Household Maintenance in Two Regions of South India, in* A HOME DIVIDED: WOMEN AND INCOME IN THE THIRD WORLD (D. Dwyer & J. Bruce eds., 1988); D.A. Per-Lee, Employment, Ingenuity and Family Life: Rajasthani Women in Delhi, India, unpublished PhD dissertation in Anthopology, American University (1981); and R.L. Blumberg, *Income Under Female vs. Male Control: Hypotheses from a Theory of Gender Stratification and Data from the Third World, in* GENDER, FAMILY AND ECONOMY: THE TRIPLE OVERLAP 97–127 (R.L. Blumberg ed., 1991).

27. S.K. Kumar, *Role of the Household Economy in Child Nutrition at Low Incomes*, Occ. Paper No. 95, Dept. of Agricultrural Economics, Cornell University, 1978.

In other words, women and children's risk of poverty and physical well-being could depend significantly on whether or not women have *direct* access to income and productive assets such as land, and not just access *mediated* through husbands or other male family members. For female-headed households without adult male support, this link between direct access to economic resources and physical well-being needs no emphasis. Such households constitute an estimated 19–20 percent of all households in India and Bangladesh.[28]

Moreover, as noted earlier, without independent resources even women from rich parental or marital homes can be economically vulnerable, in case of marital breakup or widowhood. In parts of western and northwestern India, not uncommonly, women—divorced, deserted or widowed—can be found working as agricultural laborers on the farms of their well-off brothers or brothers-in-law.[29] Similarly, in east India and Bangladesh, there are many cases of women, married into prosperous households, being left destitute after widowhood.[30] "This fact," as Omvedt observes, "perhaps . . . more than any other, shows the essential propertylessness of women *as women*."[31]

Within this general argument for women's independent access to economic resources, the case for effective rights in *land* is especially strong. Consider, for a start, the relationship between land access and poverty at the household level. In India, in 1982, an estimated 89 percent of rural households owned some land,[32] and an estimated 74 percent operated some.[33] In Bangladesh, in 1978, the percentage of rural households owning some land (arable or homestead) was 89, and those owning arable

---

28. *See* M. Buvinic & N.H. Youssef, "Women-Headed Households: The Ignored Factor in Development Planning," Report submitted to AID/WID, International Center for Research on Women, Washington, D.C., Mar. 1978, for India; and C. Safilios-Rothchild & S. Mahmud, "Women's Roles in Agriculture: Present Trends and Potential for Growth," paper produced for the Bangladesh Agricultural Sector Review, UNDP/UNIFEM, Dhaka, 1989, for Bangladesh. According to the Indian census some 10 percent of households are female-headed, but this is a significant underestimate. *See* B. Agarwal, *Work Participation of Rural Women in the Third World: Some Data and Conceptual Biases*, ECON. & POL. WEEKLY (Dec. 21, 1985), at A155–64, on reasons for the undercounting.

29. G. Omvedt, "Effects of Agricultural Development on the Status of Women," paper prepared for the International Labour Office, Tripartite Asian Regional Seminar on Rural Development and Women, Mahabeleshwar, India, 1981; personal observation of the author.

30. M.T. Cain, S.R. Khanam, & S. Nahar, *Class, Patriarchy and the Structure of Women's Work in Rural Bangladesh*, Working Paper No. 43, Center for Population Studies, The Population Council, 1979, and Vina Mazumdar, personal communication.

31. Omvedt, *supra* note 29, at 21.

32. Government of India, *A Note on Some Aspects of Household Ownership Holding: NSS 37th Round (Jan.–Dec. 1982)* and *Results on Some Aspects of Household Ownership Holding: NSS 37th Round (Jan.–Dec. 1982)*, 11 (2) SARVEKSHANA, Issue No. 33, Oct., Dept of Statistics, Ministry of Planning, pp. 1–18, S1–S175 (1987).

33. Government of India, *Thirty-Seventh Round Report on Land Holdings–2: Some Aspects of Operational Holdings*, Report No. 331, National Sample Survey Organisation (Delhi Dept. of Statistics, 1986), at 12. In these estimates, the figure for land ownership covers all land owned by the household, whether or not cultivated, including that used for non-agricultural purposes.

land was 67.[34] In Sri Lanka, in 1982, 89 percent of agricultural operators owned some land (including home gardens).[35] Although, due to high land concentration, the majority of these households across South Asia only have marginal plots, they face a significantly lower risk of absolute poverty than landless households: several studies note a negative relationship between the incidence of absolute poverty and land access (owned or operated).[36] The direct advantages of possessing land (unless the land is of very poor quality) stem from the various production possibilities it provides, such as for growing crops, fodder or trees, keeping a vegetable garden or livestock, practicing sericulture, and so on. In addition, land provides indirect benefits, such as increasing access to credit, helping agricultural labor maintain its reserve price and even push up the aggregate real wage rate,[37] and, where the land is owned, serving as a mortgageable or saleable asset during a crisis. Moreover, for widows and the elderly, ownership of land and other wealth strengthens the support they receive from relatives by increasing their bargaining power within the household. As an elderly man put it, "without property, children do not look after their parents well."[38]

However, given the noted biases in the intra-family distribution of benefits from household resources, exclusively *male* rights in land, which would render the *household* less susceptible to poverty by some average measure, will not automatically benefit all its members. And on grounds of both women's and children's welfare, there is a strong case for supporting women's effective rights in private or public land, independently of men. Although such rights are especially important as a poverty-alleviation measure for women in poor rural households, they are also relevant, as noted, for women of better-off households, given the risk of poverty that all rural women face without independent resources.

It must be emphasized that the welfare case for women's land rights stands even if the plot is too small to be economically viable on its own. Indeed, those opposing female inheritance in land often emphasize that women might end up inheriting economically non-viable holdings. In my view, this could be a problem where cultivation is seen as the *sole* basis of subsistence, but not where land-based production is one element (although a critical one) in a *diversified livelihood system*. For instance,

---

34.   F.T. Jannuzi & J.T. Peach, The Agrarian Structure of Bangladesh: An Impediment to Development 101 (1980).

35.   Government of Sri Lanka, *Sri Lanka Census of Agriculture 1982* (Colombo, Dept of Census and Statistics, Ministry of Plan Implementation, 1984) at 17.

36.   *See* I. Ali, B.M. Desai, R. Radhakrishna, & V.S. Vyas, *Indian Agriculture at 2000: Strategies for Equality*, 16 (10–12) Econ. & Pol. Weekly 409–424 (1981); K. Sundaram & S. Tendulkar, *Towards an Explanation of Inter-regional Variation in Povery and Unemployment in Rural India*, Working Paper No. 237, Delhi School of Economics (1983), and R. Gaiha & N.A. Kazmi, *Aspects of Rural Poverty in India*, 17 (2–3) Econ. of Planning 74–112 (1981).

37.   K.N. Raj & M. Tharakan, *Agrarian Reform in Kerala and its Impact on the Rural Economy—A Preliminary Assessment, in* Agrarian Reform in Contemporary Developing Countries 31–90 (A. Ghose ed., 1983).

38.   J.C. Caldwell, P.H. Reddy, & P. Caldwell, The Causes of Demographic Change: Experimental Research in South India 191 (1988).

a plot of land that does not produce enough grain for family subsistence could still support trees or provide fodder. Moreover, although forced collective farming is likely to be inefficient, cases of farmers (including groups of women farmers) voluntarily cooperating to undertake land-based joint production and/or investment activities also exist (as elaborated later).

Of course, as the industrial and service sectors of South Asian economies expand, arable land will become a less significant source of livelihood and form of property. But today the majority of South Asia's population still depends on agriculture as a primary or an important supplementary source of sustenance. And, most villagers, even those deriving their income from non-farm activities, depend on village common land and forests for fuel and other basic necessities. Moreover, in none of the South Asian countries do projections predict a rapid absorption of labor into non-farm jobs in the foreseeable future. What absorption has occured over the past two decades has been much greater for male workers than for female workers—the latter have remained substantially in agriculture, and the gender gap is growing. Today 74 percent of rural male workers, but 86 percent of rural female workers, are in agriculture.[39] Moreover, although the rural non-farm sector holds potential, its record in providing viable livelihoods has been regionally mixed, with some regions providing high returns/high wages (such as the Indian Punjab), but many others being characterized by low returns and low wages.[40] In particular, women's non-farm earnings appear characteristically low and uncertain.[41] Hence, although women's earning opportunities in the non-farm sector clearly need strengthening, for most women non-farm livelihoods can at best supplement, not substitute for, land-based livelihoods. Notably also, those who do well in the rural non-farm sector through self-employment are usually those with land.[42] Effectively, therefore, land will continue to occupy a place of primacy in South Asian livelihoods in general and female livelihood systems in particular, for quite some time to come.

Also, with sectoral shifts, although the importance of land as property may decline, income-generating property *per se* would remain a significant mediator of

39. Government of India, *Key Results on Employment and Unemployment: Fifth Quinquennial Survey, NSS Fiftieth Round (July 1993–June 1994)*, Report No. 406, National Sample Survey Organisation (Delhi: Dept. of Statistics, 1996).

40. *See, e.g.*, R. Islam, *Non-Farm Employment in Rural Asia: Issues and Evidence, in* OFF-FARM EMPLOYMENT IN THE DEVELOPMENT OF RURAL ASIA 153–73 (R.T. Shand ed., 1986), P. B. Hazell & S. Haggblade, *Rural-Urban Growth Linkages in India*, Working Paper WPS 430, Agriculture and Rural Development Department, World Bank, Washington, DC (1990), and R. Basant & B.L. Kumar, *Rural Agricultural Activities in India: A Review of Available Evidence*, 17(1–2) SOC. SCIENTIST 13–17 (1989).

41. *See, e.g.*, the case studies in Invisible Hands: Women in Home-based Production (A.M. Singh & A. Kelles-Vitanen eds., 1987), and R. Islam, *Rural Industrialisation and Employment in Asia: Issues and Evidence, in* RURAL INDUSTRIALISATION AND EMPLOYMENT IN ASIA 1–18 (New Delhi: ILO, Asian Employment Programme, 1987).

42. Islam, *Non-Farm Employment, supra* note 40; G.K. Chadha, "Non-farm Sector in India's Rural Economy: Policy, Performance and Growth Prospects," mimeo, Center for Regional Development, Jawaharlar Nehru University, Delhi (1992).

social relations and an important determinant of social status and political power. Who owns and/or controls property would therefore still be a relevant consideration; and many of the arguments for gender equality in command over landed property would apply to other types of property as well.

The Efficiency Argument

In several contexts, giving women title to land would increase output. Many women operate as household heads with the primary and sometimes sole responsibility for organizing cultivation and ensuring family subsistence, but without title to the land they are cultivating. For instance, due to long-term male outmigration many women are serving as *de facto* household heads, especially, but not only, in the hill regions of the subcontinent. Or widows are cultivating plots given to them from joint family estates (as part of their inheritance claims to their deceased husbands' lands), but the plots are still in their in-laws' names. There are also many women managing farms while their husbands take up rural non-farm occupations. And there are tribal women cultivating communal land who rarely get titles to their fields when the land is privatized, since the state typically gives the titles only to male farmers. Titling women in these circumstances and providing them infrastructural support could increase output by increasing their access to credit,[43] and to technology and information on productivity-increasing agricultural practices and inputs (in the dissemination of which both a class and a gender bias prevails).[44]

A more general issue, however, is the likely efficiency effect of women inheriting land. Female inheritance is often opposed in South Asia on the grounds that it will further reduce farm size and increase land fragmentation, and thus reduce output and also marketed surplus. Is this fear valid? Existing evidence indicates otherwise. Small-sized farms typically have a higher value of annual output per unit cultivated area than large-sized ones: this inverse size-productivity relationship, which was strong in the 1950s and 1960s (the pre-green revolution period), has sustained in the post-green revolution period, even if somewhat weakened, as studies for India, Bangladesh and Pakistan bear out.[45] Small farmers have adopted the new technology

---

43. There is considerable evidence from Asia that titling can critically enhance farmers' access to credit (in terms of sources, amounts, and terms) by enabling them to use land as collateral. *See, e.g.*, H.P. Binswanger & M. Rosenzweig, "Credit Markets, Wealth and Endowments in Rural South India," paper presented at the Eighth World Congress of the International Economic Association, New Delhi, Dec. 1–5, 1986; and G. Feder, "The Economics of Land Titling in Thailand," mimeo, World Bank, April 1989. *Also see* K.A. Saito & C.J. Weidenmann, *Agricultural Extension and Women Farmers in Africa*, World Bank Working Paper, WPS 398, Population and Human Resource Department, World Bank, Washington, D.C. (1990), on the problems women farmers face in getting credit in the absence of titles.

44. For class bias in agricultural extension, *see* B. Dasgupta, *Agrarian Change and the New Technology in India*, Report No. 77.2, United Nations Research Institute for Social Development, Geneva (1977), and on gender bias, *see* K. Kilkelly, *Women's Roles in Irrigated Agricultural Production Systems during the 1985 Yala Season: Parakrama Samudra Scheme and Giritale Scheme, Polonnaruma District*, Report, USAID, Colombia (1986).

45. R.A. BERRY & W.R. CLINE, AGRARIAN STRUCTURE AND PRODUCTIVITY IN DEVELOPING COUNTRIES

in most areas where large farmers have done so, although after a time lag.[46] The evidence on marketed surplus also does not support the skeptics' claim that this will decline because small farmers will retain a larger percentage for self-consumption.[47] In any case, an improvement in the consumption of the rural poor cannot, in itself, be seen as an inefficient outcome. Indeed, a dietary improvement may add to labor productivity.[48]

The existing evidence thus gives no reason to expect that land distribution in favor of women would reduce output on account of the size effect. And the problem of land fragmentation can arise equally with male inheritance: both cases call for land consolidation. There could, of course, be a negative output effect of female inheritance through what could be termed the "gender-transfer effect" (viz. some of the land that would have gone only to men would now go to women), insofar as women usually face some gender-specific market disadvantages as managers of farms. But again the answer lies in easing these constraints by institutional and infrastructural support to women farmers, rather than in disinheriting them.

Indeed the experience of non-governmental credit institutions such as the Grameen bank in Bangladesh suggest that women are often better credit risks than men.[49] Also, supporting women as farm managers would enlarge the talent and information pool; and in very poor households allocating resources to women could increase their productivity by improving their nutrition.

The provision of land to women could have other indirect benefits as well, such as (a) reducing migration to cities, both by women themselves and by family members dependent on them; and (b) increasing farm incomes in women's hands, which in turn could generate a higher demand for non-farm goods that are produced locally and labor-intensively, thus creating more rural jobs.[50]

(1979); B. AGARWAL, MECHANIZATION IN INDIAN AGRICULTURE: AN ANALYTICAL STUDY OF THE INDIAN PUNJAB (1983); J. BOYCE, AGRARIAN IMPASSE IN BENGAL: INSTITUTIONAL CONSTRAINTS TO TECHNOLOGICAL CHANGE (1987).

46. M. LIPTON & R. LONGHURST, NEW SEEDS AND POOR PEOPLE (1989).

47. For non-food crops the marketed surplus is often very high on farms of all size groups and for food crops the higher productivity on small farms could outweigh their higher propensity-to-consume effect, as found, for instance, in Kenya. M. Lipton, Land Reform as Commenced Business: The Evidence Against Stopping, draft paper, Institute of Develpment Studies, Sussex, 1992.

48. J. Strauss, *Does Better Nutrition Raise Farm Productivity?*, 94(2) J. POLIT. ECON. 297–320 (1986); A.B. Deolalikar, *Nutrition and Labour Productivity in Agriculture: Econometric Estimates for Rural South Asia*, 70(4) REV. ECON. & STAT. 406–413 (1988).

49. M. Hossain, "Credit for Women: A Review of Special Credit Programmes in Bangladesh," draft paper, Bangladesh Institute for Development Studies, Dhaka (1988).

50. This is partly because women's lesser mobility would confine them more than men to local markets, and it is partly derivative of the more general observation that villages with greater equality in land (and farm income) distribution in South Asia tend to generate more demand for local nonfarm products, especially through consumption linkages. Islam, *Non-Farm Employment, supra* note 40.

The Equality and Empowerment Arguments

Equality and empowerment concerns, unlike welfare and efficiency considerations, stem less from the implications of land access or deprivation in absolute terms, and more from the implications of men's and women's *relative* access to land. And they affect particularly women's ability to challenge male dominance within the home and in society.

The equality argument for land rights rests especially on two concerns. One is the larger issue of gender equality as a measure of a just society, in which equality of rights over productive resources would be an important part. The other relates to the specific link between gender equality in land rights and women's empowerment. Empowerment is defined here as a process that enhances the ability of disadvantaged ("powerless") individuals or groups to challenge and change (in their favor) existing power relationships that place them in subordinate economic, social, and political positions. Empowerment can manifest itself in acts of individual resistance as well as in group mobilization. Titling women with land could empower them economically, as well as strengthen their ability to challenge social and political gender inequities.

A telling illustration is provided by the Bodhgaya movement in Bihar (eastern India) in the late-1970s, in which women and men of landless households participated in an extended struggle for ownership rights in the land they cultivated, held illegally by a *Math* (a temple-monastery complex). During the struggle, women demanded independent land rights, not only for reasons of economic security but also because this impinged on marital relations. They feared that if land titles went only to husbands, wives would be rendered relatively even more powerless, and vulnerable to domestic violence. Their fears proved correct. Where only men received titles there was an increase in drunkenness, wife-beating and threats: "Get out of the house, the land is mine now."[51] Where women received titles they could now assert: "We had tongues but could not speak, we had feet but could not walk. Now that we have the land, we have the strength to speak and walk."[52] Similar responses were noted in China, when the Chinese Communist Party promulgated the Agrarian Reform law in 1947, which entitled women to hold separate land deeds for the first time.[53]

Land rights can also improve the treatment a women receives from other family members, by strengthening her bargaining power.[54] Although employment and other means of earning could help in similar ways, in the rural context land usually

---

51. Manimala, *Zameen Kenkar? Jote Onkar! Women's Participation in the Bodhgaya Land Struggle*, 14 MANUSHI 2, 15 (1983).

52. Alaka & Chetna, *When Women Get Land—A Report from Bodhgaya*, 40 MANUSI 25, 26 (1987).

53. W. HINTON, FANSHEN: A DOCUMENTARY OF REVOLUTION IN A CHINESE VILLAGE (1972).

54. J. Dreze, *Widows in India*, Discussion Paper No. DEP 46, The Development Economics Research Programme, London School of Economics (1990), and personal observation of author in northwest India.

offers greater security than other income sources—at the very least, a space of one's own. In the Bodhgaya case, for instance, the women being wage laborers were not economically dependent, but their husbands could still threaten them with eviction. Notably too the Bodhgaya women saw intra-household gender relations being affected not just by their own propertyless state, but by their remaining propertyless while their husbands became propertied. In other words, land titles were important to women not only for improving their economic well-being in absolute terms (the welfare argument), but also for improving their *relative* bargaining position vis-a-vis their husbands: their sense of empowerment within the home was linked to economic equality.[55]

Outside the household as well, land ownership can empower women by improving the social treatment they receive from fellow villagers, and by enabling them to bargain with employers from a stronger fall-back position.[56] Land ownership is also widely linked to rural political power.[57] Although there can be social barriers to women's participation in public decisionmaking bodies, even for women endowed with land, land rights could facilitate such participation. The support of local women's groups would also help.

Indeed in a limited sense, group action may itself empower women by enhancing their self-confidence and ability to challenge oppression, although in a larger sense it is a *means* to empowerment, wherein empowerment lies not only in the process of *challenging* gender inequity but in *eliminating* it. And collective action is likely to prove a critical means for effecting change toward gender equality in land rights, as elaborated *infra*.

While each of the above arguments for women's independent rights in land is important, it is notable that the welfare and efficiency arguments resonate more with state planners. Why? Part of the answer certainly lies in the fact that these arguments (especially those concerning welfare) focus especially on poor women, and can be subsumed within the poverty-alleviation component of planning, with special targeting towards "the most vulnerable" groups, identified as women and female children. But part of the answer must also lie in deep-rooted notions of appropriate gender relations shared by many men who make and implement policy, for whom empowering women to transform those relations into more equal ones would appear inappropriate and even threatening to existing family and kinship structures. Hence it is easier to push for changes where the goal appears to be to give poor women a slightly better deal, than where the goal is to challenge basic inequities in gender relations across classes. It is also the case that programs for health and nutrition are more readily perceived in welfare terms than programs that call for gender-redistributive land

---

55.   For elaboration on the links between women's rights in land, their bargaining position, and gender relations, *see* AGARWAL, A FIELD OF ONE'S OWN, *supra* note 17.

56.   M. MIES, K. LALITA & K. KUMARI, INDIAN WOMEN IN SUBSISTENCE AND AGRICULTRUAL LABOUR (ILO, 1986).

57.   M. Solaiman & M. Alam, "Characteristics of Candidates for Election in Three Union Parishads in Comilla Kotwali Thana," Bangladesh Agency for Rural Development, Comilla (1977); and R. SINGH, LAND, POWER AND PEOPLE: RURAL ELITE IN TRANSITION 1801–1970 (1988).

reform. It is not a coincidence that land rights have yet to become a necessary component even of women-directed poverty-alleviation schemes.

Consider now what can be learned about the association between land rights and gender relations from traditionally matrilineal and bilateral communities.

GENDER RELATIONS IN TRADITIONALLY MATRILINEAL AND BILATERAL COMMUNITIES

Historically, in some South Asian communities, women enjoyed significant rights in land, and even today they enjoy greater land rights there than elsewhere. These are communities traditionally practicing matrilineal or bilateral inheritance and concentrated in parts of northeast and south India, and Sri Lanka, as follows:

- *Northeast India:* is the home of three matrilineal tribal communities, the Garos, Khasis, and Lalungs.

- *South India:* here the Nangudi Vellalars of Tamil Nadu practiced bilateral inheritance, and several other groups in and around Kerala practiced matrilineal inheritance, including the Nayars of north and central Kerala, the Tiyyars and Mappilas of north Kerala, and the Bants of Karnataka.

- *Sri Lanka:* here all major communities practiced bilateral or matrilineal inheritance—the Sinhalese and Jaffna Tamils were bilateral and the Muslim "Moors" were matrilineal.[58]

Historical and ethnographic evidence suggests that in regions other than these, inheritance practices were essentially patrilineal.[59]

Women's land rights in the above communities fell broadly into three categories:

- In communities such as the Garos, land was a clan's communal property and could not be inherited either by individuals or by joint family units. All clan members resident in the village had use rights to this land as individuals. Responsibility for land management vested with the husband who took up residence with his wife, but a woman's contribution to field labor was substantial and critical, and she controlled the produce.

- In communities such as the Khasis, Nayars, Tiyyars, and Mappilas, land, although inherited in the female line, was held as joint family property, and there were no individual rights of alienation. Responsibility for land management vested principally with older men (usually brothers or maternal uncles). However, in decisions concerning the partition or transfer of landed property, women's concurrence was necessary.

---

58.   Although the nomenclature "Moor" (given to the Sri Lankan Muslims under Portuguese rule) has today largely been subsumed under the general category "Muslim," the term has been retained here to distinguish the group both from partilineal Sri Lankan Muslims and from matrilineal Indian Muslims (such as the Mappilas) whose inheritance practices were different.

59.   *See* AGARWAL, A FIELD OF ONE'S OWN, *supra* note 17.

- In communities such as the Sinhalese, Jaffna Tamils, and Moors, women had individual inheritance rights in land, and, among the former two groups, men too held such rights.

The picture we get of gender relations among these groups is a mixed one. On the positive side, women enjoyed considerable social independence and relative equality in marital relations. Indeed, in all the groups, a daughter's rights in land, and the fact that she either remained in her natal home after marriage or had inviolable rights to return to it if she so chose, provided her with a strong fall-back position within marriage. Women could choose their husbands (although heiresses faced some constraints) and initiate divorce. Where uxorilocality or matrilocality was the norm, as it was in many of these groups, marital breakdown led to the husband departing, sometimes (as among the Garos) with only the clothes on his back.[60] (In contrast, in patrilineal, patrilocal contexts, it was women, especially if they violated sexual norms, who faced the very real risk of being evicted and left destitute.) Norms of sexual behavior outside marriage ranged from relatively gender egalitarian (as among the Sinhalese and the matrilineal tribes of northeast India), to restricted for women (as among the Jaffna Tamils). But in comparison with Hindu and Muslim women of patrilineal groups, especially those shackled by seclusion practices in northwestern South Asia, women among all the matrilineal and bilateral groups enjoyed greater sexual freedom.

They also had considerable freedom of movement and of public interaction. Even among the (Muslim) Moors, Munck remarks: "Women move freely about the village without veils covering their faces. . . . Interaction between men and women is frequent and casual and often sexual comments are exchanged publicly."[61] This is strikingly different from women's situation among most patrilineal Muslims of the subcontinent. Daughters were also specially desired among groups such as the Nayars,[62] in marked contrast to the strong son preference among patrilineal communities in northern South Asia.

However, these favorable features were counterbalanced by less favorable ones. One, women's property rights did not alter the overall gender division of labor: domestic work and childcare were still a woman's responsibilities. Two, the range of sexual mores found among these communities indicates that rights in land did not guarantee women the same sexual freedom as men. Three, formal managerial authority over land in a number of matrilineal groups lay with men (as husbands, brothers, and maternal uncles). In practice, this would have worked in various ways depending on the

---

60.   *Uxorilocality* implies that the husband takes up residence with the wife and (with or near) her parental family. Where this is a regular practice dictated by a preferred custom, this results in institutionalized *matrilocal* residence, where the normal residence of most husbands is with or near the matrilineal kin of the wives. *Patrilocal* implies that the wife takes up residence with the husband and (with or near) his patrilineal kin.

61.   V.C. de Munck, Cross-Currents of Conflict and Cooperation in Kotabowa, unpublished PhD dissertation, Dept. of Anthopology, University of California at Riverside, 1985, at 8, 108.

62.   Personal communication, Joan Mencher, New York, 1992 (on file with author).

role women played in the household's economy, the form (individual or joint) in which property was held, and the size of the estates involved. Where women's role in production and market activities was important (as among the northeastern tribal groups), and/or where women held individual rather than joint property rights (as among Sri Lanka's bilateral groups), they exercised greater control over the land. But where women played little role in farm production, and property was held in large joint family estates collectively owned by several generations of a woman's matrilineal descendants, as among the Nayars of central Kerala and the wealthy Mappilas of north Kerala, men's managerial control over property and their overall authority in intra-household and public dealings appears to have been especially strong. This also highlights an important difference between matrilineal and patrilineal inheritance systems. In the former there is often a gender divergence between property ownership and its control, while in the latter there is convergence: men (as a gender) own as well as control the property.

Four, most importantly, in all the groups, customary institutions with jural power (such as tribal and caste councils) were monopolized by men and typically excluded women. Among matrilineally inheriting communities, this meant that despite men's restricted access to property ownership, their rights (as a gender) of control over that property on the one hand, and their access to public bodies on the other (with links between the two domains), often enabled them to consolidate social prestige and political power. The Nayar *karanavans*[63] of wealthy households and the Khasi chiefs commanded local influence in ways that the women heiresses of these communities appear not to have done as a rule. Also, among all groups, men's control of the public decision-making domain gave them critical influence over the modification of legal and social rules when external conditions began to change in significant ways, especially under British colonial rule.

In short, ownership rights in landed property clearly conferred important benefits on women, but their virtual exclusion from property management (in some groups) and from jural and overall public authority (in all groups) circumscribed the power they could derive from those rights. This holds lessons for women's struggle for land rights today, namely that women cannot derive the full advantages of land ownership if they continue to be excluded from managerial control and jural authority. And the arenas of contestation over *effective* land rights for women will therefore need to extend much beyond the courtyards of the household to encompass the complex institutions of community and state—the arenas where legal, social, and political rules are made and unmade. This is further illustrated below.

OBSTACLES TO ACHIEVING EFFECTIVE LAND RIGHTS

Today, most arable land in South Asia (as noted) is in private hands, access to which is mainly through inheritance. Women enjoy considerable property rights in

---

63.   The *karanavan* was the head of the *taravad* and manager of the joint family estate; he was usually the seniormost male member of the *taravad*. *Taravad*: the matrilineal joint family, holding property in common and often sharing a common residence.

law, but gender inequalities and anomalies remain, especially in relation to inheritance of agricultural land that is legally treated differently and more gender-unequally than other forms of property.[64] But equally critical is the noted vast gender gap between what the law promises and actual practice. Most women, as observed earlier, do not own land; even fewer exercise full control over it. A range of factors—social, administrative, and ideological—severely restrict the effective implementation of inheritance laws. These obstacles are summarized below.[65]

First, in most traditionally patrilineal communities, there is a strong male resistance to endowing women, especially daughters, with land. Apart from the reluctance to admit more contenders to the most valuable form of rural property, an important factor underlying such resistance is a structural mismatch between contemporary inheritance laws and traditional marriage practices. Among the matrilineal and bilateral communities discussed earlier, historically families sought to keep the land within the purview of the extended kin either by strict rules against land alienation by individuals, or, where such alienation was possible (as among the bilateral communities), by other means, such as post-marital residence in the village, and often an emphasis on marriage with close kin, especially cross-cousins. In fact, proximity of the post-marital residence to the natal home appears to have been virtually a necessary condition for recognizing a daughter's share in landed property.

Contemporary laws as framed by the modern state give inheritance rights to daughters as individuals among most communities, including in traditionally patrilineal, patrilocal ones. Marriage customs, however, are still under the purview of the local kin group and, on the relevant counts, have remained largely unchanged. In India this mismatch between inheritance laws and marriage practices is greatest among upper-caste Hindus of the northwest who forbid marriages with close-kin and practice village exogamy, preferring marriage alliances in distant villages. Many such communities, moreover, have social taboos against parents drawing on the economic support of married daughters even during crises. Hence, in the northern states (and especially the northwestern ones) endowing daughters is seen by Hindu parents as bringing no reciprocal economic benefit, while increasing the risk of the land passing out of the hands of the extended family. Resistance to entitling daughters tends to be greatest here. Resistance is less in south and northeast India where marriages within the village and with close kin are allowed and sought, and seeking the help of married daughters during economic crises is also possible.

Second, women in many parts of South Asia tend to forego their shares in parental land for the sake of potential economic and social support from brothers. A visit by a brother is often the only regular link a woman has with her natal home when she is married into a distant village, and especially when social taboos bar parents from accepting a married daughter's hospitality. And after the parents' deaths, the brother's home often offers the only possibility of refuge in case of marital failure or

---

64. AGARWAL, A FIELD OF ONE'S OWN, *supra* note 17; B. Agarwal, *Gender and Legal Rights in Agricultral Land in India*, 30(2) ECON. & POLIT. WEEKLY (Bombay), Mar. 25, 1995, at A–39–A–56.

65. For more detail, *see* AGARWAL, A FIELD OF ONE'S OWN, *supra* note 17.

widowhood. A woman's dependence on this support is directly related to her economic and social vulnerability. Economically, low access to personal property (especially productive assets), illiteracy, limited income-earning skills and earning opportunities, and low wages for available work can all constrain women's potential for independent economic survival. Socially, women's vulnerability is associated partly with the strength of female seclusion practices and partly with the extent of social stigma attaching to widowhood or divorce. Both economic and social factors vary in strength by community, region, and circumstance, but typically, in anticipation of such support women give up their claims in parental land. Cultural constructions of gender, including the definition of how a "good" sister should behave and the widespread feeling that it is "shameful" for a sister to claim her share, also discourage women from asserting their rights.[66] In practice, enthnographies give examples both of brothers helping a sister in need, and of their neglect and duplicity.

Third, dependence on brothers is part of a larger social context in which many aspects of rural women's relationship with the world outside the family is typically mediated through male relatives: fathers, brothers, husbands, and extended male kin. Such mediation is necessitated by a variety of factors, but particularly by the physical and social restrictions on women's mobility and behavior. In many South Asian communities these restrictions are explicit in the norms and ideology of purdah or female seclusion; in many others, they are implicit and subtle, but nevertheless effectively confine women. These restrictions are manifest not just in the veiling of women, but more commonly in the gender segregation of space and the gendered specification of behavior. In fact, strict veiling is limited to some communities and regions—being stronger among Muslims in northern South Asia and among upper-caste Hindus in northwest India than elsewhere. More pervasive are the behavioral strictures imposed upon and internalized by women from late childhood, which define where women can go, whom they can speak to and in what manner, how they should dress, and so on. Although such gendering of space and behavior is strongest in communities that explicitly endorse purdah, its more subtle manifestations constitute an implicit code of expected female behavior in large parts of the subcontinent, even where (as in South India and Nepal) purdah is not endorsed. This circumscribes rural women's interaction with men and institutions, their physical and social mobility, their domain of activity and knowledge, and their access to education and to economic (markets, banks, etc.), judicial, and administrative institutions. All this severely limits women's ability to claim and control land.

Fourth, male relatives often take pre-emptive steps to prevent women from obtaining their inheritance. Fathers have been found to leave wills favoring sons and disinheriting daughters; brothers have been known to forge wills or manipulate statements before the revenue authorities to make it appear that the woman has relinquished her right.[67] Natal kin are especially hostile to the idea of daughters and sisters inher-

---

66. P. HERSHMAN, PUNJABI KINSHIP AND MARRIAGE (1981).

67. *See, e.g.,* J.P. PARRY, CASTE AND KINSHIP IN KANGRA (1979); A.C. MAYER, CASTE AND KINSHIP IN CENTRAL INDIA—A VILLAGE AND ITS REGION (1960); E.G. JANSEN, RURAL BANGLADESH: COMPETI-

iting land, since the property can pass outside the patrilineal descent group. A widow's claims to her husband's land are viewed with less antagonism, since there is a greater chance of the land remaining with agnates: she can be persuaded to adopt the son of the deceased husband's brother if she is sonless, or to enter into a leviratic union with the husband's (usually younger) brother, or made to forfeit the property if she remarries outside the family.

Where pre-emptive methods fail, intimidation is attempted. A common tactic is to initiate expensive litigation, which few women can financially afford.[68] Some women drop their claims, others press on with the risk of having to mortgage the land to pay legal fees, thus possibly losing the land altogether. Land disputes involving women were rising in parts of the subcontinent even in the late 1950s.[69] Today direct violence is also increasingly used to deter women from filing claims or from exercising their customary rights: beatings are common and murder not unknown. Indeed, in eastern and central India, the murder of women through accusations of witchcraft, who have some land, is on the rise.[70]

Fifth, the logistics of dealing with legal, economic, and bureaucratic institutions are often formidable and work against women staking their claims; women may only decide to do so if they have male relatives who can mediate. The typically low level of education of village women, and the noted restrictions on their interaction with the extra-domestic sphere and with institutions constituted principally of men, the complicated procedures and red tape involved in dealing with judicial and administrative bodies, and so on, all work to women's disadvantage, as does their relative lack of financial resources. The problem is especially acute in communities with high female seclusion, but it is not absent even where seclusion is not prescribed.

Sixth, local (largely male) government functionaries, responsible for overseeing the recording of inheritance shares, often obstruct the implementation of laws in women's favor. Social and official prejudice tends to be particularly acute against inheritance by daughters; widows' claims (as noted) are somewhat better accepted in principle, although often violated in practice.[71]

The gap between legal ownership rights and actual ownership is only one part of the story. The other part relates to the gap between ownership and effective control, especially managerial control, attributable to a mix of factors. Patrilocal marriages in distant villages make it difficult for women to directly supervise or cultivate land they may inherit in the natal village. But problems of directly managing land

---

TION FOR SCARCE RESOURCES (1983); and H. Alavi, *Kinship in West Punjab Villages*, 6 CONTRIB. TO INDIAN SOCIOLOGY 1–27 (Dec. 1972).

68. M. Kishwar, *Toiling Without Rights: Ho Women of Singhbhum*, 22(3–5) ECON. & POL. WEEKLY (1987).

69. MAYER, *supra* note 67.

70. A.B. CHAUDHURI, THE SANTALS: RELIGION AND RITUALS (1987); Kishwar, *supra* note 68.

71. For a discussion on why there is this difference between widows and daughters, *see* Agarwal, *supra* note 21.

inherited even in the marital village (say as a widow) are compounded in many areas by factors such as the practice of purdah or the more general (implicit or explicit) gender segregation of public space and social interaction; high rates of female illiteracy; and high fertility (which increases women's childbearing and childcare responsibilities). Moreover, male control over agricultural technology, especially the plough (there are cultural taboos against women ploughing), and the noted male bias in the dissemination of information and technological inputs, disadvantage women farmers and increase their dependence on male mediation. Often added to this is the threat and practice of violence by male relatives and others interested in acquiring women's land. Pressure on women to sharecrop their land to relatives (at below market rates) is usually high, as are the difficulties of ensuring that they receive their fair share of the harvest. Some of these factors, such as gender bias in access to production inputs and information, constrain women farmers even in traditionally bilateral and matrilineal contexts.

However, the strength of these constraints to women claiming and managing land varies considerably by region. There are geographic differences in the social acceptance of women's land claims (stemming in part from differences in traditional inheritance rights); in prevailing marriage practices; in the emphasis on female seclusion and control over female sexuality; in women's freedom of movement and labor force participation; in women's literacy and fertility rates; and in the extent of land scarcity. Obstacles stemming from these factors are greatest in northwest India, Bangladesh, and Pakistan, and least in south India and Sri Lanka. In fact, four geographic zones can broadly be demarcated, ordered in terms of the strength of resistance women are likely to face in exercising their legal rights: Pakistan, northwest India, and Bangladesh fall at the high resistance end of the spectrum, and south India and Sri Lanka at the low resistance end; western, central and eastern India, and Nepal and northeast India, come in between.[72]

Over time, gender conflict over private land is likely to increase with its growing scarcity and skew in distribution. On the one hand, male family members will be increasingly reluctant to part with the land. On the other hand, the importance for women of asserting their inheritance rights will grow for several reasons, including the limited expansion of economic opportunities for non-land-related earnings, and the erosion of kin-support systems, as brothers and other relatives become less able or less willing to economically support female kin. In Bangladesh, gender conflict over land is already on the rise, with an increasing number of women asserting or planning to assert their claims;[73] and we can expect this also to be the case in other acutely land-scarce parts of South Asia.

---

72. For maps showing these cross-regional patterns, *see* AGARWAL, A FIELD OF ONE'S OWN, *supra* note 17.

73. *See, e.g.,* T. ABDULLAH & S.A. ZEIDENSTEIN, VILLAGE WOMEN OF BANGLADESH: PROSPECTS FOR CHANGE (1982); E.G. JANSEN, RURAL BANGLADESH: COMPETETION FOR SCARCE RESOURCES (1983); and J. N. Nath, Dynamics of Socio-economic Change and the Role and Status of Women in Natunpur: Case Study of Bangladesh Village, unpublished PhD dissertation, Dept. of Sociology, University of Dhaka (1984).

In the case of public land, that is, land which is under government or community jurisdiction, the obstacles are of a somewhat different nature. Here women's struggle is more directly against the consistent male bias in the distribution of land under land reform programs, resettlement schemes, and various land development projects, and only indirectly against individual family members who may be rival potential beneficiaries. Government officials typically resist the allotment of public land to women on the grounds that allotments can only be made to household heads, whom they assume are men. This bias is found even when land titles are distributed in traditionally matrilineal and bilateral communities.[74] And it is found in the policies and programs of all the political regimes in the subcontinent, including communist ones.

INTERVENTIONS FOR CHANGE: SOME CONSIDERATIONS

The discussion above indicates that gaining effective rights in land will require women to contest and struggle in many arenas—the household, the market, the community, and the state—and on diverse aspects: legal, administrative, social, and ideological. Apart from efforts to establish legal equality, there will need to be a struggle to enhance women's ability to claim and keep control over their rightful inheritance shares. This in turn will require establishing the social legitimacy of their claims; reducing gender bias in village land registration practices and village council rulings; increasing women's legal knowledge and literacy; and improving women's fall-back position so that they are better able to deal with any associated intra-family conflict, including through external support structures that would reduce women's dependence on brothers and close kin. Similarly, male bias in government distribution of public land and in infrastructural support for farmers will require contestation.

The ideological struggle to establish women's claims is likely to be especially complex. It is part of an overall struggle for changing perceptions about women's needs, roles, and abilities, in which women's movements, both local and national, even when not focusing on the specific question of land rights, have a critical role to play. This contestation over meanings could take diverse forms, including countering popular arguments against giving women land, such as those relating to land size and fragmentation, questioning the validity of female seclusion and restrictions on women's economic and social participation outside the home, and promoting women's educational programs with an empowerment perspective.

In all this, the role of collective action is likely to be primary. For instance, the local bureaucracy is more likely to accurately register individual women's claims in family land if there is collective pressure on them from gender-progressive groups, especially women's organizations. Such organizations can also play a vital supportive role in providing women with legal information and contacts with lawyers, should legal action be necessary; and in improving effective (not just nominal) female presence in village decision-making bodies. Women elected to all-women panels in vil-

---

74. AGARWAL, A FIELD OF ONE'S OWN, *supra* note 17; J. Schrijvers, *Blueprint for Undernourishment: The Mahaveli River Develpment Scheme in Sri Lanka, in* STRUCTURES OF PATRIARCHY: STATE, COMMUNITY AND HOUSEHOLD IN MODERNISING ASIA 29–51 (B. Agarwal ed., 1988).

lage councils in parts of India (especially where supported by local women's organizations), and field-level development administrators in Bangladesh, have been found to be more sensitive to women's concerns, and to give priority to local women's needs, in ways that male village council members and bureaucrats typically do not.[75] The presence of women in decision-making roles and positions of authority also has a wider ideological impact; village women are more likely to take their grievances to female representatives than to all-male bodies.

Local gender-progressive organizations could similarly strengthen women's fall-back position in intra-family conflicts over women's land claims, through economic and social support networks and programs which reduce women's dependence on male relatives, especially their brothers in whose favor women usually forfeit their claims. As a woman member of the Bangladesh Rural Advancement Committee (BRAC, a Bangladeshi development NGO which provides credit and technical support to poor village women and men, organized separately into small groups) tellingly asserted: "Well the Samity [organization] is my 'brother.'"[76] Women, after joining BRAC, have also been able to challenge purdah practices:

> We do not listen to the *mullahs* [Muslim clergy] anymore. They did not give us even a quarter kilo of rice.[77]

> They said . . . [w]e are ruining the prestige of the village and breaking *purdah*. . . . Now nobody talks ill of us. They say: "They have formed a group and now they earn money. It is good."[78]

More generally, group support can take at least two forms: through separately constituted groups that provide specialized legal and other services to village women, and through organizations comprised of village women themselves. Initiatives of both kinds would be important not only for women from landed households seeking their inheritance claims, but also for landless women seeking rights in public land by challenging male bias in government land allocations.

In this context, it is worth considering the advantages of land ownership and/or management by groups of women, rather than by women individually. Although individual ownership can allow women the freedom to bequeath, mortgage, or sell the land as they wish, it also carries the risk of the land being appropriated by rapacious moneylenders or male relatives. Moreover, individual women often do not have enough resources to invest in the land. An alternative arrangement to individual titles in the transfer of state land, or of land acquired through a land struggle, could be titles held by poor peasant women as a group—each participating woman having use rights in the land but not the right to individually dispose of it. Daughters-in-law and daugh-

---

75. R. Gandhi & N. Shah, The Issues at Stake: Theory and Practice in the Contemporary Women's Movement in India (1992); A.M. Goetz, Local Heroes, Local Despots: Exploring Fieldworker Discretion in Implementing Gender-Redistributive Development Policy, paper presented at the Development Studies Association Conference, Glaslow (1990).

76. H.I. Hunt, *Intervention and Change in the Lives of Rural Poor Women in Bangladesh: A Discussion Paper*, Bangladesh Rural Action Committee (Dhaka, Dec. 1983), at 38.

77. M.A. Chen, A Quiet Revolution: Women in Transition in Rural Bangladesh 176 (1983).

78. *Id.* at 176–77.

ters resident in the village could share these usufructuary rights; daughters leaving the village on marriage would lose them, but could reestablish their rights should they need to return to their parental homes on marital failure or widowhood. In other words, land access could be linked formally to residence, as was the case among some tribal communities (such as the Garos), the difference being that here the land would belong not to a clan but to a group of poor women.

Group ownership of land need not, however, imply joint management, just as individual ownership need not preclude joint management. Women holding joint ownership rights could either cultivate separate plots, or cultivate collectively as a group with each woman contributing labor time and sharing the returns. Or there could be some combination of individual and group management, such as individual cultivation along with joint investment in capital equipment and cooperation in terms of labor-sharing and product-marketing. Group investment through resource pooling could be advantageous even when women own land individually by reducing the resource crunch they may face at the individual level. But joint management and cultivation of small plots would provide additional benefits in the form of economies of scale and improved production efficiency. In fact, some cases of joint land management and investment by small groups of women already exist in South Asia.[79]

In such initiatives, and more generally to enhance women's ability to function as independent farmers, infrastructural support for women is critical, in the form of access to credit, production inputs, information on new agricultural practices, marketing, and so on. Again, the promotion of women's cooperatives for the provisioning of such services could prove important.

In this context it needs emphasis that it is not just an increase in women's command over economic resources, but also the *process* by which that increase occurs that has a critical bearing on gender relations. Land rights are not a "given" and will not be "provided" to most women, whether in South Asia or elsewhere, without contestation. As noted, acquiring these rights will require simultaneous struggles on both the economic and non-economic fronts and in several different arenas.

Indeed the theoretical premise of this chapter is that gender relations and women's economic, social, and political positions are the outcome of processes of contestation and bargaining between the genders. These processes may not always be explicit but are nonetheless revealed in final outcomes. They involve elements of both cooperation and conflict and take place in various arenas: the household, the market, the community, and the state—arenas which are interlinked, in that change in one impinges on the others. For instance, a strengthening of women's bargaining power in the community, say through the formation of a women's organization, has also been found to enhance women's bargaining power within the household.

---

79.   *See* CHEN, *id.*; N. SINGH, THE BANKURA STORY: RURAL WOMEN ORGANISE FOR CHANGE (ILO, 1988); and G. A. Menon, *Re-negotiating Gender: Enabling Women to Claim their Right to Land Resources*, paper presented at the NGO Forum of the U.N. Conference on Human Settlements—Habitat II, Istanbul, June, 1996.

While it is clear that various forms of collective action will be necessary to empower women to establish effective rights in land, bringing about collective action is not always easy. A number of complexities will need to be addressed,[80] including those posed by a possible conflict of interest among women arising from class differences (or differences of caste, race, etc). Complexities also arise from the fact that even to organize collectively and attend group meetings often requires women to negotiate childcare and domestic work responsibilities with household members, and challenge social norms that restrict women's public participation and mobility (such as norms of female seclusion in some communities).

Indeed, the issue of gender equality in land rights—not only in law but in practice—calls for a more multi-pronged and sustained effort than has been attempted so far on any gender-related issue in most developing countries. While undoubtedly the noted obstacles appear formidable, their very complexity and range also makes land rights a critical entry point for challenging unequal gender relations and power structures at many levels, and gives the struggle to overcome the obstacles a transformative potential.

For this and the other reasons noted, land (and more generally property) has a strategic importance for women that other gender concerns, such as employment, do not have in equal measure.

---

80.   AGARWAL, A FIELD OF ONE'S OWN, *supra* note 17.

WOMEN AND THE UNITED STATES GOVERNMENT

Marcella David*

> Every allusion to the degraded and inferior position occupied by women all over the world has been met by scorn and abuse. From the man of highest mental cultivation to the most degraded wretch who staggers in the streets do we meet ridicule, and coarse jests, freely bestowed upon those who dare assert that woman stands by the side of man, his equal. . . .
>
> —Elizabeth Cady Stanton[1]

INTRODUCTION

The relationship between the United States government and women is, like many relationships, fraught with complexity, inconsistency, misunderstanding and disappointment.[2] Yet the government's policies towards women both within and outside U.S. borders—however complex—are understandable in light of the limitations of the U.S. domestic rights regime and in light of the socio-political pressures in American society. This chapter is intended to provide the necessary context to understand the impact of these domestic limitations and pressures on U.S. policies towards gender equality.

The first section provides an introductory description of U.S. constitutional law, both generally and as it relates to women. Key policies which are at stake under the U.S. Constitution are discussed, including the doctrine of equal protection. A discussion of the attempt to amend the Constitution to incorporate the principle of gender equality is included. A brief survey of the application of constitutional policies to women in the areas of political access, family law, access to education, employment, and sexual and reproductive freedom concludes the first section.

---

* Many thanks to the editors, and to Camille de Jorna, Mimi Dane, Jane Dolkart, Mary Dudziak, Joe Knight, Ken Kress, Jean Love, Ileana Porras, Margaret Raymond, Mark Sidel and Merle Weiner for comments on previous drafts, Adrien Wing for her moral support, Hui Yu and Julia Harris for invaluable research assistance, and Sandy Cosgrove and Steve Rhodes for support services. Any errors are my own.

1. Elizabeth Cady Stanton's 1848 Seneca Falls Woman's Rights Convention Speech, *quoted in* BRADFORD MILLER, RETURNING TO SENECA FALLS: THE FIRST WOMAN'S RIGHTS CONVENTION & ITS MEANING FOR MEN & WOMEN TODAY 172 (1995).

2. A colleague notes that relationships also have many positive characteristics. That is undoubtedly true—the examples of companionship, comfort, aid, dependability and affection come to mind. However, the oppression of women has often been predicated upon those very characteristics, and it would appear that women have only gained when they have shrugged off the paternalistic cloak of protection and tradition, and the imposed role of care giver.

The second section describes the relationship between international law and U.S. domestic law. It examines the U.S. debate on whether to ratify the Convention on Elimination of Discrimination against Women (the "Women's Convention"), and key foreign policy stands on issues relating to women's rights, and describe a few of the conflicts between competing U.S. policies. Three suggestions of ways to enhance the role of the United States in advancing human rights and the rights of women conclude the second section.

DOMESTIC PERSPECTIVES

The Imperatives of American[3] Constitutional Law

The United States is a constitutional democracy composed of a republic of fifty states[4] with a unifying federal government. The U.S. Constitution, adopted over 200 years ago, is the supreme law of the land.[5] As originally adopted, the Constitution spoke primarily to the issues crucial to the newly independent democratic nation, providing a detailed blueprint for the federal government and its interaction with state governments.[6]

---

3. The eloquent "apology" of Louis Henkin is repeated here: "I use the adjective 'American' with apologies to inhabitants of other American Republics because it is often awkward to use 'United States' as an adjective." Louis Henkin, *International Human Rights and Rights in the United States, in* HUMAN RIGHTS IN INTERNATIONAL LAW: LEGAL AND POLICY ISSUES 24 n.1 (Theodor Meron ed., 1984).

4. The United States also exerts dominion over a variety of other entities, including the nation's capitol, the District of Columbia, the remaining United Nations trust territory of Palau, and a variety of commonwealths and associated nations. *See generally* 48 U.S.C.A. § 1 *et seq.* (West 1987 & Supp. 1996) (concerning "Territories and Insular Possessions"). For a perspective on the tensions of being a non-state in a republic of states, *see* Arnold Leibowitz, *The Commonwealth of Puerto Rico: Trying to Gain Dignity and Maintain Culture*, 11 GA. J. INT'L & COMP. L. 211 (1981) (regarding Puerto Rico).

5. "This Constitution, and the Laws of the United States which shall be made in Pursuance thereof; and all Treaties made, or which shall be made, under the Authority of the United States, shall be the supreme Law of the Land." U.S. CONST. art. VI, §2.

6. Articles I–III of the Constitution establish the legislative, executive and judicial branches of the federal government, and delineate the duties and powers of each branch. U.S. CONST. arts. I–III. Other articles set forth the relationships between the states and between the states and the federal government. U.S. CONST. arts. IV & VI. The almost excruciating detail provided concerning the powers of Congress, the federal legislative branch, is often attributed to the confusion arising under the predecessor to the Constitution, the Articles of Confederation (1781–89), about the relative powers of Congress and of the states. *See generally* JOHN FISKE, THE CRITICAL PERIOD OF AMERICAN HISTORY: 1783–89 (1916) (describing the tribulations of the American government under the Articles of Confederation and the impetus to adopt the federal Constitution); *see also* ANDREW C. MCLAUGHLIN, A CONSTITUTIONAL HISTORY OF THE UNITED STATES 146 (1936) (stating that "the *chief problem* of the day" was that "the distribution of powers between the [national and state governments] was imperfectly provided for in the Confederation"). *But see* Note, *The United States and the Articles of Confederation: Drifting Toward Anarchy or Inching Toward Commonwealth?*, 88 YALE L.J. 142 (1978) (challenging the conventional view that the national government under the Confederation was ineffective and unable to function).

The United States federal government consists of a triumvirate of institutions: the legislative, executive, and judicial branches, with the power of each branch held in check by the powers of the other two branches. Congress, the legislative branch, is composed of two houses of elected officials, the Senate and House of Representatives.[7] All legislation must be passed by both houses of Congress.[8] The Senate acts alone to approve judicial appointments and other key presidential appointments[9] and to consent to U.S. participation in international conventions and treaties.[10] The executive function is filled by an elected president, his or her political appointees, and an elected vice-president.[11] The executive participates in the law-making process,[12] bears primary responsibility for setting both domestic and foreign policy,[13] and serves as commander-in-chief of the armed forces.[14] Notably, the State Department is part of the executive branch, as are a variety of national commissions dealing with women's rights and civil rights in the United States.[15] The judicial branch includes a court system of various levels, of which the United States Supreme Court is the highest court,

---

7. The people of each state elect two representatives to the Senate, while the number of representatives to the House is apportioned among the states according to their population. *See* U.S. CONST. art. I, § 2 (election of representatives); U.S. CONST. art. I, § 3, *amended by* U.S. CONST. amend. XVII (election of senators).

8. *See* U.S. CONST. art. I, § 7, cl. 2.

9. *See* U.S. CONST. art. II, § 2, cl. 2.

10. *See id.* A two-thirds vote of "Senators present" is required. *Id.*

11. *See* U.S. CONST. art. II.

12. If the executive acts against legislation forwarded to her by Congress by exercising her veto powers, then Congress must reconsider the proposal and vote to override the veto by a supermajority in each house. *See* U.S. CONST. art. I, § 7, cl. 2.

13. *See* U.S. CONST. art. II, § 3.

14. *See* U.S. CONST. art. II, § 2. This power has been significant in the quest for equal rights in the United States. As noted *infra* notes 64–65 & accompanying text, significant advances in employment opportunities for minorities and women have resulted from federal government hiring policies. President Truman's decision to end racial segregation in the armed forces pre-dated any similar significant advances in the civil sector, *see* Exec. Order No. 9,981, 13 Fed. Reg. 4313 (1948), and the exemplary service of African-American servicemen provided an impetus for change in the civilian sector. President Clinton's recent attempt to permit homosexuals to serve openly in the armed forces was intended to serve as another instance where the executive's function as commander-in-chief could lead to social justice. Unfortunately the effort was unsuccessful. *See* Charles Aldinger, *Aspin Sets New Rules On Gays In Military*, REUTERS NORTH AMERICAN WIRE, July 19, 1993, *available in* LEXIS, News Library, US file; *Pentagon Sets Out Rules On Homosexuals*, REUTERS NORTH AMERICAN WIRE, Dec. 22, 1993, *available in* LEXIS, News Library, US file.

15. The President's Commission on the Status of Women, established by President John F. Kennedy in 1961, and first headed by former First Lady Eleanor Roosevelt, had a great deal of influence—both positive and negative—on the development of American discourse on gender equality. *See* CYNTHIA HARRISON, ON ACCOUNT OF SEX: THE POLITICS OF WOMEN'S ISSUES, 1945–1968 109–65 (1988). Indeed, as early as the 1920s Congress had created an agency within the Department of Labor, the Women's Bureau, which helped set policy regarding issues related to working women. *Id.* at 8–15.

and the court which bears ultimate responsibility for interpreting the Constitution.[16] Federal judges are appointed by the President, with the advice and consent of the Senate, and, once appointed, enjoy life terms subject to dismissal (known as impeachment) only in cases of extreme misconduct.[17] Accordingly, at least in theory, federal judges are insulated from everyday political concerns.

The Constitution recognizes the independence and power of state governments. State governments offer local versions of the federal legislative, executive, and judiciary branches. All states have elected executives, known as governors; however, the authority and responsibility of governors varies from state to state. Similarly, the form of state legislatures, and the method of electing legislative representatives, also varies. Today state court systems are fashioned, like the federal system, with a tier of courts headed by a "supreme" state court, which serves as the court of last resort for the state, and the court with the ultimate responsibility for interpreting the constitution and laws of the state.[18] However, state court judges may serve by appointment for life or a shorter term, or by popular election.

The framers of the Constitution anticipated that state governments would be more responsive to local initiatives and concerns than their counterpart federal institutions. As a consequence, state governments typically bear primary responsibility for policies deemed peculiarly appropriate for local governance, such as family law, public health, safety and education.[19] The power of the states in these areas was orig-

---

16. *See* U.S. CONST. art. III; Marbury v. Madison, 5 U.S. (1 Cranch) 137, 176–8 (1803) (generally regarded as holding that other branches of government must heed constitutional interpretations of the Supreme Court).

17. *See* U.S. CONST. art. III, § 1 ("Judges, both of the supreme and inferior Courts, shall hold their Offices during good Behavior").

18. It should be noted that the naming traditions for state courts vary. For example, in New York, the lowest court of general jurisdiction is the New York Supreme Court, while the "supreme" court is the New York Court of Appeals. *See* N.Y. CONST. art. VI; *see generally* DAVID D. SIEGAL, NEW YORK PRACTICE 9–24 (2d ed. 1991) (describing New York court system).

19. [S]tates were left the "responsibility for dealing, and . . . [the] authority to deal, with the whole gamut of problems cast up out of the flux of everyday life." Viewed from a Federalist perspective, the tenth and eleventh amendments ratify these understandings. The tenth amendment, providing that powers not delegated to the national government "nor prohibited . . . to the States, are reserved to the States respectively, or to the people," supports Federalist arguments that the national government may not intrude on the states' traditional sovereign functions.

Richard H. Fallon, Jr., *The Ideologies of Federal Courts Law*, 74 VA. L. REV. 1141, 1153 (1988) (citations omitted); *see also* Medtronic, Inc. v. Lohr, 116 S. Ct. 2240, 2245 (1996) ("the 'States traditionally have had great latitude under their police powers to legislate as to the protection of the lives, limbs, health, comfort, and quiet of all persons.'") (quoting Metropolitan Life Ins. Co. v. Massachusetts, 471 U.S. 724 (1985)). These areas of the law include use of local resources, *see, e.g.*, Missouri v. Holland, 252 U.S. 416 (1920), and state laws relating to domestic relations, *see, e.g.*, Barber v. Barber, 62 U.S. (21 How.) 582 (1858). While continuing to recognize the principle, the Supreme Court has recently rejected the long-held view that judicial recognition of exclusive state authority over at least one area of law, the so-called "domestic relations exception," is *constitutionally* required. *See* Ankenbrandt v. Richards, 504 U.S. 689, 697–700 (1992) (disagreeing

inally exclusive; however, the federal government has, over time, exercised concurrent or superseding authority to determine policy in many of these areas.[20] However, as originally conceived, the Constitution emphasized the importance of permitting state and local governments to set policy in these areas without federal regulation or interference.

A subsequent portion of the Constitution known as the Bill of Rights, consisting of the first ten amendments to the Constitution, sets forth certain individual rights and liberties.[21] The rights and liberties first guaranteed under the Bill of Rights also reflect the primary concerns of the time: by guaranteeing the right to free speech, freedom of the press, the right to assembly and the right to petition government, these rights were intended to ensure the power of citizens to participate in the new democracy.[22] Other rights contained in the Bill of Rights work to protect individuals from overly burdensome governmental interference.[23] Also in keeping with the overall framework of the Constitution limiting federal power, the Bill of Rights incorporates so-called "states rights" by expressly limiting the power of the federal government to interfere with the powers of the state governments.[24] The legacy of the framers' con-

---

with rationale of Barber decision, and holding that the exception is grounded in federal law and principles of federalism).

20.   For example, federal legislation now touches upon such subjects as employment discrimination, juvenile delinquency, pollution, mental health and homelessness. *See generally* Title 42 of the United States Code. The authority for the exercise of congressional authority in these areas is in some instances expressly granted. *See, e.g.*, U.S. CONST. amend. XIV, § 5 (granting Congress the power to enact legislation "appropriate" to give effect to the provisions of the amendment). In other instances, Congress' authority is based on expanded interpretations of key constitutional provisions such as the commerce clause. *See* U.S. CONST. art. 1, § 8, cl. 3; *see generally* LAURENCE H. TRIBE, AMERICAN CONSTITUTIONAL LAW 305–21 (2d ed., 1988) (discussing the expansive interpretation of the commerce clause).

21.   U.S. CONST. amends. I-X. The Bill of Rights was adopted in 1791, two years after the ratification of the Constitution.

22.   Other provisions of the Constitution speak to the concern of open and fair government. For example, the Constitution requires Congress to keep, and publish, strict records of its proceedings. *See* U.S. CONST. art. I, § 5, cl. 3.

23.   The primary concern was to curb the powers of the *federal* government over individuals. Indeed, for more than 100 years the Bill of Rights and many subsequent amendments were interpreted as only preventing federal government interference, and not state government interference with the enumerated individual rights and liberties. *See, e.g.*, Barron v. Mayor and City Council of Baltimore, 32 U.S. (7 Pet.) 243, 247 (1833) ("The question thus presented is, we think, of great importance, but not of much difficulty. The constitution was ordained and established by the people of the United States for themselves, for their own government, and not for the government of the individual states."); *Slaughter-House Cases*, 83 U.S. (16 Wall.) 36, 82 (1873) (stating "the adoption of the first eleven amendments . . . shows a prevailing sense of danger at that time from the federal power" and holding that post-Civil War amendments have only limited application to the states). This view eroded over time, so that currently most of the protections of the Bill of Rights now have been "incorporated," and are applicable to the states. *See* Duncan v. Louisiana, 391 U.S. 145, 147–50 (1968) (applying Sixth Amendment right to jury trial in criminal cases to states, and discussing the incorporation doctrine).

24.   *See* U.S. CONST. amend. X.

cept of the Constitution and the Bill of Rights, of a federal government with a sharply defined role and limited powers over states and individuals, shapes much of current U.S. constitutional doctrine.

Certain specific characteristics of the U.S. Constitution are worth keeping in mind. First, the Constitution incorporated the values of those in power in the social eras during which the Constitution and each of its amendments were adopted.[25] Thus, the text of the Constitution, as originally adopted and interpreted, incorporated the views of the white male colonists, who were in turn largely influenced by the values of eighteenth century Great Britain and other European colonial powers.[26] In accordance with those values, the Constitution, as originally drafted and interpreted, granted political and social authority to white, landed men, permitted the subjugation of women, condoned slavery and other forms of involuntary servitude, and fostered expansionist policies which contributed to the near-extermination of the indigenous populations of the American continent.[27] Not surprisingly, the Constitution incorporated the contemporaneous convictions about the proper roles for and abilities of women, and once these views were incorporated, they prevailed for generations. And so, the view of constitutional framer Thomas Jefferson that women must be excluded from the political process to "prevent depravation of morals and ambiguity of issues,"[28]

---

25.   For a detailed discussion of these issues, *see* WINNIE HAZOU, THE SOCIAL AND LEGAL STATUS OF WOMEN: A GLOBAL PERSPECTIVE (1990). *See also* THORNTON ANDERSON, CREATING THE CONSTITUTION 17–41 (1993) (discussing the influences of English law and society on the framing of the American Constitution).

26.   The men who gathered in Philadelphia in 1787 could not have envisioned [the changes in American society]. They could not have imagined, nor would they have accepted, that the document they were drafting would one day be construed by a Supreme Court to which had been appointed a woman and the descendent of an African slave.

Thurgood Marshall, *We the People: A Celebration of the Bicentennial of the United States Constitution: The Constitution: A Living Document*, 1987 How. L.J. 623, 627 (1987).

27.   *See, e.g.*, U.S. CONST. art. I, § 2, cl. 3 (recognizing the classifications of "free Persons, including those bound to Service for a Term of Years, and excluding Indians not taxed, three fifths of all other Persons").

Supreme Court Justice Taney's opinion in Scott v. Sandford, 60 U.S. (19 How.) 393, 399 (1857) discussed this provision as it applied to the "uncivilized" Indian race, noting how, "it has been found necessary, for their sake as well as our own, to regard them in a state of pupilage" to the white race. *See id.* at 404. Then, with respect to the "negro African race," the court, considering "[t]he state of public opinion in relation to that unfortunate race, which prevailed in the civilized and enlightened portions of the world at the time of the Declaration of Independence and when the Constitution was framed and adopted," *id.* at 406–07, held that negroes were regarded by the Constitution as "beings of an inferior order; and altogether unfit to associate with the white race, either in social or political relations; and so far inferior that they had no rights which the white man was bound to respect; and that the negro might justly and lawfully be reduced to slavery for his benefit." *Id.* The Court ultimately concluded that blacks were not citizens of the U.S. *See id.* at 453. That interpretation was ultimately overruled by the adoption of the Fourteenth Amendment.

For a comprehensive analysis of how racism against blacks was incorporated into early American jurisprudence, *see* A. LEON HIGGINBOTHAM, JR., IN THE MATTER OF COLOR: RACE AND THE

reverberated nearly one hundred years later in the concurring opinion of United States Supreme Court Justice Joseph P. Bradley:

> [T]he civil law, as well as nature herself, has always recognized a wide difference in the respective spheres and destinies of man and woman. Man is, or should be, woman's protector and defender. The natural and proper timidity and delicacy which belongs to the female sex evidently unfits it for many of the occupations of civil life.[29]

Over time this view of women was used to justify their exclusion not only from politics, but also from many employment opportunities,[30] and to limit their rights to property,[31] marital rights,[32] and personal integrity.[33] It is only since the turn of the century that the predominate American attitudes about the capabilities of women began to change, leading to an expansion of women's rights through constitutional amendment and constitutional interpretation.

AMERICAN LEGAL PROCESS (1978); *see also* SLAVERY AND ITS CONSEQUENCES: THE CONSTITUTION, EQUALITY AND RACE (Robert A. Goldwin & Art Kaufman eds., 1988).

28. Letter from Thomas Jefferson to Samuel Kercheval (Sept. 5, 1816) in 10 WRITINGS OF THOMAS JEFFERSON 45–6 n.1 (P. Ford ed. 1899), *quoted in* United States v. Virginia, 518 U.S. 515, 116 S. Ct. 2264, 2275 n.5 (1996).

29. Bradwell v. Illinois, 83 U.S. 130, 141 (1873). See also Muller v. Oregon, 208 U.S. 412, 422 (1908) ("her own health, [and] the well-being of the race—justify legislation to protect her from the greed as well as the passion of man").

30. *See, e.g.*, Bosley v. McLaughlin, 236 U.S. 385, 392–94 (1915) (upholding California statute prohibiting employment of women pharmacists, student nurses, and other female hospital employees—excluding regular nurses—for more than eight hours per day); Goesaert v. Cleary, 335 U.S. 464, 465–67 (1948) (upholding Michigan law which provided that no woman could obtain a bartender's license unless she was the wife or daughter of the male owner); *cf. Bradwell*, 83 U.S. at 139 (upholding decision of the Illinois' legal bar to deny women licenses to practice law).

31. *See, e.g.*, 1 BLACK. COM. 442, 445 (Sharswood's ed.) (stating that under the early common law, the "legal existence of the woman is suspended during the marriage, or at least incorporated and consolidated into that of the husband," and that, as a consequence, the wife can hold no separate interest "during the coverture"); Nolin v. Pearson, 191 Mass. 283, 284 (1906) (stating that under the common-law traditions of Massachusetts, personal property in a wife's possession upon marriage passed to her husband, and could be levied upon for his debts, or bequeathed by him to strangers, and that she could derive no benefits from, or alienate the property, without his approval) (citing cases).

32. *See, e.g.*, Dixon v. Amerman, 181 Mass. 430, 431 (1920) (stating, with reference to early British authorities, that a wife was considered the servant and chattel of her husband); De Gramm v. Jones, 6 So. 925 (Fla. 1887) (stating that a married woman may not enter into a valid contract of co-partnership); *cf.* Miskunas v. Union Carbide Corp., 399 F.2d 847 (7th Cir. 1968), *cert. denied*, 393 U.S. 1066 (1969) (upholding a state rule that husbands, and not wives, could sue for loss of consortium).

33. *See, e.g.*, State v. Oliver, 71 N.C. 60, 61 (1874) (overruling the prior acknowledged North Carolina law that a husband had the right to whip his wife provided he used a switch no larger than his thumb); Nolin v. Pearson, 191 Mass. 430, 431 (1920) (stating that under the early common law a husband had the right to moderately chastise his wife); *cf.* Southworth v. Packard, 7 Mass. 95 (1810) (holding that damages for a wife's assault might be released by her husband without her consent).

The text of the Constitution has been largely static over its 200-year history. Although the Constitution provides procedures for amendment,[34] it has been amended only sixteen times since the adoption of the Bill of Rights, and more than twenty-five years have passed since the Constitution was last amended (excepting the controversial Twenty-Seventh Amendment).[35] Indeed, several popular attempts to amend the Constitution have recently failed.[36] Of the post-Bill of Rights amendments, only nine, in whole or in part, directly address individual rights and liberties;[37] the remainder address the structure of government.

Notwithstanding the static nature of the text, the Constitution is afforded significant flexibility through its interpretation. The text of the Constitution—especially where it grants individual rights and liberties—is deliberately vague,[38] often requiring legislative initiatives to give content to the identified rights,[39] limited, as always, by any applicable constitutional principles. Although all branches of government at

---

34.   The U.S. Constitution provides that either Congress, upon a two-thirds vote of both houses, or the states, upon the application of two-thirds of the states, may propose amendments, which become valid upon the ratification of three-fourths of the states. *See* U.S. CONST. art. V. The current number of states required to ratify an amendment is thirty-eight.

35.   The Twenty-Sixth Amendment, establishing eighteen as the age to vote, was adopted in 1971. The status of the Twenty-Seventh Amendment, concerning salary increases for members of Congress, is shrouded in controversy. The amendment, first proposed as a component of the Bill of Rights, was finally ratified by the requisite proportion of states in 1992. (As the number of states increased over time from thirteen to fifty, the number of states required to amend the Constitution also increased.) Given the 201-year delay in ratification, some question the continuing validity of the amendment. *See, e.g.*, WILLIAM B. LOCKHART ET AL., THE AMERICAN CONSTITUTION 1454 (8th ed. 1996).

36.   Included in this category are the Equal Rights Amendment. *See infra notes* 117–38 and accompanying text. Recent proposals to amend the Constitution to prohibit flag desecration, and to require a federal balanced budget have failed to garner the requisite congressional support. *See* 141 Cong. Rec. S18391–02 (Dec. 12, 1995) (latest defeat of anti-flag desecration amendment; the amendment has been subsequently reintroduced); 142 Cong. Rec. S5873–04, HS903 (June 6, 1996) (defeat of balanced budget amendment; the amendment has been subsequently reintroduced).

37.   These include Amendment XIII (adopted in 1865) ending slavery; Amendment XIV (1868) guaranteeing equal protection of the laws; Amendment XV (1870) guaranteeing the right to vote regardless of race; Amendment XIX (1920) guaranteeing the right to vote regardless of sex; Amendment XXIV (1964) prohibiting poll taxes on federal elections; Amendment XXVI (1971) guaranteeing the right to vote to those over eighteen years old. In addition, Amendment XVI (1913) limited property rights by subjecting individuals to federal income taxes. The Eighteenth Amendment, adopted in 1919 and repealed in 1933 by the Twenty-First Amendment, prohibited individuals' access to acholic beverages.

38.   *See generally* A. E. Dick Howard, *The Indeterminacy of Constitutions*, 31 WAKE FOREST L. REV. 383 (1996); David A. Strauss, *Common Law and Constitutional Interpretation*, 63 U. CHI. L. REV. 877 (1996); William H. Rehnquist, *The Notion of Living Constitution*, 54 TEX. L. REV. 693, 694 (1976) ("The framers of the Constitution wisely spoke in general language and left to succeeding generations the task of applying that language to the increasingly changing environment in which they would live.").

39.   For example, the Thirteenth, Fourteenth, and Fifteenth Amendments, ending slavery and granting equal protection and other crucial rights to freed slaves, each anticipate Congressional enforcement through "appropriate legislation." *See, e.g.*, U.S. CONST. amend. XIII, § 2.

both the federal and state level participate in the development of constitutional doctrine, ultimate authority for the interpretation of the Constitution rests in the United States Supreme Court.

The justices of the Supreme Court interpret the Constitution according to a variety of interpretive techniques, of which "textualism" (the view that "principles of constitutional law must ultimately be traced to the text of the Constitution"),[40] and "originalism" (the view that "when the text is unclear the original understandings must control"),[41] are predominate—if controversial—theories.[42] Another interpretive method relies on the text but takes into account modern values and sensibilities,[43] and still other methods are advocated.[44] Over time, application of these various interpretive perspectives, in combination with the addition of new amendments, has resulted in a somewhat flexible constitutional doctrine, which has often adapted to new social realities and values—albeit slowly and imperfectly in many cases.[45]

---

40. Strauss, *supra* note 38, at 878.

41. *Id.* Many of the cases already discussed utilize this interpretative technique. *See, e.g.*, Scott v. Sandford, 60 U.S. (19 How.) 393, 412 (1857) (stating that the framers did not consider slaves or former slaves fit for citizenship); Barron v. City of Baltimore, 32 U.S. (7 Pet.) 243, 248 (1833) (stating that the framers of the Constitution intended that state governments would have greater powers than the federal government over individuals); Marbury v. Madison, 5 U.S. (1 Cranch) 137, 179 (1803) (concluding that it was the "intention of the framers" that the Supreme Court be bound to the constitutional limitations over its powers); *see also* Gregory v. Ashcroft, 501 U.S. 452, 457–60 (1996) (stating the "design" of the constitution was intended to limit the power of the federal government over local concerns such as the qualifications of state judges).

42. For an example of the debate concerning the legitimacy of originalism, *see* H. Jefferson Powell, *The Original Understanding of Original Intent*, 98 HARV. L. REV. 885 (1985) (criticizing the legitimacy of originalism); Charles A. Lofgren, *The Original Understanding of Original Intent?*, 5 CONST. COMM. 77 (1988) (criticizing Powell's critique); Jack N. Ravoke, *The Original Intention of Original Understanding*, 13 CONST. COMM. 159 (1996) (discussing both views).

43. *Compare* Marshall, *supra* note 26 (questioning the wisdom of viewing the meaning of the Constitution as being "fixed" by the framers and suggesting that the Constitution, a "living document," must evolve with modern notions of equality), *with* Michael J. Perry, *Modern Equal Protection: A Conceptualization and Appraisal*, 79 COLUM. L. REV. 1023, 1025 (1979) (arguing that analysis of the equal protection clause "should commence with the original understanding and not with some hazy 'concept of equality itself'"); *see also* United States v. Virginia, 116 S. Ct. 2264, 2292–93 (1996) (Scalia, J., dissenting) ("it is my view that when a practice not expressly prohibited by the text of the Bill of Rights bears the endorsement of a long tradition of open, widespread, and unchallenged use that dates back to the beginning of the Republic, we have no proper basis for striking it down . . . [t]he same applies, mutatis mutandis, to a practice asserted to be in violation of the post-Civil War Fourteenth Amendment.") (quotations omitted).

44. *See, e.g.*, Strauss, *supra* note 38, at 891–98, 934–35 (advocating the use of common-law principles as interpretive guidelines); *see generally* JETHRO K. LIEBERMAN, THE EVOLVING CONSTITUTION 12–19 (1992) (describing the following interpretive methods: structural, intent, contextual, historical, cannons of construction, judicial economy and necessity); Laurence H. Tribe, *On Reading the Constitution*, 1988 UTAH L. REV. 747 (discussing various interpretive techniques).

45. An example of an instance in which current trends were ignored, leading to, in the view of some scholars, disastrous results, is Justice Taney's 1857 opinion in the *Scott* case (*supra* note 27). In that opinion, the Court, ignoring a growing popular consensus that slavery was immoral, interpreted the Constitution in accordance with eighteenth-century views of the framers that blacks

Another consideration to keep in mind is the nature of the rights and liberties granted by the Constitution. Rights can be classified pursuant to a variety of paradigms. For example, some scholars speak of rights as "trumps," instances in which the government cannot impede an individual from engaging in (or not engaging in) certain activities, even against arguments of the welfare of that individual, social welfare, or social utility.[46] Other scholars classify rights as either "negative" or "positive," depending on whether the right requires the addressees of the right[47] "merely to refrain from doing something or requires them to take some positive action they might not otherwise take."[48] Depending on the level of specificity and the scope of the right, it may also be classified as "indeterminate" or "abstract," or as "aspirational."[49] While it is difficult to apply any one of these classifications to all of the rights recognized by the Constitution,[50] by and large, most rights granted by the

---

were inferior and unfit for political life. The resulting schism is often viewed as directly contributing to the start of the American Civil War. *See* Rehnquist, *supra* note 38, at 701–02 ("the great majority of antislavery groups . . . were not willing to live with the Dred Scott decision"); *see also* DON E. FEHRENBACHER, SLAVERY, LAW AND POLITICS (1981) (describing political climate leading up to the *Scott* case, and how the decision contributed to the beginning of the Civil War). Similarly, Justice Brown's 1896 opinion in Plessy v. Ferguson, 163 U.S. 537 (1896), *overruled by* Brown v. Bd. of Education of Topeka, 347 U.S. 483 (1954), which purported to apply the eighteenth-century views of the framers of the Fourteenth Amendment in its determination that segregation was constitutionally permissible, causing irreparable damage to American race relations, is now considered by some to have been "wrong the day it was decided." Planned Parenthood of Southeast Pa. v. Casey, 112 S. Ct. 2791, 2813 (1992) (opinion of Kennedy, J.).

46. *See, e.g.*, RONALD DWORKIN, TAKING RIGHTS SERIOUSLY 90–100 (1978); David T. Ozar, *Rights: What Are They and Where Do They Come From, in* PHILOSOPHICAL ISSUES IN HUMAN RIGHTS 1, 4–7 (Patricia H. Werhane et al. eds., 1986) (speaking of the "overriding" nature of rights).

47. The "addressees" of a right are the "party or parties who must act to make available the freedom or benefit identified by the right's scope." JAMES W. NICKEL, MAKING SENSE OF HUMAN RIGHTS 14 (1987).

48. *Id.* Although Nickel recognizes this popular paradigm, he considers the use of these descriptors "misleading" as applied to rights, and would only apply them to duties, given that "most rights impose on their addressees both negative and positive duties." *Id.*

49. *See generally* NICKEL, *supra* note 47, at 13–35; *see also* DWORKIN, *supra* note 46, at 90. Other common classifications include "natural," which refers to the claimed source of the right, and "utilitarian," which refers to the societal or political purpose advanced by recognition of the right. *See* David Lyons, *Utility in Rights, in* THEORIES OF RIGHTS 110 (Jeremy Waldron ed., 1984) (discussing the utilitarian principle); Margaret MacDonald, *Natural Rights, in* THEORIES OF RIGHTS, *supra*, at 21 (discussing natural rights).

50. For example, many consider the First Amendment right to freedom of speech as virtually inviolate—a "trump." *See, e.g.*, Konigsburg v. State Bar, 366 U.S. 36, 61 (1961) (Black, J. dissenting) (referring to the First Amendment as "unequivocal"). However, it may also be classified as a "negative" right in that it prohibits the government from forcing one individual "to speak or to associate with the speech of others." Pacific Gas and Electric Co. v. Public Utilities Comm'n, 475 U.S. 1, 26, 32, 33 (1986) (Rehnquist, J. dissenting); *cf.* J. M. Balkin, *Some Realism About Pluralism: Legal Realist Approaches to the First Amendment,* 1990 DUKE L.J. 375 (discussing the First Amendment as incorporating among other rights the right of access to public forums). On the other hand, while the Fourteenth Amendment right to equal protection may similarly be classified as a negative right—it requires the government to refrain from treating individuals unequally in inappropriate circumstances—it is by no means a "trump" because it is recognized

Constitution are fairly classified as negative: the Constitution enjoins undue governmental interference with certain key activities of individuals, but does not often require the government to take affirmative action to advance the abstract or aspirational goals of the right.[51]

The emphasis on negative rights naturally results from the content of the rights identified by the Constitution. The governmental framework envisioned by the framers of the Constitution provided for a unifying federal government designed to be accessible to the citizenry, yet strictly controlled against excesses by the operation of individual rights and liberties, as well as by the structural checks and balances provided by the separate spheres of power enjoyed by the three federal institutions. Accordingly, the first rights identified in the Bill of Rights—considered by some to be the linchpin of American society—are the guarantees of the First Amendment to freedom of speech, freedom of religion, a free press, the right to assembly, and the "right to petition government"—all negative rights. These rights are intended to guarantee a populace of free thinkers, able to participate in society according to their individual consciences. The remainder of the Bill of Rights erects a buffer zone between the individual (and property) and governmental interference[52]—again utilizing negative rights. In short, the rights and liberties set forth in the Bill of Rights are negative because they were intended to promote this initial vision of American society, and to ensure not only a responsive and responsible government, but also an independent citizenry.[53] Many of the subsequent amendments pick up on this theme by removing obstacles to citizenship and to the exercise of the vote.[54] One important exception is the first section of the Fourteenth Amendment, which directs its attention to the

---

that the government can indeed, when appropriate, treat people differently. *See discussion infra* text accompanying note 107.

51.   This author's so-called "fair classification" underscores Nickel's caution about the inherent difficulties of generalization (*supra* note 48): some rights are unequivocally positive, such as the "right to bear arms;" other rights can be classified as dual in nature, such as the "freedom of religion" which includes both the positive right to freely exercise your religion, *see, e.g.*, Sherbert v. Verner, 374 U.S. 398, 402–06 (1963) (holding that state cannot distribute unemployment benefits in a manner which discriminates against Seventh Day Adventists), as well as the negative right to be free from governmental establishment of religion, *see, e.g.*, Lemon v. Kurtzman, 403 U.S. 602 (1971) (holding that state's financial support of religious schools excessively "entangles" government and religion).

52.   The Bill of Rights recognizes the right to security in one's home: the Third Amendment prohibits the quartering of soldiers; the Fourth Amendment prohibits unreasonable searches and seizures. The Bill of Rights recognizes as well the right to security in one's person: The Fifth, Sixth, and Eighth amendments set forth procedures designed to protect individuals from the power of the government when investigating and prosecuting criminal cases.

53.   This emphasis on negative rights and on liberty interests was a deliberate choice of the framers. It is worth noting, however, that the drafters of the French Declaration of the Rights of Man and the Citizen, a document also adopted in 1789, made a different choice. The Declaration speaks of "rights and duties," "the common good," and "public utility." GEORGE A. BERMANN, HENRY P. DE VRIES & NINA M. GALSTON, FRENCH LAW: CONSTITUTION AND SELECTIVE LEGISLATION 2–5 (1994).

54.   *See* U.S. CONST. amends. XIV, XV, XIX, XXVI.

fundamental fairness of American society, requiring not only equal protection under the law, regardless of race, but also reiterating the need for due process under the law.[55]

Because the primary concern was to curb governmental interference, one traditional limitation on the Constitution is that its prohibitions typically apply to *governmental* action (referred to as "state action").[56] Under this principle, while the operation of federal or state legislation or policies interfering with an individual right would be invalidated under the Constitution, similar interference by another individual would be beyond constitutional reach or prohibition. For example, under current doctrine, a state that declares that African-Americans are disqualified from receiving public support available to others would be found to violate the equal protection provisions of the Fourteenth Amendment. However, the decision of a private charity to exclude African-American beneficiaries would be beyond constitutional reach.

As constitutional doctrine has evolved, the federal government has been given greater power to regulate the activities of non-state actors.[57] Important examples include federal prohibitions on race and gender discrimination by certain private employers,[58] which have survived constitutional challenge.[59] Notwithstanding this

---

54.   *See* U.S. CONST. amends. XIV, XV, XIX, XXVI.

55.   *See* U.S. CONST. amend. XIV, § 1. The primary purpose of the Fourteenth Amendment was to protect newly freed slaves. *See infra* notes 94–95 and accompanying text. Later interpretations of the amendment expanded its reach to others, including other ethnic minorities and women. *See infra* notes 106–16 and accompanying text.

56.   Consider the *Civil Rights Cases*, 109 U.S. 3, 27 (1883): "It is state action of a particular character that is prohibited. Individual invasion of individual rights is not the subject-matter of the [Fourteenth Amendment]." The Court later noted that "civil rights, such as are guaranteed by the Constitution against state aggression, cannot be impaired by the wrongful acts of individuals, unsupported by state authority." *Id*. at 17. State action may also be found where there is a close relationship between the individuals and the state, or where the individuals are filling a role normally assumed by the state. *See, e.g.*, Smith v. Allwright, 321 U.S. 649, 664–65 (1944) (where state statutes establish election system based on cooperation with political parties, actions of a political party limiting membership to "qualified" white citizens was state action governed by the constitution); Terry v. Adams, 345 U.S. 461, 472–77 (1953) (where state cedes all responsibility for primary elections to political party, racial discrimination by that political party is state action).

57.   For a discussion of how the federal government's power under the state action doctrine has evolved (and increased) over time, *see* Donald H. Regan, *The Supreme Court and State Protectionism: Making Sense of the Dormant Commerce Clause*, 84 MICH. L. REV. 1091 (1986); Donald H. Regan, *How To Think About The Federal Commerce Power and Incidentally Rewrite United States v. Lopez*, 94 MICH. L. REV. 554 (1995). For an example of cases applying this expanded view of Congressional power to permit federal action to prohibit racial discrimination by private actors, *see* Katzenbach v. McClung, 379 U.S. 294 (1964) (federal prohibition of racial discrimination in public accommodations upheld under Congress' powers to regulate national commerce).

58.   *See* Pub. L. No. 88–352, Title VII, § 701, July 2, 1964, 78 Stat 233, codified as amended in 42 U.S.C.A. §§ 2000e *et seq*. (West 1994 and Supp. 1996). Title VII applies to employers in an "industry affecting commerce," who have at least fifteen employees. *See* 42 U.S.C.A. §2000e (b).

59.   *See* Lucido v. Cravath, Swaine & Moore, 425 F. Supp. 123 (N.Y. 1977) (Title VII claim based on discrimination based on national origin surviving constitutional challenges of privacy

liberalizing trend, the traditions of United States constitutional law and of American government on all levels reflect a hesitancy to apply constitutional prohibitions in the absence of state action.

Finally, it is important to keep in mind that the Constitution is not the only source of rights in American law—indeed, in some ways it is the least significant. The Constitution provides a floor, while the creation of specific rights and entitlements is most often left to the legislative branch of the federal government, or to the states. Important congressional legislation providing specific rights and remedies to vindicate the right to equal protection are the Civil Rights Acts of 1875 and 1964, which established a variety of civil and criminal remedies to combat racial discrimination and racial violence.[60] Congressional legislation also amplified the right to vote. For example, the Voting Rights Act of 1965[61] outlawed many state practices designed to disenfranchise minorities or to dilute their voting strength;[62] it also went so far as to provide federal oversight of state election practices in several states.[63] Also significant are the many other initiatives and policies that the executive branch and Congress have supported over time. Examples include funding and support for Head Start, a targeted day care program which primarily services poor minority neighborhoods,[64] and government hiring and contracting policies that are sensitive to racial justice.[65] These initiatives are always subject to constitutional review, and some have been struck down,[66] but these policies remain a significant agent of change.[67]

---

and freedom of association rights); Weiner v. Cuyahoga Community College, 238 N.E.2d 839 (upholding constitutionality of Title VII), *aff'd*, 249 N.E.2d 907 (Ohio), *cert. denied*, 396 U.S. 1004 (1969).

60.   *See* 18 Stat. 335 (1875). Many provisions of the 1875 Act were invalidated by the Supreme Court on the grounds that Congress had exceeded its authority under the Fourteenth Amendment. *See* The Civil Rights Cases, 109 U.S. 3 (1883).

61.   *See* 42 U.S.C.A. §§ 1973 *et seq.* (West 1996).

62.   *See, e.g.*, South Carolina v. Katzenbach, 383 U.S. 301 (1966) (upholding Voting Rights Act's ban on literacy tests).

63.   *See, e.g.*, United States v. State of Louisiana, 265 F. Supp. 703 (D.C. La. 1966), *aff'd*, 386 U.S. 270 (1967) (permitting federal government program to register voters in state).

64.   *See* 42 U.S.C.A. §§ 9801 & 9831 *et seq.* (West 1996). The Head Start Program was established in 1981 and has enjoyed continued congressional support since then. *See* Congressional Press Releases, Sept. 30, 1996, Monday, "Provisions in H.R. 4278—the FY 1997 Omnibus Appropriations Bill."

65.   *See, e.g.*, 5 U.S.C.A. § 7201 (West 1996) (prohibiting discrimination on the basis of race, color, sex, or national origin and requiring the development of a federal employment minority recruitment program); 10 U.S.C.A. § 451 (West 1996) (requiring biennial reports concerning "the state of race and ethnic issues and discrimination" in the armed forces). The federal government, as an employer of millions, has great power in this regard.

66.   *See* Metro Broadcasting, Inc. v. FCC, 497 U.S. 547 (1990) (upholding congressional regulations intended to benefit minority applicants for federal broadcasting licenses); *but see* Adarand Constructor, Inc. v. Pena, 115 S. Ct. 2097 (1995) (overruling *Metro Broadcasting* and ordering lower court to strictly scrutinize federal contracting policies intended to increase participation by minority-owned businesses).

67.   *See* Thomas E. Ricks, *About Face: U.S. Infantry Surprise: It's Now Mostly White, Blacks*

This complex layer of protection provided by the Constitution, and federal legislation and policies is complemented by the protections of the state constitutions, legislation and policies. Each state has its own constitution governing the relations between the state government and its citizens. While the states are required to comply with the minimum provisions of the federal constitution, they are free to complement the Constitution by granting additional rights and liberties not recognized federally. For example, some state constitutions either include explicit provisions or have been interpreted as requiring gender equality,[68] as granting the right to education,[69] or as affording greater protections to defendants in criminal prosecutions.[70] These state constitutions are also supplemented by state legislation, initiatives and policies. While it is useful to focus on the important unifying minimum provided by the federal government—the focus of this section—these important state legal structures must also be kept in mind.

Women and the Constitution—A History

Interestingly, as originally adopted, both the Constitution and the Bill of Rights were remarkably gender-neutral, speaking nowhere of "men" or "women," but rather of "persons" and "citizens."[71] Women have always been considered to be citizens and persons under the Constitution, to whom certain fundamental rights attach.[72] However, while women have been said to enjoy "all the privileges and immunities of citizen-

---

Hold Office Jobs, WALL ST. J., Jan. 6, 1997, at A1 (stating that blacks, Hispanics, and women are disproportionately represented in office jobs and management positions, and less in the rank and file); *but see* Ian Fisher, *Blacks in Military Wrestle with Issues of Race and Justice*, N.Y. TIMES, June 17, 1997, at A1 (describing advancement of blacks in the military and suspected prejudice in current enforcement of allegations of sexual harassment against black officers).

68. *See, e.g.*, Doe v. Maher, 515 A.2d 134 (Conn. 1986) (invalidating state regulations restricting abortion funding as violative of the due process and equal protection provisions of the Connecticut state constitution).

69. *See, e.g.*, Sheff v. O'Neill, 678 A.2d 1267 (Conn. 1996) (holding that the Connecticut constitution guarantees the right to substantially equal educational opportunity).

70. *See, e.g.*, People v. Bigelow, 488 N.E.2d 451 (Ct. App. N.Y. 1985) (holding that police search permissible under federal constitution nonetheless violated defendant's rights under New York state constitution).

71. The exception is the occasional use of the pronouns "he" and "his." *See, e.g.*, U.S. CONST. art. II, § 1, cl. 1 ("The executive Power shall be vested in a President . . . [h]e shall hold his Office during the Term of four Years . . . "). *See generally* JUDITH A. BAER, WOMEN IN AMERICAN LAW: THE STRUGGLE TOWARD EQUALITY FROM THE NEW DEAL TO THE PRESENT 19–20 (2d ed. 1996) [hereinafter BAER, WOMEN] (discussing the deceptiveness of gender-neutrality in the Constitution). Later amendments began to use gender terms. Notably, the Fourteenth Amendment refers to the right of "male citizens" to vote. U.S. CONST. amend. XIV, § 2. This gender specificity was intentional, responding to the calls for women's suffrage. *See* ELEANOR FLEXNOR AND ELLEN FITZPATRICK, CENTURY OF STRUGGLE: THE WOMEN'S RIGHTS MOVEMENT IN THE UNITED STATES 136–41 (Enlarged ed. 1996) [hereinafter FLEXNOR].

72. *See* Minor v. Happersett, 88 U.S. 162–169 (1873). Of course, women who were slaves, Indians, or—in the sanitized parlance of the Constitution—"other persons" (U.S. CONST. art. I, § 2, cl. 3) had no rights under the Constitution. With the passage of the Thirteenth and Fourteenth Amendments, former slaves and all others born or naturalized in the United States were granted

ship,"[73] the scope of those privileges and immunities has been restrictively interpreted:

> Historically, the subordinate status of women has been firmly entrenched in our legal system. At common law women were conceded few rights. Constitutions were drafted on the assumption that women did not exist as legal persons. Courts classified women with children and imbeciles, denying their capacity to think and act as responsible adults and enclosing them in the bonds of protective paternalism. Over the last century, it is true, the status of women has gradually improved . . . [b]ut the development has been slow and haphazard.[74]

One significant strategy for change has been to attempt to incorporate gender equality into federal constitutional doctrine, either through direct amendment of the Constitution or by arguing for a more expansive interpretation of already existing provisions. The important successes—and failures—of these methods, and the resulting development in the constitutional doctrine of gender equality, are discussed below.

Political Life

As was previously noted, few aspects of American society are held in as high regard as the right to active participation in the civic life. Yet the right to vote was long denied to women. In the mid-1800s a New Jersey Senator declared:

> It seems to me as if the God of our race has stamped upon [the women of America] a milder, gentler nature, which not only makes them shrink from, but disqualifies them for the turmoil and battle of public life.[75]

This view was held by many, including the bench of the Supreme Court, which in 1873 held that the Constitution did not grant women the right to vote.[76] A constitutional amendment was required to overcome this settled doctrine that women were incapable of political participation, or otherwise undeserving of that privilege.

The suffrage movement was born in the mid-nineteenth century, out of the same social activism that led women to organize to campaign against slavery,[77] for educa-

---

citizenship, and accorded the "privileges and immunities of the United States." U.S. CONST. amend. XIV, § 1.

73. *Minor*, 88 U.S. at 170.

74. Barbara A. Brown et al., *The Equal Rights Amendment: A Constitutional Basis for Equal Rights for Women*, 80 YALE L.J. 871, 872 (1971).

75. Comment of Senator Frelinghuysen of New Jersey, *quoted in* FLEXNOR, *supra* note 71, at 142.

76. *See Minor*, 88 U.S. 162. A telling indication of the then prevailing attitude about the rights of women is the fact that the state of Missouri elected to forgo its right to argue its position to the Supreme Court, trusting that the Court would unhesitatingly reject the arguments of Virginia Minor. Missouri's trust in the Supreme Court was well-placed. The Court constructed a tortured rationale in support of its position, ultimately concluding that it was not a violation of the rights of women to deny them the vote because the Constitution does not grant *any* citizen the right to vote. *See id.* at 178.

77. For a historical perspective of the birth of the suffrage movement, *see generally* FLEXNOR, *supra* note 71. For the impact of the abolition movement on key figures of the suffrage movement, *see* ELISABETH GRIFFITH, IN HER OWN RIGHT: THE LIFE OF ELIZABETH CADY STANTON 25–27, 35–37, 111–12 (1984); LYNN SHERR, FAILURE IS IMPOSSIBLE: SUSAN B. ANTHONY IN HER OWN WORDS 44

tion for girls,[78] and on a variety of issues affecting women. Following the Civil War and the end of slavery, women pressed their demands for suffrage. The initial political response was overwhelmingly negative: the Fourteenth Amendment was drafted to ensure that no possible interpretation of it could lead to giving the franchise to women.[79] This put some suffragists in the position of arguing against the amendment, and against their old abolitionist allies.[80] So great, however, was the sentiment against

---

(1995); ELLEN CAROL DUBOIS, FEMINISM AND SUFFRAGE: THE EMERGENCE OF AN INDEPENDENT WOMEN'S MOVEMENT IN AMERICA 1848–1869, 21–52 (1978). An 1861 diary entry by Anthony indicated her participation in the Underground Railroad, run by fugitive slave Harriet Tubman to conduct other fugitive slaves to freedom. *See* SHERR, *supra*, at 33. *See also* KATHLEEN BARRY, SUSAN B. ANTHONY: A BIOGRAPHY OF A SINGULAR FEMINIST 62–63 (stating that Anthony "often" helped runaway slaves in the early 1850s). Cady Stanton met and married her husband through her abolition activities, and their wedding trip to London was to participate as delegates to the World Anti-Slavery Convention. *See* GRIFFITH, *supra*, at 26–35. The controversy over the participation of women at the conference galvanized Cady Stanton and others to consider the issue of women's rights. *See id.* at 36–37. *See also* FLEXNOR, *supra*, at 66–72.

Nor was the connection one sided. Famed African-American abolitionist Frederick Douglass was a consistent and staunch supporter of women's rights. *See, e.g.*, FREDERICK DOUGLASS ON WOMEN'S RIGHTS 51 (Philip S. Foner ed., 1976) [hereinafter Foner] ("'Frederick Douglass remarked that the only true basis of rights, was the capacity of individuals, and as for himself he dared not claim a right which he would not concede to women.'") *quoting* THE NORTH STAR (Rochester, N.Y.) Aug. 11, 1848.

78. *See generally* FLEXNOR *supra* note 71, at 22–37. For some of Susan B. Anthony's views on the importance of education for girls and women, *see* SHERR, *supra* note 77, at 17–27.

79. The Amendment provides:

But when the right to vote . . . [in a federal election] . . . is denied to any of the *male* inhabitants of such state, being twenty-one years of age, and citizens of the United States . . . the basis of representation therein shall be reduced in the proportion which the number of such *male* citizens shall bear to the whole number of *male* citizens twenty-one years of age in such state.

U.S. CONST. amend. XIV, § 2 (emphasis added).

80. Indeed, some suffragists, including Elizabeth Cady Stanton, argued that it was essential to give women the right to vote in order to dilute the voting strength of uneducated, less deserving blacks:

The insistence of abolitionists and Republicans that black male suffrage take precedence over female suffrage enraged Stanton. In defense she adopted an antiblack, antimale, profemale argument. According to Stanton, it was better and safer to enfranchise educated white women than former slaves or ignorant immigrants. . . . "The best interests of the nation demand that we outweigh this incoming pauperism, ignorance, and degradation, with the wealth, education, and refinement of the women of the republic," she declared.

GRIFFITH, *supra* note 77, at 124. *See also* Foner, *supra* note 77, at 26–27 (*quoting* Stanton as remarking "it becomes a serious question whether we had better stand aside and see 'Sambo' walk into the kingdom first"); *see generally* Rosalyn Terborg-Penn, *African American Women and the Woman Suffrage Movement, in* ONE WOMAN, ONE VOTE: REDISCOVERING THE WOMAN SUFFRAGE MOVEMENT 146–51 (Marjorie S. Wheeler ed., 1995); Wanda A. Hendricks, *Ida B. Wells-Barnett and the Alpha Suffrage Club of Chicago, in* ONE WOMAN, ONE VOTE, *supra*, at 268–70; "Proceedings of the American Equal Rights Association Convention, Steinway Hall, New York City, May 12, 1869" *in* Foner, *supra*, at 86–90, (debate about enfranchising black men and not women) *quoting* HISTORY OF WOMAN SUFFRAGE, vol. II, pp. 382–84, 391–92 (Elizabeth Cady

giving women the vote that soon after its adoption the Fifteenth Amendment, which guarantees the right to vote regardless of "race, color, or previous condition of servitude,"[81] was also introduced and adopted over the pleas of suffragists who wished to include "sex" in the list of impermissible grounds for denying the vote.

Over the next sixty years the battle for the vote was waged on many fronts and employed a multitude of strategies. Some activists pushed for suffrage at the state and local level, while others continued to press for a federal mandate granting women the vote in all jurisdictions (hence the slogan "universal suffrage"). The battle for universal suffrage was also fought in the courts, seeking a broadened application of existing constitutional provisions—a tactic inherently uncertain and eventually unsuccessful.[82]

The Constitution's Nineteenth Amendment granting women universal suffrage was adopted in 1920.[83] The fight to pass the Nineteenth Amendment is significant to the issue of women's rights in the U.S. on several levels. First, the women's suffrage movement, which arose out of women's concerns regarding a variety of issues, including slavery, education, child care and health, is largely viewed as the precursor to modern American feminism,[84] and is historically significant. Second, it is culturally significant that even in its nascent stages the women's movement was somewhat fragmented, with different ideals, goals, and strategies pursued by the advocates of women's rights.[85] Nor can the role that race played, and continues to play, in the quest for gender equality be underestimated. Many white suffragists, who identified them-

---

Stanton et al. eds., 1881). Susan B. Anthony had little tolerance for such views. *See* BARRY, *supra* note 77, at 320–23, 345–47.

81. U.S. CONST. amend. XV, § 1.

82. *See, e.g.,* Minor V. Happersett, 88 U.S. 162 (1874) (holding that the Constitution does not guarantee women the right to vote). Disputes over the most effective strategy (as well as other political issues) led to disputes within the leadership of the suffrage movement, and to the creation of competing women's rights organizations, the National Woman Suffrage Association, and the American Woman Suffrage Association. FLEXNOR, *supra* note 71, at 145–48, 208–17. The organizations later reconciled and combined. *Id.*

83. The Nineteenth Amendment provides: "The right of citizens of the United States to vote shall not be denied or abridged by the United States or by any State on account of sex." U.S. CONST. amend. XIX, § 1.

84. The exact meaning of "feminism" has been the subject of controversy for over one hundred years. *See, e.g.,* BECKER, THE ORIGINS OF THE EQUAL RIGHTS AMENDMENT: AMERICAN FEMINISM BETWEEN THE WARS 47–51 (1981) (describing different views of feminism); Mary Becker, *Strength in Diversity: Feminist Theoretical Approaches to Child Custody and Same-Sex Relationships,* 23 STETSON L. REV. 701, 704–14 (1994) [hereinafter Becker, *Diversity*] (same). In some circles, "feminism" is a negative term. *See, e.g.,* HARRISON, *supra* note 15, at ix–x (recognizing the invocation of the term "feminist" as an epithet or "accusation"). Here the term "feminism" is used broadly and positively, to denote the advocation of the right of women to participate in the political process, to have property and family rights, and to have broadened employment opportunities.

85. *See* SUSAN D. BECKER, *supra* note 84, at 47–64 (describing competing views of how best to advance the cause of women's rights following the adoption of the Fourteenth Amendment); *see generally* FLEXNOR, *supra* note 71, at 171–84, 208–17.

selves as the "slaves"[86] of their husbands, nonetheless considered themselves intellectually and morally superior to former slaves and the immigrant population. Their efforts to privilege white women at the expense of black and immigrant women, and to discount the unique experiences of those women, had repercussions that continue to affect the contemporary women's movement.[87] Third, the struggle itself illuminates the gap between American constitutional theory and practice: women advocating suffrage were harassed by their families, religious institutions, and public officials, notwithstanding that they were exercising the fundamental principles of freedom of speech, freedom of conscience, and political participation.[88] The cultural reality of the application of the principles of democracy expressed in the Constitution often falls short of the ideal. Finally, the suffrage movement is significant because of what it did *not* achieve: it achieved the vote, but it did not inevitably lead to equal rights for women.[89]

---

86.   While white women were not subject to the brutality of black slavery, they were in many American states considered the chattel of their husbands. *See, e.g.*, Nolin v. Pearson, 191 Mass. 283, 284 (1906) (citing cases).

87.   As critical race feminists note, the quest for equality for women often obscures or makes more difficult the quest for racial and ethnic equality under American law. *See, e.g.*, Pauli Murray, *The Negro Women's Stake in the Equal Rights Amendment*, 6 HARV. C.R.-C.L. L. REV. 253 (1971) ("All that has been said about the deprivations and frustrations of women generally . . . applies with special force to black women, who have been doubly victimized by the twin immoralities of racial and sexual bias."); *see also* Kimberle Crenshaw, *Demarginalizing the Intersection of Race and Sex*, 1989 U. CHI. LEGAL F. 139; Angela P. Harris, *Race and Essentialism in Feminist Legal Theory*, 42 STAN. L. REV. 581 (1990); Judy Scales-Trent, *Black Women and the Constitution: Finding Our Place; Asserting Our Rights*, 24 HARV. C.R.-C.L. L. REV. 9 (1989). Such tension within the women's movement is nothing new: it was noted by Sojourner Truth—arguably the first critical race feminist—at an 1851 women's rights convention held in Akron, Ohio, when she implored the other activists to remember that, although black, and destined to a life of hard service, "ain't I a woman?" FLEXNOR, *supra* note 71, at 91. Black activist and newspaper reporter Ida B. Wells-Barnett also spoke out against the prejudices of the suffragist elites. *See* Hendricks, *supra* note 80, at 263.

88.   For example, one of those objecting to the participation of women in the World Anti-Slavery Convention was Elizabeth Cady Stanton's husband, Henry Stanton, who later criticized her quest for women's suffrage. *See* GRIFFITH, *supra* note 77, at 35–37, 55. Reportedly, Cady Stanton's father, upon hearing of her plans to advocate for women's suffrage, "rushed to Seneca Falls to determine her sanity." *Id.* at 55.

89.   Why didn't universal suffrage inevitably lead to gender equality, as some of its proponents believed it would? Here are a few ideas: Women, like men, have never voted as a single block. Indeed, not all women are feminists, and even feminists split on the appropriate goals of legislative initiatives. For example: should society recognize that women, even working women, are the primary homemakers and child-care givers, and thus strive to protect them from the consequences of those economic and social sacrifices? Or should society work to remove barriers to economic and employment opportunities, on the assumption that the betterment of women requires functional equality in these areas? Are women just like men, so that equality requires no change in existing standards for jobs and other opportunities, or should standards be adjusted to provide fair representation of women in all areas of life? These conflicting views have long divided the women (and men) fighting for women's rights in America. *See* SUSAN D. BECKER, *supra* note 84, at 121–51 (describing strategies of those advocating equality under the law, and eschewing protectionist legislation in the period following the passage of the Nineteenth Amendment).

The Doctrine of Equal Protection

As noted previously, women have mounted constitutional challenges to governmental and private discrimination since the mid-nineteenth century. Those challenges have been raised under a variety of constitutional provisions, including the privileges and immunities clause of the Fourteenth Amendment.[90] The status of women has also been considered under the due process clause of the Fourteenth Amendment.[91] It is only since the 1940s that challenges to discrimination against women have been seriously entertained under the Fourteenth Amendment's equal protection clause.[92] That clause provides that no state shall "deny to any person within its jurisdiction the equal protection of the laws."[93] Despite the expansive language of the amendment, for a variety of reasons, it was not considered a viable ground on which women could seek vindication of their rights for many years.

Soon after the Fourteenth Amendment's adoption, the Supreme Court declared that "the one pervading purpose" of it and other amendments to the Constitution adopted at the close of the Civil War was to ensure "[t]he freedom of the slave race, the security and firm establishment of that freedom, and the protection of the newly-made freeman and citizens from the oppressions of those who had formerly exercised unlimited dominion over him."[94] Thus, under the approach originally announced by the Court, where discrimination was based on some characteristic other than race, there was no recourse under the Fourteenth Amendment.[95] This interpretation was

90.   The Fourteenth Amendment provides that "No State shall make or enforce any law which shall abridge the privileges or immunities of citizens of the United States." U.S. CONST. amend. XIV. Cases applying this provision to claims of gender discrimination include Minor v. Happersett, 88 U.S. (21 Wall.) 162 (1874) (upholding denial of vote to women); Bradwell v. Illinois, 83 U.S. (16 Wall.) 130 (1872) (upholding denial of admission of women to legal bar); *In re* Lockwood 154 U.S. 116 (1894) (same).

91.   That clause provides that no state shall "deprive any person of life, liberty, or property, without due process of law." U.S. CONST. amend. XIV, § 1. Cases applying this provision to gender discrimination claims include Muller v. Oregon, 208 U.S. 412 (1908) (fixing maximum hours of employment for women); Radice v. New York, 264 U.S. 292, 298 (1924) (upholding state statute regulating the working hours of female employees in restaurants); Adkins v. Children's Hospital 261 U.S. 525, 562 (1923) (invalidating state statute setting a minimum wage for adult women), *overruled by* West Coast Hotel v. Parrish, 300 U.S. 379 (1937).

92.   While earlier cases raised equal protection issues, those arguments were rejected. *See, e.g., Radice*, 264 U.S. at 296–98.

93.   U.S. CONST. amend. XIV, § 1.

94.   Slaughter-House Cases, 83 U.S. (16 Wall.) 36 (1873) (rejecting economic discrimination claims of business brought under privileges and immunities clause of the Fourteenth Amendment). For a historical perspective of the development of the equal protection doctrine, *see* Owen M. Fiss, *One Century of Anti-Discrimination*, 15 CAP. U. L. REV. 396 (1986); Michael J. Perry, *Modern Equal Protection: A Conceptualization and Appraisal*, 79 COLUM. L. REV. 1023 (1979); Laurence H. Tribe and Michael C. Dorf, *Level of Generality in the Definition of Rights*, 57 U. CHI. L. REV. 1057 (1990).

95.   Moreover, the Court's conservative interpretation of the Fourteenth Amendment rendered it unwilling to offer broad federal protections even to those claiming racial discrimination. *See, e.g.,* The Civil Rights Cases, 109 U.S. 3 (1883) (invalidating key portions of a federal statute aimed at

eventually broadened to permit claims on a variety of bases, including some types of economic classifications.[96]

Later, the Supreme Court, in its infamous 1896 holding in the case of *Plessy v. Ferguson*,[97] stated with respect to the equal protection clause that:

> it could not have been intended to abolish distinctions based upon color, or to enforce social, as distinguished from political, equality or a commingling of the two races upon terms unsatisfactory to either. Laws permitting, and even recognizing, their separation, . . . do not necessarily imply the inferiority of either race to the other, and have been generally, if not universally, recognized as within the competency of the state legislatures in the exercise of their police power.[98]

With this opinion the Court upheld laws requiring or permitting racial segregation in America. While this restrictive interpretation, like the earlier narrow reading of the scope of the Civil War amendments, was eventually overruled, together they rendered the equal protection clause an inhospitable ground upon which women—indeed, anyone, including blacks—could base constitutional claims for equal treatment.[99] Women were not the group primarily targeted by the amendment,[100] and the very nature of their complaint was the type of recognized social inequalities approved of with regard to racial discrimination.[101] Indeed, even as late as 1948, in the case of *Goesaert v. Cleary*[102] concerning a gender-based claim under the equal protection clause, the Court stated that the claim "need not detain us long."[103] Dismissing a challenge to a

---

eliminating racial discrimination in public accommodations); United States v. Cruichank, 92 U.S. 542 (1875) (disallowing the application of the federal criminal statute to persons accused of lynching two black men); *see generally* A. LEON HIGGINBOTHAM, JR., SHADES OF FREEDOM: RACIAL POLITICS AND PRESUMPTIONS OF THE AMERICAN LEGAL PROCESS (1996); J. WILLIAMSON, THE CRUCIBLE OF RACE (1984).

96.   *See* Gulf, C. & S.F. Ry. v. Ellis, 165 U.S. 150, 155 (1897). That use continues today, however, in cases where the classification is economic or social and not racial or otherwise suspect, great deference is given to the state policy. *See, e.g.*, FCC v. Beach Communications, Inc., 508 U.S. 307, 313 (1993); *see infra* note 107 and accompanying text.

97.   163 U.S. 537 (1896), *overruled by* Brown v. Bd. of Ed., 347 U.S. 483 (1954).

98.   163 U.S. at 544.

99.   Indeed, Justice Holmes referred to an equal protection argument as the "last resort of constitutional arguments." Buck v. Bell, 274 U.S. 200, 208 (1927) (rejecting a challenge to the order of forced sterilization of a mentally retarded woman).

100.   Of course, black women, like black men, could object to classifications based on their race. One of the unsuccessful plaintiffs in *The Civil Rights Cases*, 109 U.S. 3 (1883), challenging segregation of the railroads, was African-American Sally Robinson. For an interesting discussion of the background to Sally Robinson's case, *see* HIGGINBOTHAM, *supra* note 95, at 102–07.

101.   *See, e.g.*, Muller v. Oregon, 208 U.S. 412, 422 (1908) (recognizing that "the inherent difference between the two sexes" justified statutory limitations on the hours of employment of women in factories); *see also* LEO KANOWITZ, WOMEN AND THE LAW: THE UNFINISHED REVOLUTION 151–54 (1969) [hereinafter KANOWITZ, WOMEN AND THE LAW] (discussing development of the principle that "sex is a valid basis for classification").

102.   334 U.S. 464 (1948). For an excellent historical survey of the equal protection doctrine as applied to gender discrimination, *see* BAER, WOMEN, *supra* note 71, at 23–55.

103.   *Id.* at 465.

state statute restricting the ability of women to work as licensed bartenders, the Court held:

> The fact that women may now have achieved the virtues that men have long claimed as their prerogatives and now indulge in vices that men have long practiced, does not preclude the States from drawing a sharp line between the sexes.[104]

And in 1961, during the height of the American civil rights movement, the Court opined that women, despite their "enlightened emancipation" from prior restrictions, "[are] still regarded as the center of home and family life."[105] Now, however, the equal protection clause is a potent weapon in the quest for gender equality.[106]

Under current Supreme Court jurisprudence, the equal protection clause may serve as the basis for any claim of inappropriate disparate treatment, by state or federal government; however, according to the nature of the classification, the Court will vary the deference it gives to the government's legislation or policy, giving the greatest deference and the least scrutiny to "non-suspect" classifications ("suspect" classifications include racial, ethnic or religious groupings). Accordingly:

> equal protection is not a license for courts to judge the wisdom, fairness or logic of legislative choices. In areas of social and economic policy, a statutory classification that neither proceeds along suspect lines [e.g., race, national origin, religion or alienage] nor infringes fundamental constitutional rights must be upheld against equal protection challenge if there is any reasonably conceivable state of facts that could provide a rational basis for the classification. Where there are "plausible reasons" for Congress' action, "our inquiry is at an end."[107]

By contrast, where the classification indeed "proceeds along suspect lines," the Court affords little deference, subjecting the legislation or policy to "strict scrutiny." That scrutiny, the highest level of scrutiny, requires that the legislation or policy be based on a "compelling state interest," and further, that it be "narrowly tailored" to meet that interest.[108] For many years claims of gender discrimination were allocated to the deferential or "rational basis" review in recognition of some of the societal assump-

---

104. *Id.*

105. Hoyt v. Florida, 368 U.S. 57, 61 (1961) (upholding state statute which excluded women from involuntary jury service). *Cf.* Michael M. v. Superior Court, 450 U.S. 404 (1981) (upholding California statutory rape statute which penalized men, and not women, for engaging in sex with a minor); Califano v. Webster, 430 U.S. 313 (1977) (upholding statutory benefits scheme which benefited women beneficiaries); Kahn v. Shevin, 416 U.S. 351, 355 (1974) (upholding a state tax benefit for widows, but not widowers, as "reasonably designed to further the state policy of cushioning the financial impact of spousal loss upon the sex for whom the loss imposes a disproportionately heavy burden"). *But see* Orr v. Orr, 440 U.S. 268, 282–83 (1979) (invalidating statutory presumption that husbands and not wives be required to pay post-marital support); Frontiero v. Richardson, 411 U.S. 677 (1973) (invalidating federal statute which calculated military benefits on the basis of gender).

106. *See* United States v. Virginia, 116 S. Ct. 2264, 2274–76 (1996) (discussing the application of the equal protection clause to gender discrimination claims).

107. FCC v. Beach Communications, Inc., 508 U.S. 307, 313 (1993).

108. *See* Wygant v. Jackson Bd. of Ed., 476 U.S. 267, 274 (1986); Palmore v. Sidoti, 466 U.S. 429, 432–33 (1984).

tions about women's abilities and sensibilities, their appropriate family role, and appropriate employment. However, "[i]n 1971, for the first time in our Nation's history, [the Supreme Court] ruled in favor of a woman who complained that her State had denied her the equal protection of its laws."[109] That case was *Reed v. Reed.*[110]

In *Reed*, a woman's application to serve as the administrator of her deceased son's estate was rejected in favor of her husband's competing application, pursuant to a statutory requirement that "males must be preferred to females" when both are entitled to serve.[111] The Supreme Court, in a brief opinion, concluded that that "mandatory preference . . . [was] . . . the very kind of arbitrary legislative choice forbidden by the Equal Protection Clause."[112] And thus, with little fanfare, the Supreme Court finally opened the door to gender-based challenges on equal protection grounds. "[W]ithout equating gender classifications . . . to classifications based on race or national origin, the Court, in post-*Reed* decisions, has carefully inspected official action that closes a door or denies opportunity to women (or to men)."[113]

There is no universal agreement as to the exact nature of the test, although the need for some heightened scrutiny continues to be acknowledged by most. The standard is acknowledged to be something less than the "strict scrutiny" applied in racial discrimination cases.[114] Moreover, the application of heightened, but not strict, scrutiny still permits legislation which recognizes "factual generalizations about women as a class—for example, the generalization that women are physically weaker, or that they live longer than men."[115] The Court has also intimated that some social differences may serve as legitimate bases for gender-specific legislation and policies.[116]

The Equal Rights Amendment

Beginning in 1923, three years after the adoption of the Nineteenth Amendment granting women the right to vote, and continuing every year until 1971, a constitutional amendment was introduced in Congress. That amendment, the Equal Rights Amendment ("ERA"), provided that "[e]quality of rights under the law shall not be

---

109. United States v. Virginia, 116 S. Ct. at 2275.

110. 404 U.S. 71 (1971).

111. *See id.* at 72–73 (quotations omitted).

112. *Id.* at 76.

113. United States v. Virginia, 116 S. Ct. at 2275 (discussing cases).

114. For a historical discussion of the application of the equal protection clause to gender-based discrimination claims, *see generally* United States v. Virginia, 116 S. Ct. at 2274–76. The debate about the exact nature of test to be applied is discussed in the concurring opinion of Justice Wm. H. Rehnquist and the dissenting opinion of Justice Antonin Scalia. *See id.* at 2287–91, 2291–309.

115. Perry, *supra* note 43, at 1052. *See also* United States v. Virginia, 116 S. Ct. at 2276 ("Physical differences between men and women, however, are enduring.").

116. United States v. Virginia, 116 S. Ct at 2276 and n.7.

denied or abridged by the United States or by any State on account of sex."[117] The ERA was intended to provide a universal federal standard for evaluating legislation and other state action which differentiates on the basis of gender. If enacted, it would have been subject to the interpretation of the Supreme Court, providing a universal— and, it was hoped, strict—standard for review of gender-based state action.

Some feminist advocates favored amending the Constitution over "the piece-meal revision or repeal of existing federal and state laws."[118] Others believed an amendment was required to ensure that discrimination of women would be subject to the same strict scrutiny as racial discrimination.[119] It was also believed that the adoption of the ERA would signify "that the nation [was] prepared to accept and support new creative forces . . . stirring in [American] society," and thus, prepared to accept women acting in new and more powerful societal roles.[120]

For a ten-year period it seemed that America was indeed ready to commit to a future grounded in the recognition of gender equality and a new role for women. The ERA was passed by Congress in 1972, and was referred by Congress to the states for ratification.[121] Ratification by thirty-eight states was required; a seven-year deadline was placed on the ratification by Congress.[122] One state, Hawaii, ratified the ERA on the *same day* that it passed Congress.[123] Other states quickly followed suit, with thirty states ratifying the amendment within two years.[124] However, although Congress extended the original seven-year ratification deadline by three years, only five more states ratified the ERA, and the amendment failed.[125]

---

117. Over the approximately fifty years it was introduced, minor modifications were made to the text. For a discussion of the import of some of those modifications, *see* Brown, *supra* note 74, at 886–88; JANE MANSBRIDGE, WHY WE LOST THE ERA 8–11 (1986); DOROTHY MCBRIDE STETSON, WOMEN'S RIGHTS IN THE U.S.A.: POLICY DEBATES & GENDER ROLES 121–24 (1991).

118. Brown, *supra* note 74, at 875; *see also* Norman Dorsen & Susan D. Ross, *The Necessity of a Constitutional Amendment*, 6 HARV. C.R.-C.L. L. REV. 216 (1971) (because of America's history of "pervasive discrimination against women" a constitutional amendment was required "to reverse the process"); *but see* Thomas I. Emerson, *In Support of the Equal Rights Amendment*, 6 HARV. C.R.-C.L. L. REV. 225, 228 (1971) ("I feel reasonably confident that in the long run the . . . Supreme Court would reach a position very close to or identical with that of the proponents of the Equal Rights Amendment.").

119. Brown, *supra* note 74, at 884–85.

120. Brown, *supra* note 74, at 885; *see also* KANOWITZ, WOMEN AND THE LAW, *supra* note 101, at vii ("[F]or some complex sociological reason, successful attacks upon the legal aspects of social injustice . . . can often stimulate fresh concern and renewed activity beyond the strictly legal sphere.").

121. In order to be adopted, a proposed amendment must pass both houses of Congress by a two-thirds majority, and then be ratified by three-fourths of the states. *See* U.S. CONST. art. V.

122. MANSBRIDGE, *supra* note 117, at 12.

123. JANET K. BOLES, THE POLITICS OF THE EQUAL RIGHTS AMENDMENT 1–3 and Table 1.1 (1979).

124. *See id.*

125. MANSBRIDGE, *supra* note 117, at 13. Moreover, four of the states which had ratified the amendment sought to rescind their ratifications. *See* BOLES, *supra* note 123, at 3.

Why did the ERA fail? The failure of the ERA is an indication of American society's commitment to familiar gender roles and traditions, and its rejection of those "creative forces" in society who envisioned altering not only the role of women, but the face of the workforce and the nature of American family life. So intense was the attention focused on these issues that serious concerns regarding the ERA were obscured.[126] And there were many serious jurisprudential objections to the efficacy of the ERA. For example, some feminists rejected the ERA as a model of gender equality patterned on the American model of racial equality. Under American law, racial equality assumes racial neutrality or "color blindness"—that racial and ethnic differences are, or should be, irrelevant to governmental policy.[127] But, while many Americans are comfortable with both the theory and eventual reality of a color-blind society, many are not comfortable with the ideal of a gender-blind society.[128] Some object on the basis of tradition, others on grounds of physiological difference, others on theoretical grounds—rejecting a standard that assumes the rights and responsibilities of *men* should be the norm.[129] Other feminists objected to the ERA on the

---

126. As a preliminary matter, objections were raised as to whether the issue of gender equality was of constitutional significance. *See, e.g.*, Philip B. Kurland, *The Equal Rights Amendment: Some Problems of Construction*, 6 HARV. C.R.-C.L. L. REV. 243, 246–47 (1971) (arguing that the tool of constitutional amendment should be reserved for the special circumstances of changing the structure of government, reversing prior Supreme Court doctrine, or protecting minorities or the unenfranchised, and women are neither); *but see* LEO KANOWITZ, EQUAL RIGHTS: THE MALE STAKE 10 (1981) [hereinafter KANOWITZ, THE MALE STAKE] (arguing that although women are a numerical majority, they "constitute a sociological minority suffering disadvantages comparable to those endured by racial and ethnic minorities").

127. This principle was first asserted in the dissenting opinion of Justice Harlan to Plessy v. Ferguson, 163 U.S. 537 (1896), which authorized state-sponsored racial segregation. Even this first invocation of the principle was troubled:

> The white race deems itself to be the dominant race in the country. And so it is, in prestige, in achievements, in education, in wealth and in power. So, I doubt not, it will continue to be for all time. . . . But in the view of the Constitution, in the eye of the law, there is in this country no superior, dominant, ruling class of citizens. There is no caste here. Our Constitution is color-blind. . . .

Id. at 559. Since then the application of the principle of color-blindness has changed over time. For a comprehensive discussion of the historical use of the standard, see LAURENCE H. TRIBE, AMERICAN CONSTITUTIONAL LAW 1521–44 (2d ed. 1988). *See also* David A. Strauss, *The Myth of Colorblindness*, 1986 SUP. CT. REV. 99 (commenting on subtle role race plays in American society and questioning whether American society can truly achieve color-blindness).

128. *See, e.g.*, Paul A. Fruend, *The Equal Rights Amendment is Not the Way*, 6 HARV. C.R.-C.L. L. REV. 234, 240 (1971) (noting societal objections to a straight analogy to the color-blind standard); Kurland, *supra* note 126, at 246–47 (noting that as drafted the amendment would establish a "unisex" standard and discussing ramifications).

129. In commenting on the successful campaign to introduce gender-neutral language (e.g. changing "fireman" to "firefighter"), Dorothy Stetson noted: "More important is the *standard* used to determine a policy of equality. A male standard will always work against women—whose lives, because of biological and social roles, are different from the lives of most men." STETSON, *supra* note 117, at 5 (emphasis added). *See also* CATHARINE A. MACKINNON, FEMINISM UNMODIFIED: DISCOURSES ON LIFE AND LAW 9 (1987) ("Why should women have to be 'like' men to be treated as equal citizens? Why should sex inequality have to be 'like' racial inequality to be treated as invidious inequality?").

belief that the practical realities of American society require women to be the bene-ficiaries of governmental policies, policies that would likely be illegal under the ERA.[130] Because women are more likely to be homemakers and primary childcare givers than full-time workers, and because those women who do work earn less than men and are less likely to achieve the same successes, legislation favoring women in the distribution of benefits arguably better serves women than would a supposed gen-der-neutral requirement.[131]

However worthy those objections, the American debate on the ERA rarely rose to that level of sophistication. Instead, foes of the ERA, campaigning in all of the states that had yet to ratify the amendment, raised the specter of hypothetical and rad-ical specific effects of the ERA:

> They charged that it would put mothers and daughters into combat and threaten the security of homemakers. They linked the ERA with abortion, homosexuality and uni-sex bathrooms. To gain the support of those not frightened by these threats, the STOP-ERA group argued that Congress and the courts would be imposing a radical standard of justice on states.[132]

These tactics worked. While most Americans agreed with the abstract propositions that women should have equal rights with men, and that women should not be discriminated against solely because of their sex, by the end of the ratification process they no longer believed that the ERA would have the simple effect of making such discrimination ille-gal.[133] Instead, they came to believe that voting for the ERA was equivalent to voting for unisex bathrooms and women in combat.[134] The momentum to ratify the amend-ment was lost and, three states short of ratification, the ERA failed.[135]

---

130. Indeed, when considered by the Senate in 1950 and 1953, the ERA contained additional lan-guage (the so-called "Hayden rider," named for the senator who proposed it) which provided that the ERA "'shall not be construed to impair any rights, benefits, or exemptions now or hereafter con-ferred by law, upon persons of female sex.'" KANOWITZ, WOMEN AND THE LAW, *supra* note 101, at 193.

131. *See, e.g.*, Kurland, *supra* note 126, at 246–47 (noting that the ERA should not be passed without first determining whether it would put in place a "unisex" standard, or a standard which eliminates "disabilities legally imposed on women because of their sex" while leaving in place "[l]egislation purporting to afford—and in fact affording—privileges to women"). The Women's Bureau (*supra* note 15) in the 1940s and the President's Commission on the Status of Women (*id.*) in the 1960s both lobbied against the ERA on the grounds that it would deprive women in the labor force of important legal protections. HARRISON, *supra* note 15, at 15–23, 109–37.

132. STETSON, *supra* note 117, at 34. Phyllis Schlafly's group, Maine STOP ERA, ran the fol-lowing inflammatory ad:

> . . . Militant homosexuals from all over America have made the ERA a hot priority. Why? To be able to finally get homosexual marriage licenses, to adopt children and raise them to emulate their homosexual "parents" . . . Vote *NO on 6!* The Pro-Gay E.R.A.

Advertisement *quoted in* MANSBRIDGE, *supra* note 117, at 137.

133. *See* MANSBRIDGE, *supra* note 117 at 20–28, 206–11; *see also* KANOWITZ, THE MALE STAKE, *supra* note 126, at 106–14 (discussing tactics of and reactions to the ERA campaign).

134. *See* MANSBRIDGE, *supra* note 117, at 20–28, 206–11.

135. For an in-depth discussion of some of the political issues of the ratification process, *see* BAER, WOMEN, *supra* note 71, at 55–62.

Since 1984, Congress has revisited the ERA. It has been reintroduced in Congress each year since its defeat, and has been the subject of Congressional hearings;[136] however, there is currently little political support to mount another battle to amend the Constitution to incorporate gender equality. If and when America again turns its attention to the ERA, there will be a stronger jurisprudential record to rebut—or support—speculation as to the likely impact of the ERA. As discussed *supra*, the Supreme Court has increasingly turned its attention to women's rights, and its expanded equal protection analysis provides a solid basis for evaluating the anticipated impact of the ERA. Moreover, many state constitutions now include gender-equality provisions, and the issue continues to be addressed by state legislation.[137] As laws and policies are tested under these state provisions, the interpretation of those provisions by state courts and state legislatures provides further indication of how Congress and the Supreme Court would interpret a federal ERA.[138]

Breaking the Protective Hold

Many legislative policies worked to disadvantage women. Lawmakers, particularly at the state and local level, enacted civil legislation which served to exclude women from the political and the judicial processes, and limited women's opportunities for employment and economic advancement, while criminal statutes limited women's personal security.[139] Such legislation was usually enacted in the name of

---

136. *See, e.g., The Impact of the Equal Rights Amendment: Hearings Before the Subcomm. on the Constitution of the Comm. on the Judiciary of the United States Senate*, 98th Cong., 1st & 2nd Sess., Parts 1 & 2 (1983–84) [hereinafter *ERA Hearings*].

137. The Constitutions of Utah and Wyoming have always contained such provisions. *See* STETSON, *supra* note 117, at 35. Coincidentally, in the authors home state of Iowa, the State Legislature has recently considered an equal rights amendment. *See* Mike Glover, *House Passes Equal-Rights Amendment*, THE DAILY IOWAN, Jan. 29, 1997, at 3A.

138. Although dated, the analysis of the ERA in operation provided in Brown, *supra* note 74, at 920–79, is useful, as are the various perspectives contained in the *ERA Hearings, supra* note 136.

139. Included in this category are marital rape laws, *infra* notes 150–51 and accompanying text, and criminal laws about proof in rape trials which, prior to general reform begun in the 1970s, permitted defendants in rape trials to introduce evidence of prior sexual activity on the part of the complaining witness. *See* Frank Tuerkeimer, *A Reassessment and Redefinition of Rape Shield Laws*, 50 OHIO ST. L.J. 1245, 1245–47 (1989) (describing evidentiary rules prior to reform). Thus, until revised in 1974, California jury instructions provided:

> Evidence was received for the purpose of showing that the female person named in the information was a woman of unchaste character.

> A woman of unchaste character can be the victim of a forcible rape but it may be inferred that a woman who has previously consented to sexual intercourse would be more likely to consent again.

> Such evidence may be considered by you only for such bearing as it may have on the question of whether or not she gave her consent to the alleged sexual act and in judging her credibility.

Former California Jury Instruction—Criminal Instruction No. 10.06, *quoted in* Tuerkeimer, *supra* at 1245 n.3. In addition to the questionable merit of the evidentiary assumption (i.e., she consented before, she must have consented this time), these policies "undoubtedly deterred the reporting of

"protecting" the "weaker sex" from harm, or in furtherance of protecting the fabric of the family.[140] The changes in these areas have been significant, sometimes due to federal legislative or constitutional mandates, sometimes due to local initiatives, and sometimes resulting from a combination of both. The development of some of these areas of the law are described below.

Family Life

Family law worked to the disadvantage of women, albeit under the guise of protecting them. In the early nineteenth century, married women were regarded as under the protection of their husbands, so that marriage rendered women "civilly dead:"[141]

> All the legal rights and responsibilities a woman had when single transferred to her husband upon marriage. All her property, including wages, became his property. She had no right to enter into contracts or to sue or be sued. . . . Since her husband was responsible for her acts, he could restrain her and correct her behavior. The husband's obligations included paying her debts before marriage and providing support afterwards. Common-law coverture made a woman financially dependent on her husband for all her legal acts: these provisions were called a *married woman's legal disabilities.*[142]

The husband had the right to determine the disposition of all family property, to withhold it or dispose of it, in accordance with his sole wishes.[143]

Under a related doctrine called "interspousal immunity," women could not sue their husbands on any grounds.[144] Moreover, most state criminal statutes explicitly

---

vicious acts of rape" by victims who feared "having to divulge their unrelated sexual history." Note, *New Jersey Rape Shield Legislation: From Past to Present—the Pros and Cons*, 17 WOMEN'S RIGHTS L. REP. 223 (1996). Evidentiary rules known as "rape shield laws," *see, e.g.*, FED. R. EVID. 412, now prohibit the use of such evidence in nearly every jurisdiction. *See* Tuerkeimer, *supra* at 1246.

140. [H]istory discloses the fact that woman has always been dependent upon man. He established his control at the outset by superior physical strength, and this control in various forms, with diminishing intensity, has continued to the present. . . . Differentiated by these matters from the other sex, she is properly placed in a class by herself, and legislation designed for her protection may be sustained, even when like legislation is not necessary for men and could not be sustained. . . . [H]er physical structure and a proper discharge of her maternal functions—having in view not merely her own health, but the well-being of the race—justify legislation to protect her from the greed as well as the passion of man.

Muller v. Oregon, 208 U.S. 412, 422 (1908) (upholding gender-based employment restrictions).

141. *See* STETSON, *supra* note 117, at 125, 21–24. *See generally* HOMER H. CLARK, JR., THE LAW OF DOMESTIC RELATIONS IN THE UNITED STATES 286–89 (2d ed. 1988) (presenting a survey of the legal position of married women in the United States). This doctrine was not applicable to slave women, who were under the sole dominion and control of their master, and who were not permitted to legally marry.

142. STETSON, *supra* note 117, at 129 (emphasis added).

143. *See supra* note 31.

144. *See* STETSON, *supra* note 117, at 134–35. *See also* Klein v. Klein, 376 P.2d 70 (Ca. 1962) (discussing and overruling doctrine of interspousal immunity for negligence actions).

protected men from prosecution for rape in the context of marriage.[145] These provisions meant that women had little recourse against their husbands' wrongful or violent actions. Divorce was rare until the late nineteenth century.[146] When available,[147] under the principles of civil death, a woman might find herself destitute upon the termination of her marriage. Furthermore, because offspring were considered the property of the husband, she might find herself excluded from her children's lives.[148] Women were often trapped, legally and practically, in harmful relationships.

Today the doctrine of civil death has been abandoned in the United States; women may own and manage their own wealth, and may sue and be sued.[149] However, many other aspects of family law remain unchanged. Although forcible marital rape is now prohibited in most jurisdictions,[150] husbands (and in some jurisdictions, cohabitants) are still excepted from criminal liability under certain circumstances in many states.[151] Domestic abuse, once considered a private matter of family discipline, is now considered a serious social problem. But while women now have some recourse from abusive partners, many find the criminal justice system to be inadequate, indifferent, or actively hostile to their claims.[152] The level of violence against women, and the

---

145. *See generally* DIANA E. H. RUSSEL, RAPE IN MARRIAGE 17–24 (1982).

146. *See* MARY SOMERVILLE JONES, AN HISTORICAL GEOGRAPHY OF CHANGING DIVORCE LAW IN THE UNITED STATES 16–39, 204–06 (1987) (theorizing that the four-fold increase in divorce rates between the years 1890–1920 coincided with industrialization and urbanization, and with resulting increased educational and employment opportunities for women).

147. Until reform in the twentieth century, states typically permitted divorce only upon proof of "marital offenses," such as adultery, desertion (typically five years), impotence, fraud, bigamy, and consanguinity. *See id.* at 17; *see also* Michael S. Hindus & Lynne E. Withey, *The Law of Husband and Wife in Nineteenth Century America: Changing Views of Divorce, in* WOMEN AND THE LAW: A HISTORICAL PERSPECTIVE, VOL. II 133–50 (D. Kelly Weisberg ed., 1982).

148. *See generally* LEUMUEL H. FOSTER, THE LEGAL RIGHTS OF WOMEN 169–75 (1913). As this early women's legal guide noted:

> Under the common law the father has and still has the exclusive legal right to the care, custody and control of his minor children. The strict letter of the law gives the mother no rights whatever to the care or custody of her child during the life of the father, and in the event of a separation . . . the husband's right to the children is paramount and exclusive unless otherwise ordered by some court.

Id. at 169.

149. *See* Linda E. Speth, *The Married Women's Property Acts, 1839–1865: Reform, Reaction, or Revolution, in* WOMEN AND THE LAW, *supra* note 147, at 69–85 (describing civil death and reform initiatives).

150. *See, e.g.,* CAL. PENAL CODE § 262 (West 1996) (criminalizing rape of a spouse under a variety of circumstances); ARIZ. REV. STAT. ANN. § 13–1406.01 (West 1996) (criminalizing sexual assault of a spouse).

151. For example, under the California Penal Code, unless marital rape is reported to a neutral third party within a year, or is otherwise corroborated by "independent evidence," "no prosecution shall commence." CAL. PENAL CODE § 262(b). Under the Arizona Code, a first-time offense of marital rape is a low-grade felony, and the judge in his or her discretion may reduce the charges to a misdemeanor with mandatory counseling. ARIZ. REV. STAT. ANN. § 13–1406.01.

152. *See generally* DO ARRESTS AND RESTRAINING ORDERS WORK? (Eve S. Buzawa & Carl G. Buzawa eds., 1996).

failure of state criminal justice systems to adequately curb that violence, led Congress in 1994 to enact the Violence Against Women Act[153] establishing a federal right to be free from "crimes of violence motivated by gender."[154] The validity of that legislation is currently being challenged;[155] however, the enactment serves as a testament to the significance of violence against women as a continuing issue in American society.[156] It also serves as an example of an effort by Congress to use its powers under the equal protection clause to expand the civil rights of women.

Since the 1960s, divorce has become more common,[157] affording women greater opportunity to escape from repressive or violent marriages.[158] The policies related to post-marital financial support and child custody have undergone several changes, with presumptions variously favoring fathers and mothers. By the mid-1940s, women were typically favored in both child custody and financial support decisions. The common presumption in awarding custody was that children, particularly young children, would be best cared for by their mothers; in that era, men were rarely awarded custody after divorce.[159] It was also presumed that men would pay alimony to their former wives, and in some states a husband was obliged to pay alimony, regardless of the relative financial circumstances of the parties.[160]

---

153. Pub. L. No. 103–322, Title IV, Sept. 13, 1994, 108 Stat. 1902–55.

154. 42 U.S.C.A. § 13,981 (West 1996). The Act provides a civil remedy to victims of gender-based violence.

155. The constitutionality of that legislation was challenged in U.S. v. Morrison et al., 120 S. Ct. 1740 (2000). The Supreme Court, Justice Rehnquist, held that: (1) the commerce clause does not provide Congress with authority to enact the civil remedy provision of VAWA on the grounds stated, and (2) the enforcement clause of the Fourteenth Amendment does not provide Congress with authority to enact the provision on the grounds that it impermissibly regulated the actions of private actors, in violation of the state action requirement of the equal protection clause, and was also beyond Congress' very broad powers to regulate commerce. *See id.* at 785–801.

156. *See id.* at 796–97 (discussing Congress' findings and goals). It also speaks to Congress' willingness to take on this issue, and provides an example of instances where federal legislation can be used to supplement rights granted under the U.S. Constitution.

157. *See* SOMERVILLE JONES, *supra* note 146, at 143–64 (describing systematic divorce reform, including the adoption of no-fault or other liberal divorce laws, and more equitable property distribution laws in many states).

158. *See generally* LYNNE C. HALEM, DIVORCE REFORM: CHANGING LEGAL AND SOCIAL PERSPECTIVES (1980) (discussing divorce regimes from colonial to current periods); BAER, WOMEN, *supra* note 71, at 136–59 (describing divorce, support and custody law reform).

159. With regard to child custody, the adoption of the tender years presumption (the rebuttable presumption that young children should remain with their mother) and the primary caretaker doctrine (the doctrine that young children should remain with the parent most responsible for their care—most often, the mother) resulted in custody typically being awarded to the mother. *See* Andrea Charlow, *Awarding Custody: The Best Interests of the Child and Other Fictions, in* CHILD, PARENT, AND STATE: LAW AND POLICY READER 7–9 (S. Randall Humm et al. eds., 1994) (describing both legal doctrines); *see also* BAER, WOMEN, *supra* note 71, at 150–52; CLARK, *supra* note 141, at 799–800; Mary Becker, *Maternal Feelings: Myth, Taboo and Women's Studies,* 1 S. CAL. REV. L. & WOMEN'S STUD. 133, 167–72 (1992) [hereinafter Becker, *Myth*].

160. With regard to support, some states only permitted alimony (support payments) to be

Currently, the divorce laws of most states are gender neutral as to the disposition of property and custody of children.[161] Support is commonly based on "need," and those receiving support are typically required to become self-sufficient after a period of time, at which point the support will be reduced or terminated.[162] Custody is commonly decided with regard to the "best interest of the child."[163] While these changes are intended to prevent the perceived inequities of the prior presumptions in favor of women,[164] many believe that the practical effect of removing those presumptions has worked to disadvantage women and favor the husband.[165] The employment prospects of women who have supported their families as homemakers and childcare givers are usually limited, and the support often stops before they are truly economically independent. Husbands are also more likely to have greater financial stability, which sometimes permits them to establish that they will provide a better living environment for their children, a factor that might be considered in determining the best interests of the child for custody purposes.[166]

---

awarded to women. *See, e.g.,* Orr v. Orr, 440 U.S. 268 (1979) (invalidating Alabama's gender-specific alimony provision). Moreover, prior to the widespread adoption of equitable distribution laws, property settlement was linked to fault and not financial independence; this policy favored women who successfully sued husbands for divorce, granting them payments, typically until remarriage, regardless of actual financial need. *Cf. infra* note 163 and accompanying text. Of course, needy women found to have been 'at fault' were harmed by this policy. Even in the 1940s, a notable exception to these support and distribution principles was the doctrine of community property, which vests joint ownership rights in all property acquired during the marriage. *See* BAER, WOMEN, *supra* note 71, at 137.

161. *See, e.g.,* N.Y. DOM. REL. L. § 236 (Matthew Bender 1995); IOWA CODE ANN. § 598.21(3) (West 1996). It should be noted that a minority of states distribute property pursuant to the doctrine of community property, which vests joint ownership rights in all property acquired during the marriage. *See* BAER, WOMEN, *supra* note 71, at 137.

162. For example, New York law requires the court to consider the "ability of the party seeking maintenance to become self-supporting and . . . the period of time and training necessary therefor." N.Y. DOM. REL. L. § 236B6(6). *See generally* BAER, WOMEN, *supra* note 71, at 141–42.

163. *See* CLARK, *supra* note 141, at 788–89.

164. For a view disputing the perception that prior custody and divorce rules favored women, *see* BAER, WOMEN, *supra* note 71, at 139–40.

165. Mary Becker has written extensively, and provocatively, on this topic. *See* Becker, *Myth, supra* note 159, at 187–88, 192–203 (describing disadvantages of joint custody and primary caretaker standards, and proposing "maternal deference"). *See also* Becker, *Diversity, supra* note 84, at 715–25 (discussing custody standards in light of a variety of feminist theories); *see generally* Mary E. Becker, *Double Binds Facing Mothers in Abusive Families: Social Support Systems, Custody Outcomes, and Liability for the Acts of Others,* 2 U. CHI. L. SCH. ROUNDTABLE 13 (1995). With regard to support, one study indicates that immediately following a divorce women on average experience a 73 percent decline in their standard of living, while men typically experience a 42 percent increase. *See* BAER, WOMEN, *supra* note 71, at 142–44. Recent studies also indicate that fathers who choose to pursue custody have disproportionate success in winning custody. *See id.* at 152–58 (discussing research and cases).

166. *See* Mary Becker, *Myth, supra* note 159, at 177–78; BAER, WOMEN, *supra* note 71, at 154; *see generally* Charlow, *supra* note 159, at 3–11 (describing various doctrines currently used to determine custody).

Education

The United States Constitution does not include education as a basic right,[167] although several state constitutions do.[168] Thus, the question of gender equality in education is not predicated on the denial of an essential right, but rather is a question of equal treatment under the law: in this instance, the fair distribution of state resources.[169] Free public education was not widely available in the United States until the twentieth century.[170] At first, education was provided by churches, or by private schools. As communities flourished, the costs of education were distributed throughout the community by means of taxes administrated by local school boards. Eventually layers of state authority were added.

Even as public education became common, women were excluded from secondary schooling for a variety of reasons.[171] It was considered essential that women—as future wives and mothers—be versed in the rudimentary skills of reading, writing, and arithmetic. However, there was no need for them to proceed to high school:

> Why send girls to high school? Most boys did not need to go to high school; all they needed to be voters and workers they learned in grade school. Secondary school was only necessary to prepare for professions such as law, medicine, banking and engineering. Women would not be going into these male jobs and so did not need a secondary-level education.[172]

In addition, too much education was considered dangerous to the health of a woman. Influential doctors and educators of the nineteenth century opined that "'the physiological effects of hard study and academic competition with boys would interfere with the development of girls' reproductive organs'" or otherwise cause them "'life-long suffering.'"[173]

Interestingly, women's roles as homemaker and mother opened the doors of schoolhouses to them. First, as mothers, women had the primary responsibility for

---

167. San Antonio Indep. School Dist. v. Rodriquez, 411 U.S. 1, 35 (1973) ("Education . . . is not among the rights afforded explicit protection under our Federal Constitution. Nor do we find any basis for saying it is implicitly so protected.").

168. For example, the state of Texas was unusual in that its constitution provided for public schools, recognizing early that "[a] general diffusion of knowledge [is] essential to the preservation of the rights and liberties of the people." TEX. CONST. art. x, sec. 1 (1845), *quoted in Rodriquez*, 411 U.S. at 6, n.6.

169. *See, e.g., Rodriquez*, 411 U.S. 1 (considering claim by minority and poor students that the Texas state school finance system violated their rights under the equal protection clause).

170. For a useful, though skeletal, time line of the development of American public education, and the inclusion of women in education, *see* EDUCATIONAL EQUITY ix–xi. (Karen J. Maschke ed., 1997).

171. For African-American women, race was another important "reason" for their exclusion. Many states made it illegal to educate slaves. After emancipation, racial segregation of schools further limited educational opportunities for African-American women.

172. STETSON, *supra* note 117, at 103.

173. United States v. Virginia, 116 S. Ct. at 2277 n.9 (1996) (quoting recognized nineteenth century medical expert on the education of women).

teaching their sons (and daughters), and thus required sufficient training to enable them to give guidance in civics and morality. Then, as schools became more prevalent, this teaching role of women was professionalized: women would make ideal teachers (in the year or two before they got married and had families of their own).[174] They needed *some* higher education to prepare them for this task, so women were admitted to high schools and even to colleges. Finally, as society became more industrialized (and as women began to significantly outnumber men), a number of professions were deemed suitable for women; nursing, bookkeeping, and secretarial schools for women prepared them for these careers.[175] The professions such as law, engineering, business, and medicine were thought unsuitable for women and women's colleges did not offer those areas of study. Women who dared apply to men's professional colleges that offered training in these professions were typically turned away because of these views of gender roles and the custom of separate education.[176] By the late 1800s, a few state universities and professional schools began to admit women;[177] however, the uncertainty of professional employment opportunities after the completion of studies made women hesitant to pursue professional training.[178] Those women who did apply to these programs were often held to a higher standard than male applicants. Accordingly,

---

174. See Kathleen C. Berkeley, *"The Ladies Want to Bring About Reform in the Public Schools": Public Education and Women's Rights, in* EDUCATIONAL EQUITY, *supra* note 170, at 30 (describing how, in the Memphis, Tennessee, school system "marital status significantly affected the longevity of a woman's teaching career"). Women were also encouraged to become teachers by school systems eager to save on costs: in Memphis, in a year when male teachers were paid a high of $123.57 per month, the average salary paid their women counterparts was $68.11. *Id.* at 49.

175. An example is the Mississippi Industrial Institute and College for the Education of White Girls of the State of Mississippi, established in 1884. Later known as the Mississippi University for Women ("MUW"), it was maintained as a single-sex (although eventually racially integrated) school until 1982. The school had as its mission to educate girls:

> in the arts and sciences, at which such girls may acquire a thorough normal school education, together with a knowledge of kindergarten instruction, also a knowledge of telegraphy, stenography and photography; also a knowledge of drawing, painting and designing, and engraving in their industrial application; also a knowledge of fancy, practical and general needle-work; and, also a knowledge of bookkeeping . . . to promote the general objective of said Institute and College, to-wit: fitting and preparing such girls for the practical industries of their age.

MISS. CODE. ANN. Ch. XXIX, Sec. 6 (1884).

176. *See, e.g.,* United States v. Virginia, 116 S. Ct. at 2280–81 (quoting justifications for excluding women applicants from elite professional schools).

177. The law schools of the state universities of Michigan and Iowa, the law schools this author trained and teaches at, respectively, admitted women in the 1870s. Other law schools which admitted women were Union College (1870), Washington University of St. Louis, Missouri (1871), Howard University (1872) and National University in Washington, D.C. (1873). D. Kelly Weisberg, *Barred from the Bar: Women and Legal Education in the United States, 1870–1890, in* EDUCATIONAL EQUITY, *supra* note 170, at 241.

178. *See id.* In addition, faced with the expense of higher education, families often discouraged female relatives from attending college or from obtaining a professional degree, because it was assumed that, as a married lady, she would have no career outside of the home, and thus no practical use for the knowledge.

women applied to the few academic universities and professional schools that accepted far fewer women than men.[179]

As the 1960s civil rights movement flourished, women's education again became a hot issue. The thrust of the 1960s campaign remained the same: to eliminate discrimination against women in education; however, this time the issue was one of federal significance. Under the constitutional principles of federalism, and because of its grassroots development, education had always been considered a local issue not subject to federal control. However, by the 1960s, the economic reality was that the federal government subsidized schools at all levels of education, from primary school to graduate school. Using the federal purse as a policy weapon, Congress in 1972 passed Title IX of the Higher Education Amendments, which provides:

> No person in the United States shall, on the basis of sex, be excluded from participation in, be denied the benefits of, or be subjected to discrimination under any educational program or activity receiving Federal financial assistance.[180]

Within a few years, most remaining publicly funded single-sex American colleges and universities became coeducational.[181]

Yet gender equality in education remains an issue over twenty-five years after the enactment of Title IX. Title IX was subject to interpretation, and questions such as whether differences in facilities, or in support for athletic programs, constituted "exclusion from participation" in education were resolved by litigation; others issues have yet to be fully resolved.[182] In addition, Title IX included certain exceptions to its general prohibition of gender discrimination in education in order to preserve some single-sex educational opportunities. For example, all-male military schools were specifically exempted from Title IX.[183] Moreover, certain traditional men's and women's colleges,[184] and some religious schools, were also exempt from Title IX.[185] These exceptions responded to two divergent constituencies: those who wished to deny women access to certain men's schools because of stereotypical notions of women's competence, and those who wished to preserve women's colleges because

---

179. The ratio of women students is currently more reflective of the population. In the University of Iowa College of Law class of 1999, ninety-three women are enrolled out of a total class of 214 students.

180. 20 U.S.C.A. § 1681 (West 1996).

181. Title IX also applies to public elementary and high schools.

182. *See, e.g.*, Williams v. School Dist. of Bethlehem, 998 F.2d 168 (3d Cir. 1993), *cert. denied*, 114 S. Ct. 689 (1994) (discussing the application of Title IX to the question of sports teams); *see also* Glen M. Wong & Richard J. Ensor, *Sex Discrimination in Athletics: A Review of Two Decades of Accomplishments and Defeats, in* EDUCATIONAL EQUITY, *supra* note 170, at 39–87 (surveying application of Title IX to collegiate athletics); Marcia Chambers, *For Women, 25 Years of Title IX has not Leveled the Playing Field*, N.Y. TIMES, June 16, 1997, at A1 (discussing continuing disparities, particularly in collegiate athletics programs).

183. *See* 20 U.S.C.A. § 1681(4) (West 1996).

184. *See* 20 U.S.C.A.§ 1681(5) (West 1996) (exempting schools which have "traditionally and continually" been single-sex).

185. *See* 20 U.S.C.A. § 1681(3) (West 1996) (exempting religious schools "if the application . . . would not be consistent with the religious tenets of such organization").

of their belief that, under certain circumstances, women benefit from single-sex educational opportunities.[186]

Even as more schools opened to women, single-sex schools remained the chosen environment of many men and women who believe that there are great benefits derived from single-sex educational environments. Although the great bulk of these institutions are private, and therefore not subject to Title IX, a number of state supported single-sex schools existed until quite recently. For example, until 1982, the state of Mississippi operated the Mississippi University for Women ("MUW"), which offered a wide variety of academic and professional courses and provided women with the opportunity to study in an environment that they might find more appealing. The state of Virginia operated the Virginia Military Institute ("VMI") as an all-male military academy until 1996.

In 1982 and in 1996 respectively, the Supreme Court held that the single-sex policies of MUW and VMI violated the Constitution.[187] In the case of MUW, the Court considered and rejected the state's arguments that the women-only policy was an appropriate remedial measure to compensate women for past discrimination, and to provide additional training opportunities for women in an environment particularly hospitable to women.[188] Holding that the policy was based on outdated notions of gender assignment to careers, and perpetuated the stereotyped view of nursing as exclusively a "woman's job," the Court concluded those harms outweighed any possible benefits of maintaining the single-sex status.[189]

Fourteen years later the Supreme Court invalidated VMI's policy excluding women. VMI's stringent environment, intended to build character and leadership skills, was believed to be uniquely suited to men—indeed, an all-male environment was considered by the college as necessary to the success of the program.[190] The Court held that the state had no important governmental objective which was served by providing a unique "adversative" training program for men.[191] The Court further found that, even assuming that the interest was sufficiently important for the state to pursue, the state must provide similar opportunities, designed to combine a superior education with training designed to instill discipline, honor, and other leadership qualities, to

---

186. *See* BAER, WOMEN, *supra* note 71, at 242–45 (discussing studies about whether women have distinct analytical skills); *see also* United States v. Virginia, 766 F. Supp. 1407, 1411–12 (W.D. Va. 1991) *rev'd on other grounds,* 116 S. Ct. 2264 (concluding that a single-sex environment, "male or female" has educational benefits).

187. *See* Mississippi University for Women v. Hogan, 458 U.S. 718 (1982); United States v. Virginia, 116 S. Ct. 2264. For a survey of key Supreme Court decisions regarding gender discrimination in public education, *see* BAER, WOMEN, *supra* note 71, at 224–42.

188. *Hogan*, 458 U.S. at 721–22.

189. *Id.* at 755–56.

190. *Virginia*, 116 S. Ct. at 2269–271, 2279–282.

191. *Id.* at 2279. VMI's "adversative" program "features [p]hysical rigor, mental stress, absolute equality of treatment, absense of privacy, minute regulation of behavior, and indoctrination in desireable values." *Id.* at 2270 (quotations omitted).

women;[192] absent a comparable opportunity—and the Court noted that the "unique-ness" of the program made it difficult to conceive of a comparable program—VMI must admit women.[193]

In these cases the Supreme Court rejected views that it considered stereotypi-cal, that perpetuated the inferior status of women in American society, and that fore-closed women "unique" educational experiences, such as the VMI experience, to women. These decisions represented a marked improvement over the Court's prior willingness to accept societal gender constructs. However, in both cases, the Court carefully left open the question of whether state-funded single-sex education, in and of itself, violates the Constitution. Indeed, in the VMI case the Court recognized that single-sex schools provide educational diversity, and may work to "'dissipate, rather than perpetuate, traditional gender classifications.'"[194] The Court further suggested that such schools may fall within the state's discretion, if administered even-handedly, and may "advance full development of the talent and capacities" of women.[195] Although the Court has carefully avoided deciding the issue, its deferential language and the political realities of the Court's composition suggest that some single-sex programs might survive constitutional scrutiny, and that women and men seeking the benefits of studying in a single-sex environment will continue to have that opportunity.[196]

Employment Opportunities

American women have *always* worked, whether it be the grueling, thankless labor of slave women, the contributions of homemakers and farmwomen, the menial labor of maids, laundresses, the garment industry, or other work.[197] Thus, although the debate has been couched as "should women work," the question is more fairly posed as whether women should work outside of their homes, in the profession of their choice, and be paid on a scale commensurate with men with similar opportuni-ties for career advancement. Consideration of these questions has always been influ-enced by societal views of women as homemaker, wife and mother, and moral touchstone, and by the fear that family life would suffer if women worked outside of the home:

---

192. *Id.* at 2282. The alternative "ladies" program which the school had hastily established at a local women's college was found inadequate. The leadership program was less intensive—specif-ically designed to meet women's "sensibilities"—and the academic instruction was significantly less rigorous.

193. *Id.* at 2287. This conclusion necessarilty affected The Citadel, South Carolina's all-male mil-itary college, similarly based on a stringent "adversative" environment. *See* Faulkner v. Jones, 51 F.3d 440, 443–44, 447 (4th Cir. 1995).

194. *Id.* at 2276 n.7, *quoting* Brief for Twenty-Six Private Women's Colleges as Amici Curiae.

195. *See* United States v. Virginia, 116 S. Ct. at 2276.

196. Perhaps responding to these suggestions, the state of New York continued its plan to estab-lish a new girls-only high school in the fall of 1996. The school is intended to provide an educa-tional environment specifically targeted to the problems of girls in the geographic area (Harlem, a largely minority population), and to lessen the sexual pressures normally incident to a teenage environment. *See* Janine Zuniga, *East Harlem School May Be Girls-Only*, TIMES UNION (ALBANY, NY), Aug. 22, 1996, at B2, (1996 WL 9554972).

> [T]he world runs better when men and women keep in their own spheres. I do not say that women are better off, but society in general is. And that is, after all, the mysterious honor and obligation of women—to keep this planet in orbit. . . . Few jobs are worth disrupting family life for unless the family profits by it rather than the housewife herself.[198]

The middle-class fantasy of two-parent households, in which the salary of the husband is sufficient to meet the needs and desires of the family, has also driven the debate on many of these issues; that fantasy ignores the true conditions of the working class, the poor, and the middle class.[199] However benign the intentions, the collective impact of these societal policies was to limit the number of careers open to women to the most menial, undesirable, and low paying.[200]

The quest for gender equality in employment was also hampered by the fact that advocates for women's rights divided on strategy in this area perhaps more than in any other, leading to policies that were sometimes inconsistent. As the industrial revolution brought more women into the workforce, some advocates supported protective legislation limiting women's working hours and setting minimum wages, convinced that without that assistance women lacked sufficient bargaining power to secure decent wages and humane working conditions for themselves.[201] A different group of women's rights advocates argued against such protections on political and economic grounds, as both limiting the options of women, and as treating women as physically inferior.[202] The result was a hodge-podge of policies.[203]

---

197. *See* ALICE KESSLER-HARRIS, OUT TO WORK: A HISTORY OF WAGE-EARNING WOMEN IN THE UNITED STATES (1982); HAZOU, *supra* note 25, at 81–82 (describing home-work of colonial women).

198. Statement of Phyllis McGinley, *quoted in* JUDITH A. BAER, THE CHAINS OF PROTECTION: THE JUDICIAL RESPONSE TO WOMEN'S LABOR LEGISLATION 37 (1978) [hereinafter BAER, CHAINS]. *See also* Ritchie v. Wayman, 244 Ill. 509, 520–21 (1910) (taking judicial notice that "civilized countries" recognize the appropriateness of protective legislation given "the physical organization of women; . . . their maternal function; . . . the rearing and education of children; [and] the maintenance of the home").

199. *See* BAER, CHAINS, *supra* note 198, at 20–22 (describing demographic changes of women in the workforce and noting that by the early 1900s most women working in industry worked to support themselves).

200. *See generally* STETSON, *supra* note 117, at 155–57; (summarizing impact of societal views on employment opportunities of women); HAZOU, *supra* note 25, at 81–85 (same); BAER, WOMEN, *supra* note 71, at 65–69 (discussing statistics on twentieth-century employment and earnings of women).

201. *See* BAER, CHAINS, *supra* note 198, at 4–6, 14–39 (describing historical context which led to adoption of protective legislation); STETSON, *supra* note 117, at 157–61 (describing policy debate and some protective legislation); HARRISON, *supra* note 15, at 6–10 (same).

The concern was genuine—one scholar notes that at a time when organized labor had won ten-twelve hour workdays in industries dominated by men, women and children workers endured "long hours, hard labor, and dangerous conditions." BAER, CHAINS, *supra*, at 17. *See also* HAZOU, *supra* note 25, at 82–85 (describing women's hazardous working conditions and examples of serious industrial accidents).

202. *See* BECKER, *supra* note 84, at 17–22 (describing different views within early feminist movement regarding the impact of protective legislation); *see also* STETSON, *supra* note 117, at 160–62 (describing differing views in twentieth-century feminist movement); *cf.* BAER, CHAINS, *supra* note 198, at 23–29 (describing how physiological differences have been used to limit opportunities for women).

203. The hodge-podge of protective legislation also included legislation introduced by those

The Second World War, from 1939–45, changed American employment forever. To support U.S. participation in the war, women were recruited to fill manufacturing jobs critical to the war effort because the military forces had seriously depleted the male workforce. Women found themselves working in jobs previously reserved for men, and they enjoyed being liberated from job restrictions and pay limitations.[204] In addition to proving themselves capable of the work, they also proved that middle-class family life was not irreparably harmed by their work experience.[205] Despite a carefully orchestrated campaign—featuring the character "Rosie the Riveter"—that encouraged women to give their jobs "back" to returning veterans after the war, and despite the resurgence of the fantasy of middle-class family life, the seeds were sown for the next great push for women's rights in employment.

In 1963 Congress adopted the Equal Pay Act,[206] requiring that women and men performing the same job for the same employer be paid the same wage (with adjustments permitted for seniority, merit, and other conditions not related to gender). Prior to that enactment, not only were women excluded from higher-paying, more challenging jobs, they were paid less than their male counterparts in the same job, who were assumed to require higher earnings to support an entire family (the so-called "family wage"). It was presumed—often wrongly—that women were working to support only themselves or to augment their husbands' salaries.[207]

Even more far-reaching was the inclusion of women's rights in Title VII of the Civil Rights Act of 1964. The Civil Rights Act was enacted as part of the policy to secure racial equality in the United States; Title VII prohibits employment discrimi-

---

seeking to protect the interest of *male* workers, either by excluding women from certain types of work, such as bartending, creating male monopolies in those fields, or by introducing wage and hour limitations which made women less economically efficient substitutes for higher paid male workers. *See generally* BAER, CHAINS, *supra* note 198, at 7–8, 111–24.

204. *See generally* SHERNA BERGER GLUCK, ROSIE THE RIVETER REVISITED: WOMEN, THE WAR AND SOCIAL CHANGE (1988) (collecting oral histories of women working in the World War II defense industry). Women were also liberated from some societal restrictions. Stay-at-home mothers were actively encouraged to enter the workforce, and federally funded daycare was made available to some mothers. *Id.* at 13–14, 242. Married women workers were portrayed as heroines; unfortunately they were also portrayed as "super-moms," able to work and still meet all household obligations. HARRISON, *supra* note 15, at 3.

205. For Charlcia Neuman, the employment opportunities created by the war helped her family survive the waning days of the Depression. GLUCK, *supra* note 204, at 162–63. Her entire family helped out: her teenaged daughter shopped, while her husband did housework. *Id.* at 168. Charlcia, who always felt that "if married women needed to work . . . that was their choice," encouraged her daughter to attend college and pursue a career where she would be paid "good money." *Id.* at 169.

206. 29 U.S.C.A. § 206(d)(1) (West 1996).

207. Many working women were the head of their household; the assumption that they were not, and other assumptions leading to disparate pay, "depressed wages and living standards necessary for their health and efficiency." Cong. Findings, Pub. L. No. 88–3832. *See generally* HARRISON, *supra* note 15, at 89–105 (discussing enactment of Equal Pay Act); BAER, CHAINS, *supra* note 198, at 136–39 (same).

nation. With some controversy,[208] Title VII was amended to prohibit discrimination on the basis of sex as well as race, religion, and ethnicity:

> It shall be unlawful employment practice for an employer—(1) to fail or refuse to hire or to discharge any individual, or otherwise to discriminate against any individual with respect to his compensation, terms, conditions, or privileges of employment, because of such individual's race, color, religion, sex, or national origin; or (2) to limit, segregate, or classify his employees or applicants for employment in any way which would deprive or tend to deprive any individual of employment opportunities or otherwise adversely affect his status as an employee, because of such individual's race, color, religion, sex, or national origin.[209]

This section applies to employers or unions with a minimum of fifteen employees, and subject to certain other requirements. A later amendment made explicit that the prohibitions against sex discrimination include discrimination against women "on the basis of pregnancy, childbirth, or related medical conditions,"[210] closing an important gap in Title VII's protections. Title VII is partly enforced by a special investigatory and adjudicative body, the Equal Employment Opportunity Commission ("EEOC"). While the authority and responsibilities of the EEOC have expanded over time, the EEOC currently has the power to investigate complaints[211] and, upon a finding of reasonable cause to believe a violation exists, to bring suit in federal court if necessary to ensure compliance.[212] In addition, the EEOC promulgates guidelines interpreting the law, and serves an important public education function.[213] Title VII and the Equal Pay Act may also be enforced by private individuals bringing suit.[214]

The enactments of the Equal Pay Act and Title VII did not end the quest for gender-equality in employment. Title VII permits discriminatory treatment where gender is a bona fide occupational qualification ("BFOQ") "reasonably necessary to the normal operation of that particular business or enterprise."[215] The EEOC and the courts have been forced to give content to that exception, determining whether women could be excluded from serving as prison guards in a male prison, for example, or excluded

---

208. Many consider the inclusion of gender in Title VII to have been inadvertant, a joke; however:

> This description is inaccurate. It is true that . . . the author of the amendment, hoped to "[sink] the bill under gales of laughter" . . . but the amendment survived because several women members of Congress refused to join the liberals in opposing it.

BAER, CHAINS, *supra* note 198, at 136 (endnotes omitted). It is fair to say that the inclusion of gender in Title VII did not "represent[] a firm collective commitment to sexual equality" on the part of Congress. *Id.; see also* STETSON, *supra* note 117, at 165 (discussing legislative history).

209. 42 U.S.C.A. § 2000e (West 1996).

210. 42 U.S.C.A. § 2000e(k) (West 1996).

211. The power to investigate includes the power to subpoena documents and testimony. *See* 42 U.S.C.A. § 2000e–4(g) (West 1996). The complaint may be brought by an aggrieved individual, or initiated by the EEOC itself. *See* 42 U.S.C.A. § 2000e–5 (West 1996).

212. *See* 42 U.S.C.A.§ 2000e–5(f) (West 1996).

213. *See generally* 42 U.S.C.A. § 2000e–4 (West 1996).

214. *See* 42 U.S.C.A. § 2000e–5(f) (West 1996).

215. 42 U.S.C.A. § 2000e–2(e)(1) (West 1996).

from sportscasting jobs where assignments take women into men's locker rooms.[216] The exception has been interpreted narrowly to apply only when all or substantially all women would be unable to do the essential functions of the job.[217]

There has been significant success in the push to eliminate sexual harassment in the workplace. Sexual harassment is considered discriminatory treatment implicitly prohibited by Title VII:

> The courts have recognized two general types of harassment prohibited by Title VII: "quid pro quo" sexual harassment and "hostile work environment" sexual harassment. In quid pro quo sexual harassment cases, it is alleged that the performance of sexual favors is directly linked to a workplace benefit such as hiring, promotion, retention, or transfer. . . . In a hostile work environment case, it is alleged that the sexual conduct is unwelcome and sufficiently severe or pervasive to alter the conditions of employment by creating an intimidating, hostile, or offensive work environment.[218]

Sexual harassment doctrine has recently been bolstered by the recognition by some courts that in a case brought by a woman, it is appropriate to judge the hostility of a work environment against the standard of a "reasonable woman."[219] Because a successful claimant must prove both that the environment was objectively hostile, and that she subjectively perceived it as hostile,[220] utilizing this standard may be more sympathetic to women who are conditioned to silently accept certain offensive behavior.[221]

---

216. *See generally* BAER, CHAINS, *supra* note 198, at 151–67 (discussing early development of BFOQ doctrine); HAZOU, *supra* note 25, at 87–89 (same).

217. *See* Int'l Union, United Auto., Aerospace, and Agric. Implement Workers of America, UAW v. Johnson Controls, Inc., 499 U.S. 187 (1991) (describing and applying BFOQ doctrine). In *Johnson Controls* the BFOQ exception was interpreted as not permitting employers to take actions designed to substitute their own judgement as to the welfare of future children; in other words, women could not be excluded from certain areas of work on the grounds that it might harm their child-bearing capabilities.

218. TITUS E. AARON, SEXUAL HARASSMENT IN THE WORKPLACE 4 (1993) (footnotes omitted); *see also* DEBORAH L. RHODE, JUSTICE AND GENDER: SEX DISCRIMINATION AND THE LAW 231–37 (1989) (describing development of sexual harassment doctrine).

219. *See* Torres v. Pisano, No. 96–7939, 1997 U.S. App. LEXIS 12805, at *16 n.6 (2d Cir. June 3, 1997) (describing use of standard).

220. *See* Harris v. Forklift Systems, Inc., 510 U.S. 17, 21 (1993) (stating standard). As one commentator notes: "Gender differences in sexual roles have contributed to gender differences in sexual perceptions. What men often experience as fun or flirtation, women often experience as degrading and demanding. And it is male experience that has shaped the law's traditional responses to sexual harassment." RHODE, *supra* note 218, at 233 (endnotes omitted). *Cf.* Jane L. Dolkart, *Hostile Environment Harassment: Equality, Objectivity, and the Shaping of Legal Standards*, 43 EMORY L.J. 151 (1994) (arguing that plaintiffs would be best served by "[a]n individualized standard [which would] shift the focus away from stereotypes about the appropriate behavior of the victim.").

221. Infamous examples of instances where allegations of sexual harassment have been made years after the offense was committed include law professor Anita Hill's charges against then Supreme Court nominee Clarence Thomas, and Paula Jones' suit against President Clinton. In the case of Professor Hill, the reasonable woman standard might explain why, as some senators found

Despite these advances in employment discrimination law, and society's gradual acceptance of women in non-traditional roles, women (and minorities) are often frustrated by the "glass ceiling" syndrome in which their advancement is blocked by unwritten norms employed by the white male power structure. A woman may be viewed as not being a "team player" in part because she may not participate in pickup sports contests at the local gym with her male counterparts, or may be perceived as "standoffish" because she doesn't belong to the local sporting club (which may not even admit women).[222] Many men suspect that women co-workers won't carry their weight because they have children and are distracted by the demands of childrearing.[223] Deep-seated prejudice of this sort is hard for women to combat, and represents one of the serious current challenges for the women's movement.[224]

---

so difficult to believe, she continued to work with Justice Thomas despite her claimed abhorrence of his advances:

> Quite simply, she thought she'd never be believed and she'd be out of a job, branded a troublemaker or, worse, a liar.
>
> In making this choice, she was behaving like the large majority of sexual harassment victims. In 1981, the year Hill began working for Thomas, a government study of federal workers found that 42 percent of women said that they had experienced some form of sexual harassment. Various polls and studies undertaken since had found anywhere from 40 to 70 percent of women claiming to have been harassed on the job. Yet, from the early 1980s through the beginning of the next decade, one figure remained constant: fewer than 5 percent of these alleged victims filed lawsuits or lodged official complaints. . . . most women responded to harassment as Hill had— they either suffered in silence or found new jobs.

JANE MAYER & JILL ABRAMSON, STRANGE JUSTICE: THE SELLING OF CLARENCE THOMAS 223–24 (1994). The fact that the claimed harassment had been perpetrated by Thomas, then the head of the EEOC, and Clinton, then governor of the state of Arkansas—both men presumed to "know better"— makes the decision of the women to keep silent particularly credible, in this author's view.

222. *See* RHODE, supra note 218, at 171 ("Many women workers remain outside the informal networks of support, guidance, and information-exchange that are critical to advancement.").

223. *See, e.g.*, Phillips v. Martin Marietta Corp., 400 U.S. 542, 544 (1971) (Marshall, J., dissenting from denial of Supreme Court review to case where claim was whether the needs of young children could be considered a BFOQ for female, and not male, job applicants). Few woman can escape the "mommy trap"; those without children are presumed to want to have children, leading to desertion of their jobs for maternity leave. Those women are labeled "non-committed." Some of these concerns are addressed, in a non-gendered fashion, by the Family and Medical Leave Act, controversial federal legislation adopted in 1994. *See* 29 U.S.C.A.§§ 2601 et seq. (1994). Although the Act provides some job protection for any family member forced to care for ill family members or young children, women were a special focus of Congress: "[D]ue to the nature of the roles of men and women in our society, the primary responsibility for family caretaking often falls on women, and such responsibility affects the working lives of women more than it affects the working lives of men." 29 U.S.C.A.§ 2601(a)(5).

224. Another set of problems which the courts and Congress have only begun to address are complicated scenarios of discrimination, such as employers who don't discriminate against all women, but only *black* women, or lesbians. *See generally* Kathryn Adams, *Title VII and the Complex Female Subject*, 92 MICH. L. REV. 2479 (1994); Francisco Valdes, *Queers, Sissies, Dykes and Tomboys: Deconstructing the Conflation of "Sex," "Gender," and "Sexual Orientation" in Euro-American Law and Society*, 83 CALIF. L. REV. 3 (1995); Judith A. Winston, *Mirror Mirror on the Wall: Title VII, Section 1981, and the Intersection of Race and Gender in the Civil Rights*

Sexual and Reproductive Freedom

It has been asserted that "[t]he status of women is inseperable from the subject of human reproduction."[225] In keeping with colonial traditions, and consistent with traditional views of the status of women, states were free to regulate sexual activity and reproduction as they deemed appropriate, in order to promote family life or to advance local notions of public morality and decency. Women have traditionally borne the brunt of this regulation through the promulgation of laws governing prostitution, pornography, rape, and abortion, and through family law relating to the rights and duties of married and unmarried women.[226]

Reproduction was at first not widely regulated, in part because there were so few effective methods of birth control available. Contraceptive methods became more reliable and more widely available in the 1830s.[227] At the same time, social theorists began to advocate birth control over sexual restraint as a means of coping with their concerns about overpopulation and the distribution of resources. These writings ran afoul of state and federal obscenity laws.[228] The use of contraceptives was also discouraged by organized religions, on the grounds that the availability of contraceptives encouraged immoral behavior. Today many continue to link contraception with

---

Act of 1990, 79 CALIF. L. REV. 775 (1991); Note, *Asian Women and Employment Discrimination: Using Intersectionality Theory to Address Title VII claims Based on Combined Factors of Race, Gender and National Origin,* 37 B.C. L. REV. 771 (1996); *cf.* Note, *Invisible Man: Black and Male under Title VII,* 104 HARV. L. REV. 749 (1991).

225. BAER, WOMEN, *supra* note 71, at 173.

226. At the height of this regulatory fervor, states outlawed sexual relations between nonmarried persons, persons of the same sex, and between men and women who were below a certain age. However, while a husband could demand sexual relations of his wife (and use force to vindicate that right), women had no corresponding right. Even among married persons the type of sexual contact was regulated: sodomy was commonly proscribed, and still is prohibited as consensual heterosexual conduct in some states; indeed, many states mandated that those permitted to have sex could only use sexual positions deemed appropriate by the legislature. Prostitution was outlawed in theory, but tolerated in practice. However, to the extent that anti-prostitution codes were enforced, more often it was women, and not their male customers, who were apprehended, fined, jailed, and ostracized. That remains true to this day. Finally, many feminists decry current legal protection of certain types of pornography, which priviliges the free speech interests of those in the pornography industry over the interest of society in protecting women from the violence which some say is fostered by pornography. Many of these issues are addressed in the essays collected in FEMINISM & POLITICAL THEORY (Cass R. Sunstein ed., 1990).

227. Beginning in the 1840s, condoms could be mass produced using the industial rubberizing techniques. BAER, WOMEN, *supra* note 71, at 179. Of course, the effectivness of condoms as a method of contraception is dependent upon the cooperation of the male sexual partner. Not until the 1930s were "safe and reliable woman-controlled devices" available. *Id.*

228. [P]olitical leaders charged that contraceptive practices encouraged premarital and extramarital sex, which they classified along with rape, prostitution, and pornography as part of the annual moral corruption and decay of society.

STETSON, *supra* note 117, at 72; *see also* BAER, WOMEN, *supra* note 71, at 179 (discussing the federal Comstock Act and similar state "decency" legislation).

obscenity and promiscuous behavior.[229] However, the liberalization of laws regarding sexual conduct required greater flexibility in the regulation of contraception. Most states have either repealed, or no longer seriously pursue criminal enforcement of, statutes prohibiting sex between non-married persons (although many states still outlaw homosexual sex).[230] In the context of that liberalization, contraceptives have the benefit of limiting the number of children born out of wedlock and, depending on the method, of limiting the transmission of certain diseases. In addition, American society now accepts that married women and men often, for economic or other reasons, wish to limit their family size or otherwise pace the growth of their family.[231] Those choices are considered a private matter to be decided by the sexual partners without the interference of government.[232] Today the adult use of contraceptives is largely uncontroversial[233] and assumed to be a private choice of individuals.[234]

There is much controversy on the distinct reproductive issue of pregnancy termination, as opposed to pregnancy prevention. Up until the mid-1970s, abortion regulation fell entirely within the purview of the states. Most states either limited abortions

---

229. *See, e.g.,* Editorial, *Modern Morality,* WALL ST. J., June 11, 1997, 1997 WL–WSJ 2423804 ("Very simply, what we're suggesting here is that the code of sexual behavior formerly set down by established religion in the U.S. more or less kept society healthy, unlike the current manifest catastrophe.").

230. *See, e.g.,* Bowers v. Hardwick, 478 U.S. 186 (1986) (upholding Georgia's sodomy law and holding that the right to privacy does not encompass homosexual sex); *but see* Rohmer v. Evans, 116 S. Ct. 1620; 134 L.Ed. 2d 855 (1996) (invalidating amendment to Colorado state constitution which prohibited any state action designed to protect homosexuals from discrimination); *see also Rohmer,* 116 S. Ct. at 1629 (dissenting opinion of Justices Scalia, Rehnquist and Thomas, questioning the continuing validity of *Bowers* in light of *Rohmer*).

231. According to one commentator, "Until the 1960s, the American College of Obstetrics and Gynecology recommended that its members perform sterilizations only if the woman's age, multiplied by the number of living children she had, equaled at least 120." BAER, WOMEN, *supra* note 71, at 180. In addition, many hospitals also required the husband's consent. *Id.*

232. This privacy interest rises to the level of a constitutionally protected right. The Supreme Court first recognized that the Constitution, taken as a whole, creates "zones of privacy" which include sexual behavior. Griswold v. Connecticut, 381 U.S. 479 (1965); *see also* Eisenstadt v. Baird, 405 U.S. 438 (1972). In *Griswold,* the Court invalidated a particularly stringent anti-contraception law in Connecticut, which outlawed the manufacture, advertisement, distribution, and use of birth control devices; in *Eisenstadt,* the Court extended the application of *Griswold* to unmarried as well as married persons.

233. *See generally* BAER, WOMEN, *supra* note 71, at 195–99 (discussing liberalization of access to contraceptives).

234. One notable exception is the controversy surrounding the distribution of condoms in schools, and the teaching of safe-sex techniques in high-school classrooms. *See, e.g.,* Lisa O'Connor, *Behind the Debate, What's Being Taught in Sex Education,* SUN-SENTINEL, May 18, 1997 at 1A, *available in* 1997 WL 3104431 (noting that one Florida parent finds the sex education classes his children take "so loathsome that he quit his law practice to devote all his time to the issue"; his wife has sued the school district claiming the classes "promote premarital sex and homosexuality"); *but see* Karen Stram and Ted O'Meara, Editorial, *Plan Wrong for Kids at Risk— A Bill to Eliminate Access to Contraceptives is a Bad Idea,* PORTLAND PRESS HERALD, May 9, 1997, at 15A, *available in* 1997 WL 4124086 (disagreeing with efforts of the Maine state legislature to limit teen access to contraceptives).

to those necessary to save the life of the mother and/or those where the pregnancy resulted from rape, or banned them completely.[235] In 1973, the Supreme Court decided *Roe v. Wade*.[236] At stake were a variety of interests, most significantly the privacy and autonomy of women seeking safe abortions, on the one hand, and the state's interest in protecting the life, or potential life, of the unborn fetus and in safguarding the health of the woman, on the other hand.[237] In invalidating a Texas law that prohibited abortions unless necessary to save the life of the woman, the Supreme Court held that the Constitution guaranteed a woman's privacy interests and permitted her to obtain an abortion during the first trimester of pregnancy—for any reason.[238] Under *Roe*, during the second and third trimesters, the interests of the state in protecting the potential life of the fetus increases, permitting heightened regulation of abortion during the second trimester and a ban on all abortions in the final trimester, except when necessary to save the life of the woman.[239]

This pronouncement of federal constitutional policy did not end the debate.[240] Using the rhetoric of two fundamental constitutional principles, liberty ("pro-choice") and life ("pro-life"), American citizens continue to fight this battle in state legislatures and with demonstrations, vandalism, and, increasingly, violence.[241]

These tactics have had some effect. Following *Roe*, presidential candidates' campaign promises included vows to appoint judges willing to either uphold or overturn the decision.[242] Over time, the Supreme Court has become more divided on this issue,

---

235. Prior to the mid-nineteenth century, most states permitted abortions performed before "quickening"—the perceptible movement of the fetus in the woman. For a summary of the development of American abortion regulation, *see Introduction, in* ABORTION LAW IN THE UNITED STATES: FROM *ROE V. WADE* TO THE PRESENT, vol. 1, xi–xxii (Jenni Parrish ed., 1995) [hereinafter ABORTION LAW]; *see also* Roe v. Wade, 410 U.S. 113, 138–52 (1973) (same); Joseph W. Dellapenna, *The History of Abortion: Technology, Morality and Law, reprinted in* ABORTION LAW, *supra*, at vol. 3, 15–84 (same); *but see* Robert M. Byron, *An American Tragedy: The Supreme Court on Abortion, reprinted in* ABORTION LAW, *supra*, at vol. 3, 122–43 (arguing that Supreme Court's views in *Roe* about the development of abortion law in the United States was "both distorted and incomplete").

236. 410 U.S. 113 (1973).

237. *See Roe*, 410 U.S. at 152–64; *see also* BAER, WOMEN, *supra* note 71, at 200 (discussing *Roe*).

238. *See Roe*, 410 U.S. at 164. As Judith Baer notes, this is somewhat of an overstatement of the Court's opinion; for an alternative explanation, *see* BAER, WOMEN, *supra* note 71, at 203–06.

239. *See Roe*, 410 U.S. at 164–65.

240. For a collection of scholarship concerning the validity and impact of *Roe*, *see generally* ABORTION LAW, *supra* note 235, vol. 3. Particularly interesting is the alternative liberty analysis of *Roe* by Judith Jarvis Thomson, *A Defense of Abortion, originally in* 1 PHIL. & PUB. AFFAIRS 47 (1971), which equates pregnancy and the right to life to instances of medical exigency.

241. *See* Joyce Price, *Violence at Clinics Decreases*, WASH. TIMES, Jan. 23, 1997 *available in* LEXIS, News library, Curnews file, (describing 1996 decrease in violence at abortion clinics from previous highs of twenty-one arsons (1992), two bombings (1993), four murders of clinic personnel (1994), and seventy-eight death threats against clinic personnel (1993)); *see also* Bill Smith, *Picket / Counterpicket: Both Abortion Sides Claim Victory—3-Day Demonstration was Free of Violence*, ST. LOUIS POST-DISP., Aug. 6, 1995, available in LEXIS, New library, Curnews file (noting member of one "pro-life" organization had openly supported killing abortion doctors).

242. In the 1996 presidential campaign, President Clinton's promise was to keep abortion "safe,

and has increasingly permitted states to regulate abortion in ways that burden—but do not prohibit—a woman's right to decide whether to terminate her pregnancy.[243] *Roe's* formulaic trimester approach has been replaced by a flexible approach that recognizes the interest of states in regulating abortions;[244] while the essential right to an abortion is still recognized, the reasonableness of attempts to regulate the exercise of that right is now an open question. Perhaps as a result, the issue of abortion rights continues to deeply divide the nation and the feminist movement. While some attempts at outreach and compromise have been made, many believe that a woman's complete control over her sexuality and reproduction potential is crucial to women's opportunities for advancement and equality, and thus, any restriction on abortion is damaging to the interests of all women.[245]

Summary

The domestic rights of women have undergone a remarkable transformation in the 200 years since the adoption of the Bill of Rights, which incorporated contemporary views of the second-class status of women. There have been many important successes: women have gained the right of political participation; many restrictive common-law rules regarding property and marriage rights that disadvantaged women have been overruled; legislation prohibiting discrimination in education and employment, as well as laws providing recourse for victims of gender-based violence and abuse, have been established.

Yet, while the "degraded and inferior" position of women has improved, some efforts at gender equality, most notably the ERA, have been rebuffed. Two important conclusions may be drawn from this history. First, it is the courts' recognition of neg-

---

legal and rare," a promise which placed him squarely with the majority of Americans. *See Key Issues: The Candidates' Positions*, U.S.A. TODAY, Nov. 4, 1996, *available in* LEXIS, News library, Curnews file (describing Clinton's campaign promises and record). In contrast, candidate Bob Dole, his chief opponent, had to struggle with a Republican party with both moderate abortion-rights proponents and absolute abortion opponents. *See Dole's Big Tent—Seeks Tolerance in Abortion Plank*, NEWSDAY, June 7, 1996, *available in* LEXIS, News library, Curnews file (discussing Dole's unsuccessful request that the party platform include a "declaration of tolerance").

243. Examples are requirements of parental consent for minor women, waiting periods, and limits on federal funding. *See generally* BAER, WOMEN, *supra* note 71, at 206–15 (discussing state regulations, and issue of federal funding). Important state restrictions on abortions rejected by the Supreme Court include requiring consent of the husband, Planned Parenthood of Central Missouri v. Danforth, 428 U.S. 52 (1976); two-parent notification for abortions preformed on minors, Hodgson v. Minnesota, 497 U.S. 417 (1990); and hospitalization for certain routine abortion procedures, Planned Parenthood of Kansas City v. Ashcroft, 462 U.S. 476 (1983).

244. *See* Planned Parenthood of Southeastern Pennsylvania v. Casey, 505 U.S. 833 (1992).

245. It is true that pregnant women are increasingly subject to fetal protection legislation and social norms restricting their behavior. *See* Nancy Ehrenreich, *The Colonization of the Womb*, 43 DUKE L.J. 492 (1993); Lisa C. Ikemoto, *The Code of Perfect Pregnancy: At the Intersection of the Ideology of Motherhood, the Practice of Defaulting to Science, and the Interventionist Mindset of Law*, 53 OHIO ST. L.J. 1205 (1992); Dorothy E. Roberts, *Punishing Drug Addicts who have Babies: Women of Color, Equality, and the Right of Privacy*, 104 HARV. L. REV. 1419 (1991).

ative societal views of women that has always and still represents the most significant bar to the advancement of women. This first problem is augmented by the American tradition of rights and liberties, which prohibits the government from directly affecting the private behavior that underlies these views. Therefore, one may also conclude that the failure of the ERA has little legal consequence (although the failure has certainly reinforced America's gender traditions). The Supreme Court jurisprudence concerning gender equality, and that of applicable state jurisdictions, still incorporates gender views; constitutional prohibitions limiting the reach of equal protection law to state actors also serves to limit any potential legal impact of a gender equality provision. Ultimately, one may conclude that the United States will never achieve true gender equality until it is freed from the strictures of traditional gender views incorporated in the Constitution; the adoption of international rights perspectives could possibly serve to invigorate American gender relations and notions of gender equality.

INCORPORATING THE INTERNATIONAL PERSPECTIVE

> Strictly, there are no "international human rights." . . . In our international system of nation-states, human rights are to be enjoyed in national societies as rights under national law. The purpose of international law is to influence states to recognize and accept human rights, to reflect these rights in their national constitutions and laws, to respect and ensure their enjoyment through national institutions, and to incorporate them into national ways of life.
>
> —Louis Henkin[246]

If one were to measure the success of the international human rights movement solely on the basis of the standard expressed above, there would be no question as to the success of the U.S. in incorporating certain human rights into its national way of life. Yet, notwithstanding the rich domestic rights tradition described in the previous section and the incremental progress in the area of gender equality—or perhaps because of that tradition and progress—human rights activists strongly criticize American hostility towards incorporating an international view of human rights as a serious component of international policy, or as a domestic imperative.[247] In the international arena, the U.S. is a "defender" of human rights, but has refused to join most of the human rights treaties; eager to use its economic and military power to vindicate strategic and capitalistic interests, the U.S. defers to—even allies itself with—regimes well documented as abusers of human rights.[248] American domestic policy

---

246. Henkin, *supra* note 3, at 25. Some may consider this view outdated. This author believes there is continuing merit to his analysis. *See* note 249, *infra*.

247. *See, e.g.*, Thomas Buergenthal, *U.S. Human Rights Policy: A Modest Agenda for the Future*, 28 Va. J. Int'l L. 845, 846 (1988) [hereinafter Buergenthal, *Agenda*] (describing the American record on ratifying treaties as "dismal"); *cf.* William Schabas, *Invalid Reservations to the International Covenant on Civil and Political Rights: Is the United States Still a Party?*, 21 Brook. J. Int'l L. 277 (1995) (describing the international reaction to U.S. reservations to the Covenant on Civil and Political Rights).

248. "Our identification in the past with the Shah of Iran, Marcos, the Somozas, the Duvaliers, and others of like ilk has cost us dearly in terms of our long-term national interest." Buergenthal, *Agenda, supra* note 247, at 848.

often appears internally inconsistent as well: the U.S. failed to ratify the ERA, preserving the second-class status of women, yet it criticizes other countries that subjugate women. Where exactly does the U.S. stand on international human rights and the rights of women? To what can we attribute American reticence towards incorporating an international vision of human rights "into [our] national way of life"?[249] The answer is a complex combination of political imperatives, respect—some might say reverence—for American constitutional imperatives, as well as relative unfamiliarity with international human rights norms.

The U.S. Record

The strength of American recognition of and support for international human rights initiatives has varied over time.[250] In the period immediately following World War II, the United States sponsored or participated in several significant human rights initiatives, not the least of which was the formation of the United Nations, which is dedicated to "promoting and encouraging respect for human rights and for funda-

---

249. Henkin gives us a possible answer. He goes on to note that because "[t]he international law of human rights builds and depends on national law," the undertakings of a nation will depend upon its domestic law and institutions. Henkin, *supra* note 3, at 25–26. He hypothesizes that many Americans resist U.S. adoption of international human rights standards because of the dominance of, and our satisfaction with, American constitutional law and institutions. *Id.* at 50–55; *see also* Hurst Hannum & Dana Fischer, *The Political Framework, in* UNITED STATES RATIFICATION OF THE INTERNATIONAL COVENANTS ON HUMAN RIGHTS 3, 20–21 (Hurst Hannum & Dana Fischer eds., 1993) ("Promoting human rights touches on the very foundations of a State's regime, on its sources and exercise of power, on its links to its citizens"; although the authors' concern is with the possible imposition of American values on other nations, their analysis of the domestic implications is of relevance).

250. These comments are limited to the policies of the U.S. government promulgated by the legislative, judicial, and executive branches. A significant segment of the American populace has long been committed to the advancement of human rights, as evidenced by the activities of a variety of nongovernmental organizations such as Amnesty International, Human Rights Watch, The Lawyers Committee for Human Rights, Physicians for Human Rights, the International Human Rights Law Group, Peace Corp volunteers and other individual efforts, and local and state initiatives designed to advance the cause of international human rights. For example, after the federal government initially rejected calls for economic sanctions against South Africa in favor of a policy of constructive engagement, several American cities adopted their own economic sanctions aimed at ending apartheid in South Africa. *See, e.g.,* John Harrington, *Council Lifts Sanctions,* CRAIN'S, N.Y. BUS., Oct. 11–17, 1993, *available in* LEXIS, News library, Arcnws file (describing action by New York City to lift economic sanctions against South Africa following the release of Nelson Mandela); Elaine Herscher, *Berkeley Repeals Policies Against South Africa: "A Very Moving Moment" for City that Started Drive,* THE S.F. CHRON., Oct. 20, 1993, *available in* LEXIS, News library, Arcnws file (regarding Berkeley, California's sanctions against South Africa); Julie Mason, *Council Lifts Trade Sanctions Against South Africa,* THE HOUSTON CHRON. Oct. 28, 1993, *available in* LEXIS, News library, Arcnws file (regarding Houston, Texas,' sanctions against South Africa); *see generally* PAULINE BAKER, THE UNITED STATES AND SOUTH AFRICA: THE REAGAN YEARS 61–62 (1989) (describing initiatives by state and local governments). In the same spirit of local action, in July of 1995, the Iowa City Council adopted the principles of the Convention to Eliminate All Forms of Discrimination Against Women. *See* Christie Midthun, *Equal-Rights Fight Triumphs: I.C. Sets National Precedent, Adopts Discrimination Resolution,* THE DAILY IOWAN, Aug. 3, 1995, at A1.

mental freedoms for all without distinction as to race, sex, language or religion."[251] This period also saw the adoption of the Universal Declaration of Human Rights,[252] with First Lady Eleanor Roosevelt serving as a driving force behind the drafting and negotiations.[253] The Universal Declaration was intended to be quickly supplemented by a single binding agreement fleshing out the scope of international protections of human rights.[254] After some delay, two separate agreements, the International Covenant on Civil and Political Rights (ICCPR)[255] and the International Covenant on Economic, Social, and Cultural Rights (ICESCR)[256] were adopted by the United Nations in 1966.[257] The United States was an active—if at times reluctant—participant in the drafting process for those and other international human rights agreements.[258] Yet only a handful of the major modern human rights treaties—including the ICCPR, but not the ICESCR—have been ratified by the United States, and other important human rights documents, including the Convention for the Elimination of All Forms of Discrimination Against Women ("Women's Convention"),[259] languish in various points of the domestic ratification process.[260]

---

251. U.N. CHARTER art. 1, para 3.

252. *See* G.A. Res. 217 (III 1948).

253. *See* THE UNIVERSAL DECLARATION OF HUMAN RIGHTS: A COMMENTARY 10–11 (Asbjorn Eide & Theresa Swineheart eds., 1992).

254. *See* Louis Henkin, *Introduction, in* THE INTERNATIONAL BILL OF RIGHTS: THE COVENANT ON CIVIL AND POLITICAL RIGHTS 1, 8–22 (Louis Henkin ed., 1981) [hereinafter "Henkin ed."]; Vratuslav Pechota, *The Development of the Convention on Civil and Political Rights, in* Henkin ed., *supra*, at 41–43. Although the Universal Declaration was adopted as a nonbinding resolution of the U.N. General Assembly, since that time, certain core rights have been identified as binding through the force of customary international law. *See* OSCAR SCHACHTER, INTERNATIONAL LAW IN THEORY AND PRACTICE (1991) *quoted in* INTERNATIONAL HUMAN RIGHTS IN CONTEXT: LAW, POLITICS, MORALS 136–40 (Henry Steiner & Philip Alston eds., 1996) [hereinafter, Steiner] (discussing import of later U.N. General Assembly resolutions describing the Universal Declaration as obligatory, in the light of susbsequent contrary practice); THOMAS BUERGENTHAL, INTERNATIONAL HUMAN RIGHTS IN A NUTSHELL, *quoted in* Steiner, *supra*, at 143 (describing Universal Declaration as "having a normative character"); Louis B. Sohn, *The New International Law: Protection of the Rights of Individuals Rather Than States*, 32 AM. U. L. REV. 1, 14–17 (1982) (describing the legal import of the Universal Declaration and concluding that "all states" have an obligation to "fully and faithfully" observe its provisions).

255. *See* Dec. 16, 1966, 999 U.N.T.S. 171.

256. *See* Dec. 16, 1966, 993 U.N.T.S. 3.

257. *See generally* Sohn, *supra* note 254, at 19–48 (describing development of the ICCPR and ICESCR and certain provisions); NATALIE HEVENER KAUFMAN, HUMAN RIGHTS TREATIES AND THE SENATE: A HISTORY OF OPPOSITION 64–93 (1990) (same).

258. *See* Pechota, *supra* note 254, at 41–43. The United States' publicly expressed "doubt" that it could ratify a treaty containing economic, social and cultural rights contributed to the development of two separate treaties. *Id.; but see* Hannum, *supra* note 249, at 7 (noting that due to U.S. influence, "the two treaties reflect American interests and embody more American values than the United States could ever expect to renegotiate today").

259. Dec. 18, 1979, 19 I.L.M. 33 (1980).

260. *See* Todd S. Purdum, *Clinton Chides Senate for Not Approving Women's Rights Treaty*, N.Y. TIMES, Dec. 11, 1996, at A5. In addition to the Women's Convention and the ICESCR, the U.S. has

Many theories are offered to explain why international human rights initiatives did not remain a vital part of American foreign policy.[261] The interest of the executive branch[262] in pursuing international human rights as a part of American foreign policy waned considerably after the initial post-World War II initiative.[263] Some point to the Cold War and the anti-communist sentiments which fractured

---

not ratified the American Convention on Human Rights, Nov. 22, 1969, 9 I.L.M. 673 (1970) (sponsored by the Organization of American States), the Convention on the Rights of the Child (CRC), Nov. 20, 1989, 28 I.L.M. 1448 (1989); *see generally* Susan Kilbourne, *U.S. Failure to Ratify the U.N. Convention on the Rights of the Child: Playing Politics with Children's Rights,* 6 TRANSNAT'L L. & CONTEMP. PROBS. 437 (1996) (discussing arguments for and against U.S. ratification).

In addition to the ICCPR, the U.S. is a party to the Protocol Relating to the Status of Refugees, Oct. 4, 1967, 606 U.N.T.S. 267 (ratified in 1968, with reservations), the Convention on the Political Rights of Women, Mar. 31, 1953, 193 U.N.T.S. 135 (acceded to in 1976), the Convention on the Prevention and Punishment of the Crime of Genocide, Dec. 9, 1948, 78 U.N.T.S. 277 (ratified in 1988, with reservations), the International Convention on the Elimination of All Forms of Racial Discrimination, Jan. 7, 1966, 5 I.L.M. 352 (1966) (ratified in 1994, with reservations), and the Convention Against Torture and Other Cruel, Inhuman or Degrading Treatment or Punishment, Dec. 10, 1984, 23 I.L.M. 1027 (1984), *as modified,* 24 I.L.M. 535 (1985) (ratified in 1994, with reservations).

261. An important consequence of the U.S.' failure to ratify certain treaties is that it is excluded from participating in many important international human rights institutions, such as the Committee on the Elimination of Discrimination Against Women, established by the Women's Convention (art. 17), and the Committee on the Rights of the Child (pursuant to CRC art. 43). There are, however, other opportunities for the U.S. to participate in the international human rights community, opportunities which the U.S. has taken full advantage of. For example, since 1934, the U.S. has been a member of the International Labor Organization (ILO), an organization which has dedicated itself to the promotion of "universal and lasting peace" and "social justice." *ILO Constitution, Preamble, as available on* <http://www.ilo.org/public/english/about/iloconst.htm>. The ILO is recognized as playing "an extraordinary role in the multilateral efforts to secure human rights." Statement of Sen. Daniel Patrick Moynihan, *quoted in 1919–1997: The ILO Defending Human Rights.* The U.S. is also a member of the Organization of American States, which is active in the human rights arena. *See* Steiner, *supra* note 254, at 640–89 (describing Inter-American system). In addition, the U.S., as a member of the United Nations, participates in other U.N. mechanisms for vindicating human rights. *Id.* at 374–91 (describing U.N. "1235" and "1503" procedures). Thus, while U.S. commitment to human rights is limited by its failure to ratify key treaties, it does participate in the international human rights community. *Cf.* Hannum, *supra* note 249, at 14–20 (describing U.S. human rights activities).

262. In separately discussing three branches of government, the author does not intend to discount the interaction of the branches, but rather to indicate instances in which a particular branch has primary responsibility for a particular function of American international relations.

263. "In 1946 the United States enthusiastically took the lead in the new United Nations to bring human rights under the protection of that international organization. Seven years later it announced that it would no longer participate in the drafting of international covenants for that purpose." VIRGINIA PRATT, THE INFLUENCE OF DOMESTIC CONTROVERSY ON AMERICAN PARTICIPATION IN THE UNITED NATIONS COMMISSION ON HUMAN RIGHTS: 1946–1953 1 (1986). This sentiment was the result of a complex set of international political forces, as well as equally complex domestic forces, including the rising fear of a communist plot to overthrow the American government, and hostility towards the domestic civil rights movement for racial equity. *Id.* at 170–231. The hostility to international human rights treaties was expressed in Congressional efforts to alter the Constitutional provisions for the supremacy of the domestic application of international law, and calls for the U.S. to leave the United Nations (*id.*); however, despite these extremist views, as

much of whatever domestic support existed for these international undertakings,[264] and to the clash between classic political rights and "new" economic rights.[265] One can also point to the global tensions arising from the Korean War (the 1950s) and Vietnam War (late 1960s–1970s) as further contributing to the declining U.S. interest in international human rights. The administration of President Jimmy Carter (1977–81) again raised the American public awareness of international human rights,[266] but few real gains resulted from this new commitment: Carter submitted key human rights treaties to the Senate for its advice and consent to ratification— pursuant to reservations—but none were ratified during his presidency. By the time the ICCPR was ratified by the Senate in 1992, many believed the U.S. reservations rendered its ratification a nullity.[267]

The efforts of the legislative branch have been equally mixed. Key legislation passed in 1970s links U.S. foreign assistance to favorable human rights records,[268]

---

noted, the U.S. maintained some level of participation in the international human rights arena (*see* note 261, *supra*).

264. *See* Ann Elizabeth Mayer, *Reflections on the Proposed U.S. Reservations to the Women's Convention: Should the Constitution Be an Obstacle to Human Rights*, 23 HASTINGS CONST. L.Q. 727, 748–49 (1996) (describing the then-president of the American Bar Association claiming that human rights treaties are "part of a Communist plot to destroy the American way of life"); KAUF-MAN, *supra* note 257, at 9–36 (describing efforts of certain lawyers to "alert the American public to the dangers of human rights treaties").

265. *See* Pechota, *supra* note 254, at 41–42. There is some irony to U.S. reluctance to embrace certain economic and social rights, because one important force behind the U.N.'s human rights mission was the concept of the "four freedoms" advanced by American President Franklin Roosevelt, which emphasized economic and social justice as a prerequisite to world peace. Sohn, *supra* note 254, at 33–35; Hannum, *supra* note 249, at 13–14.

266. "President Carter called it the 'soul' of his foreign policy, delighting not only human rights experts but also millions of people around the world . . . Thus was ushered in the golden era of human rights." Buergenthal, *Agenda, supra* note 247, at 845–46; *but see* DAVID FORSYTHE, HUMAN RIGHTS AND U.S. FOREIGN POLICY: CONGRESS RECONSIDERED ix (1988) (comparing human rights initiatives by Congress and the executive branch between 1973 and 1984 and concluding that "it was Congress, not the Carter administration, that put international human rights back on the foreign policy agenda"); *cf.* KAUFMAN, *supra* note 257, at 149–74 (noting that the "reservations game," the practice of adding reservations and understandings to treaties to limit their impact, was "played to the hilt" by the Carter Administration).

267. *See* 138 Cong. Rec. S4781 (1991) (Senate resolution of ratification). For a comprehensive discussion of the dispute arising from the U.S. reservations, *see* Schabas, *supra* note 247. *See also* Louis Henkin, *U.S. Ratification of Human Rights Conventions: The Ghost of Senator Bricker*, 89 AM. J. INT'L L. 341 (1995) [hereinafter Henkin, *Bricker*]. The simultaneously cautious and courageous response of the ICCPR's Human Rights Committee to the U.S. reservations noted that "[o]f particular concern are widely formulated reservations which essentially render ineffective all Covenant rights which would require any change in national law." Human Rights Committee, General Comment 24 (52) ¶ 12, U.N. Doc. CCPR/C/21/Rev.1/Add.6 (1994) *as available on* <http://www.umn.edu/humanrts/gencomm/hrcom24.htm>. Although it is not clear that it has the power to do so, the Committee set forth parameters to assist states in "ensur[ing] that each and every proposed reservation is compatible with the object and purpose of the Covenant." *Id.* at ¶ 20.

268. *See* 22 U.S.C.A. § 2151n (West 1996). This statute also releases special funds to the president for carrying out special programs "to promote increased adherence to civil and political

and in the 1980s Congress overrode a presidential veto to enact legislation imposing economic sanctions on the apartheid regime of South Africa.[269] The congressional committees responsible for international affairs often hold hearings to receive input on important human rights issues.[270] Although the publicity generated by these hearings and legislative initiative is useful, often the human rights rhetoric is clouded by political objectives.[271] Taken as a whole, the congressional posture towards international human rights—and in particular, international obligations designed to vindicate international human rights standards in the U.S.—is decidedly hostile.[272] Simply put, most congressional representatives will not act to put limits on American—and Congressional—sovereignty.

U.S. courts have recognized important human rights principles as applied against other states or state actors. For example, in permitting Bosnian women rape victims to pursue a lawsuit in American courts against the Serbian leader Karadzic for violating their human rights during the civil war, one U.S. court recognized that certain "offenses against international law, such as piracy, war crimes, and genocide"[273] can

---

rights, as set forth in the Universal Declaration of Human Rights." 22 U.S.C.A. § 2151n(e). Other legislation links military assistance and U.S. votes in multilateral banking institutions (*e.g.*, the World Bank) to human rights records. *See* FORSYTHE, *supra* note 266, at 1–14, 51–79 (describing legislation and application). The reporting requirements of these statutes are important examples of the cooperation between branches of the federal government, and moreover, with nongovernmental activists. The State Department authors the reports, based on information collected from the relevant American embassies, which in turn gather information "from . . . government officials, jurists, military sources, journalists, human rights monitors, academics, and labor activists." *Preface to Country Reports on Human Rights Practices for 1996* (1997) *available on* <http://www.usis.usemb.se/human/preface.html>. The reports are then submitted to Congress for its consideration in accordance with statutory requirements. *Id.* Congress may then request additional information or critiques of the reports, as desired. *See, e.g., State Department Reports on Human Rights Practices Hearings Before the House Committee on International Relations*, Jan. 31, 1997, *available in* 1997 WL 8218672 (testimony of Stephen Rickard, Director of Amnesty International USA, Wash. Office) [hereinafter "Rickard Comments"].

269. *See* Comprehensive Anti-Apartheid Act of 1986 (Pub. L. No. 99–440, Oct. 2, 1986, 100 Stat. 1086); *see generally* BAKER, *supra* note 250, at 29–64 (describing Congress' eventual override of President Reagan's policy of constructive engagement).

270. *See, e.g., Human Rights Abuses Against Women: Hearings Before the Subcommittee on International Security, International Organizations and Human Rights of the Committee on Foreign Affairs of the House of Representatives*, 103d Cong., 1st & 2nd Sess. (1994) [hereinafter *Human Rights Hearings*] (discussing instances of international and domestic abuse of women's human rights).

271. Given that Congress is the political branch of government, it is not surprising that human rights rhetoric is used to further the political agendas of conservatives and liberals alike. *See generally* FORSYTHE, *supra* note 266, at 1–50 (assessing congressional voting patterns on human rights issues).

272. Indeed, one senator so feared domestic impact of international human rights norms that he proposed amending the Constitution to limit the impact of international agreements, and thus preserve the "sacred" nature of the American Constitution. *See* Henkin, *Bricker, supra* note 267, at 348–49; KAUFMAN, *supra* note 257, at 94–116; Mayer, *supra* note 264, at 749–50.

273. Kadic v. Karadzic, 70 F.3d 232, 240 (2d Cir. 1996) (citing THE RESTATEMENT (THIRD) OF THE FOREIGN RELATIONS LAW OF THE UNITED STATES § 702 (1987)). This position was supported by the

be enforced in domestic courts under the domestic laws.[274] However, the judiciary has rejected arguments to apply certain fundamental international human rights norms domestically; in deciding *Stanford v. Kentucky*,[275] which upheld the execution of defendants who were minors when they committed their offenses, the Supreme Court barely discussed arguments that that application of the death penalty was in violation of broadly recognized international standards.[276]

In addition to these domestic applications, American foreign policy has also been pursued in a manner that disregards key international human rights norms. The U.S. government has ignored or downplayed human rights violations by other nations in circumstances which lead to the conclusion that American diplomatic, economic, and strategic interests were afforded more weight than human suffering.[277] In those instances when the U.S. has spoken or acted to vindicate international human rights, the circumstances tend to suggest that domestic—often economic—interests, and not moral conviction, provided the motivation.[278]

United States government in its brief to the court. *See id.* at 239–40; *see also* Filartiga v. Pena, 630 F.2d 876 (2d Cir. 1980) (recognizing the right to be free of torture as a customary norm which can be enforced domestically).

274. The women claimants brought suit pursuant to the Alien Tort Statute, 28 U.S.C.A. § 1350 (West 1990). The Torture Victim Protection Act of 1991, Pub.L. No. 102–256, Mar. 12, 1992, 106 Stat. 73, provides an additional basis for vindicating foreign human rights by permitting any individual who is the victim of torture in another country to sue in U.S. courts. *See generally* Anne-Marie Burley, *The Alien Tort Statute and the Judiciary Act of 1789: A Badge of Honor*, 83 AM. J. INT'L L. 461 (1989) (discussing proposed legislation).

275. 492 U.S. 361 (1989).

276. "We emphasize that it is *American* conceptions of decency that are dispositive, rejecting the contention . . . that the sentencing practices of other countries are relevant." *Id.* at 369 n.1 (emphasis added). While three dissenting justices were willing to entertain the notion that "contemporary standards of decency in . . . other countries [are] also of relevance," *id.* at 389 (Brennan, J. dissenting), even those justices did not appear to consider the standards to be imperative norms of international law, *id.* at 389–90. Yet the execution of minors is explicitly prohibited by the ICCPR, which provides the "[s]entence of death shall not be imposed for crimes committed by persons below eighteen years of age." ICCPR art. 6(5) (one of the controversial American reservations to the ICCPR purports to limit the application of that article (*see* note 267, *supra*)). For a discussion of the clash between the execution of minors in the U.S. and U.S. obligations as a member of the Inter-American system, *see* THOMAS BUERGENTHAL ET AL., PROTECTING HUMAN RIGHTS IN THE AMERICAS 28–44 (3d ed. 1990).

277. "[T]he United States has tended to view human rights as a purely humanitarian concern to which we must pay lip service, but only after taking care of our 'real' national interests." Buergenthal, *Agenda, supra* note 247, at 848; *see also* note 339 *infra* and accompanying text.

278. For example, in the days before the 1990 Gulf War initiative, President George Bush likened Iraqi President Saddam Hussein to Adolf Hitler, and emphasized Iraq's violations of humanitarian and environmental norms, including reports of Iraqi mistreatment of Kuwaiti women and children, as the significant motivation behind American participation in efforts to halt Iraqi aggression. *See* Dan Balz & Molly Moore, *Bush Asks Nation to Back "Defensive" Mission as U.S. Forces Begin Arriving in Saudi Arabia*, THE WASH. POST, Aug. 9, 1990, *available in* 1990 WL 2116365 (discussing televised comments of President Bush); Cragg Hines & William Clayton, Jr., *Bush Hints Trial Planned for Saddam*, HOUSTON CHRON., Oct. 16, 1990, *available in* 1990 WL 6622237 (quoting President Bush as describing "'ghastly atrocities perpetrated by Saddam's

In 1974, on the occasion of the twenty-fifth anniversary of the Universal Declaration, leading human rights scholars categorized the U.S. role in the international human rights arena as "negligible,"[279] "unsatisfactory"[280] and "disturbing."[281] Little has changed in the twenty-six years since.[282] As one scholar has noted, "there is nothing peculiarly American" about the U.S. foreign policy stance which considers human rights concerns as secondary to more immediate domestic concerns.[283] However, America's standing as a world power leads human rights advocates to lament U.S. inaction:

> With all due respect, the attitude that the United States takes toward a repressive regime in, say, Central America, can have far more impact upon the lives of people

---

forces'" and hinting that an international war crimes tribunal might be convened). However, many suspected that the strategic interest and oil interests were what determined the extent of American involvement. *See, e.g.*, Alan Garr, *It's Not Worth Dying for 59–Cents-a-Litre Gas*, OTTOWA CITIZEN, Nov. 13, 1990, *available in* 1990 WL 6524165 (discussing U.S. history of cooperation with Iraq and doubting expressed humanitarian motives); Colman McCarthy, Editorial, *Ready to Kill So We Can Waste More Oil*, THE SEATTLE TIMES, Sept. 7, 1990, *available in* 1990 WL 3171403 (arguing the Gulf War is intended to "assure [U.S.] wasteful, self-indulgent way of life"). The United States' later inaction in face of Iraq's lethal quashing of the subsequent Shiite and Kurdish rebellions convinced many more that that was indeed the case. *See, e.g.*, Donald Kaul, *Kurds' Sin is not Controlling Oil*, DES MOINES REG., Apr. 12, 1991, *available in* 1991 WL 4615976 ("The former Butcher of Baghdad is dicing his opposition, women and children first, and we are standing by, like L.A. cops at a lynching."); *Were the Cynics Right? Was it all for Oil?*, ST. PETERSBURG TIMES, Apr. 12, 1991, *available in* 1991 WL 9134147 (collecting letters to the editor); *but see* John Hall, *Bush's Best Option Is Not to Intervene in Iraq's Civil Conflict*, RICHMOND NEWS LEADER, Apr. 4, 1991, *available in* 1991 WL 4748941 (defending decision to honor cease-fire agreement with Iraq).

The U.S. has been a vocal supporter, and financial backer, of the Yugoslav War Crimes Tribunal, which promises to highlight not only the crimes of genocide and ethnic cleansing, but also mass rapes; however, it has been very reluctant to commit troops already stationed in the former Yugoslavia to the task of apprehending indicted war criminals, giving rise to similar criticism. *See* Chris Hedges, *NATO Troops Kill a Serbian Suspect in War Atrocities: Another Man Arrested*, THE N.Y. TIMES, July 11, 1997, at A1 (describing first arrest by NATO forces after 18 months in Bosnia and noting "reluctan[ce]" of commanders to order arrests).

279. Jerome Shestack & Roberta Cohen, *International Human Rights: A Role for the United States*, 14 VA. J. INT'L L. 673, 676 (1974).

280. Thomas Buergenthal, *International Human Rights: The U.S. Policy and Priorities*, 14 VA. J. INT'L L. 611, 619 (1974).

281. Richard B. Lillich, *Human Rights, the National Interest, and U.S. Foreign Policy: Some Preliminary Observations*, 14 VA. J. INT'L L. 591, 593 (1974).

282. *See, e.g.*, Mayer, *supra* note 264; Jerome J. Shestack, *Human Rights in U.S. Foreign Policy: Retrospect and Prospect*, 28 VA. J. INT'L L. 907, 909 (1988) ("History underscores the fragility of the human rights role in U.S. foreign policy.").

283. Tom J. Farer, *United States Foreign Policy and the Protection of Human Rights: Observations and Proposals*, 14 VA. J. INT'L L. 623, 623 (1974); *see also* HUMAN RIGHTS WATCH, WORLD REPORT 1997 xii (1997) ("Although few governments dared to jettison human rights explicitly, the major powers settled far too often in 1996 for the facade of a human rights policy rather than a genuine effort to promote human rights.").

living under that regime than, for example, numerous petitions filed with the United Nations or the Inter-American Commission on Human Rights.[284]

U.S. explicit or tacit approval and support of violative state action has undoubtedly encouraged further violations and cost the United States opportunities to further influence the development and interpretation of important human rights norms.[285]

Understanding the U.S. Record—Treaties

Many attribute inconsistencies in American foreign policy to pure political self-interest, a calculated privileging of its interest in preserving its sovereignty and its role as a military and economic superpower. However, U.S. policy towards human rights and gender equality is also limited by principled domestic interests relating to core constitutional doctrines, including federalism, the nature of rights, and key democratic principles, that are at stake.[286]

American Governance and International Human Rights

Under the American system, it is the ratification of a treaty which has significance. Once a treaty is ratified by the Senate, it is part of federal law:

> Under the Constitution, duly-ratified treaties are the supreme law of the land, equal with enacted federal statutes. Accordingly, they displace previously adopted federal law to the extent of any inconsistency.[287]

There are limits to the domestic reach of any treaty. In order to have domestic impact, a treaty must be self-executing; otherwise it has no domestic power unless legislation is enacted to give import to its terms.[288] Even if self-executing, the Constitution places the treaties at the same level as federal legislation, and therefore, like any federal leg-

---

284. RICHARD B. LILLICH ET AL., INTERNATIONAL HUMAN RIGHTS 1029 (3d ed. 1995).

285. "[T]he United States has not exactly been a pillar of the church in the formal acceptance of . . . international consensus. Instead, it has played the role of a flying buttress supporting it from the outside." Hannum, *supra* note 249, at 21 (*citing* Louis Henkin).

286. This is an introduction to a topic covered more thoroughly in a variety of sources, including Mayer, *supra* note 264, and in KAUFMAN, *supra* note 257.

287. INITIAL REPORT OF THE UNITED STATES OF AMERICA TO THE U.N. HUMAN RIGHTS COMMITTEE UNDER THE INTERNATIONAL COVENANT ON CIVIL AND POLITICAL RIGHTS 27 (July, 1994) [hereinafter "U.S. REPORT"]. This document was prepared by the United States Department of State and as such, it is a useful statement of American views on the status of international human rights norms in the United States. For criticisms of the U.S. Report, including criticisms of the government's description of progress on sex discrimination, *see* HUMAN RIGHTS WATCH & AMERICAN CIVIL LIBERTIES UNION, HUMAN RIGHTS VIOLATIONS IN THE UNITED STATES (1993).

288. *See* People of Saipan v. United States Dept. of Interior, 502 F.2d 90 (9th Cir. 1974) (holding that whether treaty is self executing is determined on a case-by-case basis considering, among other factors, the purposes of the treaty, objectives of its creators, and the existence of domestic procedures).

289. *See* Rainey v. United States, 232 U.S. 310, 316 (1914) ("it is well settled that when a treaty is inconsistent with a subsequent act of Congress, the latter will prevail") (citing cases); *see also* RESTATEMENT (THIRD) OF THE FOREIGN RELATIONS LAW OF THE UNITED STATES § 115 (1987).

islation, treaty obligations may be superseded by a subsequent enactment.[289] The United States has made its ratification to certain human rights treaties subject to the reservation and understanding that they are not self-executing, thereby foreclosing reliance on treaty provisions under domestic law absent congressional action.[290] The understandings also state the government's view that any obligations assumed under these treaties comport with current federal constitutional doctrine. There is no question that the U.S. has sought to "pretend[] to assume international obligations [when] in fact [it] is undertaking nothing."[291]

The Senate has failed to ratify or has ratified with limitations because of certain domestic concerns about American governance which are particularly acute in connection with international human rights treaties. The Constitution provides that federal legislation, in the ordinary course, is to be enacted by both houses of Congress and signed by the President; however, the ratification of a treaty—a document drafted outside of U.S. legislative houses, with only limited participation by the U.S.—requires action by only the executive and the Senate. Yet treaties have the same status as other federal legislation. The fear, then, is that enacting treaties—particularly human rights treaties which have the potential of drastically altering or expanding the American conceptualization of rights—is anti-democratic. To many, "[t]he question . . . is whether the United States can, under its Constitution, and whether it should, having regard to fundamental principles, become a party to international legislation of this character which deals with its domestic jurisdiction."[292] One scholar has criticized these objections on the basis that:

> [T]he Constitution provides expressly for lawmaking by treaty: treaties are declared to be the supreme law of the land. The framers intended that a treaty should become law ipso facto. . . . In effect, lawmaking by treaty was to be an alternative to legislation by Congress.[293]

While this is true as a matter of law, the fundamental precept of human rights treaties—that states are bound to an international standard of care for the treatment of their own citizens—is a modern concept, outside of the expectations of the founders and thus

---

290. Examples include the ratification of the ICCPR and the Convention for the Elimination of Racial Discrimination. To date, no specific implementing legislation has been enacted, although legislation affecting these subjects has been passed.

291. Henkin, *Bricker, supra* note 267, at 344. The effect of reservations of this nature is unclear. *See* note 267 *supra* and accompanying text. The American reservations are domestic in character, and arguably do not foreclose international enforcement of any superseded obligation by other parties to the treaty. However, it is not certain by what method a violation could be vindicated on the international level, because the United States has limited the jurisdiction of the International Court of Justice with respect to some of the treaties it has ratified. *See, e.g.,* U.S. Reservations and Understandings to the Genocide Convention, Nov. 25, 1988, 28 I.L.M. 782 (1989) ("before any dispute to which the United States is a party may be submitted to the jurisdiction of the International Court of Justice . . . the specific consent of the United States is required in each case").

292. KAUFMAN, *supra* note 257, at 138–39 (quoting Senate testimony of the American Bar Association regarding ratification of the Convention Concerning Forced Labor in 1967).

293. Henkin, *Bricker, supra* note 267, at 346.

outside of their intent. Many therefore believe that treaties which change domestic law in such a fundamental manner are an impermissible circumvention of the proper legislative process, notwithstanding compliance with constitutional ratification procedures.

Another argument advanced is that, because the U.S. already provides many of the rights guaranteed in various human rights treaties, it has no need to ratify those instruments which would allow outside intervention in the domestic affairs of the U.S. This argument has persisted since the very beginning of the human rights movement:

> Peoples who do not know the meaning of freedoms are to be metamorphosed into judges of the freedoms of others. . . . To bring some people to a higher standard, those far above those standards, under the guise of precarious sacrifice to the common good, are to accept the mediocrity of the average.[294]

> I don't think the peoples of the earth are in any position where they can tell this great people on morals, politics and religion, how they should live. I still feel that we are ahead of them in that respect. . . .[295]

> . . . [W]e regard our system as a superior protection of human rights than any other system in the world.[296]

Ultimately these claims, stripped to their essentials, are simply arguments against changing American traditions. One response to this parochialism is to argue that ratification of these treaties will do little to change American domestic life.[297] That position is somewhat disingenuous, because "[t]he purpose of adhering to a treaty is to

---

294. KAUFMAN, *supra* note 257, at 43 (*quoting* Senate testimony of the American Bar Association regarding ratification of the Genocide Convention in 1950).

295. *Id*. at 45 (*quoting* statement of Senator Walter George regarding ratification of the Genocide Convention in 1950).

296. *Id*. at 184 (*quoting* statement of North Carolina Senator Jesse Helms regarding ratification of the Genocide Convention in 1985). Ironically, the voting record of Jesse Helms is singularly notable for acting to *restrict* the rights of American minorities. "Except for Jesse Helms, all current Republican U.S. senators voted in 1982 to extend [legislation protecting the access of minority populations to the political process]." DAVID BOSITIS, THE CONGRESSIONAL BLACK CAUCUS IN THE 103RD CONGRESS 55 (1994). Sen. Helms' campaigns have consistently played on the anti-black, anti-gay fears of his southern conservative constituency. *See* KATHLEEN HALL JAMIESON, DIRTY POLITICS: DECEPTION, DISTRACTION AND DEMOCRACY 83, 93–100 (1992) (describing campaigns and impact); *see generally* PAUL LUEBKE, TAR HEEL POLITICS: MYTHS AND REALITIES 26 (1990) (noting Helms had defended racial segregation early in his career, and campaigned on the promise "to say no to busing and other liberal racial reforms").

297. *See, e.g., Convention on the Elimination of All Forms of Discrimination Against Women: Hearings Before the Comm. On Foreign Relations of the United States Senate*, 103d Cong., 2d Sess. 65 (1994) ("The spirit and provisions of the Convention are similar to U.S. constitutional and statutory law. [We] recognize[] there may be some questions which will be raised before the United States Senate. Nevertheless [we do] not believe any of these problematic provisions cause practical problems.") (Statement of Bernard Hamilton, Director, Minority Rights Group); *cf. id.* at 38 ("[We] believe that the reservations, understandings and declarations proposed . . . are unnecessary and undesireable . . .") (statement of Gay McDougall, Exec. Director of the Int'l Human Rights Law Group).

undertake obligations . . . to adhere to a common international standard."[298] The internalization of modern international standards is an inevitable—and beneficial—consequence of furthering the cause of human rights for all. However addressed, these sentiments cannot be discounted as a significant philosophical and emotional bar to U.S. participation in international agreements regarding human rights.

Federalism and International Human Rights

Respect for the layered system of government, which reserves certain powers to the federal and state governments, is also offered as an explanation for American reluctance to whole heartedly participate in international conventions on human rights. The power to set national policy, including the power to set foreign policy and ratify treaties, is shared by the president and Congress. However, many other aspects of governance are reserved, in whole or in part, to the discretion of the state and local governments. Treaties, as federal law:

> also prevail over inconsistent state and local law. Where they touch on matters previously within the purview of state and local government . . . they may also serve to "federalize" the issue, thus affecting the allocation of authority between the states and the central government.[299]

Many senators are resistant to "federalizing" issues previously reserved to the states, and are particularly reluctant where the standards to be applied are not those enacted through typical means of judging national consensus—that is, through the normal federal legislative process—but rather through the ratification process; it can be done, but only at great political cost.[300] Among the areas left to state discretion are many of the issues which have been previously identified as particularly relevant to gender equality: family law, education, and most criminal laws relevant to violence against women, including assault, rape, and murder. Treaties which would "federalize"—indeed, internationalize—these issues are regarded with particular concern.[301]

Civil Rights and Human Rights

Under American jurisprudence, where a treaty provision conflicts with an existing constitutional norm, that provision is invalid.[302] Many provisions of contempo-

---

298. Louis Henkin, *The Covenant on Civil and Political Rights, in* U.S. RATIFICATION OF THE HUMAN RIGHTS TREATIES: WITH OR WITHOUT RESERVATIONS? 22 (Richard Lillich ed., 1981).

299. U.S. REPORT, *supra* note 287, at 27.

300. In *Missouri v. Holland*, 252 U.S. 416 (1920), for example, the state of Missouri strenuously objected to the operation of a duly ratified treaty which sought to limit the state's authority to issue hunting permits; a prior federal statute with the same provisions had been found an invalid usurpation of state powers. The Supreme Court upheld the treaty, holding that the president and Senate had the power to do that which Congress could not—limit the power of states over matters of local concern. *See id.*

301. *See* KAUFMAN, *supra* note 257, at 111–12, 129–32, 185–86.

302. Missouri v. Holland, 252 U.S. at 432 ("a treaty cannot be valid if it infringes the Constitution"); *see also* RESTATEMENT (THIRD) OF THE FOREIGN RELATIONS LAW OF THE UNITED STATES § 111 (1987).

rary human rights treaties conflict with provisions of the U.S. Constitution; especially problematic are those provisions which limit the right to free speech or infringe on associational or religious rights as those rights have been interpreted under U.S. law.[303] Because those provisions are presumptively invalid under domestic law, the question is raised as to whether it is appropriate for the United States to ratify treaties which will later be judged to have no domestic effect (or to make reservations limiting the domestic effect of conflicting provisions).[304]

Another concern arises from the many other provisions that do not conflict with U.S. constitutional provisions, but rather add to or expand existing rights. As discussed in the first section, the Constitution provides that it may only be amended through an extraordinarily high level of participation of the populace; indeed, the agreement of a supermajority of the states is required. Some argue that any significant expansion of constitutionally guaranteed rights through the promulgation of a treaty offends the democratic ideals of this ratification process;[305] that the treaty provisions might expand certain civil and political rights, or otherwise provide for a more inclusive society, is to some little comfort. "'It would be like an equal rights amendment enforced by the United Nations[.] . . . I don't believe in giving any power over U.S. laws to a U.N. body.'"[306]

In sum, these combined concerns render the American government (and a large segment of the American populace) hesitant to commit the U.S. to international obligations on human rights.

---

303. For example, the U.S. reservations to the ICCPR identified Article 20, which provides that war propaganda and advocacy of "national, racial, or religious hatred" which incites "discrimination, hostility or violence" be outlawed, ICCPR at art. 20, as potentially conflicting with free speech rights under the Constitution. *See* 138 Cong. Rec. S4781 § I(1) (1991); *see also* KAUFMAN, *supra* note 257, at 164–70, 184–85 (discussing proposed reservations).

304. This stems in part from the difference between so-called first-generation rights, which include the political rights and liberty interests at the heart of the American Constitution, and second- and third-generation economic, social, cultural, and group rights, which at times conflict with first-generation rights, as those rights are interpreted.

305. While one might argue that federal law often expands on constitutional rights, the federal legislative process is more tolerable in that it involves the participation of both houses. Moreover, as noted earlier, even properly enacted federal laws expanding civil rights are challenged as being beyond the scope of Congress' power.

306. Elizabeth Shogren, *Clinton Speaks Up for Treaty on Women's Rights: President Calls Senate's Failure to Ratify U.N. Anti-Discrimination Pact an Embarrassment*, L.A. TIMES, Dec. 11, 1996, *available in* 1996 WL 12764557 (quoting Phyllis Schlafly with regard to ratification of The Women's Convention); *see also* KAUFMAN, *supra* note 257, at 112 ("Our own Bill of Rights forbids the Congress to change our basic rights but as the Constitution now stands it does not prevent our basic rights from being changed by a treaty . . . . [T]his is the loophole in the Constituion . . . through which the internationalists propose to . . . by treaty law change . . . our American rights.") (quoting American Bar Association report in favor of adopting the Bricker Amendment).

The United States and the Women's Convention

The Convention for the Elimination of All Forms of Discrimination Against Women ("Women's Convention") seeks to eliminate discrimination against women[307] and encourages the equal participation of women in the civil, political, social, economic, and cultural lives of their countries.[308] The Women's Convention was adopted by the U.N. in December of 1979, and entered into force in September of 1981. The U.S. became a signatory to the Women's Convention during the Carter Administration, but the treaty was largely ignored until the Clinton Administration took office in 1993. The Women's Convention, if ratified and applied in accordance with its provisions, would significantly expand the rights of American women, and require that the government take affirmative steps to increase the participation of women in all areas of American society. For that reason, the convention is likely to never be ratified, or to be ratified subject to severely limiting reservations.[309]

Of particular concern to U.S. critics are Articles 3, 5, 6, 7, 8, and 13. Articles 3 and 5 would require the U.S. to take steps to modify the cultural behavior of men and women to combat practices which harm women or limit or discriminate against the participation of women. This implicates the right to freedom of association, as that constitutional right is currently interpreted. For example, there is some concern that the government would be required to interfere with religious practices which subjugate or limit women; those practices are currently tolerated as a component of religious freedom.[310] The reservations submitted to the full Senate thus include a reservation which would preserve "individual privacy and freedom from governmental

---

307. The U.S. "understandings" to the Civil and Political Rights Convention foreclose any reliance on that document as a basis for expanding the rights of women:

> The United States understands distinctions based on race, colour, sex, language, religion, political or other opinion, national or social origin, property, birth or other states—as those terms are used in [the Covenant]—*to be permitted when such distinctions are, at minimum, rationally related to a legitimate government objective.*

138 Cong. Rec. S4781 § II(1) (1991) (emphasis added). The Women's Convention is currently the only treaty under Senate consideration for ratification which would have a substantial impact on gender equality.

308. These goals are described in the Preamble and addressed in Parts I–IV of the convention.

309. *See Issues Relating to the United Nations Convention on the Elimination of All Forms of Discrimination Against Women: Hearing Before the Subcommittee on Terrorism, Narcotics and International Relations of the Committee on Foreign Relations of the Senate*, 100 Cong., 2d Sess. (1988) (testimony on expected domestic impact of the Women's Convention); *Convention on the Elimination of All Forms of Discrimination Against Women: Hearing Before the Committee on Foreign Relations of the Senate*, 103 Cong., 2d. Sess. (1994) [hereinafter *Foreign Relations Hearing*] (same). Other nations have joined the Women's Convention yet sought to limit its impact; indeed, the Women's Convention holds the record for number of states joining with substantive reservations. *See* Dinah Shelton, *The Applicable Law, in* U.S. RATIFICATION, *supra* note 298, at 31.

310. *See* E.E.O.C. v. Catholic University of America, 83 F.3d 455 (D.C. Cir 1996) (the court would not interfere with religious doctrine of school, even if it led to discriminatory employment practice against woman.)

interference in private conduct . . . recognized as among the fundamental values of our free and democratic society."[311] Reservations are also proposed with respect to Articles 6, 7, 8, and 13, which require signatories to take steps to "eliminate discrimination" and to ensure the participation of women in political life.[312] These obligations are also viewed as in conflict with the freedoms of speech and association, and limiting reservations are suggested.[313] Finally, the Women's Convention requires states to "pursue, by all appropriate means and without delay" the inclusion of gender equality in their national constitutions.[314] This provision represents little problem for the United States: the nation recently underwent an extended attempt to ratify the ERA through the means appropriate to amending the Constitution, thereby fulfilling the modest requirments of the text; moreover, the ERA has been reintroduced each year since its defeat (and defeated, through the appropriate measures).

In addition to concerns regarding the impairment of these constitutional interests, additional reservations address political, as distinct from constitutional, concerns. Thus, a reservation had been proposed to prevent any possible interpretation of the Women's Convention as requiring that women serve in military "direct combat" roles, or requiring that women receive certain economic benefits such as paid maternity leave or access to health care, including family planning services.[315]

Since it was first submitted for consideration in 1981, the Senate has held hearings on the impact and importance of the Women's Convention.[316] During the hearings, diverse views concerning the import of the treaty, the role of women in American society and how best to effect gender justice in American society, were expressed. Some witnesses argued against ratification at any cost, claiming the convention will be used "as a weapon against the family, the institution of marriage, and cultural and religious values, and . . . can be turned into a tool for the societal control of women."[317] Given these diverse political and jurisprudential views, it is little wonder that the treaty failed to obtain the requisite support when the ratification was submitted to a vote late in 1996. The failure to approve the Women's Convention has little domestic import; the proposed reservations would render ratification a virtual non-event. Those reservations—as well as the possible inclusion of a reservation limiting the jurisdiction of any international tribunal—would also limit any international impact of U.S. ratification.

If the Women's Convention were ratified without reservation, it would have the type of dramatic effect described by those testifying against it before the Senate. It

---

311. 140 Cong. Rec. S13927–04 (Oct. 3, 1994), *available in* 1994 WL 543936 [hereinafter Senate Recommendation].

312. *Id.*

313. *Id.*

314. The Women's Convention, art. 2(a).

315. *See* Senate Recommendation, *supra* note 311.

316. *See* note 309, *supra*.

317. *Foreign Relations Hearing, supra* note 309, at 18 (Statement of Cecilia Rolyals, President of the National Institute For Womanhood).

would force the United States to re-examine its cultural precepts of womanhood. It would also force the United States to address religious dogma and cultural practices that disadvantage women. While it is doubtful that the government would or could, under the constraints of the Constitution, directly intervene in religious affairs, under the Women's Convention certain preferences and other indirect support could be challenged. For example, under federal law, religious organizations receive certain tax benefits. With respect to religous organizations which discriminate against women in hiring or other practices, those benefits may be subject to challenge under Article 5 of the Women's Convention, which requires states to work to modify social and cultural practices based on stereotyped gender roles. The grant of important economic benefits arguably violates that undertaking, and the termination of those benefits might be an "appropriate measure" as required by Article 5.[318] The adoption of the Women's Convention would force the government to look at those practices of non-state actors which foster gender inequality, and furthermore, to examine and limit the ways in which the government explicitly or tacitly subsidizes or otherwise supports those practices.[319] In that way, the Women's Convention would have a significant impact, even greater than would the adoption of the ERA, if the ERA were interpreted pusuant to current constitutional doctrine.

Understanding the U.S. Record—Foreign Policy

In addition to the opportunities provided by its participation in international conventions and international human rights bodies, the United States government also has opportunities to advance the position of women through its foreign and domestic policy. These opportunities include American foreign aid programs, which are currently statutorily linked to human rights records,[320] vigorous investigation and rigorous reporting of human rights violations in U.S. State Department reports,[321] the use of

---

318. Such a move might be subject to constitutional challange on First Amendment grounds, but the outcome of such a challenge is not clear under current constitutional doctrine. *See* Empl. Div., Dept. Of Human Resources of Oregon v. Smith, 494 U.S. 872 (1990) (holding that attaching penalties to the use of peyote, a hallucinogenic drug, does not interfere with the exercise clause of the First Amendment). Nor would eliminating these benefits be without societal and political cost, particularly because one reason for continuing the tax benefit to religious organizations is the important charitable work they undertake.

319. In this regard, the United States would be doing no more than it often requires other states to do. For example, recent legislation requires U.S. government officials to "use the voice and vote of the United States" to limit aid to any country where FGM is practiced, and where the government "has not taken steps to implement education programs designed to prevent the practice." 22 U.S.C.A. § 262k–2 (West 1997).

320. *See* note 268, *supra*.

321. The most recent reports included the rights of women along with the rights of children and the persecution of refugees as the "major themes" of the report. *See Highlights of State Dept. Activites to Promote the Advancement of Women, available in* <http://www.state.gov/www/global/women/factsheet.html> [hereinafter *Highlights*] (discussing "integrat[ion]" of women's issues); HUMAN RIGHTS WATCH, WORLD REPORT 1996 353 (1996) (noting improved reporting of women's rights issues). While women's rights are often mentioned throughout each country report as necessary, it is significant that women's rights (along with those of children, the disabled, and oth-

trading and other economic opportunities as a coercive tool, and public statements of U.S. officials.[322] Historically, to the extent women's rights are incorporated into American foreign policy, the policy is external and prioritizes rights abuses by other countries against women living overseas—and only as long as it does not interfere with U.S. economic, political and strategic interests.

The current administration has announced a new commitment to integrating the rights of women into its foreign policy. In addition to supporting U.S. participation in the Women's Convention,[323] President Clinton highlighted women's rights as an important foreign policy initiative, acknowledging that "human rights are women's rights, and women's rights are human rights"[324] and promising:

> We cannot advance our ideals and interests unless we focus more attention on the fundamental human fights and basic needs of women and girls. . . . If women can live and work as full and equal partners in any society, then families will flourish . . . communities and nations will thrive. . . . We are putting our efforts to protect and advance women's rights where they belong—in the mainstream of American foreign policy.[325]

First Lady Hillary Rodham Clinton was a strong presence at the U.N.'s World Conference on Women held in Beijing in 1995,[326] and 1996 saw the nomination and eventual confirmation of Madeleine Albright as the first woman Secretary of State, a move which many believed signified a new emphasis on women's rights in American

---

ers subject to discrimination on the basis of race, religion, or social status) appear after discussions of political and associational rights, and rights pertaining to criminal defendants; only issues relating to worker's rights follow those related to women and other minorities. When women's rights are addressed, the reports sometimes include references to local "traditions" which, critics charge, have the "cumulative effect" of "downplay[ing] on 'cultural' grounds the culpability of the governing authorities for abuses against women." Rickard Comments, *supra* note 268 (commenting specifically on 1996 report on Afghanistan).

322. *See Human Rights Hearings, supra* note 270, at 35–41, 179–205 (testimony and statement of Hon. John Shattuck, Ass't Sec., Bureau of Human Rights and Humanitarian Affairs, Dept. of State) (describing U.S. foreign policy regarding the rights of women).

323. *See supra* text accompanying notes 307–19.

324. *President's Remarks on Signing the Proclamation on Human Rights*, Wkly, Compilation of Pres. Docs., Vol. 32, No. 50, Dec. 16, 1996, *availible in* 1996 WL 13336214 [hereinafter *Remarks*] (*quoting* First Lady Hillary Rodham Clinton and activist Julie Su). On that occasion, Human Rights Day, President Clinton directed most of his comments towards the issue of women's rights, and he honored six women who are active in vindicating women's rights both domestically and abroad. *Id.; see also* David L. Marcus, *Women's Issues Gaining Clout in U.S. Foreign Policy Agenda*, Boston Globe, Dec. 10, 1996, *available in* 1996 WL 6889328 (cataloguing administration efforts to "put women's issues on the foreign policy agenda as never before").

325. *Remarks, supra* note 324.

326. Indeed, her participation was controversial in that some thought it inappropriate that this major human rights conference was held in China, a country that has refused to recognize most first-generation civil and political rights. *See* Ann Devroy, *Hillary Clinton to Defer Decision on China Trip Until "Last Minute"*; The Wash. Post, Aug. 16, 1995, *available in* Westlaw, WASH-POST database; Reuters, *Wu Criticizes Hillary Clinton's visit to China*, The Wash. Post, Aug. 27, 1995, *available in* Westlaw, WASHPOST database.

foreign policy.[327] It may be too early to assess the extent to which these recent initiatives will "actively integrate [women's rights] into the foreign policy of the United States,"[328] or whether the U.S. will continue to make "only small steps toward integrating concern for women's human rights into its relations with abusive governments."[329] In the years since the government began to highlight international women's rights, it has not consistently matched its foreign and domestic policy to its stated goal of advancing women's rights.

On the foreign policy side, one example of this inconsistency is the government's early embrace of the revolutionary government in Afghanistan. The extremist group Taliban, on the same day that it captured control of the capital of Afghanistan in September of 1996, announced stringent new limitations on women and girls under their control: women were no longer permitted to work, and had to conform to strict dress codes; girls were no longer to report to school.[330] The United States had long been hoping for a resolution of the civil war in Afghanistan in order to restore stability to a region of strategic importance, and in the hopes that a new regime would exert control over Afghanistan's participation in the world drug trade. Thus, although the State Department quickly acknowledged that "[h]uman rights in Afghanistan, and particularly the status of women [is] a major concern," that concern was undermined by U.S. plans to meet with Taliban notwithstanding Taliban's abuse of women.[331] At no time did it appear that the American concern was truly focused on the harm to women. The State Department stated with respect to restrictions on women:

---

327. *See, e.g.*, Marcus, *supra* note 324 ("Albright's arrival as secretary of state is likely to give even more prominence to [a variety of women's issues"); Ellen Goodman, *With Albright in Power, The World May Look Different*, ALBANY TIMES UNION, Dec. 13, 1996, *available in* 1996 WL 12044091 (noting Albright's gender "may broaden the current outlook. . . . [W]hen she looks down the list of international woes—as far down as sexual slavery or child labor or genital mutilation—new priorities may rise."). It should be noted that in her capacity as U.S. delegate to the U.N. Commission on Human Rights, former U.S. Representative and past Vice-Presidential candidate, Ambassador Geraldine Ferraro, has also spoken "strongly in defense of women's rights as human rights." HUMAN RIGHTS WATCH, WORLD REPORT 1997 347 (1997).

328. Comments of Sec. of State Madeleine Albright, *quoted in Highlights, supra* note 321.

329. HUMAN RIGHTS WATCH, WORLD REPORT 1996 353 (1996).

330. *See U.S. Dept. of State Afghanistan Country Report on Human Rights Practices for 1996*, Jan. 30, 1997, § 5, <http://www.usis.usemb.se/human/AFGHANIS.htm> (describing restrictions in Taliban-controlled areas and increased incidence of violence against women throughout Afghanistan). The incidence of violence against women related to Taliban-mandated restrictions has escalated since the Taliban takeover. Women have reportedly been beaten by Taliban militiamen for inappropriate dress under Taliban strictures. *Id.* In March, Taliban religious authorities reportedly stoned a woman to death for traveling with a male who was not her relative. *See Woman Executed by Stoning*, THE FRESNO BEE, Mar. 30, 1997, *available in* 1997 WL 3895344. The woman was apparently attempting to leave the country. *Id.*

331. Regular State Department News Briefing, Nicholas Burns, U.S. State Department Spokesman, NBC Prof. Transcripts, Oct. 7, 1996, 1996 WL 11748750 at *26 [hereinafter State Dept. Briefing] (discussing planned meeting between State Department and Taliban representatives).

. . . [The restrictions] threaten to generate international isolation which would deny Afghanistan the international assistance it so badly needs. . . .[332]

. . . [W]omen are important in any economy . . . Afghanistan is no exception to that. You can't run an economy and take women out of it and be successful. . . .[333]

Although later in that same news briefing the State Department representative expressed concern for "fundamental" women's rights,[334] other statements and the government's quiet concern for a reported American $4 billion oil deal[335] led the government to continue to meet with Taliban officials. Yet, as early as 1994, Taliban's oppression of women was well documented and well known to the United States.[336]

Nearly five months after the Taliban takeover of the capital, the State Department finally admitted that, even if the group "were to take over all of the country . . . I don't *think* we would recognize them."[337] At various points the State Department explained its strategy as one of "constructive engagement;"[338] however, in light of the prior revealing statements, it is difficult to believe that a commitment to advance the rights of Afghanistan women was the sole, or even a contributing, reason behind the government's early embrace of the Taliban revolutionaries.[339] Moreover, a strategy of constructive engagement would appear to be undermined by such persistent and eager contact.

---

332. *Id.*

333. *Id.* at *27.

334. *Id.* at *29.

335. *See* Randal Ashley, *Focus on Afghanistan*, ATLANTA J. & CONST., Oct. 20, 1996, *available in* 1996 WL 8237372 (noting oil deal and that the project is not mentioned at briefings by the State Department); *see also* Charles Clover, Oil Companies Battle for Pipeline Rights, THE FINANCIAL TIMES, Apr. 4, 1997, *available in* 1997 WL 3784425 (noting strategic importance for proposed pipeline across Afghanistan, which would bypass Iran).

336. In the *U.S. Dept. of State Afghanistan Country Report on Human Rights Practices for 1995* (March 1996), the State Department reported to Congress that in every territory over which Taliban took control, "the movement . . . banned female employment and female school attendance" and enforced "strict dress codes," despite calls on the movement by U.N. agencies and officials to respect the rights of women. *Id.* at § 5. Indeed, the report noted that women had enjoyed greater rights under the Soviet Communist regime of the 1980s. *Id.; see also U.S. Dept. of State Afghanistan Country Report on Human Rights Practices for 1993* 1318 (Feb. 1994) ("The Communist regime in the 1980's officially sanctioned a wider public role for women, whose status improved, particularly in urban areas").

337. *Afghanistan's Talibans: Rights Issue May Block Deal*, DOW JONES NEWS SERVICE, Feb. 26, 1997 *available in* WL, DJNS (quoting an unidentified State Department official) (emphasis added).

338. *See, e.g., U.S. Wants Contacts with New Taliban Government in Afghanistan*, DOW JONES NEWS SERVICE, Oct. 8, 1996, *available in* WL, DJNS (*quoting* State Department spokesman Nicholas Burns):

If we hope to influence them, if we and the international community . . . hope to have any kind of effect on the Taliban's leadership . . . on its treatment of its own population . . . then we're going to have to have contact. *Id.*

339. Indeed, one critic found the government's diplomatic efforts "surprising" in light of the government's "bizarre mores of postmodern feminism." John Jennings, *Op-Ed*, THE WASH. TIMES, Oct. 25, 1996, at A23.

Ultimately, this equivocal reaction did little to advance women's rights, and instead underscored the U.S. view of women's rights as a secondary concern. Women's rights will be pursued as an American foreign policy objective only when there are no other important interests at stake:

> [Reporter]: . . . have you in any way thought better of this plan to send a diplomat to Kabul? Or at least put it on the back burner or delayed it perhaps because of this negative reporting, this thing about women's rights?
>
> [State Dept. Spokesman]: You know, our intention is to serve our national interests here. And we do have national interests in Afghanistan, so therefore . . . this argues for a continuous contact with the Taliban and others. We may not like everything that they're doing. We don't like some of what they're doing. But that doesn't mean that we should just cut them off from all contacts with the United States. We will seek contacts with them. We'll maintain contacts wherever we can have them—inside or outside of Afghanistan. That just is prudent. It's good sense. And it's the best way forward for the United States.[340]

As one women's rights advocate noted, "We're still seeing big gaps between what they say and what comes out in practice."[341] Yet the State Department is inordinately proud of its response to the upheavals in Afghanistan, and it considers itself a "leader" in defending the rights of Afghanistan's women.[342]

U.S. foreign policy with regard to women is also implicated in the application of U.S. domestic immigration policy, which may clash with U.S. recognition of human rights abuses abroad.[343] The State Department has identified "the persecution of refugees and asylum seekers" as yet another "key priorit[y] for the United States in its human rights efforts around the world."[344] A recent case which promises a positive change in American immigration policy is the case of Fauziya Kasinga,[345] a young

---

340. State Dept. Briefing, *supra* note 331, 1996 WL 11748750 at *28.

341. Comments of Regan Ralph of Human Rights Watch, *as quoted* in Marcus, *supra* note 324; *see also* Comments of Rep. Pat Schroeder, *id.* ("We're always claiming that we're changing, and we talk the talk, but we don't walk the walk."). For extensive criticisms of the U.S. recent record on women's rights, as well as highlights of certain acheivements, *see* HUMAN RIGHTS WATCH, WORLD REPORT 1997 347–49 (1997).

342. *See Highlights, supra* note 321 (with regard to Taliban abuses against women: "The State Department denounced these actions in several public statements and in contacts with Taliban representatives. Today the Department continues to take the lead in raising these issues in international fora . . .").

343. Unfortunately this is not a new problem, nor is it one unique to the United States: the Convention Relating to the Status of Regugees, 606 U.N.T.S. 267 (Jan. 31, 1967), and its subsequent protocols were a response to the widespread rejection of Jewish refugees fleeing the Holocaust. *See generally* HENRY FEINGOLD, THE POLITICS OF RESCUE: THE ROOSEVELT ADMINISTRATION AND THE HOLOCAUST 1938–1945 (1970) (describing the rejection of Jewish refugees during the Nazi build-up and World War II).

344. *Press Briefing: 1996 Country Reports on Human Rights Practices*, Jan. 30, 1997 <http://secretary.state.gov/www/statements/970130.html> (Comments of Under Secretary for Global Affairs Timothy Wirth).

345. Ms. Kasinga's story was reported in Robert L. Jackson, *Board to Hear Togo Woman's Asylum Appeal*, L.A. TIMES, Apr. 30, 1996, 1996 WL 5264819. *See also* Margo L. Ely, *A Journey*

woman from Togo, who sought asylum as a refugee from the practice of female genital mutilation ("FGM").[346] Pursuant to the discretion permitted U.S. immigration screening agents, upon her arrival in December of 1994 she was incarcerated in a criminal prison facility pending resolution of her asylum application.[347] The administrator hearing her petition denied the application on the grounds that Ms. Kasinga's story was unbelievable; although he found nothing suspicious or untruthful about her demeanor, he found her story lacked "'rationality,' 'persuasiveness,' and 'consistency.'"[348] What is troubling is that the application was opposed by the immigration service and denied by the immigration judge, even though the supposedly "unpersuasive" record included documentation describing the procedure. State Department reports on Togo describe the incidence of FGM and general human rights abuses, and an internal directive of the immigration service recognizes that "rape . . . , sexual abuse and domestic violence, infanticide and genital mutilation are forms of mistreatment primarily directed at girls and women and they may serve as evidence of past persecution" under the immigration code.[349] Moreover, the issue is one of domes-

---

Ends With Precedent-Setting Asylum Ruling, CHI. DAILY L. BULL, Aug. 12, 1996, vol. 142, no. 158; Cindy Shiner, *Persecution by Circumcision; Woman Who Fled Togo Convinced U.S. Court but Not Town Elders*, THE WASH. POST, July 3, 1996, *available in* 1996 WL 10719233.

346. "Female genital mutilation" is defined by Congress as "the removal or infibulation (or both) of the whole or part of the clitoris, the labia minora, or labia majora." 8 U.S.C.A. § 1374(c). The term "female genital mutilation" is problematic to some who believe it embodies a cultural judgement of the procedure. *See* L. Amede Obiora, *Bridges and Barricades: Rethinking Polemics and Intransigence in the Campaign Against Female Circumcision*, 47 CASE W. RES. L. REV. 275, 289–90 (1997) (this article is commented on extensively, and largely sympathetically, in a colloquium contained in that volume). On the other hand, the widely used alternative, "female circumcision," is considered objectionable to others because it suggests that this practice is similar to the cosmetic procedure undergone by men, when some forms of the practice are far more invasive and pose a serious health risk to women. *See* Bernadette Passade Cisse, *International Law Sources Applicable to Female Genital Mutilation: A Guide to Adjudicators of Refugee Claims Based on a Fear of Female Genital Mutilation*, 35 COLUM. J. TRANSNAT'L L. 429, 430–35 & n.2 (1997) (describing health risks and decision to use "FGM"); Layli Miller Bashir, *Female Genital Mutilation in the United States: An Examination of Criminal and Asylum Law*, 4 J. GENDER & L. 415, 415–24 (1997) (same).

At this time, the author has no need to debate appropriate terminology. Congress' definition of FGM excludes some of the more benign practices that advocates such as Amede Obiora would argue are not "mutilation." Moreover, because Ms. Kasinga's asylum request identified the practice as unwanted mutilation (and presumably other asylum requests will similarly characterize the practice), her acceptance of Congress' terminology is sufficient for the purposes of this analysis.

347. The United States immigration laws concerning asylum claims can be found at 8 U.S.C.A. § 1101 (West 1997).

348. In re Kasinga, 35 I.L.M. 1145 (B.I.A. June 13, 1996) (*quoting* the decision of the immigration judge).

349. *Id.* (*quoting* Coven, U.S. DEP'T OF JUSTICE, CONSIDERATIONS FOR ASYLUM OFFICERS ADJUDICATING CLAIMS FROM WOMEN (1995) [hereinafter Coven]). For a full discussion of the evidentiary issues and the legal ramifications of Ms. Kasinga's case, *see* Linda Malone & Gillian Wood, *International Decisions*, 91 AM. J. INT'L L. 121, 140–47 (1997). For a discussion of international theories which support the incorporation of violence against women into domestice asylum law, *see* Cisse, *supra* note 346; Pamela Goldberg, *Anyplace But Here: Asylum in the United States for*

tic as well as international impact: congressional hearings have been held on FGM as practiced abroad and, increasingly, in immigrant populations in the U.S.[350]

Ms. Kasinga's story has a happy ending: after she was injured in a prison riot, the national media focused considerable attention on her case and on the lawyers assisting her in her appeal of her asylum request. She was released pending decision on the appeal, and the appeals board granted her asylum petition. The media attention surrounding the case brought notice to the many circumstances where gender-related bias or violence should be taken into account, but are not. And the guidelines announced by the executive branch promise a greater sensitivity to gender issues in asylum cases.[351] The triumph of this one case is limited; the appeals board cautiously linked its decision to the specific factual circumstances of Ms. Kasinga's case, and thereby limited the breadth of its impact.[352]

Yet it is the action of Congress that is most troubling. At the same time that it enacted legislation criminalizing FGM in the U.S. and seeking to encourage foreign governments to act to end the practice abroad,[353] anti-immigration forces in Congress worked to alter the appeals process to permit summary exclusion of persons seeking asylum.[354] As noted by one senator who objected to these provisions, Fauziya Kasinga would have been returned to Togo if those provisions had been in effect when her claim was first heard.[355] The gap between American foreign policy, which vigorously

---

Women Fleeing Intimate Violence, 26 CORNELL INT'L L.J. 565 (1993); Nancy Kelly, *Gender-Related Persecution: Assuring the Asylum Claims of Women*, 26 CORNELL INT'L L.J. 625 (1993).

350. *See, e.g., Human Rights Hearings, supra* note 270, at 22–27, 159–68 (testimony and statement of Nahid Toubia, M.D., discussing FGM and calling on Congress to act to stop the practice both abroad and in the U.S.).

351. *See* Coven, *supra* note 349; *but see* Malone, *supra* note 349, at 146 (noting "the door has been opened by the Sevice's position and the Board's decision" but that as a practical matter most of those fleeing FGM will not benefit).

352. These facts include the fact that her husband was a "well-known individual" and a "friend of the police in Togo," her family's belief that she should undergo the procedure, the small size of Togo, and the overall culture of tolerance of human rights abuses in the country. *See* In re Kasinga I.L.M. 1145 (1996).

353. U.S. Secretary of State Madeleine Albright, a forceful and adept diplomat, has by her presence alone advanced women's rights. *See, e.g.*, Tyler Marshall, *Albright Blisters Balkan Leaders Diplomacy: In Strikingly Unvarnished Language, Secretary of State Tells Croat, Serb Presidents to Cooperate on Peace Accords or Pay Price*, L.A. TIMES, June, 1, 1997, A1, *available in* 1997 WL 2216166. She has also continued to encourage greater inclusion of women in positions of power, both here and abroad. *See, e.g.*, George Gedda, *Albright Champions Women's Rights Issue Emerges as Priority in Foreign Policy*, L.A. DAILY NEWS, Apr. 27, 1997, *available in* 1997 WL 4040777 (noting Sec. Albright's disappointment that in her cabinet meetings with 26 foreign presidents and cabinet ministers, she was the only woman present); 18 U.S.C.A. § 116 (criminalizing female genital mutilation in the U.S.); 22 U.S.C.A. § 262k–2 (linking foreign aid to efforts to stop female genital mutilation).

354. *See* Illegal Immigration Reform and Immigrant Responsibility Act of 1996, Pub. L. No. 104–208 (Sept. 30, 1996).

355. *See Statement of Senator Patrick Leahy on the Summary Exclusion and Asylum Provisions of the Immigration Conference Report*, GOV'T PRESS RELEASES, Sept. 25, 1996, *available in* 1996 WL 11125366.

protests abusive practices against women, and American domestic policy, which returns women fleeing the practice (or other types of abuse) to the dangerous situations, is a serious gap and, unfortunately, one which undermines the stated commitment to vindicate women's rights.

CONCLUSION

As the preceding discussion demonstrates, American constitutional law is locked in the past. There is a mythic reverence that many Americans afford the Constitution and related American traditions and social customs. There is also a compelling intellectual basis for the hesitance some have towards altering these legal and social customs through international caveat: imposing international norms on the populace through the application of the treaty process, arguably one of the less democratic methods for creating federal law under our Constitution, doesn't comport with the participatory spirit of the Constitution. Many also have a significant emotional attachment to the Constitution; for some our national identity is based on the belief that the framers of the Constitution did something enlightened and wonderful when they adopted the Constitution—a document that has endured for over 200 years, requiring only a few minor changes to reflect updated notions of racial and gender equality. Thus, many instinctively reject the idea that the American rights regime could or should be altered to meet developing international expectations. As Ann Mayer put it:

> In U.S. culture the Constitution is viewed as a kind of sacred law and the guarantor of Americans' liberties. It is revered not only as the supreme law of the land, but a law that is unquestionably superior to all other laws, including conflicting principles of international law.[356]

In sum, that which we would recognize as parochialism in others[357] to us seems natural, logical, and inevitable. However, in our quest for social justice generally, and with specific regard to the human rights of women, this reliance on traditional notions of domestic norms denies women the greater protections afforded by international standards.

Three implications of this reverence for our constitutionally tolerated, second-class status of women have been identified. Domestic constitutional doctrine, which has slowly been incorporating gender equality into the equal protection clause, must undergo further change in order to achieve gender equality; the United States' failure to ratify, without reservations, key human rights agreements including the Women's Convention, has had a deleterious effect on international human rights discourse, and has hindered domestic efforts at gender equality; American foreign policy has sent mixed messages about the importance of protecting the rights of women.[358]

---

356. Mayer, *supra* note 264, at 728. Moreover, the U.S. Constitution "the oldest constitution in the world that is still in force" is the model used for "shaping constitutionalism abroad." *Id.*

357. For example, the efforts to influence other nations to ban the practice of FGM, *see* note 353 *supra*, is made in spite of similar calls to custom and domestic legal and political realities.

358. Marcella David, author of this chapter, acknowledges: "I tend to have less invested in the

The United States must not sit on the sidelines of the debate over the development of international human rights. Rather, it should make the following commitments to the development of human rights. First, the United States should ratify the languishing human rights treaties, including the Women's Convention, with limited reservations that commit the United States to continued progress towards meeting international standards. For example, in ratifying the ICCPR, instead of reserving the right to "impose capital punishment" pursuant to "existing or future law permitting the imposition of capital punishment," the U.S. should have ratified subject to a provision limiting capital punishment to that *currently* imposed under existing law. Similarly, in the case of the Women's Convention, in place of one proposed reservation refusing to "accept any obligation . . . to enact legislation or to take any other action with respect to private conduct except as mandated by the Constitution and Laws of the United States,"[359] the United States should undertake to "promote gender equality through public information campaigns which are consistent with *current* constitutional limitations." The goal should be to advance the development of human rights in the United States vis-a-vis the international standards rather than to enshrine the American view, past, present, and future, thereby ensuring the development of a separate American view of human rights.

Second, the United States should strive for consistency in its foreign and domestic policy. This will require more than a commitment on the part of the United States to be "ideologically neutral."[360] A vast improvement would result from American evenhandedness with regard to the human rights records of all states, whether allies or not. In taking a more politically neutral, rights aggressive stance, the United States need only be a bit more cautious, and a bit more honest. Instead of immediate conciliation efforts with the revolutionary government in Afghanistan, the United States should have adopted a calculated "wait-and-see" posture, forcing Taliban to undertake and act upon certain human rights commitments in order to "earn" the most minimal diplomatic overtures. Once it became clear that the early meetings were ill-advised, the United States should have explicitly acknowledged the error, and emphasized that the repression of women was so serious as to automatically bar American acceptance of the Taliban regime.

---

constitutional mystique than some; after all, I am a woman working in a field once closed to women; I am the blending of 'inferior' negro, 'uncivilized' Indian, and caucasion blood. As a black woman, if I had been born in the last century I would be chattel twice over—as intended by the Constitution. Thus, like the late Justice Thurgood Marshall, I have less invested in maintaining the legal and social customs of our nation's founding; indeed, I would be happy to impose many of the internationally recognized human rights norms on the United States, especially those relating to gender and racial equality, corporal punishment, and some, if not all, of those relating to economic and social equality. This is notwithstanding the real risk that American society might change in ways not completely to my liking: access to reproductive services might be curtailed, the quest for economic justice might increase my tax liability, and the quest for environmental justice would undoubtedly disrupt my lifestyle. I fully acknowledge the same social and cultural differences which make it so difficult for other countries to accept that certain international human rights norms are at work in the American populace, and in my own appraisal of this subject."

359. Senate Recommendation, *supra* note 311.

360. Buergenthal, *Agenda, supra* note 247, at 847.

A commitment to international human rights will also require the United States to conform its domestic policies to its international policies. Having denounced FGM as "a severe harm to physical and psychological health of women,"[361] the United States should amend its immigration laws to include FGM as a basis for asylum.[362] The significance of that commitment will not only be felt on the international level, but it will also advance our domestic understanding of problems of gender equality.

Finally, the United States should undertake a comprehensive public information campaign educating the public about international human rights. Our government often justifies its reluctance to commit to international standards on the grounds that adoption of substantive rights by treaty promulgation represents the circumvention of constitutionally required public participation. If the argument is that it would be innappropriate to impose these norms on an unsuspecting public, there is a simple solution: education. The government has an affirmative obligation to educate the public about the alternative rights doctrines that the international community provides, and which the American government is rejecting on the public's behalf. In order to dispel our growing parochialism, the government must encourage an American rights discourse that looks beyond the boundaries of American Constitutional norms.

---

361. 8 U.S.C.A. § 1374 (West 1997).

362. Some asylum advocates do not believe a broad immigration policy admitting women fleeing from FGM will make much difference to most women subject to the practice: "They simply don't have the resources or the control over their lives to flee to a country as far away . . . as the United States." Assoc. Press., *Groups Say Case Unlikely to Alter Immigrant Flow*, THE DALLAS MORNING NEWS, June 15, 1996, at A17 (quoting Fauziya Kasinga's lead attorney).

GENERAL ETHNIC, RACIAL, AND RELIGIOUS DIFFERENCES

Janice Love and Natalie Hevener Kaufman*

At the center of recent policy discussions and scholarly debates on human rights lie fundamental challenges arising from issues of religion, race, culture, and ethnicity.[1] Scholars also increasingly acknowledge the political significance of religion, culture, and identity in wider realms of international affairs.[2] For example, the recent rise of various forms of fundamentalism across the world prompted closer attention to this particular kind of religious and cultural assertion.[3] With the end of the Cold War, there is some evidence of a new clash of cultures on matters of human rights and much more, with religion providing the basis of a new deep divide.[4]

Whereas important scholarly works explore religious, ethnic, and cultural perspectives on, and foundations for, human rights norms and standards, most of these analyses focus on particular religions or cultural expressions. For example, An-Na'im[5] and Said[6]

---

*   Lisa Panepinto, Diana Stefanova, and Ashlie Williams offered excellent and deeply appreciated assistance in the research for and preparation of this chapter.

[1]   See JACK DONNELLY, UNIVERSAL HUMAN RIGHTS IN THEORY AND PRACTICE (1989); RHODA HOWARD, HUMAN RIGHTS AND THE SEARCH FOR COMMUNITY (1995); Rhoda Howard, *Occidentalism, Human Rights, and the Obligations of Western Scholars*, 29 CANADIAN J. AFR. STUD. 110–126 (1995); ADAMANTIA POLLIS & PETER SCHWAB, HUMAN RIGHTS; CULTURAL AND IDEOLOGICAL PERSPECTIVES (1980); and A. DUNDES RENTELN, INTERNATIONAL HUMAN RIGHTS: UNIVERSALISM VERSUS RELATIVISM (1990).

[2]   See DOUGLAS JOHNSTON & CYNTHIA SAMPSON, RELIGION, THE MISSING DIMENSION OF STATECRAFT (1994).

[3]   See THE FUNDAMENTALISM PROJECT VOLUME I: FUNDAMENTALISMS OBSERVED (Martin E. Marty & R. Scott Appleby eds., 1993). *See also* Benjamin R. Barber, *Jihad vs. McWorld*, 269 ATLANTIC MONTHLY 53–63 (1992).

[4]   See Samuel P. Huntington, *The Clash of Civilizations?*, 72 FOR. AFF. 22–49 (1993); SAMUEL P. HUNTINGTON, THE CLASH OF CIVILIZATIONS & THE REMAKING OF WORLD ORDER (1996).

[5]   See ABDULLAHI AHMED AN-NA'IM, TOWARD AN ISLAMIC REFORMATION: CIVIL LIBERTIES, HUMAN RIGHTS AND INTERNATIONAL LAW (1996); Abdullahi Ahmed An-Na'im, *Toward a Cross-Cultural Approach to Defining International Standards of Human Rights: The Meaning of Cruel, Inhuman, or Degrading Treatment or Punishment, in* HUMAN RIGHTS IN CROSS-CULTURAL PERSPECTIVES: A QUEST FOR CONSENSUS 19–43 (An Na'im ed.,1992).

[6]   See Abdul Aziz Said, *Precept and Practice of Human Rights in Islam*, UNIVERSAL HUMAN RIGHTS 63–80 (1979); Abdul Aziz Said, *Human Rights in Islamic Perspectives, in* HUMAN RIGHTS: CULTURAL AND IDEOLOGICAL PERSPECTIVES (Adamantia Pollis & Peter Schwab eds., 1980).

write about Islamic prescriptions for human rights; Cahill,[7] Hollenbach,[8] Little,[9] Nolde,[10] and Van der Bent[11] examine Christian bases and frameworks; Asante[12] discusses how African humanism embodies an understanding of human rights, whereas An-Na'im and Deng[13] collect cross-cultural African perspectives; and Lo[14] provides Chinese concepts, whereas Kausikan[15] points much more broadly to all of Asia.

When institutions representing organized religious or cultural groups become active in human rights work, however, any semblance of a common and harmonious perspective on standards and policies within particular religions or cultures soon gives way to a cacophony of voices making conflicting claims. No coherent Christian chorus rises to inspire believers to clear goals, analysis, and action, just as no global call to Islamic adherents rallies the faithful to common purpose. Chinese and Korean students, among other activists in Asia, refuse to bow to various Asian governments' insistence on their region's cultural diversion from international human rights norms. And, Africans find race and culture incapable of uniting them in hotly contested rights debates.

Yet, amidst the noise, common strains can be heard. Considerable agreement exists between some Christians and some Muslims, often more so than among Christians themselves. Intragroup debates within many other religious, cultural, racial, or ethnic groups also occur, and the within group differences often loom as large or larger than the between group differences. Furthermore, some of the same issues that divide Christians also divide Muslims (or other groups) in similar ways.

No realm of human rights discussion demonstrates this division within religion and culture, accompanied by commonalities cutting across religion and culture, better than do the debates on women's rights. On issues of reproductive freedom, for example, the Holy See, representing the Roman Catholic Church, may have more in common with the self-proclaimed Islamic government of Iran than it does with some other Christian churches or institutions.

---

[7]   *See* Lisa Sowle Cahill, *Toward a Christian Theory of Human Rights*, 8 J. Relig. Ethics 277–301 (1980).

[8]   *See* David Hollenbach, Claims in Conflict: Retrieving and Renewing the Catholic Human Rights Tradition (1979).

[9]   *See* David Little, *A Christian Perspective on Human Rights, in* Human Rights in Africa: Cross Cultural Perspectives (Abdullahi A. An-Na'im & F.M. Deng eds., 1990).

[10]   *See* O. Frederick Nolde, Free and Equal: Human Rights in Ecumenical Perspective (1968).

[11]   *See* Ans Van Der Bent, Commitment to God's World: A Concise Critical Survey of Ecumenical Thought (1995).

[12]   *See* S.K.B. Asante, *Nation Building and Human Rights in Emergent Africa*, 2 Cornell Int'l L.J. 72–107 (1969).

[13]   *See* Human Rights in Africa: Cross-Cultural Perspectives (Abdullahi A. An Na'im & F.M. Deng eds., 1990).

[14]   *See* Chung-Shu Lo, *Human Rights in the Chinese Tradition, in* Unesco, Human Rights: Comments and Interpretations (1949).

[15]   *See* Bilahari Kausikan, *Asia's Different Standard*, 92 For. Pol'y 24–41 (1993).

This chapter will examine the positions of governments and other institutions in two sources: those which invoke, claim to manifest, or discuss religious or cultural authority in speeches made at the United Nations Fourth World Conference on Women in Beijing, September 1995; and those which register reservations on grounds of religion when ratifying the Convention on the Elimination of All Forms of Discrimination Against Women. Different positions within religious and cultural groups as well as between groups will be analyzed, building on categories developed by Rhoda Howard in her survey of a range of recent challenges to internationally recognized human rights norms and standards.[16] Whereas Howard applies her classification scheme to wider issues effecting the totality of human rights and their relationship to the search for community, this chapter will extend her analysis to examine women's rights in greater depth.

THE FRAMEWORK

Scholars basically agree that the widely accepted international human rights standards articulated since World War II (civil and political as well as economic, social, and cultural) have their philosophical basis in Western liberalism, which emphasizes the equality and autonomy of the individual.[17] Many who deny the universal applicability of international human rights standards base their rejection in whole or in part on the repudiation of Western culture, religion, or capitalism, especially the emphasis in each on the individual. In contrast, however, others reject international norms to accentuate further certain narrow aspects of liberalism, particularly individual freedom.

Howard groups these challenges into five categories:[18] reactive conservatism,[19] traditionalism, left collectivism, status radicalism (all of which are communitar-

---

[16]   *See* RHODA E. HOWARD, HUMAN RIGHTS AND THE SEARCH FOR COMMUNITY (1995).

[17]   *See* Natalie Hevener Kaufman, *International Law and the Status of Women: An Analysis of International Legal Instruments Related to the Treatment of Women*, 1 HARV. WOMEN'S L.J. 131–56 (1978); Rhoda E. Howard & Jack Donnelly, *Human Dignity, Human Rights, and Political Regimes*, 80 AM. POLIT. SCI. REV. 801–17 (1986); JACK DONNELLY, UNIVERSAL HUMAN RIGHTS IN THEORY AND PRACTICE (1989).

[18]   Howard creates these five categories and discusses various components of each in a number of places throughout her book, HUMAN RIGHTS AND THE SEARCH FOR COMMUNITY. The book, however, focuses more generally on communitarian perspectives as a whole as well as on the question of how modern societies might place more emphasis on community and social responsibility while preserving internationally developed human rights standards. The discussion in this chapter brings together each of the five perspectives from various sections of Howard's book and derives some of the categories' characteristics from the implications of Howard's discussion, rather than directly from her text. Furthermore, some of the labels and phraseology are ours, as is the table we construct to compare across the perspectives (particularly in the nine dimensions systematically applied to each) and, for the most part, the explicit discussion of women's rights in each. Therefore, our characterization of Howard's categories may fail to be completely faithful to her explicit or implicit definitions. If so, we regret, and accept responsibility for, such errors.

[19]   Howard's name for this category is reactionary conservative. We consider the label reactive conservatism less pejorative and thus use it instead.

ian), and radical capitalism (which is non-communitarian).[20] This classification scheme provides a useful foundation for examining religious, cultural, racial, and ethnic perspectives on human rights, and in particular, their views of women's rights. A sixth category will be added to represent the perspective of internationally agreed norms and standards on human rights, as discussed by Howard (and others). It will be demonstrated that various adherents within the same religion may identify with different perspectives in Howard's scheme, while still claiming loyalty to their common religion.

In order to more fully explore and compare each of Howard's categories, they can be defined along nine dimensions: the basis of membership in a society organized primarily according to principles established by this perspective; the basis of members' legal status in such a society; social and economic obligations; the degree of social mobility available; the source of principles of morality and justice; the nature of community or association; the significance of culture; the future vision of such a society; and its views of women's rights. The table on the framework summarizes the discussion.

International Human Rights Standards

As stated earlier, the Western liberal tradition appears in international human rights documents in the form of an emphasis on autonomy for individuals. The goal of such autonomy is the citizen's protection from the coercive powers of the state. One can most easily see the state obligation to maintain the autonomy of each of its citizens in the Universal Declaration of Human Rights as well as the International Covenant on Civil and Political Rights and the International Covenant on Economic, Social, and Cultural Rights. Howard argues:

> The citizen who is constantly afraid of the police or army cannot conduct her life as she sees fit; she cannot fulfil even her minimum social obligations—to work, to raise her family, to honor her elders—in any sort of security. To have personal autonomy also means to have the freedom to act on one's decisions and to have one's decisions respected by the state and other citizens. To have autonomy, finally, means to have privacy—to think, to consider, to resist pressures from conformist social forces. . . . Autonomy, however, does not mean complete independence or self-reliance. The autonomous individual does not live in a social vacuum, without connections with, obligations to, or claims on fellow citizens. Rather, all citizens ought to be concerned with the dignity of all fellow citizens.[21]

Non-discrimination and equality in law and political life provide an essential basis for citizens' abilities to claim all their other rights in society. No one should feel or be deemed inferior or superior on the basis of family, race, gender, etc., nor should a person's life chances or choices be ordained by some ascribed status.[22] This unequiv-

---

[20]   These dimensions represent our effort to systematize Howard's categories. Howard creates the classification scheme for the categories or perspectives, but we create the dimensions, based on her discussion of the perspectives. We hope our representation is faithful to her discussion.

[21]   HOWARD, *supra* note 16, at 17.

[22]   *Id.*

ocal and deliberate emphasis on individual rights signified by autonomy and equality, however, is balanced by prescriptions for social and economic obligation particularly for the state but, by implication, also for members.

The Universal Declaration of Human Rights and the two International Covenants only mention the members' duties and obligations to other citizens and insist on people's rights to food, clothing, housing, education, health care, social services, social security, protection for children, participation in cultural life, and to marry and found a family.[23]

Governments of societies accepting these obligations must ensure the provision of these economic and social rights. Such provision is not possible, however, without members of the society granting their government substantial resources and, in all likelihood, also themselves collectively claiming some degree of social responsibility. As Howard suggests, basic economic and social security for all citizens embodies an obligation for both the state and all its citizens to have concern and respect for one another.[24]

If societies ensure autonomy and equality of individuals, while providing basic economic and social well-being, social mobility will be very high. Members will be able to choose their level of educational attainment and occupation on the basis of merit, as well as select marriage partners and family structures with a high degree of freedom. They should also be able to create or join organizations or groups that meet their needs. Association in religious, cultural, ethnic, age, educational, neighborhood, or other groups would be voluntary. Imposition of cultural norms on individuals associated with any particular group would be mediated by people's ability to move in and out of groups at will. Therefore, the influence of a single, dominant or homogenous culture would be limited, and the principles of morality and justice governing the society would, of necessity, be secular.

Embracing mobility and voluntaristic association recognizes the reality facing virtually every society in the real world. Most cultures are (and some have always been) fairly fluid and heterogeneous; that is, for example, within the same society, people of a common religious tradition may find their group composed of people from several different ethnic or racial heritages who come together for purposes of religious ritual and activity, but who go their separate ways for ethnic or racial ritual and activity. Or similarly, people of common ethnicity may part ways to participate in different religious undertakings. Furthermore, religious, racial, ethnic or other cultural traditions may change from one time period to the next. This human rights perspective sees such heterogeneity and fluidity as desirable.

Embracing secularism means that no divine law or behavioral standards prescribed by God exist for all people in the society. God and divine law may be essen-

---

[23]   International Covenant on Economic, Social and Cultural Rights. *Adopted and opened for signature, ratification and accession by General Assembly resolution 2200A(XXI) of 16 December 1966.*

[24]   HOWARD, *supra* note 16, at 165–71, 195–203.

Framework of Human Rights Perspectives

Perspectives / Dimensions	Human Rights Standards	Radical Capitalism	Reactive Conservatism	Traditionalism	Left Collectivism	Status Radicalism
Membership	autonomous individuals	supremely autonomous individuals	group (family)	group, collectivity	group, collectivity	group, collectivity
Legal Status	non-discrimination; equality	civil & political non-discrimination; economic & social discrimination	defined by role and status in family and community	defined by role and status in family and community	defined by group	defined by group
Social and Economic Obligation	moderate (concern and respect due to all humans by state and other members); requires economic security	minimal (concern and respect to those who earn it by state and other members); no economic security	low; obligation to family high	high; responsibility and privilege allocated according to age, gender, status	high; responsibility and privilege allocated according to previous deprivation	high; responsibility and privilege allocated according to membership in previously "shamed" or "honored" group
Social Mobility	high	moderate	low	low	moderate	low
Principles of Morality and Justice	secular	secular	tradition, religion	tradition, religion	secular culture	identity, culture, ancestry
Nature of Community / Association	voluntary, non-communitarian	unimportant; privacy and self supreme	prescribed, communitarian, family	prescribed, communitarian	prescribed, communitarian; permanent hostility between groups (classes)	prescribed, communitarian; permanent hostility between groups
Significance of Culture	limited and heterogeneous	extremely limited	very high, homogeneous	absolute homogeneous	absolute homogeneous	absolute homogeneous
Preferred Solution	universal application of international standards	social closure; ignore the destitute	social closure; nostalgia for return to orderly past; condemn the destitute	return to pre-colonial, pre-capitalist communalism	national self-determination and freedom from international capitalist exploitation	creation of new culture of empathy and sharing within group

tial to the belief system and behavior of certain individuals or groups, but law governing life together in the society would be created by its citizens, not revealed by God. Furthermore, Howard asserts, "secularism means not only a denial of the authority of religion, but a rationalist, empiricist questioning of all social values."[25]

The ideal of international human rights norms posits that all societies should manifest these values and principles. Yet, each nation is likely to take a somewhat different path to accomplish them. Accepting and appreciating diverse practices across traditions and cultures of the world means that considerable variation is possible and desirable in the implementation and institutionalization of such rights. At the same time, however, the vision of protecting the wide range of human rights is one of universal application.

Women's rights within this perspective result from the recognition that "human" rights are rights of both men and women. The Universal Declaration of Human Rights asserts that "all human beings are born free and equal in dignity and rights and that everyone is entitled to all the rights and freedoms set forth therein, without distinction of any kind, including distinction based on sex."[26] The Convention on the Elimination of All Forms of Discrimination Against Women (Women's Convention) requires that states party to the treaty take, in all areas, "all appropriate measures, including legislation, to ensure the full development and advancement of women, for the purpose of guaranteeing them the exercise and enjoyment of human rights and fundamental freedoms on a basis of equality with men."[27]

More specifically, the Women's Convention provides that women have equality before the law, including in matters of property and contract. Full political rights include the right to vote and hold office at all levels of government as well as to participate in making government policy. Educational rights include equal access to all levels of education, scholarships, and vocational guidance, as well as information about family health and planning. Rights in the arena of employment include equal pay for work of equal value, maternity leave with pay and without loss of seniority, and access to social services in order that parents can combine family obligations with work. In matters of health, women should have equal access with men to health services, free health services during pregnancy, and adequate nutrition.

Marriage rights include the ability to enter marriage and choose a spouse with free consent; for men and women to have the same rights and responsibility as parents as well as throughout the marriage and its dissolution; to choose the number and spacing of children; and to change or retain one's nationality.

United Nations' world conferences on women held in 1985 (Nairobi) and 1995 (Beijing), as well as the conferences on human rights in 1993 (Vienna), on popula-

---

[25] *Id.* at 104.

[26] *Convention on the Elimination of All Forms of Discrimination Against Women.* Adopted and opened for signature, ratification and accession by General Assembly Resolution 34/180 of December 1979 at 216. U.N. Doc. A/Res/34/180 (1980), 19 INT'L LEGAL MATERIALS 33.

[27] *Id.* at 219.

tion and development in 1994 (Cairo), and on social development in 1995 (Copenhagen), added new dimensions to these rights and emphasized previously articulated ones. These include, among others: freedom from sexual violence; women's control over their fertility; access to sexual and reproductive health services; the right to safe abortion where legal; the rights of the girl child; the exercise of religious freedom; and women's full participation in social and economic development aimed at eradicating poverty.[28]

Radical Capitalism

Radical capitalism places considerably more supreme value on the autonomy of individuals, than the previous perspective. Whereas international human rights standards balance autonomy with concern and respect for each person, undergirded by economic security for all citizens, radical capitalism asserts that each individual is responsible for her or his own economic well-being, and "that anyone can rescue herself from poverty with enough effort."[29] Concern and respect is due only to those who earn it by achieving their material goals: "Material possessions become a mark of individual worth."[30]

Non-discrimination and equality hold in the civil and political spheres, with accent placed on the right to private property and privacy. Like the previous category, this perspective would remove all ascriptive barriers to achievement, thereby advocating non-discrimination and equality across gender, race and ethnicity as well.

Property may be used in any way chosen by its owner, and in emphasizing privacy, radical capitalists are "uninterested in correcting or conforming social behavior. As long as your behavior does not interfere with another's capacity to pursue her own self-interest, you are free to do as you like. . . . The private realm is completely open. Any type of behavior is permitted, and everyone is encouraged to seek the maximum happiness and gratification, just as she is encouraged to seek the maximum material wealth."[31] Maximum happiness and gratification may come through indulgence in drugs, alcohol, and sex, and members have freedom to partake.

Non-discrimination and equality, however, hold in the economic sphere only in the sense that, for the most part, individuals may exercise their entrepreneurial capabilities, if they have such. But, from the point of view of the society's social and economic obligations, "economic, social and cultural rights are considered to be superfluous."[32] Therefore, without some degree of economic security, civil and political equality may not be practically attainable, even if theoretically guaranteed.

---

[28] *See Fourth World Conference on Women, Beijing, China, Sept. 4–15, 1995, The Beijing Declaration and the Platform for Action*, U.N. Doc. DPI/1766/Wom—95–39642—February 1996—30M.

[29] HOWARD, *supra* note 16, at 3.

[30] *Id.* at 173.

[31] *Id.* at 172.

[32] *Id.* at 165.

Although this perspective would endorse the ideal of high social mobility, the reality of social mobility is not as fully attained as in the previous category. With no economic, social and cultural rights for all members, those of unequal economic capacity may have unequal access to education, occupations, or freedom of choice in marriage or family structures.

In this perspective, no religious or cultural tradition prescribes principles of morality and justice. As with the international human rights perspective, such principles stem from secular sources. Unlike the previous category, however, with supreme value placed on privacy and self-fulfillment, community becomes unimportant, and the significance of culture is extremely limited. Howard describes the long-term vision of radical capitalism as "social closure," a response to the considerable alienation that accumulates in a society where privacy and individualism gain full rein, while social responsibility with the guarantee of economic, social, and cultural rights is abandoned:

> The prosperous classes can tolerate the self-destruction of the neglected as long as it does not touch their own lives. But as self-destruction affects the wider community—through theft, drug addiction, and the spread of infectious diseases—the prosperous retreat into self-protection . . . [and they] ignore, rather than assist, the destitute.[33]

Like men living under radical capitalism, women have enormous freedom to strive for their personal satisfaction. They can own property, pursue education and occupations of their choice, associate with whom they want, partake in whatever gives them pleasure, marry whomever they choose (including other women) or not marry at all, and exercise complete reproductive freedom, including the right to abortion.

Although women may choose or set aside traditional roles as mothers and wives, those "who ask for special consideration because of their child-care responsibilities are considered to be making excessive demands on the rest of society."[34] In keeping with the lack of protection for economic, social, and cultural rights, society as a whole takes no responsibility for childcare or household work, whereas individual men might. In general, however, women and families who can pay for childcare and reproductive freedom may attain it.

Since the society essentially abandons the pursuit of community and social responsibility, women play no special role in creating or preserving culture, families or voluntary associations (as women do in some of the perspectives described below, and as all members might in the previous category). With so little emphasis on society's obligations, most violence against women falls within the realm of the private, with women having little effective recourse against their assailants.

Reactive Conservatism

Unlike the previous categories, reactive conservatism and the remaining perspectives discussed below are characterized by communitarianism. Each particular

---

[33] *Id.* at 182.

[34] *Id.* at 172.

form will be discussed in greater detail, but in general, communitarians believe that individualism encourages materialism, competition, social alienation, and social breakdown; they therefore want to emphasize community or group rights over individual rights.[35]

Groups, in this case families, form the basis of membership in society, not individuals. Reactive conservatives yearn for a restoration of an orderly, stable past where they believe that society embodied more wholesome qualities, where strong personal commitment to the family was a moral imperative. Family roles would be known, approved, and respected by all. The head of the household, husbands, would take responsibility for and be in authority over obedient wives and children. Women marry those approved by their families and have no sexual contact with any man before marriage. Women care for children, while husbands earn the family's income. Women also play crucial roles in creating and maintaining homes, culture, and community associations, but female employment outside the home would be rare.

Religion and community tradition provide the principles for morality and justice, which promote hard work, self-sacrifice, and social rectitude. A person's status and role in the family and community defines one's legal status, and members encumber high social and economic obligation to the family. Culture remains homogeneous within groups and crucial to the maintenance of order and stability. People may associate with each other within a prescribed community, but not outside of it. As Howard suggests, "the only appropriate form of happiness is that based on the maintenance of communities of self-sufficient families that share a common culture and . . . identity."[36]

The society may contain people of different races or ethnic groups, which remain communities unto themselves. Equality would not be guaranteed across groups or individuals, and reactive conservatives presume darker skinned people to be inferior to lighter skinned people. This perspective considers deference to one's superiors and elders vitally important; people know their place and usually stay in it:

> Reactive conservatives share with radical capitalists core values of hard work and individual or family economic autonomy, and both reject responsibility for nonworkers, those who by their own "fault" have not managed to acquire membership in the prosperous consumerist classes. . . . [C]onservatives agree with formal equality of opportunity but do not advocate amelioration of unequal economic conditions. . . . [T]hey deny respect to the poor. . . . [C]onservatives value hard work for its own sake as a moral good; wealth should be acquired through personal effort and discipline. The wealthy person is an autonomous being who, through his own private efforts, acquires socially acceptable goods in the marketplace.[37]

Therefore, this perspective also abandons economic, social and cultural rights, subscribing to the concept of social closure described above. Reactive conservatives, however, condemn (rather than ignore) the destitute in society, viewing them as morally bankrupt. Social mobility is necessarily low.

---

[35]   *Id.* at 5.

[36]   *Id.* at 180.

[37]   *Id.* at 179.

While their economic perspectives contain considerable commonality, reactive conservatives believe radical capitalists to be hedonistic in their insistence on individualism, the primary culprit in the breakdown of orderly and stable community according to reactive conservatives. Such individualism allows a range of unacceptable behavior: women working outside the home; women abandoning children and entire families; people not necessarily rooted in families at all; open expressions of homosexuality; widespread use of abortion as a means of birth control; the unrestricted pursuit of physical pleasures; consumption of drugs, etc.

In addition to the roles prescribed above, women also have access only to reproductive choices allowed by their husbands and religious authorities, and certainly not to abortion. Women have no individual standing in law, and here, too, violence against women falls within the realm of the private. In this perspective, women may have legal recourse against their assailants, if the assailant is from another social group, particularly an inferior one. But, like children, they have no recourse against violence perpetrated by husbands and fathers.

Traditionalism

Traditionalism shares the value of communitarianism with three other perspectives, as noted above. Together with the remaining categories, traditionalism also asserts the value of cultural absolutism. Howard makes a case for using this term instead of a softer concept, cultural relativism, which is usually employed by those adhering to this perspective and the following ones. Her analysis merits substantial quotation:

> [T]he concept of cultural relativism is used by many communitarians as a defense of their idealized way of life against the individualism and alienation that liberal human rights are thought to imply. . . . The relativism implicit in such arguments is actually a concept of cultural absolutism. Cultural absolutism declares a society's culture to be of supreme ethical value. It advocates ethnocentric adherence to one's own cultural norms as an ethically correct attitude. . . . It thus posits particular cultures as of more ethical value than any universal principle of justice. . . .

> Cultural absolutism evolves from, but is not synonymous with, cultural relativism. Cultural relativism is a method of social scientific analysis "whereby social and cultural phenomena are perceived and described in terms of scientific detachment or, ideally, from the perspective of participants in or adherents of a given culture."[38] This method of analysis evolved in the early twentieth century to counteract Westerners' nineteenth-century belief that their own white, Christian society was morally superior to all others. . . .

> Cultural relativism is not only a method, it is also an ethical stance. Relativism assumes that there is no one culture whose customs and beliefs dominate all others in a moral sense. One cannot set up a hierarchy of cultures, naming some as more advanced or more civilized than others. . . .

> But there is a difference between cultural relativism and the principle that no outsider may ever criticize any practice of a culture not her own. Relativism is now sometimes

---

[38]   David Bidney, *Cultural Relativism*, 3 Int'l Encycl. Soc. Sci. 543 (1968).

taken to such an extreme than any practice of an indigenous society can theoretically be defended merely on the grounds that it is a local custom.[39]

In advocating cultural absolutism, traditionalists yearn for a return to pre-colonial, pre-capitalist, pre-modern communal society, which they assert existed prior to Western imposition in places like the Middle East and Africa. In such a reconstituted society, groups and collectivities would form the base of membership. As with reactive conservatism, role and status in the family and community define one's legal status. Responsibility in fulfilling one's role carries certain privilege, just as privilege depends on fulfilling one's responsibilities. Rarely do participants question the unequal allocation of responsibility and privilege according to age, gender, or social status.

Religion, culture, and tradition provide the basis for principles of morality and justice. Culture is presumed to be homogeneous, with the possibility of subordinated, separate and homogeneous subcultures for people of different race or ethnicity. Social mobility would necessarily be very low. Thus, while the society would be marked by a "collectivist, nonegalitarian, and guided human existence,"[40] such a system would also provide for the possibility of a high degree of consensual, rather than competitive, decision making and "the physical and psychic security of group membership."[41]

In contrast to radical capitalism and reactive conservatism, traditionalism acknowledges the need for a certain level of social and economic well-being for the entire population, mandating some measure of economic redistribution and concern for those who encounter economic hardship (in contrast to capitalism's acquisitiveness and social closure). Therefore, those with economic resources carry obligations not to let those without such resources become completely destitute or starve.

Women's roles in traditional societies would be very much like those in reactive conservatism, with a few notable differences. Women would marry those approved by their families and have no sexual contact with any man before marriage. Women care for children, but, in contrast to the previous perspective, family members working together often earn the family income (except in the case of a few elites). Such earnings might come from agricultural activities in which women participate or even dominate, and, particularly for women, from market activities. Although women may wait for access to food or other resources (after men have taken their portion), women and children would benefit from the redistributive ethic characteristic of the society as a whole. Women also play crucial roles in creating and maintaining homes, culture, and community associations.

As with reactive conservatism, women have access only to reproductive choices allowed by their husbands and religious authorities, and certainly not to abortion. Women have no individual standing in law, and here, too, violence against women falls within the realm of the private. As in the previous category, women may have legal recourse against their assailants, if the assailant is from another social group,

---

[39]   HOWARD, *supra* note 16, at 151–152.

[40]   *Id*. at 98.

[41]   *Id*. at 90.

particularly an inferior one. But, like children, they have no recourse against violence perpetrated within the family.

Left Collectivism

Left collectivism envisions a world of self-determining national societies, each united in pursuit of the common good and free of international capitalist exploitation. Western states, transnational financial capital, and multinational corporations together create imperialism that stretches across the entire globe while penetrating each society, too. Such penetration creates internal colonial relations of dominant classes exploiting each nation's people.

Partially inspired by Marxism and its emphasis on communitarianism, left collectivism parts ways with Marx in advocating cultural absolutism. Viewing culture homogeneously, this perspective decries imperialistic destruction of whole groups of peoples and cultures and wants to regain people's rights, celebrating the cultural distinctions among peoples. Howard states that:

> This claim is made not as individuals banding together under the right to freedom of association but rather as corporate groups of suppressed cultures claiming collective rights against the dominant ethos of homogenized capitalist social relations.[42]

As a communitarian perspective, groups form both the basis of membership in the society and one's legal status. Denying the inherent value of individuals as well as civil and political liberties, left collectivism categorizes groups by imperial, racial, or gender status. Some status categories are oppressors and others are victims. Indeed, "[t]hose who previously enjoyed unfair privilege have no claim now to equitable treatment."[43] Therefore, within a system of high social and economic obligations, responsibility and privilege get allocated according to people's previous deprivation.

A centerpiece of such allocation would be economic redistribution, and the economic standing of those previously deprived of material resources and economic opportunity should improve substantially. People would not be able to move easily between groups, however, and within groups, cultural norms could proscribe individuals' choices and opportunities. Therefore, social mobility would probably be moderate.

If Marxist or socialist ideology more broadly were the sole foundation of left collectivism, the principles of morality and justice would be secular. Adherence to cultural absolutism, however, opens the door to the possibility of religious principles of morality and justice being applied in some places. In general, the emphasis on culture and people's rights suggests that this perspective would insist on certain common elements across all societies (e.g., economic redistribution and privilege for former victims) but otherwise would allow considerable variation.

---

[42] HOWARD, *supra* note 16, at 42.

[43] *Id.* at 213.

Women of color, women in "third world" countries, and poor women in rich societies, represent some of the groups left collectivists consider to be victims. Thus, in a society organized according to this perspective, women should fare well, particularly in material resources and economic opportunities. Two factors working together, however, could reinforce various inequalities for women: women's participation in every other group (e.g., racial and ethnic groups) and the emphasis on communitarianism. Would women in formerly oppressed racial, ethnic, or national groups also be considered to have been oppressed within the group as well? If so, would women of such a group then be allocated privilege vis-a-vis men in the same group? If the culture of previously oppressed group prescribes behavior for women which limits their choices and opportunities but which the group considers important for the collectivity, would women then be considered to be oppressed in the new society, or, would the emphasis on cultural absolutism deny the existence of such discrimination? For example, would a woman of one racial (or ethnic) group be allowed freely to choose a husband of a different racial (or ethnic) group? Would a woman have reproductive freedom if the collectivity placed priority on increasing its population?

No clear answers to such questions exist, and Howard does not develop this category in the same depth as she does some of the others. Therefore, the role and status of women under left collectivism cannot be clearly stated.

Status Radicalism

Status radicals desire to form new communities and new kinds of cultures characterized by empathy, shared values, and social responsibility among individuals of similar ascribed characteristics. Another label for this perspective is the politics of identity asserted by some feminists, black activists (and other groups representing people of color), indigenous populations, and gays and lesbians. Proponents argue that the social identity or status of certain categories of people carry such stigma, dishonor, and systematic denial of human rights that their oppression cannot be overcome. Therefore, group members accept the categorization imposed on them by the dominant ethos and turn an outwardly defined invidious distinction into an inwardly defined and honored cultural collectivity.

This perspective objects to the imposition of rationalism, competitiveness, and individualism on their cultures, which place a much higher value on empathy, cooperation, and the collective. In most societies at this point, proponents pursue an interim strategy of withdrawal into particular closed subcultures for psychological, if not physical, safety.

> Because the present, the concrete, is so degrading, myths of a better world—beyond or outside the current one—are developed by some status radicals. Despairing of social inclusion, separatist radicals want to withdraw from the larger society and set up their own communities.[44]

Status radicals believe that human rights, as conceived in international norms and standards, only exist for dominant groups and therefore are not relevant for sub-

---

[44]   HOWARD, *supra* note 16, at 158.

ordinated ones. Such human rights hide degradation under a facade of equality but do not really protect the degraded. As in the previous category, this perspective claims collective rights, not the freedom of individuals to voluntarily associate, but group rights for suppressed cultures.

This category shares a large number of characteristics with left collectivism including: groups forming the basis of membership in society; individual legal status defined by the collective; responsibility and privilege allocated according to previous deprivation, particularly membership in a formerly "shamed" or "honored" group; and cultural absolutism and prescribed communities, with the assumption of permanent hostility between formerly dominant and subordinate groups.

Status radicals pay little attention to matters of economic redistribution or distinctions based on class, unlike left collectivism. While the aspiration to create a new culture of empathy and sharing implies economic rights, Howard argues critically that:

> Status radicals do radical capitalists the favor of deflecting attention from the systematic abuse of economic human rights inherent in capitalist society. They pigeonhole individuals into visible status categories while ignoring class stratification. Yet in modern Western societies, to be a materially prosperous person is to have much better life chances, including a much better chance of having one's human rights protected, than a materially poor person. This advantage accrues whatever one's race, gender, or sexual orientation.[45]

If feminists or lesbians formed societies in which they shared a common identity as feminists or lesbians, presumably they would offer the highest protection possible for the human rights of women. Yet with the communitarian denial of the value of any individual rights, this may not be the case. Furthermore, collectivities based on the absolute value of culture for indigenous people or black people may or may not uphold any rights for women, depending on how the culture defines women's roles and responsibilities.

The lack of serious attention to economic matters also provides a problematic aspect of this perspective for women's human rights. Some level of material well-being for all people also provides a basic foundation for promoting, among other things, women's health and standing in the society.

Status radicalism represents the last of the perspectives Howard suggests. We move now from explication of each perspective to compare them to public positions articulated by governments and other institutions in formal documents and United Nation's arenas, positions presented in the next part of this chapter.

GOVERNMENTS' AND OTHER INSTITUTIONS' POSITIONS

Two primary sources form the basis of the following discussion on empirical representations of religious and cultural perspectives on women's human rights: governments' reservations to the Convention on the Elimination of All Forms of

---

[45]   *Id*. at 219–20.

Discrimination Against Women, and speeches made at the United Nations Fourth World Conference on Women (FWCW) in 1995 (Beijing). A few notable cases of states' domestic laws pertaining to women also help to illustrate the issues.

Government policy articulations and public presentations in U.N. arenas rarely offer a coherent philosophical position that can be neatly labeled and categorized, even for the most homogeneous of societies or even for those that tolerate little dissent. Rather, any state's policies and laws often represent a patchwork with more or less coherence, reflecting a variety of interests which contend, conflict, and perhaps compromise in the decision-making process. Furthermore, glimpses into governments' legal positions or speeches, as in the discussion below, cannot fully capture a nation's position on or philosophy of human rights (or any other issue), whether or not coherence exists; and space does not permit a thorough review of all states' policies and laws which pertain to women's rights.

Yet, speeches and official reservations to treaties make powerful public statements of strongly held sentiments in international debates where a particular government is determined to be heard. Furthermore, speeches, both by what they say and do not say, signal negotiating positions to be pursued, as well as current understandings of long-standing issues. Glimpses into a nation's domestic laws more concretely display a government's behavior back home, no matter what the politicians say at global gatherings.

The discussion below illustrates the fundamental assertion of this chapter: that different positions regarding the degree to which religious or cultural beliefs may legitimately constrain the universal application of women's human rights occur as much within religious and cultural groupings as across such groupings.

Islamic Adherents

A number of governments participating the Fourth World Conference on Women invoked or claimed to manifest Islamic positions in their statements. Some took positions that could be categorized in the framework presented here as traditionalism. Painting a picture of Islam that contrasted with traditionalism, however, others defended many elements of human rights standards. Yet a third group of governments where majorities of Muslims live made no claim to Islamic authority and ignored the issue of cultural matters altogether, choosing instead to pay full attention to further developing human rights standards for women.

---

[46]   *See* Undersecretary, Ministry of Labor and Social Affairs and Head of the Delegation of the State of Bahrain H.E. Shaikh Ahmed Bin Saqer Al Khalifa, Address at the *Fourth World Conference on Women*, Beijing, China (Sept. 4–15, 1995) (transcript available at gopher:// gopher.undp.org/1/unconfs/women/conf/gov).

[47]   *See* Presidential Advisor on Women's Affairs of Iran H.E. Ms. Shahla Habibi, Address at the *Fourth World Conference on Women*, Beijing, China (Sept. 4–15, 1995) (transcript available at gopher://gopher.undp.org/1/unconfs/women/conf/gov).

[48]   *See* State Minister for Social Planning of Sudan, Head of Delegation H.E. Mrs. Mariam

Traditionalist positions in speeches included Bahrain,[46] Iran,[47] Sudan,[48] and the United Arab Emirates,[49] all of whom asserted the Islamic religion to be their societies' basis for principles of morality and justice. They also criticized the Beijing Platform of Action (in draft form at that point) for being counter to Islamic law. In keeping with the traditionalist emphasis on prescribed community and culture, most also defined the family as the basic unit of society, proclaiming the role of mothers to be a clear and cherished one that is to be protected by the family and nation. These traditionalist articulations at the FWCW also fairly uniformly point to women's responsibility for the proper socialization of children. For example, the official from Bahrain stated:

> The family is the basis of the society; its pillars are religion, morality and patriotism; the law protects the legal entity and strengthens its ties and values, protects . . . motherhood and childhood, raises the youth and protects against exploitation and cultural, spiritual and physical negligence. This Constitutional premise stems from a Grand Islamic Heritage, based on the sound Islamic Faith. As such, the Constitution forms the basis for human rights. . . .[50]

Various references to the social and economic obligation of families and the society as a whole (e.g., for education, health care and employment opportunities for women) distinguish the positions taken by these states from the category of reactive conservatism (in which obligation to family is high but responsibility for the whole of society is low). Further investigation into the domestic legal norms for economic and social rights, however, may not confirm such a categorization.

In Beijing, the Sudanese official strongly asserted the principle of non-interference in the internal affairs of each state, one of the ways in which traditionalists hope to undermine the universal application of certain human rights norms.[51] She also pointed to controversies at the conference stemming from the "trend not to recognize cultural diversities on the global level and the tendency to impose one set of cultural values as an indispensable and solitary model." She also criticized the draft platform's "marginalization of the role of religion, spiritual heritage of humanity and ethical and moral values." Abortion, absolute sexual freedoms, and "any other form of a family other than that based on marriage between a man and a woman" also came under attack.

Sudan's statements in Beijing on the whole reflect that state's domestic legal norms that contrast starkly with international norms of human rights standards for women and clearly violate treaties such as the Women's Convention. Since 1983,

---

Osman Sir El Khatim, Address at the *Fourth World Conference on Women*, Beijing, China (Sept. 4–15, 1995) (transcript available at gopher://gopher.undp.org/1/unconfs/women/conf/gov).

[49] *See* Undersecretary in the Ministry of Labor and Social Affairs of the United Arab Emirates Mohammad Issa Suwaidi, Address at the *Fourth World Conference on Women*, Beijing, China (Sept. 4–15, 1995) (transcript available at gopher://gopher.undp.org/1/unconfs/women/ conf/gov).

[50] *See* Undersecretary, Ministry of Labor and Social Affairs and Head of the Delegation of the State of Bahrain H.E. Shaikh Ahmed Bin Saqer Al Khalifa, *supra* note 46.

[51] *See* State Minister for Social Planning of Sudan, Head of Delegation H.E. Mrs. Mariam Osman Sir El Khatim, *supra* note 48.

Sudan has adopted laws based on a traditional interpretation of the Koran. Shari'a family law provides a comprehensive set of codes governing religious rules, ethical norms, and private law. The law may be interpreted as fundamentally premised on male guardianship of the female. Men may take up to four wives and divorce them at will without any judicial authority. Women, on the other hand, can marry only one man at a time and can only divorce through judicial process. The husband controls the economic activity of his wife or wives and can prohibit her from working outside the home. A disobedient wife is not entitled to maintenance. Furthermore, a wife who leaves the home can be physically forced to return. The indirect impact is that women are socialized to be helpless and dependent from early childhood.

Citing Imam Khomeini as stating that "woman is the source of all virtues," the representative of Iran in Beijing echoed many of the same points made by the government of Sudan. This official's speech, however, went farther in proclaiming that the right of an unborn child to life far outweighs the right of women to reproductive freedom.[52]

As with Sudan, such assertions in U.N. arenas echo Iran's domestic policy positions. In Iran, the 1979 Islamic Revolution reinstated religious norms as state laws, which are in clear opposition to human rights, particularly women's rights. Within the first three weeks after the revolution, "the Family Protection Act was abolished. Polygamy once again became accepted practice, divorce became the unique right of men, and the legal age for marriage was declared to be nine years old for girls."[53]

Yet a number of other governments who also claimed to represent Islamic authority and true Islamic understandings in their public presentations at the FWCW contrasted with the positions of Iran, Sudan and other very solid traditionalists. Traditionalism lingers in the public statements of this second group of Islamic state, but they are considerably closer than the previous one to the perspective of internationally recognized human rights standards. The group consisted of Egypt, Jordan, and Pakistan.[54]

Two within this group previously submitted substantial reservations to the Women's Convention, yet in Beijing all three countries invoked very positive images of Islam's support for women's human rights as enumerated in the heritage of U.N. conferences and instruments. Although critical of it at points, they embraced this tra-

---

[52] *See* Presidential Advisor on Women's Affairs of Iran H.E. Ms. Shahla Habibi, *supra* note 47.

[53] Akram Mirhosseini, *After the Revolution: Violations of Women's Human Rights in Iran, in* WOMEN'S RIGHTS: HUMAN RIGHTS 72, 114–25 (Julie Peters & Andrea Wolper eds., 1995).

[54] *See* Ministry of Information State Information Service of Egypt Mrs. Suzanne Mubarak, Address at the *Fourth World Conference on Women*, Beijing, China (Sept. 4–15, 1995); H.R.H. Princess Basma Bint Talal of Jordan, Address at the *Fourth World Conference on Women*, Beijing, China (Sept. 4–15, 1995); Leader of the Delegation at the Fourth World Conference on Women for Pakistan Begum Shahnaz Wazir Ali, Address at the *Fourth World Conference on Women*, Beijing, China (Sept. 4–15, 1995); Prime Minister of Islamic Republic of Pakistan Mohtarma Benazir Bhutto, Address at the *Fourth World Conference on Women*, Beijing, China (Sept. 4–15, 1995); (transcripts of these speeches available at gopher://gopher.undp.org/1/unconfs/women/conf/gov).

dition and did not stand counter to it, preferring instead to interpret their own behavior within this heritage and to recount their progress towards the universal norms of human rights standards for women.

Mrs. Suzanne Mubarak, the representative of Egypt and wife of the head of state, for example, drew a distinction between the laws of the state which protect democracy, and the religion of the state, Islam. Perhaps in recognition of the features of traditionalism that remain, she also confessed that Egypt falls short of fulfilling women's rights and aspirations, noting among other obstacles, the "inherited habits and unhealthy traditions which have come down through thousands of years. These deep-seated habits are difficult to uproot quickly; at the same time it is dangerous to eliminate them by force."[55] Mrs. Mubarak also made indirect references to the need for family planning. She condemned religious extremism and, in contrast to the Sudanese representative, she praised cultural diversity within and across nations. Egypt, she asserted, is proud to be the home of both Muslims and Christians, Arab and African, the majority of whom remain true to their religious values of "peace, love and coexistence," not extremism. She states:

> [W]e are living in an era which is dominated by overpowering attempts and currents to wipe out identities, social heritage and cultural diversity. Culture diversity is an intellectual and social necessity that enriches the minds and is not any less important than bio-diversity which enriches nature. The acceptance of cultural diversity is an important stride on the way towards international democracy and understanding since it endorses the acceptance of differences between people and promotes understanding.[56]

Also praising the potential of Islam to promote the full range of internationally recognized human rights standards for women, the representative of Jordan made a similar point, arguing that those who defend culture often distort it:

> I believe that our culture and values are strong enough to withstand the hazards of the journey into modernity, yet we must strive for clarity of vision at all times. All too often, we see the true essence of our culture being distorted by elements of insecurity and defensiveness. We must be aware that such a defensive posture can never be proactive or creative, although these two qualities should always be present against the backdrop of a vibrant culture such as ours. . . .
>
> While many of us are becoming wary of the negative impact of globalization, this conference bears witness to some of the positive aspects of the global trend.[57]

The most extensive and forceful presentation in this group, however, came from Mohtarma Benazir Bhutto, then Prime Minister of the Islamic Republic of Pakistan, who introduced herself as "a Prime Minister . . . a woman and a mother. A woman proud of her cultural and religious heritage . . . (and) the first woman ever elected to head an Islamic nation."[58] She tackled the issue of culture head on, arguing:

> Muslim women have a special responsibility to help distinguish between Islamic teachings and social taboos spun by the traditions of a patriarchal society. This is a

---

55   Ministry of Information State Information Service of Egypt Mrs. Suzanne Mubarak, *id.*

56   *Id.*

57   H.R.H. Princess Basma Bint Talal of Jordan, *supra* note 54.

58   Prime Minister of Islamic Republic of Pakistan Mohtarma Benazir Bhutto, *supra* note 54.

distinction that obscurantists would not like to see. For obscurantists believe in dis-crimination. Discrimination is the first step to dictatorship and the usurpation of power.[59]

Prime Minister Bhutto then proceeded to outline extensively and in detail how Islam could support the efforts of Pakistan to promote human rights standards for women, including the need to eliminate domestic violence, abolish the dowry system, help women achieve financial independence, get rid of polygamy, and promote family planning. She applauded the draft Platform of Action, stating that it "focuses on the critical areas of concern for women and outlines an action-oriented strategy for the solution of their problems."[60]

Yet a review of reservations to the Women's Convention for two of the governments in this group reveals a more complex picture. Islamic fundamentalist groups with powerful appeals to traditionalism are strong in these countries and others. Though Egypt and Jordan ratified the Women's Convention, both share reservations to the treaty that are indicative of the strength of these groups and the incompatibility of their beliefs with the implementation of universal rights of women. Both claim immunity from Article 9, concerning the nationality of children, and Article 16, concerning discrimination against women in marriage and family relations. In addition, Egypt expressed reservations to Article 29, which would allow for international arbitration in disputes over the interpretation and application of the Convention.

Such reservations, together with the speeches from Beijing, reflect the tensions with which these governments live when addressing women's rights. The evidence presented here suggests that while Egypt and Jordan, and probably Pakistan, do not fully embrace the perspective of traditionalism, neither do they fully embrace the perspective of human rights standards.

A third group of nations illustrated by Indonesia, Malaysia, and Syria overlooked the question of Islam and, with one exception, did not address the controversy over the role of culture and religion in debates over human rights.[61] Yet all three represent majority Muslim populations. Each articulated positions in keeping with the perspective of human rights standards. Such articulations may not fully reflect domestic practice, yet the willingness of governments with large Muslim populations to affirm universal standards for women's human rights is notable.

The one mention of religion came from the Malaysian representative who commented on the family, stating:

---

[59]   *Id.*

[60]   *Id.*

[61]   *See* State Minister for the Role of Women, Head of Delegation of the Republic of Indonesia H.E. Mrs. Mien Sugandhi, Address at the *Fourth World Conference on Women*, Beijing, China (Sept. 4–15, 1995); Head of Malaysian Delegation Datin Seri Dr. Siti Hasmah Bt Haji Mohd. Ali, Address at the *Fourth World Conference on Women*, Beijing, China (Sept. 4–15, 1995); Minister of Higher Education and Head of the Syrian Delegation Dr. Salha Sankar, Address at the *Fourth World Conference on Women*, Beijing, China (Sept. 4–15, 1995); (transcripts of aforementioned speeches available at gopher://gopher.undp.org/1/unconfs/women/conf/gov).

The family has to be preserved and supported. Whilst we recognize women's great contribution to the welfare of the family and development of society, women's sex and their role in procreation cannot be the basis for discrimination. Religion also cannot be misused to justify these practices. The spirit of equality, mutuality and respect in the relationship between men and women is essential for building the foundation of a strong family.[62]

In summary, as evidenced in formal articulations in U.N. arenas and in treaty reservations, the Islamic adherents discussed here can be arrayed along a continuum between two perspectives categorized in the framework for this chapter: traditionalism and human rights standards.

The kinds of divisions that exist within Islam parallel divisions within other religions. Next to be considered is Israel, the state which claims authority for the Jewish religion.

Jewish Adherents

Though Islamic states provide the most obvious examples of the tension between traditionalism and women's rights, Judaism, as perpetuated through Israeli law, also reflects this tension. As Carmel Shalev indicates, Jewish law, *halakha*, views the world as divided into two spheres, the public and the private, and women are confined to the private sphere of the household. Though Israel professes gender equality:

recent years have brought a change of consciousness and an unveiling of the reality of Israeli women's lives. The universal issues of gender—the unequal distribution of political, economic, and physical power—appear in local form: the under representation of women in governmental, political, and financial decision-making bodies; segregation in the workplace, the devaluation of women's labor, and the feminization of poverty; the bodily abuse of women and their subordination through domestic violence, rape, sexual harassment, and pornography.[63]

In addition, though Israel ratified the Convention on the Elimination of All Forms of Discrimination Against Women in 1980, it did so while expressing two reservations. The first says that the State of Israel will not require the appointment of women as judges of religious courts where this is "prohibited by the laws of any of the religious communities in Israel." The second reservation is in regard to Article 16, which seeks to end discrimination against women in all matters relating to family and marriage relations, "to the extent that the laws on personal status which are binding on the various religious communities in Israel do not conform with the provisions of that article."[64]

The representative of the state of Israel speaking in Beijing took the opportunity to express publicly some of the stark differences of opinion which exist within that country, stating, "To my regret, there is no separation between State and Religion

---

[62]   Head of Malaysian Delegation Datin Seri Dr. Siti Hasmah Bt Haji Mohd. Ali, *supra.*

[63]   Carmel Shalev, *Women in Israel: Fighting Tradition, in* Women's Human Rights 89, 89–95 (Julie Peters & Andrea Wolper eds., 1995).

[64]   *Convention on the Elimination of All Forms of Discrimination Against Women.* Adopted and opened for signature, ratification and accession by General Assembly Resolution 34/180 of Dec. 1979 at 166. U.N. Doc. A/Res/34/180 (1980), 19 Int'l Legal Materials 33.

in our country. This creates a major problem for women in personal status law." Although some points of the country's progress were enumerated, the speech continued in a personal tone, ending with a personal vision of change which included a list typical of the perspective of the human rights standards: employment opportunities for women, enforced equal pay for equal work, childcare, political representation, etc.[65]

Such public display of a governmental representative's own personal disagreement with the traditionalism of the government's official position demonstrates that within the country and within the government, the debate over the appropriate place for religious and cultural restrictions on human rights often centers in particular on issues of women's rights.

Christian Adherents

This religious group finds itself embroiled in much the same discussion, but as was the case with Judaism, the number and range of positions presented here is necessarily more narrow than that which exists across all those who adhere to this faith. The voice with strongest claim to represent a Christian perspective among the governments gathered at the Fourth World Conference on Women was the Holy See, the Roman Catholic Church. Other churches and Christian organizations present at United Nations conferences stay confined to the category of non-governmental organizations, groups not used in the illustrations here. Therefore, this section will focus on the Roman Catholic Church (RCC) positions.

The speech delivered by Professor Mary Ann Glendon on behalf of the Delegation of the Holy See can be characterized as a mix of perspectives. The assertions on economics, education, and violence against women, and the often negative role of culture in relation to these matters, fit into the category of human rights standards. The parts on family life and family planning, abortion, and much of what is said about sexuality conform more to the perspective of traditionalism.

Calling "governments to their social duties," the RCC intervention gives considerable attention to the issue of poverty. The speaker asserted that "effective action on behalf of working mothers requires recognition of the priority of human over economic values," placing efficiency and productivity as secondary, rather than primary economic goals, and removing "all forms of the exploitation of women and young girls as cheap labour."[66]

Invoking work already accomplished at the World Summit on Social Development, Professor Glendon elaborated on a number of points in the RCC emphasis on eliminating poverty. For example, she stressed the need to find "new ways of

---

[65]   *See* Minister of Labor and Social Affairs of Israel Ora Namir, Address at the *Fourth World Conference on Women*, Beijing, China (Sept. 4–15, 1995) (transcript available at gopher://gopher.undp.org/1/unconfs/women/conf/gov).

[66]   *See* Head of the Delegation of the Holy See Prof. Mary Ann Glendon, Address at the *Fourth World Conference on Women*, Beijing, China (Sept. 4–15, 1995) (transcript available at gopher://gopher.undp.org/1/unconfs/women/conf/gov).

recognizing the economic and social value of women's unremunerated work." Noting that basic education remains key to the elimination of poverty, the speaker emphasized the fundamental commitment of the RCC both to education and to the girl child. She also registered RCC criticism of the draft platform of action for placing too little emphasis on basic public health questions such as "poor nutrition, unsafe water and those diseases that afflict millions of women each year."[67]

Furthermore, tackling the contentious subject of culture, the speaker urged: "Efforts must be strengthened to eliminate all those cultural and legal obstacles which impair the economic security of women." She applauded "the purpose of the draft Platform of Action to free women at last from the unfair burdens of cultural conditioning that have so often prevented them even from becoming conscious of their own dignity."[68]

Emphasizing the connection of culture to violence against women and girls, the RCC statement notes that violence "may be physical, sexual, psychological or moral." The statement highlights the issue of rape in war, asserting that "sexual violence as an instrument of armed conflict has stunned the conscience of humanity."[69] Then Professor Glendon pointedly linked violence to culture, stating:

> More must be done to eliminate the practice of female genital mutilation and other deplorable practices such as child prostitution, trafficking in children and their organs and child marriages. Society must also reach out to all those who have been the victims of such violence, ensuring that justice be applied to the perpetrators of such violence, as well as offering the victims holistic healing and rehabilitation into society. The question of violence experienced by women is also linked to those factors which underlie the widespread hedonistic and commercial culture which encourages the systematic exploitation of sexuality and especially reduces women to the role of sex objects. Should the Conference not condemn such attitudes, it could well be accused of condoning the very root causes of much violence against women and girls.[70]

Much of the presentation focused on these topics related to social and economic rights, all of which represent a solid affirmation of women's rights within the internationally recognized human rights standards. In this regard, in particular, the RCC official position is in sharp contrast to the perspectives of radical capitalism and reactive conservatism presented in earlier sections of this chapter. When discussing family planning, sexuality, and abortion, however, the RCC position shifts to become much more aligned with traditionalism.

Professor Glendon criticized the draft Platform of Action for being too negative in its presentation of marriage, motherhood, the family, and adherence to religion. While affirming the draft platform for its emphasis on the responsibilities of men (as well as women) in sexuality and reproduction as well as its condemnation of coercion in governments' population policies, the RCC restated its deeply held convic-

---

67 *Id.*

68 *Id.*

69 *Id.*

70 *Id.*

tions against abortion and any artificial means of birth control. Instead, the statement held high the option of "self-discipline and self-restraint" in sexuality as appropriate means for "ensuring deep respect for human life and its transmission."[71]

Using a strategy often invoked by those opposed to family planning, the RCC representative called for providing couples "with clear information about *all possible health risks* associated with family planning methods." Furthermore, abortion providers came under attack as "a vast industry that extracts its profits from the very bodies of women, while at the same time purporting to be their liberators."[72]

Again, the issue of culture is invoked in these matters, thereby criticizing social mores or cultural practices from the perspectives both of human rights standards and traditionalism. For example, the statement criticized the draft platform for not being "bold enough in acknowledging the threat to women's health arising from widespread attitudes of sexual permissiveness" or failing to sufficiently challenge societies to change "irresponsible attitudes and behavior."[73]

The actual practice of Catholic clergy and laity may deviate from the official position of the Holy See articulated in Beijing, just as governments' presentations discussed above may not fully reflect their domestic practices. Furthermore RCC public articulations do not fully represent the range of debate and perspectives contained within its own church, much less the whole Christian community. Yet the speech illustrates that this church has a great deal in common with positions taken by officials representing other religions. On particular matters within discussions of women's human rights, this commonality may be greater than that available between the RCC and other Christian churches.

CONCLUSION

This chapter attempts to accomplish two tasks. It elucidates and elaborates a framework, developed out of work initiated by Rhoda Howard, for examining six different perspectives on human rights. In particular, the chapter uses the framework to address the issues of cultural and religious differences on women's human rights. Then reservations made to the Convention on the Elimination of All Forms of Discrimination Against Women and speeches made by governments at the Fourth World Conference on Women selectively illustrated governments' positions on matters of women's human rights within the framework.

As a preliminary survey of governments' positions, the illustrations fell into only two of the six categories: human rights standards and traditionalism, with some governments expressing a mix of the two. Although thorough and systematic research on all governments' public utterances, policies, and behavior would likely yield a wider range of perspectives, all six categories would not likely be represented. To document

---

[71]   *Id.*

[72]   *Id.* [emphasis added].

[73]   *Id.*

policy advocacy for each perspective, we would need to explore positions taken by non-governmental organizations as well. In human rights, NGOs often set the stage for wider debates and project the agendas many governments will embrace in the future.

Government policies and public stances rarely represent carefully rendered and clearly articulated philosophical positions. Rather, such policies often reflect somewhat incoherent outcomes of decision-making processes where contending interests conflict and compromise. Therefore, finding some governments asserting pieces of positions from two different perspectives, as we found here, should not be surprising, although with further research we may well discover that one of the perspectives dominates or eventually overtakes the other.

Furthermore, finding that those who claim religious authority come to substantially different conclusions from others within the same religious community should be no surprise either, especially when governments invoke such authority for themselves. Yet few who consider matters of how religion and culture interact with human rights demonstrate the variety of perspectives within and across religions, implying instead that any particular religion is fairly homogeneous within its group and, on the whole, different from other religions.

This chapter seeks to accomplish the task of illustrating how, in matters of women's human rights, religions with many doctrinal and other differences find common ground, whereas adherents to any single religion may take sharply contrasting positions. Fuller documentation of this contention across a wider range of religious actors awaits further research.

INDEX

CUMULATIVE INDEX